DBS Library
73625

D1645800

Contemporary Management

Seventh Edition

Gareth R. Jones
Mays Business School
Texas A&M University

Jennifer M. George
Jesse H. Jones Graduate School of Business
Rice University

DBS Library
13/14 Aungier Street
Dublin 2
Phone: 01-4177572

McGraw-Hill Irwin

The McGraw·Hill Companies

CONTEMPORARY MANAGEMENT: GLOBAL EDITION

Published by McGraw-Hill/Irwin, a business unit of The McGraw-Hill Companies, Inc., 1221 Avenue of the Americas, New York, NY, 10020. Copyright © 2011, 2009, 2008, 2006, 2003, 2000, 1998 by The McGraw-Hill Companies, Inc. All rights reserved. No part of this publication may be reproduced or distributed in any form or by any means, or stored in a database or retrieval system, without the prior written consent of The McGraw-Hill Companies, Inc., including, but not limited to, in any network or other electronic storage or transmission, or broadcast for distance learning.

Some ancillaries, including electronic and print components, may not be available to customers outside the United States.

This book is printed on acid-free paper.

1 2 3 4 5 6 7 8 9 0 DOW/DOW 1 0 9 8 7 6 5 4 3 2 1

ISBN 978-0-07-122093-4
MHID 0-07-122093-3

DUBLIN BUSINESS SCHOOL
LIBRARY
RECEIVED
11 FEB 2014

www.mhhe.com

BRIEF CONTENTS

Part One

Management

Chapter 1
Managers and Managing 42

Chapter 2
The Evolution of Management Thought 72

Chapter 3
Values, Attitudes, Emotions, and Culture: The Manager as a Person 102

Part Two

The Environment of Management

Chapter 4
Ethics and Social Responsibility 132

Chapter 5
Managing Diverse Employees in a Multicultural Environment 162

Chapter 6
Managing in the Global Environment 186

Part Three

Decision Making, Planning, and Strategy

Chapter 7
Decision Making, Learning, Creativity, and Entrepreneurship 214

Chapter 8
The Manager as a Planner and Strategist 242

Chapter 9
Value Chain Management: Functional Strategies for Competitive Advantage 274

Part Four

Organizing and Controlling

Chapter 10
Managing Organizational Structure and Culture 302

Chapter 11
Organizational Control and Change 338

Chapter 12
Human Resource Management 368

Part Five

Leading Individuals and Groups

Chapter 13
Motivation and Performance 398

Chapter 14
Leadership 424

Chapter 15
Effective Groups and Teams 452

Part Six

Managing Critical Organizational Processes

Chapter 16
Promoting Effective Communication 480

Chapter 17
Managing Conflict, Politics, and Negotiation 510

Chapter 18
Using Advanced Information Technology to Increase Performance 534

NOTES 562

CREDITS 587

INDEX 588

NAMES 588

ORGANIZATIONS 598

GLOSSARY/SUBJECTS 601

CONTENTS

Part One | Management

Chapter 1 Managers and Managing 42

A MANAGER'S CHALLENGE

What Is High-Performance Management? 43

Topics

Overview 45

What Is Management? 45

- Achieving High Performance: A Manager's Goal 45
- Why Study Management? 46

Essential Managerial Tasks 47

- Planning 47
- Organizing 51
- Leading 51
- Controlling 52
- Performing Managerial Tasks: Mintzberg's Typology 52

Levels and Skills of Managers 53

- Levels of Management 53
- Managerial Skills 56

Recent Changes in Management Practices 59

- Restructuring and Outsourcing 59

Challenges for Management in a Global Environment 60

- Building Competitive Advantage 61
- Maintaining Ethical and Socially Responsible Standards 63
- Utilizing IT and E-Commerce 65
- Practicing Global Crisis Management 65

Chapter 2 The Evolution of Management Thought 72

A MANAGER'S CHALLENGE

Finding Better Ways to Make Cars 73

Topics

Overview 75

Scientific Management Theory 75

- Job Specialization and the Division of Labor 76
- F. W. Taylor and Scientific Management 77
- The Gilbreths 80

Administrative Management Theory 81

- The Theory of Bureaucracy 82
- Fayol's Principles of Management 84

Behavioral Management Theory 88

- The Work of Mary Parker Follett 88
- The Hawthorne Studies and Human Relations 89
- Theory X and Theory Y 90

Management Science Theory 94

Organizational Environment Theory 94

- The Open-Systems View 95
- Contingency Theory 96

Examples

Manager as a Person
Ursula Burns "Copies" Anne Mulcahy as CEO of Xerox 49

Ethics in Action
Parmalat and Self-Dealing 64

Management in Action

Summary and Review 66
Management in Action 68
Topics for Discussion and Action 68
Building Management Skills 68
Managing Ethically 69
Small Group Breakout Exercise 69
Exploring the World Wide Web 69
Be the Manager 69

Examples

Ethics in Action
Sun Tzu—Military Theory as Business Theory 79

Manager as a Person
Gottlieb Daimler and the Creation of What Became Daimler Benz 80

Management Insight
Peters and Waterman's Excellent Companies 87

Manager as a Person
Mittal Makes Millions Revitalizing Steel Industry 93

Management in Action

Summary and Review 97
Management in Action 99
Topics for Discussion and Action 99
Building Management Skills 99
Managing Ethically 99
Small Group Breakout Exercise 100
Exploring the World Wide Web 100
Be the Manager 100

Part One | Management

Chapter 3

Values, Attitudes, Emotions, and Culture: The Manager as a Person 102

A MANAGER'S CHALLENGE
Success and Failures at the Virgin Group 103

Topics

Overview 105

Enduring Characteristics: Personality Traits 105
- The Big Five Personality Traits 105
- Other Personality Traits That Affect Managerial Behavior 110

Values, Attitudes, and Moods and Emotions 111
- Values: Terminal and Instrumental 111
- Attitudes 114
- Moods and Emotions 116

Emotional Intelligence 118

Organizational Culture 119
- Managers and Organizational Culture 121
- The Role of Values and Norms in Organizational Culture 122
- Culture and Managerial Action 127

Part Two | The Environment of Management

Chapter 4

Ethics and Social Responsibility 132

A MANAGER'S CHALLENGE
Unethical Managers and the Perils of Peanut Butter 133

Topics

Overview 134

The Nature of Ethics 134
- Ethical Dilemmas 135
- Ethics and the Law 135
- Changes in Ethics over Time 136

Stakeholders and Ethics 136
- Stockholders 137
- Managers 137
- Ethics and Nonprofit Organizations 138
- Employees 139
- Suppliers and Distributors 139
- Customers 139
- Community, Society, and Nation 141
- Rules for Ethical Decision Making 143
- Why Should Managers Behave Ethically? 146

Ethics and Social Responsibility 148
- Societal Ethics 148
- Occupational Ethics 151
- Individual Ethics 151
- Organizational Ethics 152

Approaches to Social Responsibility 153
- Four Different Approaches 156
- Why Be Socially Responsible? 157
- The Role of Organizational Culture 158

Examples

Manager as a Person
Anita Roddick's Strong Social Conscience 109

Ethics in Action
Telling the Truth at Gentle Giant Moving 113

Manager as a Person
A Caring Culture at Ryla 124

Management in Action

Summary and Review 129

Management in Action 130
Topics for Discussion and Action 130
Building Management Skills 130
Managing Ethically 130
Small Group Breakout Exercise 131
Exploring the World Wide Web 131
Be the Manager 131

Examples

Ethics in Action
Whole Foods Market Practices What It Preaches 140

Ethics in Action
Digital Piracy, Ethics, and the Pirate Party of Sweden 145

Ethics in Action
Is It Right to Use Child Labor? 150

Ethics in Action
Jonathan Reckford Rebuilds Goodwill at Habitat for Humanity 154

Ethics in Action
Walmart and the Failure of Universal Ethics Standards 158

Management in Action

Summary and Review 159

Management in Action 160
Topics for Discussion and Action 160
Building Management Skills 160
Managing Ethically 160
Small Group Breakout Exercise 161
Exploring the World Wide Web 161
Be the Manager 161

Chapter 5 Managing Diverse Employees in a Multicultural Environment 162

A MANAGER'S CHALLENGE

Managing Diversity Effectively at Royal Dutch Shell 163

Topics

Overview 164

The Increasing Diversity of the Workforce and the Environment 165

Other Kinds of Diversity 168

Managers and the Effective Management of Diversity 169

Critical Managerial Roles 169

The Ethical Imperative to Manage Diversity Effectively 170

Effectively Managing Diversity Makes Good Business Sense 172

Perception 172

Factors That Influence Managerial Perception 173

Perception as a Determinant of Unfair Treatment 174

Overt Discrimination 177

How to Manage Diversity Effectively 178

Steps in Managing Diversity Effectively 178

Chapter 6 Managing in the Global Environment 186

A MANAGER'S CHALLENGE

A Turnaround at Sony Is in the Works 187

Topics

Overview 188

What Is the Global Environment? 189

The Task Environment 190

Suppliers 190

Distributors 193

Customers 194

Competitors 194

The General Environment 196

Economic Forces 197

Technological Forces 197

Sociocultural Forces 198

Demographic Forces 199

Political and Legal Forces 199

The Changing Global Environment 200

The Process of Globalization 202

Declining Barriers to Trade and Investment 204

Declining Barriers of Distance and Culture 205

Effects of Free Trade on Managers 206

The Role of National Culture 207

Cultural Values and Norms 207

Hofstede's Model of National Culture 208

National Culture and Global Management 210

Sexual Harassment 181
Forms of Sexual Harassment 181
Steps Managers Can Take to Eradicate Sexual Harassment 182

Examples

Focus on Diversity
Preventing Discrimination Based on Sexual Orientation 168
Ethics in Action
Disabled Employees Make Valuable Contributions 175

Management in Action

Summary and Review 183
Management in Action 184
Topics for Discussion and Action 184
Building Management Skills 184
Managing Ethically 184
Small Group Breakout Exercise 185
Exploring the World Wide Web 185
Be the Manager 185

Examples

Managing Globally
Why Nokia Makes Cell Phones in Romania 192
Managing Globally
Nestlé's Global Food Empire 201
Managing Globally
IKEA Is on Top of the Furniture World 202

Management in Action

Summary and Review 210
Management in Action 212
Topics for Discussion and Action 212
Building Management Skills 212
Managing Ethically 212
Small Group Breakout Exercise 213
Exploring the World Wide Web 213
Be the Manager 213

Chapter 7 Decision Making, Learning, Creativity, and Entrepreneurship 214

A MANAGER'S CHALLENGE

Decision Making in Response to Threats and Opportunities at PUMA 215

Topics

Overview 216

The Nature of Managerial Decision Making 217

- Programmed and Nonprogrammed Decision Making 217
- The Classical Model 220
- The Administrative Model 220

Steps in the Decision-Making Process 223

- Recognize the Need for a Decision 224
- Generate Alternatives 225
- Assess Alternatives 225
- Choose among Alternatives 226
- Implement the Chosen Alternative 226
- Learn from Feedback 227

Cognitive Biases and Decision Making 228

- Prior-Hypothesis Bias 228
- Representativeness Bias 229
- Illusion of Control 229
- Escalating Commitment 229
- Be Aware of Your Biases 229

Group Decision Making 230

- The Perils of Groupthink 230
- Devil's Advocacy and Dialectical Inquiry 231
- Diversity among Decision Makers 231

Chapter 8 The Manager as a Planner and Strategist 242

A MANAGER'S CHALLENGE

Japan Airlines and the Need for Planning 243

Topics

Overview 244

Planning and Strategy 245

The Nature of the Planning Process 245

- Why Planning Is Important 246
- Levels of Planning 247
- Levels and Types of Planning 247
- Time Horizons of Plans 249
- Standing Plans and Single-Use Plans 250
- Scenario Planning 250

Determining the Organization's Mission and Goals 251

- Defining the Business 251
- Establishing Major Goals 252

Formulating Strategy 253

- SWOT Analysis 253
- The Five Forces Model 254

Formulating Business-Level Strategies 257

- Low-Cost Strategy 257
- Differentiation Strategy 258

Organizational Learning and Creativity 232
Creating a Learning Organization 232
Promoting Individual Creativity 233
Promoting Group Creativity 234

Entrepreneurship and Creativity 235
Entrepreneurship and New Ventures 237
Intrapreneurship and Organizational Learning 237

Examples

Manager as a Person
Curbing Overconfidence 219

Management Insight
Decision Making in Japan 227

Ethics in Action
Microloans Give Entrepreneurs a Start 236

Management in Action

Summary and Review 238

Management in Action 240
Topics for Discussion and Action 240
Building Management Skills 240
Managing Ethically 240
Small Group Breakout Exercise 241
Exploring the World Wide Web 241
Be the Manager 241

"Stuck in the Middle" 258
Focused Low-Cost and Focused Differentiation Strategies 258

Formulating Corporate-Level Strategies 260
Concentration on a Single Industry 261
Vertical Integration 261
Diversification 263
International Expansion 265

Planning and Implementing Strategy 270

Examples

Management Insight
Carrefour: Changing What It Does 252

Manager as a Person
Douglas Conant Keeps Stirring Up Campbell Soup 255

Management Insight
Different Ways to Compete in the Soft Drink Business 259

Management Insight
How to Make Related Diversification Work 263

Managing Globally
How Samsung Became a Global Technology Leader 269

Management in Action

Summary and Review 270

Management in Action 272
Topics for Discussion and Action 272
Building Management Skills 272
Managing Ethically 272
Small Group Breakout Exercise 273
Exploring the World Wide Web 273
Be the Manager 273

Chapter 9 Value Chain Management: Functional Strategies for Competitive Advantage 274

A MANAGER'S CHALLENGE
Li & Fung's Success at Value Chain Management 275

Topics

Overview 276
Functional Strategies, the Value Chain, and Competitive Advantage 277
Functional Strategies and Value Chain Management 278
Improving Responsiveness to Customers 280
What Do Customers Want? 280
Managing the Value Chain to Increase Responsiveness to Customers 281
Customer Relationship Management 281
Improving Quality 284
Total Quality Management 284
Improving Efficiency 287
Facilities Layout, Flexible Manufacturing, and Efficiency 287
Just-in-Time Inventory and Efficiency 290
Self-Managed Work Teams and Efficiency 291
Process Reengineering and Efficiency 291
Information Systems, the Internet, and Efficiency 292
Improving Innovation 293
Two Kinds of Innovation 293
Strategies to Promote Innovation and Speed Product Development 294

Chapter 10 Managing Organizational Structure and Culture 302

A MANAGER'S CHALLENGE
Andrea Jung Reorganizes Avon's Global Structure 303

Topics

Overview 305
Designing Organizational Structure 305
The Organizational Environment 305
Strategy 306
Technology 307
Human Resources 307
Grouping Tasks into Jobs: Job Design 308
Job Enlargement and Job Enrichment 309
The Job Characteristics Model 310
Grouping Jobs into Functions and Divisions: Designing Organizational Structure 311
Functional Structure 311
Divisional Structures: Product, Market, and Geographic 312
Matrix and Product Team Designs 317

Examples

Management Insight
Tesco Adjusts to Economic Slowdown Through Its Value Chain 282

Manager as a Person
Paddy Hopkirk Improves Facilities Layout 288

Management Insight
Innovation and Product Development Are Google's Major Imperative 297

Management in Action

Summary and Review 298

Management in Action 300
Topics for Discussion and Action 300
Building Management Skills 300
Managing Ethically 300
Small Group Breakout Exercise 301
Exploring the World Wide Web 301
Be the Manager 301

Coordinating Functions and Divisions 320
- Allocating Authority 320
- Integrating and Coordinating Mechanisms 325

Organizational Culture 327
- Where Does Organizational Culture Come From? 329
- Strong, Adaptive Cultures versus Weak, Inert Cultures 331

Examples

Management Insight
Business Groups 317

Managing Globally
SK Telecom: Restructuring an Organization and Its Impact 323

Management Insight
Organizational Structure in a Large Family Business 325

Manager as a Person
Changes in Structure and Unintended Consequences 328

Management in Action

Summary and Review 333

Management in Action 334
Topics for Discussion and Action 334
Building Management Skills 334
Managing Ethically 335
Small Group Breakout Exercise 335
Exploring the World Wide Web 336
Be the Manager 336

Chapter 11 Organizational Control and Change 338

A MANAGER'S CHALLENGE

Control Systems and the Impact of Their Failure 339

Topics

Overview 341

What Is Organizational Control? 341

- The Importance of Organizational Control 341
- Control Systems and IT 342
- The Control Process 344

Output Control 347

- Financial Measures of Performance 347
- Organizational Goals 350
- Operating Budgets 350
- Problems with Output Control 351

Behavior Control 352

- Direct Supervision 352
- Management by Objectives 352
- Bureaucratic Control 355
- Problems with Bureaucratic Control 357

Clan Control 359

Organizational Change 360

- Lewin's Force-Field Theory of Change 361
- Evolutionary and Revolutionary Change 361
- Managing Change 362

Chapter 12 Human Resource Management 368

A MANAGER'S CHALLENGE

Happy Employees Provide Exceptional Service at Zappos 369

Topics

Overview 370

Strategic Human Resource Management 371

- Overview of the Components of HRM 372

Recruitment and Selection 374

- Human Resource Planning 374
- Job Analysis 375
- External and Internal Recruitment 376
- The Selection Process 378

Training and Development 381

- Types of Training 381
- Types of Development 383
- Transfer of Training and Development 383

Performance Appraisal and Feedback 384

- Types of Performance Appraisal 384
- Who Appraises Performance? 387
- Effective Performance Feedback 388

Pay and Benefits 389

- Pay Level 390
- Pay Structure 390
- Benefits 390

Labor Relations 392

- Unions 392
- Collective Bargaining 393

Examples

Management Insight
Making the Financial Figures Come Alive 349

Management Insight
Microsoft Has Problems Evaluating Its Employees 354

Ethics in Action
How Does Apple Enforce Its Rules for Product Secrecy against Its Rules for Employee Working Conditions? 358

Manager as a Person
Bayer and Innovation 364

Management in Action

Summary and Review 365

Management in Action 366
Topics for Discussion and Action 366
Building Management Skills 366
Managing Ethically 366
Small Group Breakout Exercise 367
Exploring the World Wide Web 367
Be the Manager 367

Examples

Managing Globally
Managing Human Resources at Semco 373

Focus on Diversity
Family-Friendly Benefits at Guerra DeBerry Coody 391

Management in Action

Summary and Review 393

Management in Action 395
Topics for Discussion and Action 395
Building Management Skills 395
Managing Ethically 395
Small Group Breakout Exercise 396
Exploring the World Wide Web 396
Be the Manager 396

Chapter 13 Motivation and Performance 398

A MANAGER'S CHALLENGE

Keeping Employees Motivated at Portugal Telecom 399

Topics

Overview 400
The Nature of Motivation 400
Expectancy Theory 402
Expectancy 403
Instrumentality 403
Valence 404
Bringing It All Together 404
Need Theories 406
Maslow's Hierarchy of Needs 406
Alderfer's ERG Theory 407
Herzberg's Motivator-Hygiene Theory 408
McClelland's Needs for Achievement, Affiliation, and Power 408
Other Needs 409
Equity Theory 409
Equity 409
Inequity 410
Ways to Restore Equity 410
Goal-Setting Theory 411

Chapter 14 Leadership 424

A MANAGER'S CHALLENGE

Judy McGrath Leads MTV Networks 425

Topics

Overview 426
The Nature of Leadership 427
Personal Leadership Style and Managerial Tasks 427
Leadership Styles across Cultures 429
Power: The Key to Leadership 430
Empowerment: An Ingredient in Modern Management 433
Trait and Behavior Models of Leadership 433
The Trait Model 433
The Behavior Model 434
Contingency Models of Leadership 436
Fiedler's Contingency Model 437
House's Path-Goal Theory 439
The Leader Substitutes Model 440
Bringing It All Together 440
Transformational Leadership 441
Being a Charismatic Leader 442
Stimulating Subordinates Intellectually 442
Engaging in Developmental Consideration 443
The Distinction between Transformational and Transactional Leadership 443
Gender and Leadership 443
Emotional Intelligence and Leadership 445

Learning Theories 413
Operant Conditioning Theory 413
Social Learning Theory 416
Pay and Motivation 417
Basing Merit Pay on Individual, Group, or Organizational Performance 418
Salary Increase or Bonus? 419
Examples of Merit Pay Plans 420

Examples

Management Insight
Motivating Employees at Nokia 405
Management Insight
EasyJet Rewards Employees Who Go the Extra Mile 418

Management in Action

Summary and Review 420
Management in Action 422
Topics for Discussion and Action 422
Building Management Skills 422
Managing Ethically 422
Small Group Breakout Exercise 423
Exploring the World Wide Web 423
Be the Manager 423

Examples

Ethics in Action
Servant Leadership at Zingerman's 428
Manager as a Person
Different Leadership Styles at Different Times 432
Ethics in Action
Nestlé and Leadership Training in the UK 435
Focus on Diversity
Admitting a Mistake Helps Small Business Leader 445

Management in Action

Summary and Review 446
Management in Action 448
Topics for Discussion and Action 448
Building Management Skills 448
Managing Ethically 448
Small Group Breakout Exercise 449
Exploring the World Wide Web 449
Be the Manager 449

Part Five | Leading Individuals and Groups

Chapter 15 Effective Groups and Teams 452

A MANAGER'S CHALLENGE

BMW and Innovation Teams 453

Topics

Overview 454

Groups, Teams, and Organizational Effectiveness 454
- Groups and Teams as Performance Enhancers 455
- Groups, Teams, and Responsiveness to Customers 456
- Teams and Innovation 456
- Groups and Teams as Motivators 457

Types of Groups and Teams 458
- The Top Management Team 458
- Research and Development Teams 458
- Command Groups 459
- Task Forces 459
- Self-Managed Work Teams 459
- Virtual Teams 461
- Friendship Groups 462
- Interest Groups 463

Group Dynamics 463
- Group Size, Tasks, and Roles 463
- Group Leadership 466
- Group Development over Time 466
- Group Norms 467
- Group Cohesiveness 469

Part Six | Managing Critical Organizational Processes

Chapter 16 Promoting Effective Communication 480

A MANAGER'S CHALLENGE

Singapore and Its Airline Thrive Using Strong Communication 481

Topics

Overview 482

Communication and Management 483
- The Importance of Good Communication 483
- The Communication Process 484
- The Role of Perception in Communication 486
- The Dangers of Ineffective Communication 486

Information Richness and Communication Media 487
- Face-to-Face Communication 487
- Spoken Communication Electronically Transmitted 490
- Personally Addressed Written Communication 490
- Impersonal Written Communication 493

Communication Networks 494
- Communication Networks in Groups and Teams 494
- Organizational Communication Networks 495
- External Networks 496

Managing Groups and Teams for High Performance 473
- Motivating Group Members to Achieve Organizational Goals 473
- Reducing Social Loafing in Groups 474
- Helping Groups to Manage Conflict Effectively 476

Examples

Information Technology Byte
Teams Innovate at Novartis 457

Management Insight
Self-Managed Teams at Louis Vuitton and Nucor Corporation 460

Management Insight
Singapore Airlines and Air Crew Team Building 470

Management in Action

Summary and Review 476

Management in Action 477
- Topics for Discussion and Action 477
- Building Management Skills 477
- Managing Ethically 477
- Small Group Breakout Exercise 478
- Exploring the World Wide Web 478
- Be the Manager 478

Information Technology and Communication 497
- The Internet 497
- Intranets 497
- Groupware and Collaboration Software 498

Communication Skills for Managers 501
- Communication Skills for Managers as Senders 501
- Communication Skills for Managers as Receivers 504

Examples

Managing Globally
Global Communication for Global Innovation 484

Management Insight
Know the Business Environment 488

Ethics in Action
Monitoring E-mail and Internet Use 492

Information Technology Byte
Collaborating with Wikis 500

Management in Action

Summary and Review 507

Management in Action 508
- Topics for Discussion and Action 508
- Building Management Skills 508
- Managing Ethically 508
- Small Group Breakout Exercise 509
- Exploring the World Wide Web 509
- Be the Manager 509

Chapter 17 Managing Conflict, Politics, and Negotiation 510

A MANAGER'S CHALLENGE

Bart Becht Effectively Manages Conflict at Reckitt Benckiser 511

Topics

Overview 512
Organizational Conflict 513
Types of Conflict 513
Sources of Conflict 515
Conflict Management Strategies 517
Negotiation 521
Distributive Negotiation and Integrative Bargaining 522
Strategies to Encourage Integrative Bargaining 522
Organizational Politics 523
The Importance of Organizational Politics 524
Political Strategies for Gaining and Maintaining Power 524
Political Strategies for Exercising Power 527

Chapter 18 Using Advanced Information Technology to Increase Performance 534

A MANAGER'S CHALLENGE

Technology Top Priority for Saudi Oil Firm 535

Topics

Overview 536
Information and the Manager's Job 537
Attributes of Useful Information 537
What Is Information Technology? 538
Information and Decisions 539
Information and Control 539
Information and Coordination 540
The IT Revolution 541
The Effects of Advancing IT 541
IT and the Product Life Cycle 542
The Network of Computing Power 545
Types of Management Information Systems 546
The Organizational Hierarchy: The Traditional Information System 547
Transaction-Processing Systems 547
Operations Information Systems 547
Decision Support Systems 548

NOTES 562
CREDITS 587
INDEX 588
NAMES 588
ORGANIZATIONS 598
GLOSSARY/SUBJECTS 601

Examples

Managing Globally
Ravi Kant Excels at Collaboration 517

Managing Globally
Xplane Integrates Operations in Spain 519

Management Insight
Nestlé of Switzerland and the Use of Palm Oil 522

Focus on Diversity
Indra Nooyi Builds Alliances 526

Ethics in Action
El Faro Benefits Multiple Stakeholders 529

Management in Action

Summary and Review 530
Management in Action 532
Topics for Discussion and Action 532
Building Management Skills 532
Managing Ethically 532
Small Group Breakout Exercise 533
Exploring the World Wide Web 533
Be the Manager 533

Artificial Intelligence and Expert Systems 550
Enterprise Resource Planning Systems 550
E-Commerce Systems 553

The Impact and Limitations of Information Technology 554
Strategic Alliances, B2B Network Structures, and IT 555
Flatter Structures and Horizontal Information Flows 556

Examples

Management Insight
Technology Helps Inditex Respond Fast 540

Information Technology Byte
eBay Uses IT to Develop New Ways to Sell Out-of-Fashion Clothing 544

Manager as a Person
How Judy Lewent Became One of the Most Powerful Women in Corporate America 548

Information Technology Byte
SAP's ERP System 551

Management Insight
The *Star Wars* Studio Reorganizes 557

Management in Action

Summary and Review 558
Management in Action 559
Topics for Discussion and Action 559
Building Management Skills 559
Managing Ethically 559
Small Group Breakout Exercise 560
Exploring the World Wide Web 560
Be the Manager 560

PREFACE

In the new seventh edition of our book, *Contemporary Management*, we continue our mission to provide students the most current and up-to-date account of the changes taking place in the world of business management. The fast-changing domestic and global environment continues to pressure organizations and their managers to find new and improved ways to respond in order to maintain and increase their performance. In particular, the recent global recession and financial meltdown have profoundly affected the management of both large and small companies as their managers have sought ways to increase their efficiency and effectiveness to survive in an increasingly competitive global environment.

In revising our book, we also continued our focus on making our text relevant and interesting to students–something that we know from instructor and student feedback engages them and encourages them to make the effort necessary to assimilate the text material. We continue to mirror the changes taking place in management practices by incorporating recent developments in management theory and research into our text and by providing vivid, current examples of how managers of companies large and small have responded to the changes taking place. Indeed, we have made the way managers and organizations have responded to recent economic events a focus of the new edition, and following the last edition many more examples of the opportunities and challenges facing founders, managers, and employees in small businesses are integrated into the text.

The number and complexity of the strategic, organizational, and human resource challenges facing managers and all employees have continued to increase throughout the 2000s. In most companies, managers at all levels are playing catch-up as they work toward meeting these challenges by implementing new and improved management techniques and practices. Today relatively small differences in performance between companies, such as in the speed at which they can bring new products or services to market or in how they motivate their employees to find ways to reduce costs or improve performance, can combine to give one company a significant competitive advantage over another. Managers and companies that use proven management techniques and practices in their decision making and actions increase their effectiveness over time. Companies and managers that are slower to implement new management techniques and practices find themselves at a growing competitive disadvantage that makes it even more difficult to catch up. Thus many industries have widening gaps between weaker competitors and the most successful companies, whose performance reaches new heights because their managers have made better decisions about how to use a company's resources in the most efficient and effective ways.

The challenges facing managers continue to mount as changes in the global environment, such as increasing global outsourcing and rising commodity prices, impact organizations large and small. For example, we extend our treatment of global outsourcing and examine the many managerial issues that must be addressed when millions of functional jobs in information technology, customer service, and manufacturing are sent to countries overseas. Similarly, increasing globalization means managers must respond to major differences in the legal rules and regulations and ethical values and norms that prevail in countries around the globe. Many companies and their managers, for example, have been accused of ignoring "sweatshop" working conditions under which the products they sell are manufactured abroad.

Moreover, the revolution in information technology (IT) has transformed how managers make decisions across all levels of a company's hierarchy and across all its functions and global divisions. This edition of our book continues to address these ongoing challenges as IT continues to evolve rapidly, especially in the area of mobile digital devices such as smartphones and tablet computers that can access ever more sophisticated software applications that increase their functionality. Other major challenges we continue to expand on in the new edition include the impact of the steadily increasing diversity of the workforce on companies and how this increasing diversity makes it imperative for managers to understand how and why people differ so they can effectively manage and reap the performance benefits of diversity. Similarly, across all functions and levels, managers and employees must continuously search out ways to "work smarter" and increase performance. Using new IT to improve all aspects of an organization's operations to boost efficiency and customer responsiveness is a vital part of this process. So too is the continuing need to innovate and improve the quality of goods and services, and the ways they are produced, to allow an organization to compete effectively. We have significantly revised the seventh edition of *Contemporary Management* to address these challenges to managers and their organizations.

Major Content Changes

Once again, encouraged by the increasing number of instructors and students who are using our book with each new edition, and based on the reactions and suggestions of both users and reviewers, we have revised and updated our book in the following ways. First, just as we have included pertinent new research concepts in each chapter, so too have we been careful to eliminate outdated or marginal management concepts. As usual, our goal has been to streamline our presentation and keep the focus on the changes that have been taking place that have the most impact on managers and organizations. Our goal is to avoid presenting students with excessive content in too many and too long chapters just for the sake of including outmoded management theory. In today's world of video downloads, sound bites, text messaging, and twitters, providing the best content is much more important than providing excessive content–especially when some of our students are burdened by time pressures stemming from the need to work long hours at paying jobs and personal commitments and obligations.

Second, we have added significant new management content, and have reinforced its importance by using many new relevant small and large company examples that are described in new chapter opening cases titled "A Manager's Challenge" and in the many boxed examples featuring managers and employees in companies both large and small in each chapter.

Chapter 1, for example, contains additional material on planning, with particular reference to how changing IT is affecting competition among companies; the chapter includes a new opening case about Steve Jobs and Apple, which is compared to Dell to highlight the four functions of management. It also contains an expanded discussion of outsourcing and its advantages and disadvantages and coverage of ethics and social responsibility. There is also new material about global crisis management.

Chapter 2 has updated coverage of changing manufacturing practices in the carmaking industry and of the way traditional management theories, such as Theory X and Theory Y, are being modified to suit changing conditions today.

Chapter 3 has additional material about the manager as a person and how personal characteristics of managers (and all members of an organization) influence organizational culture and effectiveness. New and updated material about, for example, changing work attitudes and job satisfaction, and recent research on moods and emotions and their implications highlights the contemporary landscape of management.

Public concern over the ethical behavior of managers has continued to increase as a result of the major problems caused by the mortgage crisis that started in 2007 and the resulting global financial crisis of 2008–2009. Chapter 4 contains updated material about the ethical issues that produced these crises and how regulators are trying to find new ways to manage and reduce the likelihood of such unethical behavior in the future. We have expanded our coverage of the many issues involved in acting and managing ethically throughout the book and especially in Chapter 4, which focuses on "Ethics and Social Responsibility." For example, we discuss new issues in ethics and ethical dilemmas, and provide more conceptual tools to help students understand better how to make ethical decisions. We have expanded coverage of issues relating to the high pay of CEOs, issues concerning regulations to protect consumer safety, and problems caused by bribery and corruption in companies around the world. Finally, we have expanded coverage of the ethics of nonprofits and their managers. Additionally, the ethical exercise at the end of every chapter continues to be a popular feature of our book.

Chapter 5, "Managing Diverse Employees in a Multicultural Environment," focuses on the effective management of the many faces of diversity in organizations for the good of all stakeholders. We have updated the text material and examples for such issues as the implication of disabilities in the workplace and how managers can take advantage of the increasing diversity of the population and workforce to reap the performance benefits that stem from diversity while ensuring that all employees are treated fairly and are not discriminated against. To address current issues in an era when many companies face discrimination lawsuits involving hundreds of millions of dollars, we discuss ways to effectively manage diversity.

Chapter 6 contains an integrated account of forces in the global environment. It has also been revised and updated to reflect the way increasing global competition and free trade have changed the global value creation process; the chapter uses competition in the global electronics industry to illustrate these issues. The chapter also has expanded discussion of issues related to global outsourcing. Finally, it has new treatment of the dynamics of global competition–particularly in relation to how companies have updated their strategies to customize products to the tastes of customers in countries around the world.

Chapter 7, "Decision Making, Learning, Creativity, and Entrepreneurship," discusses new developments in these important issues. For example, we have expanded our discussion of social entrepreneurs who seek creative ways to address social problems to improve well-being by, for example, reducing poverty, increasing literacy, and protecting the natural environment. More generally, we discuss how managers in organizations large and small can improve decision making, learning, and creativity in their organizations. For example, we discuss using contests and rewards to encourage creativity and examples of current companies that use them.

As in the last edition, Chapter 8 focuses on corporate-, global-, and business-level strategies, and Chapter 9 discusses functional strategies for managing value chain activities. These two chapters make clear the links between the different levels of strategy while maintaining a strong focus on managing operations and processes. Chapter 8 contains an updated discussion of planning and levels of strategy and a revised treatment of business-level strategy that focuses on the importance of low-cost strategies in a recession. It also contains more information about vertical integration and how companies can use forward vertical integration to raise long-term profitability. In Chapter 9 we continue to explore how companies can develop new functional-level strategies to improve efficiency, quality, innovation, and responsiveness to customers. For example, beyond increased coverage of TQM, including the Six Sigma approach, we include an expanded discussion of the importance of customer relationship management and the need to retain customers during hard economic times.

In Chapters 10 and 11 we offer new coverage of organizational structure and control and discuss how companies are confronting the need to reorganize their hierarchies and ways of doing business as the environment changes and competition increases. In Chapter 10, for example, we discuss how companies such as Avon have reorganized to improve their domestic performance–just as Nokia has reorganized its global operating structure to increase its global sales. There is increased emphasis on designing global organizational structure and the management issues surrounding it–including more coverage of organizational culture. In Chapter 11 we continue this theme by looking at how companies are changing their control systems to increase efficiency and quality, for example. The new opening case highlights the illegal trading practices that occurred at Société Générale and why the French bank lost control over its global quality standards; how to use control systems to increase quality is used as a theme throughout the chapter.

We have updated and expanded our treatment of the many ways in which managers can effectively manage and lead employees in their companies. For example, Chapter 12 includes a discussion of how treating employees well can lead to exceptional customer service, such as at Zappos, profiled in the opening case. The chapter also discusses best practices to recruit and attract outstanding employees, the importance of training and development, pay differentials, and family-friendly benefit programs. As another example, in light of the recent recession, Chapter 13 contains new coverage of how tough economic times can propel people to learn new skills and behaviors but also can lead to cuts in benefits and pay and thus limit managers' ability to provide merit pay and other performance inducements. This chapter also discusses prosocially motivated behavior and examples of people who are prosocially motivated to benefit others by a variety of factors, and more generally, discusses the many steps managers and organizations can take to create a highly motivated workforce.

Chapter 14 highlights the critical importance of effective leadership in organizations and factors that contribute to managers being effective leaders, including an updated discussion of servant leadership using the example of Zingerman's. The chapter also discusses how emotional intelligence may help leaders respond appropriately when they realize they have made a mistake, and has updated examples of how they can use reward and expert power to increase motivation and performance. Expanded and updated coverage of the effective management of teams, including virtual teams, is provided in Chapter 15. The chapter also has new coverage of the problems that arise because of a lack of leadership in teams, especially ethical issues. Chapter 16 includes updated coverage of effective communication and how, given the multitude of advances in IT, it is important to create opportunities for face-to-face communication. There is also a new discussion of social networking sites and why some managers attempt to limit employees' access to them while at work.

Chapter 17 includes an updated discussion of the vital task of effectively managing conflict and politics in organizations and how to negotiate effectively on a global level. There are many new examples of how managers can create a collaborative work context and avoid competition between individuals and groups, such as by building alliances as Indra Nooyi does at PepsiCo.

Finally, Chapter 18 has been substantially revised and updated to discuss the changing nature of companywide total computing solutions–including a new opening case that discusses the growing importance of a new drilling technology that allows Saudi Aramco to open up new sources of energy. There is also an expanded discussion of the nature of server computers and how they can be used to connect to mobile digital devices such as tablet computers and smartphones to enhance competitive advantage. The chapter also contains increased coverage of the ethical issues involved in the decision to outsource computer component and assembly operations to companies in China that do not follow the guidelines established by companies such as Apple.

We feel confident that the major changes we have made to the seventh edition of *Contemporary Management* reflect the changes that are occurring in management and the workplace; we also believe they offer an account of management that will stimulate and challenge students to think about their future as they look for opportunities in the world of organizations.

Unique Emphasis on Contemporary, Applied Management

In revising our book, we have kept at the forefront the fact that our users and reviewers are supportive of our attempts to integrate contemporary management theories and issues into the analysis of management and organizations. As in previous editions, our goal has been to distill new and classic theorizing and research into a contemporary framework that is compatible with the traditional focus on management as planning, leading, organizing, and controlling but that transcends this traditional approach.

Users and reviewers report that students appreciate and enjoy our presentation of management–a presentation that makes its relevance obvious even to those who lack exposure to a real-life management context. Students like the book's content and the way we relate management theory to real-life examples to drive home the message that management matters both because it determines how well organizations perform and because managers and organizations affect the lives of people inside and outside the organization, such as employees, customers, and shareholders.

Our contemporary approach has led us to discuss many concepts and issues that are not addressed in other management textbooks and is also illustrated by the way we organize and discuss these management issues. We have gone to great lengths to bring the manager back into the subject matter of management. That is, we have written our chapters from the perspective of current or future managers to illustrate, in a hands-on way, the problems and opportunities they face and how they can effectively meet them. For example, in Chapter 3 we provide an integrated treatment of personality, attitudes, emotions, and culture; in Chapter 4, a focus on ethics from a student's and a manager's perspective; and in Chapter 5, an in-depth treatment of effectively managing diversity and eradicating sexual harassment. In Chapters 8 and 9, our integrated treatment of strategy highlights the multitude of decisions managers must make as they perform their most important role–increasing organizational efficiency, effectiveness, and performance.

Our applied approach can also be clearly seen in the last three chapters of the book, which cover the topics of promoting effective communication; managing organizational conflict, politics, and negotiation; and using information technology in ways that increase organizational performance. These chapters provide a student-friendly, behavioral approach to understanding the management issues entailed in persuasive communication, negotiation, and implementation of advanced information systems to build competitive advantage.

Flexible Organization

Another factor of interest to instructors is how we have designed the grouping of chapters to allow instructors to teach the chapter material in the order that best suits their needs. For example, the more micro-oriented instructor can follow Chapters 1 through 5 with Chapters 12 through 16 and then use the more macro chapters. The more macro-oriented professor can follow Chapters 1 and 2 with Chapters 6 through 11, jump to 16 through 18, and then use the micro chapters, 3 through 5 and 12 through 15. Our sequencing of parts and chapters gives instructors considerable freedom to design the course that best suits their needs. Instructors are not tied to the planning, organizing, leading, and controlling framework, even though our presentation remains consistent with this approach.

ACKNOWLEDGMENTS

First, and foremost, we would like to thank Garry D. Bruton for his work on the Global Edition of *Contemporary Management*. Garry is professor of entrepreneurship at the Neeley School of Business at Texas Christian University where he holds the Fehmi Zeko Faculty Fellowship. He is one of the founders of the entrepreneurship program at TCU, which is ranked as one of the top 20 in the United States by *US News & World Report*. In 2005 Professor Bruton was the first holder of the Hall Chair in Entrepreneurship in Emerging Markets offered by the Fulbright Foundation. In addition to serving on the editorial board of several other academic journals, Garry is outgoing president of the Asia Academy of Management and editor of the *Academy of Management Perspectives*.

We are also grateful to Michael Ablassmeir, our executive editor, for his ongoing support and commitment to our project and for always finding ways to provide the resources that we need to continually improve and refine our book. Our thanks also go to Trina Hauger, our developmental editor, for so ably coordinating the book's progress; and to her and Anke Braun Weekes, our executive marketing manager, for giving us concise and timely feedback from professors and reviewers that has allowed us to shape the book to the needs of its intended market.

We also thank Cara Hawthorne and Joanne Mennemeier for executing an awe-inspiring design and Michelle Gardner for coordinating the production process. We are also grateful to the many colleagues and reviewers who gave us useful and detailed feedback, perceptive comments, and valuable suggestions for improving the manuscript.

Producing any competitive work is a challenge. Producing a truly market-driven textbook requires tremendous effort beyond simply obtaining reviews of a draft manuscript. Our goal was simple with the development of *Contemporary Management*: to be the most customer-driven principles of management text and supplement package ever published! With the goal of exceeding the expectations of both faculty and students, we executed one of the most aggressive product development plans ever undertaken in textbook publishing. Hundreds of faculty have taken part in developmental activities ranging from regional focus groups to manuscript and supplement reviews and surveys. Consequently, we're confident in assuring you and your students, our customers, that every aspect of our text and support package reflects your advice and needs. As you review it, we're confident that your reaction will be, "They listened!"

We extend our special thanks to the faculty who gave us detailed chapter-by-chapter feedback during the development of the seventh edition:

Jerry Alley, Aspen University

Charles W. Beem, Bucks County Community College

Jennifer P. Bott, Ball State University

Professor Murray Brunton, Central Ohio Technical College

Judith G. Bulin, PhD, Monroe Community College, Rochester, New York

Cheryl Cunningham, Embry-Riddle Aeronautical University–Daytona Beach

Tom Deckelman, Owens Community College

Max E. Douglas, Indiana State University

Richard Estrella, California Polytechnic University

Valerie Evans, Kansas State University

Andrea Foster, John Tyler Community College

Travis Lee Hayes, Chattanooga State Technical Community College

Samuel Hazen, Tarleton State University

Irene Joanette-Gallio, Western Nevada College

Dr. Carol Larson Jones, Professor, Cal Poly Pomona, California

Coy A. Jones, The University of Memphis

Dr. Jordan J. Kaplan, Long Island University School of Business

Renee N. King, MBA, Eastern Illinois University

Mike Knudstrup, Florida Southern College

Jim Long, Southwestern Oklahoma State University

Margaret Lucero, Texas A&M–Corpus Christi

Christy McLendon Corey, University of New Orleans

Chrisann Merriman, University of Mary Hardin–Baylor

Sandra Jeanquart Miles, DBA, SPHR, Professor, Murray State University

Carol T. Miller, Community College of Denver

Bahaudin G. Mujtaba, Nova Southeastern University

Catherine Nowicki, International Business College

John Overby, The University of Tennessee at Martin

Professor KE Overton, Houston Community College, Houston, Texas

Fernando A. Pargas, James Madison University

Marc Pendel, SPHR, Instructor, Miller College of Business, Ball State University

Susan A. Peterson, Professor of Business, Scottsdale Community College

Gregory J. Schultz, Carroll University

Marc Siegall, California State University–Chico

Randi L. Sims, Professor, Nova Southeastern University

Professor Gerald Smith, University of Northern Iowa

Marjorie Smith, Mountain State University

Dr. Susan D. Steiner, The University of Tampa

Cynthia L. Sutton, Metropolitan State College of Denver

And our thanks also go to the faculty who contributed greatly to the fourth, fifth, and sixth editions of *Contemporary Management*:

M. Ruhul Amin, Bloomsburg University of Pennsylvania

Gerald Baumgardner, Pennsylvania College of Technology

James D. Bell, Texas State University

Danielle R. Blesi, Hudson Valley Community College

Charley Braun, Marshall University

Barry Bunn, Valencia Community College

Gerald Calvasina, Southern Utah University

Bruce H. Charnov, Hofstra University

Jay Christensen-Szalanski, University of Iowa

Brad Cox, Midlands Technical College

Marian Cox Crawford, University of Arkansas–Little Rock

Teresa A. Daniel, Marshall University

Thomas W. Deckelman, Owens Community College

Richard S. DeFrank, University of Houston

Fred J. Dorn, University of Mississippi

D. Harold Doty, University of Southern Mississippi

Sandra Edwards, Northeastern State University

Scott Elston, Iowa State University

Kim Hester, Arkansas State University

Anne Kelly Hoel, University of Wisconsin–Stout

Robert C. Hoell, Georgia Southern University

Carol Larson Jones, Cal Poly Pomona, California

Gwendolyn Jones, University of Akron

Kathleen Jones, University of North Dakota

Joanne E. Kapp, Siena College

Nicholas Mathys, DePaul University

Daniel W. McAllister, University of Nevada–Las Vegas

Douglas L. Micklich, Illinois State University

Don C. Mosley Jr., University of South Alabama

Clive Muir, Stetson University

Karen Overton, Houston Community College

Gary Renz, Webster University

L. Jeff Seaton, University of Tennessee–Martin

Fred Slack, Indiana University of Pennsylvania

M. James Smas, Kent State University

Sabine Turnley, Kansas State University

Isaiah O. Ugboro, North Carolina A&T State University

Please note that these lists do not include the more than 160 faculty members who reviewed or contributed to earlier editions of the text.

Finally, we are grateful to two incredibly wonderful children, Nicholas and Julia, for being all that they are and for the joy they bring to all who know them.

Gareth R. Jones
Mays Business School
Texas A&M University

Jennifer M. George
Jesse H. Jones Graduate School of Business
Rice University

Rich and Relevant Examples

An important feature of our book is the way we use real-world examples and stories about managers and companies to drive home the applied lessons to students. Our reviewers praised the sheer range and depth of the rich, interesting examples we use to illustrate the chapter material and make it come alive. Moreover, unlike boxed material in other books, our boxes are seamlessly integrated into the text; they are an integral part of the learning experience and are not tacked on or isolated from the text itself. This is central to our pedagogical approach.

A Manager's Challenge opens each chapter, describing a chapter-related challenge and then discussing how managers in one or more organizations responded to that challenge. These vignettes help demonstrate the uncertainty and excitement surrounding the management process.

Our box features are not traditional boxes; that is, they are not disembodied from the chapter narrative. These thematic applications are fully integrated into the reading. Students will no longer be forced to decide whether or not to read boxed material. These features are interesting and engaging for students while bringing the chapter contents to life.

A MANAGER'S CHALLENGE

Success and Failures at the Virgin Group

Richard Branson is a British entrepreneur who heads the Virgin Group—a collection of over 350 different businesses. This group includes a wide range of businesses such as trains and planes, credit cards, flights in space, fitness clubs, and mega music stores. Today, he is one of the 250 richest people in the world.

Branson was, in part, motivated to focus on business since he was such a poor student. He has severe learning disabilities that hampered his success at school. But he discovered that he had a unique ability to work with, and connect to, people. His first venture, at the age 16, was to start a magazine called *Student*. The magazine was designed by students, for students and was intended to be a national magazine that connected students across Britain. Branson was unusually successful in getting many leading and interesting people to be interviewed and part of the magazine. However, his big commercial break came in 1970 when the British government abolished the Retail Price Maintenance Agreement which had limited the ability of stores to discount records. Branson saw an opportunity for his magazine to offer records cheaply by running ads for mail order delivery. Ultimately he was making more from selling records than from magazine subscriptions. Branson next opened a record store that would sell discount records directly rather than through the mail. In part, this decision was driven by the fear that a pending postal strike might hurt the mail order record business. The staff of the magazine was recruited to run the store. Branson's people skills came into play as he convinced the owner of the store to let him have the store rent free since there would be so much

Sir Richard Branson, shown here at a global symposium, is a highly successful entrepreneur. As head of the Virgin Group—a collection of more than 350 different businesses, Branson has made his mark by identifying opportunities, taking risks, and giving his employees autonomy and respect.

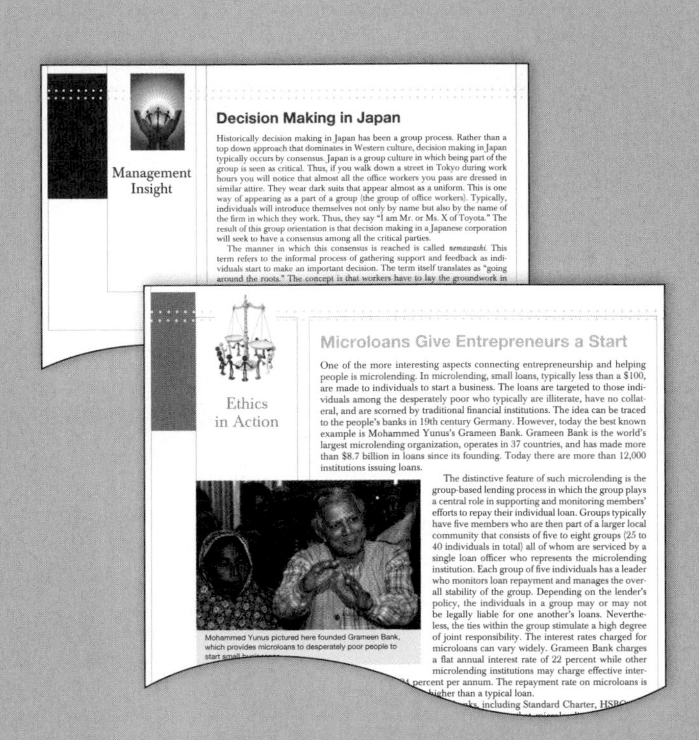

Management Insight

Decision Making in Japan

Historically decision making in Japan has been a group process. Rather than a top down approach that dominates in Western culture, decision making in Japan typically occurs by consensus. Japan is a group culture in which being part of the group is seen as critical. Thus, if you walk down a street in Tokyo during work hours you will notice that almost all the office workers you pass are dressed in similar attire. They wear dark suits that appear almost as a uniform. This is one way of appearing as a part of a group (the group of office workers). Typically, individuals will introduce themselves not only by name but also by the name of the firm in which they work. Thus, they say "I am Mr. or Ms. X of Toyota." The result of this group orientation is that decision making in a Japanese corporation will seek to have a consensus among all the critical parties.

The manner in which this consensus is reached is called *nemawashi*. This term refers to the informal process of gathering support and feedback as individuals start to make an important decision. The term itself translates as "going around the roots." The concept is that workers have to lay the groundwork in

Ethics in Action

Microloans Give Entrepreneurs a Start

One of the more interesting aspects connecting entrepreneurship and helping people is microlending. In microlending, small loans, typically less than a $100, are made to individuals to start a business. The loans are targeted to those individuals among the desperately poor who typically are illiterate, have no collateral, and are scorned by traditional financial institutions. The idea can be traced to the people's banks in 19th century Germany. However, today the best known example is Mohammed Yunus's Grameen Bank. Grameen Bank is the world's largest microlending organization, operates in 37 countries, and has made more than $8.7 billion in loans since its founding. Today there are more than 12,000 institutions issuing loans.

The distinctive feature of such microlending is the group-based lending process in which the group plays a central role in supporting and monitoring members' efforts to repay their individual loan. Groups typically have five members who are then part of a larger local community that consists of five to eight groups (25 to 40 individuals in total) all of whom are serviced by a single loan officer who represents the microlending institution. Each group of five individuals has a leader who monitors loan repayment and manages the overall stability of the group. Depending on the lender's policy, the individuals in a group may or may not be legally liable for one another's loans. Nevertheless, the ties within the group stimulate a high degree of joint responsibility. The interest rates charged for microloans can vary widely. Grameen Bank charges a flat annual interest rate of 22 percent while other microlending institutions may charge effective inter- … percent per annum. The repayment rate on microloans is … higher than a typical loan.

… including Standard Charter, HSBC …

Mohammed Yunus pictured here founded Grameen Bank, which provides microloans to desperately poor people to start small …

Additional in-depth examples appear in boxes throughout each chapter. **Management Insight** boxes illustrate the topics of the chapter, while the **Ethics in Action, Managing Globally, Focus on Diversity,** and **Information Technology Byte** boxes examine the chapter topics from each of these perspectives.

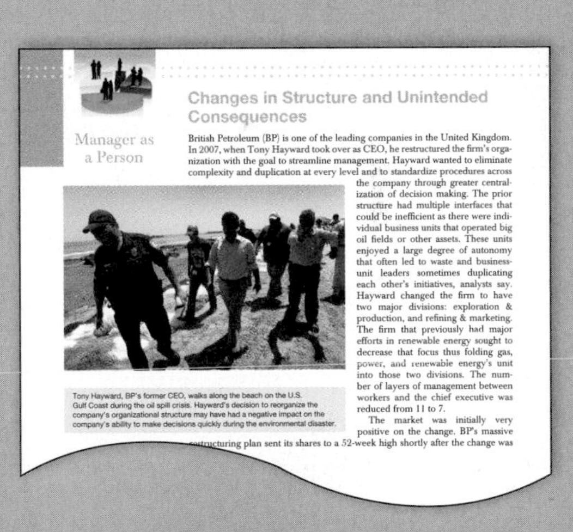

Manager as a Person

Changes in Structure and Unintended Consequences

British Petroleum (BP) is one of the leading companies in the United Kingdom. In 2007, when Tony Hayward took over as CEO, he restructured the firm's organization with the goal to streamline management. Hayward wanted to eliminate complexity and duplication at every level and to standardize procedures across the company through greater centralization of decision making. The prior structure had multiple interfaces that could be inefficient as there were individual business units that operated big oil fields or other assets. These units enjoyed a large degree of autonomy that often led to waste and business-unit leaders sometimes duplicating each other's initiatives, analysts say. Hayward changed the firm to have two major divisions: exploration & production, and refining & marketing. The firm that previously had major efforts in renewable energy sought to decrease that focus thus folding gas, power, and renewable energy's unit into those two divisions. The number of layers of management between workers and the chief executive was reduced from 11 to 7.

The market was initially very positive on the change. BP's massive restructuring plan sent its shares to a 52-week high shortly after the change was

Tony Hayward, BP's former CEO, walks along the beach on the U.S. Gulf Coast during the oil spill crisis. Hayward's decision to reorganize the company's organizational structure may have had a negative impact on the company's ability to make decisions quickly during the environmental disaster.

The **Manager as a Person** boxes focus on how real managers brought about change within their organizations. These examples allow us to reflect on how individual managers dealt with real-life, on-the-job challenges related to various chapter concepts.

Experiential Learning Features

We have given considerable time and effort to developing state-of-the-art experiential end-of-chapter learning exercises that drive home the meaning of management to students. These exercises are grouped together at the end of each chapter in a section called "Management in Action." The following activities are included at the end of every chapter:

- **Topics for Discussion and Action** are a set of chapter-related questions and points for reflection. Some ask students to research actual management issues and learn firsthand from practicing managers.
- **Building Management Skills** is a self-developed exercise that asks students to apply what they have learned from their own experience in organizations and from managers or from the experiences of others.
- **Managing Ethically** is an exercise that presents students with an ethical scenario or dilemma and asks them to think about the issue from an ethical perspective to better understand the issues facing practicing managers.
- **Small Group Breakout Exercise** is designed to allow instructors in large classes to use interactive experiential exercises.
- **Exploring the World Wide Web** requires students to actively search the Web to find the answers to a problem.
- **Be the Manager** presents a realistic scenario where a manager or organization faces some kind of challenge, problem, or opportunity. These exercises provide students with a hands-on way of solving "real" problems by applying what they've just learned in the chapter.

Assurance of Learning Ready

Many educational institutions today are focused on the notion of assurance of learning, an important element of some accreditation standards. *Contemporary Management, Seventh Edition,* is designed specifically to support your assurance of learning initiatives with a simple yet powerful solution.

Each test bank question for *Contemporary Management* maps to a specific chapter learning outcome/objective listed in the text. You can use our test bank software, EZ Test and EZ Test Online, or *Connect Management* to easily query for learning outcomes/objectives that directly relate to the learning objectives for your course. You can then use the reporting features of EZ Test to aggregate student results in similar fashion, making the collection and presentation of assurance of learning data simple and easy.

AACSB Statement

The McGraw-Hill Companies are a proud corporate member of AACSB International. To support the importance and value of AACSB accreditation, *Contemporary Management, Seventh Edition,* recognizes the curricula guidelines detailed in the AACSB standards for business accreditation by connecting selected questions in the text and/or the test bank to the six general knowledge and skill guidelines in the AACSB standards.

The statements contained in *Contemporary Management, Seventh Edition,* are provided only as a guide for the users of this textbook. The AACSB leaves content coverage and assessment within the purview of individual schools, the mission of the school, and the faculty. While *Contemporary Management* and the teaching package make no claim of any specific AACSB qualification or evaluation, we have within *Contemporary Management* labeled selected questions according to the six general knowledge and skill areas.

Integrated Learning System Great care was used in the creation of the supplementary material to accompany *Contemporary Management.* Whether you are a seasoned faculty member or a newly minted instructor, you'll find our support materials to be the most thorough and thoughtful ever created:

- **Instructor's Resource CD-ROM** The IRCD allows instructors to easily create their own custom presentations using the following resources: Instructor's Manual, Test Bank, EZ Test, and PowerPoint® presentations.
- **Instructor's Manual (IM)** The IM supporting this text has been completely updated to save instructors' time and support them in delivering the most effective course to their students. For each chapter, this manual provides a chapter overview and lecture outline with integrated PowerPoint® slides, lecture enhancers, notes for end-of-chapter materials, video cases and teaching notes, and more.
- **PowerPoint® Presentation** 40 slides per chapter feature reproductions of key tables and figures from the text as well as original content. Lecture-enhancing additions such as quick polling questions and company or video examples from outside the text can be used to generate discussion and illustrate management concepts.
- **Test Bank and EZ Test** The test bank has been thoroughly reviewed, revised, and improved. There are approximately 100 questions per chapter, including true/false, multiple-choice, and essay. Each question is tagged with learning objective, level of difficulty (corresponding to Bloom's taxonomy of educational objectives), AACSB standards, the correct answer, and page references. The new AACSB tags allow instructors to sort questions by the various standards and create reports to help give assurance that they are including recommended learning experiences in their curricula.

McGraw-Hill's flexible and easy-to-use electronic testing program **EZ Test** (found on the IRCD) allows instructors to create tests from book-specific items. It accommodates a wide range of question types, and instructors may add their own questions. Multiple versions of the test can be created, and any test can be exported for use with course management systems such as WebCT or BlackBoard. And now **EZ Test Online** (**www.eztestonline.com**) allows you to access the test bank virtually anywhere at any time, without installation, and it's even easier to use. Additionally, it allows you to administer EZ Test–created exams and quizzes online, providing instant feedback for students.

McGraw-Hill *Connect Management*

Less Managing. More Teaching. Greater Learning.

McGraw-Hill *Connect Management* is an online assignment and assessment solution that connects students with the tools and resources they'll need to achieve success.

McGraw-Hill *Connect Management* helps prepare students for their future by enabling faster learning, more efficient studying, and higher retention of knowledge.

McGraw-Hill *Connect Management* Features

Connect Management offers a number of powerful tools and features to make managing assignments easier, so faculty can spend more time teaching. With *Connect Management,* students can engage with their coursework anytime and anywhere, making the learning process more accessible and efficient. *Connect Management* offers you the features described below.

Online Interactive Applications

Online Interactive Applications are engaging tools that teach students to apply key concepts in practice. These Interactive Applications provide them with immersive, experiential learning opportunities. Students will engage in a variety of interactive scenarios to deepen critical knowledge of key course topics. They receive immediate feedback at intermediate steps throughout each exercise, as well as comprehensive feedback at the end of the assignment. All Interactive Applications are automatically scored and entered into the instructor gradebook.

Student Progress Tracking

Connect Management keeps instructors informed about how each student, section, and class is performing, allowing for more productive use of lecture and office hours. The progress-tracking function enables you to

- View scored work immediately and track individual or group performance with assignment and grade reports.
- Access an instant view of student or class performance relative to learning objectives.
- Collect data and generate reports required by many accreditation organizations, such as AACSB.

Smart Grading

When it comes to studying, time is precious. *Connect Management* helps students learn more efficiently by providing feedback and practice material when they need it, where they need it. When it comes to teaching, your time also is precious. The grading function enables you to

- Have assignments scored automatically, giving students immediate feedback on their work and side-by-side comparisons with correct answers.

- Access and review each response; manually change grades or leave comments for students to review.
- Reinforce classroom concepts with practice tests and instant quizzes.

Simple Assignment Management

With *Connect Management,* creating assignments is easier than ever, so you can spend more time teaching and less time managing. The assignment management function enables you to

- Create and deliver assignments easily with selectable end-of-chapter questions and test bank items.
- Streamline lesson planning, student progress reporting, and assignment grading to make classroom management more efficient than ever.
- Go paperless with the eBook and online submission and grading of student assignments.

Instructor Library

The *Connect Management* Instructor Library is your repository for additional resources to improve student engagement in and out of class. You can select and use any asset that enhances your lecture. The *Connect Management* Instructor Library includes

- Instructor Manual.
- PowerPoint® files.
- TestBank.
- Management Asset Gallery.
- eBook.

Student Study Center

The *Connect Management* Student Study Center is the place for students to access additional resources. The Student Study Center

- Offers students quick access to lectures, practice materials, eBooks, and more.
- Provides instant practice material and study questions, easily accessible on the go.
- Give students access to self-assessments, video materials, Manager's Hot Seat, and more.

Lecture Capture via Tegrity Campus

Increase the attention paid to lecture discussion by decreasing the attention paid to note taking. For an additional charge, Lecture Capture offers new ways for students to focus on the in-class discussion, knowing they can revisit important topics later.

McGraw-Hill *Connect Plus Management*

McGraw-Hill reinvents the textbook learning experience for the modern student with *Connect Plus Management.* A seamless integration of an eBook and

Management, Connect Plus Management provides all of the *Connect Management* features plus the following:

- An integrated eBook, allowing for anytime, anywhere access to the textbook.
- Dynamic links between the problems or questions you assign to your students and the location in the eBook where that problem or question is covered.
- A powerful search function to pinpoint and connect key concepts in a snap.

In short, *Connect Management* offers you and your students powerful tools and features that optimize your time and energies, enabling you to focus on course content, teaching, and student learning. *Connect Management* also offers a wealth of content resources for both instructors and students. This state-of-the-art, thoroughly tested system supports you in preparing students for the world that awaits.

For more information about *Connect,* go to **www.mcgrawhillconnect.com**, or contact your local McGraw-Hill sales representative.

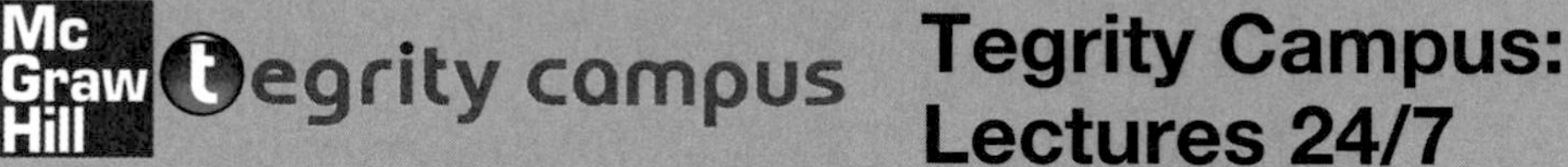

Tegrity Campus: Lectures 24/7

Tegrity Campus is a service that makes class time available 24/7 by automatically capturing every lecture in a searchable format for students to review when they study and complete assignments. With a simple one-click start-and-stop process, you capture all computer screens and corresponding audio. Students can replay any part of any class with easy-to-use browser-based viewing on a PC or Mac.

Educators know that the more students can see, hear, and experience class resources, the better they learn. In fact, studies prove it. With Tegrity Campus, students quickly recall key moments by using Tegrity Campus's unique search feature. This search helps students efficiently find what they need, when they need it, across an entire semester of class recordings. Help turn all your students' study time into learning moments immediately supported by your lecture.

Lecture Capture enables you to

- Record and distribute your lecture with a click of button.
- Record and index PowerPoint® presentations and anything shown on your computer so it is easily searchable, frame by frame.
- Offer access to lectures anytime and anywhere by computer, iPod, or mobile device.
- Increase intent listening and class participation by easing students' concerns about note taking. Lecture Capture will make it more likely you will see students' faces, not the tops of their heads.

To learn more about Tegrity, watch a two-minute Flash demo at **http://tegritycampus.mhhe.com.**

McGraw-Hill Customer Care Contact Information

At McGraw-Hill, we understand that getting the most from new technology can be challenging. That's why our services don't stop after you purchase our products. You can e-mail our product specialists 24 hours a day to get product training online. Or you can search our knowledge bank of Frequently Asked Questions on our support Web site. For customer support, call **800-331-5094,** e-mail **hmsupport@mcgraw-hill.com**, or visit **www.mhhe.com**/support. One of our technical support analysts will be able to assist you in a timely fashion.

SUPPORT MATERIALS

McGraw-Hill's Expanded Management Asset Gallery!

McGraw-Hill/Irwin Management is excited to now provide a one-stop shop for our wealth of assets, making it quick and easy for instructors to locate specific materials to enhance their courses.

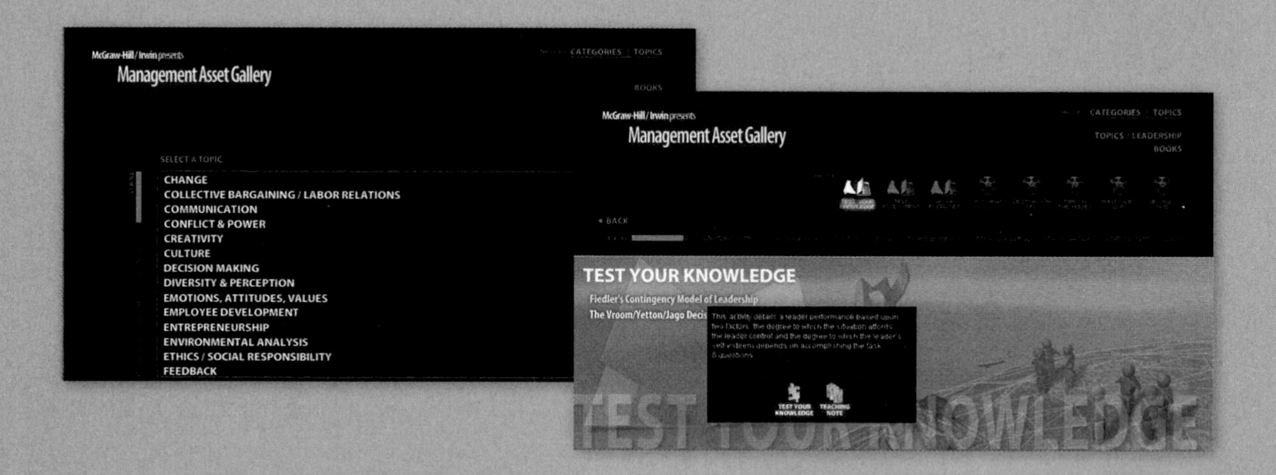

All of the following can be accessed within the Management Asset Gallery:

Manager's Hot Seat

This interactive, video-based application puts students in the manager's hot seat, builds critical thinking and decision-making skills, and allows students to apply concepts to real managerial challenges. Students watch as 15 real managers apply their years of experience when confronting unscripted issues such as bullying in the workplace, cyber loafing, globalization, intergenerational work conflicts, workplace violence, and leadership versus management.

Self-Assessment Gallery Unique among publisher-provided self-assessments, our 23 self-assessments give students background information to ensure that they understand the purpose of the assessment. Students test their values, beliefs, skills, and interests in a wide variety of areas, allowing them to personally apply chapter content to their own lives and careers.

Every self-assessment is supported with PowerPoints® and an instructor manual in the Management Asset Gallery, making it easy for the instructor to create an engaging classroom discussion surrounding the assessments.

Test Your Knowledge To help reinforce students' understanding of key management concepts, Test Your Knowledge activities give students a review of the conceptual materials followed by application-based questions to work through. Students can choose practice mode, which gives them detailed feedback after each question, or test mode, which provides feedback after the entire test has been completed. Every Test Your Knowledge activity is supported by instructor notes in the Management Asset Gallery to make it easy for the instructor to create engaging classroom discussions surrounding that materials that students have completed.

Management History Timeline This Web application allows instructors to present and students to learn the history of management in an engaging and interactive way. Management history is presented along an intuitive timeline that can be traveled through sequentially or by selected decade. With the click of a mouse, students learn the important dates, see the people who influenced the field, and understand the general management theories that have molded and shaped management as we know it today.

Video Library DVDs McGraw-Hill/Irwin offers the most comprehensive video support for the Principles of Management classroom through course library video DVDs. This discipline has library volume DVDs tailored to integrate and visually reinforce chapter concepts. The library volume DVDs contain more than 70 clips! The rich video material, organized by topic, comes from sources such as *BusinessWeek* TV, PBS, NBC, BBC, SHRM, and McGraw-Hill. Video cases and video guides are provided for some clips.

Destination CEO Videos

BusinessWeek produced video clips featuring CEOs on a variety of topics. Accompanying each clip are multiple-choice questions and discussion questions to use in the classroom or assign as a quiz.

Online Learning Center (OLC)

www.mhhe.com/jonesgeorge7e

Find a variety of online teaching and learning tools that are designed to reinforce and build on the text content. Students will have direct access to the learning tools while instructor materials are password protected.

Create Craft your teaching resources to match the way you teach! With McGraw-Hill Create, **www.mcgrawhillcreate.com**, you can easily rearrange chapters, combine material from other content sources, and quickly upload content you have written, like your course syllabus or teaching notes. Find the content you need in Create by searching through thousands of leading McGraw-Hill textbooks. Arrange your appearance by selecting the cover and adding your name, school, and course information. Order a Create book and you'll receive a complimentary print review copy in three to five business days or a complimentary electronic review copy (eComp) via e-mail in about one hour. Go to **www.mcgrawhillcreate.com** today and register. Experience how McGraw-Hill Create empowers you to teach *your* students *your* way.

AUTHORS

Gareth Jones is a Professor of Management in the Lowry Mays College and Graduate School of Business at Texas A&M University. He received his BA in Economics/Psychology and his PhD in Management from the University of Lancaster, U.K. He previously held teaching and research appointments at the University of Warwick, Michigan State University, and the University of Illinois at Urbana–Champaign. He is a frequent visitor and speaker at universities in both the United Kingdom and the United States.

He specializes in strategic management and organizational theory and is well known for his research that applies transaction cost analysis to explain many forms of strategic and organizational behavior. He is currently interested in strategy process, competitive advantage, and information technology issues. He is also investigating the relationships between ethics, trust, and organizational culture and studying the role of affect in the strategic decision-making process.

He has published many articles in leading journals of the field, and his recent work has appeared in the *Academy of Management Review,* the *Journal of International Business Studies,* and *Human Relations.* An article about the role of information technology in many aspects of organizational functioning was published in the *Journal of Management.* One of his articles won the *Academy of Management Journal's* Best Paper Award, and he is one of the most prolific authors in the *Academy of Management Review.* He is, or has served, on the editorial boards of the *Academy of Management Review,* the *Journal of Management,* and *Management Inquiry.*

Gareth Jones has used his academic knowledge to craft leading textbooks in management and three other major areas in the management discipline: organizational behavior, organizational theory, and strategic management. His books are widely recognized for their innovative, contemporary content and for the clarity with which they communicate complex, real-world issues to students.

Jennifer George is the Mary Gibbs Jones Professor of Management and Professor of Psychology in the Jesse H. Jones Graduate School of Business at Rice University. She received her BA in Psychology/Sociology from Wesleyan University, her MBA in Finance from New York University, and her PhD in Management and Organizational Behavior from New York University. Prior to joining the faculty at Rice University, she was a professor in the Department of Management at Texas A&M University.

Professor George specializes in organizational behavior and is well known for her research on mood and emotion in the workplace, their determinants, and their effects on various individual and group-level work outcomes. She is the author of many articles in leading peer-reviewed journals such as the *Academy of Management Journal,* the *Academy of Management Review,* the *Journal of Applied Psychology, Organizational Behavior and Human Decision Processes, Journal of Personality and Social Psychology,* and *Psychological Bulletin.* One of her papers won the Academy of Management's Organizational Behavior Division Outstanding Competitive Paper Award, and another paper won the Human Relations Best Paper Award. She is, or has been, on the editorial review boards of the *Journal of Applied Psychology, Academy of Management Journal, Academy of Management Review, Administrative Science Quarterly, Journal of Management, Organizational Behavior and Human Decision Processes, Organization Science, International Journal of Selection and Assessment,* and *Journal of Managerial Issues;* was a consulting editor for the *Journal of Organizational Behavior;* and was a member of the SIOP *Organizational Frontiers Series* editorial board. She is a fellow in the American Psychological Association, the American Psychological Society, and the Society for Industrial and Organizational Psychology and a member of the Society for Organizational Behavior. Professor George recently completed a six-year term as an associate editor for the *Journal of Applied Psychology.* She also has coauthored a widely used textbook titled *Understanding and Managing Organizational Behavior.*

Contemporary Management

CHAPTER 1

Managers and Managing

Learning Objectives

After studying this chapter, you should be able to:

LO1-1 Describe what management is, why management is important, what managers do, and how managers utilize organizational resources efficiently and effectively to achieve organizational goals.

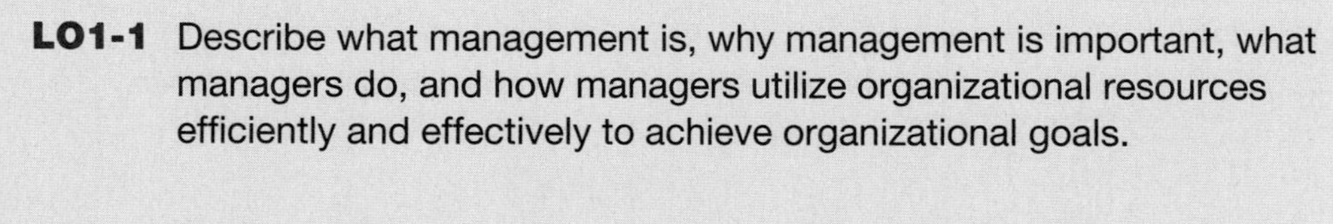

LO1-2 Distinguish among planning, organizing, leading, and controlling (the four principal managerial tasks), and explain how managers' ability to handle each one affects organizational performance.

LO1-3 Differentiate among three levels of management, and understand the tasks and responsibilities of managers at different levels in the organizational hierarchy.

LO1-4 Distinguish between three kinds of managerial skill, and explain why managers are divided into different departments to perform their tasks more efficiently and effectively.

LO1-5 Discuss some major changes in management practices today that have occurred as a result of globalization and the use of advanced information technology (IT).

LO1-6 Discuss the principal challenges managers face in today's increasingly competitive global environment.

A MANAGER'S CHALLENGE

Steve Jobs Has Changed His Approach to Management

What is high-performance management? In 1976 Steven P. Jobs sold his Volkswagen van, and his partner Steven Wozniak sold his two programmable calculators, and they used the proceeds of $1,350 to build a circuit board in Jobs's garage. So popular was the circuit board, which developed into the Apple II personal computer (PC), that in 1977 Jobs and Wozniak founded Apple Computer to make and sell it. By 1985 Apple's worldwide sales had exploded to almost $2 billion, but in the same year Jobs was forced out of the company he founded. Jobs's approach to management was a big part of the reason he lost control of Apple.

After he left Apple, Jobs started new ventures. First he founded PC maker NEXT to develop a powerful new PC that would outperform Apple's PCs. Then he founded Pixar, a computer animation company, which became a huge success after it made blockbuster movies such as *Toy Story* and *Finding Nemo,* both distributed by Walt Disney.

In both these companies Jobs developed a clear vision for managers to follow, and he built strong management teams to lead the project teams developing the new PCs and movies. Jobs saw his main task as planning the companies' future product development

Apple's CEO Steve Jobs proudly shows off his company's new iPad tablet computer in March 2010. More than 1 million iPads were sold within a month.

strategies. However, he left the actual tasks of leading and organizing to managers below him. He gave them the autonomy to put his vision into practice. In both companies he encouraged a culture of collaboration and innovation to champion creative thinking.

In 1996 Jobs convinced Apple to buy NEXT for $400 million and use its powerful operating system in new Apple PCs. Jobs began working inside Apple to lead its turnaround and was so successful that in 1997 he was asked to become its CEO. Jobs agreed and continued to put the new management skills he had developed over time to good use.

The first thing he did was create a clear vision and goals to energize and motivate Apple employees. Jobs decided that to survive, Apple had to introduce state-of-the-art, stylish PCs and related digital equipment. He instituted an across-the-board planning process and created a team structure that allowed programmers and engineers to pool their skills to develop new PCs. He delegated considerable authority to the teams, but he also established strict timetables and challenging "stretch" goals, such as bringing new products to market as quickly as possible, for these groups. One result of these efforts was Apple's sleek new line of iMac PCs, which were quickly followed by a wide range of futuristic PC-related products.[1]

In 2003 Jobs announced that Apple was starting a new service called iTunes, an online music store from which people could download songs for 99 cents. At the same time Apple introduced its iPod music player, which can store thousands of downloaded songs, and it quickly became a runaway success. Apple continually introduced new generations of the iPod, each more compact, powerful, and versatile than previous models. By 2006 Apple had gained control of 70% of the digital music player market and 80% of the online music download business, and its stock price soared to a new record level.

The next milestone in Jobs's managerial history came in 2007 when he announced that Apple would introduce the iPhone to compete directly with the popular BlackBerry. Once again he assembled a team of engineers not only to develop the new phone but to create an online iPhone applications platform where users would be able to download iPhone applications to make their phones more useful—able to surf the Web and interact with their friends. By 2010 over 2 million iPhone applications had been developed, over 2 billion applications had been downloaded by iPhone users, and Apple was the leader in the smartphone market.

In 2010 Jobs announced that Apple planned to introduce its new iPad tablet computer, which he claimed would be the best way to experience the Web, e-mail, and photos and would also have a wireless reading function to compete directly against Amazon.com's successful Kindle wireless reader.[2] Jobs organized a new engineering unit to pioneer the development of applications for its new iPad, and in spring 2010 analysts and customers were eagerly awaiting its innovative new digital tablet that could potentially revolutionize yet another industry and make Apple the most profitable company in global computers and electronics. When Apple announced on March 5 that the iPad would be released for sale on April 13, 2010, its stock rose to a record high of $219, and analysts claimed the company's stock might become worth more than Walmart's!

Overview

The history of Steve Jobs's ups and downs as founder and manager of Apple and his other companies illustrates many challenges facing people who become managers: Managing a company is a complex activity, and effective managers must possess many kinds of skills, knowledge, and abilities. Management is an unpredictable process. Making the right decision is difficult; even effective managers often make mistakes, but the most effective managers, like Jobs, learn from their mistakes and continually strive to find ways to increase their companies' performance.

In this chapter we look at what managers do and what skills and abilities they must develop to manage their organizations successfully. We also identify the different kinds of managers that organizations need and the skills and abilities they must develop to succeed. Finally, we identify some challenges managers must address if their organizations are to grow and prosper.

What Is Management?

When you think of a manager, what kind of person comes to mind? Do you see someone who, like Steve Jobs, can determine the future prosperity of a large for-profit company? Or do you see the administrator of a not-for-profit organization, such as a community college, library, or charity, or the person in charge of your local Walmart store or McDonald's restaurant, or the person you answer to if you have a part-time job? What do all these people have in common? First, they all work in organizations. **Organizations** are collections of people who work together and coordinate their actions to achieve a wide variety of goals, or desired future outcomes.[3] Second, as managers, they are the people responsible for supervising and making the most of an organization's human and other resources to achieve its goals.

organizations Collections of people who work together and coordinate their actions to achieve a wide variety of goals or desired future outcomes.

management The planning, organizing, leading, and controlling of human and other resources to achieve organizational goals efficiently and effectively.

Management, then, is the planning, organizing, leading, and controlling of human and other resources to achieve organizational goals efficiently and effectively. An organization's *resources* include assets such as people and their skills, know-how, and experience; machinery; raw materials; computers and information technology; and patents, financial capital, and loyal customers and employees.

Achieving High Performance: A Manager's Goal

LO1-1 Describe what management is, why management is important, what managers do, and how managers utilize organizational resources efficiently and effectively to achieve organizational goals.

One of the most important goals that organizations and their members try to achieve is to provide some kind of good or service that customers value or desire. The principal goal of CEO Steve Jobs is to manage Apple so it creates a continuous stream of new and improved goods and services–such as more powerful PCs, more versatile iPods and iPhones, and the ability to easily download diverse kinds of digital content from the Internet–that customers are willing to buy. In 2010 Apple led the field in many of these areas; its managers are currently working to make its new iPad the industry leader. Similarly, the principal goal of doctors, nurses, and hospital administrators is to increase their hospital's ability to make sick people well–and to do so cost-effectively. Likewise, the principal goal of each McDonald's restaurant manager is to produce burgers, salads, fries, and shakes that people want to pay for and eat so they become loyal return customers.

organizational performance A measure of how efficiently and effectively a manager uses resources to satisfy customers and achieve organizational goals.

Organizational performance is a measure of how efficiently and effectively managers use available resources to satisfy customers and achieve organizational goals. Organizational performance increases in direct proportion to increases in efficiency and effectiveness (see Figure 1.1). What are efficiency and effectiveness?

efficiency A measure of how well or how productively resources are used to achieve a goal.

Efficiency is a measure of how productively resources are used to achieve a goal.[4] Organizations are efficient when managers minimize the amount of input resources (such as labor, raw materials, and component parts) or the amount of time needed to produce a given output of goods or services. For example, McDonald's develops ever

Figure 1.1
Efficiency, Effectiveness, and Performance in an Organization

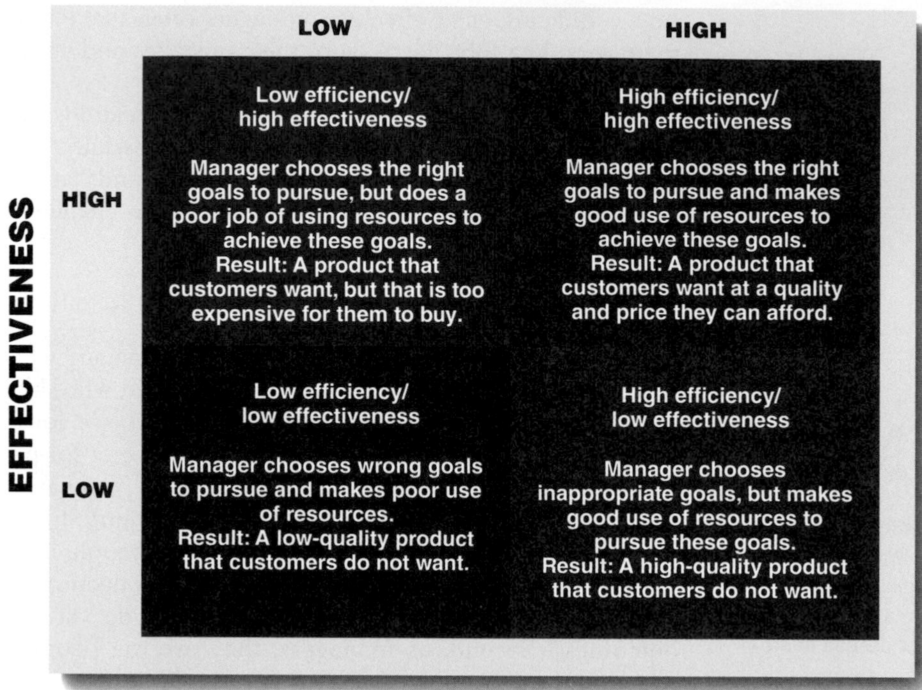

High-performing organizations are efficient *and* effective.

more efficient fat fryers that not only reduce the amount of oil used in cooking, but also speed up the cooking of french fries. Similarly Hanjin, a Korean company and one of the 10 largest shipping and logistics operations in the world, adopted changes to reduce delivery times. With Hanjin's focus on efficiency, new centralized technology systems provide more accurate monitoring of shipments. Steve Jobs instructed Apple's engineers not only to develop ever more compact, powerful, and multipurpose models of its iPod and iPhone but also to find cost-effective ways to do so, such as by outsourcing manufacturing to China. A manager's responsibility is to ensure that an organization and its members perform as efficiently as possible all the activities needed to provide goods and services to customers.

effectiveness A measure of the appropriateness of the goals an organization is pursuing and the degree to which the organization achieves those goals.

Effectiveness is a measure of the *appropriateness* of the goals that managers have selected for the organization to pursue and the degree to which the organization achieves those goals. Organizations are effective when managers choose appropriate goals and then achieve them. Some years ago, for example, managers at McDonald's decided on the goal of providing breakfast service to attract more customers. The choice of this goal has proved smart: Sales of breakfast food now account for more than 30% of McDonald's revenues and are still increasing. Jobs's goal is to create a continuous flow of innovative PC and digital entertainment products. High-performing organizations, such as Apple, McDonald's, Carrefour, Intel, Accenture, and Habitat for Humanity are simultaneously efficient and effective. Effective managers are those who choose the right organizational goals to pursue and have the skills to utilize resources efficiently.

Why Study Management?

Today more students are competing for places in business courses than ever before; the number of people wishing to pursue Master of Business Administration (MBA) degrees–today's passport to an advanced management position–either on campus or from online universities and colleges is at an all-time high. Why is the study of management currently so popular?[5]

First, in any society or culture resources are valuable and scarce; so the more efficient and effective use that organizations can make of those resources, the greater the relative well-being and prosperity of people in that society. Because managers decide how to use many of a society's most valuable resources–its skilled employees, raw materials like oil and land, computers and information systems, and financial assets–they directly impact the well-being of a society and the people in it. Understanding what managers do and how they do it is of central importance to understanding how a society creates wealth and affluence for its citizens.

Second, although most people are not managers, and many may never intend to become managers, almost all of us encounter managers because most people have jobs and bosses. Moreover, many people today work in groups and teams and have to deal with coworkers. Studying management helps people deal with their bosses and their coworkers. It reveals how to understand other people at work and make decisions and take actions that win the attention and support of the boss and coworkers. Management teaches people not yet in positions of authority how to lead coworkers, solve conflicts between them, achieve team goals, and thus increase performance.

Third, in any society, people are in competition for a very important resource–a job that pays well and provides an interesting and satisfying career; and understanding management is one important path toward obtaining this objective. In general, jobs become more interesting the more complex or responsible they are. Any person who desires a motivating job that changes over time might therefore do well to develop management skills and become promotable. A person who has been working for several years and then returns to school for an MBA can usually, after earning the degree, find a more interesting, satisfying job that pays significantly more than the previous job. Moreover, salaries increase rapidly as people move up the organizational hierarchy, whether it is a school system, a large for-profit business organization, or a not-for-profit charitable or medical institution.

Essential Managerial Tasks

The job of management is to help an organization make the best use of its resources to achieve its goals. How do managers accomplish this objective? They do so by performing four essential managerial tasks: *planning, organizing, leading,* and *controlling.* The arrows linking these tasks in Figure 1.2 suggest the sequence in which managers typically perform them. French manager Henri Fayol first outlined the nature of these managerial activities around the turn of the 20th century in *General and Industrial Management,* a book that remains the classic statement of what managers must do to create a high-performing organization.[6]

Managers at all levels and in all departments–whether in small or large companies, for-profit or not-for-profit organizations, or organizations that operate in one country or throughout the world–are responsible for performing these four tasks, which we look at next. How well managers perform these tasks determines how efficient and effective their organizations are.

Planning

planning Identifying and selecting appropriate goals; one of the four principal tasks of management.

To perform the **planning** task, managers identify and select appropriate organizational goals and courses of action; they develop *strategies* for how to achieve high performance. The three steps involved in planning are (1) deciding which goals the organization will pursue, (2) deciding what strategies to adopt to attain those goals, and (3) deciding how to allocate organizational resources to pursue the strategies that attain those goals. How well managers plan and develop strategies determines how effective and efficient the organization is–its performance level.[7]

Figure 1.2
Four Tasks of Management

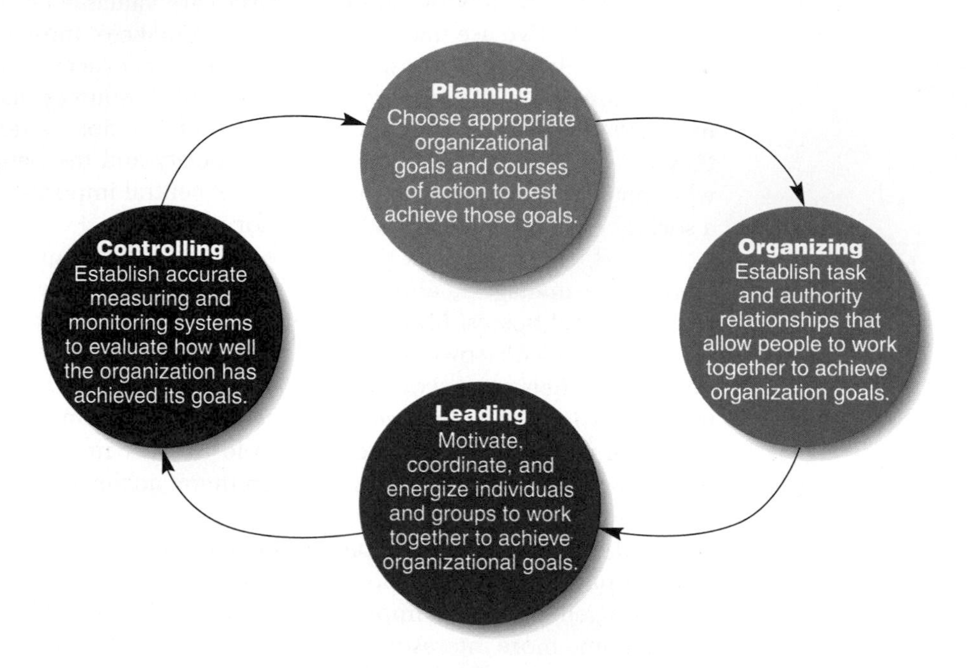

LO1-2 Distinguish among planning, organizing, leading, and controlling (the four principal managerial tasks), and explain how managers' ability to handle each one affects organizational performance.

As an example of planning in action, consider the situation confronting Michael Dell, founder and CEO of Dell Computer, who by 2010 was in a major contest with Steve Jobs to retain leadership in the PC and digital device market. In 1984 the 19-year-old Dell saw an opportunity to enter the PC market by assembling PCs and selling them directly to customers. Dell began to plan how to put his idea into practice. First, he decided that his goal was to sell an inexpensive PC, to undercut the prices charged by companies like Apple, Compaq, and HP. Second, he had to choose a course of action to achieve this goal. He decided to sell PCs directly to customers by telephone and so bypass expensive computer stores that sold Compaq and Apple PCs. He also had to decide how to obtain low-cost components and how to tell potential customers about his products. Third, he had to decide how to allocate his limited funds (he had only $5,000) to buy labor and other resources. He hired three people and worked with them around a table to assemble his PCs.

Michael Dell sits in the dorm room at the University of Texas–Austin, where he launched his personal computer company as a college freshman. When he visited, the room was occupied by freshmen Russell Smith (left) and Jacob Frith, both from Plano, Texas.

Thus to achieve his goal of making and selling low-price PCs, Dell had to plan, and as his organization grew, his plans changed and became progressively more complex. After setbacks during the 2000s that saw HP, Apple, and a new Taiwanese company, Acer, achieve competitive advantage over Dell in performance, styling, or pricing, Dell and his managers actively searched for new strategies to better compete against agile rivals and help the company regain its position as the highest-performing PC maker. In 2010 Dell was still locked in a major battle with its competitors, and its performance had not recovered despite attempts to introduce innovative new models of laptops and digital devices such as its own music player (which flopped). Dell needed a new approach to planning to compete more effectively; and new strategies Dell announced in 2010 included more powerful, customized lines of new laptops, and a plan to introduce its own smartphone and tablet computer.

strategy A cluster of decisions about what goals to pursue, what actions to take, and how to use resources to achieve goals.

As the battle between Dell, HP, Acer, and Apple suggests, the outcome of planning is a **strategy,** a cluster of decisions concerning what organizational goals to pursue, what actions to take, and how to use resources to achieve these goals. The decisions that were the outcome of Michael Dell's original planning formed a *low-cost strategy*. A low-cost strategy is a way of obtaining customers by making decisions that allow an organization to produce goods or services more cheaply than its competitors so it can charge lower prices than they do. Throughout its history, Dell has continuously refined this strategy and explored new ways to reduce costs; Dell became the most profitable PC maker as a result of its low-cost strategy, but when HP and Acer also lowered their costs it lost its competitive advantage and its profits fell. By contrast, since its founding Apple's strategy has been to deliver to customers new, exciting, and unique computer and digital products, such as its iPods, iPhones, and its new iPads–a strategy known as *differentiation*.[8] Although this strategy almost ruined Apple in the 1990s when customers bought inexpensive Dell PCs rather its premium-priced PCs, today Apple's sales have boomed as customers turn to its unique PCs and digital products. To fight back, Dell has been forced to offer more exciting, stylish products–hence its decision to introduce a new smartphone to compete with the iPhone.

Planning strategy is complex and difficult, especially because planning is done under uncertainty when the result is unknown so that success or failure are both possible outcomes of the planning process. Managers take major risks when they commit organizational resources to pursue a particular strategy. Dell enjoyed great success in the past with its low-cost strategy; but presently Apple is performing spectacularly with its differentiation strategy, and HP has enjoyed a major turnaround because by lowering its costs it now can offer customers attractive, stylish PCs at prices similar to Dell's. In Chapter 8 we focus on the planning process and on the strategies organizations can select to respond to opportunities or threats in an industry. The story of Anne Mulcahy's rise to the top at Xerox and her decision to give control of the company to its new CEO, Ursula Burns, illustrates how important the abilities to plan and create the right strategies are to a manager's career success.

Manager as a Person

Ursula Burns "Copies" Anne Mulcahy as CEO of Xerox

By the early 2000s Xerox, the well-known copier company, was near bankruptcy. The combination of aggressive Japanese competitors, which were selling low-priced copiers, and a shift toward digital copying, which made Xerox's pioneering light-lens copying process obsolete, was resulting in plummeting sales. Losing billions of dollars, Xerox's board searched for a new CEO who could revitalize the company's product line. The person they chose to plan the company's transformation was Anne Mulcahy, a 26-year Xerox veteran. Mulcahy began her career as a Xerox copier salesperson, transferred into human resource management, and then used her considerable leadership skills to work her way up the company's hierarchy to become its president.

As the new CEO, the biggest management challenge Mulcahy faced was deciding how to reduce Xerox's high operating costs. At the same time, however, she had to plan the best strategies for Xerox. Specifically, she had to decide how to best invest the company's remaining research dollars to innovate desperately needed new kinds of digital copiers that would attract customers back to the company and generate new revenues and profits. Simultaneously achieving both these objectives is one of the biggest challenges a manager can face, and how well she performed these tasks would determine Xerox's fate–indeed its survival.

Former Xerox CEO Anne Mulcahy with her handpicked successor, Ursula Burns, who became the first female African-American manager to take charge of a major U.S. corporation.

To find a solution to this problem, Mulcahy, known as an unassuming CEO who prefers to stay in the background, focused her efforts on involving and listening to Xerox's managers, employees, and customers. Mulcahy began a series of "town hall" meetings with Xerox employees, asked them for all kinds of creative input and their best efforts, but told them that tough times were ahead and that layoffs would be necessary. At the same time she emphasized that only their hard work to find ways to reduce costs could save the company. To help discover how the company should best invest its R&D budget, Mulcahy made reaching out to customers her other main priority. She insisted that managers and engineers at all levels should visit, meet, and talk to customers to uncover what they most wanted from new digital copiers–and from Xerox. During one of her initiatives, called "Focus 500," which required Xerox's top 200 managers to visit its top 500 customers, she came to increasingly appreciate the skills of Ursula Burns, who had joined Xerox four years after her and was quickly establishing her own reputation as a manager. Burns, who had started her career as a mechanical engineer, was then the manager in charge of its manufacturing and supply chain activities.

By listening closely to both employees and customers, Mulcahy and Xerox's managers and engineers gained insights that led to the development of new strategies that transformed the company's product line. Mulcahy's strategy was to spend most of the R&D budget on developing two new kinds of digital copiers: a line of digital color copying machines for use by medium-sized and large businesses and a line of low-end copiers offering print quality, speed, and prices that even Japanese competitors could not match. To shrink costs Mulcahy also reduced the number of levels in Xerox's management hierarchy, cutting 26% from corporate overhead, and streamlined its operating units, reducing the number of employees from 95,000 to 55,000. By 2007 it was clear that Mulcahy and her managers–in particular Ursula Burns, who was now Mulcahy's second in command–had devised a successful turnaround plan to save Xerox.

Continuing to work closely with customers, Mulcahy and Burns developed new strategies for Xerox based on improved products and services. In talking to Xerox customers, for example, it became clear they wanted a combination of copying software and hardware that would allow them to create highly customized documents for their own customers. Banks, retail stores, and small businesses needed personalized software to create individual client statements, for example. Mulcahy decided to grow the customized services side of Xerox's business to meet these specialized needs. She also decided to replicate Xerox's sales and customer service operations around the globe and customize them to the needs of customers in each country. The result was soaring profits.

In 2009 Mulcahy decided she would leave the position of CEO to become Xerox's chairperson, and her hand-picked successor Ursula Burns would become its next CEO. The move to transfer power from one woman CEO to another at the same company is exceptional, and Burns is also the first African-American woman to head a U.S.-based public company as large as Xerox. Ursula Burns became Xerox's CEO in July 2009, and within six months she announced a new major planning initiative. Xerox would acquire Affiliated Computer Services for $6.4 billion so Xerox could increase its push to provide highly customized customer service. Burns said the acquisition would be a major game changer because it would triple Xerox's service revenue to over $10 billion and increase total company revenues to $22 billion. Also, $400 million in cost savings were expected. Xerox's shares have climbed 40% since Burns took over as CEO, and she is busily looking for further strategies to increase Xerox's growth. Indeed, Mulcahy decided that with Burns at the helm, Xerox's future looks bright, and she decided to retire in May 2010, at which time Burns will also become its chairman.

Organizing

organizing Structuring working relationships in a way that allows organizational members to work together to achieve organizational goals; one of the four principal tasks of management.

organizational structure A formal system of task and reporting relationships that coordinates and motivates organizational members so they work together to achieve organizational goals.

Organizing is structuring working relationships so organizational members interact and cooperate to achieve organizational goals. Organizing people into departments according to the kinds of job-specific tasks they perform lays out the lines of authority and responsibility between different individuals and groups. Managers must decide how best to organize resources, particularly human resources.

The outcome of organizing is the creation of an **organizational structure,** a formal system of task and reporting relationships that coordinates and motivates members so they work together to achieve organizational goals. Organizational structure determines how an organization's resources can be best used to create goods and services. As his company grew, for example, Michael Dell faced the issue of how to structure his organization. Early on he was hiring 100 new employees a week and deciding how to design his managerial hierarchy to best motivate and coordinate managers' activities. As his organization grew to become one of the largest global PC makers, he and his managers created progressively more complex forms of organizational structure to help it achieve its goals. We examine the organizing process in detail in Chapters 10 through 12.

Leading

leading Articulating a clear vision and energizing and enabling organizational members so they understand the part they play in achieving organizational goals; one of the four principal tasks of management.

An organization's *vision* is a short, succinct, and inspiring statement of what the organization intends to become and the goals it is seeking to achieve–its desired future state. In **leading,** managers articulate a clear organizational vision for the organization's members to accomplish, and they energize and enable employees so everyone understands the part he or she plays in achieving organizational goals. Leadership involves managers using their power, personality, influence, persuasion, and communication skills to coordinate people and groups so their activities and efforts are in harmony. Leadership revolves around encouraging all employees to perform at a high level to help the organization achieve its vision and goals. Another outcome of leadership is a highly motivated and committed workforce. Employees responded well to Michael Dell's hands-on leadership style, which has resulted in a hardworking, committed workforce. Managers at Apple now

Takanobu Ito became Honda Motor Co. Ltd.'s new president and CEO effective June 2009. Ito's degree is in engineering from the Kyoto University, and he joined Honda in 1978 as a chassis design engineer. Ito was instrumental in bringing the revolutionary hybrid automobile into reality. Honda is the dominant player in the world in hybrid automobiles that combine electric and gas powered cars. In particular, he led the development of ground-breaking aluminum unibody construction. His leadership at the firm is seen as continuing the firm's focus on research and development of technologies that improve fuel efficiency and high environmental standards.

appreciate Steve Jobs's new leadership style, which is based on his willingness to delegate authority to project teams and his ability to help managers resolve differences that could easily lead to bitter disputes and power struggles. We discuss the issues involved in managing and leading individuals and groups in Chapters 13 through 16.

Controlling

controlling Evaluating how well an organization is achieving its goals and taking action to maintain or improve performance; one of the four principal tasks of management.

In **controlling,** the task of managers is to evaluate how well an organization has achieved its goals and to take any corrective actions needed to maintain or improve performance. For example, managers monitor the performance of individuals, departments, and the organization as a whole to see whether they are meeting desired performance standards. Michael Dell learned early in his career how important this is; it took Steve Jobs longer. If standards are not being met, managers seek ways to improve performance.

The outcome of the control process is the ability to measure performance accurately and regulate organizational efficiency and effectiveness. To exercise control, managers must decide which goals to measure–perhaps goals pertaining to productivity, quality, or responsiveness to customers–and then they must design control systems that will provide the information necessary to assess performance–that is, determine to what degree the goals have been met. The controlling task also helps managers evaluate how well they themselves are performing the other three tasks of management–planning, organizing, and leading–and take corrective action.

Michael Dell had difficulty establishing effective control systems because his company was growing so rapidly and he lacked experienced managers. In the 1990s Dell's costs suddenly soared because no systems were in place to control inventory, and in 1994 poor quality control resulted in a defective line of new laptop computers–some of which caught fire. To solve these and other control problems, Dell hired hundreds of experienced managers from other companies to put the right control systems in place. As a result, by 2000 Dell was able to make computers for over 10% less than its competitors, which created a major source of competitive advantage. At its peak, Dell drove competitors out of the market because it had achieved a 20% cost advantage over them.[9] However, we noted earlier that through the 2000s rivals such as HP and Acer also learned how to reduce their operating costs, and this shattered Dell's competitive advantage. Controlling, like the other managerial tasks, is an ongoing, dynamic, always-changing process that demands constant attention and action. We cover the most important aspects of the control task in Chapters 10, 11, 17, and 18.

The four managerial tasks–planning, organizing, leading, and controlling–are essential parts of a manager's job. At all levels in the managerial hierarchy, and across all jobs and departments in an organization, effective management means performing these four activities successfully–in ways that increase efficiency and effectiveness.

Performing Managerial Tasks: Mintzberg's Typology

Our discussion of managerial tasks may seem to suggest that a manager's job is highly orchestrated and that management is an orderly process in which managers rationally calculate the best way to use resources to achieve organizational goals. In reality, being a manager often involves acting emotionally and relying on gut feelings. Quick, immediate reactions to situations, rather than deliberate thought and reflection, are an important aspect of managerial action.[10] Often managers are overloaded with responsibilities and do not have time to analyze every nuance of a situation; they therefore make decisions in uncertain conditions not knowing which outcomes will be best.[11] Moreover, top managers face constantly changing situations, and a decision that seems right today may prove to be wrong tomorrow. The range of problems that managers face is enormous; managers usually must handle many problems simultaneously; and they often must make snap decisions using the intuition and experience gained through their careers to perform their jobs to the best of their abilities.[12] Henry Mintzberg, by following managers and observing what they actually *do*–hour by hour and day by day–identified 10 kinds of specific roles, or sets of job responsibilities, that capture the dynamic nature of managerial work.[13] He grouped these roles according to whether the responsibility was primarily decisional, interpersonal, or informational; they are described in Table 1.1.

Given the many complex, difficult job responsibilities managers have, it is no small wonder that many claim they are performing their jobs well if they are right just half of the time.[14] And it is understandable that many experienced managers accept failure by their subordinates as a normal part of the learning experience and a rite of passage to becoming an effective manager. Managers and their subordinates learn from both their successes and their failures.

Levels and Skills of Managers

To perform the four managerial tasks efficiently and effectively, organizations group or differentiate their managers in two main ways–by level in hierarchy and by type of skill. First, they differentiate managers according to their level or rank in the organization's hierarchy of authority. The three levels of managers are first-line managers, middle managers, and top managers–arranged in a hierarchy. Typically first-line managers report to middle managers, and middle managers report to top managers.

Second, organizations group managers into different departments (or functions) according to their specific job-related skills, expertise, and experiences, such as a manager's engineering skills, marketing expertise, or sales experience. A **department,** such as the manufacturing, accounting, engineering, or sales department, is a group of managers and employees who work together because they possess similar skills and experience or use the same kind of knowledge, tools, or techniques to perform their jobs. Within each department are all three levels of management. Next we examine why organizations use a hierarchy of managers and group them, by the jobs they perform, into departments.

department A group of people who work together and possess similar skills or use the same knowledge, tools, or techniques to perform their jobs.

LO1-3 Differentiate among three levels of management, and understand the tasks and responsibilities of managers at different levels in the organizational hierarchy.

Levels of Management

Organizations normally have three levels of management: first-line managers, middle managers, and top managers (see Figure 1.3). Managers at each level have different but related responsibilities for using organizational resources to increase efficiency and effectiveness.

At the base of the managerial hierarchy are **first-line managers,** often called *supervisors*. They are responsible for daily supervision of the nonmanagerial employees who perform the specific activities necessary to produce goods and services. First-line managers work in all departments or functions of an organization.

first-line manager A manager who is responsible for the daily supervision of nonmanagerial employees.

Examples of first-line managers include the supervisor of a work team in the manufacturing department of a car plant, the head nurse in the obstetrics department of a hospital, and the chief mechanic overseeing a crew of mechanics in the service function of a new car dealership. At Dell, first-line managers include the supervisors responsible for controlling the quality of its computers or the level of customer service provided by telephone salespeople. When Michael Dell started his company, he personally controlled the computer assembly process and thus acted as a first-line manager or supervisor.

middle manager A manager who supervises first-line managers and is responsible for finding the best way to use resources to achieve organizational goals.

Supervising the first-line managers are **middle managers,** responsible for finding the best way to organize human and other resources to achieve organizational goals. To increase efficiency, middle managers find ways to help first-line managers and nonmanagerial employees better use resources to reduce manufacturing costs or improve customer service. To increase effectiveness, middle

Table 1.1
Managerial Roles Identified by Mintzberg

Type of Role	Specific Role	Examples of Role Activities
Decisional	Entrepreneur	Commit organizational resources to develop innovative goods and services; decide to expand internationally to obtain new customers for the organization's products.
	Disturbance handler	Move quickly to take corrective action to deal with unexpected problems facing the organization from the external environment, such as a crisis like an oil spill, or from the internal environment, such as producing faulty goods or services.
	Resource allocator	Allocate organizational resources among different tasks and departments of the organization; set budgets and salaries of middle and first-level managers.
	Negotiator	Work with suppliers, distributors, and labor unions to reach agreements about the quality and price of input, technical, and human resources; work with other organizations to establish agreements to pool resources to work on joint projects.
Interpersonal	Figurehead	Outline future organizational goals to employees at company meetings; open a new corporate headquarters building; state the organization's ethical guidelines and the principles of behavior employees are to follow in their dealings with customers and suppliers.
	Leader	Provide an example for employees to follow; give direct commands and orders to subordinates; make decisions concerning the use of human and technical resources; mobilize employee support for specific organizational goals.
	Liaison	Coordinate the work of managers in different departments; establish alliances between different organizations to share resources to produce new goods and services.
Informational	Monitor	Evaluate the performance of managers in different tasks and take corrective action to improve their performance; watch for changes occurring in the external and internal environments that may affect the organization in the future.
	Disseminator	Inform employees about changes taking place in the external and internal environments that will affect them and the organization; communicate to employees the organization's vision and purpose.
	Spokesperson	Launch a national advertising campaign to promote new goods and services; give a speech to inform the local community about the organization's future intentions.

Figure 1.3
Levels of Managers

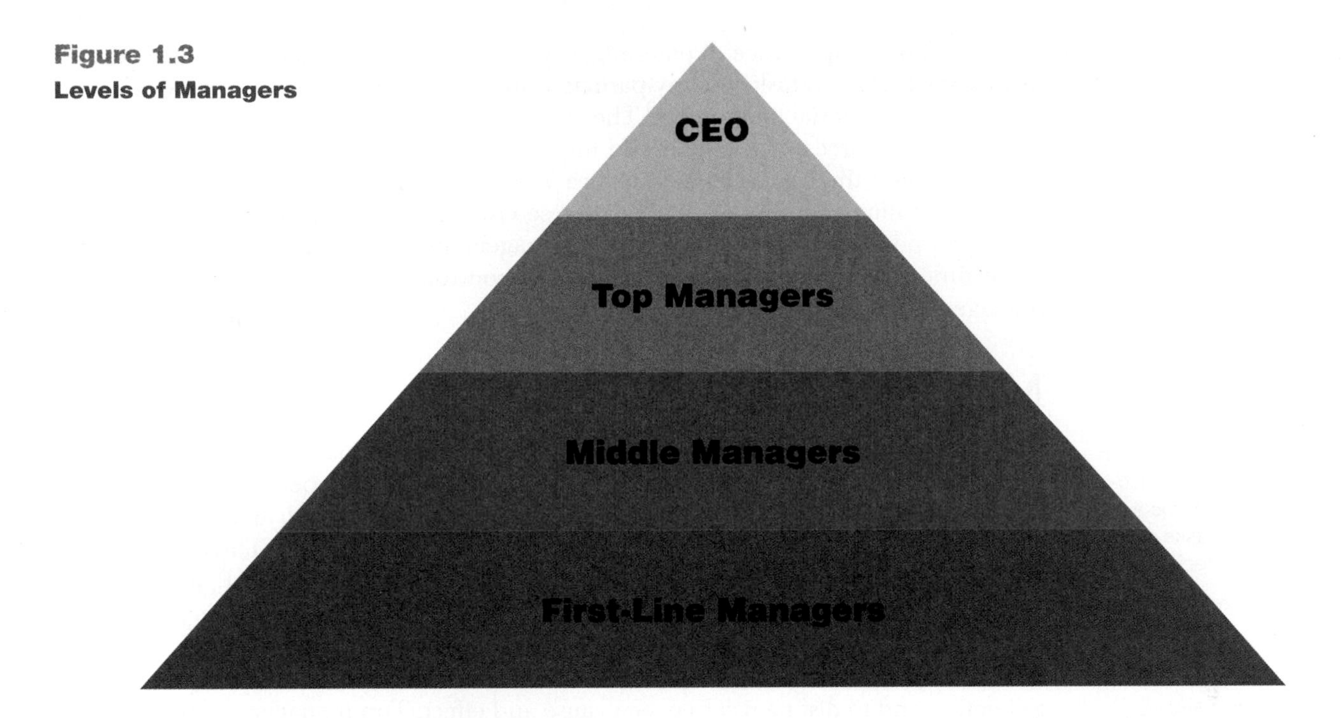

managers evaluate whether the organization's goals are appropriate and suggest to top managers how goals should be changed. Often the suggestions that middle managers make to top managers can dramatically increase organizational performance. A major part of the middle manager's job is developing and fine-tuning skills and know-how, such as manufacturing or marketing expertise, that allow the organization to be efficient and effective. Middle managers make thousands of specific decisions about the production of goods and services: Which first-line supervisors should be chosen for this particular project? Where can we find the highest-quality resources? How should employees be organized to allow them to make the best use of resources?

Behind a first-class sales force, look for the middle managers responsible for training, motivating, and rewarding the salespeople. Behind a committed staff of high school teachers, look for the principal who energizes them to find ways to obtain the resources they need to do outstanding and innovative jobs in the classroom.

top manager A manager who establishes organizational goals, decides how departments should interact, and monitors the performance of middle managers.

In contrast to middle managers, **top managers** are responsible for the performance of *all* departments.[15] They have *cross-departmental responsibility*. Top managers establish organizational goals, such as which goods and services the company should produce; they decide how the different departments should interact; and they monitor how well middle managers in each department use resources to achieve goals.[16] Top managers are ultimately responsible for the success or failure of an organization, and their performance (like that of Michael Dell or Ursula Burns) is continually scrutinized by people inside and outside the organization, such as other employees and investors.[17]

top management team A group composed of the CEO, the COO, the president, and the heads of the most important departments.

The *chief executive officer (CEO)* is a company's most senior and important manager, the one all other top managers report to. Today the term *chief operating officer (COO)* often refers to the top manager who is being groomed to take over as CEO when the current CEO, such as Anne Mulcahy of Xerox, becomes the chair of the board, retires, or leaves the company. Together the CEO and COO are responsible for developing good working relationships among the top managers of various departments (manufacturing and marketing, for example); usually these top managers have the title "vice president." A central concern of the CEO is the creation of a smoothly functioning **top management team,** a group composed of the CEO, the COO, and the vice presidents most responsible for achieving organizational goals.[18]

The relative importance of planning, organizing, leading, and controlling–the four principal managerial tasks–to any particular manager depends on the manager's position in the managerial hierarchy.[19] The amount of time managers spend planning and organizing resources to maintain and improve organizational performance increases as they ascend the hierarchy (see Figure 1.4).[20] Top managers devote most of their time to planning and organizing, the tasks so crucial to determining an organization's long-term performance. The lower that managers' positions are in the hierarchy, the more time the managers spend leading and controlling first-line managers or nonmanagerial employees.

LO1-4 Distinguish between three kinds of managerial skill, and explain why managers are divided into different departments to perform their tasks more efficiently and effectively.

Managerial Skills

Both education and experience enable managers to recognize and develop the personal skills they need to put organizational resources to their best use. Michael Dell realized from the start that he lacked sufficient experience and technical expertise in marketing, finance, and planning to guide his company alone. Thus he recruited experienced managers from other IT companies, such as IBM and HP, to help build his company. Research has shown that education and experience help managers acquire and develop three types of skills: *conceptual, human,* and *technical.*[21]

conceptual skills The ability to analyze and diagnose a situation and to distinguish between cause and effect.

Conceptual skills are demonstrated in the general ability to analyze and diagnose a situation and to distinguish between cause and effect. Top managers require the best conceptual skills because their primary responsibilities are planning and organizing.[22] By all accounts, Steve Jobs was chosen as CEO to transform Apple, and Anne Mulcahy was chosen to revive Xerox, because of their ability to identify new opportunities and mobilize managers and other resources to take advantage of those opportunities.

Formal education and training are important in helping managers develop conceptual skills. Business training at the undergraduate and graduate (MBA) levels provides many of the conceptual tools (theories and techniques in marketing, finance, and other areas) that managers need to perform their roles effectively. The study of management helps develop the skills that allow managers to understand the big picture

Figure 1.4

Relative Amount of Time That Managers Spend on the Four Managerial Tasks

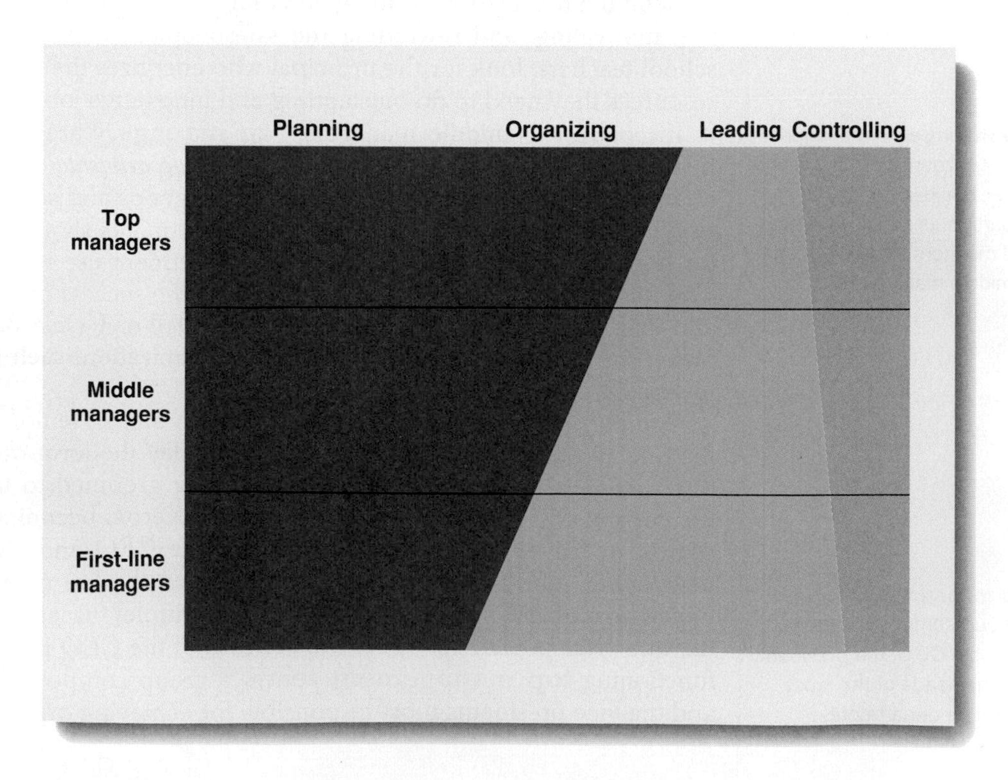

confronting an organization. The ability to focus on the big picture lets managers see beyond the situation immediately at hand and consider choices while keeping in mind the organization's long-term goals.

Today continuing management education and training, including training in advanced IT, are an integral step in building managerial skills because new theories and techniques are constantly being developed to improve organizational effectiveness, such as total quality management, benchmarking, and Web-based organization and business-to-business (B2B) networks. A quick scan through a magazine such as *BusinessWeek* or *European Business Review* reveals a host of seminars on topics such as advanced marketing, finance, leadership, and human resources management that are offered to managers at many levels in the organization, from the most senior corporate executives to middle managers. Microsoft, SAP, and many other organizations designate a portion of each manager's personal budget to be used at the manager's discretion to attend management development programs.

In addition, organizations may wish to develop a particular manager's abilities in a specific skill area–perhaps to learn an advanced component of departmental skills, such as international bond trading, or to learn the skills necessary to implement total quality management. The organization thus pays for managers to attend specialized programs to develop these skills. Indeed, one signal that a manager is performing well is an organization's willingness to invest in that manager's skill development. Similarly, many nonmanagerial employees who are performing at a high level (because they have studied management) are often sent to intensive management training programs to develop their management skills and to prepare them for promotion to first-level management positions.

human skills The ability to understand, alter, lead, and control the behavior of other individuals and groups.

Human skills include the general ability to understand, alter, lead, and control the behavior of other individuals and groups. The ability to communicate, to coordinate, and to motivate people, and to mold individuals into a cohesive team, distinguishes effective from ineffective managers. By all accounts, executives like Michael Dell possess a high level of these human skills.

Like conceptual skills, human skills can be learned through education and training, as well as be developed through experience.[23] Organizations increasingly utilize advanced programs in leadership skills and team leadership as they seek to capitalize on the advantages of self-managed teams.[24] To manage personal interactions effectively, each person in an organization needs to learn how to empathize with other people–to understand their viewpoints and the problems they face. One way to help managers understand their personal strengths and weaknesses is to have their superiors, peers, and subordinates provide feedback about their job performance. Thorough and direct feedback allows managers to develop their human skills.

technical skills The job-specific knowledge and techniques required to perform an organizational role.

Technical skills are the *job-specific* skills required to perform a particular type of work or occupation at a high level. Examples include a manager's specific manufacturing, accounting, marketing, and increasingly, IT skills. Managers need a range of technical skills to be effective. The array of technical skills managers need depends on their position in their organizations. The manager of a restaurant, for example, may need cooking skills to fill in for an absent cook, accounting and bookkeeping skills to keep track of receipts and costs and to administer the payroll, and aesthetic skills to keep the restaurant looking attractive for customers.

As noted earlier, managers and employees who possess the same kinds of technical skills typically become members of a specific department and are known as, for example, marketing managers or manufacturing managers.[25] Managers are grouped into different departments because a major part of a manager's responsibility is to monitor, train, and supervise employees so their job-specific skills and expertise increase. Obviously this is easier to do when employees with similar skills are grouped into the same department because they can learn from one another and become more skilled and productive at their particular jobs.

Figure 1.5 shows how an organization groups managers into departments on the basis of their job-specific skills. It also shows that inside each department, a managerial hierarchy of first-line, middle, and top managers emerges. At Dell, for example,

Figure 1.5
Types and Levels of Managers

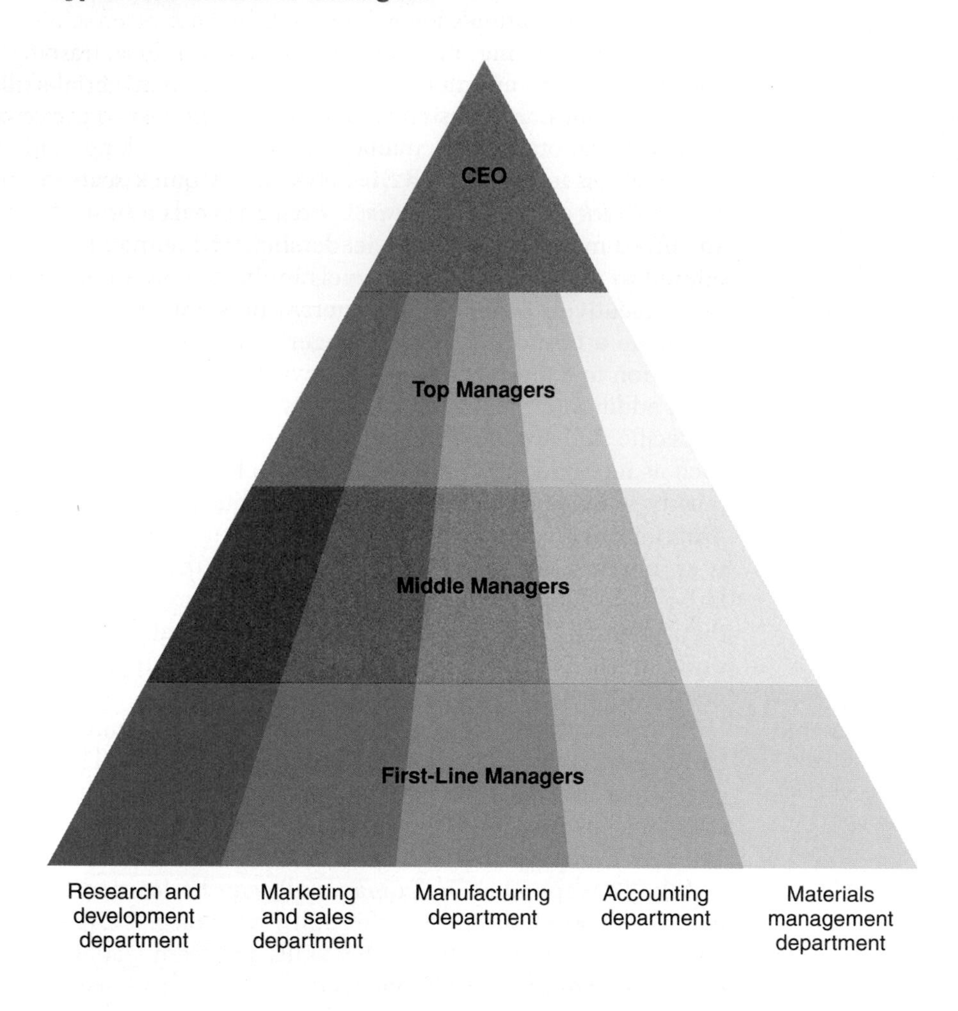

Michael Dell hired experienced top managers to take charge of the marketing, sales, and manufacturing departments and to develop work procedures to help middle and first-line managers control the company's explosive sales growth. When the head of manufacturing found he had no time to supervise computer assembly, he recruited experienced manufacturing middle managers from other companies to assume this responsibility. At Xerox, Anne Mulcahy nurtured many of her managers to develop the required functional skills, such as Ursula Burns, who used her engineering expertise to rise to become CEO.

core competency The specific set of departmental skills, knowledge, and experience that allows one organization to outperform another.

Today the term **core competency** is often used to refer to the specific set of departmental skills, knowledge, and experience that allows one organization to outperform its competitors. In other words, departmental skills that create a core competency give an organization a *competitive advantage.* Dell, for example, was the first PC maker to develop a core competency in materials management that allowed it to produce PCs at a much lower cost than its competitors–a major source of competitive advantage. Similarly, 3M is well known for its core competency in research and development (R&D) that allows it to innovate new products at a faster rate than its competitors, and Xerox has been working to develop a competency to provide a full-range service that is customized to the needs of each of the companies it serves.

Effective managers need all three kinds of skills–conceptual, human, and technical–to help their organizations perform more efficiently and effectively. The absence of even one type of managerial skill can lead to failure. One of the biggest problems that people who start small businesses confront, for example, is their lack of appropriate conceptual and human skills. Someone who has the technical skills to start a new business does not necessarily know how to manage the venture successfully. Similarly, one of the biggest problems that scientists or engineers who switch careers from research to management confront is their lack of effective human skills. Ambitious managers or prospective managers are constantly in search of the latest educational contributions to help them develop the conceptual, human, and technical skills they need to perform at a high level in today's changing and increasingly competitive global environment.

Developing new and improved skills through education and training has become a priority for both aspiring managers and the organizations they work for. As we discussed earlier, many people are enrolling in advanced management courses; major companies around the world put thousands of their employees through management programs designed to identify the employees who the company believes have the competencies that can be developed to become its future top managers. Most organizations closely link promotion to a manager's ability to acquire the competencies that a particular company believes are important.[26]

Recent Changes in Management Practices

The tasks and responsibilities of managers have been changing dramatically in recent years. Two major factors that have led to these changes are global competition and advances in information technology (IT). Stiff competition for resources from organizations both at home and abroad has put increased pressure on all managers to improve efficiency and effectiveness. Increasingly, top managers are encouraging lower-level managers to look beyond the goals of their own departments and take a cross-departmental view to find new opportunities to improve organizational performance, as Steve Jobs and Anne Mulcahy did. Modern IT gives managers at all levels and in all areas access to more and better information and improves their ability to plan, organize, lead, and control. IT also gives employees more job-related information and allows them to become more skilled, specialized, and productive.[27]

Restructuring and Outsourcing

To utilize IT to increase efficiency and effectiveness, CEOs and top management teams have been restructuring organizations and outsourcing specific organizational activities to reduce the number of employees on the payroll and make more productive use of the remaining workforce.

restructuring Downsizing an organization by eliminating the jobs of large numbers of top, middle, and first-line managers and nonmanagerial employees.

Restructuring involves simplifying, shrinking, or downsizing an organization's operations to lower operating costs, as both Dell and Xerox have been forced to do. The financial crisis that started in 2009 has forced many companies around the world–large and small, and profit and nonprofit–to find ways to reduce costs because their customers are spending less money, so their revenues decrease. Restructuring can be done by eliminating product teams, shrinking departments, and reducing levels in the hierarchy, all of which result in the loss of large numbers of jobs of top, middle, or first-line managers, as well as nonmanagerial employees. Modern IT's ability to improve efficiency has increased the amount of downsizing in recent years because IT makes it possible for fewer employees to perform a given task. IT increases each person's ability to process information and make decisions more quickly and accurately, for example. U.S. companies are spending over $100 billion a year to purchase advanced IT that can improve efficiency and effectiveness. We discuss the many dramatic effects of IT on management in Chapter 18 and throughout this book.

Restructuring, however, can produce some powerful negative outcomes. It can reduce the morale of remaining employees, who worry about their own job security–something Anne Mulcahy had to deal with at Xerox. And top managers of many downsized organizations realize that they downsized too far when their employees complain they are overworked and when increasing numbers of customers complain about poor service.[28] Dell faced this charge in the 2000s as it continued to reduce the number of its customer service representatives and outsource their jobs to India to lower costs.

outsourcing Contracting with another company, usually abroad, to have it perform an activity the organization previously performed itself.

Outsourcing involves contracting with another company, usually in a low-cost country abroad, to have it perform a work activity the organization previously performed itself, such as manufacturing, marketing, or customer service. Outsourcing increases efficiency because it lowers operating costs, freeing up money and resources that can be used in more effective ways–for example, to develop new products.

LO1-5 Discuss some major changes in management practices today that have occurred as a result of globalization and the use of advanced information technology (IT).

LO1-6 Discuss the principal challenges managers face in today's increasingly competitive global environment.

But outsourcing of jobs from one nation means that other nations gain those jobs. Thus, when Dell moves its service reps to India, there may be fewer jobs in the United States, but India gains over 12,000 new jobs.[29] Dell would send those relatively low skill jobs to India since they can be done much cheaper there. But the flow of jobs is not one way. The low skill jobs for service representatives may move to India from the United States, but there is a flow of jobs into the United States for other higher skilled activities. Thus, many Indian technology firms have research centers in the Silicon Valley. As a result there is a net positive flow of research and creative jobs into nations like the United States or other mature economies like Japan. To illustrate, Kelon is a leading Chinese refrigerator manufacturer. They make refrigerators both for their own brand and under contract or joint venture for other worldwide firms. Thus, they are a beneficiary of outsourced jobs from mature economies. But the research arm for this Chinese company is in Japan since that is the world leader for technology. Thus, low skill, low paying jobs may flow to where costs are lower, but at the same time often higher pay, higher skill jobs are flowing to the very nations that outsourced low paying jobs. Thus, outsourcing is part of the worldwide economic system in which nations focus on those things they do best.

Challenges for Management in a Global Environment

Firms now compete in a global economy. In the last 20 years, rivalry between organizations has increased radically as organizations no longer find their competition domestically (competing in a single country) but instead find they have global (from abroad) competitors. Technology now allows instant communication and has also acted to dramatically decrease the time to ship goods around the world. This allows many activities and products to flow seamlessly to any destination in the world. Consider as you look at the Internet whether you can tell where a product you may order actually comes from. The activities and products are largely indistinguishable. Once a web page is translated there is virtually no way to know where a product originates. Recently a person in Hong Kong had the experience of ordering flowers for the 98th birthday of a friend in the United States. The company providing the service was headquartered in Europe, the person taking the order over the phone was in the Philippines, while the actual flowers came from Guatemala. The flowers were delivered by a U.S. company. If a firm said it would only use suppliers from Europe it would be at a disadvantage to a firm like the one described here.

global organizations Organizations that operate and compete in more than one country.

Global organizations, organizations that operate and compete in more than one country, pressure all organizations in nations where they compete to identify better ways to use their resources and improve their performance. Consider the experience when a major retailer like Carrefour enters a new market. Carrefour, a French firm, is the world's largest retailer. It competes, around the world, directly against the U.S. firm Walmart. When Carrefour enters a new emerging economy it typically finds that retailing is calcified with little concern for the consumer. Often major retailers in such nations are owned by leading powerful families in the country. These families typically practice a type of business similar to an oligarchy in which several major firms informally agree not to have tough competition against each other. Instead, they figure they will each receive a certain percentage of customers; so, there is little reason to compete aggressively against each other. However, as Carrefour enters the market it introduces new competition as it sells products at a competitive price to gain market share, and it has a strong focus on customer service. The result is that retailing in many emerging economies is undergoing a revolution. The oligarchic firms must respond with a new focus on providing good service and selling products at competitive prices.

Even in the not-for-profit sector, global competition is spurring change. Schools, universities, police forces, and government agencies are reexamining their operations because looking at how activities are performed in other countries often reveals better ways to do them. For example, many curricula and teaching methods Japanese and European school systems use have been imported to the United States.

Today managers who make no attempt to learn from and adapt to changes in the global environment find themselves reacting rather than innovating, and their organizations often become uncompetitive and fail.[30] Four major challenges stand out for managers in today's world: building a competitive advantage, maintaining ethical standards, utilizing new information systems and technologies, and practicing global crisis management.

Building Competitive Advantage

What are the most important lessons for managers and organizations to learn if they are to reach and remain at the top of the competitive environment of business? The answer relates to the use of organizational resources to build a competitive advantage. **Competitive advantage** is the ability of one organization to outperform other organizations because it produces desired goods or services more efficiently and effectively than its competitors. The four building blocks of competitive advantage are superior *efficiency; quality; speed, flexibility,* and *innovation;* and *responsiveness to customers* (see Figure 1.6).

competitive advantage The ability of one organization to outperform other organizations because it produces desired goods or services more efficiently and effectively than they do.

Organizations increase their efficiency when they reduce the quantity of resources (such as people and raw materials) they use to produce goods or services. In today's competitive environment, organizations continually search for new ways to use their resources to improve efficiency. Many organizations are training their workforces in the new skills and techniques needed to operate heavily computerized assembly plants. Similarly, cross-training gives employees the range of skills they need to

Figure 1.6
Building Blocks of Competitive Advantage

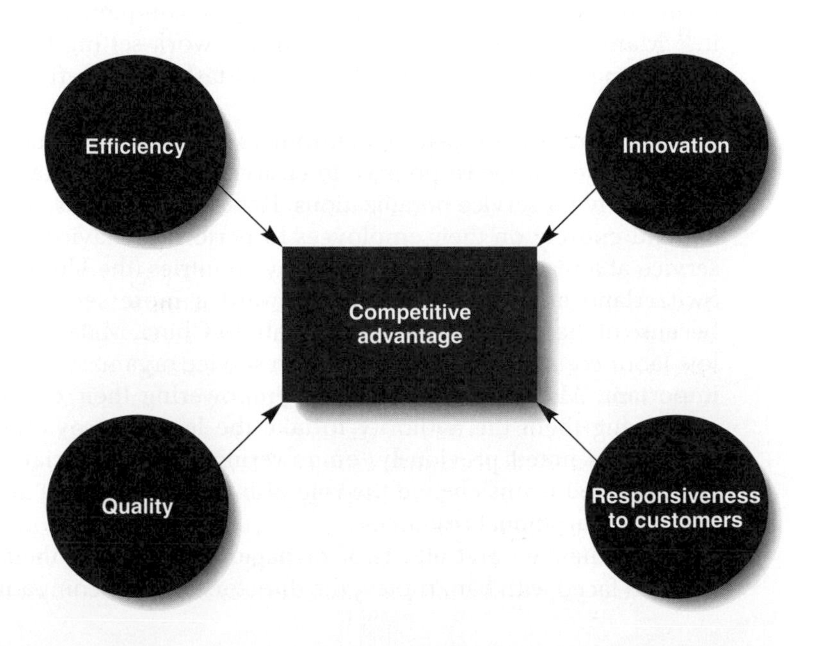

perform many different tasks; and organizing employees in new ways, such as in self-managed teams, lets them make good use of their skills. These are important steps in the effort to improve productivity. Japanese and German companies invest far more in training employees than do U.S. or Italian companies.

Managers must improve efficiency if their organizations are to compete successfully with companies operating in Mexico, China, Malaysia, and other countries where employees are paid comparatively low wages. New methods must be devised either to increase efficiency or to gain some other competitive advantage–higher-quality goods, for example–if outsourcing and the loss of jobs to low-cost countries are to be prevented.

The challenge from global organizations such as Korean electronics manufacturers, Mexican agricultural producers, and European design and financial companies also has increased pressure on companies to develop the skills and abilities of their work-forces in order to improve the quality of their goods and services. One major thrust to improving quality has been to introduce the quality-enhancing techniques known as *total quality management (TQM)*. Employees involved in TQM are often organized into quality control teams and are responsible for finding new and better ways to perform their jobs; they also must monitor and evaluate the quality of the goods they produce. We discuss ways of managing TQM successfully in Chapter 9.

Today companies can win or lose the competitive race depending on their *speed*–how fast they can bring new products to market–or their *flexibility*–how easily they can change or alter the way they perform their activities to respond to actions of their competitors. Companies that have speed and flexibility are agile competitors: Their managers have superior planning and organizing abilities; they can think ahead, decide what to do, and then speedily mobilize their resources to respond to a changing environment. We examine how managers can build speed and flexibility in their organizations in later chapters. Michael Dell and Ursula Burns are working hard to make Dell and Xerox agile companies that can react to the technological changes taking place in a digital world–their problem is how to maintain their competitive advantage against HP, Apple, Kodak, and Canon.

innovation The process of creating new or improved goods and services or developing better ways to produce or provide them.

Innovation, the process of creating new or improved goods and services that customers want or developing better ways to produce or provide goods and services, poses a special challenge. Managers must create an organizational setting in which people are encouraged to be innovative. Typically innovation takes place in small groups or teams; management decentralizes control of work activities to team members and creates an organizational culture that rewards risk taking. For example, a team composed of Apple and Nike employees came up with the idea for a new model of iPod that would be able to record and measure the distance its owner had run, among other things, and the companies formed an alliance to make it.[31] Managing innovation and creating a work setting that encourages risk taking are among the most difficult managerial tasks. Innovation is discussed in depth in Chapter 9.

Organizations compete for customers with their products and services, so training employees to be responsive to customers' needs is vital for all organizations, but particularly for service organizations. Retail stores, banks, and hospitals, for example, depend entirely on their employees to perform behaviors that result in high-quality service at a reasonable cost.[32] As many countries (the United Kingdom, Canada, and Switzerland are just a few) move toward a more service-based economy (in part because of the loss of manufacturing jobs to China, Malaysia, and other countries with low labor costs), managing behavior in service organizations is becoming increasingly important. Many organizations are empowering their customer service employees and giving them the authority to take the lead in providing high-quality customer service. As noted previously, empowering nonmanagerial employees and creating self-managed teams change the role of first-line managers and lead to more efficient use of organizational resources.

Sometimes the best efforts of managers to revitalize their organization's fortunes fail; and faced with bankruptcy, the directors of these companies are forced to appoint

turnaround management The creation of a new vision for a struggling company based on a new approach to planning and organizing to make better use of a company's resources and allow it to survive and prosper.

a new CEO who has a history of success in rebuilding a company. **Turnaround management** is the creation of a new vision for a struggling company using a new approach to planning and organizing to make better use of a company's resources and allow it to survive and eventually prosper–something Apple's Steve Jobs has excelled at. It involves developing radical new strategies such as how to reduce the number of products sold or change how they are made and distributed, or close corporate and manufacturing operations to reduce costs. Organizations that appoint turnaround CEOs are generally experiencing a crisis because they have become inefficient or ineffective; sometimes this is because of poor management over a continuing period, and sometimes it occurs because a competitor introduces a new product or technology that makes their own products unattractive to customers. For example, when Apple introduced the iPhone in 2007, sales of the former best-selling Motorola Razr cell phone plummeted because customers demand state-of-the-art products. Motorola has not recovered because it has no smartphone to compete with Apple, although it introduced new phones using Google's Android platform in 2009. BlackBerry seems to be holding its own and Nokia is fighting back, but Palm was suffering in 2010 when Dell and Microsoft announced plans to introduce their own new smartphones. What strategies will be required to make a new smartphone that can compete with the iPhone or BlackBerry?

Achieving a competitive advantage requires that managers use all their skills and expertise, as well as their companies' other resources, to find new and improved ways to improve efficiency, quality, innovation, and responsiveness to customers. We revisit this theme often as we examine the ways managers plan strategies, organize resources and activities, and lead and control people and groups to increase efficiency and effectiveness.

Maintaining Ethical and Socially Responsible Standards

Managers at all levels, especially after the recent economic crisis, are under considerable pressure to make the best use of resources to increase the level at which their organizations perform.[33] For example, top managers feel pressure from shareholders to increase the performance of the entire organization to boost its stock price, improve profits, or raise dividends. In turn, top managers may pressure middle managers to find new ways to use organizational resources to increase efficiency or quality and thus attract new customers and earn more revenues–and then middle managers hit on their department's supervisors.

Pressure to increase performance can be healthy for an organization because it leads managers to question how the organization is working, and it encourages them to find new and better ways to plan, organize, lead, and control. However, too much pressure to perform can be harmful.[34] It may induce managers to behave unethically, and even illegally, when dealing with people and groups inside and outside the organization.[35]

China has faced a series of problems in recent years with tainted milk powder for babies ultimately leading to the deaths of six children and the hospitalization of approximately 1000 more in 2008. If a child does not breast feed from its mother it will still need milk specially produced for babies. Typically, it is assumed that such powdered formula is trustworthy. However, in 2008 a number of managers of milk product firms were found to enrich the formula with a chemical called melamine. This chemical made the formula appear richer in protein than it actually was. The managers producing the formula were hoping to be able to cut costs of the milk product and increase their firms' profits. Tragically, the melamine caused kidney stones and kidney damage in the babies who consumed the formula. Perhaps as troubling as the actions of the managers was the fact that the Chinese government did not want the news of the contaminated milk product to distract from the 2008 Olympics which were on going at the time. The result was that the government did not release information on the contamination and also pressured firms not to release information on the problems. The result was no firms immediately released information on the contamination or sought to recall the product. Instead, they waited until after the Olympic games to respond to the problem.

Similarly, to secure a large foreign contract, a sales manager in a large company, such as in the defense or electronics industry, might offer bribes to foreign officials to obtain lucrative contracts–even though this is against the law. In 2010, for example, German electronic equipment maker Siemens agreed to pay $1.4 billion in fines to settle claims that it paid bribes and kickbacks to organizations around the world between 2001 and 2007.

The issue of social responsibility, discussed in Chapter 4, centers on deciding what obligations a company has toward the people and groups affected by its activities–such as employees, customers, or the cities in which it operates. Some companies have strong views about social responsibility; their managers believe they should protect the interests of others. But some managers may decide to act in an unethical way and put their own interests first, hurting others in the process. A recent example showing why managers must always keep the need to act in an ethical and socially responsible way at the forefront of their decision making is profiled in the following "Ethics in Action" box.

Ethics in Action

Parmalat and Self-Dealing

Parmalat SpA is one of Italy's largest food product companies. The firm is organized around four product areas: (1) milk, which involves the production and distribution of various types of milk: pasteurized milk and cream, Ultra High Temperature (UHT) milk and cream, flavored milk, condensed milk, milk powder, bulk milk, and Béchamel; (2) fruit-based drinks, involving the production of fruit (including concentrated) juices, soy drinks, and tea; (3) milk derivatives, including yogurt, probiotics, desserts, cheese, butter, margarine, and ice cream ingredients; and (4) other, which manufactures ice creams, ingredients, and other minor product categories. The firm has worldwide operations with approximately 140 production centers and 13,000 employees. Domestically in Italy, 5,000 Italian dairy farms are dependent on the company for the bulk of their business. The firm's sales in 2009 were approximately 4 billion euros.

Until 2003, Parmalat and its CEO played a larger than life role in the nation. The firm sponsored race cars and owned one of the most successful football teams in the football-crazy nation of Italy. All of that came to a close when, in 2003, the firm experienced the largest bankruptcy in Europe. At the heart of this bankruptcy was fraud in the firm's accounting. In the late 1990s the firm expanded aggressively using debt to fund the expansion. However, the outcome of the acquisitions was not as positive as was planned. The firm moved to use financial tools called derivatives. These financial tools allow a firm or individual to make predictions on the future movements of a wide variety of items such as monetary exchange rates, interest rates, or stock prices. However, the gains or losses can be multiplied quickly with derivatives, and thus, their use is very risky.

In 2003 the firm was unable to meet a number of its financial obligations. Specifically, it could not pay 150 million euros worth of bonds. This led to the finding that an account reflected as an asset by Parmalat of 4 billion euros at the Bank of America did not exist. Ultimately, it was discovered that an

Pictured is Calisto Tanzi, founder and former CEO of Parmalat SpA, one of Italy's largest food companies. Tanzi was sentenced to ten years in prison for his role in the multibillion euro bankruptcy of Paramalat's dairy group in 2003.

international Cayman Islands-based offshore entity called Bonlat affiliated with Parmalat had invested $6.9 billion in interest swaps. There were over 250 foreign entities discovered that were used to cover such transactions at Parmalat. Overall, it appeared that at least one billion euros disappeared on such high risk investments.

Eight managers were charged with fraud at the firm, but only the CEO was convicted and sent to prison. Today, the firm has returned to profitability. However, the bond holders, who owned bonds in the firm, received only part of the value of those bonds. These individuals, many of whom are retirees, suffered a significant loss. The company at its peak represented approximately 2% of the total economy of Italy. The potential negative impact on any nation from the corruption of a few managers is clear.

Utilizing IT and E-Commerce

As we have discussed, another important challenge for managers is to continually utilize efficient and effective new IT that can link and enable managers and employees to better perform their jobs–whatever their level in the organization. One example of how IT has changed the jobs of people at all organizational levels comes from UPS, where, until 2006, its drivers relied on maps, note cards, and their own experience to plan the fastest way to deliver hundreds of parcels each day. This changed after UPS invested over $600 million to develop a computerized route optimization system that each evening plans each of its 56,000 drivers' routes for the next day in the most efficient way by, for example, minimizing the number of left turns that waste both time and gas. The program has been incredibly successful and has been continuously updated so that by 2010 UPS drivers covered tens of million fewer miles each month while they delivered ever-increasing numbers of packages faster.

Increasingly, new kinds of IT enable not just individual employees but also self-managed teams by giving them important information and allowing virtual interactions around the globe using the Internet. Increased global coordination helps improve quality and increase the pace of innovation. Microsoft, Hitachi, IBM, and most companies now search for new IT that can help them build a competitive advantage. The importance of IT is discussed in detail in Chapters 16 and 18, and throughout the text you will find icons that alert you to examples of how IT is changing the way companies operate.

UPS Dispatch Coordinator Jim McCauley shows driver Muamer Pleh how many stops he will be making in his next delivery run—all made possible by the company's new software that allows each driver to plan the most efficient delivery route each day, which saves the company time and money.

Practicing Global Crisis Management

Today another challenge facing managers and organizations is global crisis management. The causes of global crises or disasters fall into two main categories: natural causes and human causes. Crises that arise because of natural causes include the hurricanes, tsunamis, earthquakes, famines, and diseases that have devastated so many countries in the 2000s; hardly any country has been untouched by their effects. In 2010 both Haiti and Chile experienced severe earthquakes that killed thousands of people and left tens of thousands more homeless. Despite the extensive foreign aid they have received, both these countries will probably need years to recover from these crises and rebuild their economies and infrastructure.

Human-created crises result from factors such as industrial pollution, poor attention to worker and workplace safety, global warming and the destruction of the natural habitat or environment, and geopolitical tensions and terrorism. Human-created crises, such as global warming due to emissions of carbon dioxide and other gases, may intensify the effects of natural disasters. For example, increasing global temperatures and acid rain may have increased the intensity of hurricanes, led to unusually strong rains, and contributed to lengthy droughts. Scientists believe that global warming is responsible for the rapid destruction of coral reefs, forests, animal species, and the natural habitat in many parts of the world. The shrinking polar ice caps are expected to raise the sea level by a few critical inches.

Increasing geopolitical tensions, which are partly the result of the speed of the globalization process itself, have upset the balance of world power as different countries and geographic regions attempt to protect their own economic and political interests. Rising oil prices, for example, have strengthened the bargaining power of oil-supplying countries. This has led the United States to adopt global political strategies, including its war on terrorism, to secure the supply of oil vital to protecting its national interest. In a similar way, countries in Europe have been forming contracts and allying with Russia to obtain its supply of natural gas, and Japan and China have been negotiating with Iran and Saudi Arabia. The rise of global terrorism and terrorist groups is to a large degree the result of changing political, social, and economic conditions that have made it easier for extremists to influence whole countries and cultures.

Finally, industrial pollution and limited concern for the health and safety of workers have become increasingly significant problems for companies and countries. Companies in heavy industries such as coal and steel have polluted millions of acres of land around major cities in eastern Europe and Asia; billion-dollar cleanups are necessary. The 1986 Chernobyl nuclear power plant meltdown released over 1,540 times as much radiation into the air as occurred at Hiroshima; over 50,000 people died as a result, while hundreds of thousands more have been affected.

Management has an important role to play in helping people, organizations, and countries respond to global crises; such crises provide lessons in how to plan, organize, lead, and control the resources needed to both forestall and respond effectively to a crisis. Crisis management involves making important choices about how to (1) create teams to facilitate rapid decision making and communication, (2) establish the organizational chain of command and reporting relationships necessary to mobilize a fast response, (3) recruit and select the right people to lead and work in such teams, and (4) develop bargaining and negotiating strategies to manage the conflicts that arise whenever people and groups have different interests and objectives. How well managers make such decisions determines how quickly an effective response to a crisis can be implemented, and it sometimes can prevent or reduce the severity of the crisis itself.

Summary and Review

LO1-1

WHAT IS MANAGEMENT? A manager is a person responsible for supervising the use of an organization's resources to meet its goals. An organization is a collection of people who work together and coordinate their actions to achieve a wide variety of goals. Management is the process of using organizational resources to achieve organizational goals effectively and efficiently through planning, organizing, leading, and controlling. An efficient organization makes the most productive use of its resources. An effective organization pursues appropriate goals and achieves these goals by using its resources to create goods or services that customers want.

LO1-2 **MANAGERIAL TASKS** The four principal managerial tasks are planning, organizing, leading, and controlling. Managers at all levels of the organization and in all departments perform these tasks. Effective management means managing these activities successfully.

LO1-3, 1-4 **LEVELS AND SKILLS OF MANAGERS** Organizations typically have three levels of management. First-line managers are responsible for the day-to-day supervision of nonmanagerial employees. Middle managers are responsible for developing and utilizing organizational resources efficiently and effectively. Top managers have cross-departmental responsibility. Three main kinds of managerial skills are conceptual, human, and technical. The need to develop and build technical skills leads organizations to divide managers into departments according to their job-specific responsibilities. Top managers must establish appropriate goals for the entire organization and verify that department managers are using resources to achieve those goals.

LO1-5 **RECENT CHANGES IN MANAGEMENT PRACTICES** To increase efficiency and effectiveness, many organizations have altered how they operate. Managers have restructured and downsized operations and outsourced activities to reduce costs. Companies are also empowering their workforces and using self-managed teams to increase efficiency and effectiveness. Managers are increasingly using IT to achieve these objectives.

LO1-6 **CHALLENGES FOR MANAGEMENT IN A GLOBAL ENVIRONMENT** Today's competitive global environment presents many interesting challenges to managers. One of the main challenges is building a competitive advantage by increasing efficiency; quality; speed, flexibility, and innovation; and customer responsiveness. Other challenges are behaving in an ethical and socially responsible way toward people inside and outside the organization; managing a diverse workforce; utilizing new IT; and practicing global crisis management.

Management in Action

Topics for Discussion and Action

Discussion

1. Describe the difference between efficiency and effectiveness, and identify real organizations that you think are, or are not, efficient and effective. **[LO1-1]**
2. In what ways can managers at each of the three levels of management contribute to organizational efficiency and effectiveness? **[LO1-3]**
3. Identify an organization that you believe is high-performing and one that you believe is low-performing. Give five reasons why you think the performance levels of the two organizations differ so much. **[LO1-2, 1-4]**
4. What are the building blocks of competitive advantage? Why is obtaining a competitive advantage important to managers? **[LO1-5]**
5. In what ways do you think managers' jobs have changed the most over the last 10 years? Why have these changes occurred? **[LO1-6]**

Action

6. Choose an organization such as a school or a bank; visit it; then list the different organizational resources it uses. How do managers use these resources to maintain and improve its performance? **[LO1-2, 1-4]**
7. Visit an organization, and talk to first-line, middle, and top managers about their respective management roles in the organization and what they do to help the organization be efficient and effective. **[LO1-3, 1-4]**
8. Ask a middle or top manager, perhaps someone you already know, to give examples of how he or she performs the managerial tasks of planning, organizing, leading, and controlling. How much time does he or she spend in performing each task? **[LO1-3]**
9. Try to find a cooperative manager who will allow you to follow him or her around for a day. List the roles the manager plays, and indicate how much time he or she spends performing them. **[LO1-3, 1-4]**

Building Management Skills

Thinking about Managers and Management [LO1-2, 1-3, 1-4]

Think of an organization that has provided you with work experience and the manager to whom you reported (or talk to someone who has had extensive work experience); then answer these questions:

1. Think about your direct supervisor. Of what department is he or she a member, and at what level of management is this person?
2. How do you characterize your supervisor's approach to management? For example, which particular management tasks and roles does this person perform most often? What kinds of management skills does this manager have?
3. Do you think the tasks, roles, and skills of your supervisor are appropriate for the particular job he or she performs? How could this manager improve his or her task performance? How can IT affect this?
4. How did your supervisor's approach to management affect your attitudes and behavior? For example, how well did you perform as a subordinate, and how motivated were you?
5. Think about the organization and its resources. Do its managers use organizational resources effectively? Which resources contribute most to the organization's performance?
6. Describe how the organization treats its human resources. How does this treatment affect the attitudes and behaviors of the workforce?
7. If you could give your manager one piece of advice or change one management practice in the organization, what would it be?
8. How attuned are the managers in the organization to the need to increase efficiency, quality, innovation, or responsiveness to customers? How well do you think the organization performs its prime goals of providing the goods or services that customers want or need the most?

Managing Ethically [LO1-1, 1-3]

Think about an example of unethical behavior that you observed in the past. The incident could be something you experienced as an employee or a customer or something you observed informally.

Questions

1. Either by yourself or in a group, give three reasons why you think the behavior was unethical. For example, what rules or norms were broken? Who benefited or was harmed by what took place? What was the outcome for the people involved?
2. What steps might you take to prevent such unethical behavior and encourage people to behave in an ethical way?

Small Group Breakout Exercise [LO1-2, 1-3, 1-4]

Opening a New Restaurant

Form groups of three or four people, and appoint one group member as the spokesperson who will communicate your findings to the entire class when called on by the instructor. Then discuss the following scenario:

You and your partners have decided to open a large, full-service restaurant in your local community; it will be open from 7 a.m. to 10 p.m. to serve breakfast, lunch, and dinner. Each of you is investing €50,000 in the venture, and together you have secured a bank loan for €300,000 to begin operations. You and your partners have little experience in managing a restaurant beyond serving meals or eating in restaurants, and you now face the task of deciding how you will manage the restaurant and what your respective roles will be.

1. Decide what each partner's managerial role in the restaurant will be. For example, who will be responsible for the necessary departments and specific activities? Describe your managerial hierarchy.
2. Which building blocks of competitive advantage do you need to establish to help your restaurant succeed? What criteria will you use to evaluate how successfully you are managing the restaurant?
3. Discuss the most important decisions that must be made about (a) planning, (b) organizing, (c) leading, and (d) controlling to allow you and your partners to use organizational resources effectively and build a competitive advantage.
4. For each managerial task, list the issues to solve, and decide which roles will contribute the most to your restaurant's success.

Exploring the World Wide Web [LO1-2]

Ratan Tata is one of India's leading CEOs. Go to the Internet and plug in his name, and you will find a mass of articles in leading business publications about him. Read a number of the articles in these publications. Discuss his approach to planning, organizing, leading, and controlling in his businesses. What is his approach to managing? Do you think this approach is typical of other Indian firms? What effects has his approach had on the Tata Group's performance?

Be the Manager [LO1-2, 1-5]

Problems at Achieva

You have just been called in to help managers at Achieva, a fast-growing Internet software company that specializes in business-to-business (B2B) network software. Your job is to help Achieva solve some management problems that have arisen because of its rapid growth.

Customer demand to license Achieva's software has boomed so much in just two years that more than 50 new software programmers have been added to help develop a new range of software products. Achieva's growth has been so swift that the company still operates informally, its organizational structure is loose and flexible, and programmers are encouraged to find solutions to problems as they go along. Although this structure worked well in the past, you have been told that problems are arising.

There have been increasing complaints from employees that good performance is not being recognized in the organization and that they do not feel equitably treated. Moreover, there have been complaints about getting managers to listen to their new ideas and to act on them. A bad atmosphere is developing in the company, and recently several talented employees left. Your job is to help Achieva's managers solve these problems quickly and keep the company on the fast track.

Questions

1. What kinds of organizing and controlling problems is Achieva suffering from?
2. What kinds of management changes need to be made to solve them?

CHAPTER 2

The Evolution of Management Thought

Learning Objectives

After studying this chapter, you should be able to:

LO2-1 Describe how the need to increase organizational efficiency and effectiveness has guided the evolution of management theory.

LO2-2 Explain the principle of job specialization and division of labor, and tell why the study of person–task relationships is central to the pursuit of increased efficiency.

LO2-3 Identify the principles of administration and organization that underlie effective organizations.

LO2-4 Trace the changes in theories about how managers should behave to motivate and control employees.

LO2-5 Explain the contributions of management science to the efficient use of organizational resources.

LO2-6 Explain why the study of the external environment and its impact on an organization has become a central issue in management thought.

A MANAGER'S CHALLENGE

Finding Better Ways to Make Cars

A major change in management thinking about car assembly occurred in Japan when Ohno Taiichi, a Toyota production engineer, pioneered the development of lean manufacturing in the 1960s after touring the U.S. factories of GM, Ford, and Chrysler. The management philosophy behind lean manufacturing is to continuously find methods to improve the efficiency of the production process to reduce costs, increase quality, and reduce car assembly time. Lean production is based on the idea that if workers have input and can participate in the decision-making process, their knowledge can be used to increase efficiency.

In lean manufacturing, workers work on a moving production line, but they are organized into small teams, each of which is responsible for a particular phase of car assembly, such as installing the car's transmission or electrical wiring system. Each team member is expected to learn the tasks of all members of that team, and each work group is responsible not only for assembling cars but also for finding ways to increase quality and reduce costs. By 1970 Japanese managers had applied the new lean production system so efficiently that they were producing higher-quality cars at lower prices than the U.S.

(a) The photo on top, taken in 1904 inside a Daimler Motor Company factory, is an example of the use of small-batch production, a production system in which small groups of people work together and perform all the tasks needed to assemble a product. (b) In 1913 Henry Ford revolutionized car production by pioneering mass-production manufacturing, in which a conveyor belt brings each car to the workers, and each individual worker performs a single task along the production line. Cars are still built using this system, as shown in the photo of workers along a modern computerized automobile assembly line.

carmakers they toured in the 1960s. By 1980 Japanese carmakers dominated the global market.

Another aspect of lean manufacturing is just-in-time inventory. Car manufacturers, prior to the entrance of Japanese carmakers, produced the parts that went into the automobile. The Japanese, in their lean manufacturing, moved from being automobile manufacturers to being automobile assemblers. The Japanese no longer sought to manufacture every part of the vehicle. Instead they work with a rich set of suppliers who make the parts to their specification. Working with such suppliers helps Japanese firms control costs since the smaller, more specialized firms can make the various parts cheaper. But for such a system to work they need to have sufficient parts on hand constantly or be able to have an exceptional system of parts delivery. The maintenance of excessive parts in inventory is very expensive; it ties up high levels of capital and is not very efficient. However, an inventory system that works with all the suppliers and ensures that each part is there only when needed (or just in time) offers the potential for significant cost savings. This is difficult to achieve, but the Japanese ultimately revolutionized how manufacturing in many industries occurs by developing this just-in-time system.

To compete, managers of carmakers visited Japan to learn the new manufacturing principles of lean production. Nearly all carmakers spent billions of dollars moving to lean manufacturing and just-in-time inventory. Another innovation from Japan was to employ robots on their assembly lines. The goal was to use IT to build and track the quality of cars being produced. The robots were part of this IT effort. It was felt that they would provide higher quality. Indeed, for a time it seemed that robots rather than employees would be building cars in the future. However, Toyota discovered something interesting at its first fully roboticized car plant. When only robots build cars, efficiency does not continually increase because, unlike people, robots cannot provide input to improve the work process. The optimum manufacturing methods must continuously work to find the right balance between using people, machinery, computers, and IT.

In the 2000s global car companies continued to compete fiercely to improve and perfect ways to make cars. Toyota remained the leader in pioneering new ways to manage its assembly lines to increase quality and efficiency; but other carmakers such as Hyundai, Ford, and Fiat also made major strides to close the quality gap with Japanese carmakers.

Everything changed in the carmaking business in 2009 after the economic and financial crisis led car sales to plummet, and every carmaker, including Toyota, lost billions of dollars. To stay afloat, most global carmakers had to rely on billions of dollars in assistance from their governments to stay in business because they could not pay their employees or finance their customers.

Another milestone in car-making history came in the spring of 2010 when Toyota—known as the quality leader—came under intense scrutiny because of claims that some of its cars suffered from uncontrolled acceleration due to brake defects and that it had been late in responding to owner complaints despite many accidents. This problem opened up new opportunities for other car manufacturers as they sought to establish their image of quality in consumers' minds. Now carmakers are trying to find better ways to use the hundreds of computer sensors inside each vehicle to understand how to make a car more efficiently and effectively.

Overview

As this sketch of the evolution of management thinking in global car manufacturing suggests, changes in management practices occur as managers, theorists, researchers, and customers look for ways to increase how efficiently and effectively cars are made. The driving force behind the evolution of management theory is the search for better ways to use organizational resources to make goods and services. Advances in management thought typically occur as managers and researchers find better ways to perform the principal management tasks: planning, organizing, leading, and controlling human and other organizational resources.

In this chapter we examine how management thought has evolved in modern times and the central concerns that have guided ongoing advances in management theory. First we examine the so-called classical management theories that emerged around the turn of the 20th century. These include scientific management, which focuses on matching people and tasks to maximize efficiency, and administrative management, which focuses on identifying the principles that will lead to the creation of the most efficient system of organization and management. Next we consider behavioral management theories developed both before and after World War II; these focus on how managers should lead and control their workforces to increase performance. Then we discuss management science theory, which developed during World War II and has become increasingly important as researchers have developed rigorous analytical and quantitative techniques to help managers measure and control organizational performance. Finally we discuss changes in management practices from the middle to the late 1900s and focus on the theories developed to help explain how the external environment affects the way organizations and managers operate.

By the end of this chapter you will understand how management thought and theory have evolved over time. You will also understand how economic, political, and cultural forces have affected the development of these theories and how managers and their organizations have changed their behavior as a result. In Figure 2.1 we summarize the chronology of the management theories discussed in this chapter.

Scientific Management Theory

The evolution of modern management began in the closing decades of the 19th century, after the industrial revolution had swept through Europe and America. In the new economic climate, managers of all types of organizations–political, educational, and economic–were trying to find better ways to satisfy customers' needs. Many major economic, technical, and cultural changes were taking place at this time. The introduction of steam power and the development of sophisticated machinery and equipment changed how goods were produced, particularly in the weaving and clothing industries. Small workshops run by skilled workers who produced hand-manufactured

Figure 2.1
The Evolution of Management Theory

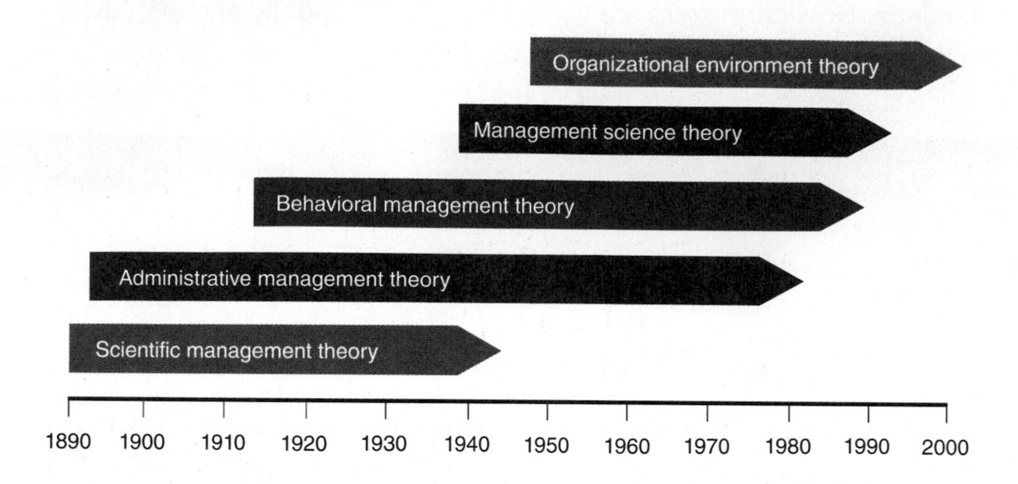

LO2-1 Describe how the need to increase organizational efficiency and effectiveness has guided the evolution of management theory.

products (a system called *crafts production*) were being replaced by large factories in which sophisticated machines controlled by hundreds or even thousands of unskilled or semiskilled workers made products. For example, raw cotton and wool, which in the past had been spun into yarn by families or whole villages working together, were now shipped to factories where workers operated machines that spun and wove large quantities of yarn into cloth.

Owners and managers of the new factories found themselves unprepared for the challenges accompanying the change from small-scale crafts production to large-scale mechanized manufacturing. Moreover, many managers and supervisors in these workshops and factories were engineers who had only a technical orientation. They were unprepared for the social problems that occur when people work together in large groups in a factory or shop system. Managers began to search for new techniques to manage their organizations' resources, and soon they began to focus on ways to increase the efficiency of the worker–task mix.

Job Specialization and the Division of Labor

LO2-2 Explain the principle of job specialization and division of labor, and tell why the study of person–task relationships is central to the pursuit of increased efficiency.

Initially management theorists were interested in why the new machine shops and factory system were more efficient and produced greater quantities of goods and services than older, crafts-style production operations. Nearly 200 years before, Adam Smith had been one of the first writers to investigate the advantages associated with producing goods and services in factories. A famous economist, Smith journeyed around England in the 1700s studying the effects of the industrial revolution.[1] In a study of factories that produced various pins or nails, Smith identified two different manufacturing methods. The first was similar to crafts-style production, in which each worker was responsible for all the 18 tasks involved in producing a pin. The other had each worker performing only one or a few of these 18 tasks.

Smith found that the performance of the factories in which workers specialized in only one or a few tasks was much greater than the performance of the factory in which each worker performed all 18 pin-making tasks. In fact, Smith found that 10 workers specializing in a particular task could make 48,000 pins a day, whereas those workers who performed all the tasks could make only a few thousand.[2] Smith reasoned that this performance difference occurred because the workers who specialized became much more skilled at their specific tasks and as a group were thus able to produce a product faster than the group of workers who each performed many tasks. Smith concluded that increasing the level of **job specialization**—the process by which a

job specialization The process by which a division of labor occurs as different workers specialize in different tasks over time.

division of labor occurs as different workers specialize in tasks–improves efficiency and leads to higher organizational performance.[3]

Armed with the insights gained from Adam Smith's observations, other managers and researchers began to investigate how to improve job specialization to increase performance. Management practitioners and theorists focused on how managers should organize and control the work process to maximize the advantages of job specialization and the division of labor.

F. W. Taylor and Scientific Management

scientific management The systematic study of relationships between people and tasks for the purpose of redesigning the work process to increase efficiency.

Frederick W. Taylor (1856–1915) is best known for defining the techniques of **scientific management,** the systematic study of relationships between people and tasks for the purpose of redesigning the work process to increase efficiency. Taylor was a manufacturing manager who eventually became a consultant and taught other managers how to apply his scientific management techniques. Taylor believed that if the amount of time and effort that each worker expends to produce a unit of output (a finished good or service) can be reduced by increasing specialization and the division of labor, the production process will become more efficient. According to Taylor, the way to create the most efficient division of labor could best be determined by scientific management techniques rather than by intuitive or informal rule-of-thumb knowledge. Based on his experiments and observations as a manufacturing manager in a variety of settings, he developed four principles to increase efficiency in the workplace:

- Principle 1: *Study the way workers perform their tasks, gather all the informal job knowledge that workers possess, and experiment with ways of improving how tasks are performed.*

To discover the most efficient method of performing specific tasks, Taylor studied in great detail and measured the ways different workers went about performing their tasks. One of the main tools he used was a time-and-motion study, which involves the careful timing and recording of the actions taken to perform a particular task. Once Taylor understood the existing method of performing a task, he then experimented to increase specialization. He tried different methods of dividing and coordinating the various tasks necessary to produce a finished product. Usually this meant simplifying jobs and having each worker perform fewer, more routine tasks, as at the pin factory or on Ford's car assembly line. Taylor also sought to find ways to improve each worker's ability to perform a particular task–for example, by reducing the number of motions workers made to complete the task, by changing the layout of the work area or the type of tools workers used, or by experimenting with tools of different sizes.

Frederick W. Taylor, founder of scientific management, and one of the first people to study the behavior and performance of people at work.

- Principle 2: *Codify the new methods of performing tasks into written rules and standard operating procedures.*

Once the best method of performing a particular task was determined, Taylor specified that it should be recorded so this procedure could be taught to all workers performing the same task. These new methods further standardized and simplified jobs–essentially making jobs even more routine. In this way efficiency could be increased throughout an organization.

- Principle 3: *Carefully select workers who possess skills and abilities that match the needs of the task, and train them to perform the task according to the established rules and procedures.*

To increase specialization, Taylor believed workers had to understand the tasks that were required and be thoroughly trained to perform the tasks at the required level. Workers who could not be trained to this level were to be transferred to a job where they were able to reach the minimum required level of proficiency.[4]

- Principle 4: *Establish a fair or acceptable level of performance for a task, and then develop a pay system that rewards performance above the acceptable level.*

To encourage workers to perform at a high level of efficiency, and to give them an incentive to reveal the most efficient techniques for performing a task, Taylor advocated that workers benefit from any gains in performance. They should be paid a bonus and receive some percentage of the performance gains achieved through the more efficient work process.[5]

By 1910 Taylor's system of scientific management had become nationally known and in many instances was faithfully and fully practiced.[6] However, managers in many organizations chose to implement the new principles of scientific management selectively. This decision ultimately resulted in problems. For example, some managers using scientific management obtained increases in performance, but rather than sharing performance gains with workers through bonuses as Taylor had advocated, they simply increased the amount of work that each worker was expected to do. Many workers experiencing the reorganized work system found that as their performance increased, managers required that they do more work for the same pay. Workers also learned that performance increases often meant fewer jobs and a greater threat of layoffs because fewer workers were needed. In addition, the specialized, simplified jobs were often monotonous and repetitive, and many workers became dissatisfied with their jobs.

Scientific management brought many workers more hardship than gain and a distrust of managers who did not seem to care about workers' well-being.[7] These dissatisfied workers resisted attempts to use the new scientific management techniques and at times even withheld their job knowledge from managers to protect their jobs and pay. It is not difficult for workers to conceal the true potential efficiency of a work system to protect their interests. Experienced machine operators, for example, can slow their machines in undetectable ways by adjusting the tension in the belts or by misaligning the gears. Workers sometimes even develop informal work rules that discourage high performance and encourage shirking as work groups attempt to identify an acceptable or fair performance level (a tactic discussed in the next section).

Charlie Chaplin tries to extricate a fellow employee from the machinery of mass production in this scene from *Modern Times.* The complex machinery is meant to represent the power that machinery has over the worker in the new work system.

Unable to inspire workers to accept the new scientific management techniques for performing tasks, some organizations increased the mechanization of the work process. For example, one reason why Henry Ford introduced moving conveyor belts in his factory was the realization that when a conveyor belt controls the pace of work (instead of workers setting their own pace), workers can be pushed to perform at higher levels–levels that they may have thought were beyond their reach. Charlie Chaplin captured this aspect of mass production in one of the opening scenes of his famous movie *Modern Times* (1936). In the film Chaplin caricatured a new factory employee fighting to work at the machine-imposed pace but losing the battle to the machine. Henry Ford also used the principles of scientific management to identify the tasks that each worker should perform on the production line and thus to determine the most effective division of labor to suit the needs of a mechanized production system.

From a performance perspective, the combination of the two management practices–(1) achieving the right worker–task specialization and (2) linking people and tasks by the speed of the production line–makes sense. It produces the huge cost savings and dramatic output increases that occur in large, organized work settings. For example, in 1908 managers at the Franklin Motor Company using scientific management principles redesigned the work process, and the output of cars increased from 100 cars a *month* to 45 cars a *day;* workers' wages, however, increased by only 90%.[8] From other perspectives, however, scientific management practices raise many concerns. While scientific management is one of the oldest management traditions in the West, there have been writings that have influenced management in other traditions far longer. The "Ethics in Action" box below highlights one of those: Sun Tzu. The use of his military ideas in business raises interesting ethics concerns.

Ethics in Action

Sun Tzu—Military Theory as Business Theory

Management theory from a Western perspective is typically based on professors or scholars who study business organizations and the work of how they operate. Frequently, however, in Chinese culture business lessons are drawn instead from military analysis. That military analysis may be drawn from someone like Mao Zedong in modern times. In the West, Mao is associated with socialism, but his writings on military issues are widely read by business people. A more popular widely read commentary on military issues comes from ancient times. *The Art of War* is attributed to philosopher and general, Sun Tzu, and was supposedly written around 500 BC. He wrote his thoughts not only on military strategy but also on planning and public administration. For many business people in China, his book today is as important as any of the Western theories we highlight in this chapter.

This portrait of Sun Tzu hangs in the China Military Museum in Beijing. A philosopher and general, Sun Tzu was believed to have written *The Art of War* around 500 BC. For many business people in China, his book is as important as any of the Western theories in use today.

The ideas of Sun Tzu do take some adjustments and interpretation of his writings by modern readers. For example, when Sun Tzu discussed keeping soldiers strong, business people today would interpret this to mean they should retain good employees and ensure that they have proper training to be successful. However, there are other points that translate very directly. For example, Sun Tzu argued that an organization grew stronger by beating the enemy. The same is also seen in business. Business success draws resources, customers, suppliers, and potential employees to the firm. Thus, success today helps to build success in the future.

The application of military writings to business can be controversial, and the ethics are debatable. However, a key point that does transfer from military writings is that business is a competition. The more one firm gains, the more another one loses. Thus, similar to the military, the goal of success in business typically comes at someone else's expense. Business does not provide a win–win setting. In a market-based system, there will be losers just as there are in military settings.

This scene from *Cheaper by the Dozen* illustrates how "efficient families," such as the Gilbreths, use formal family courts to solve problems of assigning chores to different family members and to solve disputes when they arise.

The Gilbreths

Two prominent followers of Taylor were Frank Gilbreth (1868–1924) and Lillian Gilbreth (1878–1972), who refined Taylor's analysis of work movements and made many contributions to time-and-motion study.[9] Their aims were to (1) analyze every individual action necessary to perform a particular task and break it into each of its component actions, (2) find better ways to perform each component action, and (3) reorganize each of the component actions so that the action as a whole could be performed more efficiently—at less cost in time and effort.

The Gilbreths often filmed a worker performing a particular task and then separated the task actions, frame by frame, into their component movements. Their goal was to maximize the efficiency with which each individual task was performed so that gains across tasks would add up to enormous savings of time and effort. Their attempts to develop improved management principles were captured—at times quite humorously—in the movie *Cheaper by the Dozen,* a new version of which appeared in 2004, which depicts how the Gilbreths (with their 12 children) tried to live their own lives according to these efficiency principles and apply them to daily actions such as shaving, cooking, and even raising a family.[10]

Eventually the Gilbreths became increasingly interested in the study of fatigue. They studied how physical characteristics of the workplace contribute to job stress that often leads to fatigue and thus poor performance. They isolated factors that result in worker fatigue, such as lighting, heating, the color of walls, and the design of tools and machines. Their pioneering studies paved the way for new advances in management theory.

In workshops and factories, the work of the Gilbreths, Taylor, and many others had a major effect on the practice of management. In comparison with the old crafts system, jobs in the new system were more repetitive, boring, and monotonous as a result of the application of scientific management principles, and workers became increasingly dissatisfied. Frequently the management of work settings became a game between workers and managers: Managers tried to initiate work practices to increase performance, and workers tried to hide the true potential efficiency of the work setting to protect their own well-being.[11] The story of how Gottleib Daimler founded the firm that would become Daimler Benz, one of the largest car companies in the world, is an interesting example. While Daimler was a great entrepreneur, his story that follows in the "Manager as a Person" box illustrates that the firm we know today was an outcome of the expansion that also came after his death.

Manager as a Person

Gottlieb Daimler and the Creation of What Became Daimler Benz

Daimler AG is one of the world's leading vehicle manufacturers. The firm's divisions include Mercedes-Benz Cars, Daimler Trucks, Mercedes-Benz Vans, Daimler Buses, and Daimler Financial Services. Daimler Financial Services provides financing, leasing, insurance, and fleet management to individuals and firms that buy vehicles from Daimler AG. Today, Mercedes-Benz is the oldest car brand in the world.

Pictured here is Paul Daimler driving his father Gottlieb in the first four-wheeled Daimler car, which was built in Stuttgart, Germany. Gottlieb Daimler did not live long enough to see his most successful automobile—the Mercedes--unveiled to the public in 1901.

The founder of Daimler AG was Gottlieb Daimler. Gottlieb was a gas engine builder who developed a lightweight four-stroke engine in 1884 and fitted it into a two-wheeled "motor cycle" test-bed in 1885. In 1886 he built a four-wheeled horseless carriage. Daimler produced a variety of cars but the car he is most famous for was not unveiled until 1901. He died in 1900. Thus, he was not to see his greatest success.

Daimler's Mercedes automobile was unveiled in February 1901 at the Pau Grand Prix. The name Mercedes is a Spanish name that means grace. An Austrian financial backer to Daimler was Emil Jellinek. He pushed Daimler to continue to refine his car to go faster and faster. The result was that by 1899 Daimler had engineered a car that could go an amazing 40 miles per hour–the fastest in the world. As a result of his financial support and encouragement Daimler named his car Mercedes after Jellinek's 10-year-old-daughter. This car combined many new features including a pressed-steel frame, honeycomb radiator, and gate gearchange. These innovations would become the standard in automobiles for years to come.

The appearance at the Pau Grand Prix was a disaster with the car breaking down within yards of the start. However, a few weeks later Mercedes won all major prizes at the Nice Automobile Week. Its speed and power were amazing to those who observed the car. The car's successes led some writers to argue that the Mercedes era had begun.

Following Daimler's death his long-term partner Wilhelm Maybach took over the firm. Maybach was also a great engineer and inventor who continued to refine the Mercedes automobile to make it more powerful. However, ultimately the Daimler firm would merge with another automobile firm founded by Karl Benz called Benz & Cie. The financial crisis of the late 1920s would lead the two firms (Daimler's DMG and Benz & Cie) to merge to form a single more dominant brand. Benz would remain a board member for the new firm but as is often the method in Europe the great success of the firm represents less the brilliance of a single person than great engineers continuing over time to build on the success of prior brilliant engineers.

LO2-3 Identify the principles of administration and organization that underlie effective organizations.

The scientific method was one of the first theories on management in the West. However, scientific management theory does not have a rich perspective on people. Instead, the view of people is largely as cogs in a machine. This harsh view increasingly began to be questioned. This led to a new approach to analyzing management–the Administrative Management theory.

Administrative Management Theory

Side by side with scientific managers studying the person–technology mix to increase efficiency, other managers and researchers were focusing on **administrative management,** the study of how to create an organizational structure and control system that leads to high efficiency and effectiveness. *Organizational structure* is the system of task and authority relationships that controls how employees use resources to achieve the

administrative management The study of how to create an organizational structure and control system that leads to high efficiency and effectiveness.

organization's goals. Two of the most influential early views regarding the creation of efficient systems of organizational administration were developed in Europe: Max Weber, a German sociology professor, developed one theory; and Henri Fayol, the French manager who developed the model of management introduced in Chapter 1, developed the other.

The Theory of Bureaucracy

bureaucracy A formal system of organization and administration designed to ensure efficiency and effectiveness.

Max Weber (1864–1920) wrote at the turn of the 20th century, when Germany was undergoing its industrial revolution.[12] To help Germany manage its growing industrial enterprises while it was striving to become a world power, Weber developed the principles of **bureaucracy**–a formal system of organization and administration designed to ensure efficiency and effectiveness. A bureaucratic system of administration is based on the five principles summarized in Figure 2.2:

- Principle 1: *In a bureaucracy, a manager's formal authority derives from the position he or she holds in the organization.*

authority The power to hold people accountable for their actions and to make decisions concerning the use of organizational resources.

Authority is the power to hold people accountable for their actions and to make decisions concerning the use of organizational resources. Authority gives managers the right to direct and control their subordinates' behavior to achieve organizational goals. In a bureaucratic system of administration, obedience is owed to a manager not because of any personal qualities–such as personality, wealth, or social status–but because the manager occupies a position that is associated with a certain level of authority and responsibility.[13]

- Principle 2: *In a bureaucracy, people should occupy positions because of their performance, not because of their social standing or personal contacts.*

This principle was not always followed in Weber's time and is often ignored today. Some organizations and industries are still affected by social networks in which

Figure 2.2
Weber's Principles of Bureaucracy

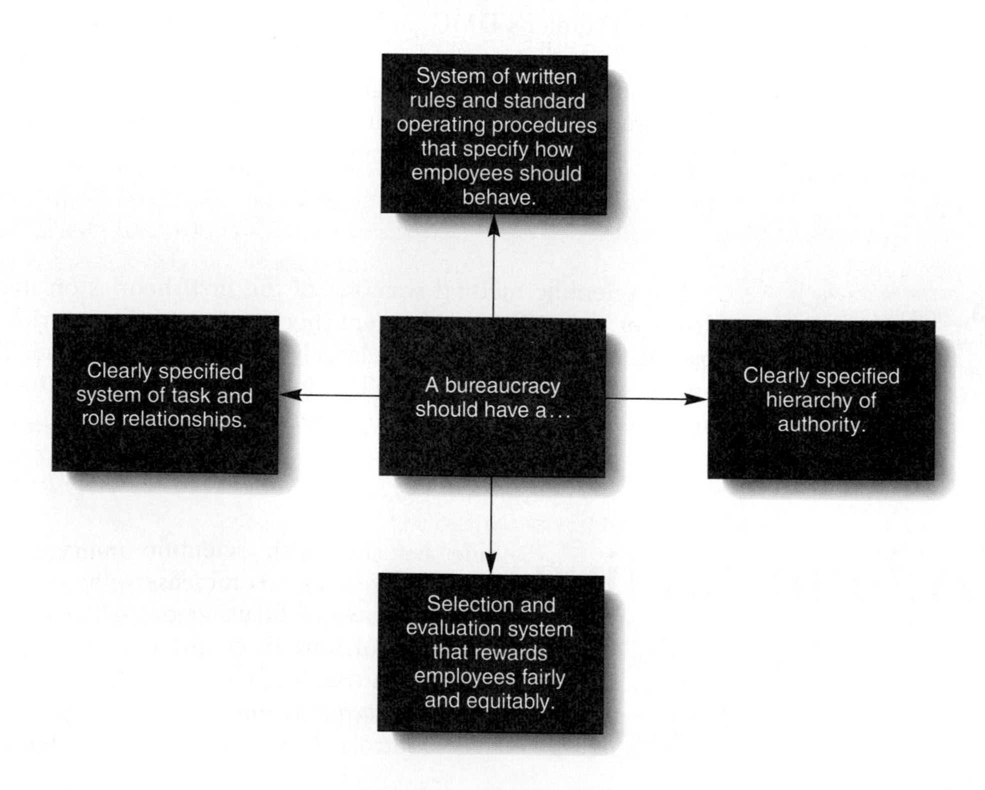

Max Weber developed the principles of bureaucracy during Germany's burgeoning industrial revolution to help organizations increase their efficiency and effectiveness.

personal contacts and relations, not job-related skills, influence hiring and promotional decisions.

- Principle 3: *The extent of each position's formal authority and task responsibilities, and its relationship to other positions in an organization, should be clearly specified.*

When the tasks and authority associated with various positions in the organization are clearly specified, managers and workers know what is expected of them and what to expect from each other. Moreover, an organization can hold all its employees strictly accountable for their actions when they know their exact responsibilities.

- Principle 4: *Authority can be exercised effectively in an organization when positions are arranged hierarchically, so employees know whom to report to and who reports to them.*[14]

Managers must create an organizational hierarchy of authority that makes it clear who reports to whom and to whom managers and workers should go if conflicts or problems arise. This principle is especially important in the armed forces, FBI, CIA, and other organizations that deal with sensitive issues involving possible major repercussions. It is vital that managers at high levels of the hierarchy be able to hold subordinates accountable for their actions.

- Principle 5: *Managers must create a well-defined system of rules, standard operating procedures, and norms so they can effectively control behavior within an organization.*

rules Formal written instructions that specify actions to be taken under different circumstances to achieve specific goals.

standard operating procedures (SOPs) Specific sets of written instructions about how to perform a certain aspect of a task.

norms Unwritten, informal codes of conduct that prescribe how people should act in particular situations and are considered important by most members of a group or organization.

Rules are formal written instructions that specify actions to be taken under different circumstances to achieve specific goals (for example, if A happens, do B). **Standard operating procedures (SOPs)** are specific sets of written instructions about how to perform a certain aspect of a task. A rule might state that at the end of the workday employees are to leave their machines in good order, and a set of SOPs would specify exactly how they should do so, itemizing which machine parts must be oiled or replaced. **Norms** are unwritten, informal codes of conduct that prescribe how people should act in particular situations and are considered important by most members of a group or organization. For example, an organizational norm in a restaurant might be that waiters should help each other if time permits.

Rules, SOPs, and norms provide behavioral guidelines that increase the performance of a bureaucratic system because they specify the best ways to accomplish organizational tasks. Companies such as McDonald's and Walmart have developed extensive rules and procedures to specify the behaviors required of their employees, such as "Always greet the customer with a smile."

Weber believed organizations that implement all five principles establish a bureaucratic system that improves organizational performance. The specification of positions and the use of rules and SOPs to regulate how tasks are performed make it easier for managers to organize and control the work of subordinates. Similarly, fair and equitable selection and promotion systems improve managers' feelings of security, reduce stress, and encourage organizational members to act ethically and further promote the interests of the organization.[15]

If bureaucracies are not managed well, however, many problems can result. Sometimes managers allow rules and SOPs, "bureaucratic red tape," to become so cumbersome that decision making is slow and inefficient and organizations cannot change. When managers rely too much on rules to solve problems and not enough on their own skills and judgment, their behavior becomes inflexible. A key challenge for managers is to use bureaucratic principles to benefit, rather than harm, an organization.

Fayol's Principles of Management

Henri Fayol (1841–1925) was the CEO of Comambault Mining. Working at the same time as Weber, but independently, Fayol identified 14 principles (summarized in Table 2.1) that he believed essential to increase the efficiency of the management process.[16] We discuss these principles in detail here because, although they were developed at the turn of the 20th century, they remain the bedrock on which much of recent management theory and research is based. In fact, as the "Management Insight" box following this discussion suggests, modern writers such as well-known management guru Tom Peters continue to extol these principles.

DIVISION OF LABOR A champion of job specialization and the division of labor for reasons already mentioned, Fayol was nevertheless among the first to point out the downside of too much specialization: boredom–a state of mind likely to diminish product quality, worker initiative, and flexibility. As a result, Fayol advocated that workers be given more job duties to perform or be encouraged to assume more responsibility for work outcomes–a principle increasingly applied today in organizations that empower their workers.

AUTHORITY AND RESPONSIBILITY Like Weber, Fayol emphasized the importance of authority and responsibility. Fayol, however, went beyond Weber's formal

Table 2.1
Fayol's 14 Principles of Management

Division of labor Job specialization and the division of labor should increase efficiency, especially if managers take steps to lessen workers' boredom.

Authority and responsibility Managers have the right to give orders and the power to exhort subordinates for obedience.

Unity of command An employee should receive orders from only one superior.

Line of authority The length of the chain of command that extends from the top to the bottom of an organization should be limited.

Centralization Authority should not be concentrated at the top of the chain of command.

Unity of direction The organization should have a single plan of action to guide managers and workers.

Equity All organizational members are entitled to be treated with justice and respect.

Order The arrangement of organizational positions should maximize organizational efficiency and provide employees with satisfying career opportunities.

Initiative Managers should allow employees to be innovative and creative.

Discipline Managers need to create a workforce that strives to achieve organizational goals.

Remuneration of personnel The system that managers use to reward employees should be equitable for both employees and the organization.

Stability of tenure of personnel Long-term employees develop skills that can improve organizational efficiency.

Subordination of individual interests to the common interest Employees should understand how their performance affects the performance of the whole organization.

Esprit de corps Managers should encourage the development of shared feelings of comradeship, enthusiasm, or devotion to a common cause.

authority, which derives from a manager's position in the hierarchy, to recognize the *informal* authority that derives from personal expertise, technical knowledge, moral worth, and the ability to lead and to generate commitment from subordinates. (The study of authority is the subject of recent research into leadership, discussed in Chapter 14.)

unity of command A reporting relationship in which an employee receives orders from, and reports to, only one superior.

UNITY OF COMMAND The principle of **unity of command** specifies that an employee should receive orders from, and report to, only one superior. Fayol believed that *dual command,* the reporting relationship that exists when two supervisors give orders to the same subordinate, should be avoided except in exceptional circumstances. Dual command confuses subordinates, undermines order and discipline, and creates havoc within the formal hierarchy of authority. Assessing any manager's authority and responsibility in a system of dual command is difficult, and the manager who is bypassed feels slighted and angry and may be uncooperative in the future.

line of authority The chain of command extending from the top to the bottom of an organization.

LINE OF AUTHORITY The **line of authority** is the chain of command extending from the top to the bottom of an organization. Fayol was one of the first management theorists to point out the importance of limiting the length of the chain of command by controlling the number of levels in the managerial hierarchy. The more levels in the hierarchy, the longer communication takes between managers at the top and bottom and the slower the pace of planning and organizing. Restricting the number of hierarchical levels to lessen these communication problems lets an organization act quickly and flexibly; this is one reason for the recent trend toward restructuring (discussed in Chapter 1).

Fayol also pointed out that when organizations are split into different departments or functions, each with its own hierarchy, it is important to allow middle and first-line managers in each department to interact with managers at similar levels in other departments. This interaction helps speed decision making because managers know each other and know whom to go to when problems arise. For cross-departmental integration to work, Fayol noted the importance of keeping one's superiors informed about what is taking place so that lower-level decisions do not harm activities taking place in other parts of the organization. One alternative to cross-departmental integration is to create cross-departmental teams controlled by a team leader (see Chapter 1).

centralization The concentration of authority at the top of the managerial hierarchy.

Henri Fayol, who maintained Weber's principles of formal organization but added recognition of the pivotal role played by informal authority.

CENTRALIZATION Fayol also was one of the first management writers to focus on **centralization,** the concentration of authority at the top of the managerial hierarchy. Fayol believed authority should not be concentrated at the top of the chain of command. One of the most significant issues that top managers face is how much authority to centralize at the top of the organization and what authority to decentralize to managers and workers at lower hierarchical levels. This important issue affects the behavior of people at all levels in the organization.

If authority is very centralized, only managers at the top make important decisions, and subordinates simply follow orders. This arrangement gives top managers great control over organizational activities and helps ensure that the organization is pursuing its strategy, but it makes it difficult for the people who are closest to problems and issues to respond to them in a timely manner. It also can reduce the motivation of middle and first-line managers and make them less flexible and adaptable because they become reluctant to make decisions on their own, even when doing so is necessary. They get used to passing the buck. As we saw in Chapter 1, the pendulum is now swinging toward decentralization as organizations seek to empower middle managers and create self-managed teams that monitor and control their own activities both to increase organizational flexibility and to reduce operating costs and increase efficiency.

unity of direction The singleness of purpose that makes possible the creation of one plan of action to guide managers and workers as they use organizational resources.

UNITY OF DIRECTION Just as there is a need for unity of command, there is also a need for **unity of direction,** the singleness of purpose that makes possible the creation of one plan of action to guide managers and workers as they use organizational resources. An organization without a single guiding plan becomes inefficient and ineffective; its activities become unfocused, and individuals and groups work at cross-purposes. Successful planning starts with top managers working as a team to craft the organization's strategy, which they communicate to middle managers, who decide how to use organizational resources to implement the strategy.

equity The justice, impartiality, and fairness to which all organizational members are entitled.

EQUITY As Fayol wrote, "For personnel to be encouraged to carry out their duties with all the devotion and loyalty of which they are capable, they must be treated with respect for their own sense of integrity, and equity results from the combination of respect and justice."[17] **Equity**–the justice, impartiality, and fairness to which all organizational members are entitled–is receiving much attention today; the desire to treat employees fairly is a primary concern of managers. (Equity theory is discussed in Chapter 13.)

order The methodical arrangement of positions to provide the organization with the greatest benefit and to provide employees with career opportunities.

ORDER Like Taylor and the Gilbreths, Fayol was interested in analyzing jobs, positions, and individuals to ensure that the organization was using resources as efficiently as possible. To Fayol, **order** meant the methodical arrangement of positions to provide the organization with the greatest benefit and to provide employees with career opportunities that satisfy their needs. Thus Fayol recommended the use of organizational charts to show the position and duties of each employee and to indicate which positions an employee might move to or be promoted into in the future. He also advocated that managers engage in extensive career planning to help ensure orderly career paths. Career planning is of primary interest today as organizations increase the resources they are willing to devote to training and developing their workforces.

initiative The ability to act on one's own without direction from a superior.

INITIATIVE Although order and equity are important means to fostering commitment and loyalty among employees, Fayol believed managers must also encourage employees to exercise **initiative,** the ability to act on their own without direction from a superior. Used properly, initiative can be a major source of strength for an organization because it leads to creativity and innovation. Managers need skill and tact to achieve the difficult balance between the organization's need for order and employees' desire for initiative. Fayol believed the ability to strike this balance was a key indicator of a superior manager.

discipline Obedience, energy, application, and other outward marks of respect for a superior's authority.

DISCIPLINE In focusing on the importance of **discipline**–obedience, energy, application, and other outward marks of respect for a superior's authority–Fayol was addressing the concern of many early managers: how to create a workforce that was reliable and hardworking and would strive to achieve organizational goals. According to Fayol, discipline results in respectful relations between organizational members and reflects the quality of an organization's leadership and a manager's ability to act fairly and equitably.

REMUNERATION OF PERSONNEL Fayol proposed reward systems including bonuses and profit-sharing plans, which are increasingly used today as organizations seek improved ways to motivate employees. Convinced from his own experience that an organization's payment system has important implications for organizational success, Fayol believed effective reward systems should be equitable for both employees and the organization, encourage productivity by rewarding well-directed effort, not be subject to abuse, and be uniformly applied to employees.

STABILITY OF TENURE OF PERSONNEL Fayol also recognized the importance of long-term employment, and this idea has been echoed by contemporary management gurus such as Tom Peters, Jeff Pfeffer, and William Ouchi. When employees stay with an organization for extended periods, they develop skills that improve the organization's ability to use its resources.

SUBORDINATION OF INDIVIDUAL INTERESTS TO THE COMMON INTEREST The interests of the organization as a whole must take precedence over the interests of any individual or group if the organization is to survive. Equitable agreements must be established between the organization and its members to ensure that employees are treated fairly and rewarded for their performance and to maintain the disciplined organizational relationships so vital to an efficient system of administration.

esprit de corps Shared feelings of comradeship, enthusiasm, or devotion to a common cause among members of a group.

ESPRIT DE CORPS As this discussion of Fayol's ideas suggests, the appropriate design of an organization's hierarchy of authority and the right mix of order and discipline foster cooperation and commitment. Likewise, a key element in a successful organization is the development of **esprit de corps,** a French expression that refers to shared feelings of comradeship, enthusiasm, or devotion to a common cause among members of a group. Esprit de corps can result when managers encourage personal, verbal contact between managers and workers and encourage communication to solve problems and implement solutions. (Today the term *organizational culture* is used to refer to these shared feelings; this concept is discussed at length in Chapter 3.)

Some of the principles that Fayol outlined have faded from contemporary management practices, but most have endured. The characteristics of organizations that Tom Peters and Robert Waterman identified as being "excellently managed" in their best-selling book *In Search of Excellence* (1982) are discussed in the following "Management Insight."[18]

Management Insight

Peters and Waterman's Excellent Companies

In the early 1980s Tom Peters and Robert Waterman identified 62 organizations that they considered to be the best-performing organizations in the United States. They asked, "Why do these companies perform better than their rivals?" and discovered that successful organizations are managed according to three sets of related principles. Those principles have a great deal in common with Fayol's principles.

First, Peters and Waterman argued, top managers of successful companies create principles and guidelines that emphasize managerial autonomy and entrepreneurship and encourage risk taking and *initiative.* For example, they allow middle managers to develop new products even though there is no assurance that these products will be winners. In high-performing organizations, top managers are closely involved in the day-to-day operations of the company, provide *unity of command* and *unity of direction,* and do not simply make isolated decisions. Top managers *decentralize authority* to lower-level managers and nonmanagerial employees and give them the freedom to get involved and the motivation to get things done.

The second approach that managers of excellent organizations use to increase performance is to create one central plan that puts organizational goals at center stage. In high-performing organizations, managers focus attention on what the organization does best, and the emphasis is on continuously improving the goods and services the organization provides to its customers. Managers of top-performing companies resist the temptation to get sidetracked into pursuing ventures outside their area of expertise just because they seem to promise a quick return. These managers also focus on customers and establish close relationships with them to learn their needs; responsiveness to customers increases competitive advantage.

The third set of management principles pertains to organizing and controlling the organization. Excellent companies establish a *division of work* and a *division of authority and responsibility* that will motivate employees to *subordinate their individual interests to the common interest.* Inherent in this approach is the belief that high performance derives from individual skills and abilities and that *equity, order, initiative,* and other indications of respect for the individual create the *esprit de corps* that fosters productive behavior. An emphasis on entrepreneurship and respect for every employee leads the best managers to create a structure that gives employees room to exercise *initiative* and motivates them to succeed. Because a simple, streamlined managerial hierarchy is best suited to achieving this outcome, top managers keep the line of *authority* as short as possible. They also decentralize authority to permit employee participation, but they keep enough control to maintain *unity of direction.*

As this insight into contemporary management suggests, the basic concerns that motivated Fayol continue to inspire management theorists.[19] The principles that Fayol and Weber set forth still provide clear and appropriate guidelines that managers can use to create a work setting that efficiently and effectively uses organizational resources. These principles remain the bedrock of modern management theory; recent researchers have refined or developed them to suit modern conditions. For example, Weber's and Fayol's concerns for equity and for establishing appropriate links between performance and reward are central themes in contemporary theories of motivation and leadership.

Behavioral Management Theory

Because the writings of Weber and Fayol were not translated into English and published in the United States until the late 1940s, American management theorists in the first half of the 20th century were unaware of the contributions of these European pioneers. American management theorists began where Taylor and his followers left off. Although their writings were different, these theorists all espoused a theme that focused on **behavioral management,** the study of how managers should personally behave to motivate employees and encourage them to perform at high levels and be committed to achieving organizational goals.

LO2-4 Trace the changes in theories about how managers should behave to motivate and control employees.

behavioral management The study of how managers should behave to motivate employees and encourage them to perform at high levels and be committed to the achievement of organizational goals.

The Work of Mary Parker Follett

If F. W. Taylor is considered the father of management thought, Mary Parker Follett (1868–1933) serves as its mother.[20] Much of her writing about management and about the way managers should behave toward workers was a response to her concern that Taylor was ignoring the human side of the organization. She pointed out that management often overlooks the multitude of ways in which employees can contribute to the organization when managers allow them to participate and exercise initiative in their everyday work lives.[21] Taylor, for example, never proposed that managers should involve workers in analyzing their jobs to identify better ways to perform tasks or should even ask workers how they felt about their jobs. Instead he used time-and-motion experts to analyze workers' jobs for them. Follett, in contrast, argued that because workers know the most about their jobs, they should be involved in job analysis and managers should allow them to participate in the work development process.

Follett proposed that "authority should go with knowledge . . . whether it is up the line or down." In other words, if workers have the relevant knowledge, then workers, rather than managers, should be in control of the work process itself, and managers should behave as coaches and facilitators–not as monitors and supervisors. In making this statement, Follett anticipated the current interest in self-managed teams and empowerment. She also recognized the importance of having managers in different departments communicate directly with each other to speed decision making. She

Mary Parker Follett, an early management thinker who advocated, "Authority should go with knowledge . . . whether it is up the line or down."

advocated what she called "cross-functioning": members of different departments working together in cross-departmental teams to accomplish projects–an approach that is increasingly used today.[22]

Fayol also mentioned expertise and knowledge as important sources of managers' authority, but Follett went further. She proposed that knowledge and expertise, and not managers' formal authority deriving from their position in the hierarchy, should decide who will lead at any particular moment. She believed, as do many management theorists today, that power is fluid and should flow to the person who can best help the organization achieve its goals. Follett took a horizontal view of power and authority, in contrast to Fayol, who saw the formal line of authority and vertical chain of command as being most essential to effective management. Follett's behavioral approach to management was very radical for its time.

The Hawthorne Studies and Human Relations

Probably because of its radical nature, Follett's work was unappreciated by managers and researchers until quite recently. Most continued to follow in the footsteps of Taylor and the Gilbreths. To increase efficiency, they studied ways to improve various characteristics of the work setting, such as job specialization or the kinds of tools workers used. One series of studies was conducted from 1924 to 1932 at the Hawthorne Works of the Western Electric Company.[23] This research, now known as the *Hawthorne studies,* began as an attempt to investigate how characteristics of the work setting–specifically the level of lighting or illumination–affect worker fatigue and performance. The researchers conducted an experiment in which they systematically measured worker productivity at various levels of illumination.

The experiment produced some unexpected results. The researchers found that regardless of whether they raised or lowered the level of illumination, productivity increased. In fact, productivity began to fall only when the level of illumination dropped to the level of moonlight–a level at which workers could presumably no longer see well enough to do their work efficiently.

Workers in a telephone manufacturing plant in 1931. Around this time, researchers at the Hawthorne Works of the Western Electric Company began to study the effects of work setting characteristics—such as lighting and rest periods—on productivity. To their surprise, they discovered that workers' productivity was affected more by the attention they received from researchers than by the characteristics of the work setting—a phenomenon that became known as the Hawthorne effect.

The researchers found these results puzzling and invited a noted Harvard psychologist, Elton Mayo, to help them. Mayo proposed another series of experiments to solve the mystery. These experiments, known as the *relay assembly test experiments,* were designed to investigate the effects of other aspects of the work context on job performance, such as the effect of the number and length of rest periods and hours of work on fatigue and monotony.[24] The goal was to raise productivity.

During a two-year study of a small group of female workers, the researchers again observed that productivity increased over time, but the increases could not be solely attributed to the effects of changes in the work setting. Gradually the researchers discovered that, to some degree, the results they were obtaining were influenced by the fact that the researchers themselves had become part of the experiment. In other words, the presence of the researchers was affecting the results because the workers enjoyed receiving attention and being the subject of study and were willing to cooperate with the researchers to produce the results they believed the researchers desired.

Subsequently it was found that many other factors also influence worker behavior, and it was not clear what was actually influencing the Hawthorne workers' behavior. However, this particular effect–which became known as the **Hawthorne effect**–seemed to suggest that workers' attitudes toward their managers affect the level of workers' performance. In particular, the significant finding was that each manager's personal behavior or leadership approach can affect performance. This finding led many researchers to turn their attention to managerial behavior and leadership. If supervisors could be trained to behave in ways that would elicit cooperative behavior from their subordinates, productivity could be increased. From this view emerged the **human relations movement,** which advocates that supervisors be behaviorally trained to manage subordinates in ways that elicit their cooperation and increase their productivity.

Hawthorne effect The finding that a manager's behavior or leadership approach can affect workers' level of performance.

human relations movement A management approach that advocates the idea that supervisors should receive behavioral training to manage subordinates in ways that elicit their cooperation and increase their productivity.

The importance of behavioral or human relations training became even clearer to its supporters after another series of experiments–the *bank wiring room experiments.* In a study of workers making telephone switching equipment, researchers Elton Mayo and F. J. Roethlisberger discovered that the workers, as a group, had deliberately adopted a norm of output restriction to protect their jobs. Workers who violated this informal production norm were subjected to sanctions by other group members. Those who violated group performance norms and performed above the norm were called "ratebusters"; those who performed below the norm were called "chiselers."

The experimenters concluded that both types of workers threatened the group as a whole. Ratebusters threatened group members because they revealed to managers how fast the work could be done. Chiselers were looked down on because they were not doing their share of the work. Work group members disciplined both ratebusters and chiselers to create a pace of work that the workers (not the managers) thought was fair. Thus a work group's influence over output can be as great as the supervisors' influence. Because the work group can influence the behavior of its members, some management theorists argue that supervisors should be trained to behave in ways that gain the goodwill and cooperation of workers so that supervisors, not workers, control the level of work group performance.

One implication of the Hawthorne studies was that the behavior of managers and workers in the work setting is as important in explaining the level of performance as the technical aspects of the task. Managers must understand the workings of the **informal organization,** the system of behavioral rules and norms that emerge in a group, when they try to manage or change behavior in organizations. Many studies have found that as time passes, groups often develop elaborate procedures and norms that bond members together, allowing unified action either to cooperate with management to raise performance or to restrict output and thwart the attainment of organizational goals.[25] The Hawthorne studies demonstrated the importance of understanding how the feelings, thoughts, and behavior of work group members and managers affect performance. It was becoming increasingly clear to researchers that understanding behavior in organizations is a complex process that is critical to increasing performance.[26] Indeed, the increasing interest in the area of management known as **organizational behavior,** the study of the factors that have an impact on how individuals and groups respond to and act in organizations, dates from these early studies.

informal organization The system of behavioral rules and norms that emerge in a group.

organizational behavior The study of the factors that have an impact on how individuals and groups respond to and act in organizations.

Theory X and Theory Y

Several studies after World War II revealed how assumptions about workers' attitudes and behavior affect managers' behavior. Perhaps the most influential approach was developed by Douglas McGregor. He proposed two sets of assumptions about how work attitudes and behaviors not only dominate the way managers think but also affect how they behave in organizations. McGregor named these two contrasting sets of assumptions *Theory X* and *Theory Y* (see Figure 2.3).[27]

Figure 2.3
Theory X versus Theory Y

THEORY X	THEORY Y
The average employee is lazy, dislikes work, and will try to do as little as possible.	Employees are not inherently lazy. Given the chance, employees will do what is good for the organization.
To ensure that employees work hard, managers should closely supervise employees.	To allow employees to work in the organization's interest, managers must create a work setting that provides opportunities for workers to exercise initiative and self-direction.
Managers should create strict work rules and implement a well-defined system of rewards and punishments to control employees.	Managers should decentralize authority to employees and make sure employees have the resources necessary to achieve organizational goals.

Source: D. McGregor, *The Human Side of Enterprise,* © 1960 by The McGraw–Hill Companies, Inc. Used with permission.

Theory X A set of negative assumptions about workers that leads to the conclusion that a manager's task is to supervise workers closely and control their behavior.

THEORY X According to the assumptions of **Theory X,** the average worker is lazy, dislikes work, and will try to do as little as possible. Moreover, workers have little ambition and wish to avoid responsibility. Thus the manager's task is to counteract workers' natural tendencies to avoid work. To keep workers' performance at a high level, the manager must supervise workers closely and control their behavior by means of "the carrot and stick"–rewards and punishments.

Managers who accept the assumptions of Theory X design and shape the work setting to maximize their control over workers' behaviors and minimize workers' control over the pace of work. These managers believe workers must be made to do what is necessary for the success of the organization, and they focus on developing rules, SOPs, and a well-defined system of rewards and punishments to control behavior. They see little point in giving workers autonomy to solve their own problems because they think the workforce neither expects nor desires cooperation. Theory X managers see their role as closely monitoring workers to ensure that they contribute to the production process and do not threaten product quality. Henry Ford, who closely supervised and managed his workforce, fits McGregor's description of a manager who holds Theory X assumptions.

Theory Y A set of positive assumptions about workers that leads to the conclusion that a manager's task is to create a work setting that encourages commitment to organizational goals and provides opportunities for workers to be imaginative and to exercise initiative and self-direction.

THEORY Y In contrast, **Theory Y** assumes that workers are not inherently lazy, do not naturally dislike work, and, if given the opportunity, will do what is good for the organization. According to Theory Y, the characteristics of the work setting determine whether workers consider work to be a source of satisfaction or punishment, and managers do not need to closely control workers' behavior to make them perform at a high level because workers exercise self-control when they are committed to organizational goals. The implication of Theory Y, according to McGregor, is that "the limits of collaboration in the organizational setting are not limits of human nature but of management's ingenuity in discovering how to realize the potential represented by its human resources."[28] It is the manager's task to create a work setting that encourages commitment to organizational goals and provides opportunities for workers to be imaginative and to exercise initiative and self-direction.

When managers design the organizational setting to reflect the assumptions about attitudes and behavior suggested by Theory Y, the characteristics of the organization are quite different from those of an organizational setting based on Theory X. Managers who believe workers are motivated to help the organization reach its goals can decentralize authority and give more control over the job to workers, both as

From the time that Dave Packard and Bill Hewlett first set up shop in a garage in 1938, they established a new people-oriented approach to management, known as the "HP Way."

individuals and in groups. In this setting, individuals and groups are still accountable for their activities; but the manager's role is not to control employees but to provide support and advice, to make sure employees have the resources they need to perform their jobs, and to evaluate them on their ability to help the organization meet its goals. Henri Fayol's approach to administration more closely reflects the assumptions of Theory Y rather than Theory X.

One company that was founded on the type of management philosophy inherent in Theory Y is the electronics company Hewlett-Packard (HP), which from its founding consistently put into practice principles derived from Theory Y. (Go to the company's Web site at www.hp.com for additional information.) Founders William Hewlett and David Packard–Bill and Dave, as they are still known throughout the organization–established a philosophy of management known as the "HP Way" that is people-oriented, stresses the importance of treating every person with consideration and respect, and offers recognition for achievements.[29]

The HP Way was based on several guiding principles. One was a policy of long-term employment, and in the past HP went to great lengths not to lay off workers. At times when fewer people were needed, rather than lay off workers, management would cut pay and shorten the workday until demand for HP products picked up. This policy strengthened employees' loyalty to the organization. Another guiding principle in the HP Way concerned how to treat members of the organization so they would feel free to be innovative and creative. HP managers believed that every employee of the company was a member of the HP team. They emphasized the need to increase communication among employees, believing that horizontal communication between peers, not just vertical communication up and down the hierarchy, is essential for creating a positive climate for innovation. So to promote communication between employees at different levels of the hierarchy, HP encouraged informality. Managers and workers were on a first-name basis with each other and with the founders, Bill and Dave. In addition, Bill and Dave pioneered the technique known as "managing by wandering around": People were expected to wander around learning what others were doing so they could tap into opportunities to develop new products or find new avenues for cooperation. Bill and Dave also pioneered the principle that employees should spend 15% of their time working on projects of their own choosing, and HP's product design engineers were told to leave their current work out in the open on their desks so anybody could see what they were doing, learn from it, or suggest ways to improve it. Bill and Dave promoted managers because of their ability to engender excitement and enthusiasm for innovation in their subordinates.[30]

HP's practices helped it become one of the leading electronics companies in the world. In 2001, however, HP, like most other high-tech companies, was experiencing major problems because of the collapse of the telecommunications industry, and the company announced that it was searching for ways to reduce costs. At first its new CEO, Carly Fiorina, did not lay off employees but asked them to accept lower salaries to help the company through this rough spot.[31] It soon became clear, however, that HP's survival was at stake as it battled with efficient global competitors such as Dell and Canon. Fiorina was forced to begin layoffs, and by 2004 HP had laid off over 40% of its employees and outsourced thousands of jobs abroad to remain competitive. In 2005 Fiorina lost her job after investors became concerned that she was pursuing the wrong strategies and that the HP Way seemed to have disappeared. She was replaced as CEO by Mark Hurd, a manager known for his cost-cutting skills;

but by 2006 HP had turned the corner, and Fiorina's efforts were shown to be the right ones for meeting the challenges HP had faced. By 2008 HP was profitable once again, and it overtook Dell to become the largest global PC maker, perhaps because of Fiorina's strategies and Hurd's prudence. Whether the company will once again choose to pursue the HP Way is open to question, however. Today Google exemplifies a company that follows Theory Y and the HP Way. It is clear that managers can view employees differently in their management efforts. Lakshmi Mittal has become very successful turning around steel businesses that governments no longer want. His approach can be seen as different from HP as discussed in the "Manager as a Person" feature.

Manager as a Person

Mittal Makes Millions Revitalizing Steel Industry

Lakshmi Niwas Mittal is the richest man in Europe and the fifth richest in the world with a personal wealth of £19.3 billion. Mittal comes from a wealthy family which concentrated on cold-rolling of sheet steels and the making of alloy steels. Cold-rolled steel occurs when the steel is rolled at room temperature so that its basic crystal arrangement is maintained. Mittal would ultimately have disagreements with his family and go out on his own to start his own steel business. He shifted his focus from cold-rolled steel to integrated mini-mills that employ scrap substitute for steelmaking. Today such mini-mills are a core part of the global steel industry. Today, Lakshmi is the world's largest steel maker. He has no connection with the family-owned steel business.

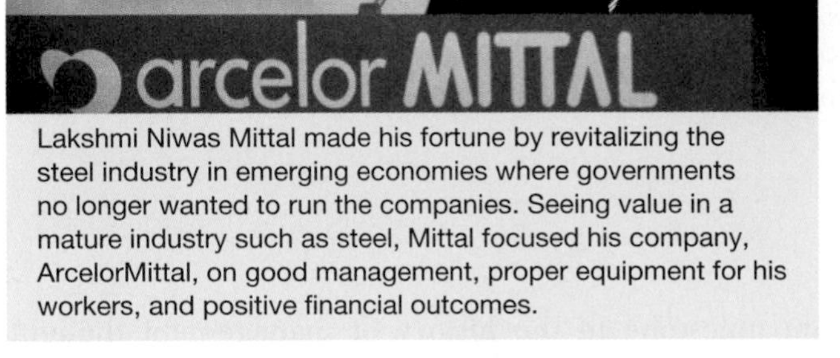

Lakshmi Niwas Mittal made his fortune by revitalizing the steel industry in emerging economies where governments no longer wanted to run the companies. Seeing value in a mature industry such as steel, Mittal focused his company, ArcelorMittal, on good management, proper equipment for his workers, and positive financial outcomes.

Mittal owns 43% of the world's largest steel company–ArcelorMittal. The key strategy that Mittal pursued in building this firm was to recognize that there were state-run steel mills in second world nations like Kazakhstan, Romania, and Poland which were poorly run and whose governments wanted to exit from ownership. Mittal bought these firms and focused on restructuring them to turn a profit. For example, in 2001 Mittal bought a Romanian steel company in Galati that was losing a million U.S. dollars a day. Mittal invested over $350 million to update the equipment. The firm then also laid off approximately 16,000 employees out of the total of 26,000. The result of these changes was that the steel production rose to approximately a $1 billion USD in revenue a year and the firm was profitable by 2004. Mittal pursued this strategy in multiple locations acquiring nearly 20 firms between 1989 and 2006.

Thus, Lakshmi Niwas Mittal has been able to generate significant personal wealth and to revitalize many stagnant industries in emerging economies. He has done so by focusing on good management and ensuring that proper equipment for the workers is present. He saw value in a mature industry that many thought had no future–steel.

Management Science Theory

LO2-5 Explain the contributions of management science to the efficient use of organizational resources.

management science theory An approach to management that uses rigorous quantitative techniques to help managers make maximum use of organizational resources.

Management science theory is a contemporary approach to management that focuses on the use of rigorous quantitative techniques to help managers make maximum use of organizational resources to produce goods and services. In essence, management science theory is a contemporary extension of scientific management, which, as developed by Taylor, also took a quantitative approach to measuring the worker–task mix to raise efficiency. There are many branches of management science; and IT, which is having a significant impact on all kinds of management practices, is affecting the tools managers use to make decisions.[32] Each branch of management science deals with a specific set of concerns:

- *Quantitative management* uses mathematical techniques–such as linear and nonlinear programming, modeling, simulation, queuing theory, and chaos theory–to help managers decide, for example, how much inventory to hold at different times of the year, where to locate a new factory, and how best to invest an organization's financial capital. IT offers managers new and improved ways of handling information so they can make more accurate assessments of the situation and better decisions.
- *Operations management* gives managers a set of techniques they can use to analyze any aspect of an organization's production system to increase efficiency. IT, through the Internet and through growing B2B networks, is transforming how managers acquire inputs and dispose of finished products.
- *Total quality management (TQM)* focuses on analyzing an organization's input, conversion, and output activities to increase product quality.[33] Once again, through sophisticated software packages and computer-controlled production, IT is changing how managers and employees think about the work process and ways of improving it.
- *Management information systems (MIS)* give managers information about events occurring inside the organization as well as in its external environment–information that is vital for effective decision making. Once again, IT gives managers access to more and better information and allows more managers at all levels to participate in the decision-making process.

All these subfields of management science, enhanced by sophisticated IT, provide tools and techniques that managers can use to help improve the quality of their decision making and increase efficiency and effectiveness. We discuss many important developments in management science theory thoroughly in this book. In particular, Chapter 9, "Value Chain Management: Functional Strategies for Competitive Advantage," focuses on how to use operations management and TQM to improve quality, efficiency, and responsiveness to customers. And Chapter 18, "Using Advanced Information Technology to Increase Performance," describes the many ways managers use information systems and technologies to improve their planning, organizing, and controlling functions.

organizational environment The set of forces and conditions that operate beyond an organization's boundaries but affect a manager's ability to acquire and utilize resources.

Organizational Environment Theory

An important milestone in the history of management thought occurred when researchers went beyond the study of how managers can influence behavior within organizations to consider how managers control the organization's relationship with its external environment, or **organizational environment**–the set of forces and conditions that operate beyond an organization's boundaries but affect a manager's ability to acquire and utilize resources. Resources in the organizational environment include the raw materials and skilled people that an organization requires to produce goods and services, as well as the support of groups, including customers who buy these goods and services and

LO2-6 Explain why the study of the external environment and its impact on an organization has become a central issue in management thought.

provide the organization with financial resources. One way of determining the relative success of an organization is to consider how effective its managers are at obtaining scarce and valuable resources.[34] The importance of studying the environment became clear after the development of open-systems theory and contingency theory during the 1960s.

The Open-Systems View

open system A system that takes in resources from its external environment and converts them into goods and services that are then sent back to that environment for purchase by customers.

One of the most influential views of how an organization is affected by its external environment was developed by Daniel Katz, Robert Kahn, and James Thompson in the 1960s.[35] These theorists viewed the organization as an **open system**–a system that takes in resources from its external environment and converts or transforms them into goods and services that are sent back to that environment, where they are bought by customers (see Figure 2.4).

At the *input stage* an organization acquires resources such as raw materials, money, and skilled workers to produce goods and services. Once the organization has gathered the necessary resources, conversion begins. At the *conversion stage* the organization's workforce, using appropriate tools, techniques, and machinery, transforms the inputs into outputs of finished goods and services such as cars, hamburgers, or flights. At the *output stage* the organization releases finished goods and services to its external environment, where customers purchase and use them to satisfy their needs. The money the organization obtains from the sales of its outputs allows the organization to acquire more resources so the cycle can begin again.

closed system A system that is self-contained and thus not affected by changes occurring in its external environment.

entropy The tendency of a closed system to lose its ability to control itself and thus to dissolve and disintegrate.

The system just described is said to be open because the organization draws from and interacts with the external environment in order to survive; in other words, the organization is open to its environment. A **closed system,** in contrast, is a self-contained system that is not affected by changes in its external environment. Organizations that operate as closed systems, that ignore the external environment, and that fail to acquire inputs are likely to experience **entropy,** which is the tendency of a closed system to lose its ability to control itself and thus to dissolve and disintegrate.

Figure 2.4
The Organization as an Open System

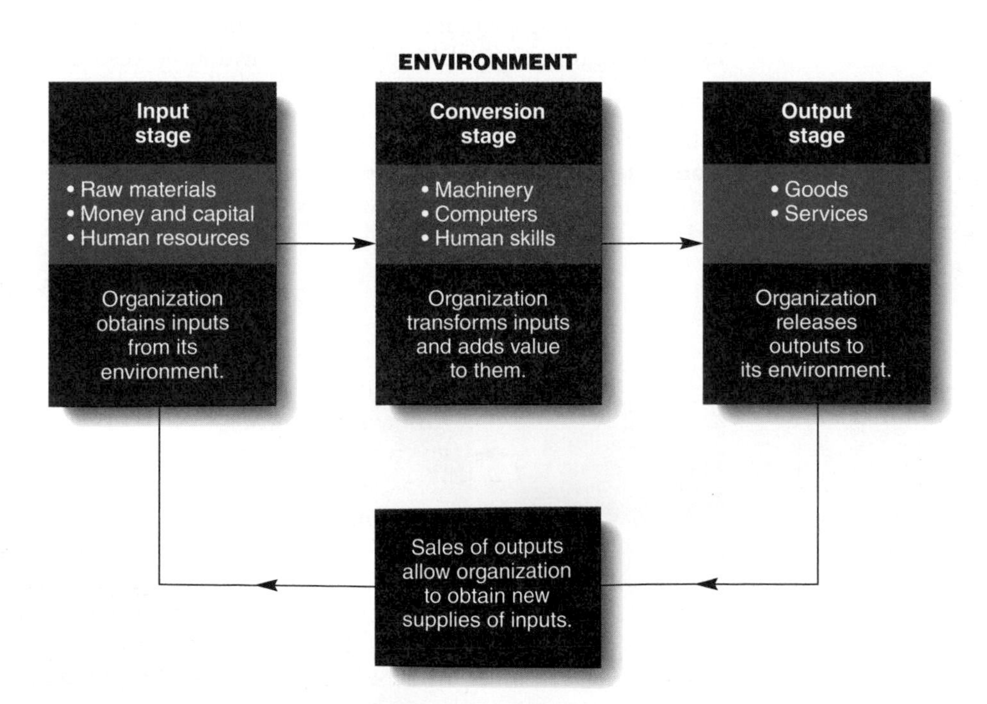

Management theorists can model the activities of most organizations by using the open-systems view. Manufacturing companies like Fiat and Siemens, for example, buy inputs such as component parts, skilled and semiskilled labor, and robots and computer-controlled manufacturing equipment; then at the conversion stage they use their manufacturing skills to assemble inputs into outputs of cars and appliances. As we discuss in later chapters, competition between organizations for resources is one of several major challenges to managing the organizational environment.

Researchers using the open-systems view are also interested in how the various parts of a system work together to promote efficiency and effectiveness. Systems theorists like to argue that the whole is greater than the sum of its parts; they mean that an organization performs at a higher level when its departments work together rather than separately. **Synergy,** the performance gains that result from the *combined* actions of individuals and departments, is possible only in an organized system. The recent interest in using teams combined or composed of people from different departments reflects systems theorists' interest in designing organizational systems to create synergy and thus increase efficiency and effectiveness.

synergy Performance gains that result when individuals and departments coordinate their actions.

Contingency Theory

Another milestone in management theory was the development of **contingency theory** in the 1960s by Tom Burns and G. M. Stalker in Britain and Paul Lawrence and Jay Lorsch in the United States.[36] The crucial message of contingency theory is that *there is no one best way to organize:* The organizational structures and the control systems that managers choose depend on (are contingent on) characteristics of the external environment in which the organization operates. According to contingency theory, the characteristics of the environment affect an organization's ability to obtain resources; and to maximize the likelihood of gaining access to resources, managers must allow an organization's departments to organize and control their activities in ways most likely to allow them to obtain resources, given the constraints of the particular environment they face. In other words, how managers design the organizational hierarchy, choose a control system, and lead and motivate their employees is contingent on the characteristics of the organizational environment (see Figure 2.5).

contingency theory The idea that the organizational structures and control systems managers choose depend on (are contingent on) characteristics of the external environment in which the organization operates.

An important characteristic of the external environment that affects an organization's ability to obtain resources is the degree to which the environment is changing. Changes in the organizational environment include changes in technology, which can lead to the creation of new products (such as compact discs) and result in the obsolescence of existing products (eight-track tapes); the entry of new competitors (such as foreign organizations that compete for available resources); and unstable economic

Figure 2.5
Contingency Theory of Organizational Design

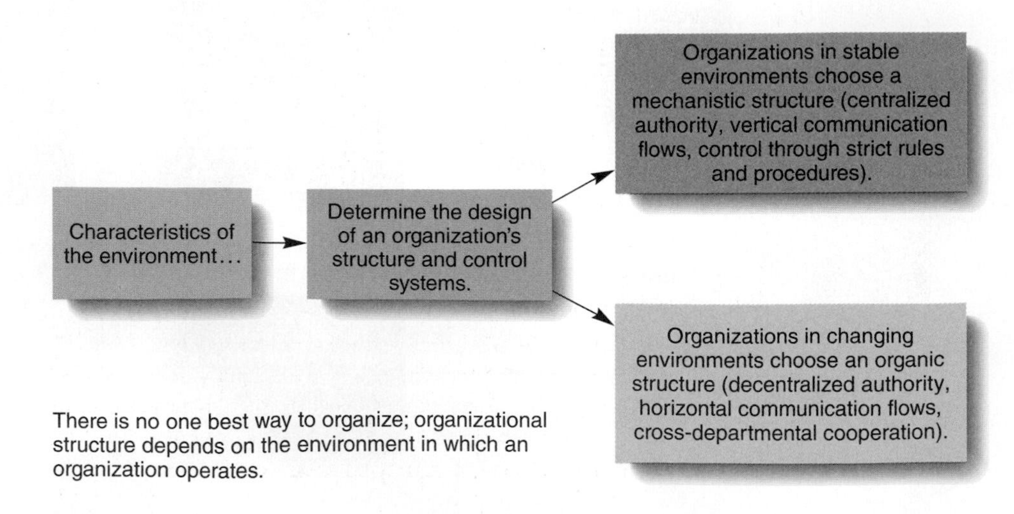

There is no one best way to organize; organizational structure depends on the environment in which an organization operates.

conditions. In general, the more quickly the organizational environment is changing, the greater are the problems associated with gaining access to resources, and the greater is managers' need to find ways to coordinate the activities of people in different departments to respond to the environment quickly and effectively.

MECHANISTIC AND ORGANIC STRUCTURES Drawing on Weber's and Fayol's principles of organization and management, Burns and Stalker proposed two basic ways in which managers can organize and control an organization's activities to respond to characteristics of its external environment: They can use a *mechanistic structure* or an *organic structure.*[37] As you will see, a mechanistic structure typically rests on Theory X assumptions, and an organic structure typically rests on Theory Y assumptions.

When the environment surrounding an organization is stable, managers tend to choose a mechanistic structure to organize and control activities and make employee behavior predictable. In a **mechanistic structure,** authority is centralized at the top of the managerial hierarchy, and the vertical hierarchy of authority is the main means used to control subordinates' behavior. Tasks and roles are clearly specified, subordinates are closely supervised, and the emphasis is on strict discipline and order. Everyone knows his or her place, and there is a place for everyone. A mechanistic structure provides the most efficient way to operate in a stable environment because it allows managers to obtain inputs at the lowest cost, giving an organization the most control over its conversion processes and enabling the most efficient production of goods and services with the smallest expenditure of resources. McDonald's restaurants operate with a mechanistic structure. Supervisors make all important decisions; employees are closely supervised and follow well-defined rules and standard operating procedures.

mechanistic structure An organizational structure in which authority is centralized, tasks and rules are clearly specified, and employees are closely supervised.

In contrast, when the environment is changing rapidly, it is difficult to obtain access to resources, and managers need to organize their activities in a way that allows them to cooperate, to act quickly to acquire resources (such as new types of inputs to produce new kinds of products), and to respond effectively to the unexpected. In an **organic structure,** authority is decentralized to middle and first-line managers to encourage them to take responsibility and act quickly to pursue scarce resources. Departments are encouraged to take a cross-departmental or functional perspective, and cross-functional teams composed of people from different departments are formed. As in Mary Parker Follett's model, the organization operates in an organic way because authority rests with the individuals, departments, and teams best positioned to control the current problems the organization is facing. As a result, managers in an organic structure can react more quickly to a changing environment than can managers in a mechanistic structure. However, an organic structure is generally more expensive to operate because it requires that more managerial time, money, and effort be spent on coordination. So it is used only when needed–when the organizational environment is unstable and rapidly changing.[38] Google, Apple, Xerox, and other companies discussed in this book are examples of companies that operate with organic structures.

organic structure An organizational structure in which authority is decentralized to middle and first-line managers and tasks and roles are left ambiguous to encourage employees to cooperate and respond quickly to the unexpected.

Summary and Review

In this chapter we examined the evolution of management theory and research over the last century. Much of the material in the rest of this book stems from developments and refinements of this work. Indeed, the rest of this book incorporates the results of the extensive research in management that has been conducted since the development of the theories discussed here.

LO2-1, 2-2 **SCIENTIFIC MANAGEMENT THEORY** The search for efficiency started with the study of how managers could improve person–task relationships to increase efficiency. The concept of job specialization and division of labor remains the basis for the design of work settings in modern organizations. New developments such as lean production and total quality management are often viewed as advances on the early scientific management principles developed by Taylor and the Gilbreths.

LO2-3 **ADMINISTRATIVE MANAGEMENT THEORY** Max Weber and Henri Fayol outlined principles of bureaucracy and administration that are as relevant to managers today as they were when developed at the turn of the 20th century. Much of modern management research refines these principles to suit contemporary conditions. For example, the increasing interest in the use of cross-departmental teams and the empowerment of workers are issues that managers also faced a century ago.

LO2-4 **BEHAVIORAL MANAGEMENT THEORY** Researchers have described many different approaches to managerial behavior, including Theories X and Y. Often the managerial behavior that researchers suggest reflects the context of their own historical eras and cultures. Mary Parker Follett advocated managerial behaviors that did not reflect accepted modes of managerial behavior at the time, and her work was largely ignored until conditions changed.

LO2-5 **MANAGEMENT SCIENCE THEORY** The various branches of management science theory provide rigorous quantitative techniques that give managers more control over each organization's use of resources to produce goods and services.

LO2-6 **ORGANIZATIONAL ENVIRONMENT THEORY** The importance of studying the organization's external environment became clear after the development of open-systems theory and contingency theory during the 1960s. A main focus of contemporary management research is to find methods to help managers improve how they use organizational resources and compete in the global environment. Strategic management and total quality management are two important approaches intended to help managers make better use of organizational resources.

Management in Action

Topics for Discussion and Action

Discussion

1. Choose a fast-food restaurant, a department store, or some other organization with which you are familiar, and describe the division of labor and job specialization it uses to produce goods and services. How might this division of labor be improved? **[LO2-1, 2-2]**
2. Apply Taylor's principles of scientific management to improve the performance of the organization you chose in topic 1. **[LO2-2]**
3. In what ways are Weber's and Fayol's ideas about bureaucracy and administration similar? How do they differ? **[LO2-3]**
4. Which of Weber's and Fayol's principles seem most relevant to the creation of an ethical organization? **[LO2-4, 2-6]**
5. Why was the work of Mary Parker Follett ahead of its time? To what degree do you think it is appropriate today? **[LO2-4, 2-5]**
6. What is contingency theory? What kinds of organizations familiar to you have been successful or unsuccessful in dealing with contingencies from the external environment? **[LO2-6]**
7. Why are mechanistic and organic structures suited to different organizational environments? **[LO2-4, 2-6]**

Action

8. Question a manager about his or her views of the relative importance of Fayol's 14 principles of management. **[LO2-3, 2-4]**
9. Visit at least two organizations in your community, and identify those that seem to operate with a Theory X or a Theory Y approach to management. **[LO2-4]**

Building Management Skills

Managing Your Own Business [LO2-2, 2-4]

Now that you understand the concerns addressed by management thinkers over the last century, use this exercise to apply your knowledge to developing your management skills.

Imagine that you are the founding entrepreneur of a software company that specializes in developing games for home computers. Customer demand for your games has increased so much that over the last year your company has grown from a busy one-person operation to one with 16 employees. In addition to yourself, you employ six software developers to produce the software, three graphic artists, two computer technicians, two marketing and sales personnel, and two secretaries. In the next year you expect to hire 30 new employees, and you are wondering how best to manage your growing company.

1. Use the principles of Weber and Fayol to decide on the system of organization and management that you think will be most effective for your growing organization. How many levels will the managerial hierarchy of your organization have? How much authority will you decentralize to your subordinates? How will you establish the division of labor between subordinates? Will your subordinates work alone and report to you or work in teams?
2. Which management approach (for example, Theory X or Y) do you propose to use to run your organization? In 50 or fewer words write a statement describing the management approach you believe will motivate and coordinate your subordinates, and tell why you think this style will be best.

Managing Ethically [LO2-3, 2-4]

Ethics in Action: How to Manage Ethical Problems
Ethics in the Global Flower-Growing Business

Every year on Valentine's Day tens of millions of roses are delivered to loved ones in the United States, and anyone who has bought roses knows that their price has been dropping. One of the main reasons for this is that global rose growing is now concentrated in poorer countries in Central and South America. Rose growing has been a boon to poor countries because the extra income women earn can mean the difference between starving or eating for their families. The hidden side of the global rose-growing business is that poorer countries tend to have lax or unenforced health and safety laws—a major reason why they have lower rose-growing costs. And many rose-growing companies are *not* considering the well-being of their workers; neither are the companies around the world that distribute and sell roses to customers. For example, almost 60% of workers of Rosas del Ecuador, a major U.S. importer, have experienced blurred vision, nausea, headaches, asthma, and other symptoms of pesticide poisoning.[39] Workers labor in hot, poorly ventilated greenhouses in which roses have been sprayed with pesticides and herbicides for long hours and safety equipment such as masks and ventilators is scarce. If workers complain, they may be fired and blacklisted, so to protect their families' well-being, workers rarely complain and thus their health remains at risk. Given this lack of protest, Canadian companies that buy its roses are often unaware of the conditions under which they are produced.

Questions

1. Use the theories discussed in the chapter to debate the ethical issues involved in the global flower-growing business.
2. In what ways do the way cars were made in the past reflect the way in which the rose-growing business is being conducted today?
3. Search the Web for changes occurring in the global flower-growing business.

Small Group Breakout Exercise [LO2-6]

Modeling an Open System

Form groups of three to five people, and appoint one group member as the spokesperson who will communicate your findings to the class when called on by the instructor. Then discuss the following scenario:

Think of an organization with which you are all familiar, such as a local restaurant, store, or bank. After choosing an organization, model it from an open-systems perspective. Identify its input, conversion, and output processes; and identify forces in the external environment that help or hurt the organization's ability to obtain resources and dispose of its goods or services.

Exploring the World Wide Web [LO2-3, 2-6]

Research Fiat's Web site (www.fiat.com), and locate and read the material about Fiat's history and evolution over time. What have been the significant stages in the company's development? What problems and issues confronted managers at these stages? What challenges face Fiat's managers now?

Be the Manager [LO 2-2, 2-4]

How to Manage a Hotel

You have been called in to advise the owners of an exclusive new luxury hotel in Italy. For the venture to succeed, hotel employees must focus on providing customers with the highest-quality customer service possible. The challenge is to devise a way of organizing and controlling employees that will promote high-quality service, that will encourage employees to be committed to the hotel, and that will reduce the level of employee turnover and absenteeism—which are typically high in the hotel business.

Questions

1. How do the various management theories discussed in this chapter offer clues for organizing and controlling hotel employees?
2. Which parts would be the most important for an effective system to organize and control employees?

CHAPTER 3

Values, Attitudes, Emotions, and Culture: The Manager as a Person

Learning Objectives

After studying this chapter, you should be able to:

LO3-1 Describe the various personality traits that affect how managers think, feel, and behave.

LO3-2 Explain what values and attitudes are and describe their impact on managerial action.

LO3-3 Appreciate how moods and emotions influence all members of an organization.

LO3-4 Describe the nature of emotional intelligence and its role in management.

LO3-5 Define organizational culture and explain how managers both create and are influenced by organizational culture.

A MANAGER'S CHALLENGE

Success and Failures at the Virgin Group

Richard Branson is a British entrepreneur who heads the Virgin Group—a collection of over 350 different businesses. This group includes a wide range of businesses such as trains and planes, credit cards, flights in space, fitness clubs, and mega music stores. Today, he is one of the 250 richest people in the world.

Branson was, in part, motivated to focus on business since he was such a poor student. He has severe learning disabilities that hampered his success at school. But he discovered that he had a unique ability to work with, and connect to, people. His first venture, at the age 16, was to start a magazine called *Student*. The magazine was designed by students, for students and was intended to be a national magazine that connected students across Britain. Branson was unusually successful in getting many leading and interesting people to be interviewed and part of the magazine. However, his big commercial break came in 1970 when the British government abolished the Retail Price Maintenance Agreement which had limited the ability of stores to discount records. Branson saw an opportunity for his magazine to offer records cheaply by running ads for mail order delivery. Ultimately he was making more from selling records than from magazine subscriptions. Branson next opened a record store that would sell discount records directly rather than through the mail. In part, this decision was driven by the fear that a pending postal strike might hurt the mail order record business. The staff of the magazine was recruited to run the store. Branson's people skills came into play as he convinced the owner of the store to let him have the store rent free since there would be so much

Sir Richard Branson, shown here at a global symposium, is a highly successful entrepreneur. As head of the Virgin Group—a collection of more than 350 different businesses, Branson has made his mark by identifying opportunities, taking risks, and giving his employees autonomy and respect.

customer traffic other shop owners in the area would benefit.

The record shop was very successful. Ultimately Branson used profits from the record store business to buy a country estate which had a recording studio. Branson began to lease time in the studio. Seeing another opportunity, he next opened Virgin Records. This studio opened up new types of music to listeners by promoting bands such as the Sex Pistols, Boy George, and Culture Club. Eventually Branson sold Virgin Records to EMI for 500 million pounds. Today he has started a new record label called V2.

Currently there is a rich set of businesses in Branson's empire. He saw that British Airlines had a near monopoly on air travel to Britain from the United States in the early 1980s. He therefore set up an all-business-class airline that would offer reasonable fares and better service from New York City to London—Virgin Atlantic. From this initial start there is now a range of airlines from Virgin Blue, to Virgin Express, to V Australia. A flight attendant on the airline suggested that Branson support a chain of bridal shops she wanted to start which, in time, he did. He then had his picture taken in a wedding dress promoting the chain of bridal stores. Branson also developed a space tourism company called Virgin Galactic. And Virgin Health Bank stores the stem cells of babies. (Such stem cells are useful if the baby ever develops serious health problems even as an adult.)

As can be imagined with such a rich array of enterprises, Branson does not have a heavy hand in managing most of them. Branson once joked, "I believe in benevolent dictatorship, provided I am the dictator." In fact, he provides the leadership and promotion of the ideas. He gives great respect and autonomy to his employees. He understands that without a solid team to run the businesses there would be little opportunity for him to be as creative and diverse as he is.

Not all of Branson's entrepreneurial efforts have been flawless. In 1971 he was charged by the British authorities with selling record stock domestically that was intended for export and as a result had not paid local tax. The result was a fine of $90,000; Branson's mother had to mortgage the family home to pay the fine. In addition, some ventures such as Virgin Trains have not been as profitable or run as well as would have been hoped. Virgin Trains came as the British government privatized trains in Britain. The trains run from London Euston to the West Midlands, North West England, North Wales and Scotland, and from Birmingham New Street to North West England and Scotland, on the West Coast Main Line. The trains have been substantially improved since the initial launch of the system but still, performance is not as high in many regards as hoped.

Richard Branson has been knighted by the Queen of England and so is now called Sir Richard Branson. This success for a person with no university education is a great accomplishment. He has been able to develop a great brand around himself based on his ability to identify opportunities, take risks, and encourage others to work hard on a given task.

Overview

In this chapter we focus on the manager as a feeling, thinking human being. We start by describing enduring characteristics that influence how managers manage, as well as how they view other people, their organizations, and the world around them. We also discuss how managers' values, attitudes, and moods play out in organizations, shaping organizational culture. By the end of this chapter, you will appreciate how the personal characteristics of managers influence the process of management in general–and organizational culture in particular.

LO3-1 Describe the various personality traits that affect how managers think, feel, and behave.

Enduring Characteristics: Personality Traits

All people, including managers, have certain enduring characteristics that influence how they think, feel, and behave both on and off the job. These characteristics are **personality traits:** particular tendencies to feel, think, and act in certain ways that can be used to describe the personality of every individual. It is important to understand the personalities of managers because their personalities influence their behavior and their approach to managing people and resources.

personality traits Enduring tendencies to feel, think, and act in certain ways.

Some managers are demanding, difficult to get along with, and highly critical of other people. Other managers may be as concerned about effectiveness and efficiency as highly critical managers but are easier to get along with, are likable, and frequently praise the people around them. Both management styles may produce excellent results, but their effects on employees are quite different. Do managers deliberately decide to adopt one or the other of these approaches to management? Although they may do so part of the time, in all likelihood their personalities account for their different approaches. Indeed, research suggests that the way people react to different conditions depends, in part, on their personalities.[1]

The Big Five Personality Traits

We can think of an individual's personality as being composed of five general traits or characteristics: extraversion, negative affectivity, agreeableness, conscientiousness, and openness to experience.[2] Researchers often consider these the Big Five personality traits.[3] Each of them can be viewed as a continuum along which every individual or, more specifically, every manager falls (see Figure 3.1).

Some managers may be at the high end of one trait continuum, others at the low end, and still others somewhere in between. An easy way to understand how these traits can affect a person's approach to management is to describe what people are like at the high and low ends of each trait continuum. As will become evident as you read about each trait, no single trait is right or wrong for being an effective manager. Rather, effectiveness is determined by a complex interaction between the characteristics of managers (including personality traits) and the nature of the job and organization in which they are working. Moreover, personality traits that enhance managerial effectiveness in one situation may impair it in another.

extraversion The tendency to experience positive emotions and moods and to feel good about oneself and the rest of the world.

EXTRAVERSION **Extraversion** is the tendency to experience positive emotions and moods and feel good about oneself and the rest of the world. Managers who are high on extraversion (often called *extraverts*) tend to be sociable, affectionate, outgoing, and friendly. Managers who are low on extraversion (often called *introverts*) tend to be less inclined toward social interactions and to have a less positive outlook. Being high on extraversion may be an asset for managers whose jobs entail especially high levels of social interaction. Managers who are low on extraversion may nevertheless be highly effective and efficient, especially when their jobs do not require much social interaction. Their quieter approach may enable them to accomplish quite a bit

Figure 3.1
The Big Five Personality Traits

Managers' personalities can be described by determining which point on each of the following dimensions best characterizes the manager in question:

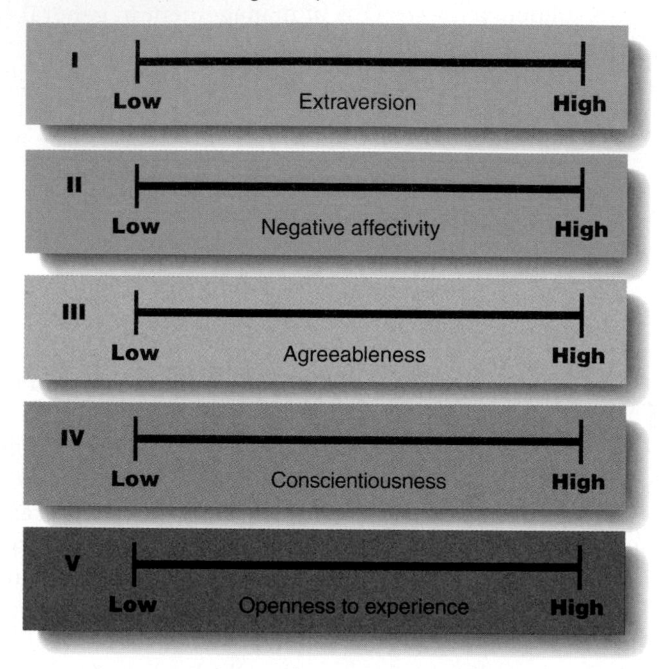

of work in limited time. See Figure 3.2 for an example of a scale that can be used to measure a person's level of extraversion.

negative affectivity The tendency to experience negative emotions and moods, to feel distressed, and to be critical of oneself and others.

NEGATIVE AFFECTIVITY **Negative affectivity** is the tendency to experience negative emotions and moods, feel distressed, and be critical of oneself and others. Managers high on this trait may often feel angry and dissatisfied and complain about their own and others' lack of progress. Managers who are low on negative affectivity do not tend to experience many negative emotions and moods and are less pessimistic and critical of themselves and others. On the plus side, the critical approach of a manager high on negative affectivity may sometimes spur both the manager and others to improve their performance. Nevertheless, it is probably more pleasant to work with a manager who is low on negative affectivity; the better working relationships that such a manager is likely to cultivate also can be an important asset. Figure 3.3 is an example of a scale developed to measure a person's level of negative affectivity.

agreeableness The tendency to get along well with other people.

AGREEABLENESS **Agreeableness** is the tendency to get along well with others. Managers who are high on the agreeableness continuum are likable, tend to be affectionate, and care about other people. Managers who are low on agreeableness may be somewhat distrustful of others, unsympathetic, uncooperative, and even at times antagonistic. Being high on agreeableness may be especially important for managers whose responsibilities require that they develop good, close relationships with others. Nevertheless, a low level of agreeableness may be an asset in managerial jobs that actually require that managers be antagonistic, such as drill sergeants and some other kinds of military managers. See Figure 3.2 for an example of a scale that measures a person's level of agreeableness.

conscientiousness The tendency to be careful, scrupulous, and persevering.

CONSCIENTIOUSNESS **Conscientiousness** is the tendency to be careful, scrupulous, and persevering.[4] Managers who are high on the conscientiousness

Figure 3.2
Measures of Extraversion, Agreeableness, Conscientiousness, and Openness to Experience

Listed below are phrases describing people's behaviors. Please use the rating scale below to describe how accurately each statement describes *you*. Describe yourself as you generally are now, not as you wish to be in the future. Describe yourself as you honestly see yourself, in relation to other people you know of the same sex as you are and roughly your same age.

1	2	3	4	5
Very inaccurate	Moderately inaccurate	Neither inaccurate nor accurate	Moderately accurate	Very accurate

____ **1.** Am interested in people.
____ **2.** Have a rich vocabulary.
____ **3.** Am always prepared.
____ **4.** Am not really interested in others.*
____ **5.** Leave my belongings around.*
____ **6.** Am the life of the party.
____ **7.** Have difficulty understanding abstract ideas.*
____ **8.** Sympathize with others' feelings.
____ **9.** Don't talk a lot.*
____ **10.** Pay attention to details.
____ **11.** Have a vivid imagination.
____ **12.** Insult people.*
____ **13.** Make a mess of things.*
____ **14.** Feel comfortable around people.
____ **15.** Am not interested in abstract ideas.*
____ **16.** Have a soft heart.
____ **17.** Get chores done right away.
____ **18.** Keep in the background.*
____ **19.** Have excellent ideas.
____ **20.** Start conversations.
____ **21.** Am not interested in other people's problems.*
____ **22.** Often forget to put things back in their proper place.*
____ **23.** Have little to say.*
____ **24.** Do not have a good imagination.*
____ **25.** Take time out for others.
____ **26.** Like order.
____ **27.** Talk to a lot of different people at parties.
____ **28.** Am quick to understand things.
____ **29.** Feel little concern for others.*
____ **30.** Shirk my duties.*
____ **31.** Don't like to draw attention to myself.*
____ **32.** Use difficult words.
____ **33.** Feel others' emotions.
____ **34.** Follow a schedule.
____ **35.** Spend time reflecting on things.
____ **36.** Don't mind being the center of attention.
____ **37.** Make people feel at ease.
____ **38.** Am exacting in my work.
____ **39.** Am quiet around strangers.*
____ **40.** Am full of ideas.

* Item is reverse-scored: 1 = 5, 2 = 4, 4 = 2, 5 = 1
Scoring: Sum responses to items for an overall scale.
Extraversion = sum of items 6, 9, 14, 18, 20, 23, 27, 31, 36, 39
Agreeableness = sum of items 1, 4, 8, 12, 16, 21, 25, 29, 33, 37
Conscientiousness = sum of items 3, 5, 10, 13, 17, 22, 26, 30, 34, 38
Openness to experience = sum of items 2, 7, 11, 15, 19, 24, 28, 32, 35, 40

Source: Lewis R. Goldberg, Oregon Research Institute, http://ipip.ori.org/ipip/. Reprinted with permission.

continuum are organized and self-disciplined; those who are low on this trait might sometimes appear to lack direction and self-discipline. Conscientiousness has been found to be a good predictor of performance in many kinds of jobs, including managerial jobs in a variety of organizations.[5] Entrepreneurs who found their own companies often are high on conscientiousness, and their persistence and determination help them to overcome obstacles and turn their ideas into successful new ventures. Figure 3.2 provides an example of a scale that measures conscientiousness.

Figure 3.3
A Measure of Negative Affectivity

Instructions: Listed below are a series of statements a person might use to describe her/his attitudes, opinions, interests, and other characteristics. If a statement is true or largely true, put a "T" in the space next to the item. Or if the statement is false or largely false, mark an "F" in the space.

Please answer every statement, even if you are not completely sure of the answer. Read each statement carefully, but don't spend too much time deciding on the answer.

____ **1.** I worry about things a lot.

____ **2.** My feelings are often hurt.

____ **3.** Small problems often irritate me.

____ **4.** I am often nervous.

____ **5.** My moods often change.

____ **6.** Sometimes I feel bad for no apparent reason.

____ **7.** I often have very strong emotions such as anger or anxiety without really knowing why.

____ **8.** The unexpected can easily startle me.

____ **9.** Sometimes, when I am thinking about the day ahead of me, I feel anxious and tense.

____ **10.** Small setbacks sometimes bother me too much.

____ **11.** My worries often cause me to lose sleep.

____ **12.** Some days I seem to be always "on edge."

____ **13.** I am more sensitive than I should be.

____ **14.** Sometimes I go from feeling happy to sad, and vice versa, for no good reason.

Scoring: Level of negative affectivity is equal to the number of items answered "True."

Source: Auke Tellegen, *Brief Manual for the Differential Personality Questionnaire,* Copyright © 1982. Paraphrased version reproduced by permission of University of Minnesota Press.

openness to experience The tendency to be original, have broad interests, be open to a wide range of stimuli, be daring, and take risks.

OPENNESS TO EXPERIENCE **Openness to experience** is the tendency to be original, have broad interests, be open to a wide range of stimuli, be daring, and take risks.[6] Managers who are high on this trait continuum may be especially likely to take risks and be innovative in their planning and decision making. Entrepreneurs who start their own businesses–like Bill Gates of Microsoft, Jeff Bezos of Amazon .com, and Anita Roddick of The Body Shop–are, in all likelihood, high on openness to experience, which has contributed to their success as entrepreneurs and managers. Managers who are low on openness to experience may be less prone to take risks and more conservative in their planning and decision making. In certain organizations and positions, this tendency might be an asset. The manager of the fiscal office in a public university, for example, must ensure that all university departments and units follow the university's rules and regulations pertaining to budgets, spending accounts, and reimbursements of expenses. Figure 3.2 provides an example of a measure of openness to experience.

Managers who come up with and implement radically new ideas are often high on openness to experience, as is true of Anita Roddick, who founded The Body Shop chain of retail stores.

Manager as a Person

Anita Roddick's Strong Social Conscience

Anita Roddick was a successful British entrepreneur who founded the well-known international chain of stores called The Body Shop. Married with two children, Roddick was looking for ways to supplement the family income while her husband was trekking in South America. The original store offered 15 products designed for women's skin. One means she used to save costs was recycled bottles to put the products in. The products themselves were popular, but over time Roddick's social consciousness became greater and she sought to have her chain of stores operate in an ethical manner. Therefore she had the chain follow several key social policies. These include:

British entrepreneur Anita Roddick, founder of The Body Shop retail chain, firmly believed that companies must have strong social consciences as part of their business strategies. Roddick was against animal testing, supported local trade, defended human rights, and used renewable resources and sustainable ingredients in her stores.

- **Against Animal Testing**—We did not test cosmetics on animals.
- **Support Community Trade**—Sought to buy natural ingredients and handcrafted products from local suppliers of those products ensuring that a fair price was paid for them.
- **Activate Self Esteem**—The firm refused to sell false promises of an unattainable ideal of beauty.
- **Defend Human Rights**—Respect and honor human rights.
- **Protect the Planet**—The firm sought to use renewable resources and sustainable raw ingredients.

Using these guiding principles, The Body Shop was able to expand to approximately 2000 stores worldwide. Ultimately Ms. Roddick developed cirrhosis of the liver that would take her life in 2007. Prior to her death she sold her company to L'Oréal for £652 million. Anita Roddick was able to see a market opportunity that also matched her personal beliefs in the value of people and how business should be operated that resulted in great success.

Successful managers occupy a variety of positions on the Big Five personality trait continua. One highly effective manager may be high on extraversion and negative affectivity; another equally effective manager may be low on both these traits; and still another may be somewhere in between. Members of an organization must understand these differences among managers because they can shed light on how managers behave and on their approach to planning, leading, organizing, or controlling. If subordinates realize, for example, that their manager is low on extraversion, they will not feel slighted when their manager seems to be aloof because they will realize that by nature he or she is simply not outgoing.

Managers themselves also need to be aware of their own personality traits and the traits of others, including their subordinates and fellow managers. A manager who knows that he has a tendency to be highly critical of other people might try to tone down his negative approach. Similarly, a manager who realizes that her chronically complaining subordinate tends to be so negative because of his personality may take all his complaints with a grain of salt and realize that things probably are not as bad as this subordinate says they are.

In order for all members of an organization to work well together and with people outside the organization, such as customers and suppliers, they must understand each other. Such understanding comes, in part, from an appreciation of some fundamental ways in which people differ from one another–that is, an appreciation of personality traits.

Other Personality Traits That Affect Managerial Behavior

Many other specific traits in addition to the Big Five describe people's personalities. Here we look at traits that are particularly important for understanding managerial effectiveness: locus of control; self-esteem; and the needs for achievement, affiliation, and power.

LOCUS OF CONTROL People differ in their views about how much control they have over what happens to and around them. The locus of control trait captures these beliefs.[7] People with an **internal locus of control** believe they themselves are responsible for their own fate; they see their own actions and behaviors as being major and decisive determinants of important outcomes such as attaining levels of job performance, being promoted, or being turned down for a choice job assignment. Some managers with an internal locus of control see the success of a whole organization resting on their shoulders. An internal locus of control also helps to ensure ethical behavior and decision making in an organization because people feel accountable and responsible for their own actions.

internal locus of control The tendency to locate responsibility for one's fate within oneself.

People with an **external locus of control** believe that outside forces are responsible for what happens to and around them; they do not think their own actions make much of a difference. As such, they tend not to intervene to try to change a situation or solve a problem, leaving it to someone else.

external locus of control The tendency to locate responsibility for one's fate in outside forces and to believe one's own behavior has little impact on outcomes.

Managers need an internal locus of control because they *are* responsible for what happens in organizations; they need to believe they can and do make a difference. Moreover, managers are responsible for ensuring that organizations and their members behave in an ethical fashion, and for this as well they need an internal locus of control–they need to know and feel they can make a difference.

SELF-ESTEEM **Self-esteem** is the degree to which individuals feel good about themselves and their capabilities. People with high self-esteem believe they are competent, deserving, and capable of handling most situations. People with low self-esteem have poor opinions of themselves, are unsure about their capabilities, and question their ability to succeed at different endeavors.[8] Research suggests that people tend to choose activities and goals consistent with their levels of self-esteem. High self-esteem is desirable for managers because it facilitates their setting and keeping high standards for themselves, pushes them ahead on difficult projects, and gives them the confidence they need to make and carry out important decisions.

self-esteem The degree to which individuals feel good about themselves and their capabilities.

NEEDS FOR ACHIEVEMENT, AFFILIATION, AND POWER Psychologist David McClelland has extensively researched the needs for achievement, affiliation, and power.[9] The **need for achievement** is the extent to which an individual has a strong desire to perform challenging tasks well and to meet personal standards for excellence. People with a high need for achievement often set clear goals for themselves and like to receive performance feedback. The **need for affiliation** is the extent to which an individual is concerned about establishing and maintaining good interpersonal relations, being liked, and having the people around him or her get along with

need for achievement The extent to which an individual has a strong desire to perform challenging tasks well and to meet personal standards for excellence.

need for affiliation The extent to which an individual is concerned about establishing and maintaining good interpersonal relations, being liked, and having other people get along.

need for power The extent to which an individual desires to control or influence others.

Confidence matters: a manager who takes difficulties in stride and can effectively lead is able to inspire subordinates while getting the job done.

one another. The **need for power** is the extent to which an individual desires to control or influence others.[10]

Research suggests that high needs for achievement and for power are assets for first-line and middle managers and that a high need for power is especially important for upper-level managers.[11] One study found that U.S. presidents with a relatively high need for power tended to be especially effective during their terms of office.[12] A high need for affiliation may not always be desirable in managers because it might lead them to try too hard to be liked by others (including subordinates) rather than doing all they can to ensure that performance is as high as it can and should be. Although most research on these needs has been done in the United States, some studies suggest that these findings may also apply to people in other countries such as India and New Zealand.[13]

Taken together, these desirable personality traits for managers–an internal locus of control, high self-esteem, and high needs for achievement and power–suggest that managers need to be take-charge people who not only believe their own actions are decisive in determining their own and their organizations' fates but also believe in their own capabilities. Such managers have a personal desire for accomplishment and influence over others.

Values, Attitudes, and Moods and Emotions

LO3-2 Explain what values and attitudes are and describe their impact on managerial action.

What are managers striving to achieve? How do they think they should behave? What do they think about their jobs and organizations? And how do they actually feel at work? We can find some answers to these questions by exploring managers' values, attitudes, and moods.

Values, attitudes, and moods and emotions capture how managers experience their jobs as individuals. *Values* describe what managers are trying to achieve through work and how they think they should behave. *Attitudes* capture their thoughts and feelings about their specific jobs and organizations. *Moods and emotions* encompass how managers actually feel when they are managing. Although these three aspects of managers' work experience are highly personal, they also have important implications for understanding how managers behave, how they treat and respond to others, and how, through their efforts, they help contribute to organizational effectiveness through planning, leading, organizing, and controlling.

Values: Terminal and Instrumental

terminal value A lifelong goal or objective that an individual seeks to achieve.

instrumental value A mode of conduct that an individual seeks to follow.

norms Unwritten, informal codes of conduct that prescribe how people should act in particular situations and are considered important by most members of a group or organization.

The two kinds of personal values are *terminal* and *instrumental.* A **terminal value** is a personal conviction about lifelong goals or objectives; an **instrumental value** is a personal conviction about desired modes of conduct or ways of behaving.[14] Terminal values often lead to the formation of **norms,** which are unwritten, informal codes of conduct, such as behaving honestly or courteously, that prescribe how people should act in particular situations and are considered important by most members of a group or organization.

Milton Rokeach, a leading researcher in the area of human values, identified 18 terminal values and 18 instrumental values that describe each person's value system

value system The terminal and instrumental values that are guiding principles in an individual's life.

(see Figure 3.4).[15] By rank ordering the terminal values from 1 (most important as a guiding principle in one's life) to 18 (least important as a guiding principle in one's life) and then rank ordering the instrumental values from 1 to 18, people can give good pictures of their **value systems**–what they are striving to achieve in life and how they want to behave.[16] (You can gain a good understanding of your own values by rank ordering first the terminal values and then the instrumental values listed in Figure 3.4.)

Several of the terminal values listed in Figure 3.4 seem to be especially important for managers–such as *a sense of accomplishment (a lasting contribution), equality (brotherhood, equal opportunity for all),* and *self-respect (self-esteem).* A manager who thinks a sense of accomplishment is of paramount importance might focus on making a lasting contribution to an organization by developing a new product that can save or prolong lives, as is true of managers at Medtronic (a company that makes medical devices such as cardiac pacemakers), or by opening a new foreign subsidiary. A manager who places equality at the top of his or her list of terminal values may be at the forefront of an organization's efforts to support, provide equal opportunities to, and capitalize on the many talents of an increasingly diverse workforce.

Other values are likely to be considered important by many managers, such *as a comfortable life (a prosperous life), an exciting life (a stimulating, active life), freedom*

Figure 3.4
Terminal and Instrumental Values

Terminal Values	Instrumental Values
A comfortable life (a prosperous life)	Ambitious (hardworking, aspiring)
An exciting life (a stimulating, active life)	Broad-minded (open-minded)
A sense of accomplishment (lasting contribution)	Capable (competent, effective)
A world at peace (free of war and conflict)	Cheerful (lighthearted, joyful)
A world of beauty (beauty of nature and the arts)	Clean (neat, tidy)
Equality (brotherhood, equal opportunity for all)	Courageous (standing up for your beliefs)
Family security (taking care of loved ones)	Forgiving (willing to pardon others)
Freedom (independence, free choice)	Helpful (working for the welfare of others)
Happiness (contentedness)	Honest (sincere, truthful)
Inner harmony (freedom from inner conflict)	Imaginative (daring, creative)
Mature love (sexual and spiritual intimacy)	Independent (self-reliant, self-sufficient)
National security (protection from attack)	Intellectual (intelligent, reflective)
Pleasure (an enjoyable, leisurely life)	Logical (consistent, rational)
Salvation (saved, eternal life)	Loving (affectionate, tender)
Self-respect (self-esteem)	Obedient (dutiful, respectful)
Social recognition (respect, admiration)	Polite (courteous, well-mannered)
True friendship (close companionship)	Responsible (dependable, reliable)
Wisdom (a mature understanding of life)	Self-controlled (restrained, self-disciplined)

Source: Milton Rokeach, *The Nature of Human Values.* Copyright © 1973 The Free Press. All rights reserved. Reprinted with permission of the Free Press, a Division of Simon & Schuster Adult Publishing Group.

(independence, free choice), and *social recognition (respect, admiration)*. The relative importance that managers place on each terminal value helps explain what they are striving to achieve in their organizations and what they will focus their efforts on.

Several of the instrumental values listed in Figure 3.4 seem to be important modes of conduct for managers, such as being *ambitious (hardworking, aspiring), broad-minded (open-minded), capable (competent, effective), responsible (dependable, reliable)*, and *self-controlled (restrained, self-disciplined)*. Moreover, the relative importance a manager places on these and other instrumental values may be a significant determinant of actual behaviors on the job. A manager who considers being *imaginative (daring, creative)* to be highly important, for example, is more likely to be innovative and take risks than is a manager who considers this to be less important (all else being equal). A manager who considers being *honest (sincere, truthful)* to be of paramount importance may be a driving force for taking steps to ensure that all members of a unit or organization behave ethically, as indicated in the following "Ethics in Action" box.

Ethics in Action

Telling the Truth at Gentle Giant Moving

Gentle Giant Moving Company, based in Somerville, Massachusetts, was founded by Larry O'Toole in 1980 and now has over $28 million in revenues and offices in multiple states.[17] Although moving is undoubtedly hard work and many people would never think about having a career in this industry, Gentle Giant's unique culture and approach to managing people have not only contributed to the company's success but also provided its employees with satisfying careers. For example, when Ryan Libby was in college, he worked for Gentle Giant during one of his summer vacations to make some extra money. Now the assistant manager for the Providence, Rhode Island, Gentle Giant Office, Libby is contemplating opening an office of his own. As he puts it, "First it was just a paycheck, and it kind of turned into a long-term career."[18]

At Gentle Giant Moving Company, employees are given leadership training, access to company outings, and the opportunity to advance to management positions.

Libby is just the kind of employee O'Toole seeks to hire–employees who start out driving moving trucks and eventually move into management positions running offices. Whereas some moving companies hire a lot of temporary help in the summer to meet seasonal demand, 60% of Gentle Giant employees are employed full-time.[19] Because the demand for moving services is lower in the winter, Gentle Giant uses this time to give employees training and leadership development activities. Of course new employees receive training in the basics of moving: packing, lifting, and carrying household goods in a safe manner. However, employees looking to advance in the company receive training in a host of other areas ranging from project management, communication, problem solving, and customer relations to leadership. An overarching goal of Gentle Giant's training efforts is inculcating in employees the importance of honesty. According to O'Toole, "We really emphasize that what matters most to us is telling the truth."[20]

Training benefits Gentle Giant's employees, customers, and the company as a whole. About one-third of the company's office and management employees started out driving moving trucks. Customers are satisfied because employees are capable, honest, and professional. And the company has continued to grow, prosper, and receive recognition in the business press as well as awards. For example, Gentle Giant was named one of the 15 Top Small Workplaces by *The Wall Street Journal* in collaboration with Winning Workplaces (a nonprofit organization that focuses on helping small and medium-size companies improve their work environments).[21]

Having fun and getting to know each other as people is also important at Gentle Giant.[22] The company holds parties and arranges outings for employees to sporting events, amusement parks, and other local attractions. Most workdays, O'Toole takes an employee out to lunch. Some college athletes are attracted to work for Gentle Giant because they see moving as a way to keep fit while at the same time having the opportunity to grow and develop on the job and move into a managerial position if they desire.[23]

All in all, managers' value systems signify what managers as individuals are trying to accomplish and become in their personal lives and at work. Thus managers' value systems are fundamental guides to their behavior and efforts at planning, leading, organizing, and controlling.

Attitudes

attitude A collection of feelings and beliefs.

An **attitude** is a collection of feelings and beliefs. Like everyone else, managers have attitudes about their jobs and organizations, and these attitudes affect how they approach their jobs. Two of the most important attitudes in this context are job satisfaction and organizational commitment.

job satisfaction The collection of feelings and beliefs that managers have about their current jobs.

JOB SATISFACTION **Job satisfaction** is the collection of feelings and beliefs that managers have about their current jobs.[24] Managers who have high levels of job satisfaction generally like their jobs, feel they are fairly treated, and believe their jobs have many desirable features or characteristics (such as interesting work, good pay and job security, autonomy, or nice coworkers). Figure 3.5 shows sample items from two scales that managers can use to measure job satisfaction. Levels of job satisfaction tend to increase as one moves up the hierarchy in an organization. Upper managers, in general, tend to be more satisfied with their jobs than entry-level employees. Managers' levels of job satisfaction can range from very low to very high.

organizational citizenship behaviors (OCBs) Behaviors that are not required of organizational members but that contribute to and are necessary for organizational efficiency, effectiveness, and competitive advantage.

In general, it is desirable for managers to be satisfied with their jobs, for at least two reasons. First, satisfied managers may be more likely to go the extra mile for their organization or perform **organizational citizenship behaviors (OCBs)**–behaviors that are not required of organizational members but that contribute to and are necessary for organizational efficiency, effectiveness, and competitive advantage.[25] Managers who are satisfied with their jobs are more likely to perform these "above and beyond the call of duty" behaviors, which can range from putting in long hours when needed to coming up with truly creative ideas and overcoming obstacles to implement them (even when doing so is not part of the manager's job), or to going out of one's way to help a coworker, subordinate, or superior (even when doing so entails considerable personal sacrifice).[26]

A second reason why it is desirable for managers to be satisfied with their jobs is that satisfied managers may be less likely to quit.[27] A manager who is highly satisfied may never even think about looking for another position; a dissatisfied manager

Figure 3.5
Sample Items from Two Measures of Job Satisfaction

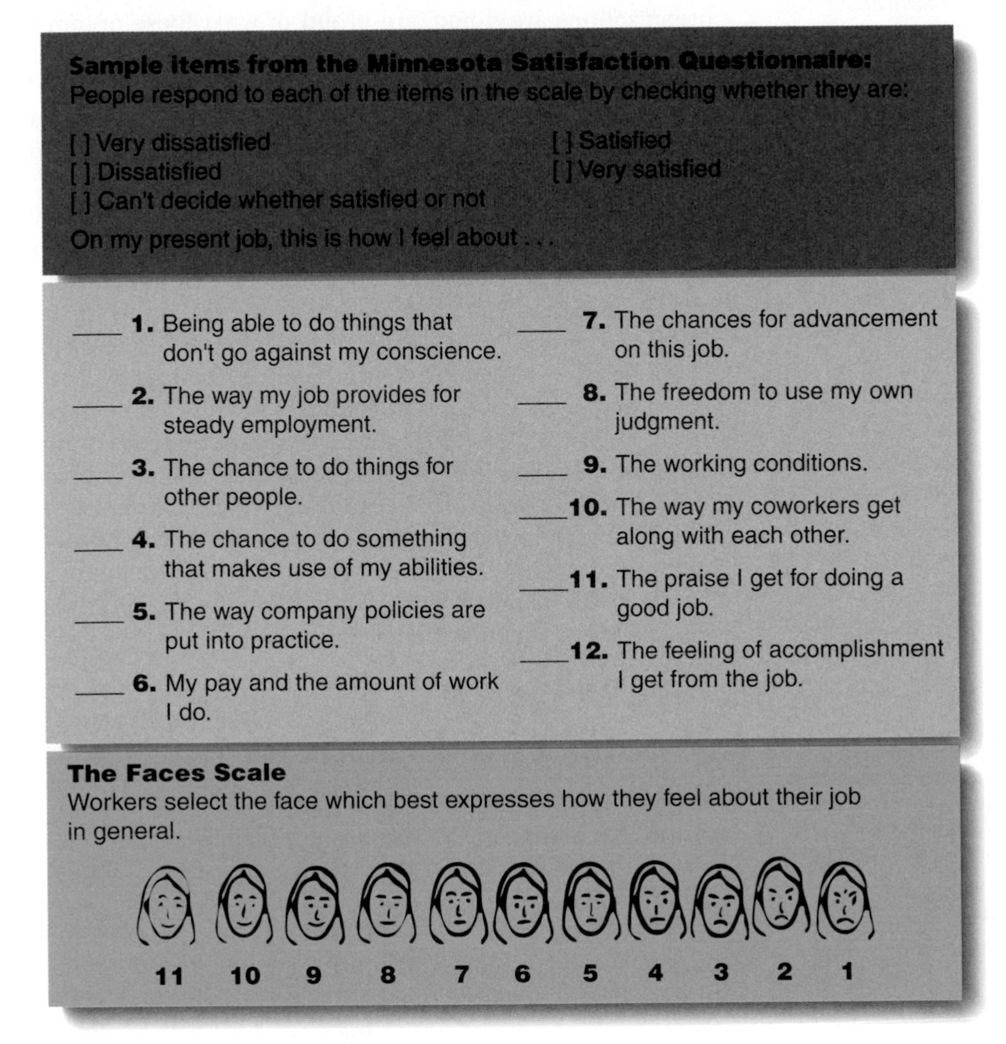
Sample items from the Minnesota Satisfaction Questionnaire:
People respond to each of the items in the scale by checking whether they are:

[ ] Very dissatisfied
[ ] Dissatisfied
[ ] Can't decide whether satisfied or not
[ ] Satisfied
[ ] Very satisfied

On my present job, this is how I feel about . . .

____ **1.** Being able to do things that don't go against my conscience.
____ **2.** The way my job provides for steady employment.
____ **3.** The chance to do things for other people.
____ **4.** The chance to do something that makes use of my abilities.
____ **5.** The way company policies are put into practice.
____ **6.** My pay and the amount of work I do.
____ **7.** The chances for advancement on this job.
____ **8.** The freedom to use my own judgment.
____ **9.** The working conditions.
____ **10.** The way my coworkers get along with each other.
____ **11.** The praise I get for doing a good job.
____ **12.** The feeling of accomplishment I get from the job.

The Faces Scale
Workers select the face which best expresses how they feel about their job in general.

11 10 9 8 7 6 5 4 3 2 1

Source: D. J. Weiss et al., *Manual for the Minnesota Satisfaction Questionnaire,* 1967, Minnesota Studies in Vocational Rehabilitation: XXII. Copyright © 1967 University of Minnesota. Copyright © 1975 by the American Psychological Association. Adapted by permission of Randall B. Dunham and J. B. Brett.

may always be on the lookout for new opportunities. Turnover can hurt an organization because it results in the loss of the experience and knowledge that managers have gained about the company, industry, and business environment.

Staying late to double-check the numbers and look ahead to tomorrow? Not a drag for a motivated, satisfied employee.

A growing source of dissatisfaction for many lower- and middle-level managers, as well as for nonmanagerial employees, is the threat of unemployment and increased workloads from organizational downsizings and layoffs. Organizations that try to improve their efficiency through restructuring and layoffs often eliminate a sizable number of first-line and middle management positions. This decision obviously hurts the managers who are laid off, and it also can reduce the job satisfaction levels of managers who remain. They might fear being the next to be let go. In addition, the workloads of remaining employees often are dramatically increased as a result of restructuring, and this can contribute to dissatisfaction.

organizational commitment The collection of feelings and beliefs that managers have about their organization as a whole.

ORGANIZATIONAL COMMITMENT **Organizational commitment** is the collection of feelings and beliefs that managers have about their organization as a whole.[28] Managers who are committed to their organizations believe in what their organizations are doing, are proud of what these organizations stand for, and feel a high degree of loyalty toward their organizations. Committed managers are more likely to go above and beyond the call of duty to help their company and are less likely to quit.[29] Organizational commitment can be especially strong when employees and managers truly believe in organizational values; it also leads to a strong organizational culture.

Organizational commitment is likely to help managers perform some of their figurehead and spokesperson roles (see Chapter 1). It is much easier for a manager to persuade others both inside and outside the organization of the merits of what the organization has done and is seeking to accomplish if the manager truly believes in and is committed to the organization. Figure 3.6 is an example of a scale that can measure a person's level of organizational commitment.

Do managers in different countries have similar or different attitudes? Differences in the levels of job satisfaction and organizational commitment among managers in different countries are likely because these managers have different kinds of opportunities and rewards and because they face different economic, political, and sociocultural forces in their organizations' general environments. Levels of organizational commitment from one country to another may depend on the extent to which countries have legislation affecting firings and layoffs and the extent to which citizens of a country are geographically mobile.

LO3-3 Appreciate how moods and emotions influence all members of an organization.

Moods and Emotions

mood A feeling or state of mind.

emotions Intense, relatively short-lived feelings.

Just as you sometimes are in a bad mood and at other times are in a good mood, so too are managers. A **mood** is a feeling or state of mind. When people are in a positive mood, they feel excited, enthusiastic, active, or elated.[30] When people are in a negative mood, they feel distressed, fearful, scornful, hostile, jittery, or nervous.[31] People who are high on extraversion are especially likely to experience positive moods; people who are high on negative affectivity are especially likely to experience negative moods. People's situations or circumstances also determine their moods; however, receiving a raise is likely to put most people in a good mood regardless of their personality traits. People who are high on negative affectivity are not always in a bad mood, and people who are low on extraversion still experience positive moods.[32]

Emotions are more intense feelings than moods, are often directly linked to whatever caused the emotion, and are more short-lived.[33] However, once whatever has triggered the emotion has been dealt with, the feelings may linger in the form of a less intense mood.[34] For example, a manager who gets very angry when a subordinate has engaged in an unethical behavior may find his anger decreasing in intensity once he has decided how to address the problem. Yet he continues to be in a bad mood the rest of the day, even though he is not directly thinking about the unfortunate incident.[35]

Research has found that moods and emotions affect the behavior of managers and all members of an organization. For example, research suggests that the subordinates of managers who experience positive moods at work may perform at somewhat higher levels and be less likely to resign and leave the organization than the subordinates of managers who do not tend to be in a positive mood at work.[36] Other research suggests that under certain conditions creativity might be enhanced by positive moods, whereas under other conditions negative moods might push people to work harder to come up with truly creative ideas.[37] Recognizing that both mood states have the potential to contribute to creativity in different ways, recent research suggests that employees may be especially likely to be creative to the extent that they experience both mood states (at different

Figure 3.6
A Measure of Organizational Commitment

People respond to each of the items in the scale by checking whether they:

[ ] Strongly disagree
[ ] Moderately disagree
[ ] Slightly disagree
[ ] Neither disagree nor agree
[ ] Slightly agree
[ ] Moderately agree
[ ] Strongly agree

____ **1.** I am willing to put in a great deal of effort beyond that normally expected in order to help this organization be successful.

____ **2.** I talk up this organization to my friends as a great organization to work for.

____ **3.** I feel very little loyalty to this organization.*

____ **4.** I would accept almost any type of job assignment in order to keep working for this organization.

____ **5.** I find that my values and the organization's values are very similar.

____ **6.** I am proud to tell others that I am part of this organization.

____ **7.** I could just as well be working for a different organization as long as the type of work was similar.*

____ **8.** This organization really inspires the very best in me in the way of job performance.

____ **9.** It would take very little change in my present circumstances to cause me to leave this organization.*

____ **10.** I am extremely glad that I chose this organization to work for over others I was considering at the time I joined.

____ **11.** There's not too much to be gained by sticking with this organization indefinitely.*

____ **12.** Often, I find it difficult to agree with this organization's policies on important matters relating to its employees.*

____ **13.** I really care about the fate of this organization.

____ **14.** For me this is the best of all possible organizations for which to work.

____ **15.** Deciding to work for this organization was a definite mistake on my part.*

Scoring: Responses to items 1, 2, 4, 5, 6, 8, 10, 13, and 14 are scored such that 1 = strongly disagree; 2 = moderately disagree; 3 = slightly disagree; 4 = neither disagree nor agree; 5 = slightly agree; 6 = moderately agree; and 7 = strongly agree. Responses to "*" items 3, 7, 9, 11, 12, and 15 are scored 7 = strongly disagree; 6 = moderately disagree; 5 = slightly disagree; 4 = neither disagree nor agree; 3 = slightly agree; 2 = moderately agree; and 1 = strongly agree. Responses to the 15 items are averaged for an overall score from 1 to 7; the higher the score, the higher the level of organizational commitment.

Source: L. W. Porter and F. J. Smith, "Organizational Commitment Questionnaire," in J. D. Cook, S. J. Hepworth, T. D. Wall, and P. B. Warr, eds., *The Experience of Work: A Compendium and Review of 249 Measures and Their Use* (New York: Academic Press, 1981), 84–86.

times) on the job and to the extent that the work environment is supportive of creativity.[38]

Other research suggests that moods and emotions may play an important role in ethical decision making. For example, researchers at Princeton University found that when people are trying to solve difficult personal moral dilemmas, the parts of their brains that are responsible for emotions and moods are especially active.[39]

More generally, emotions and moods give managers and all employees important information and signals about what is going on in the workplace.[40] Positive emotions and moods signal that things are going well and thus can lead to more expansive, and even playful, thinking. Negative emotions and moods signal that there are problems

Laugh it up: seeing the silly side can help get your brain in gear for making tougher decisions.

in need of attention and areas for improvement. So when people are in negative moods, they tend to be more detail-oriented and focused on the facts at hand.[41] Some studies suggest that critical thinking and devil's advocacy may be promoted by a negative mood, and sometimes especially accurate judgments may be made by managers in negative moods.[42]

Managers and other members of an organization need to realize that how they feel affects how they treat others and how others respond to them, including their subordinates. For example, a subordinate may be more likely to approach a manager with a somewhat unusual but potentially useful idea if the subordinate thinks the manager is in a good mood. Likewise, when managers are in very bad moods, their subordinates might try to avoid them at all costs. Figure 3.7 is an example of a scale that can measure the extent to which a person experiences positive and negative moods at work.

Emotional Intelligence

In understanding the effects of managers' and all employees' moods and emotions, it is important to take into account their levels of emotional intelligence. **Emotional intelligence** is the ability to understand and manage one's own moods and emotions and the moods and emotions of other people.[43] Managers with a high level

Figure 3.7

A Measure of Positive and Negative Mood at Work

People respond to each item by indicating the extent to which the item describes how they felt at work during the past week on the following scale:

1 = Very slightly or not at all
2 = A little
3 = Moderately
4 = Quite a bit
5 = Very much

___ **1.** Active
___ **2.** Distressed
___ **3.** Strong
___ **4.** Excited
___ **5.** Scornful
___ **6.** Hostile
___ **7.** Enthusiastic
___ **8.** Fearful
___ **9.** Peppy
___ **10.** Nervous
___ **11.** Elated
___ **12.** Jittery

Scoring: Responses to items 1, 3, 4, 7, 9, and 11 are summed for a positive mood score; the higher the score, the more positive mood is experienced at work. Responses to items 2, 5, 6, 8, 10, and 12 are summed for a negative mood score; the higher the score, the more negative mood is experienced at work.

Source: A. P. Brief, M. J. Burke, J. M. George, B. Robinson, and J. Webster, "Should Negative Affectivity Remain an Unmeasured Variable in the Study of Job Stress?" *Journal of Applied Psychology* 73 (1988), 193–98; M. J. Burke, A. P. Brief, J. M. George, L. Robinson, and J. Webster, "Measuring Affect at Work: Confirmatory Analyses of Competing Mood Structures with Conceptual Linkage in Cortical Regulatory Systems," *Journal of Personality and Social Psychology* 57 (1989), 1091–102.

LO3-4 Describe the nature of emotional intelligence and its role in management.

emotional intelligence The ability to understand and manage one's own moods and emotions and the moods and emotions of other people.

of emotional intelligence are more likely to understand how they are feeling and why, and they are more able to effectively manage their feelings. When managers are experiencing stressful feelings and emotions such as fear or anxiety, emotional intelligence lets them understand why and manage these feelings so they do not get in the way of effective decision making.[44]

Emotional intelligence also can help managers perform their important roles such as their interpersonal roles (figurehead, leader, and liaison).[45] Understanding how your subordinates feel, why they feel that way, and how to manage these feelings is central to developing strong interpersonal bonds with them.[46] Moreover, emotional intelligence has the potential to contribute to effective leadership in multiple ways[47] and can help managers make lasting contributions to society. For example, Bernard (Bernie) Goldhirsh founded *INC.* magazine in 1979, when entrepreneurs received more notoriety than respect, if they were paid attention at all.[48] Goldhirsh was an entrepreneur himself at the time, with his own publishing company. He recognized the vast contributions entrepreneurs could make to society, creating something out of nothing, and also realized firsthand what a tough task entrepreneurs faced.[49] His emotional intelligence helped him understand the challenges and frustrations entrepreneurs like himself faced and their need for support.

When Goldhirsh founded *INC.,* entrepreneurs had few sources to which they could turn for advice, guidance, and solutions to management problems. *INC.* was born to fill this gap and give entrepreneurs information and support by profiling successful and unsuccessful entrepreneurial ventures, highlighting management techniques that work, and providing firsthand accounts of how successful entrepreneurs developed and managed their businesses.[50]

Goldhirsh's emotional intelligence helped him recognize the many barriers entrepreneurs face and the emotional roller coaster of staking all one has on an idea that may or may not work. Goldhirsh believed that helping society understand the entrepreneurial process through *INC.* magazine not only helped entrepreneurs but also enlightened bankers, lawmakers, and the public at large about the role these visionaries play, the challenges they face, and the support their ventures depend on.[51]

LO3-5 Define organizational culture and explain how managers both create and are influenced by organizational culture.

Emotional intelligence helps managers understand and relate well to other people.[52] It also helps managers maintain their enthusiasm and confidence and energize subordinates to help the organization attain its goals.[53] Recent theorizing and research suggest that emotional intelligence may be especially important in awakening employee creativity.[54] Managers themselves are increasingly recognizing the importance of emotional intelligence. An example of a scale that measures emotional intelligence is provided in Figure 3.8.

Organizational Culture

Personality is a way of understanding why all managers and employees, as individuals, characteristically think and behave in different ways. However, when people belong to the same organization, they tend to share certain beliefs and values that lead them to act in similar ways.[55] **Organizational culture** comprises the shared set of beliefs, expectations, values, norms, and work routines that influence how members of an organization relate to one another and work together to achieve organizational goals. In essence, organizational culture reflects the distinctive ways in which organizational members perform their jobs and relate to others inside and outside the organization. It may, for example, be how customers in a particular hotel chain are treated from the time they are greeted at check-in until they leave; or it may be the shared work routines that research teams use to guide new product development. When organizational members share an intense commitment to cultural values, beliefs, and routines and use them to achieve their goals, a *strong* organizational culture exists.[56] When organizational members are not strongly committed to a shared system of values, beliefs, and routines, organizational culture is weak.

organizational culture The shared set of beliefs, expectations, values, norms, and work routines that influence how individuals, groups, and teams interact with one another and cooperate to achieve organizational goals.

Figure 3.8
A Measure of Emotional Intelligence

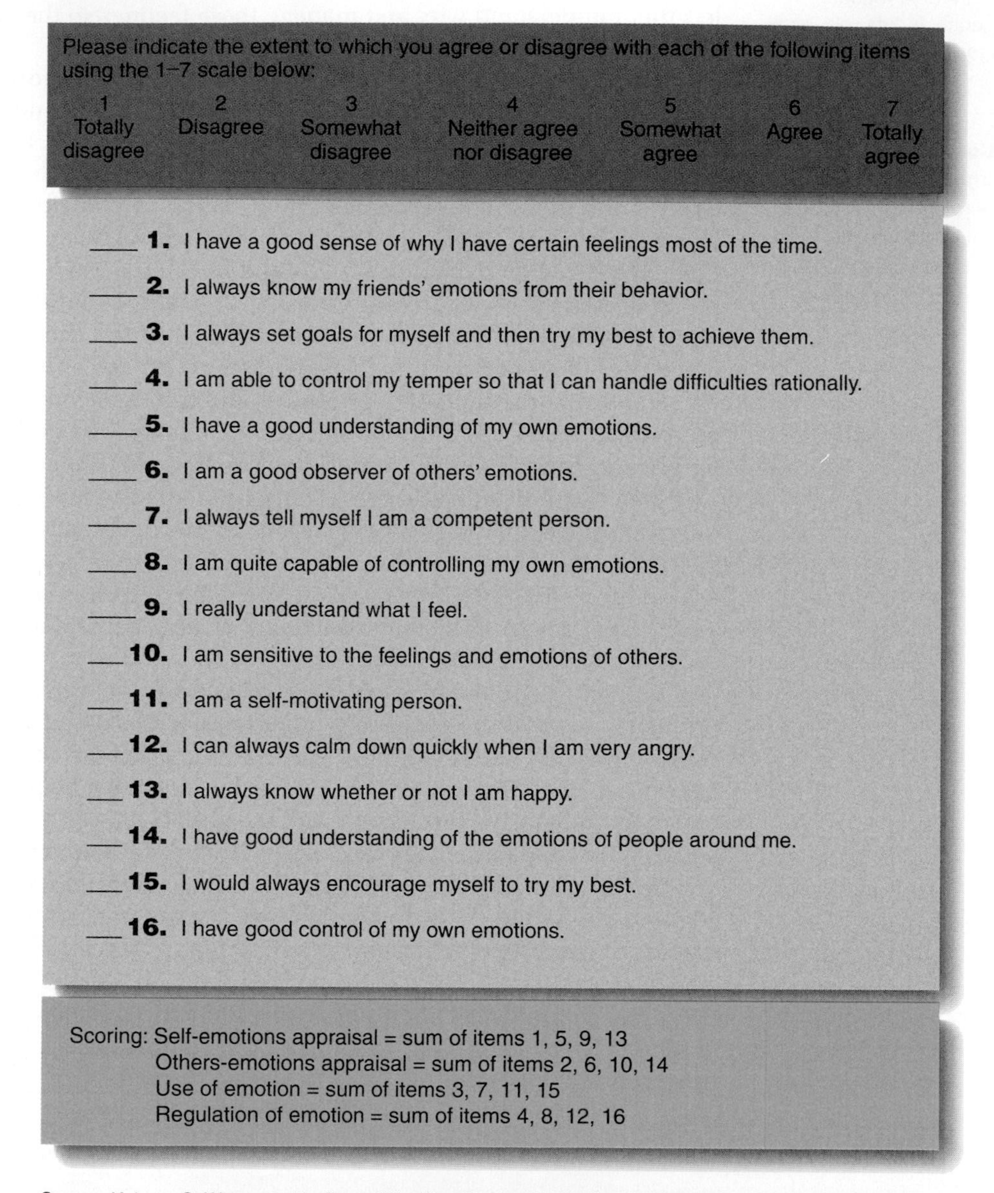
Please indicate the extent to which you agree or disagree with each of the following items using the 1–7 scale below:

1	2	3	4	5	6	7
Totally disagree	Disagree	Somewhat disagree	Neither agree nor disagree	Somewhat agree	Agree	Totally agree

____ **1.** I have a good sense of why I have certain feelings most of the time.
____ **2.** I always know my friends' emotions from their behavior.
____ **3.** I always set goals for myself and then try my best to achieve them.
____ **4.** I am able to control my temper so that I can handle difficulties rationally.
____ **5.** I have a good understanding of my own emotions.
____ **6.** I am a good observer of others' emotions.
____ **7.** I always tell myself I am a competent person.
____ **8.** I am quite capable of controlling my own emotions.
____ **9.** I really understand what I feel.
____ **10.** I am sensitive to the feelings and emotions of others.
____ **11.** I am a self-motivating person.
____ **12.** I can always calm down quickly when I am very angry.
____ **13.** I always know whether or not I am happy.
____ **14.** I have good understanding of the emotions of people around me.
____ **15.** I would always encourage myself to try my best.
____ **16.** I have good control of my own emotions.

Scoring: Self-emotions appraisal = sum of items 1, 5, 9, 13
Others-emotions appraisal = sum of items 2, 6, 10, 14
Use of emotion = sum of items 3, 7, 11, 15
Regulation of emotion = sum of items 4, 8, 12, 16

Source: K. Law, C. Wong, and L. Song, "The Construct and Criterion Validity of Emotional Intelligence and Its Potential Utility for Management Studies," *Journal of Applied Psychology* 89, no. 3 (June 2004), 496; C. S. Wong and K. S. Law, "The Effects of Leader and Follower Emotional Intelligence on Performance and Attitude: An Exploratory Study," *Leadership Quarterly* 13 (2002), 243–74.

The stronger the culture of an organization, the more one can think about it as being the "personality" of an organization because it influences the way its members behave.[57] Organizations that possess strong cultures may differ on a wide variety of dimensions that determine how their members behave toward one another and perform their jobs. For example, organizations differ in how members relate to each other (formally or informally), how important decisions are made (top-down or bottom-up), willingness to change (flexible or unyielding), innovation (creative or predictable), and playfulness (serious or serendipitous). In an innovative design firm like IDEO Product Development in Silicon Valley, employees are encouraged to adopt a playful attitude toward their work, look outside the organization to find inspiration, and adopt a flexible approach toward product design that uses multiple perspectives.[58] IDEO's culture is vastly different from that of companies such as Citibank and ExxonMobil,

IDEO employees brainstorming—informal communication, casual attire, and flexibility are all hallmarks of this organization.

in which employees treat each other in a more formal or deferential way, employees are expected to adopt a serious approach to their work, and decision making is constrained by the hierarchy of authority.

Managers and Organizational Culture

While all members of an organization can contribute to developing and maintaining organizational culture, managers play a particularly important part in influencing organizational culture[59] because of their multiple and important roles (see Chapter 1). How managers create culture is most vividly evident in start-ups of new companies. Entrepreneurs who start their own companies are typically also the startups' top managers until the companies grow and become profitable. Often referred to as the firms' founders, these managers literally create their organizations' cultures.

The founders' personal characteristics play an important role in the creation of organizational culture. Benjamin Schneider, a well-known management researcher, developed a model that helps to explain the role that founders' personal characteristics play in determining organizational culture.[60] His model, called the **attraction–selection–attrition (ASA) framework,** posits that when founders hire employees for their new ventures, they tend to be attracted to and choose employees whose personalities are similar to their own.[61] These similar employees are more likely to stay with the organization. Although employees who are dissimilar in personality might be hired, they are more likely to leave the organization over time.[62] As a result of these attraction, selection, and attrition processes, people in the organization tend to have similar personalities, and the typical or dominant personality profile of organizational members determines and shapes organizational culture.[63]

attraction–selection–attrition (ASA) framework A model that explains how personality may influence organizational culture.

For example, when David Kelley became interested in engineering and product design challenges in the late 1970s, he realized that who he was as a person meant he would not be happy working in a typical corporate environment. Kelley is high on openness to experience, driven to go where his interests take him, and not content to follow others' directives. Kelley recognized that he needed to start his own business, and with the help of other Stanford-schooled engineers and design experts, IDEO was born.[64]

From the start, IDEO's culture has embodied Kelley's spirited, freewheeling approach to work and design–from colorful and informal work spaces to an emphasis on networking and communicating with as many people as possible to understand a design problem. No project or problem is too big or too small for IDEO; the company designed the Apple Lisa computer and mouse (the precursor of the Mac) and the Palm as well as the Crest Neat Squeeze toothpaste dispenser and the Racer's Edge water bottle.[65] Kelley hates rules, job titles, big corner offices, and all the other trappings of large traditional organizations that stifle creativity. Employees who are attracted to, selected by, and remain with IDEO value creativity and innovation and embrace one of IDEO's mottos: "Fail often to succeed sooner."[66]

Although ASA processes are most evident in small firms such as IDEO, they also can operate in large companies.[67] According to the ASA model, this is a naturally occurring phenomenon to the extent that managers and new hires are free to make the kinds of choices the model specifies. However, while people tend to get along well with others who are similar to themselves, too much similarity in an organization can impair organizational effectiveness. That is, similar people tend to view conditions and events in similar ways and thus can be resistant to change. Moreover, organizations benefit from a diversity of perspectives rather than similarity in perspectives (see Chapter 5). At IDEO Kelley recognized early on how important it is to take advantage of the diverse talents and perspectives that people with different personalities, backgrounds, experiences, and education can bring to a design team. Hence IDEO's design teams include not only engineers but others who might have a unique insight into a problem, such as anthropologists, communications experts, doctors, and users of a product. When new employees are hired at IDEO, they meet many employees who have different backgrounds and characteristics; the focus is not on hiring someone who will fit in but, rather, on hiring someone who has something to offer and can "wow" different kinds of people with his or her insights.[68]

In addition to personality, other personal characteristics of managers shape organizational culture; these include managers' values, attitudes, moods and emotions, and emotional intelligence.[69] For example, both terminal and instrumental values of managers play a role in determining organizational culture. Managers who highly value freedom and equality, for example, might be likely to stress the importance of autonomy and empowerment in their organizations, as well as fair treatment for all. As another example, managers who highly value being helpful and forgiving might not only tolerate mistakes but also emphasize the importance of organizational members' being kind and helpful to one another.

Managers who are satisfied with their jobs, are committed to their organizations, and experience positive moods and emotions might also encourage these attitudes and feelings in others. The result would be an organizational culture emphasizing positive attitudes and feelings. Research suggests that attitudes like job satisfaction and organizational commitment can be affected by the influence of others. Managers are in a particularly strong position to engage in social influence given their multiple roles. Moreover, research suggests that moods and emotions can be contagious and that spending time with people who are excited and enthusiastic can increase one's own levels of excitement and enthusiasm.

The Role of Values and Norms in Organizational Culture

Shared terminal and instrumental values play a particularly important role in organizational culture. *Terminal values* signify what an organization and its employees are trying to accomplish, and *instrumental values* guide how the organization and its members achieve organizational goals. In addition to values, shared norms also are a key aspect of organizational culture. Recall that norms are unwritten, informal rules or guidelines that prescribe appropriate behavior in particular situations. For example, norms at IDEO include not being critical of others' ideas, coming up with multiple ideas before settling on one, and developing prototypes of new products.[70]

Managers determine and shape organizational culture through the kinds of values and norms they promote in an organization. Some managers, like David Kelley of IDEO, cultivate values and norms that encourage risk taking, creative responses to problems and opportunities, experimentation, tolerance of failure in order to succeed, and autonomy.[71] Top managers at organizations such as Microsoft and Google encourage employees to adopt such values to support their commitment to innovation as a source of competitive advantage.

Other managers, however, might cultivate values and norms that tell employees they should be conservative and cautious in their dealings with others and should consult their superiors before making important decisions or any changes to the status quo. Accountability for actions and decisions is stressed, and detailed records are kept to ensure that policies and procedures are followed. In settings where caution is needed–nuclear power stations, oil refineries, chemical plants, financial institutions, insurance companies–a conservative, cautious approach to making decisions might be appropriate.[72] In a nuclear power plant, for example, the catastrophic consequences of a mistake make a high level of supervision vital. Similarly, in a bank or mutual fund company, the risk of losing investors' money makes a cautious approach to investing appropriate.

Managers of different kinds of organizations deliberately cultivate and develop the organizational values and norms that are best suited to their task and general environments, strategy, or technology. Organizational culture is maintained and transmitted to organizational members through the values of the founder, the process of socialization, ceremonies and rites, and stories and language (see Figure 3.9).

VALUES OF THE FOUNDER From the ASA model just discussed, it is clear that founders of an organization can have profound and long-lasting effects on organizational culture. Founders' values inspire the founders to start their own companies and, in turn, drive the nature of these new companies and their defining characteristics. Thus an organization's founder and his or her terminal and instrumental values have a substantial influence on the values, norms, and standards of behavior that develop over time within the organization.[73] Founders set the scene for the way cultural values and norms develop because their own values guide the building of the company and they hire other managers and employees who they believe will share these values and help the organization to attain them. Moreover, new managers quickly learn from the founder what values and norms are appropriate in the organization and thus what is desired of them. Subordinates imitate the style of the founder and, in turn, transmit their values and norms to their subordinates. Gradually, over time, the founder's values and norms permeate the organization, as has been the case at Ryla, profiled in the following "Manager as a Person" box.[74]

Figure 3.9
Factors That Maintain and Transmit Organizational Culture

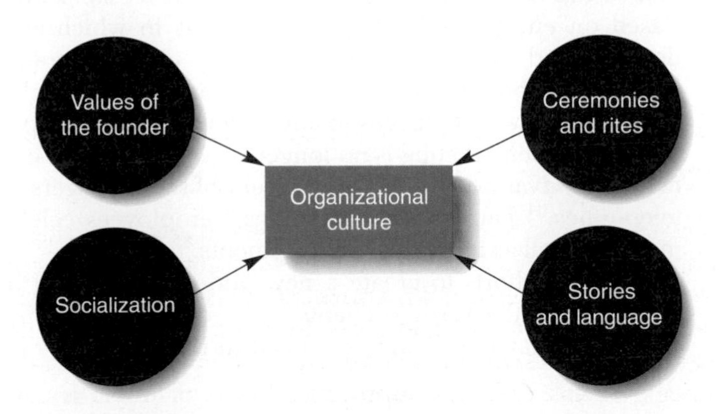

Manager as a Person

A Caring Culture at Ryla

Ryla Inc., founded by Mark Wilson in 2001, is a customer contact and business process outsourcing firm headquartered in Kennesaw, Georgia.[75] Telemarketing and customer contact organizations are notorious for high levels of turnover, dismal working conditions, and employees who are eager to abandon what they see as dead-end jobs as soon as a better opportunity comes along. Wilson imagined a different kind of customer contact business, one in which his employees would feel "like it's the best job they've ever had."[76]

Mark Wilson, shown here at Ryla's call center headquarters, demonstrates that managing for a productive work environment can also include managing for employees' well-being.

From the start, Wilson has strived to create and sustain a work environment and company culture that are true to his personal values. Treating employees with respect, fostering open communication, providing opportunities for training, growth, and development, and demonstrating commitment to the well-being of employees as well as the local community have helped Ryla to grow and prosper. Today Ryla has nearly 400 full-time employees, less than 30% annual turnover in an industry with average turnover rates over 75%, high client retention rates, and revenue growth of at least 10% per year.[77] Ryla has over a 1,500 telemarketing seat capacity and thus hires many people who are not full-time employees, as is common in this industry.[78]

Although call center work tends to be relatively routine and boring, Wilson's emphasis on both creating a caring culture and giving employees opportunities for training and advancement go a long way toward building employee loyalty.[79] Wilson maintains an open-door policy and keeps employees informed about how the business is doing.[80] He not only solicits employee suggestions for improvements but also acts on them.[81]

Ryla employees have access to a variety of benefits ranging from medical and life insurance to 401(k) plans, employee assistance programs, and aerobics classes.[82] Employees who remain with Ryla for three years and attain performance and attendance goals become eligible for stock options in the company.[83] Based on employee feedback about areas in which employees would like to develop and improve their skills, Ryla provides training and development seminars on both professional and personal topics (such as financial planning). Ryla also allows employees to advance within the company by promoting from within, so telemarketing is no longer viewed as a dead-end job with no opportunities for advancement. Eighty percent of the managers in Ryla once staffed the telephones.[84] During "Ryla Huddles," employees celebrate team accomplishments as well as individual achievements.[85]

Wilson's efforts to create a new and different kind of call center that provides excellent service to clients and a caring and supportive environment for employees have not gone unnoticed in the business community. For example,

Ryla was one of 35 finalists in *The Wall Street Journal*–Winning Workplace's Top Small Workplaces competition.[86] And it is not surprising that loyal employees like Denise Burdick, who never imagined working in telemarketing, are satisfied with their jobs and committed to Ryla.[87]

A founder who requires a great display of respect from subordinates and insists on proprieties such as formal job titles and formal dress encourages subordinates to act in this way toward their subordinates. Often a founder's personal values affect an organization's competitive advantage. For example, McDonald's founder Ray Kroc insisted from the beginning on high standards of customer service and cleanliness at McDonald's restaurants; these became core sources of McDonald's competitive advantage. Similarly, Bill Gates, the founder of Microsoft, pioneered certain cultural values in Microsoft. Employees are expected to be creative and to work hard, but they are encouraged to dress informally and to personalize their offices. Gates also established a host of company events such as cookouts, picnics, and sports events to emphasize to employees the importance of being both an individual and a team player.

SOCIALIZATION Over time, organizational members learn from each other which values are important in an organization and the norms that specify appropriate and inappropriate behaviors. Eventually organizational members behave in accordance with the organization's values and norms–often without realizing they are doing so.

organizational socialization The process by which newcomers learn an organization's values and norms and acquire the work behaviors necessary to perform jobs effectively.

Organizational socialization is the process by which newcomers learn an organization's values and norms and acquire the work behaviors necessary to perform jobs effectively.[88] As a result of their socialization experiences, organizational members internalize an organization's values and norms and behave in accordance with them not only because they think they have to but because they think these values and norms describe the right and proper way to behave.[89]

Most organizations have some kind of socialization program to help new employees learn the ropes–the values, norms, and culture of the organization. The military, for example, is well known for the rigorous socialization process it uses to turn raw recruits into trained soldiers. Organizations such as the Walt Disney Company, whether in the United States, France, Hong Kong, or Japan, also put new recruits through a rigorous training program to teach them to perform well in their jobs and play their parts in helping Disneyland visitors have fun in a wholesome theme park. New recruits at Disney are called "cast members" and attend Disney University to learn the Disney culture and their parts in it. Disney's culture emphasizes the values of safety, courtesy, entertainment, and efficiency, and these values are brought to life for newcomers at Disney University. Newcomers also learn about the attraction area they will be joining (such as Adventureland or Fantasyland) at Disney University and then receive on-the-job socialization in the area itself from experienced cast members.[90] Through organizational socialization, founders and managers of an organization transmit to employees the cultural values and norms that shape the behavior of organizational members. Thus the values and norms of founder Walt Disney live on today at Disneyland as newcomers are socialized into the Disney way.

Service with a smile and a pair of Mickey Mouse ears. Disney prides itself on training its employees around the world to carry on its founder's vision.

CEREMONIES AND RITES Another way in which managers can create or influence organizational culture is by developing organizational ceremonies and rites–formal events that recognize incidents of importance to the organization as a whole and to specific employees.[91] The most common rites that organizations use to transmit cultural norms and values to their members are rites of passage, of integration, and of enhancement (see Table 3.1).[92]

Table 3.1
Organizational Rites

Type of Rite	Example of Rite	Purpose of Rite
Rite of passage	Induction and basic training	Learn and internalize norms and values
Rite of integration	Office Christmas party	Build common norms and values
Rite of enhancement	Presentation of annual award	Motivate commitment to norms and values

Rites of passage determine how individuals enter, advance within, and leave the organization. The socialization programs developed by military organizations or by large accountancy and law firms are rites of passage. Likewise, the ways in which an organization prepares people for promotion or retirement are rites of passage.

Rites of integration, such as shared announcements of organizational successes, office parties, and company cookouts, build and reinforce common bonds among organizational members. IDEO uses many rites of integration to make its employees feel connected to one another and special. In addition to having wild "end-of-year" celebratory bashes, groups of IDEO employees periodically take time off to go to a sporting event, movie, or meal, or sometimes on a long bike ride or for a sail. These kinds of shared activities not only reinforce IDEO's culture but also can be a source of inspiration on the job (for example, IDEO has been involved in making movies such as *The Abyss* and *Free Willy*). One 35-member design studio at IDEO led by Dennis Boyle has bimonthly lunch fests with no set agenda–anything goes. While enjoying great food, jokes, and camaraderie, studio members often end up sharing ideas for their latest great products, and the freely flowing conversation that results often leads to creative insights.[93]

Rites of enhancement, such as awards dinners, newspaper releases, and employee promotions, let organizations publicly recognize and reward employees' contributions and thus strengthen their commitment to organizational values. By bonding members within the organization, rites of enhancement reinforce an organization's values and norms.

Stories and language also communicate organizational culture. Stories (whether fact or fiction) about organizational heroes and villains and their actions provide important clues about values and norms. Such stories can reveal the kinds of behaviors that are valued by the organization and the kinds of practices that are frowned on.[94] At the heart of McDonald's rich culture around the world are hundreds of stories that organizational members tell about founder Ray Kroc. Most of these stories focus on how Kroc established the strict operating values and norms that are at the heart of McDonald's culture. Kroc was dedicated to achieving perfection in McDonald's quality, service, cleanliness, and value for money (QSC&V), and these four central values permeate McDonald's culture. For example, an often retold story describes what happened when Kroc and a group of managers from the Houston region were touring various restaurants. One of the restaurants was having a bad day operationally. Kroc was incensed about the long lines of customers, and he was furious when he realized that the products customers were receiving that day were not up to his high standards. To address the problem, he jumped up and stood on the front counter to get the attention of all customers and operating crew personnel. He introduced himself, apologized for the long wait and cold food, and told the customers they could have freshly cooked food or their money back–whichever they wanted. As a result, the customers left happy; and when Kroc checked on the restaurant later, he found that his message had gotten through to its managers and crew–performance had improved. Other stories describe Kroc scrubbing dirty toilets and picking up litter inside or outside a restaurant. These and similar stories are spread around the organization by McDonald's employees. They are the stories that have helped establish Kroc as McDonald's "hero" and help to ensure that the food is hot and the restaurant clean whether it is in Berlin or Calcutta.

Because spoken language is a principal medium of communication in organizations, the characteristic slang or jargon–that is, organization-specific words or phrases–that people use to frame and describe events provides important clues about norms and values. "McLanguage," for example, is prevalent at all levels of McDonald's. Anywhere in the world a McDonald's employee described as having "ketchup in his or her blood" is someone who is truly dedicated to the McDonald's way–someone who has been completely socialized to its culture. McDonald's has an extensive training program that teaches new employees "McDonald's speak," and new employees are welcomed into the family with a formal orientation that illustrates Kroc's dedication to QSC&V.

The concept of organizational language encompasses not only spoken language but how people dress, the offices they occupy, the cars they drive, and the degree of formality they use when they address one another. For example, casual dress reflects and reinforces Microsoft's entrepreneurial culture and values. Formal business attire supports the conservative culture found in many banks, which emphasize the importance of conforming to organizational norms such as respect for authority and staying within one's prescribed role. When employees speak and understand the language of their organization's culture, they know how to behave in the organization and what is expected of them.

At IDEO, language, dress, the physical work environment, and extreme informality all underscore a culture that is adventuresome, playful, risk taking, egalitarian, and innovative. For example, at IDEO, employees refer to taking the consumers' perspective when designing products as "being left-handed." Employees dress in T-shirts and jeans, the physical work environment continually evolves and changes depending on how employees wish to personalize their workspace, no one "owns" a fancy office with a window, and rules are nonexistent.[95]

Culture and Managerial Action

While founders and managers play a critical role in developing, maintaining, and communicating organizational culture, this same culture shapes and controls the behavior of all employees, including managers themselves. For example, culture influences how managers perform their four main functions: planning, organizing, leading, and controlling. As we consider these functions, we continue to distinguish between top managers who create organizational values and norms that encourage creative, innovative behavior and top managers who encourage a conservative, cautious approach by their subordinates. We noted earlier that both kinds of values and norms can be appropriate depending on the situation and type of organization.

PLANNING Top managers in an organization with an innovative culture are likely to encourage lower-level managers to participate in the planning process and develop a flexible approach to planning. They are likely to be willing to listen to new ideas and to take risks involving the development of new products. In contrast, top managers in an organization with conservative values are likely to emphasize formal top-down planning. Suggestions from lower-level managers are likely to be subjected to a formal review process, which can significantly slow decision making. Although this deliberate approach may improve the quality of decision making in a nuclear power plant, it can have unintended consequences. In the past, at conservative IBM, the planning process became so formalized that managers spent most of their time assembling complex slide shows and overheads to defend their current positions rather than thinking about what they should do to keep IBM abreast of the changes taking place in the computer industry. When former CEO Lou Gerstner took over, he used every means at his disposal to abolish this culture, even building a brand-new campus-style headquarters to change managers' mind-sets. IBM's culture is undergoing further changes initiated by its current CEO, Samuel Palmisano.[96]

ORGANIZING What kinds of organizing will managers in innovative and in conservative cultures encourage? Valuing creativity, managers in innovative cultures are likely to try to create an organic structure–one that is flat, with few levels in the hierarchy, and one in which authority is decentralized so employees are encouraged to work together to solve ongoing problems. A product team structure may be suitable for an organization with an innovative culture. In contrast, managers in a conservative culture are likely to create a well-defined hierarchy of authority and establish clear reporting relationships so employees know exactly whom to report to and how to react to any problems that arise.

LEADING In an innovative culture, managers are likely to lead by example, encouraging employees to take risks and experiment. They are supportive regardless of whether employees succeed or fail. In contrast, managers in a conservative culture are likely to use management by objectives and to constantly monitor subordinates' progress toward goals, overseeing their every move. We examine leadership in detail in Chapter 14 when we consider the leadership styles that managers can adopt to influence and shape employee behavior.

CONTROLLING The ways in which managers evaluate, and take actions to improve, performance differ depending on whether the organizational culture emphasizes formality and caution or innovation and change. Managers who want to encourage risk taking, creativity, and innovation recognize that there are multiple potential paths to success and that failure must be accepted for creativity to thrive. Thus they are less concerned about employees' performing their jobs in a specific, predetermined manner and in strict adherence to preset goals and more concerned about employees' being flexible and taking the initiative to come up with ideas for improving performance. Managers in innovative cultures are also more concerned about long-term performance than short-term targets because they recognize that real innovation entails much uncertainty that necessitates flexibility. In contrast, managers in cultures that emphasize caution and maintenance of the status quo often set specific, difficult goals for employees, frequently monitor progress toward these goals, and develop a clear set of rules that employees are expected to adhere to.

The values and norms of an organization's culture strongly affect the way managers perform their management functions. The extent to which managers buy into the values and norms of their organization shapes their view of the world and their actions and decisions in particular circumstances. In turn, the actions that managers take can have an impact on the performance of the organization. Thus organizational culture, managerial action, and organizational performance are all linked together.

This linkage is apparent at Hewlett-Packard (HP), a leader in the electronic instrumentation and computer industries. Established in the 1940s, HP developed a culture that is an outgrowth of the strong personal beliefs of the company's founders, William Hewlett and David Packard. As discussed in Chapter 2, Bill and Dave, as they are known within the company, formalized HP's culture in 1957 in a statement of corporate objectives known as the "HP Way." The basic values informing the HP Way stress serving everyone who has a stake in the company with integrity and fairness, including customers, suppliers, employees, stockholders, and society in general. Bill and Dave helped build this culture within HP by hiring like-minded people and by letting the HP Way guide their own actions as managers.

Although the Hewlett-Packard example and our earlier example of IDEO illustrate how organizational culture can give rise to managerial actions that ultimately benefit the organization, this is not always the case. The cultures of some organizations become dysfunctional, encouraging managerial actions that harm the organization and discouraging actions that might improve performance. Recent corporate scandals at large companies like Enron, Tyco, and WorldCom show how damaging a dysfunctional culture can be to an organization and its members. For example, Enron's arrogant, "success at all costs" culture led to fraudulent behavior on the part of its top managers.[97] Unfortunately hundreds of Enron employees paid a heavy price for the unethical behavior of these top managers and the dysfunctional organizational culture. Not only did these employees lose their jobs, but many also lost their life savings in Enron stock and pension funds, which became worth just a fraction of their former value before the wrongdoing at Enron came to light. We discuss ethics and ethical cultures in depth in the next chapter.

Summary and Review

LO3-1 **ENDURING CHARACTERISTICS: PERSONALITY TRAITS** Personality traits are enduring tendencies to feel, think, and act in certain ways. The Big Five general traits are extraversion, negative affectivity, agreeableness, conscientiousness, and openness to experience. Other personality traits that affect managerial behavior are locus of control, self-esteem, and the needs for achievement, affiliation, and power.

LO3-2, 3-3, 3-4 **VALUES, ATTITUDES, AND MOODS AND EMOTIONS** A terminal value is a personal conviction about lifelong goals or objectives; an instrumental value is a personal conviction about modes of conduct. Terminal and instrumental values have an impact on what managers try to achieve in their organizations and the kinds of behaviors they engage in. An attitude is a collection of feelings and beliefs. Two attitudes important for understanding managerial behaviors include job satisfaction (the collection of feelings and beliefs that managers have about their jobs) and organizational commitment (the collection of feelings and beliefs that managers have about their organizations). A mood is a feeling or state of mind; emotions are intense feelings that are short-lived and directly linked to their causes. Managers' moods and emotions, or how they feel at work on a day-to-day basis, have the potential to impact not only their own behavior and effectiveness but also those of their subordinates. Emotional intelligence is the ability to understand and manage one's own and other people's moods and emotions.

LO3-5 **ORGANIZATIONAL CULTURE** Organizational culture is the shared set of beliefs, expectations, values, norms, and work routines that influence how members of an organization relate to one another and work together to achieve organizational goals. Founders of new organizations and managers play an important role in creating and maintaining organizational culture. Organizational socialization is the process by which newcomers learn an organization's values and norms and acquire the work behaviors necessary to perform jobs effectively.

Management in Action

Topics for Discussion and Action

Discussion

1. Discuss why managers who have different types of personalities can be equally effective and successful. **[LO3-1]**
2. How do you think these managerial styles differ between your home country and the United States? **[LO3-1]**
3. Can managers be too satisfied with their jobs? Can they be too committed to their organizations? Why or why not? **[LO3-2]**
4. Assume that you are a manager of a restaurant. Describe what it is like to work for you when you are in a negative mood. **[LO3-3]**

Action

5. Interview a manager in a local organization. Ask the manager to describe situations in which he or she is especially likely to act in accordance with his or her values. Ask the manager to describe situations in which he or she is less likely to act in accordance with his or her values. **[LO3-2]**
6. Watch a popular television show, and as you watch it, try to determine the emotional intelligence levels of the characters the actors in the show portray. Rank the characters from highest to lowest in terms of emotional intelligence. As you watched the show, what factors influenced your assessments of emotional intelligence levels? **[LO3-4]**
7. Go to an upscale clothing store and go to a clothing store that is definitely not upscale. Observe the behavior of employees in each store as well as the store's environment. In what ways are the organizational cultures in each store similar? In what ways are they different? **[LO3-5]**

Building Management Skills [LO3-5]

Diagnosing Culture

Think about the culture of the last organization you worked for, your current university, or another organization or club to which you belong. Then answer the following questions:

1. What values are emphasized in this culture?
2. What norms do members of this organization follow?
3. Who seems to have played an important role in creating the culture?
4. In what ways is the organizational culture communicated to organizational members?

Managing Ethically [LO3-1, 3-2]

Some organizations rely on personality and interest inventories to screen potential employees. Other organizations attempt to screen employees by using paper-and-pencil honesty tests.

Questions

1. Either individually or in a group, think about the ethical implications of using personality and interest inventories to screen potential employees. How might this practice be unfair to potential applicants? How might organizational members who are in charge of hiring misuse it?
2. Because of measurement error and validity problems, some relatively trustworthy people may "fail" an honesty test given by an employer. What are the ethical implications of trustworthy people "failing" honesty tests, and what obligations do you think employers should have when relying on honesty tests for screening?

Small Group Breakout Exercise [LO3-2, 3-3, 3-4, 3-5]

Making Difficult Decisions in Hard Times

Form groups of three or four people, and appoint one member as the spokesperson who will communicate your findings to the whole class when called on by the instructor. Then discuss the following scenario:

You are on the top management team of a medium-size company that manufactures cardboard boxes, containers, and other cardboard packaging materials. Your company is facing increasing levels of competition for major corporate customer accounts, and profits have declined significantly. You have tried everything you can to cut costs and remain competitive, with the exception of laying off employees. Your company has had a no-layoff policy for the past 20 years, and you believe it is an important part of the organization's culture. However, you are experiencing mounting pressure to increase your firm's performance, and your no-layoff policy has been questioned by shareholders. Even though you haven't decided whether to lay off employees and thus break with a 20-year tradition for your company, rumors are rampant in your organization that something is afoot, and employees are worried. You are meeting today to address this problem.

1. Develop a list of options and potential courses of action to address the heightened competition and decline in profitability that your company has been experiencing.
2. Choose your preferred course of action, and justify why you will take this route.
3. Describe how you will communicate your decision to employees.
4. What role will government play in these decisions?

Exploring the World Wide Web [LO3-1, 3-2, 3-5]

Go to IDEO's Web site (www.ideo.com) and read about this company. Try to find indicators of IDEO's culture that are provided on the Web site. How does the design of the Web site itself, and the pictures and words it contains, communicate the nature of IDEO's organizational culture? What kinds of people do you think would be attracted to IDEO? What kinds of people do you think would be likely to be dissatisfied with a job at IDEO?

Be the Manager [LO3-1, 3-2, 3-3, 3-4, 3-5]

You have recently been hired as the vice president for human resources in an advertising agency. One problem that has been brought to your attention is the fact that the creative departments at the agency have dysfunctionally high levels of conflict. You have spoken with members of each of these departments, and in each one it seems that a few members of the department are creating all the problems. All these individuals are valued contributors who have many creative ad campaigns to their credit. The high levels of conflict are creating problems in the departments, and negative moods and emotions are much more prevalent than positive feelings. What are you going to do to both retain valued employees and alleviate the excessive conflict and negative feelings in these departments?

CHAPTER 4

Ethics and Social Responsibility

Learning Objectives

After studying this chapter, you should be able to:

LO4-1 Explain the relationship between ethics and the law.

LO4-2 Differentiate between the claims of the different stakeholder groups that are affected by managers and their companies' actions.

LO4-3 Describe four rules that can help companies and their managers act in ethical ways.

LO4-4 Discuss why it is important for managers to behave ethically.

LO4-5 Identify the four main sources of managerial ethics.

LO4-6 Distinguish among the four main approaches toward social responsibility that a company can take.

A MANAGER'S CHALLENGE

Unethical Managers and the Perils of Peanut Butter

Why should ethics guide managers' decisions? Peanut Corporation of America (PCA) operated three plants in Virginia, Georgia, and Texas. The company produced industrial-sized containers of peanut butter. This product is a unique American food made from peanuts that are mashed until they turn into a paste. The paste was included as an ingredient in more than 3,900 products: cakes, candies, cookies, peanut crackers, ice cream, snack mixes, and pet food made by over 200 different companies, including Kellogg's and Nestlé. Also, the peanut butter was shipped to school systems and food outlets around the United States.

In 2009 a major nationwide outbreak of salmonella poisoning was traced by a U.S. governmental agency to the peanut butter produced at the PCA plant in Blakely, Georgia. PCA's contaminated peanut butter had caused over 600 illnesses and nine deaths across the United States. The 200 food makers who used or sold PCA's products were forced to recall more than 1,900 different peanut butter products. This was one of the United States' largest food recalls even though PCA accounted for only 2% of the nation's supply of peanut butter. In the immediate aftermath of the nationwide outbreak, peanut butter sales plummeted 24% across the board, and total industry losses amounted to over $1 billion. How could this tragedy and disaster have occurred?[1]

Apparently the major cause of the disaster was the unethical and illegal actions of owner and manager Stewart Parnell. The FDA investigation that took place at the PCA Georgia plant in 2009 revealed serious problems with food safety at that plant and inadequate cleaning and sanitary procedures. The investigation also revealed internal company documents that showed at least 12 instances in which the company's

Stewart Parnell, the erstwhile owner of PCA, was called before Congress to answer for poor safety standards at PCA plants. A full year later, more problems having come to light, PCA's doors are closed for good.

own tests of its products in 2007 and 2008 found they were contaminated by salmonella. Previous inspections of the plant had found dirty surfaces, grease residue, dirt buildup throughout the plant, gaps in warehouse doors large enough for rodents to enter, and major problems with the plant's routine cleaning procedures that still existed in 2009. But PCA managers had taken no steps to clean up operations or protect food safety. In fact, Parnell's poor attention to food safety was traced back to 1990, when inspectors found toxic mold in products produced in PCA's Virginia plant; the mold forced food recalls, and Parnell settled privately with the two companies whose products were affected.[2]

After interviewing employees, FDA investigators found that this long-term inattention to food safety had arisen inside PCA's processing plants because Parnell was worried about maximizing his profits, especially when prices of peanut products had started to fall. To reduce operating costs, Parnell ordered a plant manager to ship products that had already been identified as contaminated and had pleaded with health inspectors to let him "turn the raw peanuts on our floor into money." Parnell complained to his managers that the salmonella tests were costing him business, and somehow the Georgia plant received information about the dates on which the plant would be inspected—so on those days the plant was scrubbed clean.[3]

Overview

As the story of PCA and Parnell suggests, an ethical dimension is always present in management decision making that involves the production and sale of products–be they food products, cars, computers, or clothing–because managers' decisions affect people's well-being. But globally, nations, companies, and managers differ enormously in their commitment to these people, or *stakeholders*–various groups of people who may benefit or be harmed by how managers make decisions that affect them. Managers of some companies make the need to behave ethically toward stakeholders their main priority. Managers of other companies pursue their own self-interest at the expense of their stakeholders and do harm to them–such as the harm done to the millions of people around the world who work in dangerous, unsanitary conditions or who work for a pittance.

In this chapter we examine the obligations and responsibilities of managers and the companies they work for toward the people and society that are affected by their actions. First we examine the nature of ethics and the sources of ethical problems. Next we discuss the major stakeholder groups that are affected by how companies operate. We also look at four rules or guidelines managers can use to decide whether a specific business decision is ethical or unethical. Finally we consider the sources of managerial ethics and the reasons why it is important for a company to behave in a socially responsible manner. By the end of this chapter you will understand the central role of ethics in shaping the practice of management and the life of a people, society, and nation.

The Nature of Ethics

Suppose you see a person being mugged. Will you act in some way to help, even though you risk being hurt? Will you walk away? Perhaps you might not intervene but call the police? Does how you act depend on whether the person being mugged is a fit male, an elderly person, or a street person? Does it depend on whether other people are around so you can tell yourself, "Oh well, someone else will help or call the police. I don't need to"?

Ethical Dilemmas

ethical dilemma The quandary people find themselves in when they have to decide if they should act in a way that might help another person or group even though doing so might go against their own self-interest.

The situation just described is an example of an **ethical dilemma,** the quandary people find themselves in when they have to decide if they should act in a way that might help another person or group and is the right thing to do, even though doing so might go against their own self-interest.[4] A dilemma may also arise when a person has to choose between two different courses of action, knowing that whichever course he or she selects will harm one person or group even while it may benefit another. The ethical dilemma here is to decide which course of action is the lesser of two evils. Unfortunately in such situations there is not an absolutely correct answer.

People often know they are confronting an ethical dilemma when their moral scruples come into play and cause them to hesitate, debate, and reflect upon the rightness or goodness of a course of action. Moral scruples are thoughts and feelings that tell a person what is right or wrong; they are a part of a person's ethics. **Ethics** are the inner guiding moral principles, values, and beliefs that people use to analyze or interpret a situation and then decide what is the right or appropriate way to behave. Ethics also indicate what is inappropriate behavior and how a person should behave to avoid harming another person.

ethics The inner guiding moral principles, values, and beliefs that people use to analyze or interpret a situation and then decide what is the right or appropriate way to behave.

The essential problem in dealing with ethical issues, and thus solving moral dilemmas, is no absolute or indisputable rules or principles can be developed to decide whether an action is ethical or unethical. Put simply, different people or groups may dispute which actions are ethical or unethical depending on their personal self-interest and specific attitudes, beliefs, and values–concepts we discussed in Chapter 3. How, therefore, are we and companies and their managers and employees to decide what is ethical and so act appropriately toward other people and groups?

Ethics and the Law

LO4-1 Explain the relationship between ethics and the law.

The first answer to this question is that society as a whole, using the political and legal process, can lobby for and pass laws that specify what people can and cannot do. Many different kinds of laws govern business–for example, laws against fraud and deception and laws governing how companies can treat their employees and customers. Laws also specify what sanctions or punishments will follow if those laws are broken. Different groups in society lobby for which laws should be passed based on their own personal interests and beliefs about right and wrong. The group that can summon the most support can pass laws that align with its interests and beliefs. Once a law is passed, a decision about what the appropriate behavior is with regard to a person or situation is taken from the personally determined ethical realm to the societally determined legal realm. If you do not conform to the law, you can be prosecuted; and if you are found guilty of breaking the law, you can be punished. You have little say in the matter; your fate is in the hands of the court and its lawyers.

In studying the relationship between ethics and law, it is important to understand that *neither laws nor ethics are fixed principles* that do not change over time. Ethical beliefs change as time passes; and as they do so, laws change to reflect the changing ethical beliefs of a society. It was seen as ethical, and it was legal, for example, to acquire and possess slaves in ancient Rome and Greece and in Great Britain until 1819. Ethical views regarding whether slavery was morally right or appropriate changed, however. Slavery was made illegal in Great Britain when those in power decided that slavery degraded the meaning of being human. Slavery makes a statement about the value or worth of human beings and about their right to life, liberty, and the pursuit of happiness. And if we deny these rights to other people, how can we claim to have any natural rights to these things?

Moreover, what is to stop any person or group that becomes powerful enough to take control of the political and legal process from enslaving us and denying us the

Coldbath Fields Prison, London, circa 1810. The British criminal justice system around this time was severe: there were over 350 different crimes for which a person could be executed, including sheep stealing. As ethical beliefs change over time, so do laws.

right to be free and to own property? In denying freedom to others, one risks losing oneself, just as stealing from others opens the door for them to steal from us in return. "Do unto others as you would have them do unto you" is a common ethical or moral rule that people apply in such situations to decide what is the right thing to do.

Changes in Ethics over Time

While ethical beliefs lead to the development of laws and regulations to prevent certain behaviors or encourage others, laws themselves change or even disappear as ethical beliefs change. In Britain in 1830 a person could be executed for over 350 different crimes, including sheep stealing. Today the death penalty is no longer legal in Britain. Thus both ethical and legal rules are *relative:* No absolute or unvarying standards exist to determine how we should behave, and people are caught up in moral dilemmas all the time. Because of this we have to make ethical choices.

The previous discussion highlights an important issue in understanding the relationship between ethics, law, and business. Throughout the 2000s many scandals plagued major companies such as Enron, Parmalat, Lehman Brothers, and others. Managers in some of these companies clearly broke the law and used illegal means to defraud investors.

In other cases managers took advantage of loopholes in the law to divert hundreds of millions of dollars of company capital into their own personal fortunes. At WorldCom, a U.S. telecommunications firm, former CEO Bernie Ebbers used his position to place six personal friends on the 13-member board of directors. Although this is not illegal, obviously these people would vote in his favor at board meetings. As a result of their support Ebbers received huge stock options and a personal loan of over $150 million from WorldCom. In return, his supporters were well rewarded for being directors; for example, Ebbers allowed them to use WorldCom's corporate jets for a minimal cost, saving them hundreds of thousands of dollars a year.[5]

In light of these events some people said, "Well, what these people did was not illegal," implying that because such behavior was not illegal it was also not unethical. However, not being illegal does *not* make behavior ethical; such behavior is clearly unethical.[6] In many cases laws are passed *later* to close loopholes and prevent unethical people, such as Ebbers, from taking advantage of them to pursue their own self-interest at the expense of others. Like ordinary people, managers must decide what is appropriate and inappropriate as they use a company's resources to produce goods and services for customers.[7]

Stakeholders and Ethics

Just as people have to work out the right and wrong ways to act, so do companies. When the law does not specify how companies should behave, their managers must decide the right or ethical way to behave toward the people and groups affected by their actions. Who are the people or groups that are affected by a company's business decisions? If a company behaves in an ethical way, how does this benefit people and society? Conversely, how are people harmed by a company's unethical actions?

stakeholders The people and groups that supply a company with its productive resources and so have a claim on and stake in the company.

The people and groups affected by how a company and its managers behave are called its stakeholders. **Stakeholders** supply a company with its productive resources; as a result, they have a claim on and stake in the company.[8] Because stakeholders can directly benefit or be harmed by its actions, the ethics of a company and its managers are important to them. Who are a company's major stakeholders? What do they contribute to a company, and what do they claim in return? Here we examine the claims of these stakeholders–stockholders; managers; employees; suppliers and distributors; customers; and community, society, and nation-state (Figure 4.1).

Figure 4.1
Types of Company Stakeholders

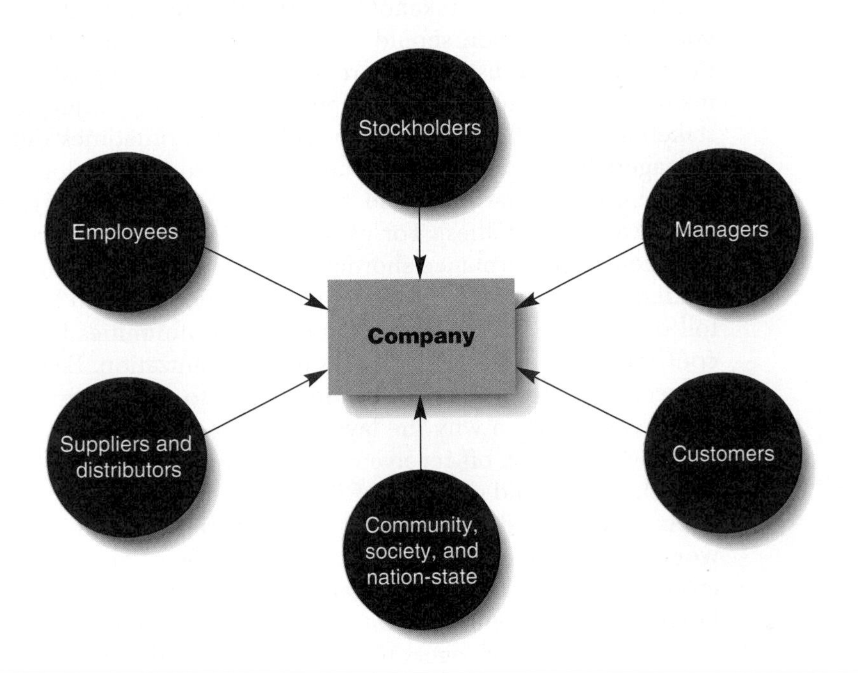

LO4-2 Differentiate between the claims of the different stakeholder groups that are affected by managers and their companies' actions.

Stockholders

Stockholders have a claim on a company because when they buy its stock or shares they become its owners. When the founder of a company decides to publicly incorporate the business to raise capital, shares of the stock of that company are issued. This stock grants its buyers ownership of a certain percentage of the company and the right to receive any future stock dividends. For example, in 2005 Microsoft decided to pay the owners of its 5 billion shares a record dividend payout of $32 billion. Bill Gates received $3.3 billion in dividends based on his stockholding, and he donated this money to the Bill and Melinda Gates Foundation, to which he has reportedly donated over $30 billion to date, with the promise of much more to come; and Warren Buffett committed in 2006 to donate at least $30 billion to the Gates Foundation over the next decade. The two richest people in the world have decided to give away a large part of their wealth to serve global ethical causes–in particular to address global health concerns such as malnutrition, malaria, tuberculosis, and AIDS.

Stockholders are interested in how a company operates because they want to maximize the return on their investment. Thus they watch the company and its managers closely to ensure that management is working diligently to increase the company's profitability.[9] Stockholders also want to ensure that managers are behaving ethically and not risking investors' capital by engaging in actions that could hurt the company's reputation. For example, in 2010 the Russian construction company Transstroi fired its CEO. Ivan Kuznetsov lost his job because of his illegal transfers of shareholder money. It is alleged that Kuznetsov illegally transferred "hundreds of millions of rubles," or millions of dollars worth of funds out of Transstroi. Federal authorities have begun prosecution of Mr. Kuznetsov.

Managers

Managers are a vital stakeholder group because they are responsible for using a company's financial, capital, and human resources to increase its performance and thus its stock price.[10] Managers have a claim on an organization because they bring to it their skills, expertise, and experience. They have the right to expect a good return or reward by investing their human capital to improve a company's performance. Such rewards include good salaries and benefits, the prospect of promotion and a career, and stock options and bonuses tied to company performance.

Managers are the stakeholder group that bears the responsibility to decide which goals an organization should pursue to most benefit stakeholders and how to make the most efficient use of resources to achieve those goals. In making such decisions, managers are frequently in the position of having to juggle the interests of different stakeholders, including themselves.[11] These sometimes difficult decisions challenge managers to uphold ethical values because some decisions that benefit certain stakeholder groups (managers and stockholders) harm other groups (individual workers and local communities). For example, in economic downturns or when a company experiences performance shortfalls, layoffs may help cut costs (thus benefiting shareholders) at the expense of the employees laid off. Such layoffs not only take a heavy toll on workers, their families, and local communities but also mean the loss of the contributions of valued employees to an organization. Because of such potential negative consequences, it is common in Europe to require firms to provide justification to the government on why the layoffs are needed. Thus, workers with permanent contracts who are laid off receive extensive compensation. BMW estimates that the cost of each worker laid off is over €12,000.[12]

As we discussed in Chapter 1, managers must be motivated and given incentives to work hard in the interests of stockholders. Their behavior must also be scrutinized to ensure they do not behave illegally or unethically, pursuing goals that threaten stockholders and the company's interests.[13] Unfortunately we have seen in the 2000s how easy it is for top managers to find ways to ruthlessly pursue their self-interest at the expense of stockholders and employees because laws and regulations are not strong enough to force them to behave ethically.

Indeed, many experts argue that the rewards given to top managers, particularly the CEO and COO, grew out of control in the 2000s. Top managers are today's "aristocrats," and through their ability to influence the board of directors and raise their own pay, they have amassed personal fortunes worth hundreds of millions of dollars.

Is it ethical for top managers to receive such large amounts of money from their companies? Do they really earn it? Remember, this money could have gone to shareholders in the form of dividends. It could also have reduced the huge salary gap between those at the top and those at the bottom of the hierarchy. Many people argue that the growing disparity between the rewards given to CEOs and to other employees is unethical and should be regulated. CEO pay has skyrocketed because CEOs are the people who set and control one another's salaries and bonuses; they can do this because they sit on the boards of other companies as outside directors. Others argue that because top managers play an important role in building a company's capital and wealth, they deserve a significant share of its profits. Some recent research has suggested that the companies whose CEO compensation includes a large percentage of stock options tend to experience big share losses more often than big gains, and that on average, company performance improves as stock option use declines.[14]

Ethics and Nonprofit Organizations

The issue of what is fair compensation for top managers is not limited to for-profit companies; it is one of many issues facing nonprofits. The many ethics scandals that have plagued companies in the 2000s might suggest that the issue of ethics is important only for profit-seeking companies, but this would be untrue.

Experts hope that the introduction of new rules and regulations to monitor and oversee how nonprofits spend their funds will result in much more value being created from the funds given by donors. After all, every cent that is spent administering a nonprofit is a cent not being used to help the people or cause for which the money was intended. Major ethical issues are involved because some badly run charities spend 70 cents of every U.S. dollar on administration costs. Clearly the directors and managers of all organizations need to carefully consider the ethical issues involved in their decision making.

Employees

A company's employees are the hundreds of thousands of people who work in its various departments and functions, such as research, sales, and manufacturing. Employees expect to receive rewards consistent with their performance. One principal way that a company can act ethically toward employees and meet their expectations is by creating an occupational structure that fairly and equitably rewards employees for their contributions. Companies, for example, need to develop recruitment, training, performance appraisal, and reward systems that do not discriminate against employees and that employees believe are fair.

Suppliers and Distributors

No company operates alone. Every company is in a network of relationships with other companies that supply it with the inputs (such as raw materials, components, contract labor, and clients) that it needs to operate. It also depends on intermediaries such as wholesalers and retailers to distribute its products to the final customers. Suppliers expect to be paid fairly and promptly for their inputs; distributors expect to receive quality products at agreed-upon prices. Once again, many ethical issues arise in how companies contract and interact with their suppliers and distributors. Important issues concerning how and when payments are made or product quality and safety specifications are governed by the contracts a company signs with its suppliers and distributors.

It is instructive to see how two major firms, Nestlé and Kellogg's, manage their relationships with suppliers to ensure that they act in an ethical way and make safe products. During 2008 Nestlé was deciding whether to continue to purchase from the now bankrupt Peanut Corporation of America (discussed at the beginning of the chapter); it has a policy of using its own inspectors to investigate potential suppliers' operating facilities. Nestlé's inspectors found rodent feces and live beetles on two separate occasions when touring PCA's plants, and the company decided to find a new peanut supplier–which saved it millions of dollars because it did not suffer from product recalls. On the other hand, Kellogg's does not use its own inspectors but relies on third parties, such as governmental inspectors, to investigate suppliers. As a result, Kellogg's continued to buy PCA's products and lost more than $70 million because it had to recall its peanut products.

The Gap is an international retailer whose stores include the Gap, Banana Republic, Old Navy, Piperlime, and Athleta brand names. The firm has over 3,000 stores in the United States, Canada, United Kingdom, France, Ireland, and Japan. To ensure that its suppliers meet key ethical standards, the company requires of its vendors the actions listed in Table 4.1.

Customers

Customers are often regarded as the most critical stakeholder group because if a company cannot attract them to buy its products, it cannot stay in business. Thus managers and employees must work to increase efficiency and effectiveness in order to create loyal customers and attract new ones. They do so by selling customers quality products at a fair price and providing good after-sales service. They can also strive to improve their products over time and provide guarantees to customers about the integrity of their products like Whole Foods Market, profiled in the following "Ethics in Action" box.

Many laws protect customers from companies that attempt to provide dangerous or shoddy products. Laws allow customers to sue a company whose product causes them injury or harm, such as a defective tire or vehicle. Other laws force companies to clearly disclose the interest rates they charge on purchases–an important hidden cost that customers frequently do not factor into their purchase decisions. Every year thousands of companies are prosecuted for breaking these laws, so "buyer beware" is an important rule customers must follow when buying goods and services.

Table 4.1
Some Principles from the Gap's Code of Vendor Conduct

As a condition of doing business with Gap Inc., each and every factory must comply with this Code of Vendor Conduct. Gap Inc. will continue to develop monitoring systems to assess and ensure compliance. If Gap Inc. determines that any factory has violated this Code, Gap Inc. may either terminate its business relationship or require the factory to implement a corrective action plan. If corrective action is advised but not taken, Gap Inc. will suspend placement of future orders and may terminate current production.

I. General Principles

Factories that produce goods for Gap Inc. shall operate in full compliance with the laws of their respective countries and with all other applicable laws, rules, and regulations.

II. Environment

Factories must comply with all applicable environmental laws and regulations. Where such requirements are less stringent than Gap Inc.'s own, factories are encouraged to meet the standards outlined in Gap Inc.'s statement of environmental principles.

III. Discrimination

Factories shall employ workers on the basis of their ability to do the job, without regard to race, color, gender, nationality, religion, age, maternity, or marital status.

IV. Forced Labor

Factories shall not use any prison, indentured, or forced labor.

V. Child Labor

Factories shall employ only workers who meet the applicable minimum legal age requirement or are at least 14 years of age, whichever is greater. Factories must also comply with all other applicable child labor laws. Factories are encouraged to develop lawful workplace apprenticeship programs for the educational benefit of their workers, provided that all participants meet both Gap Inc.'s minimum age standard of 14 and the minimum legal age requirement.

VI. Wages & Hours

Factories shall set working hours, wages, and overtime pay in compliance with all applicable laws. Workers shall be paid at least the minimum legal wage or a wage that meets local industry standards, whichever is greater. While it is understood that overtime is often required in garment production, factories shall carry out operations in ways that limit overtime to a level that ensures humane and productive working conditions.

Ethics in Action

Whole Foods Market Practices What It Preaches

The Whole Foods Market supermarket chain was founded by two hippies in Austin, Texas, in 1978 as a natural counterculture food store. Today it is the world's leading retailer of natural and organic foods, with over 285 stores in North America and the United Kingdom. Whole Foods specializes in selling chemical- and drug-free meat, poultry, and produce; its products are the "purest" possible,

Where do your grocery dollars go? Whole Foods Market's goal is to make shopping fun and socially responsible. Customers' money supports an organization that monitors its suppliers, rewards its employees, and seeks to reduce its impact on the environment.

meaning it selects the ones least adulterated by artificial additives, sweeteners, colorings, and preservatives.[15] Despite the high prices it charges for its pure produce, sales per store are growing, and its revenues had grown to over $8 billion by 2010.[16] Why has Whole Foods been so successful? Because, says founder and CEO John Mackey, of the principles he established to manage his company since its beginning–principles founded on the need to behave in an ethical and socially responsible way toward everybody affected by its business. How Whole Foods views its responsibilities to stakeholders and its approach to ethical business are depicted in Figure 4.2.

Mackey says he started his business for three reasons–to have fun, to make money, and to contribute to the well-being of other people.[17] The company's mission is based on its members' collective responsibility to the well-being of the people and groups it affects, its *stakeholders;* in order of priority, at Whole Foods these are customers, team members, investors, suppliers, the community, and the natural environment. Mackey measures his company's success by how well it satisfies the needs of these stakeholders. His ethical stance toward customers is that they are guaranteed that Whole Foods products are 100% organic, hormone-free, or as represented. To help achieve this promise, Whole Foods insists that its suppliers also behave in an ethical way so it knows, for example, that the beef it sells comes from cows pastured on grass, not corn-fed in feed lots, and the chicken it sells is from free-range hens and not from hens that have been confined in tiny cages that prevent movement.

Mackey's management approach toward "team members," as Whole Foods employees are called, is also based on a well-defined ethical position. He says, "We put great emphasis at Whole Foods on the 'Whole People' part of the company mission. We believe in helping support our team members to grow as individuals–to become 'Whole People.' We allow tremendous individual initiative at Whole Foods, and that's why our company is so innovative and creative."[18] Mackey claims that each supermarket in the chain is unique because in each one team members are constantly experimenting with new and better ways to serve customers and improve their well-being. As team members learn, they become "self-actualized" or self-fulfilled, and this increase in their well-being translates into a desire to increase the well-being of other stakeholders.

Finally, Mackey's strong views on ethics and social responsibility also serve shareholders. Mackey does not believe the object of being in business is to primarily maximize profits for shareholders; he puts customers first. He believes, however, that companies that behave ethically, and strive to satisfy the needs of customers and employees, simultaneously satisfy the needs of investors because high profits are the result of loyal customers and committed employees. Indeed, since Whole Foods issued shares to the public in 1992, the value of those shares has increased 25 times in value. Clearly, taking a strong position on ethics and social responsibility has worked so far at Whole Foods.

Community, Society, and Nation

The effects of the decisions made by companies and their managers permeate all aspects of the communities, societies, and nations in which they operate. *Community* refers to physical locations like towns or cities or to social milieus like ethnic neighborhoods in which companies are located. A community provides a company with the physical and social infrastructure that allows it to operate; its utilities and labor

Figure 4.2
Whole Foods Market's Stakeholder Approach to Ethical Business

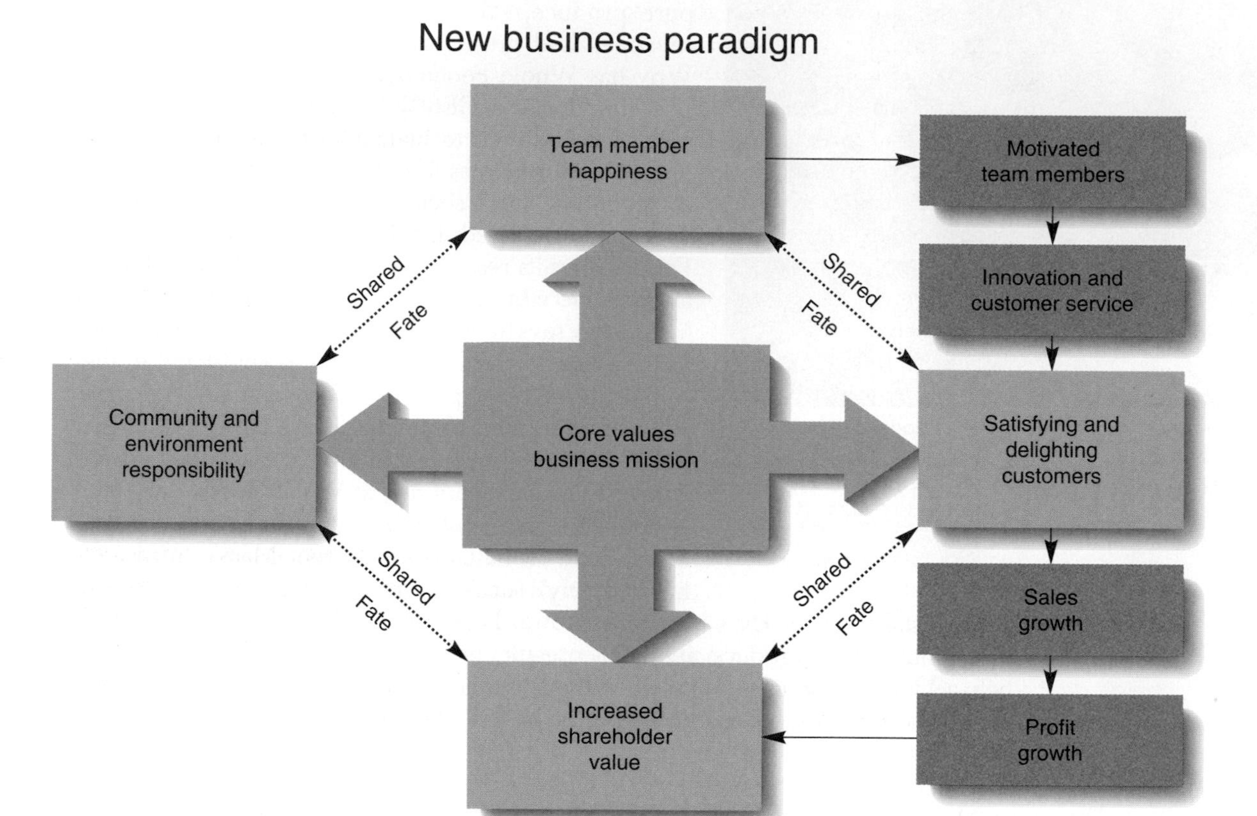

Source: www.wholefoodsmarket.com.

force; the homes in which its managers and employees live; the schools, colleges, and hospitals that serve their needs; and so on.

Through the salaries, wages, and taxes it pays, a company contributes to the economy of its town or region and often determines whether the community prospers or declines. Similarly, a company affects the prosperity of a society and a nation and, to the degree that a company is involved in global trade, all the countries it operates in and thus the prosperity of the global economy. We have already discussed the many issues surrounding global outsourcing and the loss of jobs in the United States, for example.

Although the individual effects of the way each McDonald's restaurant operates might be small, for instance, the combined effects of how all McDonald's and other fast-food companies do business are enormous. In the United States alone, over 500,000 people work in the fast-food industry, and many thousands of suppliers like farmers, paper cup manufacturers, builders, and so on depend on it for their livelihood. Small wonder then that the ethics of the fast-food business are scrutinized closely. This industry was the major lobbyer against attempts to establish a minimum wage in Hong Kong (prior to 2010 there was no minimum wage in Hong Kong), for example, because a minimum wage would substantially increase its operating costs. The minimum wage in Hong Kong was set at HK$27 per hour, or approximately US $3.50.

Business ethics are also important because the failure of a company can have catastrophic effects on a community; a general decline in business activity affects a whole nation. The decision of a large company to pull out of a community, for example, can seriously threaten the community's future. Some companies may attempt to improve their profits by engaging in actions that, although not illegal, can hurt communities and nations. One of these actions is pollution.

Rules for Ethical Decision Making

When a stakeholder perspective is taken, questions on company ethics abound.[19] What is the appropriate way to manage the claims of all stakeholders? Company decisions that favor one group of stakeholders, for example, are likely to harm the interests of others.[20] High prices charged to customers may bring high returns to shareholders and high salaries to managers in the short run. If in the long run customers turn to companies that offer lower-cost products, however, the result may be declining sales, laid-off employees, and the decline of the communities that support the high-priced company's business activity.

When companies act ethically, their stakeholders support them. For example, banks are willing to supply them with new capital, they attract highly qualified job applicants, and new customers are drawn to their products. Thus ethical companies grow and expand over time, and all their stakeholders benefit. The results of unethical behavior are loss of reputation and resources, shareholders selling their shares, skilled managers and employees leaving the company, and customers turning to the products of more reputable companies.

When making business decisions, managers must consider the claims of all stakeholders.[21] To help themselves and employees make ethical decisions and behave in ways that benefit their stakeholders, managers can use four ethical rules or principles to analyze the effects of their business decisions on stakeholders: the *utilitarian, moral rights, justice,* and *practical* rules (Figure 4.3).[22] These rules are useful guidelines that help managers decide on the appropriate way to behave in situations where it is necessary to balance a company's self-interest and the interests of its stakeholders. Remember, the right choices will lead resources to be used where they can create the most value. If all companies make the right choices, all stakeholders will benefit in the long run.[23]

Figure 4.3
Four Ethical Rules

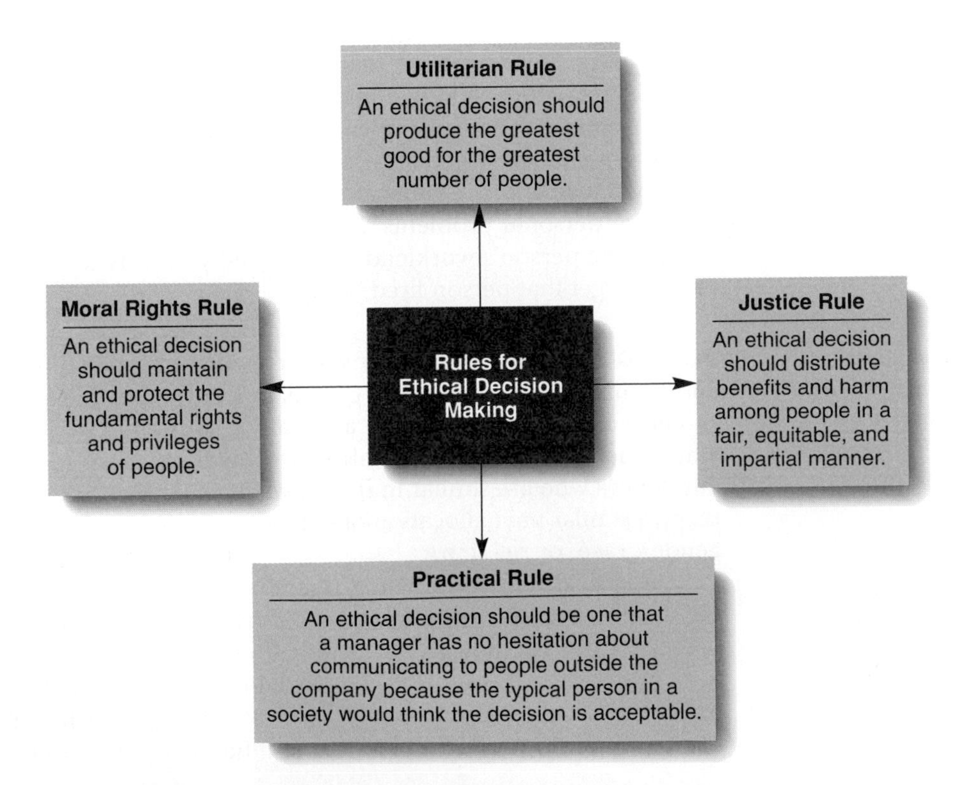

utilitarian rule An ethical decision is a decision that produces the greatest good for the greatest number of people.

UTILITARIAN RULE The **utilitarian rule** is that an ethical decision is a decision that produces the greatest good for the greatest number of people. To decide which is the most ethical course of business action, managers should first consider how different possible courses of business action would benefit or harm different stakeholders. They should then choose the course of action that provides the most benefits, or conversely the one that does the least harm, to stakeholders.[24]

The ethical dilemma for managers is this: How do you measure the benefit and harm that will be done to each stakeholder group? Moreover, how do you evaluate the rights of different stakeholder groups, and the relative importance of each group, in coming to a decision? Because stockholders own the company, shouldn't their claims be held above those of employees? For example, managers might face a choice of using global outsourcing to reduce costs and lower prices or continuing with high-cost production at home. A decision to use global outsourcing benefits shareholders and customers but will result in major layoffs that will harm employees and the communities in which they live. Typically, in a capitalist society such as the United States, the interests of shareholders are put above those of employees, so production will move abroad. This is commonly regarded as being an ethical choice because in the long run the alternative, home production, might cause the business to collapse and go bankrupt, in which case greater harm will be done to all stakeholders.

LO4-3 Describe four rules that can help companies and their managers act in ethical ways.

moral rights rule An ethical decision is one that best maintains and protects the fundamental or inalienable rights and privileges of the people affected by it.

MORAL RIGHTS RULE Under the **moral rights rule,** an ethical decision is one that best maintains and protects the fundamental or inalienable rights and privileges of the people affected by it. For example, ethical decisions protect people's rights to freedom, life and safety, property, privacy, free speech, and freedom of conscience. The adage "Do unto others as you would have them do unto you" is a moral rights principle that managers should use to decide which rights to uphold. Customers must also consider the rights of the companies and people who create the products they wish to consume.

From a moral rights perspective, managers should compare and contrast different courses of business action on the basis of how each course will affect the rights of the company's different stakeholders. Managers should then choose the course of action that best protects and upholds the rights of *all* stakeholders. For example, decisions that might significantly harm the safety or health of employees or customers would clearly be unethical choices.

The ethical dilemma for managers is that decisions that will protect the rights of some stakeholders often will hurt the rights of others. How should they choose which group to protect? For example, in deciding whether it is ethical to snoop on employees, or search them when they leave work to prevent theft, does an employee's right to privacy outweigh an organization's right to protect its property? Suppose a coworker is having personal problems and is coming in late and leaving early, forcing you to pick up the person's workload. Do you tell your boss even though you know this will probably get that person fired?

justice rule An ethical decision distributes benefits and harms among people and groups in a fair, equitable, or impartial way.

JUSTICE RULE The **justice rule** is that an ethical decision distributes benefits and harms among people and groups in a fair, equitable, or impartial way. Managers should compare and contrast alternative courses of action based on the degree to which they will fairly or equitably distribute outcomes to stakeholders. For example, employees who are similar in their level of skill, performance, or responsibility should receive similar pay; allocation of outcomes should not be based on differences such as gender, race, or religion.

The ethical dilemma for managers is to determine the fair rules and procedures for distributing outcomes to stakeholders. Managers must not give people they like bigger raises than they give to people they do not like, for example, or bend the rules to help their favorites. On the other hand, if employees want managers to act fairly toward them, then employees need to act fairly toward their companies by working hard and being loyal. Similarly, customers need to act fairly toward a company if they expect it to be fair to them–something people who illegally copy digital media should consider.

PRACTICAL RULE Each of these rules offers a different and complementary way of determining whether a decision or behavior is ethical, and all three rules should be used to sort out the ethics of a particular course of action. Ethical issues, as we just discussed, are seldom clear-cut, however, because the rights, interests, goals, and incentives of different stakeholders often conflict. For this reason many experts on ethics add a fourth rule to determine whether a business decision is ethical: The **practical rule** is that an ethical decision is one that a manager has no hesitation or reluctance about communicating to people outside the company because the typical person in a society would think it is acceptable. A business decision is probably acceptable on ethical grounds if a manager can answer yes to each of these questions:

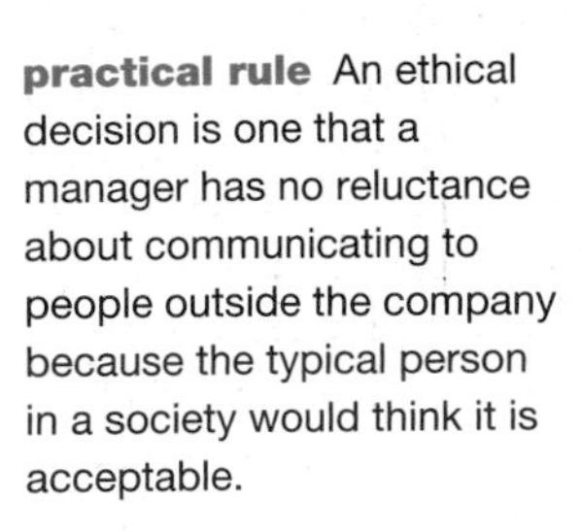

practical rule An ethical decision is one that a manager has no reluctance about communicating to people outside the company because the typical person in a society would think it is acceptable.

1. Does my decision fall within the accepted values or standards that typically apply in business activity today?
2. Am I willing to see the decision communicated to all people and groups affected by it–for example, by having it reported in newspapers or on television?
3. Would the people with whom I have a significant personal relationship, such as family members, friends, or even managers in other organizations, approve of the decision?

Applying the practical rule to analyze a business decision ensures that managers are taking into account the interests of all stakeholders.[25] After applying this rule managers can judge if they have chosen to act in an ethical or unethical way, and they must abide by the consequences. The following "Ethics in Action" box, which describes the issues surrounding individuals copying digital content from the Internet, provides a good example to test these different ethical issues. What is the right or ethical thing to do in this situation?

Ethics in Action

Digital Piracy, Ethics, and the Pirate Party of Sweden

In 2010 over 85% of all music and movies were illegally copied rather than bought. While this elevated level of piracy is lamented by high technology firms, it should not be assumed that all firms are opposed to it or see it as an ethical problem. In Sweden the third largest political part in terms of membership is the Pirate Party *(Piratpartiet)*. This party argues that efforts to limit such piracy are wrong.

Founded in 2006 by Rickard Falkvinge, the Pirate Party has three core principles:

1. Reform of copyright law–they argue that all noncommercial copying of files should be allowed.
2. Abolishment of patents.
3. Respect to right of privacy.

Thus, fundamentally the party advocates for the full and free access to movies and music rather than paying for it.

The party draws heavily from the youth of Sweden and has now spread across Europe and a variety of other nations. It now has representatives in the European parliament. The party does not define itself as a party of the left. Instead

The Pirate Party *(Piratpartiet)* is the third largest political party in Sweden. The group prides itself on supporting, among other things, abolishment of patents, repeal of copyright laws, and full and free access to movies and music.

it is willing to work with all major parties trying to enact its policies on Internet freedom.

Piratpartiet raises interesting issues. It is widely assumed that copying intellectual property is ethically wrong. But from the view of this group such activities are not wrong but instead the effort to limit these activities is wrong. From their view, free access to technology is a right that societies should not seek to limit. If intellectual property is limited, then the society cannot progress–that progress being open to all people, not only those who can pay for it.

To think how such free access may work recognize that Linux is an open source operating system that was developed by individuals and posted free on the Internet. This open source software is increasingly the operating system that firms move to employ since it is free intellectual property.

The counter ethical argument is that individuals will not generate movies or music if they cannot obtain payment for their services. The debate offers two contrasting views on the ethical issues of copying technology.

It is no easy matter to determine a fair or equitable division of the value and profit in a particular business activity. Music companies have no desire to see their revenues fall because potential customers profit from their ability to illegally copy CDs. Music companies have a responsibility to make profits so they can reward their stockholders, pay the musicians royalties on their record sales, and pay their employees' salaries. Of course they also have a responsibility toward customers–they should charge only a fair price for their CDs. In fact, since Apple opened its iTunes store in 2001 and other online music stores followed suit, billions of songs have been legally downloaded and paid for (over 10 billion from iTunes alone), which indicates that millions of customers accept their obligation to pay a fair price for the products they receive. At the same time artists and companies recognize that they must provide first-class content if customers are going to continue to purchase, rather than copy, digital content.

Why Should Managers Behave Ethically?

LO4-4 Discuss why it is important for managers to behave ethically.

Why is it so important that managers, and people in general, should act ethically and temper their pursuit of self-interest by considering the effects of their actions on others? The answer is that the relentless pursuit of self-interest can lead to a collective disaster when one or more people start to profit from being unethical because this encourages other people to act in the same way.[26] More and more people jump onto the bandwagon, and soon everybody is trying to manipulate the situation to serve their personal ends with no regard for the effects of their action on others. The situation brought about then is called the "tragedy of the commons."

Suppose that in an agricultural community there is common land that everybody has an equal right to use. Pursuing self-interest, each farmer acts to make the maximum use of the free resource by grazing his or her own cattle and sheep. Collectively all the farmers overgraze the land, which quickly becomes worn out. Then a strong wind blows away the exposed topsoil, so the common land is destroyed. The pursuit of individual self-interest with no consideration of societal interests leads to disaster for each individual and for the whole society because scarce resources are destroyed.[27] In the case of the Pirate Party, would a tragedy result if all people were to steal digital media causing the disappearance of music, movie, and book companies as creative people decided there was no point in working hard to produce original songs, stories, and so on?

We can look at the effects of unethical behavior on business activity in another way. Suppose companies and their managers operate in an unethical society, meaning one in which stakeholders routinely try to cheat and defraud one another. If stakeholders expect each other to cheat, how long will it take them to negotiate the purchase and shipment of products? When they do not trust each other, stakeholders will probably spend hours bargaining over fair prices, and this is a largely unproductive activity that reduces efficiency and effectiveness.[28] The time and effort that could be spent improving product quality or customer service are lost to negotiating and bargaining. Thus unethical behavior ruins business commerce, and society has a lower standard of living because fewer goods and services are produced, as Figure 4.4 illustrates.

trust The willingness of one person or group to have faith or confidence in the goodwill of another person, even though this puts them at risk.

On the other hand, suppose companies and their managers operate in an ethical society, meaning stakeholders believe they are dealing with others who are basically moral and honest. In this society stakeholders have a greater reason to trust others. **Trust** is the willingness of one person or group to have faith or confidence in the goodwill of another person, even though this puts them at risk (because the other might act in a deceitful way). When trust exists, stakeholders are likely to signal their good intentions by cooperating and providing information that makes it easier to exchange and price goods and services. When one person acts in a trustworthy way, this encourages others to act in the same way. Over time, as greater trust between stakeholders develops, they can work together more efficiently and effectively, which raises company performance (see Figure 4.4). As people see the positive results of acting in an honest way, ethical behavior becomes a valued social norm, and society in general becomes increasingly ethical.

Figure 4.4
Some Effects of Ethical and Unethical Behavior

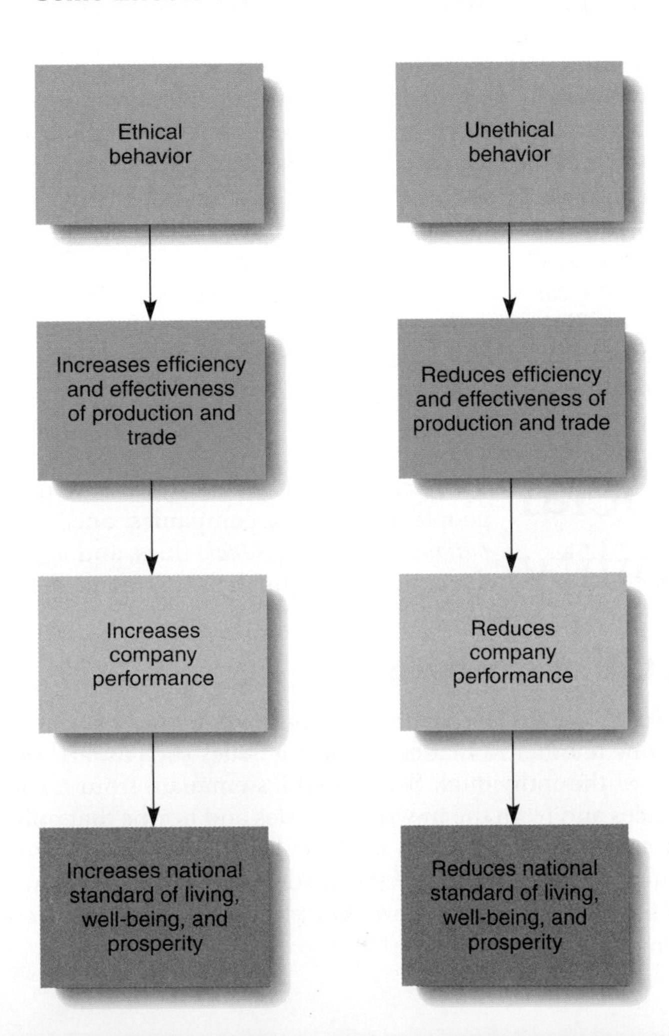

As noted in Chapter 1, a major responsibility of managers is to protect and nurture the resources under their control. Any organizational stakeholders–managers, workers, stockholders, suppliers–who advance their own interests by behaving unethically toward other stakeholders, either by taking resources or by denying resources to others, waste collective resources. If other individuals or groups copy the behavior of the unethical stakeholder, the rate at which collective resources are misused increases, and eventually few resources are available to produce goods and services. Unethical behavior that goes unpunished creates incentives for people to put their unbridled self-interests above the rights of others.[29] When this happens, the benefits that people reap from joining together in organizations disappear quickly.

reputation The esteem or high repute that individuals or organizations gain when they behave ethically.

An important safeguard against unethical behavior is the potential for loss of reputation.[30] **Reputation,** the esteem or high repute that people or organizations gain when they behave ethically, is an important asset. Stakeholders have valuable reputations that they must protect because their ability to earn a living and obtain resources in the long run depends on how they behave.

If a manager misuses resources and other parties regard that behavior as being at odds with acceptable standards, the manager's reputation will suffer. Behaving unethically in the short run can have serious long-term consequences. A manager who has a poor reputation will have difficulty finding employment with other companies. Stockholders who see managers behaving unethically may refuse to invest in their companies, and this will decrease the stock price, undermine the companies' reputations, and ultimately put the managers' jobs at risk.[31]

All stakeholders have reputations to lose. Suppliers who provide shoddy inputs find that organizations learn over time not to deal with them, and eventually, like PCA, they go out of business. Powerful customers who demand ridiculously low prices find that their suppliers become less willing to deal with them, and resources ultimately become harder for them to obtain. Workers who shirk responsibilities on the job find it hard to get new jobs when they are fired. In general, if a manager or company is known for being unethical, other stakeholders are likely to view that individual or organization with suspicion and hostility, creating a poor reputation. But a manager or company known for ethical business practices will develop a good reputation.[32]

In summary, in a complex, diverse society, stakeholders, and people in general, need to recognize they are part of a larger social group. How they make decisions and act not only affects them personally but also affects the lives of many other people. Unfortunately, for some people, the daily struggle to survive and succeed or their total disregard for others' rights can lead them to lose that bigger connection to other people. We can see our relationships to our families and friends, to our school, church, and so on. But we must go further and keep in mind the effects of our actions on other people–people who will be judging our actions and whom we might harm by acting unethically. Our moral scruples are like those "other people" but are inside our heads.

Ethics and Social Responsibility

There are four main determinants of differences in ethics between people, employees, companies, and countries: *societal* ethics, *occupational* ethics, *individual* ethics, and *organizational* ethics–especially the ethics of a company's top managers.[33] (See Figure 4.5.)

LO4-5 Identify the four main sources of managerial ethics.

Societal Ethics

societal ethics Standards that govern how members of a society should deal with one another in matters involving issues such as fairness, justice, poverty, and the rights of the individual.

Societal ethics are standards that govern how members of a society should deal with one another in matters involving issues such as fairness, justice, poverty, and the rights of the individual. Societal ethics emanate from a society's laws, customs, and practices and from the unwritten values and norms that influence how people interact with each other. People in a particular country may automatically behave ethically because they have *internalized* (made a part of their morals) certain values, beliefs, and norms that specify how they should behave when confronted with an ethical dilemma.

Figure 4.5
Sources of Ethics

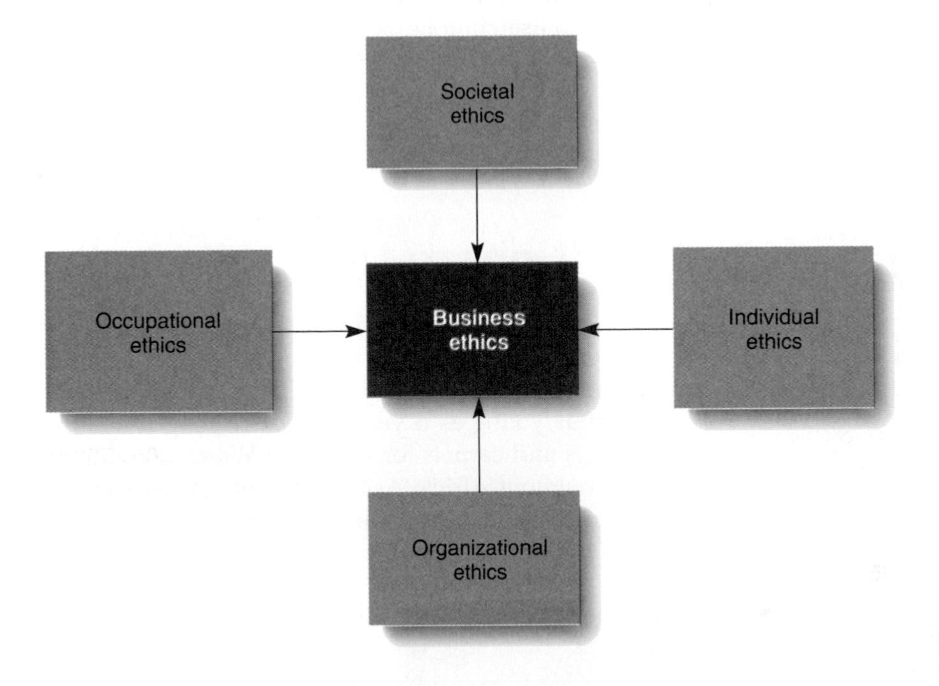

Societal ethics vary among societies. Countries like Germany, Japan, Sweden, and Switzerland are known as being some of the most ethical countries in the world, with strong values about social order and the need to create a society that protects the welfare of all their citizens. In other countries the situation is different. In many economically poor countries bribery is standard practice to get things done–such as getting a telephone installed or a contract awarded. In the United States and other economically advanced countries, bribery is considered unethical and has been made illegal.

IBM experienced the problem of different ethical standards in its Argentine division. Managers there became involved in an unethical scheme to secure a $250 million contract for IBM to provide and service the computers of one of Argentina's largest state-owned banks. After $6 million was paid to bribe the bank executives who agreed to give IBM the contract, IBM announced that it had fired the three top managers of its Argentine division. According to IBM, transactions like this, though unethical by IBM's standards, are not necessarily illegal under Argentine law. The Argentine managers were fired, however, for failing to follow IBM's organizational rules, which preclude bribery to obtain contracts in foreign countries. Moreover, bribery violates the laws of many nations. One of the key pieces of legislation is the U.S. Foreign Corrupt Practices Act, which forbids payment of bribes by U.S. companies to secure contracts abroad, makes companies liable for the actions of their foreign managers, and allows companies found in violation to be prosecuted in the United States. By firing the managers, IBM signaled that it would not tolerate unethical behavior by any of its employees, and it continues today to take a rigorous stance toward ethical issues.

In the European Union (EU), there is not an overriding law for all nations. The EU has passed a convention that lays out actions that it was hoped individual nations would follow. Historically the EU nations have been much more willing to accept payments to obtain business contracts. In some nations it was even a tax-deductible payment. However, today key EU nations such as Britain and Germany have active agencies that seek to enforce existing laws and prevent such payments or prosecute those that make such bribes.

Countries also differ widely in their beliefs about appropriate treatment for their employees. In general, the poorer a country is, the more likely employees are to be treated with little regard. One issue of particular concern on a global level is whether it is ethical to use child labor, as discussed in the following "Ethics in Action" box.

Ethics in Action

Is It Right to Use Child Labor?

In recent years, the number of companies that buy their products from low-cost foreign suppliers has been growing, and concern about the ethics associated with employing young children in factories has been increasing. In Pakistan, children as young as 6 years old work long hours in deplorable conditions to make rugs and carpets for export to Western countries. Children in poor countries throughout Africa, Asia, and South America work in similar conditions. Is it ethical to employ children in factories, and should U.S. companies buy and sell products made by these children?

Afghan boys weave a rug while their father stands nearby inside their home in Kabul, Afghanistan. Afghan rug makers contract children to make rugs, paying their families roughly $8 per yard. Making one 18-foot rug takes approximately a month, and the children often work in shifts around their schooling or other household duties.

Opinions about the ethics of child labor vary widely. Robert Reich, an economist and secretary of labor in the first Clinton administration, believed that the practice is totally reprehensible and should be outlawed on a global level. Another view, championed by *The Economist* magazine, is that while nobody wants to see children employed in factories, citizens of rich countries need to recognize that in poor countries children are often a family's breadwinners. Thus denying children employment would cause whole families to suffer, and one wrong (child labor) might produce a greater wrong (poverty). Instead *The Economist* favors regulating the conditions under which children are employed and hopes that over time, as poor countries become richer, the need for child employment will disappear.

It has been estimated that more than 300,000 children under age 14 are employed in garment factories in Guatemala, a popular low-cost location for clothing manufacturers that supply the U.S. market. These children frequently work more than 60 hours a week and often are paid less than $3 a day–close to the minimum wage in Guatemala. If these children are laid off their families will lose their major source of income.

Thus, the negative impact on the family can be immediate. However, if these children are not in school then there is virtually no hope that they ever will be able to break the cycle of poverty that is so great in Guatemala. Without an education these children will ultimately have children that do the same factory work of their parents when they were young.

The ethical challenge that faces many firms from mature economies is how to ensure that they obtain a reasonably priced product yet one that does not encourage activities such as employing children. When you go to a retailer to buy a new shirt, it will not be labeled "produced by child labor." Instead, all the shirts will look somewhat the same, but they will vary widely in price. Most consumers will choose the cheapest shirt if there is no significant difference in style or quality. Thus, child labor with its dramatically lower costs, yet poverty entrenching nature, is hard to prevent in a market driven economy.

Occupational Ethics

occupational ethics Standards that govern how members of a profession, trade, or craft should conduct themselves when performing work-related activities.

Occupational ethics are standards that govern how members of a profession, trade, or craft should conduct themselves when performing work-related activities.[34] For example, medical ethics govern how doctors and nurses should treat their patients. Doctors are expected to perform only necessary medical procedures and to act in the patient's interest, not their own self-interest. The ethics of scientific research require that scientists conduct their experiments and present their findings in ways that ensure the validity of their conclusions. Like society at large, most professional groups can impose punishments for violations of ethical standards.[35] Doctors and lawyers can be prevented from practicing their professions if they disregard professional ethics and put their own interests first.

Former investment firm owner Bernard Madoff leaves a federal court building in New York City accompanied by U.S. marshals. Madoff was convicted of running an international investment scheme that left most of his clients with little money to show for their investments with his company. Madoff's actions affected banks and businesses worldwide, with some reporting multi-billion-dollar losses.

Within an organization, occupational rules and norms often govern how employees such as lawyers, researchers, and accountants should make decisions to further stakeholder interests. Employees internalize the rules and norms of their occupational group (just as they do those of society) and often follow them automatically when deciding how to behave. Because most people tend to follow established rules of behavior, people frequently take ethics for granted. However, when occupational ethics are violated, such as when scientists fabricate data to disguise the harmful effects of products, ethical issues come to the forefront. For example, Merck scientists were accused of playing down evidence that Vioxx, a best-selling drug, increased the risk of heart attacks; the drug was pulled from the market. Top researchers in pharmaceutical companies have been accused of deliberately hiding research evidence that revealed the harmful effects of products such as Merck's Vioxx painkilling drug and Guidant's heart pacemaker, so doctors and patients could not make informed medical treatment decisions. Table 4.2 lists some failures or lapses in professional ethics according to type of functional manager.

Individual Ethics

individual ethics Personal standards and values that determine how people view their responsibilities to others and how they should act in situations when their own self-interests are at stake.

Individual ethics are personal standards and values that determine how people view their responsibilities to other people and groups and thus how they should act in situations when their own self-interests are at stake.[36] Sources of individual ethics include the influence of one's family, peers, and upbringing in general. The experiences gained over a lifetime–through membership in social institutions such as schools and religions, for example–also contribute to the development of the personal standards and values that a person uses to evaluate a situation and decide what is the morally right or wrong way to behave. However, suppose you are the son or daughter of a mobster, and your upbringing and education take place in an organized crime context; this affects how you evaluate a situation. You may come to believe that it is ethical to do anything and perform any act, up to and including murder, if it benefits your family or friends. These are your ethics. They are obviously not the ethics of the wider society and so are subject to sanction. In a similar way, managers and employees in an organization may come to believe that actions they take to promote or protect their organization are more important than any harm these actions may cause other stakeholders.

Consider the unethical way in which Jim McCormick, director of a "bomb detecting device" company based in rural Somerset, England, set out to make money by developing a bomb detector, the ADE-51, that he sold to 20 countries, including Iraq, for $40,000 each. The Iraqi government alone spent $85 million on the handheld

Table 4.2
Some Failures in Professional Ethics

For manufacturing and materials management managers:

- Releasing products that are not of a consistent quality because of defective inputs.
- Producing product batches that may be dangerous or defective and harm customers.
- Compromising workplace health and safety to reduce costs (for example, to maximize output, employees are not given adequate training to maintain and service machinery and equipment).

For sales and marketing managers:

- Knowingly making unsubstantiated product claims.
- Engaging in sales campaigns that use covert persuasive or subliminal advertising to create customer need for the product.
- Marketing to target groups such as the elderly, minorities, or children to build demand for a product.
- Having ongoing campaigns of unsolicited junk mail, spam, door-to-door, or telephone selling.

For accounting and finance managers:

- Engaging in misleading financial analysis involving creative accounting or "cooking the books" to hide salient facts.
- Authorizing excessive expenses and perks to managers, customers, and suppliers.
- Hiding the level and amount of top management and director compensation.

For human resource managers:

- Failing to act fairly, objectively, and in a uniform way toward different employees or kinds of employees because of personal factors such as personality and beliefs.
- Excessively encroaching on employee privacy through non-job-related surveillance or personality, ability, and drug testing.
- Failing to respond to employee observations and concerns surrounding health and safety violations, hostile workplace issues, or inappropriate or even illegal behavior by managers or employees.

detectors that were used at checkpoints in Baghdad. The device used a "special electronic card" to detect bombs and was powered by the users' own "kinetic energy." However, in 2010 after a tipoff, an independent computer laboratory that tested the device said the card contained only a common tag used by stores to prevent theft.[37] The ADE-51 could not possibly detect the bombs that have killed hundreds of Iraqis; as you might expect, McCormick is now being prosecuted for misrepresentation and fraud, and his device has been banned.

In general, many decisions or behaviors that one person finds unethical, such as using animals for cosmetics testing, may be acceptable to another person. If decisions or behaviors are not illegal, individuals may agree to disagree about their ethical beliefs, or they may try to impose their own beliefs on other people and make those ethical beliefs the law. In all cases, however, people should develop and follow the ethical criteria described earlier to balance their self-interests against those of others when determining how they should behave in a particular situation.

organizational ethics The guiding practices and beliefs through which a particular company and its managers view their responsibility toward their stakeholders.

Organizational Ethics

Organizational ethics are the guiding practices and beliefs through which a particular company and its managers view their responsibility toward their stakeholders. The individual ethics of a company's top managers are especially important in shaping the organization's code of ethics. Ethisphere Institute, a U.S. think tank, has highlighted Kao Corporation as one of the most ethical firms in the world. Kao operates in four basic businesses including health care products, beauty products, fabric care, and chemicals. The firm has operations around the world including Asia, North America, and Europe. The nature of the firm's products can potentially be very damaging to the environment. However, the firm has made environmental protection a key element of its actions.

Workers may behave unethically if they feel pressured to do so by the situation they are in and by unethical top managers. People typically confront ethical issues when weighing their personal interests against the effects of their actions on others. Suppose a manager knows that promotion to vice president is likely if she can secure a $100 million contract, but getting the contract requires bribing the contract giver with $1 million. The manager reasons that performing this act will ensure her career and future, and what harm would it do anyway? Bribery is common, and she knows that even if she decides not to pay the bribe, someone else surely will. So what to do? Research seems to suggest that people who realize they have the most at stake in a career sense or a monetary sense are the ones most likely to act unethically. And it is exactly in this situation that a strong code of organizational ethics can help people behave in the right or appropriate way. *The New York Times* detailed code of ethics (see nytco.com/corporate_governance/code_of_ethics/business_ethics.html), for example, was crafted by its editors to ensure the integrity and honesty of its journalists as they report sensitive information.

If a company's top managers consistently endorse the ethical principles in its corporate credo, they can prevent employees from going astray. Employees are much more likely to act unethically when a credo does not exist or is disregarded. Arthur Andersen, for example, did not follow its credo at all; its unscrupulous partners ordered middle managers to shred records that showed evidence of their wrongdoing. Although the middle managers knew this was wrong, they followed the orders because they responded to the personal power and status of the partners and not the company's code of ethics. They were afraid they would lose their jobs if they did not behave unethically, but their actions cost them their jobs anyway.

Top managers play a crucial role in determining a company's ethics. It is clearly important, then, that when making appointment decisions, the board of directors should scrutinize the reputations and ethical records of top managers. It is the responsibility of the board to decide whether a prospective CEO has the maturity, experience, and integrity needed to head a company and be entrusted with the capital and wealth of the organization, on which the fate of all its stakeholders depends. Clearly a track record of success is not enough to decide whether a top manager is capable of moral decision making; a manager might have achieved this success through unethical or illegal means. It is important to investigate prospective top managers and examine their credentials. Although the best predictor of future behavior is often past behavior, the board of directors needs to be on guard against unprincipled executives who use unethical means to rise to the top of the organizational hierarchy. For this reason it is necessary that a company's directors continuously monitor the behavior of top executives. In the 2000s this increased scrutiny has led to the dismissal of many top executives for breaking ethical rules concerning issues such as excessive personal loans, stock options, inflated expense accounts, and even sexual misconduct–as the "Ethics in Action" box on the next page discusses.

social responsibility The way a company's managers and employees view their duty or obligation to make decisions that protect, enhance, and promote the welfare and well-being of stakeholders and society as a whole.

Approaches to Social Responsibility

A company's ethics are the result of differences in societal, organizational, occupational, and individual ethics. In turn, a company's ethics determine its stance or position on social responsibility. A company's stance on **social responsibility** is the way its managers and employees view their duty or obligation to make decisions that protect, enhance, and promote the welfare

Ethics in Action

Jonathan Reckford Rebuilds Goodwill at Habitat for Humanity

Habitat for Humanity is the 17th largest U.S. nonprofit, and its mission is to build or renovate cost-effective, modest homes in partnership with families in need, who repay the organization by helping to build their own homes or the homes of others and by repaying a no-profit mortgage. Founded decades ago by Millard and Linda Fuller, it receives more than $1 billion in donations a year for its work in more than 90 countries around the world. In 2004 a scandal struck the nonprofit when Millard Fuller was accused of sexually harassing a female employee. The board brought in an investigator to review the complaint. As the investigation unfolded, the Fullers' behavior and ongoing comments about the matter were deemed divisive to the organization's work and led to their dismissal.

When Habitat for Humanity needed a new CEO, they looked to Jonathan Reckford, a Presbyterian pastor and former executive at Walt Disney and Best Buy. Reckford, pictured here with Habitat spokesperson Jimmy Carter, quickly implemented best-practice techniques in order to help Habitat perform more effectively.

In the 2000s the efficiency and effectiveness of nonprofits have been questioned, and many analysts believe that nonprofits need to introduce new management techniques to improve their level of performance. Indeed, one study estimated that nonprofits could save $100 billion by using such techniques as total quality management and benchmarking, which involve an organization's imitating a company that excels in performing some functional activity.

So Habitat's board of directors searched for a new CEO who could simultaneously help the organization continue its work and improve its performance. The person they chose was Jonathan Reckford, an ex-Walt Disney, Best Buy executive and Presbyterian pastor. Reckford relished the challenge of using his management skills to find better ways to use Habitat's $1 billion in donations and to attract more donors. Quickly Reckford began to introduce best practice techniques. For example, modeling companies like Dell and Walmart that use their huge buying power to lower their input costs, he emphasized the need for volume purchasing of building products. He introduced new kinds of output controls to provide detailed feedback on vital aspects of Habitat's performance, such as the number of new houses it built in different regions and countries and the time and cost of construction involved per house. He also introduced better human resource management practices, including creating a promotion ladder in Habitat and raising salaries to competitive levels found in other nonprofits. He decided to move a portion of Habitat's headquarters from the small city in which it had been founded to Atlanta, Georgia, to make it easier to hire skilled functional managers. Finally, he established a new set of goals and priorities for the company; and given that Reckford took over only a month after Hurricane Katrina struck, one obvious priority was to rebuild homes along the Gulf Coast. Habitat's goal was to begin construction or complete 1,000 permanent homes by the end of 2007–a feat it achieved by May 2007, upon which Reckford announced that its new goal was to build 1,000 more.[38]

Habitat for Humanity has steadily increased its international focus; for example, it already had 50 employees in place in Haiti in 2010 when the earthquake struck. Reckford, traveling with singer Ricky Martin, toured the earthquake's devastation and announced, "With more than 200,000 houses severely damaged or destroyed and 1.2 million people homeless or displaced, there is a critical need for shelter in Haiti. Based on our responses to the Asian tsunami and Hurricanes Katrina and Rita in the U.S. Gulf Coast, we are confident that we can empower families to improve their housing conditions by giving them the tools and then working alongside them. But Habitat for Humanity is in need of significant financial support so that we can help 50,000 families improve their lives."[39] In total, since its founding in 1976, Habitat has built, rehabilitated, repaired, or improved more than 350,000 houses worldwide that provide simple and affordable shelter to over 1.75 million people.

LO4-6 Distinguish among the four main approaches toward social responsibility that a company can take.

and well-being of stakeholders and society as a whole.[40] As we noted earlier, when no laws specify how a company should act toward stakeholders, managers must decide the right, ethical, and socially responsible thing to do. Differences in business ethics can lead companies to diverse positions or views on their responsibility toward stakeholders.

Many kinds of decisions signal a company's beliefs about its obligations to make socially responsible business decisions (see Table 4.3). The decision to spend money on training and educating employees–investing in them–is one such decision; so is the decision to minimize or avoid layoffs whenever possible. The decision to act promptly and warn customers when a batch of defective merchandise has been accidentally sold is another one. Companies that try to hide such problems show little regard for social responsibility.

In 2010 quality leader Toyota apologized for being slow to announce recalls to fix brake system problems on some of its vehicles, which had caused uncontrolled

Table 4.3
Forms of Socially Responsible Behavior

Managers are being socially responsible and showing their support for their stakeholders when they

- Provide severance payments to help laid-off workers make ends meet until they can find another job.
- Give workers opportunities to enhance their skills and acquire additional education so they can remain productive and do not become obsolete because of changes in technology.
- Allow employees to take time off when they need to and provide health care and pension benefits for employees.
- Contribute to charities or support various civic-minded activities in the cities or towns in which they are located. (Target and Levi Strauss both contribute 5% of their profits to support schools, charities, the arts, and other good works.)
- Decide to keep open a factory whose closure would devastate the local community.
- Decide to keep a company's operations in the United States to protect the jobs of American workers rather than move abroad.
- Decide to spend money to improve a new factory so it will not pollute the environment.
- Decline to invest in countries that have poor human rights records.
- Choose to help poor countries develop an economic base to improve living standards.

acceleration; Toyota had to deal with a public relations nightmare as a result. Part of Toyota's response was culturally driven. In Japan, good engineering is a highly valued characteristic; there is a great loss of honor when problems in a product are admitted. The culture within Japanese firms is one where there is a great hesitancy to challenge or correct a top manager. Thus, even when there is a problem, lower level managers are very reluctant to tell their superiors that they have made a mistake. Further, the relationship between business and government tends to be close so that there is not strong pressure from the government to identify problems in a product. All of these features encourage Japanese firms in their local market to be hesitant to identify any problems in a product or to publicly admit those problems. The brake problems, however, occurred in the United States where admitting problems quickly and directly is a prized characteristic. In addition there is a strong culture of identifying problems. Once the brake problem had been identified in the United States, Toyota attempted a very Japanese response to the problem. The result was not good. Firms must realize that as they compete around the world the ethics of a situation and how to respond to it are not always universal. The Japanese solution to the brake problem may have been appropriate in Japan but resulted in a perceived ethical lapse in the United States.

Four Different Approaches

obstructionist approach Companies and their managers choose *not* to behave in a socially responsible way and instead behave unethically and illegally.

The strength of companies' commitment to social responsibility can range from low to high (see Figure 4.6). At the low end of the range is an **obstructionist approach,** in which companies and their managers choose *not* to behave in a socially responsible way. Instead they behave unethically and often illegally and do all they can to prevent knowledge of their behavior from reaching other organizational stakeholders and society at large. There are many instances of such behavior. For example, tobacco companies sought to hide evidence that cigarette smoking causes lung cancer. In 2010 it was revealed that the managers of Lehman Brothers, whose bankruptcy helped propel the 2008–2009 financial crisis, used loopholes in U.K. law to hide billions of dollars of worthless assets on its balance sheet to disguise its poor financial condition.

defensive approach Companies and their managers behave ethically to the degree that they stay within the law and strictly abide by legal requirements.

A **defensive approach** indicates at least some commitment to ethical behavior.[41] Defensive companies and managers stay within the law and abide strictly by legal requirements but make no attempt to exercise social responsibility beyond what the law dictates; thus they can and often do act unethically. The managers are the kind who sell their stock in advance of other stockholders because they know their company's performance is about to fall. Although acting on inside information is illegal, it is often hard to prove because top managers have wide latitude in when they sell their shares. The founders of most dot-com companies took advantage of this legal loophole to sell billions of dollars of their dot-com shares before their stock prices collapsed. When making ethical decisions, such managers put their own interests first and commonly harm other stakeholders.

Figure 4.6
Four Approaches to Social Responsibility

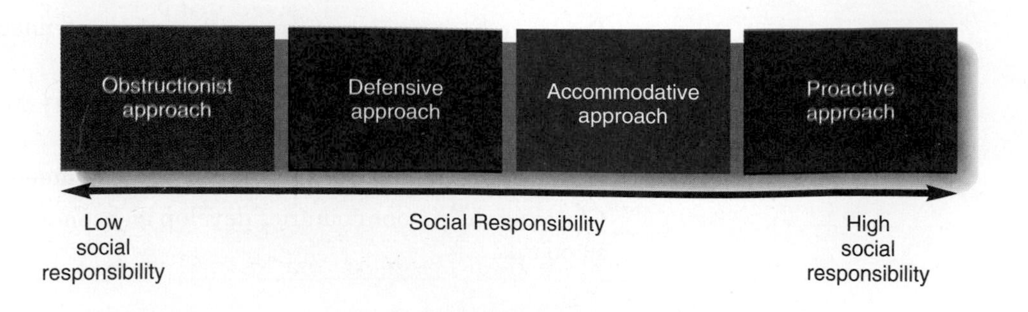

accommodative approach Companies and their managers behave legally and ethically and try to balance the interests of different stakeholders as the need arises.

An **accommodative approach** acknowledges the need to support social responsibility. Accommodative companies and managers agree that organizational members ought to behave legally and ethically, and they try to balance the interests of different stakeholders so the claims of stockholders are seen in relation to the claims of other stakeholders. Managers adopting this approach want to make choices that are reasonable in the eyes of society and want to do the right thing.

This approach is the one taken by the typical large U.S. and European company, which has the most to lose from unethical or illegal behavior. Generally, the older and more reputable a company, the more likely its managers are to curb attempts by their subordinates to act unethically. Large companies like Intel and BMW seek every way to build their companies' competitive advantage. Nevertheless, they rein in attempts by their managers to behave unethically or illegally, knowing the grave consequences such behavior can have on future profitability. Sometimes they fail, however, such as when it was revealed in 2009 that senior executives at Intel and AMD gave inside information to a hedge fund manager and received millions in kickbacks.

proactive approach Companies and their managers actively embrace socially responsible behavior, going out of their way to learn about the needs of different stakeholder groups and using organizational resources to promote the interests of all stakeholders.

Companies and managers taking a **proactive approach** actively embrace the need to behave in socially responsible ways. They go out of their way to learn about the needs of different stakeholder groups and are willing to use organizational resources to promote the interests not only of stockholders but also of the other stakeholders such as their employees and communities.

Proactive companies are often at the forefront of campaigns for causes such as a pollution-free environment; recycling and conservation of resources; the minimization or elimination of the use of animals in drug and cosmetics testing; and the reduction of crime, illiteracy, and poverty.

Why Be Socially Responsible?

Several advantages result when companies and their managers behave in a socially responsible manner. First, demonstrating its social responsibility helps a company build a good reputation. Reputation is the trust, goodwill, and confidence others have in a company that lead them to want to do business with it. The rewards for a good company reputation are increased business and improved ability to obtain resources from stakeholders.[42] Reputation thus can enhance profitability and build stockholder wealth; and behaving responsibly socially is the economically right thing to do because companies that do so benefit from increasing business and rising profits.

Wanna bike around the office complex in your blue jeans? Google's model of employee social responsibility lets you do whatever floats your boat—so the company's boat floats higher.

A second major reason for companies to act responsibly toward employees, customers, and society is that in a capitalist system companies, as well as the government, have to bear the costs of protecting their stakeholders, providing health care and income, paying taxes, and so on. So if all companies in a society act responsibly, the quality of life as a whole increases.

Moreover, how companies behave toward their employees determines many of a society's values and norms and the ethics of its citizens, as already noted. It has been suggested that if all organizations adopted a caring approach and agreed that their responsibility is to promote the interests of their employees, a climate of caring would pervade the wider society. Experts point to Japan, Sweden, Germany, the Netherlands, and Switzerland as countries where organizations are highly socially responsible and where, as a result, crime, poverty, and unemployment rates are relatively low, literacy rates are relatively high, and sociocultural values promote harmony between different groups of people. Business activity affects all aspects of people's lives, so how business behaves toward stakeholders affects how stakeholders behave toward business. You "reap what you sow," as the adage goes.

The Role of Organizational Culture

Although an organization's code of ethics guides decision making when ethical questions arise, managers can go one step further by ensuring that important ethical values and norms are key features of an organization's culture. For example, Royal Philips is a well-recognized Dutch firm that makes a wide range of products from electronics, to consumer goods, to lighting products. The firm has a well-recognized ethical standard that is led and set by its CEO Gerard Kleisterlee.

Managers' roles in developing ethical values and standards in other employees are important. Employees naturally look to those in authority to provide leadership, just as a country's citizens look to its political leaders, and managers become ethical role models whose behavior is scrutinized by subordinates. If top managers are perceived as being self-interested and not ethical, their subordinates are not likely to behave in an ethical manner. Employees may think that if it's all right for a top manager to engage in dubious behavior, it's all right for them too, and for employees this might mean slacking off, reducing customer support, and not taking supportive kinds of actions to help their company. The actions of top managers such as CEOs are scrutinized so closely for ethical improprieties because their actions represent the values of their organizations and, in the case of the president, the values of the nation.

ethics ombudsperson A manager responsible for communicating and teaching ethical standards to all employees and monitoring their conformity to those standards.

Managers can also provide a visible means of support to develop an ethical culture. Increasingly, organizations are creating the role of ethics officer, or **ethics ombudsperson,** to monitor their ethical practices and procedures. The ethics ombudsperson is responsible for communicating ethical standards to all employees, designing systems to monitor employees' conformity to those standards, and teaching managers and employees at all levels of the organization how to respond to ethical dilemmas appropriately.[43] Because the ethics ombudsperson has organizationwide authority, organizational members in any department can communicate instances of unethical behavior by their managers or coworkers without fear of retribution. This arrangement makes it easier for everyone to behave ethically. In addition, ethics ombudspeople can provide guidance when organizational members are uncertain about whether an action is ethical. Some organizations have an organizationwide ethics committee to provide guidance on ethical issues and help write and update the company code of ethics.

It should be recognized that while organizational culture that emphasizes ethics is critical as you move around the world, what is an ethical organizational culture in one setting may not be in another as the following box on Walmart illustrates.

Ethics in Action

Walmart and the Failure of Universal Ethics Standards

Walmart is the world's largest retailer. It entered the German market with great hopes but failed, in large part, due to a lack of understanding of the culture and how to adapt to the market. The firm's approach to ethics illustrates this problem.

In the United States, Walmart has a clear and definitive standard of ethics. This standard of ethics affects everything from dealings with customers, to dealings with suppliers, to supervisor/subordinate relationships. The ethical standards the firm expects are high and absolute. The Walmart Code is more than 30 typewritten pages long and very detailed.

When the firm entered Germany it expected its German subsidiary to establish similar ethical standards. However, German culture is such that standards are not as intrusive. For example, in the United States Walmart prohibits managers and subordinates from dating. Doing so can, in fact, lead to termination. The firm's fear is that subordinates can be pressured into sexual situations that they do not want to be in for fear of losing their jobs. However, in Germany such an intrusion into employees' personal lives was seen as inappropriate.

The very detailed nature of the Code and the fact that it was absolute and could lead to firing was highly resented by the Germans. Ultimately, when presented with the company's Code of Ethics, the workers at Walmart in Germany revolted and filed suit against Walmart protesting the intrusive and absolute nature of the document.

Walmart had to sell its stores in Germany at a loss and leave the country. The role of the Code of Ethics was not the sole cause, but the heavy, rule-based system that worked well in one nation was symbolic of lack of cultural understanding in another.

Summary and Review

LO4-1 **THE NATURE OF ETHICS** Ethical issues are central to how companies and their managers make decisions, and they affect not only the efficiency and effectiveness of company operations but also the prosperity of the nation. The result of ethical behavior is a general increase in company performance and in a nation's standard of living, well-being, and wealth.

An ethical dilemma is the quandary people find themselves in when they have to decide if they should act in a way that might help another person or group and is the right thing to do, even though it might go against their own self-interest. Ethics are the inner guiding moral principles, values, and beliefs that people use to analyze or interpret a situation and then decide what is the right or appropriate way to behave.

Ethical beliefs alter and change as time passes, and as they do so laws change to reflect the changing ethical beliefs of a society.

LO4-2, 4-4 **STAKEHOLDERS AND ETHICS** Stakeholders are people and groups who have a claim on and a stake in a company. The main stakeholder groups are stockholders, managers, employees, suppliers and distributors, customers, and the community, society, and nation. Companies and their managers need to make ethical business decisions that promote the well-being of their stakeholders and avoid doing them harm.

LO4-3, 4-5 To determine whether a business decision is ethical, managers can use four ethical rules to analyze it: the utilitarian, moral rights, justice, and practical rules. Managers should behave ethically because this avoids the tragedy of the commons and results in a general increase in efficiency, effectiveness, and company performance. The main determinants of differences in a manager's, company's, and country's business ethics are societal, occupational, individual, and organizational.

LO4-6 **ETHICS AND SOCIAL RESPONSIBILITY** A company's stance on social responsibility is the way its managers and employees view their duty or obligation to make decisions that protect, enhance, and promote the welfare and well-being of stakeholders and society as a whole.

There are four main approaches to social responsibility: obstructionist, defensive, accommodative, and proactive. The rewards from behaving in a socially responsible way are a good reputation, the support of all organizational stakeholders, and thus superior company performance.

Management in Action

Topics for Discussion and Action

Discussion

1. What is the relationship between ethics and the law? **[LO4-1]**
2. Why do the claims and interests of stakeholders sometimes conflict? **[LO4-2]**
3. Why should managers use ethical criteria to guide their decision making? **[LO4-3]**
4. As an employee of a company, what are some of the most unethical business practices that you have encountered in its dealings with stakeholders? **[LO4-4]**
5. What are the main determinants of business ethics? **[LO4-5]**

Action

6. Find a manager and ask about the most important ethical rules he or she uses to make the right decisions. **[LO4-3]**
7. Find an example of (a) a company that has an obstructionist approach to social responsibility and (b) one that has an accommodative approach. **[LO4-6]**

Building Management Skills

Dealing with Ethical Dilemmas [LO4-1, 4-4]

Use the chapter material to decide how you, as a manager, should respond to each of the following ethical dilemmas:

1. You are planning to leave your job to go work for a competitor; your boss invites you to an important meeting where you will learn about new products your company will be bringing out next year. Do you go to the meeting?
2. You're the manager of sales in an expensive sports car dealership. A young executive who has just received a promotion comes in and wants to buy a car that you know is out of her price range. Do you encourage the executive to buy it so you can receive a big commission on the sale?
3. You sign a contract to manage a young rock band, and that group agrees to let you produce their next seven records, for which they will receive royalties of 5%. Their first record is a smash hit and sells millions. Do you increase their royalty rate on future records?

Managing Ethically [LO4-3, 4-5]

In many countries it is common to give payments to the police for minor offenses, such as traffic tickets. The salaries of such officials are set absurdly low in part because the government expects there to be such payments. If the officers do not receive such payments they typically could not eat nor would they have housing. The same can be said to occur with officials who deal with ports of entry and importing goods. As a result it is often expected that an importer will make small payments to the officials at ports of entry when trying to bring goods into a country.

Questions

1. Is it ethical to make such payments to officials at a port of entry to ensure your goods get into the country?
2. Would you be willing, personally, to make such payments?
3. What would you do if your employer says payments or bribes are never permitted, but if you do not get your goods into a given country your performance will be judged to be negative?

Small Group Breakout Exercise

Is Chewing Gum the "Right" Thing to Do? [LO4-1, 4-3]

Form groups of three or four people, and appoint one member as the spokesperson who will communicate your findings to the class when called on by the instructor. Then discuss the following scenario:

In Europe the right to chew gum is taken for granted. Although it is often against the rules to chew gum in a high school classroom, church, and so on, it is legal to do so on the street. If you possess or chew gum on a street in Singapore, you can be arrested. Chewing gum has been made illegal in Singapore because those in power believe it creates a mess on pavements and feel that people cannot be trusted to dispose of their gum properly and thus should have no right to use it.

1. What makes chewing gum acceptable in Europe and unacceptable in Singapore?
2. How can you use ethical principles to decide when gum chewing is ethical or unethical and if and when it should be made illegal?

Exploring the World Wide Web [LO4-2, 4-5]

Go to Carrefour's Web site (www.carrefour.com) and read the information there about the company's stance on sustainability. Then search the Web for some recent stories about Carrefour's global purchasing practices and reports on the enforcement of its code of conduct.

1. What ethical principles guide Carrefour's approach to sustainability?
2. Does Carrefour appear to be doing a good job of acting on its sustainability goals?

Be the Manager [LO4-3]

Creating an Ethical Code

You are an entrepreneur who has decided to go into business and open a steak and chicken restaurant. Your business plan requires that you hire at least 20 people as chefs, waiters, and so on. As the owner, you are drawing up a list of ethical principles that each of these people will receive and must agree to when he or she accepts a job offer. These principles outline your view of what is right or acceptable behavior and what will be expected both from you and from your employees.

Create a list of the five main ethical rules or principles you will use to govern how your business operates. Be sure to spell out how these principles relate to your stakeholders; for example, state the rules you intend to follow in dealing with your employees and customers.

CHAPTER 5

Managing Diverse Employees in a Multicultural Environment

Learning Objectives

After studying this chapter, you should be able to:

LO5-1 Discuss the increasing diversity of the workforce and the organizational environment.

LO5-2 Explain the central role that managers play in the effective management of diversity.

LO5-3 Explain why the effective management of diversity is both an ethical and a business imperative.

LO5-4 Discuss how perception and the use of schemas can result in unfair treatment.

LO5-5 List the steps managers can take to effectively manage diversity.

LO5-6 Identify the two major forms of sexual harassment and how they can be eliminated.

A MANAGER'S CHALLENGE

Managing Diversity Effectively at Royal Dutch Shell

Royal Dutch Shell Oil is a Dutch company registered in the United Kingdom. The firm traces its history back to the late 1800s. Today the firm is one of the largest oil companies in the world. The firm explores for, and extracts, crude oil and natural gas; it also refines crude oil into a range of products, which are moved and marketed worldwide for domestic, industrial, and transport use. The firm has over 100,000 employees worldwide and is highly dedicated to diversity in its management; it has made a major commitment to act on that obligation. Royal Dutch Shell Chairman of the Board Jeroen van der Veer has said about the management of diversity:

"Diversity and inclusiveness are vital for winning in today's business environment. They create a competitive edge by helping us to attract and retain the best people, increase creativity and improve decision making. Most importantly, diversity and inclusiveness build trust and strengthen relationships with all of our stakeholders.

"We have made solid progress to embed diversity and inclusiveness into Group businesses, but much more needs to be done. We need to put D&I at the very heart of our business processes with greater accountability for results at business, country and individual level. By integrating diversity and inclusiveness into the mainstream of the business, we can translate our core values of honesty, integrity and respect for people into action, and improve our global performance."[1]

This commitment is seen at the firm in the expanding leadership role of women. The firm now reports that at the end of 2009, 14.0% of senior leadership positions were filled by women, up from 13.6% in 2008. In addition, 26.4% of supervisory positions (up from 24.7% in 2008) and 16.1% of management positions (up from 15.3% in 2008) were held by women.[2]

Royal Dutch Shell has taken numerous steps to manage diversity effectively throughout the global organization. Women now make up more than 14% of the company's senior managers.

The recruitment of women by Royal Dutch Shell has not been easy in a historically male business like the oil industry. However, the firm has set up strong programs in which to attract women to the firm. The business has also developed special programs to ensure that women are both developed and mentored by more senior managers to prepare them for leadership roles in the company.

Another aspect of diversity that is unique to a highly global firm like Royal Dutch Shell is that it actively seeks to ensure that local management includes a strong representation of individuals from the region in which the firm is operating. The nature of the oil business is that it is often located in very rural, poor nations. The result is that well-trained local managers are often rare and very expensive. However, if local skills and abilities of workers are not developed in a mineral extraction business, the impact on the given nation where the oil or gas is located can be negative. The local area provides the resource but often those who benefit financially from the extraction are not in that region. At some stage the oil and gas will be depleted. If the local skills and abilities are not developed then once the oil and gas is gone, the only resources from the region may be gone and there is little hope of that area ever developing economically. As a result, Royal Dutch Shell makes a concentrated effort to fill local management positions with individuals from that region. The result is that by 2009 local nationals filled more than half the senior leadership positions in 37% of the nations in which the firm operated as compared to 32% in 2008.

Royal Dutch Shell has faced a challenge in Nigeria. Nigeria's delta region is one of the major sources of oil in the world. This region in the south is populated by a variety of tribes but the largest are the Ogoni and the Ijaw. These people feel that they provide the oil from their region and suffer the resulting pollution but never benefit from the drilling activities. The oil extracted in this area provides over 80% of the revenue for the government of Nigeria. While the delta provides the revenue the residents receive no special treatment in terms of benefit; instead the money is spent throughout the nation. In addition, very little of the revenue designated for the delta area actually arrives because of corruption throughout the country. The result has been an active rebellion by locals who often target Royal Dutch Shell operations. The rebellious actions have required Royal Dutch Shell to go beyond the diversity measures of the Nigerian government to show the firm's commitment to the improvement of the delta region. Thus, Royal Dutch Shell must prove itself time and again as a responsible global citizen.

Overview

As indicated in "A Manager's Challenge," effective management of diversity means much more than hiring diverse employees. It means learning to appreciate and respond appropriately to the needs, attitudes, beliefs, and values that diverse people bring to an organization. It also means correcting misconceptions about why and how various kinds of employee groups differ from one another and finding the most effective way to use the skills and talents of diverse employees.

In this chapter we focus on the effective management of diversity. Managers need to proactively manage diversity to attract and retain the best employees and effectively compete in a diverse global environment.

LO5-1 Discuss the increasing diversity of the workforce and the organizational environment.

Sometimes well-intentioned managers inadvertently treat one group of employees differently from another group, even though there are no performance-based differences between the two groups. This chapter explores why differential treatment occurs and the steps managers and organizations can take to ensure that diversity, in all respects, is effectively managed for the good of all organizational stakeholders.

The Increasing Diversity of the Workforce and the Environment

diversity Differences among people in age, gender, race, ethnicity, religion, sexual orientation, socioeconomic background, and capabilities/disabilities.

Diversity is dissimilarities–differences–among people due to age, gender, race, ethnicity, religion, sexual orientation, socioeconomic background, education, experience, physical appearance, capabilities/disabilities, and any other characteristic that is used to distinguish between people (see Figure 5.1).

Diversity raises important ethical issues and social responsibility issues (see Chapter 4). It is also a critical issue for organizations, one that if not handled well can bring an organization to its knees, especially in our increasingly global environment. There are several reasons why diversity is such a pressing concern and issue both in the popular press and for managers and organizations:

- There is a strong ethical imperative in many societies that diverse people must receive equal opportunities and be treated fairly and justly. Unfair treatment is also illegal in many cases.
- Effectively managing diversity can improve organizational effectiveness.[3] When managers effectively manage diversity, they not only encourage other managers to treat diverse members of an organization fairly and justly but also realize that diversity is an important organizational resource that can help an organization gain a competitive advantage.
- There is substantial evidence that diverse individuals continue to experience unfair treatment in the workplace as a result of biases, stereotypes, and overt discrimination.[4]

Figure 5.1
Sources of Diversity in the Workplace

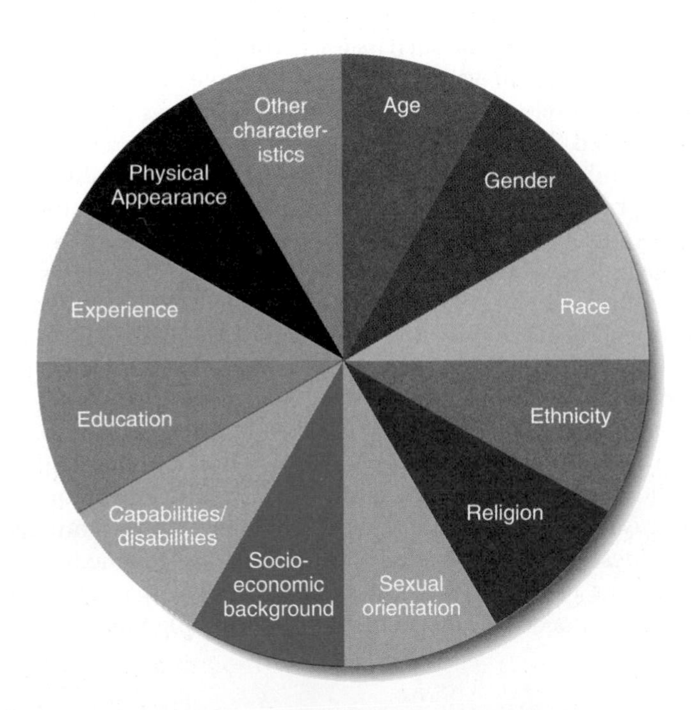

It is important to note here that organizations will face a diverse workforce in different ways. If you manage a factory in China, employees very likely will be Han Chinese; so, there is virtually no ethnic diversity. The only religious differences that may be evident at all will be if a member of the very small Muslim population in the nation is observant and wears a skull cap. Managers are more likely to face differences between workers from various regions who will group together as do workers from Yunnan province. These workers will all speak the same dominant language, Mandarin. However, they will prefer to talk among themselves in their local dialect. There will be differences in skill levels and in gender. However, the diversity issues in such an environment are far more constrained than, say, in the United States or some parts of Europe where there are significant diversity issues in terms of ethnic background and religion.

However, even in Europe there are wide differences in diversity. Table 5.1 illustrates the number of immigrants who become citizens in different EU countries. Overall in the 27 nations of the EU, approximately 6% of citizens are foreign born. This compares to the United States in which 16% of its citizens are foreign born. In some ethnic groups in the United States like Hispanics that percentage of immigrants will jump to 40%. This results in high levels of diversity in terms of ethnicity, culture, and religion and is the norm in the United States. In Europe there are some nations, such as Spain and Cyprus, that are more like the United States in that they have high levels of immigration. (Note that the high levels of immigrants in nations like Latvia in the table reflect ethnic Russians who later qualified for citizenship after the breakup of the Soviet Union. These individuals may have lived their entire lives in Latvia so do not accurately reflect immigration.)

Some countries in Europe do have significant diversity. For example, in Hungary the major ethnic group is Magyar, but there are also groups such as Romany, Serbs, Slovaks, and Germans. Thus, there is ethnic and resulting religious diversity in a nation like Hungary, although this diversity tends to be far more regionalized with different groups dominating various regions outside the capital. In the United States immigration and diversity tend to be widespread. Thus, a global firm has to be sensitive to the fact that patterns of diversity may be unique in different settings and its management must reflect this.

But being sensitive to diversity involves more than awareness of ethnic and religious diversity; other issues such as age, gender, disabilities, socioeconomic background, and sexual orientation need to be considered. The laws that regulate these issues will be different around the world. Thus, what may be legal in one setting is not in another. Each firm needs to identify what the given legal setting is and also the firm's overall policy on such issues. Some issues such as sexual orientation will be treated very differently in various settings. In some nations such as Uganda homosexuality may be severely punished; the death penalty was proposed for homosexuality but was not enacted there as of the writing of this chapter in October 2010.

It should be noted also that firms have to be sensitive not only to the laws in each setting but also the law in their home country and whether that law is extraterritorial. For example, the EU provides directives to the government of each member state on issues like gender discrimination. The member states then enforce the suggested laws often enacting them as recommended. However ensuring that the law follows European firms as they do business in other nations is up to each member nation. In the United States under Title VII it is wrong to discriminate against women. That law follows United States firms as they do business around the world; the law is written to be extraterritorial. Thus, a firm must not only understand the laws of the nations they enter but also how the laws of the firm's home nation apply.

Ultimately firms must also do what is right. A law on gender discrimination may not travel from Romania to another country, but a Romanian firm must decide what its values are. If the company standards are to maximize human value whether it is legal or not, then the firm should do what is right. Thus, the goal of most firms will be to maximize the potential of all people whether or not the firm is so driven by law.

Table 5.1
Population of Foreign Citizens, 2009

Country	Total Foreign Citizens, 000s	% of Total Population	% of Total Population from EU 27 Countries	% of Total Population from Outside the EU	Median Age, Nationals	Median Age, Foreign
EU27*	31,860.30	6.4	2.4	4.0	41.2	34.3
Belgium**	971.40	9.1	6.2	2.9	–	–
Bulgaria	23.80	0.3	0.0	0.3	41.2	39.4
Czech Republic	407.50	3.9	1.4	2.5	39.6	34.7
Denmark	320.00	5.8	2.0	3.8	41.0	32.1
Germany	7,185.90	8.8	3.1	5.7	44.5	36.6
Estonia	214.40	16.0	0.7	15.3	37.3	49.3
Ireland	504.10	11.3	8.2	3.1	33.9	33.7
Greece	929.50	8.3	1.4	6.8	42.6	34.1
Spain	5,651.00	12.3	5.0	7.4	41.1	32.6
France	3,737.50	5.8	2.0	3.8	39.3	38.3
Italy	3,891.30	6.5	1.9	4.6	43.9	32.3
Cyprus	128.20	16.1	9.8	6.3	–	–
Latvia	404.00	17.9	0.4	17.5	36.5	52.4
Lithuania	41.50	1.2	0.1	1.2	39.0	33.4
Luxembourg	214.80	43.5	37.6	6.0	43.0	34.9
Hungary	186.40	1.9	1.1	0.8	39.7	37.4
Malta	18.10	4.4	2.0	2.4	39.2	36.6
Netherlands	637.10	3.9	1.8	2.1	40.8	34.0
Austria	864.40	10.3	3.8	6.6	42.3	33.9
Poland***	35.90	0.1	0.0	0.1	37.8	42.4
Portugal	443.10	4.2	0.8	3.4	40.9	34.0
Romania	31.40	0.1	0.0	0.1	37.9	34.1
Slovenia	70.60	3.5	0.2	3.3	41.4	37.3
Slovakia	52.50	1.0	0.6	0.4	36.7	36.0
Finland	142.30	2.7	1.0	1.7	42.1	33.0
Sweden	547.70	5.9	2.8	3.2	41.3	34.0
United Kingdom**	4,020.80	6.6	2.6	3.9	–	–
Iceland	24.40	7.6	6.1	1.6	35.3	30.7
Norway	302.90	6.3	3.4	2.9	39.2	32.6
Switzerland	1,669.70	21.7	13.4	8.3	43.3	35.6
Turkey	103.80	0.1	0.1	0.1	28.5	33.4

* Estimate; ** Belgium and United Kingdom: 2008 data; *** Provisional.

Sources: Statistics from Eurostat; Simon Rogers, "Immigration to Europe: How Many Foreign Citizens Live in Each Country? Full Data and Visualisation," Data Blog, September 7, 2010, accessed at http://www.guardian.co.uk/news datablog/2010/sep/07/immigration-europe-foreign-citizens#data.

Focus on Diversity

Preventing Discrimination Based on Sexual Orientation

Although gays and lesbians have made great strides in attaining fair treatment in the workplace, much more needs to be done. In a recent study conducted by Harris Interactive Inc. (a research firm) and Witeck Communications Inc. (a marketing firm), over 40% of gay and lesbian employees indicated that they had been unfairly treated, denied a promotion, or pushed to quit their jobs because of their sexual orientation.[5] Given continued harassment and discrimination despite the progress that has been made,[6] many gay and lesbian employees fear disclosing their sexual orientation in the workplace and thus live a life of secrecy. While there are a few openly gay top managers, such as David Geffen, cofounder of DreamWorks SKG, and John deCourcey Evans, CEO and President of Opus Hotels Group of Canada,[7] many others choose not to disclose or discuss their personal lives, including long-term partners.[8]

Chubb Corporation takes diversity awareness seriously, as is evidenced by this LGBT sensitivity training session.

Thus it is not surprising that many managers are taking active steps to educate and train their employees about issues of sexual orientation. S. C. Johnson & Sons, Inc., maker of Raid insecticide and Glade air fresheners provides mandatory training to its plant managers to overturn stereotypes; and Eastman Kodak, Lehman Brothers Holdings Inc., Merck & Co., Ernst & Young, and Toronto-Dominion Bank all train managers in how to prevent sexual orientation discrimination.[9] Other organizations, such as Lucent Technologies and Microsoft, send employees to seminars conducted at prominent business schools. Many companies, such as Raytheon and IBM, provide assistance to their gay and lesbian employees through gay and lesbian support groups.[10]

The Chubb Group of Insurance Companies, a property and casualty insurance company, provides its managers with a two-hour training session to help create work environments that are safe and welcoming for lesbian, gay, bisexual, and transgender (LGBT) people.[11] The sessions are conducted by two Chubb employees; usually one of the trainers is straight and the other is gay. The sessions focus on issues that affect a manager's ability to lead diverse teams, such as assessing how safe and welcoming the workplace is for LGBT people, how to refer to gay employees' significant others, and how to respond if employees or customers use inappropriate language or behavior. The idea for the program originated from one of Chubb's employee resource groups. Managers rate the program highly and say they are better able to respond to the concerns of their LGBT employees while creating a safe and productive work environment for all.[12]

Other Kinds of Diversity

Other kinds of diversity are important in organizations, are critical for managers to deal with effectively, and also are potential sources of unfair treatment. For example, organizations and teams need members with diverse backgrounds and experiences. This is clearly illustrated by the prevalence of cross-functional teams in organizations whose members might come from various departments such as marketing, production, finance, and sales (teams are covered in depth in Chapter 15). A team responsible for developing and introducing a new product, for example, often needs the expertise of employees not only from R&D and engineering but also from marketing, sales, production, and finance.

Other types of diversity can affect how employees are treated in the workplace. For example, employees differ from each other in how attractive they are (based on the standards of the cultures in which an organization operates) and in body weight. Whether individuals are attractive or unattractive, thin or overweight, in most cases has no bearing on their job performance unless they have jobs in which physical appearance plays a role, such as modeling. Yet sometimes these physical sources of diversity end up influencing advancement rates and salaries. A recent study published in the *American Journal of Public Health* found that highly educated obese women earned approximately 30% less per year than women who were not obese and men (regardless of whether or not the men were obese).[13] Clearly managers need to ensure that all employees are treated fairly, regardless of their physical appearance.

LO5-2 Explain the central role that managers play in the effective management of diversity.

Managers and the Effective Management of Diversity

The increasing diversity of the environment–which, in turn, increases the diversity of an organization's workforce–increases the challenges managers face in effectively managing diversity. Each of the kinds of diversity just discussed presents a particular set of issues managers need to appreciate before they can respond to them effectively. Understanding these issues is not always a simple matter, as many informed managers have discovered. Research on how different groups are currently treated and the unconscious biases that might adversely affect them is vital because it helps managers become aware of the many subtle and unobtrusive ways in which diverse employee groups can come to be treated unfairly over time. Managers can take many more steps to become sensitive to the ongoing effects of diversity in their organizations, take advantage of all the contributions diverse employees can make, and prevent diverse employees from being unfairly treated.

Critical Managerial Roles

In each of their managerial roles (see Chapter 1), managers can either promote the effective management of diversity or derail such efforts; thus they are critical to this process. For example, in their interpersonal roles, managers can convey that the effective management of diversity is a valued goal and objective (figurehead role), can serve as a role model and institute policies and procedures to ensure that diverse organizational members are treated fairly (leader role), and can enable diverse individuals and groups to coordinate their efforts and cooperate with each other both inside the organization and at the organization's boundaries (liaison role). In Table 5.2 we summarize some ways managers can ensure that diversity is effectively managed as they perform their different roles.

Given the formal authority that managers have in organizations, they typically have more influence than rank-and-file employees. When managers commit to supporting diversity, their authority and positions of power and status influence other members of an organization to make a similar commitment.[14] Research on social influence supports such a link: People are likely to be influenced and persuaded by others who have high status.[15]

Moreover, when managers commit to diversity, their commitment legitimizes the diversity management efforts of others.[16] In addition, resources are devoted to such efforts, and all members of an organization believe that their diversity-related efforts are supported and valued. Consistent with this reasoning, top management commitment and rewards for the support of diversity are often cited as critical ingredients in the success of diversity management initiatives.[17] Additionally, seeing managers express confidence in the abilities and talents of diverse employees causes other organizational members to be similarly confident and helps reduce any misconceived misgivings they may have as a result of ignorance or stereotypes.[18]

Table 5.2
Managerial Roles and the Effective Management of Diversity

Type of Role	Specific Role	Example
Interpersonal	Figurehead	Convey that the effective management of diversity is a valued goal and objective.
	Leader	Serve as a role model and institute policies and procedures to ensure that diverse members are treated fairly.
	Liaison	Enable diverse individuals to coordinate their efforts and cooperate with one another.
Informational	Monitor	Evaluate the extent to which diverse employees are being treated fairly.
	Disseminator	Inform employees about diversity policies and initiatives and the intolerance of discrimination.
	Spokesperson	Support diversity initiatives in the wider community and speak to diverse groups to interest them in career opportunities.
Decisional	Entrepreneur	Commit resources to develop new ways to effectively manage diversity and eliminate biases and discrimination.
	Disturbance handler	Take quick action to correct inequalities and curtail discriminatory behavior.
	Resource allocator	Allocate resources to support and encourage the effective management of diversity.
	Negotiator	Work with organizations (e.g., suppliers) and groups (e.g., labor unions) to support and encourage the effective management of diversity.

Two other important factors emphasize why managers are so central to the effective management of diversity. The first factor is that women and ethnic minorities often start out at a slight disadvantage due to how they are perceived by others in organizations, particularly in work settings where they are a numerical minority. As Virginia Valian, a psychologist at Hunter College who studies gender, indicates, "In most organizations women begin at a slight disadvantage. A woman does not walk into the room with the same status as an equivalent man, because she is less likely than a man to be viewed as a serious professional."[19]

The second factor is that research suggests that slight differences in treatment can accumulate and result in major disparities over time. Even small differences–such as a very slight favorable bias toward men for promotions–can lead to major differences in the number of male and female managers over time.[20] Thus while women and other minorities are sometimes advised not to make "a mountain out of a molehill" when they perceive they have been unfairly treated, research conducted by Valian and others suggests that molehills (slight differences in treatment based on irrelevant distinctions such as race, gender, or ethnicity) can turn into mountains over time (major disparities in important outcomes such as promotions) if they are ignored.[21] Once again, managers have the obligation, from both an ethical and a business perspective, to prevent any disparities in treatment and outcomes due to irrelevant distinctions such as race or ethnicity.

LO5-3 Explain why the effective management of diversity is both an ethical and a business imperative.

The Ethical Imperative to Manage Diversity Effectively

Effectively managing diversity not only makes good business sense (which is discussed in the next section) but also is an ethical imperative. Two moral principles guide managers in their efforts to meet this imperative: distributive justice and procedural justice.

distributive justice A moral principle calling for fair distribution of pay, promotions, and other organizational resources based on meaningful contributions that individuals have made and not personal characteristics over which they have no control.

DISTRIBUTIVE JUSTICE The principle of **distributive justice** dictates fair distribution of pay, promotions, job titles, interesting job assignments, office space, and other organizational resources among members of an organization. These outcomes should be distributed according to the meaningful contributions that individuals have made to the organization (such as time, effort, education, skills, abilities, and performance levels) and not irrelevant personal characteristics over which individuals have no control (such as gender, race, or age).[22] Managers have an obligation to ensure that distributive justice exists in their organizations. This does not mean that all members of an organization receive identical or similar outcomes; rather, it means that members who receive more favorable outcomes than others have made substantially higher or more significant contributions to the organization.

Is distributive justice common in organizations? Probably the best way to answer this question is to say things are getting better. Fifty years ago, in the United States overt discrimination against women and minorities was common; today organizations are inching closer toward the ideal of distributive justice. Statistics comparing the treatment of women and minorities with the treatment of other employees suggest that most managers would need to take a proactive approach to achieve distributive justice in their organizations.[23] For example, across occupations, women consistently earn less than men (see Table 5.3).[24] Even in occupations dominated by women, such as sales and office occupations, men tend to earn more than women.[25] These statistics are for the United States, a nation with some of the strongest laws against discrimination in the world. Thus, the wage difference is likely even greater in other parts of the world.

In many countries, managers have not only an ethical obligation to strive to achieve distributive justice in their organizations but also a legal obligation to treat all employees fairly. They risk being sued by employees who believe they are not being fairly treated.

procedural justice A moral principle calling for the use of fair procedures to determine how to distribute outcomes to organizational members.

PROCEDURAL JUSTICE The principle of **procedural justice** requires that managers use fair procedures to determine how to distribute outcomes to organizational members.[26] This principle applies to typical procedures such as appraising subordinates' performance, deciding who should receive a raise or a promotion, and deciding whom to lay off when an organization is forced to downsize. Procedural

Table 5.3
Weekly Earnings by Sex and Occupation in 2009 in the United States

Median Weekly Earning for Full-Time Workers in 2009

Occupation	Men	Women	Women's Earnings as a Percentage of Men's
Management, professional, and related	$1,248	$907	73
Service	524	418	80
Sales and office	737	590	80
Natural resources, construction, and maintenance	727	542	75
Production, transportation, and material moving	648	472	73

Source: "Table 7. Median Usual Weekly Earnings of Full-Time Wage and Salary Workers by Occupation and Sex, Annual Wages," http://data.bls.gov/cgi-bin/print.pl/news.release/wkyeng.t07.htm, February 9, 2010.

justice exists, for example, when managers (1) carefully appraise a subordinate's performance, (2) take into account any environmental obstacles to high performance beyond the subordinate's control, such as lack of supplies, machine breakdowns, or dwindling customer demand for a product, and (3) ignore irrelevant personal characteristics such as the subordinate's age or ethnicity. Like distributive justice, procedural justice is necessary not only to ensure ethical conduct but also to avoid costly lawsuits.

Effectively Managing Diversity Makes Good Business Sense

Diverse organizational members can be a source of competitive advantage, helping an organization provide customers with better goods and services.[27] The variety of points of view and approaches to problems and opportunities that diverse employees provide can improve managerial decision making. Suppose the Budget Gourmet frozen food company is trying to come up with creative ideas for new frozen meals that will appeal to health-conscious, time-conscious customers tired of the same old frozen fare. Most people would agree that a diverse group is likely to have a wider range of creative ideas that are applicable in a diversity of settings. Although this example is simplistic, it underscores one way in which diversity can lead to a competitive advantage.

Just as the workforce is becoming increasingly diverse, so too are the customers who buy an organization's goods or services. In an attempt to suit local customers' needs and tastes, organizations often vary the selection of products available in stores in different cities and regions.[28]

Diverse members of an organization are likely to be attuned to what goods and services diverse segments of the market want and do not want. Automakers, for example, are increasingly assigning women to their design teams to ensure that the needs and desires of female customers are taken into account in new car design.

Another way that effective management of diversity can improve profitability is by increasing retention of valued employees, which decreases the costs of hiring replacements for those who quit as well as ensures that all employees are highly motivated. In terms of retention, given the current legal environment, more and more organizations are attuned to the need to emphasize the importance of diversity in hiring. Once hired, if diverse employees think they are being unfairly treated, however, they will be likely to seek opportunities elsewhere. Thus recruiting diverse employees has to be followed up by ongoing effective management of diversity to retain valued organizational members.

If diversity is not effectively managed and turnover rates are higher for members of groups who are not treated fairly, profitability will suffer on several counts. Not only are the future contributions of diverse employees lost when they quit, but the organization also has to bear the costs of hiring replacement workers. Moreover, additional costs from failing to effectively manage diversity stem from time lost due to the barriers diverse members of an organization perceive as thwarting their progress and advancement.[29] Effectively managing diversity makes good business sense for another reason. More and more, managers and organizations concerned about diversity are insisting that their suppliers also support diversity.[30]

LO5-4 Discuss how perception and the use of schemas can result in unfair treatment.

Effectively managing diversity is a necessity on both ethical and business grounds. This brings us to the question of why diversity presents managers and all of us with so many challenges–a question we address in the next section on perception.

Perception

Most people tend to think that the decisions managers make in organizations and the actions they take are the result of objective determination of the issues involved and the surrounding situation. However, each manager's interpretation of a situation or even of another person is precisely that–an interpretation. Nowhere are the effects of perception more likely to lead to different interpretations than in the area of diversity. This is because each person's interpretation of a situation, and subsequent response to it, is affected by his or her own age, race, gender, religion, socioeconomic status, capabilities, and sexual orientation. For example, different managers may see the same 21-year-old, black, male, gay, gifted, and talented subordinate in different ways: One may see a creative maverick with a great future in the organization, while another may see a potential troublemaker who needs to be watched closely.

perception The process through which people select, organize, and interpret what they see, hear, touch, smell, and taste to give meaning and order to the world around them.

Perception is the process through which people select, organize, and interpret sensory input–what they see, hear, touch, smell, and taste–to give meaning and order to the world around them.[31] All decisions and actions of managers are based on their subjective perceptions. When these perceptions are relatively accurate–close to the true nature of what is actually being perceived–good decisions are likely to be made and appropriate actions taken. Managers of fast-food restaurant chains such as McDonald's and Pizza Hut accurately perceived that their customers were becoming more health-conscious in the 1980s and 1990s and added salad bars and low-fat entrées to their menus. Managers at Kentucky Fried Chicken and Burger King took much longer to perceive this change in what customers wanted.

One reason why McDonald's is so successful is that its managers go to great lengths to make sure their perceptions of what customers want are accurate. McDonald's has over 14,880 restaurants outside the United States that generate over $14.1 billion in annual revenues.[32] Key to McDonald's success in these diverse markets are managers' efforts to perceive accurately a country's culture and taste in food and then to act on these perceptions. For instance, McDonald's serves veggie burgers in Holland and black currant shakes in Poland.[33]

When managers' perceptions are relatively inaccurate, managers are likely to make bad decisions and take inappropriate actions, which hurt organizational effectiveness. Bad decisions concerning diversity for reasons of age, ethnicity, or sexual orientation include (1) not hiring qualified people, (2) failing to promote top-performing subordinates, who subsequently may take their skills to competing organizations, and (3) promoting poorly performing managers because they have the same "diversity profile" as the manager or managers making the decision.

Factors That Influence Managerial Perception

Several managers' perceptions of the same person, event, or situation are likely to differ because managers differ in personality, values, attitudes, and moods (see Chapter 3). Each of these factors can influence how someone perceives a person or situation. An older middle manager who is high on openness to experience is likely to perceive the recruitment of able young managers as a positive learning opportunity; a similar middle manager who is low on openness to experience may perceive able younger subordinates as a threat. A manager who has high levels of job satisfaction and organizational commitment may perceive a job transfer to another department or geographic location that has very different employees (age, ethnicity, and so on) as an opportunity to learn and develop new skills. A dissatisfied, uncommitted manager may perceive the same transfer as a demotion.

Managers' and all organizational members' perceptions of one another also are affected by their past experiences with and acquired knowledge about people, events, and situations–information that is organized into preexisting schemas. **Schemas** are abstract knowledge structures stored in memory that allow people to organize and interpret information about a person, an event, or a situation.[34] Once a person develops a schema for a kind of person or event, any newly encountered person or situation that is related to the schema activates it, and information is processed in ways consistent with the information stored in the schema. Thus people tend to perceive others by using the expectations or preconceived notions contained

schema An abstract knowledge structure that is stored in memory and makes possible the interpretation and organization of information about a person, event, or situation.

in their schemas.[35] Once again, these expectations are derived from past experience and knowledge.

People tend to pay attention to information that is consistent with their schemas and to ignore or discount inconsistent information. Thus schemas tend to be reinforced and strengthened over time because the information attended to is seen as confirming the schemas. This also results in schemas being resistant to change.[36] This does not mean schemas never change; if that were the case, people could never adapt to changing conditions and learn from their mistakes. Rather, it suggests that schemas are slow to change and that a considerable amount of contradictory information needs to be encountered for people to change their schemas.

Schemas that accurately depict the true nature of a person or situation are functional because they help people make sense of the world around them. People typically confront so much information that it is not possible to make sense of it without relying on schemas. Schemas are dysfunctional when they are inaccurate because they cause managers and all members of an organization to perceive people and situations inaccurately and assume certain things that are not necessarily true.

gender schemas Preconceived beliefs or ideas about the nature of men and women and their traits, attitudes, behaviors, and preferences.

Psychologist Virginia Valian refers to inaccurate preconceived notions of men and women as gender schemas. **Gender schemas** are a person's preconceived notions about the nature of men and women and their traits, attitudes, behaviors, and preferences.[37] Research suggests that among white, middle-class Americans, the following gender schemas are prevalent: Men are action-oriented, assertive, independent, and task-focused; women are expressive, nurturing, and oriented toward caring of other people.[38] Any schemas such as these–which assume a single visible characteristic such as gender causes a person to possess specific traits and tendencies–are bound to be inaccurate. For example, not all women are alike and not all men are alike, and many women are more independent and task-focused than men. Gender schemas can be learned in childhood and are reinforced in a number of ways in society. For instance, while young girls may be encouraged by their parents to play with toy trucks and tools (stereotypically masculine toys), boys generally are not encouraged, and sometimes are actively discouraged, from playing with dolls (stereotypically feminine toys).[39] As children grow up, they learn that occupations dominated by men have higher status than occupations dominated by women.

Perception as a Determinant of Unfair Treatment

Even though most people would agree that distributive justice and procedural justice are desirable goals, diverse organizational members are sometimes treated unfairly, as previous examples illustrate. Why is this problem occurring? One important overarching reason is inaccurate perceptions. To the extent that managers and other members of an organization rely on inaccurate schemas such as gender schemas to guide their perceptions of each other, unfair treatment is likely to occur.

stereotype Simplistic and often inaccurate beliefs about the typical characteristics of particular groups of people.

Gender schemas are a kind of **stereotype,** which is composed of simplistic and often inaccurate beliefs about the typical characteristics of particular groups of people. Stereotypes are usually based on a visible characteristic such as a person's age, gender, or race.[40] Managers who allow stereotypes to influence their perceptions assume erroneously that a person possesses a whole host of characteristics simply because the person happens to be an Asian woman, a white man, or a lesbian, for example. African men are often stereotyped as good athletes, Hispanic women as subservient, or Shanghai women as strong-willed.[41] Obviously there is no reason to assume that every African man is a good athlete or that every Hispanic woman is subservient. Stereotypes, however, lead people to make such erroneous assumptions. A manager who accepts stereotypes might, for example, decide not to promote a highly capable Hispanic woman into a management position because the manager is certain that she will not be assertive enough to supervise others.

A recent study suggests that stereotypes might hamper the progress of mothers in their organizations when they are seeking to advance in positions that are traditionally held by men. According to the study, based on gender stereotypes, people tend to view mothers as less competent in terms of skills and capabilities related to advancing in such positions.[42]

People with disabilities might also be unfairly treated due to stereotypes.[43] Although the ADA requires (as mentioned previously) that organizations provide disabled employees with accommodations, employment rates of people with disabilities have declined in recent years. As profiled in the following "Ethics in Action" box, a number of organizations have not only provided employment opportunities for disabled adults but also have benefited from their valuable contributions.[44]

Ethics in Action

Disabled Employees Make Valuable Contributions

Some large organizations in the United States like Home Depot and Walgreens actively recruit disabled employees to work in positions such as cashiers, maintenance workers, greeters, shelf stockers, and floor workers that help customers find items. Home Depot, for example, works with a nonprofit agency called Ken's Kids, founded by parents of disabled adults, to recruit and place disabled employees in its stores. Thus far, working with Ken's Kids has enabled Home Depot to recruit and place around 100 disabled adults in over 50 of its stores.[45]

Often, when given the opportunity, disabled employees make valuable contributions to their organizations. Walgreens recently opened an automated distribution center in Anderson, South Carolina, in which more than 40% of its 264 employees are disabled.[46] For disabled employees like 18-year-old Harrison Mullinax, who has autism and checks in merchandise to be distributed to drugstores with a bar code scanner, having a regular job is a godsend. Randy Lewis, senior vice president of distribution and logistics at Walgreens, thought about hiring workers with disabilities when Walgreens was considering using technology to increase automation levels in a distribution center. Lewis, the father of a young adult son who has autism, was aware of how difficult it can be for young adults like his son to find employment. Various accommodations were made, like redesigning workstations and computer displays to suit employees' needs, and employees received appropriate training in how to do their jobs. Some days, disabled employees are actually the most productive in the center. As Lewis puts it, "One thing we found is they can all do the job. . . . What surprised us is the environment that it's created. It's a building where everybody helps each other out."[47]

Walgreens is a large organization, but small organizations also have benefited from the valuable contributions of disabled employees. Habitat International, founded by current CEO David Morris and his father Saul over 20 years ago, is a manufacturer and contractor of indoor–outdoor carpet and artificial grass and a supplier to home improvement companies like Lowe's and Home Depot.[48] Habitat's profits have steadily increased over the years, and the factory's defect rate is less than 0.5%.[49]

Morris attributes Habitat's success to its employees, 75% of whom have either a physical or a mental disability or both.[50] Habitat has consistently provided employment opportunities to people with disabilities such as Down syndrome, schizophrenia, or cerebral palsy.[51] The company has also hired the homeless,

The first clue that Habitat isn't your run-of-the mill factory may be the gigantic animal sculptures at the plant entrance in Chattanooga, Tennessee. The Habitat team produces the sculptures, which can also be seen at restaurants, parks, garden centers, medical centers, museums, and other sites.

recovering alcoholics, and non-English-speaking refugees from other countries. And these employees were relied on by plant manager Connie Presnell when she needed to fill a rush order by assigning it to a team of her fastest workers.[52] Habitat pays its employees regionally competitive wages and has low absence and turnover rates. Employees who need accommodations to perform their jobs are provided them, and Habitat has a highly motivated, satisfied, and committed workforce.[53]

While Habitat has actually gained some business from clients who applaud its commitment to diversity, Habitat's ethical values and social responsibility have also led the company to forgo a major account when stereotypes reared their ugly heads. A few years ago CEO Morris dropped the account of a distribution company because its representatives had made derogatory comments about his employees. Although it took Habitat two years to regain the lost revenues from this major account, Morris had no regrets.[54] Habitat's commitment to diversity and fair treatment is a win–win situation; the company is thriving, and so are its employees.[55]

bias The systematic tendency to use information about others in ways that result in inaccurate perceptions.

Inaccurate perceptions leading to unfair treatment of diverse members of an organization also can be due to biases. **Biases** are systematic tendencies to use information about others in ways that result in inaccurate perceptions. Because of the way biases operate, people often are unaware that their perceptions of others are inaccurate. There are several types of biases.

The *similar-to-me effect* is the tendency to perceive others who are similar to ourselves more positively than we perceive people who are different.[56] The similar-to-me effect is summed up by the saying, "Birds of a feather flock together." It can lead to unfair treatment of diverse employees simply because they are different from the managers who are perceiving them, evaluating them, and making decisions that affect their future in the organization.

The salience effect focuses extra attention on a person who stands out from the group mold. Part of being a good manager includes being aware of these sorts of tendencies and actively working against them.

Managers (particularly top managers) are likely to be men. Although these managers may endorse the principles of distributive and procedural justice, they may unintentionally fall into the trap of perceiving other men more positively than they perceive women and minorities. This is the similar-to-me effect. Being aware of this bias as well as using objective information about employees' capabilities and performance as much as possible in decision making about job assignments, pay raises, promotions, and other outcomes can help managers avoid the similar-to-me effect.

Social status–a person's real or perceived position in a society or an organization–can be the source of another bias. The *social status effect* is the tendency to perceive individuals with high social status more positively than we perceive those with low social status. A high-status person may be perceived as smarter and more believable, capable, knowledgeable, and responsible than a low-status person, even in the absence of objective information about either person.

Imagine being introduced to two people at a company party. Both are men in their late 30s, and you learn that one is a member of the company's top management team and the other is a supervisor in the mailroom. From this information alone, you might assume that the top manager is smarter, more capable, more responsible, and even more interesting than the mailroom supervisor. Because women and minorities have traditionally had lower social status than men, the social status effect may lead some people to perceive women and minorities less positively than they perceive men.

Have you ever stood out in a crowd? Maybe you were the only man in a group of women; or maybe you were dressed formally for a social gathering, and everyone else was in jeans. Salience (that is, conspicuousness) is another source of bias. The *salience effect* is the tendency to focus attention on individuals who are conspicuously different from us. When people are salient, they often feel as though all eyes are watching them, and this perception is not far from the mark. Salient individuals are more often the object of attention than are other members of a work group, for example. A manager who has six white subordinates and one Hispanic subordinate reporting to her may inadvertently pay more attention to the Hispanic in group meetings because of the salience effect.

Individuals who are salient are often perceived to be primarily responsible for outcomes and operations and are evaluated more extremely in either a positive or a negative direction.[57] Thus when the Hispanic subordinate does a good job on a project, she receives excessive praise, and when she misses a deadline, she is excessively chastised.

Overt Discrimination

overt discrimination Knowingly and willingly denying diverse individuals access to opportunities and outcomes in an organization.

Inaccurate schemas and perceptual biases can lead well-meaning managers and organizational members to unintentionally discriminate against others. On the other hand, **overt discrimination,** or knowingly and willingly denying diverse individuals access to opportunities and outcomes in an organization, is intentional and deliberate. Overt discrimination is both unethical and illegal. Unfortunately, just as some managers steal from their organizations, others engage in overt discrimination.

Despite all the advances that have been made, allegations of overt discrimination based on gender, race, age, and other forms of diversity continue to occur in the United States. For example in the United States, Nike recently settled a class action lawsuit filed on behalf of 400 African-American employees of its Chicago Niketown store.[58] Employees claimed that managers used racial slurs when referring to African-American employees and customers, gave African-American employees lower-paying jobs, made unwarranted accusations of theft, and had security personnel monitor employees and customers based on race.[59] Although Nike denied the allegations, as part of the settlement, Nike agreed to pay current and former employees $7.6 million and also agreed to promote effective management of diversity, partly by providing diversity training to all managers and supervisors in the store.[60]

Overt discrimination continues to be a problem around the world. For example, although Japan passed its first Equal Employment Opportunity Law in 1985 and Japanese women are increasingly working in jobs once dominated by men, professional Japanese women have continued to find it difficult to advance in their careers and assume managerial positions.[61] Women make up almost half of the Japanese workforce, but only around 10% of managerial positions in business and government are occupied by women, according to the International Labor Organization agency of the United Nations.[62]

According to the United Nations Development Program's gender empowerment measure, which assesses the participation of women in a country's politics and economy, Japan is the most unequal of the world's wealthy nations when it comes to women.[63] Takako Ariishi has witnessed women's struggle in Japan firsthand. As an employee of a family-owned manufacturing business that supplies parts to Nissan,[64] Ariishi was fired by her own father (who was then president of the company) when she had a son (her father claimed that her son would be his successor as president).

Nonetheless, when Ariishi's father died, she took over as company president. Her company is one of 160 Nissan suppliers in Japan, and the heads of these companies meet twice a year; Arrishi is the only woman among the 160 presidents, and the first time the group met, she was asked to wait in a separate room with the secretaries. Miiko Tsuda, an employee of a tutoring company, indicates that she is paid less than her male coworkers, and she is often asked to push elevator buttons and make tea for male coworkers. Only 5 of the company's 300 management employees are women.[65]

How to Manage Diversity Effectively

Various kinds of barriers arise to managing diversity effectively in organizations. Some barriers originate in the person doing the perceiving; others are based on the information and schemas that have built up over time concerning the person being perceived. To overcome these barriers and effectively manage diversity, managers (and other organizational members) must possess or develop certain attitudes and values and the skills needed to change other people's attitudes and values.

LO5-5 List the steps managers can take to effectively manage diversity.

Steps in Managing Diversity Effectively

Managers can take a number of steps to change attitudes and values and promote the effective management of diversity. Here we describe these steps, some of which we have referred to previously (see Table 5.4).

SECURE TOP MANAGEMENT COMMITMENT As we mentioned earlier in the chapter, top management's commitment to diversity is crucial for the success of any diversity-related initiatives. Top managers need to develop the correct ethical values and performance- or business-oriented attitudes that allow them to make appropriate use of their human resources.

STRIVE TO INCREASE THE ACCURACY OF PERCEPTIONS One aspect of developing the appropriate values and attitudes is to take steps to increase the accuracy of perceptions. Managers should consciously attempt to be open to other points of view and perspectives, seek them out, and encourage their subordinates to do the same.[66] Organizational members who are open to other perspectives put their own beliefs and knowledge to an important reality test and will be more inclined to modify or change them when necessary. Managers should not be afraid to change their views

Table 5.4
Promoting the Effective Management of Diversity

- Secure top management commitment.
- Increase the accuracy of perceptions.
- Increase diversity awareness.
- Increase diversity skills.
- Encourage flexibility.
- Pay close attention to how employees are evaluated.
- Consider the numbers.
- Empower employees to challenge discriminatory behaviors, actions, and remarks.
- Reward employees for effectively managing diversity.
- Provide training utilizing a multipronged, ongoing approach.
- Encourage mentoring of diverse employees.

about a person, issue, or event; moreover, they should encourage their subordinates to be open to changing their views in the light of disconfirming evidence. Additionally, managers and all members of an organization should strive to avoid making snap judgments about people; rather, judgments should be made only when sufficient and relevant information has been gathered.[67]

INCREASE DIVERSITY AWARENESS It is natural for managers and other members of an organization to view other people from their own perspective because their own feelings, thoughts, attitudes, and experiences guide their perceptions and interactions. The ability to appreciate diversity, however, requires that people become aware of other perspectives and the various attitudes and experiences of others. Many diversity awareness programs in organizations strive to increase managers' and workers' awareness of (1) their own attitudes, biases, and stereotypes and (2) the differing perspectives of diverse managers, subordinates, coworkers, and customers. Diversity awareness programs often have these goals:[68]

- Providing organizational members with accurate information about diversity.
- Uncovering personal biases and stereotypes.
- Assessing personal beliefs, attitudes, and values and learning about other points of view.
- Overturning inaccurate stereotypes and beliefs about different groups.
- Developing an atmosphere in which people feel free to share their differing perspectives and points of view.
- Improving understanding of others who are different from oneself.

Sometimes simply taking the time to interact with someone who is different in some way can increase awareness. When employees and managers are at social functions or just having lunch with a coworker, often the people they interact with are those they feel most comfortable with. If all members of an organization make an effort to interact with people they ordinarily would not, mutual understanding is likely to be enhanced.[69]

In large organizations, top managers are often far removed from entry-level employees–they may lack a real understanding and appreciation for what these employees do day in and day out, the challenges and obstacles they face, and the steps that can be taken to improve effectiveness. Recognizing this fact, some managers have taken concrete steps to improve their understanding of the experiences, attitudes, and perspectives of frontline employees.

INCREASE DIVERSITY SKILLS Efforts to increase diversity skills focus on improving how managers and their subordinates interact with each other and improving their ability to work with different kinds of people.[70] An important issue here is being able to communicate with diverse employees. Diverse organizational members may have different communication styles, may differ in their language fluency, may use words differently, may differ in the nonverbal signals they send through facial expressions and body language, and may differ in how they perceive and interpret information. Managers and their subordinates must learn to communicate effectively with one another if an organization is to take advantage of the skills and abilities of its diverse workforce. Educating organizational members about differences in ways of communicating is often a good starting point.

Diversity education can help managers and subordinates gain a better understanding of how people may interpret certain kinds of comments. Diversity education also can help employees learn how to resolve misunderstandings. Organizational members should feel comfortable enough to "clear the air" and solve communication difficulties and misunderstandings as they occur rather than letting problems grow and fester without acknowledgment.

ENCOURAGE FLEXIBILITY Managers and their subordinates must learn how to be open to different approaches and ways of doing things. This does not mean organizational members have to suppress their personal styles. Rather, it means they must be open to, and not feel threatened by, different approaches and perspectives and must have the patience and flexibility needed to understand and appreciate diverse perspectives.[71]

To the extent feasible, managers should also be flexible enough to incorporate the differing needs of diverse employees. Earlier we mentioned that religious diversity suggests that people of certain religions might need time off for holidays that are traditionally workdays. Managers need to anticipate and respond to such needs with flexibility (perhaps letting people skip the lunch hour so they can leave work early). Moreover, flexible work hours, the option to work from home, and cafeteria-style benefit plans (see Chapter 12) are just a few of the many ways in which managers can respond to the differing needs of diverse employees while enabling those employees to be effective contributors to an organization.

PAY CLOSE ATTENTION TO HOW ORGANIZATIONAL MEMBERS ARE EVALUATED Whenever feasible, it is desirable to rely on objective performance indicators (see Chapter 12) because they are less subject to bias. When objective indicators are not available or are inappropriate, managers should ensure that adequate time and attention are focused on the evaluation of employees' performance and that evaluators are held accountable for their evaluations.[72] Vague performance standards should be avoided.[73]

CONSIDER THE NUMBERS Looking at the numbers of members of different minority groups and women in various positions, at various levels in the hierarchy, in locations that differ in their desirability, and in any other relevant categorizations in an organization can tell managers important information about potential problems and ways to rectify them.[74] If members of certain groups are underrepresented in particular kinds of jobs or units, managers need to understand why this is the case and resolve any problems they might uncover.

EMPOWER EMPLOYEES TO CHALLENGE DISCRIMINATORY BEHAVIORS, ACTIONS, AND REMARKS When managers or employees witness another organizational member being unfairly treated, they should be encouraged to speak up and rectify the situation. Top managers can make this happen by creating an organizational culture (see Chapter 3) that has zero tolerance for discrimination. As part of such a culture, organizational members should feel empowered to challenge discriminatory behavior, whether the behavior is directed at them or they witness it being directed at another employee.[75]

REWARD EMPLOYEES FOR EFFECTIVELY MANAGING DIVERSITY If effective management of diversity is a valued organizational objective, then employees should be rewarded for their contributions to this objective.[76] For example, after settling a major race discrimination lawsuit, Coca-Cola Company now ties managers' pay to their achievement of diversity goals.

PROVIDE TRAINING UTILIZING A MULTIPRONGED, ONGOING APPROACH Many managers use a multipronged approach to increase diversity awareness and skills in their organizations; they use films and printed materials supplemented by experiential exercises to uncover hidden biases and stereotypes. Sometimes simply providing a forum for people to learn about and discuss their differing attitudes, values, and experiences can be a powerful means of increasing awareness. Also useful are role-plays that enact problems resulting from lack of awareness and show the increased understanding that comes from appreciating others' viewpoints. Accurate information and training experiences can debunk stereotypes. Group exercises, role-plays, and diversity-related experiences can help organizational members develop the skills they need to work effectively with a variety of people. Many organizations hire outside consultants to provide diversity training, in addition to utilizing their own in-house diversity experts.[77]

Ah, the power of a listening ear. The mentoring process allows a newer employee the chance to gain an edge through informal conversation.

ENCOURAGE MENTORING OF DIVERSE EMPLOYEES

Unfortunately minorities continue to be less likely to attain high-level positions in their organizations; and for those who do attain them, the climb up the corporate ladder typically takes longer. David Thomas, a professor at the Harvard Business School, has studied the careers of minorities in corporate America. One of his major conclusions is that mentoring is very important for minorities, most of whom have reached high levels in their organizations by having a solid network of mentors and contacts.[78] **Mentoring** is a process by which an experienced member of an organization (the mentor) provides advice and guidance to a less experienced member (the protégé) and helps the less experienced member learn how to advance in the organization and in his or her career.

mentoring A process by which an experienced member of an organization (the mentor) provides advice and guidance to a less experienced member (the protégé) and helps the less experienced member learn how to advance in the organization and in his or her career.

According to Thomas, effective mentoring is more than providing instruction, offering advice, helping build skills, and sharing technical expertise. Of course these aspects of mentoring are important and necessary. However, equally important is developing a high-quality, close, and supportive relationship with the protégé. Emotional bonds between a mentor and a protégé can enable a protégé, for example, to express fears and concerns, and sometimes even reluctance to follow a mentor's advice. The mentor can help the protégé build his or her confidence and feel comfortable engaging in unfamiliar work behaviors.[79]

Pat Carmichael, a senior vice president at JPMorgan Chase, has mentored hundreds of protégés throughout her career and exemplifies effective mentoring.[80] She encourages her protégés to seek difficult assignments and feedback from their supervisors. She also helps her protégés build networks of contacts and has an extensive network herself. She serves as both a coach and a counselor to her protégés and encourages them to seek opportunities to address their weaknesses and broaden their horizons.[81]

Sexual Harassment

LO5-6 Identify the two major forms of sexual harassment and how they can be eliminated.

Sexual harassment seriously damages both the people who are harassed and the reputation of the organization in which it occurs. Sexual harassment victims can be women or men, and their harassers do not necessarily have to be of the opposite sex.[82] However, women are the most frequent victims of sexual harassment, particularly those in male-dominated occupations or those who occupy positions stereotypically associated with certain gender relationships, such as a female secretary reporting to a male boss. In 2010 Mark McInnes, CEO of Australia's largest retailer David Jones, resigned over sexual harassment charges. Though it occurs less frequently, men can also be victims of sexual harassment.

Forms of Sexual Harassment

There are two basic forms of sexual harassment: quid pro quo sexual harassment and hostile work environment sexual harassment. **Quid pro quo sexual harassment** occurs when a harasser asks or forces an employee to perform sexual favors to keep a job, receive a promotion, receive a raise, obtain some other work-related opportunity, or avoid receiving negative consequences such as demotion or dismissal.[83] This "Sleep with me, honey, or you're fired" form of harassment is the more extreme type and leaves no doubt in anyone's mind that sexual harassment has taken place.[84]

quid pro quo sexual harassment Asking for or forcing an employee to perform sexual favors in exchange for receiving some reward or avoiding negative consequences.

Hostile work environment sexual harassment is more subtle. It occurs when organizational members face an intimidating, hostile, or offensive work environment because of their sex.[85] Lewd jokes, sexually oriented comments or innuendos,

hostile work environment sexual harassment Telling lewd jokes, displaying pornography, making sexually oriented remarks about someone's personal appearance, and other sex-related actions that make the work environment unpleasant.

vulgar language, displays of pornography, displays or distribution of sexually oriented objects, and sexually oriented remarks about one's physical appearance are examples of hostile work environment sexual harassment.[86] A hostile work environment interferes with organizational members' ability to perform their jobs effectively and has been deemed illegal by the courts.

Steps Managers Can Take to Eradicate Sexual Harassment

Managers have an ethical obligation to eradicate sexual harassment in their organizations. There are many ways to accomplish this objective. Here are four initial steps managers can take to deal with the problem:[87]

- *Develop and clearly communicate a sexual harassment policy endorsed by top management.* This policy should include prohibitions against both quid pro quo and hostile work environment sexual harassment. It should contain (1) examples of types of behavior that are unacceptable, (2) a procedure for employees to use to report instances of harassment, (3) a discussion of the disciplinary actions that will be taken when harassment has taken place, and (4) a commitment to educate and train organizational members about sexual harassment.
- *Use a fair complaint procedure to investigate charges of sexual harassment.* Such a procedure should (1) be managed by a neutral third party, (2) ensure that complaints are dealt with promptly and thoroughly, (3) protect and fairly treat victims, and (4) ensure that alleged harassers are fairly treated.
- *When it has been determined that sexual harassment has taken place, take corrective actions as soon as possible.* These actions can vary depending on the severity of the harassment. When harassment is extensive, prolonged, of a quid pro quo nature, or severely objectionable in some other manner, corrective action may include firing the harasser.
- *Provide sexual harassment education and training to all organizational members, including managers.* The majority of *Fortune* 500 firms currently provide this education and training for their employees. For example, managers at DuPont developed DuPont's "A Matter of Respect" program to help educate employees about sexual harassment and eliminate its occurrence. The program includes a four-hour workshop in which participants are given information that defines sexual harassment, sets forth the company's policy against it, and explains how to report complaints and access a 24-hour hotline. Participants watch video clips showing actual instances of harassment. One clip shows a saleswoman having dinner with a male client who, after much negotiating, seems about to give her company his business when he suddenly suggests that they continue their conversation in his hotel room. The saleswoman is confused about what to do. Will she be reprimanded if she says no and the deal is lost? After watching a video, participants discuss what they have seen, why the behavior is inappropriate, and what organizations can do to alleviate the problem.[88] Throughout the program, managers stress to employees that they do not have to tolerate sexual harassment or get involved in situations in which harassment is likely to occur.

Barry S. Roberts and Richard A. Mann, experts on business law and authors of several books on the topic, suggest a number of additional factors that managers and all members of an organization need to keep in mind about sexual harassment:[89]

- Every sexual harassment charge should be taken seriously.
- Employees who go along with unwanted sexual attention in the workplace can be sexual harassment victims.
- Employees sometimes wait before they file complaints of sexual harassment.
- An organization's sexual harassment policy should be communicated to each new employee and reviewed with current employees periodically.

- Suppliers and customers need to be familiar with an organization's sexual harassment policy.
- Managers should give employees alternative ways to report incidents of sexual harassment.
- Employees who report sexual harassment must have their rights protected; this includes being protected from any potential retaliation.
- Allegations of sexual harassment should be kept confidential; those accused of harassment should have their rights protected.
- Investigations of harassment charges and any resultant disciplinary actions need to proceed in a timely manner.
- Managers must protect employees from sexual harassment from third parties they may interact with while performing their jobs, such as suppliers or customers.[90]

Summary and Review

LO5-1 **THE INCREASING DIVERSITY OF THE WORKFORCE AND THE ENVIRONMENT** Diversity is dissimilarity or differences among people. Diversity is a pressing concern for managers and organizations for business and ethical reasons. There are multiple forms of diversity such as age, gender, race and ethnicity, religion, capabilities/disabilities, socioeconomic background, sexual orientation, and physical appearance.

LO5-2, 5-3 **MANAGERS AND THE EFFECTIVE MANAGEMENT OF DIVERSITY** Both the workforce and the organizational environment are increasingly diverse, and effectively managing this diversity is an essential component of management. In each of their managerial roles, managers can encourage the effective management of diversity, which is both an ethical and a business imperative.

LO5-4 **PERCEPTION** Perception is the process through which people select, organize, and interpret sensory input to give meaning and order to the world around them. It is inherently subjective. Schemas guide perception; when schemas are based on a single visible characteristic such as race or gender, they are stereotypes and highly inaccurate, leading to unfair treatment. Unfair treatment also can result from biases and overt discrimination.

LO5-5 **HOW TO MANAGE DIVERSITY EFFECTIVELY** Managers can take many steps to effectively manage diversity. Effective management of diversity is an ongoing process that requires frequent monitoring.

LO5-6 **SEXUAL HARASSMENT** Two forms of sexual harassment are quid pro quo sexual harassment and hostile work environment sexual harassment. Steps that managers can take to eradicate sexual harassment include development and communication of a sexual harassment policy endorsed by top management, use of fair complaint procedures, prompt corrective action when harassment occurs, and sexual harassment training and education.

Management in Action

Topics for Discussion and Action

Discussion

1. Discuss why violations of the principles of distributive and procedural justice continue to occur in modern organizations. What can managers do to uphold these principles in their organizations? **[LO5-2, 5-3, 5-4, 5-5]**
2. Why do workers who test positive for HIV sometimes get discriminated against? **[LO5-1, 5-4]**
3. Why would some employees resent accommodations made for employees with disabilities? **[LO5-1, 5-4]**
4. Discuss the ways in which schemas can be functional and dysfunctional. **[LO5-4]**
5. Discuss an occasion when you may have been treated unfairly because of stereotypical thinking. What stereotypes were applied to you? How did they result in your being treated unfairly? **[LO5-4]**
6. Why is it important to consider the numbers of different groups of employees at various levels in an organization's hierarchy? **[LO5-5]**
7. Think about a situation in which you would have benefited from mentoring but a mentor was not available. What could you have done to try to get the help of a mentor in this situation? **[LO5-5]**

Action

8. Choose a *Fortune* 500 company not mentioned in the chapter. Conduct research to determine what steps this organization has taken to effectively manage diversity and eliminate sexual harassment. **[LO5-2, 5-5, 5-6]**

Building Management Skills **[LO5-1, 5-2, 5-3, 5-4, 5-5, 5-6]**

Solving Diversity-Related Problems

Think about the last time that you (1) were treated unfairly because you differed from a decision maker on a particular dimension of diversity or (2) observed someone else being treated unfairly because that person differed from a decision maker on a particular dimension of diversity. Then answer these questions:

1. Why do you think the decision maker acted unfairly in this situation?
2. In what ways, if any, were biases, stereotypes, or overt discrimination involved in this situation?
3. Was the decision maker aware that he or she was acting unfairly?
4. What could you or the person who was treated unfairly have done to improve matters and rectify the injustice on the spot?
5. Was any sexual harassment involved in this situation? If so, what kind was it?
6. If you had authority over the decision maker (that is, if you were his or her manager or supervisor), what steps would you take to ensure that the decision maker no longer treated diverse individuals unfairly?

Managing Ethically **[LO5-1, 5-2, 5-3, 5-5]**

Some companies require that their employees work long hours and travel extensively. Employees with young children, employees taking care of elderly relatives, and employees who have interests outside the workplace sometimes find that their careers are jeopardized if they try to work more reasonable hours or limit their work-related travel. Some of these employees feel that it is unethical for their managers to expect so much of them in the workplace and not understand their needs as parents and caregivers.

Questions

1. Either individually or in a group, think about the ethical implications of requiring long hours and extensive amounts of travel for some jobs.
2. What obligations do you think managers and companies have to enable employees to have balanced lives and meet nonwork needs and demands?

Small Group Breakout Exercise [LO5-1, 5-2, 5-3, 5-4, 5-5]

Determining If a Problem Exists

Form groups of three or four people, and appoint one member as the spokesperson who will communicate your findings to the whole class when called on by the instructor. Then discuss the following scenario:

You and your partners own and manage a local chain of restaurants, with moderate to expensive prices, that are open for lunch and dinner during the week and for dinner on weekends. Your staff is diverse, and you believe that you are effectively managing diversity. Yet on visits to the different restaurants you have noticed that your African employees tend to congregate together and communicate mainly with each other. The same is true for your Hispanic employees and your white employees. You are meeting with your partners today to discuss this observation.

1. Discuss why the patterns of communication that you observed might be occurring in your restaurants.
2. Discuss whether your observation reflects an underlying problem. If so, why? If not, why not?
3. Discuss whether you should address this issue with your staff and in your restaurants. If so, how and why? If not, why not?

Exploring the World Wide Web [LO5-1, 5-2, 5-3, 5-5, 5-6]

Go to the European Union's Web sites that deal with employment issues, diversity, and sexual harassment. After reviewing these Web sites, develop a list of tips to help managers effectively manage diversity and avoid costly lawsuits.

Be the Manager [LO5-1, 5-2, 5-3, 5-4, 5-5]

You are Maria Herrera and have been recently promoted to the position of director of financial analysis for a medium-sized consumer goods firm. During your first few weeks on the job, you took the time to have lunch with each of your subordinates to try to get to know them better. You have 12 direct reports who are junior and senior financial analysts who support different product lines. Susan Epstein, one of the female financial analysts you had lunch with, made the following statement: "I'm so glad we finally have a woman in charge. Now, hopefully things will get better around here." You pressed Epstein to elaborate, but she clammed up. She indicated that she didn't want to unnecessarily bias you and that the problems were pretty self-evident. In fact, Epstein was surprised that you didn't know what she was talking about and jokingly mentioned that perhaps you should spend some time undercover, observing her group and their interactions with others.

You spoke with your supervisor and the former director, who had been promoted and had volunteered to be on call if you had any questions. Neither man knew of any diversity-related issues in your group. In fact, your supervisor's response was, "We've got a lot of problems, but fortunately that's not one of them."

What are you going to do to address this issue?

CHAPTER 6

Managing in the Global Environment

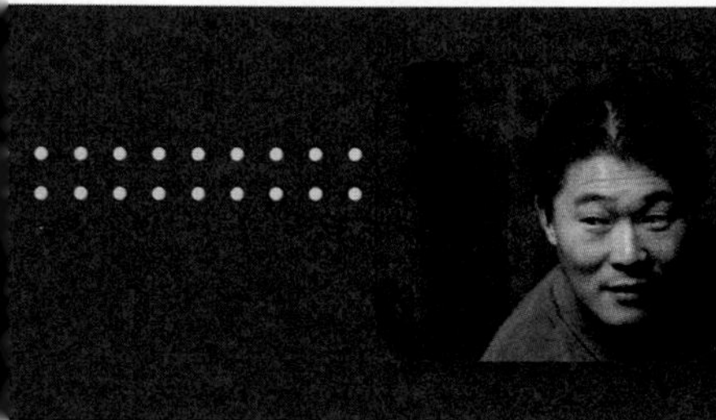

Learning Objectives

After studying this chapter, you should be able to:

LO6-1 Explain why the ability to perceive, interpret, and respond appropriately to the global environment is crucial for managerial success.

LO6-2 Differentiate between the global task and global general environments.

LO6-3 Identify the main forces in the global task and general environments, and describe the challenges that each force presents to managers.

LO6-4 Explain why the global environment is becoming more open and competitive, and identify the forces behind the process of globalization that increase the opportunities, complexities, challenges, and threats managers face.

LO6-5 Discuss why national cultures differ and why it is important that managers be sensitive to the effects of falling trade barriers and regional trade associations on the political and social systems of nations around the world.

A MANAGER'S CHALLENGE

A Turnaround at Sony Is in the Works

By 2005 Sony was in big trouble; and at this crucial point in their company's history, Sony's Japanese top managers turned to a **gaijin*****, or non-Japanese, executive to lead their company.*** Their choice was Sir Howard Stringer, a Welshman, the previous head of Sony's North American operations who had been instrumental in cutting costs and increasing the profits of Sony's U.S. division. Once he became CEO in 2005, Stringer faced the immediate problem of reducing Sony's operating costs, which were double those of its competitors even as it was losing its technological leadership. Stringer had to make many radical strategic decisions.

Japan is a country where large companies traditionally had a policy of lifetime employment, but Stringer made it clear that layoffs were inevitable. Within five years he cut Sony's Japanese workforce by over 25,000 employees and closed 12 factories to reduce costs. Stringer also recognized how the extensive power struggles among the top managers of Sony's different product divisions were hurting the company, and he made it clear that these problems had to stop. Many top divisional managers, including the manager of Sony's successful PlayStation division, ignored Stringer; they were replaced, and he worked steadily to downsize Sony's bloated corporate headquarters staff and to change its culture. In Stringer's own words, the culture or "business of Sony has been management, not making products." In 2009 Stringer announced he would take charge of the Japanese company's struggling core electronics group and would add the title of president to his existing roles as chairman and CEO as he reorganized Sony's divisions. He also replaced four more top executives with

Sir Howard Stringer, flanked by two younger executives, shows off new Sony products. Stringer's embrace of those outside Japan may help turn the flagging multinational around.

young managers who had held positions outside Japan and were "familiar with the digital world." In the future, according to Stringer, managers must prioritize new products and invest in only those with the greatest chance of success so Sony could reduce its out-of-control R&D costs.

Stringer worked hard to bring the realities of global competition to the forefront at Sony—along with the need to deal with them quickly. Beyond his internal problems, he also pushed for major changes in how Sony picked its suppliers. Stringer's goal was to reduce the number of Sony's parts suppliers from 2,500 to 1,200 to cut purchasing costs by over $5 billion or 20%. This would require cooperation between divisions because in the past each division made its own purchasing decisions. In the future Sony will centralize purchasing to negotiate cheaper prices by increasing the amount of business it does with its remaining suppliers.

By 2010 Sony's financial results suggested that Stringer's initiatives were finally paying off; he had stemmed Sony's huge losses, and its products were selling better. For example, PlayStation 3 sales jumped more than 40% after a 25% price cut and continued to outperform Nintendo's Wii. Although Sony still expected to lose money in 2010, Stringer expected Sony to become profitable by 2011. To help ensure this Stringer also took charge of a newly created networked products and services group that included its Vaio computers, Walkman media players, Sony's PlayStation gaming console, and the software and online services to support these products. Stringer's goal was for Sony to regain its global leadership in making the premium, differentiated digital products that command high prices and result in good profit margins. In 2010 Sony announced a major initiative to push into new technologies such as 3D LCD TVs, tablet computers, digital viewers, and action gaming and introduced a new motion controller for its PlayStation.[1] But competitors such as Apple, Samsung, and Panasonic were also competing in these markets, so global rivalry was likely to remain intense.

Overview

Top managers of a global company like Sony operate in an environment where they compete with other companies for scarce and valuable resources. Managers of companies large and small have found that to survive and prosper in the 21st century, most organizations must become **global organizations** that operate and compete not only domestically, at home, but also globally, in countries around the world. Operating in the global environment is uncertain and unpredictable because it is complex and changes constantly.

LO6-1 Explain why the ability to perceive, interpret, and respond appropriately to the global environment is crucial for managerial success.

LO6-2 Differentiate between the global task and global general environments.

If organizations are to adapt successfully to this changing environment, their managers must learn to understand the forces that operate in it and how these forces give rise to opportunities and threats. In this chapter we examine why the environment, both domestically and globally, has become more open, vibrant, and competitive. We examine how forces in the task and general environments affect global organizations and their managers. By the end of this chapter, you will appreciate the changes that are taking place in the environment and understand why it is important

global organization An organization that operates and competes in more than one country.

for managers to develop a global perspective as they strive to increase organizational efficiency and effectiveness.

What Is the Global Environment?

global environment The set of global forces and conditions that operate beyond an organization's boundaries but affect a manager's ability to acquire and utilize resources.

The **global environment** is a set of forces and conditions in the world outside an organization's boundary that affect how it operates and shape its behavior.[2] These forces change over time and thus present managers with *opportunities* and *threats.* Some changes in the global environment, such as the development of efficient new production technology, the availability of lower-cost components, or the opening of new global markets, create opportunities for managers to make and sell more products, obtain more resources and capital, and thereby strengthen their organization. In contrast, the rise of new global competitors, a global economic recession, or an oil shortage poses threats that can devastate an organization if managers are unable to sell its products so that revenues and profits plunge. The quality of managers' understanding of forces in the global environment and their ability to respond appropriately to those forces, such as Sony's managers' ability to make and sell the electronic products customers around the world want to buy, are critical factors affecting organizational performance.

In this chapter we explore the nature of these forces and consider how managers can respond to them. To identify opportunities and threats caused by forces in the environment, it is helpful for managers to distinguish between the *task environment* and the more encompassing *general environment* (see Figure 6.1).

Figure 6.1
Forces in the Global Environment

task environment The set of forces and conditions that originate with suppliers, distributors, customers, and competitors and affect an organization's ability to obtain inputs and dispose of its outputs because they influence managers daily.

The **task environment** is the set of forces and conditions that originate with global suppliers, distributors, customers, and competitors; these forces and conditions affect an organization's ability to obtain inputs and dispose of its outputs. The task environment contains the forces that have the most *immediate* and *direct* effect on managers because they pressure and influence managers daily. When managers turn on the radio or television, arrive at their offices in the morning, open their mail, or look at their computer screens, they are likely to learn about problems facing them because of changing conditions in their organization's task environment.

general environment The wide-ranging global, economic, technological, sociocultural, demographic, political, and legal forces that affect an organization and its task environment.

The **general environment** includes the wide-ranging global, economic, technological, sociocultural, demographic, political, and legal forces that affect the organization and its task environment. For the individual manager, opportunities and threats resulting from changes in the general environment are often more difficult to identify and respond to than are events in the task environment. However, changes in these forces can have major impacts on managers and their organizations.

The Task Environment

Forces in the task environment result from the actions of suppliers, distributors, customers, and competitors both at home and abroad (see Figure 6.1). These four groups affect a manager's ability to obtain resources and dispose of outputs daily, weekly, and monthly and thus have a significant impact on short-term decision making.

LO6-3 Identify the main forces in the global task and general environments, and describe the challenges that each force presents to managers.

Suppliers

suppliers Individuals and organizations that provide an organization with the input resources it needs to produce goods and services.

Suppliers are the individuals and companies that provide an organization with the input resources (such as raw materials, component parts, or employees) it needs to produce goods and services. In return, the suppliers receive payment for those goods and services. An important aspect of a manager's job is to ensure a reliable supply of input resources.

Take Acer, for example, one of the world's largest computer makers from Taiwan. Acer has many suppliers of component parts such as microprocessors (Intel and AMD). It also has suppliers of preinstalled software, including operating system and specific applications software (Microsoft). Acer's providers of capital, such as banks and financial institutions, are also important suppliers.

Acer has several suppliers of labor. One source is the educational institutions that train future Acer employees and therefore provide the company with skilled workers. Another is trade unions, organizations that represent employee interests and can control the supply of labor by exercising the right of unionized workers to strike. Unions also can influence the terms and conditions under which labor is employed. Most of Acer's plants are in China where, even if there are unions, they typically are very weak. However, in other settings unions can be very strong. For example, it is the law in Germany that unions are typically represented on the board of directors of publicly traded firms. In organizations and industries where unions are strong, however, such as the transportation industry, an important part of a manager's job is negotiating and administering agreements with unions and their representatives.

Changes in the nature, number, or type of suppliers produce opportunities and threats to which managers must respond if their organizations are to prosper. For example, a major supplier-related threat that confronts managers arises when suppliers' bargaining position is so strong that they can raise the prices of the inputs they supply to the organization. A supplier's bargaining position is especially strong when (1) the supplier is the sole source of an input and (2) the input is vital to the organization.[3] For example, for 17 years G. D. Searle was the sole supplier of NutraSweet, the artificial sweetener used in most diet soft drinks. Not only was NutraSweet an important ingredient in diet soft drinks, but it also was one for which there was no acceptable substitute (saccharin and other artificial sweeteners raised

The purchasing activities of global companies have become increasingly complicated in recent years. More than 700 suppliers around the world produce parts for Boeing's new Dreamliner.

health concerns). Searle earned its privileged position because it invented and held the patent for NutraSweet, and patents prohibit other organizations from introducing competing products for 17 years. As a result Searle was able to demand a high price for NutraSweet, charging twice the price of an equivalent amount of sugar; and paying that price raised the costs of soft drink manufacturers such as Coca-Cola and PepsiCo. When Searle's patent expired many other companies introduced products similar to NutraSweet, and prices fell.[4] In the 2000s Splenda, which was made by McNeil Nutritionals, owned by Tate & Lyle, a British company, replaced NutraSweet as the artificial sweetener of choice, and NutraSweet's price fell further; Splenda began to command a high price from soft drink companies.[5]

In contrast, when an organization has many suppliers for a particular input, it is in a relatively strong bargaining position with those suppliers and can demand low-cost, high-quality inputs from them. Often an organization can use its power with suppliers to force them to reduce their prices, as Acer frequently does. Acer, for example, is constantly searching for low-cost suppliers to keep its PC prices competitive. At a global level, organizations can buy products from suppliers overseas or become their own suppliers by manufacturing their products abroad.

It is important that managers recognize the opportunities and threats associated with managing the global supply chain. On one hand, gaining access to low-cost products made abroad represents an opportunity for companies from mature economies to lower their input costs. On the other hand, managers who fail to use low-cost overseas suppliers create a threat and put their organizations at a competitive disadvantage.[6] Levi Strauss, for example, was slow to realize that it could not compete with the low-priced jeans sold by Walmart and other retailers, and it was eventually forced to close all its U.S. jean factories and outsource manufacturing to low-cost overseas suppliers to cut the price of its jeans to a competitive level. Now it sells its low-priced jeans in Walmart.

A common problem facing managers of large global companies such as Sony and Acer is managing the development of a global supplier network that will allow their companies to keep costs down and quality high. For example, Boeing's 777 jet was originally built using 132,500 engineered components made by 545 global suppliers.[7] Although Boeing made the majority of these parts, eight Japanese suppliers made parts for the 777 fuselage, doors, and wings; a Singapore supplier made the doors for the plane's forward landing gear; and three Italian suppliers produced its wing flaps. Boeing decided to buy so many inputs from global suppliers because these suppliers were the best in the world at performing their particular activities, and Boeing's goal was to produce a high-quality final product–a vital requirement for aircraft safety and reliability.[8]

The purchasing activities of global companies have become increasingly complicated as a result of the development of a whole range of skills and competencies in different countries around the world. It is clearly in companies' interests to search out the lowest-cost, best-quality suppliers. IT and the Internet are continually making it easier for companies to coordinate complicated, long-distance exchanges involving the purchasing of inputs and the disposal of outputs–something Sony has taken advantage of as it trims the number of its suppliers to reduce costs.

global outsourcing The purchase or production of inputs or final products from overseas suppliers to lower costs and improve product quality or design.

Global outsourcing occurs when a company contracts with suppliers in other countries to make the various inputs or components that go into its products or to assemble the final products to reduce costs. For example, Apple contracts with companies in Taiwan to make inputs such as the chips, batteries, and LCD displays that power its digital devices; then it contracts with Chinese outsourcing companies such as Foxconn to assemble its final products–such as iPods, iPhones, and iPads. Apple outsources the distribution of its products around the world by contracting with companies such as FedEx or DHL. However, one of the costs associated with such supplier networks is that when a supplier does something for which it may be criticized, often the larger and better known firm that is buying the output to sell to consumers receives the negative publicity. For example, Foxconn suffered a number of suicides among employees due to the high work levels expected, but it was Apple that was criticized.

Global outsourcing has grown enormously to take advantage of national differences in the cost and quality of resources such as labor or raw materials that can significantly reduce manufacturing costs or increase product quality or reliability. Today such global exchanges are becoming so complex that some companies specialize in managing other companies' global supply chains. Global companies use the services of overseas intermediaries or brokers, which are located close to potential suppliers, to find the suppliers that can best meet the needs of a particular company. They can design the most efficient supply chain for a company to outsource the component and assembly operations required to produce its final products. Because these suppliers are located in thousands of cities in many countries, finding them is difficult. Li & Fung, based in Hong Kong, is one broker that has helped hundreds of global companies to outsource their component or assembly operations to suitable overseas suppliers, especially suppliers in mainland China.[9]

Although outsourcing to take advantage of low labor costs has helped many companies perform better, in the late 2000s its risks have also become apparent, especially when issues such as reliability, quality, and speed are important. For example, the introduction of Boeing's 787 Dreamliner plane was delayed for over two years because the company, encouraged by the success of its 777 outsourcing program, increased its reliance on companies. To design and make the 787, Boeing turned to its suppliers early in the development process to gain access to foreign ingenuity and cut costs. Boeing uses 50 U.S. suppliers but also 23 suppliers abroad, many of whom had problems in meeting Boeing's delivery requirements.

Design and quality issues arose, such as in 2008 when Boeing announced that an Italian supplier had stopped production of two sections of the fuselage because of structural design problems. The Dreamliner finally took its inaugural flight in 2010.[10] By contrast, in 2010 Hanes Brands (HBI), the underwear maker, announced an agreement to sell its yarn and thread operations to Parkdale, a large-scale yarn manufacturer based in Gastonia, North Carolina. In the future Parkdale will be HBI's yarn supplier in North America; because yarn is a simple product to make, HBI did not need to look outside the United States. Clearly outsourcing decisions need to be carefully considered given the nature of a company's products.[11] On the other hand, some companies do not outsource production; they prefer to establish their own factories in countries around the world, as the example of Nokia in the following "Managing Globally" box suggests.

Managing Globally

Why Nokia Makes Cell Phones in Romania

Nokia is still the world's largest cell phone maker, although it has been fighting hard to maintain its lead as the popularity of smartphones has soared and companies like Apple, BlackBerry, Samsung, and now Google and Microsoft are competing for the lucrative smartphone segment of the market. While these other companies outsource their cell phone production to Asian companies, Nokia does not. Indeed, one reason for Nokia's continuing dominance in cell phones is

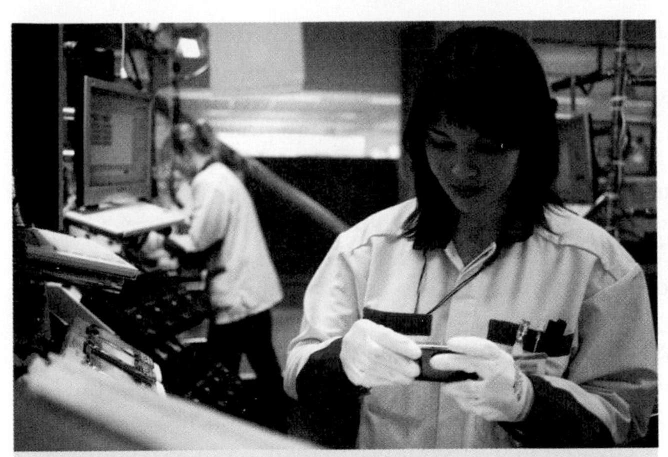

Nokia goes global by establishing operations in Romania. The plant has already performed beyond management's expectations, resulting in pay raises and more jobs for the area.

its skills in global supply chain management, which allow it to provide low-cost phones that are customized to the needs of customers in different world regions. To achieve this, Nokia's global strategy is to make its phones in the world region where they are to be sold; so Nokia has built state-of-the-art factories in Germany, Brazil, China, and India, and in 2008 it opened a new plant in Romania to make phones for the expanding eastern European and Russian market.

A major reason for beginning operations in Romania is low labor costs. Skilled Romanian engineers can be hired for a quarter of what they would earn in Finland or Germany, and production line employees can expect to earn about US$450 a month–a fraction of what Nokia's German employees earn. In fact, once Nokia's Romanian factory was running, Nokia closed its factory in Bochum, Germany, in 2008 because it was too expensive to operate in a highly competitive global environment.

Opening a new factory in a new country is a complex process; and to increase the chances its new factory would operate efficiently, Nokia's managers adopted several strategies. First they worked to create a culture in the factory that is attractive to its new Romanian employees so they will stay with the company and learn the skills required to make it operate more efficiently over time. For example, the factory's cafeteria offers free food, and there are gyms, sports facilities, and (of course) a Finnish sauna. In addition, although managers from other countries run the plant at present, Nokia hopes that within a few years most of the factory's managers and supervisors will be Romanian. Its goal is to create a career ladder that will motivate employees to perform at a high level and so be promoted.

At the same time Nokia is hardheaded about how efficiently it expects its Romanian factory to operate because all its factories are required to operate at the same level of efficiency that its *most* efficient global factory has achieved. Thus Nokia has created a compensation plan for factory managers based on the *collective* performance of all its factories. This means managers in all its factories will see their bonuses reduced if just one factory in any country performs below expectations. This is a tough approach, but its purpose is to encourage all managers to develop more efficient manufacturing techniques, which, when learned in one factory, must be shared with all other factories around the world for managers to obtain their bonuses. Nokia's goal is that efficiency will improve constantly over time as managers are encouraged to find better ways to operate and then share this knowledge across the company.

Just six months after it opened in June 2008 the Romanian plant reached the 1 million handset produced milestone. The plant's efficiency has exceeded Nokia's expectations–so much so that Nokia opened a new cell phone accessory factory next to the plant and has hired hundreds of new workers who received a 9% salary increase in 2010 because of their high productivity. In 2010 Nokia was contemplating opening a plant in Argentina to serve the booming South American market.[12]

Distributors

distributors Organizations that help other organizations sell their goods or services to customers.

Distributors are organizations that help other organizations sell their goods or services to customers. The decisions managers make about how to distribute products to customers can have important effects on organizational performance. For example, package delivery companies such as DHL from Germany have become vital distributors for the millions of items bought online and shipped to customers by dot-com companies.

The changing nature of distributors and distribution methods can bring opportunities and threats for managers. If distributors become so large and powerful that they can control customers' access to a particular organization's goods and services, they can threaten the organization by demanding that it reduce the prices of its goods and services.[13] For example, the huge retail distributor Carrefour from France controls its suppliers' access to millions of customers and thus can demand that its suppliers reduce their prices to keep its business. If an organization such as Procter & Gamble refuses to reduce its prices, Carrefour might respond by buying products only from Procter & Gamble's competitors–companies such as Unilever and Colgate.

It is illegal for distributors to collaborate or collude to keep prices high and thus maintain their power over buyers; however, this frequently happens. In the early 2000s several European drug companies conspired to keep the price of vitamins artificially high. In 2005 the three largest global makers of flash memory, including Samsung, were found guilty of price fixing (they collaborated to keep prices high). All these companies paid hundreds of millions of dollars in fines, and many of their top executives were sentenced to jail terms.

Customers

customers Individuals and groups that buy the goods and services an organization produces.

Customers are the individuals and groups that buy the goods and services an organization produces. For example, Acer's customers can be segmented into several distinct groups: (1) individuals who purchase PCs for home use, (2) small companies, (3) large companies, and (4) government agencies and educational institutions. Changes in the number and types of customers or in customers' tastes and needs create opportunities and threats. An organization's success depends on its responsiveness to customers–whether it can satisfy their needs. In the PC industry, customers are demanding thinner computers, better graphics and speed, and increased wireless and Internet connections–and lower prices–and PC makers must respond to the changing types and needs of customers, such as by introducing tablet computers. A university, too, must adapt to the changing needs of its customers. For example, if more Mandarin-speaking students enroll, additional classes in English as a second language may need to be scheduled. A manager's ability to identify an organization's main customer groups, and make the products that best satisfy their particular needs, is a crucial factor affecting organizational and managerial success.

Today many products have gained global customer acceptance. This consolidation is occurring both for consumer goods and for business products and has created enormous opportunities for managers. The worldwide acceptance of Coca-Cola, Apple iPods, McDonald's hamburgers, Sony Playstation and Nokia cell phones is a sign that the tastes and preferences of customers in different countries may not be so different after all.[14] Likewise, large global markets exist for business products such as telecommunications equipment, electronic components, and computer and financial services.

Competitors

competitors Organizations that produce goods and services that are similar to a particular organization's goods and services.

One of the most important forces an organization confronts in its task environment is competitors. **Competitors** are organizations that produce goods and services that are similar and comparable to a particular organization's goods and services. In other words, competitors are organizations trying to attract the same customers. In the laptop computer market, Acer competes against Lenovo from China, Hewlett Packard and Dell from the United States, and Toshiba from Japan.

Rivalry between competitors is potentially the most threatening force managers must deal with. A high level of rivalry typically results in price competition, and falling prices reduce customer revenues and profits. In the early 2000s competition in the PC industry became intense as many firms aggressively cut costs and prices to increase their global market share.[15] IBM had to exit the PC business after it lost billions in its battle against low-cost rivals.

Although extensive rivalry between existing competitors is a major threat to profitability, so is the potential for new competitors to enter the task environment. **Potential competitors** are organizations that are not presently in a task environment but have the resources to enter if they so choose. In 2010 Amazon.com, for example, was not in the retail furniture or large appliance business, but it could enter these businesses if its managers decided it could profitably sell such products online. When new competitors enter an industry, competition increases, and prices and profits decrease.

potential competitors Organizations that presently are not in a task environment but could enter if they so choose.

BARRIERS TO ENTRY In general, the potential for new competitors to enter a task environment (and thus increase competition) is a function of barriers to entry.[16] **Barriers to entry** are factors that make it difficult and costly for a company to enter a particular task environment or industry.[17] In other words, the more difficult and costly it is to enter the task environment, the higher are the barriers to entry. The higher the barriers to entry, the fewer the competitors in an organization's task environment and thus the lower the threat of competition. With fewer competitors, it is easier to obtain customers and keep prices high.

barriers to entry Factors that make it difficult and costly for an organization to enter a particular task environment or industry.

Barriers to entry result from three main sources: economies of scale, brand loyalty, and government regulations that impede entry (see Figure 6.2). **Economies of scale** are the cost advantages associated with large operations. Economies of scale result from factors such as manufacturing products in very large quantities, buying inputs in bulk, or making more effective use of organizational resources than do competitors by fully utilizing employees' skills and knowledge. If organizations already in the task environment are large and enjoy significant economies of scale, their costs are lower than the costs that potential entrants will face, and newcomers will find it expensive to enter the industry. Amazon.com, for example, enjoys significant economies of scale relative to most other dot-com companies because of its highly efficient distribution system.[18]

economies of scale Cost advantages associated with large operations.

Brand loyalty is customers' preference for the products of organizations currently in the task environment. If established organizations enjoy significant brand loyalty, a new entrant will find it difficult and costly to obtain a share of the market. Newcomers must bear huge advertising costs to build customer awareness of the goods or services they intend to provide.[19] Today Google and Amazon.com are worldwide brands that have high levels of loyalty. As a result, these sites have some of the highest Web site hit rates, which allows them to increase their marketing revenues.

brand loyalty Customers' preference for the products of organizations currently existing in the task environment.

In some cases, *government regulations* function as a barrier to entry at both the industry and the country levels. Many industries that were deregulated, such as air transport, trucking, utilities, and telecommunications, experienced a high level of new entry after deregulation; this forced existing companies in those industries to operate more efficiently or risk being put out of business. At the national and global

Figure 6.2
Barriers to Entry and Competition

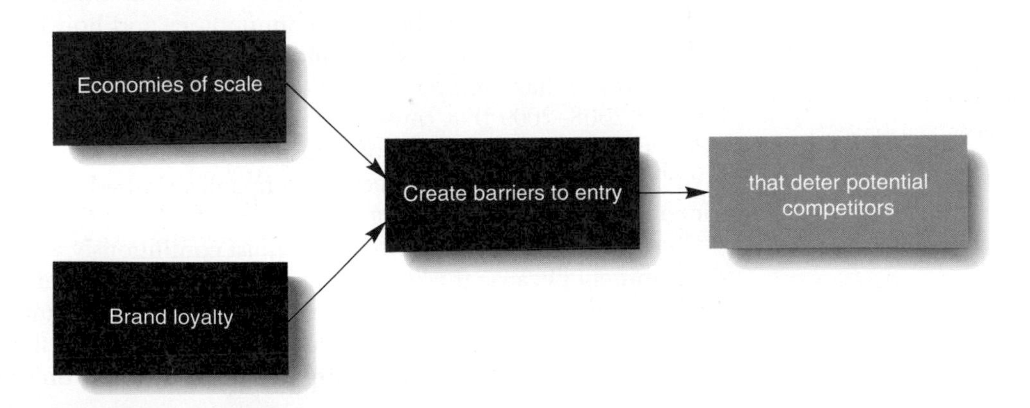

The tyranny of the lower price. A Japanese businessman purchases a frozen, U.S.-sourced rice O-bento lunch at a Nippon Tokyo store. Nippon's importing practices have angered Japanese rice farmers.

levels, administrative barriers are government policies that create barriers to entry and limit imports of goods by overseas companies. Japan is well known for the many ways in which it attempts to restrict the entry of overseas competitors or lessen their impact on Japanese firms. Japan has come under intense pressure to relax and abolish regulations such as those governing the import of rice, for example.

The Japanese rice market, like many other Japanese markets, was closed to overseas competitors until 1993 to protect Japan's thousands of high-cost, low-output rice farmers. Rice cultivation is expensive in Japan because of the country's mountainous terrain, and Japanese consumers have always paid high prices for rice. Under overseas pressure, the Japanese government opened the market; but overseas competitors are allowed to export to Japan only 8% of its annual rice consumption to protect its farmers.

In the 2000s, however, an alliance between organic rice grower Lundberg Family Farms of California and the Nippon Restaurant Enterprise Co. found a new way to break into the Japanese rice market. Because there is no tariff on rice used in processed foods, Nippon converts the U.S. organic rice into "O-bento," an organic hot boxed lunch packed with rice, vegetables, chicken, beef, and salmon, all imported from the United States. The lunches, which cost about US$4 compared to a Japanese rice bento that costs about US$9, are sold at railway stations and other outlets throughout Japan and have become very popular. A storm of protest from Japanese rice farmers arose because the entry of U.S. rice growers forced them to leave their rice fields idle or grow less profitable crops. Other overseas companies are increasingly forming alliances with Japanese companies to find new ways to break into the high-priced Japanese market, and little by little, Japan's restrictive trade practices are being whittled away.

In summary, intense rivalry among competitors creates a task environment that is highly threatening and makes it increasingly difficult for managers to gain access to the resources an organization needs to make goods and services. Conversely, low rivalry results in a task environment where competitive pressures are more moderate and managers have greater opportunities to acquire the resources they need to make their organizations effective.

The General Environment

Economic, technological, sociocultural, demographic, political, and legal forces in the general environment often have important effects on forces in the task environment that determine an organization's ability to obtain resources–effects that managers may not be aware of. For example, the sudden, dramatic upheavals in the mortgage and banking industry that started in 2007 were brought about by a combination of the development of complex new financial lending instruments called derivatives; a speculative boom in commodities and housing prices; and lax government regulation that allowed unethical bankers and financial managers to exploit the derivatives to make immense short-term profits. These events triggered the economic crisis of 2008–2009 that caused stock markets around the world to plummet, devastating the retirement savings of hundreds of millions of ordinary people, and caused layoffs of millions of employees as companies slashed their workforces because customers reduced their spending.

The implication is clear: Managers must continuously analyze forces in the general environment because these forces affect ongoing decision making and planning. How well managers can perform this task determines how quickly an organization can respond to the changes taking place. Next we discuss the major forces in the general environment and examine their impact on an organization's task environment.

Economic Forces

economic forces Interest rates, inflation, unemployment, economic growth, and other factors that affect the general health and well-being of a nation or the regional economy of an organization.

Economic forces affect the general health and well-being of a country or world region. They include interest rates, inflation, unemployment, and economic growth. Economic forces produce many opportunities and threats for managers. Low levels of unemployment and falling interest rates give people more money to spend, and as a result organizations can sell more goods and services. Good economic times affect the supply of resources that become easier or more inexpensive to acquire, and organizations have an opportunity to flourish. High-tech companies enjoyed this throughout the 1990s as computer and electronics companies like Sony made record profits as the global economy boomed because of advances in IT and growing global trade.

In contrast, worsening macroeconomic conditions, like those in the late 2000s, pose a major threat because they reduce managers' ability to gain access to the resources their organizations need to survive and prosper. Profit-seeking organizations such as hotels and retail stores have fewer customers during economic downturns; hotel rates dropped by 14% in 2009 compared to 2008, for example, just as retail sales plunged. Nonprofits such as charities and colleges also saw donations decline by more than 20% because of the economic downturn.

Poor economic conditions make the environment more complex and managers' jobs more difficult and demanding. Companies often need to reduce the number of their managers and employees, streamline their operations, and identify ways to acquire and use resources more efficiently and effectively. Successful managers realize the important effects that economic forces have on their organizations, and they pay close attention to what is occurring in the economy at the national and regional levels to respond appropriately.

Technological Forces

technology The combination of skills and equipment that managers use in designing, producing, and distributing goods and services.

technological forces Outcomes of changes in the technology managers use to design, produce, or distribute goods and services.

Technology is the combination of tools, machines, computers, skills, information, and knowledge that managers use to design, produce, and distribute goods and services; **technological forces** are outcomes of changes in that technology. The overall pace of technological change has accelerated greatly in the last decades because technological advances in microprocessors and computer hardware and software have spurred technological advances in most businesses and industries. The effects of changing technological forces are still increasing in magnitude.[20]

Technological forces can have profound implications for managers and organizations. Technological change can make established products obsolete–for example, cathode-ray tube (CRT) computer monitors and televisions (such as Sony's Trinitron), bound sets of encyclopedias, and even newspapers–forcing managers to find new ways to satisfy customer needs. Although technological change can threaten an organization, it also can create a host of new opportunities for designing, making, or distributing new and better kinds of goods and services. Ever more powerful microprocessors developed by Intel and AMD, which now have 8 or 12 processing cores on each chip, are continuing the IT revolution that has spurred demand for all kinds of new digital computing devices and services and has affected the competitive position of all high-tech companies. Will Google devastate Microsoft, for example, just as Microsoft devastated IBM in the 1990s? Managers must move quickly to respond to such changes if their organizations are to survive and prosper.

Changes in IT are altering the nature of work itself within organizations, including that of the manager's job. Today telecommuting, videoconferencing, and text messaging are everyday activities that let managers supervise and coordinate geographically dispersed employees. Salespeople in many companies work from home offices and commute electronically to work. They communicate with other employees through companywide electronic communication networks using PCs and webcams to orchestrate "face-to-face" meetings with coworkers across the country or globe.

Sociocultural Forces

sociocultural forces Pressures emanating from the social structure of a country or society or from the national culture.

social structure The traditional system of relationships established between people and groups in a society.

Sociocultural forces are pressures emanating from the social structure of a country or society or from the national culture, such as the concern for diversity, discussed in the previous chapter. Pressures from both sources can either constrain or facilitate the way organizations operate and managers behave. **Social structure** is the traditional system of relationships established between people and groups in a society. Societies differ substantially in social structure. In societies that have a high degree of social stratification, there are many distinctions among individuals and groups. Caste systems in India and Tibet and the recognition of numerous social classes in Great Britain and France produce a multilayered social structure in each of those countries. In contrast, social stratification is lower in relatively egalitarian New Zealand and in Australia, where the social structure reveals few distinctions among people. Most top managers in France come from the upper classes of French society, but top managers in Australia come from all strata of Australian society.

national culture The set of values that a society considers important and the norms of behavior that are approved or sanctioned in that society.

Societies also differ in the extent to which they emphasize the individual over the group. Such differences may dictate how managers need to motivate and lead employees. **National culture** is the set of values that a society considers important and the norms of behavior that are approved or sanctioned in that society. Societies differ substantially in the values and norms they emphasize. For example, in the United States individualism is highly valued, and in Korea and Japan individuals are expected to conform to group expectations.[21] National culture, discussed at length later in this chapter, also affects how managers motivate and coordinate employees and how organizations do business. Ethics, an important aspect of national culture, were discussed in detail in Chapter 4.

Social structure and national culture not only differ across societies but also change within societies over time. In Germany, attitudes toward the roles of women, sex, marriage, and gays and lesbians changed in each past decade. Many people in Asian countries such as Hong Kong, Singapore, Korea, and even China think the younger generation is far more individualistic than previous generations. Currently, throughout much of eastern Europe, new values that emphasize individualism and entrepreneurship are replacing communist values based on collectivism and obedience to the state. The pace of change is accelerating.

Pick your poison. The American trend towards fitness has prompted traditional soft drink manufacturers to expand their offerings into a staggering array of energy drinks.

Individual managers and organizations must be responsive to changes in, and differences among, the social structures and national cultures of all the countries in which they operate. In today's increasingly integrated global economy, managers are likely to interact with people from several countries, and many managers live and work abroad. Effective managers are sensitive to differences between societies and adjust their behavior accordingly.

Managers and organizations also must respond to social changes within a society. In the last decades, for example, Europeans have become increasingly interested in their personal health and fitness. Managers who recognized this trend early and took advantage of the opportunities that resulted from it were able to reap significant gains for their organizations such as chains of health clubs. PepsiCo used the opportunity presented by the fitness trend and took market share from archrival Coca-Cola by being the first to introduce diet colas and fruit-based soft drinks. Then Quaker Oats made Gatorade the most popular energy drink, and now others like Red Bull, Monster, and Rockstar are increasing in popularity. The health trend, however, did not offer opportunities to all companies; to some it posed a threat. Tobacco companies came under intense pressure due to consumers' greater awareness of negative health impacts from smoking. The rage for "low-carb" foods in the 2000s increased demand for meat and protein, and bread and pasta companies suffered–until the 2008 recession boosted the sale of inexpensive products such as macaroni and cheese and hamburger helper.

Demographic Forces

demographic forces Outcomes of changes in, or changing attitudes toward, the characteristics of a population, such as age, gender, ethnic origin, race, sexual orientation, and social class.

Demographic forces are outcomes of changes in, or changing attitudes toward, the characteristics of a population, such as age, gender, ethnic origin, race, sexual orientation, and social class. Like the other forces in the general environment, demographic forces present managers with opportunities and threats and can have major implications for organizations. We examined the nature of these challenges in depth in our discussion of diversity in Chapter 5.

Today most industrialized nations are experiencing the aging of their populations as a consequence of falling birth and death rates and the aging of the baby boom generation. Consequently, the absolute number of older people has increased substantially, which has generated opportunities for organizations that cater to older people such as the home health care, recreation, and medical industries, which have seen an upswing in demand for their services. The aging of the population also has several implications for the workplace. Most significant are a relative decline in the number of young people joining the workforce and an increase in the number of active employees who are postponing retirement beyond the traditional age of 65. Indeed, the financial crisis of 2008–2009 has made it impossible for millions of older people to retire because their savings have been decimated. These changes suggest that organizations need to find ways to motivate older employees and use their skills and knowledge–an issue that many Western societies have yet to tackle.

Political and Legal Forces

political and legal forces Outcomes of changes in laws and regulations, such as deregulation of industries, privatization of organizations, and increased emphasis on environmental protection.

Political and legal forces are outcomes of changes in laws and regulations. They result from political and legal developments that take place within a nation, within a world region, or across the world and significantly affect managers and organizations everywhere. Political processes shape a nation's laws and the international laws that govern the relationships between nations. Laws constrain the operations of organizations and managers and thus create both opportunities and threats.[22] For example, throughout much of the industrialized world there has been a strong trend toward deregulation of industries previously controlled by the state and privatization of organizations once owned by the state.

Another important political and legal force affecting managers and organizations is the political integration of countries that has been taking place during the past decades.[23] Increasingly, nations are forming political unions that allow free exchange of resources and capital. The growth of the European Union (EU) is one example: Common laws govern trade and commerce between EU member countries, and the European Court has the right to examine the business of any global organization and to approve any proposed mergers between overseas companies that operate inside the EU. For example, Microsoft's anticompetitive business practices came under scrutiny, and it was fined hundreds of millions for its uncompetitive practice of bundling its Internet Explorer Web browser with its software. As part of its agreement with the European Court, Microsoft agreed that from spring 2010 forward it would ship its Windows 7 software with a choice of 10 Web browsers (such as Chrome, Safari, and Mozilla). Also in 2010, after months of delay, the court allowed the merger between Oracle and Sun to proceed providing the companies followed some strict competitive guidelines.

Indeed, international agreements to abolish laws and regulations that restrict and reduce trade between countries have been having profound effects on global organizations. The falling legal trade barriers create enormous opportunities for companies to sell goods and services internationally. But by allowing overseas companies to compete in a nation's domestic market for customers, falling trade barriers also pose a serious threat because they increase competition in the task environment. Between 1980 and 2010, for example, Japanese companies increased their share of the U.S. car market from around 20% to 40%; Taiwanese companies' share grew from 2% to 7%. In essence, removing legal restrictions on global trade has the same effect as deregulating industries and removing restrictions against competition: It increases the intensity of competition in the task environment and forces conservative, slow-moving companies to become more efficient, improve product quality, and learn new values and norms to compete in the global environment.

Deregulation, privatization, and the removal of legal barriers to trade are just a few of the many ways in which changing political and legal forces can challenge organizations and managers. Others include increased emphasis on environmental protection and the preservation of endangered species, increased emphasis on workplace safety, and legal constraints against discrimination on the basis of race, gender, or age. Managers face major challenges when they seek to take advantage of the opportunities created by changing political, legal, and economic forces.

The Changing Global Environment

LO6-4 Explain why the global environment is becoming more open and competitive, and identify the forces behind the process of globalization that increase the opportunities, complexities, challenges, and threats managers face.

The 21st century has banished the idea that the world is composed of distinct national countries and markets that are separated physically, economically, and culturally. Managers need to recognize that companies compete in a truly global marketplace, which is the source of the opportunities and threats they must respond to. Managers continually confront the challenges of global competition such as establishing operations in a country abroad, obtaining inputs from suppliers abroad, or managing in a different national culture.[24] (See Figure 6.3.)

In essence, as a result of falling trade barriers, managers view the global environment as open—that is, as an environment in which companies are free to buy goods and services from, and sell goods and services to, whichever companies and countries they choose. They also are free to compete against each other to attract customers around the world. All large companies must establish an international network of operations and subsidiaries to build global competitive advantage. Coca-Cola and PepsiCo, for example, have competed aggressively for decades to develop the strongest global

Figure 6.3
The Global Environment

soft drink empire, just as Toyota and Honda have built hundreds of car plants around the world to provide the vehicles that global customers like. This is also true in the food processing industry, as the following "Managing Globally" box suggests.

Managing Globally

Nestlé's Global Food Empire

Nestlé is the world's largest food company. In 2009 its sales increased by 4%, and it enjoyed record profits of over $100 billion; globally it had over 190,000 employees and 500 factories in 80 countries. It makes and sells over 8,000 food products, including such popular brands as Kit-Kat chocolate bars, Taster's Choice coffee, Carnation Instant milk, and Stouffer's Foods. At its corporate headquarters in Vevey, Switzerland, CEO Peter Brabeck-Latmathe, who has been in charge since 1997, is responsible for Nestlé's improving global performance and has faced and managed many global challenges.[25]

From the beginning Brabeck worked to increase Nestlé's revenues and profits by entering new attractive national markets in both developed and emerging nations as trade barriers fell. He continued the ambitious global expansion that Nestlé began in the 1990s, when, for example, it bought the U.S. food companies Carnation and Buitoni Pasta, the British chocolate maker Rowntree, the French bottled water company Perrier, and the Mexican food maker Ortega. Under Brabeck, Nestlé spent $18 billion to acquire U.S. companies Ralston Purina, Dreyer's Ice Cream, and Chef America. Brabeck's intention was not only to develop these food brands in the United States but also to customize their products to suit the tastes of customers in countries around the world. He was particularly anxious to enter emerging markets such as those in eastern Europe, India, and Asia to take advantage of the enormous numbers of potential new customers in these regions. In this way Nestlé could leverage its well-known brand image and products around the world to drive up its performance.

Increasing global product sale revenues was only the first part of Brabeck's global business model, however. He was also anxious to increase Nestlé's operating efficiency and reduce the cost of managing its global operations. As you can imagine, with over 500 factories the costs of organizing Nestlé's global activities were enormous. Brabeck benchmarked its operating costs to those of competitors such as Kraft Foods and Unilever and found that Nestlé's costs were significantly higher than theirs. Brabeck cut the workforce by 20%, closed 150 factories, and reduced operating costs by over 12%. Nestlé was also using advanced IT both to reduce the number of its global suppliers and to negotiate more favorable supply contracts with them–moves that significantly cut purchasing costs. Brabeck also designed Nestlé's new streamlined operating structure and IT to increase the flow of information between its food products units and all the countries in which it sells its products. His goal was to capitalize on a prime source of its competitive advantage: superior innovation.

Nescafé anywhere, anytime. Nestlé's expanded operations and benchmarked processes make it a force to be reckoned with.

Thus Brabeck's global strategy for Nestlé was driven by three main goals: (1) Expand Nestlé's range of products, and offer them to new and existing customers in countries throughout the world; (2) find lower-cost ways to make and sell these products; and (3) speed up Nestlé's product innovation by leveraging its expertise across its food businesses to create more attractive food products that would increase its global market share. In addition, many customers around the world have been demanding more nutritious food products. So Brabeck adopted what he called an "organic approach" to developing Nestlé's products. Brabeck claimed his company was engaged in a "transformation" that would lead it to become the "world's leading nutrition, health, and wellness" food company that made consumer health and safety its prime concern.[26]

In the next section we first explain how this open global environment is the result of globalization and the flow of capital around the world. Next we examine how specific economic, political, and legal changes, such as the lowering of barriers to trade and investment, have increased globalization and led to greater interaction and exchanges between organizations and countries. Then we discuss how declining barriers of distance and culture have also increased the pace of globalization, and we consider the specific implications of these changes for managers and organizations. Finally we note that nations still differ widely from each other because they have distinct cultural values and norms and that managers must appreciate these differences to compete successfully across countries.

The Process of Globalization

globalization The set of specific and general forces that work together to integrate and connect economic, political, and social systems *across* countries, cultures, or geographical regions so that nations become increasingly interdependent and similar.

Perhaps the most important reason why the global environment has become more open and competitive is the increase in globalization. **Globalization** is the set of specific and general forces that work together to integrate and connect economic, political, and social systems *across* countries, cultures, or geographic regions. The result of globalization is that nations and peoples become increasingly *interdependent* because the same forces affect them in similar ways. The fates of peoples in different countries become interlinked as the world's markets and businesses become increasingly interconnected. And as nations become more interdependent, they become more similar to one another in the sense that people develop a similar liking for products as diverse as cell phones, iPods, blue jeans, soft drinks, sports teams, Japanese cars, and foods such as curry, green tea, and Colombian coffee. One outcome of globalization is that the world is becoming a "global village": Products, services, or people can become well known throughout the world–something IKEA, with its range of furniture designed to appeal to customers around the world, is taking advantage of, as the following "Managing Globally" box describes.

Managing Globally

IKEA Is on Top of the Furniture World

IKEA is the largest furniture chain in the world, and in 2010 the Swedish company operated over 267 stores in 25 countries. In 2009 IKEA sales soared to over US$33 billion, or over 20% of the global furniture market; but to its managers and employees this was just the tip of the iceberg. They believed IKEA was poised for massive growth throughout the world in the coming decade because it could provide what the average customer wanted: well-designed and well-made contemporary furniture at an affordable price. IKEA's ability to provide customers with affordable furniture is the result of its approach to globalization, to how it treats its global employees and operates its global store empire. In a nutshell, IKEA's global approach focuses on simplicity, attention to detail, cost consciousness, and responsiveness in every aspect of its operations and behavior.

Need a new kitchen table? How about a cute rug to go with it, and while you're at it, a cookie sheet, too? Options await you at any one of the thousands of IKEA stores worldwide.

IKEA's global approach derives from the personal values and beliefs of its founder, Ingvar Kamprad, about how companies should treat their employees and customers. Kamprad, who is in his early 80s (and in 2010 ranked as the 11th richest person in the world), was born in Smaland, a poor Swedish province whose citizens are known for being entrepreneurial, frugal, and hardworking. Kamprad definitely absorbed these values–when he entered the furniture business, he made them the core of his management approach. He teaches store managers and employees his values; his beliefs about the need to operate in a no-frills, cost-conscious way; and his view that they are all in business "together," by which he means that every person who works in his global empire plays an essential role and has an obligation to everyone else.

What does Kamprad's approach mean in practice? All IKEA employees fly coach class on business trips, stay in inexpensive hotels, and keep traveling expenses to a minimum. And IKEA stores operate on the simplest rules and procedures possible, with employees expected to cooperate to solve problems and get the job done. Many famous stories circulate about the frugal Kamprad, such as that even he always flies coach class and that when he takes a soda can from the minibar in a hotel room, he replaces it with one bought in a store–despite the fact that he is a multibillionaire.

IKEA's employees see what Kamprad's global approach means as soon as they are recruited to work in a store in one of the many countries in which the company operates. They start learning about IKEA's global corporate culture by performing jobs at the bottom of the ladder, and they are quickly trained to perform all the various jobs involved in store operations. During this process they internalize IKEA's global values and norms, which center on the importance the company attaches to their taking the initiative and responsibility for solving problems and for focusing on customers. Employees are rotated between departments and sometimes stores, and rapid promotion is possible for those who demonstrate the enthusiasm and togetherness that show they have bought into IKEA's global culture.

Most of IKEA's top managers rose from its ranks, and the company holds "breaking the bureaucracy weeks" in which managers are required to work in stores and warehouses for a week each year to make sure they and all employees stay committed to IKEA's global values. No matter which country they operate in, all employees wear informal clothes to work at IKEA–Kamprad has always worn an open-neck shirt–and there are no marks of status such as executive dining rooms or private parking places. Employees believe that if they buy into IKEA's work values, behave in ways that keep its growing global operations streamlined and efficient, and focus on being one step ahead of potential problems, they will share in its success. Promotion, training, above-average pay, a generous store bonus system, and the personal well-being that comes from working in a company where people feel valued are some of the rewards that Kamprad pioneered to build and strengthen IKEA's global approach.

Whenever IKEA enters a new country, it sends its most experienced store managers to establish its global approach in its new stores. When IKEA first entered the United States, the attitude of U.S. employees puzzled its managers. Despite their obvious drive to succeed and good education, employees seemed reluctant to take initiative and assume responsibility. IKEA's managers discovered that their U.S. employees were afraid mistakes would result in the loss of their jobs, so the managers strove to teach employees the "IKEA way." The approach paid off: The United States has become the company's second best country market, and IKEA plans to open many more U.S. stores, as well as stores around the world, over the next decade.[27]

But what drives or spurs globalization? What makes companies like IKEA, Toyota, or Microsoft want to venture into an uncertain global environment? The answer is that the path of globalization is shaped by the ebb and flow of *capital*–valuable wealth-generating assets or resources that people move through companies, countries, and world regions to seek their greatest returns or profits. Managers, employees, and companies like IKEA and Sony are motivated to try to profit or benefit by using their skills to make products customers around the world want to buy. The four principal forms of capital that flow between countries are these:

- *Human capital:* the flow of people around the world through immigration, migration, and emigration.
- *Financial capital:* the flow of money capital across world markets through overseas investment, credit, lending, and aid.
- *Resource capital:* the flow of natural resources, parts, and components between companies and countries, such as metals, minerals, lumber, energy, food products, microprocessors, and auto parts.
- *Political capital:* the flow of power and influence around the world using diplomacy, persuasion, aggression, and force of arms to protect the right or access of a country, world region, or political bloc to the other forms of capital.

Most of the economic advances associated with globalization are the result of these four capital flows and the interactions between them, as nations compete on the world stage to protect and increase their standards of living and to further the political goals and social causes that are espoused by their societies' cultures. The next sections look at the factors that have increased the rate at which capital flows between companies and countries. In a positive sense the faster the flow, the more capital is being utilized where it can create the most value, in the sense of people moving to where their skills earn them more money, or investors switching to the stocks or bonds that give them higher dividends or interest, or companies finding lower-cost sources of inputs. In a negative sense, however, a fast flow of capital also means that individual countries or world regions can find themselves in trouble when companies and investors move their capital to invest it in more productive ways in other countries or world regions–often those with lower labor costs or rapidly expanding markets. When capital leaves a country, the results are higher unemployment, recession, and a lower standard of living for its people.

Declining Barriers to Trade and Investment

One of the main factors that has speeded globalization by freeing the movement of capital has been the decline in barriers to trade and investment, discussed earlier. During the 1920s and 1930s many countries erected formidable barriers to international trade and investment in the belief that this was the best way to promote their economic well-being. Many of these barriers were high tariffs on imports of manufactured goods. A **tariff** is a tax that a government imposes on goods imported into one country from another. The aim of import tariffs is to protect domestic industries and jobs, such as those in the auto or steel industry, from overseas competition by raising the price of these products from abroad. In 2009, for example, the U.S. government increased the tariffs on vehicle tires imported from China to protect U.S. tire makers from unfair competition; China vigorously protested that the price of its tires was fair and it would retaliate by increasing tariffs on U.S. imports of chicken and other products.

tariff A tax that a government imposes on imported or, occasionally, exported goods.

The reason for removing tariffs is that, very often, when one country imposes an import tariff, others follow suit and the result is a series of retaliatory moves as countries progressively raise tariff barriers against each other. In the 1920s this behavior depressed world demand and helped usher in the Great Depression of the 1930s and massive unemployment. During the 2008–2009 economic crisis, the governments of most countries worked hard not to fall into the trap of raising tariffs to protect jobs and industries in the short run because they knew the long-term consequences of this would be the loss of even more jobs. Governments of countries that resort to raising tariff barriers ultimately reduce employment and undermine the economic growth of their countries because capital and resources will always move to their most highly valued use–wherever that is in the world.[28]

GATT AND THE RISE OF FREE TRADE After World War II, advanced Western industrial countries, having learned from the Great Depression, committed themselves to the goal of removing barriers to the free flow of resources and capital between countries. This commitment was reinforced by acceptance of the principle that free trade, rather than tariff barriers, was the best way to foster a healthy domestic economy and low unemployment.[29]

free-trade doctrine The idea that if each country specializes in the production of the goods and services that it can produce most efficiently, this will make the best use of global resources.

The **free-trade doctrine** predicts that if each country agrees to specialize in the production of the goods and services that it can produce most efficiently, this will make the best use of global capital resources and will result in lower prices.[30] For example, if Indian companies are highly efficient in the production of textiles and U.S. companies are highly efficient in the production of computer software, then under a free-trade agreement capital would move to India and be invested there to produce textiles, while capital from around the world would flow to the United States and be invested in its innovative computer software companies. Consequently, prices of both textiles and software should fall because each product is being produced where it can be made at the lowest cost, benefiting consumers and making the best use of scarce capital. This doctrine is also responsible for the increase in global outsourcing and the loss of millions of U.S. jobs in textiles and manufacturing as capital has been invested in factories in Asian countries such as China and Malaysia. However, millions of U.S. jobs have also been created because of new capital investments in the high-tech, IT, and service sectors, which in theory should offset manufacturing job losses in the long run.

Historically countries that accepted this free-trade doctrine set as their goal the removal of barriers to the free flow of goods, services, and capital between countries. They attempted to achieve this through an international treaty known as the General Agreement on Tariffs and Trade (GATT). In the half-century since World War II, there have been eight rounds of GATT negotiations aimed at lowering tariff barriers. The last round, the Uruguay Round, involved 117 countries and was completed in December 1993. This round succeeded in lowering tariffs by over 30% from the previous level. It also led to the dissolving of GATT and its replacement by the World Trade Organization (WTO), which continues the struggle to reduce tariffs and has more power to sanction countries that break global agreements.[31] On average, the tariff barriers among the governments of developed countries declined from over 40% in 1948 to about 3% today, causing a dramatic increase in world trade.[32]

Declining Barriers of Distance and Culture

Historically, barriers of distance and culture also closed the global environment and kept managers focused on their domestic market. The management problems Unilever, the huge British-based soap and detergent maker, experienced at the turn of the 20th century illustrate the effect of these barriers.

Founded in London during the 1880s by William Lever, Unilever had a worldwide reach by the early 1900s and operated subsidiaries in most major countries of the British Empire, including India, Canada, and Australia. Lever had a very hands-on, autocratic management style and found his far-flung business empire difficult to control. The reason for Lever's control problems was that communication over great distances was difficult. It took six weeks to reach India by ship from England, and international telephone and telegraph services were unreliable.

Another problem Unilever encountered was the difficulty of doing business in societies that were separated from Britain by barriers of language and culture. Different countries have different sets of national beliefs, values, and norms, and Lever found that a management approach that worked in Britain did not necessarily work in India or Persia (now Iran). As a result, management practices had to be tailored to suit each unique national culture. After Lever's death in 1925, top management at Unilever lowered or *decentralized* (see Chapter 10) decision-making authority to the managers of the various national subsidiaries so they could develop a management approach that suited the country in which they were operating. One result of this strategy was that the subsidiaries grew distant and remote from one another, which reduced Unilever's performance.[33]

Since the end of World War II, a continuing stream of advances in communications and transportation technology has worked to reduce the barriers of distance and culture that affected Unilever and all global organizations. Over the last decades, global communication has been revolutionized by developments in satellites, digital technology, the Internet and global computer networks, and video teleconferencing that allow transmission of vast amounts of information and make reliable, secure, and instantaneous communication possible between people and companies anywhere in the world.[34] This revolution has made it possible for a global organization–a tiny garment factory in Li & Fung's network or a huge company such as Sony or Unilever–to do business anywhere, anytime, and to search for customers and suppliers around the world.

One of the most important innovations in transportation technology that has opened the global environment has been the growth of commercial jet travel. New York is now closer in travel time to Tokyo than it was to Philadelphia in the days of the 13 colonies–a fact that makes control of far-flung international businesses much easier today than in William Lever's era. In addition to speeding travel, modern communications and transportation technologies have also helped reduce the cultural distance between countries. The Internet and its millions of Web sites facilitate the development of global communications networks and media that are helping to create a worldwide culture above and beyond unique national cultures. Moreover, television networks such as CNN, MTV, ESPN, BBC, and HBO can now be received in many countries, and Hollywood films are shown throughout the world.

Effects of Free Trade on Managers

The lowering of barriers to trade and investment and the decline of distance and culture barriers has created enormous opportunities for companies to expand the market for their goods and services through exports and investments in overseas countries. The shift toward a more open global economy has created not only more opportunities to sell goods and services in markets abroad but also the opportunity to buy more from other countries. For example, the success of clothing companies such as Lands' End has been based on its managers' willingness to import low-cost clothing and bedding from overseas manufacturers. Lands' End works closely with manufacturers in Hong Kong, Malaysia, Taiwan, and China to make the clothing that its managers decide has the quality and styling its customers want at a price they will pay.[35] A manager's job is more challenging in a dynamic global environment because of the increased intensity of competition that goes hand in hand with the lowering of barriers to trade and investment.

REGIONAL TRADE AGREEMENTS The growth of regional trade agreements such as the North American Free Trade Agreement (NAFTA) also presents opportunities and threats for managers and their organizations. In North America, NAFTA, which became effective in 1994, had the aim of abolishing the tariffs on 99% of the goods traded between Mexico, Canada, and the United States by 2004. Although it did not achieve this lofty goal, NAFTA has removed most barriers on the cross-border flow of resources, giving, for example, financial institutions and retail businesses in Canada and the United States unrestricted access to the Mexican marketplace. After NAFTA was signed, there was a flood of investment into Mexico from the United States, as well as many other countries such as Japan. Similarly major U.S. retail chains have expanded their operations in Mexico; Walmart, for example, is stocking many more products from Mexico in its U.S. stores, and its Mexican store chain is also expanding rapidly. Today, Walmart is the largest retailer in Mexico.

The establishment of free-trade areas creates an opportunity for manufacturing organizations because it lets them reduce their costs. They can do this either by shifting production to the lowest-cost location within the free-trade area (for example, U.S. auto and textile companies shifting production to Mexico) or by serving the whole region from one location rather than establishing separate operations in each country. Some managers, however, view regional free-trade agreements as a threat because they expose a company based in one member country to increased competition from companies based in the other member countries. NAFTA has had this effect; today Mexican managers in some industries face the threat of head-to-head competition against efficient U.S. and Canadian companies. But the opposite is true as well: U.S. and Canadian managers are experiencing threats in labor-intensive industries, such as the flooring tile and textile industries, where Mexican businesses have a cost advantage.

The Role of National Culture

Despite evidence that countries are becoming more similar because of globalization, and that the world may become "a global village," the cultures of different countries still vary widely because of vital differences in their values, norms, and attitudes. As noted earlier, national culture includes the values, norms, knowledge, beliefs, moral principles, laws, customs, and other practices that unite the citizens of a country.[36] National culture shapes individual behavior by specifying appropriate and inappropriate behavior and interaction with others. People learn national culture in their everyday lives by interacting with those around them. This learning starts at an early age and continues throughout their lives.

Cultural Values and Norms

values Ideas about what a society believes to be good, right, desirable, or beautiful.

The basic building blocks of national culture are values and norms. **Values** are beliefs about what a society considers to be good, right, desirable, or beautiful–or their opposites. They provide the basic underpinnings for notions of individual freedom, democracy, truth, justice, honesty, loyalty, social obligation, collective responsibility, the appropriate roles for men and women, love, sex, marriage, and so on. Values are more than merely abstract concepts; they are invested with considerable emotional significance. People argue, fight, and even die over values such as freedom or dignity.

Although deeply embedded in society, values are not static and change over time; but change is often the result of a slow and painful process. For example, the value systems of many formerly communist states such as Russia and Romania are undergoing significant changes as those countries move away from a value system that emphasizes the state and toward one that emphasizes individual freedom. Social turmoil often results when countries undergo major changes in their values.

norms Unwritten, informal codes of conduct that prescribe how people should act in particular situations and are considered important by most members of a group or organization.

mores Norms that are considered to be central to the functioning of society and to social life.

Norms are unwritten, informal codes of conduct that prescribe appropriate behavior in particular situations and are considered important by most members of a group or organization. They shape the behavior of people toward one another. Two types of norms play a major role in national culture: mores and folkways. **Mores** are norms that are considered to be of central importance to the functioning of society and to social life. Accordingly, the violation of mores brings serious retribution. Mores include proscriptions against murder, theft, adultery, and incest. In many societies mores have been enacted into law. Thus all advanced societies have laws against murder and theft. However, there are many differences in mores from one society to another.[37] In the United States, for example, drinking alcohol is widely accepted; but in Saudi Arabia consumption of alcohol is viewed as a serious violation of social mores and is punishable by imprisonment.

folkways The routine social conventions of everyday life.

Folkways are the routine social conventions of everyday life. They concern customs and practices such as dressing appropriately for particular situations, good social manners, eating with the correct utensils, and neighborly behavior. Although folkways define how people are expected to behave, violation of folkways is not a serious or moral matter. People who violate folkways are often thought to be eccentric or ill-mannered, but they are not usually considered immoral or wicked. In many countries, strangers are usually excused for violating folkways because they are unaccustomed to local behavior; but if they repeat the violation they are censured because they are expected to learn appropriate behavior. Hence the importance of managers working in countries abroad to gain wide experience.

LO6-5 Discuss why national cultures differ and why it is important that managers be sensitive to the effects of falling trade barriers and regional trade associations on the political and social systems of nations around the world.

Hofstede's Model of National Culture

Researchers have spent considerable time and effort identifying similarities and differences in the values and norms of different countries. One model of national culture was developed by Geert Hofstede.[38] As a psychologist for IBM, Hofstede collected data on employee values and norms from more than 100,000 IBM employees in 64 countries. Based on his research, Hofstede developed five dimensions along which national cultures can be placed (see Figure 6.4).[39]

individualism A worldview that values individual freedom and self-expression and adherence to the principle that people should be judged by their individual achievements rather than by their social background.

collectivism A worldview that values subordination of the individual to the goals of the group and adherence to the principle that people should be judged by their contribution to the group.

INDIVIDUALISM VERSUS COLLECTIVISM The first dimension, which Hofstede labeled "individualism versus collectivism," has a long history in human thought. **Individualism** is a worldview that values individual freedom and self-expression and adherence to the principle that people should be judged by their individual achievements rather than by their social background. In Western countries, individualism usually includes admiration for personal success, a strong belief in individual rights, and high regard for individual entrepreneurs.[40]

In contrast, **collectivism** is a worldview that values subordination of the individual to the goals of the group and adherence to the principle that people should be judged by their contribution to the group. Collectivism was widespread in communist countries but has become less prevalent since the collapse of communism in most of those countries. Japan is a noncommunist country where collectivism is highly valued.

Collectivism in Japan traces its roots to the fusion of Confucian, Buddhist, and Shinto thought that occurred during the Tokugawa period in Japanese history (1600–1870s).[41] A central value that emerged during this period was strong attachment

Figure 6.4
Hofstede's Model of National Culture

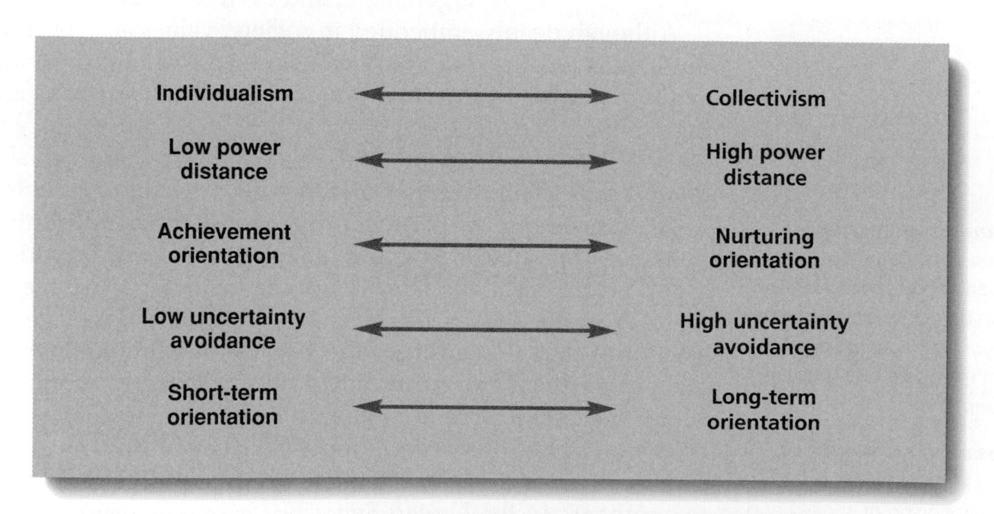

Source: G. Hofstede, B. Nevijen, D. D. Ohayv, and G. Sanders, "Measuring Organizational Cultures: A Qualitative and Quantitative Study across Twenty Cases," *Administrative Science Quarterly* 35, no. 2 (June 1990), pp. 286–316. Approval of request for permission to reprint. © Johnson Graduate School of Management, Cornell University.

to the group–whether a village, a work group, or a company. Strong identification with the group is said to create pressures for collective action in Japan, as well as strong pressure for conformity to group norms and a relative lack of individualism.[42]

Managers must realize that organizations and organizational members reflect their national culture's emphasis on individualism or collectivism. Indeed, one of the major reasons why Japanese and American management practices differ is that Japanese culture values collectivism and U.S. culture values individualism.[43]

power distance The degree to which societies accept the idea that inequalities in the power and well-being of their citizens are due to differences in individuals' physical and intellectual capabilities and heritage.

POWER DISTANCE By **power distance** Hofstede meant the degree to which societies accept the idea that inequalities in the power and well-being of their citizens are due to differences in individuals' physical and intellectual capabilities and heritage. This concept also encompasses the degree to which societies accept the economic and social differences in wealth, status, and well-being that result from differences in individual capabilities.

Societies in which inequalities are allowed to persist or grow over time have *high power distance.* In high-power-distance societies, workers who are professionally successful amass wealth and pass it on to their children, and, as a result, inequalities may grow over time. In such societies, the gap between rich and poor, with all the attendant political and social consequences, grows very large. In contrast, in societies with *low power distance,* large inequalities between citizens are not allowed to develop. In low-power-distance countries, the government uses taxation and social welfare programs to reduce inequality and improve the welfare of the least fortunate. These societies are more attuned to preventing a large gap between rich and poor and minimizing discord between different classes of citizens.

Advanced Western countries such as the United States, Germany, the Netherlands, and the United Kingdom have relatively low power distance and high individualism. Economically poor Latin American countries such as Guatemala and Panama, and Asian countries such as Malaysia and the Philippines, have high power distance and low individualism.[44] These findings suggest that the cultural values of richer countries emphasize protecting the rights of individuals and, at the same time, provide a fair chance of success to every member of society.

achievement orientation A worldview that values assertiveness, performance, success, and competition.

nurturing orientation A worldview that values the quality of life, warm personal friendships, and services and care for the weak.

ACHIEVEMENT VERSUS NURTURING ORIENTATION Societies that have an **achievement orientation** value assertiveness, performance, success, competition, and results. Societies that have a **nurturing orientation** value the quality of life, warm personal relationships, and services and care for the weak. Japan and the United States tend to be achievement-oriented; the Netherlands, Sweden, and Denmark are more nurturing-oriented.

uncertainty avoidance The degree to which societies are willing to tolerate uncertainty and risk.

UNCERTAINTY AVOIDANCE Societies as well as individuals differ in their tolerance for uncertainty and risk. Societies low on **uncertainty avoidance** (such as the United States and Hong Kong) are easygoing, value diversity, and tolerate differences in personal beliefs and actions. Societies high on uncertainty avoidance (such as Japan and France) are more rigid and skeptical about people whose behaviors or beliefs differ from the norm. In these societies, conformity to the values of the social and work groups to which a person belongs is the norm, and structured situations are preferred because they provide a sense of security.

long-term orientation A worldview that values thrift and persistence in achieving goals.

short-term orientation A worldview that values personal stability or happiness and living for the present.

LONG-TERM VERSUS SHORT-TERM ORIENTATION The last dimension that Hofstede described is orientation toward life and work.[45] A national culture with a **long-term orientation** rests on values such as thrift (saving) and persistence in achieving goals. A national culture with a **short-term orientation** is concerned with maintaining personal stability or happiness and living for the present. Societies with a long-term orientation include Taiwan and Hong Kong, well known for their high rate of per capita savings. The United States and France have a short-term orientation, and their citizens tend to spend more and save less.

National Culture and Global Management

Differences among national cultures have important implications for managers. First, because of cultural differences, management practices that are effective in one country might be troublesome in another. General Electric's managers learned this while trying to manage Tungsram, a Hungarian lighting products company GE acquired for $150 million. GE was attracted to Tungsram, widely regarded as one of Hungary's best companies, because of Hungary's low wage rates and the possibility of using the company as a base from which to export lighting products to western Europe. GE transferred some of its best managers to Tungsram and hoped it would soon become a leader in Europe. Unfortunately many problems arose.

One problem resulted from major misunderstandings between the American managers and the Hungarian workers. The Americans complained that the Hungarians were lazy; the Hungarians thought the Americans were pushy. The Americans wanted strong sales and marketing functions that would pamper customers. In the prior command economy, sales and marketing activities were unnecessary. In addition, Hungarians expected GE to deliver Western-style wages, but GE came to Hungary to take advantage of the country's low-wage structure.[46] As Tungsram's losses mounted, GE managers had to admit that, because of differences in basic attitudes between countries, they had underestimated the difficulties they would face in turning Tungsram around. Nevertheless, by 2001 these problems had been solved, and the increased efficiency of GE's Hungarian operations made General Electric a major player in the European lighting market, causing it to invest another US$1 billion.[47]

Often management practices must be tailored to suit the cultural contexts within which an organization operates. An approach effective in Hungary might not work in Japan, the United States, or Mexico because of differences in national culture. For example, U.S.-style pay-for-performance systems that emphasize the performance of individuals might not work well in Japan, where individual performance in pursuit of group goals is the value that receives emphasis.

Managers doing business with individuals from another country must be sensitive to the value systems and norms of that country and behave accordingly. For example, Friday is the Islamic Sabbath. Thus it would be impolite and inappropriate for a U.S. manager to schedule a busy day of activities for Saudi Arabian managers on a Friday.

A culturally diverse management team can be a source of strength for an organization participating in the global marketplace. Compared to organizations with culturally homogeneous management teams, organizations that employ managers from a variety of cultures have a better appreciation of how national cultures differ, and they tailor their management systems and behaviors to the differences.[48] Indeed, one advantage that many Western companies have over their Japanese competitors is greater willingness to create global teams composed of employees from different countries around the world who can draw on and share their different cultural experiences and knowledge to provide service that is customized to the needs of companies in different countries.

Summary and Review

LO6-1

WHAT IS THE GLOBAL ENVIRONMENT? The global environment is the set of forces and conditions that operate beyond an organization's boundaries but affect a manager's ability to acquire and use resources. The global environment has two components: the task environment and the general environment.

LO6-2, 6-3

THE TASK ENVIRONMENT The task environment is the set of forces and conditions that originate with global suppliers, distributors, customers, and competitors and influence managers daily. The opportunities and threats associated with forces in the task environment become more complex as a company expands globally.

LO6-2, 6-3 **THE GENERAL ENVIRONMENT** The general environment comprises wide-ranging global economic, technological, sociocultural, demographic, political, and legal forces that affect an organization and its task environment.

LO6-4, 6-5 **THE CHANGING GLOBAL ENVIRONMENT** In recent years there has been a marked shift toward a more open global environment in which capital flows more freely as people and companies search for new opportunities to create profit and wealth. This has hastened the process of globalization. Globalization is the set of specific and general forces that work together to integrate and connect economic, political, and social systems across countries, cultures, or geographic regions so that nations become increasingly interdependent and similar. The process of globalization has been furthered by declining barriers to international trade and investment and declining barriers of distance and culture.

Management in Action

Topics for Discussion and Action

Discussion

1. Why is it important for managers to understand the forces in the global environment that are acting on them and their organizations? **[LO6-1]**
2. Which organization is likely to face the most complex task environment—a biotechnology company trying to develop a cure for cancer or a large retailer like Carrefour? Why? **[LO6-2, 6-3]**
3. The population is aging because of declining birth rates, declining death rates, and the aging of the baby boom generation. What might some of the implications of this demographic trend be for (a) a pharmaceutical company and (b) the home construction industry? **[LO6-1, 6-2, 6-3]**
4. How do political, legal, and economic forces shape national culture? What characteristics of national culture do you think have the most important effect on how successful a country is in doing business abroad? **[LO6-3, 6-5]**
5. After the expansion of the EU to Poland many German companies shifted production operations to Poland to take advantage of lower labor costs and worker protection. As a result, they cut their costs and were better able to survive in an increasingly competitive global environment. Was their behavior ethical—that is, did the ends justify the means? **[LO6-4]**

Action

6. Choose an organization, and ask a manager in that organization to list the number and strengths of forces in the organization's task environment. Ask the manager to pay particular attention to identifying opportunities and threats that result from pressures and changes in customers, competitors, and suppliers. **[LO6-1, 6-2, 6-3]**

Building Management Skills

Analyzing an Organization's Environment [LO6-1, 6-2, 6-3]

Pick an organization with which you are familiar. It can be an organization in which you have worked or currently work or one that you interact with regularly as a customer (such as the college you are attending). For this organization do the following:

1. Describe the main forces in the global task environment that are affecting the organization.
2. Describe the main forces in the global general environment that are affecting the organization.
3. Explain how environmental forces affect the job of an individual manager within this organization. How do they determine the opportunities and threats that its managers must confront?

Managing Ethically [LO6-4, 6-5]

In recent years the number of European companies that buy their inputs from low-cost overseas suppliers has been growing, and concern about the ethics associated with employing young children in factories has been increasing. In Pakistan and India, children as young as six years old work long hours to make rugs and carpets for export to Western countries or clay bricks for local use. In countries like Malaysia and in Central America, children and teenagers routinely work long hours in factories and sweatshops to produce the clothing that is found in most European discount and department stores.

Questions

1. Either by yourself or in a group, discuss whether it is ethical to employ children in factories and whether European companies should buy and sell products made by these children. What are some arguments for and against child labor?
2. If child labor is an economic necessity, what methods could be employed to make it as ethical a practice as possible? Or is it simply unethical?

Small Group Breakout Exercise

How to Enter the Copying Business [LO6-1, 6-2]

Form groups of three to five people, and appoint one group member as the spokesperson who will communicate your findings to the whole class when called on by the instructor. Then discuss the following scenario:

You and your partners have decided to open a small printing and copying business. Your business will compete with companies like FedEx Kinko's. You know that over 50% of small businesses fail in their first year, so to increase your chances of success, you have decided to perform a detailed analysis of the task environment of the copying business to discover what opportunities and threats you will encounter.

1. Decide what you must know about (a) your future customers, (b) your future competitors, and (c) other critical forces in the task environment if you are to be successful.
2. Evaluate the main barriers to entry into the copying business.
3. Based on this analysis, list some steps you would take to help your new copying business succeed.

Exploring the World Wide Web [LO6-2, 6-3, 6-4]

Go to Fuji Films' Web site (www.fujifilm.com), click on "About Us," "History," and then "Corporate History," and consider how Fuji's global activities have expanded over time.

1. How would you characterize the way Fuji manages the global environment? For example, how has Fuji responded to the needs of customers in different countries?
2. How have increasing global competition and declining barriers of distance and culture affected Fuji's global operations?

Be the Manager [LO6-1, 6-2]

The Changing Environment of Retailing

You are the new manager of a major clothing store that is facing a crisis. This clothing store has been the leader in its market for the last 15 years. In the last three years, however, two other major clothing store chains have opened, and they have steadily been attracting customers away from your store—your sales are down 30%. To find out why, your store surveyed former customers and learned that they perceive your store as not keeping up with changing fashion trends and new forms of customer service. In examining how the store operates, you found out that the 10 purchasing managers who buy the clothing and accessories for the store have been buying from the same clothing suppliers and have become reluctant to try new ones. Moreover, salespeople rarely, if ever, make suggestions for changing how the store operates, and they don't respond to customer requests; the culture of the store has become conservative and risk-averse.

Questions

1. Analyze the major forces in the task environment of a retail clothing store.
2. Devise a program that will help other managers and employees to better understand and respond to their store's task environment.

CHAPTER 7

Decision Making, Learning, Creativity, and Entrepreneurship

Learning Objectives

After studying this chapter, you should be able to:

LO7-1 Understand the nature of managerial decision making, differentiate between programmed and nonprogrammed decisions, and explain why nonprogrammed decision making is a complex, uncertain process.

LO7-2 Describe the six steps managers should take to make the best decisions, and explain how cognitive biases can lead managers to make poor decisions.

LO7-3 Identify the advantages and disadvantages of group decision making, and describe techniques that can improve it.

LO7-4 Explain the role that organizational learning and creativity play in helping managers to improve their decisions.

LO7-5 Describe how managers can encourage and promote entrepreneurship to create a learning organization, and differentiate between entrepreneurs and intrapreneurs.

A MANAGER'S CHALLENGE

Decision Making in Response to Threats and Opportunities at PUMA

Why is decision making of paramount importance in organizations? When Jochen Zeitz took over as CEO of PUMA AG in 1993 at the age of 30, the company was facing major threats.[1] PUMA AG, based in the small German sneaker-producing town of Herzogenaurach,[2] had lost money for the past eight years, and PUMA North America was facing imminent bankruptcy. The company's cash levels were low, and it was no match for major industry leaders like Adidas (Adidas and PUMA were both founded in Herzogenaurach by two brothers who have long competed with each other), Reebok, and Nike.[3]

Facing tough decisions about how to turn around the company's fortunes, Zeitz decided that rather than trying to compete based on the performance capabilities of its athletic shoes and equipment, PUMA would focus more on style, colors, and lines of shoes. Essentially Zeitz saw a potential opportunity in trying to start up a new division focus on experimental fashion and sport as lifestyle.

Zeitz's bold decision to pursue the world of fashion and style contributed to PUMA becoming the major athletic apparel company it is today.[4] Recognizing the importance of creative designs and products, he decided to start a new division called "sport lifestyle"

The decisions CEO Jochen Zeitz has made at PUMA and the daily decisions he and other managers continue to make are key contributors to PUMA's success today.

led by Antonio Bertone, a then 21-year-old skateboarder.[5] The division was asked to create experimental fashion products. In 1998 Bertone partnered with German fashion designer Jil Sander to turn PUMA's traditional 1960s-style cleated soccer shoe into a trendy fashion sneaker using funky colors and suede. At first this experimental product line received a lot of skepticism from industry experts and retailers alike; famed soccer player Pelé had worn PUMA cleats, and it was unthinkable to many that PUMA would succeed in the world of fashion. As Zeitz indicates, "It took a while—and from my perspective, a lot of energy—to protect this new little child [the lifestyle group] of PUMA from getting killed. . . . Eventually, it became the entire company."[6]

Customers loved the retro look and edgy colors of the new sneakers, which are now sold in a variety of venues ranging from the Foot Locker to high-end stores like Barneys to upscale department stores. PUMA has its own showcase boutique in the meatpacking district of Manhattan and over 70 stores around the world.[7]

Zeitz continues to pursue new opportunities at PUMA—reinventing traditional products to combine performance with style—and continues to partner with creative thinkers such as Xuly Bet, born in Mali and now a Paris fashion designer, and Yasuhiro Mihara of Japan to create new products.[8] Designers Philippe Starck and Alexander McQueen both created product lines for PUMA. PUMA partnered with the BMW Mini to make a new driving shoe; and PUMA's Mostro shoe continues to be a top seller.[9]

Former skateboarder Bertone is now based in Boston as PUMA's global director of brand management. Now a top manager, Bertone continues to make decisions to seize opportunities for creative and innovative product lines such as the limited-edition line called Thrift (products made from vintage clothing) and Mongolian Shoe BBQ (shoes that can be customized online).

Overview

The "Manager's Challenge" illustrates how decision making can have a profound influence on organizational effectiveness. The decisions managers make at all levels in companies large and small can have a dramatic impact on the growth and prosperity of these companies and the well-being of their employees, customers, and other stakeholders. Yet such decisions can be difficult to make because they are fraught with uncertainty.

LO7-1 Understand the nature of managerial decision making, differentiate between programmed and nonprogrammed decisions, and explain why nonprogrammed decision making is a complex, uncertain process.

In this chapter we examine how managers make decisions, and we explore how individual, group, and organizational factors affect the quality of the decisions they make and ultimately determine organizational performance. We discuss the nature of managerial decision making and examine some models of the decision-making process that help reveal the complexities of successful decision making. Then we outline the main steps of the decision-making process; in addition, we explore the biases that may cause capable managers to make poor decisions both as individuals and as members of a group. Next we examine how managers can promote organizational learning and creativity and improve the quality of decision making throughout an organization. Finally we discuss the important role of entrepreneurship in promoting organizational creativity, and we differentiate between entrepreneurs and intrapreneurs. By the end of this chapter you will appreciate the critical role of management decision making in creating a high-performing organization.

The Nature of Managerial Decision Making

Every time managers act to plan, organize, direct, or control organizational activities, they make a stream of decisions. In opening a new restaurant, for example, managers have to decide where to locate it, what kinds of food to provide, which people to employ, and so on. Decision making is a basic part of every task managers perform. In this chapter we study how these decisions are made.

As we discussed in the last three chapters, one of the main tasks facing a manager is to manage the organizational environment. Forces in the external environment give rise to many opportunities and threats for managers and their organizations. In addition, inside an organization managers must address many opportunities and threats that may arise as organizational resources are used. To deal with these opportunities and threats, managers must make decisions–that is, they must select one solution from a set of alternatives. **Decision making** is the process by which managers respond to opportunities and threats by analyzing the options and making determinations, or *decisions,* about specific organizational goals and courses of action. Good decisions result in the selection of appropriate goals and courses of action that increase organizational performance; bad decisions lower performance.

decision making The process by which managers respond to opportunities and threats by analyzing options and making determinations about specific organizational goals and courses of action.

Decision making in response to opportunities occurs when managers search for ways to improve organizational performance to benefit customers, employees, and other stakeholder groups. In "A Manager's Challenge," Jochen Zeitz turned around PUMA's fortunes by the decisions he made in response to opportunities. *Decision making in response to threats* occurs when events inside or outside the organization adversely affect organizational performance and managers search for ways to increase performance.[10] When Zeitz become CEO of PUMA, high production costs and an ineffective distribution system were threats that prompted Zeitz to make a number of decisions to improve the performance and viability of the company.[11] Decision making is central to being a manager, and whenever managers engage in planning, organizing, leading, and controlling–their four principal tasks–they are constantly making decisions.

Managers are always searching for ways to make better decisions to improve organizational performance. At the same time they do their best to avoid costly mistakes that will hurt organizational performance.

Programmed and Nonprogrammed Decision Making

Regardless of the specific decisions a manager makes, the decision-making process is either programmed or nonprogrammed.[12]

PROGRAMMED DECISION MAKING **Programmed decision making** is a *routine,* virtually automatic process. Programmed decisions are decisions that have been made so many times in the past that managers have developed rules or guidelines to be applied when certain situations inevitably occur. Programmed decision making takes place when a school principal asks the school board to hire a new teacher whenever student enrollment increases by 40 students; when a manufacturing supervisor hires new workers whenever existing workers' overtime increases by more than 10%; and when an office manager orders basic office supplies, such as paper and pens, whenever the inventory of supplies drops below a certain level. Furthermore, in the last example, the office manager probably orders the same amount of supplies each time.

programmed decision making Routine, virtually automatic decision making that follows established rules or guidelines.

This decision making is called *programmed* because office managers, for example, do not need to repeatedly make new judgments about what should be done. They can rely on long-established decision rules such as these:

- *Rule 1:* When the storage shelves are three-quarters empty, order more copy paper.
- *Rule 2:* When ordering paper, order enough to fill the shelves.

Managers can develop rules and guidelines to regulate all routine organizational activities. For example, rules can specify how a worker should perform a certain task,

Programmed decisions allow warehouse supervisors such as this one to develop simple rubrics so the job is done consistently and with less error.

and rules can specify the quality standards that raw materials must meet to be acceptable. Most decision making that relates to the day-to-day running of an organization is programmed decision making. Examples include deciding how much inventory to hold, when to pay bills, when to bill customers, and when to order materials and supplies. Programmed decision making occurs when managers have the information they need to create rules that will guide decision making. There is little ambiguity involved in assessing when the stockroom is empty or counting the number of new students in class.

NONPROGRAMMED DECISION MAKING Suppose, however, managers are not certain that a course of action will lead to a desired outcome. Or in even more ambiguous terms, suppose managers are not even sure what they are trying to achieve. Obviously rules cannot be developed to predict uncertain events.

nonprogrammed decision making Nonroutine decision making that occurs in response to unusual, unpredictable opportunities and threats.

Nonprogrammed decision making is required for these *nonroutine* decisions. Nonprogrammed decisions are made in response to unusual or novel opportunities and threats. Nonprogrammed decision making occurs when there are no ready-made decision rules that managers can apply to a situation. Rules do not exist because the situation is unexpected or uncertain and managers lack the information they would need to develop rules to cover it. Examples of nonprogrammed decision making include decisions to invest in a new technology, develop a new kind of product, as Jochen Zeitz did in "A Manager's Challenge," launch a new promotional campaign, enter a new market, expand internationally, or start a new business.

intuition Feelings, beliefs, and hunches that come readily to mind, require little effort and information gathering, and result in on-the-spot decisions.

reasoned judgment A decision that requires time and effort and results from careful information gathering, generation of alternatives, and evaluation of alternatives.

How do managers make decisions in the absence of decision rules? They may rely on their **intuition**–feelings, beliefs, and hunches that come readily to mind, require little effort and information gathering, and result in on-the-spot decisions.[13] Or they may make **reasoned judgments**–decisions that require time and effort and result from careful information gathering, generation of alternatives, and evaluation of alternatives. "Exercising" one's judgment is a more rational process than "going with" one's intuition. For reasons that we examine later in this chapter, both intuition and judgment often are flawed and can result in poor decision making. Thus the likelihood of error is much greater in nonprogrammed decision making than in programmed decision making.[14] In the remainder of this chapter, when we talk about decision making, we are referring to *nonprogrammed* decision making because it causes the most problems for managers and is inherently challenging.

Sometimes managers have to make rapid decisions and don't have time to carefully consider the issues involved. They must rely on their intuition to quickly respond to a pressing concern. For example, when fire chiefs, captains, and lieutenants manage firefighters battling dangerous, out-of-control fires, they often need to rely on their expert intuition to make on-the-spot decisions that will protect the lives of the firefighters and save the lives of others, contain the fires, and preserve property–decisions made in emergency situations entailing high uncertainty, high risk, and rapidly changing conditions.[15] In other cases managers do have time to make reasoned judgments, but there are no established rules to guide their decisions, such as when deciding whether to proceed with a proposed merger.

Regardless of the circumstances, making nonprogrammed decisions can result in effective or ineffective decision making. As indicated in the "Manager as a Person" box on the next page, managers have to be on their guard to avoid being overconfident in decisions that result from either intuition or reasoned judgment.

The classical and administrative decision-making models reveal many of the assumptions, complexities, and pitfalls that affect decision making. These models help reveal the factors that managers and other decision makers must be aware of to improve the quality of their decision making. Keep in mind, however, that the

Manager as a Person

Curbing Overconfidence

Should managers be confident in their intuition and reasoned judgments?[16] Decades of research by Nobel Prize winner Daniel Kahneman, his longtime collaborator the late Amos Tversy, and other researchers suggests that managers (like all people) tend to be overconfident in the decisions they make, whether based on intuition or reasoned judgment. And with overconfidence comes failure to evaluate and rethink the wisdom of the decisions one makes and failure to learn from mistakes.[17]

Kahneman distinguishes between the intuition of managers who are truly expert in the content domain of a decision and the intuition of managers who have some knowledge and experience but are not true experts.[18] Although the intuition of both types can be faulty, that of experts is less likely to be flawed. This is why fire captains can make good decisions and why expert chess players can make good moves, in both cases without spending much time or deliberating carefully on what, for nonexperts, is a complicated set of circumstances. What distinguishes expert managers from those with limited expertise is that the experts have extensive experience under conditions in which they receive quick and clear feedback about the outcomes of their decisions.[19]

Unfortunately managers who have some experience in a content area but are not true experts tend to be overly confident in their intuition and their judgments.[20] As Kahneman puts it, "People jump to statistical conclusions on the basis of very weak evidence. We form powerful intuitions about trends and about the replicability of results on the basis of information that is truly inadequate."[21] Not only do managers, and all people, tend to be overconfident about their intuition and judgments, but they also tend not to learn from mistakes. Compounding this undue optimism is the human tendency to be overconfident in one's own abilities and influence over unpredictable events. Surveys have found that the majority of people think they are above average, make better decisions, and are less prone to making bad decisions than others (of course it is impossible for most people to be above average on any dimension).[22]

Examples of managerial overconfidence abound. Research has consistently found that mergers tend to turn out poorly–postmerger profitability declines, stock prices drop, and so forth. For example, Chrysler had the biggest profits of the three largest automakers in the United States when it merged with Daimler; the merger was a failure, and both Chrysler and Daimler would have been better off if it never had happened.[23] So one would imagine that top executives and boards of directors would learn from this research and from articles in the business press about the woes of merged companies (such as the AOL–Time Warner merger).[24] Evidently not. According to a recent study by Hewitt Associates, top executives and board members are, if anything, planning to increase their involvement in mergers over the next few years. These top managers seem to overconfidently believe that they can succeed where others have failed.[25]

Jeffrey Pfeffer, a professor at Stanford University's Graduate School of Business, suggests that managers can avoid the perils of overconfidence by critically evaluating the decisions they have made and the outcomes of those decisions. They should admit to themselves when they have made a mistake and really learn from their mistakes (rather than dismissing them as flukes or situations out of their control). In addition, managers should be leery of too much agreement at the top. As Pfeffer puts it, "If two people agree all the time, one of them is redundant."[26]

classical and administrative models are just guides that can help managers understand the decision-making process. In real life the process is typically not cut-and-dried, but these models can help guide a manager through it.

The Classical Model

classical decision-making model A prescriptive approach to decision making based on the assumption that the decision maker can identify and evaluate all possible alternatives and their consequences and rationally choose the most appropriate course of action.

optimum decision The most appropriate decision in light of what managers believe to be the most desirable consequences for the organization.

One of the earliest models of decision making, the **classical model,** is *prescriptive,* which means it specifies how decisions *should* be made. Managers using the classical model make a series of simplifying assumptions about the nature of the decision-making process (see Figure 7.1). The premise of the classical model is that once managers recognize the need to make a decision, they should be able to generate a complete list of *all* alternatives and consequences and make the best choice. In other words, the classical model assumes managers have access to *all* the information they need to make the **optimum decision,** which is the most appropriate decision possible in light of what they believe to be the most desirable consequences for the organization. Furthermore, the classical model assumes managers can easily list their own preferences for each alternative and rank them from least to most preferred to make the optimum decision.

The Administrative Model

administrative model An approach to decision making that explains why decision making is inherently uncertain and risky and why managers usually make satisfactory rather than optimum decisions.

James March and Herbert Simon disagreed with the underlying assumptions of the classical model of decision making. In contrast, they proposed that managers in the real world do *not* have access to all the information they need to make a decision. Moreover, they pointed out that even if all information were readily available, many managers would lack the mental or psychological ability to absorb and evaluate it correctly. As a result, March and Simon developed the **administrative model** of decision making to explain why decision making is always an inherently uncertain and risky process–and why managers can rarely make decisions in the manner prescribed by the classical model. The administrative model is based on three important concepts: *bounded rationality, incomplete information,* and *satisficing.*

BOUNDED RATIONALITY March and Simon pointed out that human decision-making capabilities are bounded by people's cognitive limitations–that is, limitations in their ability to interpret, process, and act on information.[27] They argued that the limitations of human intelligence constrain the ability of decision makers to determine

Figure 7.1
The Classical Model of Decision Making

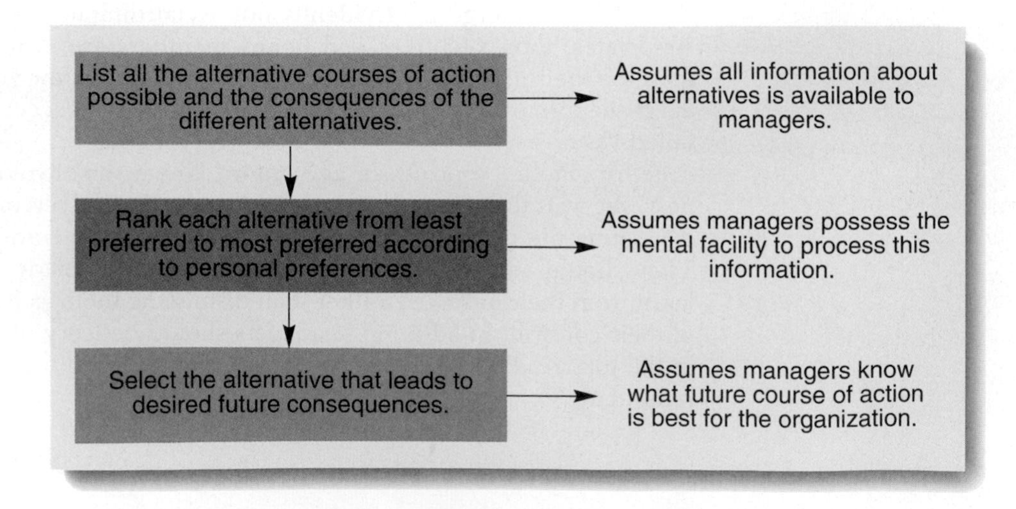

bounded rationality Cognitive limitations that constrain one's ability to interpret, process, and act on information.

the optimum decision. March and Simon coined the term **bounded rationality** to describe the situation in which the number of alternatives a manager must identify is so great and the amount of information so vast that it is difficult for the manager to even come close to evaluating it all before making a decision.[28]

INCOMPLETE INFORMATION Even if managers had unlimited ability to evaluate information, they still would not be able to arrive at the optimum decision because they would have incomplete information. Information is incomplete because the full range of decision-making alternatives is unknowable in most situations, and the consequences associated with known alternatives are uncertain.[29] In other words, information is incomplete because of risk and uncertainty, ambiguity, and time constraints (see Figure 7.2).

risk The degree of probability that the possible outcomes of a particular course of action will occur.

uncertainty Unpredictability.

RISK AND UNCERTAINTY As we saw in Chapter 6, forces in the organizational environment are constantly changing. **Risk** is present when managers know the possible outcomes of a particular course of action and can assign probabilities to them. For example, managers in the biotechnology industry know that new drugs have a 10% probability of successfully passing advanced clinical trials and a 90% probability of failing. These probabilities reflect the experiences of thousands of drugs that have gone through advanced clinical trials. Thus when managers in the biotechnology industry decide to submit a drug for testing, they know that there is only a 10% chance that the drug will succeed, but at least they have some information on which to base their decision.

When **uncertainty** exists, the probabilities of alternative outcomes *cannot* be determined and future outcomes are *unknown*. Managers are working blind. Because the probability of a given outcome occurring is not known, managers have little information to use in making a decision. For example, in 1993, when Apple Computer introduced the Newton, its personal digital assistant (PDA), managers had no idea what the probability of a successful product launch for a PDA might be. Because Apple was the first to market this totally new product, there was no body of well-known data that Apple's managers could draw on to calculate the probability of a successful launch. Uncertainty plagues most managerial decision making.[30] Although Apple's initial launch of its PDA was a disaster due to technical problems, an improved version was more successful. In fact, Apple created the PDA market that has boomed during the 2000s as new and different wireless products have been introduced.

Decision making in parts of Europe can be more complex than in either Asia or North America. All regions require that firms report large amounts of data on their environmental activities. However, there are now requirements in Denmark, France,

Figure 7.2
Why Information Is Incomplete

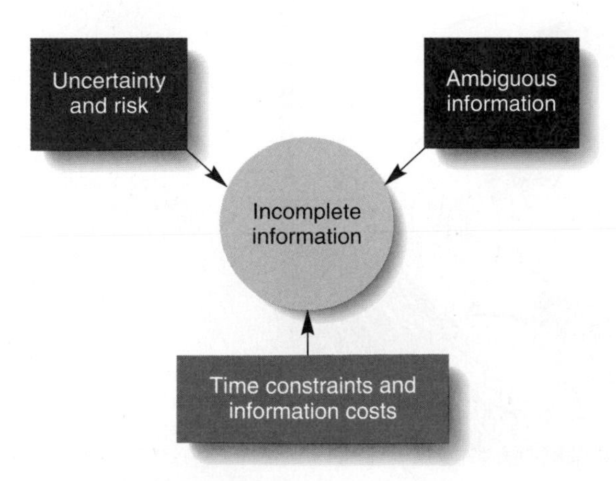

and Sweden that firms report on their impact on sustainability. This requirement may soon be adopted by the United Kingdom. This reporting requires that firms tell about their impact on the environment. Particularly, they have to report on their carbon footprint. A carbon footprint is the amount of carbon that went into producing a given product. Thus, the decision making is not simply about the economics of the project or product but also what the environmental impact of that decision is. Thus, consider a product like Danish cheese. The product may be sold profitably in a region far from Europe, such as the Middle East. The purely economic rationale may push a firm, therefore, to sell the product in the Middle East. However, the product most likely will have to be flown to the Middle East, which has a major negative environmental impact as it generates large amounts of greenhouse gases. Therefore, a firm would have two decisions–whether it will make a profit and whether the activity negatively impacts the environment. The firm may still decide to sell the cheese, but it will need to consider the environment and address this impact in its reporting.

The model for most such reporting is the Global Reporting Initiative (GRI). This organization has developed the world's most widely used sustainability reporting framework. This framework is developed by interested firms and other parties joining together to develop methods relevant to both business and the broader community. There are more than 1000 major firms that now also follow these guidelines voluntarily. The environmental reporting requires a firm to provide information on issues like energy consumed, energy saved due to conservation, percentage of recycled materials employed, water used in processes, habitats disturbed, and greenhouse gases emitted, among other issues. It should also be noted that the GRI includes reporting not only on environmental issues but also in other domains such as labor relations.

The issue also involves the potential taxation of companies emitting pollution. European nations appear ready to tax pollution emitted. Such taxes will be tied to the amount of pollution emitted with each unit of pollution taxed at a given level. The requirement of environmental reporting and taxation are not prevalent in North America or Asia. Managers in these regions are often environmentally concerned; however, they have more flexibility in decision making since they do not have formal requirements on such issues to fulfill, as of today.

ambiguous information Information that can be interpreted in multiple and often conflicting ways.

AMBIGUOUS INFORMATION A second reason why information is incomplete is that much of the information managers have at their disposal is **ambiguous information.** Its meaning is not clear–it can be interpreted in multiple and often conflicting ways.[31] Take a look at Figure 7.3. Do you see a young woman or an old

Figure 7.3
Ambiguous Information: Young Woman or Old Woman?

woman? In a similar fashion, managers often interpret the same piece of information differently and make decisions based on their own interpretations.

TIME CONSTRAINTS AND INFORMATION COSTS The third reason why information is incomplete is that managers have neither the time nor the money to search for all possible alternative solutions and evaluate all the potential consequences of those alternatives. Consider the situation confronting a Ford Motor Company purchasing manager who has one month to choose a supplier for a small engine part. There are over 100,000 potential suppliers worldwide for this part. Given the time available, the purchasing manager cannot contact all potential suppliers and ask each for its terms (price, delivery schedules, and so on). Moreover, even if the time were available, the costs of obtaining the information, including the manager's own time, would be prohibitive.

SATISFICING March and Simon argued that managers do not attempt to discover every alternative when faced with bounded rationality, an uncertain future, unquantifiable risks, considerable ambiguity, time constraints, and high information costs. Rather, they use a strategy known as **satisficing,** which is exploring a limited sample of all potential alternatives.[32] When managers satisfice, they search for and choose acceptable, or satisfactory, ways to respond to problems and opportunities rather than trying to make the optimal decision.[33] In the case of the Ford purchasing manager's search, for example, satisficing may involve asking a limited number of suppliers for their terms, trusting that they are representative of suppliers in general, and making a choice from that set. Although this course of action is reasonable from the perspective of the purchasing manager, it may mean that a potentially superior supplier is overlooked.

satisficing Searching for and choosing an acceptable, or satisfactory, response to problems and opportunities, rather than trying to make the best decision.

March and Simon pointed out that managerial decision making is often more art than science. In the real world, managers must rely on their intuition and judgment to make what seems to them to be the best decision in the face of uncertainty and ambiguity.[34] Moreover, managerial decision making is often fast-paced; managers use their experience and judgment to make crucial decisions under conditions of incomplete information. Although there is nothing wrong with this approach, decision makers should be aware that human judgment is often flawed. As a result, even the best managers sometimes make poor decisions.[35]

Steps in the Decision-Making Process

Using the work of March and Simon as a basis, researchers have developed a step-by-step model of the decision-making process and the issues and problems that managers confront at each step. Perhaps the best way to introduce this model is to examine the real-world nonprogrammed decision making of Scott McNealy at a crucial point in Sun Microsystems' history. McNealy was a founder of Sun Microsystems and was the chairman of the board of directors until Sun was acquired by Oracle in 2010.[36]

LO7-2 Describe the six steps managers should take to make the best decisions, and explain how cognitive biases can lead managers to make poor decisions.

In early August 1985, Scott McNealy, then CEO of Sun Microsystems[37] (a hardware and software computer workstation manufacturer focused on network solutions), had to decide whether to go ahead with the launch of the new Carrera workstation computer, scheduled for September 10. Sun's managers had chosen the date nine months earlier when the development plan for the Carrera was first proposed. McNealy knew it would take at least a month to prepare for the September 10 launch, and the decision could not be put off.

Customers were waiting for the new machine, and McNealy wanted to be the first to provide a workstation that took advantage of Motorola's powerful 16-megahertz 68020 microprocessor. Capitalizing on this opportunity would give Sun a significant edge over Apollo, its main competitor in the workstation market. McNealy knew, however, that committing to the September 10 launch date was risky. Motorola was having production problems with the 16-megahertz 68020 microprocessor and could not guarantee Sun a steady supply of these chips. Moreover, the operating system software was not completely free of bugs.

If Sun launched the Carrera on September 10, the company might have to ship some machines with software that was not fully operational, was likely to crash the system, and utilized Motorola's less powerful 12-megahertz 68020 microprocessor instead of the 16-megahertz version.[38] Of course Sun could later upgrade the microprocessor and operating system software in any machines purchased by early customers, but the company's reputation would suffer. If Sun did not go ahead with the September launch, the company would miss an important opportunity.[39] Rumors were circulating in the industry that Apollo would be launching a new machine of its own in December.

McNealy clearly had a difficult decision to make. He had to decide quickly whether to launch the Carrera, but he did not have all the facts. He did not know, for example, whether the microprocessor or operating system problems could be resolved by September 10; nor did he know whether Apollo was going to launch a competing machine in December. But he could not wait to find these things out–he had to make a decision. We'll see what he decided later in the chapter.

Many managers who must make important decisions with incomplete information face dilemmas similar to McNealy's. Managers should consciously follow six steps to make a good decision (see Figure 7.4).[40] We review these steps in the remainder of this section.

Recognize the Need for a Decision

The first step in the decision-making process is to recognize the need for a decision. Scott McNealy recognized this need, and he realized a decision had to be made quickly.

Some stimuli usually spark the realization that a decision must be made. These stimuli often become apparent because changes in the organizational environment result in new kinds of opportunities and threats. This happened at Sun Microsystems. The September 10 launch date had been set when it seemed that Motorola chips would be readily available. Later, with the supply of chips in doubt and bugs remaining in the system software, Sun was in danger of failing to meet its launch date.

The stimuli that spark decision making are as likely to result from the actions of managers inside an organization as they are from changes in the external environment.[41] An organization possesses a set of skills, competencies, and resources in its

Figure 7.4
Six Steps in Decision Making

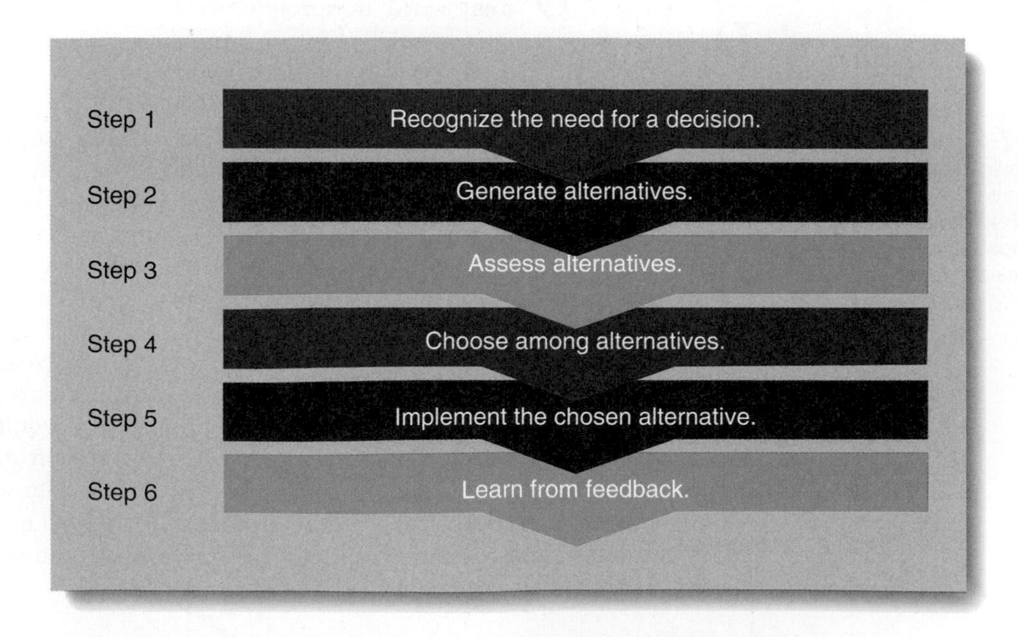

employees and in departments such as marketing, manufacturing, and research and development. Managers who actively pursue opportunities to use these competencies create the need to make decisions. Managers thus can be proactive or reactive in recognizing the need to make a decision, but the important issue is that they must recognize this need and respond in a timely and appropriate way.[42]

Generate Alternatives

Having recognized the need to make a decision, a manager must generate a set of feasible alternative courses of action to take in response to the opportunity or threat. Management experts cite failure to properly generate and consider different alternatives as one reason why managers sometimes make bad decisions.[43] In the Sun Microsystems decision, the alternatives seemed clear: to go ahead with the September 10 launch or to delay the launch until the Carrera was 100% ready for market introduction. Often, however, the alternatives are not so obvious or so clearly specified.

One major problem is that managers may find it difficult to come up with creative alternative solutions to specific problems. Perhaps some of them are used to seeing the world from a single perspective–they have a certain "managerial mind-set." Many managers find it difficult to view problems from a fresh perspective. According to best-selling management author Peter Senge, we all are trapped within our personal mental models of the world–our ideas about what is important and how the world works.[44] Generating creative alternatives to solve problems and take advantage of opportunities may require that we abandon our existing mind-sets and develop new ones–something that usually is difficult to do.

The importance of getting managers to set aside their mental models of the world and generate creative alternatives is reflected in the growth of interest in the work of authors such as Peter Senge and Edward de Bono, who have popularized techniques for stimulating problem solving and creative thinking among managers.[45] Later in this chapter, we discuss the important issues of organizational learning and creativity in detail.

Assess Alternatives

Once managers have generated a set of alternatives, they must evaluate the advantages and disadvantages of each one.[46] The key to a good assessment of the alternatives is to define the opportunity or threat exactly and then specify the criteria that *should* influence the selection of alternatives for responding to the problem or opportunity. One reason for bad decisions is that managers often fail to specify the criteria that are important in reaching a decision.[47] In general, successful managers use four criteria to evaluate the pros and cons of alternative courses of action (see Figure 7.5):

1. *Legality:* Managers must ensure that a possible course of action will not violate any domestic or international laws or government regulations.
2. *Ethicalness:* Managers must ensure that a possible course of action is ethical and will not unnecessarily harm any stakeholder group. Many decisions managers make may help some organizational stakeholders and harm others (see Chapter 4). When examining alternative courses of action, managers need to be clear about the potential effects of their decisions.
3. *Economic feasibility:* Managers must decide whether the alternatives are economically feasible–that is, whether they can be accomplished given the organization's performance goals. Typically managers perform a cost–benefit analysis of the various alternatives to determine which one will have the best net financial payoff.
4. *Practicality:* Managers must decide whether they have the capabilities and resources required to implement the alternative, and they must be sure the alternative will not threaten the attainment of other organizational goals. At first glance an alternative might seem economically superior to other alternatives; but if managers realize it is likely to threaten other important projects, they might decide it is not practical after all.

Figure 7.5
General Criteria for Evaluating Possible Courses of Action

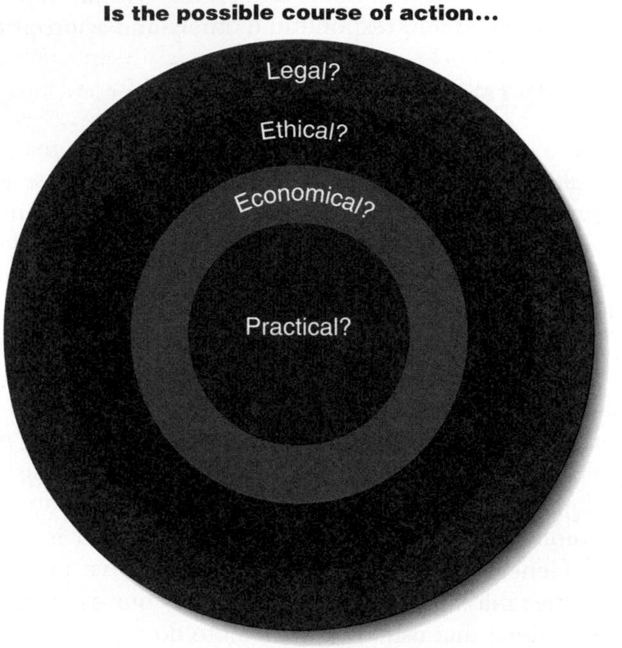

Is the possible course of action...

Legal?
Ethical?
Economical?
Practical?

Often a manager must consider these four criteria simultaneously. Scott McNealy framed the problem at hand at Sun Microsystems quite well. The key question was whether to go ahead with the September 10 launch date. Two main criteria were influencing McNealy's choice: the need to ship a machine that was as "complete" as possible (the *practicality* criterion) and the need to beat Apollo to market with a new workstation (the *economic feasibility* criterion). These two criteria conflicted. The first suggested that the launch should be delayed; the second, that the launch should go ahead. McNealy's actual choice was based on the relative importance that he assigned to these two criteria. In fact, Sun Microsystems went ahead with the September 10 launch, which suggests that McNealy thought the need to beat Apollo to market was the more important criterion.

Choose among Alternatives

Once the set of alternative solutions has been carefully evaluated, the next task is to rank the various alternatives (using the criteria discussed in the previous section) and make a decision. When ranking alternatives, managers must be sure *all* the information available is brought to bear on the problem or issue at hand. As the Sun Microsystems case indicates, however, identifying all *relevant* information for a decision does not mean the manager has *complete* information; in most instances, information is incomplete.

Perhaps more serious than the existence of incomplete information is the often-documented tendency of managers to ignore critical information, even when it is available. We discuss this tendency in detail later when we examine the operation of cognitive biases and groupthink.

Implement the Chosen Alternative

Once a decision has been made and an alternative has been selected, it must be implemented, and many subsequent and related decisions must be made. After a course of action has been decided–say, to develop a new line of women's clothing–thousands of subsequent decisions are necessary to implement it. These decisions would involve recruiting dress designers, obtaining fabrics, finding high-quality manufacturers, and signing contracts with clothing stores to sell the new line.

Although the need to make subsequent decisions to implement the chosen course of action may seem obvious, many managers make a decision and then fail to act on it. This is the same as not making a decision at all. To ensure that a decision is implemented, top managers must assign to middle managers the responsibility for making the follow-up decisions necessary to achieve the goal. They must give middle managers sufficient resources to achieve the goal, and they must hold the middle managers accountable for their performance. If the middle managers succeed in implementing the decision, they should be rewarded; if they fail, they should be subject to sanctions.

Learn from Feedback

The final step in the decision-making process is learning from feedback. Effective managers always conduct a retrospective analysis to see what they can learn from past successes or failures. Managers who do not evaluate the results of their decisions do not learn from experience; instead they stagnate and are likely to make the same mistakes again and again.[48] To avoid this problem, managers must establish a formal procedure with which they can learn from the results of past decisions. The procedure should include these steps:

1. Compare what actually happened to what was expected to happen as a result of the decision.
2. Explore why any expectations for the decision were not met.
3. Derive guidelines that will help in future decision making.

Managers who always strive to learn from past mistakes and successes are likely to continuously improve the decisions they make. A significant amount of learning can take place when the outcomes of decisions are evaluated, and this assessment can produce enormous benefits. As the following "Management Insight" box describes, decision making in Japanese firms is typically a group process, which can take too much time and cause problems, as Toyota found out in early 2010.

Management Insight

Decision Making in Japan

Historically decision making in Japan has been a group process. Rather than a top-down approach that dominates Western culture, decision making in Japan typically occurs by consensus. Japan is a group culture in which being part of the group is seen as critical. Thus, if you walk down a street in Tokyo during work hours you will notice that almost all the office workers you pass are dressed in similar attire. They wear dark suits that appear almost as a uniform. This is one way of behaving as a part of a group (the group of office workers). Typically, individuals will introduce themselves not only by name but also by the name of the firm in which they work. Thus, they say "I am Mr. or Ms. X of Toyota." The result of this cultural orientation is that decision making in a Japanese corporation will seek to reach consensus among all the critical parties.

The manner in which this consensus is reached is called *nemawashi.* This term refers to the informal process of gathering support and feedback as individuals start to make an important decision. The term itself translates as "going around the roots." The concept is that workers have to lay the groundwork in order to build a consensus decision. The result of such decision making is that there is great commitment to the decision once it is made. However, arriving at a decision takes a great deal of time. In today's rapidly changing environment, such slow and painstaking decision making can be detrimental.

To illustrate the potential drawbacks of such a decision-making process, consider the response of Toyota to the recent problems with unintended acceleration in their cars. The problems became identified in January 2010. The firm's response was slow and highly criticized. For example, it took two weeks for the CEO of Toyota, the grandson of the firm's founder, to respond to the problems publicly. In Japan it is uncommon for firms to be attacked for quality problems. Thus, when the questions began to arise it was a new experience for a firm with a strong safety record. The consensus decision making required that lower level employees not bring these problems to the firm's leadership. Instead, in a consensus process the questions needed to rise up through the organization. Thus, it is not surprising that top management was probably unaware of the problems until they had festered for several weeks. Even when Toyota did make a response it was seen as weak. Again, a consensus process makes strong decisive action difficult for a firm like Toyota. Over time Toyota developed a strong response to the problems of unintended acceleration. However, the consensus method of decision making, while building strong support for the final decision, had made the firm's response slow and caused serious damage to the brand.[49]

Cognitive Biases and Decision Making

In the 1970s psychologists Daniel Kahneman and Amos Tversky suggested that because all decision makers are subject to bounded rationality, they tend to use **heuristics,** which are rules of thumb that simplify the process of making decisions.[50] Kahneman and Tversky argued that rules of thumb are often useful because they help decision makers make sense of complex, uncertain, and ambiguous information. Sometimes, however, the use of heuristics can lead to systematic errors in the way decision makers process information about alternatives and make decisions. **Systematic errors** are errors that people make over and over and that result in poor decision making. Because of cognitive biases, which are caused by systematic errors, otherwise capable managers may end up making bad decisions.[51] Four sources of bias that can adversely affect the way managers make decisions are prior hypotheses, representativeness, the illusion of control, and escalating commitment (see Figure 7.6).

heuristics Rules of thumb that simplify decision making.

systematic errors Errors that people make over and over and that result in poor decision making.

Prior-Hypothesis Bias

prior-hypothesis bias A cognitive bias resulting from the tendency to base decisions on strong prior beliefs even if evidence shows that those beliefs are wrong.

Decision makers who have strong prior beliefs about the relationship between two variables tend to make decisions based on those beliefs *even when presented with evidence that their beliefs are wrong.* In doing so, they fall victim to **prior-hypothesis bias.** Moreover, decision makers tend to seek and use information that is consistent with their prior beliefs and to ignore information that contradicts those beliefs.

Figure 7.6
Sources of Cognitive Bias at the Individual and Group Levels

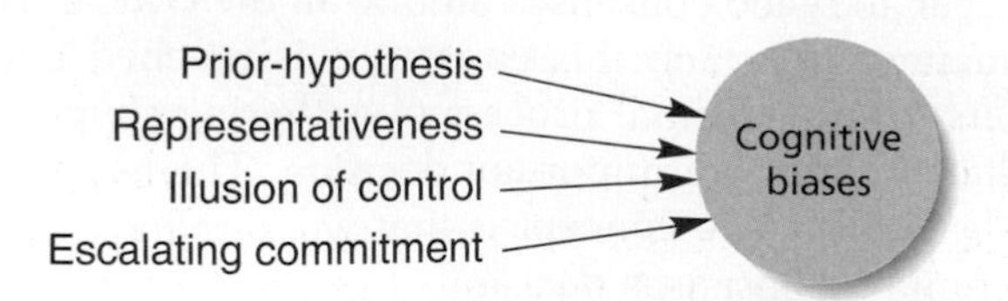

Representativeness Bias

representativeness bias A cognitive bias resulting from the tendency to generalize inappropriately from a small sample or from a single vivid event or episode.

Many decision makers inappropriately generalize from a small sample or even from a single vivid case or episode; these are instances of the **representativeness bias.** Consider the case of a bookstore manager in the southeast United States who decided to partner with a local independent school for a "Book Day": Students and parents from the school would be encouraged to buy books at the bookstore as a fund-raiser for the school, and the bookstore would share a small portion of proceeds from these sales with the school. After quite a bit of planning, the Book Day generated lackluster sales and publicity for the store. When other public and independent schools approached the manager with similar proposals for fund-raising and Book Days, the manager declined based on her initial bad experience. As a result, she lost real opportunities to expand sales and gain word-of-mouth advertising and publicity for her store; her initial bad experience was the result of an inadvertent scheduling snafu at the school, whereby a key rugby game was scheduled the same day as the Book Day.

Illusion of Control

illusion of control A source of cognitive bias resulting from the tendency to overestimate one's own ability to control activities and events.

Other errors in decision making result from the **illusion of control,** which is the tendency of decision makers to overestimate their ability to control activities and events. Top managers seem particularly prone to this bias. Having worked their way to the top of an organization, they tend to have an exaggerated sense of their own worth and are overconfident about their ability to succeed and to control events.[52] The illusion of control causes managers to overestimate the odds of a favorable outcome and, consequently, to make inappropriate decisions. As mentioned earlier, most mergers turn out unfavorably; yet time and time again, top managers overestimate their abilities to combine companies with vastly different cultures in a successful merger.[53]

Escalating Commitment

escalating commitment A source of cognitive bias resulting from the tendency to commit additional resources to a project even if evidence shows that the project is failing.

Having already committed significant resources to a course of action, some managers commit more resources to the project *even if they receive feedback that the project is failing.*[54] Feelings of personal responsibility for a project apparently bias the analysis of decision makers and lead to this **escalating commitment.** The managers decide to increase their investment of time and money in a course of action and even ignore evidence that it is illegal, unethical, uneconomical, or impractical (see Figure 7.5). Often the more appropriate decision would be to cut their losses and run.

An example of escalating commitment was Sony's development of the Betamax. The video recording system was a direct competitor to VHS. The Betamax system was released in 1975 and became the industry leader in this field. However, it would ultimately be replaced by VHS technology. Sony had been given the opportunity to join with JVC and Matsushita to promote the VHS technology. It is common in Japan for firms to cooperate in many technology areas such as this under guidance of the Japanese Ministry of Trade and Industry. However, Sony felt it had made too much commitment and refused to compromise. This commitment to Betamax continued to grow as price wars between firms supporting the VHS technology competed against Sony with a higher priced and higher quality product. Ultimately after significant losses, Sony introduced its own VCR player–the technology that evolved from VHS. However, Sony continued to manufacture the Betamax; as a matter of fact, the last Betamax was produced in 2002.

Be Aware of Your Biases

How can managers avoid the negative effects of cognitive biases and improve their decision-making and problem-solving abilities? Managers must become aware of biases and their effects, and they must identify their own personal style of making decisions.[55] One useful way for managers to analyze their decision-making style is to review two decisions that they made recently–one decision that turned out well and one that turned out poorly. Problem-solving experts recommend that managers start by determining how much time to spend on each of the decision-making steps, such as gathering information to identify the pros and cons of alternatives or ranking the alternatives, to make sure they spend sufficient time on each step.[56]

Another recommended technique for examining decision-making style is for managers to list the criteria they typically use to assess and evaluate alternatives–the heuristics (rules of thumb) they typically employ, their personal biases, and so on–and then critically evaluate the appropriateness of these different factors.

Many individual managers are likely to have difficulty identifying their own biases, so it is often advisable for managers to scrutinize their own assumptions by working with other managers to help expose weaknesses in their decision-making style. In this context, the issue of group decision making becomes important.

Group Decision Making

LO7-3 Identify the advantages and disadvantages of group decision making, and describe techniques that can improve it.

Many (or perhaps most) important organizational decisions are made by groups or teams of managers rather than by individuals. Group decision making is superior to individual decision making in several respects. When managers work as a team to make decisions and solve problems, their choices of alternatives are less likely to fall victim to the biases and errors discussed previously. They are able to draw on the combined skills, competencies, and accumulated knowledge of group members and thereby improve their ability to generate feasible alternatives and make good decisions. Group decision making also allows managers to process more information and to correct one another's errors. And in the implementation phase, all managers affected by the decisions agree to cooperate. When a group of managers makes a decision (as opposed to one top manager making a decision and imposing it on subordinate managers), the probability that the decision will be implemented successfully increases. (We discuss how to encourage employee participation in decision making in Chapter 14.)

When everyone agrees right off the bat, chances are high that the lack of conflict is in fact groupthink and more critical evaluation is needed.

Some potential disadvantages are associated with group decision making. Groups often take much longer than individuals to make decisions. Getting two or more managers to agree to the same solution can be difficult because managers' interests and preferences are often different. In addition, just like decision making by individual managers, group decision making can be undermined by biases. A major source of group bias is *groupthink.*

The Perils of Groupthink

groupthink A pattern of faulty and biased decision making that occurs in groups whose members strive for agreement among themselves at the expense of accurately assessing information relevant to a decision.

Groupthink is a pattern of faulty and biased decision making that occurs in groups whose members strive for agreement among themselves at the expense of accurately assessing information relevant to a decision.[57] When managers are subject to groupthink, they collectively embark on a course of action without developing appropriate criteria to evaluate alternatives. Typically a group rallies around one central manager, such as the CEO, and the course of action that manager supports. Group members become blindly committed to that course of action without evaluating its merits. Commitment is often based on an emotional, rather than an objective, assessment of the optimal course of action.

When groupthink occurs, pressures for agreement and harmony within a group have the unintended effect of discouraging individuals from raising issues that run counter to majority opinion.

Devil's Advocacy and Dialectical Inquiry

The existence of cognitive biases and groupthink raises the question of how to improve the quality of group and individual decision making so managers make decisions that are realistic and are based on thorough evaluation of alternatives. Two techniques known to counteract groupthink and cognitive biases are devil's advocacy and dialectic inquiry (see Figure 7.7).[58]

devil's advocacy Critical analysis of a preferred alternative, made in response to challenges raised by a group member who, playing the role of devil's advocate, defends unpopular or opposing alternatives for the sake of argument.

dialectical inquiry Critical analysis of two preferred alternatives in order to find an even better alternative for the organization to adopt.

Devil's advocacy is a critical analysis of a preferred alternative to ascertain its strengths and weaknesses before it is implemented.[59] Typically one member of the decision-making group plays the role of devil's advocate. The devil's advocate critiques and challenges the way the group evaluated alternatives and chose one over the others. The purpose of devil's advocacy is to identify all the reasons that might make the preferred alternative unacceptable after all. In this way, decision makers can be made aware of the possible perils of recommended courses of action.

Dialectical inquiry goes one step further. Two groups of managers are assigned to a problem, and each group is responsible for evaluating alternatives and selecting one of them.[60] Top managers hear each group present its preferred alternative, and then each group critiques the other's position. During this debate, top managers challenge both groups' positions to uncover potential problems and perils associated with their solutions. The goal is to find an even better alternative course of action for the organization to adopt.

Both devil's advocacy and dialectical inquiry can help counter the effects of cognitive biases and groupthink.[61] In practice, devil's advocacy is probably easier to implement because it involves less managerial time and effort than does dialectical inquiry.

Diversity among Decision Makers

Another way to improve group decision making is to promote diversity in decision-making groups (see Chapter 5).[62] Bringing together managers of both genders from various ethnic, national, and functional backgrounds broadens the range of life experiences and opinions that group members can draw on as they generate, assess, and choose among alternatives. Moreover, diverse groups are sometimes less prone to groupthink because group members already differ from each other and thus are less subject to pressures for uniformity.

Figure 7.7
Devil's Advocacy and Dialectical Inquiry

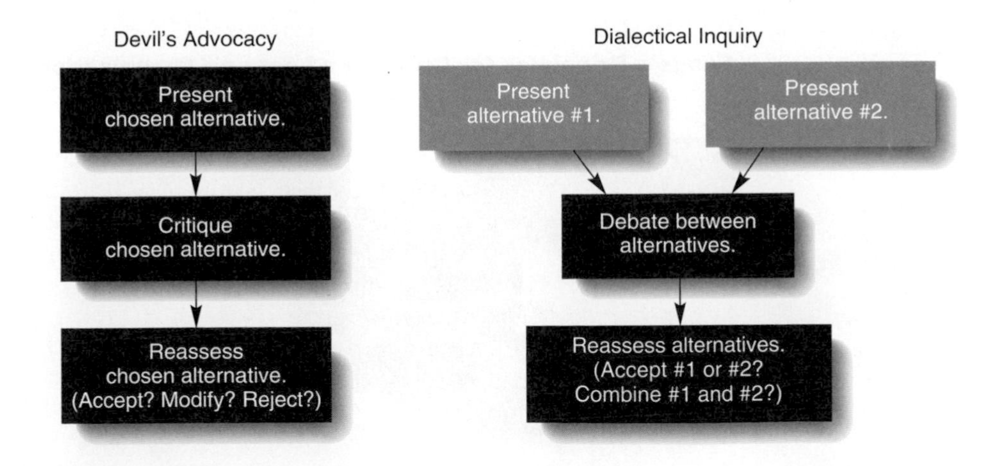

Organizational Learning and Creativity

The quality of managerial decision making ultimately depends on innovative responses to opportunities and threats. How can managers increase their ability to make nonprogrammed decisions that will allow them to adapt to, modify, and even drastically alter their task environments so they can continually increase organizational performance? The answer is by encouraging organizational learning.[63]

LO7-4 Explain the role that organizational learning and creativity play in helping managers to improve their decisions.

Organizational learning is the process through which managers seek to improve employees' desire and ability to understand and manage the organization and its task environment so employees can make decisions that continuously raise organizational effectiveness.[64] A **learning organization** is one in which managers do everything possible to maximize the ability of individuals and groups to think and behave creatively and thus maximize the potential for organizational learning to take place. At the heart of organizational learning is **creativity,** which is the ability of a decision maker to discover original and novel ideas that lead to feasible alternative courses of action. Encouraging creativity among managers is such a pressing organizational concern that many organizations hire outside experts to help them develop programs to train their managers in the art of creative thinking and problem solving.

organizational learning The process through which managers seek to improve employees' desire and ability to understand and manage the organization and its task environment.

learning organization An organization in which managers try to maximize the ability of individuals and groups to think and behave creatively and thus maximize the potential for organizational learning to take place.

creativity A decision maker's ability to discover original and novel ideas that lead to feasible alternative courses of action.

Creating a Learning Organization

How do managers go about creating a learning organization? Learning theorist Peter Senge identified five principles for creating a learning organization (see Figure 7.8):[65]

1. For organizational learning to occur, top managers must allow every person in the organization to develop a sense of *personal mastery*. Managers must empower employees and allow them to experiment, create, and explore what they want.
2. As part of attaining personal mastery, organizations need to encourage employees to develop and use *complex mental models*–sophisticated ways of thinking that challenge them to find new or better ways of performing a task–to deepen their understanding of what is involved in a particular activity. Here Senge argued that managers must encourage employees to develop a taste for experimenting and risk taking.[66]
3. Managers must do everything they can to promote group creativity. Senge thought that *team learning* (learning that takes place in a group or team) is more important than individual learning in increasing organizational learning. He pointed out that most important decisions are made in subunits such as groups, functions, and divisions.

Figure 7.8
Senge's Principles for Creating a Learning Organization

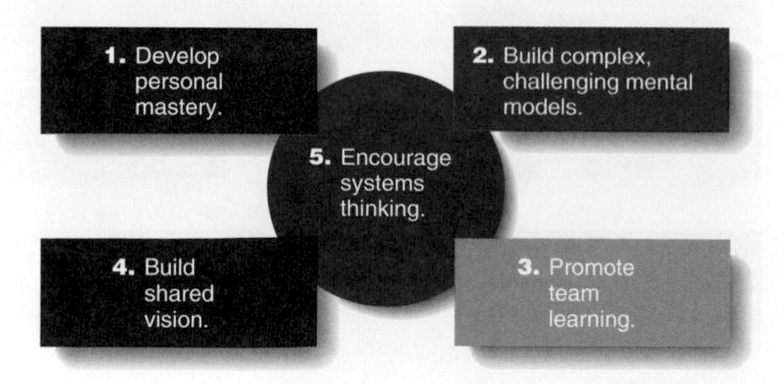

4. Managers must emphasize the importance of *building a shared vision*–a common mental model that all organizational members use to frame problems or opportunities.
5. Managers must encourage *systems thinking* (a concept drawn from systems theory, discussed in Chapter 2). Senge emphasized that to create a learning organization, managers must recognize the effects of one level of learning on another. Thus, for example, there is little point in creating teams to facilitate team learning if managers do not also take steps to give employees the freedom to develop a sense of personal mastery.

Building a learning organization requires that managers change their management assumptions radically. Developing a learning organization is neither a quick nor an easy process. Senge worked with Unilever Europe to help managers make Unilever Europe a learning organization. Why would Unilever Europe want this? Top management believed that to compete successfully, Unilever Europe must improve its members' ability to be creative and make the right decisions.

Increasingly, managers are being called on to promote global organizational learning. For example, managers at Walmart have used the lessons derived from its failures and successes in one country to promote global organizational learning across the many countries in which it now operates. For instance, when Walmart entered Malaysia, it was convinced customers there would respond to its one-stop shopping format. It found, however, that Malaysians enjoy the social experience of shopping in a lively market or bazaar and thus did not like the impersonal efficiency of the typical Walmart store. As a result, Walmart learned the importance of designing store layouts to appeal specifically to the customers of each country in which it operates.

When purchasing and operating a chain of stores in another country, such as the British ASDA chain, Walmart now strives to retain what customers value in the local market while taking advantage of its own accumulated organizational learning. For example, Walmart improved ASDA's information technology used for inventory and sales tracking in stores and enrolled ASDA in Walmart's global purchasing operations, which has enabled the chain to pay less for certain products, sell them for less, and, overall, significantly increase sales. At the same time Walmart empowered local ASDA managers to run the stores; as the president of ASDA indicates, "This is still essentially a British business in the way it's run day to day."[67] Clearly global organizational learning is essential for companies such as Walmart that have significant operations in multiple countries.

Promoting Individual Creativity

Research suggests that when certain conditions are met, managers are more likely to be creative. People must be given the opportunity and freedom to generate new ideas.[68] Creativity declines when managers look over the shoulders of talented employees and try to "hurry up" a creative solution. How would you feel if your boss said you had one week to come up with a new product idea to beat the competition? Creativity results when employees have an opportunity to experiment, to take risks, and to make mistakes and learn from them. And employees must not fear that they will be looked down on or penalized for ideas that might at first seem outlandish; sometimes those ideas yield truly innovative products and services.[69] Highly innovative companies such as Google, Apple, and Facebook are well known for the wide degree of freedom they give their managers and employees to experiment and develop innovative goods and services.[70]

Once managers have generated alternatives, creativity can be fostered by giving them constructive feedback so they know how well they are doing. Ideas that seem to be going nowhere can be eliminated and creative energies refocused in other directions. Ideas that seem promising can be promoted, and help from other managers can be obtained.[71]

Top managers must stress the importance of looking for alternative solutions and should visibly reward employees who come up with creative ideas. Being creative can be demanding and stressful. Employees who believe they are working on important, vital issues are motivated to put forth the high levels of effort that creativity demands. Creative people like to receive the acclaim of others, and innovative organizations have many kinds of ceremonies and rewards to recognize creative employees.

Promoting Group Creativity

To encourage creativity at the group level, organizations can use group problem-solving techniques that promote creative ideas and innovative solutions. These techniques can also prevent groupthink and help managers uncover biases. Here we look at three group decision-making techniques: *brainstorming,* the *nominal group technique,* and the *Delphi technique.*

BRAINSTORMING *Brainstorming* is a group problem-solving technique in which managers meet face-to-face to generate and debate a wide variety of alternatives from which to make a decision.[72] Generally from 5 to 15 managers meet in a closed-door session and proceed like this:

These ad agency employees are conducting a brainstorming session. Brainstorming can be used to generate multiple ideas and solutions for problems.

- One manager describes in broad outline the problem the group is to address.
- Group members share their ideas and generate alternative courses of action.
- As each alternative is described, group members are not allowed to criticize it; everyone withholds judgment until all alternatives have been heard. One member of the group records the alternatives on a flip chart.
- Group members are encouraged to be as innovative and radical as possible. Anything goes; and the greater the number of ideas put forth, the better. Moreover, group members are encouraged to "piggyback" or build on each other's suggestions.
- When all alternatives have been generated, group members debate the pros and cons of each and develop a short list of the best alternatives.

Brainstorming is very useful in some problem-solving situations–for example, when managers are trying to find a name for a new perfume or car model. But sometimes individuals working alone can generate more alternatives. The main reason for the loss of productivity in brainstorming appears to be **production blocking,** which occurs because group members cannot always simultaneously make sense of all the alternatives being generated, think up additional alternatives, and remember what they were thinking.[73]

production blocking A loss of productivity in brainstorming sessions due to the unstructured nature of brainstorming.

nominal group technique A decision-making technique in which group members write down ideas and solutions, read their suggestions to the whole group, and discuss and then rank the alternatives.

NOMINAL GROUP TECHNIQUE To avoid production blocking, the **nominal group technique** is often used. It provides a more structured way of generating alternatives in writing and gives each manager more time and opportunity to come up with potential solutions. The nominal group technique is especially useful when an issue is controversial and when different managers might be expected to champion different courses of action. Generally a small group of managers meets in a closed-door session and adopts the following procedures:

- One manager outlines the problem to be addressed, and 30 or 40 minutes are allocated for group members, working individually, to write down their ideas and solutions. Group members are encouraged to be innovative.
- Managers take turns reading their suggestions to the group. One manager writes all the alternatives on a flip chart. No criticism or evaluation of alternatives is allowed until all alternatives have been read.

- The alternatives are then discussed, one by one, in the sequence in which they were proposed. Group members can ask for clarifying information and critique each alternative to identify its pros and cons.
- When all alternatives have been discussed, each group member ranks all the alternatives from most preferred to least preferred, and the alternative that receives the highest ranking is chosen.[74]

Delphi technique A decision-making technique in which group members do not meet face-to-face but respond in writing to questions posed by the group leader.

entrepreneur An individual who notices opportunities and decides how to mobilize the resources necessary to produce new and improved goods and services.

LO7-5 Describe how managers can encourage and promote entrepreneurship to create a learning organization, and differentiate between entrepreneurs and intrapreneurs.

DELPHI TECHNIQUE Both the nominal group technique and brainstorming require that managers meet to generate creative ideas and engage in joint problem solving. What happens if managers are in different cities or in different parts of the world and cannot meet face-to-face? Videoconferencing is one way to bring distant managers together to brainstorm. Another way is to use the **Delphi technique,** which is a written approach to creative problem solving.[75] The Delphi technique works like this:

- The group leader writes a statement of the problem and a series of questions to which participating managers are to respond.
- The questionnaire is sent to the managers and departmental experts who are most knowledgeable about the problem. They are asked to generate solutions and mail the questionnaire back to the group leader.
- A team of top managers records and summarizes the responses. The results are then sent back to the participants, with additional questions to be answered before a decision can be made.
- The process is repeated until a consensus is reached and the most suitable course of action is apparent.

Entrepreneurship and Creativity

Entrepreneurs are individuals who notice opportunities and decide how to mobilize the resources necessary to produce new and improved goods and services. Entrepreneurs make all of the planning, organizing, leading, and controlling decisions necessary to start new business ventures. Thus entrepreneurs are an important source of creativity in the organizational world. These people, such as David Filo and Jerry Yang (founders of Yahoo!), make vast fortunes when their businesses succeed. Or they are among the millions of people who start new business ventures only to lose their money when they fail. Despite the fact that an estimated 80% of small businesses fail in the first three to five years, by some estimates 38% of men and 50% of women in today's workforce want to start their own companies.[76]

social entrepreneur An individual who pursues initiatives and opportunities and mobilizes resources to address social problems and needs in order to improve society and well-being through creative solutions.

Social entrepreneurs are individuals who pursue initiatives and opportunities to address social problems and needs in order to improve society and well-being, such as reducing poverty, increasing literacy, protecting the natural environment, or reducing substance abuse.[77] Social entrepreneurs seek to mobilize resources to solve social problems through creative solutions.[78]

As indicated in the "Ethics in Action" box on the next page, although social entrepreneurs often face challenges in raising funds to support their initiatives, their options are increasing thanks to the concept of microlending.

intrapreneur A manager, scientist, or researcher who works inside an organization and notices opportunities to develop new or improved products and better ways to make them.

Many managers, scientists, and researchers employed by companies engage in entrepreneurial activity, and they are an important source of organizational creativity. They are involved in innovation, developing new and improved products and ways to make them, which we describe in detail in Chapter 9. Such employees notice opportunities for either quantum or incremental product improvements and are responsible for managing the product development process. These individuals are known as **intrapreneurs** to distinguish them from entrepreneurs who start their own businesses. But in general, entrepreneurship involves creative decision making that gives customers new or improved goods and services.

Ethics in Action

Microloans Give Entrepreneurs a Start

A heartening and very interesting example of entrepreneurship helping people is microlending. In microlending, small loans, typically less than $100, are made to individuals to start a business. The loans are targeted to those individuals among the desperately poor who usually are illiterate, have no collateral, and are scorned by traditional financial institutions. The idea can be traced to the people's banks in 19th century Germany. However, today the best known example is Mohammed Yunus's Grameen Bank. Grameen Bank is the world's largest microlending organization, operates in 37 countries, and has made more than $8.7 billion in loans since its founding. Today there are more than 12,000 institutions issuing loans.

Mohammed Yunus pictured here founded Grameen Bank, which provides microloans to desperately poor people to start small businesses.

The distinctive feature of such microlending is the group-based lending process in which the group plays a central role in supporting and monitoring members' efforts to repay their individual loan. Groups typically have five members who are then part of a larger local community that consists of five to eight groups (25 to 40 individuals in total) all of whom are serviced by a single loan officer who represents the microlending institution. Each group of five individuals has a leader who monitors loan repayment and manages the overall stability of the group. Depending on the lender's policy, the individuals in a group may or may not be legally liable for one another's loans. Nevertheless, the ties within the group stimulate a high degree of joint responsibility. The interest rates charged for microloans can vary widely. Grameen Bank charges a flat annual interest rate of 22% while other microlending institutions may charge effective interest rates as high as 94% per annum. The repayment rate on microloans is typically over 90%–much higher than a typical loan.

Recently large multinational banks, including Standard Charter, HSBC, and Deutsche Bank, have recognized the opportunities that microlending presents and entered the business directly or through intermediaries. Despite rapid entry, estimates suggest that the industry can still grow. It is estimated that in 2008 as many as half of the world's 3 billion poor were eligible for microloans. As a result, the current US$17 billion in loans outstanding represents 10% of the potential microfinance market.[79]

There is an interesting relationship between entrepreneurs and intrapreneurs. Many managers with intrapreneurial talents become dissatisfied if their superiors decide neither to support nor to fund new product ideas and development efforts that the managers think will succeed. What do intrapreneurial managers who feel they are getting nowhere do? Often they decide to leave their current organizations and start their own companies to take advantage of their new product ideas! In other words, intrapreneurs become entrepreneurs and found companies that often compete with the companies they left. To avoid losing these individuals, top managers must find ways to facilitate the entrepreneurial spirit of their most creative employees. In the remainder of this section we consider issues involved in promoting successful entrepreneurship in both new and existing organizations.

Entrepreneurship and New Ventures

The fact that a significant number of entrepreneurs were frustrated intrapreneurs provides a clue about the personal characteristics of people who are likely to start a new venture and bear all the uncertainty and risk associated with being an entrepreneur.

CHARACTERISTICS OF ENTREPRENEURS Entrepreneurs are likely to possess a particular set of the personality characteristics we discussed in Chapter 3. First, they are likely to be high on the personality trait of *openness to experience,* meaning they are predisposed to be original, to be open to a wide range of stimuli, to be daring, and to take risks. Entrepreneurs also are likely to have an *internal locus of control,* believing that they are responsible for what happens to them and that their own actions determine important outcomes such as the success or failure of a new business. People with an external locus of control, in contrast, would be unlikely to leave a secure job in an organization and assume the risk associated with a new venture.

Intrapreneurs face unique challenges in balancing their championing of new ideas with the company's overall need for stability.

Entrepreneurs are likely to have a high level of *self-esteem* and feel competent and capable of handling most situations–including the stress and uncertainty surrounding a plunge into a risky new venture. Entrepreneurs are also likely to have a high *need for achievement* and have a strong desire to perform challenging tasks and meet high personal standards of excellence.

ENTREPRENEURSHIP AND MANAGEMENT Given that entrepreneurs are predisposed to activities that are somewhat adventurous and risky, in what ways can people become involved in entrepreneurial ventures? One way is to start a business from scratch. Taking advantage of modern IT, many people are starting solo ventures.

When people who go it alone succeed, they frequently need to hire other people to help them run the business. Michael Dell, for example, began his computer business as a college student and within weeks had hired several people to help him assemble computers from the components he bought from suppliers. From his solo venture grew Dell Computer.

Some entrepreneurs who start a new business have difficulty deciding how to manage the organization as it grows; **entrepreneurship** is *not* the same as management. Management encompasses all the decisions involved in planning, organizing, leading, and controlling resources. Entrepreneurship is noticing an opportunity to satisfy a customer need and then deciding how to find and use resources to make a product that satisfies that need. When an entrepreneur has produced something customers want, entrepreneurship gives way to management because the pressing need becomes providing the product both efficiently and effectively. Frequently a founding entrepreneur lacks the skills, patience, and experience to engage in the difficult and challenging work of management. Some entrepreneurs find it hard to delegate authority because they are afraid to risk their company by letting others manage it. As a result they become overloaded, and the quality of their decision making declines. Other entrepreneurs lack the detailed knowledge necessary to establish state-of-the-art information systems and technology or to create the operations management procedures that are vital to increase the efficiency of their organizations' production systems. Thus, to succeed, it is necessary to do more than create a new product; an entrepreneur must hire managers who can create an operating system that will let a new venture survive and prosper.

entrepreneurship The mobilization of resources to take advantage of an opportunity to provide customers with new or improved goods and services.

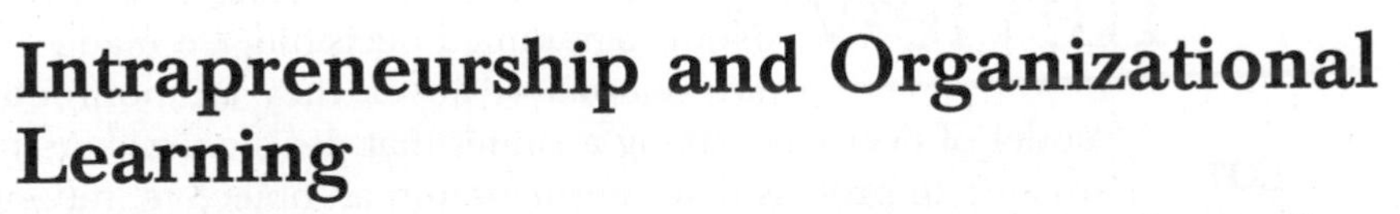

Intrapreneurship and Organizational Learning

The intensity of competition today, particularly from agile, small companies, has made it increasingly important for large, established organizations to promote and encourage intrapreneurship to raise their level of innovation and organizational learning. As we discussed earlier, a learning organization encourages all employees to identify opportunities and solve problems, thus enabling the organization to continuously experiment, improve, and increase its ability to provide customers with new and improved goods and services. The higher the level of intrapreneurship, the higher will be the level of learning and innovation. How can organizations promote organizational learning and intrapreneurship?

product champion A manager who takes "ownership" of a project and provides the leadership and vision that take a product from the idea stage to the final customer.

PRODUCT CHAMPIONS One way to promote intrapreneurship is to encourage individuals to assume the role of **product champion,** a manager who takes "ownership" of a project and provides the leadership and vision that take a product from the idea stage to the final customer. 3M, a company well known for its attempts to promote intrapreneurship, encourages all its managers to become product champions and identify new product ideas. A product champion becomes responsible for developing a business plan for the product. Armed with this business plan, the champion appears before 3M's product development committee, a team of senior 3M managers who probe the strengths and weaknesses of the plan to decide whether it should be funded. If the plan is accepted, the product champion assumes responsibility for product development.

skunkworks A group of intrapreneurs who are deliberately separated from the normal operation of an organization to encourage them to devote all their attention to developing new products.

SKUNKWORKS The idea behind the product champion role is that employees who feel ownership for a project are inclined to act like outside entrepreneurs and go to great lengths to make the project succeed. Using skunkworks and new venture divisions can also strengthen this feeling of ownership. A **skunkworks** is a group of intrapreneurs who are deliberately separated from the normal operation of an organization–for example, from the normal chain of command–to encourage them to devote all their attention to developing new products. The idea is that if these people are isolated, they will become so intensely involved in a project that development time will be relatively brief and the quality of the final product will be enhanced. The term *skunkworks* was coined at the Lockheed Corporation, which formed a team of design engineers to develop special aircraft.

REWARDS FOR INNOVATION To encourage managers to bear the uncertainty and risk associated with the hard work of entrepreneurship, it is necessary to link performance to rewards. Increasingly companies are rewarding intrapreneurs on the basis of the outcome of the product development process. Intrapreneurs are paid large bonuses if their projects succeed, or they are granted stock options that can make them millionaires if their products sell well. Both Microsoft and Google, for example, have made hundreds of their employees multimillionaires as a result of the stock options they were granted as part of their reward packages. In addition to receiving money, successful intrapreneurs can expect to receive promotion to the ranks of top management. Most of 3M's top managers, for example, reached the executive suite because they had a track record of successful entrepreneurship. Organizations must reward intrapreneurs equitably if they wish to prevent them from leaving and becoming outside entrepreneurs who might form a competitive new venture. Nevertheless, intrapreneurs frequently do so.

Summary and Review

THE NATURE OF MANAGERIAL DECISION MAKING Programmed decisions are routine decisions made so often that managers have developed decision rules to be followed automatically. Nonprogrammed decisions are made in response to situations that are unusual or novel; they are nonroutine decisions. The classical model of decision making assumes that decision makers have complete information, are able to process that information in an objective, rational manner, and make optimum decisions. March and Simon argued that managers exhibit bounded rationality, rarely have access to all the information they need to make optimum decisions, and consequently satisfice and rely on their intuition and judgment when making decisions.

LO7-1

LO7-2 **STEPS IN THE DECISION-MAKING PROCESS** When making decisions, managers should take these six steps: recognize the need for a decision, generate alternatives, assess alternatives, choose among alternatives, implement the chosen alternative, and learn from feedback.

LO7-2 **COGNITIVE BIASES AND DECISION MAKING** Most of the time managers are fairly good decision makers. On occasion, however, problems can result because human judgment can be adversely affected by the operation of cognitive biases that result in poor decisions. Cognitive biases are caused by systematic errors in the way decision makers process information and make decisions. Sources of these errors include prior hypotheses, representativeness, the illusion of control, and escalating commitment. Managers should undertake a personal decision audit to become aware of their biases and thus improve their decision making.

LO7-3 **GROUP DECISION MAKING** Many advantages are associated with group decision making, but there are also several disadvantages. One major source of poor decision making is groupthink. Afflicted decision makers collectively embark on a dubious course of action without questioning the assumptions that underlie their decision. Managers can improve the quality of group decision making by using techniques such as devil's advocacy and dialectical inquiry and by increasing diversity in the decision-making group.

LO7-4 **ORGANIZATIONAL LEARNING AND CREATIVITY** Organizational learning is the process through which managers seek to improve employees' desire and ability to understand and manage the organization and its task environment so employees can make decisions that continuously raise organizational effectiveness. Managers must take steps to promote organizational learning and creativity at the individual and group levels to improve the quality of decision making.

LO7-5 **ENTREPRENEURSHIP** Entrepreneurship is the mobilization of resources to take advantage of an opportunity to provide customers with new or improved goods and services. Entrepreneurs find new ventures of their own. Intrapreneurs work inside organizations and manage the product development process. Organizations need to encourage intrapreneurship because it leads to organizational learning and innovation.

Management in Action

Topics for Discussion and Action

Discussion

1. What are the main differences between programmed decision making and nonprogrammed decision making? **[LO7-1]**
2. In what ways do the classical and administrative models of decision making help managers appreciate the complexities of real-world decision making? **[LO7-1]**
3. Why do capable managers sometimes make bad decisions? What can individual managers do to improve their decision-making skills? **[LO7-1, 7-2]**
4. In what kinds of groups is groupthink most likely to be a problem? When is it least likely to be a problem? What steps can group members take to ward off groupthink? **[LO7-3]**
5. What is organizational learning, and how can managers promote it? **[LO7-4]**
6. What is the difference between entrepreneurship and intrapreneurship? **[LO7-5]**

Action

7. Ask a manager to recall the best and the worst decisions he or she ever made. Try to determine why these decisions were so good or so bad. **[LO7-1, 7-2, 7-3]**
8. Think about an organization in your local community or your university, or an organization that you are familiar with, that is doing poorly. Now think of questions managers in the organization should ask stakeholders to elicit creative ideas for turning around the organization's fortunes. **[LO7-4]**

Building Management Skills [LO7-1, 7-2, 7-4]

How Do You Make Decisions?

Pick a decision you made recently that has had important consequences for you. It may be your decision about which college to attend, which major to select, whether to take a part-time job, or which part-time job to take. Using the material in this chapter, analyze how you made the decision:

1. Identify the criteria you used, either consciously or unconsciously, to guide your decision making.
2. List the alternatives you considered. Were they all possible alternatives? Did you unconsciously (or consciously) ignore some important alternatives?
3. How much information did you have about each alternative? Were you making the decision on the basis of complete or incomplete information?
4. Try to remember how you reached the decision. Did you sit down and consciously think through the implications of each alternative, or did you make the decision on the basis of intuition? Did you use any rules of thumb to help you make the decision?
5. In retrospect, do you think your choice of alternative was shaped by any of the cognitive biases discussed in this chapter?
6. Having answered the previous five questions, do you think in retrospect that you made a reasonable decision? What, if anything, might you do to improve your ability to make good decisions in the future?

Managing Ethically [LO7-3]

It was highlighted that in Europe there is increasing pressure to include the impact on sustainability into business decisions. While this is the case in Europe there is not worldwide pressure to conduct such an analysis on all decisions. In fact consider that in North America today, air pollution rates are increasing not because of local pollution but because of air pollution from China.

Questions

1. Is it appropriate for firms to consider sustainability in their decision making if not all their competitors in the world do so?
2. What will be the impact on the firm's competitiveness if it does consider sustainability but other companies do not?
3. Is sustainability something that firms themselves should pursue or should this be something that only occurs when required by governments?

Small Group Breakout Exercise [LO7-3, 7-4]

Brainstorming

Form groups of three or four people, and appoint one member as the spokesperson who will communicate your findings to the class when called on by the instructor. Then discuss the following scenario:

You and your partners are trying to decide which kind of restaurant to open in a centrally located shopping area that has just been built in your city. The problem confronting you is that the city already has many restaurants that provide different kinds of food at all price ranges. You have the resources to open any type of restaurant. Your challenge is to decide which type is most likely to succeed.

Use brainstorming to decide which type of restaurant to open. Follow these steps:

1. As a group, spend 5 or 10 minutes generating ideas about the alternative restaurants that the members think will be most likely to succeed. Each group member should be as innovative and creative as possible, and no suggestions should be criticized.
2. Appoint one group member to write down the alternatives as they are identified.
3. Spend the next 10 or 15 minutes debating the pros and cons of the alternatives. As a group, try to reach a consensus on which alternative is most likely to succeed.

After making your decision, discuss the pros and cons of the brainstorming method, and decide whether any production blocking occurred.

When called on by the instructor, the spokesperson should be prepared to share your group's decision with the class, as well as the reasons for the group's decision.

Exploring the World Wide Web [LO7-4]

Go to www.brainstorming.co.uk. This Web site contains "Training on Creativity Techniques" and "Creativity Puzzles." Spend at least 30 minutes on the training and/or puzzles. Think about what you have learned. Come up with specific ways in which you can be more creative in your thinking and decision making based on what you have learned.

Be the Manager [LO7-1, 7-2, 7-3, 7-4, 7-5]

You are a top manager who was recently hired by an oil field services company in Bahrain to help it respond more quickly and proactively to potential opportunities in its market. You report to the chief operating officer (COO), who reports to the CEO, and you have been on the job for eight months. Thus far you have come up with three initiatives you carefully studied, thought were noteworthy, and proposed and justified to the COO. The COO seemed cautiously interested when you presented the proposals, and each time he indicated he would think about them and discuss them with the CEO because considerable resources were involved. Each time you never heard back from the COO, and after a few weeks elapsed, you casually asked the COO if there was any news on the proposal in question. For the first proposal, the COO said, "We think it's a good idea, but the timing is off. Let's shelve it for the time being and reconsider it next year." For the second proposal, the COO said, "Mike [the CEO] reminded me that we tried that two years ago and it wasn't well received in the market. I am surprised I didn't remember it myself when you first described the proposal, but it came right back to me once Mike mentioned it." For the third proposal, the COO simply said, "We're not convinced it will work."

You believe your three proposed initiatives are viable ways to seize opportunities in the marketplace, yet you cannot proceed with any of them. Moreover, for each proposal, you invested considerable time and even worked to bring others on board to support the proposal, only to have it shot down by the CEO. When you interviewed for the position, both the COO and the CEO claimed they wanted "an outsider to help them step out of the box and innovate." Yet your experience to date has been just the opposite. What are you going to do?

CHAPTER 8

The Manager as a Planner and Strategist

Learning Objectives

After studying this chapter, you should be able to:

LO8-1 Identify the three main steps of the planning process and explain the relationship between planning and strategy.

LO8-2 Describe some techniques managers can use to improve the planning process so they can better predict the future and mobilize organizational resources to meet future contingencies.

LO8-3 Differentiate between the main types of business-level strategies and explain how they give an organization a competitive advantage that may lead to superior performance.

LO8-4 Differentiate between the main types of corporate-level strategies and explain how they are used to strengthen a company's business-level strategy and competitive advantage.

LO8-5 Describe the vital role managers play in implementing strategies to achieve an organization's mission and goals.

A MANAGER'S CHALLENGE

Japan Airlines and the Need for Planning

One of the leading airlines in Asia is Japan Airlines (JAL). In 2009 the airline was worth approximately 1,950 billion yen or 1.3 billion USD. The firm has gone from one of the great symbols of Japanese quality to a firm in bankruptcy. These troubles were driven by environmental changes that JAL was unable to keep up with through its planning.

The firm began in 1951 with 100 million yen in capital. The airline was encouraged by the government to fill the need for transportation following the World War. Initially it served domestic routes only and grew quickly; by 1954 it began offering international flights. The airline industry at this time was heavily regulated. The government encouraged the development of the airline industry by allocating routes in ways that limited competition and ensured each airline a critical mass of customers. JAL became the principal international airline of Japan during this time. The airline developed a strategic planning process during this time, but the key activity that decided profitability was the relationship with the government so the actual use of strategic planning was limited.

However, by 1987 the economic environment had changed dramatically. Rather than choosing national champions, the Japanese view of business had moved to be more free-market oriented, and firms began to compete against each other for customers. As a result the Japanese government deregulated the airline industry. All Nippon Airways (ANA) and Japan Air System (JAS) moved quickly to offer international flights. International flights tend to be more profitable than domestic routes. Many of the costs in the airline industry are fixed; the cost of the plane is largely the same if it flies full or nearly empty. Thus, once a flight obtains enough customers to reach the break-even point, the rest is

Missteps in the strategic planning process cost Japan Airlines (JAL) its profitability, which has led to the company filing bankruptcy. Although it continues to operate, JAL's future is unclear.

nearly complete profit. The strategy of JAL during this time was high quality and high price. The new entrants began to compete on price. The profit position of JAL began to deteriorate.

As JAL's position continued to decline the firm strategically decided to cut costs. The response was slow in coming but ultimately the firm became very aggressive in its cost cutting particularly in terms of staff. Staff is one of the few areas where an airline can control costs as the costs of the plane and fuel are fixed. The airline made aggressive moves, such as hiring cabin crew as contract labor rather than full-time employees. This change allowed the airline not to pay retirement, thus giving JAL greater flexibility in releasing staff. However, JAL still wanted to be perceived as the high quality option in Japan, and many of the staff changes resulted in poor service. Thus, the airline was seen as stuck in the middle–charging for quality service but not delivering it.

The strategic planning efforts at JAL also led to other corporate responses. One was to set up a low cost subsidiary for Japanese residents going on Asian holidays. Another response for JAL was to purchase JAS. The goal was to cut the costs by creating a critical mass. However, integrating the two firms proved to be difficult. The airline also sold a hotel that was creating losses. The forward integration into the hotel industry had proven not to be a good investment.

The outcome of these various problems was that by 2010 the airline filed bankruptcy. The firm continues to fly at this time but faces a difficult future. During all of its troubles the firm has had a strategic planning process but has proven unable to use the process to reinvigorate the airline as it moves from a protected national carrier to a competitive firm. The airline proved unwilling to take on direct competition in this domain. The firm was slow to recognize the nature of the threats and their potential impact. Once the firm recognized the problems, its actions gave mixed signals on its strategy with no clear direction for the future.

Overview

As the opening case suggests, in a fast-changing competitive environment managers must continually evaluate how well products are meeting customer needs, and they must engage in thorough, systematic planning to find new strategies to better meet those needs. This chapter explores the manager's role both as planner and as strategist. First, we discuss the nature and importance of planning, the kinds of plans managers develop, and the levels at which planning takes place. Second, we discuss the three major steps in the planning process: (1) determining an organization's mission and major goals, (2) choosing or formulating strategies to realize the mission and goals, and (3) selecting the most effective ways to implement and put these strategies into action. We also examine several techniques, such as scenario planning and SWOT analysis, that can help managers improve the quality of their planning; and we discuss a range of strategies managers can use to give their companies a competitive advantage over their rivals. By the end of this chapter, you will understand the vital role managers carry out when they plan, develop, and implement strategies to create a high-performing organization.

Planning and Strategy

LO8-1 Identify the three main steps of the planning process and explain the relationship between planning and strategy.

planning Identifying and selecting appropriate goals and courses of action; one of the four principal tasks of management.

strategy A cluster of decisions about what goals to pursue, what actions to take, and how to use resources to achieve goals.

Planning, as we noted in Chapter 1, is a process managers use to identify and select appropriate goals and courses of action for an organization.[1] The organizational plan that results from the planning process details the goals of the organization and the specific strategies managers will implement to attain those goals. Recall from Chapter 1 that a **strategy** is a cluster of related managerial decisions and actions to help an organization attain one of its goals. Thus planning is both a goal-making and a strategy-making process.

In most organizations, planning is a three-step activity (see Figure 8.1). The first step is determining the organization's mission and goals. A **mission statement** is a broad declaration of an organization's overriding purpose, what it is seeking to achieve from its activities; this statement also identifies what is *unique or important* about its products to its employees and customers; finally it *distinguishes or differentiates* the organization in some ways from its competitors. (Two examples of mission statements, those created by Cisco Systems and Hyundai, are illustrated later in Figure 8.4.)

The second step is formulating strategy. Managers analyze the organization's current situation and then conceive and develop the strategies necessary to attain the organization's mission and goals. The third step is implementing strategy. Managers decide how to allocate the resources and responsibilities required to implement the strategies among people and groups within the organization.[2] In subsequent sections of this chapter we look in detail at the specifics of these steps. But first we examine the general nature and purpose of planning.

The Nature of the Planning Process

mission statement A broad declaration of an organization's purpose that identifies the organization's products and customers and distinguishes the organization from its competitors.

Essentially, to perform the planning task, managers (1) establish and discover where an organization is at the *present time;* (2) determine where it should be in the future, its *desired future state;* and (3) decide how to *move it forward* to reach that future state. When managers plan, they must forecast what may happen in the future to decide what to do in the present. The better their predictions, the more effective will be the strategies they formulate to take advantage of future opportunities and counter emerging competitive threats in the environment. As previous chapters noted, however, the external environment is uncertain and complex, and managers typically must deal with incomplete information and bounded rationality. This is why planning and strategy making

Figure 8.1
Three Steps in Planning

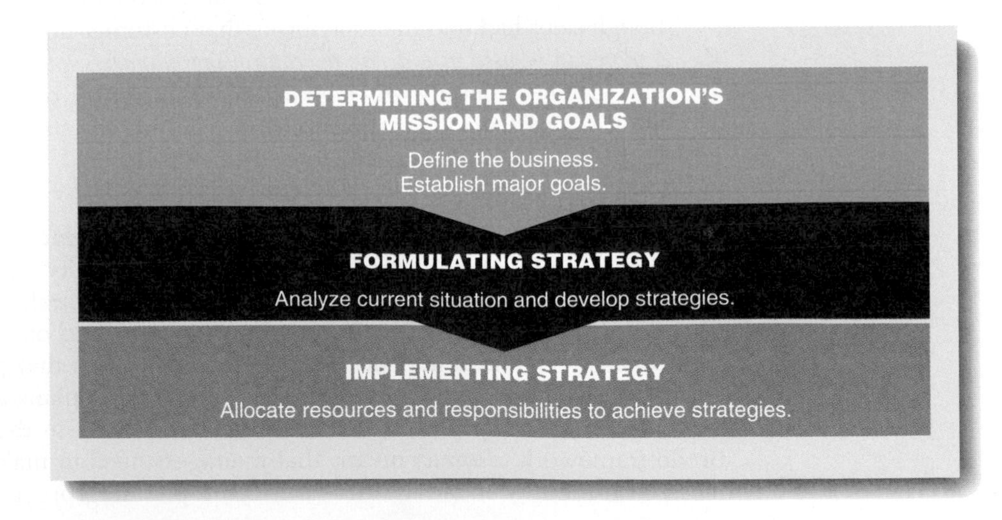

are so difficult and risky; and if managers' predictions are wrong and strategies fail, organizational performance falls.

Why Planning Is Important

Almost all managers participate in some kind of planning because they must try to predict future opportunities and threats and develop a plan and strategies that will result in a high-performing organization. Moreover, the absence of a plan often results in hesitations, false steps, and mistaken changes of direction that can hurt an organization or even lead to disaster. Planning is important for four main reasons:

1. *Planning is necessary to give the organization a sense of direction and purpose.*[3] A plan states what goals an organization is trying to achieve and what strategies it intends to use to achieve them. Without the sense of direction and purpose that a formal plan provides, managers may interpret their own specific tasks and jobs in ways that best suit themselves. The result will be an organization that is pursuing multiple and often conflicting goals and a set of managers who do not cooperate and work well together. By stating which organizational goals and strategies are important, a plan keeps managers on track so they use the resources under their control efficiently and effectively.
2. *Planning is a useful way of getting managers to participate in decision making about the appropriate goals and strategies for an organization.* Effective planning gives all managers the opportunity to participate in decision making. At Intel, for example, top managers, as part of their annual planning process, regularly request input from lower-level managers to determine what the organization's goals and strategies should be.
3. *A plan helps coordinate managers of the different functions and divisions of an organization to ensure that they all pull in the same direction and work to achieve its desired future state.* Without a well-thought-out plan, for example, it is possible that the manufacturing function will make more products than the sales function can sell, resulting in a mass of unsold inventory. In fact, this happened to the currently high-flying Internet equipment supplier Cisco Systems. In the early 2000s it was able to sell all the routers it produced; but in 2003 Cisco found it had over $2 billion of inventory that its sales force could not sell because customers now wanted new kinds of optical routers that Cisco had not planned to develop–even though sales had told manufacturing that customer needs were changing.
4. *A plan can be used as a device for controlling managers within an organization.* A good plan specifies not only which goals and strategies the organization is committed to but also *who* bears the responsibility for putting the strategies into action to attain the goals. When managers know they will be held accountable for attaining a goal, they are motivated to do their best to make sure the goal is achieved.

A group of managers meets to plot their company's strategy. Their ability to assess opportunities and challenges and to forecast the future doesn't just depend on brilliance. Such tools as SWOT analysis can significantly bolster the accuracy of their predictions.

Henri Fayol, the originator of the model of management we discussed in Chapter 1, said that effective plans should have four qualities: unity, continuity, accuracy, and flexibility.[4] *Unity* means that at any time only one central, guiding plan is put into operation to achieve an organizational goal; more than one plan to achieve a goal would cause confusion and disorder. *Continuity* means that planning is an ongoing process in which managers build and refine previous plans and continually modify plans at all levels–corporate, business, and functional–so they fit together into one broad framework. *Accuracy* means that managers need to make every attempt to collect and use all available information in the planning process. Of course managers must recognize that uncertainty exists and that information is almost always incomplete (for reasons we discussed in Chapter 7). Despite the need for continuity and accuracy, however, Fayol emphasized that the planning process should be *flexible* enough so plans can be altered and changed if the situation changes; managers must not be bound to a static plan.

Levels of Planning

In large organizations planning usually takes place at three levels of management: corporate, business or division, and department or functional. Consider how General Electric (GE) operates. One of the world's largest global organizations, GE competes in over 150 different businesses or industries.[5] GE has three main levels of management: corporate level, business or divisional level, and functional level (see Figure 8.2). At the corporate level are CEO and Chairman Jeffrey Immelt, his top management team, and their corporate support staff. Together they are responsible for planning and strategy making for the organization as a whole.

Below the corporate level is the business level. At the business level are the different *divisions* or *business units* of the company that compete in distinct industries; GE has over 150 divisions, including GE Aircraft Engines, GE Financial Services, GE Lighting, GE Motors, and GE Plastics. Each division or business unit has its own set of *divisional managers* who control planning and strategy for their particular division or unit. So, for example, GE Lighting's divisional managers plan how to operate globally to reduce costs while meeting the needs of customers in different countries.

Going down one more level, each division has its own set of *functions* or *departments,* such as manufacturing, marketing, human resource management (HRM), and research and development (R&D). For example, GE Aircraft has its own marketing function, as do GE Lighting and GE Motors. Each division's *functional managers* are responsible for the planning and strategy making necessary to increase the efficiency and effectiveness of their particular function. So, for example, GE Lighting's marketing managers are responsible for increasing the effectiveness of its advertising and sales campaigns in different countries to improve lightbulb sales.

Levels and Types of Planning

As just discussed, planning at GE, as at all other large organizations, takes place at each level. Figure 8.3 shows the link between these three levels and the three steps in the planning and strategy-making process illustrated in Figure 8.1.

corporate-level plan Top management's decisions pertaining to the organization's mission, overall strategy, and structure.

corporate-level strategy A plan that indicates in which industries and national markets an organization intends to compete.

business-level plan Divisional managers' decisions pertaining to divisions' long-term goals, overall strategy, and structure.

business-level strategy A plan that indicates how a division intends to compete against its rivals in an industry.

The **corporate-level plan** contains top management's decisions concerning the organization's mission and goals, overall (corporate-level) strategy, and structure (see Figure 8.3). **Corporate-level strategy** specifies in which industries and national markets an organization intends to compete and why. One of the goals stated in GE's corporate-level plan is that GE should be first or second in market share in every industry in which it competes. A division that cannot attain this goal may be sold to another company. GE Medical Systems was sold to Thompson of France for this reason. Another GE goal is to acquire other companies that can help a division build its market share to reach its corporate goal of being first or second in an industry.

In general, corporate-level planning and strategy are the primary responsibility of top or corporate managers.[6] The corporate-level goal of GE is to be the first or second leading company in every industry in which it competes. Jeffrey Immelt and his top management team decide which industries GE should compete in to achieve this goal. The corporate-level plan provides the framework within which divisional managers create their business-level plans. At the business level, the managers of each division create a **business-level plan** that details (1) the long-term divisional goals that will allow the division to meet corporate goals and (2) the division's business-level strategy and structure necessary to achieve divisional goals. **Business-level strategy** outlines the specific methods a division, business unit, or organization will use to compete effectively against its rivals in an industry. Managers at GE's lighting division

Figure 8.2
Levels of Planning at General Electric

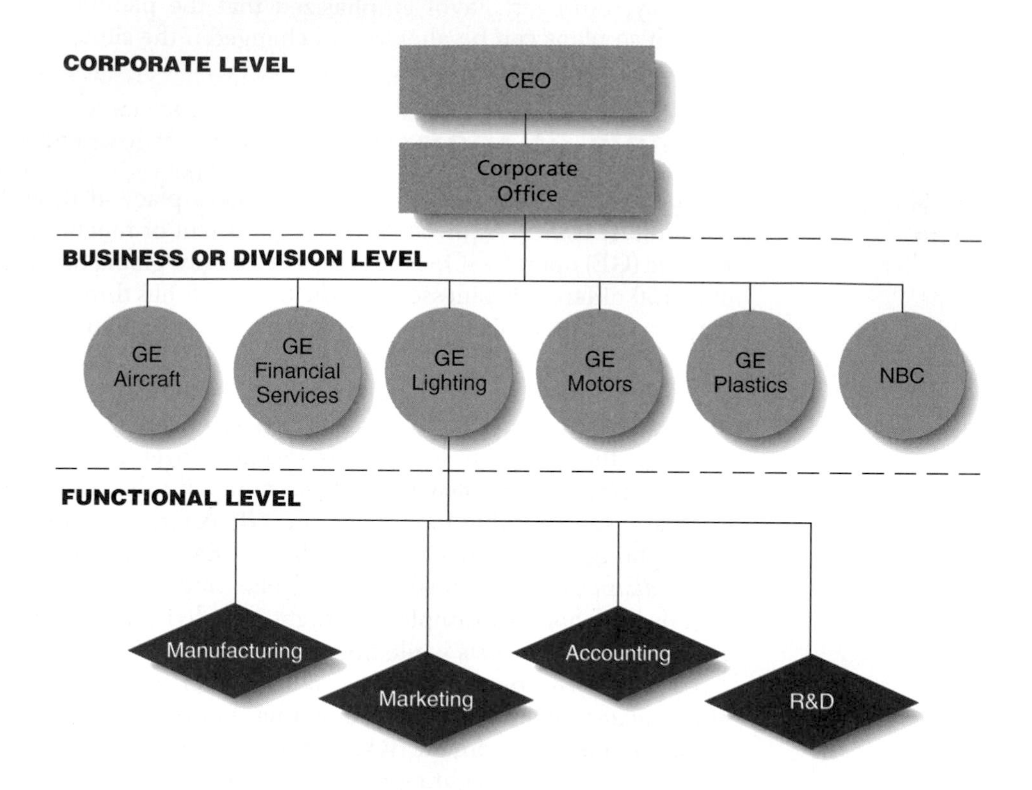

Figure 8.3
Levels and Types of Planning

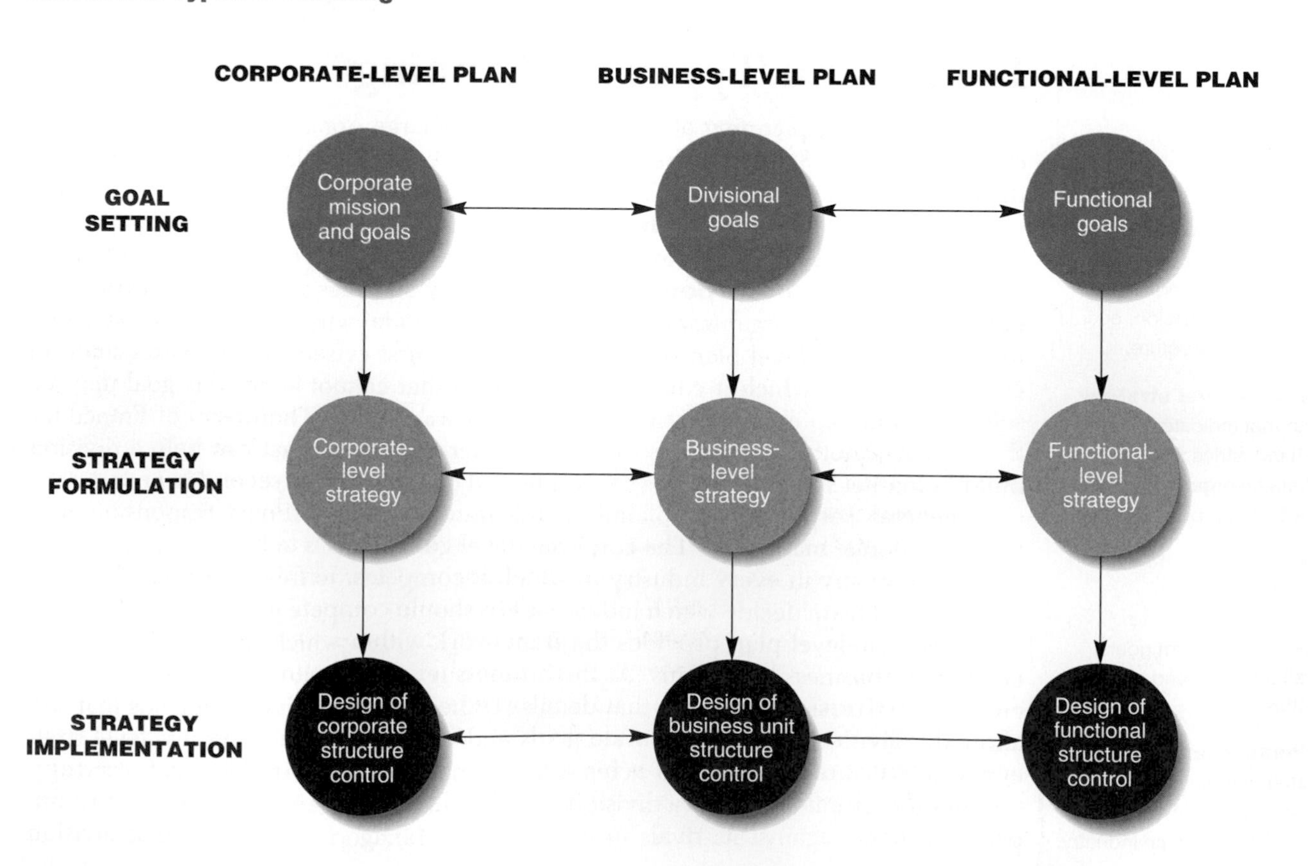

(currently number two in the global lighting industry, behind the Dutch company Philips NV) develop strategies designed to help their division take over the number one spot and better contribute to GE's corporate goals. The lighting division's specific strategies might focus on ways to reduce costs in all departments to lower prices and so gain market share from Philips. For example, GE has expanded its European lighting operations in Hungary, which is a low-cost location.[7]

functional-level plan Functional managers' decisions pertaining to the goals that they propose to pursue to help the division attain its business-level goals.

functional-level strategy A plan of action to improve the ability of each of an organization's functions to perform its task-specific activities in ways that add value to an organization's goods and services.

At the functional level, the business-level plan provides the framework within which functional managers devise their plans. A **functional-level plan** states the goals that the managers of each function will pursue to help their division attain its business-level goals, which, in turn, will allow the entire company to achieve its corporate goals. **Functional-level strategy** is a plan of action that managers of individual functions (such as manufacturing or marketing) can follow to improve the ability of each function to perform its task-specific activities in ways that add value to an organization's goods and services and thereby increase the value customers receive. Thus, for example, consistent with the lighting division's strategy of driving down costs, its manufacturing function might adopt the goal "To reduce production costs by 20% over the next three years," and functional strategies to achieve this goal might include (1) investing in state-of-the-art European production facilities and (2) developing an electronic global business-to-business network to reduce the costs of inputs and inventory holding. The many ways in which managers can use functional-level strategy to strengthen business-level strategy are discussed in detail in Chapter 9.

In the planning process, it is important to ensure that planning across the three different levels is *consistent*–functional goals and strategies should be consistent with divisional goals and strategies, which, in turn, should be consistent with corporate goals and strategies, and vice versa. When consistency is achieved, the whole company operates in harmony; activities at one level reinforce and strengthen those at the other levels, increasing efficiency and effectiveness. To help accomplish this, each function's plan is linked to its division's business-level plan, which, in turn, is linked to the corporate plan. Although few organizations are as large and complex as GE, most plan in the same way as GE and have written plans, which are frequently updated, to guide managerial decision making.

Time Horizons of Plans

time horizon The intended duration of a plan.

Plans differ in their **time horizons,** the periods of time over which they are intended to apply or endure. Managers usually distinguish among *long-term plans,* with a time horizon of five years or more; *intermediate-term plans,* with a horizon between one and five years; and *short-term plans,* with a horizon of one year or less.[8] Typically corporate- and business-level goals and strategies require long- and intermediate-term plans, and functional-level goals and strategies require intermediate- and short-term plans.

Although most companies operate with planning horizons of five years or more, this does not mean that managers undertake major planning exercises only once every five years and then "lock in" a specific set of goals and strategies for that period. Most organizations have an annual planning cycle that is usually linked to the annual financial budget (although a major planning effort may be undertaken only every few years). So a corporate- or business-level plan that extends over several years is typically treated as a *rolling plan*–a plan that is updated and amended every year to take account of changing conditions in the external environment. Thus the time horizon for an organization's 2009 corporate-level plan might be 2014; for the 2010 plan it might be 2015; and so on. The use of rolling plans is essential because of the high rate of change in the environment and the difficulty of predicting competitive conditions five years in the future. Rolling plans enable managers to make midcourse corrections if environmental changes warrant or to change the thrust of the plan altogether if it no longer seems appropriate. The use of rolling plans allows managers to plan flexibly without losing sight of the need to plan for the long term.

Standing Plans and Single-Use Plans

Another distinction often made between plans is whether they are standing plans or single-use plans. Managers create standing and single-use plans to help achieve an organization's specific goals. *Standing plans* are used in situations in which programmed decision making is appropriate. When the same situations occur repeatedly, managers develop policies, rules, and standard operating procedures (SOPs) to control the way employees perform their tasks. A policy is a general guide to action; a rule is a formal, written guide to action; and a standing operating procedure is a written instruction describing the exact series of actions that should be followed in a specific situation. For example, an organization may have a standing plan about ethical behavior by employees. This plan includes a policy that all employees are expected to behave ethically in their dealings with suppliers and customers; a rule that requires any employee who receives from a supplier or customer a gift worth more than US$20 to report the gift; and an SOP that obliges the recipient of the gift to make the disclosure in writing within 30 days.

In contrast, *single-use plans* are developed to handle nonprogrammed decision making in unusual or one-of-a-kind situations. Examples of single-use plans include *programs,* which are integrated sets of plans for achieving certain goals, and *projects,* which are specific action plans created to complete various aspects of a program.

LO8-2 Describe some techniques managers can use to improve the planning process so they can better predict the future and mobilize organizational resources to meet future contingencies.

Scenario Planning

Earlier we noted that effective plans have four qualities: unity, continuity, accuracy, and flexibility. One of the most widely used planning methods or techniques that can help managers create plans that have these qualities is scenario planning. **Scenario planning** (also known as *contingency planning*) is the generation of multiple forecasts of future conditions followed by an analysis of how to respond effectively to each of those conditions.

scenario planning The generation of multiple forecasts of future conditions followed by an analysis of how to respond effectively to each of those conditions.

As we know all too well, oil and gas prices are unpredictable. Oil industry managers therefore sometimes use scenario planning to deal with this chaotic market.

As noted previously, planning is about trying to forecast and predict the future in order to be able to anticipate future opportunities and threats. The future, however, is inherently unpredictable. How can managers best deal with this unpredictability? This question preoccupied managers at Royal Dutch Shell, the third largest global oil company, in the 1980s. In 1984 oil was US$30 a barrel, and most analysts and managers, including Shell's, believed it would hit US$50 per barrel by 1990. Although these high prices guaranteed high profits, Shell's top managers decided to conduct a scenario-planning exercise. Shell's corporate and divisional managers were told to use scenario planning to generate different future scenarios of conditions in the oil market and then to develop a set of plans that detailed how they would respond to these opportunities and threats if any such scenario occurred.

One scenario assumed that oil prices would fall to US$15 per barrel, and managers had to decide what they should do in such a case. Managers went to work with the goal of creating a plan consisting of a series of recommendations. The final plan included proposals to cut oil exploration costs by investing in new technologies, to accelerate investments in cost-efficient oil-refining facilities, and to weed out unprofitable gas stations.[9] In reviewing these proposals, top management came to the conclusion that even if oil prices continued to rise, all of these actions would benefit Shell and increase its profit margin. So they decided to put the cost-cutting plan into action. As it happened, in the mid-1980s oil prices did not rise; they collapsed to US$15 a barrel, but Shell, unlike its competitors, had already taken steps to be profitable in a low-oil-price world. Consequently, by 1990 the company was twice as profitable as its major competitors.

As this example suggests, because the future is unpredictable–the US$30-a-barrel oil level was not reached again until the early 2000s, for example–the best way to improve planning is first to generate "multiple futures," or scenarios of the future, based on different assumptions about conditions that *might prevail* in the future and then to develop different plans that detail what a company should do if one of these scenarios occurs. Scenario planning is a learning tool that raises the quality of the planning process and can bring real benefits to an organization.[10] Shell's success with scenario planning influenced many other companies to adopt similar systems. By 1990 more than 50% of *Fortune* 500 companies were using some version of scenario planning, and the number has increased since then. A major advantage of scenario planning is its ability not only to anticipate the challenges of an uncertain future but also to educate managers to think about the future–*to think strategically.*[11]

Determining the Organization's Mission and Goals

As we discussed earlier, determining the organization's mission and goals is the first step of the planning process. Once the mission and goals are agreed upon and formally stated in the corporate plan, they guide the next steps by defining which strategies are appropriate.[12] Figure 8.4 presents the missions and goals of two companies: Cisco and Hyundai Motors.

Defining the Business

To determine an organization's *mission*–the overriding reason it exists to provide customers with goods or services they value–managers must first *define its business* so they can identify what kind of value customers are receiving. To define the business,

Figure 8.4
Three Mission Statements

COMPANY	MISSION STATEMENT
Cisco	Cisco solutions provide competitive advantage to our customers through more efficient and timely exchange of information, which in turn leads to cost savings, process efficiencies, and closer relationships with our customers, prospects, business partners, suppliers, and employees.
Hyundai Motors	To create exceptional automotive value for our customers by harmoniously blending safety, quality, and efficiency. With our diverse team, we will provide responsible stewardship to our community and environment while achieving stability and security now and for future generations.

managers must ask three related questions about a company's products: (1) *Who* are our customers? (2) *What* customer needs are being satisfied? (3) *How* are we satisfying customer needs?[13] Managers ask these questions to identify the customer needs that the organization satisfies and how the organization satisfies those needs. Answering these questions helps managers identify not only the customer needs they are satisfying now but also the needs they should try to satisfy in the future and who their true competitors are. All this information helps managers plan and establish appropriate goals. In the following "Management Insight" box, the case of Carrefour shows the importance of reshaping strategies as part of the planning process.

Management Insight

Carrefour: Changing What It Does

Carrefour is the largest retailer in the world but is fundamentally reshaping its strategy. The firm began in the 1950s in France. However, today it operates in over 35 countries around the world. The concept of a hypermarket is one that the firm pioneered. A hypermarket is one in which not only food is sold but also other items such as clothing–items that historically were sold only in department stores.

Carrefour's effort to reshape its strategy has taken a variety of forms. One has been to move from selling other firms' products to selling more of its own in-house brands. The focus on in-house brands will allow the firm to cut prices for consumers; an in-house brand can cost up to 50% less than an international brand of the same quality. International brands like Kraft or Nestlé have to invest heavily in developing brand recognition. The result is that their products are more costly than an in-house brand. A retailer sells those brands because consumers are drawn to the store for them not for the retailer's name. However, Carrefour now believes it has a strong brand identity and it no longer has to offer such premium branded products. Instead, it can rely on in-house brands. Another retailer that uses this model very successfully in furniture sales is IKEA. There is evidence of success in this approach as sales are up at Carrefour.

Carrefour is also withdrawing from less profitable markets to concentrate its development on markets that offer the greatest potential. For example, the firm has decided to withdraw from Thailand, Singapore, and Malaysia to concentrate its Asia development in China. The firm similarly withdrew from Portugal to focus on other markets where it had a more dominant position. Thus, even as the largest retailer in the world and a successful firm, Carrefour must continually update its strategy as the environment around it evolves.[14]

Establishing Major Goals

Once the business is defined, managers must establish a set of primary goals to which the organization is committed. Developing these goals gives the organization a sense of direction or purpose. In most organizations, articulating major goals is the job of the CEO, although other managers have input into the process. The best statements of organizational goals are ambitious–that is, they *stretch* the organization and require that each of its members work to improve company performance.[15] The role of **strategic leadership,** the ability of the CEO and top managers to convey a compelling vision of what they want to achieve to their subordinates, is important here. If subordinates buy into the vision and model their behaviors on their leaders, they

strategic leadership The ability of the CEO and top managers to convey a compelling vision of what they want the organization to achieve to their subordinates.

develop a willingness to undertake the hard, stressful work that is necessary for creative, risk-taking strategy making.[16] Many popular books such as *Built to Last* provide lucid accounts of strategic leaders establishing "big, hairy, audacious goals (BHAGs)" that serve as rallying points to unite their subordinates.[17]

Although goals should be challenging, they should also be realistic. Challenging goals give managers at all levels an incentive to look for ways to improve organizational performance, but a goal that is clearly unrealistic and impossible to attain may prompt managers to give up.[18]

Finally, the time period in which a goal is expected to be achieved should be stated. Time constraints are important because they emphasize that a goal must be attained within a reasonable period; they inject a sense of urgency into goal attainment and act as a motivator.

Formulating Strategy

In **strategy formulation** managers work to develop the set of strategies (corporate, divisional, and functional) that will allow an organization to accomplish its mission and achieve its goals.[19] Strategy formulation begins with managers systematically analyzing the factors or forces inside an organization, and outside in the global environment, that affect the organization's ability to meet its goals now and in the future. SWOT analysis and the five forces model are two handy techniques managers can use to analyze these factors.

strategy formulation The development of a set of corporate, business, and functional strategies that allow an organization to accomplish its mission and achieve its goals.

SWOT analysis A planning exercise in which managers identify organizational strengths (S) and weaknesses (W) and environmental opportunities (O) and threats (T).

SWOT Analysis

SWOT analysis is a planning exercise in which managers identify *internal* organizational strengths (S) and weaknesses (W) and *external* environmental opportunities (O) and threats (T). Based on a SWOT analysis, managers at the different levels of the organization select the corporate, business, and functional strategies to best position the organization to achieve its mission and goals (see Figure 8.5). In Chapter 6 we discussed forces in the task and general environments that have the potential to affect an organization. We noted that changes in these forces can produce opportunities that an organization might take advantage of and threats that may harm its current situation.

The first step in SWOT analysis is to identify an organization's strengths and weaknesses. Table 8.1 lists many important strengths (such as high-quality skills in marketing and in research and development) and weaknesses (such as rising manufacturing

Figure 8.5
Planning and Strategy Formulation

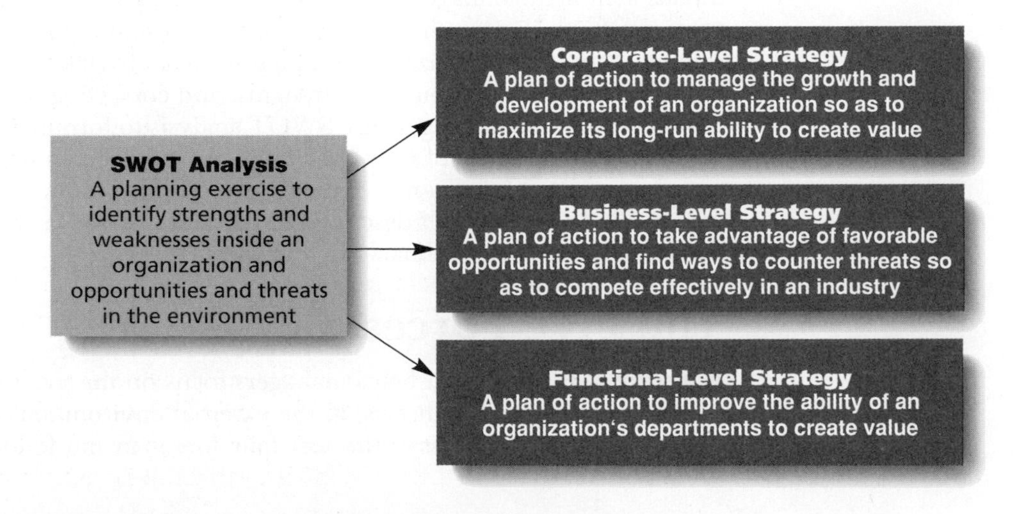

Table 8.1
Questions for SWOT Analysis

Potential Strengths	Potential Opportunities	Potential Weaknesses	Potential Threats
Well-developed strategy?	Expand core business(es)?	Poorly developed strategy?	Attacks on core business(es)?
Strong product lines?	Exploit new market segments?	Obsolete, narrow product lines?	Increase in domestic competition?
Broad market coverage?	Widen product range?	Rising manufacturing costs?	Increase in foreign competition?
Manufacturing competence?	Extend cost or differentiation advantage?	Decline in R&D innovations?	Change in consumer tastes?
Good marketing skills?	Diversify into new growth businesses?	Poor marketing plan?	Fall in barriers to entry?
Good materials management systems?	Expand into foreign markets?	Poor materials management systems?	Rise in new or substitute products?
R&D skills and leadership?	Apply R&D skills in new areas?	Loss of customer goodwill?	Increase in industry rivalry?
Human resource competencies?	Enter new related businesses?	Inadequate human resources?	New forms of industry competition?
Brand-name reputation?	Vertically integrate forward?	Loss of brand name?	Potential for takeover?
Cost of differentiation advantage?	Vertically integrate backward?	Growth without direction?	Changes in demographic factors?
Appropriate management style?	Overcome barriers to entry?	Loss of corporate direction?	Changes in economic factors?
Appropriate organizational structure?	Reduce rivalry among competitors?	Infighting among divisions?	Downturn in economy?
Appropriate control systems?	Apply brand-name capital in new areas?	Loss of corporate control?	Rising labor costs?
Ability to manage strategic change?	Seek fast market growth?	Inappropriate organizational structure and control systems?	Slower market growth?
Others?	Others?	High conflict and politics?	Others?
		Others?	

costs and outdated technology). The task facing managers is to identify the strengths and weaknesses that characterize the present state of their organization.

The second step in SWOT analysis begins when managers embark on a full-scale SWOT planning exercise to identify potential opportunities and threats in the environment that affect the organization now or may affect it in the future. Examples of possible opportunities and threats that must be anticipated (many of which were discussed in Chapter 6) are listed in Table 8.1. Scenario planning is often used to strengthen this analysis.

With the SWOT analysis completed, and strengths, weaknesses, opportunities, and threats identified, managers can continue the planning process and determine specific strategies for achieving the organization's mission and goals. The resulting strategies should enable the organization to attain its goals by taking advantage of opportunities, countering threats, building strengths, and correcting organizational weaknesses. To appreciate how managers use SWOT analysis to formulate strategy, consider how Douglas Conant, CEO of Campbell Soup since 2001, has used it to find strategies to turn around the performance of the troubled food products maker in the 2000s (see next page). In fact, his self-described mission was to take a "bad" company and lift its performance to "extraordinary" by the end of 2011.[20]

The Five Forces Model

A well-known model that helps managers focus on the five most important competitive forces, or potential threats, in the external environment is Michael Porter's five forces model. We discussed the first four forces in the following list in Chapter 6.

Manager as a Person

Douglas Conant Keeps Stirring Up Campbell Soup

Campbell Soup Co., one of the oldest and best-known global food companies, saw demand for its major product, condensed soup, plummet by 30% between 1998 and 2004 as customers switched from high-salt, processed soups to more healthful low-fat, low-salt varieties. Campbell's profits and stock price plunged as its condensed soup business collapsed, and in 2001 its directors brought in a new CEO, Douglas Conant, to help the troubled company. Conant decided it was necessary to develop a three-year turnaround plan to help the company strengthen its market position against aggressive competitors such as General Mills, whose Progresso Soup division had attracted away many Campbell customers with its innovative new lines of healthful soup.

One of Conant's first actions was to initiate a thorough SWOT planning exercise. *External analysis* of the environment identified the growth of the organic and health food segment of the food market and the increasing number of other kinds of convenience foods as a threat to Campbell's core soup business. It also revealed three growth opportunities: (1) the growing market for health and sports drinks, in which Campbell already was a competitor with its V8 juice; (2) the growing market for quality bread and cookies, in which Campbell competed with its Pepperidge Farm brand; and (3) chocolate products, where Campbell's Godiva brand had enjoyed increasing sales throughout the 1990s.

With the analysis of the environment complete, Conant turned his attention to his organization's resources and capabilities. His *internal analysis* of Campbell identified a number of major weaknesses. These included staffing levels that were too high relative to its competitors and high costs associated with manufacturing its soups because of the use of outdated machinery. Also, Conant noted that Campbell had a conservative culture in which people seemed to be afraid to take risks—something that was a real problem in an industry where customer tastes are always changing and new products must be developed constantly. At the same time, the SWOT analysis identified an enormous strength: Campbell enjoyed huge economies of scale because of the enormous quantity of food products that it makes, and it also had a first-rate R&D division capable of developing exciting new food products.

Douglas Conant, CEO of Campbell's, has revitalized the company through SWOT analysis. From SWOT analysis he has learned how to innovate successful new food products, and Campbell's has emerged as a leader in the low-carb, health-conscious, and luxury-food market segments.

Using the information from this SWOT analysis, Conant and his managers decided that Campbell needed to use its product development skills to revitalize its core products and modify or reinvent them in ways that would appeal to increasingly health-conscious and busy consumers. Conant stressed convenience with microwaveable soups and cans that open with a pull. The recipes became more healthful for its soups, V8 drinks, and Pepperidge Farm snacks because Conant needed to expand Campbell's share of the health, sports, snack, and luxury food market segments. Also, to increase sales, Campbell needed to tap into new food outlets, such as corporate cafeterias, college dining halls, and other mass eateries, to expand consumers' access to its foods. Finally, Conant decided to decentralize authority to managers at lower levels in the organization and make them responsible for developing new soup, bread, and chocolate products that met customers' changing needs. In this way he hoped to revitalize Campbell's slow-moving culture and speed the flow of improved and new products to the market.

Conant's turnaround included questioning if the firm's highly profitable Godiva chocolate brand was still a good fit for the company. He decided it had become a weakness, and in 2008 he sold it for $850 million.[21] He used some of the proceeds of this sale to build new company strengths. For example, he invested in R&D to develop the skills needed to customize Campbell's brands to the needs of customers in countries such as India and China–a move that spearheaded global expansion into major soup-eating nations.

Under Conant, Campbell's profits and stock price have increased each year during the 2000s; and with a culture of innovation permeating the organization, in 2010 its future looks even brighter. Thanks to his leadership employees are more engaged and involved, sales are up, and many new leaders and managers have been promoted to change the company's culture and stretch its employees. How does Conant himself encourage employees to perform at a high level? Obviously he rewards good performance, but he also sends around 20 daily "thank-you" e-mail messages to employees at every level of the organization to show he understands how everyone can contribute to help the company meet its goals and mission over the next three years.

Porter identified these five factors as major threats because they affect how much profit organizations competing within the same industry can expect to make:

- *The level of rivalry among organizations in an industry:* The more that companies compete against one another for customers–for example, by lowering the prices of their products or by increasing advertising–the lower is the level of industry profits (low prices mean less profit).
- *The potential for entry into an industry:* The easier it is for companies to enter an industry–because, for example, barriers to entry, such as brand loyalty, are low–the more likely it is for industry prices and therefore industry profits to be low.
- *The power of large suppliers:* If there are only a few large suppliers of an important input, then suppliers can drive up the price of that input, and expensive inputs result in lower profits for companies in an industry.
- *The power of large customers:* If only a few large customers are available to buy an industry's output, they can bargain to drive down the price of that output. As a result, industry producers make lower profits.
- *The threat of substitute products:* Often the output of one industry is a substitute for the output of another industry (plastic may be a substitute for steel in some applications, for example; similarly, bottled water is a substitute for cola). When a substitute for their product exists, companies cannot demand high prices for it or customers will switch to the substitute, and this constraint keeps their profits low.

Porter argued that when managers analyze opportunities and threats, they should pay particular attention to these five forces because they are the major threats an organization will encounter. It is the job of managers at the corporate, business, and functional levels to formulate strategies to counter these threats so an organization can manage its task and general environments, perform at a high level, and generate high profits. At Campbell, Conant performed such analysis to identify the opportunities and threats stemming from the actions of food industry rivals. For example, as noted earlier, General Mill's Progresso Soups division developed more healthful kinds of soups, and this increased rivalry and lowered Campbell's sales and profits until it successfully developed new lines of healthful soups. Both companies have been affected by the threat of rising global food prices as the costs of wheat, corn, rice, and dairy products have increased. Both companies are striving to reduce operating costs to limit food price increases because the company with the lowest prices will attract the most customers and gain a competitive advantage–especially during the recent recession.

Today competition is tough in most industries, whether companies make cars, soup, computers, or dolls. The term **hypercompetition** applies to industries that are characterized by permanent, ongoing, intense competition brought about by advancing technology or changing customer tastes and fads and fashions.[22] Clearly, planning and strategy formulation are much more difficult and risky when hypercompetition prevails in an industry.

hypercompetition Permanent, ongoing, intense competition brought about in an industry by advancing technology or changing customer tastes.

Formulating Business-Level Strategies

Michael Porter, the researcher who developed the five forces model, also developed a theory of how managers can select a business-level strategy–a plan to gain a competitive advantage in a particular market or industry.[23]Porter argued that business-level strategy creates a competitive advantage because it allows an organization (or a division of a company) to *counter and reduce* the threat of the five industry forces. That is, successful business-level strategy reduces rivalry, prevents new competitors from entering the industry, reduces the power of suppliers or buyers, and lowers the threat of substitutes–and this raises prices and profits.

LO8-3 Differentiate between the main types of business-level strategies and explain how they give an organization a competitive advantage that may lead to superior performance.

According to Porter, to obtain these higher profits managers must choose between two basic ways of increasing the value of an organization's products: *differentiating the product* to increase its value to customers or *lowering the costs* of making the product. Porter also argues that managers must choose between serving the whole market or serving just one segment or part of a market. Based on those choices, managers choose to pursue one of four business-level strategies: low cost, differentiation, focused low cost, or focused differentiation (see Table 8.2).

Low-Cost Strategy

low-cost strategy Driving the organization's costs down below the costs of its rivals.

With a **low-cost strategy,** managers try to gain a competitive advantage by focusing the energy of all the organization's departments or functions on driving the company's costs down below the costs of its industry rivals. This strategy, for example, would require that manufacturing managers search for new ways to reduce production costs, R&D managers focus on developing new products that can be manufactured more cheaply, and marketing managers find ways to lower the costs of attracting customers. According to Porter, companies pursuing a low-cost strategy can sell a product for less than their rivals sell it and yet still make a good profit because of their lower costs. Thus such organizations enjoy a competitive advantage based on their low prices. For

Table 8.2
Porter's Business-Level Strategies

	Number of Market Segments Served	
Strategy	**Many**	**Few**
Low cost	✓	
Focused low cost		✓
Differentiation	✓	
Focused differentiation		✓

example, Carrefour's move to in-house brands was clearly an effort to become the low cost leader. Also, when existing companies have low costs and can charge low prices, it is difficult for new companies to enter the industry because entering is always an expensive process.

Differentiation Strategy

differentiation strategy Distinguishing an organization's products from the products of competitors on dimensions such as product design, quality, or after-sales service.

With a **differentiation strategy,** managers try to gain a competitive advantage by focusing all the energies of the organization's departments or functions on *distinguishing* the organization's products from those of competitors on one or more important dimensions, such as product design, quality, or after-sales service and support. Often the process of making products unique and different is expensive. This strategy, for example, frequently requires that managers increase spending on product design or R&D to differentiate products, and costs rise as a result. Organizations that successfully pursue a differentiation strategy may be able to charge a *premium price* for their products; the premium price lets organizations pursuing a differentiation strategy recoup their higher costs. Marks & Spencer is a well-known retail company that pursues a strategy of differentiation. The firm spends money to advertise, differentiate, and create a unique image for their products. Also, differentiation makes industry entry difficult because new companies have no brand name to help them compete and customers don't perceive other products to be close substitutes, so this also allows premium pricing and results in high profits.

"Stuck in the Middle"

According to Porter's theory, managers cannot simultaneously pursue both a low-cost strategy and a differentiation strategy. Porter identified a simple correlation: Differentiation raises costs and thus necessitates premium pricing to recoup those high costs. According to Porter, managers must choose between a low-cost strategy and a differentiation strategy. He refers to managers and organizations that have not made this choice as being "stuck in the middle."

Organizations stuck in the middle tend to have lower levels of performance than do those that pursue a low-cost or a differentiation strategy. To avoid being stuck in the middle, top managers must instruct departmental managers to take actions that will result in either low cost or differentiation.

However, exceptions to this rule can be found. In many organizations managers have been able to drive costs below those of rivals and simultaneously differentiate their products from those offered by rivals.[24] For example, Toyota's production system is the most efficient–and still one of the most reliable–of any global carmaker, as we discuss in the next chapter. This efficiency gives Toyota a low-cost advantage over its rivals in the global car industry. At the same time, Toyota has differentiated its cars from those of rivals on the basis of superior design and quality. This superiority allows the company to charge a premium price for many of its popular models.[25] Thus Toyota seems to be simultaneously pursuing both a low-cost and a differentiated business-level strategy. This example suggests that although Porter's ideas may be valid in most cases, very well managed companies such as Cisco, Campbell, and Toyota may have both low costs and differentiated products–and so make the highest profits of any company in an industry.

Focused Low-Cost and Focused Differentiation Strategies

focused low-cost strategy Serving only one segment of the overall market and trying to be the lowest-cost organization serving that segment.

Both the differentiation strategy and the low-cost strategy are aimed at serving many or most segments of a particular market, such as for cars, toys, foods, or computers. Porter identified two other business-level strategies that aim to serve the needs of customers in only one or a few market segments.[26] Managers pursuing a **focused low-cost strategy** serve one or a few segments of the overall market and aim to

focused differentiation strategy Serving only one segment of the overall market and trying to be the most differentiated organization serving that segment.

make their organization the lowest-cost company serving that segment. By contrast, managers pursuing a **focused differentiation strategy** serve just one or a few segments of the market and aim to make their organization the most differentiated company serving that segment.

Companies pursuing either of these strategies have chosen to *specialize* in some way by directing their efforts at a particular kind of customer (such as serving the needs of babies or affluent customers) or even the needs of customers in a specific geographic region (customers in northern Europe). BMW, for example, pursues a focused differentiation strategy, producing cars exclusively for higher-income customers. By contrast, Toyota pursues a differentiation strategy and produces cars that appeal to consumers in almost all segments of the car market, from basic transportation (Toyota Corolla) through the middle of the market (Toyota Camry) to the high-income end of the market (Lexus). An interesting example of how a company pursuing a focused low-cost strategy, by specializing in one market segment, can compete with powerful differentiators is profiled in the following "Management Insight" box.

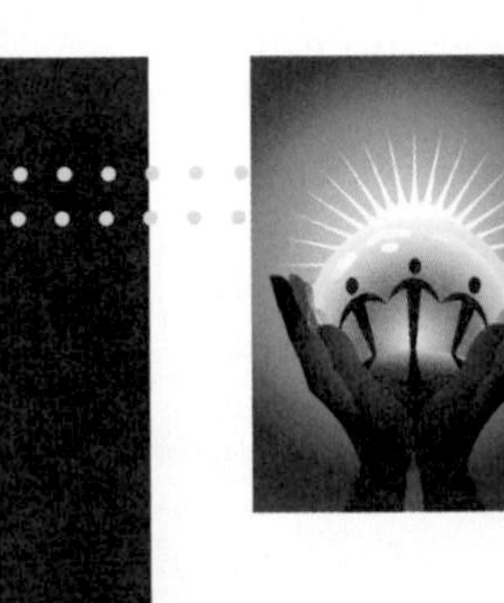

Management Insight

Different Ways to Compete in the Soft Drink Business

"Coke" and "Pepsi" are household names worldwide. Together Coca-Cola and PepsiCo control over 70% of the global soft drink market and over 75% of the U.S. soft drink market. Their success can be attributed to the differentiation strategies they developed to produce and promote their products–strategies that have made them two of the most profitable global organizations. There are several parts to their differentiation strategies. First, both companies built global brands by manufacturing the soft drink concentrate that gives cola its flavor but then selling the concentrate in a syrup form to bottlers throughout the world. The bottlers are responsible for producing and distributing the actual cola. They add carbonated water to the syrup, package the resulting drinks, and distribute them to vending machines, supermarkets, restaurants, and other retail outlets. The bottlers must also sign an exclusive agreement that prohibits them from bottling or distributing the products of competing soft drink companies. This creates a barrier to entry that helps prevent new companies from entering the industry.

Second, Coca-Cola and PepsiCo charge the bottlers a premium price for the syrup; they then invest a large part of the profits in advertising to build and maintain brand awareness. The hundreds of millions they spend on advertising to develop a global brand name help Coca-Cola and PepsiCo differentiate their products so consumers are more likely to buy a Coke or a Pepsi than a less well-known cola. Moreover, brand loyalty allows both companies to charge a premium or comparatively high price for what is, after all, merely colored water and flavoring.

In the last decade the global soft drink environment has undergone a major change, however, because of Gerald Pencer, a Canadian entrepreneur who came up with a new strategy for competing against these powerful differentiators. Pencer's strategy was to produce a high-quality, low-priced cola, manufactured and bottled by the Cott Corporation, of which he was CEO at the time, but to sell it as the private-label house brand of major retail stores such as Walmart (Sam's Cola brand) and

"I'll have a Coke" may not be as easy a decision for much longer, as Cott and other competitors wedge lower-cost sodas into the big retail chains.

supermarket chains such as Kroger's (Big K brand), thus bypassing the bottlers. Pencer could implement his focused low-cost strategy and charge a low price for his soft drinks because he did not need to spend on advertising (the retail stores did that) and because Cott's soft drinks are distributed by the store chains and retailers using their efficient national distribution systems, such as the nationwide trucking system developed by giant retailer Walmart. Retailers are willing to do this because Cott's low-cost soft drinks allow them to make much more profit than they receive from selling Coke or Pepsi. At the same time, the products build their store brand image.

Pencer implemented this plan first in Canada and then quickly expanded into the United States as retailers' demand for his products grew. He went on to supply the international market by offering to sell soft drink concentrate to global retailers at prices lower than Coca-Cola and PepsiCo. By 2004 Cott was the world's largest supplier of retailer-branded carbonated soft drinks.[27] It has manufacturing facilities in Canada, the United States, and the United Kingdom, and a syrup concentrate production plant in Columbus, Georgia, that supply most of the private-label grocery store, drugstore, mass merchandising, and convenience store chains in these countries. However, note that while Cott is the leading supplier of retailer-branded sodas, it is still focusing on its low-cost strategy. It makes no attempt to compete with Coke and Pepsi, which pursue differentiation strategies and whose brand-name sodas dominate the global soda market. Indeed, in 2010 both these companies announced plans to buy back their bottlers at a cost of billions of dollars because this would increase their long-term profits–a strategy known as vertical integration, discussed later in the chapter.[28] But Cott is its own bottler; it knows the value of this strategy.

Formulating Corporate-Level Strategies

LO8-4 Differentiate between the main types of corporate-level strategies and explain how they are used to strengthen a company's business-level strategy and competitive advantage.

Once managers have formulated the business-level strategies that will best position a company, or a division of a company, to compete in an industry and outperform its rivals, they must look to the future. If their planning has been successful the company will be generating high profits, and their task now is to plan how to invest these profits to increase performance over time.

Recall that *corporate-level strategy* is a plan of action that involves choosing in which industries and countries a company should invest its resources to achieve its mission and goals. In choosing a corporate-level strategy, managers ask, How should the growth and development of our company be managed to increase its ability to create value for customers (and thus increase its performance) over the long run? Managers of effective organizations actively seek new opportunities to use a company's resources to create new and improved and services for customers. Examples of organizations whose product lines are growing rapidly are Google and Apple, whose managers pursue any feasible opportunity to use their companies' skills to provide customers with new products.

In addition, some managers must help their organizations respond to threats due to changing forces in the task or general environment that have made their business-level strategies less effective and reduced profits. For example, customers may no longer be buying the kinds of goods and services a company is producing (high-salt soup, or bulky CRT televisions), or other organizations may have entered the market and attracted away customers (this happened to Sony in the 2000s after Apple and Samsung began to produce better portable music players, laptops, and flat-screen LCD televisions). Top managers aim to find corporate strategies that can help the organization strengthen its business-level strategies and thus respond to these changes and improve performance.

The principal corporate-level strategies that managers use to help a company grow and keep it at the top of its industry, or to help it retrench and reorganize to stop its decline, are (1) concentration on a single industry, (2) vertical integration, (3) diversification, and (4) international expansion. An organization will benefit from pursuing any of these strategies only when the strategy helps further increase the value of the organization's goods and services so more customers buy them. Specifically, to increase the value of goods and services, a corporate-level strategy must help a company, or one of its divisions, either (1) lower the costs of developing and making products or (2) increase product differentiation so more customers want to buy the products even at high or premium prices. Both of these outcomes strengthen a company's competitive advantage and increase its performance.

Concentration on a Single Industry

concentration on a single industry Reinvesting a company's profits to strengthen its competitive position in its current industry.

Most growing companies reinvest their profits to strengthen their competitive position in the industry in which they are currently operating; in doing so, they pursue the corporate-level strategy of **concentration on a single industry.** Most commonly, an organization uses its functional skills to develop new kinds of products, or it expands the number of locations in which it uses those skills. For example, Apple continuously introduces improved iPods and mobile wireless devices such as the iPhone and iPad, whereas McDonald's, which began as one restaurant, focused all its efforts on using its resources to quickly expand across the globe. On the other hand, concentration on a single industry becomes an appropriate corporate-level strategy when managers see the need to *reduce* the size of their organizations to increase performance. Managers may decide to get out of certain industries when, for example, the business-level strategy pursued by a particular division no longer works and the division has lost its competitive advantage. To improve performance, managers can sell off low-performing divisions, concentrate remaining organizational resources in one industry, and try to develop new products customers want to buy. For example, Campbell sold its Godiva chocolate division and invested the proceeds in its core food and snack divisions.

Vertical Integration

vertical integration Expanding a company's operations either backward into an industry that produces inputs for its products or forward into an industry that uses, distributes, or sells its products.

When an organization is performing well in its industry, managers often see new opportunities to create value either by producing the inputs it uses to make its products or by distributing and selling its products to customers. **Vertical integration** is a corporate-level strategy in which a company expands its business operations either backward into an industry that produces inputs for its products (*backward vertical integration*) or forward into a new industry that uses, distributes, or sells the company's products (*forward vertical integration*).[29] A steel company that buys iron ore mines and enters the raw materials industry to supply the ore needed to make steel is engaging in backward vertical integration. A PC maker that decides to enter the retail industry and open a chain of company-owned retail outlets to sell its PCs is engaging in forward integration. For example, Apple entered the retail industry when it set up a chain of Apple stores to sell its computers and other electronic devices.

Figure 8.6 illustrates the four main stages in a typical raw material to customer value chain; value is added to the product at each stage by the activities involved in each industry. For a company based in the assembly stage, backward integration would involve establishing a new division in the intermediate manufacturing or raw material production industries; and forward integration would involve establishing a new division to distribute its products to wholesalers or a retail division to sell directly to customers. A division at one stage or one industry receives the product produced by the division in the previous stage or industry, transforms it in some way–adding value–and then transfers the output at a higher price to the division at the next stage in the chain.

As an example of how this industry value chain works, consider the cola segment of the soft drink industry. In the raw material industry, suppliers include sugar companies

Figure 8.6
Stages in a Vertical Value Chain

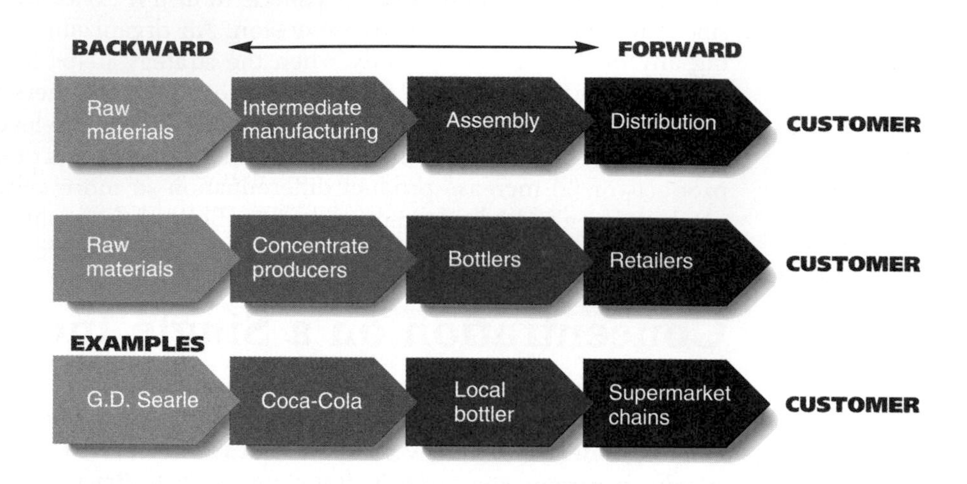

and manufacturers of artificial sweeteners such as NutraSweet and Splenda, which are used in diet colas. These companies sell their products to companies in the soft drink industry that make concentrate–such as Coca-Cola and PepsiCo, which mix these inputs with others to produce the cola concentrate. In the process, they add value to these inputs. The concentrate producers then sell the concentrate to companies in the bottling and distribution industry, which add carbonated water to the concentrate and package the resulting drinks–again adding value to the concentrate. Next the bottlers distribute and sell the soft drinks to retailers and fast-food chains such as McDonald's. Companies in the retail industry add value by making the product accessible to customers, and they profit from direct sales to customers. Thus value is added at each stage in the raw material to consumer chain.

The reason managers pursue vertical integration is that it allows them either to add value to their products by making them special or unique or to lower the costs of making and selling them. An example of using forward vertical integration to increase differentiation is Apple's decision to open its own stores to make its unique products more accessible to customers who could try them out before they bought them. An example of using forward vertical integration to lower costs is Matsushita's decision to open company-owned stores to sell its Panasonic and JVC products and thus keep the profit that otherwise would be earned by independent retailers.[30] So too is Coca-Cola and PepsiCo's decision to buy their bottlers so they can better differentiate their products and lower costs in the future.

Although vertical integration can strengthen an organization's competitive advantage and increase its performance, it can also reduce an organization's flexibility to respond to changing environmental conditions and create threats that must be countered by changing the organization's strategy. For example, IBM used to produce most of the components of its mainframe computers. Although this made sense in the past when IBM enjoyed a major competitive advantage, it became a major handicap for the company in the 1990s when the increasing use of organizationwide networks of PCs cut demand for mainframes. IBM had lost its competitive advantage and found itself with an excess capacity problem in its component operations. Closing down this capacity by exiting the computer components industry cost IBM over $5 billion.[31]

Thus, when considering vertical integration as a strategy to add value, managers must be careful because sometimes it may *reduce* a company's ability to create value when the environment changes. This is why so many companies now outsource the production of component parts to other companies and, like IBM, have exited the components industry–by vertically *disintegrating* backward. IBM, however, found a profitable new opportunity for forward vertical integration in the 2000s: It entered the IT consulting services industry to provide advice to large companies about how to install and manage their computer hardware and software, which has become the major source of IBM's profitability in the 2000s.[32]

Diversification

diversification Expanding a company's business operations into a new industry in order to produce new kinds of valuable goods or services.

Diversification is the corporate-level strategy of expanding a company's business operations into a new industry in order to produce new kinds of valuable goods or services.[33] Examples include PepsiCo's diversification into the snack food business with the purchase of Frito Lay. There are two main kinds of diversification: related and unrelated.

related diversification Entering a new business or industry to create a competitive advantage in one or more of an organization's existing divisions or businesses.

synergy Performance gains that result when individuals and departments coordinate their actions.

RELATED DIVERSIFICATION **Related diversification** is the strategy of entering a new business or industry to create a competitive advantage in one or more of an organization's existing divisions or businesses. Related diversification can add value to an organization's products if managers can find ways for its various divisions or business units to share their valuable skills or resources so that synergy is created.[34] **Synergy** is obtained when the value created by two divisions cooperating is greater than the value that would be created if the two divisions operated separately and independently. For example, suppose two or more divisions of a diversified company can use the same manufacturing facilities, distribution channels, or advertising campaigns–that is, share functional activities. Each division has to invest fewer resources in a shared functional activity than it would have to invest if it performed the functional activity by itself. Related diversification can be a major source of cost savings when divisions share the costs of performing a functional activity.[35] Similarly, if one division's R&D skills can improve another division's products and increase their differentiated appeal, this synergy can give the second division an important competitive advantage over its industry rivals–so the company as a whole benefits from diversification. To illustrate, when Coca-Cola bought the British firm Innocent Drinks, which made fruit and smoothie beverages, it was able to obtain such synergies.

In addition, the divisions can share the research costs of developing new and improved products, such as finding more absorbent material, that increase both products' differentiated appeal. This is something that is also at the heart of 3M's corporate strategy, which is discussed in the following "Management Insight" box.

Management Insight

How to Make Related Diversification Work

3M is a 100-year-old industrial giant that in 2009 generated over US$23 billion in revenues and over US$6 billion in profits from its more than 50,000 individual products, ranging from sandpaper and adhesive tape to medical devices, office supplies, and electronic components.[36] From the beginning, 3M has pursued related diversification and created new businesses by leveraging its skills in research and development. Today the company is composed of more than 40 separate divisions positioned in six major business groups: transportation, health care, industrial, consumer and office, electronics and communications,

How did we ever survive without Post-it Notes? 3M's intense focus on solving customer problems results in new products that sell well, including countless variations of the original sticky note.

and specialty materials. The company currently operates with the goal of producing 40% of sales revenues from products introduced within the previous four years. Its CEO George Buckley's mission was to "kick-start growth," and he has achieved this by increasing spending on R&D to almost US$1 billion or about 6% of sales.[37]

How does 3M do it? First, the company is a science-based enterprise with a strong tradition of innovation and risk taking. Risk taking is encouraged, and failure is not punished but is seen as a natural part of the process of creating new products and business.[38] Second, 3M's management is relentlessly focused on the company's customers and the problems they face. Many of 3M's products have come from helping customers to solve difficult problems. Third, managers set stretch goals that require the company to create new products and businesses at a rapid rate. Fourth, employees are given considerable autonomy to pursue their own ideas; indeed, 15% of employees' time can be spent working on projects of their own choosing without management approval. Many products have resulted from this autonomy, including the ubiquitous Post-it Notes. Fifth, while products belong to business units and business units are responsible for generating profits, the technologies belong to every unit within the company. Anyone at 3M is free to try to develop new applications for a technology developed by its business units. Finally, 3M organizes many companywide meetings where researchers from its different divisions are brought together to share the results of their work. It also implemented an IT system that promotes the sharing of technological knowledge between researchers so new opportunities can be identified.

In sum, to pursue related diversification successfully, managers search for new businesses where they can use the existing skills and resources in their departments and divisions to create synergies, add value to new products and businesses, and improve their competitive position and that of the entire company. In addition, managers may try to acquire a company in a new industry because they believe it possesses skills and resources that will improve the performance of one or more of their existing divisions. If successful, such skill transfers can help an organization to lower its costs or better differentiate its products because they create synergies between divisions.

unrelated diversification Entering a new industry or buying a company in a new industry that is not related in any way to an organization's current businesses or industries.

UNRELATED DIVERSIFICATION Managers pursue **unrelated diversification** when they establish divisions or buy companies in new industries that are *not* linked in any way to their current businesses or industries. One main reason for pursuing unrelated diversification is that sometimes managers can buy a poorly performing company, transfer their management skills to that company, turn around its business, and increase its performance–all of which create value.

Another reason for pursuing unrelated diversification is that purchasing businesses in different industries lets managers engage in *portfolio strategy,* which is apportioning financial resources among divisions to increase financial returns or spread risks among different businesses, much as individual investors do with their own portfolios. For example, managers may transfer funds from a rich division (a "cash cow") to a new and promising division (a "star") and, by appropriately allocating money between divisions, create value. Though used as a popular explanation in the 1980s for unrelated diversification, portfolio strategy ran into increasing criticism in the 1990s because it simply does not work.[39] Why? As managers expand the scope of their organization's operations and enter more and more industries, it becomes increasingly difficult for top managers to be knowledgeable about all of the organization's diverse businesses. Managers do not have the time to process all of the information required to adequately assess the strategy and performance of each division, and so the performance of the entire company often falls.

While unrelated diversification is largely discouraged in mature economies, it should be recognized that in emerging economies unrelated diversification is the norm and in fact leads to better performance. In most emerging economies there is an absence of institutional supports for business. Thus, the legal system often does not work as efficiently as it does in the mature economies of Europe or North America. This can create situations where contracts cannot be enforced, among other problems. In addition, the banking system may not be fully developed so gaining access to resources can be difficult. In such settings, rather than concentrating on a single industry, the corporation will diversify into a variety of businesses. These diverse businesses then conduct trade with and support each other. Thus, the profitable businesses in one area will help to fund the new enterprises in another area. The various affiliations often deal with each other. And when outside customers do business with the various affiliated businesses, these customers are hesitant not to fulfill their obligations under the contract since they will lose the opportunity not only to do business with one firm in the future but also all the firms associated with that corporation. Thus, the unrelated businesses act to support each other in ways that may not be necessary in a mature economy in Europe or North America. The result is that in emerging economies unrelated diversified firms typically outperform related firms.

International Expansion

As if planning whether to vertically integrate, diversify, or concentrate on the core business were not a difficult enough task, corporate-level managers also must decide on the appropriate way to compete internationally. A basic question confronts the managers of any organization that needs to sell its products abroad and compete in more than one national market: To what extent should the organization customize features of its products and marketing campaign to different national conditions?[40]

If managers decide that their organization should sell the same standardized product in each national market in which it competes, and use the same basic marketing approach, they adopt a **global strategy.**[41] Such companies undertake little, if any, customization to suit the specific needs of customers in different countries. But if managers decide to customize products and marketing strategies to specific national conditions, they adopt a **multidomestic strategy.** Matsushita, with its Panasonic and JVC brands, has traditionally pursued a global strategy, selling the same basic TVs, camcorders, and DVD and MP3 players in every country in which it does business and often using the same basic marketing approach. Unilever, the European food and household products company, has pursued a multidomestic strategy. Thus, to appeal to German customers, Unilever's German division sells a different range of food products and uses a different marketing approach than its North American division.

global strategy Selling the same standardized product and using the same basic marketing approach in each national market.

multidomestic strategy Customizing products and marketing strategies to specific national conditions.

Both global and multidomestic strategies have advantages and disadvantages. The major advantage of a global strategy is the significant cost savings associated with not having to customize products and marketing approaches to different national conditions. For example, Rolex watches and Chanel or Armani clothing or accessories or perfume are all products that can be sold using the same marketing across many countries by simply changing the language. Thus companies can save a significant amount of money. The major disadvantage of pursuing a global strategy is that by ignoring national differences, managers may leave themselves vulnerable to local competitors that differentiate their products to suit local tastes.

Global food makers Kellogg's and Nestlé learned this when they entered the Indian processed food market, which is worth over US$100 billion a year. These companies did not understand how to customize their products to the tastes of the Indian market and initially suffered large losses. When Kellogg's launched its breakfast cereals in India, for example, it failed to understand that most Indians eat cooked breakfasts because milk is normally not pasteurized. Today, with the growing availability of pasteurized or canned milk, it offers exotic cereals made from basmati rice and flavored with mango to appeal to customers. Similarly, Nestlé's Maggi noodles failed to please

Indian customers until it gave them a "masala" or mixed curry spice flavor; today its noodles have become a staple in Indian school lunches.

The advantages and disadvantages of a multidomestic strategy are the opposite of those of a global strategy. The major advantage of a multidomestic strategy is that by customizing product offerings and marketing approaches to local conditions, managers may be able to gain market share or charge higher prices for their products. The major disadvantage is that customization raises production costs and puts the multidomestic company at a price disadvantage because it often has to charge prices higher than the prices charged by competitors pursuing a global strategy. Obviously the choice between these two strategies calls for trade-offs.

Managers at Gillette, the well-known razor blade maker that is now part of Procter & Gamble (P&G), created a strategy that combined the best features of both international strategies. Gillette has always been a global organization because its managers quickly saw the advantages of selling its core product, razor blades, in as many countries as possible. Gillette's strategy over the years has been pretty constant: Find a new country with a growing market for razor blades, form a strategic alliance with a local razor blade company and take a majority stake in it, invest in a large marketing campaign, and then build a modern factory to make razor blades and other products for the local market. For example, when Gillette entered Russia after the breakup of the Soviet Union, it saw a huge opportunity to increase sales. It formed a joint venture with a local company called Leninets Concern, which made a razor known as the Sputnik, and then with this base began to import its own brands into Russia. When sales grew sharply, Gillette decided to offer more products in the market and built a new plant in St. Petersburg.[42]

A study in contrasts. Matsushita, with its Panasonic brand (shown on the top), has largely pursued a global strategy, selling the same basic TVs and DVD players in every market and using a similar marketing message. Unilever, on the other hand, has pursued a multidomestic strategy, tailoring its product line and marketing approach to specific locations. On the bottom, the CEO of Hindustan Unilever, Keki Dadiseth, holds a box of Surf detergent designed for local customers.

In establishing factories in countries where labor and other costs are low and then distributing and marketing its products to countries in that region of the world, Gillette pursued a global strategy. However, all of Gillette's research and development and design activities are located in the United States. As it develops new kinds of razors, it equips its foreign factories to manufacture them when it decides that local customers are ready to trade up to the new product. So, for example, Gillette's latest razor may be introduced in a country abroad years later than in the United States. Thus Gillette is customizing its products to the needs of different countries and so also pursues a multidomestic strategy.

By pursuing this kind of international strategy, Gillette achieves low costs and still differentiates and customizes its product range to suit the needs of each country or world region.[43]

CHOOSING A WAY TO EXPAND INTERNATIONALLY

As we have discussed, a more competitive global environment has proved to be both an opportunity and a threat for organizations and managers. The opportunity is that organizations that expand globally can open new markets, reach more customers, and gain access to new sources of raw materials and to low-cost suppliers of inputs. The threat is that organizations that expand globally are likely to encounter new competitors in the foreign countries they enter and must respond to new political, economic, and cultural conditions.

Before setting up foreign operations, managers of companies need to analyze the forces in the environment of a particular country (such as Korea or Brazil) to choose the right method to expand and respond to those forces in the most appropriate way. In general, four basic ways to operate in the global environment are importing and exporting, licensing and franchising, strategic alliances, and wholly owned foreign subsidiaries. We briefly discuss each one, moving from the lowest level of foreign involvement and investment required of a global organization and its managers, and the least amount of risk, to the high end of the spectrum (see Figure 8.7).[44]

exporting Making products at home and selling them abroad.

IMPORTING AND EXPORTING The least complex global operations are exporting and importing. A company engaged in **exporting** makes products at home and sells them abroad. An organization might sell its own products abroad or allow a local organization in the foreign country to distribute its products. Few risks are associated with exporting because a company does not have to invest in developing manufacturing facilities abroad. It can further reduce its investment abroad if it allows a local company to distribute its products.

importing Selling products at home that are made abroad.

A company engaged in **importing** sells products at home that are made abroad (products it makes itself or buys from other companies). In many cases the appeal of a product–Irish crystal, French wine, Italian furniture, or Indian silk–is that it is made abroad. The Internet has made it much easier for companies to tell potential foreign buyers about their products; detailed product specifications and features are available online, and informed buyers can communicate easily with prospective sellers.

licensing Allowing a foreign organization to take charge of manufacturing and distributing a product in its country or world region in return for a negotiated fee.

LICENSING AND FRANCHISING In **licensing,** a company (the licenser) allows a foreign organization (the licensee) to take charge of both manufacturing and distributing one or more of its products in the licensee's country or world region in return for a negotiated fee. Chemical maker DuPont might license a local factory in India to produce nylon or Teflon. The advantage of licensing is that the licenser does not have to bear the development costs associated with opening up in a foreign country; the licensee bears the costs. The risks associated with this strategy are that the company granting the license has to give its foreign partner access to its technological know-how and so risks losing control of its secrets.

franchising Selling to a foreign organization the rights to use a brand name and operating know-how in return for a lump-sum payment and a share of the profits.

Whereas licensing is pursued primarily by manufacturing companies, franchising is pursued primarily by service organizations. In **franchising,** a company (the franchiser) sells to a foreign organization (the franchisee) the rights to use its brand name and operating know-how in return for a lump-sum payment and share of the franchiser's profits. Hilton Hotels might sell a franchise to a local company in Chile to operate hotels under the Hilton name in return for a franchise payment. The advantage of franchising is that the franchiser does not have to bear the development costs of overseas expansion and avoids the many problems associated with setting up foreign operations. The downside is that the organization that grants the franchise may lose control over how the franchisee operates, and product quality may fall. In this way franchisers, such as Hilton, Avis, and McDonald's, risk losing their good names. A firm's reputation will suffer over time if quality is not maintained. Once again, the Internet facilitates communication between partners and allows them to better meet each other's expectations.

Figure 8.7
Four Ways to Expand Internationally

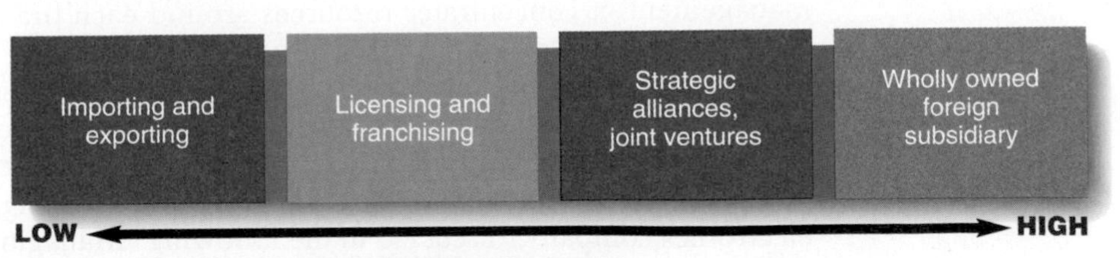

strategic alliance An agreement in which managers pool or share their organization's resources and know-how with a foreign company, and the two organizations share the rewards and risks of starting a new venture.

joint venture A strategic alliance among two or more companies that agree to jointly establish and share the ownership of a new business.

wholly owned foreign subsidiary Production operations established in a foreign country independent of any local direct involvement.

STRATEGIC ALLIANCES One way to overcome the loss-of-control problems associated with exporting, licensing, and franchising is to expand globally by means of a strategic alliance. In a **strategic alliance,** managers pool or share their organization's resources and know-how with those of a foreign company, and the two organizations share the rewards or risks of starting a new venture in a foreign country.

A strategic alliance can take the form of a written contract between two or more companies to exchange resources, or it can result in the creation of a new organization. A **joint venture** is a strategic alliance among two or more companies that agree to jointly establish and share the ownership of a new business.[45] An organization's level of involvement abroad increases in a joint venture because the alliance normally involves a capital investment in production facilities abroad in order to produce goods or services outside the home country. Risk, however, is reduced. The Internet and global teleconferencing provide the increased communication and coordination necessary for global partners to work together. For example, Coca-Cola and Nestlé formed a joint venture to market their teas, coffees, and health-oriented beverages in more than 50 countries.[46] Similarly, BP Amoco and Italy's ENI formed a joint venture to build a $2.5 billion gas liquefaction plant in Egypt.[47]

WHOLLY OWNED FOREIGN SUBSIDIARIES When managers decide to establish a **wholly owned foreign subsidiary,** they invest in establishing production operations in a foreign country independent of any local direct involvement. Many Japanese car component companies, for example, have established their own operations in the United States to supply U.S.-based Japanese carmakers such as Toyota and Honda with high-quality car components.

Operating alone, without any direct involvement from foreign companies, an organization receives all of the rewards and bears all of the risks associated with operating abroad.[48] This method of international expansion is much more expensive than the others because it requires a higher level of foreign investment and presents managers with many more threats. However, investment in a foreign subsidiary or division offers significant advantages: It gives an organization high potential returns because the organization does not have to share its profits with a foreign organization, and it reduces the level of risk because the organization's managers have full control over all aspects of their foreign subsidiary's operations. Moreover, this type of investment allows managers to protect their technology and know-how from foreign organizations. Large, well-known companies like DuPont, General Motors, and P&G, which have plenty of resources, make extensive use of wholly owned subsidiaries. Recall from Chapter 6 that Nokia establishes a wholly owned manufacturing subsidiary in each world region to make the mobile phones it sells in that region.

Obviously, global companies can use many of these different corporate strategies simultaneously to create the most value and strengthen their competitive position. We discussed earlier how P&G pursues related diversification at the global level while it pursues an international strategy that is a mixture of global and multidomestic. P&G also pursues vertical integration: It operates factories that make many of the specialized chemicals used in its products; it operates in the container industry and makes the thousands of different glass and plastic bottles and jars that contain its products; it prints its own product labels; and it distributes its products using its own fleet of trucks. Although P&G is highly diversified, it still puts the focus on its core individual product lines because it is famous for pursuing brand management–it concentrates resources around each brand, which in effect is managed as a "separate company." So P&G is trying to add value in every way it can from its corporate and business strategies. At the business level, for example, P&G aggressively pursues differentiation and charges premium prices for its products. However, it also strives to lower its costs and pursues the corporate-level strategies just discussed to achieve this. The way in which Samsung, the second largest global electronics company (discussed in the following "Managing Globally" box), chose to expand globally also illustrates the complex issues surrounding developing the right strategies to expand globally.

Managing Globally

How Samsung Became a Global Technology Leader

In the 2000s Samsung Electronics, based in Seoul, Korea, became the second most profitable global technology company after Microsoft. Samsung accomplished this when its CEO Lee Kun Hee decided to develop and build competencies first in low-cost manufacturing, and second in R&D, and then use them to make new and improved products for customers the world over.

Samsung's core industry is the consumer electronics industry; in the 1990s its engineers studied how companies such as Sony, Panasonic, Motorola, and Nokia had innovated products such as the Walkman, home video recorders, high-quality televisions, and cell phones. Then they imitated this technology but used Samsung's low-cost advantage to make lower-priced versions of these products that they could sell at lower prices. For example, Samsung decided to enter the cell phone industry and to make lower-cost phones than companies such as Nokia and Motorola. Samsung also entered the semiconductor industry in which it worked to make the lowest-cost memory chips; soon it became the global cost leader. It also entered markets for other digital products such as cameras, printers, and storage devices.

As this Samsung employee demonstrates, the invention of color screens hit a sweet spot in the digital phone market; now we can't live without carrying around detailed photos of our dogs, friends, and workplaces.

Samsung was pursuing the corporate-level strategy of related diversification; its goal was to increase its profitability by using and developing its core competencies in product development and manufacturing to enter new industries and produce attractive new products for global customers. Samsung's strategy was successful and profitable, but it was not playing in the same league as Sony or Nokia, for example. CEO Hee decided to adopt new strategies that would allow his company to compete head-to-head with leading global electronics companies to make it a global technology leader. Now Samsung's goal was not to imitate technology innovated by Sony, Nokia, and so on, but for its engineers to develop the R&D skills necessary to develop leading-edge technologies, such as LCD displays, to create products more advanced than those of its competitors.[49]

Within a decade, SE became the leading supplier of advanced flash memory chips and LCD screens–premium-priced products that it sold to other global electronics makers, including Japanese flat screen TV makers such as Sony. Samsung also developed a new core competence in global marketing. For example, in the early 2000s Samsung was first to realize customers wanted color screens for their cell phones to play games and built-in cameras to send photographs to their friends. Both of these incremental advances allowed Samsung to increase its share of the cell phone market; it has become the second largest cell phone maker after Nokia.[50]

Today Samsung has become one of the most innovative global electronics makers; however, like most other electronics companies it has been forced to find ways to reduce costs because of the global recession. In 2009 Samsung's new CEO Lee Yoon Woo announced a major restructuring that would consolidate its four global divisions into two to reduce costs but still speed product development. Samsung's semiconductor and LCD display businesses are now combined into a new Device Solutions Division, and its television, mobile phone, and consumer electronics products such as printers and computers are in the Digital Media and Communications Division. Because all of Samsung's products use in-house chips and LCD displays, this means that while SE is pursuing related diversification, it is also using its low-cost skills to benefit from vertical integration as it continues its rapid global expansion.

Planning and Implementing Strategy

LO8-5 Describe the vital role managers play in implementing strategies to achieve an organization's mission and goals.

After identifying appropriate business and corporate strategies to attain an organization's mission and goals, managers confront the challenge of putting those strategies into action. Strategy implementation is a five-step process:

1. Allocating responsibility for implementation to the appropriate individuals or groups.
2. Drafting detailed action plans that specify how a strategy is to be implemented.
3. Establishing a timetable for implementation that includes precise, measurable goals linked to the attainment of the action plan.
4. Allocating appropriate resources to the responsible individuals or groups.
5. Holding specific individuals or groups responsible for the attainment of corporate, divisional, and functional goals.

The planning process goes beyond just identifying effective strategies; it also includes plans to ensure that these strategies are put into action. Normally the plan for implementing a new strategy requires the development of new functional strategies, the redesign of an organization's structure, and the development of new control systems; it might also require a new program to change an organization's culture. These are issues we address in the next three chapters.

Summary and Review

LO8-1, 8-2 **PLANNING** Planning is a three-step process: (1) determining an organization's mission and goals; (2) formulating strategy; and (3) implementing strategy. Managers use planning to identify and select appropriate goals and courses of action for an organization and to decide how to allocate the resources they need to attain those goals and carry out those actions. A good plan builds commitment for the organization's goals, gives the organization a sense of direction and purpose, coordinates the different functions and divisions of the organization, and controls managers by making them accountable for specific goals. In large organizations planning takes place at three levels: corporate, business or divisional, and functional or departmental. Long-term plans have a time horizon of five years or more; intermediate-term plans, between one and five years; and short-term plans, one year or less.

LO8-1, 8-2, 8-3, 8-4 **DETERMINING MISSION AND GOALS AND FORMULATING STRATEGY** Determining the organization's mission requires that managers define the business of the organization and establish major goals. Strategy formulation requires that managers perform a SWOT analysis and then choose appropriate strategies at the corporate, business, and functional levels. At the business level, managers are responsible for developing a successful low-cost and/or differentiation strategy, either for the whole market or a particular segment of it. At the functional level, departmental managers develop strategies to help the organization either add value to its products by differentiating them or lower the costs of value creation. At the corporate level, organizations use strategies such as concentration on a single industry, vertical integration, related and unrelated diversification, and international expansion to strengthen their competitive advantage by increasing the value of the goods and services provided to customers.

LO8-5 **IMPLEMENTING STRATEGY** Strategy implementation requires that managers allocate responsibilities to appropriate individuals or groups; draft detailed action plans that specify how a strategy is to be implemented; establish a timetable for implementation that includes precise, measurable goals linked to the attainment of the action plan; allocate appropriate resources to the responsible individuals or groups; and hold individuals or groups accountable for the attainment of goals.

Management in Action

Topics for Discussion and Action

Discussion

1. Describe the three steps of planning. Explain how they are related. **[LO8-1]**
2. How can scenario planning help managers predict the future? **[LO8-2]**
3. What is the relationship among corporate-, business-, and functional-level strategies, and how do they create value for an organization? **[LO8-3, 8-4]**
4. Pick an industry and identify four companies in the industry that pursue one of the four main business-level strategies (low-cost, focused low-cost, and so on). **[LO8-2, 8-3]**
5. What is the difference between vertical integration and related diversification? **[LO8-4]**

Action

6. Ask a manager about the kinds of planning exercises he or she regularly uses. What are the purposes of these exercises, and what are their advantages or disadvantages? **[LO8-1, 8-2]**
7. Ask a manager to identify the corporate- and business-level strategies used by his or her organization. **[LO8-3, 8-4]**

Building Management Skills

How to Analyze a Company's Strategy [LO8-3, 8-4]

Pick a well-known business organization that has received recent press coverage and that provides annual reports at its Web site. From the information in the articles and annual reports, answer these questions:

1. What is (are) the main industry(ies) in which the company competes?
2. What business-level strategy does the company seem to be pursuing in this industry? Why?
3. What corporate-level strategies is the company pursuing? Why?
4. Have there been any major changes in its strategy recently? Why?

Managing Ethically [LO8-2, 8-5]

A few years ago, IBM announced that it had fired the three top managers of its Argentine division because of their involvement in a scheme to secure a $250 million contract for IBM to provide and service the computers of one of Argentina's largest state-owned banks. The three executives paid $14 million of the contract money to a third company, CCR, which paid nearly $6 million to phantom companies. This $6 million was then used to bribe the bank executives who agreed to give IBM the contract.

These bribes are not necessarily illegal under Argentine law. Moreover, the three managers argued that all companies have to pay bribes to get new business contracts, and they were not doing anything that managers in other companies were not.

Questions

1. Either by yourself or in a group decide if the business practice of paying bribes is ethical or unethical.
2. Should IBM allow its foreign divisions to pay bribes if all other companies are doing so?
3. If bribery is common in a particular country, what effect would this likely have on the nation's economy and culture?

Small Group Breakout Exercise

Low Cost or Differentiation? [LO8-2, 8-3]

Form groups of three or four people, and appoint one member as the spokesperson who will communicate your findings to the class when called on by the instructor. Then discuss the following scenario:

You are a team of managers of a major national clothing chain, and you have been charged with finding a way to restore your organization's competitive advantage. Recently your organization has been experiencing increasing competition from two sources. First, discount stores such as Carrefour have been undercutting your prices because they sell in-house brand clothing whereas you buy most of yours from high-quality domestic suppliers. Discount stores have been attracting your customers who buy at the low end of the price range. Second, small boutiques opening near business centers provide high-price designer clothing and are attracting your customers at the high end of the market. Your company has become stuck in the middle, and you have to decide what to do: Should you start to buy abroad so you can lower your prices and pursue a low-cost strategy? Should you focus on the high end of the market and become more of a differentiator? Or should you try to pursue both a low-cost strategy and a differentiation strategy?

1. Using scenario planning, analyze the pros and cons of each alternative.
2. Think about the various clothing retailers in your local malls and city, and analyze the choices they have made about how to compete along the low-cost and differentiation dimensions.

Exploring the World Wide Web [LO8-1, 8-3, 8-4]

Go to Google (www.google.com) and click on About Google; then click on Corporate Info and explore this Web page. For example, click on Technology, Business, Culture, Milestones, and the Ten Things that guide Google's corporate philosophy.

1. How would you describe Google's mission and goals?
2. What business-level strategies is Google pursuing? Why?
3. What corporate-level strategies is Google pursuing? Why?

Be the Manager [LO8-2, 8-3]

A group of investors in your city is considering opening a new upscale supermarket to compete with the major supermarket chains that are currently dominating the city's marketplace. They have called you in to help them determine what kind of upscale supermarket they should open. In other words, how can they best develop a competitive advantage against existing supermarket chains?

Questions

1. List the supermarket chains in your city, and identify their strengths and weaknesses.
2. What business-level strategies are these supermarkets currently pursuing?
3. What kind of supermarket would do best against the competition? What kind of business-level strategy should it pursue?

CHAPTER 9

Value Chain Management: Functional Strategies for Competitive Advantage

Learning Objectives

After studying this chapter, you should be able to:

LO9-1 Explain the role of functional strategy and value chain management in achieving superior quality, efficiency, innovation, and responsiveness to customers.

LO9-2 Describe what customers want, and explain why it is so important for managers to be responsive to their needs.

LO9-3 Explain why achieving superior quality is so important, and understand the challenges facing managers and organizations that seek to implement total quality management.

LO9-4 Explain why achieving superior efficiency is so important, and understand the different kinds of techniques that need to be employed to increase efficiency.

LO9-5 Differentiate between two forms of innovation, and explain why innovation and product development are crucial components of the search for competitive advantage.

A MANAGER'S CHALLENGE

Li & Fung's Success at Value Chain Management

Li & Fung is one of the world's major consumer goods supply chain management companies. The firm started in 1906 in Guangzhou, China. However, with the communist takeover of China following World War II, the firm moved to Hong Kong. The company engages in a variety of activities that include both directly providing goods and sourcing of goods from others as the firm seeks to help firms manage their value chain.

In the 1980s and 1990s China became the world's factory. The prices for goods produced there were dramatically cheaper than in the rest of the world. Even today after rapid increases in wages an hourly wage is 80 U.S. pennies per hour. The costs in the 1980s and 1990s were even cheaper. However, as firms sought to take advantage of these lower costs and source their products from China, they found that the culture and political setting were very different than anything they were familiar with. Li & Fung rose to help fill that gap. The firm helps major companies to source a product from someone else, or Li & Fung will produce the product themselves for the given business.

To help source products from others, Li & Fung has relationships with more than 15,000 suppliers. Li & Fung identifies these firms and ensures their capabilities. When customer firms come to Li & Fung, they help those customers to connect with the suppliers, and Li & Fung receives a fee from the customers to help identify potential suppliers. They also receive fees if contracts are signed and if there is a need to monitor that contract for the customer. However, Li & Fung also has its own manufacturing capabilities. The firm works with major retailers such as Walmart to produce garments, for example. Li & Fung has its own design capabilities, so a firm

Managing Director William Fung, *left*, Chairman Victor Fung, *center*, and President Bruce Rockowitz, *right*, of Li & Fung Ltd. attend the company's 2010 annual general meeting in Hong Kong.

like Walmart can come to Li & Fung and make their request. Then Li & Fung will design and produce the desired product to Walmart's specifications. Thus, Li & Fung can ensure that customers around the world are able to develop the products they want either through others or through Li & Fung itself.

However, the management of the value chain does not end with the creation of the product. For a fee Li & Fung can also generate export documentation and perform shipping consolidation. Anyone can arrange shipping; however, the more that is shipped, the cheaper the cost of the shipping. Li & Fung's size results in the consolidation of shipping of various parties thereby reducing costs. Thus Li & Fung is able to provide customers a rich set of activities that ensure that they can source products in China, and the value chain will still be maximized so that value is enhanced. These services whether they be product design and development, raw material and factory sourcing, production planning and management, quality assurance and export documentation, or shipping consolidation, all help firms take advantage of internationalization to generate the most efficient and profitable value chain possible.

One interesting aspect of Li & Fung that locals in Hong Kong use to illustrate the good fortune of the company is that the firm's CEO, William Fung, was booked on United Airlines Flight 175 on September 11, 2001.[1] This flight was to leave New York and go to Los Angeles. At the last minute Fung changed planes and went to San Francisco instead. Flight 175 was one of the flights that al-Qaeda used to attack the World Trade Center in New York and killed thousands of people. His last-minute decision saved his life and has allowed the firm to continue to prosper. Today the firm has more than 14,000 employees worldwide and sales moving close to the goal of $20 billion per year. The firm is not standing still, however. Today the firm continues to look for new sourcing opportunities in places such as Africa.

Overview

In this chapter we focus on the functional-level strategies managers can use to achieve superior efficiency, quality, innovation, and responsiveness to customers and so build competitive advantage. We also examine the nature of an organization's value chain and discuss how the combined or cooperative efforts of managers across the value chain are required if an organization is to achieve its mission and goal of maximizing the amount of value its products provide customers. By the end of this chapter, you will understand the vital role value chain management plays in building competitive advantage and creating a high-performing organization.

Functional Strategies, the Value Chain, and Competitive Advantage

As we noted in Chapter 8, managers can use two basic business-level strategies to add value to an organization's products and achieve a competitive advantage over industry rivals. First, managers can pursue a *low-cost strategy* and lower the costs of creating value to attract customers by keeping product prices as low as or lower than competitors' prices. Second, managers can pursue a *differentiation strategy* and add value to a product by finding ways to make it superior in some way to the products of other companies. If they are successful, and customers see greater value in the product, then like Sony or a similar high-end brand they can charge a premium or higher price for the product. The four specific ways in which managers can lower costs and/or increase differentiation to obtain a competitive advantage were mentioned in Chapter 1 and are reviewed here; how organizations seek to achieve them is the topic of this chapter. (See Figure 9.1.)

LO9-1 Explain the role of functional strategy and value chain management in achieving superior quality, efficiency, innovation, and responsiveness to customers.

1. *Achieve superior efficiency.* Efficiency is a measure of the amount of inputs required to produce a given amount of outputs. The fewer the inputs required to produce a given output, the higher is efficiency and the lower the cost of outputs. For example, in the 1990s Toyota was the leader in global supply chain management and had a major cost advantage over its rivals, but in the 2000s its rivals adopted more efficient manufacturing methods and significantly reduced their costs.
2. *Achieve superior quality.* Quality means producing goods and services that have attributes–such as design, styling, performance, and reliability–that customers perceive as being superior to those found in competing products.[2] Providing high-quality products creates a brand-name reputation for an organization's products, and this enhanced reputation allows it to charge higher prices. In the PC industry, for example, Toshiba's reputation for making reliable PCs allowed it to outperform its rivals, and even today this still gives it some advantage over them.
3. *Achieve superior innovation, speed, and flexibility.* Anything new or better about the way an organization operates or the goods and services it produces is the result of innovation. Successful innovation gives an organization something *unique* or different about its products that rivals lack–more sophisticated products, production processes, or strategies and structures that strengthen its competitive advantage. Innovation adds value to products and allows the organization to further differentiate itself from rivals and attract customers willing to pay a premium price for unique products.

Figure 9.1
Four Ways to Create a Competitive Advantage

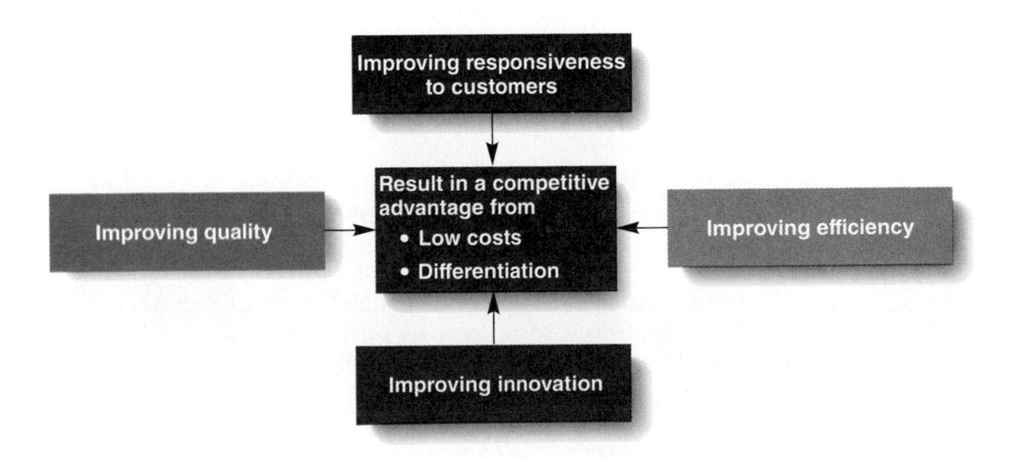

4. *Attain superior responsiveness to customers.* An organization that is responsive to customers tries to satisfy their needs and give them *exactly* what they want. An organization that treats customers better than its rivals do also provides a valuable service some customers may be willing to pay a higher price for. Managers can increase responsiveness by providing excellent after-sales service and support and by working to provide improved products or services to customers in the future.

Functional Strategies and Value Chain Management

functional-level strategy A plan of action to improve the ability of each of an organization's functions to perform its task-specific activities in ways that add value to an organization's goods and services.

value chain The coordinated series or sequence of functional activities necessary to transform inputs such as new product concepts, raw materials, component parts, or professional skills into the finished goods or services customers value and want to buy.

value chain management The development of a set of functional-level strategies that support a company's business-level strategy and strengthen its competitive advantage.

Functional-level strategy is a plan of action to improve the ability of each of an organization's functions or departments (such as manufacturing or marketing) to perform its task-specific activities in ways that add value to an organization's goods and services. A company's **value chain** is the coordinated series or sequence of functional activities necessary to transform inputs such as new product concepts, raw materials, component parts, or professional skills into the finished goods or services customers value and want to buy (see Figure 9.2). Each functional activity along the chain *adds value* to the product when it lowers costs or gives the product differentiated qualities that increase the price a company can charge for it.

Value chain management is the development of a set of functional-level strategies that support a company's business-level strategy and strengthen its competitive advantage. Functional managers develop the strategies that increase efficiency, quality, innovation, and/or responsiveness to customers and thus strengthen an organization's competitive advantage. So the better the fit between functional- and business-level strategies, the greater will be the organization's competitive advantage, and the better able the organization is to achieve its mission and goal of maximizing the amount of value it gives customers. Each function along the value chain has an important role to play in value creation.

As Figure 9.2 suggests, the starting point of the value chain is often the search for new and improved products that will better appeal to customers, so the activities of the product development and marketing functions become important. *Product development* is the engineering and scientific research activities involved in innovating new or improved products that add value to a product. For example, Apple has been a leader in developing new kinds of mobile digital devices that have become so popular among buyers that its products are rapidly imitated by its competitors. Once a new product has been developed, the *marketing function's* task is to persuade customers that the product meets their needs and convince them to buy it. Marketing

Figure 9.2
Functional Activities and the Value Chain

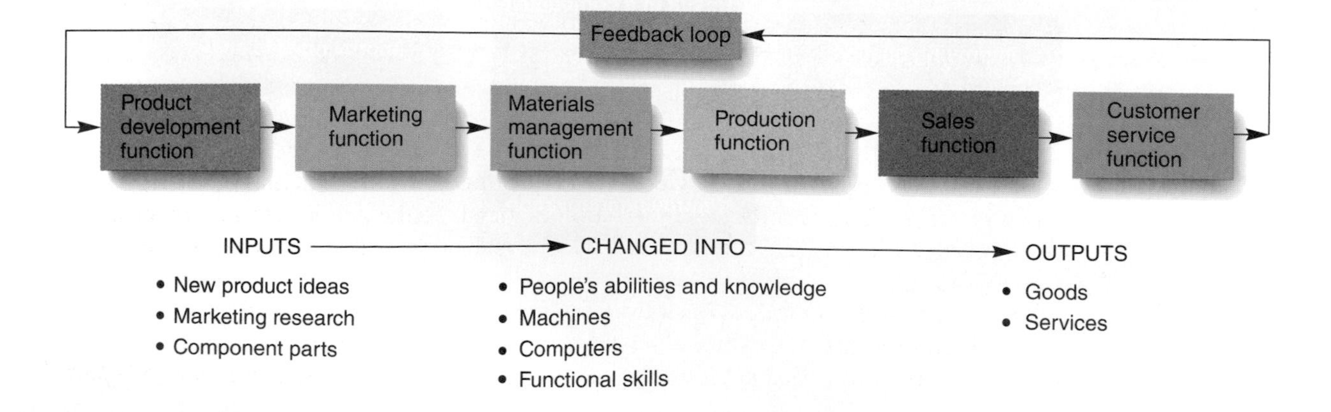

can help create value through brand positioning and advertising that increase customer perceptions of the utility of a company's product. For example, the French company Perrier persuaded U.S. customers that carbonated bottled water is worth $2 per liter–much more than the 75 cents it costs to purchase a gallon of spring water. Perrier's marketing function developed strategies that made customers want to buy the product, and other major companies such as Coca-Cola and PepsiCo rushed to bring out their own bottled water labels to capitalize on customers' growing appetite for "differentiated" bottled water.

Even the best-designed product can fail if the marketing function hasn't devised a careful plan to persuade people to buy it and try it out–or to make sure customers really want it. For this reason, marketing often conducts consumer research to discover unmet customer product needs and to find better ways to tailor existing products to satisfy customer needs. Marketing then presents its suggestions to product development, which performs its own research to discover how best to design and make the new or improved products.

At the next stage of the value chain, the *materials management function* controls the movement of physical materials from the procurement of inputs through production and to distribution and delivery to the customer. The efficiency with which this is carried out can significantly lower costs and create more value. Toyota has the most efficient materials management function in the auto industry. By tightly controlling the flow of goods from its suppliers through its stores and into the hands of customers, Toyota has eliminated the need to hold large inventories of goods. Lower inventories mean lower costs and hence greater value creation.

The *production function* is responsible for creating, assembling, or providing a good or service–for transforming inputs into outputs. For physical products, when we talk about production, we generally mean manufacturing and assembly. For services such as banking or retailing, production takes place when the service is actually provided or delivered to the customer (for example, when a bank originates a loan for a customer, it is engaged in "production" of the loan). By performing its activities efficiently, the production function helps to lower costs. For example, the efficient production operations of Honda and Toyota have made them more profitable than competitors such as Renault, Volkswagen, and Chrysler. The production function can also perform its activities in a way that is consistent with high product quality, which leads to differentiation (and higher value) and to lower costs.

At the next stage in the value chain, the *sales function* plays a crucial role in locating customers and then informing and persuading them to buy the company's products. Personal selling–that is, direct face-to-face communication by salespeople with existing and potential customers to promote a company's products–is a crucial value chain activity. Which products retailers choose to stock, for example, or which drugs doctors choose to prescribe often depend on the salesperson's ability to inform and persuade customers that his or her company's product is superior and thus the best choice.

Finally, the role of the *customer service function* is to provide after-sales service and support. This function can create a perception of superior value in the minds of customers by solving customer problems and supporting customers after they have purchased the product. For example, FedEx can get its customers' parcels to any point in the world within 24 hours, thereby lowering the cost of its own value creation activities. Finally, customer service controls the electronic systems for tracking sales and inventory, pricing products, selling products, dealing with customer inquiries, and so on, all of which can greatly increase responsiveness to customers. Indeed, an important activity of sales and customer service is to tell product development and marketing why a product is meeting or not meeting customers' needs so the product can be redesigned or improved. Hence a feedback loop links the end of the value chain to its beginning (see Figure 9.2).

In the rest of this chapter we examine the functional strategies used to manage the value chain to improve quality, efficiency, innovation, and responsiveness to customers. Notice, however, that achieving superior quality, efficiency, and innovation is *part* of attaining superior responsiveness to customers. Customers want value for their money, and managers who develop functional strategies that result in a value chain capable of creating innovative, high-quality, low-cost products best deliver this value to customers. For this reason, we begin by discussing how functional managers can increase responsiveness to customers.

Improving Responsiveness to Customers

All organizations produce outputs–goods or services–that are consumed by customers, who, in buying these products, provide the monetary resources most organizations need to survive. Because customers are vital to organizational survival, managers must correctly identify their customers and pursue strategies that result in products that best meet their needs. This is why the marketing function plays such an important part in the value chain, and good value chain management requires that marketing managers focus on defining their company's business in terms of the customer *needs* it is satisfying and not by the *type of products* it makes–or the result can be disaster.[3] For example, Kodak's managers said "no thanks" when the company was offered the rights to "instant photography," which was later marketed by Polaroid. Why did they make this mistake? Because the managers adopted a product-oriented approach to their business that didn't put the needs of customers first. Kodak's managers believed their job was to sell high-quality, glossy photographs to people; why would they want to become involved in instant photography, which results in inferior-quality photographs? In reality, Kodak was not satisfying people's needs for high-quality photographs; it was satisfying the need customers had to *capture and record the images of their lives*–their birthday parties, weddings, graduations, and so on. And people wanted those images quickly so they could share them right away with other people–which is why today digital photography has taken off. In the 2000s Kodak was in serious trouble because its film-based photographic business had declined sharply; it lost billions while striving to position itself in the digital market to give customers what they want.

Kodak fell behind in the digital camera market by focusing more on products than on customers.

What Do Customers Want?

Given that satisfying customer demand is central to the survival of an organization, an important question is "What do customers want?" Although specifying *exactly* what customers want is not possible because their needs vary from product to product, it is possible to identify some general product attributes or qualities that most customers prefer:

1. A lower price to a higher price.
2. High-quality products to low-quality products.
3. Quick service and good after-sales support to slow service and poor after-sales support.
4. Products with many useful or valuable features to products with few features.
5. Products that are, as far as possible, customized or tailored to their unique needs.

LO9-2 Describe what customers want, and explain why it is so important for managers to be responsive to their needs.

Managers know that the more desired product attributes a company's value chain builds into its products, the higher the price that must be charged to cover the costs of developing and making the product. So what do managers of a customer-responsive organization do? They try to develop functional strategies that allow the organization's value chain to deliver to customers either *more* desired product attributes for the *same price* or the *same* product attributes for a *lower price*.[4] In general, new IT has allowed many organizations to offer new models of products with more attributes

Passengers queue up at a Ryanair ticket and information counter in Madrid, Spain. The airline's operating system is geared toward satisfying customer demand for low-priced, reliable, and convenient air travel, making it one of the most successful airlines in recent years and the third largest airline in Europe.

at a price similar to or even lower than that of earlier models, and so in the last decade customers have been able to choose from a wider variety of higher-quality products and receive quicker customer service.

Managing the Value Chain to Increase Responsiveness to Customers

Because satisfying customers is so important, managers try to design and improve the way their value chains operate so they can supply products that have the desired attributes–quality, cost, and features. For example, the need to respond to customer demand for competitively priced, quality cars drove U.S. carmakers like Ford and GM to imitate Japanese companies and copy how Toyota and Honda perform their value chain activities. Today the imperative of satisfying customer needs shapes the activities of U.S. carmakers materials management and manufacturing functions. As an example of the link between responsiveness to customers and an organization's value chain, consider how Ryanair of Ireland operates.[5]

The major reason for Ryanair's success is that it has pursued functional strategies that improve how its value chain operates to give customers what they want. Ryanair started in 1985 directly challenging the duopoly that British Airlines and Aer Lingus had flying between the two nations. The airline dramatically expanded in 1997 as deregulation came to Europe. Today, it is the third largest airline in Europe. Ryanair commands high customer loyalty precisely because it can deliver products in Europe that have all the desired attributes: reliability, convenience, and low price. In each of its functions, Ryanair's strategies revolve around finding ways to lower costs. For example, Ryanair allows customers to fly in standing room seats. These seats literally require that the passenger stand the entire trip, but they can be purchased for as little as $6 per flight. The firm examined the possibility of charging passengers to use the toilet. It decided not to do this, but the company will aggressively pursue any way to cut costs. All this translates into low prices for customers.

Ryanair's convenience comes from its scheduling multiple flights every day between its popular locations. Frequently flights on Ryanair may be listed as arriving in a major city. In fact, they locate their operations in a smaller city that is relatively close to the major city but which has much cheaper rates. Thus, if you fly Ryanair to Milan you will land about 47 kilometers away in Bergamo. In sum, value chain management has given Ryanair a competitive advantage in the airline industry.

Although managers must seek to improve their responsiveness to customers by improving how the value chain operates, they should not offer a level of responsiveness to customers that results in costs becoming *too high*–something that threatens an organization's future performance and survival. For example, a company that customizes every product to the unique demands of individual customers is likely to see its costs grow out of control.

Customer Relationship Management

customer relationship management (CRM) A technique that uses IT to develop an ongoing relationship with customers to maximize the value an organization can deliver to them over time.

One functional strategy managers can use to get close to customers and understand their needs is **customer relationship management (CRM).** CRM is a technique that uses IT to develop an ongoing relationship with customers to maximize the value an organization can deliver to them over time. In the 2000s most large companies had installed sophisticated CRM IT to track customers' changing demands for a company's products; this became a vital tool to maximize responsiveness to

Management Insight

Tesco Adjusts to Economic Slowdown Through Its Value Chain

Tesco is one of the United Kingdom's largest retailers. The firm sells both groceries and clothing and is well known for low cost prices and innovations such as home delivery. The key to the development of this strategy for the firm was to lower costs through the use of private labels. Private labeling occurs when a firm uses its own brands rather than large international brands. Thus, the clothing would not come from a major company like Levi Strauss; the jeans would have the retailer's name or a brand name only associated with that retailer. The same would occur in food–rather than a soup brand like Campbell's, the retailer would have its own private label. In a recession low cost providers can gain market share as consumers focus more on lower costs. However, for a low cost manufacturer like Tesco, one issue becomes how to lower costs further to gain even greater market share. The key to this strategic effort is a firm's value chain.

The key to sourcing of goods like clothing for Tesco is the firm's international sourcing center in Hong Kong. This center is responsible for designing, sourcing, overseeing production, quality controlling, and customs documentation for 50,000 Tesco product lines. Tesco uses more than 800 suppliers across 1,200 factories to source these products. These factories are in 44 countries, although the vast majority of them are located in China. To control costs in these sourcing efforts Tesco is seeking to lower costs by finding cheaper inputs into garments. The firm also aggressively negotiates with suppliers. As the economy slowed many suppliers were willing to cut prices to maintain customers. It is estimated that more than 20,000 factories closed in south China as a result of the economic recession. Those that stayed in business often did so by lowering their prices. While prices were often lowered Tesco maintained an active set of technical audits to ensure that quality was maintained.

Shoppers enter and exit a Tesco Store in Dandong, China. One of the UK's largest retailers, Tesco was able to adjust to the global economic downturn by the use of private labeling. This strategy helped reduce costs and strengthen the company's value chain.

One key aspect of Tesco's supply chain that is undergoing revision is an effort to reduce the firm's carbon footprint. The carbon footprint is the amount of carbon that is produced in generating a product. As you can imagine in shipping a product from China to the United Kingdom, the carbon footprint can be significant. Therefore, the firm seeks to limit packaging around products and looks for ways to produce them more efficiently. The goal is to reduce the carbon footprint of the firm 30% by 2020. To help communicate this process to the public, the firm also makes this information available on many products on its Web site. Thus, Tesco is seeking constantly to revise its value chain not only to control costs but also to reduce the firm's impact on the environment.[6]

customers. CRM IT monitors, controls, and links each of the functional activities involved in marketing, selling, and delivering products to customers, such as monitoring the delivery of products through the distribution channel, monitoring salespeople's selling activities, setting product pricing, and coordinating after-sales service.

CRM systems have three interconnected components: sales and selling, after-sales service and support, and marketing.

Suppose a sales manager has access only to sales data that show the total sales revenue each salesperson generated in the last 30 days. This information does not break down how much revenue came from sales to existing customers versus sales to new customers. What important knowledge is being lost? First, if most revenues are earned from sales to existing customers, this suggests that the money being spent by a company to advertise and promote its products is not attracting new customers and so is being wasted. Second, important dimensions involved in sales are pricing, financing, and order processing. In many companies, to close a deal, a salesperson has to send the paperwork to a central sales office that handles matters such as approving the customer for special financing and determining specific shipping and delivery dates. In some companies, different departments handle these activities, and it can take a long time to get a response from them; this keeps customers waiting–something that often leads to lost sales. Until CRM systems were introduced, these kinds of problems were widespread and resulted in missed sales and higher operating costs. Today the sales and selling CRM software contains *best sales practices* that analyze this information and then recommend ways to improve how the sales process operates.

Standard Bank is the largest bank in South Africa ranked by assets and earnings. The firm has 2200 service representatives to address customer needs. In a given year the bank has over 40 million customer interactions. The firm, in 2009, introduced a new CRM system to help manage these interactions. Specifically, the firm re-engineered key business processes from a customer perspective so that each customer received a tailored response to his/her request whether it came by telephone, Web, email, or instant messaging. The new system allowed for all required information to be obtained in a single central view by the bank's service representatives. The effort was to create a setting where the customer could use a mixture of self-service, virtual agent, and/or human support to solve a problem.

The preparation of the plan for the new system took three years, and implementation occurred in three controlled phases. Phases one and two were completed on time and within budget; preparations for phase three are well under way. Only 24 months after implementing the new system, the project will be cost neutral with a projected overall savings of approximately US $ 30 million. First call resolution increased significantly and all inquiries improved by 30%. The average handling time of inquiries decreased and training time of service representatives was reduced by two weeks. Moreover, the bank had a better understanding of its customers' behavior and demographics, which is critical in a highly diverse market like South Africa.[7]

When a company implements after-sales service and support CRM software, salespeople are required to input detailed information about their follow-up visits to customers. Because the system tracks and documents every customer's case history, salespeople have instant access to a record of everything that occurred during previous phone calls or visits. They are in a much better position to respond to customers' needs and build customer loyalty, so a company's after-sales service improves.

A CRM system can also identify the top 10 reasons for customer complaints. Sales managers can then work to eliminate the sources of these problems and improve after-sales support procedures. The CRM system also identifies the top 10 best service and support practices, which can then be taught to all sales reps.

Finally, as a CRM system processes information about changing customer needs, this improves marketing in many ways. Marketing managers, for example, have access to detailed customer profiles, including data about purchases and the reasons why individuals were or were not attracted to a company's products. Armed with this knowledge, marketing can better identify customers and the specific product attributes they desire. It may become clear, for example, that a targeted customer group has a specific need that is not satisfied by a product–such as a need for a cell phone containing a 20-megapixel video camera and a GPS system. With real-time information, marketing can work with product development to redesign the product to better meet customer needs. In sum, a CRM system is a comprehensive method of gathering crucial information about how customers respond to a company's products. It is a powerful functional strategy used to align a company's products with customer needs.

Improving Quality

LO9-3 Explain why achieving superior quality is so important, and understand the challenges facing managers and organizations that seek to implement total quality management.

As noted earlier, high-quality products possess attributes such as superior design, features, reliability, and after-sales support; these products are designed to better meet customer requirements.[8] Quality is a concept that can be applied to the products of both manufacturing and service organizations–goods such as an Acer computer or services such as Ryanair flight service or customer service in an HSBC branch. Why do managers seek to control and improve the quality of their organizations' products?[9] There are two reasons (see Figure 9.3).

First, customers usually prefer a higher-quality product to a lower-quality product. So an organization able to provide, *for the same price,* a product of higher quality than a competitor's product is serving its customers better–it is being more responsive to its customers. Often providing high-quality products creates a brand-name reputation for an organization's products. This enhanced reputation may allow the organization to charge more for its products than its competitors can charge, and thus it makes greater profits. For example, in 2009 Lexus, Toyota's high-end brand, was ranked number one, as it has been for over a decade, on the J. D. Power list of the 10 most reliable carmakers.[10] The high quality of Lexus vehicles enables the company to charge higher prices for its cars than the prices charged by rival carmakers.

The second reason for trying to boost product quality is that higher product quality can increase efficiency and thereby lower operating costs and boost profits. Achieving high product quality lowers operating costs because of the effect of quality on employee productivity: Higher product quality means less employee time is wasted in making defective products that must be discarded or in providing substandard services, and thus less time has to be spent fixing mistakes. This translates into higher employee productivity, which means lower costs.

Total Quality Management

total quality management (TQM) A management technique that focuses on improving the quality of an organization's products and services.

At the forefront of the drive to improve product quality is a functional strategy known as total quality management.[11] **Total quality management (TQM)** focuses on improving the quality of an organization's products and stresses that *all* of an organization's value chain activities should be directed toward this goal. TQM requires the

Figure 9.3
The Impact of Increased Quality on Organizational Performance

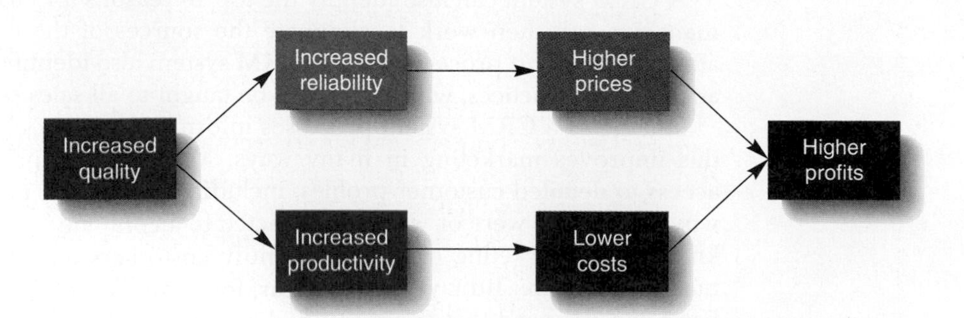

cooperation of managers in every function of an organization and across functions.[12] To show how TQM works, we next describe the way that Citibank used the technique. Then, using Citibank as an example, we look at the 10 steps that are necessary for managers to implement a successful TQM program.

In the 2000s Citibank's top managers decided the bank could retain and expand its customer base only if it could increase customer loyalty, so they decided to implement a TQM program to better satisfy customer needs. As the first step in its TQM effort, Citibank identified the factors that dissatisfy its customers. When analyzing the complaints, it found that most concerned the time it took to complete a customer's request, such as responding to an account problem or getting a loan. So Citibank's managers began to examine how they handled each kind of customer request. For each distinct request, they formed a cross-functional team that broke down the request into the steps required, between people and departments, to complete the response. In analyzing the steps, teams found that many of them were unnecessary and could be replaced by using the right information systems. They also found that delays often occurred because employees did not know how to handle a request. They were not being given the right kind of training, and when they couldn't handle a request, they simply put it aside until a supervisor could deal with it.

Citibank's second step to increase its responsiveness was to implement an organizationwide TQM program. Managers and supervisors were charged with reducing the complexity of the work process and finding the most effective way to process each particular request, such as a request for a loan. Managers were also charged with training employees to answer each specific request. The results were remarkable. For example, in the loan department the TQM program reduced by 75% the number of handoffs necessary to process a request. The department's average response time dropped from several hours to 30 minutes. What are the 10 steps in TQM that made this possible?

1. *Build organizational commitment to quality.* TQM will do little to improve the performance of an organization unless all employees embrace it, and this often requires a change in an organization's culture.[13] At Citibank the process of changing culture began at the top. First a group of top managers, including the CEO, received training in TQM from consultants from Motorola. Each member of the top management group was then given the responsibility of training a group at the next level in the hierarchy, and so on down through the organization until all 100,000 employees had received basic TQM training.
2. *Focus on the customer.* TQM practitioners see a focus on the customer as the starting point.[14] According to TQM philosophy, the customer, not managers in quality control or engineering, defines what quality is. The challenge is fourfold: (1) to identify what customers want from the good or service that the company provides; (2) to identify what the company actually provides to customers; (3) to identify any gap between what customers want and what they actually get (the quality gap); and (4) to formulate a plan for closing the quality gap. The efforts of Citibank managers to increase responsiveness to customers illustrate this aspect of TQM well.
3. *Find ways to measure quality.* Another crucial element of TQM is the development of a measuring system that managers can use to evaluate quality. Devising appropriate measures is relatively easy in manufacturing companies, where quality can be measured by criteria such as defects per million parts. It is more difficult in service companies, where outputs are less tangible. However, with a little creativity, suitable quality measures can be devised as they were by managers at Citibank. Similarly, at L. L. Bean, the mail-order retailer, managers use the percentage of orders that are correctly filled as one of their quality measures.
4. *Set goals and create incentives.* Once a measure has been devised, managers' next step is to set a challenging quality goal and to create incentives for reaching that goal. At Citibank the CEO set an initial goal of reducing customer complaints by 50%. One way of creating incentives to attain a goal is to link rewards, such as bonus pay and promotional opportunities, to the goal.

5. *Solicit input from employees.* Employees are a major source of information about the causes of poor quality, so it is important that managers establish a system for soliciting employee suggestions about improvements that can be made. At most companies, like Citibank, this is an ongoing endeavor–the process never stops.
6. *Identify defects and trace them to their source.* A major source of product defects is the production system; a major source of service defects is poor customer service procedures. TQM preaches the need for managers to identify defects in the work process, trace those defects back to their source, find out why they occurred, and make corrections so they do not occur again. Today IT makes quality measurement much easier.

inventory The stock of raw materials, inputs, and component parts that an organization has on hand at a particular time.

just-in-time (JIT) inventory system A system in which parts or supplies arrive at an organization when they are needed, not before.

7. *Introduce just-in-time inventory systems.* **Inventory** is the stock of raw materials, inputs, and component parts that an organization has on hand at a particular time. When the materials management function designs a **just-in-time (JIT) inventory system,** parts or supplies arrive at the organization when they are needed, not before. Also, under a JIT inventory system, defective parts enter an organization's operating system immediately; they are not warehoused for months before use. This means defective inputs can be quickly spotted. JIT is discussed more later in the chapter.
8. *Work closely with suppliers.* A major cause of poor-quality finished goods is poor-quality component parts. To decrease product defects, materials managers must work closely with suppliers to improve the quality of the parts they supply. Managers at Xerox worked closely with suppliers to get them to adopt TQM programs, and the result was a huge reduction in the defect rate of component parts. Managers also need to work closely with suppliers to get them to adopt a JIT inventory system, also required for high quality.
9. *Design for ease of production.* The more steps required to assemble a product or provide a service, the more opportunities there are for making a mistake. It follows that designing products that have fewer parts or finding ways to simplify providing a service should be linked to fewer defects or customer complaints. For example, Acer continually redesigns the way it assembles its computers to reduce the number of assembly steps required, and it constantly searches for new ways to reduce the number of components that have to be linked together. The consequence of these redesign efforts was a continuous fall in assembly costs and marked improvement in product quality during the 1990s.
10. *Break down barriers between functions.* Successful implementation of TQM requires substantial cooperation between the different value chain functions. Materials managers have to cooperate with manufacturing managers to find high-quality inputs that reduce manufacturing costs; marketing managers have to cooperate with manufacturing so customer problems identified by marketing can be acted on; information systems have to cooperate with all other functions of the company to devise suitable IT training programs; and so on.

In essence, to increase quality, all functional managers need to cooperate to develop goals and spell out exactly how they will be achieved. Managers should embrace the philosophy that mistakes, defects, and poor-quality materials are not acceptable and should be eliminated. Functional managers should spend more time working with employees and providing them with the tools they need to do the job. Managers should create an environment in which employees will not be afraid to report problems or recommend improvements. Output goals and targets need to include not only numbers or quotas but also some indicators of quality to promote the production of defect-free output. Functional managers also need to train employees in new skills to keep pace with changes in the workplace. Finally, achieving better quality requires that managers develop organizational values and norms centered on improving quality.

Six Sigma A technique used to improve quality by systematically improving how value chain activities are performed and then using statistical methods to measure the improvement.

SIX SIGMA One TQM technique called **Six Sigma** has gained increasing popularity in the last decade, particularly because of the well-publicized success GE enjoyed as a result of implementing it across its operating divisions. The goal of Six Sigma is to improve a company's quality to only three defects per million by systematically altering the way all the processes involved in value chain activities are performed, and then carefully measuring how much improvement has been made using statistical methods. Six Sigma shares with TQM its focus on improving value chain processes to increase quality; but it differs because TQM emphasizes top-down organizationwide employee involvement, whereas the Six Sigma approach is to create teams of expert change agents, known as "green belts and black belts," to take control of the problem-finding and problem-solving process and then to train other employees in implementing solutions.

Improving Efficiency

LO9-4 Explain why achieving superior efficiency is so important, and understand the different kinds of techniques that need to be employed to increase efficiency.

The third goal of value chain management is to increase the efficiency of the various functional activities. The fewer the input resources required to produce a given volume of output, the higher will be the efficiency of the operating system. So efficiency is a useful measure of how well an organization uses all its resources–such as labor, capital, materials, or energy–to produce its outputs, or goods and services. Developing functional strategies to improve efficiency is an extremely important issue for managers because increased efficiency lowers production costs, which lets an organization make a greater profit or attract more customers by lowering its price. Several important functional strategies are discussed here.

Facilities Layout, Flexible Manufacturing, and Efficiency

The strategies managers use to lay out or design an organization's physical work facilities also determine its efficiency. First, the way in which machines and workers are organized or grouped together into workstations affects the efficiency of the operating system. Second, a major determinant of efficiency is the cost associated with setting up the equipment needed to make a particular product. **Facilities layout** is the strategy of designing the machine–worker interface to increase operating system efficiency. **Flexible manufacturing** is a strategy based on the use of IT to reduce the costs associated with the product assembly process or the way services are delivered to customers. For example, this might be how computers are made on a production line or how patients are routed through a hospital.

facilities layout The strategy of designing the machine–worker interface to increase operating system efficiency.

flexible manufacturing The set of techniques that attempt to reduce the costs associated with the product assembly process or the way services are delivered to customers.

FACILITIES LAYOUT The way in which machines, robots, and people are grouped together affects how productive they can be. Figure 9.4 shows three basic ways of arranging workstations: product layout, process layout, and fixed-position layout.

In a *product layout,* machines are organized so that each operation needed to manufacture a product or process a patient is performed at workstations arranged in a fixed sequence. In manufacturing, workers are stationary in this arrangement, and a moving conveyor belt takes the product being worked on to the next workstation so that it is progressively assembled. Mass production is the familiar name for this layout; car assembly lines are probably the best-known example. It used to be that product layout was efficient only when products were created in large quantities; however, the introduction of modular assembly lines controlled by computers is making it efficient to make products in small batches.

In a *process layout,* workstations are not organized in a fixed sequence. Rather, each workstation is relatively self-contained, and a product goes to whichever workstation is needed to perform the next operation to complete the product. Process layout is often suited to manufacturing settings that produce a variety of custom-made products, each tailored to the needs of a different kind of customer. For example, a custom furniture manufacturer might use a process layout so different teams of workers can produce different styles of chairs or tables made from different kinds of woods and finishes. Such a layout also describes how a patient might go through a hospital from emergency room to X-ray room, to operating room, and so on. A process layout

Figure 9.4
Three Facilities Layouts

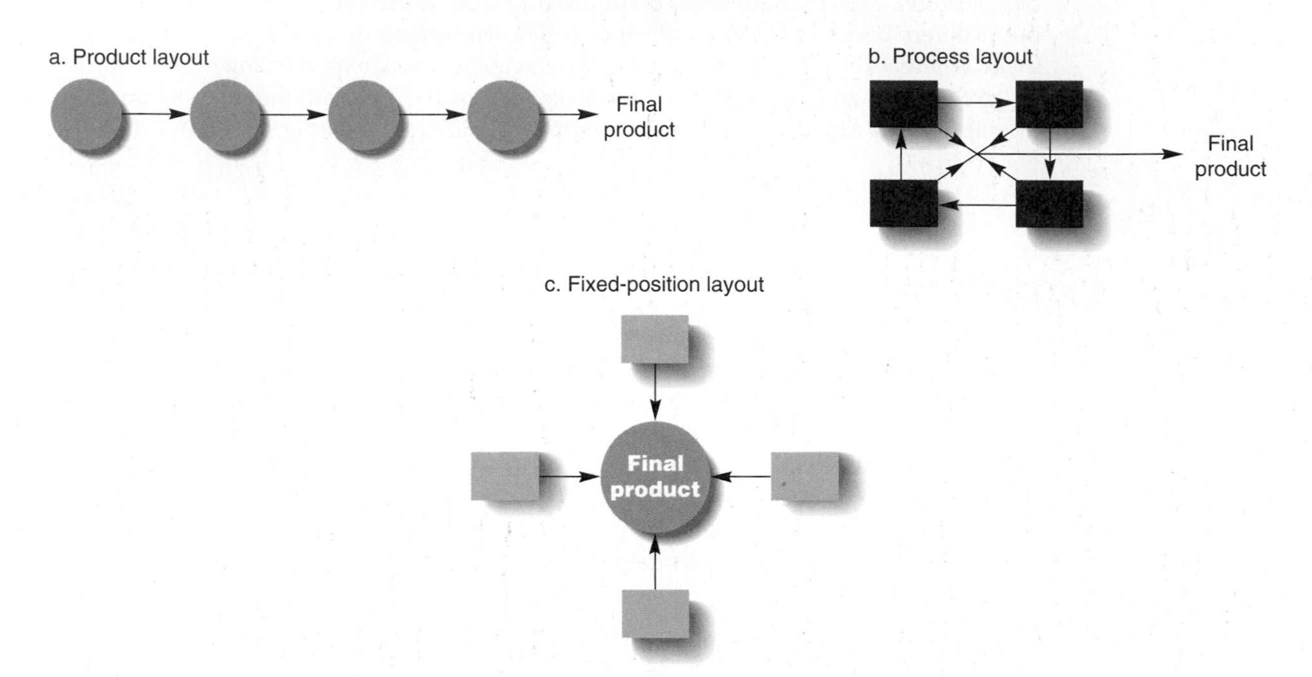

provides the flexibility needed to change a product, whether it is a PC or a patient's treatment. Such flexibility, however, often reduces efficiency because it is expensive.

In a *fixed-position layout,* the product stays in a fixed position. Its component parts are produced in remote workstations and brought to the production area for final assembly. Increasingly, self-managed teams are using fixed-position layouts. Different teams assemble each component part and then send the parts to the final assembly team, which makes the final product. A fixed-position layout is commonly used for products such as jet airliners, mainframe computers, and gas turbines–products that are complex and difficult to assemble or so large that moving them from one workstation to another would be difficult. The effects of moving from one facilities layout to another can be dramatic, as the following "Manager as a Person" box suggests.

Manager as a Person

Paddy Hopkirk Improves Facilities Layout

Paddy Hopkirk established his car accessories business in Bedfordshire, England, shortly after he had shot to car-racing fame by winning the famous Monte Carlo Rally. Sales of Hopkirk's accessories, such as bicycle racks and axle stands, were always brisk; but Hopkirk was the first to admit that his operating system left a lot to be desired, so he invited consultants to help reorganize the system.

After analyzing his factory's operating system, the consultants realized that the source of the problem was the facilities layout Hopkirk had established. Over time, as sales grew, Hopkirk simply added new workstations to the operating

Figure 9.5
Changing a Facilities Layout[15]

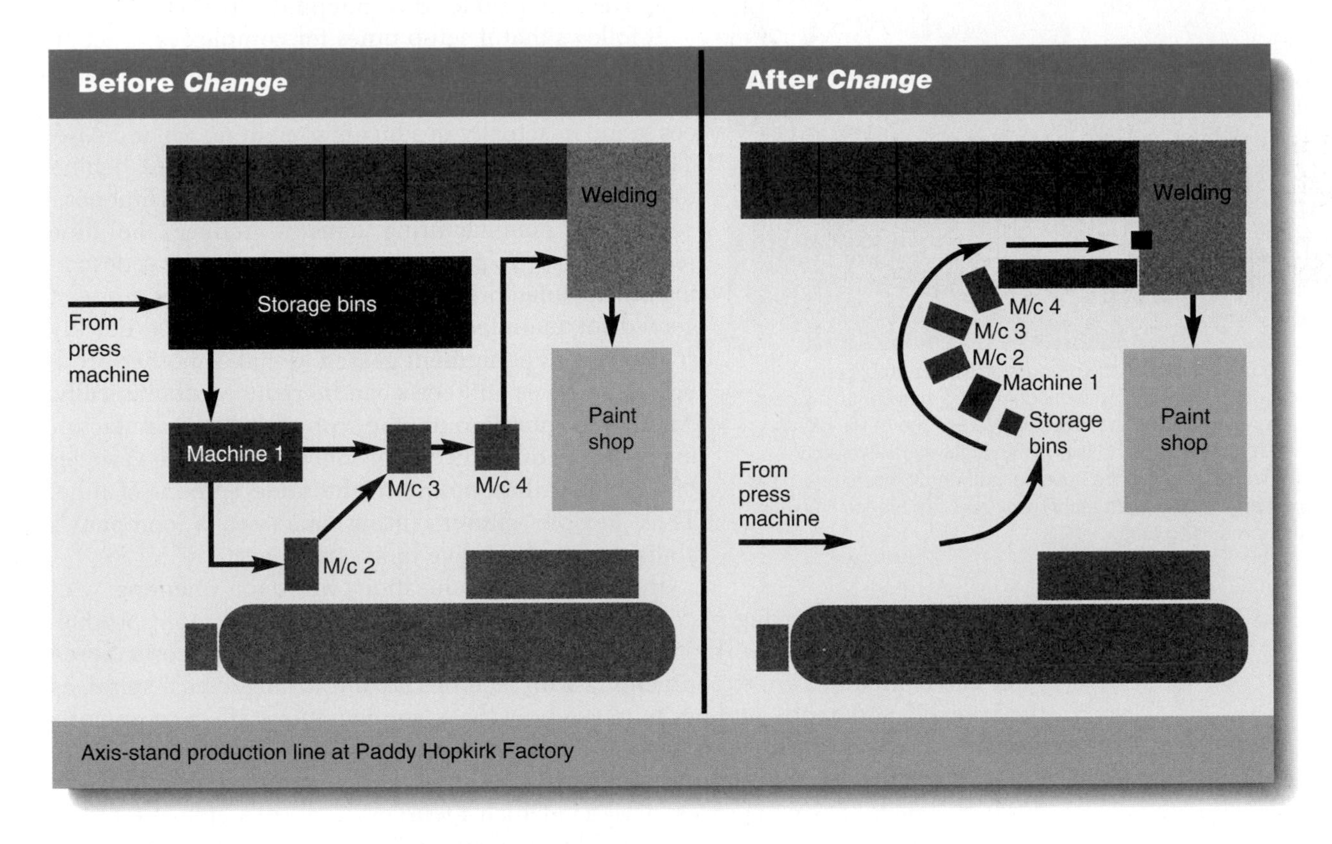

Axis-stand production line at Paddy Hopkirk Factory

system as they were needed. The result was a process layout in which the product being assembled moved in the irregular sequences shown in the "Before Change" half of Figure 9.5. The consultants suggested that to save time and effort, the workstations should be reorganized into the sequential product layout shown in the "After Change" illustration.

Once this change was made, the results were dramatic. One morning the factory was an untidy sprawl of workstations surrounded by piles of crates holding semifinished components. Two days later, when the 170-person workforce came back to work, the machines had been brought together into tightly grouped workstations arranged in the fixed sequence shown in the illustration. The piles of components had disappeared, and the newly cleared floor space was neatly marked with color-coded lines mapping out the new flow of materials between workstations.

In the first full day of production, efficiency increased by as much as 30%. The space needed for some operations had been cut in half, and work in progress had been cut considerably. Moreover, the improved layout allowed some jobs to be combined, freeing operators for deployment elsewhere in the factory. An amazed Hopkirk exclaimed, "I was expecting a change but nothing as dramatic as this . . . it is fantastic."[16]

FLEXIBLE MANUFACTURING In a manufacturing company, a major source of costs is setting up the equipment needed to make a particular product. One of these costs is that of production forgone because nothing is produced while the equipment is being set up. For example, components manufacturers often need as much as half a day to set up automated production equipment when switching from production of one component part (such as a washer ring for the steering column of a car) to another (such as a washer

Housing units move on the production line as employees of Toyota Motor Corporation work during the installation process at the company's Kasugai Housing Works, one of the plants of Toyota home-brand houses on Kasugai, Aichi Prefecture, Japan. Toyota entered the housing industry 30 years ago where it applies the plant technology and experience it gained through producing cars.

ring for the steering column of a truck). During this half-day, a manufacturing plant is not producing anything, but employees are paid for this "nonproductive" time.

It follows that if setup times for complex production equipment can be reduced, so can setup costs, and efficiency will rise; that is, the time that plant and employees spend in actually producing something will increase. This simple insight has been the driving force behind the development of flexible manufacturing techniques.

Flexible manufacturing aims to reduce the time required to set up production equipment.[17] By redesigning the manufacturing process so production equipment geared for manufacturing one product can be quickly replaced with equipment geared to make another product, setup times and costs can be reduced dramatically. Another favorable outcome from flexible manufacturing is that a company can produce many more varieties of a product than before in the same amount of time. Thus flexible manufacturing increases a company's ability to be responsive to its customers.

Increasingly, organizations are experimenting with new designs for operating systems that not only allow workers to be more productive but also make the work process more flexible, thus reducing setup costs. Some Japanese companies are experimenting with facilities layouts arranged as a spiral, as the letter *Y,* and as the number 6, to see how these configurations affect setup costs and worker productivity. At a camcorder plant in Kohda, Japan, for example, Sony changed from a fixed-position layout in which 50 workers sequentially built a camcorder to a flexible spiral process design in which 4 workers perform all the operations necessary to produce the camcorder. This new layout lets the most efficient workers work at the highest pace, and it reduces setup costs because workers can easily switch from one model to another, increasing efficiency by 10%.[18]

An interesting example of a company that built a new factory to obtain the benefits from flexible manufacturing is the German company Igus Inc. Igus makes over 28,000 polymer bearings and energy supply cable products used in applications the world over. Increasing global competition led Igus managers to realize they needed to build a new factory that could handle the company's rapidly growing product line. At Igus new products are often introduced daily, so flexibility is the company's prime requirement. Moreover, because many of its products are highly customized, the specific and changing needs of its customers drive new product development.

Igus's new factory was designed for flexibility. As big as three football fields, the factory has nothing tied down or bolted to the floor. All the machines, computers, and equipment can be moved and repositioned to suit changing product requirements. Moreover, all Igus employees are trained to be flexible and can perform many of the necessary production tasks. For example, when one new product line proved popular with customers, its employees and production operations were relocated four times as it grew into larger spaces. Igus can change its operating system at a moment's notice and with minimal disruption; and because the company operates seven days a week, 24 hours a day, these changes are constant. Igus's decision to create a flexible factory of the future has paid off as its global sales have more than tripled in the 2000s.

Just-in-Time Inventory and Efficiency

As noted earlier, a just-in-time inventory system gets components to the assembly line just as they are needed and thus drives down costs. In a JIT inventory system, component parts travel from suppliers to the assembly line in a small wheeled container known as a *kanban.* Assembly-line workers empty the kanbans, which are sent back to the suppliers as the signal to produce another small batch of component parts, and so the process repeats itself. This system can be contrasted with a just-in-case view of inventory, which leads an organization to stockpile excess inputs in a warehouse in case it needs them to meet sudden upturns in demand.

JIT inventory systems have major implications for efficiency. Great cost savings can result from increasing inventory turnover and reducing inventory holding costs, such as warehousing and storage costs and the cost of capital tied up in inventory. Although companies that manufacture and assemble products can obviously use JIT to great advantage, so can service organizations.[19] Walmart, the biggest retailer in the United States, uses JIT systems to replenish the stock in its stores at least twice a week. Many Walmart stores receive daily deliveries. Walmart's main competitors typically restock every two weeks. Walmart can maintain the same service levels as these competitors but at one-fourth the inventory holding cost. Faster inventory turnover has helped Walmart achieve an efficiency-based competitive advantage in the retailing industry.[20]

Self-Managed Work Teams and Efficiency

Another functional strategy to increase efficiency in the United States and Europe is the use of self-managed work teams.[21] A typical self-managed team consists of 5 to 15 employees who produce an entire product instead of just parts of it.[22] Team members learn all team tasks and move from job to job. The result is a flexible workforce because team members can fill in for absent coworkers. The members of each team also assume responsibility for scheduling work and vacations, ordering materials, and hiring new members–previously all responsibilities of first-line managers. Because people often respond well to greater autonomy and responsibility, the use of empowered self-managed teams can increase productivity and efficiency. Moreover, cost savings arise from eliminating supervisors and creating a flatter organizational hierarchy, which further increase efficiency.

The effect of introducing self-managed teams is often an increase in efficiency of 30% or sometimes much more. After the introduction of flexible manufacturing technology and self-managed teams, a GE plant in Salisbury, North Carolina, increased efficiency by 250% compared with other GE plants producing the same products.[23] However, it should be realized that the impact of self-managed work teams is not consistent around the world. While such teams have been shown to be effective in settings that are culturally similar to the United States and parts of Europe, such groups have much lower success rates in other settings. For example, in Thailand workers expect managers to manage; management should not come from the workers. Such a view is consistent with high levels of power distance as in the discussion of Hofstede. The result is that the impact of self-managed teams is typically not positive in such settings.[24]

Process Reengineering and Efficiency

The value chain is a collection of functional activities or business processes that transforms one or more kinds of inputs to create an output that is of value to the customer.[25] **Process reengineering** involves the fundamental rethinking and radical redesign of business processes (and thus the *value chain*) to achieve dramatic improvements in critical measures of performance such as cost, quality, service, and speed.[26] Order fulfillment, for example, can be thought of as a business process: When a customer's order is received (the input), many different functional tasks must be performed as necessary to process the order, and then the ordered goods are delivered to the customer (the output). Process reengineering boosts efficiency when it reduces the number of order fulfillment tasks that must be performed, or reduces the time they take, and so reduces operating costs.

process reengineering
The fundamental rethinking and radical redesign of business processes to achieve dramatic improvement in critical measures of performance such as cost, quality, service, and speed.

For an example of process reengineering in practice, consider how Ford used it. One day a manager from Ford was working at its Japanese partner Mazda and discovered that Mazda had only five people in its accounts payable department. The Ford manager was shocked because Ford's U.S. operation had 500 employees in accounts payable. He reported his discovery to Ford's U.S. managers, who decided to form a task force to study this difference.

Ford managers discovered that procurement began when the purchasing department sent a purchase order to a supplier and sent a copy of the purchase order to Ford's accounts payable department. When the supplier shipped the goods and they arrived at Ford, a clerk at the receiving dock completed a form describing the goods and sent the form to accounts payable. The supplier, meanwhile, sent accounts payable an invoice. Thus accounts payable received three documents relating to these goods: a copy of the original purchase order, the receiving document, and the invoice. If the information in all three was in agreement (most of the time it was), a clerk in accounts payable issued payment. Occasionally, however, all three documents did not agree. And Ford discovered that accounts payable clerks spent most of their time straightening out the 1% of instances in which the purchase order, receiving document, and invoice contained conflicting information.[27]

Ford managers decided to reengineer the procurement process to simplify it. Now when a buyer in the purchasing department issues a purchase order to a supplier, that buyer also enters the order into an online database. As before, suppliers send goods to the receiving dock. When the goods arrive, the clerk at the receiving dock checks a computer terminal to see whether the received shipment matches the description on the purchase order. If it does, the clerk accepts the goods and pushes a button on the terminal keyboard that tells the database the goods have arrived. Receipt of the goods is recorded in the database, and a computer automatically issues and sends a check to the supplier. If the goods do not correspond to the description on the purchase order in the database, the clerk at the dock refuses the shipment and sends it back to the supplier.

Payment authorization, which used to be performed by accounts payable, is now accomplished at the receiving dock. The new process has come close to eliminating the need for an accounts payable department. In some parts of Ford, the size of the accounts payable department has been cut by 95%. By reducing the head count in accounts payable, the reengineering effort reduced the amount of time wasted on unproductive activities, thereby increasing the efficiency of the total organization.

Information Systems, the Internet, and Efficiency

With the rapid spread of computers, the explosive growth of the Internet and corporate intranets, and high-speed digital Internet technology, the information systems function is moving to center stage in the quest for operating efficiencies and a lower cost structure. The impact of information systems on productivity is wide-ranging and potentially affects all other activities of a company. For example, Cisco Systems has been able to realize significant cost savings by moving its ordering and customer service functions online. The company has just 300 service agents handling all its customer accounts, compared to the 900 it would need if sales were not handled online. The difference represents an annual savings of US $30 million a year. Moreover, without automated customer service functions, Cisco calculates that it would need at least 1,000 additional service engineers, which would cost around US $75 million.

All large companies today use the Internet to manage the value chain, feeding real-time information about order flow to suppliers, which use this information to schedule their own production to provide components on a just-in-time basis. This approach reduces the costs of coordination both between the company and its customers and between the company and its suppliers. Using the Internet to automate customer and supplier interactions substantially reduces the number of employees required to manage these interfaces, which significantly reduces costs. This trend extends beyond high-tech companies. Banks and financial service companies are finding that they can substantially reduce costs by moving customer accounts and support functions online. Such a move reduces the need for customer service representatives, bank tellers, stockbrokers, insurance agents, and others. For example, it costs about US $1 when a customer executes a transaction at a bank, such as shifting money from one account to another; over the Internet the same transaction costs about US $0.01.

Improving Innovation

As discussed in Chapter 6, *technology* comprises the skills, know-how, experience, body of scientific knowledge, tools, machines, computers, and equipment used in the design, production, and distribution of goods and services. Technology is involved in all functional activities, and the rapid advance of technology today is a significant factor in managers' attempts to improve how their value chains innovate new kinds of goods and services or ways to provide them.

LO9-5 Differentiate between two forms of innovation, and explain why innovation and product development are crucial components of the search for competitive advantage.

Two Kinds of Innovation

Two principal kinds of innovation can be identified based on the nature of the technological change that brings them about. **Quantum product innovation** results in the development of new, often radically different, kinds of goods and services because of fundamental shifts in technology brought about by pioneering discoveries. Examples are the creation of the Internet and the World Wide Web that have revolutionized the computer, cell phone, and media/music industries, and biotechnology, which has transformed the treatment of illness by creating new, genetically engineered medicines. McDonald's development of the principles behind the provision of fast food also qualifies as a quantum product innovation.

quantum product innovation The development of new, often radically different, kinds of goods and services because of fundamental shifts in technology brought about by pioneering discoveries.

Incremental product innovation results in gradual improvements and refinements of existing products over time as existing technologies are perfected and functional managers, like those at Dell, Toyota, and McDonald's, learn how to perform value chain activities in better ways–ways that add more value to products. For example, since their debut, Google's staffers have made thousands of incremental improvements to the company's search engine, Chrome Internet browser, and Android operating system–changes that have enhanced their capabilities enormously such as by giving them the ability to work on all kinds of mobile devices and making them available in many different languages.

incremental product innovation The gradual improvement and refinement of existing products that occurs over time as existing technologies are perfected.

Quantum product innovations are relatively rare; most managers' activities focus on incremental product innovations that result from ongoing technological advances. For example, every time Acer puts a new, faster Intel chip into a PC, or Google improves its search engine's capability, the company is making incremental product innovations. Similarly, every time car engineers redesign a car model, and every time McDonald's managers work to improve the flavor and texture of burgers, fries, and salads, their product development efforts are intended to lead to incremental product innovations. Incremental innovation is frequently as important as–or even more important than–quantum innovation in raising a company's performance. Indeed, as discussed next, it is often managers' ability to successfully manage incremental product development that results in success or failure in an industry.

The need to speed innovation and quickly develop new and improved products becomes especially important when the technology behind the product is advancing rapidly. This is because the first companies in an industry to adopt the new technology will be able to develop products that better meet customer needs and gain a "first-mover" advantage over their rivals. Indeed, managers who do not quickly adopt and apply new technologies to innovate products may soon find they have no customers for their products–and destroy their organizations. In sum, the greater the rate of technological change in an industry, the more important it is for managers to innovate.

Strategies to Promote Innovation and Speed Product Development

product development The management of the value chain activities involved in bringing new or improved goods and services to the market.

There are several ways in which managers can promote innovation and encourage the development of new products. **Product development** is the management of the value chain activities involved in bringing new or improved goods and services to the market. Inditex is an integrated Spanish company. The firm is a major garment manufacturer that is vertically integrated with its own retailer called Zara. Inditex designs its own garments domestically in Spain. Through complete control of its value chain, the firm has the ability to design the product, manufacture it in Spain, Portugal, and Morocco, and have it on Zara's shelves within three weeks. This approach to innovation of products relies not on cost but on speed and innovation. While other designers create garments up to a year in advance and shipping the product can take months, Inditex's response is immediate. The Zara stores' managers receive up to 70% of their salary in sales commission. Thus, when they see a need for a new product or a new design, they can send that idea instantly to the more than three hundred designers on staff. The product then goes to garment factories that are close by and very responsive.[28]

INVOLVE BOTH CUSTOMERS AND SUPPLIERS Many new products fail when they reach the marketplace because they were designed with scant attention to customer needs. Successful product development requires inputs from more than just an organization's members; also needed are inputs from customers and suppliers. In some cases companies have found it worthwhile to include customer representatives as peripheral members of their product development teams. Boeing, for example, has included its customers, the major airlines, in the design of its most recent commercial jet aircraft, the 787 Dreamliner. Boeing builds a mockup of the aircraft's cabin and then, over a period of months, allows each airline's representatives to experiment with repositioning the galleys, seating, aisles, and bathrooms to best meet the needs of their particular airline. Boeing has learned a great deal from this process.

stage-gate development funnel A planning model that forces managers to choose among competing projects so organizational resources are not spread thinly over too many projects.

ESTABLISH A STAGE-GATE DEVELOPMENT FUNNEL One of the most common mistakes managers make in product development is trying to fund too many new projects at any one time. This approach spreads the activities of the different value chain functions too thinly over too many different projects. As a consequence, no single project is given the functional resources and attention required.

One strategy for solving this problem is for managers to develop a structured process for evaluating product development proposals and deciding which to support and which to reject. A common solution is to establish a **stage-gate development funnel,** a technique that forces managers to choose among competing projects so functional resources are not spread thinly over too many projects. The funnel gives functional managers control over product development and allows them to intervene and take corrective action quickly and appropriately (see Figure 9.6).

Cross-functionality at its best. Here, two research scientists, an executive, and a marketing manager put their heads together to figure out what's next.

At stage 1 the development funnel has a wide mouth, so top managers initially can encourage employees to come up with as many new product ideas as possible. Managers can create incentives for employees to come up with ideas. Many organizations run "bright-idea programs" that reward employees whose ideas eventually make it through the development process. Other organizations allow research scientists to devote a certain amount of work time to their own projects. Top managers at 3M, for example, have a 15% rule: They expect a research scientist to spend 15% of the workweek working on a project of his or her own choosing. Ideas may be submitted by individuals or by groups. Brainstorming (see Chapter 7) is a technique that managers frequently use to encourage new ideas.

Figure 9.6
A Stage–Gate Development Funnel

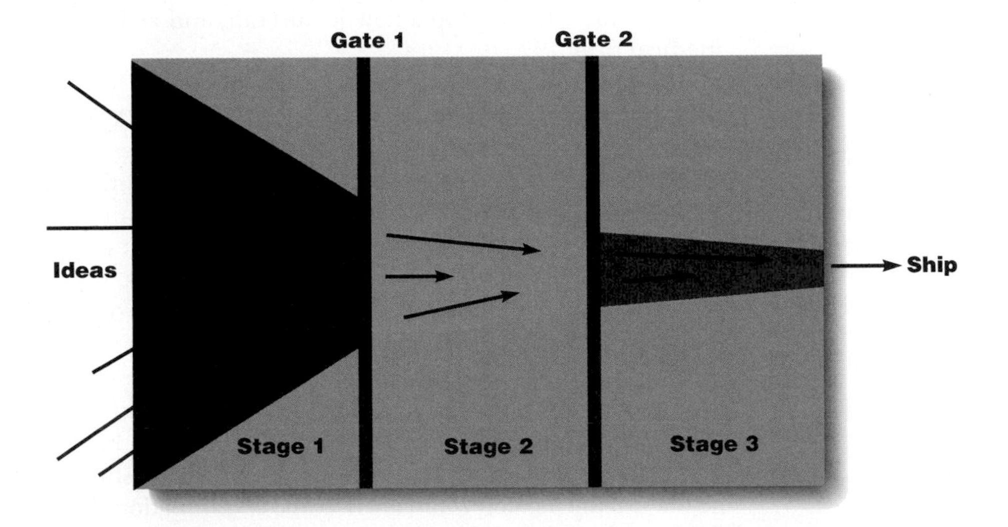

New product ideas are written up as brief proposals. The proposals are submitted to a cross-functional team of managers, who evaluate each proposal at gate 1. The cross-functional team considers a proposal's fit with the organization's strategy and its technical feasibility. Proposals that are consistent with the strategy of the organization and are judged technically feasible pass through gate 1 and into stage 2. Other proposals are turned down (although the door is often left open for reconsidering a proposal later).

The primary goal in stage 2 is to draft a detailed product development plan. The **product development plan** specifies all of the relevant information that managers need to decide whether to go ahead with a full-blown product development effort. The product development plan should include strategic and financial objectives, an analysis of the product's market potential, a list of desired product features, a list of technological requirements, a list of financial and human resource requirements, a detailed development budget, and a time line that contains specific milestones (for example, dates for prototype completion and final launch).

product development plan A plan that specifies all of the relevant information that managers need in order to decide whether to proceed with a full-blown product development effort.

A cross-functional team of managers normally drafts this plan. Good planning requires a good strategic analysis (see Chapter 8), and team members must be prepared to spend considerable time in the field with customers, trying to understand their needs. Drafting a product development plan generally takes about three months. Once completed, the plan is reviewed by a senior management committee at gate 2 (see Figure 9.6). These managers focus on the details of the plan to see whether the proposal is attractive (given its market potential) and viable (given the technological, financial, and human resources that would be needed to develop the product). Senior managers making this review keep in mind all other product development efforts currently being undertaken by the organization. One goal at this point is to ensure that limited organizational resources are used to their maximum effect.

At gate 2 projects are rejected, sent back for revision, or allowed to pass through to stage 3, the development phase. Product development starts with the formation of a cross-functional team that is given primary responsibility for developing the product. In some companies, at the beginning of stage 3 top managers and cross-functional team members sign a **contract book,** a written agreement that details factors such as responsibilities, resource commitments, budgets, time lines, and development milestones. Signing the contract book is viewed as the symbolic launch of a product development effort. The contract book is also a document against which actual development progress can be measured. At 3M, for example, team members and top management negotiate a contract and sign a contract book at the launch of a development effort, thereby signaling their commitment to the objectives contained in the contract.

contract book A written agreement that details product development factors such as responsibilities, resource commitments, budgets, time lines, and development milestones.

The stage 3 development effort can last anywhere from 6 months to 10 years, depending on the industry and type of product. Some electronics products have development cycles of 6 months, but it takes from 3 to 5 years to develop a new car, about 5 years to develop a new jet aircraft, and as long as 10 years to develop a new medical drug.

ESTABLISH CROSS-FUNCTIONAL TEAMS A smooth-running cross-functional team also seems to be a critical component of successful product development, as the experience of Zara suggests. Marketing, engineering, and manufacturing personnel are **core members** of a successful product development team–the people who have primary responsibility for the product development effort. Other people besides core members work on the project when the need arises, but the core members (generally from three to six individuals) stay with the project from inception to completion of the development effort (see Figure 9.7).

core members The members of a team who bear primary responsibility for the success of a project and who stay with a project from inception to completion.

The reason for using a cross-functional team is to ensure a high level of coordination and communication among managers in different functions.

If a cross-functional team is to succeed, it must have the right kind of leadership and it must be managed effectively. To be successful, a product development team needs a team leader who can rise above a functional background and take a cross-functional view. In addition to having effective leadership, successful cross-functional product development teams have several other key characteristics. Often core members of successful teams are located close to one another, in the same office space, to foster a sense of shared mission and commitment to a development program. Successful teams develop a clear sense of their objectives and how they will be achieved, the purpose again being to create a sense of shared mission. The way in which Google uses many of these strategies to promote innovation is discussed in the "Management Insight" box on the next page.

Google prospers because of its founders' ability to create a culture that encourages staffers to be innovative and because of their willingness to delegate authority for product development to managers and staffers. Managing innovation is an increasingly

Figure 9.7
Members of a Cross-Functional Product Development Team

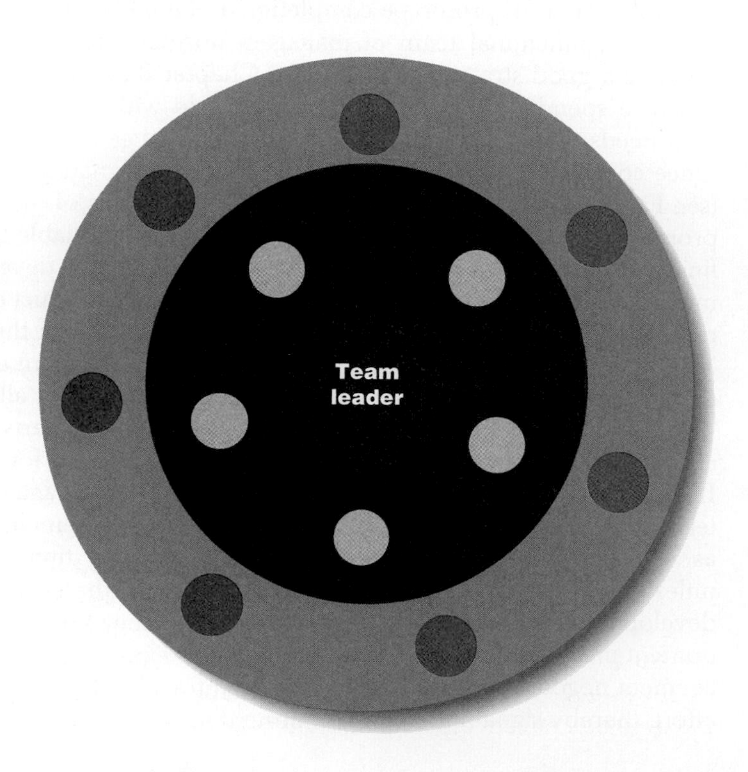

Management Insight

Innovation and Product Development Are Google's Major Imperative

The history of Google, the Internet search engine company, began in 1995 when two Stanford graduate computer science students, Sergey Brin and Larry Page, decided to collaborate to develop a new kind of search engine technology.[29] They understood the limitations of existing search engines, and by 1998 they had developed a superior engine that they felt was ready to go online. They raised US $1 million from family, friends, and risk-taking "angel" investors to buy the hardware necessary to connect Google to the Internet.

At first Google answered 10,000 inquiries a day, but in a few months it was answering 500,000. By fall 1999 it was handling 3 million; by fall 2000, 60 million; and by spring 2001, 100 million per day. In the 2000s Google became the dominant search engine, handling around 75% of inquiries by 2010; it is one of the top five most used Internet companies, and rivals like Microsoft are working hard to catch up and beat Google at its own game.

From the beginning, Google employees have worked in "high-density clusters," which contributes to their camaraderie and cooperative innovations—whether they're sitting on therapeutic bouncy balls or ergonomic office chairs.

Google's explosive growth is largely due to the culture of innovation its founders cultivated from the start. Although by 2010 Google had grown to 15,000 employees worldwide, its founders claim that Google still maintains a small-company feel because its culture empowers its employees, who are called staffers or "Googlers," to create the best software possible. Brin and Page created Google's innovative culture in several ways.

From the beginning, lacking space and seeking to keep operating costs low, Google staffers worked in "high-density clusters." Three or four employees, each equipped with a high-powered Linux workstation, shared a desk, couch, and chairs that were large rubber balls, working together to improve the company's technology. Even when Google moved into more spacious surroundings at its "Googleplex" headquarters building, staffers continued to work in shared spaces. Google designed the building so staffers constantly meet one another in its funky lobby; in its Google Café, where everyone eats together; in its state-of-the-art recreational facilities; and in its "snack rooms," equipped with bins packed with cereals, gummi bears, yogurt, carrots, and make-your-own cappuccino. Google also created many social gatherings of employees, such as a TGIF open meetings and a twice weekly outdoor roller hockey game where staffers are encouraged to bring down the founders.[30]

All this attention to creating what might be the "grooviest" company headquarters in the world did not come about by chance. Brin and Page knew that Google's most important strength would be its ability to attract the best software engineers in the world and then motivate them to perform well. Common offices, lobbies, cafés, and so on bring staffers into close contact with one another, develop collegiality, and encourage them to share new ideas with their colleagues and to constantly improve Google's search engine technology and find new ways to expand the company. The freedom Google gives its staffers to pursue new ideas is a clear indication of its founders' desire to empower them to be innovative and to look off the beaten path for new ideas. Finally, recognizing that staffers who innovate important new software applications should be rewarded for their achievements, Google's founders give them stock in the company, effectively making staffers its owners as well.

Their focus on innovation did not blind Brin and Page to the need to build a viable competitive strategy so Google could compete effectively in the cutthroat search engine market. They recognized, however, that they lacked business experience; they had never had to craft strategies to compete with giants like Microsoft and Yahoo. Moreover, they also had never been responsible for building a strong set of value chain functions. So they recruited a team of talented and experienced functional managers to help them manage their company. They also decided to give responsibility for the company's value chain management to a new CEO, Eric Schmidt, who came from Novell, where he had been in charge of strategic planning and technology development.

Brin and Page's understanding that successful product development requires building a strong organizational architecture has paid off. In August 2004 Google went public, and its shares, which were sold at US $85, were worth over US $100 each by the end of the first day of trading, US $500 by 2006, and a staggering US $750 in 2007 before falling back to around US $550 in spring 2010 after the recession. This has made Brin and Page's stake in the company worth billions; clearly it can pay to focus on innovation.

important aspect of a manager's job in an era of dramatic changes in advanced IT. Promoting successful new product development is difficult and challenging, and some product development efforts are much more successful than others. Google is performing at a high level, while thousands of other dot-coms, including many search engine companies such as Magellan and Openfind, have gone out of business.

In sum, managers need to recognize that successful innovation and product development cut across roles and functions and require a high level of cooperation. They should recognize the importance of common values and norms in promoting the high levels of cooperation and cohesiveness necessary to build a culture for innovation. They also should reward successful innovators and make heroes of the employees and teams who develop successful new products. Finally, managers should fully utilize the product development techniques just discussed to guide the process.

Summary and Review

LO9-1 **VALUE CHAIN MANAGEMENT AND COMPETITIVE ADVANTAGE** To achieve high performance, managers try to improve their responsiveness to customers, the quality of their products, and the efficiency of their organization. To achieve these goals, managers can use a number of value chain management techniques to improve the way an organization operates.

LO9-2 **IMPROVING RESPONSIVENESS TO CUSTOMERS** To achieve high performance in a competitive environment, it is imperative that the organization's value chain be managed to produce outputs that have the attributes customers desire. A central task of value chain management is to develop new and improved operating systems that enhance the ability of the organization to economically deliver more of the product attributes that customers desire for the same price. Techniques such as CRM and TQM, JIT, flexible manufacturing, and process reengineering are popular because they promise to do this. As important as responsiveness to customers is, however, managers need to recognize that there are limits to how responsive an organization can be and still cover its costs.

LO9-3 **IMPROVING QUALITY** Managers seek to improve the quality of their organization's output because doing so enables them to better serve customers, to raise prices, and to lower production costs. Total quality management focuses on improving the quality of an organization's products and services and stresses that all of an organization's operations should be directed toward this goal. Putting TQM into practice requires having an organizationwide commitment to TQM, having a strong customer focus, finding ways to measure quality, setting quality improvement goals, soliciting input from employees about how to improve product quality, identifying defects and tracing them to their source, introducing just-in-time inventory systems, getting suppliers to adopt TQM practices, designing products for ease of manufacture, and breaking down barriers between functional departments.

LO9-4 **IMPROVING EFFICIENCY** Improving efficiency requires one or more of the following: the introduction of a TQM program, the adoption of flexible manufacturing technologies, the introduction of just-in-time inventory systems, the establishment of self-managed work teams, and the application of process reengineering. Top management is responsible for setting the context within which efficiency improvements can take place by, for example, emphasizing the need for continuous improvement. Functional-level managers bear prime responsibility for identifying and implementing efficiency-enhancing improvements in operating systems.

LO9-5 **IMPROVING PRODUCT INNOVATION** When technology is changing, managers must quickly innovate new and improved products to protect their competitive advantage. Some value chain strategies managers can use to achieve this are (1) involving both customers and suppliers in the development process; (2) establishing a stage–gate development funnel for evaluating and controlling different product development efforts; and (3) establishing cross-functional teams composed of individuals from different functional departments, and giving each team a leader who can rise above his or her functional background.

Management in Action

Topics for Discussion and Action

Discussion

1. What is CRM, and how can it help improve responsiveness to customers? **[LO9-2]**

2. What are the main challenges in implementing a successful total quality management program? **[LO9-3]**

3. What is efficiency, and what are some strategies managers can use to increase it? **[LO9-4]**

4. Why is it important for managers to pay close attention to value chain management if they wish to be responsive to their customers? **[LO9-1, 9-2]**

5. What is innovation, and what are some strategies managers can use to develop successful new products? **[LO9-5]**

Action

6. Ask a manager how responsiveness to customers, quality, efficiency, and innovation are defined and measured in his or her organization. **[LO9-1, 9-2]**

7. Go to a local store, restaurant, or supermarket, observe how customers are treated, and list the ways in which you think the organization is being responsive or unresponsive to the needs of its customers. How could this business improve its responsiveness to customers? **[LO9-1, 9-2]**

Building Management Skills

Managing the Value Chain **[LO9-1, 9-2]**

Choose an organization with which you are familiar—one that you have worked in or patronized or one that has received extensive coverage in the popular press. The organization should be involved in only one industry or business. Answer these questions about the organization:

1. What is the output of the organization?

2. Describe the value chain activities that the organization uses to produce this output.

3. What product attributes do customers of the organization desire?

4. Try to identify improvements that might be made to the organization's value chain to boost its responsiveness to customers, quality, efficiency, and innovation.

Managing Ethically **[LO9-1, 9-4]**

After implementing efficiency-improving techniques, many companies commonly lay off hundreds or thousands of employees whose services are no longer required. And frequently remaining employees must perform more tasks more quickly—a situation that can generate employee stress and other work-related problems. Also, these employees may experience guilt because they stayed while many of their colleagues and friends were fired.

Questions

1. Either by yourself or in a group, think through the ethical implications of using a new functional strategy to improve organizational performance.

2. What criteria would you use to decide which kind of strategy is ethical to adopt and how far to push employees to raise the level of their performance?

3. How big a layoff, if any, is acceptable? If layoffs are acceptable, what could be done to reduce their harm to employees?

Small Group Breakout Exercise

How to Compete in the Sandwich Business [LO9-1, 9-2]

Form groups of three or four people, and appoint one member as the spokesperson who will communicate your findings to the class when called on by the instructor. Then discuss the following scenario:

You and your partners are thinking about opening a new kind of small restaurant that will compete head-to-head with major restaurant groups. These groups have good brand-name recognition, so it is vital that you find some source of competitive advantage for your new small restaurant, and you are meeting to brainstorm ways of obtaining such a competitive advantage.

1. Identify what your restaurant will focus on and what customers will want from a restaurant like yours.
2. In what ways do you think you will be able to improve on the operations and processes of existing restaurants and increase responsiveness to customers through better product quality, efficiency, or innovation?

Exploring the World Wide Web [LO9-3, 9-4]

In 2010 Toyota was accused of allowing its desire for rapid global growth to undermine its commitment to quality and safety in the design of its vehicles, creating problems such as the design failure of the acceleration and braking systems in some of its vehicles. Search the Web for articles about the Toyota recalls and investigations.

1. How have the recalls that Toyota announced in early 2010 affected current public opinion about the company's record for quality and reliability?
2. How has Toyota changed its strategies toward value chain management as a result of these quality and safety problems?

Be the Manager [LO9-1, 9-3, 9-4, 9-5]

How to Build Flat-Panel Displays

You are the top manager of a start-up company that will produce innovative new flat-screen displays for PC makers like Acer. The flat-screen display market is highly competitive, so there is considerable pressure to reduce costs. Also, PC makers are demanding ever-higher quality and better features to please customers. In addition, they demand that delivery of your product meets their production schedule needs. Functional managers want your advice on how to best meet these requirements, especially because they are in the process of recruiting new workers and building a production facility.

Questions

1. What kinds of techniques discussed in the chapter can help your functional managers to increase efficiency?
2. In what ways can these managers develop a program to increase quality and innovation?

CHAPTER 10

Managing Organizational Structure and Culture

Learning Objectives

After studying this chapter, you should be able to:

LO10-1 Identify the factors that influence managers' choice of an organizational structure.

LO10-2 Explain how managers group tasks into jobs that are motivating and satisfying for employees.

LO10-3 Describe the types of organizational structures managers can design, and explain why they choose one structure over another.

LO10-4 Explain why managers must coordinate jobs, functions, and divisions using the hierarchy of authority and integrating mechanisms.

LO10-5 List the four sources of organizational culture, and explain why and how a company's culture can lead to competitive advantage.

A MANAGER'S CHALLENGE

Andrea Jung Reorganizes Avon's Global Structure

How should managers organize to improve performance? In 2007 Andrea Jung, CEO of Avon, found that the company's rapid global expansion had given Avon's managers too much autonomy. They had gained so much authority to control operations in their respective countries and world regions that they had made decisions to benefit their own divisions—and these decisions had hurt the performance of the whole company. Avon's country-level managers from Poland to Mexico ran their own factories, made their own product development decisions, and developed their own advertising campaigns. And these decisions were often based on poor marketing knowledge and with little concern for operating costs; their goal was to increase sales as fast as possible. Also, when too much authority is decentralized to managers lower in an organization's hierarchy, these managers often recruit more managers to help them build their country "empires." The result was that Avon's global organizational hierarchy had exploded—it had risen from 7 levels to 15 levels of managers in a decade as tens of thousands of extra managers were hired around the globe.[1] Because Avon's profits were rising fast, Jung had not paid enough attention to the way Avon's organizational structure was becoming taller and taller—just as it was getting wider and wider as it established new divisions in new countries to expand cosmetics sales.

By 2008 Jung realized she had to lay off thousands of Avon's global managers and restructure its organizational hierarchy to reduce costs and increase profitability. She embarked on a program to take away the authority of Avon's country-level managers and to transfer authority to global regional and corporate headquarters managers to

Andrea Jung, here addressing a stellar group of women leaders in the White House, has seen her tough streamlining decisions in the short term begin to pay off over the longer haul.

streamline decision making and reduce costs. She cut out seven levels of management and laid off 25% of Avon's global managers in its 114 worldwide markets. Then, using teams of expert managers from corporate headquarters, she examined all of Avon's functional activities, country by country, to find out why its costs had risen so quickly and what could be done to bring them under control. The duplication of marketing efforts in countries around the world was one source of these high costs. In Mexico one team found that country managers' desire to expand their empires led to the development of a staggering 13,000 different products! Not only had this led product development costs to soar; it had also caused major marketing problems—how could Avon's Mexican sales reps learn about the differences between so many products to help customers choose the right ones for them?

In Avon's new structure, the goal is to centralize all major new product development. Avon still develops over 1,000 new products a year, but in the future while the input from different country managers will be used to customize products to country needs in terms of fragrance, packaging, and so on, R&D will be performed in the United States. Similarly, Avon's present strategy is to develop marketing campaigns targeted toward the average global customer but that can be easily customized to a particular country or world region by, for example, using the appropriate language or nationality of the models. Other initiatives have been to increase the money spent on global marketing, which had not kept pace with Avon's rapid global expansion, and to hire more Avon salespeople in developing nations to attract more customers. Today Avon has recruited over 400,000 reps in China alone![2]

Country-level managers now are responsible for managing this army of Avon reps and for making sure that marketing dollars are directed toward the right channels for maximum impact. However, they no longer have authority to engage in major product development or build new manufacturing capacity—or to hire new managers without the agreement of regional or corporate level managers. The balance of control has changed at Avon, and Jung and all her managers are now firmly focused on making operational decisions in the best interests of the whole company.

Jung's efforts to streamline the company's organizational structure have worked; but the recession necessitated more restructuring, and the company began another program of downsizing. Jung's focus has been on realigning its global value chain operations, particularly in Western Europe and Latin America; and Avon has increased its use of outsourcing, by outsourcing its call centers and transaction processing functions. As a result of these initiatives, approximately 4,000 more global positions will be lost by 2012; but Jung hopes that by then with its new streamlined structure Avon will be able to expand rapidly again when the economy has recovered—analysts claim the prospects for the company in China alone are "outstanding." Avon's share price had recovered by 2010. Clearly, paying attention to organizing is important in determining a company's long-term profitability.

Overview

As the example of Avon suggests, when the environment changes because, for example, customer tastes change, or because agile competitors have developed new strategies to outperform their rivals, a company often has to change its organizational structure and move to one better suited to its new environment. How an organization is designed also affects employees' behavior and how well the organization operates; and with competition heating up in the cosmetics industry, the challenge facing Avon's Andrea Jung was to identify the best way to organize people and resources to increase efficiency and effectiveness.

organizational architecture The organizational structure, control systems, culture, and human resource management systems that together determine how efficiently and effectively organizational resources are used.

In Part 4 of this book, we examine how managers can organize and control human and other resources to create high-performing organizations. To organize and control (two of the four tasks of management identified in Chapter 1), managers must design an organizational architecture that makes the best use of resources to produce the goods and services customers want. **Organizational architecture** is the combination of organizational structure, culture, control systems, and human resource management (HRM) systems that together determine how efficiently and effectively organizational resources are used.

organizational structure A formal system of task and reporting relationships that coordinates and motivates organizational members so they work together to achieve organizational goals.

By the end of this chapter, you will be familiar not only with various forms of organizational structures and cultures but also with various factors that determine the organizational design choices that managers make. Then, in Chapters 11 and 12, we examine issues surrounding the design of an organization's control systems and HRM systems.

Designing Organizational Structure

Organizing is the process by which managers establish the structure of working relationships among employees to allow them to achieve organizational goals efficiently and effectively. **Organizational structure** is the formal system of task and job reporting relationships that determines how employees use resources to achieve organizational goals.[3] *Organizational culture,* discussed in Chapter 3, is the shared set of beliefs, values, and norms that influence how people and groups work together to achieve organizational goals. **Organizational design** is the process by which managers create a specific type of organizational structure and culture so a company can operate in the most efficient and effective way–as Andrea Jung did for Avon.[4]

LO10-1 Identify the factors that influence managers' choice of an organizational structure.

Once a company decides what kind of work attitudes and behaviors it wants from its employees, managers create a particular arrangement of task and authority relationships, and promote specific cultural values and norms, to obtain these desired attitudes and behaviors. The challenge facing all companies is to design a structure and culture that (1) *motivate* managers and employees to work hard and to develop supportive job behaviors and attitudes and (2) *coordinate* the actions of employees, groups, functions, and divisions to ensure they work together efficiently and effectively.

organizational design The process by which managers make specific organizing choices that result in a particular kind of organizational structure.

As noted in Chapter 2, according to contingency theory, managers design organizational structures to fit the factors or circumstances that are affecting the company the most and causing the most uncertainty.[5] Thus there is no one best way to design an organization: Design reflects each organization's specific situation, and researchers have argued that in some situations stable, mechanistic structures may be most appropriate while in others flexible, organic structures might be the most effective. Four factors are important determinants of the type of organizational structure or culture managers select: the nature of the organizational environment, the type of strategy the organization pursues, the technology (and particularly information technology) the organization uses, and the characteristics of the organization's human resources (see Figure 10.1).[6]

The Organizational Environment

In general, the more quickly the external environment is changing and the greater the uncertainty within it, the greater are the problems managers face in trying to gain access to scarce resources. In this situation, to speed decision making and communication

Figure 10.1
Factors Affecting Organizational Structure

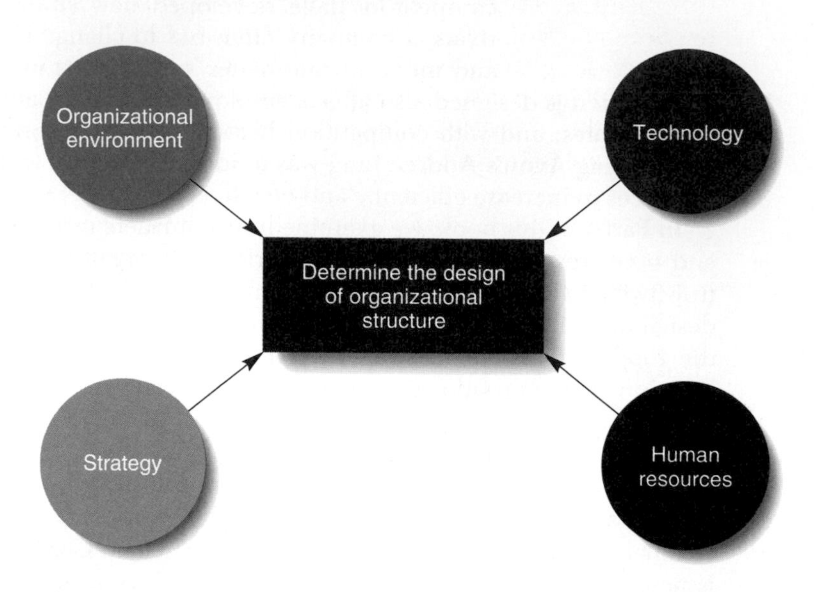

and make it easier to obtain resources, managers typically make organizing choices that result in more flexible structures and entrepreneurial cultures.[7] They are likely to decentralize authority, empower lower-level employees to make important operating decisions, and encourage values and norms that emphasize change and innovation–a more organic from of organizing.

In contrast, if the external environment is stable, resources are readily available, and uncertainty is low, then less coordination and communication among people and functions are needed to obtain resources. Managers can make organizing choices that bring more stability or formality to the organizational structure and can establish values and norms that emphasize obedience and being a team player. Managers in this situation prefer to make decisions within a clearly defined hierarchy of authority and to use detailed rules, standard operating procedures (SOPs), and restrictive norms to guide and govern employees' activities–a more mechanistic form of organizing.

As we discussed in Chapter 6, change is rapid in today's marketplace, and increasing competition both at home and abroad is putting greater pressure on managers to attract customers and increase efficiency and effectiveness. Consequently, interest in finding ways to structure organizations–such as through empowerment and self-managed teams–to allow people and departments to behave flexibly has been increasing.

Strategy

Chapter 8 suggests that once managers decide on a strategy, they must choose the right means to implement it. Different strategies often call for the use of different organizational structures and cultures. For example, a differentiation strategy aimed at increasing the value customers perceive in an organization's goods and services usually succeeds best in a flexible structure with a culture that values innovation; flexibility facilitates a differentiation strategy because managers can develop new or innovative products quickly–an activity that requires extensive cooperation among functions or departments. In contrast, a low-cost strategy that is aimed at driving down costs in all functions usually fares best in a more formal structure with more conservative norms, which gives managers greater control over the activities of an organization's various departments.[8]

In addition, at the corporate level, when managers decide to expand the scope of organizational activities by vertical integration or diversification, for example, they need to design a flexible structure to provide sufficient coordination among the different business divisions.[9] As discussed in Chapter 8, many companies have been divesting businesses because managers have been unable to create a competitive advantage to keep them up to speed in fast-changing industries. By moving to a more flexible structure, managers gain more control over their different businesses. Finally, expanding internationally and operating in many different countries challenges managers to create organizational structures that allow organizations to be flexible on a global level.[10] As we discuss later, managers can group their departments or divisions in several ways to allow them to effectively pursue an international strategy.

Technology

Recall that technology is the combination of skills, knowledge, machines, and computers that are used to design, make, and distribute goods and services. As a rule, the more complicated the technology that an organization uses, the more difficult it is to regulate or control it because more unexpected events can arise. Thus the more complicated the technology, the greater is the need for a flexible structure and progressive culture to enhance managers' ability to respond to unexpected situations–and give them the freedom and desire to work out new solutions to the problems they encounter. In contrast, the more routine the technology, the more appropriate is a formal structure because tasks are simple and the steps needed to produce goods and services have been worked out in advance.

What makes a technology routine or complicated? One researcher who investigated this issue, Charles Perrow, argued that two factors determine how complicated or nonroutine technology is: task variety and task analyzability.[11] *Task variety* is the number of new or unexpected problems or situations that a person or function encounters in performing tasks or jobs. *Task analyzability* is the degree to which programmed solutions are available to people or functions to solve the problems they encounter. Nonroutine or complicated technologies are characterized by high task variety and low task analyzability; this means many varied problems occur and solving these problems requires significant nonprogrammed decision making. In contrast, routine technologies are characterized by low task variety and high task analyzability; this means the problems encountered do not vary much and are easily resolved through programmed decision making.

Examples of nonroutine technology are found in the work of scientists in an R&D laboratory who develop new products or discover new drugs, and they are seen in the planning exercises an organization's top management team uses to chart the organization's future strategy. Examples of routine technology include typical mass-production or assembly operations, where workers perform the same task repeatedly and where managers have already identified the programmed solutions necessary to perform a task efficiently. Similarly, in service organizations such as fast-food restaurants, the tasks that crew members perform in making and serving fast food are routine.

LO10-2 Explain how managers group tasks into jobs that are motivating and satisfying for employees.

Human Resources

A final important factor affecting an organization's choice of structure and culture is the characteristics of the human resources it employs. In general, the more highly skilled its workforce, and the greater the number of employees who work together in groups or teams, the more likely an organization is to use a flexible, decentralized structure and a professional culture based on values and norms that foster employee autonomy and self-control. Highly skilled employees, or employees who have internalized strong professional values and norms of behavior as part of their training, usually desire greater freedom and autonomy and dislike close supervision.

Flexible structures, characterized by decentralized authority and empowered employees, are well suited to the needs of highly skilled people. Similarly, when people work in teams, they must be allowed to interact freely and develop norms to guide their own work interactions, which also is possible in a flexible organizational structure. Thus, when designing organizational structure and culture, managers must pay close attention to the needs of the workforce and to the complexity and kind of work employees perform.

In summary, an organization's external environment, strategy, technology, and human resources are the factors to be considered by managers seeking to design the best structure and culture for an organization. The greater the level of uncertainty in the organization's environment, the more complex its strategy and technologies, and the more highly qualified and skilled its workforce, the more likely managers are to design a structure and a culture that are flexible, can change quickly, and allow employees to be innovative in their responses to problems, customer needs, and so on. The more stable the organization's environment, the less complex and more well understood its strategy or technology, and the less skilled its workforce, the more likely managers are to design an organizational structure that is formal and controlling and a culture whose values and norms prescribe how employees should act in particular situations.

Later in the chapter we discuss how managers can create different kinds of organizational cultures. First, however, we discuss how managers can design flexible or formal organizational structures. The way an organization's structure works depends on the organizing choices managers make about three issues:

- How to group tasks into individual jobs.
- How to group jobs into functions and divisions.
- How to allocate authority and coordinate or integrate functions and divisions.

Grouping Tasks into Jobs: Job Design

job design The process by which managers decide how to divide tasks into specific jobs.

The first step in organizational design is **job design,** the process by which managers decide how to divide into specific jobs the tasks that have to be performed to provide customers with goods and services. Managers at McDonald's, for example, have decided how best to divide the tasks required to provide customers with fast, cheap food in each McDonald's restaurant. After experimenting with different job arrangements, McDonald's managers decided on a basic division of labor among chefs and food servers. Managers allocated all the tasks involved in actually cooking the food (putting oil in the fat fryers, opening packages of frozen french fries, putting beef patties on the grill, making salads, and so on) to the job of chef. They allocated all the tasks involved in giving the food to customers (such as greeting customers, taking orders, putting fries and burgers into bags, adding salt, pepper, and napkins, and taking money) to food servers. In addition, they created other jobs–the job of dealing with drive-through customers, the job of keeping the restaurant clean, and the job of overseeing employees and responding to unexpected events. The result of the job design process is a *division of labor* among employees, one that McDonald's managers have discovered through experience is most efficient.

Establishing an appropriate division of labor among employees is a critical part of the organizing process, one that is vital to increasing efficiency and effectiveness. At McDonald's, the tasks associated with chef and food server were split into different jobs because managers found that, for the kind of food McDonald's serves, this approach was most efficient. It is efficient because when each employee is given fewer tasks to perform (so that each job becomes more specialized), employees become more productive at performing the tasks that constitute each job.

At Subway, the roles of chef and server are combined into one, making the job "larger" than the jobs of McDonald's more specialized food servers. The idea behind job enlargement is that increasing the range of tasks performed by the worker will reduce boredom.

At Subway, a sandwich shop found in 92 countries, managers chose a different kind of job design. At Subway there is no division of labor among the people who make the sandwiches, wrap the sandwiches, give them to customers, and take the money. The roles of chef and food server are combined into one. This different division of tasks and jobs is efficient for Subway and not for McDonald's because Subway serves a limited menu of mostly submarine-style sandwiches that are prepared to order. Subway's production system is far simpler than McDonald's; McDonald's menu is much more varied, and its chefs must cook many different kinds of foods.

Managers of every organization must analyze the range of tasks to be performed and then create jobs that best allow the organization to give customers the goods and services they want. In deciding how to assign tasks to individual jobs, however, managers must be careful not to take **job simplification,** the process of reducing the number of tasks that each worker performs, too far.[12] Too much job simplification may reduce efficiency rather than increase it if workers find their simplified jobs boring and monotonous, become demotivated and unhappy, and, as a result, perform at a low level.

job simplification The process of reducing the number of tasks that each worker performs.

Job Enlargement and Job Enrichment

In an attempt to create a division of labor and design individual jobs to encourage workers to perform at a higher level and be more satisfied with their work, several researchers have proposed ways other than job simplification to group tasks into jobs: job enlargement and job enrichment.

job enlargement Increasing the number of different tasks in a given job by changing the division of labor.

Job enlargement is increasing the number of different tasks in a given job by changing the division of labor.[13] For example, because Subway food servers make the food as well as serve it, their jobs are "larger" than the jobs of McDonald's food servers. The Subway employee performs the whole process of making the sandwich, including baking the bread. In contrast, the McDonald's employee performs one specific task, such as cooking the hamburgers. The idea behind job enlargement is that increasing the range of tasks performed by a worker will reduce boredom and fatigue and may increase motivation to perform at a high level–increasing both the quantity and the quality of goods and services provided.

job enrichment Increasing the degree of responsibility a worker has over his or her job.

Job enrichment is increasing the degree of responsibility a worker has over a job by, for example, (1) empowering workers to experiment to find new or better ways of doing the job, (2) encouraging workers to develop new skills, (3) allowing workers to decide how to do the work and giving them the responsibility for deciding how to respond to unexpected situations, and (4) allowing workers to monitor and measure their own performance.[14] The idea behind job enrichment is that increasing workers' responsibility increases their involvement in their jobs and thus improves their interest in the quality of the goods they make or the services they provide.

In general, managers who make design choices that increase job enrichment and job enlargement are likely to increase the degree to which people behave flexibly rather than rigidly or mechanically. Narrow, specialized jobs are likely to lead people to behave in predictable ways; workers who perform a variety of tasks and who are allowed and encouraged to discover new and better ways to perform their jobs are likely to act flexibly and creatively. Thus managers who enlarge and enrich jobs create a flexible organizational structure, and those who simplify jobs create a more formal structure. If workers are grouped into self-managed work teams, the organization is likely to be flexible because team members provide support for each other and can learn from one another.

LO10-3 Describe the types of organizational structures managers can design, and explain why they choose one structure over another.

The Job Characteristics Model

J. R. Hackman and G. R. Oldham's job characteristics model is an influential model of job design that explains in detail how managers can make jobs more interesting and motivating.[15] Hackman and Oldham's model (see Figure 10.2) also describes the likely personal and organizational outcomes that will result from enriched and enlarged jobs.

According to Hackman and Oldham, every job has five characteristics that determine how motivating the job is. These characteristics determine how employees react to their work and lead to outcomes such as high performance and satisfaction and low absenteeism and turnover:

- *Skill variety:* The extent to which a job requires that an employee use a wide range of different skills, abilities, or knowledge. Example: The skill variety required by the job of a research scientist is higher than that called for by the job of a McDonald's food server.
- *Task identity:* The extent to which a job requires that a worker perform all the tasks necessary to complete the job, from the beginning to the end of the production process. Example: A craftsworker who takes a piece of wood and transforms it into a custom-made desk has higher task identity than does a worker who performs only one of the numerous operations required to assemble a flat-screen TV.
- *Task significance:* The degree to which a worker feels his or her job is meaningful because of its effect on people inside the organization, such as coworkers, or on people outside the organization, such as customers. Example: A teacher who sees the effect of his or her efforts in a well-educated and well-adjusted student enjoys high task significance compared to a dishwasher who monotonously washes dishes as they come to the kitchen.
- *Autonomy:* The degree to which a job gives an employee the freedom and discretion needed to schedule different tasks and decide how to carry them out. Example: Salespeople who have to plan their schedules and decide how to allocate their time among different customers have relatively high autonomy compared to assembly-line workers, whose actions are determined by the speed of the production line.
- *Feedback:* The extent to which actually doing a job provides a worker with clear and direct information about how well he or she has performed the job. Example: An air traffic controller whose mistakes may result in a midair collision receives

Figure 10.2
The Job Characteristics Model

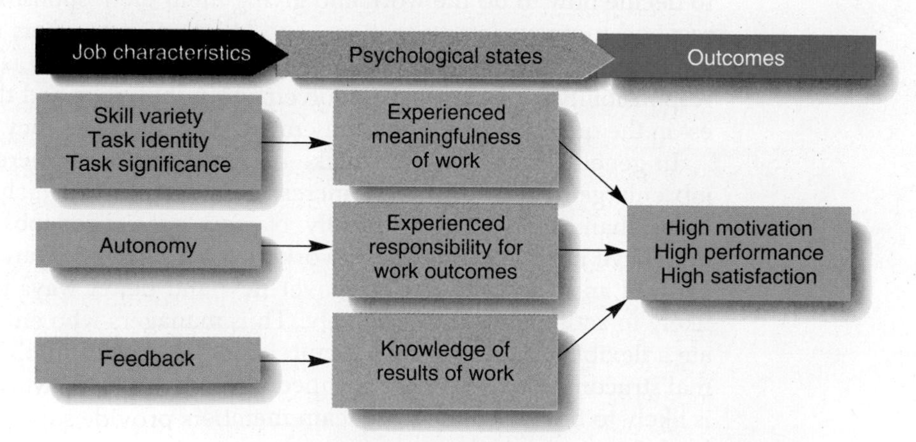

Source: J. Richard Hackman and Greg R. Oldham, *Work Redesign*, 1st edition, © 1980. Reproduced by permission of Pearson Education, Inc., Upper Saddle River, New Jersey.

immediate feedback on job performance; a person who compiles statistics for a business magazine often has little idea of when he or she makes a mistake or does a particularly good job.

Hackman and Oldham argue that these five job characteristics affect an employee's motivation because they affect three critical psychological states (see Figure 10.2). The more employees feel that their work is *meaningful* and that they are *responsible for work outcomes and responsible for knowing how those outcomes affect others,* the more motivating work becomes and the more likely employees are to be satisfied and to perform at a high level. Moreover, employees who have jobs that are highly motivating are called on to use their skills more and to perform more tasks, and they are given more responsibility for doing the job. All of the foregoing are characteristic of jobs and employees in flexible structures where authority is decentralized and where employees commonly work with others and must learn new skills to complete the range of tasks for which their group is responsible.

Grouping Jobs into Functions and Divisions: Designing Organizational Structure

Once managers have decided which tasks to allocate to which jobs, they face the next organizing decision: how to group jobs together to best match the needs of the organization's environment, strategy, technology, and human resources. Typically managers first decide to group jobs into departments and then design a *functional structure* to use organizational resources effectively. As an organization grows and becomes more difficult to control, managers must choose a more complex organizational design, such as a divisional structure or a matrix or product team structure. The different way in which managers can design organizational structure are discussed next. Selecting and designing an organizational structure to increase efficiency and effectiveness is a significant challenge. As noted in Chapter 8, managers reap the rewards of a well-thought-out strategy only if they choose the right type of structure to implement the strategy. The ability to make the right kinds of organizing choices is often what differentiates effective from ineffective managers and creates a high-performing organization.

Functional Structure

A *function* is a group of people, working together, who possess similar skills or use the same kind of knowledge, tools, or techniques to perform their jobs. Manufacturing, sales, and research and development are often organized into functional departments. A **functional structure** is an organizational structure composed of all the departments that an organization requires to produce its goods or services. Figure 10.3 shows the functional structure for Affilips N.V., a copper, aluminum, nickel, and lead alloys manufacturer in Belgium. The firm is well known for its use of recycled material.

functional structure An organizational structure composed of all the departments that an organization requires to produce its goods or services.

Purchasing, environmental, security, R&D, production, quality, finance, and personnel are the major functions of the firm. Each job inside a function exists because it helps the function perform the activities necessary for high organizational performance.

There are several advantages to grouping jobs according to function. First, when people who perform similar jobs are grouped together, they can learn from observing one another and thus become more specialized and can perform at a higher level. The tasks associated with one job often are related to the tasks associated with another job, which encourages cooperation within a function.

Second, when people who perform similar jobs are grouped together, it is easier for managers to monitor and evaluate their performance.[16] Imagine if marketing experts, purchasing experts, and real estate experts were grouped together in one function and

Figure 10.3
The Functional Structure of Affilips N.V. in Tienen, Belgium

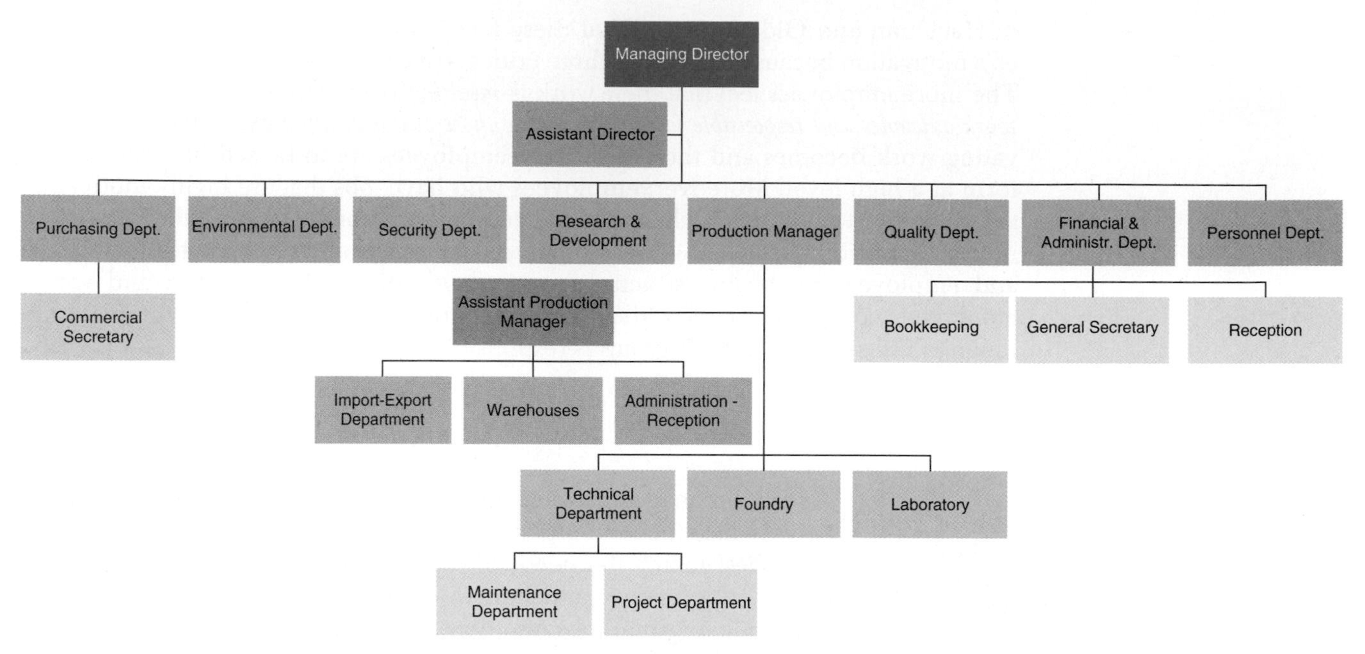

Source: Affilips: Organization Chart, *Welcome to Affilips*, http://www.affilips.com/organization.html, accessed October 19, 2010.

supervised by a manager from merchandising. Obviously the merchandising manager would not have the expertise to evaluate all these different people appropriately. A functional structure allows workers to evaluate how well coworkers are performing their jobs, and if some workers are performing poorly, more experienced workers can help them develop new skills.

Finally, managers appreciate functional structure because it lets them create the set of functions they need to scan and monitor the competitive environment and obtain information about how it is changing.[17] With the right set of functions in place, managers are in a good position to develop a strategy that allows the organization to respond to its changing situation.

As an organization grows, and particularly as its task environment and strategy change because it is beginning to produce a wider range of goods and services for different kinds of customers, several problems can make a functional structure less efficient and effective.[18] First, managers in different functions may find it more difficult to communicate and coordinate with one another when they are responsible for several different kinds of products, especially as the organization grows both domestically and internationally. Second, functional managers may become so preoccupied with supervising their own specific departments and achieving their departmental goals that they lose sight of organizational goals. If that happens, organizational effectiveness will suffer because managers will be viewing issues and problems facing the organization only from their own, relatively narrow, departmental perspectives.[19] Both of these problems can reduce efficiency and effectiveness.

Divisional Structures: Product, Market, and Geographic

divisional structure An organizational structure composed of separate business units within which are the functions that work together to produce a specific product for a specific customer.

As the problems associated with growth and diversification increase over time, managers must search for new ways to organize their activities to overcome the problems associated with a functional structure. Most managers of large organizations choose a **divisional structure** and create a series of business units to produce a specific kind

Affilips N.V., an alloys manufacturer in Belgium, organizes its operations by function, which means that employees can more easily learn from one another and improve the service they provide to customers.

of product for a specific kind of customer. Each *division* is a collection of functions or departments that work together to produce the product. The goal behind the change to a divisional structure is to create smaller, more manageable units within the organization. There are three forms of divisional structure (see Figure 10.4).[20] When managers organize divisions according to the *type of good or service* they provide, they adopt a product structure. When managers organize divisions according to the *area of the country or world* they operate in, they adopt a geographic structure. When managers organize divisions according to *the type of customer* they focus on, they adopt a market structure.

PRODUCT STRUCTURE Imagine the problems that managers at Affilips N.V. would encounter if they decided to diversify into producing and selling cars, fast food, and health insurance–in addition to home furnishings–and tried to use their existing set of functional managers to oversee the production of all four kinds of products. No manager would have the necessary skills or abilities to oversee those four products. No individual marketing manager, for example, could effectively market cars, fast food, health insurance, and home furnishings at the same time. To perform a functional activity successfully, managers must have experience in specific markets or industries. Consequently, if managers decide to diversify into new industries or to expand their range of products, they commonly design a product structure to organize their operations (see Figure 10.4a).

product structure An organizational structure in which each product line or business is handled by a self-contained division.

Using a **product structure,** managers place each distinct product line or business in its own self-contained division and give divisional managers the responsibility for devising an appropriate business-level strategy to allow the division to compete effectively in its industry or market.[21] Each division is self-contained because it has a complete set of all the functions–marketing, R&D, finance, and so on–that it needs to produce or provide goods or services efficiently and effectively. Functional managers report to divisional managers, and divisional managers report to top or corporate managers.

Grouping functions into divisions focused on particular products has several advantages for managers at all levels in the organization. First, a product structure allows functional managers to specialize in only one product area, so they can build expertise and fine-tune their skills in this particular area. Second, each division's managers

Figure 10.4
Product, Market, and Geographic Structures

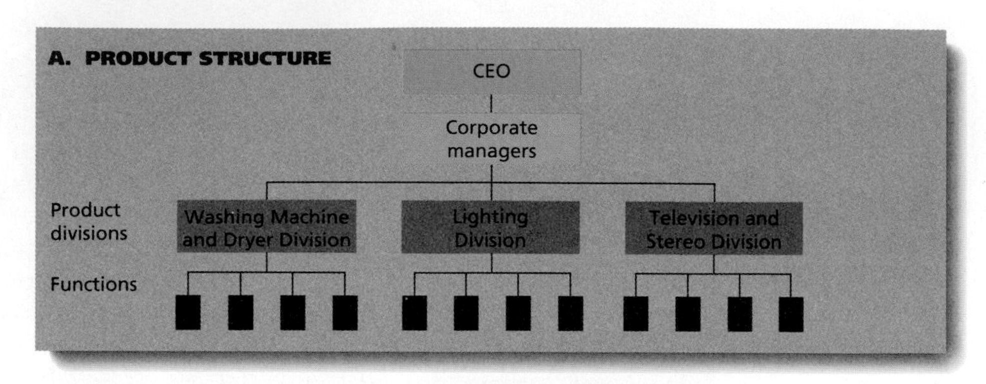

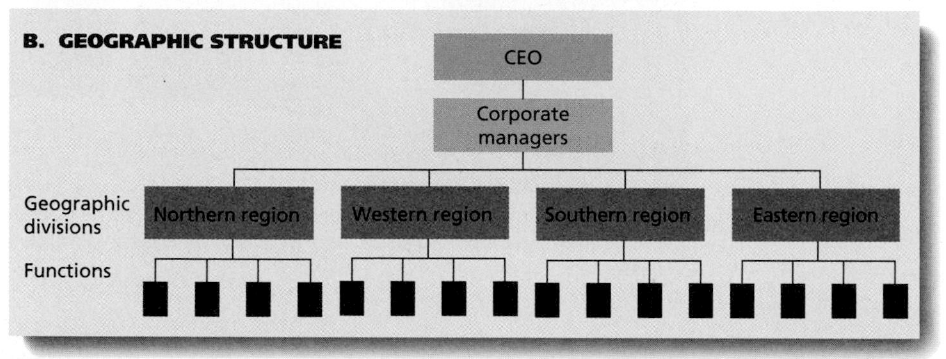

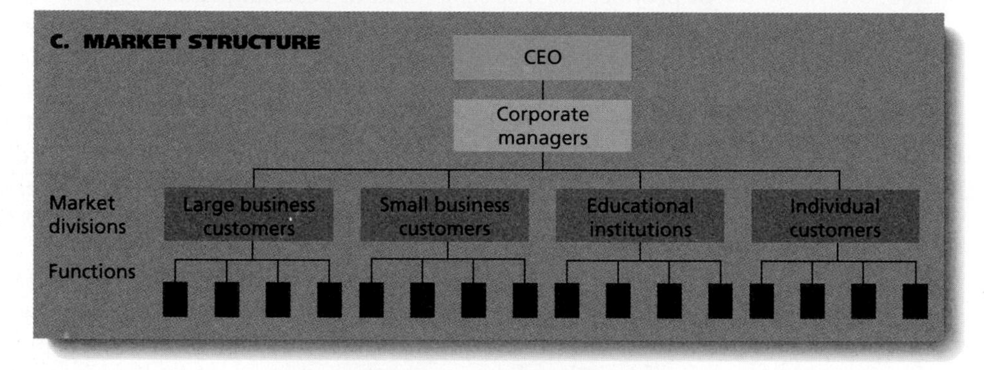

can become experts in their industry; this expertise helps them choose and develop a business-level strategy to differentiate their products or lower their costs while meeting the needs of customers. Third, a product structure frees corporate managers from the need to supervise directly each division's day-to-day operations; this latitude lets corporate managers create the best corporate-level strategy to maximize the organization's future growth and ability to create value. Corporate managers are likely to make fewer mistakes about which businesses to diversify into or how to best expand internationally, for example, because they can take an organizationwide view.[22] Corporate managers also are likely to evaluate better how well divisional managers are doing, and they can intervene and take corrective action as needed.

The extra layer of management, the divisional management layer, can improve the use of organizational resources. Moreover, a product structure puts divisional managers close to their customers and lets them respond quickly and appropriately to the changing task environment. One pharmaceutical company that successfully adopted a new product structure to better organize its activities is GlaxoSmithKline, a British pharmaceutical firm. The need to innovate new kinds of prescription drugs to boost performance is a continual battle for pharmaceutical companies. In the

When Glaxo Wellcome and SmithKline Beecham merged, managers resolved the problem of how to coordinate the activities of thousands of research scientists by organizing them into product divisions focusing on clusters of diseases.

2000s many of these companies have been merging to try to increase their research productivity, and one of them, GlaxoSmithKline, was created from the merger between Glaxo Wellcome and SmithKline Beecham.[23] Prior to the merger, both companies experienced a steep decline in the number of new prescription drugs their scientists were able to invent. The problem facing the new company's top managers was how to best use and combine the talents of the scientists and researchers from both of the former companies to allow them to quickly innovate exciting new drugs.

Top managers realized that after the merger there would be enormous problems associated with coordinating the activities of the thousands of research scientists who were working on hundreds of different kinds of drug research programs. Understanding the problems associated with large size, the top managers decided to group the researchers into eight product divisions to allow them to focus on particular clusters of diseases such as heart disease or viral infections. The members of each product division were told they would be rewarded based on the number of new prescription drugs they were able to invent and the speed with which they could bring these new drugs to the market. GlaxoSmithKline's new product structure worked well; its research productivity doubled after the reorganization, and a record number of new drugs moved into clinical trials.[24]

GEOGRAPHIC STRUCTURE When organizations expand rapidly both at home and abroad, functional structures can create special problems because managers in one central location may find it increasingly difficult to deal with the different problems and issues that may arise in each region of a country or area of the world. In these cases, a **geographic structure,** in which divisions are broken down by geographic location, is often chosen (see Figure 10.4b).

geographic structure An organizational structure in which each region of a country or area of the world is served by a self-contained division.

In adopting a *global geographic structure,* such as shown in Figure 10.5a, managers locate different divisions in each of the world regions where the organization operates. To illustrate, you can see the organizational chart for the Telefónica Group of Argentina in Figure 10.5a. The firm is in 25 countries and these countries are organized into three geographical regions: Spain, Latin America, and Europe. Under each regional group would be a complete set of functional areas. Managers are most likely to do this when they pursue a multidomestic strategy because customer needs vary widely by country or world region. For example, if products that appeal to U.S. customers do not sell in Europe, the Pacific Rim, or South America, managers must customize the products to meet the needs of customers in those different world regions; a global geographic structure with global divisions will allow them to do this.

In contrast, to the degree that customers abroad are willing to buy the same kind of product or slight variations thereof, managers are more likely to pursue a global strategy. In this case they are more likely to use a global product structure. In a *global product structure,* each product division, not the country and regional managers, takes responsibility for deciding where to manufacture its products and how to market them in countries worldwide (see Figure 10.5b). Product division managers manage their own global value chains and decide where to establish foreign subsidiaries to distribute and sell their products to customers in foreign countries. As we noted at the beginning of this chapter, an organization's strategy is a major determinant of its structure both at home and abroad; and in Chapter 6 we discussed how Nokia took a commanding lead in global cell phone sales because of its strategy of customizing phones to the needs of local users and assembling the phones in a factory located in a country within the world region where the phones are to be sold. Nokia's most important function is its design and engineering function, which spearheads its global new product development efforts. And to allow this function, and the company, to

Figure 10.5
Global Geographic and Global Product Structures

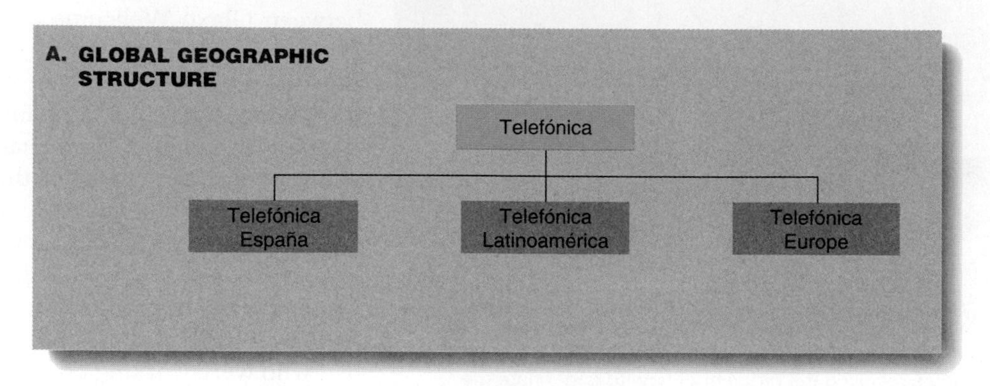

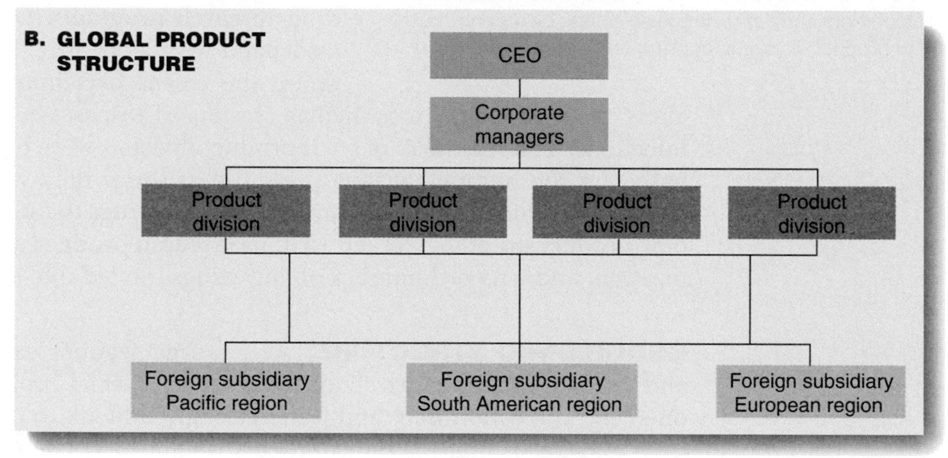

Source: Telefónica, "About Telefónica, Our Organization, Our Structure," http://www.telefonica.com/en/about_telefonica/html/estrucorganiz/estrucgrupo.shtml, accessed October 20, 2010.

perform most effectively, Nokia adopted a global structure to organize its design activities.

Nokia was the first cell phone manufacturer to recognize that the needs of customers differ markedly in different countries of the world. In Western countries, for example, the style of the phone is paramount, as is its ability to offer users services like e-mail and video downloading, and Nokia is developing advanced smartphones to compete with Apple. In India customers also value style, and they buy a cell phone as a status symbol and so are willing to pay a premium price for it. But in China customers want a bargain–the phone has to be at the right price point if customers are to buy the entry-level version or be enticed to spend more for premium features. How did Nokia discover how much needs diverge among customers in different countries?

Click, click, click. Nokia can pride itself on its forward-thinking momentum, which prompted it to develop regionally based products.

Its top managers decided that the engineers in its vast central design studio in Finland should be in charge of basic cell phone R&D and monitoring changing global forces in technology and changing customer demand for services such as video downloads, touch screens, colors, and so forth. However, to get close to customers in different countries, top managers decided to open nine different geographic design studios in various world regions and countries, such as India and China, where Nokia hopes to generate the most sales revenues. Engineers in these geographic studios, aided by marketing experts, determine the most important country-specific customer preferences.[25] These preferences are then transmitted back to Nokia's Finnish design headquarters, where they are incorporated into the studio's knowledge about changing global preferences for faster Internet service, touch screens, and so on. The result is a range of phones that share much in common but that can be highly customized to the needs of customers in different regions and countries. So Nokia uses a global divisional structure to facilitate its global design and manufacturing competencies as it attempts to remain ahead in the fiercely competitive global cell phone market.

MARKET STRUCTURE Sometimes the pressing issue facing managers is to group functions according to the type of customer buying the product in order to tailor the products the organization offers to each customer's unique demands. A PC maker such as Dell, for example, has several kinds of customers, including large businesses (which might demand networks of computers linked to a mainframe computer), small companies (which may need just a few PCs linked together), educational users in schools and universities (which might want thousands of independent PCs for their students), and individual users (who may want a high-quality multimedia PC so they can play the latest video games).

market structure An organizational structure in which each kind of customer is served by a self-contained division; also called *customer structure.*

To satisfy the needs of diverse customers, a company might adopt a **market structure,** which groups divisions according to the particular kinds of customers they serve (see Figure 10.4c). A market structure lets managers be responsive to the needs of their customers and allows them to act flexibly in making decisions in response to customers' changing needs. All kinds of organizations need to continually evaluate their structures, as is suggested in the following "Management Insight" box, which examines the concept of business groups.

Matrix and Product Team Designs

Moving to a product, market, or geographic divisional structure allows managers to respond more quickly and flexibly to the particular circumstances they confront. However, when information technology or customer needs are changing rapidly and the environment is uncertain, even a divisional structure may not give managers enough flexibility to respond to the environment quickly. To operate effectively under these conditions, managers must design the most flexible kind of organizational structure available: a matrix structure or a product team structure (see Figure 10.6).

Management Insight

Business Groups

Around the world a dominant form of business, not present in North America and limited in Europe, is the business group. Business groups are a set of legally independent entities bound by economic and social ties. These ties lead firms in the group to support one another, for example, by purchasing from each other. In addition they own one another's stock. Thus, rather than widespread stock ownership there is cross ownership within the business group. The best-known business groups are those in Japan, the *keiretsu*, and Korea, the *chaebol*.

To illustrate the keiretsu in Japan, consider the impact of the Mitsubishi group on the Japanese economy. There are over 160 firms in the Mitsubishi group. To begin, Mitsubishi Bank is the largest commercial banking company in the world, with assets of nearly US$820 billion. Next, Meiji Mutual, a Mitsubishi Group member, is the sixth largest mutual life insurance company worldwide, with assets of more than US$90 billion. Mitsubishi Motors is among world's top ten vehicle producers, while Mitsubishi Chemical is among world's top ten chemical companies. Mitsubishi Electric is one of the top ten electronics companies, and one of the fifty largest industrial companies in the world. Mitsubishi Heavy Industries is the largest industrial and farm equipment manufacturer in the world. Other core group members include Mitsubishi Materials (the twelfth largest metals company on earth), Kirin Brewery (the fourth largest beverage company), Mitsubishi Oil (the twenty-eighth petroleum refiner), and Asahi Glass (third in building materials).

This is only a sampling of the Mitsubishi firms. In total the Mitsubishi Group is estimated to contribute about 11% of the Japanese economy.

Figure 10.6
Matrix and Product Team Structures

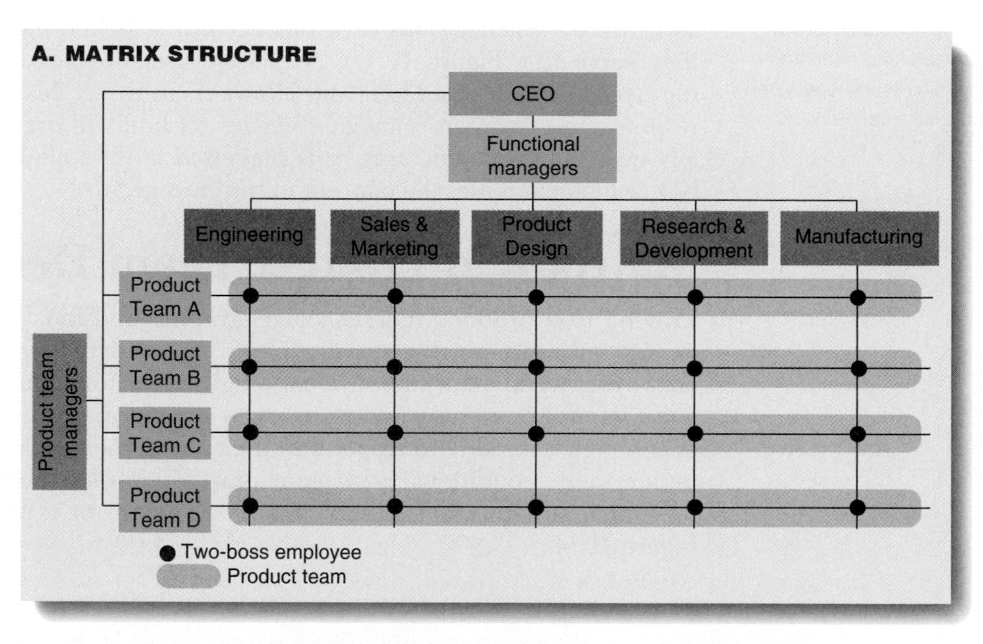

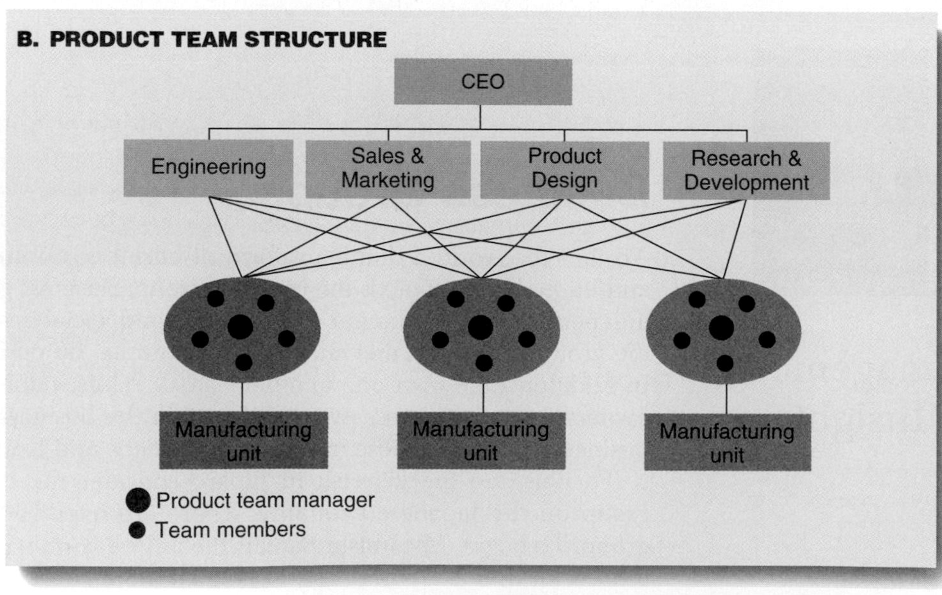

MATRIX STRUCTURE In a **matrix structure,** managers group people and resources in two ways simultaneously: by function and by product.[26] Employees are grouped by *functions* to allow them to learn from one another and become more skilled and productive. In addition, employees are grouped into *product teams* in which members of different functions work together to develop a specific product. The result is a complex network of reporting relationships among product teams and functions that makes the matrix structure very flexible (see Figure 10.6a). Each person in a product team reports to two managers: (1) a functional boss, who assigns individuals to a team and evaluates their performance from a functional perspective, and (2) the boss of the product team, who evaluates their performance on the team. Thus team members are known as *two-boss employees.* The functional employees assigned to product teams change over time as the specific skills that the team needs change. At the beginning of the product development process, for example, engineers and R&D specialists are assigned to a product team because their skills are needed to develop new products. When a provisional design has been established, marketing experts are assigned to the team to gauge how customers will respond to the new product. Manufacturing personnel join when it is time to find the most efficient way to produce the product. As their specific jobs are completed, team members leave and are reassigned to new teams. In this way the matrix structure makes the most use of human resources.

matrix structure An organizational structure that simultaneously groups people and resources by function and by product.

To keep the matrix structure flexible, product teams are empowered and team members are responsible for making most of the important decisions involved in product development.[27] The product team manager acts as a facilitator, controlling the financial resources and trying to keep the project on time and within budget. The functional managers try to ensure that the product is the best it can be to maximize its differentiated appeal.

High-tech companies that operate in environments where new product development takes place monthly or yearly have used matrix structures successfully for many years, and the need to innovate quickly is vital to the organization's survival. The flexibility afforded by a matrix structure lets managers keep pace with a changing and increasingly complex environment.[28]

PRODUCT TEAM STRUCTURE The dual reporting relationships that are at the heart of a matrix structure have always been difficult for managers and employees to deal with. Often the functional boss and the product boss make conflicting demands on team members, who do not know which boss to satisfy first. Also, functional and product team bosses may come into conflict over precisely who is in charge of which team members and for how long. To avoid these problems, managers have devised a way of organizing people and resources that still allows an organization to be flexible but makes its structure easier to operate: a product team structure.

The **product team structure** differs from a matrix structure in two ways: (1) It does away with dual reporting relationships and two-boss employees, and (2) functional employees are permanently assigned to a cross-functional team that is empowered to bring a new or redesigned product to market. A **cross-functional team** is a group of managers brought together from different departments to perform organizational tasks. When managers are grouped into cross-functional teams, the artificial boundaries between departments disappear, and a narrow focus on departmental goals is replaced with a general interest in working together to achieve organizational goals. The results of such changes have been dramatic: Ford can introduce a new model of car in two years.

product team structure An organizational structure in which employees are permanently assigned to a cross-functional team and report only to the product team manager or to one of his or her direct subordinates.

cross-functional team A group of managers brought together from different departments to perform organizational tasks.

Members of a cross-functional team report only to the product team manager or to one of his or her direct subordinates. The heads of the functions have only an informal, advisory relationship with members of the product teams–the role of functional managers is only to counsel and help team members, share knowledge among teams, and provide new technological developments that can help improve each team's performance (see Figure 10.6b).[29]

Increasingly, organizations are making empowered cross-functional teams an essential part of their organizational architecture to help them gain a competitive advantage in fast-changing organizational environments.

Coordinating Functions and Divisions

The more complex the structure a company uses to group its activities, the greater are the problems of *linking and coordinating* its different functions and divisions. Coordination becomes a problem because each function or division develops a different orientation toward the other groups that affects how it interacts with them. Each function or division comes to view the problems facing the company from its own perspective; for example, they may develop different views about the major goals, problems, or issues facing a company.

At the functional level, the manufacturing function typically has a short-term view; its major goal is to keep costs under control and get the product out the factory door on time. By contrast, the product development function has a long-term viewpoint because developing a new product is a relatively slow process and high product quality is seen as more important than low costs. Such differences in viewpoint may make manufacturing and product development managers reluctant to cooperate and coordinate their activities to meet company goals. At the divisional level, in a company with a product structure, employees may become concerned more with making *their* division's products a success than with the profitability of the entire company. They may refuse, or simply not see, the need to cooperate and share information or knowledge with other divisions.

The problem of linking and coordinating the activities of different functions and divisions becomes more acute as the number of functions and divisions increases. We look first at how managers design the hierarchy of authority to coordinate functions and divisions so they work together effectively. Then we focus on integration and examine the different integrating mechanisms managers can use to coordinate functions and divisions.

Allocating Authority

As organizations grow and produce a wider range of goods and services, the size and number of their functions and divisions increase. To coordinate the activities of people, functions, and divisions and to allow them to work together effectively, managers must develop a clear hierarchy of authority.[30] **Authority** is the power vested in a manager to make decisions and use resources to achieve organizational goals by virtue of his or her position in an organization. The **hierarchy of authority** is an organization's *chain of command*–the relative authority that each manager has–extending from the CEO at the top, down through the middle managers and first-line managers, to the nonmanagerial employees who actually make goods or provide services. Every manager, at every level of the hierarchy, supervises one or more subordinates. The term **span of control** refers to the number of subordinates who report directly to a manager.

authority The power to hold people accountable for their actions and to make decisions concerning the use of organizational resources.

hierarchy of authority An organization's chain of command, specifying the relative authority of each manager.

span of control The number of subordinates who report directly to a manager.

Figure 10.7 shows a simplified picture of the hierarchy of authority and the span of control of managers in McDonald's in 2008. At the top of the hierarchy is Jim Skinner, CEO and vice chairman of McDonald's board of directors, who took control in 2004.[31] Skinner is the manager who has ultimate responsibility for McDonald's performance, and he has the authority to decide how to use organizational resources to benefit McDonald's stakeholders.[32] Don Thompson, next in line, is president and COO and is responsible for overseeing all of McDonald's global restaurant operations. Thompson reports directly to Skinner, as does chief financial officer Peter Bensen. Unlike the other managers, Bensen is not a line manager, someone in the direct line or chain of command who has formal authority over people and resources. Rather, Bensen is a staff manager, responsible for one of McDonald's specialist

Figure 10.7
The Hierarchy of Authority and Span of Control at McDonald's Corporation

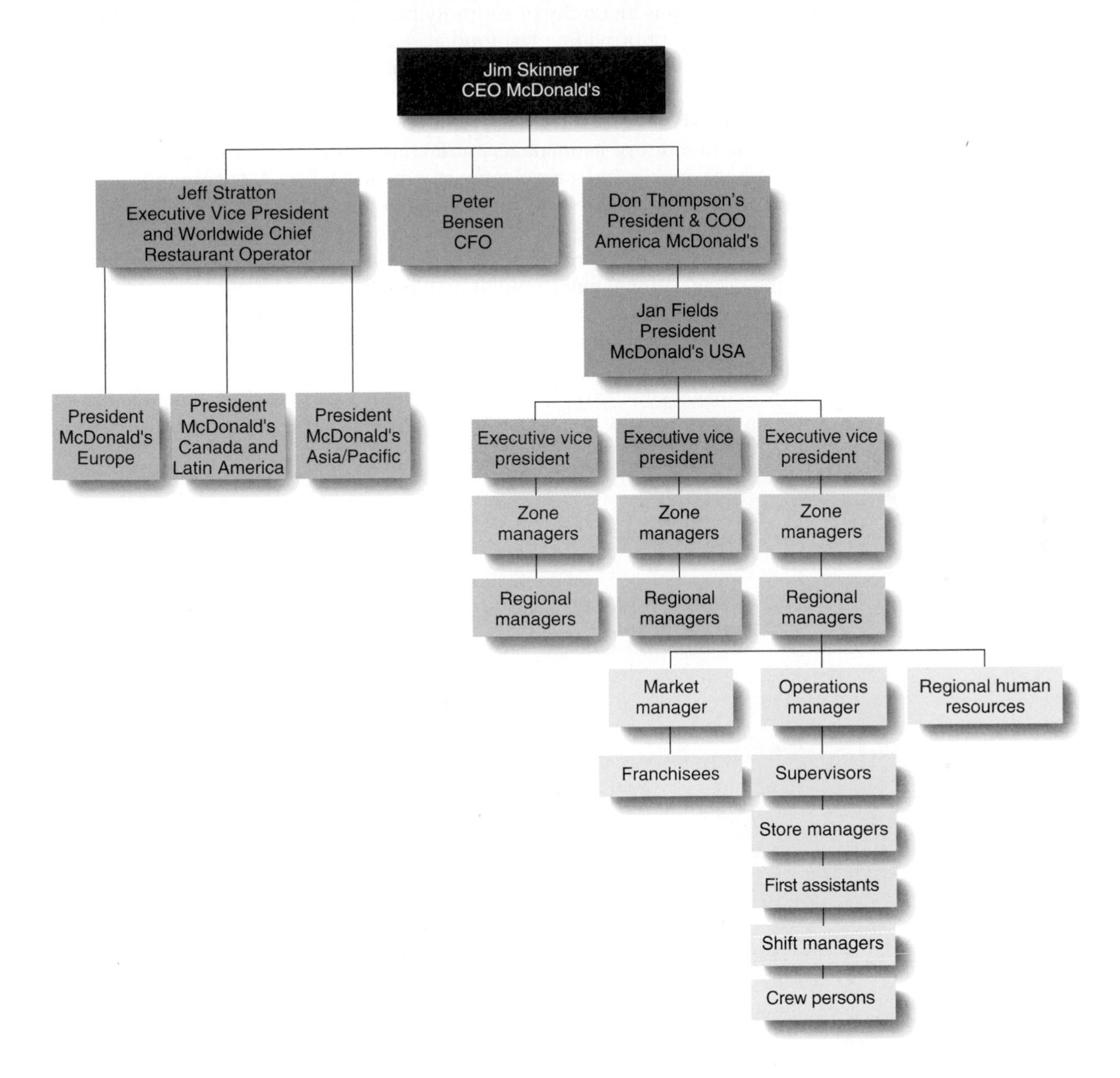

functions, finance. Worldwide chief operations officer Jeff Stratton is responsible for overseeing all functional aspects of McDonald's overseas operations, which are headed by the presidents of world regions: Europe; Canada and Latin America; and Asia/Pacific, Middle East, and Africa. Jan Fields is president of McDonald's U.S. operations and reports to Thompson.

Managers at each level of the hierarchy confer on managers at the next level down the authority to decide how to use organizational resources. Accepting this authority, those lower-level managers are accountable for how well they make those decisions. Managers who make the right decisions are typically promoted, and organizations motivate managers with the prospects of promotion and increased responsibility within the chain of command.

Below Fields are the other main levels or layers in the McDonald's domestic chain of command–executive vice presidents of its West, Central, and East regions, zone managers, regional managers, and supervisors. A hierarchy is also evident in each company-owned McDonald's restaurant. At the top is the store manager; at lower levels are the first assistant, shift managers, and crew personnel. McDonald's managers have decided that this hierarchy of authority best allows the company to pursue its business-level strategy of providing fast food at reasonable prices–and its stock price has exploded in the 2000s as its performance has increased.

TALL AND FLAT ORGANIZATIONS As an organization grows in size (normally measured by the number of its managers and employees), its hierarchy of authority normally lengthens, making the organizational structure taller. A *tall* organization has many levels of authority relative to company size; a *flat* organization has fewer levels relative to company size (see Figure 10.8).[33] As a hierarchy becomes taller, problems that make the organization's structure less flexible and slow managers' response to changes in the organizational environment may result.

Communication problems may arise when an organization has many levels in the hierarchy. It can take a long time for the decisions and orders of upper-level managers to reach managers further down in the hierarchy, and it can take a long time for top managers to learn how well their decisions worked. Feeling out of touch, top managers may want to verify that lower-level managers are following

Figure 10.8
Tall and Flat Organizations

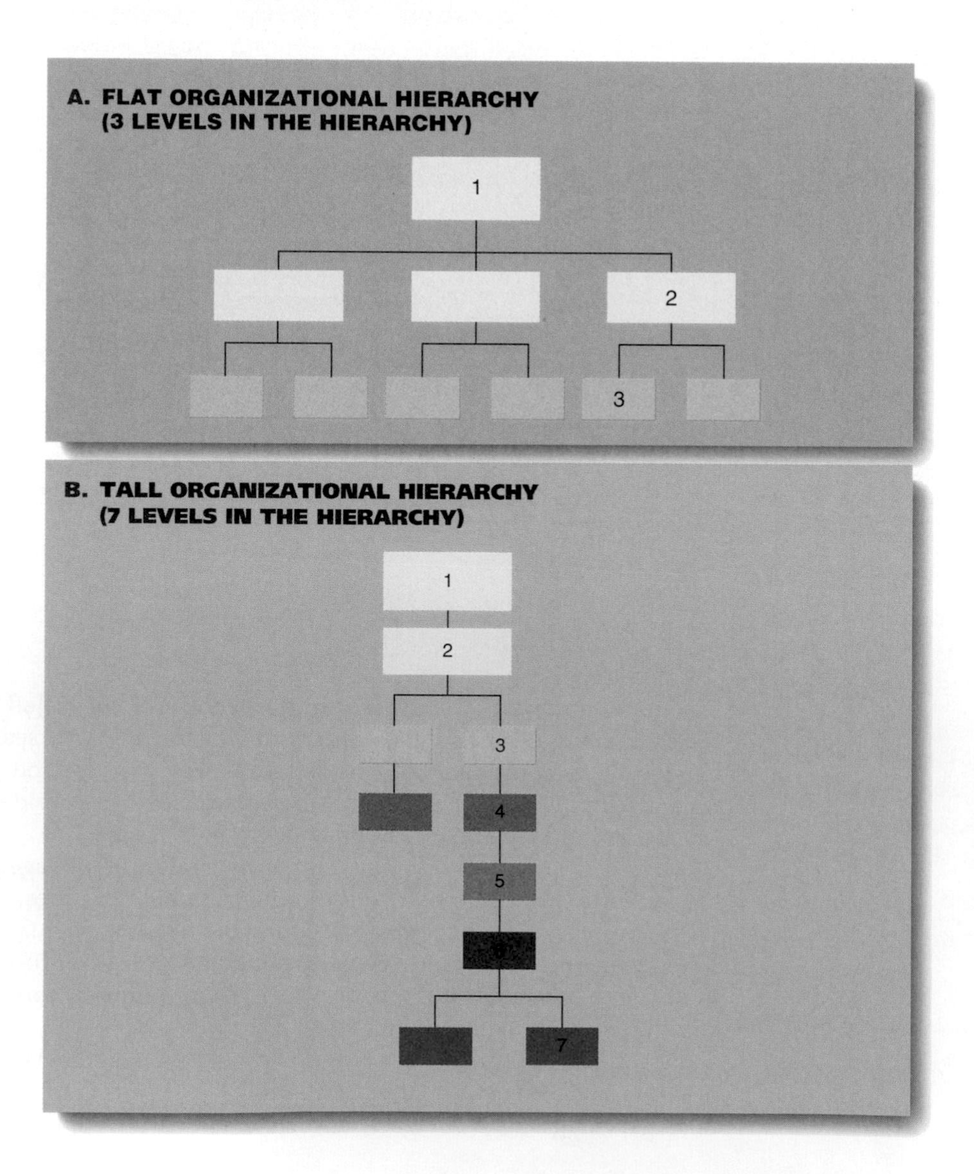

orders and may require written confirmation from them. Middle managers, who know they will be held strictly accountable for their actions, start devoting too much time to the process of making decisions to improve their chances of being right. They might even try to avoid responsibility by making top managers decide what actions to take.

Another communication problem that can result is the distortion of commands and messages being transmitted up and down the hierarchy, which causes managers at different levels to interpret what is happening differently. Distortion of orders and messages can be accidental, occurring because different managers interpret messages from their own narrow, functional perspectives. Or distortion can be intentional, occurring because managers low in the hierarchy decide to interpret information in a way that increases their own personal advantage.

THE MINIMUM CHAIN OF COMMAND To ward off the problems that result when an organization becomes too tall and employs too many managers, top managers need to ascertain whether they are employing the right number of middle and first-line managers and whether they can redesign their organizational architecture to reduce the number of managers. Top managers might well follow a basic organizing principle–the principle of the minimum chain of command–which states that top managers should always construct a hierarchy with the fewest levels of authority necessary to efficiently and effectively use organizational resources. This is something Andrea Jung learned expensively at Avon.

Effective managers constantly scrutinize their hierarchies to see whether the number of levels can be reduced–for example, by eliminating one level and giving the responsibilities of managers at that level to managers above and by empowering employees below. The need to empower workers is increasing as companies work to reduce the number of middle managers to lower costs and to compete with low-cost overseas competitors, as the following "Managing Globally" box suggests.

Managing Globally

SK Telecom: Restructuring an Organization and Its Impact

SK Telecom is a leading cell phone provider in Korea. However, in recent years the firm faced strong pressure on its revenue as cell phone saturation has grown. In an effort to address this problem, the firm realized it needed to change the organization of the firm and, in turn, the firm's culture. The Korean culture is strongly connected to Confucianism, which stresses hierarchy and respect for order. The firm's organizational structure was consistent with this culture. SK Telecom employed a five-staff-rank system of managers with a rigid top-down structure. The employees typically addressed each other by their title and then last name. In meetings lower-ranking employees were not permitted to question decisions. In October 2006, SK Telecom revamped its organizational structure in hopes of spurring more risk taking and creativity in the firm.

The company's first move was to eliminate five levels of management. Instead, it moved to a flatter organizational structure with greater decentralization of decision making in which there were only three levels of management. In addition, the firm moved to change how employees addressed each other; the firm required employees to simply address each other as "Manager." The firm maintained the very top titles but all levels below vice president were combined into a single category: team leader.

To help change the culture the firm also created new reward mechanisms that reinforced the new structure. One key change was that promotion became based on ability rather than seniority. Before the restructuring it was typical that promotions were based solely on seniority. SK Telecom began to place individuals in their 20s to lead projects for the firm. Previously individuals had to be in their 30s to have such responsibility. Some of the employees also saw their bonus structure change as bonuses are now based on creativity. Other changes that were made to reinforce the new structure included simple things like relaxing the dress code so that a more casual and innovative environment would result. The firm reports over 80% satisfaction by employees in the new environment in anonymous surveys.[34]

decentralizing authority Giving lower-level managers and nonmanagerial employees the right to make important decisions about how to use organizational resources.

CENTRALIZATION AND DECENTRALIZATION OF AUTHORITY Another way in which managers can keep the organizational hierarchy flat is by **decentralizing authority**–that is, by giving lower-level managers and nonmanagerial employees the right to make important decisions about how to use organizational resources.[35] If managers at higher levels give lower-level employees the responsibility of making important decisions and only *manage by exception,* then the problems of slow and distorted communication noted previously are kept to a minimum. Moreover, fewer managers are needed because their role is not to make decisions but to act as coach and facilitator and to help other employees make the best decisions. In addition, when decision-making authority is low in the organization and near the customer, employees are better able to recognize and respond to customer needs.

Decentralizing authority allows an organization and its employees to behave in a flexible way even as the organization grows and becomes taller. This is why managers are so interested in empowering employees, creating self-managed work teams, establishing cross-functional teams, and even moving to a product team structure. These design innovations help keep the organizational architecture flexible and responsive to complex task and general environments, complex technologies, and complex strategies.

Although more and more organizations are taking steps to decentralize authority, *too much* decentralization has certain disadvantages. If divisions, functions, or teams are given too much decision-making authority, they may begin to pursue their own goals at the expense of organizational goals. Managers in engineering design or R&D, for example, may become so focused on making the best possible product they fail to realize that the best product may be so expensive few people are willing or able to buy it. Also, too much decentralization can cause lack of communication among functions or divisions; this prevents the synergies of cooperation from ever materializing, and organizational performance suffers.

Top managers must seek the balance between centralization and decentralization of authority that best meets the four major contingencies an organization faces (see Figure 10.1). If managers are in a stable environment, are using well-understood technology, and are producing stable kinds of products (such as cereal, canned soup, or books), there is no pressing need to decentralize authority, and managers at the top can maintain control of much of organizational decision making.[36] However, in uncertain, changing environments where high-tech companies are producing state-of-the-art products, top managers must often empower employees and allow teams to make important strategic decisions so the organization can keep up with the changes taking place. No matter what its environment, a company that fails to control the balance between centralization and decentralization will find its performance suffering. The following "Management Insight" box profiles the organizational structure in a large family business.

Management Insight

Organizational Structure in a Large Family Business

The Emami Group is an Indian conglomerate that has an aggregate turnover of about US$170 million. The group owns consumer goods, paper and newsprint, writing instruments, edible oil, agriculture, biodiesel plants, hospitals, pharmaceuticals, cement, coal, real estate, and retail. Emami's founders were two childhood friends, R. S. Agarwal and R. S. Goenka. They have a major concern for the transition to the next generation across two families. Therefore, they have structured the organization to facilitate such a transition.

Agarwal has three children, and Goenka has two. To ensure that the two families work together in all lines of business, they seek to have one child from each family involved in the management of the various lines of business. For example, Aditya, the elder son of Agarwal, and Manish, the younger son of Goenka, together run the hospital, edible oil, biodiesel, and paper businesses. Mohan, Goenka's elder son, and Harsh, Agarwal's youngest child, are spearheading the company's forays into new areas such as cement, power production, and coal. Sureka, Agarwal's daughter, heads new brands in consumer products. Concerns about including both families in the business structure go beyond the children of the founders: Prashant, Goenka's nephew, heads Emami international business.

To reinforce this structure, the families take other actions to ensure that they have strong interconnections so information is shared among all of the members of the two families. Some of these information-sharing methods are formal. For example, they have a family forum each month to ensure that all issues of concern are addressed in a more formal manner. However, there are also informal methods that support the organizational goal of full information sharing. For example, all children of the two families are next to each other at corporate headquarters. Their offices have walls of glass, so no one can hide from the others. The families also still have lunch with each other every day. Both families stay in multi-storied houses on the same lane in their home city. Finally, the two families, the founders and their spouses, their children and spouses, and the founders' grandchildren always take an annual vacation, during the Puja holidays in October.

The founders both have set up a formal structure to support communication in the firm and have also set up informal methods to support that formal structure. Overall, the business group looks well placed to be able to transition to the next generation when the time comes.[37]

Integrating and Coordinating Mechanisms

LO10-4 Explain why managers must coordinate jobs, functions, and divisions using the hierarchy of authority and integrating mechanisms.

Much coordination takes place through the hierarchy of authority. However, several problems are associated with establishing contact among managers in different functions or divisions. As discussed earlier, managers from different functions and divisions may have different views about what must be done to achieve organizational goals. But if the managers have equal authority (as functional managers typically do), the only manager who can tell them what to do is the CEO, who has the ultimate authority to resolve conflicts. The need to solve everyday conflicts, however, wastes top management time and slows strategic decision making; indeed, one sign of a poorly performing structure is the number of problems sent up the hierarchy for top managers to solve.

integrating mechanisms Organizing tools that managers can use to increase communication and coordination among functions and divisions.

To increase communication and coordination among functions or between divisions and to prevent these problems from emerging, top managers incorporate various **integrating mechanisms** into their organizational architecture. The greater the complexity of an organization's structure, the greater is the need for coordination among people, functions, and divisions to make the organizational structure work efficiently and effectively.[38] Thus when managers adopt a divisional, matrix, or product team structure, they must use complex integrating mechanisms to achieve organizational goals. Several integrating mechanisms are available to managers to increase communication and coordination.[39] Figure 10.9 lists these mechanisms, as well as examples of the individuals or groups who might use them.

LIAISON ROLES Managers can increase coordination among functions and divisions by establishing liaison roles. When the volume of contacts between two functions increases, one way to improve coordination is to give one manager in each function or division the responsibility for coordinating with the other. These managers may meet daily, weekly, monthly, or as needed. A liaison role is illustrated in Figure 10.9; the small dot represents the person within a function who has responsibility for coordinating with the other function. Coordinating is part of the liaison's full-time job, and usually an informal relationship develops between the people involved, greatly easing strains between functions. Furthermore, liaison roles provide a way of transmitting information across an organization, which is important in large organizations whose employees may know no one outside their immediate function or division.

task force A committee of managers from various functions or divisions who meet to solve a specific, mutual problem; also called *ad hoc committee.*

TASK FORCES When more than two functions or divisions share many common problems, direct contact and liaison roles may not provide sufficient coordination. In these cases, a more complex integrating mechanism, a **task force,** may be appropriate (see Figure 10.9). One manager from each relevant function or division is assigned to a task force that meets to solve a specific, mutual problem; members are responsible for reporting to their departments on the issues addressed and the solutions recommended. Task forces are often called *ad hoc committees* because they are temporary; they may meet on a regular basis or only a few times. When the problem or issue is solved, the task force is no longer needed; members return to their normal roles in their departments or are assigned to other task forces. Typically task force members also perform many of their normal duties while serving on the task force.

Figure 10.9
Types and Examples of Integrating Mechanisms

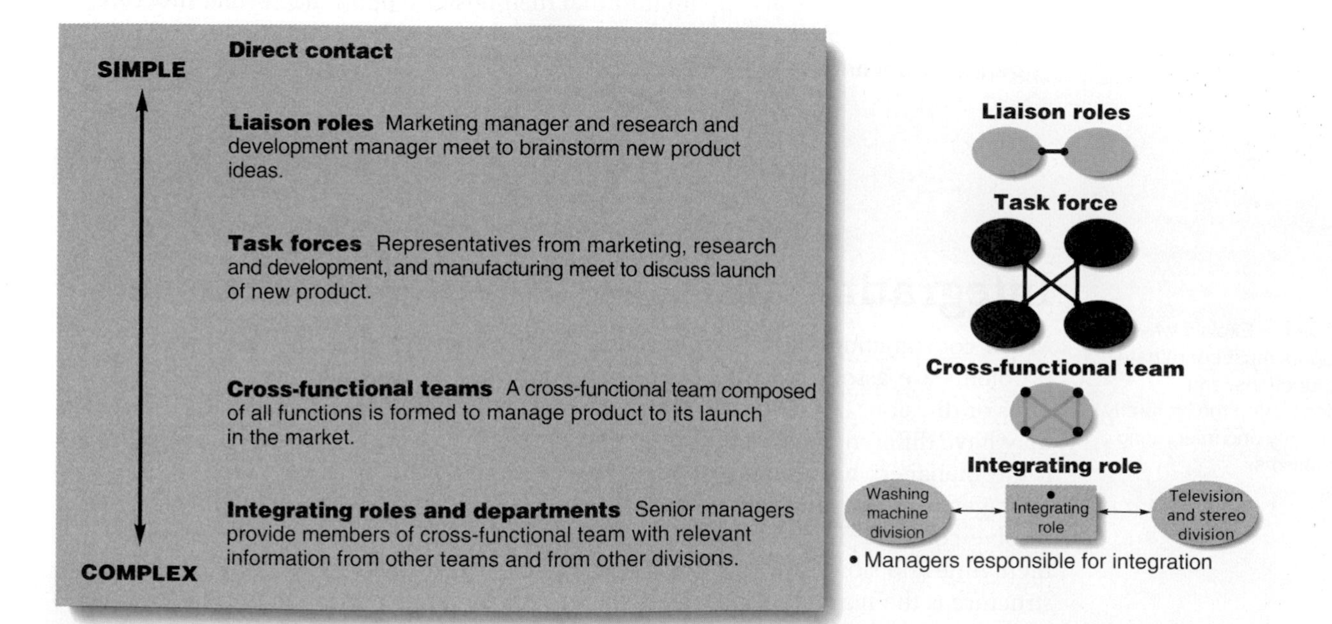

CROSS-FUNCTIONAL TEAMS In many cases the issues addressed by a task force are recurring problems, such as the need to develop new products or find new kinds of customers. To address recurring problems effectively, managers are increasingly using permanent integrating mechanisms such as cross-functional teams. An example of a cross-functional team is a new product development committee that is responsible for the choice, design, manufacturing, and marketing of a new product. Such an activity obviously requires a great deal of integration among functions if new products are to be successfully introduced, and using a complex integrating mechanism such as a cross-functional team accomplishes this. As discussed earlier, in a product team structure people and resources are grouped into permanent cross-functional teams to speed products to market. These teams assume long-term responsibility for all aspects of development and making the product.

INTEGRATING ROLES An integrating role is a role whose only function is to increase coordination and integration among functions or divisions to achieve performance gains from synergies. Usually managers who perform integrating roles are experienced senior managers who can envisage how to use the resources of the functions or divisions to obtain new synergies. One study found that DuPont, the giant chemical company, had created 160 integrating roles to coordinate the different divisions of the company and improve corporate performance.[40] The more complex an organization and the greater the number of its divisions, the more important integrating roles are.

In summary, to keep an organization responsive to changes in its task and general environments as it grows and becomes more complex, managers must increase coordination among functions and divisions by using complex integrating mechanisms. Managers must decide on the best way to organize their structures–that is, choose the structure that allows them to make the best use of organizational resources.

Organizational Culture

The second principal issue in organizational design is to create, develop, and maintain an organization's culture. As we discussed in Chapter 3, **organizational culture** is the shared set of beliefs, expectations, values, and norms that influence how members of an organization relate to one another and cooperate to achieve organizational goals. Culture influences the work behaviors and attitudes of individuals and groups in an organization because its members adhere to shared values, norms, and expected standards of behavior. Employees *internalize* organizational values and norms and then let these values and norms guide their decisions and actions.[41]

organizational culture The shared set of beliefs, expectations, values, and norms that influence how members of an organization relate to one another and cooperate to achieve organizational goals.

A company's culture is a result of its pivotal or guiding values and norms. A company's *values* are the shared standards that its members use to evaluate whether they have helped the company achieve its vision and goals. The values a company might adopt include any or all of the following standards: excellence, stability, predictability, profitability, economy, creativity, morality, and usefulness. A company's *norms* specify or prescribe the kinds of shared beliefs, attitudes, and behaviors that its members should observe and follow. Norms are informal, but powerful, rules about how employees should behave or conduct themselves in a company if they are to be accepted and help it to achieve its goals. Norms can be equally as constraining as the formal written rules contained in a company's handbook. Companies might encourage workers to adopt norms such as working hard, respecting traditions and authority, and being courteous to others; being conservative, cautious, and a "team player"; being creative and courageous and taking risks; or being honest and frugal and maintaining high personal standards. Norms may also prescribe certain specific behaviors such as keeping one's desk tidy, cleaning up at the end of the day, taking one's turn to bring doughnuts, and even wearing jeans on Fridays.

Ideally a company's norms help the company achieve its values. For example, a new computer company whose culture is based on values of excellence and innovation may try to attain this high standard by encouraging workers to adopt norms about being creative, taking risks, and working hard now and looking long-term for rewards (this combination of values and norms leads to an *entrepreneurial* culture in a company). On the other hand, a bank or insurance company that has values of stability and predictability may emphasize norms of cautiousness and obedience to authority (the result of adopting these values and norms would be a *stable, conservative* culture in a company).

Over time, members of a company learn from one another how to perceive and interpret various events that happen in the work setting and to respond to them in ways that reflect the company's guiding values and norms. This is why organizational culture is so important: When a strong and cohesive set of organizational values and norms is in place, employees focus on what is best for the organization in the long run–all their decisions and actions become oriented toward helping the organization perform well. For example, a teacher spends personal time after school coaching and counseling students; an R&D scientist works 80 hours a week, evenings, and weekends to help speed up a late project; or a salesclerk at a department store runs after a customer who left a credit card at the cash register. The following "Manager as a Person" box profiles embattled CEO Tony Hayward of British Petroleum, whose decision to streamline management had some unintended consequences.

Manager as a Person

Changes in Structure and Unintended Consequences

British Petroleum (BP) is one of the leading companies in the United Kingdom. In 2007, when Tony Hayward took over as CEO, he restructured the firm's organization with the goal to streamline management. Hayward wanted to eliminate complexity and duplication at every level and to standardize procedures across the company through greater centralization of decision making. The prior structure had multiple interfaces that could be inefficient as there were individual business units that operated big oil fields or other assets. These units enjoyed a large degree of autonomy that often led to waste and business-unit leaders sometimes duplicating each other's initiatives, analysts say. Hayward changed the firm to have two major divisions: exploration & production, and refining & marketing. The firm that previously had major efforts in renewable energy sought to decrease that focus thus folding gas, power, and renewable energy's unit into those two divisions. The number of layers of management between workers and the chief executive was reduced from 11 to 7.

Tony Hayward, BP's former CEO, walks along the beach on the U.S. Gulf Coast during the oil spill crisis. Hayward's decision to reorganize the company's organizational structure may have had a negative impact on the company's ability to make decisions quickly during the environmental disaster.

The market was initially very positive on the change. BP's massive restructuring plan sent its shares to a 52-week high shortly after the change was implemented. However, the firm's structure was questioned following the 2010 oil spill in the Gulf of Mexico. BP's centralized decision making was efficient when there was a normal decision-making environment. However, during the early stages of the oil spill crisis, the local unit looked to Britain for key decisions. The result was delayed decision making and poor public relations during the early stages of the crisis. The firm ultimately rallied and addressed the problem aggressively.[42–44]

LO10-5 List the four sources of organizational culture, and explain why and how a company's culture can lead to competitive advantage.

Where Does Organizational Culture Come From?

In managing organizational architecture, some important questions that arise are these: Where does organizational culture come from? Why do different companies have different cultures? Why might a culture that for many years helped an organization achieve its goals suddenly harm the organization?

Organizational culture is shaped by the interaction of four main factors: the personal and professional characteristics of people within the organization, organizational ethics, the nature of the employment relationship, and the design of its organizational structure (see Figure 10.10). These factors work together to produce different cultures in different organizations and cause changes in culture over time.

CHARACTERISTICS OF ORGANIZATIONAL MEMBERS The ultimate source of organizational culture is the people who make up the organization. If you want to know why organizational cultures differ, look at how the characteristics of their members differ. Organizations A, B, and C develop distinctly different cultures because they attract, select, and retain people who have different values, personalities, and ethics.[45] Recall the attraction–selection–attrition model from Chapter 3. People may

Figure 10.10
Sources of an Organization's Culture

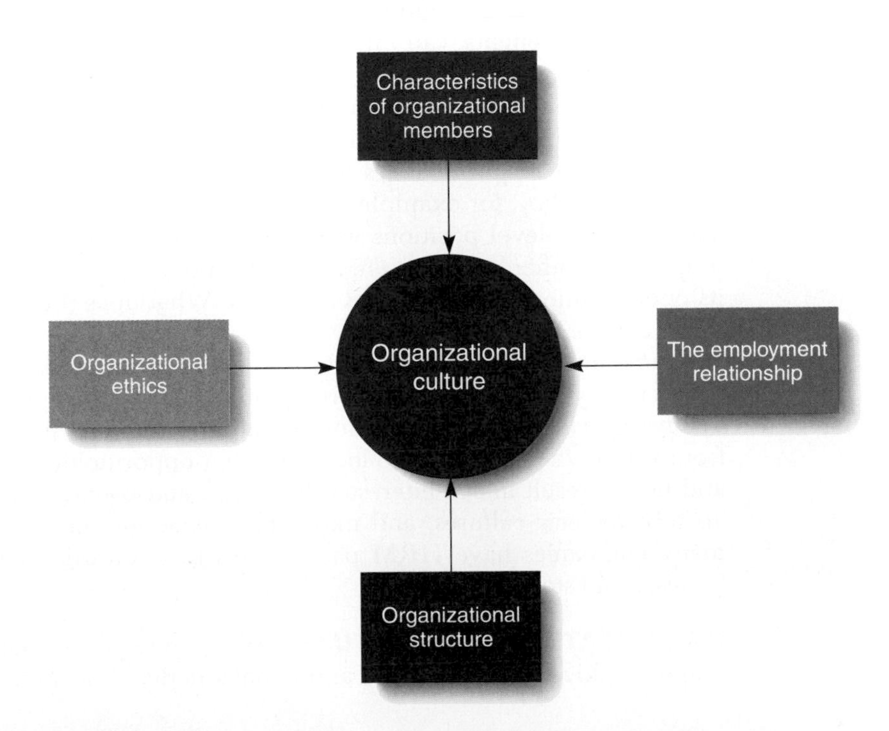

be attracted to an organization whose values match theirs; similarly, an organization selects people who share its values. Over time, people who do not fit in leave. The result is that people inside the organization become more similar, the values of the organization become more pronounced and clear-cut, and the culture becomes distinct from those of similar organizations.[46]

The fact that an organization's members become similar over time and come to share the same values may actually hinder their ability to adapt and respond to changes in the environment.[47] This happens when the organization's values and norms become so strong and promote so much cohesiveness in members' attitudes that the members begin to misperceive the environment.[48] Companies such as SAP, Bayer and Toshiba need a strong set of values that emphasize innovation and hard work; they also need to be careful their success doesn't lead members to believe their company is the best in the business. Companies frequently make this mistake. One famous example is the CEO of Digital Equipment, who in the 1990s laughed off the potential threat posed by PCs to his powerful minicomputers, claiming, "Personal computers are just toys." This company no longer exists.

organizational ethics The moral values, beliefs, and rules that establish the appropriate way for an organization and its members to deal with each other and with people outside the organization.

ORGANIZATIONAL ETHICS The managers of an organization can set out purposefully to develop specific cultural values and norms to control how its members behave. One important class of values in this category stems from **organizational ethics,** which are the moral values, beliefs, and rules that establish the appropriate way for an organization and its members to deal with each other and with people outside the organization. Recall from Chapter 4 that ethical values rest on principles stressing the importance of treating organizational stakeholders fairly and equitably. Managers and employees are constantly making choices about the right, or ethical, thing to do; and to help them make ethical decisions, top managers purposefully implant ethical values into an organization's culture.[49] Consequently ethical values, and the rules and norms that embody them, become an integral part of an organization's culture and determine how its members will manage situations and make decisions.

THE EMPLOYMENT RELATIONSHIP A third factor shaping organizational culture is the nature of the employment relationship a company establishes with its employees via its human resource policies and practices. Recall from Chapter 1 our discussion of the changing relationship between organizations and their employees due to the growth of outsourcing and employment of contingent workers. Like a company's hiring, promotion, and layoff policies, human resource policies, along with pay and benefits, can influence how hard employees will work to achieve the organization's goals, how attached they will be to the organization, and whether they will buy into its values and norms.[50] As we discuss in Chapter 12, an organization's human resource policies are a good indicator of the values in its culture concerning its responsibilities to employees. Consider the effects of a company's promotion policy, for example: A company with a policy of promoting from within will fill higher-level positions with employees who already work for the organization. On the other hand, a company with a policy of promotion from without will fill its open positions with qualified outsiders. What does this say about each organization's culture?

Promoting from within will bolster strong values and norms that build loyalty, align employees' goals with the organization, and encourage employees to work hard to advance within the organization. If employees see no prospect of being promoted from within, they are likely to look for better opportunities elsewhere, cultural values and norms result in self-interested behavior, and cooperation and cohesiveness fall. To rebuild their cultures, and make their remaining employees feel like "owners," many companies have HRM pay policies that reward superior performance with bonuses and stock options.[51]

ORGANIZATIONAL STRUCTURE We have seen how the values and norms that shape employee work attitudes and behaviors derive from an organization's people, ethics, and HRM policies. A fourth source of cultural values comes from the organization's structure. *Different kinds of structure give rise to different kinds of culture;* so to create a certain culture, managers often need to design a particular type of structure. Tall and highly centralized structures give rise to totally different sets of norms, rules, and cultural values than do structures that are flat and decentralized. In a tall, centralized organization people have little personal autonomy, and norms that focus on being cautious, obeying authority, and respecting traditions emerge because predictability and stability are desired goals. In a flat, decentralized structure people have more freedom to choose and control their own activities, and norms that focus on being creative and courageous and taking risks appear, giving rise to a culture in which innovation and flexibility are desired goals.

Whether a company is centralized or decentralized also leads to the development of different kinds of cultural values. By decentralizing authority and empowering employees, an organization can establish values that encourage and reward creativity or innovation. In doing this, an organization signals employees that it's okay to be innovative and do things their own way–as long as their actions are consistent with the good of the organization. Conversely, in some organizations it is important that employees do not make decisions on their own and that their actions be open to the scrutiny of superiors. In cases like this, centralization can be used to create cultural values that reinforce obedience and accountability. For example, in nuclear power plants, values that promote stability, predictability, and obedience to authority are deliberately fostered to prevent disasters.[52] Through norms and rules, employees are taught the importance of behaving consistently and honestly, and they learn that sharing information with supervisors, especially information about mistakes or errors, is the only acceptable form of behavior.[53]

An organization that seeks to manage and change its culture must take a hard look at all four factors that shape culture: the characteristics of its members, its ethical values, its human resource policies, and its organizational structure. However, changing a culture can be difficult because of the way these factors interact and affect one another.[54] Often a major reorganization is necessary for a cultural change to occur, as we discuss in the next chapter.

Strong, Adaptive Cultures versus Weak, Inert Cultures

Many researchers and managers believe that employees of some organizations go out of their way to help the organization because it has a strong and cohesive organizational culture–an adaptive culture that controls employee attitudes and behaviors. *Adaptive cultures* are those whose values and norms help an organization to build momentum and to grow and change as needed to achieve its goals and be effective. By contrast, *inert cultures* are those whose values and norms fail to motivate or inspire employees; they lead to stagnation and, often, failure over time. What leads to a strong adaptive culture or one that is inert and hard to change?

Researchers have found that organizations with strong adaptive cultures, like 3M, SAP and Microsoft, invest in their employees. They demonstrate their commitment to their members by, for example, emphasizing the long-term nature of the employment relationship and trying to avoid layoffs. These companies develop long-term career paths for their employees and spend a lot of money on training and development to increase employees' value to the organization. In these ways, terminal and instrumental values pertaining to the worth of human resources encourage the development of supportive work attitudes and behaviors.

In adaptive cultures employees often receive rewards linked directly to their performance and to the performance of the company as a whole. Sometimes employee stock ownership plans (ESOPs) are developed in which workers as a group are allowed to buy a significant percentage of their company's stock. Workers who are owners of the company have additional incentive to develop skills that allow them to perform highly and search actively for ways to improve quality, efficiency, and performance.

Some organizations, however, develop cultures with values that do not include protecting and increasing the worth of their human resources as a major goal. Their employment practices are based on short-term employment according to the needs of the organization and on minimal investment in employees who perform simple, routine tasks. Moreover, employees are not often rewarded on the basis of their performance and thus have little incentive to improve their skills or otherwise invest in the organization to help it achieve goals. If a company has an inert culture, poor working relationships frequently develop between the organization and its employees, and instrumental values of noncooperation, laziness, and loafing and work norms of output restriction are common.

Moreover, an adaptive culture develops an emphasis on entrepreneurship and respect for the employee and allows the use of organizational structures, such as the cross-functional team structure, that empower employees to make decisions and motivate them to succeed. By contrast, in an inert culture, employees are content to be told what to do and have little incentive or motivation to perform beyond minimum work requirements. As you might expect, the emphasis is on close supervision and hierarchical authority, which result in a culture that makes it difficult to adapt to a changing environment.

Nokia, discussed earlier, is a good example of a company in which managers strive to create an adaptive culture.[55] Nokia's top managers have always believed that Nokia's cultural values are based on the Finnish character: Finns are down-to-earth, rational, straightforward people. They are also friendly and democratic people who do not believe in a rigid hierarchy based either on a person's authority or on social class. Nokia's culture reflects these values because innovation and decision making are pushed right down to the bottom line, to teams of employees who take up the challenge of developing the ever-smaller and more sophisticated phones for which the company is known. Bureaucracy is kept to a minimum at Nokia; its adaptive culture is based on informal and personal relationships and norms of cooperation and teamwork.

To help strengthen its culture, Nokia built a futuristic open-plan steel and glass building just outside Helsinki. Here, in an open environment, its R&D employees can work together to innovate new kinds of cell phones focused on Nokia's company mission to produce phones that are more versatile, cheaper, and easier to use than competitor's phones. This is the "Nokia Way"–a system of cultural values and norms that can't be written down but is always present in the values that cement people together and in the language and stories its members use to orient themselves to the company. Yet, as we noted before, Nokia is the cell phone company that is most sensitive to the need to appreciate the values, norms, and tastes of other nations. So the Nokia Way is not just confined to Finland; the company has taken it to every country around the globe in which it operates.

Another company with an adaptive culture is GlaxoSmithKline, the prescription drug maker discussed earlier in the chapter. Much of GSK's success can be attributed to its ability to recruit the best research scientists because its adaptive culture nurtures scientists and emphasizes values and norms of innovation. Scientists are given great freedom to pursue intriguing ideas even if the commercial payoff is questionable. Moreover, researchers are inspired to think of their work as a quest to alleviate human disease and suffering worldwide, and GSK has a reputation as an ethical company whose values put people above profits.

Although the experience of Nokia and GSK suggests that organizational culture can give rise to managerial actions that ultimately benefit the organization, this is not always the case. The cultures of some organizations become dysfunctional, encouraging managerial actions that harm the organization and discouraging actions that might improve performance.[56] For example, Sunflower Electric Power, an electricity generation and transmission cooperative, almost went bankrupt in the early 2000s. A committee of inquiry set up to find the source of the problem put the blame on Sunflower's CEO and decided he had created an abusive culture based on fear and blame that encouraged managers to fight over and protect their turf–an inert culture. The

CEO was fired, and a new CEO was appointed to change the cooperative's culture, which he found hard to do because his top managers were so used to the old values and norms. With the help of consultants, he changed values and norms to emphasize cooperation, teamwork, and respect for others–which involved firing many top managers. Clearly, managers can influence how their organizational culture develops over time.

Summary and Review

LO10-1 **DESIGNING ORGANIZATIONAL STRUCTURE** The four main determinants of organizational structure are the external environment, strategy, technology, and human resources. In general, the higher the level of uncertainty associated with these factors, the more appropriate is a flexible, adaptable structure as opposed to a formal, rigid one.

LO10-2 **GROUPING TASKS INTO JOBS** Job design is the process by which managers group tasks into jobs. To create more interesting jobs, and to get workers to act flexibly, managers can enlarge and enrich jobs. The job characteristics model is a tool that managers can use to measure how motivating or satisfying a particular job is.

LO10-3 **ORGANIZATIONAL STRUCTURE: GROUPING JOBS INTO FUNCTIONS AND DIVISIONS** Managers can choose from many kinds of organizational structures to make the best use of organizational resources. Depending on the specific organizing problems they face, managers can choose from functional, product, geographic, market, matrix, product team, and hybrid structures.

LO10-4 **COORDINATING FUNCTIONS AND DIVISIONS** No matter which structure managers choose, they must decide how to distribute authority in the organization, how many levels to have in the hierarchy of authority, and what balance to strike between centralization and decentralization to keep the number of levels in the hierarchy to a minimum. As organizations grow, managers must increase integration and coordination among functions and divisions. Four integrating mechanisms that facilitate this are liaison roles, task forces, cross-functional teams, and integrating roles.

LO10-5 **ORGANIZATIONAL CULTURE** Organizational culture is the set of values, norms, and standards of behavior that control how individuals and groups in an organization interact with one another and work to achieve organizational goals. The four main sources of organizational culture are member characteristics, organizational ethics, the nature of the employment relationship, and the design of organizational structure. How managers work to influence these four factors determines whether an organization's culture is strong and adaptive or is inert and difficult to change.

Management in Action

Topics for Discussion and Action

Discussion

1. Would a flexible or a more formal structure be appropriate for these organizations? (a) A large department store, (b) a Big Five accounting firm, (c) a biotechnology company. Explain your reasoning. **[LO10-1, 10-2]**

2. Using the job characteristics model as a guide, discuss how a manager can enrich or enlarge subordinates' jobs. **[LO10-2]**

3. How might a salesperson's job or a secretary's job be enlarged or enriched to make it more motivating? **[LO10-2, 10-3]**

4. When and under what conditions might managers change from a functional to (a) a product, (b) a geographic, or (c) a market structure? **[LO10-1, 10-3]**

5. How do matrix structure and product team structure differ? Why is product team structure more widely used? **[LO10-1, 10-3, 10-4]**

6. What is organizational culture, and how does it affect the way employees behave? **[LO10-5]**

Action

7. Find and interview a manager and identify the kind of organizational structure that his or her organization uses to coordinate its people and resources. Why is the organization using that structure? Do you think a different structure would be more appropriate? Which one? **[LO10-1, 10-3, 10-4]**

8. With the same or another manager, discuss the distribution of authority in the organization. Does the manager think that decentralizing authority and empowering employees is appropriate? **[LO10-1, 10-3]**

9. Interview some employees of an organization, and ask them about the organization's values and norms, the typical characteristics of employees, and the organization's ethical values and socialization practices. Using this information, try to describe the organization's culture and the way it affects how people and groups behave. **[LO10-1, 10-5]**

Building Management Skills

Understanding Organizing [LO10-1, 10-2, 10-3]

Think of an organization with which you are familiar, perhaps one you have worked for—such as a store, restaurant, office, church, or school. Then answer the following questions:

1. Which contingencies are most important in explaining how the organization is organized? Do you think it is organized in the best way?

2. Do you think national culture will impact these choices?

3. Can you think of any ways in which a typical job could be enlarged or enriched?

4. What kind of organizational structure does the organization use? If it is part of a chain, what kind of structure does the entire organization use? What other structures discussed in the chapter might allow the organization to operate more effectively? For example, would the move to a product team structure lead to greater efficiency or effectiveness? Why or why not?

5. How many levels are there in the organization's hierarchy? Is authority centralized or decentralized? Describe the span of control of the top manager and of middle or first-line managers.

6. Is the distribution of authority appropriate for the organization and its activities? Would it be possible to flatten the hierarchy by decentralizing authority and empowering employees?

7. What are the principal integrating mechanisms used in the organization? Do they provide sufficient coordination among individuals and functions? How might they be improved?

8. Now that you have analyzed the way this organization is structured, what advice would you give its managers to help them improve how it operates?

Managing Ethically [LO10-1, 10-3, 10-5]

Suppose an organization is downsizing and laying off many of its middle managers. Some top managers charged with deciding whom to terminate might decide to keep the subordinates they like, and who are obedient to them, rather than the ones who are difficult or the best performers. They might also decide to lay off the most highly paid subordinates even if they are high performers. Think of the ethical issues involved in designing a hierarchy, and discuss the following issues.

Questions

1. What are the laws in your country on layoffs? Can a manager in your home country lay off an employee simply because they choose to?
2. Some people argue that employees who have worked for an organization for many years have a claim on the organization at least as strong as that of its shareholders. What do you think of the ethics of this position—can employees claim to "own" their jobs if they have contributed significantly to the organization's past success? How does a socially responsible organization behave in this situation?

Small Group Breakout Exercise

Bob's Appliances [LO10-1, 10-3]

Form groups of three or four people, and appoint one member as the spokesperson who will communicate your findings to the class when called on by the instructor. Then discuss the following scenario:

Bob's Appliances sells and services household appliances such as washing machines, dishwashers, ranges, and refrigerators. Over the years, the company has developed a good reputation for the quality of its customer service, and many local builders patronize the store. However, large retailers are also providing an increasing range of appliances. Moreover, to attract more customers these stores also carry a complete range of consumer electronics products—LCD TVs, computers, and digital devices. Bob Lange, the owner of Bob's Appliances, has decided that if he is to stay in business, he must widen his product range and compete directly with the chains.

In 2007 he decided to build a 20,000-square-foot store and service center, and he is now hiring new employees to sell and service the new line of consumer electronics. Because of his company's increased size, Lange is not sure of the best way to organize the employees. Currently he uses a functional structure; employees are divided into sales, purchasing and accounting, and repair. Bob is wondering whether selling and servicing consumer electronics is so different from selling and servicing appliances that he should move to a product structure (see the figure on the next page) and create separate sets of functions for each of his two lines of business.[57]

You are a team of local consultants whom Bob has called in to advise him as he makes this crucial choice. Which structure do you recommend? Why?

FUNCTIONAL STRUCTURE

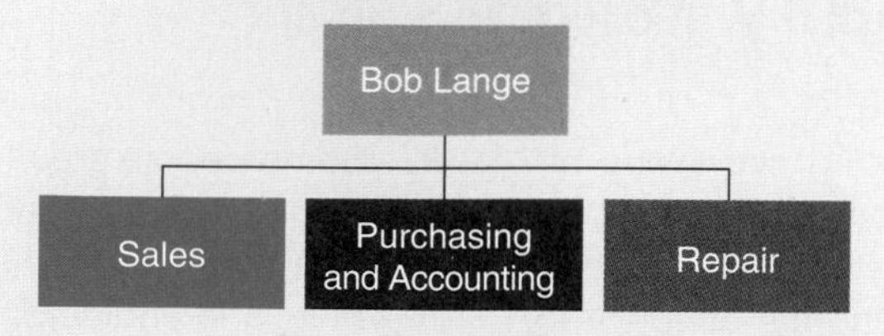

PRODUCT STRUCTURE

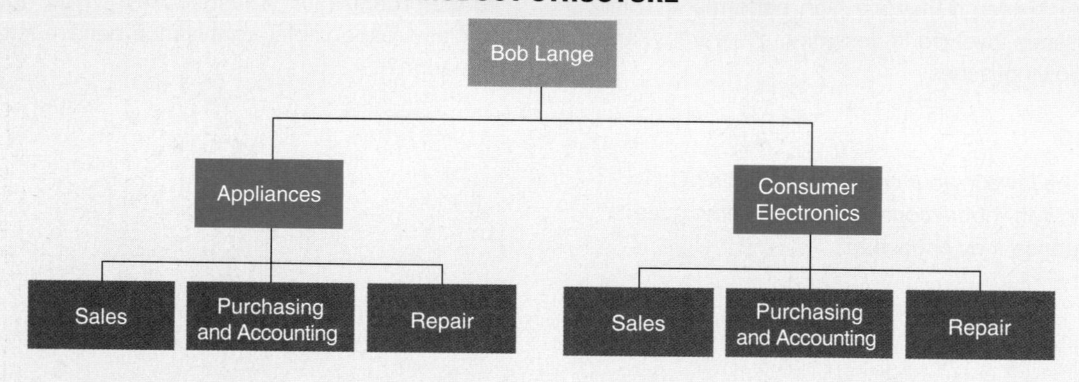

Exploring the World Wide Web [LO10-3]

Go to the Web site of Kraft, the food services company (www.kraft.com). Click on "Corporate Information" and then explore its brands—especially its takeover of Cadbury's.

1. Given the way it describes its brands, what kind of divisional structure do you think Kraft uses? Why do you think it uses this structure?
2. Click on featured brands, and look at products like its Oreo cookies. How is Kraft managing its different brands to increase global sales? What do you think are the main challenges Kraft faces in managing its global food business to improve performance?

Be the Manager [LO10-1, 10-3, 10-5]

Speeding Up Web Site Design

You have been hired by a Web site design, production, and hosting company whose new animated Web site designs are attracting a lot of attention and many customers. Currently employees are organized into different functions such as hardware, software design, graphic art, and Web site hosting, as well as functions such as marketing and human resources. Each function takes its turn to work on a new project from initial customer request to final online Web site hosting.

The problem the company is experiencing is that it typically takes one year from the initial idea stage to the time a Web site is up and running; the company wants to shorten this time by half to protect and expand its market niche. In talking to other managers, you discover that they believe the company's current functional structure is the source of the problem—it is not allowing employees to develop Web sites fast enough to satisfy customers' demands. They want you to design a better structure.

Questions

1. Discuss how you can improve the way the current functional structure operates so it speeds Web site development.
2. Discuss the pros and cons of moving to a (a) multidivisional, (b) matrix, and (c) product team structure to reduce Web site development time.
3. Which of these structures do you think is most appropriate, and why?
4. What kind of culture would you help create to make the company's structure work more effectively?

CHAPTER 11

Organizational Control and Change

Learning Objectives

After studying this chapter, you should be able to:

LO11-1 Define organizational control and explain how it increases organizational effectiveness.

LO11-2 Describe the four steps in the control process and the way it operates over time.

LO11-3 Identify the main output controls, and discuss their advantages and disadvantages as means of coordinating and motivating employees.

LO11-4 Identify the main behavior controls, and discuss their advantages and disadvantages as a means of coordinating and motivating employees.

LO11-5 Discuss the relationship between organizational control and change, and explain why managing change is a vital management task.

A MANAGER'S CHALLENGE

Control Systems and the Impact of Their Failure

Jerome Kerviel is a young man in his 30s who, in late 2010, received a three-year sentence for fraud and a fine of approximately US$7 billion. The sentence and fine were issued for fraudulent trading of stocks that took place over a two-year period. The fine of US$7 billion reflects the amount of money that he lost for one of France's oldest and most respected banks. The illegal trading started small but ultimately represented major unauthorized trades. The control systems of the bank, those systems that make sure the employees and the firm are doing what they are suppose to do, failed. If these systems had worked as they were intended, this problem would not have been created; or at the very least the control systems should have prevented the fraudulent activities from continuing for as long as they did.

In the summer of 2000 Kerviel went to work for the Société Générale, one France's oldest banks founded in the 1860s. Kerviel had undergraduate and master's degrees in finance. He began his work as a compliance officer with responsibility to ensure all laws were followed but moved quickly to trade derivatives. A derivative can take several forms. One type of derivative is a financial product in which the firm employs complex mathematical equations to determine when there are small differences in the amount a stock or another financial instrument trades at and the amount it theoretically should trade at. Ultimately the market will respond and the stock or other instrument will reach its theoretical value. The value gained may be pennies or fractions of pennies but when traded in large volumes a great deal of money can be made by taking advantage of such small inefficiencies in the market.

Société Générale's failure to implement strong control systems allowed trader Jerome Kerviel to trade stocks fraudulently over a two-year period. His actions ultimately caused a US$7 billion loss for the bank and a three-year prison sentence for Kerviel.

Kerviel's illegal trades were not approved by the management of the firm. His trades did not require that he put up extensive capital. Big banks typically do not have to put up the same collateral that ordinary stock buyers have to in making such trades since they are seen as reliable. As a result, Kerviel only had to put up a few hundred thousand U.S. dollars to buy the stock even though its value exceeded that. He then sold the stock and took the profit. Using leverage in this way, with a move of less than 1% in the right direction he could have sold the stock, closing out his position at a significant profit. However, if the market moved in the wrong direction, his losses could be big. Kerviel made enormous gambles on what would happen in the market such as investing US$43 billion in Euro Stoxx indexes, US$23 billion on the German Dax, and US$2.5 billion on the UK's FTSE. The most problematic investment was 140,000 Dax futures contracts in which he made predictions on the future prices of stock, equivalent to roughly an entire day's worth of trading on the German futures exchange. It is estimated that Kerviel at one time had bought stock greater than the entire capital of the bank. Kerviel's experience as a compliance officer helped him to hide the trades. Ultimately, the illegal trades were noticed as some reports did not align as they should have. The bank had to sell Kerviel's unsold shares.

When the bank found the fraud they sought to quietly sell the stock, but the market was already in decline. The nature of the stock market is that selling large amounts of stock can scare the market and make stock prices drop. When the bank's problems were discovered there were even greater drops in value; the day the problem became public knowledge the French Cac 40 and the German Dax 30 were both down 7% and London's FTSE 100 5.5%. The result was that the shares when sold created an approximately US$7 billion loss for the bank.

The bank's control systems should have prevented this activity from ever taking place. The culture that any organization establishes helps to prevent or allow employees' behaviors to take place. Kerviel, in his defense trial, argued that the culture of the bank encouraged excessive risk taking. He even argued that some officers of the bank knew what he was doing but accepted it since he was making money for the bank although there was no direct evidence of such knowledge. Beyond that there should have been control systems in place to tell when stocks actually were traded—either sold or bought. There also should have been controls in place to tell when a stock was owned by the bank. However, these controls were not in place and as a result the bank suffered a massive loss. French regulators later fined the bank US$4 million dollars for poor control systems but the losses suffered were far greater. Today Société Générale is a candidate for takeover due to its weakened state.[1]

Overview

As we discussed in Chapter 10, the first task facing managers is to establish a structure of task and job reporting relationships that allows organizational members to use resources most efficiently and effectively. Structure alone, however, does not provide the incentive or motivation for people to behave in ways that help achieve organizational goals. When managers choose how to influence, shape, and regulate the activities of organizational divisions, functions, and employees to achieve the organization's mission and goals, they establish the second foundation of organizational architecture: organizational control. An organization's structure provides the organization with a skeleton, but its control systems give it the muscles, sinews, nerves, and sensations that allow managers to regulate and govern its activities. The control systems also give managers specific feedback on how well the organization and its members are performing. The managerial functions of organizing and controlling are inseparable, and effective managers must learn to make them work together in a harmonious way.

In this chapter, we look in detail at the nature of organizational control and describe the main steps in the control process. We also discuss the different types of control systems that are available to managers to shape and influence organizational activities–*output control, behavior control,* and *clan control.*[2] Finally, we discuss the important issue of organizational change, which is possible only when managers have put in place a control system that allows them to adjust the way people and groups behave and alter or transform the way the organization operates. Control is the essential ingredient that is needed to bring about and manage organizational change efficiently and effectively. By the end of this chapter, you will appreciate the different forms of control available to managers and understand why developing an appropriate control system is vital to increasing organizational performance.

What Is Organizational Control?

As noted in Chapter 1, *controlling* is the process whereby managers monitor and regulate how efficiently and effectively an organization and its members are performing the activities necessary to achieve organizational goals. As discussed in previous chapters, when planning and organizing, managers develop the organizational strategy and structure that they hope will allow the organization to use resources most effectively to create value for customers. In controlling, managers monitor and evaluate whether the organization's strategy and structure are working as intended, how they could be improved, and how they might be changed if they are not working.

LO11-1 Define organizational control and explain how it increases organizational effectiveness.

Control, however, does not mean just reacting to events after they have occurred. It also means keeping an organization on track, anticipating events that might occur, and then changing the organization to respond to whatever opportunities or threats have been identified. Control is concerned with keeping employees motivated, focused on the important problems confronting the organization, and working together to make the changes that will help an organization improve its performance over time.

The Importance of Organizational Control

To understand the importance of organizational control, consider how it helps managers obtain superior efficiency, quality, responsiveness to customers, and innovation–the four building blocks of competitive advantage.

To determine how efficiently they are using their resources, managers must be able to accurately measure how many units of inputs (raw materials, human resources, and so on) are being used to produce a unit of output. Managers also must be able to measure how many units of outputs (goods and services) are being produced. A control system contains the measures or yardsticks that let managers assess how efficiently the organization is producing goods and services. Moreover, if managers experiment with changing how the organization produces goods and services to find a more efficient way of producing them, these measures tell managers how successful they have been. For example, when managers at Toyota decided to manufacture different cars on the same production line, they used measures such as time taken to change over from one car to another, and cost savings per car produced, to evaluate how well the new method worked. Without a control system in place, managers have no idea how well their organization is performing and how its performance can be improved–information that is becoming increasingly important in today's highly competitive environment.

Today much of the competition among organizations centers on increasing the quality of goods and services. In the car industry, for example, cars within each price range compete in features, design, and reliability. Thus whether a customer will buy a Ford Taurus, GM Grand Prix, Toyota Camry, or Honda Accord depends significantly on the quality of each product. Organizational control is important in determining the quality of goods and services because it gives managers feedback on product quality. If the managers of carmakers consistently measure the number of customer complaints and the number of new cars returned for repairs, or if school principals measure how many students drop out of school or how achievement scores on nationally based tests vary over time, they have a good indication of how much quality they have built into their product–be it an educated student or a car that does not break down. Effective managers create a control system that consistently monitors the quality of goods and services so they can continuously improve quality–an approach to change that gives them a competitive advantage.

Managers can help make their organizations more responsive to customers if they develop a control system that allows them to evaluate how well customer contact employees perform their jobs. Monitoring employee behavior can help managers find ways to increase employees' performance levels, perhaps by revealing areas in which skill training can help employees or in which new procedures can allow employees to perform their jobs better. Also, when employees know their behaviors are being monitored, they have more incentive to be helpful and consistent in how they act toward customers. To improve customer service, for example, Toyota regularly surveys customers about their experiences with particular Toyota dealers. If a dealership receives too many customer complaints, Toyota's managers investigate the dealership to uncover the sources of the problems and suggest solutions; if necessary, they might even threaten to reduce the number of cars a dealership receives to force the dealer to improve the quality of its customer service.

Finally, controlling can raise the level of innovation in an organization. Successful innovation takes place when managers create an organizational setting in which employees feel empowered to be creative and in which authority is decentralized to employees so they feel free to experiment and take control of their work activities. Deciding on the appropriate control systems to encourage risk taking is an important management challenge; organizational culture is vital in this regard. To encourage work teams at Toyota to perform at a high level, top managers monitored the performance of each team, for example, by examining how each team reduced costs or increased quality–and used a bonus system related to performance to reward each team. The team manager then evaluated each team member's individual performance, and the most innovative employees received promotions and rewards based on their superior performance.

Control Systems and IT

control systems Formal target-setting, monitoring, evaluation, and feedback systems that provide managers with information about how well the organization's strategy and structure are working.

Control systems are formal target-setting, monitoring, evaluation, and feedback systems that provide managers with information about whether the organization's strategy and structure are working efficiently and effectively.[3] Effective control systems alert managers when something is going wrong and give them time to respond to opportunities and threats. An effective control system has three

Who would you rather buy a new car from? A company that reinforces and rewards employee responsiveness, consistency, and know-how in customer care, or a company that doesn't?

characteristics: It is flexible enough to allow managers to respond as necessary to unexpected events; it provides accurate information about organizational performance; and it gives managers information in a timely manner because making decisions on the basis of outdated information is a recipe for failure.

New forms of IT have revolutionized control systems because they facilitate the flow of accurate and timely information up and down the organizational hierarchy and between functions and divisions. Today employees at all levels of the organization routinely feed information into a company's information system or network and start the chain of events that affect decision making in some other part of the organization. This could be the department store clerk whose scanning of purchased clothing tells merchandise managers what kinds of clothing need to be reordered or the salesperson in the field who feeds into a wireless laptop the information necessary to inform marketing about customers' changing needs.

feedforward control
Control that allows managers to anticipate problems before they arise.

Control and information systems are developed to measure performance at each stage in the process of transforming inputs into finished goods and services (see Figure 11.1). At the input stage, managers use **feedforward control** to anticipate problems before they arise so problems do not occur later during the conversion process.[4] For example, by giving stringent product specifications to suppliers in advance (a form of performance target), an organization can control the quality of the inputs it receives from its suppliers and thus avoid potential problems during the conversion process. Also, IT can be used to keep in contact with suppliers and to monitor their progress. Similarly, by screening job applicants, often by viewing their résumés electronically and using several interviews to select the most highly skilled people, managers can lessen the chance that they will hire people who lack the necessary skills or experience to perform effectively. In general, the development of management information systems promotes feedforward control that gives managers timely information about changes in the task and general environments that may impact their organization later on. Effective managers always monitor trends and changes in the external environment to try to anticipate problems. (We discuss management information systems in detail in Chapter 18.)

Figure 11.1
Three Types of Control

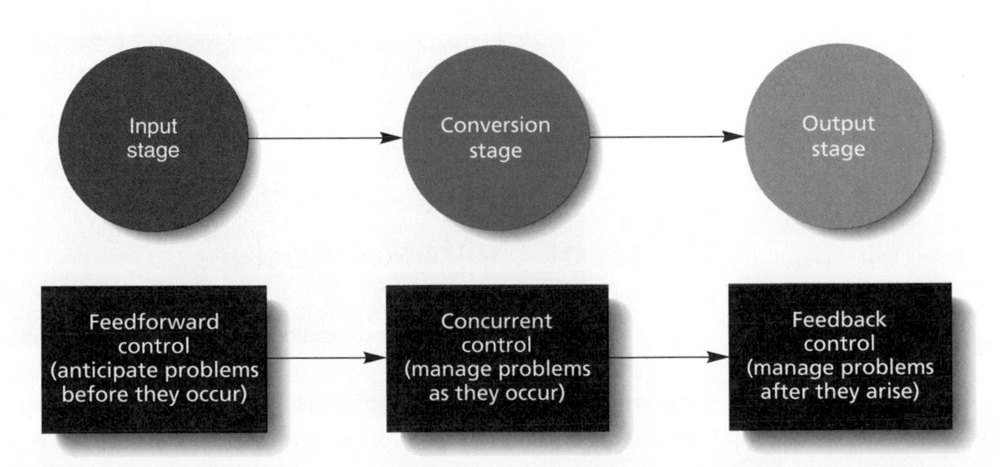

concurrent control Control that gives managers immediate feedback on how efficiently inputs are being transformed into outputs so managers can correct problems as they arise.

At the conversion stage, **concurrent control** gives managers immediate feedback on how efficiently inputs are being transformed into outputs so managers can correct problems as they arise. Concurrent control through IT alerts managers to the need to react quickly to whatever is the source of the problem, be it a defective batch of inputs, a machine that is out of alignment, or a worker who lacks the skills necessary to perform a task efficiently. Concurrent control is at the heart of total quality management programs (discussed in Chapter 9), in which workers are expected to constantly monitor the quality of the goods or services they provide at every step of the production process and inform managers as soon as they discover problems. Historically one of the strengths of Toyota's production system, for example, is that individual workers have the authority to push a button to stop the assembly line whenever they discover a quality problem. When all problems are corrected the result is a finished product that is much more reliable. Recent safety problems, however, call into question whether the focus on quality remains.

feedback control Control that gives managers information about customers' reactions to goods and services so corrective action can be taken if necessary.

At the output stage, managers use **feedback control** to provide information about customers' reactions to goods and services so corrective action can be taken if necessary. For example, a feedback control system that monitors the number of customer returns alerts managers when defective products are being produced, and a management information system (MIS) that measures increases or decreases in relative sales of different products alerts managers to changes in customer tastes so they can increase or reduce the production of specific products.

The Control Process

LO11-2 Describe the four steps in the control process and the way it operates over time.

The control process, whether at the input, conversion, or output stage, can be broken down into four steps: establishing standards of performance, and then measuring, comparing, and evaluating actual performance (see Figure 11.2).[5]

- Step 1: *Establish the standards of performance, goals, or targets against which performance is to be evaluated.*

At step 1 in the control process managers decide on the standards of performance, goals, or targets that they will use in the future to evaluate the performance of the entire organization or part of it (such as a division, a function, or an individual). The standards of performance that managers select measure efficiency, quality, responsiveness to customers, and innovation.[6] If managers decide to pursue a low-cost strategy, for example, they need to measure efficiency at all levels in the organization.

Figure 11.2
Four Steps in Organizational Control

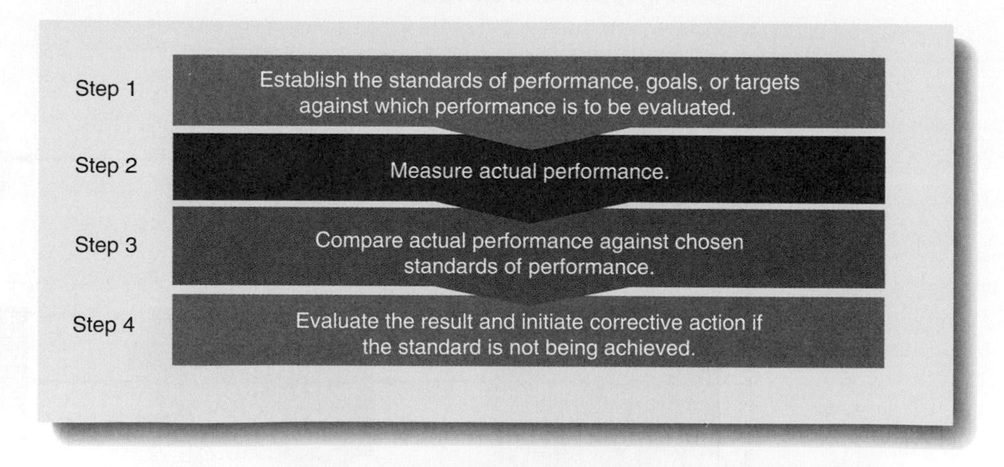

At the corporate level, a standard of performance that measures efficiency is operating costs, the actual costs associated with producing goods and services, including all employee-related costs. Top managers might set a corporate goal of "reducing operating costs by 10% for the next three years" to increase efficiency. Corporate managers might then evaluate divisional managers for their ability to reduce operating costs within their respective divisions, and divisional managers might set cost-saving targets for functional managers. Thus performance standards selected at one level affect those at the other levels, and ultimately the performance of individual managers is evaluated in terms of their ability to reduce costs.

The number of standards or indicators of performance that an organization's managers use to evaluate efficiency, quality, and so on can run into the thousands or hundreds of thousands. Managers at each level are responsible for selecting standards that will best allow them to evaluate how well the part of the organization they are responsible for is performing.[7] Managers must be careful to choose standards of performance that let them assess how well they are doing with all four building blocks of competitive advantage. If managers focus on just one standard (such as efficiency), and ignore others (such as determining what customers really want and innovating a new line of products to satisfy them), managers may end up hurting their organization's performance.

- Step 2: *Measure actual performance.*

Once managers have decided which standards or targets they will use to evaluate performance, the next step in the control process is to measure actual performance. In practice, managers can measure or evaluate two things: (1) the actual ***outputs*** that result from the behavior of their members and (2) the ***behaviors*** themselves (hence the terms ***output control*** and ***behavior control*** used in this chapter).[8]

Sometimes both outputs and behaviors can be easily measured. Measuring outputs and evaluating behavior is relatively easy in a fast-food restaurant, for example, because employees are performing routine tasks. Managers at Carrefour are rigorous in using output control to measure how fast inventory flows through stores. Similarly, managers of a fast-food restaurant can easily measure outputs by counting how many customers their employees serve, the time each transaction takes, and how much money each customer spends. Managers can easily observe each employee's behavior and quickly take action to solve any problems that may arise.

When an organization and its members perform complex, nonroutine activities that are intrinsically hard to measure, it is more challenging for managers to measure outputs or behavior.[9] It is difficult, for example, for managers in charge of R&D departments at SAP or Bayer, or at Microsoft, to measure performance or to evaluate the performance of individual members because it can take several years to determine whether the new products that engineers and scientists are developing will be profitable. Moreover, it is impossible for a manager to measure how creative an engineer or scientist is by watching his or her actions.

In general, the more nonroutine or complex organizational activities are, the harder it is for managers to measure outputs or behaviors.[10] Outputs, however, are usually easier to measure than behaviors because they are more tangible and objective. Therefore, the first kind of performance measures that managers tend to use are those that measure outputs. Then managers develop performance measures or standards that allow them to evaluate behaviors to determine whether employees at all levels are working toward organizational goals. Some simple behavior measures are (1) whether employees come to work on time and (2) whether employees consistently follow the established rules for greeting and serving customers. The various types of output and behavior control and how they are used at the different organizational levels–corporate, divisional, functional, and individual–are discussed in detail subsequently.

- Step 3: *Compare actual performance against chosen standards of performance.*

During step 3, managers evaluate whether–and to what extent–performance deviates from the standards of performance chosen in step 1. If performance is higher than expected, managers might decide they set performance standards too low and may raise them for the next period to challenge their subordinates.[11] Managers at Japanese companies are well known for the way they try to improve performance in manufacturing settings by constantly raising performance standards to motivate managers and workers to find new ways to reduce costs or increase quality; Chapter 9 discussed how companies can use TQM from an organizational control perspective.

However, if performance is too low and standards were not reached, or if standards were set so high that employees could not achieve them, managers must decide whether to take corrective action.[12] It is easy to take corrective action when the reasons for poor performance can be identified–for instance, high labor costs. To reduce costs, managers can search for low-cost overseas suppliers, invest more in technology, or implement cross-functional teams. More often, however, the reasons for poor performance are hard to identify. Changes in the environment, such as the emergence of a new global competitor, a recession, or an increase in interest rates, might be the source of the problem. Within an organization, perhaps the R&D function underestimated the problems it would encounter in developing a new product or the extra costs of doing unforeseen research–or as at Toyota, the faulty design of just one component in thousands slipped through the cracks. If managers are to take any form of corrective action, step 4 is necessary.

- Step 4: *Evaluate the result and initiate corrective action (that is, make changes) if the standard is not being achieved.*

The final step in the control process is to evaluate the results and bring about change as appropriate. Whether or not performance standards have been met, managers can learn a great deal during this step. If managers decide the level of performance is unacceptable, they must try to change how work activities are performed to solve the problem. Sometimes performance problems occur because the work standard was too high–for example, a sales target was too optimistic and impossible to achieve. In this case, adopting more realistic standards can reduce the gap between actual performance and desired performance.

However, if managers determine that something in the situation is causing the problem, then to raise performance they will need to change how resources are utilized.[13] Perhaps the latest technology is not being used; perhaps workers lack the advanced training needed to perform at a higher level; perhaps the organization needs to buy its inputs or assemble its products abroad to compete against low-cost rivals; perhaps it needs to restructure itself or reengineer its work processes using Six Sigma to increase efficiency.

The simplest example of a control system is the thermostat in a home. By setting the thermostat, you establish the standard of performance with which actual temperature is to be compared. The thermostat contains a sensing or monitoring device, which measures the actual temperature against the desired temperature. Whenever there is a difference between them, the furnace or air-conditioning unit is activated to bring the temperature back to the standard. In other words, corrective action is initiated. This is a simple control system: It is entirely self-contained, and the target (temperature) is easy to measure.

Establishing targets and designing measurement systems are much more difficult for managers because the high level of uncertainty in the organizational environment means managers rarely know what might happen in the future. Thus it is vital for managers to design control systems to alert them to problems quickly so they can be dealt with before they become threatening. Another issue is that managers are not just concerned about bringing the organization's performance up to some predetermined standard; they want to push that standard forward to encourage employees at all levels to find new ways to raise performance.

Figure 11.3
Three Organizational Control Systems

Type of control	Mechanisms of control
Output control	Financial measures of performance Organizational goals Operating budgets
Behavior control	Direct supervision Management by objectives Rules and standard operating procedures
Clan control	Values Norms Socialization

In the following sections, we consider three important types of control systems that managers use to coordinate and motivate employees to ensure that they pursue superior efficiency, quality, innovation, and responsiveness to customers: output control, behavior control, and clan control (see Figure 11.3). Managers use all three to shape, regulate, and govern organizational activities, no matter what specific organizational structure is in place. However, as Figure 11.3 suggests, an important element of control is embedded in organizational culture, which is discussed later.

Output Control

All managers develop a system of output control for their organizations. First they choose the goals or output performance standards or targets that they think will best measure efficiency, quality, innovation, and responsiveness to customers. Then they measure to see whether the performance goals and standards are being achieved at the corporate, divisional, functional, and individual employee levels of the organization. The three main mechanisms that managers use to assess output or performance are financial measures, organizational goals, and operating budgets.

LO11-3 Identify the main output controls, and discuss their advantages and disadvantages as means of coordinating and motivating employees.

Financial Measures of Performance

Top managers are most concerned with overall organizational performance and use various financial measures to evaluate it. The most common are profit ratios, liquidity ratios, leverage ratios, and activity ratios. They are discussed here and summarized in Table 11.1.[14]

- *Profit ratios* measure how efficiently managers are using the organization's resources to generate profits. *Return on investment (ROI),* an organization's net income before taxes divided by its total assets, is the most commonly used financial performance measure because it allows managers of one organization to compare performance with that of other organizations. ROI lets managers assess an organization's competitive advantage. *Operating margin* is calculated by dividing a company's operating profit (the amount it has left after all the costs of making the product and running the business have been deducted) by sales revenues. This measure tells managers how efficiently an organization is using its resources; every successful attempt to reduce costs will be reflected in increased operating profit, for example. Also, operating margin is a means of comparing one year's performance to another; for example, if managers discover operating margin has

Table 11.1
Four Measures of Financial Performance

Profit Ratios			
Return on investment	=	$\frac{\text{Net profit before taxes}}{\text{Total assets}}$	Measures how well managers are using the organization's resources to generate profits.
Operating margin	=	$\frac{\text{Total operating profit}}{\text{Sales revenues}}$	A measure of how much percentage profit a company is earning on sales; the higher the percentage, the better a company is using its resources to make and sell the product.
Liquidity Ratios			
Current ratio	=	$\frac{\text{Current assets}}{\text{Current liabilities}}$	Do managers have resources available to meet claims of short-term creditors?
Quick ratio	=	$\frac{\text{Current assets} - \text{Inventory}}{\text{Current liabilities}}$	Can managers pay off claims of short-term creditors without selling inventory?
Leverage Ratios			
Debt-to-assets ratio	=	$\frac{\text{Total debt}}{\text{Total assets}}$	To what extent have managers used borrowed funds to finance investments?
Times-covered ratio	=	$\frac{\text{Profit before interest and taxes}}{\text{Total interest charges}}$	Measures how far profits can decline before managers cannot meet interest changes. If this ratio declines to less than 1, the organization is technically insolvent.
Activity Ratios			
Inventory turnover	=	$\frac{\text{Cost of good sold}}{\text{Inventory}}$	Measures how efficiently managers are turning inventory over so that excess inventory is not carried.
Days sales outstanding	=	$\frac{\text{Current accounts receivable}}{\text{Sales for period divided by days in period}}$	Measures how efficiently managers are collecting revenues from customers to pay expenses.

improved by 5% from one year to the next, they know their organization is building a competitive advantage.

- *Liquidity ratios* measure how well managers have protected organizational resources to be able to meet short-term obligations. The *current ratio* (current assets divided by current liabilities) tells managers whether they have the resources available to meet the claims of short-term creditors. The *quick ratio* shows whether they can pay these claims without selling inventory.
- *Leverage ratios,* such as the *debt-to-assets ratio* and the *times-covered ratio,* measure the degree to which managers use debt (borrow money) or equity (issue new shares) to finance ongoing operations. An organization is highly leveraged if it uses more debt than equity. Debt can be risky when net income or profit fails to cover the interest on the debt–as some people learn too late when their paychecks do not allow them to pay off their credit cards.
- *Activity ratios* show how well managers are creating value from organizational assets. *Inventory turnover* measures how efficiently managers are turning inventory over so excess inventory is not carried. *Days sales outstanding* reveals how efficiently managers are collecting revenue from customers to pay expenses.

The objectivity of financial measures of performance is the reason why so many managers use them to assess the efficiency and effectiveness of their organizations. When an organization fails to meet performance standards such as ROI, revenue, or stock price targets, managers know they must take corrective action. Thus financial controls tell managers when a corporate reorganization might be necessary, when they should sell off divisions and exit businesses, or when they should rethink their corporate-level strategies.[15] Today financial controls are taught to all organizational employees, as the following "Management Insight" box describes.

Although financial information is an important output control, financial information by itself does not tell managers all they need to know about the four building blocks of competitive advantage. Financial results inform managers about the results of decisions they have already made; they do not tell managers how to find new opportunities to build competitive advantage in the future. To encourage a future-oriented approach, top managers must establish organizational goals that encourage middle and first-line managers to achieve superior efficiency, quality, innovation, and responsiveness to customers.

Management Insight

Making the Financial Figures Come Alive

You might think financial control is the province of top managers and employees lower in the organization don't need to worry about the numbers or about how their specific activities affect those numbers. However, some top managers make a point of showing employees exactly how their activities affect financial ratios, and they do so because employees' activities directly affect a company's costs and its sales revenues. One of those managers is Michael Dell, founder of one of the world's major technology firms.

Dell goes to enormous lengths to convince employees that they need to watch every dime spent in making the PCs that have made his company so prosperous, as well as in saying every word or making every phone call or service call that is needed to sell or repair them. Dell believes all his managers need to have at their fingertips detailed information about Dell's cost structure, including assembly costs, selling costs, and after-sales costs, in order to squeeze out every cent of operating costs. One good reason for this is that Dell puts a heavy emphasis on the operating margin financial ratio in measuring his company's performance. Dell doesn't care about how much profits or sales are growing individually; he cares about how these two figures work together because only if profits are growing faster than sales is the company increasing its long-run profitability by operating more efficiently and effectively.

Michael Dell prepares to work the phone lines at Dell's U.S. customer service call center. Dell's emphasis on productivity everywhere means he has no qualms about sitting in an entry-level position for a day both to learn what his employees face and to better teach them.

So he insists that his managers search for every way possible to reduce costs or make customers happier and then help employees learn the new procedures to achieve these goals. At Dell's boot camp for new employees in Austin, Texas, he has been known to bring financial charts that show employees how each minute spent on performing some job activity, or how each mistake made in assembling or packing a PC, affects bottom-line profitability. In the early 2000s Dell's repeated efforts to reduce costs and build customer loyalty boosted its efficiency and operating margins; today, as it battles rivals such as HP and Acer, it is even more important that its employees understand how their specific behaviors affect Dell's bottom-line financial performance. In the 2000s all kinds of companies are training employees at all levels in how their specific job activities, and the way their functions operate, affect the financial ratios used to judge how well an organization is performing.

Organizational Goals

Once top managers consult with lower-level managers and set the organization's overall goals, they establish performance standards for the divisions and functions. These standards specify for divisional and functional managers the level at which their units must perform if the organization is to achieve its overall goals.[16] Each division is given a set of specific goals to achieve (see Figure 11.4). Divisional managers then develop a business-level strategy (based on achieving superior efficiency or innovation) that they hope will allow them to achieve that goal.[17] In consultation with functional managers, they specify the functional goals that the managers of different functions need to achieve to allow the division to achieve its goals. For example, sales managers might be evaluated for their ability to increase sales; materials management managers, for their ability to increase the quality of inputs or lower their costs; R&D managers, for the number of products they innovate or the number of patents they receive. In turn, functional managers establish goals that first-line managers and nonmanagerial employees need to achieve to allow the function to achieve its goals.

Output control is used at every level of the organization, and it is vital that the goals set at each level harmonize with the goals set at other levels so managers and other employees throughout the organization work together to attain the corporate goals that top managers have set.[18] It is also important that goals be set appropriately so managers are motivated to accomplish them. If goals are set at an impossibly high level, managers might work only half-heartedly to achieve them because they are certain they will fail. In contrast, if goals are set so low that they are too easy to achieve, managers will not be motivated to use all their resources as efficiently and effectively as possible. Research suggests that the best goals are specific, difficult goals–goals that challenge and stretch managers' ability but are not out of reach and do not require an impossibly high expenditure of managerial time and energy. Such goals are often called *stretch goals.*

Deciding what is a specific, difficult goal and what is a goal that is too difficult or too easy is a skill that managers must develop. Based on their own judgment and work experience, managers at all levels must assess how difficult a certain task is, and they must assess the ability of a particular subordinate manager to achieve the goal. If they do so successfully, challenging, interrelated goals–goals that reinforce one another and focus on achieving overall corporate objectives–will energize the organization.

Operating Budgets

operating budget A budget that states how managers intend to use organizational resources to achieve organizational goals.

Once managers at each level have been given a goal or target to achieve, the next step in developing an output control system is to establish operating budgets that regulate how managers and workers attain their goals. An **operating budget** is a

Figure 11.4
Organizationwide Goal Setting

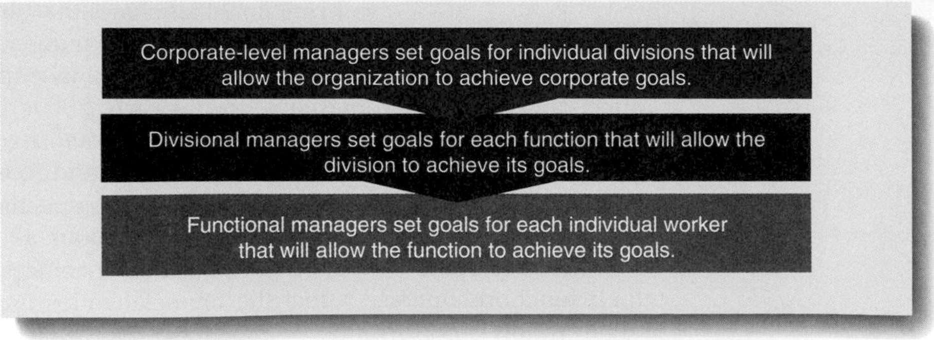

Corporate-level managers set goals for individual divisions that will allow the organization to achieve corporate goals.

Divisional managers set goals for each function that will allow the division to achieve its goals.

Functional managers set goals for each individual worker that will allow the function to achieve its goals.

blueprint that states how managers intend to use organizational resources to achieve organizational goals efficiently. Typically managers at one level allocate to subordinate managers a specific amount of resources to produce goods and services. Once they have been given a budget, these lower-level managers must decide how to allocate money for different organizational activities. They are then evaluated for their ability to stay within the budget and to make the best use of available resources. For example, managers at GE's washing machine division might have a budget of US$50 million to spend on developing and selling a new line of washing machines. They must decide how much money to allocate to the various functions such as R&D, engineering, and sales so the division generates the most customer revenue and makes the biggest profit.

Large organizations often treat each division as a singular or stand-alone responsibility center. Corporate managers then evaluate each division's contribution to corporate performance. Managers of a division may be given a fixed budget for resources and be evaluated on the amount of goods or services they can produce using those resources (this is a cost or expense budget approach). Alternatively, managers may be asked to maximize the revenues from the sales of goods and services produced (a revenue budget approach). Or managers may be evaluated on the difference between the revenues generated by the sales of goods and services and the budgeted cost of making those goods and services (a profit budget approach). Japanese companies' use of operating budgets and challenging goals to increase efficiency is instructive in this context.

In summary, three components–objective financial measures, challenging goals and performance standards, and appropriate operating budgets–are the essence of effective output control. Most organizations develop sophisticated output control systems to allow managers at all levels to keep accurate account of the organization so they can move quickly to take corrective action as needed.[19] Output control is an essential part of management.

Problems with Output Control

When designing an output control system, managers must be careful to avoid some pitfalls. For example, they must be sure the output standards they create motivate managers at all levels and do not cause managers to behave in inappropriate ways to achieve organizational goals.

Suppose top managers give divisional managers the goal of doubling profits over a three-year period. This goal seems challenging and reachable when it is jointly agreed upon, and in the first two years profits go up by 70%. In the third year, however, an economic recession hits and sales plummet. Divisional managers think it is increasingly unlikely that they will meet their profit goal. Failure will mean losing the substantial monetary bonus tied to achieving the goal. How might managers behave to try to preserve their bonuses?

Perhaps they might find ways to reduce costs because profit can be increased either by raising sales revenues or reducing costs. Thus divisional managers might cut back on expensive research activities, delay machinery maintenance, reduce marketing expenditures, and lay off middle managers and workers to reduce costs so that at the end of the year they will make their target of doubling profits and receive their bonuses. This tactic might help them achieve a short-run goal–doubling profits–but such actions could hurt long-term profitability or ROI (because a cutback in R&D can reduce the rate of product innovation, a cutback in marketing will lead to the loss of customers, and so on).

The message is clear: Although output control is a useful tool for keeping managers and employees at all levels motivated and the organization on track, it is only a guide to appropriate action. Managers must be sensitive in how they use output control and must constantly monitor its effects at all levels in the organization–and on customers and other stakeholders.

Behavior Control

LO11-4 Identify the main behavior controls, and discuss their advantages and disadvantages as a means of coordinating and motivating employees.

Organizational structure by itself does not provide any mechanism that motivates managers and nonmanagerial employees to behave in ways that make the structure work–or even improve how it works–hence the need for control. Put another way, managers can develop an organizational structure that has the right grouping of divisions and functions, and an effective chain of command, but it will work as designed *only* if managers also establish control systems that motivate and shape employee behavior in ways that *match* this structure.[20] Output control is one method of motivating employees; behavior control is another method. This section examines three mechanisms of behavior control that managers can use to keep subordinates on track and make organizational structures work as they are designed to work: direct supervision, management by objectives, and rules and standard operating procedures (see Figure 11.3).

Direct Supervision

The most immediate and potent form of behavior control is direct supervision by managers who actively monitor and observe the behavior of their subordinates, teach subordinates the behaviors that are appropriate and inappropriate, and intervene to take corrective action as needed. Moreover, when managers personally supervise subordinates, they lead by example and in this way can help subordinates develop and increase their own skill levels. (Leadership is the subject of Chapter 14.)

Direct supervision allows managers at all levels to become personally involved with their subordinates and allows them to mentor subordinates and develop their management skills. Thus control through personal supervision can be an effective way of motivating employees and promoting behaviors that increase efficiency and effectiveness.[21]

Nevertheless, certain problems are associated with direct supervision. First, it is expensive because a manager can personally manage only a relatively small number of subordinates effectively. Therefore, if direct supervision is the main kind of control being used in an organization, a lot of managers will be needed and costs will increase. For this reason, output control is usually preferred to behavior control; indeed, output control tends to be the first type of control that managers at all levels use to evaluate performance. Second, direct supervision can *demotivate* subordinates. This occurs if employees feel they are under such close scrutiny that they are not free to make their own decisions or if they feel they are not being evaluated in an accurate and impartial way. Team members and other employees may start to pass the buck, avoid responsibility, and cease to cooperate with other team members if they feel their manager is not accurately evaluating their performance and is favoring some people over others.

Third, as noted previously, for many jobs personal control through direct supervision is simply not feasible. The more complex a job is, the more difficult it is for a manager to evaluate how well a subordinate is performing. The performance of divisional and functional managers, for example, can be evaluated only over relatively long periods (which is why an output control system is developed), so it makes little sense for top managers to continually monitor their performance. However, managers can still communicate the organization's mission and goals to their subordinates and reinforce the values and norms in the organization's culture through their own personal style.

management by objectives (MBO) A goal-setting process in which a manager and each of his or her subordinates negotiate specific goals and objectives for the subordinate to achieve and then periodically evaluate the extent to which the subordinate is achieving those goals.

Management by Objectives

To provide a framework within which to evaluate subordinates' behavior and, in particular, to allow managers to monitor progress toward achieving goals, many organizations implement some version of management by objectives. **Management by objectives (MBO)** is a formal system of evaluating subordinates on their ability to achieve specific organizational goals or performance standards and to meet operating budgets.[22] Most organizations use some form of MBO system because it is pointless to establish goals and then fail to evaluate whether they are being achieved. Management by objectives involves three specific steps:

- Step 1: *Specific goals and objectives are established at each level of the organization.*

MBO starts when top managers establish overall organizational objectives, such as specific financial performance goals or targets. Then objective setting cascades down throughout the organization as managers at the divisional and functional levels set their goals to achieve corporate objectives.[23] Finally first-level managers and employees jointly set goals that will contribute to achieving functional objectives.

- Step 2: *Managers and their subordinates together determine the subordinates' goals.*

An important characteristic of management by objectives is its participatory nature. Managers at every level sit down with each of the subordinate managers who report directly to them, and together they determine appropriate and feasible goals for the subordinate and bargain over the budget that the subordinate will need to achieve his or her goals. The participation of subordinates in the objective-setting process is a way of strengthening their commitment to achieving their goals and meeting their budgets.[24] Another reason why it is so important for subordinates (both individuals and teams) to participate in goal setting is that doing so enables them to tell managers what they think they can realistically achieve.[25]

- Step 3: *Managers and their subordinates periodically review the subordinates' progress toward meeting goals.*

Once specific objectives have been agreed on for managers at each level, managers are accountable for meeting those objectives. Periodically they sit down with their subordinates to evaluate their progress. Normally salary raises and promotions are linked to the goal-setting process, and managers who achieve their goals receive greater rewards than those who fall short. (The issue of how to design reward systems to motivate managers and other organizational employees is discussed in Chapter 13.)

In the companies that have decentralized responsibility for the production of goods and services to empowered teams and cross-functional teams, management by objectives works somewhat differently. Managers ask each team to develop a set of goals and performance targets that the team hopes to achieve–goals that are consistent with organizational objectives. Managers then negotiate with each team to establish its final goals and the budget the team will need to achieve them. The reward system is linked to team performance, not to the performance of any one team member.

Cypress Semiconductor offers an interesting example of how IT can be used to manage the MBO process quickly and effectively. In the fast-moving semiconductor business, a premium is placed on organizational adaptability. At Cypress, CEO T. J. Rodgers was facing a problem: How could he control his growing, 1,500-employee organization without developing a bureaucratic management hierarchy? Rodgers believed that a tall hierarchy hinders the ability of an organization to adapt to changing conditions. He was committed to maintaining a flat and decentralized organizational structure with a minimum of management layers. At the same time he needed to control his employees to ensure that they performed in a manner consistent with the goals of the company.[26] How could he achieve this without resorting to direct supervision and the lengthy management hierarchy that it implies?

To solve this problem, Rodgers implemented an online information system through which he can monitor what every employee and team is doing in his fast-moving and decentralized organization. Each employee maintains a list of 10 to 15 goals, such as "Meet with marketing for new product launch" or "Make sure to check with customer X." Noted next to each goal are when it was agreed upon, when it is due to be finished, and whether it has been finished. All this information is stored on a central computer. Rodgers claims that he can review the goals of all employees in about four hours and that he does so each week.[27] How is this possible? He *manages by exception* and looks only for employees who are falling behind. He then calls them, not to scold but to ask whether there is anything he can do to help them get the job done. It takes only about half an hour each week for employees to review and update their lists. This system allows Rodgers to exercise control over his organization without resorting to the expensive layers of a management hierarchy and direct supervision.

MBO does not always work out as planned, however. Managers and their subordinates at all levels must believe that performance evaluations are accurate and fair. Any suggestion that personal biases and political objectives play a part in the evaluation process can lower or even destroy MBO's effectiveness as a control system. This is why many organizations work so hard to protect the integrity of their systems. Microsoft has experienced problems with its performance evaluation system, as the following "Management Insight" box suggests.

Management Insight

Microsoft Has Problems Evaluating Its Employees

From its beginning, Microsoft organized its software engineers into small work groups and teams so team members could cooperate, learning from and helping each other, and so speed the development of innovative software. Each team works on a subset of the thousands of programs that together make up its Windows operating system and applications software, which is loaded on over 90% of PCs today.[28] In the past, much of Microsoft's reward system was based on team performance; employees of successful teams that quickly developed innovative software received valuable stock options and other benefits. Microsoft's team-based reward system encouraged team members to work together intensively and cooperate to meet team goals. At the same time, the contributions of exceptional team members were recognized; these individuals received rewards such as promotion to become the managers or leaders of new teams as the company grew.

Microsoft ran into serious problems when it was developing its Vista operating system. Vista was scheduled to come out in the summer of 2006, but unforeseen delays had put the project six months behind schedule, delaying its planned launch until spring 2007. Why? Many analysts blamed the delay on the new performance evaluation system Microsoft had introduced, which, because it was primarily based on individual performance contributions, was hurting team performance. As Microsoft grew over time (it now employs over 100,000 people), it developed a more and more rigid performance evaluation system that became increasingly based on each engineer's individual performance. The manager of each team was expected to rate the performance of each team member on a scale of 2.5, 3.0, and so on to 5, the highest individual performance rating. Microsoft adopted this system to try to increase the perceived fairness of its evaluation system.

Employees still worked principally in teams, however, and the new emphasis on individual performance negatively affected the relationships among team members because members were aware that they were in competition for the highest ratings. For example, when confronted with a situation in which they could help other team members but doing so might hurt their own personal performance evaluations, they behaved self-interestedly, and this hurt overall team performance. Moreover, Microsoft is highly secretive about employees' performance evaluations, current salaries, and raises: Employees are told *not* to share such information and can get fired if they do.[29] To make matters worse, the way these evaluations were made

Microsoft employees revamped their work cubicles to allow for greater face-to-face contact and better communication, which improves their ability to cooperate with each other to achieve team goals.

by team managers was also highly secretive. And employees believed that when the managers of different teams met to discuss which teams (as a unit) had achieved the highest level of team performance, these evaluations were distorted by favoritism. Specifically, leaders of the teams who were liked by *their* managers (often because the leaders actively support their managers) received higher team evaluations than did leaders of teams who were not perceived as supportive by their managers. Because evaluations were biased by personal likes and dislikes, the performance evaluation system was regarded as being highly political.

Increasingly, engineers and teams perceived that they were being evaluated not objectively–by the results achieved–but subjectively, by the ability of an engineer or team leader to "make the right pitch" and gain the favor of his or her direct superior. As a result, team members increasingly pursued their own interests at the expense of others, and so team performance was declining across the organization.[30] As you can imagine, when team members feel that their personal performance contributions are not being adequately recognized, and that even the performance of different teams is not being judged fairly, many performance problems arise. And one of these problems was that many of Microsoft's best software engineers left to join rivals such as Google or create their own start-up organizations as a result of their failure to achieve the recognition they thought they deserved at Microsoft.[31]

In developing its new Windows 7 operating system Microsoft was careful to make team performance a more important element of its promotion and reward evaluations. Indeed, it now lets team members contribute to the evaluation process and allows them to evaluate their team leaders' performance using the 360-degree performance appraisal technique discussed in the next chapter.

Clearly, when people work in teams, each member's contribution to the team, and each team's contribution to the goals of the organization, must be fairly evaluated. This is no easy thing to do. It depends on managers' ability to create an organizational control system that measures performance accurately and fairly and links performance evaluations to rewards so employees stay motivated and coordinate their activities to achieve the organization's mission and goals. Microsoft's problem was that the changes it made to its control system (new performance evaluation measures) as the company grew hurt its ability to motivate its employees.

Bureaucratic Control

bureaucratic control
Control of behavior by means of a comprehensive system of rules and standard operating procedures.

When direct supervision is too expensive and management by objectives is inappropriate, managers might turn to another mechanism to shape and motivate employee behavior: bureaucratic control. **Bureaucratic control** is control by means of a comprehensive system of rules and standard operating procedures (SOPs) that shapes and regulates the behavior of divisions, functions, and individuals. In Chapter 2 we discussed Weber's theory of bureaucracy and noted that all organizations use bureaucratic rules and procedures but some use them more than others.[32] Recall that rules and SOPs are formal, written instructions that specify a series of actions that employees should follow to achieve a given end; in other words, if *A* happens, then do *B* and *C*.

Rules and SOPs guide behavior and specify what employees are to do when they confront a problem that needs a solution. It is the responsibility of a manager to develop rules that allow employees to perform their activities efficiently and effectively. Rules and SOPs also clarify people's expectations about one another and prevent misunderstandings over responsibility or the use of power. Such guidelines can prevent a supervisor from arbitrarily increasing a subordinate's workload and prevent a subordinate from ignoring tasks that are a legitimate part of the job.

When employees follow the rules that managers have developed, their behavior is *standardized*–actions are performed the same way time and time again–and the outcomes of their work are predictable. And to the degree that managers can make employees' behavior predictable, there is no need to monitor the outputs of behavior because *standardized behavior leads to standardized outputs,* such as goods and services of the same uniform quality. Suppose a worker at Toyota comes up with a way to attach exhaust pipes that reduces the number of steps in the assembly process and increases efficiency. Always on the lookout for ways to standardize and improve procedures, managers make this idea the basis of a new rule that says, "From now on, the procedure for attaching the exhaust pipe to the car is as follows." If all workers follow the rule to the letter, every car will come off the assembly line with its exhaust pipe attached in the new way, and there will be no need to check exhaust pipes at the end of the line.

In practice, mistakes and lapses of attention happen, so output control is used at the end of the line, and each car's exhaust system is given a routine inspection. However, the number of quality problems with the exhaust system is minimized because the rule (bureaucratic control) is being followed. Service organizations such as retail stores, fast-food restaurants, and home improvement stores also attempt to standardize employee behavior, such as customer service quality, by instructing employees in the correct way to greet customers or the appropriate way to serve and bag food. Employees are trained to follow the rules that have proved to be most effective in a particular situation, and the better trained the employees are, the more standardized is their behavior and the more trust managers can have that outputs (such as food quality) will be consistent. An interesting example of how creating the wrong rules can reduce performance occurred at Gateway (now part of Taiwan-based PC maker Acer), which saw its customer satisfaction rating plummet as a result of its new rules. Managers at Gateway discovered that the reason for rising customer dissatisfaction was the new rules they had created to reduce the increasing costs of after-sales service. When customers installed additional software on their new Gateway computers, this often caused problems with the software already installed on the PC. It often took customer reps considerable time to iron out the problems, and Gateway was spending millions of dollars in employee time to solve these problems. To reduce costs, managers told its service reps to inform customers that if they installed any other software on their machines, this would invalidate Gateway's warranty. This infuriated customers who obviously had the right to install other software. Gateway also began to reward customer reps based on how quickly they handled customer calls; the more calls they handled in an hour or day, the higher their bonuses. The effect of these changes was to motivate customer reps to keep service calls short. Customers resented this treatment, and when Gateway's managers realized what was happening, they went back to the old system and customer satisfaction soared. As Gateway's and Toyota's managers discovered, to prevent unexpected problems, it is necessary to carefully choose and evaluate the rules and policies used to control employees' behavior.

In contrast to the situation at Gateway, Dave Lilly, an ex-nuclear submarine commander, chose the right rules for siteROCK, whose business is hosting and managing other companies' Web sites to keep them running and error-free. A customer's Web site that goes down or runs haywire is the enemy. To maximize his employees' performance and increase their ability to respond to unexpected online events, Lilly decided they needed a comprehensive set of rules and SOPs to cover the main known problems.[33] Lilly insisted that every problem-solving procedure should be written down and recorded. siteROCK's employees developed over 30 thick binders that list all the processes and checklists they need to follow when an unexpected event happens. Moreover, again drawing from his military experience, Lilly instituted a "two-person rule": Whenever the unexpected happens, each employee must immediately tell a coworker and the two together should attempt to solve the problem. The goal is simple: Use the rules to achieve a quick resolution of a complex issue. If the existing rules don't work, employees must experiment; and when they find a solution, it is turned into a new rule to be included in the procedures book to aid the future decision making of all employees in the organization.

Looks like even Mickey Mouse approves! Bob Iger's redesign of Disney's methods of innovation and planning lets employees get moving faster on new ideas.

Problems with Bureaucratic Control

Like all organizations, Toyota makes extensive use of bureaucratic control because rules and SOPs effectively control routine organizational activities. With a bureaucratic control system in place, managers can manage by exception and intervene and take corrective action only when necessary. However, managers need to be aware of a number of problems associated with bureaucratic control because such problems can reduce organizational effectiveness.[34]

First, establishing rules is always easier than discarding them. Organizations tend to become overly bureaucratic over time as managers do everything according to the rule book. If the amount of red tape becomes too great, decision making slows and managers react sluggishly to changing conditions. This can imperil an organization's survival if agile new competitors emerge.

Second, because rules constrain and standardize behavior and lead people to behave in predictable ways, people might become so used to automatically following rules that they stop thinking for themselves. Thus too much standardization can actually *reduce* the level of learning taking place in an organization and get the organization off track if managers and workers focus on the wrong issues. An organization thrives when its members are constantly thinking of new ways to increase efficiency, quality, and customer responsiveness. By definition, new ideas do not come from blindly following standardized procedures. Similarly, the pursuit of innovation implies a commitment by managers to discover new ways of doing things; innovation, however, is incompatible with extensive bureaucratic control.

Consider, for example, what happened at Walt Disney, which has amusement park operations in the United States, France, and Hong Kong, plus retail operations around the world. (The Disneyland in Japan is a license, and as a result, Disney itself does not operate the park.) In 2006, Bob Iger became CEO of the troubled company. Bob Iger had been COO of Disney under CEO Michael Eisner, and he had noticed how Disney was plagued by slow decision making that had led to made many mistakes in putting its new strategies into action. Its Disney stores were losing money; its Internet properties were flops; and even its theme parks seemed to have lost their luster as few new rides or attractions were introduced. Iger believed one of the main reasons for Disney's declining performance was that it had become too tall and bureaucratic and its top managers were following financial rules that did not lead to innovative strategies.

One of Iger's first moves to turn around the performance of the poorly performing company was to dismantle Disney's central strategic planning office. In this office several levels of managers were responsible for sifting through all the new ideas and innovations sent up by Disney's different business divisions, such as theme parks, movies, and gaming, and then deciding which ones to present to the CEO. Iger saw the strategic planning office as a bureaucratic bottleneck that reduced the number of ideas coming from below. So he dissolved the office and reassigned its managers back to the different business units.[35] The result of cutting an unnecessary layer in Disney's hierarchy has been that more new ideas are generated by its different business units. The level of innovation has increased because managers are more willing to speak out and champion their ideas when they know they are dealing directly with the CEO and a top management team searching for innovative ways to improve performance–rather than a layer of strategic planning bureaucrats concerned only with the bottom line.[36]

Managers must always be sensitive about the way they use bureaucratic control. It is most useful when organizational activities are routine and well understood and when employees are making programmed decisions. Bureaucratic control is much less useful in situations where nonprogrammed decisions have to be made and managers have to react quickly to changes in the task environment. There are also ethical issues involved in the way managers create and enforce bureaucratic rules and SOPs, as the following "Ethics in Action" box suggests.

Ethics in Action

How Does Apple Enforce Its Rules for Product Secrecy against Its Rules for Employee Working Conditions?

Apple has rules that govern all its value chain activities, but consider how it enforces the rules about protecting the secrets of its innovative new products compared to how it enforces the rules about protecting the rights of its employees overseas who make those products. Today all Apple products are assembled by huge specialist outsourcing companies abroad, such as Foxconn International, which operates several huge factories in mainland China, some of which employ over 300,000 employees. Foxconn is a subsidiary of Taiwan's giant outsourcer, Hon Hai Precision Industry.

Your iPhone's cool new features may entail more than you think; Apple's emphasis on secrecy and isolation within its outsourced factories appears to also open the door to unsavory labor practices.

Apple has long been known for its concern with protecting the details of its new products until their launch. Its concern for secrecy led it to sue a college student who published a Web site that contained details of its future products; it has also brought legal action against many bloggers who reveal details about its new products. Even in its own U.S. product development units, Apple is known for its strict rules preventing engineers from discussing their own projects with other engineers not involved in those projects to stop the flow of information across its employees. Apple has also developed stern rules governing how its outsourcers behave to protect the secrecy of its products.

To keep its business, outsourcers like Foxconn have to go to extreme lengths to follow Apple's rules protecting the details of its new products and follow stringent security guidelines in their manufacturing plants. For example, Apple dictates that the final product should not be assembled until as late as possible to meet its launch date; so while workers learn how to assemble each component, they have no idea what collection of final components will go into the final product. Also, outsourcers control their factories to make it easier to enforce such rules. For example, Foxconn's massive plant in Longhua, China, employs over 350,000 workers who are discouraged from leaving the plant because it offers them a full array of inexpensive services such as canteens, dormitories, and recreational facilities. If they leave the plant they are searched, and metal detectors are used to ensure they do not take components with them. Workers are scanned when they return as well, as are the truck drivers who bring components to the plant and anyone else who wishes to enter. Apple's contracts always include a confidentiality clause with stiff penalties in the event of a security breach, and Apple performs surprise factory inspections to ensure that outsourcers follow its rules.

To protect the security of its products Apple insists on elaborate operating rules to build walls around the assembly plants of its contractors. But these same walls make it much more difficult to enforce the extensive and well-publicized rules Apple has developed regarding the fair and equitable treatment of employees who work in these gigantic "sweatshops." For example, in 2006, after reporters claimed Hon Hai, Foxconn's owner, was not following Apple's rules regarding employee treatment, Apple audited Hon Hai's facilities. It found many violations whose nature was never publicly disclosed. The company has been repeatedly criticized for allowing its products to be made at plants with poor employment practices–despite the fact that it claims to enforce many rules governing how they should be treated. In 2010 Apple announced that new audits had revealed that child labor had been used in Chinese factories that made its iPods and other electronic devices: "In each of the three facilities, we required a review of all employment records for the year as well as a complete analysis of the hiring process to clarify how under-age people had been able to gain employment." Also, Apple admitted that sweatshop conditions existed inside the factories making its products, and at least 55 of the 102 factories had ignored Apple's rule that employees should not work more than 60 hours per week. Apple said one of its factories had repeatedly falsified its records to conceal child labor practices and long employee hours; it terminated all contracts with that factory: "When we investigated, we uncovered records and conducted worker interviews that revealed excessive working hours and seven days of continuous work."

To use output control and behavior control, managers must be able to identify the outcomes they want to achieve and the behaviors they want employees to perform to achieve those outcomes. For many of the most important and significant organizational activities, however, output control and behavior control are inappropriate for several reasons:

- A manager cannot evaluate the performance of workers such as doctors, research scientists, or engineers by observing their daily behavior.
- Rules and SOPs are of little use in telling a doctor how to respond to an emergency situation or a scientist how to discover something new.
- Output controls such as the amount of time a surgeon takes for each operation or the costs of making a discovery are crude measures of the quality of performance.

How can managers attempt to control and regulate the behavior of their subordinates when personal supervision is of little use, when rules cannot be developed to tell employees what to do, and when outputs and goals cannot be measured at all or can be measured usefully only over long periods?

Clan Control

clan control The control exerted on individuals and groups in an organization by shared values, norms, standards of behavior, and expectations.

One source of control increasingly being used by organizations is **clan control,** which takes advantage of the power of internalized values and norms to guide and constrain employee attitudes and behavior in ways that increase organizational performance.[37] The first function of a control system is to shape the behavior of organizational members to ensure that they are working toward organizational goals and to take corrective action if those goals are not being met. The second function of control, however, is to keep organizational members focused on thinking about what is best for their organization in the future and to keep them looking for new opportunities to use organizational resources to create value. Clan control serves this dual function of keeping organizational members goal-directed while open to new opportunities because it takes advantage of the power of organizational culture, discussed in the previous chapter.

Organizational culture functions as a kind of control system because managers can deliberately try to influence the kind of values and norms that develop in an organization–values and norms that specify appropriate and inappropriate behaviors and so determine the way its members behave.[38] We discussed the sources of organizational culture and the way managers can help create different kinds of cultures in Chapter 10, so there is no need to repeat this discussion here.

Organizational Change

As we have discussed, many problems can arise if an organization's control systems are not designed correctly. One of these problems is that an organization cannot change or adapt in response to a changing environment unless it has effective control over its activities. Companies can lose this control over time, as happened to Societe Generale, discussed in the opening case; or they can change in ways that make them more effective. **Organizational change** is the movement of an organization away from its present state toward some preferred future state to increase its efficiency and effectiveness.

organizational change The movement of an organization away from its present state and toward some preferred future state to increase its efficiency and effectiveness.

LO11-5 Discuss the relationship between organizational control and change, and explain why managing change is a vital management task.

Interestingly enough, there is a fundamental tension or need to balance two opposing forces in the control process that influences how organizations change. As just noted, organizations and their managers need to be able to control their activities and make their operations routine and predictable. At the same time, however, organizations have to be responsive to the need to change, and managers and employees have to "think on their feet" and realize when they need to depart from routines to be responsive to unpredictable events. In other words, even though adopting the right set of output and behavior controls is essential for improving efficiency, because the environment is dynamic and uncertain employees also need to feel that they have the autonomy to depart from routines as necessary to increase effectiveness. (See Figure 11.5.)

For this reason many researchers believe that the highest-performing organizations are those that are constantly changing–and thus become experienced at doing so–in their search to become more efficient and effective. Companies like Toyota are constantly changing the mix of their activities to move forward even as they seek to make their existing operations more efficient.

Figure 11.5
Organizational Control and Change

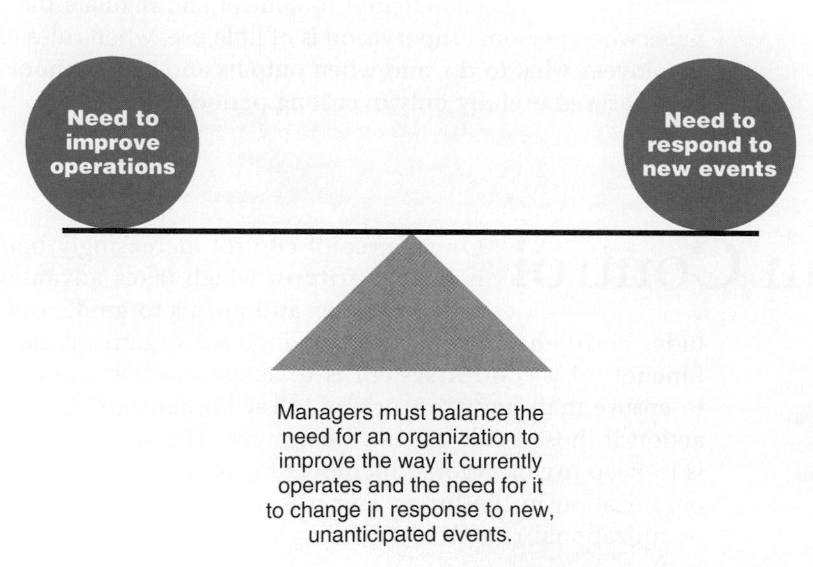

Lewin's Force-Field Theory of Change

Researcher Kurt Lewin developed a theory about organizational change. According to his *force-field theory,* a wide variety of forces arise from the way an organization operates–from its structure, culture, and control systems–that make organizations resistant to change. At the same time a wide variety of forces arise from changing task and general environments that push organizations toward change. These two sets of forces are always in opposition in an organization.[39] When the forces are evenly balanced, the organization is in a state of inertia and does not change. To get an organization to change, managers must find a way to *increase* the forces for change, *reduce* resistance to change, or do *both* simultaneously. Any of these strategies will overcome inertia and cause an organization to change.

Figure 11.6 illustrates Lewin's theory. An organization at performance level P1 is in balance: Forces for change and resistance to change are equal. Management, however, decides that the organization should strive to achieve performance level P2. To get to level P2, managers must *increase* the forces for change (the increase is represented by the lengthening of the up arrows), *reduce* resistance to change (the reduction is represented by the shortening of the down arrows), or both. If managers pursue any of the three strategies successfully, the organization will change and reach performance level P2. Before we look in more detail at the techniques managers can use to overcome resistance and facilitate change, we need to look at the types of change they can implement to increase organizational effectiveness.

Evolutionary and Revolutionary Change

Managers continually face choices about how best to respond to the forces for change. There are several types of change that managers can adopt to help their organizations achieve desired future states.[40] In general, types of change fall into two broad categories: evolutionary change and revolutionary change.[41]

evolutionary change Change that is gradual, incremental, and narrowly focused.

Evolutionary change is gradual, incremental, and narrowly focused. Evolutionary change is not drastic or sudden but, rather, is a constant attempt to improve, adapt, and adjust strategy and structure incrementally to accommodate changes taking place in the environment.[42] Sociotechnical systems theory and total quality management, or kaizen, are two instruments of evolutionary change. Such improvements might entail using technology in a better way or reorganizing the work process.

Some organizations, however, need to make major changes quickly. Faced with drastic, unexpected changes in the environment (for example, a new technological

Figure 11.6
Lewin's Force-Field Model of Change

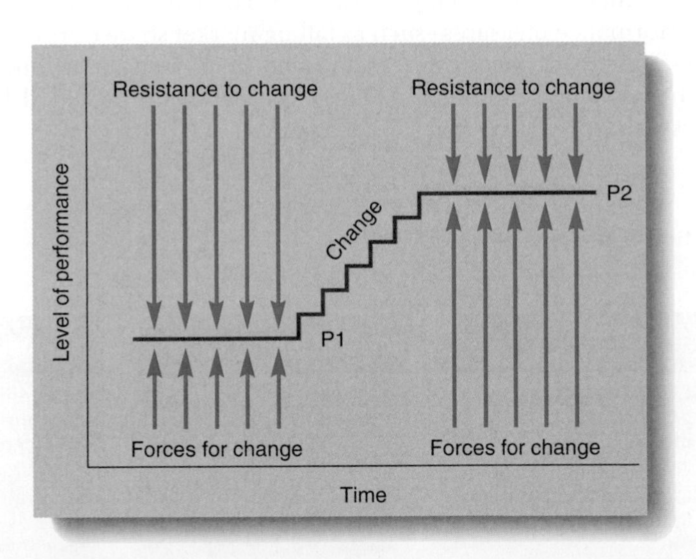

breakthrough) or with an impending disaster resulting from mismanagement, an organization might need to act quickly and decisively. In this case, revolutionary change is called for.

revolutionary change Change that is rapid, dramatic, and broadly focused.

Revolutionary change is rapid, dramatic, and broadly focused. Revolutionary change involves a bold attempt to quickly find new ways to be effective. It is likely to result in a radical shift in ways of doing things, new goals, and a new structure for the organization. The process has repercussions at all levels in the organization–corporate, divisional, functional, group, and individual. Reengineering, restructuring, and innovation are three important instruments of revolutionary change.

Managing Change

The need to constantly search for ways to improve efficiency and effectiveness makes it vital that managers develop the skills necessary to manage change effectively. Several experts have proposed a model of change that managers can follow to implement change successfully–that is, to move an organization away from its present state and toward some desired future state to increase its efficiency and effectiveness.[43] Figure 11.7 outlines the steps in this process. In the rest of this section we examine each one.

ASSESSING THE NEED FOR CHANGE Organizational change can affect practically all aspects of organizational functioning, including organizational structure, culture, strategies, control systems, and groups and teams, as well as the human resource management system and critical organizational processes such as communication, motivation, and leadership. Organizational change can alter how managers carry out the critical tasks of planning, organizing, leading, and controlling and the ways they perform their managerial roles.

Deciding how to change an organization is a complex matter because change disrupts the status quo and poses a threat, prompting employees to resist attempts to alter work relationships and procedures. Organizational learning–the process through which managers try to increase organizational members' abilities to understand and appropriately respond to changing conditions–can be an important impetus for change and can help all members of an organization, including managers, effectively make decisions about needed changes.

Assessing the need for change calls for two important activities: recognizing that there is a problem and identifying its source. Sometimes the need for change is obvious, such as when an organization's performance is suffering. Often, however, managers have trouble determining that something is going wrong because problems develop gradually; organizational performance may slip for a number of years before a problem becomes obvious. Thus during the first step in the change process, managers need to recognize that there is a problem that requires change.

Often the problems that managers detect have produced a gap between desired performance and actual performance. To detect such a gap, managers need to look at performance measures–such as falling market share or profits, rising costs, or employees' failure to meet their established goals or stay within budgets–which indicate whether change is needed. These measures are provided by organizational control systems, discussed earlier in the chapter.

Figure 11.7
Four Steps in the Organizational Change Process

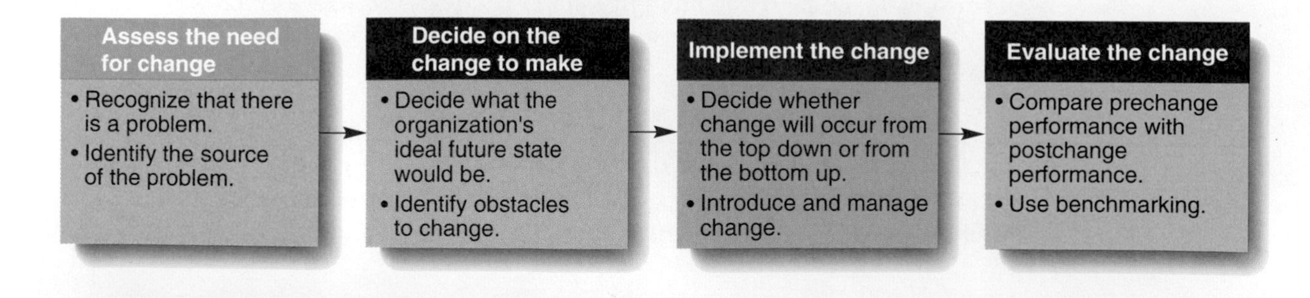

To discover the source of the problem, managers need to look both inside and outside the organization. Outside the organization, they must examine how changing environmental forces may be creating opportunities and threats that are affecting internal work relationships. Perhaps the emergence of low-cost competitors abroad has led to conflict among different departments that are trying to find new ways to gain a competitive advantage. Managers also need to look within the organization to see whether its structure is causing problems between departments. Perhaps a company does not have integrating mechanisms in place to allow different departments to respond to low-cost competition.

DECIDING ON THE CHANGE TO MAKE Once managers have identified the source of the problem, they must decide what they think the organization's ideal future state would be. In other words, they must decide where they would like their organization to be in the future–what kinds of goods and services it should be making, what its business-level strategy should be, how the organizational structure should be changed, and so on. During this step, managers also must plan how to attain the organization's ideal future state.

This step in the change process also includes identifying obstacles or sources of resistance to change. Managers must analyze the factors that may prevent the company from reaching its ideal future state. Obstacles to change are found at the corporate, divisional, departmental, and individual levels of the organization.

Corporate-level changes in an organization's strategy or structure, even seemingly trivial changes, may significantly affect how divisional and departmental managers behave. Suppose that to compete with low-cost foreign competitors, top managers decide to increase the resources spent on state-of-the-art machinery and reduce the resources spent on marketing or R&D. The power of manufacturing managers would increase, and the power of marketing and R&D managers would fall. This decision would alter the balance of power among departments and might increase conflict as departments fight to retain their status in the organization. An organization's present strategy and structure are powerful obstacles to change.

Whether a company's culture is adaptive or inert facilitates or obstructs change. Organizations with entrepreneurial, flexible cultures, such as high-tech companies, are much easier to change than are organizations with more rigid cultures, such as those sometimes found in large, bureaucratic organizations like the military.

The same obstacles to change exist at the divisional and departmental levels. Division managers may differ in their attitudes toward the changes that top managers propose and, if their interests and power seem threatened, will resist those changes. Managers at all levels usually fight to protect their power and control over resources. Given that departments have different goals and time horizons, they may also react differently to the changes other managers propose. When top managers are trying to reduce costs, for example, sales managers may resist attempts to cut back on sales expenditures if they believe that problems stem from manufacturing managers' inefficiencies.

At the individual level, too, people often resist change because it brings uncertainty and stress. For example, individuals may resist the introduction of a new technology because they are uncertain about their abilities to learn it and effectively use it.

These obstacles make organizational change a slow process. Managers must recognize the potential obstacles to change and take them into consideration. Some obstacles can be overcome by improving communication so all organizational members are aware of the need for change and of the nature of the changes being made. Empowering employees and inviting them to participate in planning for change also can help overcome resistance and allay employees' fears. In addition, managers can sometimes overcome resistance by emphasizing group or shared goals such as increased organizational efficiency and effectiveness. The larger and more complex an organization is, the more complex is the change process.

top-down change A fast, revolutionary approach to change in which top managers identify what needs to be changed and then move quickly to implement the changes throughout the organization.

IMPLEMENTING THE CHANGE Generally managers implement–that is, introduce and manage–change from the top down or from the bottom up.[44] **Top-down change** is implemented quickly: Top managers identify the need for change, decide what to do, and then move quickly to implement the changes throughout the organization. For example, top managers may decide to restructure and downsize the organization and then give divisional and departmental managers specific goals to achieve. With top-down change, the emphasis is on making the changes quickly and dealing with problems as they arise; it is revolutionary in nature.

bottom-up change A gradual or evolutionary approach to change in which managers at all levels work together to develop a detailed plan for change.

Bottom-up change is typically more gradual or evolutionary. Top managers consult with middle and first-line managers about the need for change. Then, over time, managers at all levels work to develop a detailed plan for change. A major advantage of bottom-up change is that it can co-opt resistance to change from employees. Because the emphasis in bottom-up change is on participation and on keeping people informed about what is going on, uncertainty and resistance are minimized. Creating change can be difficult in a mature organization. Bayer AG is a German firm that illustrates the multiple levels on which such change must occur in order to be successful, as the following "Manager as a Person" box describes.

Manager as a Person

Bayer and Innovation

Bayer AG, a German firm, is one of the world's oldest pharmaceutical companies; it was founded in the 1860s. The pharmaceutical product the firm is best known for is aspirin. In fact the name "Aspirin" is a trademarked name by Bayer in many nations. While the firm is best known for its aspirin, however, it is, in fact, a widely diversified firm. Bayer AG was created as a holding company in 2003 that wholly owns a variety of other firms. The firms that Bayer AG owns include: Bayer CropScience AG; Bayer HealthCare AG; Bayer Material Science AG, Bayer Chemicals AG, and the three service limited companies Bayer Technology Services GmbH, Bayer Business Services GmbH, and Bayer Industry Services GmbH & Co. OHG. Bayer separated these units so that each can be judged individually on their performance. In addition, it makes change and adaptation much easier to have all the related business in one area. Thus, if Bayer wants to shift the direction of the chemical business it is easier and more direct to have those business activities concentrated in a separate unit.

While separate units help make change easier it is still difficult to introduce change in a large mature firm. One result of this recognition is that Bayer AG has created a new unit, Bayer Innovation GmbH. This new firm is located on Merowinger Square in Düsseldorf. This location is purposefully away from the corporate headquarters in Leverkusen. The firm wants new innovations to be nurtured and encouraged. Too often in a mature firm such innovations are seen as a threat to someone or a prize to be fought over.

One product that illustrates the manner in which the new unit works is a catheter, a narrow plastic tube that helps deliver medicines to patients in the hospital. There are approximately 13 million catheter treatments every year in hospitals around the world. Approximately one in 20 of those patients receiving medicine through a catheter will develop an infection at the point where the tube enters the body. This infection will kill approximately 26,000 people every year. Bayer has developed a catheter that has antibiotics inside it so that there is less chance of infection. Thus, this is a very simple product that has massive potential for growth. Placing such a product in a large unit, however, can result in the product not receiving the attention a new product needs to be successful. Placing the product in a separate unit allows the product to be supported and developed until it reaches a sufficient level and then it will be moved into the health care firm. There are other similar products that are in the process of being supported such as a skin repair kit that is a gel that helps the skin to naturally repair itself.

Again, this is a relatively simple idea with huge potential but which will take special attention to grow to the stage where it can survive in a large organization.

Dr. Marijn E. Dekkers (51), currently President and CEO of U.S. laboratory equipment manufacturer Thermo Fisher Scientific Inc., became the new CEO of Bayer AG on October 1, 2010. He has stated his strong commitment to maintaining the innovation orientation of Bayer.[45]

benchmarking The process of comparing one company's performance on specific dimensions with the performance of other, high-performing organizations.

EVALUATING THE CHANGE The last step in the change process is to evaluate how successful the change effort has been in improving organizational performance.[46] Using measures such as changes in market share, in profits, or in the pharmaceutical company Pfizer's case the ability of its scientists to innovate new drugs, managers compare how well an organization is performing after the change with how well it was performing before. Managers also can use **benchmarking,** comparing their performance on specific dimensions with the performance of high-performing organizations to decide how successful a change effort has been.

In summary, organizational control and change are closely linked because organizations operate in environments that are constantly changing; so managers must be alert to the need to change their strategies and structures. Managers of high-performing organizations are attuned to the need to continually modify the way they operate, and they adopt techniques like empowered work groups and teams, benchmarking, and global outsourcing to remain competitive in a global world.

Summary and Review

LO11-1, 11-2 **WHAT IS ORGANIZATIONAL CONTROL?** Controlling is the process whereby managers monitor and regulate how efficiently and effectively an organization and its members are performing the activities necessary to achieve organizational goals. Controlling is a four-step process: (1) establishing performance standards, (2) measuring actual performance, (3) comparing actual performance against performance standards, and (4) evaluating the results and initiating corrective action if needed.

LO11-3 **OUTPUT CONTROL** To monitor output or performance, managers choose goals or performance standards that they think will best measure efficiency, quality, innovation, and responsiveness to customers at the corporate, divisional, departmental or functional, and individual levels. The main mechanisms that managers use to monitor output are financial measures of performance, organizational goals, and operating budgets.

LO11-4 **BEHAVIOR CONTROL** In an attempt to shape behavior and induce employees to work toward achieving organizational goals, managers use direct supervision, management by objectives, and bureaucratic control by means of rules and standard operating procedures.

CLAN CONTROL Clan control is the control exerted on individuals and groups by shared values, norms, and prescribed standards of behavior. An organization's culture is deliberately fashioned to emphasize the values and norms top managers believe will lead to high performance.

LO11-5 **ORGANIZATIONAL CHANGE** There is a need to balance two opposing forces in the control process that influences the way organizations change. On one hand, managers need to be able to control organizational activities and make their operations routine and predictable. On the other hand, organizations have to be responsive to the need to change, and managers must understand when they need to depart from routines to be responsive to unpredictable events. The four steps in managing change are (1) assessing the need for change, (2) deciding on the changes to make, (3) implementing change, and (4) evaluating the results of change.

Management in Action

Topics for Discussion and Action

Discussion

1. What is the relationship between organizing and controlling? **[LO11-1]**
2. How do output control and behavior control differ? **[LO11-2, 11-3]**
3. Why is it important for managers to involve subordinates in the control process? **[LO11-3, 11-4]**
4. What kind of controls would you expect to find most used in (a) a hospital, (b) the Navy, and (c) a city police force? Why? **[LO11-2, 11-3, 11-4]**
5. What are the main obstacles to organizational change? What techniques can managers use to overcome these obstacles? **[LO11-1, 11-5]**

Action

6. Ask a manager to list the main performance measures that he or she uses to evaluate how well the organization is achieving its goals. **[LO11-1, 11-3, 11-4]**
7. Ask the same or a different manager to list the main forms of output control and behavior control that he or she uses to monitor and evaluate employee behavior. **[LO11-3, 11-4]**

Building Management Skills

Understanding Controlling [LO11-1, 11-3, 11-4]

For this exercise you will analyze the control systems used by a real organization such as a department store, restaurant, hospital, police department, or small business. Your objective is to uncover all the different ways in which managers monitor and evaluate the performance of the organization and employees.

1. At what levels does control take place in this organization?
2. Which output performance standards (such as financial measures and organizational goals) do managers use most often to evaluate performance at each level?
3. Does the organization have a management by objectives system in place? If it does, describe it. If it does not, speculate about why not.
4. How important is behavior control in this organization? For example, how much of managers' time is spent directly supervising employees? How formalized is the organization? Do employees receive a book of rules to teach them how to perform their jobs?
5. What kind of culture does the organization have? What are the values and norms? What effect does the organizational culture have on the way employees behave or treat customers?
6. Based on this analysis, do you think there is a fit between the organization's control systems and its culture? What is the nature of this fit? How could it be improved?
7. If the organization is part of a multinational firm, how might control systems vary in different nations?

Managing Ethically [LO11-1, 11-5]

Some managers and organizations go to great lengths to monitor their employees' behavior, and they keep extensive records about employees' behavior and performance. Some organizations also seem to possess norms and values that cause their employees to behave in certain ways.

Questions

1. Either by yourself or in a group, think about the ethical implications of organizations' monitoring and collecting information about their employees. What kinds of information is it ethical or unethical to

collect? Why? Should managers and organizations tell subordinates they are collecting such information?

2. What if the government wants the firm to gather such information about employees? What should be the response of the firm?

Small Group Breakout Exercise

How Best to Control the Sales Force? [LO11-1, 11-3, 11-5]

Form groups of three or four people, and appoint one member as the spokesperson who will communicate your findings to the class when called on by the instructor. Then discuss the following scenario:

You are the regional sales managers of an organization that supplies high-quality windows and doors to building supply centers nationwide. Over the last three years, the rate of sales growth has slackened. There is increasing evidence that, to make their jobs easier, salespeople are primarily servicing large customer accounts and ignoring small accounts. In addition, the salespeople are not dealing promptly with customer questions and complaints, and this inattention has resulted in poor after-sales service. You have talked about these problems, and you are meeting to design a control system to increase both the amount of sales and the quality of customer service.

1. Design a control system that you think will best motivate salespeople to achieve these goals.
2. What relative importance do you put on (a) output control, (b) behavior control, and (c) organizational culture in this design?

Exploring the World Wide Web [LO11-1, 11-5]

Go to the Web site of Google. Look at pages such as "Jobs at Google," "Life at Google," "Company Overview," and "Our Culture."

1. How would you expect Google's values and norms to affect its employees' behavior?
2. How does Google design its organizational structure and workspace to shape its culture?

Be the Manager

You have been asked by your company's CEO to find a way to improve the performance of its teams of Web design and Web hosting specialists and programmers. Each team works on a different aspect of Web site production; and while each is responsible for the quality of its own performance, its performance also depends on how well the other teams perform. Your task is to create a control system that will help to increase the performance of each team separately and facilitate cooperation among the teams. This is necessary because the various projects are interlinked and affect one another just as the different parts of a car must fit together. Because competition in the Web site production market is intense, it is imperative that each Web site is up and running as quickly as possible and incorporates all the latest advances in Web site software technology.

Questions

1. What kind of output controls will best facilitate positive interactions both within the teams and among the teams?
2. What kind of behavior controls will best facilitate positive interactions both within the teams and among the teams?
3. How would you help managers develop a culture to promote high team performance?

CHAPTER 12

Human Resource Management

Learning Objectives

After studying this chapter, you should be able to:

LO12-1 Explain why strategic human resource management can help an organization gain a competitive advantage.

LO12-2 Describe the steps managers take to recruit and select organizational members.

LO12-3 Discuss the training and development options that ensure organizational members can effectively perform their jobs.

LO12-4 Explain why performance appraisal and feedback is such a crucial activity, and list the choices managers must make in designing effective performance appraisal and feedback procedures.

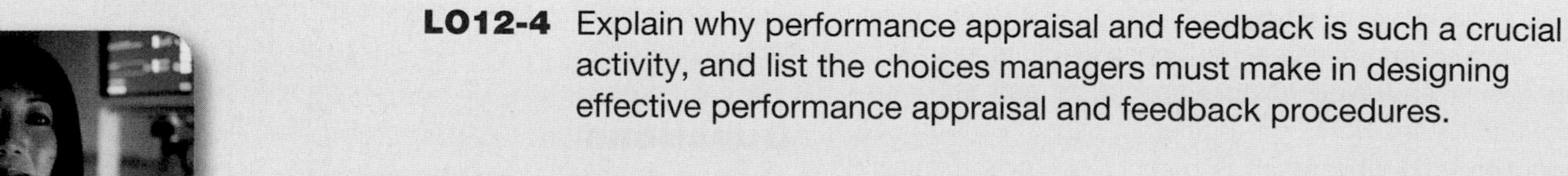

LO12-5 Explain the issues managers face in determining levels of pay and benefits.

LO12-6 Understand the role that labor relations play in the effective management of human resources.

A MANAGER'S CHALLENGE

Happy Employees Provide Exceptional Service at Zappos

How can managers ensure that employees will provide excellent service and be happy doing so? Zappos, founded in 1999 as a struggling online shoe shop, rode out the dot-com bust to earn US$1 billion in sales in 2008 and be ranked 15th on *Fortune* magazine's list of the One Hundred Best Companies to Work For in 2010; in 2009 Zappos was ranked 23rd.[1] In 2009 Amazon.com purchased Zappos for shares worth US$1.2 billion.[2] As a wholly owned subsidiary of Amazon, Zappos continues to be led by its long-standing CEO Tony Hsieh; Hsieh was the initial primary investor who kept Zappos afloat as a start-up and became its CEO in 2000.[3]

Key to Zappos's success is a focus on people—having happy employees provide exceptional service to customers.[4] In fact, Hsieh's own experiences helped him realize the importance of employees being happy and having fun at work.

Customers receive free shipping on products both ways (for purchases and returns), and Zappos has a 365-day return policy. Its Web site prominently displays a toll-free telephone number that customers can call to speak to a member of the Customer Loyalty Team (CLT) 24 hours a day, seven days a week.[5] CLT members have great autonomy to keep customers happy the way they think is best. Their call times are not monitored, and they do not read from scripts. They make decisions on their own, such as providing refunds for defective goods or sending flowers to a customer who had a death in the family, without having to consult a manager. And they strive to make personal connections with their customers. Some calls last for hours, and team members regularly send personal notes to customers.[6] Providing exceptional service that leads to repeat business from happy customers and good word-of-mouth advertising is central to Zappos's approach to business.[7]

Mission: create fun and a little weirdness, accomplished! If you'd like to work in a T-shirt surrounded by your favorite plants, a plastic skull, and personalized balloons while getting the chance to develop your business savvy, check out Zappos's job openings.

Equally central is having a happy workforce of satisfied employees who actually want to come to work each day and have fun on and off the job.[8] Thus Hsieh and other managers at Zappos go to great lengths to ensure that the Zappos core values and unique culture are maintained and strengthened. The core values of Zappos are these: "1. Deliver WOW through Service; 2. Embrace and Drive Change; 3. Create Fun and a Little Weirdness; 4. Be Adventurous, Creative, and Open-Minded; 5. Pursue Growth and Learning; 6. Build Open and Honest Relationships with Communication; 7. Build a Positive Team and Family Spirit; 8. Do More with Less; 9. Be Passionate and Determined; 10. Be Humble."[9]

Because of the importance of having happy employees, Zappos goes to great lengths to effectively manage human resources. Potential new hires are interviewed by human resources, to make sure they will work well in Zappos's culture and support its values, as well as by the department doing the hiring, to determine their suitability for the position they are interviewing for. If human resources and the hiring manager disagree in their assessments of an applicant, Hsieh interviews the applicant himself and makes the final decision.[10]

Newly hired employees receive extensive training. For example, the CLT new hires who answer calls have two weeks of classroom training followed by two weeks of training in answering calls. Once the training is completed, they are given the opportunity to receive $2,000 and pay for the time they spent in training if they want to quit.[11] This way only new hires who want to stay with the company remain.

Experienced employees are encouraged to continue to grow and develop on the job. For example, employees who have worked at Zappos for two or fewer years have over 200 hours of classroom training and development during their work hours and are required to read nine books about business. More experienced employees receive training and development in such areas as financial planning and speaking in public. Zappos has a company library well stocked with multiple copies of business books and books about personal growth and development for employees to borrow and read. As Hseih indicates, "The vision is that three years from now, almost all our hires will be entry-level people. . . . We'll provide them with training and mentorship, so that within five to seven years, they can become senior leaders within the company."[12]

Overview

LO12-1 Explain why strategic human resource management can help an organization gain a competitive advantage.

Managers are responsible for acquiring, developing, protecting, and utilizing the resources an organization needs to be efficient and effective. One of the most important resources in all organizations is human resources–the people involved in producing and distributing goods and services. Human resources include all members of an organization, ranging from top managers to entry-level employees. Effective managers like Tony Hsieh in "A Manager's Challenge" realize how valuable human resources are and take active steps to make sure their organizations build and fully utilize their human resources to gain a competitive advantage.

human resource management (HRM) Activities that managers engage in to attract and retain employees and to ensure that they perform at a high level and contribute to the accomplishment of organizational goals.

This chapter examines how managers can tailor their human resource management system to their organization's strategy and structure. We discuss in particular the major components of human resource management: recruitment and selection, training and development, performance appraisal, pay and benefits, and labor relations. By the end of this chapter you will understand the central role human resource management plays in creating a high-performing organization.

Strategic Human Resource Management

Organizational architecture (see Chapter 10) is the combination of organizational structure, control systems, culture, and a human resource management system that managers develop to use resources efficiently and effectively. **Human resource management (HRM)** includes all the activities managers engage in to attract and retain employees and to ensure that they perform at a high level and contribute to the accomplishment of organizational goals. These activities make up an organization's human resource management system, which has five major components: recruitment and selection, training and development, performance appraisal and feedback, pay and benefits, and labor relations (see Figure 12.1).

strategic human resource management The process by which managers design the components of an HRM system to be consistent with each other, with other elements of organizational architecture, and with the organization's strategy and goals.

Strategic human resource management is the process by which managers design the components of an HRM system to be consistent with each other, with other elements of organizational architecture, and with the organization's strategy and goals.[13] The objective of strategic HRM is the development of an HRM system that enhances an organization's efficiency, quality, innovation, and responsiveness to customers–the four building blocks of competitive advantage. At Zappos in "A Manager's Challenge," HRM practices ensure that all employees provide excellent customer service.

As part of strategic human resource management, some managers have adopted "Six Sigma" quality improvement plans. These plans ensure that an organization's products and services are as free of errors or defects as possible through a variety of

Figure 12.1
Components of a Human Resource Management System

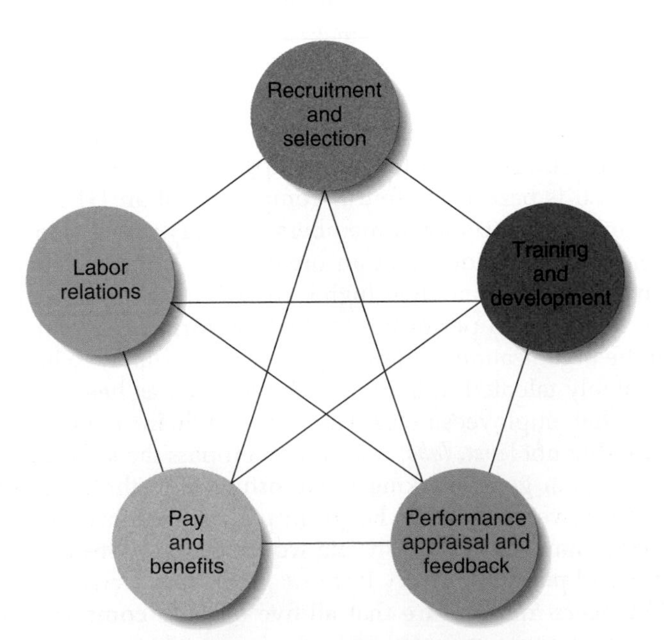

Each component of an HRM system influences the others, and all five must fit together.

human resource–related initiatives. Jack Welch, former CEO of General Electric Company, has indicated that these initiatives have saved his company millions of dollars.

Overview of the Components of HRM

Managers use *recruitment and selection,* the first component of an HRM system, to attract and hire new employees who have the abilities, skills, and experiences that will help an organization achieve its goals. Microsoft Corporation, for example, has the goal of remaining the premier computer software company in the world. To achieve this goal, managers at Microsoft realize the importance of hiring only the best software designers: Hundreds of highly qualified candidates are interviewed and rigorously tested. This careful attention to selection has contributed to Microsoft's competitive advantage. Microsoft has little trouble recruiting top programmers because candidates know they will be at the forefront of the industry if they work for Microsoft.[14]

After recruiting and selecting employees, managers use the second component, *training and development,* to ensure that organizational members develop the skills and abilities that will enable them to perform their jobs effectively in the present and the future. Training and development compose an ongoing process; changes in technology and the environment, as well as in an organization's goals and strategies, often require that organizational members learn new techniques and ways of working. At Microsoft, newly hired program designers receive on-the-job training by joining small teams that include experienced employees who serve as mentors or advisers. New recruits learn firsthand from team members how to go about developing computer systems that are responsive to customers' programming needs.[15]

The third component, *performance appraisal and feedback,* serves two different purposes in HRM. First, performance appraisal can give managers the information they need to make good human resources decisions–decisions about how to train, motivate, and reward organizational members.[16] Thus the performance appraisal and feedback component is a kind of *control system* that can be used with management by objectives (discussed in Chapter 11). Second, feedback from performance appraisal serves a developmental purpose for members of an organization. When managers regularly evaluate their subordinates' performance, they can provide employees with valuable information about their strengths and weaknesses and the areas in which they need to concentrate. Performance appraisal and feedback can flow both down and up an organizational structure. HCL Technologies is an Indian firm that provides a wide range of technology solutions from creating infrastructure for clients to writing software. HCL has an extensive human resource Web site that seeks to provide an easy means to solve all human resource problems. The Web site has questions that each employee must answer each week, and the total evaluation of the manager is then published. Those managers who consistently get poor evaluations by employees will have a human resource intervention.[17]

On the basis of performance appraisals, managers distribute *pay* to employees, which is part of the fourth component of an HRM system. By rewarding high-performing organizational members with pay raises, bonuses, and the like, managers increase the likelihood that an organization's most valued human resources will be motivated to continue their high levels of contribution to the organization. Moreover, if pay is linked to performance, high-performing employees are more likely to stay with the organization, and managers are more likely to fill positions that become open with highly talented individuals. *Benefits* such as health insurance are important outcomes that employees receive by virtue of their membership in an organization.

Last, but not least, *labor relations* encompass the steps that managers take to develop and maintain good working relationships with the labor unions that may represent their employees' interests. For example, an organization's labor relations component can help managers establish safe working conditions and fair labor practices in their offices and plants.

Managers must ensure that all five of these components fit together and complement their company's structure and control systems.[18] For example, if managers decide to decentralize authority and empower employees, they need to invest in training and development to ensure that lower-level employees have the knowledge and expertise they need to make the decisions that top managers would make in a more centralized structure.

Each of the five components of HRM influences the others (see Figure 12.1).[19] The kinds of people that the organization attracts and hires through recruitment and selection, for example, determine (1) the kinds of training and development that are necessary, (2) the way performance is appraised, and (3) the appropriate levels of pay and benefits. Managers at Microsoft ensure that their organization has highly qualified program designers by (1) recruiting and selecting the best candidates, (2) guiding new hires with experienced team members, (3) appraising program designers' performance in terms of their individual contributions and their teams' performance, and (4) basing programmers' pay on individual and team performance.

Effectively managing human resources helps ensure that both customers and employees are satisfied and loyal, as illustrated in the following "Managing Globally" box.

Managing Globally

Managing Human Resources at Semco

Ricardo Semler was 21 years old (and one of the youngest graduates from the Harvard Business School MBA program) when he took his father's place as head of the family business, Semco, based in São Paolo, Brazil, in 1984.[20] His father, Antonio, had founded Semco in 1954 as a machine shop; the company went on to become a manufacturer of marine pumps for the shipbuilding industry, with US$4 million a year in revenues when Ricardo Semler took over. Today Semco's revenues are over US$200 million a year from a diverse set of businesses ranging from industrial machinery, cooling towers, and facility management to environmental consulting and Web-based HRM outsourcing and inventory management services. Semco prides itself on being a premier provider of goods and services in its markets and has loyal customers.[21]

Ricardo Semler recognizes that Semco's success hinges on its employees.

Semler is the first to admit that Semco's track record of success is due to its human resources–its employees. In fact, Semler so firmly believes in Semco's employees that he and the other top managers are reluctant to tell employees what to do. Semco has no rules, regulations, or organizational charts; hierarchy is eschewed; and workplace democracy rules the day. Employees have levels of autonomy unheard of in other companies, and flexibility and trust are built into every aspect of human resource management at Semco.[22]

Human resource practices at Semco revolve around maximizing the contributions employees make to the company, and this begins by hiring individuals who want to, can, and will contribute. Semco strives to ensure that all selection decisions are based on relevant and complete information. Job candidates are first interviewed as a group; the candidates meet many employees, receive a tour of the company, and interact with potential coworkers. This gives Semco a chance to size up candidates in ways more likely to reveal their true natures, and it gives the candidates a chance to learn about Semco. When finalists are identified from the pool, multiple Semco employees interview each one five or six more times to choose the best person(s) to be hired. The result is that both Semco and new hires make informed decisions and are mutually committed to making the relationship a success.[23]

Once hired, entry-level employees participate in the Lost in Space program, in which they rotate through different positions and units of their own choosing for about a year.[24] In this way, the new hires learn about their options and can decide where their interests lie, and the units they work in learn about the new hires. At the end of the year, the new employees may be offered a job in one of the units in which they worked, or they may seek a position elsewhere in Semco. Seasoned Semco employees are also encouraged to rotate positions and work in different parts of the company to keep them fresh, energized, and motivated and to give them the opportunity to contribute in new ways as their interests change.[25]

Performance is appraised at Semco in terms of results; all employees and managers must demonstrate that they are making valuable contributions and deserve to be "rehired." For example, each manager's performance is anonymously appraised by all the employees who report to him or her, and the appraisals are made publicly available in Semco. Employees also can choose how they are paid from a combination of 11 different compensation options, ranging from fixed salaries, bonuses, and profit sharing to royalties on sales or profits and arrangements based on meeting annual self-set goals. Flexibility in compensation promotes risk taking and innovation, according to Semler, and maximizes returns to employees in terms of their pay and to the company in terms of revenues and profitability.[26] Flexibility, autonomy, the ability to change jobs often, and control of working hours and even compensation are some of the ways by which Semler strives to ensure that employees are loyal and involved in their work because they *want* to be; turnover at Semco is less than 1% annually.[27] And with human resource practices geared toward maximizing contributions and performance, Semco is well poised to continue to provide value to its customers.

Recruitment and Selection

LO12-2 Describe the steps managers take to recruit and select organizational members.

recruitment Activities that managers engage in to develop a pool of qualified candidates for open positions.

selection The process that managers use to determine the relative qualifications of job applicants and their potential for performing well in a particular job.

human resource planning Activities that managers engage in to forecast their current and future needs for human resources.

Recruitment includes all the activities managers engage in to develop a pool of qualified candidates for open positions.[28] **Selection** is the process by which managers determine the relative qualifications of job applicants and their potential for performing well in a particular job. Before actually recruiting and selecting employees, managers need to engage in two important activities: human resource planning and job analysis (Figure 12.2).

Human Resource Planning

Human resource planning includes all the activities managers engage in to forecast their current and future human resource needs. Current human resources are the employees an organization needs today to provide high-quality goods and services to customers. Future human resource needs are the employees the organization will need at some later date to achieve its longer-term goals.

Figure 12.2
The Recruitment and Selection System

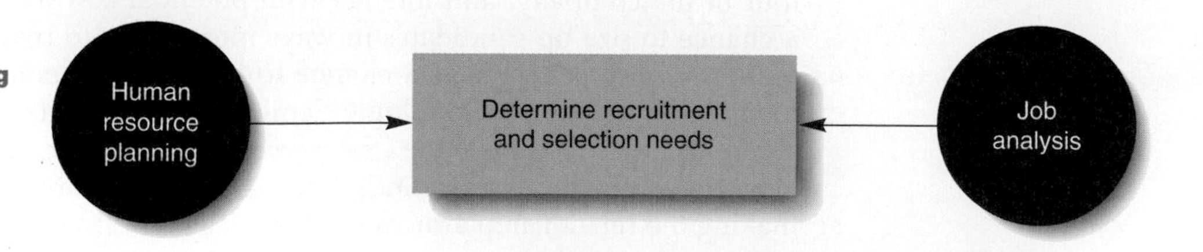

As part of human resource planning, managers must make both demand forecasts and supply forecasts. *Demand forecasts* estimate the qualifications and numbers of employees an organization will need given its goals and strategies. *Supply forecasts* estimate the availability and qualifications of current employees now and in the future, as well as the supply of qualified workers in the external labor market.

outsource To use outside suppliers and manufacturers to produce goods and services.

As a result of their human resource planning, managers sometimes decide to **outsource** to fill some of their human resource needs. Instead of recruiting and selecting employees to produce goods and services, managers contract with people who are not members of their organization to produce goods and services. Managers in publishing companies, for example, frequently contract with freelance editors to copyedit books that they intend to publish.

Two reasons why human resource planning sometimes leads managers to outsource are flexibility and cost. First, outsourcing can give managers increased flexibility, especially when accurately forecasting human resource needs is difficult, human resource needs fluctuate over time, or finding skilled workers in a particular area is difficult. Frequently in Europe or parts of Asia work is also outsourced to avoid long-term employment commitments. In these settings if employees are hired as full time, the employer makes a substantial commitment. To lay off an employee a firm may have to receive permission from the government and will have to pay the employee compensation. In Germany that compensation is estimated to be around 12,000 euros.[29] Second, outsourcing can sometimes allow managers to use human resources at a lower cost. When work is outsourced, costs can be lower for a number of reasons: The organization does not have to provide benefits to workers; managers can contract for work only when the work is needed; and managers do not have to invest in training. Outsourcing can be used for functional activities such as after-sales service on appliances and equipment, legal work, and the management of information systems.[30]

Outsourcing has disadvantages, however.[31] When work is outsourced, managers may lose some control over the quality of goods and services. Also, individuals performing outsourced work may have less knowledge of organizational practices, procedures, and goals and less commitment to an organization than regular employees. In addition, unions resist outsourcing because it has the potential to eliminate some of their members.

A major trend reflecting the increasing globalization of business is the outsourcing of office work, computer programming, and technical jobs from the United States and countries in western Europe, with high labor costs, to countries like India and China, with low labor costs.[32] For example, computer programmers in India and China earn a fraction of what their European counterparts earn. Outsourcing (or *offshoring,* as it is also called when work is outsourced to other countries) has also expanded into knowledge-intensive work such as engineering, research and development, and the development of computer software. According to a recent study conducted by The Conference Board and Duke University's Offshoring Research Network, more than half of U.S. companies surveyed have some kind of offshoring strategy related to knowledge-intensive work and innovation.[33] Why are so many companies engaged in offshoring, and why are companies that already offshore work planning to increase the extent of offshoring? While cost savings continue to be a major motivation for offshoring, managers also want to take advantage of an increasingly talented global workforce and be closer to the growing global marketplace for goods and services.[34]

Job Analysis

job analysis Identifying the tasks, duties, and responsibilities that make up a job and the knowledge, skills, and abilities needed to perform the job.

Job analysis is a second important activity that managers need to undertake prior to recruitment and selection.[35] **Job analysis** is the process of identifying (1) the tasks, duties, and responsibilities that make up a job (the *job description*) and (2) the knowledge, skills, and abilities needed to perform the job (the *job specifications*).[36] For each job in an organization, a job analysis needs to be done.

Job analysis can be done in a number of ways, including observing current employees as they perform the job or interviewing them. Often managers rely on questionnaires compiled by jobholders and their managers. The questionnaires ask about the skills and abilities needed to perform the job, job tasks and the amount of time spent on them, responsibilities, supervisory activities, equipment used, reports prepared, and decisions made.[37] The Position Analysis Questionnaire (PAQ) is a comprehensive standardized questionnaire that many managers rely on to conduct job analyses.[38] It focuses on behaviors jobholders perform, working conditions, and job characteristics and can be used for a variety of jobs.[39] The PAQ contains 194 items organized into six divisions: (1) information input (where and how the jobholder acquires information to perform the job), (2) mental processes (reasoning, decision making, planning, and information processing activities that are part of the job), (3) work output (physical activities performed on the job and machines and devices used), (4) relationships with others (interactions with other people that are necessary to perform the job), (5) job context (the physical and social environment of the job), and (6) other job characteristics (such as work pace).[40] A trend, in some organizations, is toward more flexible jobs in which tasks and responsibilities change and cannot be clearly specified in advance. For these kinds of jobs, job analysis focuses more on determining the skills and knowledge workers need to be effective and less on specific duties.

After managers have completed human resource planning and job analyses for all jobs in an organization, they will know their human resource needs and the jobs they need to fill. They will also know what knowledge, skills, and abilities potential employees need to perform those jobs. At this point, recruitment and selection can begin.

External and Internal Recruitment

As noted earlier, recruitment is what managers do to develop a pool of qualified candidates for open positions.[41] They traditionally have used two main types of recruiting: external and internal, which are now supplemented by recruiting over the Internet.

EXTERNAL RECRUITING When managers recruit externally to fill open positions, they look outside the organization for people who have not worked for the organization previously. There are multiple means through which managers can recruit externally: advertisements in newspapers and magazines, open houses for students and career counselors at high schools and colleges or on-site at the organization, career fairs at colleges, and recruitment meetings with groups in the local community.

Many large organizations send teams of interviewers to college campuses to recruit new employees. External recruitment can also take place through informal networks, as occurs when current employees inform friends about open positions in their companies or recommend people they know to fill vacant spots. Some organizations use employment agencies for external recruitment, and some external recruitment takes place simply through walk-ins–job hunters coming to an organization and inquiring about employment possibilities.

Many colleges and universities hold job fairs to connect employers with students looking for jobs.

With all the downsizing and corporate layoffs that have taken place in recent years, you might think external recruiting would be a relatively easy task for managers. However, it often is not, because even though many people may be looking for jobs, many jobs that are open require skills and abilities that these job hunters do not have. Managers needing to fill vacant positions and job hunters seeking employment opportunities are increasingly relying on the Internet to connect with each other through employment Web sites such as Monster.com[42] and JobLine International.[43]

External recruiting has both advantages and disadvantages for managers. Advantages include having access to a potentially large applicant pool, being able to attract people who have the skills, knowledge, and abilities that an organization needs to achieve its goals, and being able to bring in newcomers who may have a fresh approach to problems and be up to date on the latest technology. These advantages have to be weighed against the disadvantages, including the relatively high costs of external recruitment. Employees recruited externally also lack knowledge about the inner workings of the organization and may need to receive more training than those recruited internally. Finally, when employees are recruited externally, there is always uncertainty concerning whether they will actually be good performers.

INTERNAL RECRUITING When recruiting is internal, managers turn to existing employees to fill open positions. Employees recruited internally are either seeking **lateral moves** (job changes that entail no major changes in responsibility or authority levels) or promotions. Internal recruiting has several advantages. First, internal applicants are already familiar with the organization (including its goals, structure, culture, rules, and norms). Second, managers already know the candidates; they have considerable information about their skills and abilities and actual behavior on the job. Third, internal recruiting can help boost levels of employee motivation and morale, both for the employee who gets the job and for other workers. Those who are not seeking a promotion or who may not be ready for one can see that promotion is a possibility in the future; or a lateral move can alleviate boredom once a job has been fully mastered and can also be a useful way to learn new skills. Finally, internal recruiting is normally less time-consuming and expensive than external recruiting.

lateral move A job change that entails no major changes in responsibility or authority levels.

Given the advantages of internal recruiting, why do managers rely on external recruiting as much as they do? The answer lies in the disadvantages of internal recruiting–among them, a limited pool of candidates and a tendency among those candidates to be set in the organization's ways. Often the organization simply does not have suitable internal candidates. Sometimes, even when suitable internal applicants are available, managers may rely on external recruiting to find the very best candidate or to help bring new ideas and approaches into their organization. When organizations are in trouble and performing poorly, external recruiting is often relied on to bring in managerial talent with a fresh approach.

HONESTY IN RECRUITING At times, when trying to recruit the most qualified applicants, managers may be tempted to paint rosy pictures of both the open positions and the organization as a whole. They may worry that if they are honest about advantages and disadvantages, they either will not be able to fill positions or will have fewer or less qualified applicants. A manager trying to fill a secretarial position, for example, may emphasize the high level of pay and benefits the job offers and fail to mention the fact that the position is usually a dead-end job offering few opportunities for promotion.

Research suggests that painting a rosy picture of a job and the organization is not a wise recruiting strategy. Recruitment is more likely to be effective when managers give potential applicants an honest assessment of both the advantages and the disadvantages of the job and organization. Such an assessment is called a **realistic job preview (RJP)**.[44] RJPs can reduce the number of new hires who quit when their jobs and organizations fail to meet their unrealistic expectations, and they help applicants decide for themselves whether a job is right for them.

realistic job preview (RJP) An honest assessment of the advantages and disadvantages of a job and organization.

Take the earlier example of the manager trying to recruit a secretary. The manager who paints a rosy picture of the job might have an easy time filling it but might hire a secretary who expects to be promoted quickly to an administrative assistant position. After a few weeks on the job, the secretary may realize that a promotion is unlikely no matter how good his or her performance, become dissatisfied, and look for and accept another job. The manager then has to recruit, select, and train another new secretary. The manager could have avoided this waste of valuable organizational resources by using a realistic job preview. The RJP would have increased the likelihood of hiring a secretary who was comfortable with few promotional opportunities and subsequently would have been satisfied to remain on the job.

The Selection Process

Once managers develop a pool of applicants for open positions through the recruitment process, they need to find out whether each applicant is qualified for the position and likely to be a good performer. If more than one applicant meets these two conditions, managers must further determine which applicants are likely to be better performers than others. They have several selection tools to help them sort out the relative qualifications of job applicants and appraise their potential for being good performers in a particular job. These tools include background information, interviews, paper-and-pencil tests, physical ability tests, performance tests, and references (see Figure 12.3).[45]

The recruitment process can be very extensive. For example, at Singapore Airlines the recruitment process for cabin crews involves:

- An initial screening based on age ranges, academic qualifications, and physical attributes.
- Three rounds of interviews which examine characteristics such as cheerfulness, friendliness, humility, English language competence, and the fit with the airline's core values; uniform checks that assess the look in the airline's *sarong kabaya;* a water confidence test that requires candidates to jump from a height of 3 meters; a psychometric test, and even attendance at a tea party to observe applicants' interaction style and demeanor.

The selection rate is 3 to 4% of total applicants; thus, out of 16,000 applicants, only 500 to 600 new cabin-crew members are hired annually to replace 10% turnover.[46]

BACKGROUND INFORMATION To aid in the selection process, managers obtain background information from job applications and from résumés. Such information might include the highest levels of education obtained, college majors and minors, type of college or university attended, years and type of work experience, and mastery of foreign languages. Background information can be helpful both to screen out applicants who are lacking key qualifications (such as a college degree) and to determine which qualified applicants are more promising than others. For example, applicants with a BS may be acceptable, but those who also have an MBA may be preferable.

Figure 12.3
Selection Tools

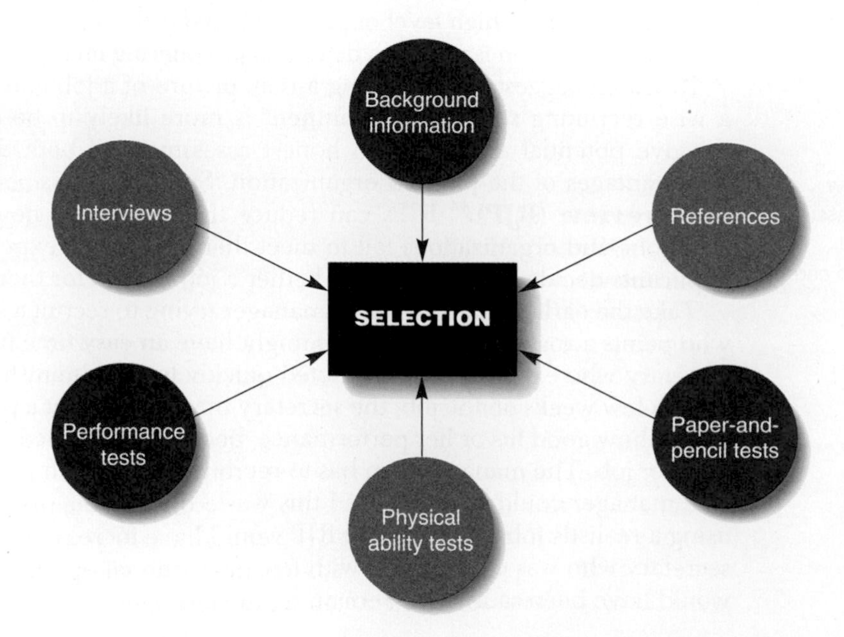

Increasing numbers of organizations are performing background checks to verify the background information prospective employees provide (and also to uncover any negative information such as crime convictions).[47] According to ADP Employer Services, an outsourcing company that performs payroll and human resource functions for organizations, more and more companies are performing background checks on prospective employees and are uncovering inaccuracies, inconsistencies, and negative information such as prior convictions or driving violations.[48] According to a recent survey ADP conducted, about half of all background checks turn up an inconsistency between the education and credentials applicants list and the information other sources (such as universities or prior employers) provide. And in some cases, background checks reveal convictions and driving violations.[49]

INTERVIEWS Virtually all organizations use interviews during the selection process, as is true at Zappos in "A Manager's Challenge." Interviews may be structured or unstructured. In a *structured interview,* managers ask each applicant the same standard questions (such as "What are your unique qualifications for this position?" and "What characteristics of a job are most important to you?"). Particularly informative questions may be those that prompt an interviewee to demonstrate skills and abilities needed for the job by answering the question. Sometimes called *situational interview questions,* these often present interviewees with a scenario they would likely encounter on the job and ask them to indicate how they would handle it.[50] For example, applicants for a sales job may be asked to indicate how they would respond to a customer who complains about waiting too long for service, a customer who is indecisive, and a customer whose order is lost.

An *unstructured interview* proceeds more like an ordinary conversation. The interviewer feels free to ask probing questions to discover what the applicant is like and does not ask a fixed set of questions determined in advance. In general, structured interviews are superior to unstructured interviews because they are more likely to yield information that will help identify qualified candidates, are less subjective, and may be less influenced by the interviewer's biases.

Practically all organizations use some kind of interview during the selection process.

Even when structured interviews are used, however, the potential exists for the interviewer's biases to influence his or her judgment. Recall from Chapter 5 how the similar-to-me effect can cause people to perceive others who are similar to themselves more positively than those who are different and how stereotypes can result in inaccurate perceptions. Interviewers must be trained to avoid these biases and sources of inaccurate perceptions as much as possible. Many of the approaches to increasing diversity awareness and diversity skills described in Chapter 5 are used to train interviewers to avoid the effects of biases and stereotypes. In addition, using multiple interviewers can be advantageous because their individual biases and idiosyncrasies may cancel one another out.[51]

When conducting interviews, managers cannot ask questions that are irrelevant to the job in question; otherwise their organizations run the risk of costly lawsuits. It is inappropriate and illegal, for example, to inquire about an interviewee's spouse or to ask questions about whether an interviewee plans to have children.

Managers can use interviews at various stages in the selection process. Some use interviews as initial screening devices; others use them as a final hurdle that applicants must jump. Regardless of when they are used, managers typically use other selection tools in conjunction with interviews because of the potential for bias and for inaccurate assessments of interviewees. Even though training and structured interviews can eliminate the effects of some biases, interviewers can still come to erroneous conclusions about interviewees' qualifications. Interviewees, for example, who make a bad initial impression or are overly nervous in the first minute or two of an interview tend to be judged more harshly than less nervous candidates, even if the rest of the interview goes well.

PAPER-AND-PENCIL TESTS The two main kinds of paper-and-pencil tests used for selection purposes are ability tests and personality tests. *Ability tests* assess the extent to which applicants possess the skills necessary for job performance, such as verbal comprehension or numerical skills. Autoworkers hired by General Motors, Chrysler, and Ford, for example, are typically tested for their ability to read and to do mathematics.[52]

Personality tests measure personality traits and characteristics relevant to job performance. Some retail organizations, for example, give job applicants honesty tests to determine how trustworthy they are. The use of personality tests (including honesty tests) for hiring purposes is controversial. Some critics maintain that honesty tests do not really measure honesty (that is, they are not valid) and can be faked by job applicants. Before using any paper-and-pencil tests for selection purposes, managers must have sound evidence that the tests are actually good predictors of performance on the job in question. Managers who use tests without such evidence may be subject to costly discrimination lawsuits.

PHYSICAL ABILITY TESTS For jobs requiring physical abilities, such as firefighting, garbage collecting, and package delivery, managers use physical ability tests that measure physical strength and stamina as selection tools. Autoworkers are typically tested for mechanical dexterity because this physical ability is an important skill for high job performance in many auto plants.[53]

PERFORMANCE TESTS *Performance tests* measure job applicants' performance on actual job tasks. Applicants for secretarial positions, for example, typically are required to complete a keyboarding test that measures how quickly and accurately they type. Applicants for middle and top management positions are sometimes given short-term projects to complete–projects that mirror the kinds of situations that arise in the job being filled–to assess their knowledge and problem-solving capabilities.[54]

Assessment centers, first used by AT&T, take performance tests one step further. In a typical assessment center, about 10 to 15 candidates for managerial positions participate in a variety of activities over a few days. During this time they are assessed for the skills an effective manager needs–problem-solving, organizational, communication, and conflict resolution skills. Some of the activities are performed individually; others are performed in groups. Throughout the process, current managers observe the candidates' behavior and measure performance. Summary evaluations are then used as a selection tool.

REFERENCES Applicants for many jobs are required to provide references from former employers or other knowledgeable sources (such as a college instructor or adviser) who know the applicants' skills, abilities, and other personal characteristics. These individuals are asked to provide candid information about the applicant. References are often used at the end of the selection process to confirm a decision to hire. Yet the fact that many former employers are reluctant to provide negative information in references sometimes makes it difficult to interpret what a reference is really saying about an applicant.

In fact, several recent lawsuits filed by applicants who felt that they were unfairly denigrated or had their privacy invaded by unfavorable references from former employers have caused managers to be increasingly wary of providing any negative information in a reference, even if it is accurate. For jobs in which the jobholder is responsible for the safety and lives of other people, however, failing to provide accurate negative information in a reference does not just mean that the wrong person might get hired; it may also mean that other people's lives will be at stake.

reliability The degree to which a tool or test measures the same thing each time it is used.

THE IMPORTANCE OF RELIABILITY AND VALIDITY Whatever selection tools a manager uses need to be both reliable and valid. **Reliability** is the degree to which a tool or test measures the same thing each time it is administered. Scores on a selection test should be similar if the same person is assessed with the same tool on two different days; if there is quite a bit of variability, the tool is unreliable. For interviews, determining reliability is more complex because the dynamic is personal interpretation. That is why the reliability of interviews can be increased if two or more different qualified interviewers interview the same candidate. If the interviews are reliable, the interviewers should come to similar conclusions about the interviewee's qualifications.

validity The degree to which a tool or test measures what it purports to measure.

Validity is the degree to which a tool measures what it purports to measure–for selection tools, it is the degree to which the test predicts performance on the tasks or job in question. Does a physical ability test used to select firefighters, for example, actually predict on-the-job performance? Do assessment center ratings actually predict managerial performance? Do keyboarding tests predict secretarial performance? These are all questions of validity. Honesty tests, for example, are controversial because it is not clear that they validly predict honesty in such jobs as retailing and banking.

Managers have an ethical and legal obligation to use reliable and valid selection tools. Yet reliability and validity are matters of degree rather than all-or-nothing characteristics. Thus managers should strive to use selection tools in such a way that they can achieve the greatest degree of reliability and validity. For ability tests of a particular skill, managers should keep up to date on the latest advances in the development of valid paper-and-pencil tests and use the test with the highest reliability and validity ratings for their purposes. Regarding interviews, managers can improve reliability by having more than one person interview job candidates.

LO12-3 Discuss the training and development options that ensure organizational members can effectively perform their jobs.

Training and Development

Training and development help to ensure that organizational members have the knowledge and skills needed to perform jobs effectively, take on new responsibilities, and adapt to changing conditions. **Training** focuses primarily on teaching organizational members how to perform their current jobs and helping them acquire the knowledge and skills they need to be effective performers. **Development** focuses on building the knowledge and skills of organizational members so they are prepared to take on new responsibilities and challenges. Training tends to be used more frequently at lower levels of an organization; development tends to be used more frequently with professionals and managers. The training process in many firms can be quite extensive. For example, at Singapore Airlines new recruits undertake intensive four-month training courses, the longest and most comprehensive in the industry. The training is holistic and includes not only safety and functional issues but also beauty care, gourmet food and wine appreciation, and the art of conversation. Additionally there are training tools for the seven core functional areas: cabin crew, flight operations, commercial training, IT, security, airport services, and engineering.

training Teaching organizational members how to perform their current jobs and helping them acquire the knowledge and skills they need to be effective performers.

development Building the knowledge and skills of organizational members so they are prepared to take on new responsibilities and challenges.

After training there is a six-month probationary period when 75% of trainees are offered a five-year contract and 20% have their probation extended; the rest of the recruits are disqualified. There is a 29-month comprehensive online training program prior to any promotion and a training program that requires job rotation for management. Annually approximately 9,000 employees have some sort of development training.[55]

Before creating training and development programs, managers should perform a **needs assessment** to determine which employees need training or development and what type of skills or knowledge they need to acquire (see Figure 12.4).[56]

needs assessment An assessment of which employees need training or development and what type of skills or knowledge they need to acquire.

Types of Training

There are two types of training: classroom instruction and on-the-job training.

CLASSROOM INSTRUCTION Through classroom instruction, employees acquire knowledge and skills in a classroom setting. This instruction may take place within the organization or outside it, such as through courses at local colleges and universities.

Figure 12.4
Training and Development

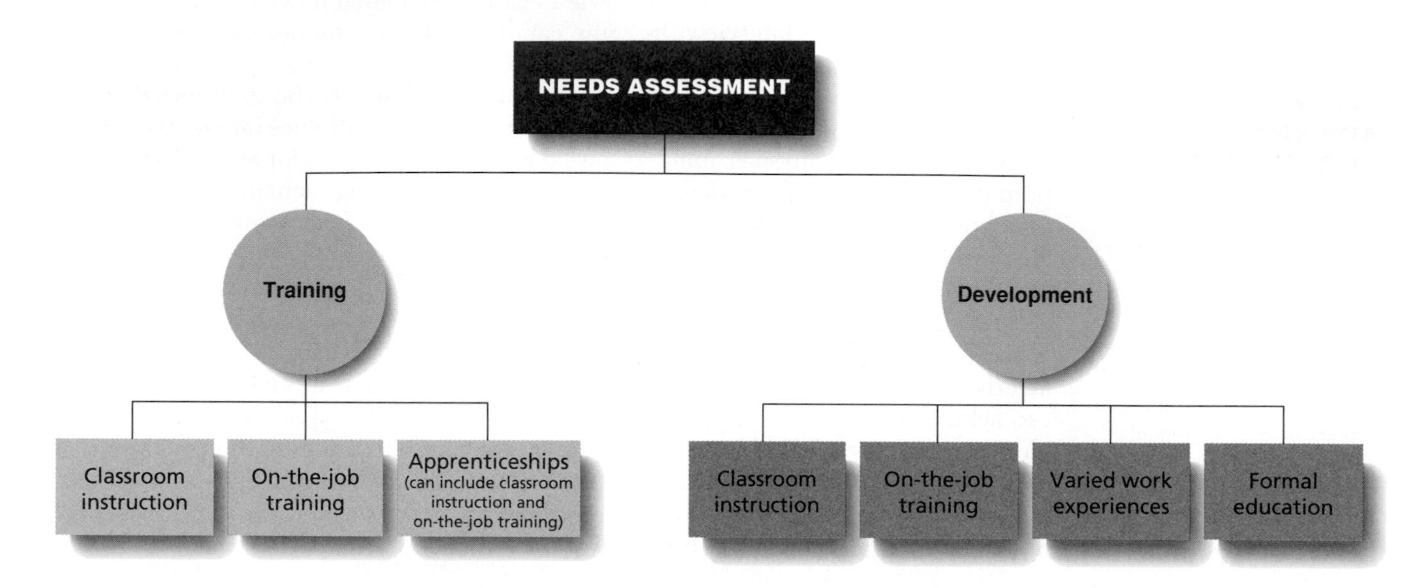

Many organizations establish their own formal instructional divisions–some are even called "colleges"–to provide needed classroom instruction.

Classroom instruction frequently uses videos and role playing in addition to traditional written materials, lectures, and group discussions. *Videos* can demonstrate appropriate and inappropriate job behaviors. For example, by watching an experienced salesperson effectively deal with a loud and angry customer, inexperienced salespeople can develop skills in handling similar situations. During *role playing,* trainees either directly participate in or watch others perform actual job activities in a simulated setting.

on-the-job training Training that takes place in the work setting as employees perform their job tasks.

Simulations also can be part of classroom instruction, particularly for complicated jobs that require an extensive amount of learning and in which errors carry a high cost. In a simulation, key aspects of the work situation and job tasks are duplicated as closely as possible in an artificial setting. For example, air traffic controllers are trained by simulations because of the complicated nature of the work, the extensive amount of learning involved, and the very high costs of air traffic control errors.

At many restaurants, new employees receive on-the-job training by shadowing more experienced waiters and waitresses as they go about their work.

ON-THE-JOB TRAINING In **on-the-job training,** learning occurs in the work setting as employees perform their job tasks. On-the-job training can be provided by coworkers or supervisors or can occur simply as jobholders gain experience and knowledge from doing the work. The supervisor of a new bus driver for a campus bus system may ride the bus for a week to ensure that the driver has learned the routes and follows safety procedures. Chefs learn to create new and innovative dishes by experimenting with different combinations of ingredients and cooking techniques. For all on-the-job training, employees learn by doing.

Managers often use on-the-job training on a continuing basis to ensure that their subordinates keep up to date with changes in goals, technology, products, or customer needs and desires. For example, Metalúrgica

Gerdau S.A. is a Brazilian steel company that invests more than 60 hours of ongoing training for each employee.[57]

Types of Development

Although both classroom instruction and on-the-job training can be used for development as well as training, development often includes additional activities such as varied work experiences and formal education.

VARIED WORK EXPERIENCES Top managers need to develop an understanding of, and expertise in, a variety of functions, products and services, and markets. To develop executives who will have this expertise, managers frequently make sure that employees with high potential have a wide variety of different job experiences, some in line positions and some in staff positions. Varied work experiences broaden employees' horizons and help them think about the big picture. For example, one- to three-year stints overseas are being used increasingly to provide managers with international work experiences. With organizations becoming more global, managers need to understand the different values, beliefs, cultures, regions, and ways of doing business in different countries.

Another development approach is mentoring. (Recall from Chapter 5 that a *mentor* is an experienced member of an organization who provides advice and guidance to a less experienced member, called a *protégé*.) Having a mentor can help managers seek out work experiences and assignments that will contribute to their development and can enable them to gain the most possible from varied work experiences.[58] Although some mentors and protégés hook up informally, organizations have found that formal mentoring programs can be valuable ways to contribute to the development of managers and all employees.

Formal mentoring programs ensure that mentoring takes place in an organization, structure the process, and make sure diverse organizational members have equal access to mentors. Participants receive training, efforts are focused on matching mentors and protégés so meaningful developmental relationships ensue, and organizations can track reactions and assess the potential benefits of mentoring. Formal mentoring programs can also ensure that diverse members of an organization receive the benefits of mentoring.

FORMAL EDUCATION Many large corporations reimburse employees for tuition expenses they incur while taking college courses and obtaining advanced degrees. This is not just benevolence on the part of the employer or even a simple reward given to the employee; it is an effective way to develop employees who can take on new responsibilities and more challenging positions. For similar reasons, corporations spend thousands of dollars sending managers to executive development programs such as executive MBA programs. In these programs, experts teach managers the latest in business and management techniques and practices.

To save time and travel costs, some managers rely on *long-distance learning* to formally educate and develop employees. Using videoconferencing technologies, business schools such as the Harvard Business School, the University of Michigan, and Babson College teach courses on video screens in corporate conference rooms. Business schools also customize courses and degrees to fit the development needs of employees in a particular company and/or a particular geographic region.[59]

LO12-4 Explain why performance appraisal and feedback is such a crucial activity, and list the choices managers must make in designing effective performance appraisal and feedback procedures.

Transfer of Training and Development

Whenever training and development take place off the job or in a classroom setting, it is vital for managers to promote the transfer of the knowledge and skills acquired *to the actual work situation.* Trainees should be encouraged and expected to use their newfound expertise on the job.

Performance Appraisal and Feedback

The recruitment/selection and training/development components of a human resource management system ensure that employees have the knowledge and skills needed to be effective now and in the future. Performance appraisal and feedback complement recruitment, selection, training, and development. **Performance appraisal** is the evaluation of employees' job performance and contributions to the organization. **Performance feedback** is the process through which managers share performance appraisal information with their subordinates, give subordinates an opportunity to reflect on their own performance, and develop, with subordinates, plans for the future. Before performance feedback, performance appraisal must take place. Performance appraisal could take place without providing performance feedback, but wise managers are careful to provide feedback because it can contribute to employee motivation and performance.

performance appraisal The evaluation of employees' job performance and contributions to their organization.

performance feedback The process through which managers share performance appraisal information with subordinates, give subordinates an opportunity to reflect on their own performance, and develop, with subordinates, plans for the future.

Performance appraisal and feedback contribute to the effective management of human resources in several ways. Performance appraisal gives managers important information on which to base human resource decisions.[60] Decisions about pay raises, bonuses, promotions, and job moves all hinge on the accurate appraisal of performance. Performance appraisal can also help managers determine which workers are candidates for training and development and in what areas. Performance feedback encourages high levels of employee motivation and performance. It lets good performers know that their efforts are valued and appreciated. It also lets poor performers know that their lackluster performance needs improvement. Performance feedback can give both good and poor performers insight on their strengths and weaknesses and ways in which they can improve their performance in the future.

Types of Performance Appraisal

Performance appraisal focuses on the evaluation of traits, behaviors, and results.[61]

TRAIT APPRAISALS When trait appraisals are used, managers assess subordinates on personal characteristics that are relevant to job performance, such as skills, abilities, or personality. A factory worker, for example, may be evaluated based on her ability to use computerized equipment and perform numerical calculations. A social worker may be appraised based on his empathy and communication skills.

Three disadvantages of trait appraisals often lead managers to rely on other appraisal methods. First, possessing a certain personal characteristic does not ensure that the personal characteristic will actually be used on the job and result in high performance. For example, a factory worker may possess superior computer and numerical skills but be a poor performer due to low motivation. The second disadvantage of trait appraisals is linked to the first. Because traits do not always show a direct association with performance, workers and courts of law may view them as unfair and potentially discriminatory. The third disadvantage of trait appraisals is that they often do not enable managers to give employees feedback they can use to improve performance. Because trait appraisals focus on relatively enduring human characteristics that change only over the long term, employees can do little to change their behavior in response to performance feedback from a trait appraisal. Telling a social worker that he lacks empathy says little about how he can improve his interactions with clients, for example. These disadvantages suggest that managers should use trait appraisals only when they can demonstrate that the assessed traits are accurate and important indicators of job performance.

How'm I doing? Sitting down for an honest and open performance appraisal with your immediate supervisor can help keep you on track.

BEHAVIOR APPRAISALS Through behavior appraisals, managers assess how workers perform their jobs–the actual actions and behaviors that workers exhibit on the job. Whereas trait appraisals assess what workers *are like,* behavior appraisals assess what workers *do.* For example, with a behavior appraisal, a manager might evaluate a social worker on the extent to which he looks clients in the eye when talking with them, expresses sympathy when they are upset, and refers them to community counseling and support groups geared toward the specific problems they are encountering. Behavior appraisals are especially useful when *how* workers perform their jobs is important. In educational organizations such as high schools, for example, the numbers of classes and students taught are important, but also important is how they are taught or the methods teachers use to ensure that learning takes place.

Behavior appraisals have the advantage of giving employees clear information about what they are doing right and wrong and how they can improve their performance. And because behaviors are much easier for employees to change than traits, performance feedback from behavior appraisals is more likely to lead to improve performance.

RESULTS APPRAISALS For some jobs, *how* people perform the job is not as important as *what* they accomplish or the results they obtain. With results appraisals, managers appraise performance by the results or the actual outcomes of work behaviors. Take the case of two new car salespeople. One salesperson strives to develop personal relationships with her customers. She spends hours talking to them and frequently calls them to see how their decision-making process is going. The other salesperson has a much more hands-off approach. He is very knowledgeable, answers customers' questions, and then waits for them to come to him. Both salespersons sell, on average, the same number of cars, and the customers of both are satisfied with the service they receive, according to postcards the dealership mails to customers asking for an assessment of their satisfaction. The manager of the dealership appropriately uses results appraisals (sales and customer satisfaction) to evaluate the salespeople's performance because it does not matter which behavior salespeople use to sell cars as long as they sell the desired number and satisfy customers. If one salesperson sells too few cars, however, the manager can give that person performance feedback about his or her low sales.

objective appraisal An appraisal that is based on facts and is likely to be numerical.

subjective appraisal An appraisal that is based on perceptions of traits, behaviors, or results.

OBJECTIVE AND SUBJECTIVE APPRAISALS Whether managers appraise performance in terms of traits, behaviors, or results, the information they assess is either *objective* or *subjective.* **Objective appraisals** are based on facts and are likely to be numerical–the number of cars sold, the number of meals prepared, the number of times late, the number of audits completed. Managers often use objective appraisals when results are being appraised because results tend to be easier to quantify than traits or behaviors. When *how* workers perform their jobs is important, however, subjective behavior appraisals are more appropriate than results appraisals.

Subjective appraisals are based on managers' perceptions of traits, behaviors, or results. Because subjective appraisals rest on managers' perceptions, there is always the chance that they are inaccurate (see Chapter 5). This is why both researchers and managers have spent considerable time and effort on determining the best way to develop reliable and valid subjective measures of performance.

Some of the more popular subjective measures such as the graphic rating scale, the behaviorally anchored rating scale (BARS), and the behavior observation scale (BOS) are illustrated in Figure 12.5.[62] When graphic rating scales are used, performance is assessed along a continuum with specified intervals. With a BARS, performance is assessed along a scale with clearly defined scale points containing examples of specific behaviors. A BOS assesses performance by how often specific behaviors are performed. Many managers may use both objective and subjective appraisals. For example, a salesperson may be appraised both on the dollar value of sales (objective) and the quality of customer service (subjective).

Figure 12.5
Subjective Measures of Performance

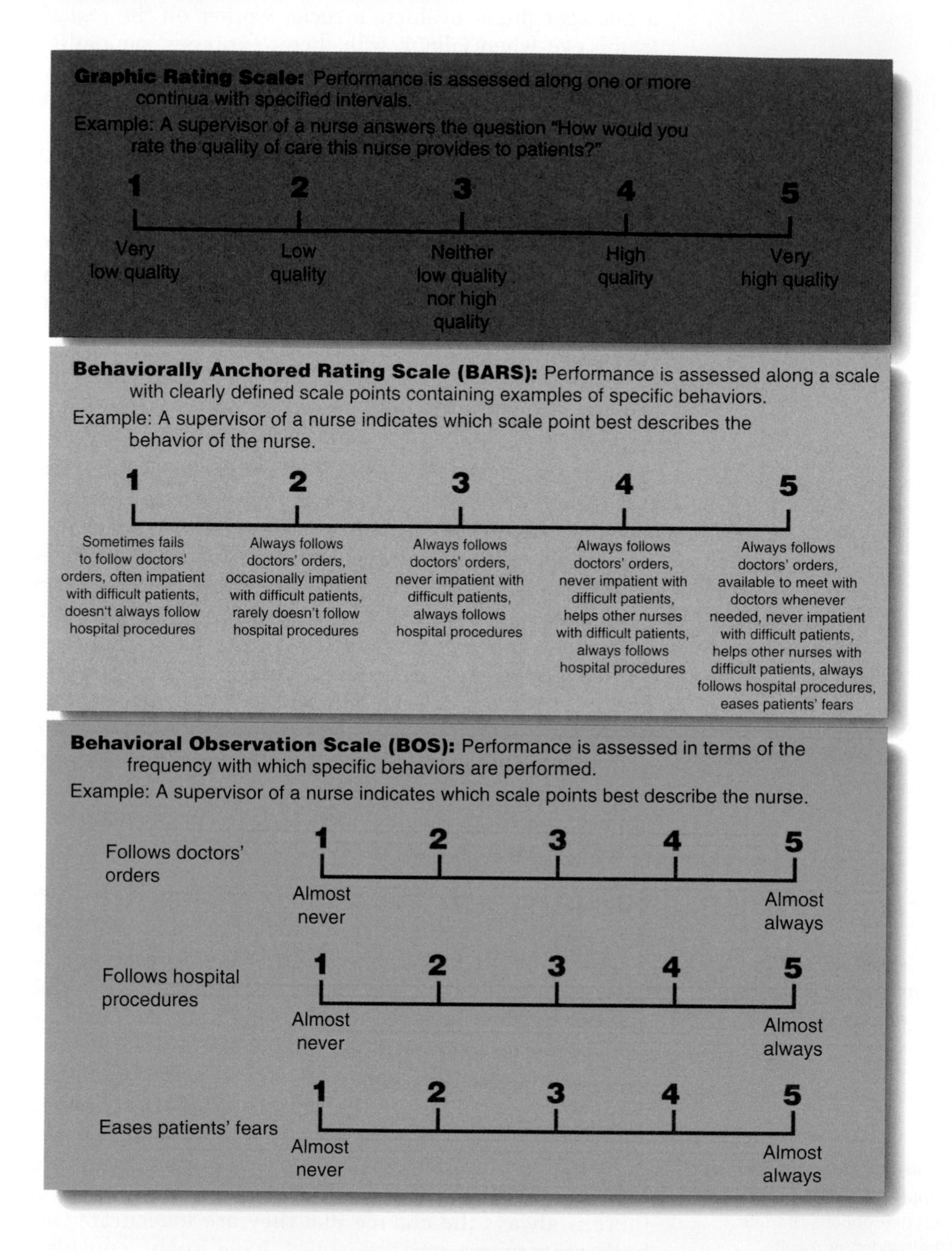

In addition to subjective appraisals, some organizations employ *forced rankings* whereby supervisors must rank their subordinates and assign them to different categories according to their performance (which is subjectively appraised). For example, middle managers at Ford Motor Company are ranked by their supervisors in a forced distribution from A to C, with 10% of them receiving A ratings, 80% receiving B ratings, and 10% receiving C ratings.[63] The first year an employee receives a C, he or she does not receive a bonus, and after two years of C performance, a demotion or even firing is possible. However, in some European nations such forced ranking systems are seen as inconsistent with building a group effort. Rather than seeing the group as a team and encouraging its members, the forced ranking system means someone in the team must be judged as a poor. Thus, forced ranking systems are more likely to be seen in nations such as the United States than in team-oriented environments such as Scandinavia.

Who Appraises Performance?

We have been assuming that managers or the supervisors of employees evaluate performance. This is a reasonable assumption: Supervisors are the most common appraisers of performance.[64] Performance appraisal is an important part of most managers' job duties. Managers are responsible for not only motivating their subordinates to perform at a high level but also making many decisions hinging on performance appraisals, such as pay raises or promotions. Appraisals by managers can be usefully augmented by appraisals from other sources (see Figure 12.6).

SELF, PEERS, SUBORDINATES, AND CLIENTS When self-appraisals are used, managers supplement their evaluations with an employee's assessment of his or her own performance. Peer appraisals are provided by an employee's coworkers. Especially when subordinates work in groups or teams, feedback from peer appraisals can motivate team members while giving managers important information for decision making. A growing number of companies are having subordinates appraise their managers' performance and leadership as well. And sometimes customers or clients assess employee performance in terms of responsiveness to customers and quality of service. Although appraisals from these sources can be useful, managers need to be aware of potential issues that may arise when they are used. Subordinates sometimes may be inclined to inflate self-appraisals, especially if organizations are downsizing and they are worried about job security. Managers who are appraised by their subordinates may fail to take needed but unpopular actions out of fear that their subordinates will appraise them negatively. Some of these potential issues can be mitigated to the extent that there are high levels of trust in an organization.

360-degree appraisal A performance appraisal by peers, subordinates, superiors, and sometimes clients who are in a position to evaluate a manager's performance.

360-DEGREE PERFORMANCE APPRAISALS To improve motivation and performance, some organizations include 360-degree appraisals and feedback in their performance appraisal systems, especially for managers. In a **360-degree appraisal** a variety of people, beginning with the manager and including peers or coworkers, subordinates, superiors, and sometimes even customers or clients, appraise a manager's performance. The manager receives feedback based on evaluations from these multiple sources.

Figure 12.6
Who Appraises Performance?

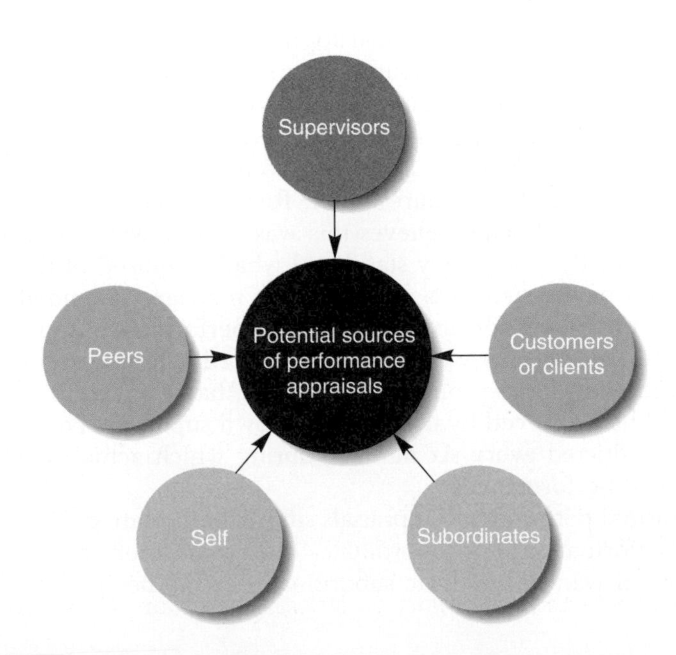

The growing number of companies using 360-degree appraisals and feedback include the British firm Alliance Unichem. For 360-degree appraisals and feedback to be effective, there has to be trust throughout an organization. More generally, trust is a critical ingredient in any performance appraisal and feedback procedure. In addition, research suggests that 360-degree appraisals should focus on behaviors rather than traits or results and that managers need to carefully select appropriate raters. Moreover, appraisals tend to be more honest when made anonymously and when raters have been trained in how to use 360-degree appraisal forms.[65] Additionally, managers need to think carefully about the extent to which 360-degree appraisals are appropriate for certain jobs and be willing to modify any appraisal system they implement if they become aware of unintended problems it creates.[66]

Even when 360-degree appraisals are used, it is sometimes difficult to design an effective process by which subordinates' feedback can be communicated to their managers; but advances in information technology can solve this problem. For example, ImproveNow.com has online questionnaires that subordinates fill out to evaluate the performance of their managers and give the managers feedback. Each subordinate of a particular manager completes the questionnaire independently, all responses are tabulated, and the manager is given specific feedback on behaviors in a variety of areas, such as rewarding good performance, looking out for subordinates' best interests and being supportive, and having a vision for the future.[67]

Effective Performance Feedback

formal appraisal An appraisal conducted at a set time during the year and based on performance dimensions and measures that were specified in advance.

For the appraisal and feedback component of a human resource management system to encourage and motivate high performance, managers must give their subordinates feedback. To generate useful information to feed back to their subordinates, managers can use both formal and informal appraisals. **Formal appraisals** are conducted at set times during the year and are based on performance dimensions and measures that have been specified in advance. A salesperson, for example, may be evaluated by his or her manager twice a year on the performance dimensions of sales and customer service, sales being objectively measured from sales reports, and customer service being measured with a BARS (see Figure 12.5).

Managers in most large organizations use formal performance appraisals on a fixed schedule dictated by company policy, such as every six months or every year. An integral part of a formal appraisal is a meeting between the manager and the subordinate in which the subordinate is given feedback on performance. Performance feedback lets subordinates know which areas they are excelling in and which areas need improvement; it should also tell them *how* they can improve their performance.

Realizing the value of formal appraisals, managers in many large corporations have committed substantial resources to updating their performance appraisal procedures and training low-level managers in how to use them and provide accurate feedback to employees. Top managers at the German pharmaceutical company Hoffmann-La Roche Inc., for example, spent US$1.5 million updating and improving their performance appraisal procedures. Alan Rubino, vice president of human resources for Hoffmann-La Roche, believes this was money well spent because "people need to know exactly where they stand and what's required of them." Before Hoffmann-La Roche's new system was implemented, managers attended a three-day training and development session to improve their performance appraisal skills. The new procedures call for every manager and subordinate to develop a performance plan for subordinates for the coming year–a plan that is linked to the company's strategy and goals and approved by the manager's own superiors. Formal performance appraisals are conducted every six months, during which actual performance is compared to planned performance.[68]

Formal performance appraisals supply both managers and subordinates with valuable information; but subordinates often want more frequent feedback, and managers often want to motivate subordinates as the need arises. For these reasons many

informal appraisal An unscheduled appraisal of ongoing progress and areas for improvement.

companies, including Hoffman-La Roche, supplement formal performance appraisal with frequent **informal appraisals,** for which managers and their subordinates meet as the need arises to discuss ongoing progress and areas for improvement. Moreover, when job duties, assignments, or goals change, informal appraisals can give workers timely feedback concerning how they are handling their new responsibilities.

Managers often dislike providing performance feedback, especially when the feedback is negative, but doing so is an important managerial activity.[69] Here are some guidelines for giving effective performance feedback that contributes to employee motivation and performance:

- *Be specific and focus on behaviors or outcomes that are correctable and within a worker's ability to improve.* Example: Telling a salesperson that he is too shy when interacting with customers is likely to lower his self-confidence and prompt him to become defensive. A more effective approach would be to give the salesperson feedback about specific behaviors to engage in–greeting customers as soon as they enter the department, asking customers whether they need help, and volunteering to help customers find items.
- *Approach performance appraisal as an exercise in problem solving and solution finding, not criticizing.* Example: Rather than criticizing a financial analyst for turning in reports late, the manager helps the analyst determine why the reports are late and identify ways to better manage her time.
- *Express confidence in a subordinate's ability to improve.* Example: Instead of being skeptical, a first-level manager tells a subordinate that he is confident that the subordinate can increase quality levels.
- *Provide performance feedback both formally and informally.* Example: The staff of a preschool receives feedback from formal performance appraisals twice a year. The school director also provides frequent informal feedback such as complimenting staff members on creative ideas for special projects, noticing when they do a particularly good job handling a difficult child, and pointing out when they provide inadequate supervision.
- *Praise instances of high performance and areas of a job in which a worker excels.* Example: Rather than focusing on just the negative, a manager discusses the areas her subordinate excels in as well as the areas in need of improvement.
- *Avoid personal criticisms and treat subordinates with respect.* Example: An engineering manager acknowledges her subordinates' expertise and treats them as professionals. Even when the manager points out performance problems to subordinates, she refrains from criticizing them personally.
- *Agree to a timetable for performance improvements.* Example: A first-level manager and his subordinate decide to meet again in one month to determine whether quality levels have improved.

In following these guidelines, managers need to remember *why* they are giving performance feedback: to encourage high levels of motivation and performance. Moreover, the information that managers gather through performance appraisal and feedback helps them determine how to distribute pay raises and bonuses.

Pay and Benefits

LO12-5 Explain the issues managers face in determining levels of pay and benefits.

Pay includes employees' base salaries, pay raises, and bonuses and is determined by a number of factors such as characteristics of the organization and the job and levels of performance. Employee *benefits* are based on membership in an organization (and not necessarily on the particular job held) and include sick days, vacation days, and medical and life insurance. In Chapter 13 we discuss how pay can motivate organizational members to perform at a high level, as well as the different kinds of pay plans managers can use to help an organization achieve its goals and gain a competitive advantage. As you will learn, it is important to link pay to behaviors or results that contribute to organizational effectiveness. Next we focus on establishing an organization's pay level and pay structure.

Pay Level

pay level The relative position of an organization's pay incentives in comparison with those of other organizations in the same industry employing similar kinds of workers.

Pay level is a broad comparative concept that refers to how an organization's pay incentives compare, in general, to those of other organizations in the same industry employing similar kinds of workers. Managers must decide if they want to offer relatively high wages, average wages, or relatively low wages. High wages help ensure that an organization is going to be able to recruit, select, and retain high performers, but high wages also raise costs. Low wages give an organization a cost advantage but may undermine the organization's ability to select and recruit high performers and to motivate current employees to perform at a high level. Either of these situations may lead to inferior quality or inadequate customer service.

In determining pay levels, managers should take into account their organization's strategy. A high pay level may prohibit managers from effectively pursuing a low-cost strategy. But a high pay level may be worth the added costs in an organization whose competitive advantage lies in superior quality and excellent customer service.

Pay Structure

pay structure The arrangement of jobs into categories reflecting their relative importance to the organization and its goals, levels of skill required, and other characteristics.

cafeteria-style benefit plan A plan from which employees can choose the benefits they want.

After deciding on a pay level, managers have to establish a pay structure for the different jobs in the organization. A **pay structure** clusters jobs into categories reflecting their relative importance to the organization and its goals, levels of skill required, and other characteristics managers consider important. Pay ranges are established for each job category. Individual jobholders' pay within job categories is then determined by factors such as performance, seniority, and skill levels.

There are some interesting global differences in pay structures. Large corporations based in the United States tend to pay their CEOs and top managers higher salaries than do their European or Japanese counterparts. Also, the pay differential between employees at the bottom of the corporate hierarchy and those higher up is much greater in U.S. companies than in European or Japanese companies.[70] The average CEO in the United States typically earns over 360 times what the average hourly worker earns.[71] Is a pay structure with such a huge pay differential ethical? Shareholders and the public are increasingly asking this very question and asking large corporations to rethink their pay structures.[72] Also troubling are the millions of dollars in severance packages that some CEOs receive when they leave their organizations. When many workers are struggling to find and keep jobs and make ends meet, more and more people are questioning whether it is ethical for some top managers to be making so much money.[73]

Some organizations seek to promote employee wellness by providing on-site fitness centers.

Benefits

Organizations are legally required to provide certain benefits to their employees.

In some organizations, top managers determine which benefits might best suit the employees and organization and offer the same benefit package to all employees. Other organizations, realizing that employees' needs and desires might differ, offer **cafeteria-style benefit plans** that let employees themselves choose the benefits they want. Cafeteria-style benefit plans sometimes help managers deal with employees who feel unfairly treated because they are unable to take advantage of certain benefits available to other employees who, for example, have children. Some organizations have success with cafeteria-style benefit plans; others find them difficult to manage.

The nature of these benefits varies widely around the world. In Europe it is common that health care is provided by the government. Thus, there is little need for private health insurance in nations such as Finland. However, there are other nations where health care relies almost exclusively on private insurance such as the United States. (The recent law passed in 2010 in the United States provides some level of government support for health care, but it is unclear at this stage what the actual impact of that law will be.) In settings such as Asia, one of the greatest motivators and desired benefits is support to pursue education. However, in other nations such as Germany, education is free at state universities, and there are very few private universities. Therefore, a firm has to generate an appropriate set of benefits for each setting.

For working parents, family-friendly benefits are especially attractive, as profiled in the following "Focus on Diversity" box.

Focus on Diversity

Family-Friendly Benefits at Guerra DeBerry Coody

Guerra DeBerry Coody is a small public relations and advertising firm based in San Antonio, Texas.[74] Founded in 1995, the firm has 61 employees and over US$50 million in annual revenues. Recently Guerra DeBerry Coody was named a "Top Small Workplace" by *The Wall Street Journal* and Winning Workplaces, a nonprofit organization. Employees at Guerra DeBerry Coody nominated their employer for this award.[75] In some societies, it is typical to offer family-friendly benefits but not in the United States.

Guerra DeBerry Coody offers family-friendly benefits such as child care.

Guerra DeBerry Coody provides on-site employee child care until employees' children enter kindergarten, with the firm covering 85% of the cost and employees paying US$20 per day per child.[76] Employees can spend time with their children during the workday–employees often eat with their children, play with them, and settle them down for naps. The on-site child care center has a ratio of 1 child care worker for every 2 children enrolled, and around 11 children are currently enrolled. Employees with older children can bring their children to work after school if they wish. Senior account supervisor Patti Tanner sometimes has her two young teenage children come to the office after school. She indicates, "I don't even have any angst about having them here because I know it's completely and totally accepted."[77]

Guerra DeBerry Coody provides other benefits that help employees deal with the multiple demands and obligations in their lives. For example, employees can apply for interest-free loans from the company. Employees also have the options of working from home, telecommuting, and adopting flexible work schedules. Guerra DeBerry Coody provides free health insurance for all its employees, and those with dependents needing coverage can purchase it for around US$125–US$200 per month. The company also contributes to a 401(k) retirement plan for its employees.[78] As Frank Guerra, one of the founding partners of Guerra DeBerry Coody and its current CEO, indicated upon the firm being named a "Top Small Workplace," "With or without this recognition we are so proud that we have the ability to offer our employees a family-friendly work environment where everyone has a vested interest in each other and in the business, caring for one another like family."[79]

LO12-6 Understand the role that labor relations play in the effective management of human resources.

Same-sex domestic partner benefits are also being used to attract and retain valued employees. Gay and lesbian workers are reluctant to work for companies that do not provide the same kinds of benefits for their partners as those provided for partners of the opposite sex.[80]

Labor Relations

Labor relations are the activities managers engage in to ensure that they have effective working relationships with the labor unions that represent their employees' interests.

labor relations The activities managers engage in to ensure that they have effective working relationships with the labor unions that represent their employees' interests.

Unions

Unions exist to represent workers' interests in organizations. Given that managers have more power than rank-and-file workers and that organizations have multiple stakeholders, there is always the potential that managers might take steps that benefit one set of stakeholders such as shareholders while hurting another such as employees. For example, managers may decide to speed up a production line to lower costs and increase production in the hopes of increasing returns to shareholders. Speeding

Members of IG Metall, Germany's largest labor union, protest at the harbor in Hamburg, Germany. The union members were demonstrating against the government's austerity measures.

up the line, however, could hurt employees forced to work at a rapid pace and may increase the risk of injuries. Also, employees receive no additional pay for the extra work they are performing. Unions would represent workers' interests in a scenario such as this one.

Unions and their strength vary widely around the world. In China and typically in all communist countries, there are not independent unions. The workers are represented by the Communist party, so there is not supposed to be a reason for unions. This approach has changed in recent years, and there are now unions for international firms in China. But the unions are typically very passive and have as much to do with having government representation at the factory as representing the workers. In other nations, such as Germany, unions continue to be strong. The Metal Workers Union today has more than 3 million members and is quite active. In Latin American countries, such as Colombia, unions are legal but under constant threat with more than 2,500 union organizers killed since the 1980s.

Unions also organize differently according to their home nation. In Germany unions are formed along industrial lines so that all workers at one firm belong to the same union regardless of their individual occupations. In the United States unions are organized around professions so that in a large plant such as Boeing there are multiple unions including teamsters, electricians, and machinists. In contrast, in other locations such as France, unions principally organize for political issues and organize around political parties. French workers can choose to belong to the communist union or another political party's union group. Thus, a firm operating in different parts of the world needs to understand each setting and the nature of the local labor organization.

Collective Bargaining

collective bargaining Negotiations between labor unions and managers to resolve conflicts and disputes about issues such as working hours, wages, benefits, working conditions, and job security.

Collective bargaining is negotiation between labor unions and managers to resolve conflicts and disputes about important issues such as working hours, wages, working conditions, and job security. Before sitting down with management to negotiate, union members sometimes go on strike to drive home their concerns to managers. Once an agreement that union members support has been reached (sometimes with the help of a neutral third party called a *mediator*), union leaders and managers sign a contract spelling out the terms of the collective bargaining agreement. We discuss conflict and negotiation in depth in Chapter 17, but some brief observations are in order here because collective bargaining is an ongoing consideration in labor relations.

The signing of a contract, for example, does not finish the collective bargaining process. Disagreement and conflicts can arise over the interpretation of the contract. In such cases, a neutral third party called an *arbitrator* is usually called in to resolve the conflict. An important component of a collective bargaining agreement is a *grievance procedure* through which workers who believe they are not being fairly treated are allowed to voice their concerns and have their interests represented by the union. Workers who think they were unjustly fired in violation of a union contract, for example, may file a grievance, have the union represent them, and get their jobs back if an arbitrator agrees with them. Union members sometimes go on strike when managers make decisions that the members think will hurt them and are not in their best interests.

Summary and Review

LO12-1 **STRATEGIC HUMAN RESOURCE MANAGEMENT** Human resource management (HRM) includes all the activities managers engage in to ensure that their organizations can attract, retain, and effectively use human resources. Strategic HRM is the process by which managers design the components of a human resource management system to be consistent with each other, with other elements of organizational architecture, and with the organization's strategies and goals.

LO12-2 **RECRUITMENT AND SELECTION** Before recruiting and selecting employees, managers must engage in human resource planning and job analysis. Human resource planning includes all the activities managers engage in to forecast their current and future needs for human resources. Job analysis is the process of identifying (1) the tasks, duties, and responsibilities that make up a job and (2) the knowledge, skills, and abilities needed to perform the job. Recruitment includes all the activities managers engage in to develop a pool of qualified applicants for open positions. Selection is the process by which managers determine the relative qualifications of job applicants and their potential for performing well in a particular job.

LO12-3 **TRAINING AND DEVELOPMENT** Training focuses on teaching organizational members how to perform effectively in their current jobs. Development focuses on broadening organizational members' knowledge and skills so they are prepared to take on new responsibilities and challenges.

LO12-4 **PERFORMANCE APPRAISAL AND FEEDBACK** Performance appraisal is the evaluation of employees' job performance and contributions to the organization. Performance feedback is the process through which managers share performance appraisal information with their subordinates, give them an opportunity to reflect on their own performance, and develop with them plans for the future. Performance appraisal gives managers useful information for decision making. Performance feedback can encourage high levels of motivation and performance.

LO12-5 **PAY AND BENEFITS** Pay level is the relative position of an organization's pay incentives in comparison with those of other organizations in the same industry employing similar workers. A pay structure clusters jobs into categories according to their relative importance to the organization and its goals, the levels of skill required, and other characteristics. Pay ranges are then established for each job category. Organizations are legally required to provide certain benefits to their employees; other benefits are provided at the discretion of employers.

LO12-6 **LABOR RELATIONS** Labor relations include all the activities managers engage in to ensure that they have effective working relationships with the labor unions that represent their employees' interests. The National Labor Relations Board oversees union activity. Collective bargaining is the process through which labor unions and managers resolve conflicts and disputes and negotiate agreements.

Management in Action

Topics for Discussion and Action

Discussion

1. Discuss why it is important for human resource management systems to be in sync with an organization's strategy and goals and with each other. **[LO12-1]**
2. Discuss why training and development are ongoing activities for all organizations. **[LO12-3]**
3. Describe the type of development activities you think middle managers are most in need of. **[LO12-3]**
4. Evaluate the pros and cons of 360-degree performance appraisals and feedback. Would you like your performance to be appraised in this manner? Why or why not? **[LO12-4]**
5. Discuss why two restaurants in the same community might have different pay levels. **[LO12-5]**
6. Explain why union membership is becoming more diverse. **[LO12-6]**

Action

7. Interview a manager in a local organization to determine how that organization recruits and selects employees. **[LO12-2]**

Building Management Skills

Analyzing Human Resource Systems **[LO12-1, 12-2, 12-3, 12-4, 12-5]**

Think about your current job or a job you have had in the past. If you have never had a job, interview a friend or family member who is currently working. Answer the following questions about the job you have chosen:

1. How are people recruited and selected for this job? Are the recruitment and selection procedures the organization uses effective or ineffective? Why?
2. What training and development do people who hold this job receive? Are the training and development appropriate? Why or why not?
3. How is performance of this job appraised? Does performance feedback contribute to motivation and high performance on this job?
4. What levels of pay and benefits are provided on this job? Are these levels appropriate? Why or why not?

Managing Ethically **[LO12-4, 12-5]**

Accor is the world's largest hotel chain. The company includes a variety of brands from the low-end Etap to the high-end Mercure. The firm has more than 150,000 employees worldwide.

Questions

1. Is it appropriate to pay a manager of the low-end hotel brand in a firm like Accor less than at the high-end hotel if the number of rooms at both hotels is the same?
2. Is it appropriate to pay managers in a worldwide organization less if they reside in a low-income country (i.e., should a manager earn less in Guatemala than in France)?
3. What would happen if you move a manager from France to Guatemala? Should you change their pay?

Small Group Breakout Exercise [LO12-1, 12-2, 12-3, 12-4, 12-5]

Building a Human Resource Management System

Form groups of three or four people, and appoint one group member as the spokesperson who will communicate your findings to the class when called on by the instructor. Then discuss the following scenario:

You and your three partners are engineers who minored in business at college and have decided to start a consulting business. Your goal is to provide manufacturing process engineering and other engineering services to large and small organizations. You forecast that there will be an increased use of outsourcing for these activities. You discussed with managers in several large organizations the services you plan to offer, and they expressed considerable interest. You have secured funding to start your business and now are building the HRM system. Your human resource planning suggests that you need to hire between five and eight experienced engineers with good communication skills, two clerical/secretarial workers, and two MBAs who between them have financial, accounting, and human resource skills. You are striving to develop your human resources in a way that will enable your new business to prosper.

1. Describe the steps you will take to recruit and select (a) the engineers, (b) the clerical/secretarial workers, and (c) the MBAs.
2. Describe the training and development the engineers, the clerical/secretarial workers, and the MBAs will receive.
3. Describe how you will appraise the performance of each group of employees and how you will provide feedback.
4. Describe the pay level and pay structure of your consulting firm.

Exploring the World Wide Web [LO12-2]

Go to www.net-temps.com, a Web site geared toward temporary employment. Imagine that you have to take a year off from college and are seeking a one-year position. Guided by your own interests, use this Web site to learn about your options and possible employment opportunities.

1. What are the potential advantages of online job searching and recruiting? What are the potential disadvantages?
2. Would you ever rely on a Web site like this to help you find a position? Why or why not?

Be the Manager [LO12-4]

You are Walter Michaels and have just received some disturbing feedback. You are the director of human resources for Maxi Vision Inc., a medium-size window and glass door manufacturer. You recently initiated a 360-degree performance appraisal system for all middle and upper managers at Maxi Vision, including yourself but excluding the most senior executives and the top management team.

You were eagerly awaiting the feedback you would receive from the managers who report to you; you had recently implemented several important initiatives that affected them and their subordinates, including a complete overhaul of the organization's performance appraisal system. While the managers who report to you were evaluated based on 360-degree appraisals, their subordinates were evaluated using a 20-question BARS scale you recently created that focuses on behaviors. Conducted annually, appraisals are an important input into pay raise and bonus decisions.

You were so convinced that the new performance appraisal procedures were highly effective that you hoped your own subordinates would mention them in their feedback to you. And boy did they! You were amazed to learn that the managers *and* their subordinates thought the new BARS scales were unfair, inappropriate, and a waste of time. In fact, the managers' feedback to you was that their own performance was suffering, based on the 360-degree appraisals they received, because their subordinates hated the new appraisal system and partially blamed their bosses, who were part of management. Some managers even admitted giving all their subordinates approximately the same scores on the scales so their pay raises and bonuses would not be affected by their performance appraisals.

You couldn't believe your eyes when you read these comments. You spent so much time developing what you thought was the ideal rating scale for this group of employees. Evidently, for some unknown reason, they wouldn't give it a chance. Your own supervisor is aware of these complaints and said that it was a top priority for you to fix "this mess" (with the implication that you were responsible for creating it). What are you going to do?

CHAPTER 13

Motivation and Performance

Learning Objectives

After studying this chapter, you should be able to:

LO13-1 Explain what motivation is and why managers need to be concerned about it.

LO13-2 Describe from the perspectives of expectancy theory and equity theory what managers should do to have a highly motivated workforce.

LO13-3 Explain how goals and needs motivate people and what kinds of goals are especially likely to result in high performance.

LO13-4 Identify the motivation lessons that managers can learn from operant conditioning theory and social learning theory.

LO13-5 Explain why and how managers can use pay as a major motivation tool.

A MANAGER'S CHALLENGE

Keeping Employees Motivated at Portugal Telecom

Portugal Telecom is a telecommunications firm with a long history of fostering innovation and steady growth. For example, the firm was among the first in the world to offer prepaid cell phone service. Recognizing the world-class competition it faces and the need to change how it operates, Portugal Telecom is prepared to meet the challenge with several initiatives. Most importantly, according to its CEO Zeinal Bava, the company places a strong focus on fostering a culture that nurtures innovation in its employees.

One way the company motivates workers is by utilizing an internal communications system. The system uses teaser ads and emails to build interest among employees to increase their innovation efforts. Employees are rewarded not only for originating an idea but also for evaluating, critiquing, and/or improving upon an idea.

To reward employees, Portugal Telecom created its own currency called "Opens." Employees can accumulate Opens and redeem them for significant prizes. For example, in 2004 employees could redeem their Opens for a ticket to the company's courtesy room at the official venue of the European Soccer Championship or a similar room at the Soccer World Cup. Since soccer is Portugal's national sport, these rewards were particularly valuable to employees.

Workers can also invest Opens in innovation projects. The company wants to seek the wisdom of its employees. However, the firm realizes not everyone can generate an idea; highly creative individuals are more likely to provide such advances. As a result, Portugal Telecomm allows employees to invest their Opens in good innovative ideas. Individuals decide which concept is best and invest their Opens in those ideas. If the idea is successful, their Opens are

Portugal Telecom's commitment to fostering innovation among its employees has paid off for the telecommunications firm. By creating an internal communications system that uses teaser ads and emails to build interest, the company motivates employees to increase their innovation efforts.

multiplied but if the idea fails, the employees face the loss of their investment. Thus workers view their choices as important and having consequences, and at the same time the company gains more value through the Opens investment as a vote of confidence in good and innovative ideas. Portugal Telecom's communication system keeps everyone informed and even motivates the previously unmotivated, since the rewards might be a great seat at a soccer game or a paid vacation.[1]

Overview

Even with the best strategy in place and an appropriate organizational architecture, an organization will be effective only if its members are motivated to perform at a high level. Zeinal Bava of Portugal Telecom in "A Manager's Challenge" clearly realizes this. One reason why leading is such an important managerial activity is that it entails ensuring that each member of an organization is motivated to perform highly and help the organization achieve its goals. When managers are effective, the outcome of the leading process is a highly motivated workforce. A key challenge for managers of organizations both large and small is to encourage employees to perform at a high level.

In this chapter we describe what motivation is, where it comes from, and why managers need to promote high levels of it for an organization to be effective and achieve its goals. We examine important theories of motivation: expectancy theory, need theories, equity theory, goal-setting theory, and learning theories. Each gives managers important insights about how to motivate organizational members. The theories are complementary in that each focuses on a different aspect of motivation. Considering all the theories together helps managers gain a rich understanding of the many issues and problems involved in encouraging high levels of motivation throughout an organization. Last, we consider the use of pay as a motivation tool. By the end of this chapter you will understand what it takes to have a highly motivated workforce.

The Nature of Motivation

LO13-1 Explain what motivation is and why managers need to be concerned about it.

motivation Psychological forces that determine the direction of a person's behavior in an organization, a person's level of effort, and a person's level of persistence.

intrinsically motivated behavior Behavior that is performed for its own sake.

Motivation may be defined as psychological forces that determine the direction of a person's behavior in an organization, a person's level of effort, and a person's level of persistence in the face of obstacles.[2] The *direction of a person's behavior* refers to the many possible behaviors a person could engage in. For example, employees at Portugal Telecom are encouraged to be creative and meet customers' needs. *Effort* refers to how hard people work. *Persistence* refers to whether, when faced with roadblocks and obstacles, people keep trying or give up. Setbacks and obstacles are part of research and development work.

Motivation is central to management because it explains *why* people behave the way they do in organizations.[3] Motivation also explains why a waiter is polite or rude and why a kindergarten teacher really tries to get children to enjoy learning or just goes through the motions. It explains why some managers truly put their organizations' best interests first whereas others are more concerned with maximizing their salaries and why—more generally—some workers put forth twice as much effort as others.

Motivation can come from *intrinsic* or *extrinsic* sources. **Intrinsically motivated behavior** is behavior that is performed for its own sake; the source of motivation is actually performing the behavior, and motivation comes from doing the work itself. Many managers are intrinsically motivated; they derive a sense of accomplishment and achievement from helping the organization achieve its goals and gain competitive advantages. Jobs that are interesting and challenging or high on the five characteristics described by the job characteristics model (see Chapter 10) are more likely to lead to intrinsic motivation than are jobs that are boring or do not use a person's skills and abilities. An elementary school teacher who really enjoys teaching children, a computer programmer who loves solving programming problems, and a commercial photographer who relishes taking creative photographs are all intrinsically motivated. For these individuals, motivation comes from performing their jobs–teaching children, finding bugs in computer programs, and taking pictures.

extrinsically motivated behavior Behavior that is performed to acquire material or social rewards or to avoid punishment.

Extrinsically motivated behavior is behavior that is performed to acquire material or social rewards or to avoid punishment; the source of motivation is the consequences of the behavior, not the behavior itself. A car salesperson who is motivated by receiving a commission on all cars sold, a lawyer who is motivated by the high salary and status that go along with the job, and a factory worker who is motivated by the opportunity to earn a secure income are all extrinsically motivated. Their motivation comes from the consequences they receive as a result of their work behaviors.

Child care often attracts those with a highly intrinsic motivation, such as the preschool worker above.

People can be intrinsically motivated, extrinsically motivated, or both intrinsically and extrinsically motivated.[4] A top manager who derives a sense of accomplishment and achievement from managing a large corporation and strives to reach year-end targets to obtain a hefty bonus is both intrinsically and extrinsically motivated. Similarly, a nurse who enjoys helping and taking care of patients and is motivated by having a secure job with good benefits is both intrinsically and extrinsically motivated. At Portugal Telecom, employees are both extrinsically motivated, because of the opportunity to receive rewards, and intrinsically motivated, because of the opportunity to do interesting work. Whether workers are intrinsically motivated, extrinsically motivated, or both depends on a wide variety of factors: (1) workers' own personal characteristics (such as their personalities, abilities, values, attitudes, and needs), (2) the nature of their jobs (such as whether they have been enriched or where they are on the five core characteristics of the job characteristics model), and (3) the nature of the organization (such as its structure, its culture, its control systems, its human resource management system, and the ways in which rewards such as pay are distributed to employees).

prosocially motivated behavior Behavior that is performed to benefit or help others.

In addition to being intrinsically or extrinsically motivated, some people are prosocially motivated by their work.[5] **Prosocially motivated behavior** is behavior that is performed to benefit or help others.[6] Behavior can be prosocially motivated in addition to being extrinsically and/or intrinsically motivated. An elementary school teacher who not only enjoys the process of teaching young children (has high intrinsic motivation) but also has a strong desire to give children the best learning experience possible and help those with learning disabilities overcome their challenges, and who keeps up with the latest research on child development and teaching methods in an effort to continually improve the effectiveness of his teaching, has high prosocial motivation in addition to high intrinsic motivation. A surgeon who specializes in organ transplants and enjoys the challenge of performing complex operations, has a strong desire to help her patients regain their health and extend their lives through successful organ transplants, and also is motivated by the relatively high income she earns has high intrinsic, prosocial, and extrinsic motivation. Recent preliminary research suggests that when workers have high prosocial motivation, also having high intrinsic motivation can be especially beneficial for job performance.[7]

outcome Anything a person gets from a job or organization.

Regardless of whether people are intrinsically, extrinsically, or prosocially motivated, they join and are motivated to work in organizations to obtain certain outcomes. An **outcome** is anything a person gets from a job or organization. Some outcomes, such as autonomy, responsibility, a feeling of accomplishment, and the pleasure of doing interesting or enjoyable work, result in intrinsically motivated behavior. Outcomes such as improving the lives or well-being of other people and doing good by

Figure 13.1
The Motivation Equation

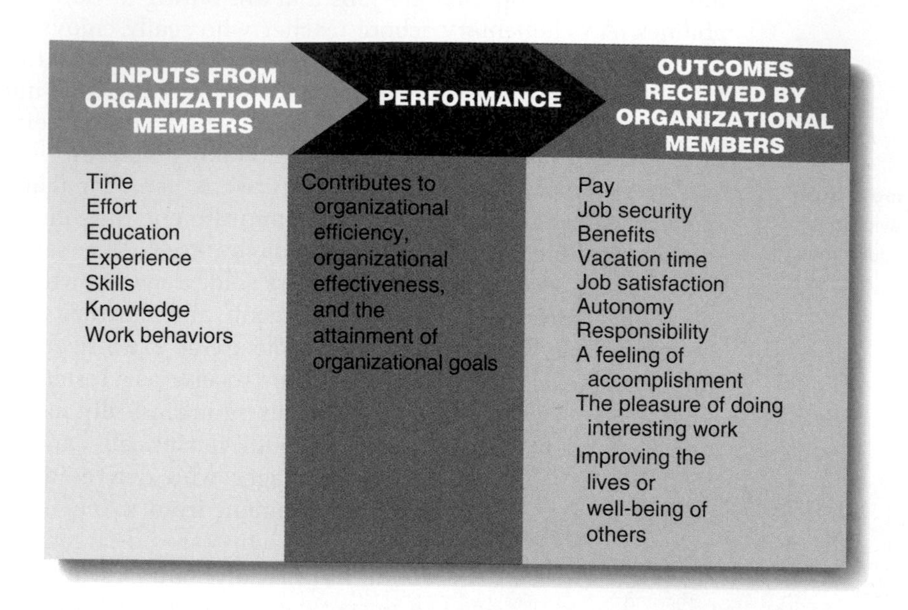

helping others result in prosocially motivated behavior. Other outcomes, such as pay, job security, benefits, and vacation time, result in extrinsically motivated behavior.

input Anything a person contributes to his or her job or organization.

Organizations hire people to obtain important inputs. An **input** is anything a person contributes to the job or organization, such as time, effort, education, experience, skills, knowledge, and actual work behaviors. Inputs such as these are necessary for an organization to achieve its goals. Managers strive to motivate members of an organization to contribute inputs–through their behavior, effort, and persistence–that help the organization achieve its goals. How do managers do this? They ensure that members of an organization obtain the outcomes they desire when they make valuable contributions to the organization. Managers use outcomes to motivate people to contribute their inputs to the organization. Giving people outcomes when they contribute inputs and perform well aligns the interests of employees with the goals of the organization as a whole because when employees do what is good for the organization, they personally benefit.

LO13-2 Describe from the perspectives of expectancy theory and equity theory what managers should do to have a highly motivated workforce.

This alignment between employees and organizational goals as a whole can be described by the motivation equation depicted in Figure 13.1. Managers seek to ensure that people are motivated to contribute important inputs to the organization, that these inputs are put to good use or focused in the direction of high performance, and that high performance results in workers' obtaining the outcomes they desire.

expectancy theory The theory that motivation will be high when workers believe that high levels of effort lead to high performance and high performance leads to the attainment of desired outcomes.

Each of the theories of motivation discussed in this chapter focuses on one or more aspects of this equation. Each theory focuses on a different set of issues that managers need to address to have a highly motivated workforce. Together, the theories provide a comprehensive set of guidelines for managers to follow to promote high levels of employee motivation. Effective managers, such as Zeinal Bava in "A Manager's Challenge," tend to follow many of these guidelines, whereas ineffective managers often fail to follow them and seem to have trouble motivating organizational members.

Expectancy Theory

Expectancy theory, formulated by Victor H. Vroom in the 1960s, posits that motivation is high when workers believe that high levels of effort lead to high performance and high performance leads to the attainment of desired outcomes. Expectancy theory is one of the most popular theories of work motivation

Figure 13.2
Expectancy, Instrumentality, and Valence

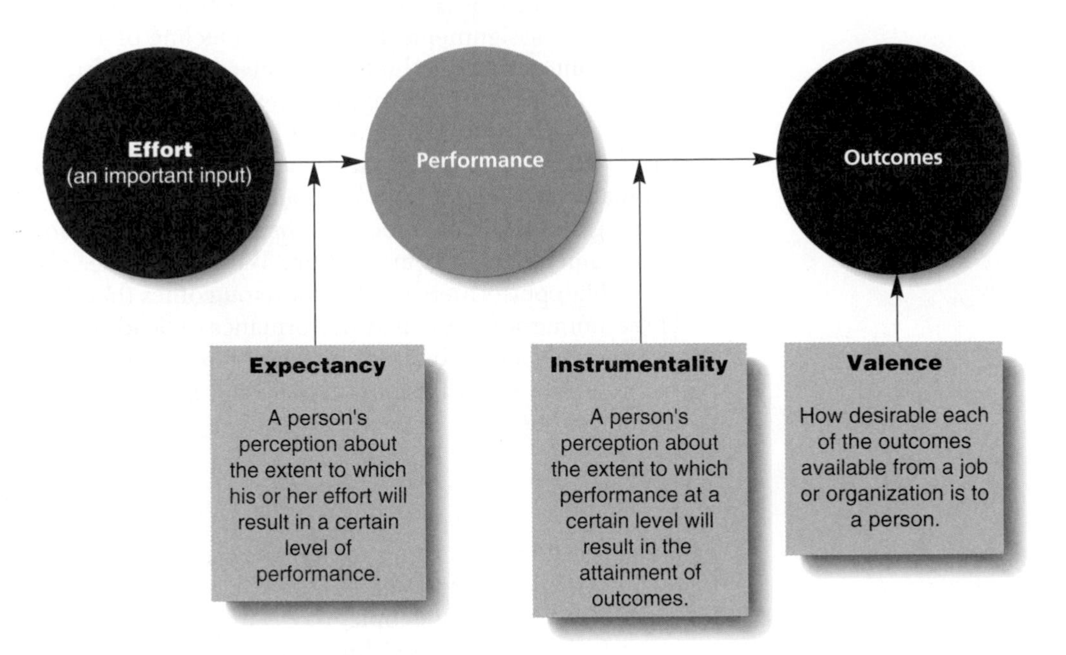

because it focuses on all three parts of the motivation equation: inputs, performance, and outcomes. Expectancy theory identifies three major factors that determine a person's motivation: *expectancy, instrumentality,* and *valence* (see Figure 13.2).[8]

Expectancy

expectancy In expectancy theory, a perception about the extent to which effort results in a certain level of performance.

Expectancy is a person's perception about the extent to which effort (an input) results in a certain level of performance. A person's level of expectancy determines whether he or she believes that a high level of effort results in a high level of performance. People are motivated to put forth a lot of effort on their jobs only if they think that their effort will pay off in high performance–that is, if they have high expectancy. Think about how motivated you would be to study for a test if you thought that no matter how hard you tried, you would get a D. Think about how motivated a marketing manager would be who thought that no matter how hard he or she worked, there was no way to increase sales of an unpopular product. In these cases, expectancy is low, so overall motivation is also low.

Members of an organization are motivated to put forth a high level of effort only if they think that doing so leads to high performance.[9] In other words, in order for people's motivation to be high, expectancy must be high. Thus, in attempting to influence motivation, managers need to make sure their subordinates believe that if they do try hard, they can actually succeed. One way managers can boost expectancies is through expressing confidence in their subordinates' capabilities.

In addition to expressing confidence in subordinates, other ways for managers to boost subordinates' expectancy levels and motivation is by providing training so people have the expertise needed for high performance and increasing their levels of autonomy and responsibility as they gain experience so they have the freedom to do what it takes to perform at a high level.

Instrumentality

instrumentality In expectancy theory, a perception about the extent to which performance results in the attainment of outcomes.

Expectancy captures a person's perceptions about the relationship between effort and performance. **Instrumentality,** the second major concept in expectancy theory, is a person's perception about the extent to which performance at a certain level results in the attainment of outcomes (see Figure 13.2). According to expectancy theory, employees are motivated to perform at a high level only if they think high performance will lead to (or is *instrumental* for attaining) outcomes such as pay, job security, interesting job assignments, bonuses, or a feeling of accomplishment. In other words, instrumentalities must be high for motivation to be high–people must perceive that because of their high performance they will receive outcomes.[10]

Managers promote high levels of instrumentality when they link performance to desired outcomes. In addition, managers must clearly communicate this linkage to subordinates. By making sure that outcomes available in an organization are distributed to organizational members on the basis of their performance, managers promote high instrumentality and motivation. When outcomes are linked to performance in this way, high performers receive more outcomes than low performers.

These immigrants see high performance as leading to many important outcomes such as income, a comfortable existence, family security, and the autonomy provided by working in a small business. Their high instrumentality contributes to their high motivation to succeed.

Valence

Although all members of an organization must have high expectancies and instrumentalities, expectancy theory acknowledges that people differ in their preferences for outcomes. For many people, pay is the most important outcome of working. For others, a feeling of accomplishment or enjoying one's work is more important than pay. The term **valence** refers to how desirable each of the outcomes available from a job or organization is to a person. To motivate organizational members, managers need to determine which outcomes have high valence for them–are highly desired–and make sure that those outcomes are provided when members perform at a high level. Providing employees with highly valent outcomes not only can contribute to high levels of motivation but also has the potential to reduce turnover.

valence In expectancy theory, how desirable each of the outcomes available from a job or organization is to a person.

Bringing It All Together

According to expectancy theory, high motivation results from high levels of expectancy, instrumentality, and valence (see Figure 13.3). If any one of these factors is low, motivation is likely to be low. No matter how tightly desired outcomes are linked to performance, if a person thinks it is practically impossible to perform at a high level,

Figure 13.3
Expectancy Theory

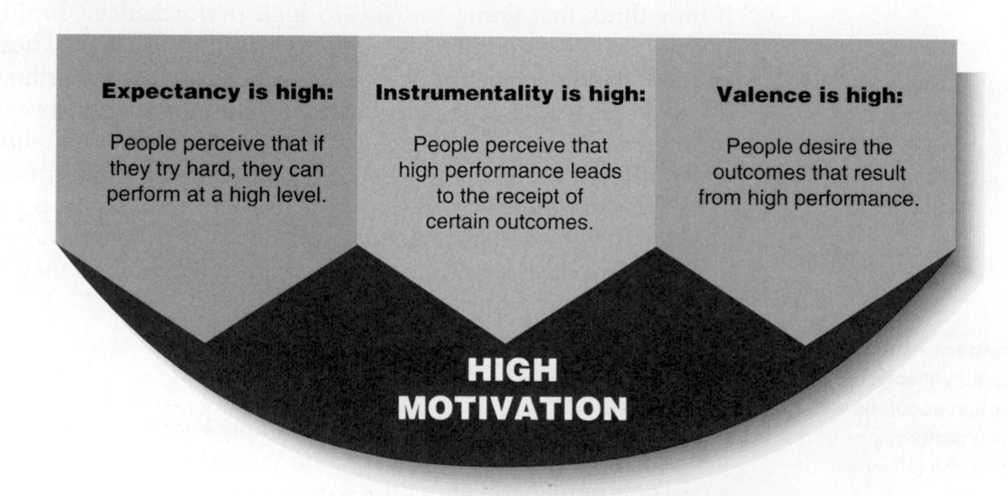

motivation to perform at a high level will be exceedingly low. Similarly, if a person does not think outcomes are linked to high performance, or if a person does not desire the outcomes that are linked to high performance, motivation to perform at a high level will be low.

Effective managers realize the importance of high levels of expectancy, instrumentality, and valence and take concrete steps to ensure that their employees are highly motivated. This has certainly been the case at Nokia as profiled in the following "Management Insight" box.

Management Insight

Motivating Employees at Nokia

With more than 50,000 employees at 16 factories in nine countries, and research and development facilities in 11 countries, Finland-based Nokia is the largest maker of mobile telephones in the world. Nokia's people policies have played a key role in helping the company reach its 40% share of the global handset market and industry-leading profit margins of 20 to 25%, at a time of technological change and intense competition from Asian manufacturers. Central to this success are the firm's employees and their motivation.

Nokia Employee Value Proposition summarizes the firm's commitment to its employees. The firm describes this proposition as "a concrete employment offering for each employee from the very first Nokia day onwards." It comprises four elements to motivate and engage the employee and maintain his or her satisfaction and well-being at work. The first element is called the Nokia way and values. The firm stresses it is a flat organization that wishes to ensure employees respect each other and also provide high service to their customers. Performance-based rewards are the second motivational element. Nokia's total compensation package is tailored to each country and typically consists of benefits such as an annual base salary, incentives, bonuses, possible participation in an equity plan, and other local benefits. Nokia's total compensation is based on a pay-for-performance philosophy. Results through consistent performance and proven, relevant competencies are rewarded.

Two Nokia employees talk to a local woman about her cell phone usage at the Budaburam Refugee Camp in Ghana. Nokia's commitment to ensuring employees' professional and personal growth is an integral part of motivating employees to be successful.

The third element is to ensure employees' professional and personal growth. Nokia employees are encouraged to create their own development plans, take part in on-the-job training, and take advantage of learning opportunities provided by the company. The Nokia performance-management system, named Investing in People (IIP), is closely aligned to the company's strategy and planning processes. It involves formalized discussions between employees and their managers twice a year. Employees are encouraged to "own" their IIP, to understand what is expected of them, and how their individual achievements support the company's overall strategy.

Finally Nokia strives for their employees to have a work–life balance. The various aspects may alter by country according to local needs, legislation, employment market, and common practices. Typically, they include telecommuting, mobile working, flexible working hours, sabbaticals, study leave, health-care services, and recreational activities. The Nokia Helping Hands volunteering initiative gives employees the chance to contribute time, effort and expertise in a global network of community causes.[11]

LO13-3 Explain how goals and needs motivate people and what kinds of goals are especially likely to result in high performance.

Need Theories

need A requirement or necessity for survival and well-being.

need theories Theories of motivation that focus on what needs people are trying to satisfy at work and what outcomes will satisfy those needs.

A **need** is a requirement or necessity for survival and well-being. The basic premise of **need theories** is that people are motivated to obtain outcomes at work that will satisfy their needs. Need theory complements expectancy theory by exploring in depth which outcomes motivate people to perform at a high level. Need theories suggest that to motivate a person to contribute valuable inputs to a job and perform at a high level, a manager must determine what needs the person is trying to satisfy at work and ensure that the person receives outcomes that help to satisfy those needs when the person performs at a high level and helps the organization achieve its goals.

There are several need theories. Here we discuss Abraham Maslow's hierarchy of needs, Clayton Alderfer's ERG theory, Frederick Herzberg's motivator-hygiene theory, and David McClelland's needs for achievement, affiliation, and power. These theories describe needs that people try to satisfy at work. In doing so, they give managers insights about what outcomes motivate members of an organization to perform at a high level and contribute inputs to help the organization achieve its goals.

Maslow's hierarchy of needs An arrangement of five basic needs that, according to Maslow, motivate behavior. Maslow proposed that the lowest level of unmet needs is the prime motivator and that only one level of needs is motivational at a time.

Maslow's Hierarchy of Needs

Psychologist Abraham Maslow proposed that all people seek to satisfy five basic kinds of needs: physiological needs, safety needs, belongingness needs, esteem needs, and self-actualization needs (see Table 13.1).[12] He suggested that these needs constitute a **hierarchy of needs,** with the most basic or compelling needs–physiological and safety needs–at the bottom. Maslow argued that these lowest-level needs must be met before a person strives to satisfy needs higher up in the hierarchy, such as self-esteem needs. Once a need is satisfied, Maslow proposed, it ceases to operate as a source of motivation.

Table 13.1
Maslow's Hierarchy of Needs

	Needs	Description	Examples of How Managers Can Help People Satisfy These Needs at Work
Highest-level needs	**Self-actualization needs**	The needs to realize one's full potential as a human being.	By giving people the opportunity to use their skills and abilities to the fullest extent possible.
↑	**Esteem needs**	The needs to feel good about oneself and one's capabilities, to be respected by others, and to receive recognition and appreciation.	By granting promotions and recognizing accomplishments.
	Belongingness needs	Needs for social interaction, friendship, affection, and love.	By promoting good interpersonal relations and organizing social functions such as company picnics and holiday parties.
↓	**Safety needs**	Needs for security, stability, and a safe environment.	By providing job security, adequate medical benefits, and safe working conditions.
Lowest-level needs (most basic or compelling)	**Physiological needs**	Basic needs for things such as food, water, and shelter that must be met in order for a person to survive.	By providing a level of pay that enables a person to buy food and clothing and have adequate housing.

The lowest level of unsatisfied needs motivates behavior; once this level of needs is satisfied, a person tries to satisfy the needs at the next level.

The lowest level of *unmet* needs in the hierarchy is the prime motivator of behavior; if and when this level is satisfied, needs at the next highest level in the hierarchy motivate behavior.

Although this theory identifies needs that are likely to be important sources of motivation for many people, research does not support Maslow's contention that there is a need hierarchy or his notion that only one level of needs is motivational at a time.[13] Nevertheless, a key conclusion can be drawn from Maslow's theory: People try to satisfy different needs at work. To have a motivated workforce, managers must determine which needs employees are trying to satisfy in organizations and then make sure that individuals receive outcomes that satisfy their needs when they perform at a high level and contribute to organizational effectiveness. By doing this, managers align the interests of individual members with the interests of the organization as a whole. By doing what is good for the organization (that is, performing at a high level), employees receive outcomes that satisfy their needs.

In our increasingly global economy, managers must realize that citizens of different countries might differ in the needs they seek to satisfy through work.[14] Some research suggests, for example, that people in Greece and Japan are especially motivated by safety needs and that people in Sweden, Norway, and Denmark are motivated by belongingness needs.[15] In less developed countries with low standards of living, physiological and safety needs are likely to be the prime motivators of behavior. As countries become wealthier and have higher standards of living, needs related to personal growth and accomplishment (such as esteem and self-actualization) become important motivators of behavior.

Alderfer's ERG Theory

Alderfer's ERG theory The theory that three universal needs—for existence, relatedness, and growth—constitute a hierarchy of needs and motivate behavior. Alderfer proposed that needs at more than one level can be motivational at the same time.

Clayton **Alderfer's ERG theory** collapsed the five categories of needs in Maslow's hierarchy into three universal categories–existence, relatedness, and growth–also arranged in a hierarchy (see Table 13.2). Alderfer agreed with Maslow that as lower-level needs become satisfied, a person seeks to satisfy higher-level needs. Unlike Maslow, however, Alderfer believed that a person can be motivated by needs at more than one level at the same time. A cashier in a supermarket, for example, may be motivated by both existence needs and relatedness needs. The existence needs motivate the cashier to come to work regularly and not make mistakes so his job will be secure and he will be able to pay his rent and buy food. The relatedness needs

Table 13.2
Alderfer's ERG Theory

	Needs	Description	Examples of How Managers Can Help People Satisfy These Needs at Work
Highest-level needs ↑	**Growth needs**	The needs for self-development and creative and productive work.	By allowing people to continually improve their skills and abilities and engage in meaningful work.
↕	**Relatedness needs**	The needs to have good interpersonal relations, to share thoughts and feelings, and to have open two-way communication.	By promoting good interpersonal relations and by providing accurate feedback.
↓ **Lowest-level needs**	**Existence needs**	Basic needs for food, water, clothing, shelter, and a secure and safe environment.	By promoting enough pay to provide for the basic necessities of life and safe working conditions.

As lower-level needs are satisfied, a person is motivated to satisfy higher-level needs. When a person is unable to satisfy higher-level needs (or is frustrated), motivation to satisfy lower-level needs increases.

motivate the cashier to become friends with some of the other cashiers and have a good relationship with the store manager. Alderfer also suggested that when people experience *need frustration* or are unable to satisfy needs at a certain level, they will focus more intently on satisfying the needs at the next lowest level in the hierarchy.[16]

As with Maslow's theory, research does not support some of the specific ideas outlined in ERG theory, such as the existence of the three-level need hierarchy that Alderfer proposed.[17] However, for managers, the important message from ERG theory is the same as that from Maslow's theory: Determine what needs your subordinates are trying to satisfy at work, and make sure they receive outcomes that satisfy these needs when they perform at a high level to help the organization achieve its goals.

Herzberg's Motivator-Hygiene Theory

Adopting an approach different from Maslow's and Alderfer's, Frederick Herzberg focused on two factors: (1) outcomes that can lead to high levels of motivation and job satisfaction and (2) outcomes that can prevent people from being dissatisfied. According to **Herzberg's motivator-hygiene theory,** people have two sets of needs or requirements: motivator needs and hygiene needs.[18] *Motivator needs* are related to the nature of the work itself and how challenging it is. Outcomes such as interesting work, autonomy, responsibility, being able to grow and develop on the job, and a sense of accomplishment and achievement help to satisfy motivator needs. To have a highly motivated and satisfied workforce, Herzberg suggested, managers should take steps to ensure that employees' motivator needs are being met.

Herzberg's motivator-hygiene theory A need theory that distinguishes between motivator needs (related to the nature of the work itself) and hygiene needs (related to the physical and psychological context in which the work is performed) and proposes that motivator needs must be met for motivation and job satisfaction to be high.

Hygiene needs are related to the physical and psychological context in which the work is performed. Hygiene needs are satisfied by outcomes such as pleasant and comfortable working conditions, pay, job security, good relationships with coworkers, and effective supervision. According to Herzberg, when hygiene needs are not met, workers are dissatisfied, and when hygiene needs are met, workers are not dissatisfied. Satisfying hygiene needs, however, does not result in high levels of motivation or even high levels of job satisfaction. For motivation and job satisfaction to be high, motivator needs must be met.

Many research studies have tested Herzberg's propositions, and, by and large, the theory fails to receive support.[19] Nevertheless, Herzberg's formulations have contributed to our understanding of motivation in at least two ways. First, Herzberg helped to focus researchers' and managers' attention on the important distinction between intrinsic motivation (related to motivator needs) and extrinsic motivation (related to hygiene needs), covered earlier in the chapter. Second, his theory prompted researchers and managers to study how jobs could be designed or redesigned so they are intrinsically motivating.

McClelland's Needs for Achievement, Affiliation, and Power

need for achievement The extent to which an individual has a strong desire to perform challenging tasks well and to meet personal standards for excellence.

need for affiliation The extent to which an individual is concerned about establishing and maintaining good interpersonal relations, being liked, and having the people around him or her get along with each other.

need for power The extent to which an individual desires to control or influence others.

Psychologist David McClelland extensively researched the needs for achievement, affiliation, and power.[20] The **need for achievement** is the extent to which an individual has a strong desire to perform challenging tasks well and to meet personal standards for excellence. People with a high need for achievement often set clear goals for themselves and like to receive performance feedback. The **need for affiliation** is the extent to which an individual is concerned about establishing and maintaining good interpersonal relations, being liked, and having the people around him or her get along with each other. The **need for power** is the extent to which an individual desires to control or influence others.[21]

Although each of these needs is present in each of us to some degree, their importance in the workplace depends on the position one occupies. For example, research suggests that high needs for achievement and for power are assets for first-line and middle managers and that a high need for power is especially important for upper managers.[22] One study found that U.S. presidents with a relatively high need for power tended to be especially effective during their terms of office.[23] A high need for affiliation may not always be desirable in managers and other leaders because it might lead them to try too hard to be liked by others (including subordinates) rather than doing all they can to ensure that performance is as high as it can and should be. Although most research on these needs has been done in the United States, some studies suggest that the findings may be applicable to people in other countries as well, such as India and New Zealand.[24]

Other Needs

Clearly more needs motivate workers than the needs described by these four theories. For example, more and more workers are feeling the need for work–life balance and time to take care of their loved ones while simultaneously being highly motivated at work. Interestingly enough, recent research suggests that being exposed to nature (even just being able to see some trees from an office window) has many salutary effects, and a lack of such exposure can impair well-being and performance.[25] Thus having some time during the day when one can at least see nature may be another important need. Managers of successful companies often strive to ensure that as many of their valued employees' needs as possible are satisfied in the workplace.

Equity Theory

LO13-2 Describe from the perspectives of expectancy theory and equity theory what managers should do to have a highly motivated workforce.

equity theory A theory of motivation that focuses on people's perceptions of the fairness of their work outcomes relative to their work inputs.

equity The justice, impartiality, and fairness to which all organizational members are entitled.

Equity theory is a theory of motivation that concentrates on people's perceptions of the fairness of their work *outcomes* relative to, or in proportion to, their work *inputs*. Equity theory complements expectancy and need theories by focusing on how people perceive the relationship between the outcomes they receive from their jobs and organizations and the inputs they contribute. Equity theory was formulated in the 1960s by J. Stacy Adams, who stressed that what is important in determining motivation is the *relative* rather than the *absolute* levels of outcomes a person receives and inputs a person contributes. Specifically, motivation is influenced by the comparison of one's own outcome–input ratio with the outcome–input ratio of a referent.[26] The *referent* could be another person or a group of people who are perceived to be similar to oneself; the referent also could be oneself in a previous job or one's expectations about what outcome–input ratios should be. In a comparison of one's own outcome–input ratio to a referent's ratio, one's *perceptions* of outcomes and inputs (not any objective indicator of them) are key.

Equity

Equity exists when a person perceives his or her own outcome–input ratio to be equal to a referent's outcome–input ratio. Under conditions of equity (see Table 13.3), if a referent receives more outcomes than you receive, the referent contributes proportionally more inputs to the organization, so his or her outcome–input ratio still equals your ratio. Maria Sanchez and Claudia King, for example, both work in a shoe store in a large mall. Sanchez is paid more per hour than King but also contributes more inputs, including being responsible for some of the store's bookkeeping, closing the store, and periodically depositing cash in the bank. When King compares her outcome–input ratio to Sanchez's (her referent's), she perceives the ratios to be equitable because Sanchez's higher level of pay (an outcome) is proportional to her higher level of inputs (bookkeeping, closing the store, and going to the bank).

Similarly, under conditions of equity, if you receive more outcomes than a referent, your inputs are perceived to be proportionally higher. Continuing with our example, when Sanchez compares her outcome–input ratio to King's (her referent's) ratio, she

Table 13.3
Equity Theory

Condition	Person		Referent	Example
Equity	Outcomes / Inputs	=	Outcomes / Inputs	An engineer perceives that he contributes more inputs (time and effort) and receives proportionally more outcomes (a higher salary and choice job assignments) than his referent.
Underpayment inequity	Outcomes / Inputs	< (less than)	Outcomes / Inputs	An engineer perceives that he contributes more inputs but receives the same outcomes as his referent.
Overpayment inequity	Outcomes / Inputs	> (greater than)	Outcomes / Inputs	An engineer perceives that he contributes the same inputs but receives more outcomes than his referent.

perceives them to be equitable because her higher level of pay is proportional to her higher level of inputs.

When equity exists, people are motivated to continue contributing their current levels of inputs to their organizations to receive their current levels of outcomes. If people wish to increase their outcomes under conditions of equity, they are motivated to increase their inputs.

Inequity

inequity Lack of fairness.

Inequity, or lack of fairness, exists when a person's outcome–input ratio is not perceived to be equal to a referent's. Inequity creates pressure or tension inside people and motivates them to restore equity by bringing the two ratios back into balance.

underpayment inequity The inequity that exists when a person perceives that his or her own outcome–input ratio is less than the ratio of a referent.

overpayment inequity The inequity that exists when a person perceives that his or her own outcome–input ratio is greater than the ratio of a referent.

There are two types of inequity: underpayment inequity and overpayment inequity (see Table 13.3). **Underpayment inequity** exists when a person's own outcome–input ratio is perceived to be *less* than that of a referent. In comparing yourself to a referent, you think you are *not* receiving the outcomes you should be, given your inputs. **Overpayment inequity** exists when a person perceives that his or her own outcome–input ratio is *greater* than that of a referent. In comparing yourself to a referent, you think you are receiving *more* outcomes than you should be, given your inputs.

Ways to Restore Equity

According to equity theory, both underpayment inequity and overpayment inequity create tension that motivates most people to restore equity by bringing the ratios back into balance.[27] When people experience *underpayment* inequity, they may be motivated to lower their inputs by reducing their working hours, putting forth less effort on the job, or being absent; or they may be motivated to increase their outcomes by asking for a raise or a promotion. Susan Chu, a financial analyst at a large corporation, noticed that she was working longer hours and getting more work accomplished than a coworker who had the same position, yet they both received the exact same pay and other outcomes. To restore equity, Chu decided to stop coming in early and staying late. Alternatively, she could have tried to restore equity by trying to increase her outcomes, perhaps by asking her boss for a raise.

When people experience underpayment inequity and other means of equity restoration fail, they can change their perceptions of their own or the referent's inputs or outcomes. For example, they may realize that their referent is really working on more difficult projects than they are or that they really take more time off from work than their referent does. Alternatively, if people who feel they are underpaid have other employment options, they may leave the organization. As an example, John Steinberg, an assistant principal in a high school, experienced underpayment inequity when he realized all the other assistant principals of high schools in his school district had received promotions to the position of principal even though they had been in their jobs for a shorter time than he had. Steinberg's performance had always been appraised as being high, so after his repeated requests for a promotion went unheeded, he found a job as a principal in a different school district.

When people experience *overpayment* inequity, they may try to restore equity by changing their perceptions of their own or their referent's inputs or outcomes. Equity can be restored when people realize they are contributing more inputs than they originally thought. Equity also can be restored by perceiving the referent's inputs to be lower or the referent's outcomes to be higher than one originally thought. When equity is restored in this way, actual inputs and outcomes are unchanged, and the person being overpaid takes no real action. What is changed is how people think about or view their or the referent's inputs and outcomes. For instance, Mary McMann experienced overpayment inequity when she realized she was being paid $2 an hour more than a coworker who had the same job as she did in a record store and who contributed the same amount of inputs. McMann restored equity by changing her perceptions of her inputs. She realized she worked harder than her coworker and solved more problems that came up in the store.

Experiencing either overpayment or underpayment inequity, you might decide that your referent is not appropriate because, for example, the referent is too different from yourself. Choosing a more appropriate referent may bring the ratios back into balance. Angela Martinez, a middle manager in the engineering department of a chemical company, experienced overpayment inequity when she realized she was being paid quite a bit more than her friend, who was a middle manager in the marketing department of the same company. After thinking about the discrepancy for a while, Martinez decided that engineering and marketing were so different that she should not be comparing her job to her friend's job even though they were both middle managers. Martinez restored equity by changing her referent; she picked a middle manager in the engineering department as a new referent.

Motivation is highest when as many people as possible in an organization perceive that they are being equitably treated–their outcomes and inputs are in balance. Top contributors and performers are motivated to continue contributing a high level of inputs because they are receiving the outcomes they deserve. Mediocre contributors and performers realize that if they want to increase their outcomes, they have to increase their inputs. Managers of effective organizations, like SAS, realize the importance of equity for motivation and performance and continually strive to ensure that employees believe they are being equitably treated.

LO13-3 Explain how goals and needs motivate people and what kinds of goals are especially likely to result in high performance.

The dot-com boom, its subsequent bust, and two recessions, along with increased global competition, have resulted in some workers putting in longer and longer working hours (increasing their inputs) without any increase in their outcomes. For those whose referents are not experiencing a similar change, perceptions of inequity are likely.

Goal-Setting Theory

goal-setting theory A theory that focuses on identifying the types of goals that are most effective in producing high levels of motivation and performance and explaining why goals have these effects.

Goal-setting theory focuses on motivating workers to contribute their inputs to their jobs and organizations; in this way it is similar to expectancy theory and equity theory. But goal-setting theory takes this focus a step further by considering as well how managers can ensure that organizational members focus their inputs in the direction of high performance and the achievement of organizational goals.

Ed Locke and Gary Latham, the leading researchers for goal-setting theory, suggested that the goals organizational members strive to attain are prime determinants of their motivation and subsequent performance. A *goal* is what a person is trying to accomplish through his or her efforts and behaviors.[28] Just as you may have a goal to get a good grade in this course, so do members of an organization have goals they strive to meet.

Goal-setting theory suggests that to stimulate high motivation and performance, goals must be *specific* and *difficult*.[29] Specific goals are often quantitative—a salesperson's goal to sell $200 worth of merchandise per day, a scientist's goal to finish a project in one year, a CEO's goal to reduce debt by 40% and increase revenues by 20%, a restaurant manager's goal to serve 150 customers per evening. In contrast to specific goals, vague goals such as "doing your best" or "selling as much as you can" do not have much motivational impact.

Difficult goals are hard but not impossible to attain. In contrast to difficult goals, easy goals are those that practically everyone can attain, and moderate goals are goals that about one-half of the people can attain. Both easy and moderate goals have less motivational power than difficult goals.

Regardless of whether specific, difficult goals are set by managers, workers, or teams of managers and workers, they lead to high levels of motivation and performance. When managers set goals for their subordinates, their subordinates must accept the goals or agree to work toward them; also, they should be committed to them or really want to attain them. Some managers find that having subordinates participate in the actual setting of goals boosts their acceptance of and commitment to the goals. In addition, organizational members need to receive *feedback* about how they are doing; feedback can often be provided by the performance appraisal and feedback component of an organization's human resource management system (see Chapter 12). More generally, goals and feedback are integral components of performance management systems such as management by objectives (see Chapter 11).

Specific, difficult goals can encourage people to exert high levels of effort and to focus efforts in the right direction.

Specific, difficult goals affect motivation in two ways. First, they motivate people to contribute more inputs to their jobs. Specific, difficult goals cause people to put forth high levels of effort, for example. Just as you would study harder if you were trying to get an A in a course instead of a C, so too will a salesperson work harder to reach a $200 sales goal instead of a $100 sales goal. Specific, difficult goals also cause people to be more persistent than easy, moderate, or vague goals when they run into difficulties. Salespeople who are told to sell as much as possible might stop trying on a slow day, whereas having a specific, difficult goal to reach causes them to keep trying.

A second way in which specific, difficult goals affect motivation is by helping people focus their inputs in the right direction. These goals let people know what they should be focusing their attention on, be it increasing the quality of customer service or sales or lowering new product development times. The fact that the goals are specific and difficult also frequently causes people to develop *action plans* for reaching them.[30] Action plans can include the strategies to attain the goals and timetables or schedules for the completion of different activities crucial to goal attainment. Like the goals themselves, action plans also help ensure that efforts are focused in the right direction and that people do not get sidetracked along the way.

Although specific, difficult goals have been found to increase motivation and performance in a wide variety of jobs and organizations both in the United States and abroad, recent research suggests that they may detract from performance under certain conditions. When people are performing complicated and challenging tasks that require them to focus on a considerable amount of learning, specific, difficult goals may actually impair performance.[31] Striving to reach such goals may direct some of a person's attention away from learning about the task and toward trying to figure out how to achieve the goal. Once a person has learned the task and it no longer seems complicated or difficult, then the assignment of specific, difficult goals is likely to have its usual effects. Additionally, for work that is very creative and uncertain, specific, difficult goals may be detrimental.

LO13-4 Identify the motivation lessons that managers can learn from operant conditioning theory and social learning theory.

Learning Theories

The basic premise of **learning theories** as applied to organizations is that managers can increase employee motivation and performance by how they link the outcomes that employees receive to the performance of desired behaviors and the attainment of goals. Thus learning theory focuses on the linkage between performance and outcomes in the motivation equation (see Figure 13.1).

learning theories Theories that focus on increasing employee motivation and performance by linking the outcomes that employees receive to the performance of desired behaviors and the attainment of goals.

Learning can be defined as a relatively permanent change in a person's knowledge or behavior that results from practice or experience.[32] Learning takes place in organizations when people learn to perform certain behaviors to receive certain outcomes. For example, a person learns to perform at a higher level than in the past or to come to work earlier because he or she is motivated to obtain the outcomes that result from these behaviors, such as a pay raise or praise from a supervisor.

learning A relatively permanent change in knowledge or behavior that results from practice or experience.

Of the different learning theories, operant conditioning theory and social learning theory provide the most guidance to managers in their efforts to have a highly motivated workforce.

Operant Conditioning Theory

According to **operant conditioning theory,** developed by psychologist B. F. Skinner, people learn to perform behaviors that lead to desired consequences and learn not to perform behaviors that lead to undesired consequences.[33] Translated into motivation terms, Skinner's theory means that people will be motivated to perform at a high level and attain their work goals to the extent that high performance and goal attainment allow them to obtain outcomes they desire. Similarly, people avoid performing behaviors that lead to outcomes they do not desire. By linking the performance of *specific behaviors* to the attainment of *specific outcomes,* managers can motivate organizational members to perform in ways that help an organization achieve its goals.

operant conditioning theory The theory that people learn to perform behaviors that lead to desired consequences and learn not to perform behaviors that lead to undesired consequences.

Operant conditioning theory provides four tools that managers can use to motivate high performance and prevent workers from engaging in absenteeism and other behaviors that detract from organizational effectiveness. These tools are positive reinforcement, negative reinforcement, extinction, and punishment.[34]

POSITIVE REINFORCEMENT **Positive reinforcement** gives people outcomes they desire when they perform organizationally functional behaviors. These desired outcomes, called *positive reinforcers,* include any outcomes that a person desires, such as pay, praise, or a promotion. Organizationally functional behaviors are behaviors that contribute to organizational effectiveness; they can include producing high-quality goods and services, providing high-quality customer service, and meeting deadlines. By linking positive reinforcers to the performance of functional behaviors, managers motivate people to perform the desired behaviors.

positive reinforcement Giving people outcomes they desire when they perform organizationally functional behaviors.

NEGATIVE REINFORCEMENT **Negative reinforcement** also can encourage members of an organization to perform desired or organizationally functional behaviors. Managers using negative reinforcement actually eliminate or remove undesired outcomes once the functional behavior is performed. These undesired outcomes, called *negative reinforcers,* can range from a manager's constant nagging or criticism to unpleasant assignments or the ever-present threat of losing one's job. When negative reinforcement is used, people are motivated to perform behaviors because they want to stop receiving or avoid undesired outcomes. Managers who try to encourage salespeople to sell more by threatening them with being fired are using negative reinforcement. In this case, the negative reinforcer is the threat of job loss, which is removed once the functional behavior is performed.

negative reinforcement Eliminating or removing undesired outcomes when people perform organizationally functional behaviors.

Whenever possible, managers should try to use positive reinforcement. Negative reinforcement can create a very unpleasant work environment and even a negative culture in an organization. No one likes to be nagged, threatened, or exposed to other kinds of negative outcomes. The use of negative reinforcement sometimes causes subordinates to resent managers and try to get back at them.

IDENTIFYING THE RIGHT BEHAVIORS FOR REINFORCEMENT Even managers who use positive reinforcement (and refrain from using negative reinforcement) can get into trouble if they are not careful to identify the right behaviors to reinforce–behaviors that are truly functional for the organization. Doing this is not always as straightforward as it might seem. First, it is crucial for managers to choose behaviors over which subordinates have control; in other words, subordinates must have the freedom and opportunity to perform the behaviors that are being reinforced. Second, it is crucial that these behaviors contribute to organizational effectiveness.

EXTINCTION Sometimes members of an organization are motivated to perform behaviors that detract from organizational effectiveness. According to operant conditioning theory, all behavior is controlled or determined by its consequences; one way for managers to curtail the performance of dysfunctional behaviors is to eliminate whatever is reinforcing the behaviors. This process is called **extinction.**

extinction Curtailing the performance of dysfunctional behaviors by eliminating whatever is reinforcing them.

Suppose a manager has a subordinate who frequently stops by his office to chat–sometimes about work-related matters but at other times about various topics ranging from politics to last night's football game. The manager and the subordinate share certain interests and views, so these conversations can get quite involved, and both seem to enjoy them. The manager, however, realizes that these frequent and sometimes lengthy conversations are causing him to stay at work later in the evenings to make up for the time he loses during the day. The manager also realizes that he is reinforcing his subordinate's behavior by acting interested in the topics the subordinate brings up and responding at length to them. To extinguish this behavior, the manager stops acting interested in these non-work-related conversations and keeps his responses polite and friendly but brief. No longer being reinforced with a pleasurable conversation, the subordinate eventually ceases to be motivated to interrupt the manager during working hours to discuss non-work-related issues.

PUNISHMENT Sometimes managers cannot rely on extinction to eliminate dysfunctional behaviors because they do not have control over whatever is reinforcing the behavior or because they cannot afford the time needed for extinction to work. When employees are performing dangerous behaviors or behaviors that are illegal or unethical, the behavior needs to be eliminated immediately. Sexual harassment, for example, is an organizationally dysfunctional behavior that cannot be tolerated. In such cases managers often rely on **punishment,** which is administering an undesired or negative consequence to subordinates when they perform the dysfunctional behavior. Punishments used by organizations range from verbal reprimands to pay cuts, temporary suspensions, demotions, and firings. Punishment, however, can have some unintended side effects–resentment, loss of self-respect, a desire for retaliation–and should be used only when necessary.

punishment Administering an undesired or negative consequence when dysfunctional behavior occurs.

To avoid the unintended side effects of punishment, managers should keep in mind these guidelines:

- Downplay the emotional element involved in punishment. Make it clear that you are punishing a person's performance of a dysfunctional behavior, not the person himself or herself.
- Try to punish dysfunctional behaviors as soon after they occur as possible, and make sure the negative consequence is a source of punishment for the individuals involved. Be certain that organizational members know exactly why they are being punished.
- Try to avoid punishing someone in front of others because this can hurt a person's self-respect and lower esteem in the eyes of coworkers as well as make coworkers feel uncomfortable.[35] Even so, making organizational members aware that an individual who has committed a serious infraction has been punished can sometimes be effective in preventing future infractions and teaching all members of the organization that certain behaviors are unacceptable. For example, when organizational members are informed that a manager who has sexually harassed subordinates has been punished, they learn or are reminded of the fact that sexual harassment is not tolerated in the organization.

Figure 13.4
Five Steps in OB MOD

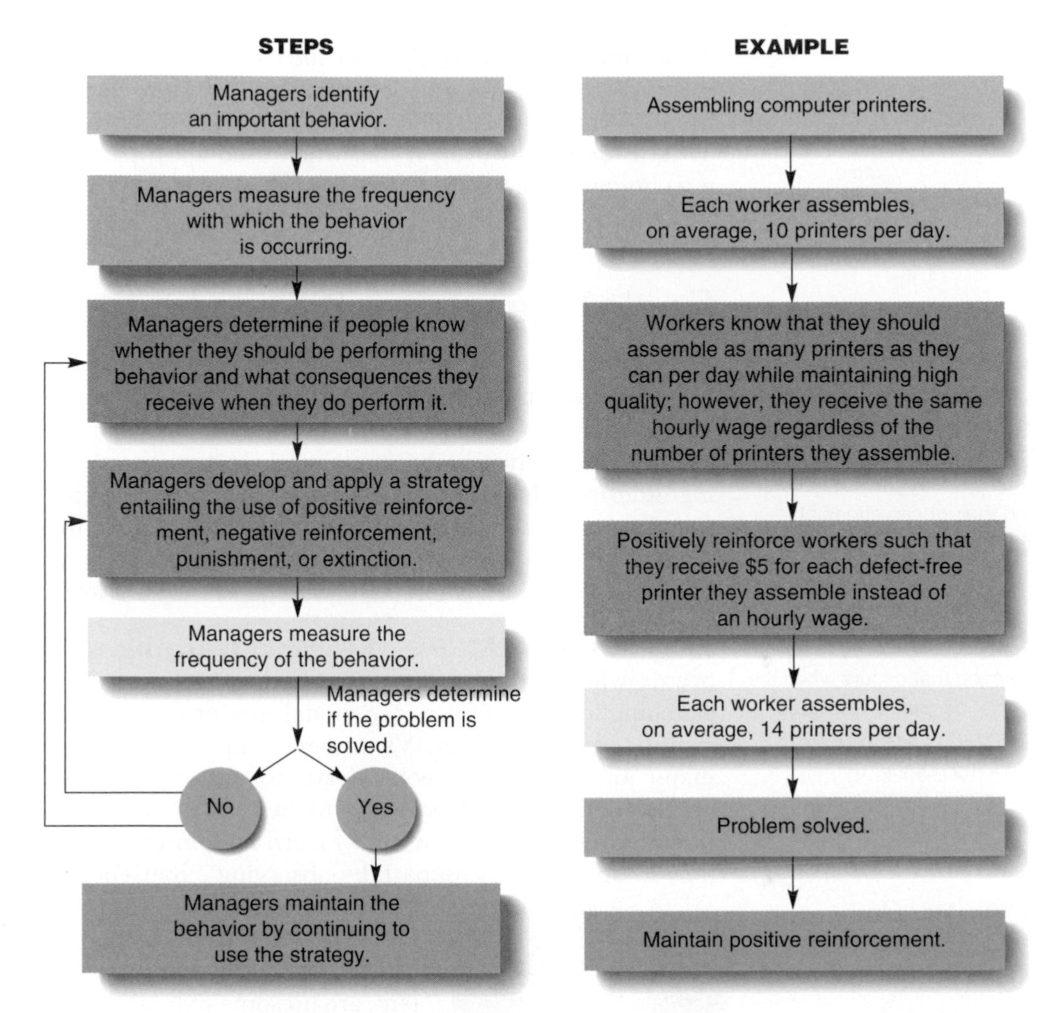

Source: Adapted from *Organizational Behavior Modification and Beyond* by F. Luthans and R. Kreitner (Scott, Foresman, 1985). With permission of the authors.

Managers and students alike often confuse negative reinforcement and punishment. To avoid such confusion, keep in mind the two major differences between them. First, negative reinforcement is used to promote the performance of functional behaviors in organizations; punishment is used to stop the performance of dysfunctional behaviors. Second, negative reinforcement entails the *removal* of a negative consequence when functional behaviors are performed; punishment entails the *administration* of negative consequences when dysfunctional behaviors are performed.

organizational behavior modification (OB MOD) The systematic application of operant conditioning techniques to promote the performance of organizationally functional behaviors and discourage the performance of dysfunctional behaviors.

ORGANIZATIONAL BEHAVIOR MODIFICATION When managers systematically apply operant conditioning techniques to promote the performance of organizationally functional behaviors and discourage the performance of dysfunctional behaviors, they are engaging in **organizational behavior modification (OB MOD).**[36] OB MOD has been successfully used to improve productivity, efficiency, attendance, punctuality, safe work practices, customer service, and other important behaviors in a wide variety of organizations such as banks, department stores, factories, hospitals, and construction sites.[37] The five basic steps in OB MOD are described in Figure 13.4.

OB MOD works best for behaviors that are specific, objective, and countable, such as attendance and punctuality, making sales, or putting telephones together, all of which lend themselves to careful scrutiny and control. OB MOD may be questioned because of its lack of relevance to certain work behaviors (for example, the many work behaviors that are not specific, objective, and countable). Some people also have questioned it on ethical grounds. Critics of OB MOD suggest that it is overly controlling and robs workers of their dignity, individuality, freedom of choice, and even creativity. Supporters counter that OB MOD is a highly effective means of promoting organizational efficiency. There is some merit to both sides of this argument. What is clear, however, is that when used appropriately, OB MOD gives managers a technique to motivate the performance of at least some organizationally functional behaviors.[38]

Social Learning Theory

social learning theory A theory that takes into account how learning and motivation are influenced by people's thoughts and beliefs and their observations of other people's behavior.

Social learning theory proposes that motivation results not only from direct experience of rewards and punishments but also from a person's thoughts and beliefs. Social learning theory extends operant conditioning's contribution to managers' understanding of motivation by explaining (1) how people can be motivated by observing other people performing a behavior and being reinforced for doing so (*vicarious learning*), (2) how people can be motivated to control their behavior themselves (*self-reinforcement*), and (3) how people's beliefs about their ability to successfully perform a behavior affect motivation (*self-efficacy*).[39] We look briefly at each of these motivators.

vicarious learning Learning that occurs when the learner becomes motivated to perform a behavior by watching another person performing it and being reinforced for doing so; also called *observational learning.*

VICARIOUS LEARNING **Vicarious learning,** often called *observational learning,* occurs when a person (the learner) becomes motivated to perform a behavior by watching another person (the model) performing the behavior and being positively reinforced for doing so. Vicarious learning is a powerful source of motivation on many jobs in which people learn to perform functional behaviors by watching others. Salespeople learn how to help customers, medical school students learn how to treat patients, law clerks learn how to practice law, and nonmanagers learn how to be managers, in part, by observing experienced members of an organization perform these behaviors properly and be reinforced for them. In general, people are more likely to be motivated to imitate the behavior of models who are highly competent, are (to some extent) experts in the behavior, have high status, receive attractive reinforcers, and are friendly or approachable.[40]

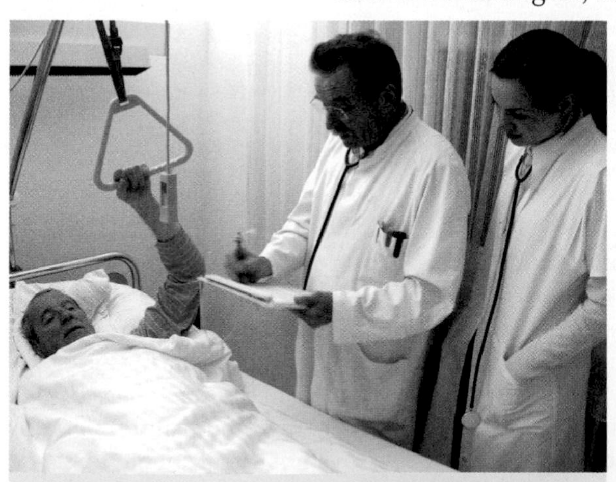

How do you treat *that*? When medical students enter residency, their education becomes entirely vicarious, as they shadow a full physician on his or her rounds.

To promote vicarious learning, managers should strive to have the learner meet the following conditions:

- The learner observes the model performing the behavior.
- The learner accurately perceives the model's behavior.
- The learner remembers the behavior.
- The learner has the skills and abilities needed to perform the behavior.
- The learner sees or knows that the model is positively reinforced for the behavior.[41]

self-reinforcer Any desired or attractive outcome or reward that a person gives to himself or herself for good performance.

SELF-REINFORCEMENT Although managers are often the providers of reinforcement in organizations, sometimes people motivate themselves through self-reinforcement. People can control their own behavior by setting goals for themselves and then reinforcing themselves when they achieve the goals.[42] **Self-reinforcers** are any desired or attractive outcomes or rewards that people can give to themselves for good performance, such as a feeling of accomplishment, going to a movie, having dinner out, buying a new CD, or taking time out for a golf game. When members of an organization control their own behavior through self-reinforcement, managers do not need to spend as much time as they ordinarily would trying to motivate and control behavior through the administration of consequences because subordinates are controlling and motivating themselves. In fact, this self-control is often referred to as the *self-management of behavior*.

When employees are highly skilled and are responsible for creating new goods and services, managers typically rely on self-control and self-management of behavior, as is the case at Google. Employees at Google are given the flexibility and autonomy to experiment, take risks, and sometimes fail as they work on new projects. They are encouraged to learn from their failures and apply what they learn to subsequent projects.[43] Google's engineers are given one day a week to work on their own projects that they are highly involved with, and new products such as Google News often emerge from these projects.[44]

self-efficacy A person's belief about his or her ability to perform a behavior successfully.

SELF-EFFICACY **Self-efficacy** is a person's belief about his or her ability to perform a behavior successfully.[45] Even with all the most attractive consequences or reinforcers hinging on high performance, people are not going to be motivated if they do not think they can actually perform at a high level. Similarly, when people control their own behavior, they are likely to set for themselves difficult goals that will lead to outstanding accomplishments only if they think they can reach those goals. Thus self-efficacy influences motivation both when managers provide reinforcement and when workers themselves provide it.[46] The greater the self-efficacy, the greater is the motivation and performance. Verbal persuasion such as a manager expressing confidence in an employee's ability to reach a challenging goal, as well as a person's own past performance and accomplishments and the accomplishments of other people, plays a role in determining a person's self-efficacy.

Pay and Motivation

LO13-5 Explain why and how managers can use pay as a major motivation tool.

In Chapter 12 we discussed how managers establish a pay level and structure for an organization as a whole. Here we focus on how, once a pay level and structure are in place, managers can use pay to motivate employees to perform at a high level and attain their work goals. Pay is used to motivate entry-level workers, first-line and middle managers, and even top managers such as CEOs. Pay can be used to motivate people to perform behaviors that help an organization achieve its goals, and it can be used to motivate people to join and remain with an organization.

Each of the theories described in this chapter alludes to the importance of pay and suggests that pay should be based on performance:

- *Expectancy theory:* Instrumentality, the association between performance and outcomes such as pay, must be high for motivation to be high. In addition, pay is an outcome that has high valence for many people.
- *Need theories:* People should be able to satisfy their needs by performing at a high level; pay can be used to satisfy several different kinds of needs.
- *Equity theory:* Outcomes such as pay should be distributed in proportion to inputs (including performance levels).
- *Goal-setting theory:* Outcomes such as pay should be linked to the attainment of goals.
- *Learning theories:* The distribution of outcomes such as pay should be contingent on the performance of organizationally functional behaviors.

As these theories suggest, to promote high motivation, managers should base the distribution of pay to organizational members on performance levels so that high performers receive more pay than low performers (other things being equal).[47] At General Mills, for example, the pay of all employees, ranging from mailroom clerks to senior managers, is based, at least in part, on performance.[48] A compensation plan basing pay on performance is often called a **merit pay plan.**

merit pay plan A compensation plan that bases pay on performance.

In tough economic times, when organizations lay off employees and pay levels and benefits of those who are at least able to keep their jobs may be cut while their responsibilities are often increased,[49] managers are often limited in the extent to which they can use merit pay, if at all.[50] Nonetheless, in such times, managers can still try to recognize top performers, as indicated in the following "Management Insight" box.

Management Insight

EasyJet Rewards Employees Who Go the Extra Mile

EasyJet Airline Company Limited is a British airline headquartered at London's Luton Airport. The airline carries more passengers than any other United Kingdom-based airline, operating domestic and international scheduled services on 500 routes between 118 European, North African, and West Asian airports. In 2006 EasyJet wanted to create a motivation program for its 5,500 employees that reinforced its strategy. This strategy focuses on keeping costs low while maintaining safety. At the same time, the firm seeks to ensure that there is adequate customer service. To achieve these aims, the airline introduced the Gem awards, which stands for "going the extra mile." Employees can nominate one another or a whole team for behavior that supports that strategy. This can include highlighting a particular hazard, taking action to keep customers safe, or an example of great customer service.

Employees at EasyJet vie for the Gem award, which stands for "going the extra mile." This motivation program has been very successful and supports the company's overall strategy of providing low cost air travel with care and convenience.

A judging panel of managers votes on the nominations for the award, and winners receive vouchers to spend on travel, gifts, and shopping. Since the awards were established, the company has received more than 1,500 nominations and awarded more than $125,000 USD of benefits to staff. Andy Turnbull, organizational development manager, says the program is designed to reward staff who live out the company values and deliver "low cost with care and convenience." The motivational program has been very successful and supports the strategy of the firm.[51]

Once managers have decided to use a merit pay plan, they face two important choices: whether to base pay on individual, group, or organizational performance and whether to use salary increases or bonuses.

Basing Merit Pay on Individual, Group, or Organizational Performance

Managers can base merit pay on individual, group, or organizational performance. When individual performance (such as the monetary value of merchandise a sales person sells, the number of loudspeakers a factory worker assembles, and a lawyer's billable hours) can be accurately determined, individual motivation is likely to be highest when pay is based on individual performance.[52] When members of an organization work closely together and individual performance cannot be accurately determined (as in a team of computer programmers developing a single software package), pay cannot be based on individual performance, and a group- or organization-based plan must be used. When the attainment of organizational goals hinges on members' working closely together and cooperating with each other (as in a small construction company that builds custom homes), group- or organization-based plans may be more appropriate than individual-based plans.[53]

It is possible to combine elements of an individual-based plan with a group- or organization-based plan to motivate each individual to perform highly and, at the same time, motivate all individuals to work well together, cooperate with one another, and help one another as needed.

Salary Increase or Bonus?

Managers can distribute merit pay to people in the form of a salary increase or a bonus on top of regular salaries. Although the dollar amount of a salary increase or bonus might be identical, bonuses tend to have more motivational impact for at least three reasons. First, salary levels are typically based on performance levels, cost-of-living increases, and so forth, from the day people start working in an organization, which means the absolute level of the salary is based largely on factors unrelated to *current* performance. A 5% merit increase in salary, for example, may seem relatively small in comparison to one's total salary. Second, a current salary increase may be affected by other factors in addition to performance, such as cost-of-living increases or across-the-board market adjustments. Third, because organizations rarely reduce salaries, salary levels tend to vary less than performance levels do. Related to this point is the fact that bonuses give managers more flexibility in distributing outcomes. If an organization is doing well, bonuses can be relatively high to reward employees for their contributions. However, unlike salary increases, bonus levels can be reduced when an organization's performance lags. All in all, bonus plans have more motivational impact than salary increases because the amount of the bonus can be directly and exclusively based on performance.[54] Consistent with the lessons from motivation theories, bonuses can be linked directly to performance and vary from year to year and employee to employee.

employee stock option A financial instrument that entitles the bearer to buy shares of an organization's stock at a certain price during a certain period or under certain conditions.

In addition to receiving pay raises and bonuses, high-level managers and executives are sometimes granted employee stock options. **Employee stock options** are financial instruments that entitle the bearer to buy shares of an organization's stock at a certain price during a certain period or under certain conditions.[55] For example, in addition to salaries, stock options are sometimes used to attract high-level managers. The exercise price is the stock price at which the bearer can buy the stock, and the vesting conditions specify when the bearer can actually buy the stock at the exercise price. The option's exercise price is generally set equal to the market price of the stock on the date it is granted, and the vesting conditions might specify that the manager has to have worked at the organization for 12 months or perhaps met some performance target (perhaps an increase in profits) before being able to exercise the option. In high-technology firms and start-ups, options are sometimes used in a similar fashion for employees at various levels in the organization.[56]

From a motivation standpoint, stock options are used not so much to reward past individual performance but, rather, to motivate employees to work in the future for the good of the company as a whole. This is true because stock options issued at current stock prices have value in the future only if an organization does well and its stock price appreciates; thus giving employees stock options should encourage them to help the organization improve its performance over time.[57] At high-technology start-ups and dot-coms, stock options have often motivated potential employees to leave promising jobs in larger companies and work for the start-ups. In the late 1990s and early 2000s, many dot-commers were devastated to learn not only that their stock options were worthless, because their companies went out of business or were doing poorly, but also that they were unemployed. Unfortunately stock options have also led to unethical behavior; for example, sometimes individuals seek to artificially inflate the value of a company's stock to increase the value of stock options.

Examples of Merit Pay Plans

Managers can choose among several merit pay plans, depending on the work that employees perform and other considerations. Using *piece-rate pay,* an individual-based merit plan, managers base employees' pay on the number of units each employee produces, whether televisions, computer components, or welded auto parts.

Using *commission pay,* another individual-based merit pay plan, managers base pay on a percentage of sales. Managers at the successful real estate company Re/Max International Inc. use commission pay for their agents, who are paid a percentage of their sales. Some department stores, such as Neiman Marcus, use commission pay for their salespeople.

Examples of organizational-based merit pay plans include the Scanlon plan and profit sharing. The *Scanlon plan* (developed by Joseph Scanlon, a union leader in a steel and tin plant in the 1920s) focuses on reducing expenses or cutting costs; members of an organization are motivated to come up with and implement cost-cutting strategies because a percentage of the cost savings achieved during a specified time is distributed to the employees.[58] Under *profit sharing,* employees receive a share of an organization's profits. Regardless of the specific kind of plan that is used, managers should always strive to link pay to the performance of behaviors that help an organization achieve its goals.

Japanese managers in large corporations have long shunned merit pay plans in favor of plans that reward seniority. However, more and more Japanese companies are adopting merit-based pay due to its motivational benefits; among such companies are SiteDesign,[59] Tokio Marine and Fire Insurance, and Hissho Iwai, a trading organization.[60]

Summary and Review

THE NATURE OF MOTIVATION Motivation encompasses the psychological forces within a person that determine the direction of the person's behavior in an organization, the person's level of effort, and the person's level of persistence in the face of obstacles. Managers strive to motivate people to contribute their inputs to an organization, to focus these inputs in the direction of high performance, and to ensure that people receive the outcomes they desire when they perform at a high level. **LO13-1**

LO13-2 **EXPECTANCY THEORY** According to expectancy theory, managers can promote high levels of motivation in their organizations by taking steps to ensure that expectancy is high (people think that if they try, they can perform at a high level), instrumentality is high (people think that if they perform at a high level, they will receive certain outcomes), and valence is high (people desire these outcomes).

LO13-3 **NEED THEORIES** Need theories suggest that to motivate their workforces, managers should determine what needs people are trying to satisfy in organizations and then ensure that people receive outcomes that satisfy these needs when they perform at a high level and contribute to organizational effectiveness.

LO13-2 **EQUITY THEORY** According to equity theory, managers can promote high levels of motivation by ensuring that people perceive that there is equity in the organization or that outcomes are distributed in proportion to inputs. Equity exists when a person perceives that his or her own outcome–input ratio equals the outcome–input ratio of a referent. Inequity motivates people to try to restore equity.

LO13-3 **GOAL-SETTING THEORY** Goal-setting theory suggests that managers can promote high motivation and performance by ensuring that people are striving to achieve specific, difficult goals. It is important for people to accept the goals, be committed to them, and receive feedback about how they are doing.

LO13-4 **LEARNING THEORIES** Operant conditioning theory suggests that managers can motivate people to perform highly by using positive reinforcement or negative reinforcement (positive reinforcement being the preferred strategy). Managers can motivate people to avoid performing dysfunctional behaviors by using extinction or punishment. Social learning theory suggests that people can also be motivated by observing how others perform behaviors and receive rewards, by engaging in self-reinforcement, and by having high levels of self-efficacy.

LO13-5 **PAY AND MOTIVATION** Each of the motivation theories discussed in this chapter alludes to the importance of pay and suggests that pay should be based on performance. Merit pay plans can be individual-, group-, or organization-based and can entail the use of salary increases or bonuses.

Management in Action

Topics for Discussion and Action

Discussion

1. Discuss why two people with similar abilities may have very different expectancies for performing at a high level. **[LO13-2]**
2. Describe why some people have low instrumentalities even when their managers distribute outcomes based on performance. **[LO13-2]**
3. Analyze how professors try to promote equity to motivate students. **[LO13-2]**
4. Describe three techniques or procedures that managers can use to determine whether a goal is difficult. **[LO13-3]**
5. Discuss why managers should always try to use positive reinforcement instead of negative reinforcement. **[LO13-4]**

Action

6. Interview three people who have the same kind of job (such as salesperson, waiter/waitress, or teacher), and determine what kinds of needs each is trying to satisfy at work. **[LO13-3]**
7. Interview a manager in an organization in your community to determine the extent to which the manager takes advantage of vicarious learning to promote high motivation among subordinates. **[LO13-3]**

Building Management Skills

Diagnosing Motivation **[LO13-1, 13-2, 13-3, 13-4]**

Think about the ideal job that you would like to obtain upon graduation. Describe this job, the kind of manager you would like to report to, and the kind of organization you would be working in. Then answer the following questions:

1. What would be your levels of expectancy and instrumentality on this job? Which outcomes would have high valence for you on this job? What steps would your manager take to influence your levels of expectancy, instrumentality, and valence?
2. Whom would you choose as a referent on this job? What steps would your manager take to make you feel that you were being equitably treated? What would you do if, after a year on the job, you experienced underpayment inequity?
3. What goals would you strive to achieve on this job? Why? What role would your manager play in determining your goals?
4. What needs would you strive to satisfy on this job? Why? What role would your manager play in helping you satisfy these needs?
5. What behaviors would your manager positively reinforce on this job? Why? What positive reinforcers would your manager use?
6. Would there be any vicarious learning on this job? Why or why not?
7. To what extent would you be motivated by self-control on this job? Why?
8. What would be your level of self-efficacy on this job? Why would your self-efficacy be at this level? Should your manager take steps to boost your self-efficacy? If not, why not? If so, what would these steps be?

Managing Ethically **[LO13-5]**

Sometimes pay is so contingent upon performance that it creates stress for employees. Imagine a salesperson who knows that if sales targets are not met, she or he will not be able to make a house mortgage payment or pay the rent.

Questions

1. Either individually or in a group, think about the ethical implications of closely linking pay to performance.
2. Under what conditions might contingent pay be most stressful, and what steps can managers take to try to help their subordinates perform effectively and not experience excessive amounts of stress?

Small Group Breakout Exercise

Increasing Motivation [LO13-1, 13-2, 13-3, 13-4, 13-5]

Form groups of three or four people, and appoint one member as the spokesperson who will communicate your findings to the class when called on by the instructor. Then discuss the following scenario:

You and your partners own a chain of 15 dry-cleaning stores in a medium-size town. All of you are concerned about a problem in customer service that has surfaced recently. When any one of you spends the day, or even part of the day, in a particular store, clerks seem to provide excellent customer service, spotters make sure all stains are removed from garments, and pressers do a good job of pressing difficult items such as silk blouses. Yet during those same visits customers complain to you about such things as stains not being removed and items being poorly pressed in some of their previous orders; indeed, several customers have brought garments in to be redone. Customers also sometimes comment on having waited too long for service on previous visits. You and your partners are meeting today to address this problem.

1. Discuss the extent to which you believe that you have a motivation problem in your stores.
2. Given what you have learned in this chapter, design a plan to increase the motivation of clerks to provide prompt service to customers even when they are not being watched by a partner.
3. Design a plan to increase the motivation of spotters to remove as many stains as possible even when they are not being watched by a partner.
4. Design a plan to increase the motivation of pressers to do a top-notch job on all clothes they press, no matter how difficult.

Exploring the World Wide Web [LO13-1, 13-2, 13-3, 13-4, 13-5]

If you had the chance to choose which well-known corporation you would work for, which would it be? Now go to the Web site of that company and find out as much as you can about how it motivates employees. Also, using Google and other search engines, try to find articles in the news about this company. Based on what you have learned, would this company still be your top choice? Why or why not?

Be the Manager [LO13-1, 13-2, 13-3, 13-4, 13-5]

You supervise a team of marketing analysts who work on different snack products in a large food products company. The marketing analysts have recently received undergraduate degrees in business or liberal arts and have been on the job between one and three years. Their responsibilities include analyzing the market for their respective products, including competitors; tracking current marketing initiatives; and planning future marketing campaigns. They also need to prepare quarterly sales and expense reports for their products and estimated budgets for the next three quarters; to prepare these reports, they need to obtain data from financial and accounting analysts assigned to their products.

When they first started on the job, you took each marketing analyst through the reporting cycle, explaining what needs to be done and how to accomplish it and emphasizing the need for timely reports. Although preparing the reports can be tedious, you think the task is pretty straightforward and easily accomplished if the analysts plan ahead and allocate sufficient time for it. When reporting time approaches, you remind the analysts through e-mail messages and emphasize the need for accurate and timely reports in team meetings.

You believe this element of the analysts' jobs couldn't be more straightforward. However, at the end of each quarter, the majority of the analysts turn their reports in a day or two late, and, worse yet, your own supervisor (to whom the reports are eventually turned in) has indicated that information is often missing and sometimes the reports contain errors. Once you started getting flak from your supervisor about this problem, you decided you had better fix things quickly. You met with the marketing analysts, explained the problem, told them to turn the reports in to you a day or two early so you could look them over, and more generally emphasized that they really needed to get their act together. Unfortunately things have not improved much, and you are spending more and more of your own time doing the reports. What are you going to do?

CHAPTER 14

Leadership

Learning Objectives

After studying this chapter, you should be able to:

LO14-1 Explain what leadership is, when leaders are effective and ineffective, and the sources of power that enable managers to be effective leaders.

LO14-2 Identify the traits that show the strongest relationship to leadership, the behaviors leaders engage in, and the limitations of the trait and behavior models of leadership.

LO14-3 Explain how contingency models of leadership enhance our understanding of effective leadership and management in organizations.

LO14-4 Describe what transformational leadership is, and explain how managers can engage in it.

LO14-5 Characterize the relationship between gender and leadership and explain how emotional intelligence may contribute to leadership effectiveness.

A MANAGER'S CHALLENGE

Judy McGrath Leads MTV Networks

How can a manager continuously transform a hip company in a rapidly changing environment? Judy McGrath is the chairperson and CEO of MTV Networks, a unit of Viacom, home to the original MTV as well as MTV2, mtvU, MTV Tr3s, Nickelodeon, VH1, VH1 Classic, VH1 Soul, CMT, Comedy Central, LOGO, Nick at Nite, Noggin, TV Land, CMT, the N, Spike TV, Atom, AddictingGames.com, Shockwave.com, GameTrailers.com, Harmonix, Neopets, Quizilla, Xfire, Y2M, and MTVN International.[1] MTV Networks is accessed by more than 440 million households in over 165 viewing territories.

McGrath is one of only five women who have been included on *Fortune* magazine's list of the "50 Most Powerful Women in Business" every year since the magazine started the list; in 2009 she was ranked 20th.[2] In 2009 she also made *Forbes'* list of "The 100 Most Powerful Women in Business," was awarded the AWRT Achievement Award, and topped the list of the 2009 Billboard Women In Music Power Players list.[3]

Her personal leadership style emphasizes empowering all members of the MTV organization as well as its viewers. According to McGrath, creativity and innovation stem from employees at all ranks, leaders and managers should listen to employees' ideas, and change must be the rule of the day in a dynamic environment.[4] She has also strived to empower the MTV viewing audience and raise viewers' awareness about important social concerns with award-winning programming such as the *Fight For Your Rights* series [for example, "Take a Stand against Violence," "Protect Yourself" (an AIDS awareness initiative), and "Take a Stand against Discrimination"].[5]

McGrath networks daily with wide-ranging contacts, keeping up with the latest developments in the industry and pop culture and

Chairperson and CEO Judy McGrath successfully leads the complex organization that is MTV Networks.

always on the lookout for new ideas and opportunities. She is visionary and can see possibilities and opportunities where others might see just risks or potential downsides. She works hard, perseveres, and believes that anything is possible. Under her leadership, MTV has launched scores of successful new programs, all of which were risky and could have failed. As she puts it, "Falling flat on your face is a great motivator. The smartest thing we can do when confronted by something truly creative is to get out of the way."[6] That is what McGrath did when two producers came to her with the idea of filming people going through their day-to-day lives (with a soundtrack, of course, of new music); so started reality TV and MTV's *The Real World* series, which is in its 23rd season.[7]

McGrath faces new challenges as she leads MTV forward. MTV's programming is now part of the media establishment, and in an era of broadband, iPods, and online everything, she realizes that MTV cannot rest on its laurels: It must continually transform itself to maintain its hip and edgy focus and continue to appeal to its audience. Thus McGrath has pushed MTV to deliver services from multiple digital platforms ranging from cell phones to new broadband channels to video games.[8]

To spearhead this digital transformation, McGrath is expanding from MTV's tradition of developing its own offerings to seeking partnerships and acquisitions. For example, MTV Networks has partnered with Microsoft to offer a digital music download service called URGE.[9] MTV has purchased Web sites such as IFILM, which is devoted to amateur short movies, and Neopets (popular with the younger set). McGrath is seeking synergies between digital acquisitions such as these and MTV's existing lineup. For example, IFILM debuted a show on VH1, and Nickelodeon has developed products for Neopets.[10]

Overview

LO14-1 Explain what leadership is, when leaders are effective and ineffective, and the sources of power that enable managers to be effective leaders.

Judy McGrath exemplifies the many facets of effective leadership. In Chapter 1 we explained that one of the four primary tasks of managers is leading. Thus it should come as no surprise that leadership is a key ingredient in effective management. When leaders are effective, their subordinates or followers are highly motivated, committed, and high-performing. When leaders are ineffective, chances are good that their subordinates do not perform up to their capabilities, are demotivated, and may be dissatisfied as well. CEO Judy McGrath is a leader at the very top of an organization, but leadership is an important ingredient for managerial success at all levels of organizations: top management, middle management, and first-line management. Moreover, leadership is a key ingredient of managerial success for organizations large and small.

In this chapter we describe what leadership is and examine the major leadership models that shed light on the factors that contribute to a manager's being an effective leader. We look at trait and behavior models, which focus on what leaders are like and what they do, and contingency models–Fiedler's contingency model, path–goal theory, and the leader substitutes model–each of which takes into account the complexity surrounding leadership and the role of the situation in leader effectiveness. We also describe how managers can use transformational leadership to dramatically affect their organizations. By the end of this chapter, you will appreciate the many factors and issues that managers face in their quest to be effective leaders.

The Nature of Leadership

leadership The process by which an individual exerts influence over other people and inspires, motivates, and directs their activities to help achieve group or organizational goals.

leader An individual who is able to exert influence over other people to help achieve group or organizational goals.

Leadership is the process by which a person exerts influence over other people and inspires, motivates, and directs their activities to help achieve group or organizational goals.[11] The person who exerts such influence is a **leader.** When leaders are effective, the influence they exert over others helps a group or organization achieve its performance goals. When leaders are ineffective, their influence does not contribute to, and often detracts from, goal attainment. As "A Manager's Challenge" makes clear, Judy McGrath is taking multiple steps to inspire and motivate MTV's employees so they help MTV achieve its goals.

Beyond facilitating the attainment of performance goals, effective leadership increases an organization's ability to meet all the contemporary challenges discussed throughout this book, including the need to obtain a competitive advantage, the need to foster ethical behavior, and the need to manage a diverse workforce fairly and equitably. Leaders who exert influence over organizational members to help meet these goals increase their organizations' chances of success.

In considering the nature of leadership, we first look at leadership styles and how they affect managerial tasks and at the influence of culture on leadership styles. We then focus on the key to leadership, *power,* which can come from a variety of sources. Finally we consider the contemporary dynamic of empowerment and how it relates to effective leadership.

Personal Leadership Style and Managerial Tasks

A manager's *personal leadership style*–that is, the specific ways in which a manager chooses to influence other people–shapes how that manager approaches planning, organizing, and controlling (the other principal tasks of managing). Consider Judy McGrath's personal leadership style in "A Manager's Challenge": She is down to earth, nurturing of employees and talent, and at the same time decisive and visionary. She empowers employees, encourages them to be creative and take risks, and fosters an inclusive culture at MTV Networks.[12]

Managers at all levels and in all kinds of organizations have their own personal leadership styles that determine not only how they lead their subordinates but also how they perform the other management tasks. Developing an effective personal leadership style often is a challenge for managers at all levels in an organization. This challenge is often exacerbated when times are tough, due, for example, to an economic downturn or a decline in customer demand. The recession in the late 2000s provided many managers with just such a challenge.

Although leading is one of the four principal tasks of managing, a distinction is often made between managers and leaders. When this distinction is made, managers are thought of as those organizational members who establish and implement procedures and processes to ensure smooth functioning and who are accountable for goal accomplishment.[13] Leaders look to the future, chart the course for the organization, and attract, retain, motivate, inspire, and develop relationships with employees based on trust and mutual respect.[14] Leaders provide meaning and purpose, seek innovation rather than stability, and impassion employees to work together to achieve the leaders' vision.[15]

As part of their personal leadership style, some leaders strive to truly serve others. Robert Greenleaf, who was director of management research at AT&T and upon his

servant leader A leader who has a strong desire to serve and work for the benefit of others.

retirement in 1964 embarked on a second career focused on writing, speaking, and consulting, came up with the term *servant leadership* to describe these leaders.[16] **Servant leaders,** above all else, have a strong desire to serve and work for the benefit of others.[17] Servant leaders share power with followers and strive to ensure that followers' most important needs are met, they are able to develop as individuals, and their well-being is enhanced, and that attention is paid to those who are least well-off in a society.[18] Greenleaf founded a nonprofit organization called the Greenleaf Center for Servant Leadership (formerly called the Center for Applied Ethics) to foster leadership focused on service to others, power sharing, and a sense of community between organizations and their multiple stakeholders.[19] Some entrepreneurs strive to incorporate servant leadership into their personal leadership styles, as profiled in the following "Ethics in Action" box.

Ethics in Action

Servant Leadership at Zingerman's

Ari Weinzweig and Paul Saginaw founded Zingerman's Delicatessen in Ann Arbor, Michigan, in 1982.[20] Food lovers at heart, Weinzweig and Saginaw delighted in finding both traditional and exotic foods from around the world, making delicious sandwiches to order, and having extensive selections of food items ranging from olives, oils, and vinegars to cheeses, smoked fish, and salami. As their business grew, and to maintain an intimate atmosphere with excellent customer service, Weinzweig and Saginaw expanded from their original deli into a community of related businesses called Zingerman's Community of Businesses. In addition to the original deli, Zingerman's Community of Businesses now includes a mail-order business, a bakery, a catering business, a creamery, a restaurant, a wholesale coffee business, and a training business and has combined annual revenues of about $30 million.[21] From the start, Weinzweig and

Paul Saginaw (left) and Ari Weinzweig have incorporated servant leadership into their personal leadership styles at Zingerman's.

Saginaw have been devoted to excellent customer service, great food, and a commitment to people and community.[22]

As part of their commitment to people and community, Weinzweig and Saginaw have incorporated servant leadership into their personal leadership styles. As their business has grown and prospered, they have realized that increasing success means greater responsibility to serve others. They strive to treat their employees as well as they treat their customers and give their employees opportunities for growth and development on the job. They have also realized that when their own needs or desires differ from what is best for their company, they should do what is best for the company.[23]

To this day, the cofounders encourage their employees to let them know how they can help them and what they can do for them. And given Zingerman's culture of mutual respect and trust, employees do not hesitate to communicate how their leaders can serve them in many and varied ways. For example, when Weinzweig visits the Zingerman's Roadhouse restaurant and the staff is very busy, they may ask him to help out by serving customers or cleaning off tables. As he indicates, "People give me assignments all the time. Sometimes I'm the note-taker. Sometimes I'm the cleaner-upper. . . . Sometimes I'm on my hands and knees wiping up what people spilled."[24]

Weinzweig and Saginaw also have a strong sense of commitment to serving the local community; Zingerman's founded the nonprofit organization Food Gatherers to eliminate hunger and distribute food to the needy, and Food Gatherers is now an independent nonprofit responsible for the Washtenaw County Food Bank with over 5,000 volunteers and a 19-member staff.[25] On Zingerman's 20th anniversary, 13 nonprofit community organizations in Ann Arbor erected a plaque next to Zingerman's Delicatessen with a dedication that read, "Thank you for feeding, sheltering, educating, uplifting, and inspiring an entire community."[26] Clearly, for Weinzweig and Saginaw, leadership entails being of service to others.[27]

Leadership Styles across Cultures

Some evidence suggests that leadership styles vary not only among individuals but also among countries or cultures. Some research indicates that European managers tend to be more humanistic or people-oriented than both Japanese and American managers. The collectivistic culture in Japan places prime emphasis on the group rather than the individual, so the importance of individuals' own personalities, needs, and desires is minimized. Organizations in the United States tend to be very profit-oriented and thus tend to downplay the importance of individual employees' needs and desires. Many countries in Europe have a more individualistic perspective than Japan and a more humanistic perspective than the United States, and this may result in some European managers' being more people-oriented than their Japanese or American counterparts. European managers, for example, tend to be reluctant to lay off employees, and when a layoff is absolutely necessary, they take careful steps to make it as painless as possible.[28]

Another cross-cultural difference occurs in time horizons. While managers in any one country often differ in their time horizons, there are also national differences. For example, U.S. organizations tend to have a short-term profit orientation, and thus U.S. managers' personal leadership styles emphasize short-term performance. Japanese organizations tend to have a long-term growth orientation, so Japanese managers' personal leadership styles emphasize long-term performance. Justus Mische, a personnel manager at the European organization Hoechst, suggests that "Europe, at least the big international firms in Europe, have a philosophy between the Japanese, long term, and the United States, short term."[29] Research on these and other global aspects of leadership is in its infancy; as it continues, more cultural differences in managers' personal leadership styles may be discovered.

Power: The Key to Leadership

No matter what one's leadership style, a key component of effective leadership is found in the *power* the leader has to affect other people's behavior and get them to act in certain ways.[30] There are several types of power: legitimate, reward, coercive, expert, and referent power (see Figure 14.1).[31] Effective leaders take steps to ensure that they have sufficient levels of each type and that they use the power they have in beneficial ways.

legitimate power The authority that a manager has by virtue of his or her position in an organization's hierarchy.

LEGITIMATE POWER **Legitimate power** is the authority a manager has by virtue of his or her position in an organization's hierarchy. Personal leadership style often influences how a manager exercises legitimate power. Take the case of Carol Loray, who is a first-line manager in a greeting card company and leads a group of 15 artists and designers. Loray has the legitimate power to hire new employees, assign projects to the artists and designers, monitor their work, and appraise their performance. She uses this power effectively. She always makes sure her project assignments match the interests of her subordinates as much as possible so they will enjoy their work. She monitors their work to make sure they are on track but does not engage in close supervision, which can hamper creativity. She makes sure her performance appraisals are developmental, providing concrete advice for areas where improvements could be made. Recently Loray negotiated with her manager to increase her legitimate power so she can now initiate and develop proposals for new card lines.

reward power The ability of a manager to give or withhold tangible and intangible rewards.

REWARD POWER **Reward power** is the ability of a manager to give or withhold tangible rewards (pay raises, bonuses, choice job assignments) and intangible rewards (verbal praise, a pat on the back, respect). As you learned in Chapter 13, members of an organization are motivated to perform at a high level by a variety of rewards. Being able to give or withhold rewards based on performance is a major source of power that allows managers to have a highly motivated workforce. Managers of

Figure 14.1
Source of Managerial Power

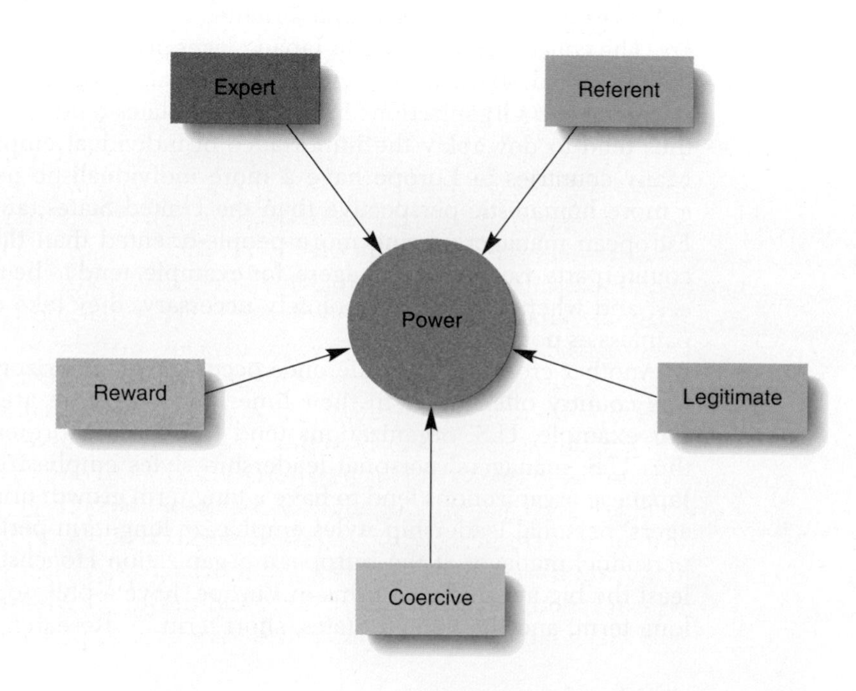

salespeople in retail organizations like Metro from Germany; Carrefour from France; and A.S. Watson & Company from Hong Kong and in car dealerships such as Mazda and Volvo often use their reward power to motivate their subordinates. Subordinates in organizations such as these often receive commissions on whatever they sell and rewards for the quality of their customer service, which motivate them to do the best they can.

Effective managers use their reward power to show appreciation for subordinates' good work and efforts. Ineffective managers use rewards in a more controlling manner (wielding the "stick" instead of offering the "carrot") that signals to subordinates that the manager has the upper hand. Managers also can take steps to increase their reward power. Carol Loray had the legitimate power to appraise her subordinates' performance, but she lacked the reward power to distribute raises and end-of-year bonuses until she discussed with her own manager why this would be a valuable motivational tool for her to use. Loray now receives a pool of money each year for salary increases and bonuses and has the reward power to distribute them as she sees fit.

coercive power The ability of a manager to punish others.

COERCIVE POWER **Coercive power** is the ability of a manager to punish others. Punishment can range from verbal reprimands to reductions in pay or working hours to actual dismissal. In the previous chapter we discussed how punishment can have negative side effects, such as resentment and retaliation, and should be used only when necessary (for example, to curtail a dangerous behavior). Managers who rely heavily on coercive power tend to be ineffective as leaders and sometimes even get fired themselves. William J. Fife is one example; he was fired from his position as CEO of Giddings and Lewis Inc., a U.S. manufacturer of factory equipment, because of his overreliance on coercive power. In meetings Fife often verbally criticized, attacked, and embarrassed top managers. Realizing how destructive Fife's use of punishment was for them and the company, these managers complained to the board of directors, who, after a careful consideration of the issues, asked Fife to resign.[32]

Excessive use of coercive power seldom produces high performance and is questionable ethically. Sometimes it amounts to a form of mental abuse, robbing workers of their dignity and causing excessive levels of stress. Overuse of coercive power can even result in dangerous working conditions. Better results and, importantly, an ethical workplace that respects employee dignity can be obtained by using reward power.

expert power Power that is based on the special knowledge, skills, and expertise that a leader possesses.

EXPERT POWER **Expert power** is based on the special knowledge, skills, and expertise that a leader possesses. The nature of expert power varies, depending on the leader's level in the hierarchy. First-level and middle managers often have technical expertise relevant to the tasks their subordinates perform. Their expert power gives them considerable influence over subordinates. Carol Loray has expert power: She is an artist herself and has drawn and designed some of her company's top-selling greeting cards. Judy McGrath in "A Manager's Challenge" has expert power from over 25 years' experience in the media industry, as well as from her efforts to stay attuned to pop culture through extensive networking, reading, and ever-ready openness for the new and the quirky. As indicated in the "Manager as a Person" box on the next page, the kinds of positions that leaders with expert power assume depends on who they are as individuals and the kinds of challenges that appeal to them.

Some top managers derive expert power from their technical expertise. Craig Barrett, chairman of the board of directors of Intel from 2005 to 2009, has a PhD in materials science from Stanford University and is very knowledgeable about the ins and outs of Intel's business–producing semiconductors and microprocessors.[33] Similarly, Bill Gates, chairman of Microsoft, and CEO Steve Ballmer have expertise in software design; and Tachi Yamada, president of the Bill and Melinda Gates Foundation's Global Health Program, has an MD and was previously chairman of research and development at GlaxoSmithKline.[34] Many top-level managers, however, lack technical expertise and derive their expert power from their abilities as

Manager as a Person

Different Leadership Styles at Different Times

Novartis is one of the world's largest pharmaceutical firms with more than US$36 billion in sales. The firm is the creation of a merger that occurred in 1996 of two very large pharmaceutical firms, Ciba-Geigy and Sandoz. The oldest of these firms was Geigy, which was formed in the 1750s. Ciba-Geigy was formed in a merger in the 1970s, and then this firm merged with Sandoz in the 1990s. In addition to these large mergers there have been a number of acquisitions of smaller firms that have occurred to create the Novartis that exists today.

In 2010 the CEO, who had overseen the merger of Ciba-Geigy and Sandoz to create Novartis and a number of other acquisitions in an effort to grow the firm, retired. The selection of the new CEO presented the firm two stark choices among the leading candidates. One candidate was Joe Jimenez, a 50-year-old American who worked at U.S. consumer-products companies before joining Novartis in 2007. The other candidate was Joerg Reinhardt, a German scientist who helped develop Novartis's vaccine business during a 28-year career with the company. The two candidates offered contrasts–one had been with the firm most of his adult life and the other only a few years. One candidate was technically an expert in one of pharmaceutical industry's key domains, while the other had previously worked with consumer goods such as food.

The board chose to go with Joe Jimenez. The board felt it needed technical expertise not expertise in pharmaceuticals. The board felt it needed operational expertise on how to increase efficiency in the large firm. The result of mergers and acquisitions was large and profitable, but the board feared not as efficient as it needed to be. Thus, the board decided the company needed someone who could operate the large pharmaceutical business in an efficient manner–the efficiency not necessarily being any different than any other consumer manufacturing process. Thus, the technical knowledge needed was not scientific but operational.

decision makers, planners, and strategists. Jack Welch, the former well-known leader and CEO of General Electric, summed it up this way: "The basic thing that we at the top of the company know is that we don't know the business. What we have, I hope, is the ability to allocate resources, people, and dollars."[35]

Effective leaders take steps to ensure that they have an adequate amount of expert power to perform their leadership roles. They may obtain additional training or education in their fields, make sure they keep up with the latest developments and changes in technology, stay abreast of changes in their fields through involvement in professional associations, and read widely to be aware of momentous changes in the organization's task and general environments. Expert power tends to be best used in a guiding or coaching manner rather than in an arrogant, high-handed manner.

referent power Power that comes from subordinates' and coworkers' respect, admiration, and loyalty.

REFERENT POWER **Referent power** is more informal than the other kinds of power. Referent power is a function of the personal characteristics of a leader; it is the power that comes from subordinates' and coworkers' respect, admiration, and loyalty. Leaders who are likable and whom subordinates wish to use as a role model are especially likely to possess referent power, as is true of Judy McGrath in "A Manager's Challenge." Managers can take steps to increase their referent power, such as taking time to get to know their subordinates and showing interest in and concern for them.

Empowerment: An Ingredient in Modern Management

empowerment The expansion of employees' knowledge, tasks, and decision-making responsibilities.

More and more managers today are incorporating into their personal leadership styles an aspect that at first glance seems to be the opposite of being a leader. In Chapter 1 we described how **empowerment**–the process of giving employees at all levels the authority to make decisions, be responsible for their outcomes, improve quality, and cut costs–is becoming increasingly popular in organizations. When leaders empower their subordinates, the subordinates typically take over some responsibilities and authority that used to reside with the leader or manager, such as the right to reject parts that do not meet quality standards, the right to check one's own work, and the right to schedule work activities. Empowered subordinates are given the power to make some decisions that their leaders or supervisors used to make.

An empowered employee, like this auto assembly line worker, can halt the production process to correct an error rather than wasting time and money by waiting for a supervisor.

Empowerment might seem to be the opposite of effective leadership because managers are allowing subordinates to take a more active role in leading themselves. In actuality, however, empowerment can contribute to effective leadership for several reasons:

- Empowerment increases a manager's ability to get things done because the manager has the support and help of subordinates who may have special knowledge of work tasks.
- Empowerment often increases workers' involvement, motivation, and commitment, and this helps ensure that they are working toward organizational goals.
- Empowerment gives managers more time to concentrate on their pressing concerns because they spend less time on day-to-day supervision.

Effective managers like Judy McGrath realize the benefits of empowerment. The personal leadership style of managers who empower subordinates often entails developing subordinates' ability to make good decisions as well as being their guide, coach, and source of inspiration. Empowerment is a popular trend in the United States and Europe at companies as diverse as United Parcel Service (a package delivery company) and Boots Group, a U.K. retailer, and is a part of servant leadership. Empowerment is being attempted around the world.[36] For instance, companies in South Korea (such as Samsung, Hyundai, and Daewoo), in which decision making typically was centralized with the founding families, are now seeking to empower managers at lower levels to make decisions.[37]

LO14-2 Identify the traits that show the strongest relationship to leadership, the behaviors leaders engage in, and the limitations of the trait and behavior models of leadership.

Trait and Behavior Models of Leadership

Leading is such an important process in all organizations–nonprofit organizations, government agencies, and schools, as well as for-profit corporations–that it has been researched for decades. Early approaches to leadership, called the *trait model* and the *behavior model,* sought to determine what effective leaders are like as people and what they do that makes them so effective.

The Trait Model

The trait model of leadership focused on identifying the personal characteristics that cause effective leadership. Researchers thought effective leaders must have certain personal qualities that set them apart from ineffective leaders and from people who never become leaders. Decades of research (beginning in the 1930s) and hundreds of studies indicate that certain personal characteristics do appear to be associated with effective leadership. (See Table 14.1 for a list of these.)[38] Notice that although this model is called the "trait" model, some of the personal characteristics that it identifies are not personality traits per se but, rather, are concerned with a leader's skills, abilities, knowledge, and expertise. As "A Manager's Challenge" shows, Judy McGrath certainly appears to possess many of these characteristics (such as intelligence, knowledge and expertise, self-confidence, high energy, and integrity and honesty). Leaders who do not possess these traits may be ineffective.

Traits alone are not the key to understanding leader effectiveness, however. Some effective leaders do not possess all these traits, and some leaders who possess them are not effective in their leadership roles. This lack of a consistent relationship between leader traits and leader effectiveness led researchers to shift their attention away from traits and to search for new explanations for effective leadership. Rather than focusing on what leaders are like (the traits they possess), researchers began looking at what effective leaders actually do–in other words, at the behaviors that allow effective leaders to influence their subordinates to achieve group and organizational goals.

The Behavior Model

After extensive study in the 1940s and 1950s, researchers at The Ohio State University identified two basic kinds of leader behaviors that many leaders in the United States, Germany, and other countries engaged in to influence their subordinates: *consideration* and *initiating structure.*[39]

consideration Behavior indicating that a manager trusts, respects, and cares about subordinates.

CONSIDERATION Leaders engage in **consideration** when they show their subordinates that they trust, respect, and care about them. Managers who truly look out for the well-being of their subordinates, and do what they can to help subordinates feel good and enjoy their work, perform consideration behaviors. In "A Manager's Challenge," Judy McGrath engages in consideration when she listens to employees and fosters an inclusive, nurturing culture at MTV Networks.

Table 14.1
Traits and Personal Characteristics Related to Effective Leadership

Trait	Description
Intelligence	Helps managers understand complex issues and solve problems.
Knowledge and expertise	Help managers make good decisions and discover ways to increase efficiency and effectiveness.
Dominance	Helps managers influence their subordinates to achieve organizational goals.
Self-confidence	Contributes to managers' effectively influencing subordinates and persisting when faced with obstacles or difficulties.
High energy	Helps managers deal with the many demands they face.
Tolerance for stress	Helps managers deal with uncertainty and make difficult decisions.
Integrity and honesty	Help managers behave ethically and earn their subordinates' trust and confidence.
Maturity	Helps managers avoid acting selfishly, control their feelings, and admit when they have made a mistake.

initiating structure Behavior that managers engage in to ensure that work gets done, subordinates perform their jobs acceptably, and the organization is efficient and effective.

INITIATING STRUCTURE Leaders engage in **initiating structure** when they take steps to make sure that work gets done, subordinates perform their jobs acceptably, and the organization is efficient and effective. Assigning tasks to individuals or work groups, letting subordinates know what is expected of them, deciding how work should be done, making schedules, encouraging adherence to rules and regulations, and motivating subordinates to do a good job are all examples of initiating structure.[40] Michael Teckel, the manager of an upscale store selling imported men's and women's shoes in a European city, engages in initiating structure when he establishes weekly work, lunch, and break schedules to ensure that the store has enough salespeople on the floor. Teckle also initiates structure when he discusses the latest shoe designs with his subordinates so they are knowledgeable with customers, when he encourages adherence to the store's refund and exchange policies, and when he encourages his staff to provide high-quality customer service and to avoid a hard-sell approach.

Initiating structure and consideration are independent leader behaviors. Leaders can be high on both, low on both, or high on one and low on the other. Many effective leaders, like Judy McGrath of MTV Networks, engage in both of these behaviors.

Ethics in Action

Nestlé and Leadership Training in the UK

BusinessWeek ranks Nestlé as one of the top 20 companies in the world for leadership. The Swiss firm is one of the largest consumer product companies in the world with sales of more than 100 billion US dollars and more than 275,000 employees worldwide. Leadership development is a key part of this effort.

According to Edward Marsh, head of talent and organization development, "Leadership at Nestlé is about a long-term commitment to growing the business while growing people, and our leadership development efforts continue to stress the importance of learning from real, often international, experience, supported in more innovative ways aligned to people's changing aspirations and personal circumstances. This may include more short-term assignments, global projects, and even weekly commutes, as well as peer coaching and mentoring. Executive education will continue to play a supporting role."

Nestlé UK implemented a training program called Lead2Win, which focuses on how to make employees more effective leaders.

The firm operates in a relatively decentralized manner for leadership training. Each nation runs its own training programs picking the combination of classroom, Internet, and seminar presentations that work best for that unit. The United Kingdom and Ireland unit of Nestlé began a new program in 2009 called Lead2Win that is tailored to the needs of that market.

The training gives the managers a new language so that they all can communicate more effectively and new skills that support the vision for Nestlé UK. The training takes eight days of learning, which address six program objectives including identifying what it is to be a leader and increasing leadership accountability; creating collaboration across divisions; delivering clear business results; and managing and leading through change. The total program with all of its different elements takes 18 months for participants to graduate from a program. The goal is that all 1,200 plus employees in leadership roles in the Nestlé UK unit complete the training.[41]

Leadership researchers have identified leader behaviors similar to consideration and initiating structure. Researchers at the University of Michigan, for example, identified two categories of leadership behaviors, *employee-centered behaviors* and *job-oriented behaviors,* that correspond roughly to consideration and initiating structure, respectively.[42] Models of leadership popular with consultants also tend to zero in on these two kinds of behaviors. For example, Robert Blake and Jane Mouton's Managerial Grid focuses on *concern for people* (similar to consideration) and *concern for production* (similar to initiating structure). Blake and Mouton advise that effective leadership often requires both a high level of concern for people and a high level of concern for production.[43] As another example, Paul Hersey and Kenneth Blanchard's model focuses on *supportive behaviors* (similar to consideration) and *task-oriented behaviors* (similar to initiating structure). According to Hersey and Blanchard, leaders need to consider the nature of their subordinates when trying to determine the extent to which they should perform these two behaviors.[44]

You might expect that effective leaders and managers would perform both kinds of behaviors, but research has found that this is not necessarily the case. The relationship between performance of consideration and initiating-structure behaviors and leader effectiveness is not clear-cut. Some leaders are effective even when they do not perform consideration or initiating-structure behaviors, and some leaders are ineffective even when they perform both kinds of behaviors. Like the trait model of leadership, the behavior model alone cannot explain leader effectiveness. Realizing this, researchers began building more complicated models of leadership, focused not only on the leader and what he or she does but also on the situation or context in which leadership occurs.

Contingency Models of Leadership

LO14-3 Explain how contingency models of leadership enhance our understanding of effective leadership and management in organizations.

Simply possessing certain traits or performing certain behaviors does not ensure that a manager will be an effective leader in all situations calling for leadership. Some managers who seem to possess the right traits and perform the right behaviors turn out to be ineffective leaders. Managers lead in a wide variety of situations and organizations and have various kinds of subordinates performing diverse tasks in a multiplicity of environmental contexts. Given the wide variety of situations in which leadership occurs, what makes a manager an effective leader in one situation (such as certain traits or behaviors) is not necessarily what that manager needs to be equally effective in a different situation. An effective army general might not be an effective university president; an effective restaurant manager might not be an effective clothing store manager; an effective football team coach might not be an effective fitness center manager; and an effective first-line manager in a manufacturing company might not be an effective middle manager. The traits or behaviors that may contribute to a manager's being an effective leader in one situation might actually result in the same manager being an ineffective leader in another situation.

Contingency models of leadership take into account the situation or context within which leadership occurs. According to contingency models, whether or not a manager is an effective leader is the result of the interplay between what the manager is like, what he or she does, and the situation in which leadership takes place. Contingency models propose that whether a leader who possesses certain traits or performs certain behaviors is effective depends on, or is contingent on, the situation or context. In this section we discuss three prominent contingency models developed to shed light on what makes managers effective leaders: Fred Fiedler's contingency model, Robert House's path–goal theory, and the leader substitutes model. As you will see, these leadership models are complementary; each focuses on a somewhat different aspect of effective leadership in organizations.

Fiedler's Contingency Model

Fred E. Fiedler was among the first leadership researchers to acknowledge that effective leadership is contingent on, or depends on, the characteristics of the leader *and* of the situation. Fiedler's contingency model helps explain why a manager may be an effective leader in one situation and ineffective in another; it also suggests which kinds of managers are likely to be most effective in which situations.[45]

LEADER STYLE As with the trait approach, Fiedler hypothesized that personal characteristics can influence leader effectiveness. He used the term *leader style* to refer to a manager's characteristic approach to leadership and identified two basic leader styles: *relationship-oriented* and *task-oriented.* All managers can be described as having one style or the other.

relationship-oriented leaders Leaders whose primary concern is to develop good relationships with their subordinates and to be liked by them.

task-oriented leaders Leaders whose primary concern is to ensure that subordinates perform at a high level.

Relationship-oriented leaders are primarily concerned with developing good relationships with their subordinates and being liked by them. Relationship-oriented managers focus on having high-quality interpersonal relationships with subordinates. This does not mean, however, that the job does not get done when such leaders are at the helm. But it does mean that the quality of interpersonal relationships with subordinates is a prime concern for relationship-oriented leaders.

Task-oriented leaders are primarily concerned with ensuring that subordinates perform at a high level and focus on task accomplishment. While task-oriented leaders also may be concerned about having good interpersonal relationships with their subordinates, task accomplishment is their prime concern.

In his research, Fiedler measured leader style by asking leaders to rate the coworker with whom they have had the most difficulty working (called the least preferred coworker or LPC) on a number of dimensions, such as whether the person is boring or interesting, gloomy or cheerful, enthusiastic or unenthusiastic, cooperative or uncooperative. Relationship-oriented leaders tend to describe the LPC in relatively positive terms; their concern for good relationships leads them to think well of others. Task-oriented leaders tend to describe the LPC in negative terms; their concern for task accomplishment causes them to think badly about others who make getting the job done difficult. Thus relationship-oriented and task-oriented leaders are sometimes referred to as high-LPC and low-LPC leaders, respectively.

SITUATIONAL CHARACTERISTICS According to Fiedler, leadership style is an enduring characteristic; managers cannot change their style, nor can they adopt different styles in different kinds of situations. With this in mind, Fiedler identified three situational characteristics that are important determinants of how favorable a situation is for leading: leader–member relations, task structure, and position power. When a situation is favorable for leading, it is relatively easy for a manager to influence subordinates so they perform at a high level and contribute to organizational efficiency and effectiveness. In a situation unfavorable for leading, it is much more difficult for a manager to exert influence.

leader–member relations The extent to which followers like, trust, and are loyal to their leader; a determinant of how favorable a situation is for leading.

task structure The extent to which the work to be performed is clear-cut so that a leader's subordinates know what needs to be accomplished and how to go about doing it; a determinant of how favorable a situation is for leading.

LEADER–MEMBER RELATIONS The first situational characteristic Fiedler described, **leader–member relations,** is the extent to which followers like, trust, and are loyal to their leader. Situations are more favorable for leading when leader–member relations are good.

TASK STRUCTURE The second situational characteristic Fiedler described, **task structure,** is the extent to which the work to be performed is clear-cut so that a leader's subordinates know what needs to be accomplished and how to go about doing it. When task structure is high, the situation is favorable for leading. When task structure is low, goals may be vague, subordinates may be unsure of what they should be doing or how they should do it, and the situation is unfavorable for leading.

Task structure was low for Geraldine Laybourne when she was a top manager at Nickelodeon, the children's television network. It was never precisely clear what would appeal to her young viewers, whose tastes can change dramatically, or how

Developing good relations with employees can make the "situation" more favorable for leading.

to motivate her subordinates to come up with creative and novel ideas.[46] In contrast, Herman Mashaba, founder of Black Like Me, a hair care products company based in South Africa, seemed to have relatively high task structure when he started his company. His company's goals were to produce and sell inexpensive hair care products to native Africans, and managers accomplished these goals by using simple yet appealing packaging and distributing the products through neighborhood beauty salons.[47]

POSITION POWER The third situational characteristic Fiedler described, **position power,** is the amount of legitimate, reward, and coercive power a leader has by virtue of his or her position in an organization. Leadership situations are more favorable for leading when position power is strong.

position power The amount of legitimate, reward, and coercive power that a leader has by virtue of his or her position in an organization; a determinant of how favorable a situation is for leading.

COMBINING LEADER STYLE AND THE SITUATION By considering all possible combinations of good and poor leader–member relations, high and low task structure, and strong and weak position power, Fiedler identified eight leadership situations, which vary in their favorability for leading (see Figure 14.2). After extensive research, he determined that relationship-oriented leaders are most effective in moderately favorable situations (IV, V, VI, and VII in Figure 14.2) and task-oriented leaders are most effective in situations that are either very favorable (I, II, and III) or very unfavorable (VIII).

PUTTING THE CONTINGENCY MODEL INTO PRACTICE Recall that, according to Fiedler, leader style is an enduring characteristic that managers cannot change. This suggests that for managers to be effective, either managers need to be placed in leadership situations that fit their style or situations need to be changed to suit the managers. Situations can be changed, for example, by giving a manager more position power or taking steps to increase task structure, such as by clarifying goals.

Take the case of Mark Compton, a relationship-oriented leader employed by a small construction company, who was in a very unfavorable situation and was having a rough time leading his construction crew. His subordinates did not trust him to look out for their well-being (poor leader–member relations); the construction jobs he supervised tended to be novel and complex (low task structure); and he had no control over the rewards and disciplinary actions his subordinates received (weak position power). Recognizing the need to improve matters, Compton's supervisor

Figure 14.2
Fielder's Contingency Theory of Leadership

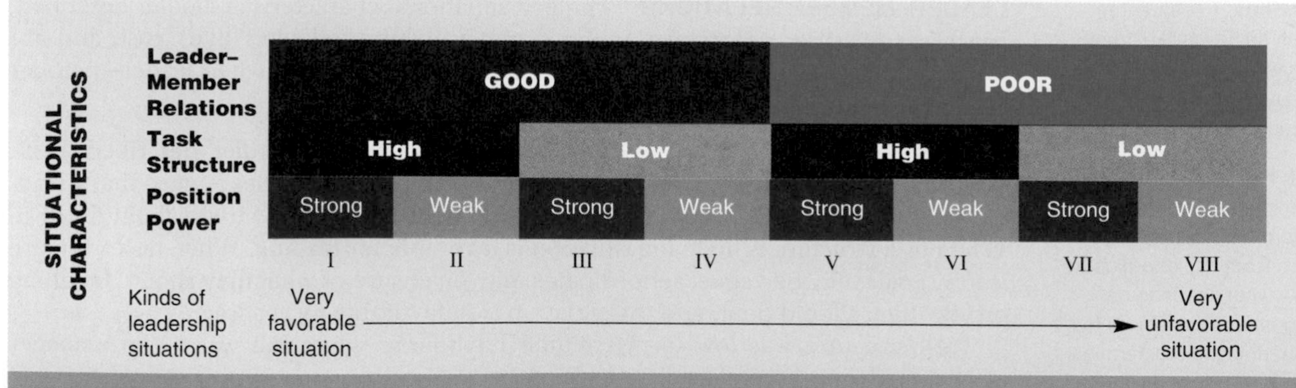

gave him the power to reward crew members with bonuses and overtime work as he saw fit and to discipline crew members for poor-quality work and unsafe on-the-job behavior. As his leadership situation improved to moderately favorable, so too did Compton's effectiveness as a leader and the performance of his crew.

Research studies tend to support some aspects of Fiedler's model but also suggest that, like most theories, it needs some modifications.[48] Some researchers have questioned what the LPC scale really measures. Others find fault with the model's premise that leaders cannot alter their styles. That is, it is likely that at least some leaders can diagnose the situation they are in and, when their style is inappropriate for the situation, modify their style so that it is more in line with what the leadership situation calls for.

House's Path–Goal Theory

path–goal theory A contingency model of leadership proposing that leaders can motivate subordinates by identifying their desired outcomes, rewarding them for high performance and the attainment of work goals with these desired outcomes, and clarifying for them the paths leading to the attainment of work goals.

In what he called **path–goal theory,** leadership researcher Robert House focused on what leaders can do to motivate their subordinates to achieve group and organizational goals.[49] The premise of path–goal theory is that effective leaders motivate subordinates to achieve goals by (1) clearly identifying the outcomes that subordinates are trying to obtain from the workplace, (2) rewarding subordinates with these outcomes for high performance and the attainment of work goals, and (3) clarifying for subordinates the *paths* leading to the attainment of work *goals.* Path–goal theory is a contingency model because it proposes that the steps managers should take to motivate subordinates depend on both the nature of the subordinates and the type of work they do.

Based on the expectancy theory of motivation (see Chapter 13), path–goal theory gives managers three guidelines to being effective leaders:

1. *Find out what outcomes your subordinates are trying to obtain from their jobs and the organization.* These outcomes can range from satisfactory pay and job security to reasonable working hours and interesting and challenging job assignments. After identifying these outcomes, the manager should have the *reward power* needed to distribute or withhold the outcomes.
2. *Reward subordinates for high performance and goal attainment with the outcomes they desire.*
3. *Clarify the paths to goal attainment for subordinates, remove any obstacles to high performance, and express confidence in subordinates' capabilities.* This does not mean that a manager needs to tell subordinates what to do. Rather, it means that a manager needs to make sure subordinates are clear about what they should be trying to accomplish and have the capabilities, resources, and confidence levels needed to be successful.

Path–goal theory identifies four kinds of leadership behaviors that motivate subordinates:

- *Directive behaviors* are similar to initiating structure and include setting goals, assigning tasks, showing subordinates how to complete tasks, and taking concrete steps to improve performance.
- *Supportive behaviors* are similar to consideration and include expressing concern for subordinates and looking out for their best interests.
- *Participative behaviors* give subordinates a say in matters and decisions that affect them.
- *Achievement-oriented behaviors* motivate subordinates to perform at the highest level possible by, for example, setting challenging goals, expecting that they be met, and believing in subordinates' capabilities.

Which of these behaviors should managers use to lead effectively? The answer to this question depends, or is contingent on, the nature of the subordinates and the kind of work they do.

Directive behaviors may be beneficial when subordinates are having difficulty completing assigned tasks, but they might be detrimental when subordinates are independent thinkers who work best when left alone. *Supportive* behaviors are often advisable when subordinates are experiencing high levels of stress. *Participative* behaviors can be particularly effective when subordinates' support of a decision is required. *Achievement-oriented* behaviors may increase motivation levels of highly capable subordinates who are bored from having too few challenges, but they might backfire if used with subordinates who are already pushed to their limit.

The Leader Substitutes Model

leadership substitute A characteristic of a subordinate or of a situation or context that acts in place of the influence of a leader and makes leadership unnecessary.

The leader substitutes model suggests that leadership is sometimes unnecessary because substitutes for leadership are present. A **leadership substitute** is something that acts in place of the influence of a leader and makes leadership unnecessary. This model suggests that under certain conditions managers do not have to play a leadership role–members of an organization sometimes can perform at a high level without a manager exerting influence over them.[50] The leader substitutes model is a contingency model because it suggests that in some situations leadership is unnecessary.

Take the case of David Cotsonas, who teaches English at a foreign language school in Cyprus, an island in the Mediterranean Sea. Cotsonas is fluent in Greek, English, and French; is an excellent teacher; and is highly motivated. Many of his students are businesspeople who have some rudimentary English skills and wish to increase their fluency to be able to conduct more of their business in English. He enjoys not only teaching them English but also learning about the work they do, and he often keeps in touch with his students after they finish his classes. Cotsonas meets with the director of the school twice a year to discuss semiannual class schedules and enrollments.

With practically no influence from a leader, Cotsonas is a highly motivated top performer at the school. In his situation, leadership is unnecessary because substitutes for leadership are present. Cotsonas's teaching expertise, his motivation, and his enjoyment of his work all are substitutes for the influence of a leader–in this case the school's director. If the school's director were to try to influence how Cotsonas performs his job, Cotsonas would probably resent this infringement on his autonomy, and it is unlikely that his performance would improve because he is already one of the school's best teachers.

As in Cotsonas's case, *characteristics of subordinates*–such as their skills, abilities, experience, knowledge, and motivation–can be substitutes for leadership.[51] *Characteristics of the situation or context*–such as the extent to which the work is interesting and enjoyable–also can be substitutes. When work is interesting and enjoyable, as it is for Cotsonas, jobholders do not need to be coaxed into performing because performing is rewarding in its own right. Similarly, when managers *empower* their subordinates or use *self-managed work teams* (discussed in detail in Chapter 15), the need for leadership influence from a manager is decreased because team members manage themselves.

Substitutes for leadership can increase organizational efficiency and effectiveness because they free up some of managers' valuable time and allow managers to focus their efforts on discovering new ways to improve organizational effectiveness. The director of the language school, for example, was able to spend much of his time making arrangements to open a second school in Rhodes, an island in the Aegean Sea, because of the presence of leadership substitutes, not only for Cotsonas but for most other teachers at the school as well.

Bringing It All Together

Effective leadership in organizations occurs when managers take steps to lead in a way that is appropriate for the situation or context in which leadership occurs and for the subordinates who are being led. The three contingency models of leadership just discussed help managers focus on the necessary ingredients for effective leadership. They are complementary in that each one looks at the leadership question from

Table 14.2
Contingency Models of Leadership

Model	Focus	Key Contingencies
Fiedler's contingency model	Describes two leader styles, relationship-oriented and task-oriented, and the kinds of situations in which each kind of leader will be most effective.	Whether a relationship-oriented or a task-oriented leader is effective is contingent on the situation.
House's path–goal theory	Describes how effective leaders motivate their followers.	The behaviors that managers should engage in to be effective leaders are contingent on the nature of the subordinates and the work they do.
Leader substitutes model	Describes when leadership is unnecessary.	Whether leadership is necessary for subordinates to perform highly is contingent on characteristics of the subordinates and the situation.

a different angle. Fiedler's contingency model explores how a manager's leadership style needs to be matched to that person's leadership situation for maximum effectiveness. House's path–goal theory focuses on how managers should motivate subordinates and describes the specific kinds of behaviors managers can engage in to have a highly motivated workforce. The leadership substitutes model alerts managers to the fact that sometimes they do not need to exert influence over subordinates and thus can free up their time for other important activities. Table 14.2 recaps these three contingency models of leadership.

Transformational Leadership

LO14-4 Describe what transformational leadership is, and explain how managers can engage in it.

Time and time again, throughout business history, certain leaders seem to literally transform their organizations, making sweeping changes to revitalize and renew operations. Transformational leaders are people whose leadership style allows them to make dramatic changes in an organization. This leadership style should not be confused with charisma. In fact, in some settings charisma is not a valued characteristic. For example, in Germany charisma is associated with the rise of Hitler. He was a very charismatic person who created a horrific government that almost destroyed all of Europe including the holocaust for Jews and other groups. As a result, charisma is not a characteristic that is valued. However, the nation still has great transformational leaders. It should be recognized that in general transformational leadership, and all styles of leadership, will be impacted by the cultural setting in which they appear.[52]

transformational leadership Leadership that makes subordinates aware of the importance of their jobs and performance to the organization and aware of their own needs for personal growth and that motivates subordinates to work for the good of the organization.

Transformational leadership occurs when managers change (or transform) their subordinates in three important ways:[53]

1. *Transformational managers make subordinates aware of how important their jobs are for the organization and how necessary it is for them to perform those jobs as best they can so the organization can attain its goals.* An example of transformational leadership is Heinrich von Pierer, CEO of Siemens. His analogy is that leadership should not try to turn a supertanker, which is very difficult. Instead, the firm must empower lots of managers so that the firm becomes like a flotilla of small, nimble boats.
2. *Transformational managers make their subordinates aware of the subordinates' own needs for personal growth, development, and accomplishment.* This transformational leadership often takes different forms in Europe than in the United States. In the United States success is associated strictly with increased profits. This can lead to a focus

on employee reduction. But in Europe the focus is often on transforming a business to be successful. This often takes investment and the return may be less than it could be if workers were fired–but the transformation is often better for the community. Such a transformation and view of what the firm wants to achieve requires the leadership of the firm to help subordinates understand this vision. Thus, Siemens in Germany invested in revitalizing a turbine plant in Berlin rather than closing the plant and moving it to a new location.[54]

3. *Transformational managers motivate their subordinates to work for the good of the organization as a whole, not just for their own personal gain or benefit.* The transformation of the Siemens turbine plant in Berlin required all parties including workers and their union representatives to understand the transformation necessary to keep the plant open and revitalized.

When managers transform their subordinates in these three ways, subordinates trust the managers, are highly motivated, and help the organization achieve its goals. How do managers such as von Pierer transform subordinates and produce dramatic effects in their organizations? There are at least three ways in which transformational leaders can influence their followers: by being a charismatic leader, by intellectually stimulating subordinates, and by engaging in developmental consideration (see Table 14.3).

Being a Charismatic Leader

charismatic leader An enthusiastic, self-confident leader who is able to clearly communicate his or her vision of how good things could be.

Transformational managers are **charismatic leaders.** They have a vision of how good things could be in their work groups and organizations that is in contrast with the status quo. Their vision usually entails dramatic improvements in group and organizational performance as a result of changes in the organization's structure, culture, strategy, decision making, and other critical processes and factors. This vision paves the way for gaining a competitive advantage. From "A Manager's Challenge," it is clear that part of Judy McGrath's vision for MTV Networks is increasing its digital offerings and transforming MTV into a truly digital company.

Charismatic leaders are excited and enthusiastic about their vision and clearly communicate it to their subordinates, as does Judy McGrath. The excitement, enthusiasm, and self-confidence of a charismatic leader contribute to the leader's being able to inspire followers to enthusiastically support his or her vision.[55] People often think of charismatic leaders or managers as being "larger than life." The essence of charisma, however, is having a vision and enthusiastically communicating it to others. Thus managers who appear to be quiet and earnest can also be charismatic.

Stimulating Subordinates Intellectually

Transformational managers openly share information with their subordinates so they are aware of problems and the need for change. The manager causes subordinates to view problems in their groups and throughout the organization from a different

Table 14.3
Transformational Leadership

Transformational managers
- Are charismatic.
- Intellectually stimulate subordinates.
- Engage in developmental consideration.

Subordinates of transformational managers
- Have increased awareness of the importance of their jobs and high performance.
- Are aware of their own needs for growth, development, and accomplishment.
- Work for the good of the organization and not just their own personal benefit.

perspective, consistent with the manager's vision. Whereas in the past subordinates might not have been aware of some problems, may have viewed problems as a "management issue" beyond their concern, or may have viewed problems as insurmountable, the transformational manager's **intellectual stimulation** leads subordinates to view problems as challenges that they can and will meet and conquer. The manager engages and empowers subordinates to take personal responsibility for helping to solve problems.[56]

intellectual stimulation Behavior a leader engages in to make followers be aware of problems and view these problems in new ways, consistent with the leader's vision.

Engaging in Developmental Consideration

developmental consideration Behavior a leader engages in to support and encourage followers and help them develop and grow on the job.

When managers engage in **developmental consideration,** they not only perform the consideration behaviors described earlier, such as demonstrating true concern for the well-being of subordinates, but go one step further. The manager goes out of his or her way to support and encourage subordinates, giving them opportunities to enhance their skills and capabilities and to grow and excel on the job.[57]

All organizations, no matter how large or small, successful or unsuccessful, can benefit when their managers engage in transformational leadership. Moreover, while the benefits of transformational leadership are often most apparent when an organization is in trouble, transformational leadership can be an enduring approach to leadership, leading to long-term organizational effectiveness.

The Distinction between Transformational and Transactional Leadership

transactional leadership Leadership that motivates subordinates by rewarding them for high performance and reprimanding them for low performance.

Transformational leadership is often contrasted with transactional leadership. In **transactional leadership,** managers use their reward and coercive powers to encourage high performance. When managers reward high performers, reprimand or otherwise punish low performers, and motivate subordinates by reinforcing desired behaviors and extinguishing or punishing undesired ones, they are engaging in transactional leadership.[58] Managers who effectively influence their subordinates to achieve goals, yet do not seem to be making the kind of dramatic changes that are part of transformational leadership, are engaging in transactional leadership.

Many transformational leaders engage in transactional leadership. They reward subordinates for a job well done and notice and respond to substandard performance. But they also have their eyes on the bigger picture of how much better things could be in their organizations, how much more their subordinates are capable of achieving, and how important it is to treat their subordinates with respect and help them reach their full potential.

Research has found that when leaders engage in transformational leadership, their subordinates tend to have higher levels of job satisfaction and performance.[59] Additionally, subordinates of transformational leaders may be more likely to trust their leaders and their organizations and feel that they are being fairly treated, and this, in turn, may positively influence their work motivation (see Chapter 13).[60]

LO14-5 Characterize the relationship between gender and leadership and explain how emotional intelligence may contribute to leadership effectiveness.

Gender and Leadership

The increasing number of women entering the ranks of management, as well as the problems some women face in their efforts to be hired as managers or promoted into management positions, has prompted researchers to explore the relationship between gender and leadership. Although there are relatively more women in management positions today than there were 10 years ago, there are still relatively few women in top management and, in some organizations, even in middle management.

When women do advance to top management positions, special attention often is focused on them and the fact that they are women. For example, women CEOs of large companies are still rare; those who make it to the top post, such as

Indra Nooyi of PepsiCo,[61] Judy McGrath of MTV Networks, and Andrea Jung of Avon,[62] are salient. As business writer Linda Tischler puts it, "In a workplace where women CEOs of major companies are so scarce . . . they can be identified, like rock stars, by first name only."[63] Although women have certainly made inroads into leadership positions in organizations, they continue to be underrepresented in top leadership posts. For example, only 2.5% of board members of Germany's largest firms are women. Only 11% of all listed firms in Europe have female board members.[64]

A widespread stereotype of women is that they are nurturing, supportive, and concerned with interpersonal relations. Men are stereotypically viewed as being directive and focused on task accomplishment. Such stereotypes suggest that women tend to be more relationship-oriented as managers and engage in more consideration behaviors, whereas men are more task-oriented and engage in more initiating-structure behaviors. Does the behavior of actual male and female managers bear out these stereotypes? Do women managers lead in different ways than men do? Are male or female managers more effective as leaders?

Research suggests that male and female managers who have leadership positions in organizations behave in similar ways.[65] Women do not engage in more consideration than men, and men do not engage in more initiating structure than women. Research does suggest, however, that leadership style may vary between women and men. Women tend to be somewhat more participative as leaders than are men, involving subordinates in decision making and seeking their input.[66] Male managers tend to be less participative than are female managers, making more decisions on their own and wanting to do things their own way. Moreover, research suggests that men tend to be harsher when they punish their subordinates than do women.[67]

There are at least two reasons why female managers may be more participative as leaders than are male managers.[68] First, subordinates may try to resist the influence of female managers more than they do the influence of male managers. Some subordinates may never have reported to a woman before; some may incorrectly see a management role as being more appropriate for a man than for a woman; and some may just resist being led by a woman. To overcome this resistance and encourage subordinates' trust and respect, women managers may adopt a participative approach.

A second reason why female managers may be more participative is that they sometimes have better interpersonal skills than male managers.[69] A participative approach to leadership requires high levels of interaction and involvement between a manager and his or her subordinates, sensitivity to subordinates' feelings, and the ability to make decisions that may be unpopular with subordinates but necessary for goal attainment. Good interpersonal skills may help female managers have the effective interactions with their subordinates that are crucial to a participative approach.[70] To the extent that male managers have more difficulty managing interpersonal relationships, they may shy away from the high levels of interaction with subordinates necessary for true participation.

The key finding from research on leader behaviors, however, is that male and female managers do *not* differ significantly in their propensities to perform different leader behaviors. Even though they may be more participative, female managers do not engage in more consideration or less initiating structure than male managers.

Perhaps a question even more important than whether male and female managers differ in the leadership behaviors they perform is whether they differ in effectiveness. Consistent with the findings for leader behaviors, research suggests that across different kinds of organizational settings, male and female managers tend to be *equally effective* as leaders.[71] Thus there is no logical basis for stereotypes favoring male managers and leaders or for the existence of the "glass ceiling" (an invisible barrier that seems to prevent women from advancing as far as they should in some organizations). Because women and men are equally effective as leaders, the increasing number of women in the workforce should result in a larger pool of highly qualified candidates for management positions in organizations, ultimately enhancing organizational effectiveness.[72]

Emotional Intelligence and Leadership

Do the moods and emotions leaders experience on the job influence their behavior and effectiveness as leaders? Research suggests this is likely to be the case. For example, one study found that when store managers experienced positive moods at work, salespeople in their stores provided high-quality customer service and were less likely to quit.[73] Another study found that groups whose leaders experienced positive moods had better coordination, whereas groups whose leaders experienced negative moods exerted more effort; members of groups with leaders in positive moods also tended to experience more positive moods themselves; and members of groups with leaders in negative moods tended to experience more negative moods.[74]

A leader's level of emotional intelligence (see Chapter 3) may play a particularly important role in leadership effectiveness.[75] For example, emotional intelligence may help leaders develop a vision for their organizations, motivate their subordinates to commit to this vision, and energize them to enthusiastically work to achieve this vision. Moreover, emotional intelligence may enable leaders to develop a significant identity for their organization and instill high levels of trust and cooperation throughout the organization while maintaining the flexibility needed to respond to changing conditions.[76]

Emotional intelligence also plays a crucial role in how leaders relate to and deal with their followers, particularly when it comes to encouraging followers to be creative.[77] Creativity in organizations is an emotion-laden process; it often entails challenging the status quo, being willing to take risks and accept and learn from failures, and doing much hard work to bring creative ideas to fruition in terms of new products, services, or procedures and processes when uncertainty is bound to be high.[78] Leaders who are high on emotional intelligence are more likely to understand all the emotions surrounding creative endeavors, to be able to awaken and support the creative pursuits of their followers, and to provide the kind of support that enables creativity to flourish in organizations.[79]

Leaders, like people everywhere, sometimes make mistakes. Emotional intelligence may also help leaders respond appropriately when they realize they have made a mistake. Recognizing, admitting, and learning from mistakes can be especially important for entrepreneurs who start their own businesses, as profiled in the following "Focus on Diversity" box.

Focus on Diversity

Admitting a Mistake Helps Small Business Leader

Things seemed to be going well for Maureen Borzacchiello, CEO of Creative Display Solutions, located in Garden City, New York.[80] She founded her small business in 2001 to provide displays, graphics, and exhibits for use in trade shows and at events for companies ranging from American Express, FedEx, and General Electric to JetBlue Airways, AIG, and The Weather Channel.[81] Her company was growing, and she had received an award from the nonprofit organization, Count Me In for Women's Economic Independence.[82]

However, in 2006 she realized she had overextended her business financially. A large investment in inventory coupled with a sizable lease commitment, the need for office space renovations, the purchase of new furniture, and the addition of three new employees brought her to the point where she lacked the cash to pay her employees their regular salaries. When she had made these

Leadership means taking on responsibility for one's (and one's company's) mistakes, learning how to do better, and maintaining honesty with employees, as Maureen Borzacchiello exemplifies.

decisions, she thought she and her husband (who also works in the company) would be able to generate the revenues to cover the expenditures. But her brother-in-law unexpectedly passed away, and their involvement in family matters meant they weren't able to get new accounts as quickly as she had thought they would.[83]

Still confident that if she could get through this tough period, she would be able to get her business back on track, Borzacchiello decided to be honest with her employees about the company's current financial problems, why they occurred, and how she would strive to prevent such problems in the future. She met with her employees and told them, "All I can tell you is that I apologize. . . . We were so focused on accelerating growth that I didn't see it coming."[84] She admitted she needed to better understand her company's financial situation and daily cash flow, reassured employees that the company would be back on square footing in two to three months, and promised she would pay much more attention to ongoing financial performance and cash flow in the future.[85]

Borzacchiello also told employees that she and her husband would take no money out of the business for their own salaries until the financial problems were resolved. By being honest and open with employees, Borzacchiello gained their commitment and support. All employees decided to work shorter hours, and two employees were willing to have their hourly pay rates cut.[86] True to her promise, within two months all employees were able to return to their regular work hours; and by the beginning of 2007, Creative Display Solutions had over $1 million in revenues (which was more than double its revenues at the time of the financial problems).[87] To this day Creative Display Solutions remains a profitable business; and by 2010 its list of clients included more than 600 companies.[88] Clearly Borzacchiello effectively handled the temporary crisis her company faced by admitting and apologizing for her mistake and being open and honest with employees about her company's future prospects.[89]

Summary and Review

LO14-1 **THE NATURE OF LEADERSHIP** Leadership is the process by which a person exerts influence over other people and inspires, motivates, and directs their activities to help achieve group or organizational goals. Leaders can influence others because they possess power. The five types of power available to managers are legitimate power, reward power, coercive power, expert power, and referent power. Many managers are using empowerment as a tool to increase their effectiveness as leaders.

LO14-2 **TRAIT AND BEHAVIOR MODELS OF LEADERSHIP** The trait model of leadership describes personal characteristics or traits that contribute to effective leadership. However, some managers who possess these traits are not effective leaders, and some managers who do not possess all the traits are nevertheless effective leaders. The behavior model of leadership describes two kinds of behavior that most leaders engage in: consideration and initiating structure.

LO14-3 **CONTINGENCY MODELS OF LEADERSHIP** Contingency models take into account the complexity surrounding leadership and the role of the situation in determining whether a manager is an effective leader. Fiedler's contingency model explains why managers may be effective leaders in one situation and ineffective in another. According to Fiedler's model, relationship-oriented leaders are most effective in situations that are moderately favorable for leading, and task-oriented leaders are most effective in situations that are very favorable or very unfavorable for leading. House's path–goal theory describes how effective managers motivate their subordinates by determining what outcomes their subordinates want, rewarding subordinates with these outcomes when they achieve their goals and perform at a high level, and clarifying the paths to goal attainment. Managers can engage in four kinds of behaviors to motivate subordinates: directive, supportive, participative, and achievement-oriented behaviors. The leader substitutes model suggests that sometimes managers do not have to play a leadership role because their subordinates perform at a high level without the manager having to exert influence over them.

LO14-4 **TRANSFORMATIONAL LEADERSHIP** Transformational leadership occurs when managers have dramatic effects on their subordinates and on the organization as a whole, and inspire and energize subordinates to solve problems and improve performance. These effects include making subordinates aware of the importance of their own jobs and high performance; making subordinates aware of their own needs for personal growth, development, and accomplishment; and motivating subordinates to work for the good of the organization and not just their own personal gain. Managers can engage in transformational leadership by being charismatic leaders, by intellectually stimulating subordinates, and by engaging in developmental consideration. Transformational managers also often engage in transactional leadership by using their reward and coercive powers to encourage high performance.

LO14-5 **GENDER AND LEADERSHIP** Female and male managers do not differ in the leadership behaviors they perform, contrary to stereotypes suggesting that women are more relationship-oriented and men more task-oriented. Female managers sometimes are more participative than male managers, however. Research has found that women and men are equally effective as managers and leaders.

LO14-5 **EMOTIONAL INTELLIGENCE AND LEADERSHIP** The moods and emotions leaders experience on the job, and their ability to effectively manage these feelings, can influence their effectiveness as leaders. Moreover, emotional intelligence can contribute to leadership effectiveness in multiple ways, including encouraging and supporting creativity among followers.

Management in Action

Topics for Discussion and Action

Discussion

1. Describe the steps managers can take to increase their power and ability to be effective leaders. **[LO14-1]**
2. Think of specific situations in which it might be especially important for a manager to engage in consideration and in initiating structure. **[LO14-2]**
3. For your current job or for a future job you expect to hold, describe what your supervisor could do to strongly motivate you to be a top performer. **[LO14-3]**
4. Discuss why managers might want to change the behaviors they engage in, given their situation, their subordinates, and the nature of the work being done. Do you think managers can readily change their leadership behaviors? Why or why not? **[LO14-3]**
5. Describe what transformational leadership is, and explain how managers can engage in it. **[LO14-4]**
6. How do you think leadership in your home country may differ from that in the United States? **[LO14-5]**
7. Imagine that you are working in an organization in an entry-level position after graduation and have come up with what you think is a great idea for improving a critical process in the organization that relates to your job. In what ways might your supervisor encourage you to implement your idea? How might your supervisor discourage you from even sharing your idea with others? **[LO14-4, 14-5]**

Action

8. Interview a manager to find out how the three situational characteristics that Fiedler identified affect his or her ability to provide leadership. **[LO14-3]**
9. Find a company that has dramatically turned around its fortunes and improved its performance. Determine whether a transformational manager was behind the turnaround and, if one was, what this manager did. **[LO14-4]**

Building Management Skills

Analyzing Failures of Leadership **[LO14-1, 14-2, 14-3, 14-4]**

Think about a situation you are familiar with in which a leader was very ineffective. Then answer the following questions:

1. What sources of power did this leader have? Did the leader have enough power to influence his or her followers?
2. What kinds of behaviors did this leader engage in? Were they appropriate for the situation? Why or why not?
3. From what you know, do you think this leader was a task-oriented leader or a relationship-oriented leader? How favorable was this leader's situation for leading?
4. What steps did this leader take to motivate his or her followers? Were these steps appropriate or inappropriate? Why?
5. What signs, if any, did this leader show of being a transformational leader?

Managing Ethically [LO14-1]

Managers who verbally criticize their subordinates, put them down in front of their coworkers, or use the threat of job loss to influence behavior are exercising coercive power.

Questions

1. Either alone or in a group, think about the ethical implications of the use of coercive power.
2. To what extent do managers and organizations have an ethical obligation to put limits on the amount of coercive power that is exercised?

Small Group Breakout Exercise

Improving Leadership Effectiveness [LO14-1, 14-2, 14-3, 14-4]

Form groups of three to five people, and appoint one member as the spokesperson who will communicate your findings and conclusions to the class when called on by the instructor. Then discuss the following scenario:

You are a team of human resource consultants who have been hired by Carla Caruso, an entrepreneur who has started her own interior decorating business. A highly competent and creative interior decorator, Caruso has established a working relationship with most of the major home builders in her community. At first she worked on her own as an independent contractor. Then because of a dramatic increase in the number of new homes being built, she became swamped with requests for her services and decided to start her own company.

She hired a secretary–bookkeeper and four interior decorators, all of whom are highly competent. Caruso still does decorating jobs herself and has adopted a hands-off approach to leading the four decorators who report to her because she feels that interior design is a very personal, creative endeavor. Rather than pay the decorators on some kind of commission basis (such as a percentage of their customers' total billings), she pays them a premium salary, higher than average, so they are motivated to do what's best for a customer's needs and not what will result in higher billings and commissions.

Caruso thought everything was going smoothly until customer complaints started coming in. The complaints ranged from the decorators' being hard to reach, promising unrealistic delivery times, and being late for or failing to keep appointments to their being impatient and rude when customers had trouble making up their minds. Caruso knows her decorators are competent and is concerned that she is not effectively leading and managing them. She wonders, in particular, if her hands-off approach is to blame and if she should change the manner in which she rewards or pays her decorators. She has asked for your advice.

1. Analyze the sources of power that Caruso has available to her to influence the decorators. What advice can you give her to either increase her power base or use her existing power more effectively?
2. Given what you have learned in this chapter (for example, from the behavior model and path–goal theory), does Caruso seem to be performing appropriate leader behaviors in this situation? What advice can you give her about the kinds of behaviors she should perform?
3. What steps would you advise Caruso to take to increase the decorators' motivation to deliver high-quality customer service?
4. Would you advise Caruso to try to engage in transformational leadership in this situation? If not, why not? If so, what steps would you advise her to take?

Exploring the World Wide Web [LO14-1, 14-2, 14-3, 14-4, 14-5]

Go to the Web site of the Center for Creative Leadership (www.ccl.org). Spend some time browsing through the site to learn more about this organization, which specializes in leadership. Then click on "Customized Services" and then "Coaching Services." Read about the different coaching programs and options the center provides. How do you think leaders might benefit from coaching? What kinds of leaders/managers may find coaching especially beneficial? Do you think coaching services such as those provided by the Center for Creative Leadership can help leaders become more effective? Why or why not?

Be the Manager [LO14-1, 14-2, 14-3, 14-4, 14-5]

You are the CEO of a medium-size company that makes window coverings. Your company has a real cost advantage in terms of being able to make custom window coverings at costs that are relatively low in the industry. However, the performance of your company has been lackluster. To make needed changes and improve performance, you met with the eight other top managers in your company and charged them with identifying problems and missed opportunities in each of their areas and coming up with an action plan to address the problems and take advantage of opportunities.

Once you gave the managers the okay, they were charged with implementing their action plans in a timely fashion and monitoring the effects of their initiatives monthly for the next 8 to 12 months.

You approved each of the managers' action plans, and a year later most of the managers were reporting that their initiatives had been successful in addressing the problems and opportunities they had identified a year ago. However, overall company performance continues to be lackluster and shows no signs of improvement. You are confused and starting to question your leadership capabilities and approach to change. What are you going to do to improve the performance and effectiveness of your company?

CHAPTER 15

Effective Groups and Teams

Learning Objectives

After studying this chapter, you should be able to:

LO15-1 Explain why groups and teams are key contributors to organizational effectiveness.

LO15-2 Identify the different types of groups and teams that help managers and organizations achieve their goals.

LO15-3 Explain how different elements of group dynamics influence the functioning and effectiveness of groups and teams.

LO15-4 Explain why it is important for groups and teams to have a balance of conformity and deviance and a moderate level of cohesiveness.

LO15-5 Describe how managers can motivate group members to achieve organizational goals and reduce social loafing in groups and teams.

A MANAGER'S CHALLENGE

BMW and Innovation Teams

Karl Friedrich Rapp is the founder of BMW (Bavarian Motor Works). The firm originally made aircraft engines for the military. After the armistice following World War I, the peace treaty specified that Germany could no longer make aircraft engines. At that time the firm began building engines for trucks and boats. It was not until 1921 that the firm built its first motorcycle and in 1928 its first car. Today, BMW sells over 1.25 million cars a year. A key part of that success is innovation, and teams are central to the innovation success of the firm.

BMW innovation employs lateral management techniques. Lateral management of the firm involves the teams managing themselves rather than the typical top-down system of management. There is still a hierarchy to set strategic goals but the day-to-day management happens through teams. Such a system requires that the workers interact extensively with each other to be successful. This interaction is dependent on informal human networks of employees as much as it is on formal cross-functional teams. The informal means for all workers to interact includes a coffee break at 4 p.m. on Friday afternoon at BMW R&D center in Munich in which all engineers, designers, and managers meet to talk.

Cross-functional teams look messy and inefficient, but they are more effective at problem solving. Companies such as BMW that leverage workers' tacit knowledge through such networks "are widely ahead of their competitors." In part cross-functional teams work because they allow the firm to make changes far faster than a competitor can. By shifting effective management of day-to-day operations to such human networks, the speed with which knowledge can move laterally through companies is faster and better than old hierarchies. In part it is this same ability to move information

At BMW's Research and Innovation Center in Munich, lateral management techniques have been a key to the company's success and innovation. Engineers, designers, and managers meet informally on Friday afternoons to talk and interact with team members.

quickly that allows entrepreneurial firms to be so successful in adapting and moving to take advantage of opportunities. Such arrangements also help to ensure that there is less resistance to ideas once change is instituted.

Culture plays a critical part in the success of this effort. Workers at the Bavarian automaker are encouraged from their first day on the job to build a network or web of personal ties to speed problem solving and innovation, be it in R&D, design, production, or marketing. Those ties run across divisions and up and down the chain of command. There are limited formal meetings or stamps of approval needed when new ideas are generated. Instead, the key to success in the organization is stressed to the new employee that pushing fresh ideas is paramount. They want the employees to get used to the idea that asking for forgiveness is often better than asking for permission when it comes to a new idea.

The firm has identified people who are particularly critical to this process. These people function as nodes by serving in two or more informal networks. In this process they help to connect different networks and the knowledge that they hold. The identification of these individuals helps the firm to ensure that key information flows across the firm when it is needed.[1]

Overview

BMW is not alone in using groups and teams to improve organizational effectiveness. Managers in companies large and small are using groups and teams to enhance performance, increase responsiveness to customers, spur innovation, and motivate employees. In this chapter we look in detail at how groups and teams can contribute to organizational effectiveness and the types of groups and teams used in organizations. We discuss how different elements of group dynamics influence the functioning and effectiveness of groups, and we describe how managers can motivate group members to achieve organizational goals and reduce social loafing in groups and teams. By the end of this chapter you will appreciate why the effective management of groups and teams is a key ingredient for organizational performance and effectiveness.

Groups, Teams, and Organizational Effectiveness

A **group** may be defined as two or more people who interact with each other to accomplish certain goals or meet certain needs.[2] A **team** is a group whose members work *intensely* with one another to achieve a specific common goal or objective. As these definitions imply, all teams are groups, but not all groups are teams. The two characteristics that distinguish teams from groups are the *intensity* with which team members work together and the presence of a *specific, overriding team goal or objective.*

group Two or more people who interact with each other to accomplish certain goals or meet certain needs.

Recall from "A Manager's Challenge" that teamwork is critical to innovation at BMW. In contrast, the accountants who work in a small CPA firm are a group: They may interact with one another to achieve goals such as keeping up to date on the latest changes in accounting rules and regulations, maintaining a smoothly functioning office, satisfying clients, and attracting new clients.

LO15-1 Explain why groups and teams are key contributors to organizational effectiveness.

But they are not a team because they do not work intensely with one another. Each accountant concentrates on serving the needs of his or her own clients.

team A group whose members work intensely with one another to achieve a specific common goal or objective.

Because all teams are also groups, whenever we use the term *group* in this chapter, we are referring to both groups *and* teams. As you might imagine, because members of teams work intensely together, teams can sometimes be difficult to form, and it may take time for members to learn how to effectively work together. Groups and teams can help an organization gain a competitive advantage because they can (1) enhance its performance, (2) increase its responsiveness to customers, (3) increase innovation, and (4) increase employees' motivation and satisfaction (see Figure 15.1). In this section we look at each of these contributions in turn.

Groups and Teams as Performance Enhancers

synergy Performance gains that result when individuals and departments coordinate their actions.

One of the main advantages of using groups is the opportunity to obtain a type of **synergy:** People working in a group can produce more or higher-quality outputs than would have been produced if each person had worked separately and all their individual efforts were later combined. The essence of synergy is captured in the saying "The whole is more than the sum of its parts." Factors that can contribute to synergy in groups include the ability of group members to bounce ideas off one another, to correct one another's mistakes, to solve problems immediately as they arise, to bring a diverse knowledge base to bear on a problem or goal, and to accomplish work that is too vast or all-encompassing for any individual to achieve on his or her own.

Getting multiple perspectives and departmental inputs on one project at once unravels snafus before they start and gets a better product out the door faster.

To take advantage of the potential for synergy in groups, managers need to make sure that groups are composed of members who have complementary skills and knowledge relevant to the group's work.

To promote synergy, managers need to empower their subordinates and be coaches, guides, and resources for groups while refraining from playing a more directive or supervisory role. The potential for synergy in groups may be why more and more managers are incorporating empowerment into their personal leadership styles (see Chapter 14).

When tasks are complex and involve highly sophisticated and rapidly changing technologies, achieving synergies in teams often hinges on having the appropriate mix of

Figure 15.1
Groups' and Teams' Contributions to Organizational Effectiveness

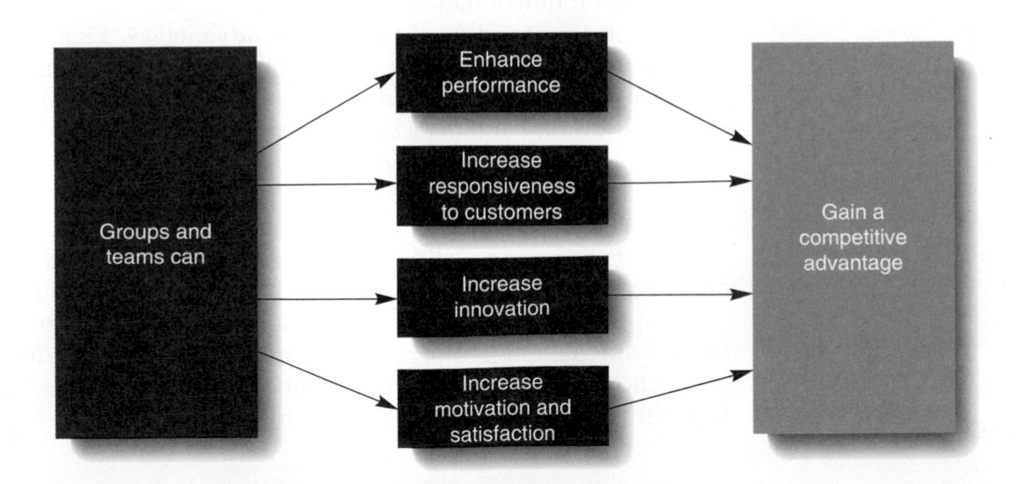

backgrounds and areas of expertise represented on the team. In large organizations with operations in many states and countries, managers can rely on databases and software applications to determine which employees might have the expertise needed on a particular team or for a certain project.

Groups, Teams, and Responsiveness to Customers

Being responsive to customers is not always easy. In manufacturing organizations, for example, customers' needs and desires for new and improved products have to be balanced against engineering constraints, production costs and feasibilities, government safety regulations, and marketing challenges. In service organizations such as hospitals, being responsive to patients' needs and desires for prompt, high-quality medical care and treatment has to be balanced against meeting physicians' needs and desires and keeping health care costs under control. Being responsive to customers often requires the wide variety of skills and expertise found in different departments and at different levels in an organization's hierarchy. Sometimes, for example, employees at lower levels in an organization's hierarchy, such as sales representatives for a computer company, are closest to its customers and the most attuned to their needs. However, lower-level employees like salespeople often lack the technical expertise needed for new product ideas; such expertise is found in the research and development department. Bringing salespeople, research and development experts, and members of other departments together in a group or cross-functional team can enhance responsiveness to customers. Consequently, when managers form a team, they must make sure the diversity of expertise and knowledge needed to be responsive to customers exists within the team; this is why cross-functional teams are so popular.

In a cross-functional team, the expertise and knowledge in different organizational departments are brought together in the skills and knowledge of the team members. Managers of high-performing organizations are careful to determine which types of expertise and knowledge are required for teams to be responsive to customers, and they use this information in forming teams.

Teams and Innovation

Innovation–the creative development of new products, new technologies, new services, or even new organizational structures–is a topic we discuss in detail in Chapter 18. Often an individual working alone does not possess the extensive and diverse skills, knowledge, and expertise required for successful innovation. Managers can better encourage innovation by creating teams of diverse individuals who together have the knowledge relevant to a particular type of innovation, rather than by relying on individuals working alone.

Using teams to innovate has other advantages. First, team members can often uncover one another's errors or false assumptions; an individual acting alone would not be able to do this. Second, team members can critique one another's approaches and build off one another's strengths while compensating for weaknesses–an advantage of devil's advocacy and dialectical inquiry, discussed in Chapter 7.

To further promote innovation, managers can empower teams and make their members fully responsible and accountable for the innovation process. The manager's role is to provide guidance, assistance, coaching, and the resources team members need and *not* to closely direct or supervise their activities.

To speed innovation, managers also need to form teams in which each member brings some unique resource to the team, such as engineering prowess, knowledge of production, marketing expertise, or financial savvy. Successful innovation sometimes requires that managers form teams with members from different countries and cultures.

Novartis uses teams to spur innovation at its manufacturing plants, as described in the following "Information Technology Byte" box.

Information Technology Byte

Teams Innovate at Novartis

Novartis is one of the world's largest pharmaceutical companies. The pharmaceutical industry is dependent on the continuous innovation of new products. Novartis, a Swiss company, employed cross-functional teams at its major manufacturing sites. These teams then sought to identify radical new ways to redesign the processes to make the plant more efficient. Each team first toured the manufacturing site to ensure they had a full understanding of the production processes and how work flowed through them. Then in a half-day meeting, the teams learned about just-in-time (JIT) inventory principles and how they could improve drug production at their sites. Next, teams brainstormed to come up with revised processes that incorporated JIT concepts. The idea was for employees to invent creative solutions with no constraints on their thinking. Overall the teams have been very innovative and helped to improve what the firm does. To illustrate, part of the innovative process was to think of new ways to manage the firm including changing the company's organizational structure to increase speed and reduce waste. Novartis, as a result of the teams' suggestions, eliminated traditional functions and departments at its manufacturing sites and replaced them with process-oriented organizations (i.e., teams aligned around products). The aim was to streamline and empower manufacturing teams. To illustrate the change, most of the sites historically had between five and eight levels of management, and now they have three.[3]

Groups and Teams as Motivators

Managers often form groups and teams to accomplish organizational goals and then find that using groups and teams brings additional benefits. Members of groups, and especially members of teams (because of the higher intensity of interaction in teams), are likely to be more satisfied than they would have been if they were working on their own. The experience of working alongside other highly charged and motivated people can be stimulating and motivating: Team members can see how their efforts and expertise directly contribute to the achievement of team and organizational goals, and they feel personally responsible for the outcomes or results of their work. The increased motivation and satisfaction that can accompany the use of teams can also lead to other outcomes, such as lower turnover.

Working in a group or team can also satisfy organizational members' needs for engaging in social interaction and feeling connected to other people. For workers who perform highly stressful jobs, such as hospital emergency and operating room staff, group membership can be an important source of social support and motivation. Family members or friends may not be able to fully understand or appreciate some sources of work stress that these group members experience firsthand. Moreover, group members may cope better with work stressors when they can share them with other members of their group. In addition, groups often devise techniques to relieve stress, such as the telling of jokes among hospital operating room staff.

Why do managers in all kinds of organizations rely so heavily on groups and teams? Effectively managed groups and teams can help managers in their quest for high performance, responsiveness to customers, and employee motivation. Before explaining how managers can effectively manage groups, however, we will describe the types of groups that are formed in organizations.

Types of Groups and Teams

LO15-2 Identify the different types of groups and teams that help managers and organizations achieve their goals.

To achieve their goals of high performance, responsiveness to customers, innovation, and employee motivation, managers can form various types of groups and teams (see Figure 15.2). **Formal groups** are those managers establish to achieve organizational goals. The formal work groups are *cross-functional* teams composed of members from different departments, and *cross-cultural* teams composed of members from different cultures or countries, such as the teams at global carmakers. As you will see, some of the groups discussed in this section also can be considered to be cross-functional (if they are composed of members from different departments) or cross-cultural (if they are composed of members from different countries or cultures).

Sometimes organizational members, managers or nonmanagers, form groups because they feel that groups will help them achieve their own goals or meet their own needs (for example, the need for social interaction). Groups formed in this way are **informal groups.** Four nurses who work in a hospital and have lunch together twice a week constitute an informal group.

formal group A group that managers establish to achieve organizational goals.

informal group A group that managers or nonmanagerial employees form to help achieve their own goals or meet their own needs.

The Top Management Team

A central concern of the CEO and president of a company is to form a **top management team** to help the organization achieve its mission and goals. Top management teams are responsible for developing the strategies that result in an organization's competitive advantage; most have between five and seven members. In forming their top management teams, CEOs are well advised to stress diversity in expertise, skills, knowledge, and experience. Thus many top management teams are also cross-functional teams: They are composed of members from different departments, such as finance, marketing, production, and engineering. Diversity helps ensure that the top management team will have all the background and resources it needs to make good decisions. Diversity also helps guard against *groupthink*–faulty group decision making that results when group members strive for agreement at the expense of an accurate assessment of the situation (see Chapter 7).

top management team A group composed of the CEO, the president, and the heads of the most important departments.

Research and Development Teams

Managers in pharmaceuticals, computers, electronics, electronic imaging, and other high-tech industries often create **research and development teams** to develop new products. Managers select R&D team members on the basis of their expertise and experience in a certain area. Sometimes R&D teams are cross-functional teams with members from departments such as engineering, marketing, and production in addition to members from the research and development department.

research and development team A team whose members have the expertise and experience needed to develop new products.

Figure 15.2
Types of Groups and Teams in Organizations

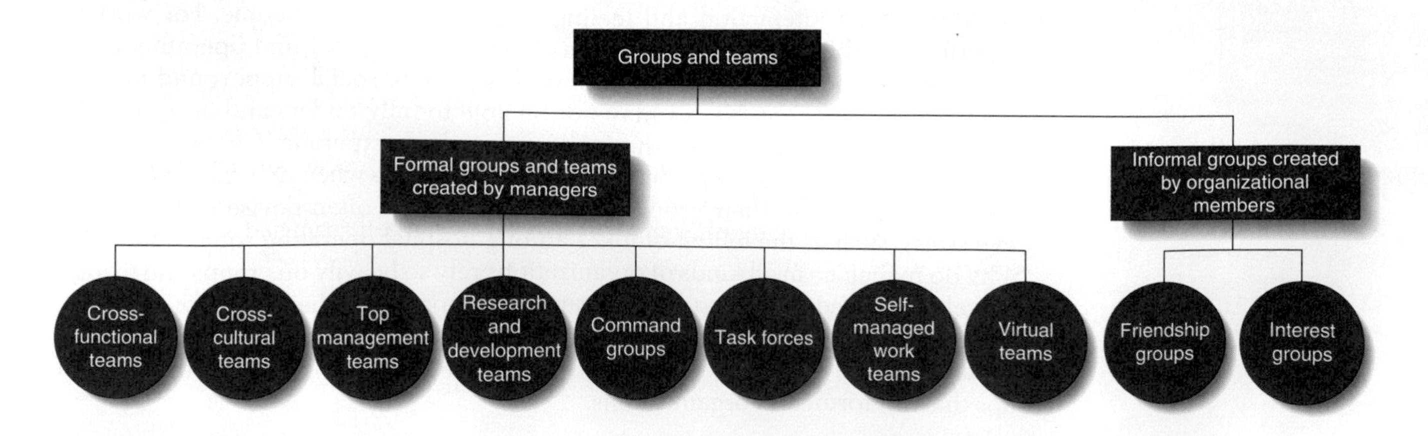

Command Groups

command group A group composed of subordinates who report to the same supervisor; also called *department* or *unit.*

Subordinates who report to the same supervisor compose a **command group.** When top managers design an organization's structure and establish reporting relationships and a chain of command, they are essentially creating command groups. Command groups, often called *departments* or *units,* perform a significant amount of the work in many organizations. In order to have command groups that help an organization gain a competitive advantage, managers not only need to motivate group members to perform at a high level but also need to be effective leaders. An example of command group is workers on an automobile assembly line in the Ford Motor Company or BMW who report to the same first-line manager.

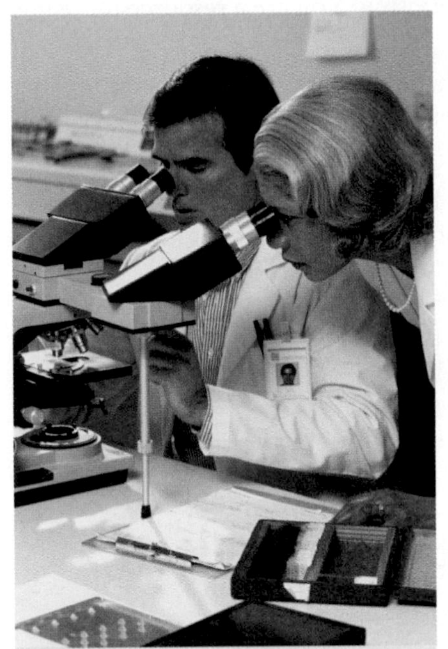

Figuring out if the new pharmaceutical drug is a go takes a strong R&D team made up of medical experts who know the science as well as the market needs.

Task Forces

Managers form **task forces** to accomplish specific goals or solve problems in a certain time period; task forces are sometimes called *ad hoc committees.* For example, Michael Rider, owner and top manager of a chain of six gyms and fitness centers, created a task force composed of the general managers of the six gyms to determine whether the fitness centers should institute a separate fee schedule for customers who wanted to use the centers only for aerobics classes (and not use other facilities such as weights, steps, tracks, and swimming pools). The task force was given three months to prepare a report summarizing the pros and cons of the proposed change in fee schedules. After the task force completed its report and reached the conclusion that the change in fee structure probably would reduce revenues rather than increase them and thus should not be implemented, it was disbanded. As in Rider's case, task forces can be a valuable tool for busy managers who do not have the time to personally explore an important issue in depth.

Sometimes managers need to form task forces whose work, so to speak, is never done. The task force may be addressing a long-term or enduring problem or issue facing an organization, such as how to most usefully contribute to the local community or how to make sure the organization provides opportunities for potential employees with disabilities. Task forces that are relatively permanent are often referred to as *standing committees.* Membership in standing committees changes over time. Members may have, for example, a two- or three-year term on the committee, and memberships expire at varying times so there are always some members with experience on the committee. Managers often form and maintain standing committees to make sure important issues continue to be addressed.

task force A committee of managers or nonmanagerial employees from various departments or divisions who meet to solve a specific, mutual problem; also called *ad hoc committee.*

Self-Managed Work Teams

self-managed work team A group of employees who supervise their own activities and monitor the quality of the goods and services they provide.

Self-managed work teams are teams in which members are empowered and have the responsibility and autonomy to complete identifiable pieces of work. On a day-to-day basis, team members decide what the team will do, how it will do it, and which members will perform which specific tasks.[4] Managers assign self-managed work teams' overall goals (such as assembling defect-free computer keyboards) but let team members decide how to meet those goals. Managers usually form self-managed work teams to improve quality, increase motivation and satisfaction, and lower costs. Often, by creating self-managed work teams, they combine tasks that individuals working separately used to perform, so the team is responsible for the whole set of tasks that yields an identifiable output or end product.

Managers can take a number of steps to ensure that self-managed work teams are effective and help an organization achieve its goals:[5]

- Give teams enough responsibility and autonomy to be truly self-managing. Refrain from telling team members what to do or solving problems for them even if you (as a manager) know what should be done.

- Make sure a team's work is sufficiently complex so it entails a number of different steps or procedures that must be performed and results in some kind of finished end product.
- Carefully select members of self-managed work teams. Team members should have the diversity of skills needed to complete the team's work, have the ability to work with others, and want to be part of a team.
- As a manager, realize that your role vis-à-vis self-managed work teams calls for guidance, coaching, and supporting, not supervising. You are a resource for teams to turn to when needed.
- Analyze what type of training team members need, and provide it. Working in a self-managed work team often requires that employees have more extensive technical and interpersonal skills.

Managers in a wide variety of organizations have found that self-managed work teams help the organization achieve its goals,[6] as profiled in the following "Management Insight" box.

Management Insight

Self-Managed Teams at Louis Vuitton and Nucor Corporation

While there clearly are cultural impacts in different nations, there are also similarities in many settings when it comes to teams. Managers at the French company Louis Vuitton, the most profitable luxury brand in the world, and managers at Nucor Corporation, the largest producer of steel and biggest recycler in the United States, have succeeded in effectively using self-managed teams to produce luxury accessories and steel, respectively. Self-managed teams at both companies not only are effective but truly excel and have helped make the companies leaders in their respective industries.[7]

Teams with between 20 and 30 members make Vuitton handbags and accessories. The teams work on only one product at a time; a team with 24 members might produce about 120 handbags per day. Team members are empowered to take ownership of the goods they produce, are encouraged to suggest improvements, and are kept up to date on key facts such as products' selling prices and popularity. As Thierry Nogues, a team leader at a Vuitton factory in Ducey, France, puts it, "Our goal is to make everyone as multiskilled and autonomous as possible."[8]

A team member assembles classic Louis Vuitton bags at the company's fine leather goods factory in the Normandy town of Ducey in France.

Production workers at Nucor are organized into teams ranging in size from 8 to 40 members based on the kind of work the team is responsible for, such as rolling steel or operating a furnace. Team members have considerable autonomy to make decisions and creatively respond to problems and opportunities, and there are relatively few layers in the corporate hierarchy, supporting the empowerment of teams.[9] Teams develop their own informal rules for behavior and make their own decisions. As long as team members follow organizational rules and policies (such as those for safety) and meet quality standards, they are free to govern themselves. Managers act as coaches or advisers rather than supervisors, helping teams when needed.[10]

To ensure that production teams are motivated to help Nucor achieve its goals, team members are eligible for weekly bonuses based on the team's performance. Essentially, these production workers receive base pay that does not vary and are eligible to receive weekly bonus pay that can average from 80% to 150% of their regular pay.[11] The bonus rate is predetermined by the work a team performs and the capabilities of the machinery they use. Given the immediacy of the bonus and its potential magnitude, team members are motivated to perform at a high level, develop informal rules that support high performance, and strive to help Nucor reach its goals. Moreover, because all members of a team receive the same amount of weekly bonus money, they are motivated to do their best for the team, cooperate, and help one another out.[12] Of course, in tough economic times such as the recession in the late 2000s, Nucor's production workers' bonuses fall as demand for Nucor's products drops. Nonetheless, Nucor has been able to avoid laying off employees (unlike a lot of other large corporations).[13]

Crafting a luxury handbag and making steel joists couldn't be more different from each other in certain ways. Yet the highly effective self-managed teams at Louis Vuitton and Nucor share some fundamental qualities. These teams really do take ownership of their work and are highly motivated to perform effectively. Team members have the skills and knowledge they need to be effective, they are empowered to make decisions about their work, and they know their teams are making vital contributions to their organizations.[14]

Sometimes employees have individual jobs but also are part of a self-managed team that is formed to accomplish a specific goal or work on an important project. Employees need to perform their own individual job tasks and also actively contribute to the self-managed team so the team achieves its goal.

Sometimes self-managed work teams can run into trouble. Members may be reluctant to discipline one another by withholding bonuses from members who are not performing up to par or by firing members.[15] Team members do not feel comfortable assuming this role, and managers end up handling these tasks.[16] One reason for team members' discomfort may be the close personal relationships they sometimes develop with one another. In addition, members of self-managed work teams may sometimes take longer to accomplish tasks, such as when team members have difficulties coordinating their efforts.

Virtual Teams

virtual team A team whose members rarely or never meet face-to-face but, rather, interact by using various forms of information technology such as e-mail, computer networks, telephone, fax, and videoconferences.

Virtual teams are teams whose members rarely or never meet face-to-face but, rather, interact by using various forms of information technology such as e-mail, text messaging, computer networks, telephone, fax, and videoconferences. As organizations become increasingly global, and as the need for specialized knowledge increases due to advances in technology, managers can create virtual teams to solve problems or explore opportunities without being limited by team members needing to work in the same geographic location.[17]

Take the case of an organization that has manufacturing facilities in Australia, Canada, the United States, and Mexico and is encountering a quality problem in a complex manufacturing process. Each of its facilities has a quality control team headed by a quality control manager. The vice president for production does not try to solve the problem by forming and leading a team at one of the four manufacturing facilities; instead she forms and leads a virtual team composed of the quality control managers of the four plants and the plants' general managers. When these team members communicate via e-mail, the company's networking site, and videoconferencing, a wide array of knowledge and experience is brought to solve the problem.

The principal advantage of virtual teams is that they enable managers to disregard geographic distances and form teams whose members have the knowledge, expertise, and experience to tackle a particular problem or take advantage of a specific opportunity.[18] Virtual teams also can include members who are not actually employees of the organization itself; a virtual team might include members of a company that is used for outsourcing. More and more companies, including BP PLC, Nokia Corporation, and Ogilvy & Mather, are using virtual teams.[19]

Members of virtual teams rely on two forms of information technology: synchronous technologies and asynchronous technologies.[20] *Synchronous technologies* let virtual team members communicate and interact with one another in real time simultaneously and include videoconferencing, teleconferencing, and electronic meetings. *Asynchronous technologies* delay communication and include e-mail, electronic bulletin boards, and Internet Web sites. Many virtual teams use both kinds of technology depending on what projects they are working on.

Increasing globalization is likely to result in more organizations relying on virtual teams to a greater extent.[21] One challenge members of virtual teams face is building a sense of camaraderie and trust among team members who rarely, if ever, meet face-to-face. To address this challenge, some organizations schedule recreational activities, such as ski trips, so virtual team members can get together. Other organizations make sure virtual team members have a chance to meet in person soon after the team is formed and then schedule periodic face-to-face meetings to promote trust, understanding, and cooperation in the teams.[22] The need for such meetings is underscored by research suggesting that while some virtual teams can be as effective as teams that meet face-to-face, virtual team members might be less satisfied with teamwork efforts and have fewer feelings of camaraderie or cohesion. (Group cohesiveness is discussed in more detail later in the chapter.)[23]

Research also suggests that it is important for managers to keep track of virtual teams and intervene when necessary by, for example, encouraging members of teams who do not communicate often enough to monitor their team's progress and making sure team members actually have the time, and are recognized for, their virtual teamwork.[24] Additionally, when virtual teams are experiencing downtime or rough spots, managers might try to schedule face-to-face team time to bring team members together and help them focus on their goals.[25]

Researchers at the London Business School, including Professor Lynda Gratton, recently studied global virtual teams to try to identify factors that might help such teams be effective.[26] Based on their research, Gratton suggests that when forming virtual teams, it is helpful to include a few members who already know each other, other members who are well connected to people outside the team, and when possible, members who have volunteered to be a part of the team.[27] It is also advantageous for companies to have some kind of online site where team members can learn more about each other and the kinds of work they are engaged in, and in particular, a shared online workspace that team members can access around the clock.[28] Frequent communication is beneficial. Additionally, virtual team projects should be perceived as meaningful, interesting, and important by their members to promote and sustain their motivation.[29]

Friendship Groups

friendship group An informal group composed of employees who enjoy one another's company and socialize with one another.

The groups described so far are formal groups created by managers. **Friendship groups** are informal groups composed of employees who enjoy one another's company and socialize with one another. Members of friendship groups may have lunch together, take breaks together, or meet after work for meals, sports, or other activities. Friendship groups help satisfy employees' needs for interpersonal interaction,

A recycling interest group organizes like-minded colleagues to help pick up the slack where formal organization may be lacking.

can provide needed social support in times of stress, and can contribute to people's feeling good at work and being satisfied with their jobs. Managers themselves often form friendship groups. The informal relationships that managers build in friendship groups can often help them solve work-related problems because members of these groups typically discuss work-related matters and offer advice.

Interest Groups

Employees form informal **interest groups** when they seek to achieve a common goal related to their membership in an organization. Employees may form interest groups, for example, to encourage managers to consider instituting flexible working hours, providing on-site child care, improving working conditions, or more proactively supporting environmental protection. Interest groups can give managers valuable insights into the issues and concerns that are foremost in employees' minds. They also can signal the need for change.

interest group An informal group composed of employees seeking to achieve a common goal related to their membership in an organization.

Group Dynamics

How groups function and, ultimately, their effectiveness hinge on group characteristics and processes known collectively as *group dynamics*. In this section we discuss five key elements of group dynamics: group size, tasks, and roles; group leadership; group development; group norms; and group cohesiveness.

Group Size, Tasks, and Roles

LO15-3 Explain how different elements of group dynamics influence the functioning and effectiveness of groups and teams.

Managers need to take group size, group tasks, and group roles into account as they create and maintain high-performing groups and teams.

GROUP SIZE The number of members in a group can be an important determinant of members' motivation and commitment and group performance. There are several advantages to keeping a group relatively small–between two and nine members. Compared with members of large groups, members of small groups tend to (1) interact more with each other and find it easier to coordinate their efforts, (2) be more motivated, satisfied, and committed, (3) find it easier to share information, and (4) be better able to see the importance of their personal contributions for group success. A disadvantage of small rather than large groups is that members of small groups have fewer resources available to accomplish their goals.

Large groups–with 10 or more members–also offer some advantages. They have more resources at their disposal to achieve group goals than small groups do. These resources include the knowledge, experience, skills, and abilities of group members as well as their actual time and effort. Large groups also let managers obtain the advantages stemming from the **division of labor**–splitting the work to be performed into particular tasks and assigning tasks to individual workers. Workers who specialize in particular tasks are likely to become skilled at performing those tasks and contribute significantly to high group performance.

division of labor Splitting the work to be performed into particular tasks and assigning tasks to individual workers.

The disadvantages of large groups include the problems of communication and coordination and the lower levels of motivation, satisfaction, and commitment that members of large groups sometimes experience. It is clearly more difficult to share information with, and coordinate the activities of, 16 people rather than 8 people. Moreover, members of large groups might not think their efforts are really needed and sometimes might not even feel a part of the group.

In deciding on the appropriate size for any group, managers attempt to gain the advantages of small group size and, at the same time, form groups with sufficient resources to accomplish their goals and have a well-developed division of labor. As a general rule of thumb, groups should have no more members than necessary to achieve a division of labor and provide the resources needed to achieve group goals. In R&D teams, for example, group size is too large when (1) members spend more time communicating what they know to others than applying what they know to solve problems and create new products, (2) individual productivity decreases, and (3) group performance suffers.[30]

task interdependence The degree to which the work performed by one member of a group influences the work performed by other members.

pooled task interdependence The task interdependence that exists when group members make separate and independent contributions to group performance.

GROUP TASKS The appropriate size of a high-performing group is affected by the kind of tasks the group is to perform. An important characteristic of group tasks that affects performance is **task interdependence**–the degree to which the work performed by one member of a group influences the work performed by other members.[31] As task interdependence increases, group members need to interact more frequently and intensely with one another, and their efforts have to be more closely coordinated if they are to perform at a high level. Management expert James D. Thompson identified three types of task interdependence: pooled, sequential, and reciprocal (see Figure 15.3).[32]

POOLED TASK INTERDEPENDENCE **Pooled task interdependence** exists when group members make separate and independent contributions to group performance; overall group performance is the sum of the performance of the individual members (see Figure 15.3a). Examples of groups that have pooled task interdependence include a group of teachers in an elementary school, a group of salespeople in a department

Figure 15.3
Types of Task Interdependence

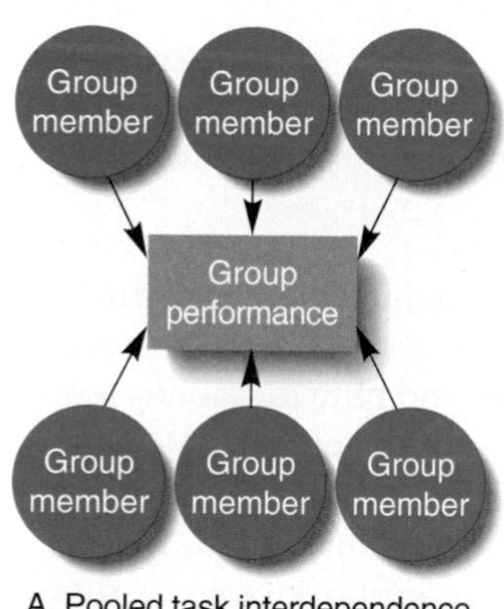

A. Pooled task interdependence

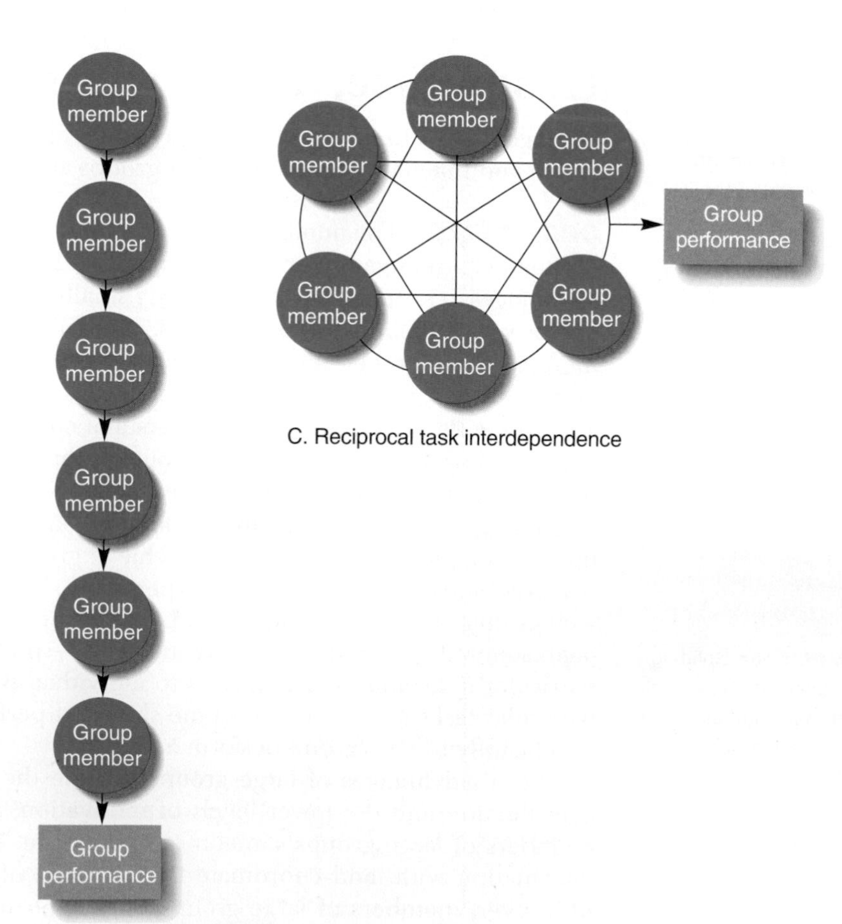

B. Sequential task interdependence

C. Reciprocal task interdependence

store, a group of secretaries in an office, and a group of custodians in an office building. In these examples, group performance, whether it be the number of children who are taught and the quality of their education, the dollar value of sales, the amount of secretarial work completed, or the number of offices cleaned, is determined by summing the individual contributions of group members.

For groups with pooled interdependence, managers should determine the appropriate group size primarily from the amount of work to be accomplished. Large groups can be effective because group members work independently and do not have to interact frequently with one another. Motivation in groups with pooled interdependence will be highest when managers reward group members based on individual performance.

sequential task interdependence The task interdependence that exists when group members must perform specific tasks in a predetermined order.

SEQUENTIAL TASK INTERDEPENDENCE **Sequential task interdependence** exists when group members must perform specific tasks in a predetermined order; certain tasks have to be performed before others, and what one worker does affects the work of others (see Figure 15.3b). Assembly lines and mass-production processes are characterized by sequential task interdependence.

When group members are sequentially interdependent, group size is usually dictated by the needs of the production process–for example, the number of steps needed in an assembly line to efficiently produce a DVD player. With sequential interdependence, it is difficult to identify individual performance because one group member's performance depends on how well others perform their tasks. A slow worker at the start of an assembly line, for example, causes all workers further down to work slowly. Thus managers are often advised to reward group members for group performance. Group members will be motivated to perform at a high level because if the group performs well, each member will benefit. In addition, group members may put pressure on poor performers to improve so group performance and rewards do not suffer.

reciprocal task interdependence The task interdependence that exists when the work performed by each group member is fully dependent on the work performed by other group members.

RECIPROCAL TASK INTERDEPENDENCE **Reciprocal task interdependence** exists when the work performed by each group member is fully dependent on the work performed by other group members; group members have to share information, intensely interact with one another, and coordinate their efforts in order for the group to achieve its goals (see Figure 15.3c). In general, reciprocal task interdependence characterizes the operation of teams, rather than other kinds of groups. The task interdependence of R&D teams, top management teams, and many self-managed work teams is reciprocal.

When group members are reciprocally interdependent, managers are advised to keep group size relatively small because of the necessity of coordinating team members' activities. Communication difficulties can arise in teams with reciprocally interdependent tasks because team members need to interact frequently with one another and be available when needed. As group size increases, communication difficulties increase and can impair team performance.

When a group's members are reciprocally interdependent, managers also are advised to reward group members on the basis of group performance. Individual levels of performance are often difficult for managers to identify, and group-based rewards help ensure that group members will be motivated to perform at a high level and make valuable contributions to the group. Of course, if a manager can identify instances of individual performance in such groups, they too can be rewarded to maintain high levels of motivation. Microsoft and many other companies reward group members for their individual performance as well as for the performance of their group.

group role A set of behaviors and tasks that a member of a group is expected to perform because of his or her position in the group.

GROUP ROLES A **group role** is a set of behaviors and tasks that a member of a group is expected to perform because of his or her position in the group. Members of cross-functional teams, for example, are expected to perform roles relevant to their special areas of expertise. The roles of members of top management teams are shaped primarily by their areas of expertise–production, marketing, finance, research and development–but members of top management teams also typically draw on their broad expertise as planners and strategists.

First the steak, then the green beans, then the carefully drizzled béarnaise; gourmet kitchens where the presentation is an integral part of the experience exemplify sequential task interdependence.

In forming groups and teams, managers need to clearly communicate to group members the expectations for their roles in the group, what is required of them, and how the different roles in the group fit together to accomplish group goals. Managers also need to realize that group roles often change and evolve as a group's tasks and goals change and as group members gain experience and knowledge. Thus, to get the performance gains that come from experience or "learning by doing," managers should encourage group members to take the initiative to assume additional responsibilities as they see fit and modify their assigned roles. This process, called **role making,** can enhance individual and group performance.

role making Taking the initiative to modify an assigned role by assuming additional responsibilities.

In self-managed work teams and some other groups, group members themselves are responsible for creating and assigning roles. Many self-managed work teams also pick their own team leaders. When group members create their own roles, managers should be available to group members in an advisory capacity, helping them effectively settle conflicts and disagreements. At Johnsonville Foods, for example, the position titles of first-line managers have been changed to "advisory coach" to reflect the managers' new role vis-à-vis the self-managed work teams they oversee.[33]

Group Leadership

All groups and teams need leadership. Indeed, as we discussed in detail in Chapter 14, effective leadership is a key ingredient for high-performing groups, teams, and organizations. Sometimes managers assume the leadership role in groups and teams, as is the case in many command groups and top management teams. Or a manager may appoint a member of a group who is not a manager to be group leader or chairperson, as is the case in a task force or standing committee. In other cases, group or team members may choose their own leaders, or a leader may emerge naturally as group members work together to achieve group goals. When managers empower members of self-managed work teams, they often let group members choose their own leaders. Some self-managed work teams find it effective to rotate the leadership role among their members. Whether or not leaders of groups and teams are managers, and whether they are appointed by managers (often referred to as *formal leaders*) or emerge naturally in a group (often referred to as *informal leaders*), they play an important role in ensuring that groups and teams perform up to their potential.

Group Development over Time

As many managers overseeing self-managed teams have learned, it sometimes takes a self-managed work team two or three years to perform up to its true capabilities.[34] As their experience suggests, what a group is capable of achieving depends in part on its stage of development. Knowing that it takes considerable time for self-managed work teams to get up and running has helped managers have realistic expectations for new teams and know that they need to give new team members considerable training and guidance.

Although every group's development over time is unique, researchers have identified five stages of group development that many groups seem to pass through (see Figure 15.4).[35] In the first stage, *forming,* members try to get to know one another and reach a common understanding of what the group is trying to accomplish and how group members should behave. During this stage, managers should strive to make each member feel that he or she is a valued part of the group.

In the second stage, *storming,* group members experience conflict and disagreements because some members do not wish to submit to the demands of other group members. Disputes may arise over who should lead the group. Self-managed work teams can be particularly vulnerable during the storming stage. Managers need to keep an eye on groups at this stage to make sure conflict does not get out of hand.

Figure 15.4
Five Stages of Group Development

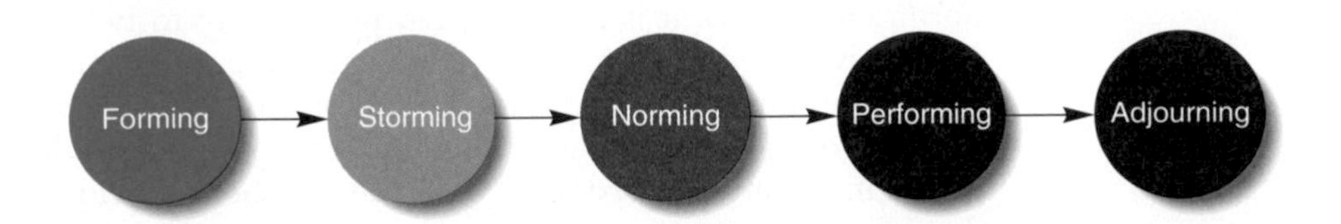

During the third stage, *norming,* close ties between group members develop, and feelings of friendship and camaraderie emerge. Group members arrive at a consensus about what goals they should seek to achieve and how group members should behave toward one another. In the fourth stage, *performing,* the real work of the group gets accomplished. Depending on the type of group in question, managers need to take different steps at this stage to help ensure that groups are effective. Managers of command groups need to make sure that group members are motivated and that they are effectively leading group members. Managers overseeing self-managed work teams have to empower team members and make sure teams are given enough responsibility and autonomy at the performing stage.

The last stage, *adjourning,* applies only to groups that eventually are disbanded, such as task forces. During adjourning a group is dispersed. Sometimes adjourning takes place when a group completes a finished product, such as when a task force evaluating the pros and cons of providing on-site child care produces a report supporting its recommendation.

Managers should have a flexible approach to group development and should keep attuned to the different needs and requirements of groups at the various stages.[36] Above all else, and regardless of the stage of development, managers need to think of themselves as *resources* for groups. Thus managers always should strive to find ways to help groups and teams function more effectively.

LO15-4 Explain why it is important for groups and teams to have a balance of conformity and deviance and a moderate level of cohesiveness.

Group Norms

All groups, whether top management teams, self-managed work teams, or command groups, need to control their members' behaviors to ensure that the group performs at a high level and meets its goals. Assigning roles to each group member is one way to control behavior in groups. Another important way in which groups influence members' behavior is through the development and enforcement of group norms.[37] **Group norms** are shared guidelines or rules for behavior that most group members follow. Groups develop norms concerning a wide variety of behaviors, including working hours, the sharing of information among group members, how certain group tasks should be performed, and even how members of a group should dress.

group norms Shared guidelines or rules for behavior that most group members follow.

Managers should encourage members of a group to develop norms that contribute to group performance and the attainment of group goals. For example, group norms dictating that each member of a cross-functional team should always be available for the rest of the team when his or her input is needed, return phone calls as soon as possible, inform other team members of travel plans, and give team members a phone number at which he or she can be reached when traveling on business help to ensure that the team is efficient, performs at a high level, and achieves its goals. A norm in a command group of secretaries that dictates that secretaries who happen to have a light workload in any given week should help out secretaries with heavier workloads helps to ensure that the group completes all assignments in a timely and efficient manner. And a norm in a top management team that dictates that team members should always consult with one another before making major decisions helps to ensure that good decisions are made with a minimum of errors.

CONFORMITY AND DEVIANCE Group members conform to norms for three reasons: (1) They want to obtain rewards and avoid punishments. (2) They want to imitate group members whom they like and admire. (3) They have internalized the norm and believe it is the right and proper way to behave.[38] Consider the case of Robert King, who conformed to his department's norm of attending a fund-raiser for a community food bank. King's conformity could be due to (1) his desire to be a member of the group in good standing and to have friendly relationships with other group members (rewards), (2) his copying the behavior of other members of the department whom he respects and who always attend the fund-raiser (imitating other group members), or (3) his belief in the merits of supporting the activities of the food bank (believing that is the right and proper way to behave).

Failure to conform, or deviance, occurs when a member of a group violates a group norm. Deviance signals that a group is not controlling one of its member's behaviors. Groups generally respond to members who behave defiantly in one of three ways:[39]

1. The group might try to get the member to change his or her deviant ways and conform to the norm. Group members might try to convince the member of the need to conform, or they might ignore or even punish the deviant. For example, in a U.S. foods plant Liz Senkbiel, a member of a self-managed work team responsible for weighing sausages, failed to conform to a group norm dictating that group members should periodically clean up an untidy interview room. Because Senkbiel refused to take part in the team's cleanup efforts, team members reduced her monthly bonus significantly for a two-month period.[40] Senkbiel clearly learned the costs of deviant behavior in her team.
2. The group might expel the member.
3. The group might change the norm to be consistent with the member's behavior.

This last alternative suggests that some deviant behavior can be functional for groups. Deviance is functional for a group when it causes group members to evaluate norms that may be dysfunctional but are taken for granted by the group. Often group members do not think about why they behave in a certain way or why they follow certain norms. Deviance can cause group members to reflect on their norms and change them when appropriate.

Consider a group of receptionists in a beauty salon who followed the norm that all appointments would be handwritten in an appointment book and, at the end of each day, the receptionist on duty would enter the appointments into the salon's computer system, which printed out the hairdressers' daily schedules. One day a receptionist decided to enter appointments directly into the computer system when they were being made, bypassing the appointment book. This deviant behavior caused the other receptionists to think about why they were using the appointment book at all. After consulting with the owner of the salon, the group changed its norm. Now appointments are entered directly into the computer, which saves time and reduces scheduling errors.

ENCOURAGING A BALANCE OF CONFORMITY AND DEVIANCE To effectively help an organization gain a competitive advantage, groups and teams need the right balance of conformity and deviance (see Figure 15.5). A group needs a certain level of conformity to ensure that it can control members' behavior and channel it in the direction of high performance and group goal accomplishment. A group also needs a certain level of deviance to ensure that dysfunctional norms are discarded and replaced with functional ones. Balancing conformity and deviance is a pressing concern for all groups, whether they are top management teams, R&D teams, command groups, or self-managed work teams.

The extent of conformity and reactions to deviance within groups are determined by group members themselves. The three bases for conformity just described are powerful forces that more often than not result in group members' conforming to norms. Sometimes these forces are so strong that deviance rarely occurs in groups, and when it does, it is stamped out.

Figure 15.5
Balancing Conformity and Deviance in Groups

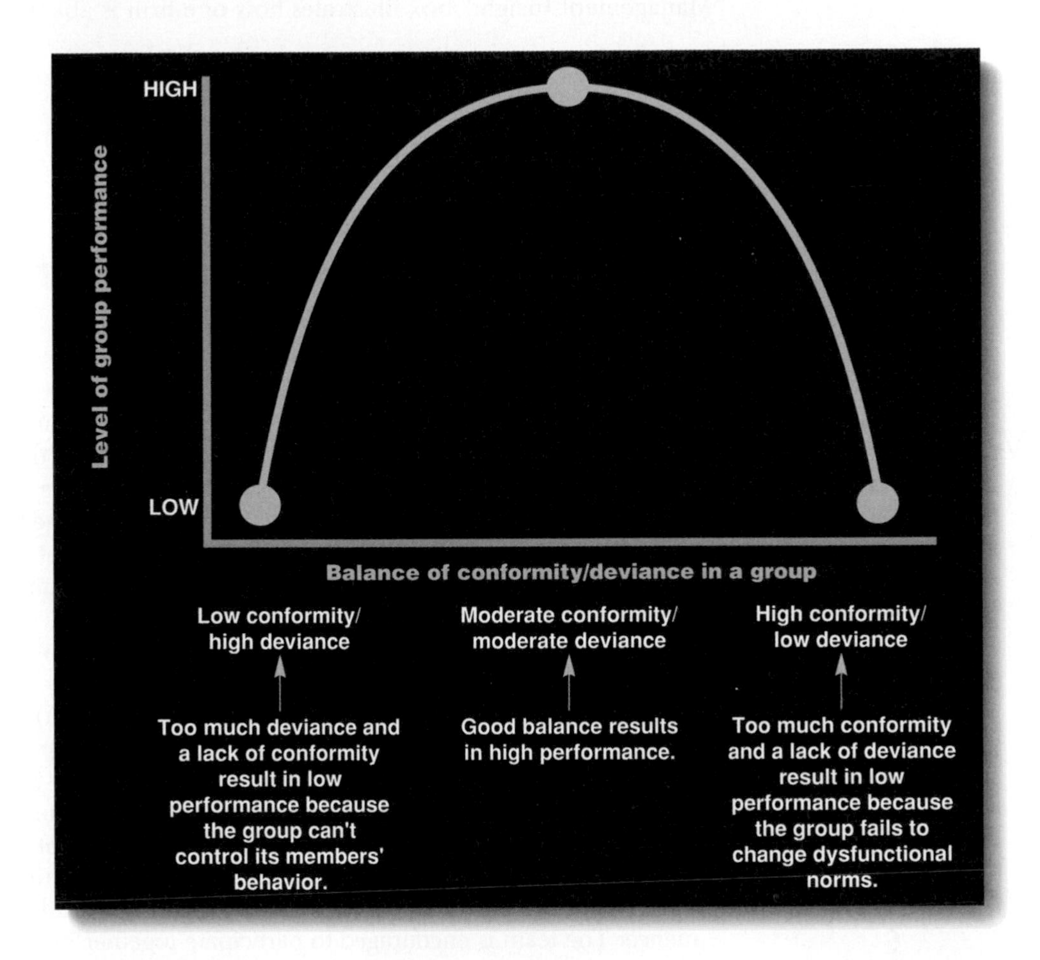

Managers can take several steps to ensure adequate tolerance of deviance in groups so group members are willing to deviate from dysfunctional norms and, when deviance occurs in their group, reflect on the appropriateness of the violated norm and change the norm if necessary. First, managers can be role models for the groups and teams they oversee. When managers encourage and accept employees' suggestions for changes in procedures, do not rigidly insist that tasks be accomplished in a certain way, and admit when a norm they once supported is no longer functional, they signal to group members that conformity should not come at the expense of needed changes and improvements. Second, managers should let employees know that there are always ways to improve group processes and performance levels and thus opportunities to replace existing norms with norms that will better enable a group to achieve its goals and perform at a high level. Third, managers should encourage members of groups and teams to periodically assess the appropriateness of their norms.

Group Cohesiveness

group cohesiveness The degree to which members are attracted to or loyal to their group.

Another important element of group dynamics that affects group performance and effectiveness is **group cohesiveness,** which is the degree to which members are attracted to or loyal to their group or team.[41] When group cohesiveness is high, individuals strongly value their group membership, find the group appealing, and have strong desires to remain a part of the group. When group cohesiveness is low, group members do not find their group particularly appealing and have little desire to retain their group membership. Research suggests that managers should strive to have a moderate level of cohesiveness in the groups and teams they manage because that is most likely to contribute to an organization's competitive advantage. It often takes great efforts to encourage the group to develop such cohesiveness. The following "Management Insight" box illustrates how one firm is able to do this.

Management Insight

Singapore Airlines and Air Crew Team Building

In the airline industry, service is critical. The most direct delivery of customer service comes from the airline attendants that serve on the flights. It is critical that these individuals work well as a team in order to deliver the best service possible. Singapore Airlines is consistently rated as a top service provider in the airline industry, in large part because of the teamwork among the flight crew. The formation of successful service delivery teams among the flight crew takes special care by Singapore Airlines. They are successful not only working together well but also looking for ways to improve service constantly.

Singapore Airlines begins by taking their 6,600 crew members and forming teams of 13 workers. These teams fly together as much as possible, allowing them to build camaraderie and better understand each other's personalities and capacities. The teams will spend 60 to 70% of the time flying together. Team leaders act as counselors to team members; the leaders are to help the employees and solve any problems they (the leaders) see. The leaders also point out improvement areas, evaluate crew, monitor development, and provide feedback. The team leader is central to retraining needs and promotion of employees.

"Check trainers" oversee 12–13 teams and often fly with them to inspect performance. The team is encouraged to participate together in activities outside of work such as attending plays, eating out, or engaging in sports. The goal is to have the team truly know and understand each other very well. [42]

CONSEQUENCES OF GROUP COHESIVENESS There are three major consequences of group cohesiveness: level of participation within a group, level of conformity to group norms, and emphasis on group goal accomplishment (see Figure 15.6).[43]

LEVEL OF PARTICIPATION WITHIN A GROUP As group cohesiveness increases, the extent of group members' participation within the group increases. Participation contributes to group effectiveness because group members are actively involved in the group, ensure that group tasks get accomplished, readily share information with each other, and have frequent and open communication (the important topic of communication is covered in depth in Chapter 16).

A moderate level of group cohesiveness helps ensure that group members actively participate in the group and communicate effectively with one another. The reason why managers may not want to encourage high levels of cohesiveness is illustrated by the example of two cross-functional teams responsible for developing new toys. Members of the highly cohesive Team Alpha often have lengthy meetings that usually start with non-work-related conversations and jokes, meet more often than most of the other cross-functional teams in the company, and spend a good portion of their time communicating the ins and outs of their department's contribution to toy development to other team members. Members of the moderately cohesive Team Beta generally have efficient meetings in which ideas are communicated and discussed as needed, do not meet more often than necessary, and share the ins and outs of their expertise with one another to the extent needed for the development process. Teams Alpha and Beta have both developed some top-selling toys. However, it generally takes Team Alpha 30% longer to do so than Team Beta. This is why too much cohesiveness can be too much of a good thing.

LEVEL OF CONFORMITY TO GROUP NORMS Increasing levels of group cohesiveness result in increasing levels of conformity to group norms, and when cohesiveness becomes high, there may be so little deviance in groups that group members conform to norms even when they are dysfunctional. In contrast, low cohesiveness can result in too much deviance and undermine the ability of a group to control its members' behaviors to get things done.

Teams Alpha and Beta in the toy company both had the same norm for toy development. It dictated that members of each team would discuss potential ideas for new toys, decide on a line of toys to pursue, and then have the team member from R&D design a prototype. Recently a new animated movie featuring a family of rabbits produced by a small film company was an unexpected hit, and major toy companies were scrambling to reach licensing agreements to produce toy lines featuring the rabbits. The top management team in the toy company assigned Teams Alpha and Beta to develop the new toy lines quickly to beat the competition.

Members of Team Alpha followed their usual toy development norm even though the marketing expert on the team believed the process could have been streamlined to save time. The marketing expert on Team Beta urged the team to deviate from its toy development norm. She suggested that the team not have R&D develop prototypes but, instead, modify top-selling toys the company already made to feature rabbits and then reach a licensing agreement with the film company based on the high sales potential (given the company's prior success). Once the licensing agreement was signed, the company could take the time needed to develop innovative and unique rabbit toys with more input from R&D.

As a result of the willingness of the marketing expert on Team Beta to deviate from the norm for toy development, the toy company obtained an exclusive licensing agreement with the film company and had its first rabbit toys on the shelves of stores in a record three months. Groups need a balance of conformity and deviance, so a moderate level of cohesiveness often yields the best outcome, as it did in the case of Team Beta.

EMPHASIS ON GROUP GOAL ACCOMPLISHMENT As group cohesiveness increases, the emphasis placed on group goal accomplishment also increases within a group. A strong emphasis on group goal accomplishment, however, does not always lead to organizational effectiveness. For an organization to be effective and gain a competitive advantage, the different groups and teams in the organization must cooperate with one another and be motivated to achieve *organizational goals,* even if doing so sometimes comes at the expense of the achievement of group goals. A moderate level of cohesiveness motivates group members to accomplish both group and organizational goals. High levels of cohesiveness can cause group members to be so focused on group goal accomplishment that they may strive to achieve group goals no matter what–even when doing so jeopardizes organizational performance.

At the toy company, the major goal of the cross-functional teams was to develop new toy lines that were truly innovative, utilized the latest in technology, and were in some way fundamentally distinct from other toys on the market. When it came to the rabbit project, Team Alpha's high level of cohesiveness contributed to its continued emphasis on its group goal of developing an innovative line of toys; thus the team stuck with its usual design process. Team Beta, in contrast, realized that developing the new line of toys quickly was an important organizational goal that should take precedence over the group's goal of developing groundbreaking new toys, at least in the short term. Team Beta's moderate level of cohesiveness contributed to team members' doing what was best for the toy company in this case.

FACTORS LEADING TO GROUP COHESIVENESS Four factors contribute to the level of group cohesiveness (see Figure 15.6).[44] By influencing these *determinants of group cohesiveness,* managers can raise or lower the level of cohesiveness to promote moderate levels of cohesiveness in groups and teams.

GROUP SIZE As we mentioned earlier, members of small groups tend to be more motivated and committed than members of large groups. Thus to promote cohesiveness in groups, when feasible, managers should form groups that are small to medium in size (about 2 to 15 members). If a group is low in cohesiveness and large in size, managers might want to consider dividing the group in half and assigning different tasks and goals to the two newly formed groups.

EFFECTIVELY MANAGED DIVERSITY In general, people tend to like and get along with others who are similar to themselves. It is easier to communicate with someone, for example, who shares your values, has a similar background, and has had similar experiences. However, as discussed in Chapter 5, diversity in groups, teams, and organizations can help an organization gain a competitive advantage. Diverse groups often come up with more innovative and creative ideas. One reason why cross-functional teams are so popular in organizations like Hallmark Cards is that the diverse expertise represented in the teams results in higher levels of team performance.

In forming groups and teams, managers need to make sure the diversity in knowledge, experience, expertise, and other characteristics necessary for group goal accomplishment is represented in the new groups. Managers then have to make sure this diversity in group membership is effectively managed so groups will be cohesive (see Chapter 5).

GROUP IDENTITY AND HEALTHY COMPETITION When group cohesiveness is low, managers can often increase it by encouraging groups to develop their own identities or personalities and engage in healthy competition. This is precisely what managers did at one company that manufactures engine valves, gears, truck axles, and circuit breakers. Managers created self-managed work teams to cut costs and improve performance. They realized, however, that the teams would have to be cohesive to ensure that they would strive to achieve their goals. Managers promoted group identity by having the teams give themselves names such as "The Hoods," "The Worms," and "Scrap Attack" (a team striving to reduce costly scrap metal waste by 50%). Healthy competition among groups was promoted by displaying measures of each team's

Figure 15.6
Sources and Consequences of Group Cohesiveness

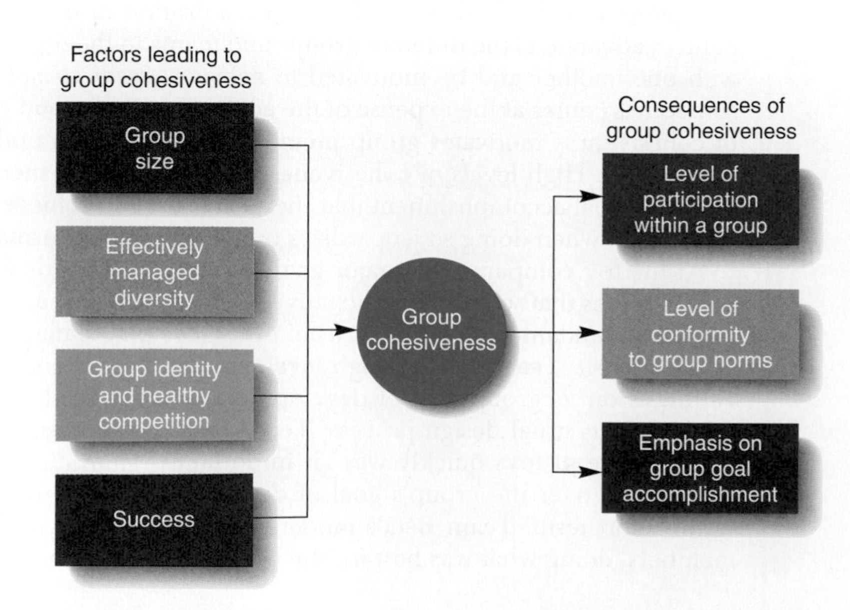

performance and the extent to which teams met their goals on a large TV screen in the cafeteria and by rewarding team members for team performance.[45]

If groups are too cohesive, managers can try to decrease cohesiveness by promoting organizational (rather than group) identity and making the organization as a whole the focus of the group's efforts. Organizational identity can be promoted by making group members feel that they are valued members of the organization and by stressing cooperation across groups to promote the achievement of organizational goals. Excessive levels of cohesiveness also can be reduced by reducing or eliminating competition among groups and rewarding cooperation.

SUCCESS When it comes to promoting group cohesiveness, there is more than a grain of truth to the saying "Nothing succeeds like success." As groups become more successful, they become increasingly attractive to their members, and their cohesiveness tends to increase. When cohesiveness is low, managers can increase cohesiveness by making sure a group can achieve some noticeable and visible successes.

Consider a group of salespeople in the housewares department of a medium-size department store. The housewares department was recently moved to a corner of the store's basement. Its remote location resulted in low sales because of infrequent customer traffic in that part of the store. The salespeople, who were generally evaluated favorably by their supervisors and were valued members of the store, tried various initiatives to boost sales, but to no avail. As a result of this lack of success and the poor performance of their department, their cohesiveness started to plummet. To increase and preserve the cohesiveness of the group, the store manager implemented a group-based incentive across the store. In any month, members of the group with the best attendance and punctuality records would have their names and pictures posted on a bulletin board in the cafeteria and would each receive a gift certificate. The housewares group frequently had the best records, and their success on this dimension helped to build and maintain their cohesiveness. Moreover, this initiative boosted attendance and discouraged lateness throughout the store.

Managing Groups and Teams for High Performance

Now that you understand why groups and teams are so important for organizations, the types of groups managers create, and group dynamics, we consider some additional steps managers can take to make sure groups and teams perform at a high level and contribute to organizational effectiveness. Managers striving to have top-performing groups and teams need to (1) motivate group members to work toward the achievement of organizational goals, (2) reduce social loafing, and (3) help groups manage conflict effectively.

LO15-5 Describe how managers can motivate group members to achieve organizational goals and reduce social loafing in groups and teams.

Motivating Group Members to Achieve Organizational Goals

When work is difficult, tedious, or requires a high level of commitment and energy, managers cannot assume group members will always be motivated to work toward the achievement of organizational goals. Consider a group of house painters who paint the interiors and exteriors of new homes for a construction company and are paid on an hourly basis. Why should they strive to complete painting jobs quickly and efficiently if doing so will just make them feel more tired at the end of the day and they will not receive any tangible benefits? It makes more sense for the painters to adopt a relaxed approach, to take frequent breaks, and to work at a leisurely pace. This relaxed approach, however, impairs the construction company's ability to gain a competitive advantage because it raises costs and increases the time needed to complete a new home.

Managers can motivate members of groups and teams to achieve organizational goals by making sure the members themselves benefit when the group or team performs highly. For example, if members of a self-managed work team know they will receive a weekly bonus based on team performance, they will be motivated to perform at a high level.

Managers often rely on some combination of individual and group-based incentives to motivate members of groups and teams to work toward the achievement of organizational goals. When individual performance within a group can be assessed, pay is often determined by individual performance or by both individual and group performance. When individual performance within a group cannot be accurately assessed, group performance should be the key determinant of pay levels. Many companies that use self-managed work teams base team members' pay in part on team performance.[46] A major challenge for managers is to develop a fair pay system that will lead to both high individual motivation and high group or team performance.

Other benefits managers can make available to high-performance group members–in addition to monetary rewards–include extra resources such as equipment and computer software, awards and other forms of recognition, and choice of future work assignments. For example, members of self-managed work teams that develop new software at companies such as Microsoft often value working on interesting and important projects; members of teams that have performed at a high level are rewarded by being assigned to interesting and important new projects.

Reducing Social Loafing in Groups

social loafing The tendency of individuals to put forth less effort when they work in groups than when they work alone.

We have been focusing on the steps managers can take to encourage high levels of performance in groups. Managers, however, need to be aware of an important downside to group and team work: the potential for social loafing, which reduces group performance. **Social loafing** is the tendency of individuals to put forth less effort when they work in groups than when they work alone.[47] Have you ever worked on a group project in which one or two group members never seemed to be pulling their weight? Have you ever worked in a student club or committee in which some members always seemed to be missing meetings and never volunteered for activities? Have you ever had a job in which one or two of your coworkers seemed to be slacking off because they knew you or other members of your work group would make up for their low levels of effort? If so, you have witnessed social loafing in action.

Social loafing can occur in all kinds of groups and teams and in all kinds of organizations. It can result in lower group performance and may even prevent a group from attaining its goals. Fortunately managers can take steps to reduce social loafing and sometimes completely eliminate it; we will look at three (see Figure 15.7):

1. *Make individual contributions to a group identifiable.* Some people may engage in social loafing when they work in groups because they think they can hide in the crowd–no one will notice if they put forth less effort than they should. Other people may think if they put forth high levels of effort and make substantial contributions to the group, their contributions will not be noticed and they will receive no rewards for their work–so why bother.[48]

One way that managers can effectively eliminate social loafing is by making individual contributions to a group identifiable so group members perceive that low and high levels of effort will be noticed and individual contributions evaluated.[49] Managers can accomplish this by assigning specific tasks to group members and holding them accountable for their completion. Take the case of a group of eight employees responsible for reshelving returned books in a large public library. The head librarian was concerned that there was always a backlog of seven or eight carts of books to be reshelved, even though the employees never seemed to be particularly busy and some even found time to sit down and read newspapers and magazines. The librarian decided to try to eliminate the apparent social loafing by

Figure 15.7
Three Ways to Reduce Social Loafing

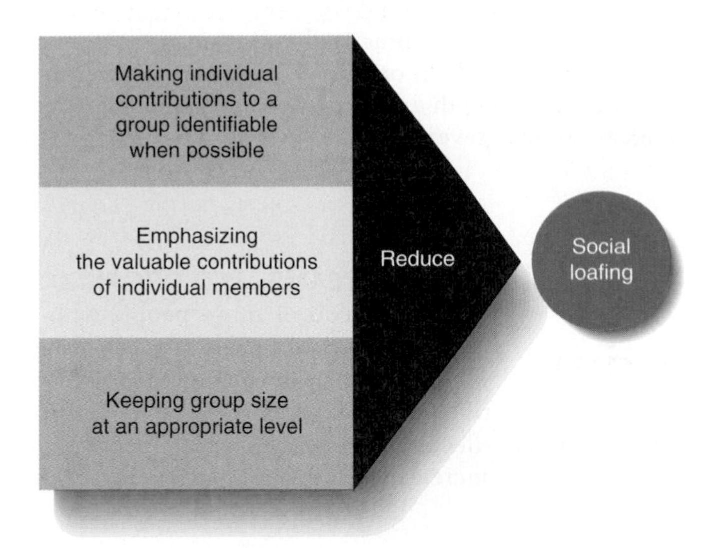

assigning each employee sole responsibility for reshelving a particular section of the library. Because the library's front desk employees sorted the books by section on the carts as they were returned, holding the shelvers responsible for particular sections was easily accomplished. Once the shelvers knew the librarian could identify their effort or lack thereof, there were rarely any backlogs of books to be reshelved.

Sometimes the members of a group can cooperate to eliminate social loafing by making individual contributions identifiable. For example, in a small security company, members of a self-managed work team who assemble control boxes for home alarm systems start each day by deciding who will perform which tasks that day and how much work each member and the group as a whole should strive to accomplish. Each team member knows that, at the end of the day, the other team members will know exactly how much he or she has accomplished. With this system in place, social loafing never occurs in the team. Remember, however, that in some teams, individual contributions cannot be made identifiable, as in teams whose members are reciprocally interdependent.

2. *Emphasize the valuable contributions of individual members.* Another reason why social loafing may occur is that people sometimes think their efforts are unnecessary or unimportant when they work in a group. They feel the group will accomplish its goals and perform at an acceptable level whether or not they personally perform at a high level. To counteract this belief, when managers form groups, they should assign individuals to a group on the basis of the valuable contributions that *each* person can make to the group as a whole. Clearly communicating to group members why each person's contributions are valuable to the group is an effective means by which managers and group members themselves can reduce or eliminate social loafing.[50] This is most clearly illustrated in cross-functional teams, where each member's valuable contribution to the team derives from a personal area of expertise. By emphasizing why each member's skills are important, managers can reduce social loafing in such teams.
3. *Keep group size at an appropriate level.* Group size is related to the causes of social loafing we just described. As size increases, identifying individual contributions becomes increasingly difficult, and members are increasingly likely to think their individual contributions are not important. To overcome this, managers should form groups with no more members than are needed to accomplish group goals and perform at a high level.[51]

Helping Groups to Manage Conflict Effectively

At some point or other, practically all groups experience conflict either within the group (*intragroup* conflict) or with other groups (*intergroup* conflict). In Chapter 17 we discuss conflict in depth and explore ways to manage it effectively. As you will learn, managers can take several steps to help groups manage conflict and disagreements.

Summary and Review

LO15-1 **GROUPS, TEAMS, AND ORGANIZATIONAL EFFECTIVENESS** A group is two or more people who interact with each other to accomplish certain goals or meet certain needs. A team is a group whose members work intensely with one another to achieve a specific common goal or objective. Groups and teams can contribute to organizational effectiveness by enhancing performance, increasing responsiveness to customers, increasing innovation, and being a source of motivation for their members.

LO15-2 **TYPES OF GROUPS AND TEAMS** Formal groups are groups that managers establish to achieve organizational goals; they include cross-functional teams, cross-cultural teams, top management teams, research and development teams, command groups, task forces, self-managed work teams, and virtual teams. Informal groups are groups that employees form because they believe the groups will help them achieve their own goals or meet their needs; they include friendship groups and interest groups.

LO15-3 **GROUP DYNAMICS** Key elements of group dynamics are group size, tasks, and roles; group leadership; group development; group norms; and group cohesiveness. The advantages and disadvantages of large and small groups suggest that managers should form groups with no more members than are needed to provide the group with the human resources it needs to achieve its goals and use a division of labor. The type of task interdependence that characterizes a group's work gives managers a clue about the appropriate size of the group. A group role is a set of behaviors and tasks that a member of a group is expected to perform because of his or her position in the group. All groups and teams need leadership.

LO15-3, 15-4 Five stages of development that many groups pass through are forming, storming, norming, performing, and adjourning. Group norms are shared rules for behavior that most group members follow. To be effective, groups need a balance of conformity and deviance. Conformity allows a group to control its members' behavior to achieve group goals; deviance provides the impetus for needed change.

LO15-4 Group cohesiveness is the attractiveness of a group or team to its members. As group cohesiveness increases, so do the level of participation and communication within a group, the level of conformity to group norms, and the emphasis on group goal accomplishment. Managers should strive to achieve a moderate level of group cohesiveness in the groups and teams they manage.

LO15-5 **MANAGING GROUPS AND TEAMS FOR HIGH PERFORMANCE** To make sure groups and teams perform at a high level, managers need to motivate group members to work toward the achievement of organizational goals, reduce social loafing, and help groups to effectively manage conflict. Managers can motivate members of groups and teams to work toward the achievement of organizational goals by making sure members personally benefit when the group or team performs at a high level.

Management in Action

Topics for Discussion and Action

Discussion

1. Why do all organizations need to rely on groups and teams to achieve their goals and gain a competitive advantage? **[LO15-1]**
2. What kinds of employees would prefer to work in a virtual team? What kinds of employees would prefer to work in a team that meets face-to-face? **[LO15-2]**
3. Think about a group that you are a member of, and describe that group's current stage of development. Does the development of this group seem to be following the forming, storming, norming, performing, and adjourning stages described in the chapter? **[LO15-3]**
4. Think about a group of employees who work in a fast food restaurant. What type of task interdependence characterizes this group? What potential problems in the group should the restaurant manager be aware of and take steps to avoid? **[LO15-3]**
5. Discuss the reasons why too much conformity can hurt groups and their organizations. **[LO15-4]**
6. Why do some groups have very low levels of cohesiveness? **[LO15-4]**
7. Imagine that you are the manager of a hotel. What steps will you take to reduce social loafing by members of the cleaning staff who are responsible for keeping all common areas and guest rooms spotless? **[LO15-5]**

Action

8. Interview one or more managers in an organization in your local community to identify the types of groups and teams that the organization uses to achieve its goals. What challenges do these groups and teams face? **[LO15-2]**

Building Management Skills

Diagnosing Group Failures **[LO15-1, 15-2, 15-3, 15-4, 15-5]**

Think about the last dissatisfying or discouraging experience you had as a member of a group or team. Perhaps the group did not accomplish its goals, perhaps group members could agree about nothing, or perhaps there was too much social loafing. Now answer the following questions:

1. What type of group was this?
2. Were group members motivated to achieve group goals? Why or why not?
3. How large was the group, what type of task interdependence existed in the group, and what group roles did members play?
4. What were the group's norms? How much conformity and deviance existed in the group?
5. How cohesive was the group? Why do you think the group's cohesiveness was at this level? What consequences did this level of group cohesiveness have for the group and its members?
6. Was social loafing a problem in this group? Why or why not?
7. What could the group's leader or manager have done differently to increase group effectiveness?
8. What could group members have done differently to increase group effectiveness?

Managing Ethically **[LO15-1, 15-2, 15-3, 15-4, 15-5]**

Some self-managed teams encounter a vexing problem: One or more members engage in social loafing, and other members are reluctant to try to rectify the situation. Social loafing can be especially troubling if team members' pay is based on team performance and social loafing reduces the team's performance and thus the pay of all members (even the highest performers). Even if managers are aware of the problem, they may be reluctant to take action because the team is supposedly self-managing.

Questions

1. Either individually or in a group, think about the ethical implications of social loafing in a self-managed team.
2. Do managers have an ethical obligation to step in when they are aware of social loafing in a self-managed team? Why or why not? Do other team members have an obligation to try to curtail the social loafing? Why or why not?

Small Group Breakout Exercise

Creating a Cross-Functional Team [LO15-1, 15-2, 15-3, 15-4, 15-5]

Form groups of three or four people, and appoint one member as the spokesperson who will communicate your findings to the class when called on by the instructor. Then discuss the following scenario:

You are a group of managers in charge of food services for a large publicly funded university. Recently a survey of students, faculty, and staff was conducted to evaluate customer satisfaction with the food services provided by the university's eight cafeterias. The results were disappointing, to put it mildly. Complaints ranged from dissatisfaction with the type and range of meals and snacks provided, operating hours, and food temperature to frustration about unresponsiveness to current concerns about healthful diets and the needs of vegetarians. You have decided to form a cross-functional team that will further evaluate reactions to the food services and will develop a proposal for changes to be made to increase customer satisfaction.

1. Indicate who should be on this important cross-functional team, and explain why.
2. Describe the goals the team should strive to achieve.
3. Describe the different roles that will need to be performed on this team.
4. Describe the steps you will take to help ensure that the team has a good balance between conformity and deviance and has a moderate level of cohesiveness.

Exploring the World Wide Web [LO15-1, 15-2, 15-3, 15-4, 15-5]

Many consultants and organizations provide team-building services to organizations. Although some managers and teams have found these services to be helpful, others have found them to be a waste of time and money—another consulting fad that provides no real performance benefits. Search online for team-building services, and examine the Web sites of a few consultants/companies. Based on what you have read, what might be some advantages and disadvantages of team-building services? For what kinds of problems/issues might these services be beneficial, and when might they have little benefit or perhaps even do more harm than good?

Be the Manager [LO15-1, 15-2, 15-3, 15-4, 15-5]

You were recently hired in a boundary-spanning role for the global unit of an educational and professional publishing company. The company is headquartered in New York (where you work) and has divisions in multiple countries. Each division is responsible for translating, manufacturing, marketing, and selling a set of books in its country. Your responsibilities include interfacing with managers in each of the divisions in your region (Central and South America), overseeing their budgeting and financial reporting to headquarters, and leading a virtual team consisting of the top managers in charge of each of the divisions in your region. The virtual team's mission is to promote global learning, explore new potential opportunities and markets, and address ongoing problems. You communicate directly with division managers via telephone and e-mail, as well as written reports, memos, and faxes. When virtual team meetings are convened, videoconferencing is often used.

After your first few virtual team meetings, you noticed that the managers seemed to be reticent about speaking up. Interestingly enough, when each manager communicates with you individually, primarily in telephone conversations and e-mails, she or he tends to be forthcoming and frank, and you feel you have a good rapport with each of them. However, getting the managers to communicate with one another as a virtual team has been a real challenge. At the last meeting you tried to prompt some of the managers to raise issues relevant to the agenda that you knew were on their minds from your individual conversations with them. Surprisingly, the managers skillfully avoided informing their teammates about the heart of the issues in question. You are confused and troubled. Although you feel your other responsibilities are going well, you know your virtual team is not operating like a team at all; and no matter what you try, discussions in virtual team meetings are forced and generally unproductive. What are you going to do to address this problem?

CHAPTER 16

Promoting Effective Communication

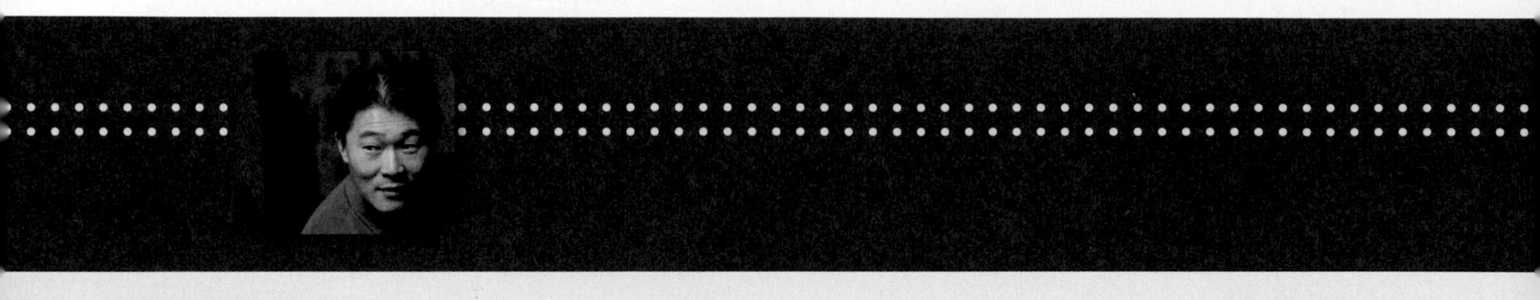

Learning Objectives

After studying this chapter, you should be able to:

LO16-1 Explain why effective communication helps an organization gain a competitive advantage.

LO16-2 Describe the communication process, and explain the role of perception in communication.

LO16-3 Define information richness, and describe the information richness of communication media available to managers.

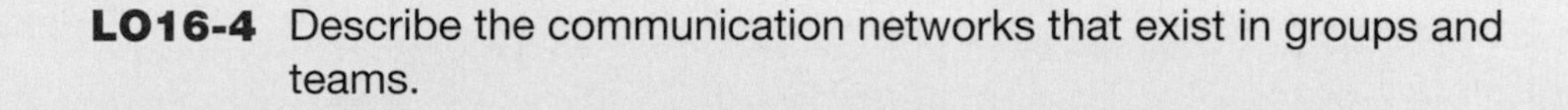

LO16-4 Describe the communication networks that exist in groups and teams.

LO16-5 Explain how advances in technology have given managers new options for managing communication.

LO16-6 Describe important communication skills that managers need as senders and as receivers of messages and why it is important to understand differences in linguistic styles.

A MANAGER'S CHALLENGE

Singapore and Its Airline Thrive Using Strong Communication

Singapore Airlines is one of the most respected airlines in the world, consistently appearing in the list generated by* Fortune *magazine as one of the world's most admired companies. The history of the firm and the nation of Singapore are intertwined. The firm began in 1947 as Malayan Airways. This name reflects the fact that Singapore was initially part of the Malaysian Federation when independence was granted by the British in the 1960s. However, difficulty between Singapore and Malaysia resulted in the city of Singapore being expelled from the Federation in 1965, and the nation of Singapore was created.

Singapore today is a city/state with a population of approximately 4.8 million people. The nation is predominately ethnic Chinese but also has large ethnic Malay and Indian populations. Singapore has grown from relative poverty to one of the richest nations in the world with a per capita income of approximately $50,000 per person, one of the top ten in the world. Thus, both the airline and the nation are now centers of quality and success.

For a nation to be able to transform itself in only 25 years from an emerging economy to a major mature economy is a key accomplishment; central to this accomplishment is extensive communication by the government to the people. The government set an initial and clear goal to develop into a mature economy and a relatively rich nation. That aspiration and mission were clearly communicated to the population. Associated with the goal were steps the government felt would have to be accomplished. For example, the government felt that a clean environment was important to develop the tourist trade. The government spent extensive resources educating the public on issues such as cleanliness. Singapore is famous today for not allowing individuals to chew

Strong communication has helped both Singapore Airlines and the nation of Singapore to thrive in a global environment.

gum freely; the fear is that people will stick the gum in any convenient place rather than throw it away, resulting in a mess. Another aspect of this growth plan was that the government decided that communication with the world was so critical that English became the standard education language in the nation. The result was exceptional levels of English that allow Singaporeans to communicate very well in almost any business situation worldwide.

The transformation of Singapore Airlines was similar to the transformation of the nation. The airline began as a small regional airline with service consistent with that status. Just as the government set the goal to become one of the leading economic powers in the world, Singapore Airlines desired to be one of the leading airlines in the world. Central to the accomplishment of this goal was communication in the firm. For example, the airline developed extensive print and electronic communications to all employees. The print publications include the companywide publication called *Outlook.* This publication is, in turn, supplemented with publications tailored to specific employees, such as cabin crew and pilots. For example, the Cabin Crew Division produces *Highpoint* (a monthly newsletter with cabin crew events and passenger comments) and *Cabin Crew Circulars* (bi-weekly updates on service procedures, rules and regulations, security and safety guidelines). In addition, Singapore Airlines sends out electronic news through a cabin crew online portal and mass email updates for urgent announcements. The Senior Vice President of the Cabin Crew meets with all the cabin crews every two weeks to get feedback and to provide verbal communication on the firm's actions and to reinforce core values of the firm such as service. Importantly, just as the government ensures that individuals in Singapore learn English, the firm also emphasizes that staff have excellent English skills so that they serve customers in any of the 38 nations where Singapore Airlines flies.

Thus, Singapore Airlines and the nation of Singapore have largely developed together. Both set high goals and ensured through communication that employees and citizens understand those goals and the actions necessary to achieve them. The result has been that the airline and the nation have moved from a position of weakness to world leaders.[1]

Overview

Even with all the advances in information technology that are available to managers, ineffective communication continues to take place in organizations. Ineffective communication is detrimental for managers, employees, and organizations; it can lead to poor performance, strained interpersonal relations, poor service, and dissatisfied customers. For an organization to be effective and gain a competitive advantage, managers at all levels need to be good communicators.

In this chapter we describe the nature of communication and the communication process and explain why all managers and their subordinates need to be effective communicators. We describe the communication media available to managers and the factors they need to consider in selecting a communication medium for each message they send. We consider the communication networks organizational members rely on, and we explore how advances in information technology have expanded managers' range of communication options. We describe the communication skills that help managers be effective senders and receivers of messages. By the end of this chapter you will appreciate the nature of communication and the steps managers can take to ensure that they are effective communicators.

LO16-1 Explain why effective communication helps an organization gain a competitive advantage.

Communication and Management

Communication is the sharing of information between two or more individuals or groups to reach a common understanding.[2] First and foremost, no matter how electronically based, communication is a human endeavor and involves individuals and groups. Second, communication does not take place unless a common understanding is reached. Thus when you call a business to speak to a person in customer service or billing and are bounced between endless automated messages and menu options and eventually hang up in frustration, communication has not taken place.

communication The sharing of information between two or more individuals or groups to reach a common understanding.

The Importance of Good Communication

In Chapter 1 we described how an organization can gain a competitive advantage when managers strive to increase efficiency, quality, responsiveness to customers, and innovation. Good communication is essential for attaining each of these four goals and thus is a necessity for gaining a competitive advantage.

Managers can *increase efficiency* by updating the production process to take advantage of new and more efficient technologies and by training workers to operate the new technologies and to expand their skills. Good communication is necessary for managers to learn about new technologies, implement them in their organizations, and train workers in how to use them. Similarly, *improving quality* hinges on effective communication. Managers need to communicate to all members of an organization the meaning and importance of high quality and the routes to attaining it. Subordinates need to communicate quality problems and suggestions for increasing quality to their superiors, and members of self-managed work teams need to share their ideas on improving quality with one another.

Good communication can also help increase *responsiveness to customers.* When the organizational members who are closest to customers, such as department store salespeople and bank tellers, are empowered to communicate customers' needs and desires to managers, managers can better respond to these needs. Managers, in turn, must communicate with other organizational members to determine how best to respond to changing customer preferences.

Innovation, which often takes place in cross-functional teams, also requires effective communication. Members of a cross-functional team developing a new electronic game, for example, must effectively communicate with one another to develop a game that customers will want to play; that will be engaging, interesting, and fun; and that can potentially lead to sequels. Members of the team also must communicate with managers to secure the resources they need for developing the game and to keep managers informed of progress on the project. Innovation in organizations is increasingly taking place on a global level, making effective communication all the more important, as illustrated in the "Managing Globally" box on the next page.

Effective communication is necessary for managers and all members of an organization to increase efficiency, quality, responsiveness to customers, and innovation and thus gain a competitive advantage for the organization. Managers therefore must understand the communication process well if they are to perform effectively. This impact is so great that some firms such as Tata Chemical of India feel communication is so critical that they have created a Communications Effectiveness Index (CEI) to measure the effectiveness of their communications and its impact on these activities.

Managing Globally

Global Communication for Global Innovation

GE Healthcare (headquartered in the United Kingdom) is a provider of medical technology and services and makes medical imaging, diagnostic, and monitoring systems such as CT scanners. With over 46,000 employees around the world, GE Healthcare has approximately $17 billion in revenues.[3] To make the best scanners that meet the needs of doctors and patients around the world with next-generation technology, new product development and manufacturing are truly global endeavors at GE Healthcare Technologies. Consider the LightSpeed VCT scanner series (*VCT* stands for "volume controlled tomography"), which costs in the millions and is among the quickest and highest-resolution scanners available in the world.[4] The LightSpeed can perform a full-body scan in under 10 seconds and yields a three-dimensional picture of patients' hearts within five heartbeats.[5]

As GE Healthcare learned, conference calls and e-mails can stand in the gap, but nothing replaces getting managers together for face-to-face conversations and problem solving.

The LightSpeed was developed through global collaboration. GE managers not only spoke with doctors (including cardiologists and radiologists) around the world to find out what their needs were and what kinds of tests they would perform with the LightSpeed but also gathered information about differences among patients in various countries. Engineers in Hino (Japan), Buc (France), and Waukesha, Wisconsin (US), developed the electronics for the LightSpeed. Other parts, such as the automated table that patients lie on, are made in Beijing (China) and Hino. Software for the LightSpeed was written in Haifa (Israel), Bangalore (India), Buc, and Waukesha.[6]

Effective global communication was a challenge and a necessity to successfully develop the LightSpeed series. As Brian Duchinsky, GE's general manager for global CT, put it, "If we sat around in this cornfield west of Milwaukee, we wouldn't come up with the same breadth of good ideas. But yet, getting six countries on the phone to make a decision can be a pain."[7]

GE managers facilitated effective communication in a number of ways–participating in daily conference calls, making sure teams in different countries depended on one another, developing an internal Web site devoted to the LightSpeed, encouraging teams to ask one another for help, and holding face-to-face meetings in different locations. Although much communication took place electronically, such as through conference calls, face-to-face meetings were also important. As Bob Armstrong, GE's general manager for engineering, indicated, "You need to get your people together in one place if you want them to really appreciate how good everyone is, and how good you are as a team."[8]

The Communication Process

LO16-2 Describe the communication process, and explain the role of perception in communication.

The communication process consists of two phases. In the *transmission phase,* information is shared between two or more individuals or groups. In the *feedback phase,* a common understanding is ensured. In both phases, a number of distinct stages must occur for communication to take place (see Figure 16.1).[9]

Figure 16.1
The Communication Process

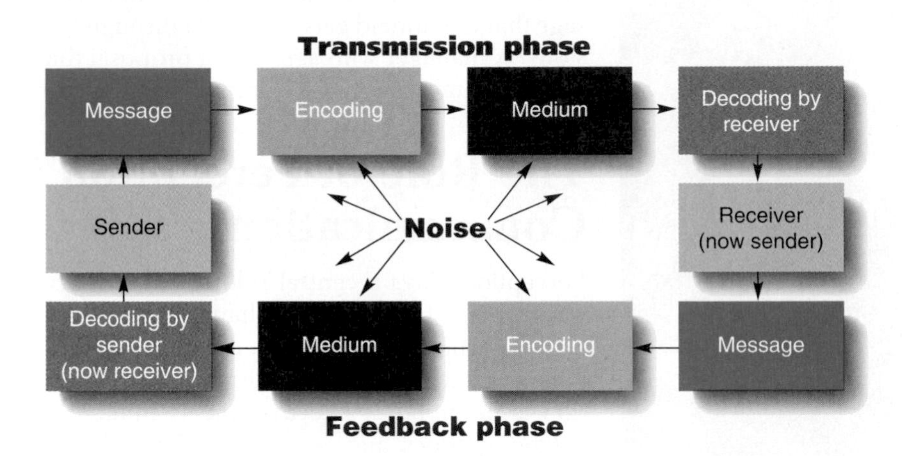

sender The person or group wishing to share information.

message The information that a sender wants to share.

encoding Translating a message into understandable symbols or language.

noise Anything that hampers any stage of the communication process.

receiver The person or group for which a message is intended.

medium The pathway through which an encoded message is transmitted to a receiver.

decoding Interpreting and trying to make sense of a message.

verbal communication The encoding of messages into words, either written or spoken.

nonverbal communication The encoding of messages by means of facial expressions, body language, and styles of dress.

Starting the transmission phase, the **sender,** the person or group wishing to share information with some other person or group, decides on the **message,** what information to communicate. Then the sender translates the message into symbols or language, a process called **encoding;** often messages are encoded into words. **Noise** is a general term that refers to anything that hampers any stage of the communication process.

Once encoded, a message is transmitted through a medium to the **receiver,** the person or group for which the message is intended. A **medium** is simply the pathway, such as a phone call, a letter, a memo, or face-to-face communication in a meeting, through which an encoded message is transmitted to a receiver. At the next stage, the receiver interprets and tries to make sense of the message, a process called **decoding.** This is a critical point in communication.

The feedback phase is initiated by the receiver (who becomes a sender). The receiver decides what message to send to the original sender (who becomes a receiver), encodes it, and transmits it through a chosen medium (see Figure 16.1). The message might contain a confirmation that the original message was received and understood or a restatement of the original message to make sure it has been correctly interpreted, or it might include a request for more information. The original sender decodes the message and makes sure a common understanding has been reached. If the original sender determines that a common understanding has not been reached, sender and receiver cycle through the whole process as many times as needed to reach a common understanding. Feedback eliminates misunderstandings, ensures that messages are correctly interpreted, and enables senders and receivers to reach a common understanding.

The encoding of messages into words, written or spoken, is **verbal communication.** We can also encode messages without using written or spoken language. **Nonverbal communication** shares information by means of facial expressions (smiling, raising an eyebrow, frowning, dropping one's jaw), body language (posture, gestures, nods, and shrugs), and even style of dress (casual, formal, conservative, trendy).

Nonverbal communication can be used to back up or reinforce verbal communication. Just as a warm and genuine smile can back up words of appreciation for a job well done, a concerned facial expression can back up words of sympathy for a personal problem. In such cases, the congruence between the verbal and the nonverbal communication helps to ensure that a common understanding is reached.

If a picture is worth a thousand words, so too is nonverbal communication; facial expressions, body language, posture, and eye contact all send powerful messages.

Sometimes when members of an organization decide not to express a message verbally, they inadvertently do so nonverbally. People tend to have less control over nonverbal communication, and often a verbal message that is withheld gets expressed through body language or facial expressions. A manager who agrees to a proposal that she or he actually does not like may unintentionally communicate her or his disfavor by grimacing.

The Role of Perception in Communication

Perception plays a central role in communication and affects both transmission and feedback. In Chapter 5 we defined *perception* as the process through which people select, organize, and interpret sensory input to give meaning and order to the world around them. We mentioned that perception is inherently subjective and is influenced by people's personalities, values, attitudes, and moods as well as by their experience and knowledge. When senders and receivers communicate with each other, they are doing so based on their own subjective perceptions. The encoding and decoding of messages and even the choice of a medium hinge on the perceptions of senders and receivers.

In addition, perceptual biases can hamper effective communication. Recall from Chapter 5 that *biases* are systematic tendencies to use information about others in ways that result in inaccurate perceptions. In Chapter 5 we described a number of biases that can cause unfair treatment of diverse members of an organization. The same biases also can lead to ineffective communication. For example, *stereotypes*–simplified and often inaccurate beliefs about the characteristics of particular groups of people–can interfere with the encoding and decoding of messages.

Suppose a manager stereotypes older workers as being fearful of change. When this manager encodes a message to an older worker about an upcoming change in the organization, she may downplay the extent of the change so as not to make the older worker feel stressed. The older worker, however, fears change no more than do his younger colleagues and thus decodes the message to mean that only a minor change is going to be made. The older worker fails to adequately prepare for the change, and his performance subsequently suffers because of his lack of preparation for the change. Clearly this ineffective communication was due to the manager's inaccurate assumptions about older workers. Instead of relying on stereotypes, effective managers strive to perceive other people accurately by focusing on their actual behaviors, knowledge, skills, and abilities. Accurate perceptions, in turn, contribute to effective communication.

The Dangers of Ineffective Communication

Because managers must communicate with others to perform their various roles and tasks, managers spend most of their time communicating, whether in meetings, in telephone conversations, through e-mail, or in face-to-face interactions. Indeed, some experts estimate that managers spend approximately 85% of their time engaged in some form of communication.[10]

Effective communication is so important that managers cannot just be concerned that they themselves are effective communicators; they also have to help their subordinates be effective communicators. When all members of an organization can communicate effectively with one another and with people outside the organization, the organization is much more likely to perform highly and gain a competitive advantage.

When managers and other members of an organization are ineffective communicators, organizational performance suffers and any competitive advantage the organization might have is likely to be lost. Moreover, poor communication sometimes can be downright dangerous and even lead to tragic and unnecessary loss of human life. For example, researchers from Harvard University recently studied the causes of mistakes, such as a patient receiving the wrong medication, in two large hospitals in the Boston area. They discovered that some mistakes in hospitals occur because of communication problems–physicians' not having the information they need to correctly order medications for their patients or nurses' not having the information they need to correctly administer medications. The researchers concluded that some of the responsibility for these mistakes lies with hospital management, which has not taken active steps to improve communication.[11]

Communication problems in airplane cockpits and between flying crews and air traffic controllers are unfortunately all too common, sometimes with deadly consequences. In the late 1970s two jets collided in Tenerife (one of the Canary Islands) because of miscommunication between a pilot and the control tower, and 600 people were killed. The tower radioed to the pilot, "Clipper 1736 report clear of runway." The pilot mistakenly interpreted this message to mean that he was cleared for takeoff.[12] Unfortunately communication problems persist in the airline industry.

Information Richness and Communication Media

LO16-3 Define information richness, and describe the information richness of communication media available to managers.

information richness The amount of information that a communication medium can carry and the extent to which the medium enables the sender and receiver to reach a common understanding.

To be effective communicators, managers (and other members of an organization) need to select an appropriate communication medium for each message they send. Should a change in procedures be communicated to subordinates in a memo sent through e-mail? Should a congratulatory message about a major accomplishment be communicated in a letter, in a phone call, or over lunch? Should a layoff announcement be made in a memo or at a plant meeting? Should the members of a purchasing team travel to Europe to cement a major agreement with a new supplier, or should they do so through faxes? Managers deal with these questions day in and day out.

There is no one best communication medium for managers to rely on. In choosing a communication medium for any message, managers need to consider three factors. The first and most important is the level of information richness that is needed. **Information richness** is the amount of information a communication medium can carry and the extent to which the medium enables the sender and receiver to reach a common understanding.[13] The communication media that managers use vary in their information richness (see Figure 16.2).[14] Media high in information richness can carry an extensive amount of information and generally enable receivers and senders to come to a common understanding.

The second factor that managers need to take into account in selecting a communication medium is the *time* needed for communication because managers' and other organizational members' time is valuable. Managers at United Parcel Service, for example, dramatically reduced the amount of time they spent on communicating by using videoconferences instead of face-to-face communication, which required that managers travel overseas.[15]

The third factor that affects the choice of a communication medium is the *need for a paper or electronic trail* or some kind of written documentation that a message was sent and received. A manager may wish to document in writing, for example, that a subordinate was given a formal warning about excessive lateness.

In the remainder of this section we examine four types of communication media that vary along these three dimensions (information richness, time, and paper or electronic trail).[16]

Face-to-Face Communication

Face-to-face communication is the medium that is highest in information richness. When managers communicate face-to-face, they not only can take advantage of verbal communication but also can interpret each other's nonverbal signals such as facial

Figure 16.2
The Information Richness of Communication Media

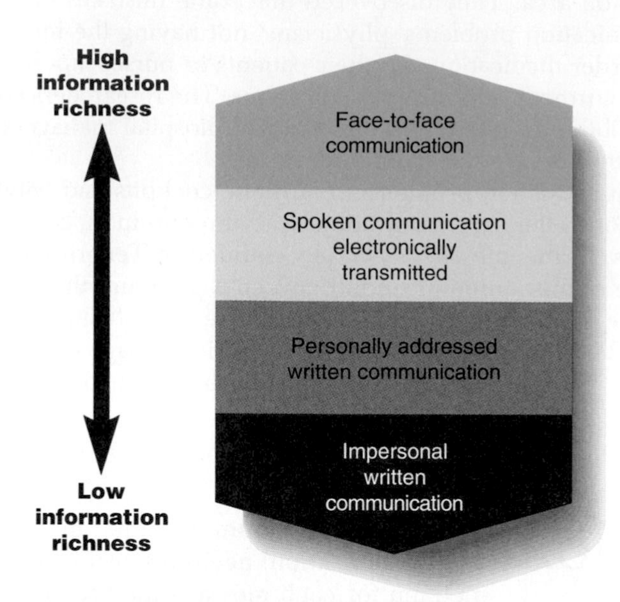

expressions and body language. A look of concern or puzzlement can sometimes say more than a thousand words, and managers can respond to such nonverbal signals on the spot. Face-to-face communication also enables managers to receive instant feedback. Points of confusion, ambiguity, or misunderstanding can be resolved, and managers can cycle through the communication process as many times as needed to reach a common understanding.

With the growing proliferation of electronic forms of communication, such as e-mail, some managers fear that face-to-face communication is being shortchanged to the detriment of building common understandings and rapport.[17] Moreover, some messages that really should be communicated face-to-face or at least in a phone conversation, and messages that are more efficiently communicated in this manner, are nonetheless sent electronically.[18] As indicated in the following "Management Insight" box, managers need to carefully consider whether face-to-face communication is being shortchanged in their organizations and, if it is, take steps to rectify the situation.

Management Insight

Know the Business Environment

Communication around the world often has different impacts based on whether a person comes from a high or low context environment. High and low context refers to the fact that in some cultures the context in which something is said may have greater importance than the content of what is said. However, in other cultures, it is the content of what is said that matters–not the context.

To illustrate, in cultures such as the United States, Australia, Germany, and the United Kingdom, it is the content of what is said that matters. This would be a low context culture. This focus on content is illustrated in a number of ways. For example, let's say a business proposal is made in a low context country. This leads to meetings where the new business activity is proposed; the meetings focus strictly on the proposed activity, how it will be put into operation, and the potential profit from the endeavor.

In contrast, in high context settings such as China or the Middle East, who makes the proposal and how they present it is as critical, or more so, than the proposal itself. For example, in high context settings business people typically do not present a business proposal directly unless they already have clear relationships with those involved. Instead, initial meetings focus on getting to know each other. In this "pre-proposal" phase, individuals in high context cultures want to know not only about you and your family but whom else you know. The very fact that you met with someone and that person acknowledged your idea can have powerful signaling impact on others. Thus, all communications are set in the context of who says what. This is in contrast to the low context setting, which focuses almost exclusively on the content.

Allowing opportunities for face-to-face communication can be especially important when trying to effectively communicate with employees located in other countries. For example, Greg Caltabiano, CEO of Teknovus Inc., which is based in California, and has offices in Asia, arranges for U.S. employees to go to Asia and Asian employees to come to the United States to engage in face-to-face communication to build mutual understanding.[19]

management by wandering around A face-to-face communication technique in which a manager walks around a work area and talks informally with employees about issues and concerns.

Management by wandering around is a face-to-face communication technique that is effective for many managers at all levels in an organization.[20] Rather than scheduling formal meetings with subordinates, managers walk around work areas and talk informally with employees about issues and concerns that both employees and managers may have. These informal conversations give managers and subordinates important information and at the same time foster the development of positive relationships. William Hewlett and David Packard, founders and former top managers of Hewlett-Packard, found management by wandering around to be a highly effective way of communicating with their employees.

Because face-to-face communication is highest in information richness, you might think it should always be the medium of choice for managers. This is not the case, however, because of the amount of time it can take and the lack of a paper or electronic trail resulting from it. For messages that are important, personal, or likely to be misunderstood, it is often well worth managers' time to use face-to-face communication and, if need be, supplement it with some form of written communication documenting the message.

Advances in information technology are giving managers new communication media that are close substitutes for face-to-face communication. Many organizations, such as Hewlett-Packard, are using *videoconferences* to capture some of the advantages of face-to-face communication (such as access to facial expressions) while saving time and money because managers in different locations do not have to travel to meet with one another. During a videoconference, managers in two or more locations communicate with each other over large TV or video screens; they not only hear each other but also see each other throughout the meeting.

In addition to saving travel costs, videoconferences sometimes have other advantages. Managers at Hewlett-Packard have found that videoconferences have shortened new product development time by 30% for similar reasons. Videoconferences also seem to lead to more efficient meetings. Some managers have found that their meetings are 20% to 30% shorter when videoconferences are used instead of face-to-face meetings.[21]

Taking videoconferences a leap forward, Cisco Systems has developed its TelePresence line of products, enabling individuals and teams in different locations to communicate live and in real time over the Internet with high-definition, life-size video and excellent audio that make it feel like all participants, no matter where they are, are in the same room.[22] One morning Cisco CEO John Chambers was able to

Videoconferencing allows these remotely based teams to see each other around the conference table, the next best thing to actually being in the same office space.

participate in meetings with employees and teams in India, Japan, Cleveland, and London in less than four hours by using TelePresence.[23] Other companies, such as HP, have developed similar products. What distinguishes these products from older videoconferencing systems is the lack of transmission delay and the sharp, clear, life-size video quality.[24]

Spoken Communication Electronically Transmitted

After face-to-face communication, spoken communication electronically transmitted over phone lines (and the World Wide Web) is second highest in information richness (see Figure 16.2). Although managers communicating over the telephone do not have access to body language and facial expressions, they do have access to the tone of voice in which a message is delivered, the parts of the message the sender emphasizes, and the general manner in which the message is spoken, in addition to the actual words themselves. Thus telephone conversations can convey extensive amounts of information. Managers can ensure that mutual understanding is reached because they can get quick feedback over the phone and answer questions. When Greg Caltabiano, CEO of Teknovus Inc., wanted to improve communication between engineers in United States who design semiconductors for fiber optic networks and employees and customers in Asia, he encouraged the engineers to communicate via the telephone instead of by e-mail.[25]

Voice mail systems and answering machines also allow managers to send and receive verbal electronic messages over telephone lines. Voice mail systems are companywide systems that let senders record messages for members of an organization who are away from their desks and allow receivers to access their messages even when hundreds of miles away from the office. Such systems are obviously a necessity when managers are frequently out of the office, and managers on the road are well advised to periodically check their voice mail.

Personally Addressed Written Communication

Lower in information richness than electronically transmitted verbal communication is personally addressed written communication (see Figure 16.2). One advantage of face-to-face communication and electronically transmitted verbal communication is that they both tend to demand attention, which helps ensure that receivers pay attention. Personally addressed written communications, such as memos and letters, also have this advantage. Because they are addressed to a particular person, the chances are good that the person will actually pay attention to (and read) them. Moreover, the sender can write the message in a way that the receiver is most likely to understand. Like voice mail, written communication does not enable a receiver to have his or her questions answered immediately; but when messages are clearly written and feedback is provided, common understandings can still be reached.

Even if managers use face-to-face communication, sending a follow-up in writing is often necessary for messages that are important or complicated and need to be referred to later on. E-mail also fits into this category of communication media because senders and receivers are communicating through personally addressed written words. The words, however, appear on their computer screens rather than on paper. E-mail is so widespread in the business world that some managers find they have to deliberately take time out from managing their e-mail to get their work done, think about pressing concerns, and come up with new and innovative ideas.[26] According to the Radacati Group, an independent market research firm, the average e-mail account in corporations today receives about 18 megabytes of e-mail and attachments per workday; the volume of e-mail is expected to increase over time.[27] To help their employees effectively manage e-mail, a growing number of organizations are instituting training programs to help employees learn how to more effectively use e-mail by sending clearer messages, avoiding e-mail copies to multiple parties who do not really need to see it, and writing clear and informative subject lines.[28] For example, Capital One trains employees to (1) write clear subject lines so recipients know why they are receiving a message and can easily search for it and retrieve it later, and (2) convey information clearly and effectively in the e-mail body.[29]

Ultimately, for messages that are sensitive or potentially misunderstood, or that require the give-and-take of a face-to-face or telephone conversation, relying on e-mail can take considerably more time to reach a common understanding.[30] Additionally, given the lack of nonverbal cues, tone of voice, and intonation in e-mail, senders need to be aware of the potential for misunderstandings.[31] For example, Kristin Byron, a professor of management at Syracuse University, suggests that recipients may have a tendency to perceive some of the e-mail they receive as more negative than the senders intended, based on her research.[32] Senders who are rushed, for example, may send short, curt messages lacking greeting and closing lines because they are so busy.[33] Recipients, however, might read something more negative into messages like these.[34]

The growing popularity of e-mail has also enabled many workers and managers to become *telecommuters*–people who are employed by organizations and work out of offices in their own homes. There are over 34 million telecommuters in the United States.[35] Many telecommuters indicate that the flexibility of working at home lets them be more productive and, at the same time, be closer to their families and not waste time traveling to and from the office.[36] In a study conducted by Georgetown University, 75% of the telecommuters surveyed said their productivity increased, and 83% said their home life improved once they started telecommuting.[37]

Managers need to develop a clear, written policy specifying what company e-mail can and should be used for and what is out of bounds. Managers also should clearly communicate this policy to all members of the organization, as well as tell them what procedures will be used when e-mail abuse is suspected and what consequences will result if the abuse is confirmed. According to a survey conducted by the ePolicy Institute, of the 79% of companies that have an e-mail policy, only about 54% actually give employees training and education to ensure that they understand it.[38] Training and education are important to ensure that employees know not only what the policy is but also what it means for their own e-mail use.

Additionally, e-mail policies should specify how much personal e-mail is appropriate and when the bounds of appropriateness have been overstepped. Just as employees make personal phone calls while on the job (and sometimes have to), so too do they send and receive personal e-mail. In fact, according to Waterford Technologies, a provider of e-mail management and archive services based in Irvine, California, about one-third of e-mail to and from companies is personal or not work-related.[39] Clearly, banning all personal e-mail is impractical and likely to have negative consequences for employees and their organizations (such as lower levels of job satisfaction and increased personal phone conversations). Some companies limit personal e-mail to certain times of the day or a certain amount of time per day; others have employees create lists of contacts from whom they want to receive e-mail at work (family members, children, baby-sitters); still others want personal e-mail to be sent and received through Web-based systems like Gmail and Hotmail rather than the corporate e-mail system.[40]

What about surfing the Internet on company time? According to a study conducted by Websense, approximately half of the employees surveyed indicated that they surfed the Web at work, averaging about two hours per week.[41] Most visited news and travel sites, but about 22% of the male respondents and 12% of the female respondents indicated that they visited pornographic Web sites.[42] Of all those surveyed, 56% said they sent personal e-mail at work. The majority of those surveyed felt that sending personal e-mail and surfing the Web had no effect on their performance, and 27% thought that doing so improved their productivity.[43] Other statistics suggest that while overall there is more Internet use at home than at work, individuals who use the Internet at work spend more time on it and visit more sites than do those who use it at home.[44] As indicated in the following "Ethics in Action" box, personal e-mail and Internet surfing at work present managers with some challenging ethical dilemmas.

Ethics in Action

Monitoring E-mail and Internet Use

A growing number of companies provide managers and organizations with tools to track the Web sites their employees visit and the e-mail they send. For example, Stellar Technologies Inc., based in Naples, Florida, sells software that managers can access anywhere to find out exactly how much time employees have spent at specific Web sites.[45] Currently a majority of large corporations monitor their employees' e-mail; the percentage is higher among high-technology organizations. Most of the organizations that monitor e-mail tell their employees about the monitoring.[46] However, the means by which they let employees know are not necessarily effective. For example, putting information about e-mail monitoring in an employee handbook might be ineffective if most employees do not read the handbook.[47]

Monitoring employees raises concerns about privacy.[48] Most employees would not like to have their bosses listening to their phone conversations; similarly, some believe that monitoring e-mail and tracking Internet use are an invasion of privacy.[49] Given the increasingly long working hours of many employees, should personal e-mail and Internet use be closely scrutinized? Clearly, when illegal and unethical e-mail use is suspected, such as sexually harassing coworkers or divulging confidential company information, monitoring may be called for. But should it be a normal part of organizational life, even when there are no indications of a real problem?

Surf YouTube or finish that spreadsheet? The spreadsheet might just win out, especially when companies realize that intrusive monitoring policies often backfire on employee performance.

Essentially this dilemma involves issues of trust. Procter & Gamble does not monitor individuals unless there appears to be a need to do so. P&G has close to 140,000 employees working in 80 countries, and the different countries have different laws and different internal organizational rules and norms.[50] Rather than monitoring individuals to see if they are abiding by the particular standards of the location where they work, P&G monitors electronic communication at its work sites in the aggregate to spot patterns. As Sandy Hughes, head of P&G's Global Privacy Council, puts it, "At some level, you have to trust your employees are going to be doing the right things."[51] Interestingly, some research suggests that people are less likely to lie in e-mail than they are in phone calls or face-to-face conversations.[52]

Impersonal Written Communication

Impersonal written communication is lowest in information richness but is well suited for messages that need to reach many receivers. Because such messages are not addressed to particular receivers, feedback is unlikely, so managers must make sure messages sent by this medium are written clearly in language that all receivers will understand.

Managers often find company newsletters useful vehicles for reaching large numbers of employees. Many managers give their newsletters catchy names to spark employee interest and also to inject a bit of humor into the workplace.[53] Increasing numbers of companies are distributing their newsletters online. For example, IBM's employee newsletter w3 is distributed to employees online and is updated daily.[54]

Managers can use impersonal written communication for various messages, including announcements of rules, regulations, policies, newsworthy information, changes in procedures, and the arrival of new organizational members. Impersonal written communication also can convey instructions about how to use machinery or how to process work orders or customer requests. For these kinds of messages, the paper or electronic trail left by this communication medium can be valuable for employees.

Just as with personal written communication, impersonal written communication can be delivered and retrieved electronically, and this is increasingly the case in companies large and small. Unfortunately the ease with which electronic messages can spread has led to their proliferation. Many managers' and workers' electronic in-boxes are so backlogged that often they do not have time to read all the electronic work-related information available to them. The problem with such **information overload** is the potential for important information to be ignored or overlooked (even that which is personally addressed) while tangential information receives attention. Moreover, information overload can result in thousands of hours and millions of dollars in lost productivity.

information overload The potential for important information to be ignored or overlooked while tangential information receives attention.

Some managers and organizations use blogs to communicate with employees, investors, customers, and the general public.[55] A **blog** is a Web site on which an individual, group, or organization posts information, commentary, and opinions and to which readers can often respond with their own commentary and opinions.[56] Some top managers write their own blogs, and some companies such as Cisco Systems and Oracle have corporate blogs.[57] Just as organizations have rules and guidelines about employee e-mail and Internet use, a growing number of organizations are instituting employee guidelines for blogs.[58] At IBM over 25,000 employees have blogs on IBM's internal computer network.[59] Guidelines for the use of blogs include following IBM's code of conduct (especially with regard to confidentiality, respect, and privacy), refraining from criticizing competitors, and refraining from mentioning customers' names without obtaining prior permission; bloggers must also reveal their own identity on their blogs (anonymous blogs are not permitted).[60]

blog A Web site on which an individual, group, or organization posts information, commentary, and opinions and to which readers can often respond with their own commentary and opinions.

A **social networking site** such as Facebook or Twitter is a Web site that enables people to communicate with others with whom they might have some common interest or connection. Participants in these sites create customized profiles and communicate with networks of other participants.[61] Millions of people communicate via social networking sites.[62] These sites offer a valuable means for companies such as the Irish retailer, Primark, to highlight their products. While communication through social networking sites can be work-related, some managers are concerned that their employees are wasting valuable time at work communicating with their friends through these sites. According to a recent study sponsored by Robert Half Technology, over 50% of the U.S. companies included in the study prohibit employees from accessing social networking sites such as Twitter, MySpace, LinkedIn, and Facebook while at work.[63] Around 19% of the companies permit communicating through social networking sites for work-related reasons, and 16% permit some personal communication through these sites. Just 10% of the companies surveyed permit full use of social networking sites while on the job.[64]

social networking site A Web site that enables people to communicate with others with whom they have some common interest or connection.

LO16-4 Describe the communication networks that exist in groups and teams.

Communication Networks

Although various communication media are used, communication in organizations tends to flow in certain patterns. The pathways along which information flows in groups and teams and throughout an organization are called **communication networks.** The type of communication network that exists in a group depends on the nature of the group's tasks and the extent to which group members need to communicate with one another to achieve group goals.

communication networks The pathways along which information flows in groups and teams and throughout the organization.

Communication Networks in Groups and Teams

As you learned in Chapter 15, groups and teams, whether they are cross-functional teams, top management teams, command groups, self-managed work teams, or task forces, are the building blocks of organizations. Four kinds of communication networks can develop in groups and teams: the wheel, the chain, the circle, and the all-channel network (see Figure 16.3).

WHEEL NETWORK In a wheel network, information flows to and from one central member of the group. Other group members do not need to communicate with one another to perform at a high level, so the group can accomplish its goals by directing all communication to and from the central member. Wheel networks are often found in command groups with pooled task interdependence. Picture a group of taxi drivers who report to the same dispatcher, who is also their supervisor. Each

Figure 16.3
Communication Networks in Groups and Teams

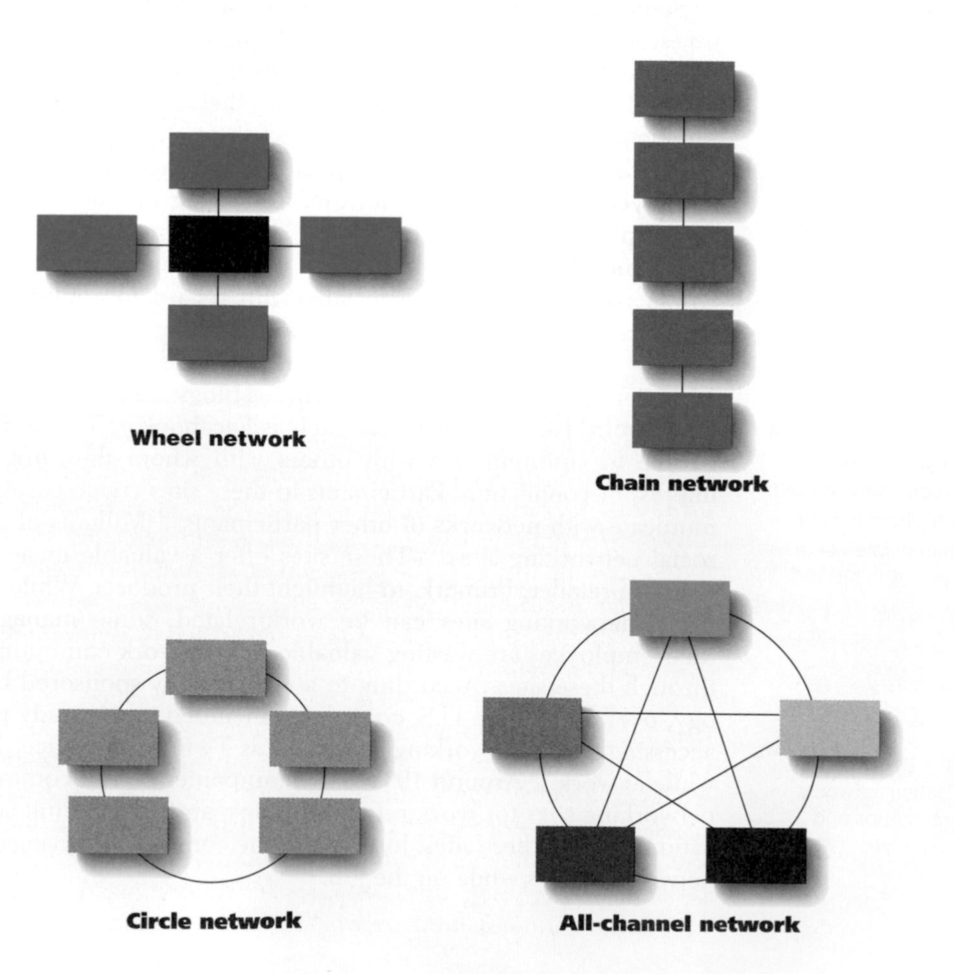

All-channel networks, like this team, are structured around the premise that in a small enough group, if everyone talks with everyone else, things can get done faster.

driver needs to communicate with the dispatcher, but the drivers do not need to communicate with one another. In groups such as this, the wheel network results in efficient communication, saving time without compromising performance. Although found in groups, wheel networks are not found in teams because they do not allow the intense interactions characteristic of teamwork.

CHAIN NETWORK In a chain network, members communicate with one another in a predetermined sequence. Chain networks are found in groups with sequential task interdependence, such as in assembly-line groups. When group work has to be performed in a predetermined order, the chain network is often found because group members need to communicate with those whose work directly precedes and follows their own. Like wheel networks, chain networks tend not to exist in teams because of the limited amount of interaction among group members.

CIRCLE NETWORK In a circle network, group members communicate with others who are similar to them in experiences, beliefs, areas of expertise, background, office location, or even where they sit when the group meets. Members of task forces and standing committees, for example, tend to communicate with others who have similar experiences or backgrounds. People also tend to communicate with people whose offices are next to their own. Like wheel and chain networks, circle networks are most often found in groups that are not teams.

ALL-CHANNEL NETWORK An all-channel network is found in teams. It is characterized by high levels of communication: Every team member communicates with every other team member. Top management teams, cross-functional teams, and self-managed work teams frequently have all-channel networks. The reciprocal task interdependence often found in such teams requires information flows in all directions. Computer software specially designed for use by work groups can help maintain effective communication in teams with all-channel networks because it gives team members an efficient way to share information.

Organizational Communication Networks

An organization chart may seem to be a good summary of an organization's communication network, but often it is not. An organization chart summarizes the *formal* reporting relationships in an organization and the formal pathways along which communication takes place. Often, however, communication is *informal* and flows around issues, goals, projects, and ideas instead of moving up and down the organizational hierarchy in an orderly fashion. Thus an organization's communication network includes not only the formal communication pathways summarized in an organization chart but also informal communication pathways along which a great deal of communication takes place (see Figure 16.4).

Communication can and should occur across departments and groups as well as within them and up and down and sideways in the corporate hierarchy. Communication up and down the corporate hierarchy is often called *vertical* communication. Communication among employees at the same level in the hierarchy, or sideways, is called *horizontal* communication. Managers obviously cannot determine in advance what an organization's communication network will be, nor should they try to. Instead, to accomplish goals and perform at a high level, organizational members should be free to communicate with whomever they need to contact. Because organizational goals change over time, so too do organizational communication networks. Informal communication networks can contribute to an organization's competitive

Figure 16.4
Formal and Informal Communication Networks in an Organization

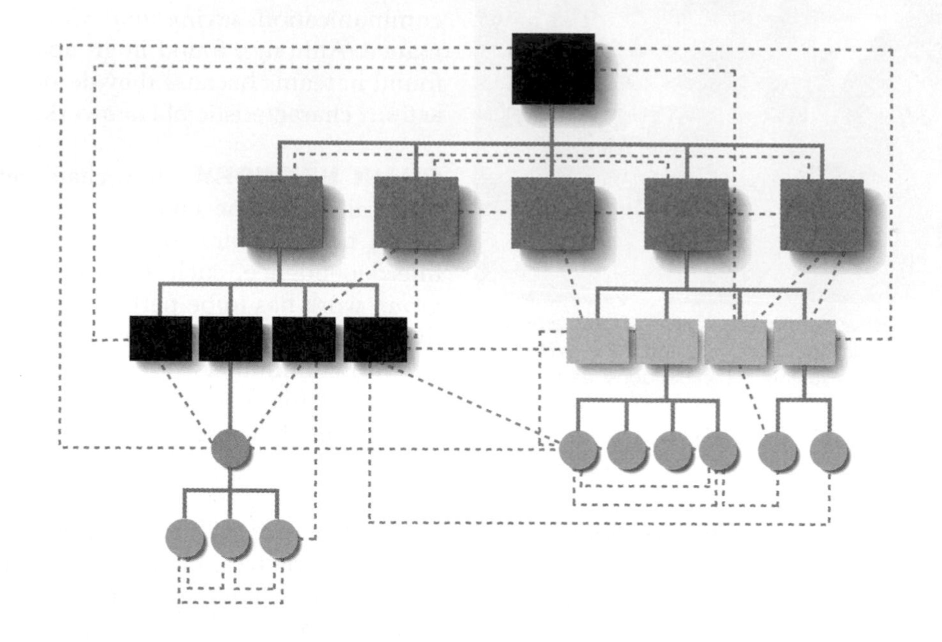

—— Formal pathways of communication summarized in an organization chart.

------ Informal pathways along which a great deal of communication takes place.

advantage because they help ensure that organizational members have the information they need when they need it to accomplish their goals.

When Reynolds Bish took over as CEO of the British firm Kofax, he realized he needed to use all such channels. The change in CEO can be a high stress period for employees and other key stakeholders in the organization. In this particular case, stress was high because Bish previously was the CEO of Kofax's major competitor. Realizing the stress this placed on the employees at Kofax, Bish established both formal and informal methods to communicate his vision with them. He met with all employees in formal settings such as meetings; however he also traveled around the world making a point to meet informally with individuals in casual settings to communicate his vision for the firm. Finally, he made sure to meet personally with all new hires so that the seeds of his vision could be planted anew with people coming into the organization.[65]

grapevine An informal communication network along which unofficial information flows.

The **grapevine** is an informal organizational communication network along which unofficial information flows quickly, if not always accurately.[66] People in an organization who seem to know everything about everyone are prominent in the grapevine. Information spread over the grapevine can be about issues of either a business nature (an impending takeover) or a personal nature (the CEO's separation from his wife).

External Networks

In addition to participating in networks within an organization, managers, professional employees, and those with work-related ties outside their employing organization often are part of external networks whose members span a variety of companies. For example, scientists working in universities and in corporations often communicate in networks formed around common underlying interests in a particular topic or subfield. As another example, physicians working throughout the country belong to specialty professional associations that help them keep up to date on the latest advances in their fields. For some managers and professionals, participation in such interest-oriented networks is as important as, or even more important than, participation in internal company networks. Networks of contacts who are working in the same discipline or field or who have similar expertise and knowledge can be very helpful, for example, when an individual wants to change jobs or find a job after a layoff. Unfortunately, as a result of discrimination and stereotypes, some of these networks are off-limits to certain individuals due to gender or race. For example, the term *old boys' network* alludes to the fact that networks of contacts for job leads, government contracts, or venture capital funding have sometimes been dominated by men and less welcoming of women.[67]

Information Technology and Communication

Advances in information technology have dramatically increased managers' abilities to communicate with others as well as to quickly access information to make decisions. Advances that are having major impacts on managerial communication include the Internet, intranets, groupware, and collaboration software. However, managers must not forget that communication is essentially a human endeavor, no matter how much it may be facilitated by information technology.

LO16-5 Explain how advances in technology have given managers new options for managing communication.

The Internet

Internet A global system of computer networks.

The **Internet** is a global system of computer networks that is easy to join and is used by employees of organizations around the world to communicate inside and outside their companies. Table 16.1 lists the 20 countries with the most Internet users.[68]

On the Internet, the World Wide Web is the "business district" with multimedia capabilities. Companies' home pages on the Web are like offices that potential customers can visit. In attractive graphic displays on home pages, managers communicate information about the goods and services they offer, why customers should want to purchase them, how to purchase them, and where to purchase them. By surfing the Web and visiting competitors' home pages, managers can see what their competitors are doing.[69] Each day hundreds of new companies add themselves to the growing number of organizations on the World Wide Web.[70] According to one study, the six "Web-savviest" nations (taking into account use of broadband connections) in descending order are Denmark, Great Britain, Sweden, Norway, Finland, and the United States.[71] By all counts, use of the Internet for communication is burgeoning.

Intranets

intranet A companywide system of computer networks.

Growing numbers of managers are finding that the technology on which the World Wide Web and the Internet are based has enabled them to improve communication within their own companies. These managers use this technology to share information within their own companies through company networks called **intranets.** Intranets are being used at many companies including Chevron, Goodyear, Levi Strauss, Pfizer, and Motorola.[72]

Intranets allow employees to have many kinds of information at their fingertips. Directories, manuals, inventory figures, product specifications, information about customers, biographies of top managers and the board of directors, global sales figures, meeting minutes, annual reports, delivery schedules, and up-to-the-minute revenue, cost, and profit figures are just a few examples of the information that can be shared through intranets. Intranets can be accessed with different kinds of computers so that all members of an organization can be linked together. Intranets are protected from unwanted intrusions, by hackers or by competitors, by firewall security systems that ask users to provide passwords and other identification before they are allowed access.[73]

Table 16.1
Top 20 Countries in Internet Usage as of September 30, 2009

Country	Internet Users
China	360,000,000
United States	227,719,000
Japan	95,979,000
India	81,000,000
Brazil	67,510,400
Germany	54,229,325
United Kingdom	46,683,900
Russia	45,250,000
France	43,100,134
South Korea	37,475,800
Iran	32,200,000
Italy	30,026,400
Indonesia	30,000,000
Spain	29,093,984
Mexico	27,600,000
Turkey	26,500,000
Canada	25,086,000
Philippines	24,000,000
Vietnam	21,963,117
Poland	20,020,362

Source: "Top 20 Countries with the Highest Number of Internet Users," Internet World Stats Usage and Population Statistics, www.internetworldstats.com/top20.htm, March 15, 2010. Used by permission.

The advantage of intranets lies in their versatility as a communication medium. They can be used for a number of different purposes by people who may have little expertise in computer software and programming. While some managers complain that the Internet is too crowded and the World Wide Web too glitzy, informed managers are realizing that using the Internet's technology to create their own computer networks may be one of the Internet's biggest contributions to organizational effectiveness.

Groupware and Collaboration Software

groupware Computer software that enables members of groups and teams to share information with one another.

Groupware is computer software that enables members of groups and teams to share information with one another to improve their communication and performance. In some organizations, such as the Bank of Montreal, managers have had success in introducing groupware into the organization; in other organizations, such as the advertising agency Young & Rubicam, managers have encountered considerable resistance to groupware.[74] Even in companies where the introduction of groupware has been successful, some employees resist using it. Some clerical and secretarial workers at the Bank of Montreal, for example, were dismayed to find that their neat and accurate files were being consolidated into computer files that would be accessible to many of their coworkers.

Managers are most likely to be able to successfully use groupware as a communication medium in their organizations when certain conditions are met:[75]

1. The work is group- or team-based, and members are rewarded, at least in part, for group performance.

2. Groupware has the full support of top management.
3. The culture of the organization stresses flexibility and knowledge sharing, and the organization does not have a rigid hierarchy of authority.
4. Groupware is used for a specific purpose and is viewed as a tool that enables group or team members to work more effectively together, not as a personal source of power or advantage.
5. Employees receive adequate training in the use of computers and groupware.[76]

Employees are likely to resist using groupware and managers are likely to have a difficult time implementing it when people are working primarily on their own and are rewarded for individual performance.[77] Under these circumstances, information is often viewed as a source of power, and people are reluctant to share information with others by means of groupware.

Consider three salespeople who sell insurance policies in the same geographic area; each is paid based on the number of policies he or she sells and on his or her retention of customers. Their supervisor invested in groupware and encouraged them to use it to share information about their sales, sales tactics, customers, insurance providers, and claim histories. The supervisor told the salespeople that having all this information at their fingertips would allow them to be more efficient as well as sell more policies and provide better service to customers.

Even though they received extensive training in how to use the groupware, the salespeople never got around to using it. Why? They all were afraid that giving away their secrets to their coworkers might reduce their own commissions. In this situation, the salespeople were essentially competing with one another and thus had no incentive to share information. Under such circumstances, a groupware system may not be a wise choice of communication medium. Conversely, had the salespeople been working as a team and had they received bonuses based on team performance, groupware might have been an effective communication medium.

For an organization to gain a competitive advantage, managers need to keep up to date on advances in information technology such as groupware. But managers should not adopt these or other advances without first considering carefully how the advance in question might improve communication and performance in their particular groups, teams, or whole organization. Moreover, managers need to keep in mind that all of these advances in IT are tools for people to use to facilitate effective communication; they are not replacements for face-to-face communication.

collaboration software Groupware that promotes and facilitates collaborative, highly interdependent interactions and provides an electronic meeting site for communication among team members.

Collaboration software is groupware that aims to promote collaborative, highly interdependent interactions among members of a team and provide the team with an electronic meeting site for communication.[78] Collaboration software gives members of a team an online work site where they can post, share, and save data, reports, sketches, and other documents; keep calendars; have team-based online conferences; and send and receive messages. The software can also keep and update progress reports, survey team members about different issues, forward documents to managers, and let users know which of their team members are also online and at the site.[79] Having an integrated online work area can help organize and centralize the work of a team, help ensure that information is readily available as needed, and also help team members make sure important information is not overlooked. Collaboration software can be much more efficient than e-mail or instant messaging for managing ongoing team collaboration and interaction that is not face-to-face. Moreover, when a team does meet face-to-face, all documents the team might need in the meeting are just a click away.[80]

For work that is truly team-based, entails a number of highly interdependent yet distinct components, and involves team members with distinct areas of expertise who need to closely coordinate their efforts, collaboration software can be a powerful communication tool. The New York–based public relations company Ketchum Inc. uses collaboration software for some of its projects. For example, Ketchum managed public relations, marketing, and advertising for a new charitable program that Fireman's Fund Insurance Co. undertook. By using the eRoom software provided by

Documentum (a part of EMC Corporation), Ketchum employees working on the project at six different locations, employee representatives from Fireman's, and a graphics company that was designing a Web site for the program were able to share plans, documents, graphic designs, and calendars at an online work site.[81] Members of the Ketchum–Fireman team got e-mail alerts when something had been modified or added to the site. As Ketchum's chief information officer Andy Roach puts it, "The fact that everyone has access to the same document means Ketchum isn't going to waste time on the logistics and can focus on the creative side."[82]

Another company taking advantage of collaboration software is Honeywell International Inc. Managers at Honeywell decided to use the SharePoint collaboration software provided by Microsoft, in part because it can be integrated with other Microsoft software such as Outlook.[83] For example, if a team using SharePoint makes a change to the team's calendar, that change will be automatically made in team members' Outlook calendars.[84] Clearly collaboration software has the potential to enhance communication efficiency and effectiveness in teams.

Wikis, a result of the open-source software movement, are a free or very low-cost form of collaboration software that a growing number of organizations are using. Wikis enable the organizations not only to promote collaboration and better communication but also to cut back on the use of e-mail,[85] as indicated in the following "Information Technology Byte" box.

Information Technology Byte

Collaborating with Wikis

According to Postini Inc., an e-mail filtering company in the United States, approximately 10% of all e-mail sent and received is legitimate.[86] And while many organizations have invested in filtering software to keep spam from flooding employees' in-boxes, according to the Gartner Group (an Internet research firm), 60% of messages that make their way into employees' in-boxes are spam.[87] Darren Lennard, a managing director at Dresdner Kleinwort Wasserstein, an investment bank in London, was receiving approximately 250 e-mail messages a day, of which only 15% were relevant to his job. Every day Lennard's first and last activities were to clear out his in-box on his BlackBerry–until frustration got the better of him, after a long and grueling workday, and he smashed his BlackBerry on the kitchen countertop in his home.[88]

Lennard is not alone in his frustration. J. P. Rangaswani, global chief information officer at Dresdner, who particularly dislikes use of copies on e-mail, wants to reduce the reliance on e-mail communication at the bank. He is taking steps to implement the use of collaboration software and other electronic forms of communication such as instant messaging and RSS (really simple syndication, which enables users to subscribe for information they require). In fact many organizations such as Yahoo!, Eastman Kodak, and Walt Disney are trying to reduce their reliance on e-mail by turning to other software tools that promote effective communication and collaboration.[89] While e-mail is likely to continue to be extensively used for one-on-one communication, for communication that involves collaboration within and between groups and teams, the use of other, more efficient and effective software tools is likely to dramatically increase in the coming years.[90]

In particular, wikis (in Hawaiian, the word *wiki* means "fast"), which are relatively easy to use and low-cost or free, are becoming increasingly popular as collaborative communication tools.[91] A wiki uses server software to enable users to create and revise Web pages quickly on a company intranet or through a hosted

Internet site. Users who are authorized to access a wiki can log on to it and edit and update data, as well as see what other authorized users have contributed. Wikis enable collaboration in real time, and they keep a history so users can see what changes were made to, for example, a spreadsheet or a proposal.[92] Some Web-based collaboration software providers such as Basecamp provide customers with a wiki as part of their services.[93]

Dresdner has found that e-mail pertaining to projects that use wikis has been reduced by about 75%, and even meeting times have been significantly lowered.[94] Lennard recently created a wiki to figure out how to increase profits on a certain kind of trade. In the past he would send e-mail with attachments to multiple colleagues, have to integrate and make sense of all the responses he received back from them, and then perhaps follow up with subsequent e-mail. Instead, on the wiki page he created, colleagues contributed ideas, commented on each others' ideas, and revised and edited in real time. Lennard estimates that what would have taken about two weeks to accomplish through e-mail took about two days using a wiki.[95]

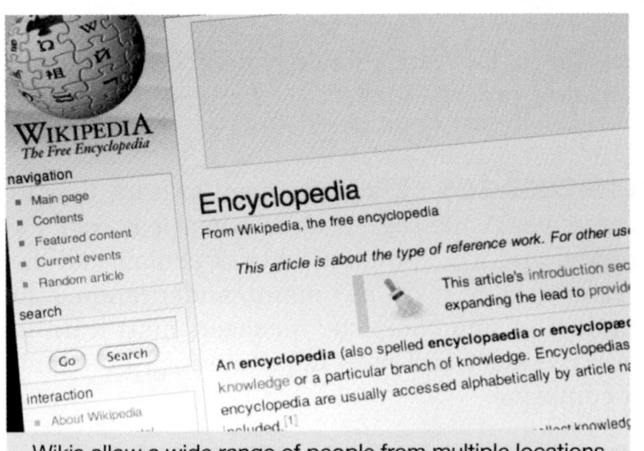

Wikis allow a wide range of people from multiple locations to contribute their specific skills and knowledge to the same task, resulting in a truly collaborative process.

Even though IBM has its own collaboration software, Lotus Notes, IBM employees rely on wikis for collaboration to such a great extent that IBM created Wiki Central to manage the wikis. Wiki Central manages over 20,000 IBM wikis and has over 100,000 users.[96] For example, some teams use wikis to coordinate the development of computer software. Wiki Central also gives employees tools to improve and enhance the functioning of their wikis, such as the "polling widget" (used for electronic voting) and the "rating widget" (used to evaluate proposals).[97] Clearly managers have multiple options to ensure efficient, effective, and collaborative communication.[98]

Communication Skills for Managers

Some of the barriers to effective communication in organizations have their origins in senders. When messages are unclear, incomplete, or difficult to understand, when they are sent over an inappropriate medium, or when no provision for feedback is made, communication suffers. Other communication barriers have their origins in receivers. When receivers pay no attention to or do not listen to messages or when they make no effort to understand the meaning of a message, communication is likely to be ineffective. Sometimes advanced information technology, such as automated phone systems, can hamper effective communication to the extent that the human element is missing.

To overcome these barriers and effectively communicate with others, managers (as well as other organizational members) must possess or develop certain communication skills. Some of these skills are particularly important when managers *send* messages; others are critical when managers *receive* messages. These skills help ensure that managers will be able to share information, will have the information they need to make good decisions and take action, and will be able to reach a common understanding with others.

LO16-6 Describe important communication skills that managers need as senders and as receivers of messages and why it is important to understand differences in linguistic styles.

Communication Skills for Managers as Senders

Organizational effectiveness depends on the ability of managers (as well as other organizational members) to effectively send messages to people both inside and outside the organization. Table 16.2 summarizes seven communication skills that help

Table 16.2
Seven Communication Skills for Managers as Senders of Messages

- Send messages that are clear and complete.
- Encode messages in symbols that the receiver understands.
- Select a medium that is appropriate for the message.
- Select a medium that the receiver monitors.
- Avoid filtering and information distortion.
- Ensure that a feedback mechanism is built into messages.
- Provide accurate information to ensure that misleading rumors are not spread.

ensure that when managers send messages, they are properly understood and the transmission phase of the communication process is effective. Let's see what each skill entails.

SEND CLEAR AND COMPLETE MESSAGES Managers need to learn how to send a message that is clear and complete. A message is clear when it is easy for the receiver to understand and interpret, and it is complete when it contains all the information that the sender and receiver need to reach a common understanding. In striving to send messages that are both clear and complete, managers must learn to anticipate how receivers will interpret messages and must adjust messages to eliminate sources of misunderstanding or confusion.

ENCODE MESSAGES IN SYMBOLS THE RECEIVER UNDERSTANDS Managers need to appreciate that when they encode messages, they should use symbols or language that the receiver understands. When sending messages in English to receivers whose native language is not English, for example, it is important to use common vocabulary and to avoid using clichés that, when translated, may make little sense and sometimes are either comical or insulting. **Jargon,** specialized language that members of an occupation, group, or organization develop to facilitate communication among themselves, should never be used when communicating with people outside the occupation, group, or organization.

jargon Specialized language that members of an occupation, group, or organization develop to facilitate communication among themselves.

SELECT A MEDIUM APPROPRIATE FOR THE MESSAGE As you have learned, when relying on verbal communication, managers can choose from a variety of communication media, including face-to-face communication in person, written letters, memos, newsletters, phone conversations, e-mail, voice mail, faxes, and videoconferences. When choosing among these media, managers need to take into account the level of information richness required, time constraints, and the need for a paper or electronic trail. A primary concern in choosing an appropriate medium is the nature of the message. Is it personal, important, nonroutine, and likely to be misunderstood and in need of further clarification? If it is, face-to-face communication is likely to be in order.

SELECT A MEDIUM THE RECEIVER MONITORS Another factor that managers need to take into account when selecting a communication medium is whether the medium is one that the receiver monitors. Managers differ in the communication media they pay attention to. Many managers simply select the medium that they themselves use the most and are most comfortable with, but doing this can often lead to ineffective communication. Managers who dislike telephone conversations and too many face-to-face interactions may prefer to use e-mail, send many e-mail messages per day, and check their own e-mail often. Managers who prefer to communicate with people in person or over the phone may have e-mail addresses but may be less likely to respond to e-mail messages. No matter how much a manager likes e-mail, sending e-mail to someone who does not respond to e-mail may be futile. Learning which managers like things in writing and which prefer face-to-face interactions and then using the appropriate medium enhances the chance that receivers will actually receive and pay attention to messages.

A related consideration is whether receivers have disabilities that hamper their ability to decode certain messages. A blind receiver, for example, cannot read a written message. Managers should ensure that employees with disabilities have resources available to communicate effectively with others. For example, deaf employees can effectively communicate over the telephone by using text-typewriters that have a screen and a keyboard on which senders can type messages. The message travels along the phone lines to special operators called *communication assistants,* who translate the typed message into words that the receiver can listen to. The receiver's spoken replies are translated into typewritten text by the communication assistants and appear on the sender's screen. The communication assistants relay messages back and forth to each sender and receiver.[99] Additionally, use of fax and e-mail instead of phone conversations can aid deaf employees.

filtering Withholding part of a message because of the mistaken belief that the receiver does not need or will not want the information.

AVOID FILTERING AND INFORMATION DISTORTION **Filtering** occurs when senders withhold part of a message because they (mistakenly) think the receiver does not need the information or will not want to receive it. Filtering can occur at all levels in an organization and in both vertical and horizontal communication. Rank-and-file workers may filter messages they send to first-line managers, first-line managers may filter messages to middle managers, and middle managers may filter messages to top managers. Such filtering is most likely to take place when messages contain bad news or problems that subordinates are afraid they will be blamed for. Managers need to hear bad news and be aware of problems as soon as they occur so they can take swift steps to rectify the problem and limit the damage it may have caused.

Some filtering takes place because of internal competition in organizations or because organizational members fear their power and influence will be diminished if others have access to some of their specialized knowledge. By increasing levels of trust in an organization, taking steps to motivate all employees (and the groups and teams they belong to) to work together to achieve organizational goals, and ensuring that employees realize that when the organization reaches its goals and performs effectively, they too will benefit, this kind of filtering can be reduced.

information distortion Changes in the meaning of a message as the message passes through a series of senders and receivers.

Information distortion occurs when the meaning of a message changes as the message passes through a series of senders and receivers. Some information distortion is accidental–due to faulty encoding and decoding or to a lack of feedback. Other information distortion is deliberate. Senders may alter a message to make themselves or their groups look good and to receive special treatment.

Managers themselves should avoid filtering and distorting information. But how can they eliminate these barriers to effective communication throughout their organization? They need to establish trust throughout the organization. Subordinates who trust their managers believe they will not be blamed for things beyond their control and will be treated fairly. Managers who trust their subordinates give them clear and complete information and do not hold things back.

INCLUDE A FEEDBACK MECHANISM IN MESSAGES Because feedback is essential for effective communication, managers should build a feedback mechanism into the messages they send. They either should include a request for feedback or indicate when and how they will follow up on the message to make sure it was received and understood. When managers write letters and memos or send faxes, they can request that the receiver respond with comments and suggestions in a letter, memo, or fax; schedule a meeting to discuss the issue; or follow up with a phone call. By building feedback mechanisms such as these into their messages, managers ensure that they get heard and are understood.

rumors Unofficial pieces of information of interest to organizational members but with no identifiable source.

PROVIDE ACCURATE INFORMATION **Rumors** are unofficial pieces of information of interest to organizational members but with no identifiable source. Rumors spread quickly once they are started, and usually they concern topics that organizational members think are important, interesting, or amusing. Rumors, however, can be misleading and can harm individual employees and their organizations when they are false, malicious, or unfounded. Managers can halt the spread of misleading rumors by giving organizational members accurate information about matters that concern them.

Providing accurate information is especially important in tough economic times like the recession in the late 2000s.[100] During a recession, employees are sometimes laid off or find their working hours or pay levels cut back and often experience high levels of stress. When managers give employees accurate information, this can help reduce their stress levels as well as motivate them to find ways to help their companies weather the tough times.[101] Moreover, when the economy does turn around, employees who received accurate information from their bosses may be more likely to remain with their organizations rather than pursue other opportunities.

Table 16.3
Three Communication Skills for Managers as Receivers of Messages

- Pay attention.
- Be a good listener.
- Be empathetic.

Communication Skills for Managers as Receivers

Managers receive as many messages as they send. Thus managers must possess or develop communication skills that allow them to be effective receivers of messages. Table 16.3 summarizes three of these important skills, which we examine here in greater detail.

PAY ATTENTION Because of their multiple roles and tasks, managers often are overloaded and forced to think about several things at once. Pulled in many different directions, they sometimes do not pay sufficient attention to the messages they receive. To be effective, however, managers should always pay attention to messages they receive, no matter how busy they are. When discussing a project with a subordinate, an effective manager focuses on the project and not on an upcoming meeting with his or her own boss. Similarly, when managers are reading written communication, they should focus on understanding what they are reading; they should not be sidetracked into thinking about other issues.

BE A GOOD LISTENER Managers (and all other members of an organization) can do several things to be good listeners. First, managers should refrain from interrupting senders in the middle of a message so senders do not lose their train of thought and managers do not jump to erroneous conclusions based on incomplete information. Second, managers should maintain eye contact with senders so senders feel their listeners are paying attention; doing this also helps managers focus on what they are hearing. Third, after receiving a message, managers should ask questions to clarify points of ambiguity or confusion. Fourth, managers should paraphrase, or restate in their own words, points senders make that are important, complex, or open to alternative interpretations; this is the feedback component so critical to successful communication.

This manager demonstrates that he is paying attention to what his employee is asking for with his eye contact, engaged posture, and focus.

Managers, like most people, often like to hear themselves talk rather than listen to others. Part of being a good communicator, however, is being a good listener–an essential communication skill for managers as receivers of messages transmitted face-to-face and over the telephone.

BE EMPATHETIC Managers should also be empathetic. Receivers are empathetic when they try to understand how the sender feels and try to interpret a message from the sender's perspective, rather than viewing the message from only their own point of view.

CROSS-CULTURAL DIFFERENCES Managers from Japan tend to be more formal in their conversations and more deferential toward upper-level managers and people with high status than are managers from the United States. Japanese managers do not mind extensive pauses in conversations when they are thinking things through or when they think further conversation might be detrimental. In contrast, U.S. managers (even managers from regions of the United States where pauses tend to be long) find lengthy pauses disconcerting and feel obligated to talk to fill the silence.[102]

Another cross-cultural difference in linguistic style concerns the appropriate physical distance separating speakers and listeners in business-oriented conversations.[103] The distance between speakers and listeners is greater in the United States, for example, than it is in Brazil or Saudi Arabia. Citizens of different countries also vary in how direct or indirect they are in conversations and the extent to which they take individual credit for accomplishments. Japanese culture, with its collectivist or group orientation, tends to encourage linguistic styles in which group rather than individual accomplishments are emphasized. The opposite tends to be true in the United States.

These and other cross-cultural differences in linguistic style can and often do lead to misunderstandings. For example, when a team of American managers presented a proposal for a joint venture to Japanese managers, the Japanese managers were silent as they thought about the implications of what they had just heard. The American managers took this silence as a sign that the Japanese managers wanted more information, so they went into more detail about the proposal. When they finished, the Japanese were silent again, not only frustrating the Americans but also making them wonder whether the Japanese were interested in the project. The American managers suggested that if the Japanese already had decided they did not want to pursue the project, there was no reason for the meeting to continue. The Japanese were bewildered. They were trying to carefully think out the proposal, yet the Americans thought they were not interested!

Communication misunderstandings and problems like this can be overcome if managers learn about cross-cultural differences in linguistic styles. If the American managers and the Japanese managers had realized that periods of silence are viewed

Cross-cultural differences in linguistic style can lead to misunderstandings.

differently in Japan and in the United States, their different linguistic styles might have been less troublesome barriers to communication. Before managers communicate with people from abroad, they should try to find out as much as they can about the aspects of linguistic style that are specific to the country or culture in question. Expatriate managers who have lived in the country in question for an extended time can be good sources of information about linguistic styles because they are likely to have experienced firsthand some of the differences that citizens of a country are not aware of. Finding out as much as possible about cultural differences also can help managers learn about differences in linguistic styles because the two are often closely linked.

GENDER DIFFERENCES Research conducted by Tannen and other linguists has found that the linguistic styles of men and women differ in practically every culture or language.[104] Men and women take their own linguistic styles for granted and thus do not realize when they are talking with someone of a different gender that differences in their styles may lead to ineffective communication.

In the United States, women tend to downplay differences between people, are not overly concerned about receiving credit for their own accomplishments, and want to make everyone feel more or less on an equal footing so that even poor performers or low-status individuals feel valued. Men, in contrast, tend to emphasize their own superiority and are not reluctant to acknowledge differences in status.

The gender differences in linguistic style that Tannen and other linguists have uncovered are general tendencies evident in *many* women and men, not in *all* women and men.

Where do gender differences in linguistic style come from? Tannen suggests they begin developing in early childhood. Girls and boys tend to play with children of their own gender, and the ways in which girls and boys play are quite different. Girls play in small groups, engage in a lot of close conversation, emphasize how similar they are to one another, and view boastfulness negatively. Boys play in large groups, emphasize status differences, expect leaders to emerge who boss others around, and give one another challenges to try to meet. These differences in styles of play and interaction result in different linguistic styles when boys and girls grow up and communicate as adults. The ways in which men communicate emphasize status differences and play up relative strengths; the ways in which women communicate emphasize similarities and downplay individual strengths.[105]

Interestingly, gender differences are also turning up in how women and men use e-mail and electronic forms of communication. For example, Susan Herring, a researcher at Indiana University, has found that in public electronic forums such as message boards and chat rooms, men tend to make stronger assertions, be more sarcastic, and be more likely to use insults and profanity than women, whereas women are more likely to be supportive, agreeable, and polite.[106] David Silver, a researcher at the University of Washington, has found that women are more expressive electronic communicators and encourage others to express their thoughts and feelings, while men are briefer and more to the point.[107] Interestingly enough, some men find e-mail to be a welcome way to express their feelings to people they care about. For example, real estate broker Mike Murname finds it easier to communicate with, and express his love for, his grown children via e-mail.[108]

MANAGING DIFFERENCES IN LINGUISTIC STYLES Managers should not expect to change people's linguistic styles and should not try to. To be effective, managers need to understand differences in linguistic styles. Knowing, for example, that some women are reluctant to speak up in meetings not because they have nothing to contribute but because of their linguistic style should lead managers to ensure that these women have a chance to talk. And a manager who knows certain people are reluctant to take credit for ideas can be careful to give credit where it is deserved. As Tannen points out, "Talk is the lifeblood of managerial work, and understanding that different people have different ways of saying what they mean will make it possible to take advantage of the talents of people with a broad range of linguistic styles."[109]

Summary and Review

LO16-1, 16-2 **COMMUNICATION AND MANAGEMENT** Communication is the sharing of information between two or more individuals or groups to reach a common understanding. Good communication is necessary for an organization to gain a competitive advantage. Communication occurs in a cyclical process that entails two phases, transmission and feedback.

LO16-3 **INFORMATION RICHNESS AND COMMUNICATION MEDIA** Information richness is the amount of information a communication medium can carry and the extent to which the medium enables the sender and receiver to reach a common understanding. Four categories of communication media, in descending order of information richness, are face-to-face communication (includes videoconferences), electronically transmitted spoken communication (includes voice mail), personally addressed written communication (includes e-mail), and impersonal written communication.

LO16-4 **COMMUNICATION NETWORKS** Communication networks are the pathways along which information flows in an organization. Four communication networks found in groups and teams are the wheel, the chain, the circle, and the all-channel network. An organization chart summarizes formal pathways of communication, but communication in organizations is often informal, as is true of communication through the grapevine.

LO16-5 **INFORMATION TECHNOLOGY AND COMMUNICATION** The Internet is a global system of computer networks that managers around the world use to communicate within and outside their companies. The World Wide Web is the multimedia business district on the Internet. Intranets are internal communication networks that managers can create to improve communication, performance, and customer service. Intranets use the same technology that the Internet and World Wide Web are based on. Groupware is computer software that enables members of groups and teams to share information with one another to improve their communication and performance.

LO16-6 **COMMUNICATION SKILLS FOR MANAGERS** There are various barriers to effective communication in organizations. To overcome these barriers and effectively communicate with others, managers must possess or develop certain communication skills. As senders of messages, managers should send messages that are clear and complete, encode messages in symbols the receiver understands, choose a medium appropriate for the message and monitored by the receiver, avoid filtering and information distortion, include a feedback mechanism in the message, and provide accurate information to ensure that misleading rumors are not spread. Communication skills for managers as receivers of messages include paying attention, being a good listener, and being empathetic. Understanding linguistic styles is also an essential communication skill for managers. Linguistic styles can vary by geographic region, gender, and country or culture. When these differences are not understood, ineffective communication can occur.

Management in Action

Topics for Discussion and Action

Discussion

1. Which medium (or media) do you think would be appropriate for each of the following kinds of messages that a subordinate could receive from his or her boss: (a) a raise, (b) not receiving a promotion, (c) an error in a report prepared by the subordinate, (d) additional job responsibilities, and (e) the schedule for company holidays for the upcoming year? Explain your choices. **[LO16-3]**
2. Discuss the pros and cons of using the Internet and World Wide Web for communication within and between organizations. **[LO16-1, 16-2, 16-3, 16-5]**
3. Why do some organizational members resist using groupware? **[LO16-5]**
4. Why do some managers find it difficult to be good listeners? **[LO16-6]**
5. Explain why subordinates might filter and distort information about problems and performance shortfalls when communicating with their bosses. What steps can managers take to eliminate filtering and information distortion? **[LO16-6]**
6. Explain why differences in linguistic style, when not understood by senders and receivers of messages, can lead to ineffective communication. **[LO16-6]**

Action

7. Interview a manager in an organization in your community to determine with whom he or she communicates on a typical day, what communication media he or she uses, and which typical communication problems the manager experiences. **[LO16-1, 16-2, 16-3, 16-4, 16-5, 16-6]**

Building Management Skills

Diagnosing Ineffective Communication **[LO16-1, 16-2, 16-3, 16-4, 16-5, 16-6]**

Think about the last time you experienced very ineffective communication with another person—someone you work with, a classmate, a friend, a member of your family. Describe the incident. Then answer the following questions:

1. Why was your communication ineffective in this incident?
2. What stages of the communication process were particularly problematic and why?
3. Describe any filtering or information distortion that occurred.
4. Do you think differences in linguistic styles adversely affected the communication that took place? Why or why not?
5. How could you have handled this situation differently so communication would have been effective?

Managing Ethically **[LO16-3, 16-5]**

Many employees use their company's Internet connections and e-mail systems to visit Web sites and send personal e-mail and instant messages.

Questions

1. Either individually or in a group, explore the ethics of using an organization's Internet connection and e-mail system for personal purposes at work and while away from the office. Should employees have some rights to use this resource? When does their behavior become unethical?
2. Some companies track how their employees use the company's Internet connection and e-mail system. Is it ethical for managers to read employees' personal e-mail or to record Web sites that employees visit? Why or why not?
3. Some governments such as China's monitor the Internet closely. Should a firm help the government with such monitoring of employee Internet activity?

Small Group Breakout Exercise

Reducing Resistance to Advances in Information Technology [LO16-5]

Form groups of three or four people, and appoint one member as the spokesperson who will communicate your findings to the class when called on by the instructor. Then discuss the following scenario:

You are a team of managers in charge of information and communication in a large consumer products corporation. Your company has already implemented many advances in information technology. Managers and workers have access to e-mail, the Internet, your company's own intranet, groupware, and collaboration software.

Many employees use the technology, but the resistance of some is causing communication problems. A case in point is the use of groupware and collaboration software. Many teams in your organization have access to groupware and are encouraged to use it. While some teams welcome this communication tool and actually have made suggestions for improvements, others are highly resistant to sharing documents in their teams' online workspaces.

Although you do not want to force people to use the technology, you want them to at least try it and give it a chance. You are meeting today to develop strategies for reducing resistance to the new technologies.

1. One resistant group of employees is made up of top managers. Some of them seem computer-phobic and are highly resistant to sharing information online, even with sophisticated security precautions in place. What steps will you take to get these managers to have more confidence in electronic communication?
2. A second group of resistant employees consists of middle managers. Some middle managers resist using your company's intranet. Although these managers do not resist the technology per se and do use electronic communication for multiple purposes, they seem to distrust the intranet as a viable way to communicate and get things done. What steps will you take to get these managers to take advantage of the intranet?
3. A third group of resistant employees is made up of members of groups and teams who do not want to use the groupware that has been provided to them. You think the groupware could improve their communication and performance, but they seem to think otherwise. What steps will you take to get these members of groups and teams to start using groupware?

Exploring the World Wide Web [LO16-5]

Atos Origin is a global information technology company that provides IT services to major corporations to improve, facilitate, integrate, and manage operations, information, and communication across multiple locations. Visit Atos Origin's Web site at www.atosorigin.com, and read about this company and the services it provides to improve communication. Then read the case studies on the Web site (listed under "Business Insights"). How can companies like Atos Origin help managers improve communication effectiveness in their organizations? What kinds of organizations and groups are most likely to benefit from services provided by Atos Origin? Why is it beneficial for some organizations to contract with firms like Atos Origin for their IT and communication needs rather than meet these needs internally with their own employees?

Be the Manager [LO16-1, 16-2, 16-3, 16-6]

You supervise support staff for an Internet merchandising organization that sells furniture over the Internet. You always thought that you needed to expand your staff, and just when you were about to approach your boss with such a request, business slowed. Thus your plan to try to add new employees to your staff is on hold.

However, you have noticed a troubling pattern of communication with your staff. Ordinarily, when you want a staff member to work on a task, you e-mail that subordinate the pertinent information. For the last few months, your e-mail requests have gone unheeded, and your subordinates seem to respond to your requests only after you visit them in person and give them a specific deadline. Each time they apologize for not getting to the task sooner but say they are so overloaded with requests that they sometimes even stop answering their phones. Unless someone asks for something more than once, your staff seems to feel the request is not that urgent and can be put on hold. You think this state of affairs is dysfunctional and could lead to serious problems down the road. Also, you are starting to realize that your subordinates seem to have no way of prioritizing tasks—hence some very important projects you asked them to complete were put on hold until you followed up with them about the tasks. Knowing you cannot add employees to your staff in the short term, what are you going to do to improve communication with your overloaded staff?

CHAPTER 17

Managing Conflict, Politics, and Negotiation

Learning Objectives

After studying this chapter, you should be able to:

LO17-1 Explain why conflict arises, and identify the types and sources of conflict in organizations.

LO17-2 Describe conflict management strategies that managers can use to resolve conflict effectively.

LO17-3 Understand the nature of negotiation and why integrative bargaining is more effective than distributive negotiation.

LO17-4 Describe ways in which managers can promote integrative bargaining in organizations.

LO17-5 Explain why managers need to be attuned to organizational politics, and describe the political strategies that managers can use to become politically skilled.

A MANAGER'S CHALLENGE

Bart Becht Effectively Manages Conflict at Reckitt Benckiser

How can managers effectively manage conflict while promoting innovation in global organizations? When Reckitt & Colman, a British company that made cleaning products for household use, merged with Benckiser, a Dutch company that made consumer products, Reckitt Benckiser came into existence and has been led ever since by Bart Becht, its current CEO.[1] Reckitt Benckiser, headquartered in Slough, England, is a global company that makes and sells products for personal care, household use, and health. Although some people have never heard of this company, many are familiar with what it calls its Powerbrands—brands like Vanish, Calgon, Woolite, Lysol, Air Wick, Muxinex, and Clearasil.[2] Employing 23,000 people in over 60 countries, Reckitt Benckiser sells its products in approximately 80 countries.[3]

Often mergers run into problems because employees from the different companies are used to working in different organizational cultures, have different perspectives and outlooks, and find it difficult to work synergistically together.[4] When two companies are based in different countries with different national cultures, potential problems and conflicts can be exacerbated. After the merger Becht deliberately assigned managers to work in countries other than those of their origin and continues to do so to this day. For example, an American manager oversees operations in Germany, an Italian manager oversees operations in the United Kingdom, a Dutch manager oversees operations in the United States, and an Indian manager oversees operations in China. In each country in which Reckitt Benckiser has operations, multiple nationalities are represented along with local citizens. The 400 top managers at Reckitt Benckiser are from 53 different countries.[5]

Essentially, working in a variety of countries over one's career is normal at Reckitt

Bart Becht relocates managers at Reckitt Benckiser to oversee operations in countries other than their place of origin, believing that doing so can eliminate turf battles and promote cross-cultural innovation.

Benckiser. Becht believes that experience working and living in other countries promotes creativity, innovation, and global entrepreneurship as well as ongoing learning and development. And it also can help prevent dysfunctional conflict and an "us versus them" mentality between employees of different nationalities. By living and working in several different countries, and by having several nationalities represented in every location, employees not only learn to respect and appreciate each other but also come up with new ideas based on their different perspectives and experiences.[6]

Even though Becht is Dutch, he does not speak his native language when he is with other Dutch employees at Reckitt Benckiser because this would make other employees feel left out.[7] Since so many nationalities and languages are represented in Reckitt Benckiser, Becht felt the need to have one language—English—used in all meetings. As he puts it, "We are one team with one language. English isn't most people's native language, and often our English isn't pretty. But the way we see it, it doesn't matter as long as you give a view."[8]

While recognizing that conflict due to cultural misunderstanding is dysfunctional, Becht believes in constructive conflict and everyone speaking his or her mind on work-related matters. Employees are expected and encouraged to come to meetings prepared with facts, speak their minds, and defend their positions. Becht knows that sometimes those who might disagree with the majority on a project or idea for a new product might have the best insights and be sources of real creativity and innovation.[9]

Becht strives to achieve win–win solutions to conflicts and disagreements whereby all parties can express and defend their positions, everyone's voice is listened to, and real collaboration takes place. When conflicts occur, rather than strive for consensus by convincing those in the minority to accept the majority's decision, Becht strives for consensus in terms of implementation. Thus once a decision has been made, everyone works together to effectively implement it, including those who might have been in the minority by not supporting it. Those in the minority, however, are permitted to continue to develop their ideas and run small experiments to determine if they are on the right track for an innovative product that will be appealing to Reckitt Benckiser's consumers.[10]

Overview

Successful leaders such as Bart Becht in "A Manager's Challenge" can effectively use their power to influence others and to manage conflict to achieve win–win solutions. In Chapter 14 we described how managers, as leaders, influence other people to achieve group and organizational goals and how managers' sources of power enable them to exert such influence. In this chapter we describe why managers need to develop the skills necessary to manage organizational conflict, politics, and negotiation if they are going to be effective and achieve their goals, as does Bart Becht.

We describe conflict and the strategies managers can use to resolve it effectively. We discuss one major conflict resolution technique, negotiation, in detail, outlining the steps managers can take to be good negotiators. Then we discuss the nature of organizational politics and the political strategies managers can use to maintain and expand their power and use it effectively. By the end of this chapter, you will appreciate why managers must develop the skills necessary to manage these important organizational processes if they are to be effective and achieve organizational goals.

Organizational Conflict

LO17-1 Explain why conflict arises, and identify the types and sources of conflict in organizations.

Organizational conflict is the discord that arises when the goals, interests, or values of different individuals or groups are incompatible and those individuals or groups block or thwart one another's attempts to achieve their objectives.[11] Conflict is an inevitable part of organizational life because the goals of different stakeholders such as managers and workers are often incompatible. Organizational conflict also can exist between departments and divisions that compete for resources or even between managers who may be competing for promotion to the next level in the organizational hierarchy.

organizational conflict The discord that arises when the goals, interests, or values of different individuals or groups are incompatible and those individuals or groups block or thwart one another's attempts to achieve their objectives.

It is important for managers to develop the skills necessary to manage conflict effectively. In addition, the level of conflict present in an organization has important implications for organizational performance. Figure 17.1 illustrates the relationship between organizational conflict and performance. At point A there is little or no conflict, and organizational performance suffers. Lack of conflict in an organization often signals that managers emphasize conformity at the expense of new ideas, resist change, and strive for agreement rather than effective decision making. As the level of conflict increases from point A to point B, organizational effectiveness is likely to increase. When an organization has an optimum level of conflict, as does Reckitt Benckiser in "A Manager's Challenge" (point B), managers are likely to be open to, and encourage, a variety of perspectives; look for ways to improve organizational functioning and effectiveness; and view debates and disagreements as a necessary ingredient of effective decision making and innovation. As the level of conflict increases from point B to point C, conflict escalates to the point where organizational performance suffers. When an organization has a dysfunctionally high level of conflict, managers are likely to waste organizational resources to achieve their own ends, to be more concerned about winning political battles than about doing what will lead to a competitive advantage for their organization, and to try to get even with their opponents rather than make good decisions.

Just another manic Monday? Inappropriately handling legitimate conflict can create lasting damage within one's work group.

Conflict is a force that needs to be managed rather than eliminated.[12] Managers should never try to eliminate all conflict but, rather, should try to keep conflict at a moderate and functional level to promote change efforts that benefit the organization. Additionally, managers should strive to keep conflict focused on substantive, task-based issues and minimize conflict based on personal disagreements and animosities. To manage conflict,[13] managers must understand the types and sources of conflict and be familiar with strategies that can be effective in dealing with it.

Types of Conflict

There are several types of conflict in organizations: interpersonal, intragroup, intergroup, and interorganizational (see Figure 17.2).[14] Understanding how these types differ can help managers deal with conflict.

INTERPERSONAL CONFLICT Interpersonal conflict is conflict between individual members of an organization, occurring because of differences in their goals

Figure 17.1
The Effect of Conflict on Organizational Performance

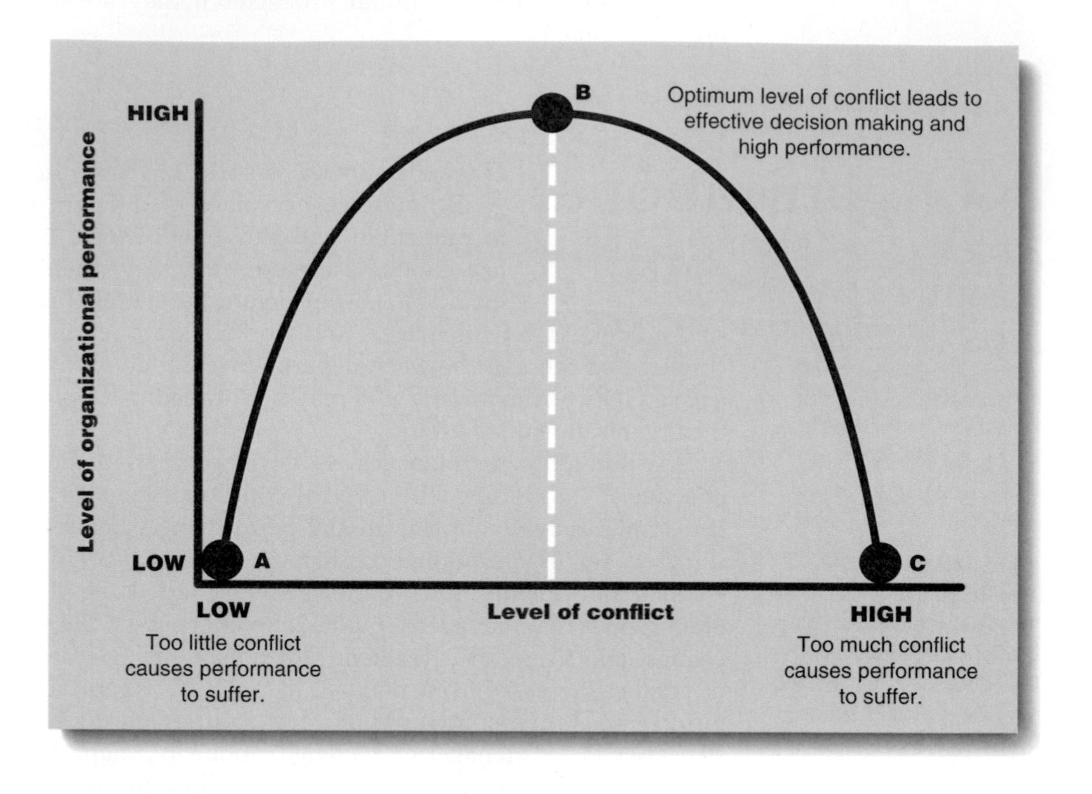

Figure 17.2
Types of Conflict in Organizations

or values. Two managers may experience interpersonal conflict when their values concerning protection of the environment differ. One manager may argue that the organization should do only what is required by law. The other manager may counter that the organization should invest in equipment to reduce emissions even though the organization's current level of emissions is below the legal limit.

INTRAGROUP CONFLICT Intragroup conflict arises within a group, team, or department. When members of the marketing department in a clothing company disagree about how they should spend budgeted advertising dollars for a new line of men's designer jeans, they are experiencing intragroup conflict. Some of the members want to spend all the money on advertisements in magazines. Others want to devote half of the money to billboards and ads in city buses and subways.

INTERGROUP CONFLICT Intergroup conflict occurs between groups, teams, or departments. R&D departments, for example, sometimes experience intergroup conflict with production departments. Members of the R&D department may develop a new product that they think production can make inexpensively by using existing manufacturing capabilities. Members of the production department, however, may disagree and believe that the costs of making the product will be much higher. Managers of departments usually play a key role in managing intergroup conflicts such as this.

INTERORGANIZATIONAL CONFLICT Interorganizational conflict arises across organizations. Sometimes interorganizational conflict occurs when managers in one organization feel that another organization is not behaving ethically and is threatening the well-being of certain stakeholder groups.

Sources of Conflict

Conflict in organizations springs from a variety of sources. The ones we examine here are different goals and time horizons, overlapping authority, task interdependencies, different evaluation or reward systems, scarce resources, and status inconsistencies (see Figure 17.3).[15]

DIFFERENT GOALS AND TIME HORIZONS Recall from Chapter 10 that an important managerial activity is organizing people and tasks into departments and divisions to accomplish an organization's goals. Almost inevitably this grouping creates departments and divisions that have different goals and time horizons, and the result can be conflict. Production managers, for example, usually concentrate on efficiency and cost cutting; they have a relatively short time horizon and focus on producing quality goods or services in a timely and efficient manner. In contrast, marketing managers focus on sales and responsiveness to customers. Their time horizon is longer than that of production because they are trying to be responsive not only to customers' needs today but also to their changing needs in the future to build long-term customer loyalty. These fundamental differences between marketing and production often breed conflict.

Figure 17.3
Sources of Conflict in Organizations

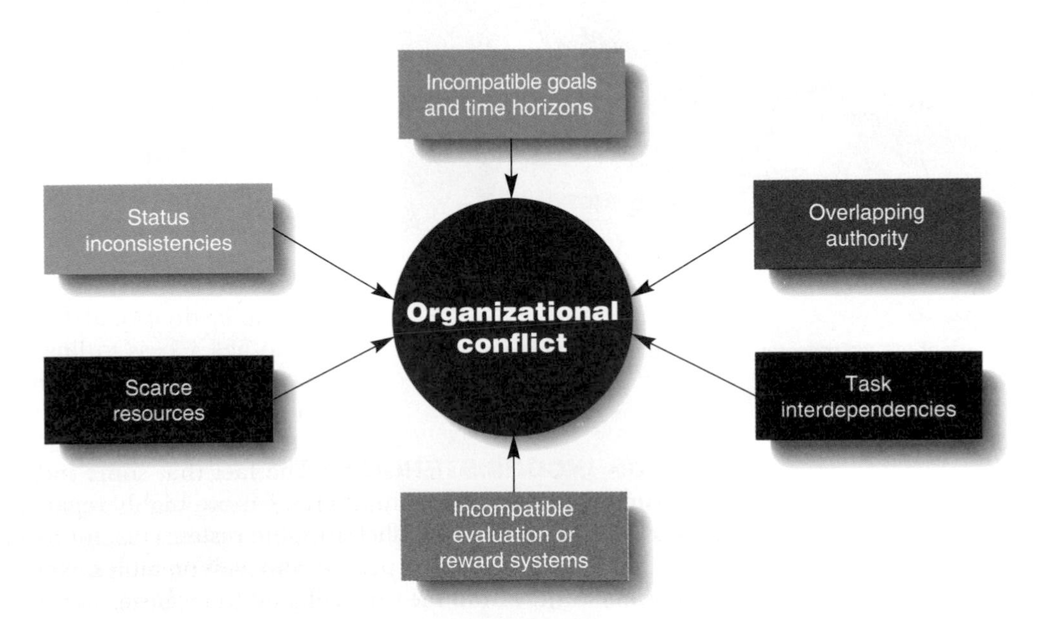

Suppose production is behind schedule in its plan to produce a specialized product for a key customer. The marketing manager believes the delay will reduce sales of the product and therefore insists that the product be delivered on time even if saving the production schedule means increasing costs by paying production workers overtime. The production manager says that she will happily schedule overtime if marketing will pay for it. Both managers' positions are reasonable from the perspective of their own departments, and conflict is likely.

OVERLAPPING AUTHORITY When two or more managers, departments, or functions claim authority for the same activities or tasks, conflict is likely.[16] Overlapping authority and the resulting conflict is often a problem in family businesses where roles may be unclear. For example, a family member may be placed in a leadership role during a time of transition, but other members may be more suited to lead the company. Consider a setting like Europe's where family businesses are tremendously strong. As a matter of fact, there are so many businesses that are over 300 years old they have formed their own organization, the Tercentenarians Club. How does a business that has survived centuries resolve its conflicts?

TASK INTERDEPENDENCIES Have you ever been assigned a group project for one of your classes and had one group member who consistently failed to get things done on time? This probably created some conflict in your group because other group members were dependent on the late member's contributions to complete the project. Whenever individuals, groups, teams, or departments are interdependent, the potential for conflict exists.[17] With differing goals and time horizons, the managers of marketing and production come into conflict precisely because the departments are interdependent. Marketing is dependent on production for the goods it markets and sells, and production is dependent on marketing to create demand for the things it makes.

DIFFERENT EVALUATION OR REWARD SYSTEMS How interdependent groups, teams, or departments are evaluated and rewarded can be another source of conflict.[18] Production managers, for example, are evaluated and rewarded for their success in staying within budget or lowering costs while maintaining quality. So they are reluctant to take any steps that will increase costs, such as paying workers high overtime rates to finish a late order for an important customer. Marketing managers, in contrast, are evaluated and rewarded for their success in generating sales and satisfying customers. So they often think overtime pay is a small price to pay for responsiveness to customers. Thus conflict between production and marketing is rarely unexpected.

Whenever groups or teams are interdependent, the potential for conflict exists.

SCARCE RESOURCES Management is the process of acquiring, developing, protecting, and using the resources that allow an organization to be efficient and effective (see Chapter 1). When resources are scarce, management is more difficult and conflict is likely.[19] For example, divisional managers may be in conflict over who has access to financial capital, and organizational members at all levels may be in conflict over who gets raises and promotions.

STATUS INCONSISTENCIES The fact that some individuals, groups, teams, or departments within an organization are more highly regarded than others in the organization can also create conflict. In some restaurants, for example, the chefs have relatively higher status than the people who wait on tables. Nevertheless, the chefs receive customers' orders from the waitstaff, and the waitstaff can return to the chefs food that

LO17-2 Describe conflict management strategies that managers can use to resolve conflict effectively.

their customers or they think is not acceptable. This status inconsistency–high-status chefs taking orders from low-status waitstaff–can be the source of considerable conflict between chefs and the waitstaff. For this reason, some restaurants require that the waitstaff put orders on a spindle, thereby reducing the amount of direct order giving from the waitstaff to the chefs.[20]

compromise A way of managing conflict in which each party is concerned about not only its own goal accomplishment but also the goal accomplishment of the other party and is willing to engage in a give-and-take exchange and make concessions.

collaboration A way of managing conflict in which both parties try to satisfy their goals by coming up with an approach that leaves them both better off and does not require concessions on issues that are important to either party.

Conflict Management Strategies

If an organization is to achieve its goals, managers must be able to resolve conflicts in a functional manner. *Functional conflict resolution* means the conflict is settled by compromise or by collaboration between the parties in conflict (later in the chapter we discuss other, typically less functional ways in which conflicts are sometimes resolved).[21] **Compromise** is possible when each party is concerned about not only its own goal accomplishment but also the goal accomplishment of the other party and is willing to engage in a give-and-take exchange and to make concessions until a reasonable resolution of the conflict is reached. **Collaboration** is a way of handling conflict in which the parties try to satisfy their goals without making any concessions but, instead, come up with a way to resolve their differences that leaves them both better off.[22] Bart Becht, from "A Manager's Challenge," excels at using collaboration to resolve conflicts; so does Ravi Kant, Managing Director of Tata Motors Ltd.,[23] as profiled in the following "Managing Globally" box.

Managing Globally

Ravi Kant Excels at Collaboration

Ravi Kant, managing director of Tata Motors Ltd., used collaboration to address a conflict he faced as executive director of Tata Motors' commercial vehicles unit.[24] The commercial vehicles unit of Tata Motors, the biggest automobile manufacturer in India, was interested in acquiring Daewoo's truck division based in Gunsan, South Korea, to increase its capabilities.[25] The Korean truck division was doing poorly, and an auction was being held in Korea to sell off the unit. When Kant traveled to Korea, he realized that there was resistance among some managers and employees at the Daewoo truck division to being potentially taken over by Tata Motors; they were concerned about what such a takeover would mean for the future of their company.[26]

Ravi Kant lowered cross-cultural tensions in the Tata Motors' acquisition of Daewoo's truck division by meeting the Korean company's employees on their own turf.

Kant arranged for Tata managers who were trying to negotiate the deal to take lessons in the Korean language so they could better communicate with the Koreans.[27] He had brochures and other documents about Tata translated into Korean. Tata managers made presentations to multiple parties involved in the auction, including Daewoo managers and employees, the head of the local auto association, Gunsun's mayor, and government decision makers in Seoul, Korea, including the prime minister. In these presentations, Tata managers indicated that if Tata were to win the auction, Daewoo employees would be able to keep their jobs, and efforts would focus on building the Daewoo truck unit into a key exporter while integrating it into Tata Motors (and the larger Tata Group of which it is a part). Kant and Tata's efforts paid off; Tata purchased Daewoo's truck division for $102 million.[28] As Kwang-Ok Chae, CEO of Tata Daewoo,[29] indicated, "Tata had done its homework in everything needed to do business here."[30]

Throughout the process, Tata managers showed respect for Daewoo employees and managers.[31] At Tata Daewoo a joint board of directors was created, and Kwang-Ok Chae retained his top management position as CEO of the company.[32] When Kant requested that two Tata top managers advise him, Chae made them a part of his top management team. Together Indian and Korean managers focused on ways to increase Tata Daewoo's product line and exports. Although Daewoo had focused on the Korean market, today Tata Daewoo is a major exporter of heavy trucks, and its revenues have increased substantially since the acquisition.[33] Tata Daewoo is the second biggest manufacturer of heavy-duty trucks in Korea and now exports trucks to over 60 countries, including countries in the Middle East, South Africa, Eastern Europe, and Southeast Asia.[34]

Clearly, the process of acquiring a company can be fraught with the potential for conflict, which if not effectively managed can harm both the acquiring company and the company being acquired. The collaborative way in which the acquisition that created Tata Daewoo was handled made both parties better off. Tata Daewoo is now a successful company, employees' and managers' jobs are secure, and the Tata Group as a whole is better off as a result of the acquisition. As Choi Jai Choon, a South Korean labor union leader, indicated, "It's turned out to be a win–win situation."[35]

In addition to compromise and collaboration, there are three other ways in which conflicts are sometimes handled: accommodation, avoidance, and competition.[36] When **accommodation** takes place, one party to the conflict simply gives in to the demands of the other party. Accommodation typically takes place when one party has more power than the other and can pursue its goal attainment at the expense of the weaker party. From an organizational perspective, accommodation is often ineffective: The two parties are not cooperating with each other, they are unlikely to want to cooperate in the future, and the weaker party who gives in or accommodates the more powerful party might look for ways to get back at the stronger party in the future.

accommodation An ineffective conflict-handling approach in which one party, typically with weaker power, gives in to the demands of the other, typically more powerful, party.

When conflicts are handled by **avoidance,** the parties to a conflict try to ignore the problem and do nothing to resolve the disagreement. Avoidance is often ineffective because the real source of the disagreement has not been addressed, conflict is likely to continue, and communication and cooperation are hindered.

avoidance An ineffective conflict handling approach in which the parties try to ignore the problem and do nothing to resolve their differences.

Competition occurs when each party to a conflict tries to maximize its own gain and has little interest in understanding the other party's position and arriving at a solution that will allow both parties to achieve their goals. Competition can actually escalate levels of conflict as each party tries to outmaneuver the other. As a way of handling conflict, competition is ineffective for the organization because the two sides to a conflict are more concerned about winning the battle than cooperating to arrive at a solution that is best for the organization and acceptable to both sides. Handling conflicts through accommodation, avoidance, or competition is ineffective from an organizational point of view because the parties do not cooperate with each other and work toward a mutually acceptable solution to their differences.

competition An ineffective conflict handling approach in which each party tries to maximize its own gain and has little interest in understanding the other party's position and arriving at a solution that will allow both parties to achieve their goals.

When the parties to a conflict are willing to cooperate with each other and, through compromise or collaboration, devise a solution that each finds acceptable, an organization is more likely to achieve its goals.[37] Conflict management strategies that managers can use to ensure that conflicts are resolved in a functional manner focus on individuals and on the organization as a whole. Next we describe four strategies that focus on individuals: increasing awareness of the sources of conflict, increasing diversity awareness and skills, practicing job rotation or temporary assignments, and using permanent transfers or dismissals when necessary. We also describe two strategies that focus on the organization as a whole: changing an organization's structure or culture and directly altering the source of conflict.

STRATEGIES FOCUSED ON INDIVIDUALS

INCREASING AWARENESS OF THE SOURCES OF CONFLICT Sometimes conflict arises because of communication problems and interpersonal misunderstandings. For example, different linguistic styles (see Chapter 16) may lead some men in work teams to talk more, and take more credit for ideas, than women in those teams. These communication differences can cause conflict when the men incorrectly assume that the women are uninterested or less capable because they participate less and the women incorrectly assume that the men are bossy and are not interested in their ideas because they seem to do all the talking. By increasing people's awareness of this source of conflict, managers can help resolve conflict functionally. Once men and women realize that the source of their conflict is different linguistic styles, they can take steps to interact with each other more effectively. The men can give the women more chances to provide input, and the women can be more proactive in providing this input.

Sometimes personalities clash in an organization. In these situations, too, managers can help resolve conflicts functionally by increasing organizational members' awareness of the source of their difficulties. For example, some people who are not inclined to take risks may come into conflict with those who are prone to taking risks. The non-risk takers might complain that those who welcome risk propose outlandish ideas without justification, whereas the risk takers might complain that their innovative ideas are always getting shot down. When both types of people are made aware that their conflicts are due to fundamental differences in their ways of approaching problems, they will likely be better able to cooperate in coming up with innovative ideas that entail only moderate levels of risk.

INCREASING DIVERSITY AWARENESS AND SKILLS Interpersonal conflicts also can arise because of diversity. Older workers may feel uncomfortable or resentful about reporting to a younger supervisor, a Hispanic may feel singled out in a group of non-Hispanic workers, or a female top manager may feel that members of her predominantly male top management team band together whenever one of them disagrees with one of her proposals. Whether or not these feelings are justified, they are likely to cause recurring conflicts. Many of the techniques we described in Chapter 5 for increasing diversity awareness and skills can help managers effectively manage diversity and resolve conflicts that originate in differences among organizational members.

Increasing diversity awareness and skills can be especially important when organizations expand globally and seek to successfully integrate operations in other countries, as illustrated in the following "Managing Globally" box.

Managing Globally

Xplane Integrates Operations in Spain

Xplane is a small consulting and design firm with global headquarters in Portland, Oregon, and an additional U.S. office in St. Louis, Missouri.[38] When Dave Gray, founder and chairman of the company, decided to expand operations by acquiring a small firm in Madrid, Spain, with around six employees, in the hopes of expanding operations in Europe as well as building capabilities to serve companies in Spanish-speaking countries, he learned firsthand the importance of increasing diversity awareness and skills. Misunderstandings and conflict arose, ranging from a St. Louis employee inadvertently insulting Spanish employees during a dinner in Madrid to Spanish employees feeling excluded from communications and not integrated within Xplane's operations.[39] For

Xplane learned that plane tickets plus technology were needed to integrate Spanish and American workers; this infrastructure enables the company to continue expanding in Europe.

example, Stephen O'Flynn, who is a project manager in the Madrid office and originally came from Ireland, felt that some employees in the two U.S. offices almost seemed to forget that the company had a third office in Spain.[40]

Gray realized that given cultural differences and the geographic distance between the U.S. and Spanish offices, it was vital to both improve communication across offices and provide more opportunities for employees in the different offices to interact with each other and establish a common understanding. Company e-mail, for example, should not be sent just to U.S. employees but also to employees in Spain. The company changed to a Web-based phone system so employees would need to dial only 4 digits (rather than 13) to make calls between Spain and the United States.[41] Wikis were created with photos of all employees. O'Flynn frequently called employees in Portland and St. Louis to discuss projects with them and encouraged other employees in the Madrid office to similarly reach out. As he indicates, "I did a lot of brokering to get people talking."[42]

Gray also realized that it was important for U.S. and Spanish employees to have a chance to interact face-to-face and for more extended periods than a phone conversation, a dinner, or one-shot meeting in either country. To accomplish this, he created an exchange program for employees.[43] As part of the program, employees in each country can visit and work with their counterparts in the other country to build relationships, increase their diversity awareness and skills, and learn from each other. For example, a U.S. employee can stay in an apartment rented by Xplane in Madrid for a week and work with employees in the Spanish office. Similarly, a Spanish employee can stay in an apartment rented by Xplane in Portland and work with employees in Portland for a week.[44] As Xplane CEO Aric Wood indicated, "We tried to close the gap through technology, but ultimately we had to buy a lot of airline tickets."[45] By taking steps to increase diversity awareness and skills and foster effective communication, managers like Wood not only help alleviate sources of misunderstanding and potential conflict but also increase their chances of reaping the benefits that different perspectives and points of view can bring. The Madrid office is now Xplane's global headquarters; on April 1, 2010, Xplane opened an additional European office in Amsterdam in the Netherlands.[46]

PRACTICING JOB ROTATION OR TEMPORARY ASSIGNMENTS Sometimes conflicts arise because individual organizational members simply do not understand the work activities and demands that others in an organization face. A financial analyst, for example, may be required to submit monthly reports to a member of the accounting department. These reports have a low priority for the analyst, who typically turns them in a couple of days late. On each due date the accountant calls the financial analyst, and conflict ensues as the accountant describes in detail why she must have the reports on time and the financial analyst describes everything else he needs to do. In situations such as this, job rotation or temporary assignments, which expand organizational members' knowledge base and appreciation of other departments, can be a useful way of resolving the conflict. If the financial analyst spends some time working in the accounting department, he may appreciate better the need for timely reports. Similarly, a temporary assignment in the finance department may help the accountant realize the demands a financial analyst faces and the need to streamline unnecessary aspects of reporting.

USING PERMANENT TRANSFERS OR DISMISSALS WHEN NECESSARY Sometimes when other conflict resolution strategies do not work, managers may need to take more drastic steps, including permanent transfers or dismissals.

Suppose two first-line managers who work in the same department are always at each other's throats; frequent bitter conflicts arise between them even though they both seem to get along well with other employees. No matter what their supervisor does to increase their understanding of each other, the conflicts keep occurring. In this case the supervisor may want to transfer one or both managers so they do not have to interact as frequently.

STRATEGIES FOCUSED ON THE WHOLE ORGANIZATION

CHANGING AN ORGANIZATION'S STRUCTURE OR CULTURE Conflict can signal the need for changes in an organization's structure or culture. Sometimes managers can effectively resolve conflict by changing the organizational structure they use to group people and tasks.[47] As an organization grows, for example, the *functional structure* (composed of departments such as marketing, finance, and production) that was effective when the organization was small may cease to be effective, and a shift to a *product structure* might effectively resolve conflicts (see Chapter 10).

Sometimes managers may need to take steps to change an organization's culture to resolve conflict (see Chapter 3). Norms and values in an organizational culture might inadvertently promote dysfunctionally high levels of conflict that are difficult to resolve. For instance, norms that stress respect for formal authority may create conflict that is difficult to resolve when an organization creates self-managed work teams and managers' roles and the structure of authority in the organization change. Values stressing individual competition may make it difficult to resolve conflicts when organizational members need to put others' interests ahead of their own. In circumstances such as these, taking steps to change norms and values can be an effective conflict resolution strategy.

negotiation A method of conflict resolution in which the parties consider various alternative ways to allocate resources to come up with a solution acceptable to all of them.

third-party negotiator An impartial individual with expertise in handling conflicts and negotiations who helps parties in conflict reach an acceptable solution.

ALTERING THE SOURCE OF CONFLICT When the source of conflict is overlapping authority, different evaluation or reward systems, or status inconsistencies, managers can sometimes effectively resolve the conflict by directly altering its source. For example, managers can clarify the chain of command and reassign tasks and responsibilities to resolve conflicts due to overlapping authority.

LO17-3 Understand the nature of negotiation and why integrative bargaining is more effective than distributive negotiation.

Negotiation

Negotiation is a particularly important conflict resolution technique for managers and other organizational members in situations where the parties to a conflict have approximately equal levels of power. During **negotiation** the parties to a conflict try to come up with a solution acceptable to themselves by considering various alternative ways to allocate resources to each other.[48] Sometimes the sides involved in a conflict negotiate directly with each other. Other times a **third-party negotiator** is relied on. Third-party negotiators are impartial individuals who are not directly involved in the conflict and have special expertise in handling conflicts and negotiations;[49] they are relied on to help the two negotiating parties reach an acceptable resolution of their conflict.[50] When a third-party negotiator acts as a **mediator,** his or her role in the negotiation process is to facilitate an effective negotiation between the two parties; mediators do not force either party to make concessions, nor can they force an agreement to resolve a conflict. **Arbitrators,** on the other hand, are third-party negotiators who can impose what they believe is a fair solution to a dispute that both parties are obligated to abide by.[51]

mediator A third-party negotiator who facilitates negotiations but has no authority to impose a solution.

arbitrator A third-party negotiator who can impose what he or she thinks is a fair solution to a conflict that both parties are obligated to abide by.

Management Insight

Nestlé of Switzerland and the Use of Palm Oil

Negotiations to end conflict can take many forms. In early 2010, the environmental group Greenpeace launched a campaign against Nestlé of Switzerland. Nestlé is one of the largest food manufacturers in the world. The campaign criticized Nestlé for its links with an Indonesian palm oil producer accused of illegal deforestation. Nestlé found itself under attack in many ways. For example, the firm's Facebook page had postings where the word Killer was substituted for KitKat. Greenpeace posted a video on You Tube showing an office worker biting into a KitKat containing an orangutan finger that dripped blood onto a computer keyboard.

In response Nestlé negotiated with The Forest Trust (TFT), a global not-for-profit group that is helping the company audit the suppliers of its palm oil. TFT assisted Nestlé in establishing requirements for the palm oil suppliers and a code of compliance with which to evaluate the suppliers. The resulting agreement ensures that Nestlé will cancel contracts with any firm found to be clearing rainforests to produce the palm oil. These measures have quieted Greenpeace for the time, although the group continues to be vigilant in monitoring Nestlé's activities.[52]

Distributive Negotiation and Integrative Bargaining

distributive negotiation Adversarial negotiation in which the parties in conflict compete to win the most resources while conceding as little as possible.

integrative bargaining Cooperative negotiation in which the parties in conflict work together to achieve a resolution that is good for them both.

There are two major types of negotiation–distributive negotiation and integrative bargaining.[53] In **distributive negotiation,** the two parties perceive that they have a "fixed pie" of resources that they need to divide.[54] They take a competitive, adversarial stance. Each party realizes that he or she must concede something but is out to get the lion's share of the resources.[55] The parties see no need to interact with each other in the future and do not care if their interpersonal relationship is damaged or destroyed by their competitive negotiation.[56] In distributive negotiations, conflicts are handled by competition.

In **integrative bargaining,** the parties perceive that they might be able to increase the resource pie by trying to come up with a creative solution to the conflict. They do not view the conflict competitively, as a win-or-lose situation; instead they view it cooperatively, as a win–win situation in which both parties can gain. Trust, information sharing, and the desire of both parties to achieve a good resolution of the conflict characterize integrative bargaining.[57] In integrative bargaining, conflicts are handled through collaboration and/or compromise.

LO17-4 Describe ways in which managers can promote integrative bargaining in organizations.

Strategies to Encourage Integrative Bargaining

Managers in all kinds of organizations can rely on five strategies to facilitate integrative bargaining and avoid distributive negotiation: emphasizing superordinate goals; focusing on the problem, not the people; focusing on interests, not demands; creating new options for joint gain; and focusing on what is fair (see Table 17.1).[58]

EMPHASIZING SUPERORDINATE GOALS *Superordinate goals* are goals that both parties agree to regardless of the source of their conflict. Increasing organizational effectiveness, increasing responsiveness to customers, and gaining a competitive advantage are just a few of the many superordinate goals that members of an organization can emphasize during integrative bargaining. Superordinate goals help parties in conflict to keep in mind the big picture and the fact that they are working together for a larger purpose or goal despite their disagreements.

Table 17.1
Negotiation Strategies for Integrative Bargaining

- Emphasize superordinate goals.
- Focus on the problem, not the people.
- Focus on interests, not demands.
- Create new options for joint gain.
- Focus on what is fair.

FOCUSING ON THE PROBLEM, NOT THE PEOPLE People who are in conflict may not be able to resist the temptation to focus on the other party's shortcomings and weaknesses, thereby personalizing the conflict. Instead of attacking the problem, the parties to the conflict attack each other. This approach is inconsistent with integrative bargaining and can easily lead both parties into a distributive negotiation mode. All parties to a conflict need to keep focused on the problem or on the source of the conflict and avoid the temptation to discredit one another.

Integrative bargaining brings all parties to the table in order to create a solution based on honest assessment of the problem and a willingness to honor others' interests and values.

FOCUSING ON INTERESTS, NOT DEMANDS Demands are *what* a person wants; interests are *why* the person wants them. When two people are in conflict, it is unlikely that the demands of both can be met. Their underlying interests, however, can be met, and meeting them is what integrative bargaining is all about.

CREATING NEW OPTIONS FOR JOINT GAIN Once two parties to a conflict focus on their interests, they are on the road to achieving creative solutions to the conflict that will benefit them both. This win–win scenario means that rather than having a fixed set of alternatives from which to choose, the two parties can come up with new alternatives that might even expand the resource pie.

FOCUSING ON WHAT IS FAIR Focusing on what is fair is consistent with the principle of distributive justice, which emphasizes the fair distribution of outcomes based on the meaningful contributions that people make to organizations (see Chapter 5). It is likely that two parties in conflict will disagree on certain points and prefer different alternatives that each party believes may better serve his or her own interests or maximize his or her own outcomes. Emphasizing fairness and distributive justice will help the two parties come to a mutual agreement about what the best solution is to the problem.

When managers pursue these five strategies and encourage other organizational members to do so, they are more likely to be able to effectively resolve their conflicts through integrative bargaining. In addition, throughout the negotiation process, managers and other organizational members need to be aware of, and on their guard against, the biases that can lead to faulty decision making (see Chapter 7).[59]

LO17-5 Explain why managers need to be attuned to organizational politics, and describe the political strategies that managers can use to become politically skilled.

Organizational Politics

Managers must develop the skills necessary to manage organizational conflict for an organization to be effective. Suppose, however, that top managers are in conflict over the best strategy for an organization to pursue or the best structure to adopt to use organizational resources efficiently. In such situations resolving conflict is often difficult, and the parties to the conflict resort to organizational politics and political strategies to try to resolve the conflict in their favor.

organizational politics Activities that managers engage in to increase their power and to use power effectively to achieve their goals and overcome resistance or opposition.

political strategies Tactics that managers use to increase their power and to use power effectively to influence and gain the support of other people while overcoming resistance or opposition.

Organizational politics are the activities that managers (and other members of an organization) engage in to increase their power and to use power effectively to achieve their goals and overcome resistance or opposition.[60] Managers often engage in organizational politics to resolve conflicts in their favor.

Political strategies are the specific tactics that managers (and other members of an organization) use to increase their power and to use power effectively to influence and gain the support of other people while overcoming resistance or opposition. Political strategies are especially important when managers are planning and implementing major changes in an organization: Managers need not only to gain support for their change initiatives and influence organizational members to behave in new ways but also to overcome often strong opposition from people who feel threatened by the change and prefer the status quo. By increasing their power, managers are better able to make needed changes. In addition to increasing their power, managers also must make sure they use their power in a way that actually enables them to influence others.

The Importance of Organizational Politics

The term *politics* has a negative connotation for many people. Some may think that managers who are political have risen to the top not because of their own merit and capabilities but because of whom they know. Or people may think that political managers are self-interested and wield power to benefit themselves, not their organization. There is a grain of truth to this negative connotation. Some managers do appear to misuse their power for personal benefit at the expense of their organization's effectiveness.

Nevertheless, organizational politics are often a positive force. Managers striving to make needed changes often encounter resistance from individuals and groups who feel threatened and wish to preserve the status quo. Effective managers engage in politics to gain support for and implement needed changes. Similarly, managers often face resistance from other managers who disagree with their goals for a group or for the organization and with what they are trying to accomplish. Engaging in organizational politics can help managers overcome this resistance and achieve their goals.

Indeed, managers cannot afford to ignore organizational politics. Everyone engages in politics to a degree–other managers, coworkers, and subordinates, as well as people outside an organization, such as suppliers. Those who try to ignore politics might as well bury their heads in the sand because in all likelihood they will be unable to gain support for their initiatives and goals.

Political Strategies for Gaining and Maintaining Power

Managers who use political strategies to increase and maintain their power are better able to influence others to work toward the achievement of group and organizational goals. (Recall from Chapter 14 that legitimate, reward, coercive, expert, and referent powers help managers influence others as leaders.) By controlling uncertainty, making themselves irreplaceable, being in a central position, generating resources, and building alliances, managers can increase their power (see Figure 17.4).[61] We next look at each of these strategies.

CONTROLLING UNCERTAINTY Uncertainty is a threat for individuals, groups, and whole organizations and can interfere with effective performance and goal attainment. For example, uncertainty about job security is threatening for many workers and may cause top performers (who have the best chance of finding another job) to quit and take a more secure position with another organization. When an R&D department faces uncertainty about customer preferences, its members may waste

Figure 17.4
Political Strategies for Increasing Power

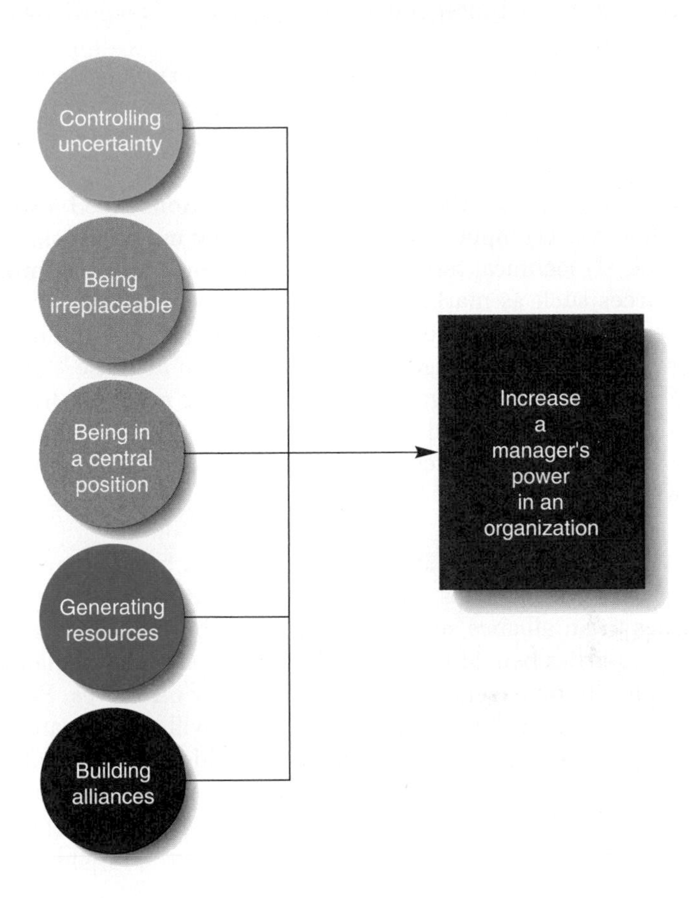

valuable resources to develop a product, such as smokeless cigarettes, that customers do not want. When top managers face uncertainty about global demand, they may fail to export products to countries that want them and thus may lose a source of competitive advantage.

Managers who can control and reduce uncertainty for other managers, teams, departments, and the organization as a whole are likely to see their power increase.[62] Managers of labor unions gain power when they can eliminate uncertainty over job security for workers. Marketing and sales managers gain power when they can eliminate uncertainty for other departments such as R&D by accurately forecasting customers' changing preferences. Top managers gain power when they are knowledgeable about global demand for an organization's products. Managers who can control uncertainty are likely to be in demand and be sought after by other organizations.

MAKING ONESELF IRREPLACEABLE Managers gain power when they have valuable knowledge and expertise that allow them to perform activities no one else can handle. This is the essence of being irreplaceable.[63] The more central these activities are to organizational effectiveness, the more power managers gain from being irreplaceable.

BEING IN A CENTRAL POSITION Managers in central positions are responsible for activities that are directly connected to an organization's goals and sources of competitive advantage and often are located in central positions in important communication networks in an organization.[64] Managers in key positions have control over crucial organizational activities and initiatives and have access to important information.

Other organizational members depend on them for their knowledge, expertise, advice, and support, and the success of the organization as a whole is seen as riding on these managers. These consequences of being in a central position are likely to increase managers' power.

Managers who are outstanding performers, have a wide knowledge base, and have made important and visible contributions to their organizations are likely to be offered central positions that will increase their power.

GENERATING RESOURCES Organizations need three kinds of resources to be effective: (1) input resources such as raw materials, skilled workers, and financial capital; (2) technical resources such as machinery and computers; and (3) knowledge resources such as marketing, information technology, or engineering expertise. To the extent that a manager can generate one or more of these kinds of resources for an organization, that manager's power is likely to increase.[65] In universities, for example, professors who win large grants to fund their research, from associations such as the National Science Foundation and the Army Research Institute, gain power because of the financial resources they generate for their departments and the university as a whole.

BUILDING ALLIANCES When managers build alliances, they develop mutually beneficial relationships with people both inside and outside the organization. The parties to an alliance support one another because doing so is in their best interests, and all parties benefit from the alliance. Alliances give managers power because they provide the managers with support for their initiatives. Partners to alliances provide support because they know the managers will reciprocate when their partners need support. Alliances can help managers achieve their goals and implement needed changes in organizations because they increase managers' levels of power. As illustrated in the following "Focus on Diversity" box, many powerful top managers such as Indra Nooyi, chair and CEO of PepsiCo, are particularly skilled when it comes to building alliances.[66]

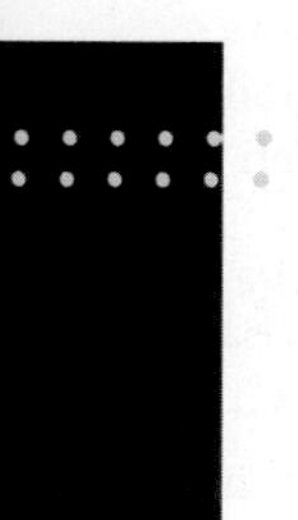

Focus on Diversity

Indra Nooyi Builds Alliances

By all counts Indra Nooyi is a powerful business leader.[67] As CEO and chair of PepsiCo, she oversees a company with over $43 billion in revenues and over 198,000 employees; Pepsi-Cola, Lay's, Doritos, Tropicana, Mountain Dew, Gatorade, and Quaker are among Pepsi's many well-known brands.[68] She effectively uses her vision for PepsiCo, "Performance with Purpose," both to motivate and guide Pepsi employees and to communicate PepsiCo's stance on important issues such as health, obesity, and protecting the natural environment around the world.[69] In 2008 she was included in *Time* magazine's list of "The World's Most Influential People";[70] in 2007, 2008, and 2009 she was ranked the most powerful woman in business by *Fortune* magazine.[71]

Nooyi, born and raised in India, was senior vice president of strategic planning at PepsiCo before assuming the top post on October 1, 2006.[72] When the PepsiCo board of directors was deciding who would be the next CEO of the company, two senior executives at PepsiCo were under consideration, Nooyi and Michael White, vice chairman.[73] When Nooyi found out the board had chosen her, one of her top priorities was to ensure that White would stay at PepsiCo, the two would maintain the great relationship they had with each other that had evolved from years of working together, and she would have

Indra Nooyi skillfully expanded the CEO table when she assumed the reins at PepsiCo; by openly asking for help from other key executives and previous CEOs, she has ensured that she isn't flying blind.

his support and advice.[74] At the time White was on vacation at his beach house in Cape Cod, Massachusetts. Nooyi flew to Cape Cod and the two walked on the beach, had ice cream together, and even played a duet (Nooyi and White both are fond of music, and in this case he played the piano and she sang). Prior to leaving Cape Cod, she told White, "Tell me whatever I need to do to keep you, and I will."[75] Ultimately White decided to remain at PepsiCo as CEO of PepsiCo International as well as vice chairman of PepsiCo.[76] At a meeting announcing Nooyi's appointment, Nooyi told employees, "I treat Mike as my partner. He could easily have been CEO." White said, "I play the piano and Indra sings."[77] In 2009 White retired from PepsiCo.[78]

Nooyi also excels at gaining the support of PepsiCo's employees.[79] She is down-to-earth, sincere, and genuine in her interactions with employees and also comfortable just being herself; she has been known to walk barefoot in the halls of PepsiCo on occasion and sometimes sings at gatherings. Celebrations for employees' birthdays include a cake. Nooyi, as a mother of two daughters, also recognizes how employees' families are affected by their work and what a great source of support families can be.[80]

Of course Nooyi faces a number of challenges at PepsiCo as she strives to make the company more globally focused (and less focused on the United States), make more healthful food products, protect the natural environment, and look out for the well-being of employees in a troubled economy with rising prices for ingredients in PepsiCo's products.[81] Her exceptional skills at building alliances and gaining support will help. As she indicates, ". . . you give the team of people a set of objectives and goals and get them all to buy into it, and they can move mountains."[82]

Many powerful top managers focus on building alliances not only inside their organizations but also with individuals, groups, and organizations in the task and general environments on which their organizations depend for resources. These individuals, groups, and organizations enter alliances with managers because doing so is in their best interests and they know they can count on the managers' support when they need it. When managers build alliances, they need to be on their guard to ensure that everything is aboveboard, ethical, and legal.

Political Strategies for Exercising Power

Politically skilled managers not only understand, and can use, the five strategies to increase their power; they also appreciate strategies for exercising their power. These strategies generally focus on how managers can use their power *unobtrusively*.[83] When managers exercise power unobtrusively, other members of an organization may not be aware that the managers are using their power to influence them. They may think they support these managers for a variety of reasons: because they believe it is the rational or logical thing to do, because they believe doing so is in their own best interests, or because they believe the position or decision the managers are advocating is legitimate or appropriate.

The unobtrusive use of power may sound devious, but managers typically use this strategy to bring about change and achieve organizational goals. Political strategies for exercising power to gain the support and concurrence of others include relying

Figure 17.5
Political Strategies for Exercising Power

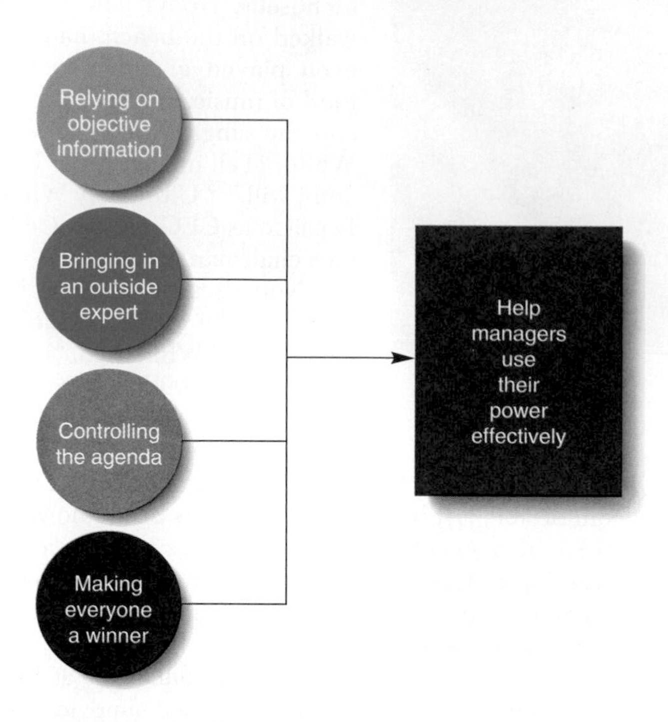

on objective information, bringing in an outside expert, controlling the agenda, and making everyone a winner (see Figure 17.5).[84]

RELYING ON OBJECTIVE INFORMATION Managers require the support of others to achieve their goals, implement changes, and overcome opposition. One way for a manager to gain this support and overcome opposition is to rely on objective information that supports the manager's initiatives. Reliance on objective information leads others to support the manager because of the facts; objective information causes others to believe that what the manager is proposing is the proper course of action. By relying on objective information, politically skilled managers unobtrusively exercise their power to influence others.

BRINGING IN AN OUTSIDE EXPERT Bringing in an outside expert to support a proposal or decision can, at times, provide managers with some of the same benefits that the use of objective information does. It lends credibility to a manager's initiatives and causes others to believe that what the manager is proposing is the appropriate or rational thing to do.

Although you might think consultants and other outside experts are neutral or objective, they sometimes are hired by managers who want them to support a certain position or decision in an organization. For instance, when managers face strong opposition from others who fear that a decision will harm their interests, the managers may bring in an outside expert. They hope this expert will be perceived as a neutral observer to lend credibility and "objectivity" to their point of view. The support of an outside expert may cause others to believe that a decision is indeed the right one. Of course sometimes consultants and other outside experts actually are brought into organizations *to be* objective and guide managers on the appropriate course of action.

CONTROLLING THE AGENDA Managers also can exercise power unobtrusively by controlling the agenda–influencing which alternatives are considered or even whether a decision is made.[85] When managers influence the alternatives that are considered, they can make sure that each considered alternative is acceptable to them and that undesirable alternatives are not in the feasible set. In a hiring context, for example, managers can exert their power unobtrusively by ensuring that job candidates whom they do not find acceptable do not make their way onto the list of finalists for an open position. They do this by making sure that these candidates' drawbacks or deficiencies are communicated to everyone involved in making the hiring decision. When three finalists for an open position are discussed and evaluated in a hiring meeting, a manager may seem to exert little power or influence and just go along with what the rest of the group wants. However, the manager may have exerted power in the hiring process unobtrusively by controlling which candidates made it to the final stage.

Sometimes managers can prevent a decision from being made. The manager can exert influence by not including the proposal on the agenda for the committee's next meeting. Alternatively, the manager could place the proposal at the end of the agenda for the meeting and feel confident that the committee will run out of time and not get to the last items on the agenda because that is what always happens. Either approach enables the manager to unobtrusively exercise power. Committee members do not perceive this manager as trying to influence them to turn down the proposal. Rather, the manager has made the proposal into a nonissue that is not even considered.

MAKING EVERYONE A WINNER Often, politically skilled managers can exercise their power unobtrusively because they make sure that everyone whose support they need benefits personally from providing that support. By making everyone a winner, a manager can influence other organizational members because these members see supporting the manager as being in their best interest.

When top managers turn around troubled companies, some organizational members and parts of the organization are bound to suffer due to restructurings that often entail painful layoffs. However, the power of the turnaround CEO often accelerates as it becomes clear that the future of the company is on surer footing and the organization and its stakeholders are winners as a result of the change effort.

Making everyone a winner not only is an effective way of exercising power but, when used consistently and forthrightly, can increase managers' power and influence over time. That is, when a manager actually does make everyone a winner, all stakeholders will see it as in their best interests to support the manager and his or her initiatives. When managers who make everyone a winner have strong ethical values, everyone really is a winner, as profiled in the following "Ethics in Action" box.

Ethics in Action

El Faro Benefits Multiple Stakeholders

When Estuardo Porras was taking business classes at Pepperdine University in Malibu, California, in the 1990s, he was surprised to see the high prices that Starbucks charged for coffee.[86] In his native country of Guatemala, coffee used to be the major export until prices declined in the 1980s due to a large influx of low-cost coffee beans coming on the market from countries like Vietnam. Porras had a vision of returning to Guatemala, resurrecting an old coffee plantation, and operating it in a socially responsible way that protected the natural environment, looked out for and contributed to the well-being of the workers who operated it and the local community, and produced high-quality coffee beans that a socially responsible organization like Starbucks would be interested in purchasing.[87]

Porras returned to Guatemala, borrowed $1.25 million from his father, who had recently sold a Coca-Cola bottling company, and transformed an abandoned plantation called El Faro into a marvel of environmental sustainability, social responsibility, and effectiveness.[88] El Faro protects the natural environment, helps a poor community, and produces high-quality arabica coffee used by specialty coffee companies like Starbucks. And because of Starbucks' commitment to purchasing coffee beans from growers that abide by ethical social and environmental values, El Faro can sell all the coffee beans it grows that meet Starbucks' standards for more than the beans would sell for on the general commodity export market.[89]

El Faro is located near a volcano, and the ash from the volcano provides excellent soil for growing coffee. Coffee beans are fermented in recycled water, and the casings from the beans are eaten by earthworms, yielding an organic fertilizer. Much of the work on the plantation is done by hand.[90] El Faro supports a free elementary school for children in the local community and buses older children to a high school in the vicinity. Employees receive free health care after they have been with El Faro for three months; the care is provided in the plantation's medical office, staffed by a part-time doctor and full-time nurse. They also receive 15 days of paid vacation annually. Many of El Faro's full-time employees and their families live on the plantation; El Faro also has part-time employees.[91]

Fermenting coffee beans in recycled water is just one of the many areas in which Estuardo Porras has transformed El Faro into a productive, environmentally responsible enterprise.

Porras initially sold El Faro's coffee beans on the commodity export market while persistently trying to make inroads at Starbucks by sending letters and coffee samples to no avail. Eventually an exporter who bought beans from El Faro persuaded two coffee buyers from Starbucks to visit the plantation. After a tour and coffee tasting, the buyers were so delighted with what they saw and tasted that they ordered coffee from El Faro that day and gave Porras the opportunity to participate in a program that gives long-terms contracts to growers who are socially responsible.[92]

Summary and Review

ORGANIZATIONAL CONFLICT Organizational conflict is the discord that arises when the goals, interests, or values of different individuals or groups are incompatible and those individuals or groups block or thwart each other's attempts to achieve their objectives. Four types of conflict arising in organizations are interpersonal conflict, intragroup conflict, intergroup conflict, and interorganizational conflict. Sources of conflict in organizations include different goals and time horizons, overlapping authority, task interdependencies, different evaluation or reward systems, scarce resources, and status inconsistencies. Conflict management strategies focused on individuals include increasing awareness of the sources of conflict, increasing diversity awareness and skills, practicing job rotation or temporary assignments, and using permanent transfers or dismissals when necessary. Strategies focused on the whole organization include changing an organization's structure or culture and altering the source of conflict.

LO17-1, 17-2

LO17-3, 17-4

NEGOTIATION Negotiation is a conflict resolution technique used when parties to a conflict have approximately equal levels of power and try to come up with an acceptable way to allocate resources to each other. In distributive negotiation, the parties perceive that there is a fixed level of resources for them to allocate, and they compete to receive as much as possible at the expense of the other party, not caring about their relationship in the future. In integrative bargaining, both parties perceive that they may be able to increase the resource pie by coming up with a creative solution to the conflict, trusting each other, and cooperating with each other to achieve a win–win resolution. Five strategies that managers can use to facilitate integrative bargaining are to emphasize superordinate goals; focus on the problem, not the people; focus on interests, not demands; create new options for joint gain; and focus on what is fair.

LO17-5 **ORGANIZATIONAL POLITICS** Organizational politics are the activities that managers (and other members of an organization) engage in to increase their power and to use power effectively to achieve their goals and overcome resistance or opposition. Effective managers realize that politics can be a positive force that enables them to make needed changes in an organization. Five important political strategies for gaining and maintaining power are controlling uncertainty, making oneself irreplaceable, being in a central position, generating resources, and building alliances. Political strategies for effectively exercising power focus on how to use power unobtrusively and include relying on objective information, bringing in an outside expert, controlling the agenda, and making everyone a winner.

Management in Action

Topics for Discussion and Action

Discussion

1. Discuss why too little conflict in an organization can be just as detrimental as too much conflict. **[LO17-1]**
2. Why are compromise and collaboration more effective ways of handling conflict than accommodation, avoidance, and competition? **[LO17-2]**
3. Why should managers promote integrative bargaining rather than distributive negotiation? **[LO17-3]**
4. How can managers promote integrative bargaining? **[LO17-4]**
5. Why do organizational politics affect practically every organization? **[LO17-5]**
6. Why do effective managers need good political skills? **[LO17-5]**
7. What steps can managers take to ensure that organizational politics are a positive force leading to a competitive advantage, not a negative force leading to personal advantage at the expense of organizational goal attainment? **[LO17-5]**
8. Think of a member of an organization whom you know and who is particularly powerful. What political strategies does this person use to increase his or her power? **[LO17-5]**
9. Why is it best to use power unobtrusively? How are people likely to react to power that is exercised obtrusively? **[LO17-5]**

Action

10. Interview a manager in a local organization to determine the kinds of conflicts that occur in his or her organization and the strategies that are used to manage them. **[LO17-1, 17-2]**

Building Management Skills [LO17-1, 17-2]

Effective and Ineffective Conflict Resolution

Think about two recent conflicts that you had with other people—one conflict that you felt was effectively resolved (C1) and one that you felt was ineffectively resolved (C2). The other people involved could be coworkers, students, family members, friends, or members of an organization that you are a member of. Answer the following questions:

1. Briefly describe C1 and C2. What type of conflict was involved in each of these incidents?
2. What was the source of the conflict in C1 and in C2?
3. What conflict management strategies were used in C1 and in C2?
4. What could you have done differently to more effectively manage conflict in C2?
5. How was the conflict resolved in C1 and in C2?

Managing Ethically [LO17-5]

One political strategy managers can engage in is controlling the agenda by subtly influencing which alternatives are considered or even whether a decision is up for discussion. Some employees believe this can be unethical and can prevent important issues from being raised and points of view from being expressed.

Questions

1. Either individually or in a group, think about the ethical implications of controlling the agenda as a political strategy.
2. What steps can managers and organizations take to ensure that this strategy does not result in important issues and differing points of view being suppressed in an organization?
3. Do you think that the views of controlling the agenda would be different in various countries? Discuss how this view of managing may vary in different nations.

Small Group Breakout Exercise [LO17-3, 17-4]

Negotiating a Solution

Form groups of three or four people. One member of your group will play the role of Jane Rister, one member will play the role of Michael Schwartz, and one or two members will be observer(s) and spokesperson(s) for your group.

Jane Rister and Michael Schwartz are assistant managers in a large department store. They report directly to the store manager. Today they are meeting to discuss some important problems they need to solve but about which they disagree.

The first problem hinges on the fact that either Rister or Schwartz needs to be on duty whenever the store is open. For the last six months, Rister has taken most of the least desirable hours (nights and Saturdays; in their country the department store must stay closed on Sunday). They are planning their schedules for the next six months. Rister thought Schwartz would take more of the undesirable times, but Schwartz has informed Rister that his wife has just gotten a nursing job that requires her to work weekends, so he needs to stay home weekends to take care of their infant daughter.

The second problem concerns a department manager who has had a hard time retaining salespeople in his department. The turnover rate in his department is twice that in the other store departments. Rister thinks the manager is ineffective and wants to replace him. Schwartz thinks the high turnover is just a fluke and the manager is effective.

The last problem concerns Rister's and Schwartz's vacation schedules. Both managers want to take off the week of their nation's biggest holiday, but one of them needs to be in the store whenever it is open.

1. The group members playing Rister and Schwartz assume their roles and negotiate a solution to these three problems.
2. Observers take notes on how Rister and Schwartz negotiate solutions to their problems.
3. Observers determine the extent to which Rister and Schwartz use distributive negotiation or integrative bargaining to resolve their conflicts.
4. When called on by the instructor, observers communicate to the rest of the class how Rister and Schwartz resolved their conflicts, whether they used distributive negotiation or integrative bargaining, and their actual solutions.

Exploring the World Wide Web [LO17-1, 17-2]

Think of a major conflict in the business world that you have read about in the newspaper in the past few weeks. Then search on the Web for magazine and newspaper articles presenting differing viewpoints and perspectives on the conflict. Based on what you have read, how are the parties to this conflict handling it? Is their approach functional or dysfunctional, and why?

Be the Manager [LO17-1, 17-2, 17-3, 17-4, 17-5]

You are a middle manager in a large corporation, and lately you feel that you are caught between a rock and a hard place. Times are tough; your unit has experienced layoffs; your surviving subordinates are overworked and demoralized; and you feel that you have no meaningful rewards, such as the chance for a pay raise, bonus, or promotion, to motivate them with. Your boss keeps increasing the demands on your unit as well as the unit's responsibilities. Moreover, you believe that you and your subordinates are being unfairly blamed for certain problems beyond your control. You believe that you have the expertise and skills to perform your job effectively and also that your subordinates are capable and effective in their jobs. Yet you feel that you are on shaky ground and powerless given the current state of affairs. What are you going to do?

CHAPTER 18

Using Advanced Information Technology to Increase Performance

Learning Objectives

After studying this chapter, you should be able to:

LO18-1 Differentiate between data and information, and explain how the attributes of useful information allow managers to make better decisions.

LO18-2 Describe three reasons why managers must have access to information to perform their tasks and roles effectively.

LO18-3 Describe the computer hardware and software innovations that created the IT revolution and changed the way managers behave.

LO18-4 Differentiate among seven performance-enhancing kinds of management information systems.

LO18-5 Explain how IT is helping managers build strategic alliances and network structures to increase efficiency and effectiveness.

A MANAGER'S CHALLENGE

Technology Top Priority for Saudi Oil Firm

Saudi Aramco is a state-owned business that is the largest oil company in the world. It is estimated that it produces approximately 3.5 billion barrels of oil a year and has reserves of over 1.2 trillion proven barrels of oil, with the potential for greater recovery as technology improves of another 700 billion barrels. Often it is assumed that a state-owned business will be managed poorly and skimp on the investment in technology since it is a long-term investment and the state prefers immediate returns instead. Aramco challenges that assumption.

The new CEO of the firm, Khalid al Falih, has made the focus on technology one of his central concerns. The result is that today Aramco is one of the technological leaders in the field. It is estimated that the firm has 34 teraflops, or 34 trillion floating point operations per second, of computing capacity. This represents a 300-fold increase in computing capacity since 1999. This computing power is approximately the same as 30,000 desktop computers. The goals of this technology are to most efficiently and thoroughly take advantage of oil reserves.

In the oil industry, the percentage of oil recovered is critical. Thus, the oil is in the ground but not all of it can be easily removed for use. Historically wells were drilled vertically. Saudi Aramco's increased technological capability allows directed drilling, which means that wells can be drilled vertically, horizontally, and multilaterally in difficult geologic environments. Also, natural gas can be recovered using this technology.

This new drilling technology has opened up the potential to drill in areas it was assumed would never be drilled—cities. In

Aramco, Saudi Arabia's state-owned oil company, believes that cutting-edge technology provides the firm with a strategic advantage when it comes to developing new sources of energy.

the United States and Europe cities are often built over reserves of gas and oil. However, it is not acceptable to drill multiple places around a city due to the population and negative impact it may have in highly populated or historical areas. This new technology allows the well to be drilled outside the city limits, which typically is not obvious to most people. From this single well it is then possible to drill vertically and horizontally to open new areas and obtain high levels of production. This approach allows oil and gas wells to be drilled in relatively unobtrusive ways that may pull oil and gas from the center of a city. The well itself is a considerable distance away but drilling horizontally the well now reaches an area that has the gas over which large populations live. Removing the oil and gas from these areas has no negative impact on the people but can reduce a nation's needs for imports and also become a revenue stream for local governments.

Aramco's focus on technology has also allowed the firm to develop new technologies that open up rich new sources of energy; for example, extra heavy oil, tar sands, and bitumen. These do not represent most of the oil in Saudi Arabia. However, techniques to open up such sources impact the overall environment and world energy picture. Aramco has made a strong commitment to develop technology to open up these domains in an environmentally safe manner. Aramco leadership and the culture of the firm are committed to developing cutting edge technology and to employ it in a manner that helps the environment and the oil industry.[1]

Overview

In a world in which business activities of all kinds are increasingly conducted through the Internet, the challenge facing managers is to continually update and improve their use of advancing IT to increase organizational performance. Managers must work to adopt the most effective IT solutions for their employees and customers or risk being surpassed by more effective rivals who have developed superior IT competencies. Google and Apple have become two of the most valuable companies in the world because they provide advanced IT solutions that increase people's ability to access, search, and use the potential of the World Wide Web and communicate with others. There are enormous opportunities for managers of all kinds of organizations to find new ways to use IT to use organizational resources more efficiently and effectively.

In this chapter we begin by looking at the relationship between information and the manager's job and then examine the ongoing IT revolution. Then we discuss six types of management information systems, each of which is based on a different sort of IT, which can help managers perform their jobs more efficiently and effectively. Next we examine the impact of rapidly evolving IT on managers' jobs and on an organization's competitive advantage. By the end of this chapter, you will understand how new developments in IT are profoundly shaping managers' tasks and roles and the way organizations operate.

Information and the Manager's Job

data Raw, unsummarized, and unanalyzed facts.

information Data that are organized in a meaningful fashion.

Managers cannot plan, organize, lead, and control effectively unless they have access to information. Information is the source of the knowledge and intelligence they need to make the right decisions. Information, however, is not the same as data.[2] **Data** are raw, unsummarized, and unanalyzed facts such as volume of sales, level of costs, or number of customers. **Information** is data that are organized in a meaningful fashion, such as in a graph showing the changes in sales volume or costs over time. Data alone do not tell managers anything; information, in contrast, can communicate a great deal of useful knowledge to the person who receives it–such as a manager who sees sales falling or costs rising. The distinction between data and information is important because one purpose of IT is to help managers transform data into information to make better managerial decisions.

To further clarify the difference between data and information, consider a supermarket manager who must decide how much shelf space to allocate to two breakfast cereal brands: Dentist's Delight and Sugar Supreme. Most supermarkets use checkout scanners to record individual sales and store the data on a computer. Accessing this computer, the manager might find that Dentist's Delight sells 50 boxes per day and Sugar Supreme sells 25 boxes per day. These raw data, however, are of little help in helping the manager decide how to allocate shelf space. The manager also needs to know how much shelf space each cereal currently occupies and how much profit each cereal generates for the supermarket.

LO18-1 Differentiate between data and information, and explain how the attributes of useful information allow managers to make better decisions.

Suppose the manager discovers that Dentist's Delight occupies 10 feet of shelf space and Sugar Supreme occupies 4 feet and that Dentist's Delight generates 20 cents of profit a box while Sugar Supreme generates 40 cents of profit a box. By putting these three bits of data together (number of boxes sold, amount of shelf space, and profit per box), the manager gets some useful information on which to base a decision: Dentist's Delight generates $1 of profit per foot of shelf space per day [(50 boxes × $.20)/10 feet], and Sugar Supreme generates $2.50 of profit per foot of shelf space per day [(25 boxes × $.40)/4 feet]. Armed with this information, the manager might decide to allocate less shelf space to Dentist's Delight and more to Sugar Supreme.

Attributes of Useful Information

Four factors determine the usefulness of information to a manager: quality, timeliness, completeness, and relevance (see Figure 18.1).

Figure 18.1
Factors Affecting the Usefulness of Information

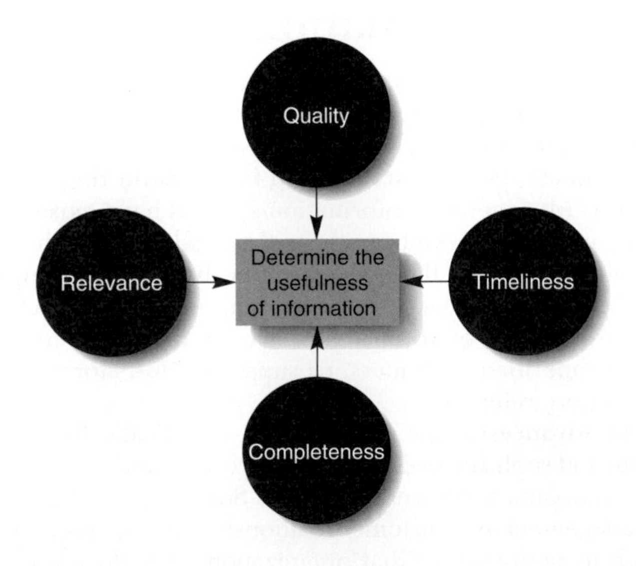

QUALITY Accuracy and reliability determine the quality of information.[3] The greater its accuracy and reliability, the higher is the quality of information. Modern IT gives managers access to high-quality real-time information that they can use to improve long-term decision making and alter short-term operating decisions, such as how much of a particular product to make daily or monthly. Supermarket managers, for example, use handheld bar code readers linked to a server to monitor and record how demand for particular products such as milk, chicken, or bread changes daily so they know how to restock their shelves to ensure the products are always available.

TIMELINESS Information that is timely is available when it is required to allow managers to make the optimal decision–not after the decision has been made. In today's rapidly changing world, the need for timely information often means information must be available on a real-time basis–hence the enormous growth in the demand for PDAs such as smartphones.[4] **Real-time information** is information that reflects current changes in business conditions. In an industry that experiences rapid changes, real-time information may need to be updated frequently.

real-time information Frequently updated information that reflects current conditions.

Airlines use real-time information about the number of flight bookings and competitors' prices to adjust their prices hourly to maximize their revenues. Thus, for example, the fare for flights from London to Rome might change from one hour to the next as fares are reduced to fill empty seats and raised when most seats have been sold. Airlines use real-time information about reservations to adjust fares at the last possible moment to fill planes and maximize revenues. Airlines make more than 100,000 fare changes each day.[5] Obviously the managers who make such pricing decisions need real-time information about current market demand.

COMPLETENESS Information that is complete gives managers all the information they need to exercise control, achieve coordination, or make an effective decision. Recall from Chapter 7, however, that managers rarely have access to complete information. Instead, because of uncertainty, ambiguity, and bounded rationality, they have to make do with incomplete information.[6] One function of IT is to increase the completeness of managers' information.

RELEVANCE Information that is relevant is useful and suits a manager's particular needs and circumstances. Irrelevant information is useless and may actually hurt the performance of a busy manager who has to spend valuable time determining whether information is relevant. Given the massive amounts of information that managers are now exposed to and their limited information-processing capabilities, a company's information systems designers need to ensure that managers receive only relevant information.

information technology The set of methods or techniques for acquiring, organizing, storing, manipulating, and transmitting information.

management information system (MIS) A specific form of IT that managers utilize to generate the specific, detailed information they need to perform their roles effectively.

What Is Information Technology?

Information technology (IT) is the set of methods or techniques for acquiring, organizing, storing, manipulating, and transmitting information.[7] A **management information system (MIS)** is a specific form of IT that managers select and use to generate the specific, detailed information they need to perform their roles effectively. Management information systems have existed for as long as there have been organizations, which is a long time indeed–merchants in ancient Egypt used clay tablets to record their transactions. Before the computing age, most systems were paper-based: Clerks recorded important information on paper documents (often in duplicate or triplicate) in words and numbers; sent copies of the documents to superiors, customers, or suppliers; and stored other copies in filing cabinets for future reference.

LO18-2 Describe three reasons why managers must have access to information to perform their tasks and roles effectively.

Rapid advances in the power of IT–specifically the development of ever more powerful and sophisticated computer hardware and software–have had a fundamental impact on organizations and managers. Some recent IT developments, such as inventory management and customer relationship management (CRM) systems, contribute so much to performance that organizations that do *not* adopt it, or that implement

Charts and graphs may be the clichéd centerpieces of managerial meetings, but the data they represent are key for making informed decisions.

it ineffectively, become uncompetitive compared with organizations that do adopt it.[8] In the 2000s much of the increasing productivity and efficiency of business in general has been attributed to the way organizations and their employees use advancing IT to improve their performance.

Managers need information for three reasons: to make effective decisions, to control the activities of the organization, and to coordinate the activities of the organization. Next we examine these uses of information in detail.

Information and Decisions

Much of management (planning, organizing, leading, and controlling) is about making decisions. For example, the marketing manager must decide what price to charge for a product, what distribution channels to use, and what promotional messages to emphasize to maximize sales. The manufacturing manager must decide how much of a product to make and how to make it. The purchasing manager must decide from whom to purchase inputs and what inventory of inputs to hold. The human relations manager must decide how much employees should be paid, how they should be trained, and what benefits they should be given. The engineering manager must make decisions about new product design. Top managers must decide how to allocate scarce financial resources among competing projects, how best to structure and control the organization, and what business-level strategy the organization should be pursuing. And regardless of their functional orientation, all managers have to make decisions about matters such as what performance evaluation to give to a subordinate.

To make effective decisions, managers need information both from inside the organization and from external stakeholders. When deciding how to price a product, for example, marketing managers need information about how consumers will react to different prices. They need information about unit costs because they do not want to set the price below the cost of production. And they need information about competitive strategy because pricing strategy should be consistent with an organization's competitive strategy. Some of this information will come from outside the organization (for example, from consumer surveys) and some from inside the organization (information about production costs comes from manufacturing). As this example suggests, managers' ability to make effective decisions rests on their ability to acquire and process information.

Information and Control

As discussed in Chapter 11, controlling is the process through which managers regulate how efficiently and effectively an organization and its members perform the activities necessary to achieve its stated goals.[9] Managers achieve control over organizational activities by taking four steps (see Figure 11.2 on page 344): (1) They establish measurable standards of performance or goals; (2) they measure actual performance; (3) they compare actual performance against established goals; and (4) they evaluate the results and take corrective action if necessary.[10] The package delivery company DHL, for example, has a delivery goal: to deliver over 90% of the overnight packages it picks up by noon the next day.[11] DHL has thousands of stations (branch offices that coordinate the pickup and delivery of packages in a particular area) that are responsible for the physical pickup and delivery of packages. DHL managers monitor the delivery performance of these stations regularly; if they find that the goal is not being attained, they determine why and take corrective action if necessary.

To achieve control over any organizational activity, managers must have information. To control ground station activities, a DHL manager might need to know what percentage of packages each station delivers by noon. To obtain this information the manager uses DHL's own IT. All packages to be shipped to the stations have been scanned with handheld scanners by the drivers who pick them up; then all this information is sent wirelessly through servers to DHL headquarters' mainframe computer. When the packages are scanned again at delivery, this information is also transmitted through its computer network. Managers can access this information to quickly discover what percentage of packages were delivered by noon of the day after they were picked up, and also how this information breaks down station by station so they can take corrective action if necessary.

Management information systems are used to control all divisional and functional operations. In accounting, for example, information systems are used to monitor expenditures and compare them against budgets.[12] To track expenditures against budgets, managers need information about current expenditures, broken down by relevant organizational units; accounting IT is designed to give managers this information. An example of IT used to monitor and control the daily activities of employees is the online MBO information system used by T. J. Rodgers at Cypress Semiconductor, discussed in Chapter 11. Rodgers implemented IT that allows him to review the goals of all his employees in about four hours.[13] At first glance it might seem that advances in IT would have a limited impact on the business of a clothing retailer; however, this assumption would be incorrect, as the following "Management Insight" box suggests.

Technology Helps Inditex Respond Fast

The retailer Inditex of Spain has been highlighted elsewhere in the text. You will recall that this garment company designs its own clothes, manufactures them in Spain, Portugal, or Morocco, and then sells them in one of approximately 4,500 stores. The clothes typically cost more as the cost for labor in Spain and Portugal is, at a minimum, approximately US$1200 a month as compared to US$200 for a worker in China. But the firm is able to prosper with a differentiation strategy because of the fast response with which it offers changes rapidly as customers demand new things.

Central to Inditex's ability to be so responsive is technology. The firm has a centralized IT infrastructure that enhances its demand-driven business model. Its system is designed to allow tracking of over 300,000 new stock-keeping units each year. The centralized design and production center has removed the need for expensive communication networks and distribution infrastructure, allowing goods to be shipped directly to stores. Inditex uses employee computer-aided design technology to refine prototypes. This technology allows designers to send specifications directly to cutting machines and other equipment in the production process, which limits errors and increases productivity. PDAs give managers the ability to update inventory. The tight fit between the firm's strategy and its technology allows the strategy to be enacted in the most efficient manner.[14]

Information and Coordination

Coordinating department and divisional activities to achieve organizational goals is another basic task of management. As an example of the size of the coordination task that managers face, consider the coordination effort necessary to build Boeing's 787

Dreamliner jet aircraft, which is assembled from over 3 million individual parts.[15] Managers at Boeing have to coordinate the production and delivery of all these parts so every part arrives at Boeing's Everett, Washington, facility exactly when it is needed (for example, the wings should arrive before the engines). To achieve this high level of coordination, managers need information about which global supplier is producing what part, and when it will be produced. To meet this need, managers at Boeing created global IT that links Boeing to all its suppliers and can track the flow of 3 million components through the production process around the world in real time–an immense task. Indeed, as we noted in earlier chapters Boeing's IT system could not match the enormous complexity of the task, and the launch of its new airliner was delayed until 2010 because of IT glitches that affected communication with suppliers.

Managers face increasing coordination problems in managing their global supply chains to take advantage of national differences in production costs. Li & Fung has been highlighted as a key source of value-chain management skills. A key means by which they are able to do this is through IT. Managers in all types of firms must adopt ever more sophisticated IT that helps them coordinate the flow of materials, semifinished goods, and finished products throughout the world. Consider, for example, how Bose, which manufactures some of the world's highest-quality speakers, manages its global supply chain. Bose purchases almost all the components for its speakers, and about half of these components come from suppliers around the world, mainly in Asia. The challenge for managers is to coordinate this global supply chain to minimize Bose's inventory and transportation costs, which is achieved when components arrive at Bose's assembly plant just in time to enter the production process. Bose also has to remain responsive to customer demands, which means its suppliers have to be able to respond quickly to changes in Bose's demand for specific kinds of components and increase or decrease production as needed.

The responsibility for coordinating the supply chain to simultaneously minimize inventory and transportation costs and respond quickly to changing customer demands belongs to Bose's logistics managers. They contracted with W. N. Procter, a Boston-based supply chain manager, to use its proprietary logistics IT, ProcterLink, to give Bose the real-time information it needs to track components parts as they move through the global supply chain.[16] When a shipment leaves a supplier it is logged into ProcterLink, and from this point on Bose can track the supplies as they move around the globe toward Massachusetts, which allows Bose to fine-tune its production scheduling so components enter the assembly process exactly when they are needed.

How well this system works was illustrated when one Japanese customer unexpectedly doubled its order for Bose speakers. Bose had to gear up its manufacturing in a hurry, but many of its components were stretched out across long distances. By using ProcterLink, Bose was able to locate the needed parts in its supply chain. It broke them out of the normal delivery chain and moved them by air freight to get them to the assembly line in time to meet the accelerated schedule so Bose could meet the needs of its customer.

The IT Revolution

Advances in IT have enabled managers to make gigantic leaps in the way they can collect more timely, complete, relevant, and high-quality information and use it in more effective ways. To better understand the ongoing revolution in IT that has transformed companies such as Inditex and Bose, allowing them to improve their responsiveness to customers, minimize costs, and improve their competitive position, we need to examine several key aspects of advanced IT.

LO18-3 Describe the computer hardware and software innovations that created the IT revolution and changed the way managers behave.

The Effects of Advancing IT

The IT revolution began with the development of the first computers–the hardware of IT–in the 1950s. The language of computers is a digital language of zeros and ones. Words, numbers, images, and sound can all be expressed in zeros and ones. Each letter in the alphabet has its own unique code of zeros and ones, as does each number, each color, and each sound. For example, the digital code for the number 20 is 10100. In the language of computers it takes a lot of zeros and ones to express even a simple sentence, to say nothing of complex color graphics or moving video images. Nevertheless, modern computers can read, process, and store trillions of instructions per second (an *instruction* is a line of software code) and thus vast amounts of zeros and ones. This awesome number-crunching power forms the foundation of the ongoing IT revolution.

The products and services that result from advancing IT are all around us–ever more powerful microprocessors and PCs, high-bandwidth wireless smartphones, sophisticated word-processing software, ever-expanding computer networks, inexpensive digital cameras and camcorders, and more and more useful online information and retailing services that did not exist a generation ago. These products are commonplace and are being continuously improved. Many managers and companies that helped develop the new IT have reaped enormous gains.

However, while many companies have benefited from advancing IT, others have been threatened. Traditional landline telephone companies and long-distance companies the world over have seen their market dominance threatened by new companies offering Internet, broadband, and wireless telephone technology. They have been forced to respond by buying wireless cell phone companies, building their own high-powered broadband networks, and forming alliances with other companies. So advancing IT is both an opportunity and a threat, and managers have to move quickly to protect their companies and maintain their competitive advantage.[17] To illustrate, consider the telecommunication industry in the United States. In 2010 Sprint, which had lost millions of customers to its rivals (especially AT&T with its iPhone franchise), began to champion its new WiMAX, 4G broadband network and new Android-based smartphones from Samsung. Sprint claimed its new IT would give customers much faster Internet service than AT&T's iPhone customers have received because AT&T's outdated broadband network could not keep up with customer demands for access to the Web. To fight back, in 2010 AT&T announced it would spend $2 billion more to upgrade its U.S. network and was working with Apple to make software changes that would allow iPhone and iPad applications to work faster on its network to improve the quality of customer service. Clearly, developing the right strategies to provide advanced IT solutions is a complicated process.

On one hand, IT helps create new product opportunities that managers and their organizations can take advantage of–such as online travel and vacation booking. On the other hand, IT creates new and improved products that reduce or destroy demand for older, established products–such as the services provided by bricks-and-mortar travel agents. Walmart, by developing its own sophisticated proprietary IT, has been able to reduce retailing costs so much that it has put hundreds of thousands of small and medium-size stores out of business. Similarly, thousands of small, specialized bookstores have closed in the last decade as a result of advances in IT that made online bookselling possible.

IT and the Product Life Cycle

product life cycle The way demand for a product changes in a predictable pattern over time.

When IT is advancing, organizational survival requires that managers quickly adopt and apply it. One reason for this is how IT affects the length of the **product life cycle,** which is the way demand for a product changes in a predictable pattern over time.[18] In general, the product life cycle consists of four stages: the embryonic, growth, maturity, and decline stages (see Figure 18.2). In the *embryonic stage* a product has yet to gain widespread acceptance; customers are unsure what a product, such as a new smartphone, has to offer, and demand for it is minimal. As a product, like Apple's iPod, becomes accepted by customers (although many products do *not,* recall the discussion of Sony's Betamax technology and how the VCR won over Betamax customers), demand takes off and the product enters its growth stage. In the *growth stage* many consumers are entering the market and buying the product for the first

Figure 18.2
A Product Life Cycle

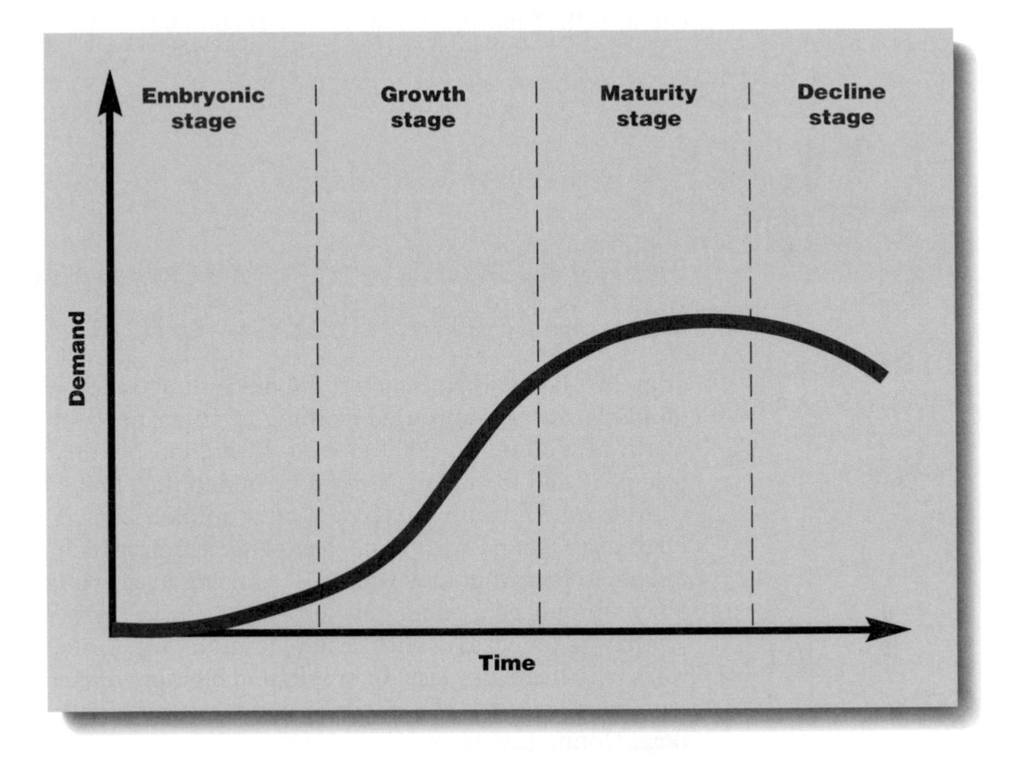

time, and demand increases rapidly. This is the stage Apple iPods were in and its iPhones are currently in–and Apple hopes its new iPad (launched in April 2010) will quickly reach the growth stage. Of course this will depend on the value customers see in the collection of IT applications that the iPad offers them–and how fast competitors move to offer similar and less expensive tablet computers.

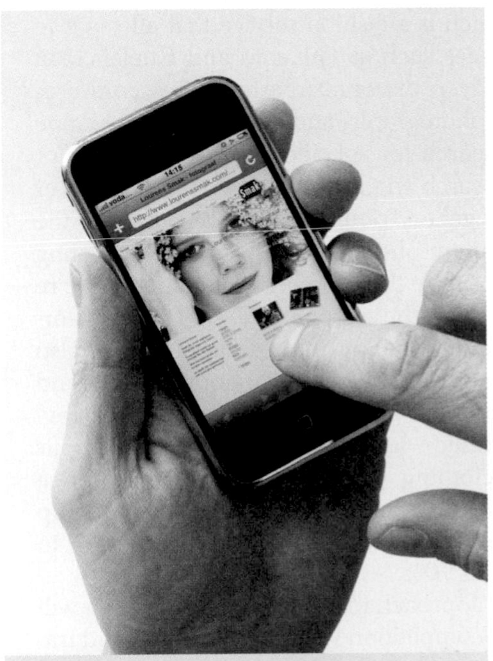

Apple's iPhone 4 claims that it changes everything, again. Boasting the revolutionary FaceTime app and HD video, Steve Jobs may not be exaggerating. Need one in your hot little hands? Get ready to fork over $200–$300.

The growth stage ends and the *maturity stage* begins when market demand peaks because most customers have already bought the product (there are relatively few first-time buyers left). At this stage, demand is typically replacement demand. In the PC market, for example, people who already have a PC trade up to a more powerful model. The iPod is currently in this stage; its users decide whether or not to trade up to a more powerful version that offer greater capabilities. Products such as laptops and smartphones and services such as Internet broadband and digital TV services are currently in this stage.

Once demand for a product starts to fall, the *decline stage* begins; this typically occurs when advancing IT leads to the development of a more advanced product, making the old one obsolete, such as when the iPod destroyed Sony's Walkman franchise. In general, demand for every generation of a digital device such as a PC, cell phone, or MP3 music player falls off when the current leaders' technology is superseded by new products that incorporate the most recent IT advances. For example, 3G or 4G smartphones and tablet computers with broadband capability permit superfast Web browsing and downloading of videos, books, and all kinds of digital media. Thus one reason the IT revolution has been so important for managers is that advances in IT are one of the most significant determinants of the length of a product's life cycle, and therefore of competition in an industry.[19] In more and more industries advances in IT are shortening product life cycles as customers jump on the latest fad or fashion–such as the iPad in 2010. Will iPad technology hurt Amazon.com's Kindle book reader, which was the leader in book downloading and reading in 2009? In the clothing industry, which also has a short product life cycle because of quickly changing customer tastes, IT makes it possible to introduce new fashions much more quickly–or dispose of outdated clothing, as the following "Information Technology Byte" feature discusses.

Information Technology Byte

eBay Uses IT to Develop New Ways to Sell Out-of-Fashion Clothing

eBay Inc. is the world's largest online clothing seller; every year it sells millions of articles of new and used clothing in all shapes and sizes–it sold $7.1 billion worth of clothing in 2009 to over 10 million buyers. Until now the merchandise provided by its sellers has determined the choice of clothing it can offer its customers. And with an average of 20 million listings in the clothing category, eBay's site can be hard to navigate and search, which makes it difficult for customers to find what they want. Recognizing its growing problems in April 2010, eBay announced a major new initiative to drive up its online clothing sales.

eBay planned to launch a new fashion "microsite," Fashion.ebay.com, and work with the major fashion brands and clothing makers to sell their overstocked merchandise. It has already worked out contracts with companies such as Hugo Boss, Donna Karan, and Zara to act as sellers in what essentially will be an online outlet mall, and eBay hopes to encourage all major clothing brands to join its initiative. Currently, to dispose of their excess inventory, clothing makers set up their own bricks-and-mortar stores in outlet malls or sell to discount retail stores.

eBay's new microsite will offer several new ways of selling to customers online. It has developed "flash sales," which are sales of a small selection of fashion merchandise for only short periods to encourage buyers to purchase quickly. In March 2010 it also launched "Fashion Vault," which is a fashion service that allows it to compete with online private sales companies such as Gilt.com and Ruelala.com to sell trendy clothing and accessories at deep discounts. Fashion.ebay.com uses a selling format that employs gallery-style photographs and a better search engine that will make it easier for customers to search for specific styles of fashion. For example, its new IT features an improved search engine to allow shoppers to better find brands, fashion trends, and prices; its gallery photographs let buyers see the items they are interested in–but also offer them photographs of similar competing products to improve their buying experience. "We're really transforming the experience," said Lorrie Norrington, president of eBay marketplaces, which also include such e-commerce sites as Shopping.com and Kijiji and accounted for 61% of the company's revenue of $8.7 billion last year. "We're playing to our strengths" in clothing, she said.[20] In 2010 fixed-price selling accounted for over half of eBay's revenues, up from 35% two years ago, and Norrington expects it to grow as much as 70%.

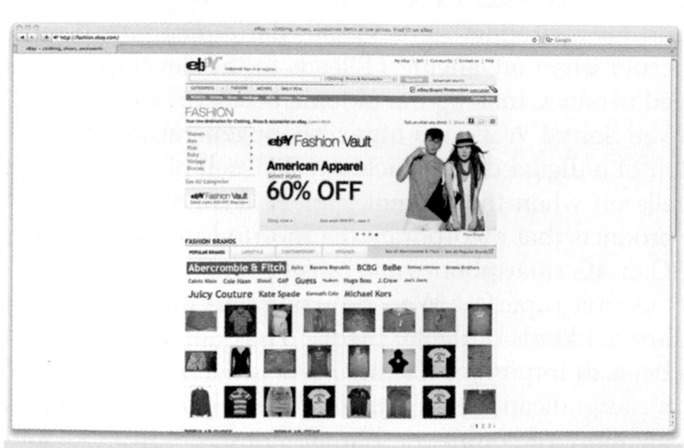

eBay's Fashion Vault Web site is just one of the IT initiatives the company is rolling out in order to compete with other online fashion retailers.

eBay's new approach to online fashion retailing will put it in direct competition with Amazon.com and traditional retailers. The company plans to transfer all the IT innovations it has made to develop and launch its fashion microsite into other product categories, including home and garden, technology, and media, to increase sales. So far, early signs from its big push into fashion have been positive. According to eBay managers, many clothing makers have expressed interest in its new outlet mall because they see the site as a more efficient way to get rid of excess inventory in the clothing market–where the life cycles of fashions are very short, often only months, so that cost savings from fast inventory turnaround are substantial.

The message for managers is clear: The shorter a product's life cycle because of advancing IT, the more important it is to innovate products quickly and continuously. A PC company that cannot develop a new and improved product line every three to six months will soon find itself in trouble. Increasingly managers are trying to outdo their rivals by being the first to market with a product that incorporates some advance in IT, such as advanced stability or steering control that prevents vehicle wrecks.[21] In sum, the tumbling price of information brought about by advances in IT is at the heart of the IT revolution. So how can managers use all this computing power to their advantage?

The Network of Computing Power

The tumbling price of computing power and applications has allowed all kinds of organizations, large and small, to invest more to develop a network of computer servers. Companies can buy networks of server racks that are customized with the mix of hardware and software applications that best meets the needs of their current value chain management activities. The typical organizationwide computing **network** that has emerged over time is a four-tier network solution that consists of "external" PDAs such as netbooks, smartphones, and tablet computers, connected to desktops and laptops, and then through "internal" rack servers to a company's mainframe (see Figure 18.3). Through wireless and wired communication an employee with the necessary permissions can hook into a company's IT system from any location–in the office, at home, on a boat, on the beach, in the air–anywhere a wireless or wired link can be established.

network Interlinked computers that exchange information.

The internal network is composed of "client" desktop and laptop PCs connected by Ethernet to the company's system of rack servers. The client computers that are linked directly to a server constitute a *local area network* (LAN), and most companies have many LANs–for example, one in every division and function. Large companies that need immense processing power have a mainframe computer at the center or hub of the network that can quickly process vast amounts of information, issue commands, and coordinate computing devices at the other levels. The mainframe can also handle electronic communications between servers and PCs situated in different LANs, and the mainframe can connect to the mainframes of other companies. The mainframe is the master computer that controls the operations of all the other types of computers and digital devices as needed and can link them into one integrated system. It also provides the connection to the *external* IT networks outside the organization; for example, it gives a user access to an organization's cloud computing services–but with high security and reliability and only from recognized and protected computing devices. For instance, a manager with a PDA or PC hooked into a four-tier system can access data and software stored in the local server, in the mainframe, or through the Internet to a cloud-based computing solution hosted by an outsourcer whose B&M database might be located anywhere in the world.

Just as computer hardware has been advancing rapidly, so has computer software. *Operating system software* tells the computer hardware how to run. *Applications software,* such as programs for word processing, spreadsheets, graphics, and database management, is developed for a specific task or use. The increase in the power of computer hardware has allowed software developers to write increasingly powerful programs that are also increasingly user-friendly. By harnessing the rapidly growing power of microprocessors, applications software has vastly increased the ability of managers to acquire, organize, and transmit information. In doing so, it also has improved the

Figure 18.3
A Four-Tier Information System with Cloud Computing

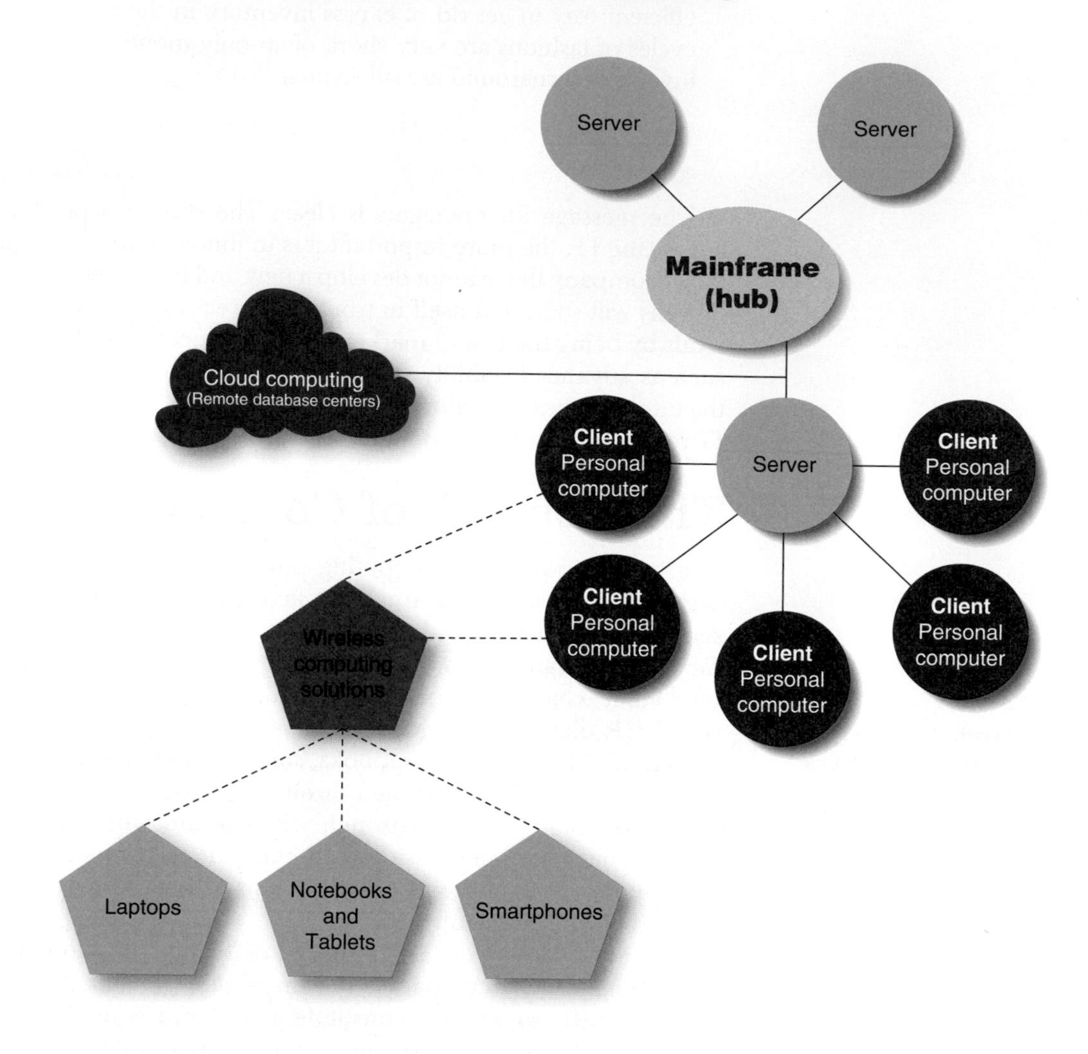

ability of managers to coordinate and control the activities of their organization and to make better decisions, as discussed earlier.

Types of Management Information Systems

LO18-4 Differentiate among seven performance-enhancing kinds of management information systems.

Advances in IT have continuously increased managers' ability to obtain the information they need to make better decisions and coordinate and control organizational resources. Next we discuss six types of management information systems (MIS) that have been particularly helpful to managers as they perform their management tasks: transaction-processing systems, operations information systems, decision support systems, expert systems, enterprise resource planning systems, and e-commerce systems (see Figure 18.4). These MIS systems are arranged along a continuum according to the sophistication of the IT they are based on–IT that determines their ability to give managers the information they need to make nonprogrammed decisions. (Recall from Chapter 7 that nonprogrammed decision making occurs in response to unusual, unpredictable opportunities and threats.) We examine each of these systems after focusing on the management information system that preceded them all: the organizational hierarchy.

Figure 18.4
Six Computer-Based Management Information Systems

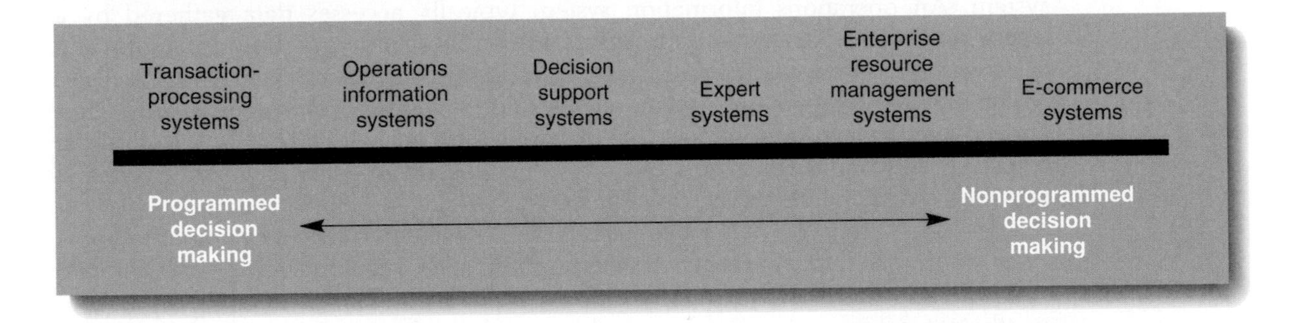

The Organizational Hierarchy: The Traditional Information System

Traditionally managers have used the organizational hierarchy as the main way to gather the information necessary to make decisions and coordinate and control organizational activities (see Chapter 10 for a detailed discussion of organizational structure and hierarchy).

Although hierarchy is a useful information system, it has several drawbacks, as we noted in Chapter 10. First, when too many layers of managers exist it takes a long time for information and requests to travel up the hierarchy and for decisions and answers to travel back down. The slow communication can reduce the timeliness and usefulness of the information and prevent a quick response to changing market conditions.[22] Second, information can be distorted as it moves from one layer of management to another, and information distortion reduces the quality of information.[23] Third, managers have only a limited span of control; so as an organization grows larger and its hierarchy lengthens, more managers must be hired, and this makes the hierarchy an expensive information system. The popular idea that companies with tall management hierarchies are bureaucratic and unresponsive to the needs of their customers arises from the inability of tall hierarchies to effectively process data and give managers timely, complete, relevant, and high-quality information. The management hierarchy is still the best information system available today–the one that results in the best decisions–*if* managers have access to the other kinds of MIS systems discussed next.

Transaction-Processing Systems

transaction-processing system A management information system designed to handle large volumes of routine, recurring transactions.

A **transaction-processing system** is an MIS designed to handle large volumes of routine, recurring transactions (see Figure 18.4). Transaction-processing systems began to appear in the early 1960s with the advent of commercially available mainframe computers. They were the first type of computer-based IT adopted by many organizations, and today they are commonplace. Bank managers use a transaction-processing system to record deposits into, and payments out of, bank accounts. Supermarket managers use a transaction-processing system to record the sale of items and to track inventory levels. More generally, most managers in large organizations use a transaction-processing system to handle tasks such as payroll preparation and payment, customer billing, and payment of suppliers.

operations information system A management information system that gathers, organizes, and summarizes comprehensive data in a form that managers can use in their nonroutine coordinating, controlling, and decision-making tasks.

Operations Information Systems

Many types of MIS followed hard on the heels of transaction-processing systems in the 1960s as companies like IBM advanced IT. An **operations information system** is an MIS that gathers comprehensive data, organizes them, and summarizes them in a form that is of value to managers. Whereas a transaction-processing system processes routine transactions, an operations information system gives managers information they can use in their nonroutine coordinating, controlling, and decision-making tasks. Most operations information systems are coupled with a transaction-processing system. An operations information system typically accesses data gathered by a transaction-processing system, processes those data into useful information, and organizes that information into a form accessible to managers. Managers often use an operations information system to get sales, inventory, accounting, and other performance-related information. For example, the information that T. J. Rodgers at Cypress Semiconductors gets about individual employee goals and performance is provided by an operations information system.

DHL uses technology extensively to track packages. Allowing a customer to know exactly where to find a package when approximately 1.5 billion packages are shipped to 120,000 locations around the world can be difficult. Thus, the company is constantly introducing new technology such as the ability for drivers to send the information scanned immediately onto cellular networks where it goes to the main computer rather than the industry standard of scanning information into a storage device that is later downloaded. The generation of extensive information on packages, however, also generates extensive information on the performance of its employees. Thus, the firm can judge with great accuracy the time for all pickups and the efficiency of its drivers. The firm's technology emphasis similarly allows managers to track how quickly customer service can answer a call, and number of calls handled per hour. As a result, the technology not only helps in addressing the immediate task at hand but also alerts managers to problems such as an underperforming employee or unit so that the manager can intervene to help solve problems.

Decision Support Systems

decision support system An interactive computer-based management information system that managers can use to make nonroutine decisions.

A **decision support system** provides computer-built models that help managers make better nonprogrammed decisions.[24] Recall from Chapter 7 that nonprogrammed decisions are those that are relatively unusual or novel, such as decisions to invest in new productive capacity, develop a new product, launch a new promotional campaign, enter a new market, or expand internationally. Whereas an operations information system organizes important information for managers, a decision support system gives managers model-building capability and the chance to manipulate information in a variety of ways. Managers might use a decision support system to help them decide whether to cut prices for a product. The decision support system might contain models of how customers and competitors would respond to a price cut. Managers could run these models and use the results as an *aid* to decision making.

The stress on the word *aid* is important–in the final analysis a decision support system is not meant to make decisions for managers. Rather, its function is to give managers valuable information they can use to improve the quality of their decisions. A good example of a sophisticated decision support system, one developed by Judy Lewent, the first woman to become the chief financial officer of a major U.S. company, is profiled in the following "Manager as a Person" box.

Manager as a Person

How Judy Lewent Became One of the Most Powerful Women in Corporate America

With annual sales of over $27 billion, Merck is one of the world's largest developers and marketers of advanced pharmaceuticals.[25] The company spends over $3 billion a year on R&D to develop new drugs–an expensive and difficult process

Judy Lewent's Research Planning Model has allowed Merck to more strategically develop promising new drugs while avoiding pitfalls, thus sharpening the company's focus and allowing it to roll out such programs as an HIV/AIDS prevention initiative in China, pictured here.

that is fraught with risks. Most new drug ideas fail to make it through the development process. It takes an average of $300 million and 10 years to bring a new drug to market, and 7 out of 10 new drugs fail to make a profit for the developing company.

Given the costs, risks, and uncertainties involved in the new drug development process, Judy Lewent, the former director of capital analysis at Merck, decided to develop a decision support system that could help managers make more effective R&D investment decisions. Her aim was to give Merck's top managers the information they needed to evaluate proposed R&D projects on a case-by-case basis. The system that Lewent and her staff developed is referred to in Merck as the "Research Planning Model."[26] At the heart of this decision support system is a sophisticated model. The input variables to the model include data on R&D spending, manufacturing costs, selling costs, and demand conditions. The relationships among the input variables are modeled by several equations that factor in the probability of a drug's making it through the development process and to market. The outputs of this modeling process are the revenues, cash flows, and profits that a project might generate.

The model Lewent developed did not use a single value for an input variable, nor did it compute a single value for each output. Rather, a range is specified for each input variable (such as high, medium, and low R&D spending); then the computer randomly samples repeatedly from the range of values for each input variable to produce a probability distribution of values for each output. So, for example, instead of reporting that a proposed R&D project will yield a profit of $500 million, the decision support system produces a probability distribution. It might state that although $500 million is the most likely profit, there is a 25% chance that the profit will be less than $300 million and a 25% chance that it will be greater than $700 million.

Merck used Lewent's decision support system to evaluate all its proposed R&D investment decisions; of course, in recent years as IT advances have become commonplace, it has improved upon and refined her system. But Lewent's reward for her innovation was promotion to the chief financial officer of Merck, and she became one of the most powerful women in corporate America.

Most decision support systems are geared toward aiding middle managers in the decision-making process. For example, a loan manager at a bank might use a decision support system to evaluate the credit risk involved in lending money to a particular client. Rarely does a top manager use a decision support system. One reason for this is that most electronic management information systems have not yet become sophisticated enough to handle effectively the ambiguous types of problems facing top managers. To improve this situation, IT experts have been developing a variant of the decision support system: an executive support system.

executive support system A sophisticated version of a decision support system that is designed to meet the needs of top managers.

An **executive support system** is a sophisticated version of a decision support system that is designed to meet the needs of top managers. One defining characteristic of executive support systems is user-friendliness. Many of them include simple pull-down menus to take a manager through a decision analysis problem. Moreover, they may contain stunning graphics and other visual and interactive features to encourage top managers to use them.[27] Increasingly, executive support systems are used to link top managers virtually so they can function as a team; this type of executive support system is called a **group decision support system.**

group decision support system An executive support system that links top managers so they can function as a team.

Ultimately top managers' intuition, judgment, and integrity will always be needed to decide whether to pursue the course of action suggested by an MIS. There are always many different issues to be factored into a decision, not least of which are its ethical implications.

Artificial Intelligence and Expert Systems

artificial intelligence Behavior performed by a machine that, if performed by a human being, would be called "intelligent."

expert system A management information system that employs human knowledge, embedded in a computer, to solve problems that ordinarily require human expertise.

Artificial intelligence has been defined as behavior by a machine that, if performed by a human being, would be called "intelligent."[28] Artificial intelligence has already made it possible to write programs that can solve problems and perform simple tasks. For example, software programs variously called *software agents, softbots,* or *knowbots* can be used to perform simple managerial tasks such as sorting through reams of data or incoming e-mail messages to look for important ones. The interesting feature of these programs is that from "watching" a manager sort through such data they can "learn" what his or her preferences are. Having done this, they can take over some of this work from the manager, freeing time for the manager to work on other tasks. Most of these programs are still in the development stage, but they may be commonplace within a decade.[29]

Expert systems, the most advanced management information systems available, incorporate artificial intelligence in their design.[30] An **expert system** is a system that employs human knowledge, embedded in computer software, to solve problems that ordinarily require human expertise.[31] Mimicking human expertise (and intelligence) requires IT that can at a minimum (1) recognize, formulate, and solve a problem; (2) explain the solution; and (3) learn from experience.

Artificial intelligence takes to the boards. Chess expert Garry Kasparov squares off against IBM's chess-playing computer Deep Blue. In 1997 Deep Blue and Kasparov traded wins, ending in a decisive victory for the computer—after it had been reprogrammed.

Recent developments in artificial intelligence that go by names such as "fuzzy logic" and "neural networks" have resulted in computer programs that, in a primitive way, try to mimic human thought processes. Although artificial intelligence is still at an early stage of development, an increasing number of business applications are beginning to emerge in the form of expert systems.

Enterprise Resource Planning Systems

To achieve high performance, it is not sufficient just to develop an MIS inside each of a company's functions or divisions to provide better information and knowledge. It is also vital that managers in the different functions and divisions have access to information about the activities of managers in other functions and divisions. The greater the flow of information and knowledge among functions and divisions, the more learning can take place, and this builds a company's stock of knowledge and expertise. This knowledge and expertise are the source of its competitive advantage and profitability.

enterprise resource planning (ERP) systems Multimodule application software packages that coordinate the functional activities necessary to move products from the design stage to the final customer stage.

In the last 25 years, another revolution has taken place in IT as software companies have worked to develop enterprise resource planning systems, which essentially incorporate most MIS aspects just discussed, as well as much more. **Enterprise resource planning (ERP) systems** are multimodule application software packages that allow a company to link and coordinate the entire set of functional activities and operations necessary to move products from the initial design stage to the final customer stage. Essentially ERP systems (1) help each individual function improve its functional-level skills and (2) improve integration among all functions so they work together to build a competitive advantage for the company. Today choosing and designing an ERP system to improve how a company operates is the biggest challenge facing the IT function inside a company. To understand why almost every large global company has installed an ERP system in the last few decades, it is necessary to return to the concept of the value chain, introduced in Chapter 8.

Recall that a company's value chain is composed of the sequence of functional activities that are necessary to make and sell a product. The value chain idea focuses attention on the fact that each function, in sequence, performs its activities to add or contribute value to a product. After one function has made its contribution, it hands the product over to the next function, which makes its own contribution, and so on down the line.

The primary activity of marketing, for example, is to uncover new or changing customer needs or new groups of customers and then decide what kinds of products should be developed to appeal to those customers. It shares or "hands off" its information to product development, where engineers and scientists work to develop and design the new products. In turn, manufacturing and materials management work to find ways to make the new products as efficiently as possible. Then sales is responsible for finding the best way to convince customers to buy these products.

The value chain is useful in demonstrating the sequence of activities necessary to bring products to the market successfully. In an IT context, however, it suggests the enormous amount of information and communication that needs to link and coordinate the activities of all the various functions. Installing an ERP system for a large company can cost tens of millions of dollars. The following "Information Technology Byte" feature discusses the ERP system designed and sold by the German IT company SAP.

Information Technology Byte

SAP's ERP System

SAP, the world's leading supplier of ERP software, introduced the world's first ERP system in 1973. So great was the demand for its software that it had to train thousands of consultants from companies like IBM, HP, Accenture, and Cap Gemini to install and customize its software to meet the needs of companies in different industries throughout the world. Why?

SAP's ERP was demanded by companies because it can manage all the stages of the value chain, and strengthen them both individually and jointly when they work together. SAP's software has modules specifically devoted to each of a company's core functional activities. Each module contains a set of "best practices," the optimum way to perform a specific functional activity that increases efficiency, quality, innovation, and responsiveness to customers. SAP's ERP is therefore "the expert system of expert systems." SAP claims that when a company reconfigures its IT system to make SAP's software work, it can achieve productivity gains of 30% to 50%, which amounts to many billions of dollars of savings for large companies.[32]

For each function in the value chain, SAP installs its software module on a function's LAN. Each function then inputs its data into that module in the way specified by SAP. For example, the sales function inputs all the information about customer needs required by SAP's sales module, and the materials management function inputs information about the product specifications it requires from suppliers into SAP's materials management module. These modules give functional managers real-time feedback on ongoing developments in their particular functional activity, such as daily changes in sales of leading products. Each SAP module functions as an expert system that can reason through the information functional employees continually input into it through their laptops or other computers. It recommends new strategies that managers can use to improve functional operations. However, the magic of ERP does not stop there.

SAP's ERP software also connects across functions. Managers in all functions have access to other functions' expert systems, and SAP's software is designed to alert managers when their functional activities will be affected by changes taking place in another function. Thus SAP's ERP system lets managers across the organization better coordinate their activities–a major source of competitive advantage. Moreover, SAP software on corporate mainframe computers takes the information from all the different functional and divisional expert systems and creates a companywide ERP system that shows top managers an overview of the operations of the whole company.

In sum, SAP's ERP system creates a sophisticated top-level expert system that can reason through the huge volume of information provided by the company's functions. It can recognize and diagnose common problems and issues in that information and develop and recommend organizationwide solutions for those problems. Using this information, top managers can improve the fit between their strategies and the changing environment.

As an example of how an ERP system works, let's examine how SAP's software helps managers coordinate their activities to speed product development. Suppose marketing has discovered some new unmet customer need, has suggested what kind of product needs to be developed, and forecasts that the demand for the product will be 40,000 units a year. With SAP's IT, engineers in product development use their expert system to work out how to design the new product in a way that builds in quality at the lowest possible cost. Manufacturing managers, watching product development's progress, work simultaneously to find the best way to make the product, and thus use their expert system to find out how to keep operating costs at a minimum.

Remember that SAP's IT gives all the other functions access to this information; they can tap into what is going on between marketing and manufacturing in real time. So materials management managers watching manufacturing make its plans can simultaneously plan how to order supplies of inputs or components from global suppliers or how and when to ship the final product to customers to keep costs at a minimum. At the same time, HRM is tied into the ERP system and uses its expert system to forecast the type and cost of the labor that will be required to carry out the activities in the other functions–for example, the number of manufacturing employees who will be required to make the product or the number of salespeople who will be needed to sell the product to achieve the 40,000 sales forecast.

How does this build competitive advantage and profitability? First, it speeds up product development; companies can bring products to market much more quickly, thereby generating higher sales revenues. Second, SAP's IT focuses on how to drive down operating costs while keeping quality high. Third, SAP's IT is oriented toward the final customer; its CRM module watches how customers respond to the new product and then feeds back this information quickly to the other functions.

To see what this means in practice, let's jump ahead three months and suppose that the CRM component of SAP's ERP software reports that actual sales are 20% below target. Further, the software has reasoned that the problem is occurring because the product lacks a crucial feature that customers want. The product is a smartphone, for example, and customers demand a built-in digital camera. Sales decides this issue deserves major priority and alerts managers in all the other functions about the problem. Now managers can begin to decide how to manage this unexpected situation.

Engineers in product development, for example, use their expert system to work out how much it would cost, and how long it would take, to modify the product so it includes the missing feature, the digital camera, that customers require. Managers in other functions watch the engineers' progress through the ERP system and can make suggestions for improvement. In the meantime, manufacturing managers know about the slow sales and have already cut back on production to avoid a buildup of the unsold product in the company's warehouse. They are also planning how to phase out this product and introduce the next version, with the digital camera, to keep costs as low as possible. Similarly, materials management managers are contacting digital camera makers to find out how much such a camera will cost and when it can be supplied. Meanwhile marketing managers are researching how they missed this crucial product feature and are developing new sales forecasts to estimate demand for the modified product. They announce a revised sales forecast of 75,000 units of the modified product.

It takes the engineers one month to modify the product; but because SAP's IT has been providing information about the modified product to managers in manufacturing and materials management, the product reaches the market only two months later. Within weeks, the sales function reports that early sales figures for the product have greatly exceeded even marketing's revised forecast. The company knows it has a winning product, and top managers give the go-ahead for manufacturing to build a second production line to double production of the product. All the other functions are expecting this decision; in fact, they have already been experimenting with their SAP modules to find out how long it will take them to respond to such a move. Each function gives the others its latest information so they can all adjust their functional activities accordingly.

This quick and responsive action is possible because of the ERP system that gives a company better control of its manufacturing and materials management activities. Quality is increased because a greater flow of information between functions allows a better-designed product. Innovation is speeded because a company can rapidly change its products to suit the needs of customers. Finally, responsiveness to customers improves because using its CRM software module, sales can better manage and react to customers' changing needs and provide better service and support to back up the sales of the product. ERP's ability to promote competitive advantage is the reason why managers in so many companies, large and small, are moving to find the best ERP solution for their particular companies.

e-commerce Trade that takes place between companies, and between companies and individual customers, using IT and the Internet.

business-to-business (B2B) commerce Trade that takes place between companies using IT and the Internet to link and coordinate the value chains of different companies.

B2B marketplace An Internet-based trading platform set up to connect buyers and sellers in an industry.

business-to-customer (B2C) commerce Trade that takes place between a company and individual customers using IT and the Internet.

E-Commerce Systems

E-commerce is trade that takes place between companies, and between companies and individual customers, using IT and the Internet. **Business-to-business (B2B) commerce** is trade that takes place between companies using IT and the Internet to link and coordinate the value chains of different companies. (See Figure 18.5.) The goal of B2B commerce is to increase the profitability of making and selling goods and services. B2B commerce increases profitability because it lets companies reduce operating costs and may improve product quality. A principal B2B software application is **B2B marketplaces,** which are Internet-based trading platforms that have been set up in many industries to connect buyers and sellers. To participate in a B2B marketplace, companies adopt a common software standard that allows them to search for and share information with one another. Then companies can work together over time to find ways to reduce costs or improve quality.

Business-to-customer (B2C) commerce is trade that takes place between a company and individual customers using IT and the Internet. Using IT to connect directly to the customer means companies can avoid having to use intermediaries, such as wholesalers and retailers, who capture a significant part of the profit in the value chain. The use of Web sites and online stores also lets companies give their customers much more information about the value of their products. This often allows them to attract more customers and thus generate higher sales revenues.

In the 2000s computer software makers, including Microsoft, Oracle, SAP, and IBM, have rushed to make their products work seamlessly with the Internet to respond to global companies' growing demand for e-commerce software. Previously their software was configured to work only on a particular company's intranet; today

Figure 18.5
Types of E-Commerce

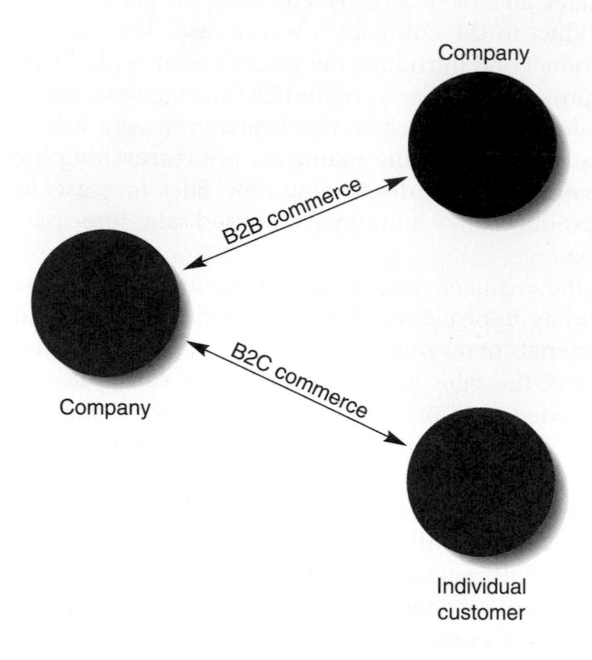

their software must be able to network a company's IT systems to other companies, such as their suppliers and distributors.

The challenge facing managers now is to select e-commerce software that allows seamless exchange of information between companies anywhere in the world. The stakes are high because global competitive advantage goes to the company first with a major new technological advance. For example, SAP rushed to update its ERP modules to allow transactions over the Internet, and today all its modules have full Internet capability. However, Oracle, IBM, and many small specialist companies have also developed ways to provide advanced Internet applications at a lower price, so SAP faces increased global competition.

In summary, by using advanced types of MIS, managers have more control over a company's activities and operations and can work to improve its competitive advantage and profitability. Today the IT function is becoming increasingly important because IT managers select which kind of hardware and software a company will use and then train other functional managers and employees how to use it.

LO18-5 Explain how IT is helping managers build strategic alliances and network structures to increase efficiency and effectiveness.

The Impact and Limitations of Information Technology

Advances in IT and management information systems are having important effects on managers and organizations. By improving the ability of managers to coordinate and control the activities of the organization and by helping managers make more effective decisions, modern IT has become a central component of any organization's structure. And evidence that IT can be a source of competitive advantage is growing; organizations that do not adopt leading-edge IT are likely to be at a competitive disadvantage. In this section we examine how the rapid advances in IT are affecting organizational structure and competitive advantage. We also examine problems associated with implementing management information systems effectively, as well as the limitations of MIS.

Strategic Alliances, B2B Network Structures, and IT

strategic alliance An agreement in which managers pool or share their organization's resources and know-how with a foreign company, and the two organizations share the rewards and risks of starting a new venture.

B2B network structure A series of global strategic alliances that an organization creates with suppliers, manufacturers, and distributors to produce and market a product.

Recently, increasing globalization and the use of new IT have brought about two innovations that are sweeping through U.S. and European companies: electronically managed strategic alliances and B2B network structures. A **strategic alliance** is a formal agreement that commits two or more companies to exchange or share their resources in order to produce and market a product.[33] Most commonly, strategic alliances are formed because the companies share similar interests and believe they can benefit from cooperating. For example, global carmakers such as Honda have formed many strategic alliances with particular suppliers of inputs such as car axles, gearboxes, and air-conditioning systems. Over time these car companies work closely with their suppliers to improve the efficiency and effectiveness of the inputs so that the final product–the car produced–is of higher quality and often can be produced at lower cost. Honda have also established alliances with many different global suppliers because both companies now make several car models that are assembled and sold in many countries around the world.

Throughout the 1990s, the growing sophistication of IT with global intranets and teleconferencing made it much easier to manage strategic alliances and allow managers to share information and cooperate. One outcome of this has been the growth of strategic alliances into an IT-based network structure. A **B2B network structure** is a formal series of global strategic alliances that one or several organizations create with suppliers, manufacturers, and distributors to produce and market a product. Network structures allow an organization to manage its global value chain in order to find new ways to reduce costs and increase the quality of products–without incurring the high costs of operating a complex organizational structure (such as the costs of employing many managers). More and more U.S. and European companies are relying on global network structures to gain access to low-cost foreign sources of inputs, as discussed in Chapter 6. Shoemakers such as Nike and Adidas are two companies that have used this approach extensively.

Nike is the largest and most profitable sports shoe manufacturer in the world. The key to Nike's success is the network structure that Nike founder and CEO Philip Knight created to allow his company to produce and market shoes. As noted in Chapter 8, the most successful companies today are trying to pursue simultaneously a low-cost and a differentiation strategy. Knight decided early that to do this at Nike he needed to focus his company's efforts on the most important functional activities, such as product design and engineering, and leave the others, such as manufacturing, to other organizations.

By far the largest function at Nike's headquarters is the design and engineering function, whose members pioneered innovations in sports shoe design such as the air pump and Air Jordans that Nike introduced so successfully. Designers use computer-aided design (CAD) to design Nike shoes, and they electronically store all new product information, including manufacturing instructions. When the designers have finished their work, they electronically transmit the blueprints for the new products to a network of Southeast Asian suppliers and manufacturers with which Nike has formed strategic alliances.[34] Instructions for the design of a new sole may be sent to a supplier in Taiwan; instructions for the leather uppers, to a supplier in Malaysia. The suppliers produce the shoe parts and send them for final assembly to a manufacturer in China with which Nike has established another strategic alliance. From China the shoes are shipped to distributors throughout the world. Ninety-nine percent of the over 100 million pairs of shoes that Nike makes each year are made in Southeast Asia.

This network structure gives Nike two important advantages. First, Nike can quickly respond to changes in sports shoe fashion. Using its global IT system, Nike literally can change the instructions it gives each of its suppliers overnight, so that within a few weeks its foreign manufacturers are producing new kinds of shoes.[35] Any alliance partners that fail to perform up to Nike's standards are replaced with new partners through the regular B2B marketplace.

Second, Nike's costs are low because wages in Southeast Asia are a fraction of what they are in the North America, and this difference gives Nike a low-cost advantage. Also, Nike's ability to outsource and use foreign manufacturers to produce all its shoes abroad allows Knight to keep the organization's U.S. structure flat and flexible. Nike can use a relatively inexpensive functional structure to organize its activities.

The use of network structures is increasing rapidly as organizations recognize the many opportunities they offer to reduce costs and increase organizational flexibility. The push to lower costs has led to the development of B2B marketplaces in which most or all of the companies in an industry (for example, carmakers) use the same software platform to link to each other and establish industry specifications and standards. Then these companies jointly list the quantity and specifications of the inputs they require and invite bids from the thousands of potential suppliers around the world. Suppliers also use the same software platform, so electronic bidding, auctions, and transactions are possible between buyers and sellers around the world. The idea is that high-volume standardized transactions can help drive down costs at the industry level. Also, quality will increase as these relationships become more stable as a B2B network structure develops.

Flatter Structures and Horizontal Information Flows

Rapid advances in IT have been associated with a "delayering" (flattening) of the organizational hierarchy, a move toward greater decentralization and horizontal information flows within organizations, and the concept of the boundaryless organization.[36] By electronically giving managers high-quality, timely, relevant, and relatively complete information, modern management information systems have reduced the need for tall management hierarchies.

Modern IT has reduced the need for a hierarchy to function as a means of coordinating and controlling organizational activities. Also, by reducing the need for hierarchy, modern IT can directly increase an organization's efficiency because fewer employees are required to perform organizational activities.

The ability of IT to flatten structure and facilitate the flow of horizontal information between employees has led many researchers and consultants to popularize the idea of a **boundaryless organization.** Such an organization is composed of people linked by IT–computers, faxes, computer-aided design systems, and video teleconferencing–who may rarely, if ever, see one another face-to-face. People are utilized when their services are needed, but they are not formal members of an organization; they are functional experts who form an alliance with an organization, fulfill their contractual obligations, and then move on to the next project.

boundaryless organization An organization whose members are linked by computers, faxes, computer-aided design systems, and video teleconferencing and who rarely, if ever, see one another face-to-face.

Large consulting companies, such as Accenture and McKinsey & Co., use their global consultants in this way. Consultants are connected by laptops to an organization's **knowledge management system**–its company-specific virtual information system that systematizes the knowledge of its employees and facilitates the sharing and integrating of expertise within and between functions and divisions through real-time, interconnected IT. Knowledge management systems let employees share their knowledge and expertise and give them virtual access to other employees who have the expertise to solve the problems they encounter as they perform their jobs.

knowledge management system A company-specific virtual information system that systematizes the knowledge of its employees and facilitates the sharing and integrating of their expertise.

Despite their usefulness, IT in general and management information systems in particular have some limitations. A serious potential problem is that in all the enthusiasm for MIS, communication via computer networks might lose the vital human element of communication. There is a strong argument that electronic communication should support face-to-face communication rather than replacing it. For example, it would be wrong to make a judgment about an individual's performance merely by "reading the numbers" provided by an MIS. Instead the numbers should be used to alert managers to individuals who may have a performance problem. The nature of this problem should then be explored in a face-to-face meeting, during which more detailed information can be gathered. One drawback of using IT, such as e-mail and teleconferencing, is that employees may spend too much time watching their computer screens and communicating electronically–and little time interacting directly with other employees.[37] If this occurs, important and relevant information may not be obtained because of the lack of face-to-face contact, and the quality of decision making may fall. As the following "Management Insight" box suggests, the experience of George Lucas and his high-tech digital media illustrates how IT must be woven with personal face-to-face contact to get the most performance-enhancing benefits.

Management Insight

The *Star Wars* Studio Reorganizes

The *Star Wars* movies are some of the best known in the world, and George Lucas, the director who writes and produces them, is famous for pioneering special effects. But in the 2000s competition from other special effects companies intensified, and there is a huge market for new video games; thus pressure is increasing on all companies to make the best use of their resources. So what do you do if you manage a special effects company that has many different units staffed by talented engineers who are so distant from each other that they have no incentive to cooperate and share their knowledge? This was the problem confronting CEO Lucas and Micheline Chua, the president and COO of Lucas Arts: how to better use the talents of their creative digital artists and engineers who worked autonomously–often connected to their coworkers mainly by videoconferencing systems.[38]

George Lucas with a pair of storm troopers from *Star Wars*. Lucas's special effects studio faced real challenges in getting his company's digital artists and special effects crews to work together to compete in the video game industry.

By 2008 Lucas and Chau realized they were losing valuable synergies between their various groups. They especially needed to make more use of the Industrial Light & Magic (ILM) Group, the unit responsible for the special effects behind the *Star Wars* movies and many other movies whose directors rely on its services to make their state-of-the-art special effects. How do you make different groups cooperate, especially when they each contain hundreds of talented design artists who value their autonomy and are proud of their own achievements?

The answer for Lucas was to build a new state-of-the-art $250 million office complex in the Presidio, a former army base and now a national park that has spectacular views of San Francisco Bay. In this modernistic, futuristic building everything–its rooms, facilities, and recreational areas–has been designed to facilitate communication and cooperation between people, but especially between different units.[39] Both the ILM and Lucas Arts units have been thrust together, for example, and their members who now work face-to-face have been told to build a common digital platform that will allow each unit to learn from and take advantage of the skills and knowledge of the other. To increase its performance, Lucas Arts needs these experts to collaborate to develop the state-of-the-art movies, and especially video games, on which its future profitability depends. Indeed, the gaming market is booming in the 2000s as the Nintendo Wii and its competitors compete to develop games that customers want, and these often rely on state-of-the-art graphics that only companies like Lucas can produce.

Apparently both units have learned to work together and take advantage of the open, inviting lounges and work areas where designers can meet personally to share their skills and knowledge. One recent result of their cooperation was the video game *Star Wars: The Force Unleashed.* The gaming group credits the ILM group with providing the technology for the incredible lighting, facial, and movement effects that have made the game so popular. Who knows what might happen as the members of these units develop the personal relationships and networks necessary to create the next generation of digital technology for movies and gaming? One result has been the special effects in the blockbuster *Iron Man 2* movie in 2010.

Summary and Review

LO18-1, 18-2 **INFORMATION AND THE MANAGER'S JOB** Computer-based IT is central to the operation of most organizations. By giving managers high-quality, timely, relevant, and relatively complete information, properly implemented IT can improve managers' ability to coordinate and control the operations of an organization and to make effective decisions. Moreover, IT can help the organization attain a competitive advantage through its beneficial impact on productivity, quality, innovation, and responsiveness to customers. Thus modern IT is an indispensable management tool.

LO18-3 **THE IT REVOLUTION** Over the last 30 years there have been rapid advances in the power, and rapid declines in the cost, of IT. Falling prices, wireless communication, computer networks, and software developments have all radically improved the power and efficacy of computer-based IT.

LO18-4 **TYPES OF MANAGEMENT INFORMATION SYSTEMS** Traditionally managers used the organizational hierarchy as the main system for gathering the information they needed to coordinate and control the organization and to make effective decisions. Today managers use six main types of computer-based information systems. Listed in ascending order of sophistication, they are transaction-processing systems, operations information systems, decision support systems, expert systems, enterprise resource planning systems, and e-commerce systems.

LO18-5 **THE IMPACT AND LIMITATIONS OF IT** Modern IT has changed organizational structure in many ways. Using IT, managers can create electronic strategic alliances and form a B2B network structure. A network structure, based on some shared form of IT, can be formed around one company, or a number of companies can join together to create an industry B2B network. Modern IT also makes organizations flatter and encourages more horizontal cross-functional communication. As this increasingly happens across the organizational boundary, the term *boundaryless organizations* has been coined to refer to virtual organizations whose members are linked electronically.

Management in Action

Topics for Discussion and Action

Discussion

1. To be useful, information must be of high quality, be timely, be relevant, and be as complete as possible. Why does a tall management hierarchy, when used as a management information system, have negative effects on these desirable attributes? **[LO18-1]**
2. What is the relationship between IT and competitive advantage? **[LO18-2]**
3. Because of the growth of high-powered, low-cost wireless communications and IT such as videoconferencing, many managers soon may not need to come into the office to do their jobs. They will be able to work at home. What are the pros and cons of such an arrangement? **[LO18-3, 18-4]**
4. Many companies have reported that it is difficult to implement advanced management information systems such as ERP systems. Why do you think this is so? How might the roadblocks to implementation be removed? **[LO18-4]**
5. How can IT help in the new product development process? **[LO18-4]**
6. Why is face-to-face communication between managers still important in an organization? How will face-to-face communication be different around the world? Will technology impact such communication differently in various settings? How? **[LO18-4, 18-5]**

Action

7. Ask a manager to describe the main kinds of IT that he or she uses on a routine basis at work. **[LO18-1, 18-4]**
8. Compare the pros and cons of using a network structure to perform organizational activities versus performing all activities in-house or within one organizational hierarchy. **[LO18-3, 18-4, 18-5]**
9. What are the advantages and disadvantages of business-to-business networks? **[LO18-5]**

Building Management Skills

Analyzing Management Information Systems [LO18-3, 18-4]

Choose an organization about which you have some direct knowledge. It may be an organization you worked for in the past or are in contact with now (such as the college or school you attend). For this organization, answer the following questions:

1. Describe the management information systems that are used to coordinate and control organizational activities and to help make decisions.
2. Do you think that the organization's existing MIS gives managers high-quality, timely, relevant, and relatively complete information? Why or why not?
3. How might advanced IT improve the competitive position of this organization? In particular, try to identify the impact that a new MIS might have on the organization's efficiency, quality, innovation, and responsiveness to customers.

Managing Ethically [LO18-1, 18-2]

The use of management information systems, such as ERPs, often gives employees access to confidential information from all functions and levels of an organization. Employees can see important information about the company's products that is of great value to competitors. As a result, many companies monitor employees' use of the intranet and Internet to prevent an employee from acting unethically, such as by selling this information to competitors. On the other hand, with access to this information employees might discover that their company has been engaging in unethical or even illegal practices.

Questions

1. Ethically speaking, how far should a company go to protect its proprietary information, given that it needs to also protect the privacy of its employees? What steps can it take?
2. When is it ethical for employees to give information about a company's unethical or illegal practices to a third party, such as a newspaper or government agency?

Small Group Breakout Exercise

Using New Management Information Systems [LO18-2, 18-4]

Form groups of three or four people, and appoint one member as the spokesperson who will communicate your findings to the class when called on by the instructor. Then discuss the following scenario:

You are a team of managing partners of a large management consulting company. You are responsible for auditing your firm's MIS to determine whether it is appropriate and up to date. To your surprise, you find that although your organization has a wireless e-mail system in place and consultants are connected into a powerful local area network (LAN) at all times, most of the consultants (including partners) are not using this technology. It seems that most important decision making still takes place through the organizational hierarchy.

Given this situation, you are concerned that your organization is not exploiting the opportunities offered by new IT to obtain a competitive advantage. You have discussed this issue and are meeting to develop an action plan to get consultants to appreciate the need to learn about and use the new IT.

1. What advantages can you tell consultants they will obtain when they use the new IT?
2. What problems do you think you may encounter in convincing consultants to use the new IT?
3. What steps might you take to motivate consultants to learn to use the new technology?

Exploring the World Wide Web [LO18-2, 18-5]

Go to DHL's Web site (the specific page is http://www.dhl.com/en/mail/mail_essentials/dm_guide/case_studies.html). Scroll through the featured case studies. Read about how DHL used its IT and logistics systems to help companies and answer the following questions:

1. What are the main ways in which DHL can use its IT and logistics skills to help its clients?
2. In what specific ways does DHL's IT help these companies improve their efficiency, quality, innovation, and responsiveness to customers as well as the companies' performance?

Be the Manager [LO18-4]

You are one of the managers of a small specialty maker of custom tables, chairs, and cabinets. You have been charged with finding ways to use IT and the Internet to identify new business opportunities that can improve your company's competitive advantage, such as ways to reduce costs or attract customers.

Questions

1. What are the various forces in a specialty furniture maker's task environment that have the most effect on its performance?
2. What kinds of IT or MIS can help the company better manage these forces?
3. In what ways can the Internet help this organization improve its competitive position?

Notes

Chapter 1

1. www.apple.com, 2010.
2. Ibid.
3. G. R. Jones, *Organizational Theory, Design, and Change* (Upper Saddle River, NJ: Pearson, 2008).
4. J. P. Campbell, "On the Nature of Organizational Effectiveness," in P. S. Goodman, J. M. Pennings, et al., *New Perspectives on Organizational Effectiveness* (San Francisco: Jossey-Bass, 1977).
5. M. J. Provitera, "What Management Is: How It Works and Why It's Everyone's Business," *Academy of Management Executive* 17 (August 2003), 152–54.
6. H. Fayol, *General and Industrial Management* (New York: IEEE Press, 1984). Fayol actually identified five different managerial tasks, but most scholars today believe these four capture the essence of Fayol's ideas.
7. P. F. Drucker, *Management Tasks, Responsibilities, and Practices* (New York: Harper & Row, 1974).
8. www.apple.com, press release, 2003.
9. G. McWilliams, "Lean Machine–How Dell Fine-Tunes Its PC Pricing to Gain Edge in a Slow Market," *The Wall Street Journal*, June 8, 2001, A1.
10. R. H. Guest, "Of Time and the Foreman," *Personnel* 32 (1955), 478–86.
11. L. Hill, *Becoming a Manager: Mastery of a New Identity* (Boston: Harvard Business School Press, 1992).
12. Ibid.
13. H. Mintzberg, "The Manager's Job: Folklore and Fact," *Harvard Business Review*, July–August 1975, 56–62.
14. H. Mintzberg, *The Nature of Managerial Work* (New York: Harper & Row, 1973).
15. J. Kotter, *The General Managers* (New York: Free Press, 1992).
16. C. P. Hales, "What Do Managers Do? A Critical Review of the Evidence," *Journal of Management Studies*, January 1986, 88–115; A. I. Kraul, P. R. Pedigo, D. D. McKenna, and M. D. Dunnette, "The Role of the Manager: What's Really Important in Different Management Jobs," *Academy of Management Executive*, November 1989, 286–93.
17. A. K. Gupta, "Contingency Perspectives on Strategic Leadership," in D. C. Hambrick, ed., *The Executive Effect: Concepts and Methods for Studying Top Managers* (Greenwich, CT: JAI Press, 1988), 147–78.
18. D. G. Ancona, "Top Management Teams: Preparing for the Revolution," in J. S. Carroll, ed., *Applied Social Psychology and Organizational Settings* (Hillsdale, NJ: Erlbaum, 1990); D. C. Hambrick and P. A. Mason, "Upper Echelons: The Organization as a Reflection of Its Top Managers," *Academy of Management Journal* 9 (1984), 193–206.
19. T. A. Mahony, T. H. Jerdee, and S. J. Carroll, "The Jobs of Management," *Industrial Relations* 4 (1965), 97–110; L. Gomez-Mejia, J. McCann, and R. C. Page, "The Structure of Managerial Behaviors and Rewards," *Industrial Relations* 24 (1985), 147–54.
20. W. R. Nord and M. J. Waller, "The Human Organization of Time: Temporal Realities and Experiences," *Academy of Management Review* 29 (January 2004), 137–40.
21. R. L. Katz, "Skills of an Effective Administrator," *Harvard Business Review*, September–October 1974, 90–102.
22. Ibid.
23. P. Tharenou, "Going Up? Do Traits and Informal Social Processes Predict Advancing in Management," *Academy of Management Journal* 44 (October 2001), 1005–18.
24. C. J. Collins and K. D. Clark, "Strategic Human Resource Practices, Top Management Team Social Networks, and Firm Performance: The Role of Human Resource Practices in Creating Organizational Competitive Advantage," *Academy of Management Journal* 46 (December 2003), 740–52.
25. R. Stewart, "Middle Managers: Their Jobs and Behaviors," in J. W. Lorsch, ed., *Handbook of Organizational Behavior* (Englewood Cliffs, NJ: Prentice-Hall, 1987), 385–91.
26. S. C. de Janasz, S. E. Sullivan, and V. Whiting, "Mentor Networks and Career Success: Lessons for Turbulent Times," *Academy of Management Executive* 17 (November 2003), 78–92.
27. K. Labich, "Making Over Middle Managers," *Fortune*, May 8, 1989, 58–64.
28. B. Wysocki, "Some Companies Cut Costs Too Far, Suffer from Corporate Anorexia," *The Wall Street Journal*, July 5, 1995, A1.
29. www.dell.com, 2008, 2010.
30. A. Shama, "Management under Fire: The Transformation of Management in the Soviet Union and Eastern Europe," *Academy of Management Executive* 10 (1993), 22–35.
31. www.apple.com, 2010; www.nike.com, 2010.
32. K. Seiders and L. L. Berry, "Service Fairness: What It Is and Why It Matters," *Academy of Management Executive* 12 (1998), 8–20.
33. T. Donaldson, "Editor's Comments: Taking Ethics Seriously–A Mission Now More Possible," *Academy of Management Review* 28 (July 2003), 363–67.
34. C. Anderson, "Values-Based Management," *Academy of Management Executive* 11 (1997), 25–46.
35. W. H. Shaw and V. Barry, *Moral Issues in Business*, 6th ed. (Belmont, CA: Wadsworth, 1995); T. Donaldson, *Corporations and Morality* (Englewood Cliffs, NJ: Prentice-Hall, 1982).

Chapter 2

1. A. Smith, *The Wealth of Nations* (London: Penguin, 1982).
2. Ibid., 110.
3. J. G. March and H. A. Simon, *Organizations* (New York: Wiley, 1958).
4. L. W. Fry, "The Maligned F. W. Taylor: A Reply to His Many Critics," *Academy of Management Review* 1 (1976), 124–29.
5. F. W. Taylor, *Shop Management* (New York: Harper, 1903); F. W. Taylor, *The Principles of Scientific Management* (New York: Harper, 1911).
6. J. A. Litterer, *The Emergence of Systematic Management as Shown by the Literature from 1870–1900* (New York: Garland, 1986).
7. H. R. Pollard, *Developments in Management Thought* (New York: Crane, 1974).
8. D. Wren, *The Evolution of Management Thought* (New York: Wiley, 1994), 134.
9. F. B. Gilbreth, *Primer of Scientific Management* (New York: Van Nostrand Reinhold, 1912).
10. F. B. Gilbreth Jr. and E. G. Gilbreth, *Cheaper by the Dozen* (New York: Crowell, 1948).
11. D. Roy, "Efficiency and the Fix: Informal Intergroup Relations in a Piece Work Setting," *American Journal of Sociology* 60 (1954), 255–66.
12. M. Weber, *From Max Weber: Essays in Sociology*, ed. H. H. Gerth and C. W. Mills (New York: Oxford University Press, 1946); M. Weber, *Economy and Society*, ed. G. Roth and C. Wittich (Berkeley: University of California Press, 1978).
13. C. Perrow, *Complex Organizations*, 2nd ed. (Glenview, IL: Scott, Foresman, 1979).
14. Weber, *From Max Weber*, 331.
15. See Perrow, *Complex Organizations*, chap. 1, for a detailed discussion of these issues.

16. H. Fayol, *General and Industrial Management* (New York: IEEE Press, 1984).
17. Ibid., 79.
18. T. J. Peters and R. H. Waterman Jr., *In Search of Excellence: Lessons from America's Best-Run Companies* (New York: Harper & Row, 1982).
19. R. E. Eccles and N. Nohira, *Beyond the Hype: Rediscovering the Essence of Management* (Boston: Harvard Business School Press, 1992).
20. L. D. Parker, "Control in Organizational Life: The Contribution of Mary Parker Follett," *Academy of Management Review* 9 (1984), 736–45.
21. P. Graham, *M. P. Follett–Prophet of Management: A Celebration of Writings from the 1920s* (Boston: Harvard Business School Press, 1995).
22. M. P. Follett, *Creative Experience* (London: Longmans, 1924).
23. E. Mayo, *The Human Problems of Industrial Civilization* (New York: Macmillan, 1933); F. J. Roethlisberger and W. J. Dickson, *Management and the Worker* (Cambridge: Harvard University Press, 1947).
24. D. W. Organ, "Review of *Management and the Worker,* by F. J. Roethlisberger and W. J. Dickson," *Academy of Management Review* 13 (1986), 460–64.
25. D. Roy, "Banana Time: Job Satisfaction and Informal Interaction," *Human Organization* 18 (1960), 158–61.
26. For an analysis of the problems in distinguishing cause from effect in the Hawthorne studies and in social settings in general, see A. Carey, "The Hawthorne Studies: A Radical Criticism," *American Sociological Review* 33 (1967), 403–16.
27. D. McGregor, *The Human Side of Enterprise* (New York: McGraw-Hill, 1960).
28. Ibid., 48.
29. Peters and Waterman, *In Search of Excellence.*
30. J. Pitta, "It Had to Be Done and We Did It," *Forbes,* April 26, 1993, 148–52.
31. Press release, www.hp.com, June 2001.
32. T. Dewett and G. R. Jones, "The Role of Information Technology in the Organization: A Review, Model, and Assessment," *Journal of Management* 27 (2001), 313–46.
33. W. E. Deming, *Out of the Crisis* (Cambridge: MIT Press, 1986).
34. J. D. Thompson, *Organizations in Action* (New York: McGraw-Hill, 1967).
35. D. Katz and R. L. Kahn, *The Social Psychology of Organizations* (New York: Wiley, 1966); Thompson, *Organizations in Action.*
36. T. Burns and G. M. Stalker, *The Management of Innovation* (London: Tavistock, 1961); P. R. Lawrence and J. R. Lorsch, *Organization and Environment* (Boston: Graduate School of Business Administration, Harvard University, 1967).
37. Burns and Stalker, *The Management of Innovation.*
38. C. W. L. Hill and G. R. Jones, *Strategic Management: An Integrated Approach,* 8th ed. (Florence, KY: Cengage, 2010).
39. J. Bohr, "Deadly Roses," *The Battalion,* February 13, 2006, 3.

Chapter 3

1. J. M. Digman, "Personality Structure: Emergence of the Five-Factor Model," *Annual Review of Psychology* 41 (1990), 417–40; R. R. McCrae and P. T. Costa, "Validation of the Five-Factor Model of Personality across Instruments and Observers," *Journal of Personality and Social Psychology* 52 (1987), 81–90; R. R. McCrae and P. T. Costa, "Discriminant Validity of NEO-PIR Facet Scales," *Educational and Psychological Measurement* 52 (1992), 229–37.
2. Digman, "Personality Structure"; McCrae and Costa, "Validation of the Five-Factor Model"; McCrae and Costa, "Discriminant Validity"; R. P. Tett and D. D. Burnett, "A Personality Trait-Based Interactionist Model of Job Performance," *Journal of Applied Psychology* 88, no. 3 (2003), 500–17; J. M. George, "Personality, Five-Factor Model," in S. Clegg and J. R. Bailey, eds., *International Encyclopedia of Organization Studies* (Thousand Oaks, CA: Sage, 2007).
3. L. A. Witt and G. R. Ferris, "Social Skills as Moderator of Conscientiousness–Performance Relationship: Convergent Results across Four Studies," *Journal of Applied Psychology* 88, no. 5 (2003), 809–20; M. J. Simmering, J. A. Colquitte, R. A. Noe, and C. O. L. H. Porter, "Conscientiousness, Autonomy Fit, and Development: A Longitudinal Study," *Journal of Applied Psychology* 88, no. 5 (2003), 954–63.
4. M. R. Barrick and M. K. Mount, "The Big Five Personality Dimensions and Job Performance: A Meta-Analysis," *Personnel Psychology* 44 (1991), 1–26; S. Komar, D. J. Brown, J. A. Komar, and C. Robie, "Faking and the Validity of Conscientiousness: A Monte Carlo Investigation," *Journal of Applied Psychology* 93 (2008), 140–54.
5. Digman, "Personality Structure"; McCrae and Costa, "Validation of the Five-Factor Model"; McCrae and Costa, "Discriminant Validity."
6. E. McGirt, "The Dirtiest Mind in Business: How Filth Met Opportunity and Created a Franchise," *Fast Company* 122 (February 2008), 64, www.fastcompany.com/magazine/122/the-dirtiest-mind-in-business_Printer_Friendl . . . , January 23, 2008; Dirty Jobs: About the Show; Discovery Channel, "Get Down and Dirty," http://dsc.discovery.com/fansites/dirtyjobs/about/about-print.html, February 3, 2010.
7. J. Brockner, *Self-Esteem at Work* (Lexington, MA: Lexington Books, 1988).
8. D. C. McClelland, *Human Motivation* (Glenview, IL: Scott, Foresman, 1985); D. C. McClelland, "How Motives, Skills, and Values Determine What People Do," *American Psychologist* 40 (1985), 812–25; D. C. McClelland, "Managing Motivation to Expand Human Freedom," *American Psychologist* 33 (1978), 201–10.
9. D. G. Winter, *The Power Motive* (New York: Free Press 1973).
10. M. J. Stahl, "Achievement, Power, and Managerial Motivation: Selecting Managerial Talent with the Job Choice Exercise," *Personnel Psychology* 36 (1983), 775–89; D. C. McClelland and D. H. Burnham, "Power Is the Great Motivator," *Harvard Business Review* 54 (1976), 100–10.
11. R. J. House, W. D. Spangler, and J. Woycke, "Personality and Charisma in the U.S. Presidency: A Psychological Theory of Leader Effectiveness," *Administrative Science Quarterly* 36 (1991), 364–96.
12. G. H. Hines, "Achievement, Motivation, Occupations and Labor Turnover in New Zealand," *Journal of Applied Psychology* 58 (1973), 313–17; P. S. Hundal, "A Study of Entrepreneurial Motivation: Comparison of Fast- and Slow-Progressing Small Scale Industrial Entrepreneurs in Punjab, India," *Journal of Applied Psychology* 55 (1971), 317–23.
13. M. Rokeach, *The Nature of Human Values* (New York: Free Press 1973).
14. Rokeach, *The Nature of Human Values.*
15. Rokeach, *The Nature of Human Values.*
16. K. K. Spors, "Top Small Workplaces 2007: Gentle Giant Moving," *The Wall Street Journal,* October 1, 2007, R4–R5; "Gentle Giant Sees Revenue Boost, *Boston Business Journal,* January 15, 2008, www.gentlegiant.com/news-011508-1.htm, February 5, 2008; Company History: Gentle Giant Moving Company, "Company History," http://www.gentlegiant.com/history.php, February 3, 2010; "Massachusetts Moving Company Gentle Giant Moving Company Celebrates 30 Years in Operation," January 25, 2010, http://www.gentlegiant.com/press/press20100125.php, February 3, 2010.

17. Spors, "Top Small Workplaces 2007: Gentle Giant Moving."
18. Spors, "Top Small Workplaces 2007: Gentle Giant Moving."
19. Spors, "Top Small Workplaces 2007: Gentle Giant Moving."
20. Spors, "Top Small Workplaces 2007: Gentle Giant Moving"; "Gentle Giant Receives Top Small Workplace Award," www.gentlegiant.com/topsmallworkplace.htm, January 5, 2008; "Corporate Overview," http://www.gentlegiant.com/company.php, February 3, 2010.
21. Spors, "Top Small Workplaces 2007: Gentle Giant Moving."
22. Spors, "Top Small Workplaces 2007: Gentle Giant Moving."
23. A. P. Brief, *Attitudes In and Around Organizations* (Thousand Oaks, CA: Sage, 1998).
24. P. S. Goodman, "U.S. Job Losses in December Dim Hopes for Quick Upswing," *The New York Times*, http://www.nytimes.com/2010/01/09/business/economy/09jobs.html?pagewanted=print, February 3, 2010; U.S. Bureau of Labor Statistics, Economic News Release Employment Situations Summary, http://data.bls.gov/cgi-bin/print.pl/news.release/empsit.nr0.htm, February 3, 2010; B. Steverman, "Layoffs: Short-Term Profits, Long-Term Problems," *BusinessWeek*, http://www.businessweek.com/print/investor/content/jan2010/pi20100113_133780.htm, February 3, 2010.
25. J. M. George and A. P. Brief, "Feeling Good–Doing Good: A Conceptual Analysis of the Mood at Work–Organizational Spontaneity Relationship," *Psychological Bulletin* 112 (1992), 310–29.
26. W. H. Mobley, "Intermediate Linkages in the Relationship between Job Satisfaction and Employee Turnover," *Journal of Applied Psychology* 62 (1977), 237–40.
27. C. Hymowitz, "Though Now Routine, Bosses Still Stumble during Layoff Process," *The Wall Street Journal*, June 25, 2007, B1; J. Brockner, "The Effects of Work Layoffs on Survivors: Research, Theory and Practice," in B. M. Staw and L. L. Cummings, eds., *Research in Organizational Behavior*, vol. 10 (Greenwich, CT: JAI Press, 1988), 213–55.
28. J. E. Mathieu and D. M. Zajac, "A Review and Meta-Analysis of the Antecedents, Correlates, and Consequences of Organizational Commitment," *Psychological Bulletin* 108 (1990), 171–94.
29. D. Watson and A. Tellegen, "Toward a Consensual Structure of Mood," *Psychological Bulletin* 98 (1985), 219–35.
30. Watson and Tellegen, "Toward a Consensual Structure of Mood."
31. J. M. George, "The Role of Personality in Organizational Life: Issues and Evidence," *Journal of Management* 18 (1992), 185–213.
32. H. A. Elfenbein, "Emotion in Organizations: A Review and Theoretical Integration," in J. P. Walsh and A. P. Brief, eds., *The Academy of Management Annals*, vol. 1 (New York: Lawrence Erlbaum Associates, 2008), 315–86.
33. J. P. Forgas, "Affect in Social Judgments and Decisions: A Multi-Process Model," in M. Zanna, ed., *Advances in Experimental and Social Psychology*, vol. 25 (San Diego, CA: Academic Press, 1992), 227–75; J. P. Forgas and J. M. George, "Affective Influences on Judgments and Behavior in Organizations: An Information Processing Perspective," *Organizational Behavior and Human Decision Processes* 86 (2001), 3–34; J. M. George, "Emotions and Leadership: The Role of Emotional Intelligence," *Human Relations* 53 (2000), 1027–55; W. N. Morris, *Mood: The Frame of Mind* (New York: Springer-Verlag, 1989).
34. George, "Emotions and Leadership."
35. J. M. George and K. Bettenhausen, "Understanding Prosocial Behavior, Sales Performance, and Turnover: A Group Level Analysis in a Service Context," *Journal of Applied Psychology* 75 (1990), 698–709.
36. George and Brief, "Feeling Good–Doing Good"; J. M. George and J. Zhou, "Understanding When Bad Moods Foster Creativity and Good Ones Don't: The Role of Context and Clarity of Feelings," paper presented at the Academy of Management Annual Meeting, 2001; A. M. Isen and R. A. Baron, "Positive Affect as a Factor in Organizational Behavior," in B. M. Staw and L. L. Cummings, eds., *Research in Organizational Behavior*, vol. 13 (Greenwich, CT: JAI Press, 1991), 1–53.
37. J. M. George and J. Zhou, "Dual Tuning in a Supportive Context: Joint Contributions of Positive Mood, Negative Mood, and Supervisory Behaviors to Employee Creativity," *Academy of Management Journal*, 50 (2007), 605–22; J. M. George, "Creativity in Organizations," in J. P. Walsh and A. P. Brief, eds., *The Academy of Management Annals*, vol. 1 (New York: Lawrence Erlbaum Associates, 2008), 439–77.
38. J. D. Greene, R. B. Sommerville, L. E. Nystrom, J. M. Darley, and J. D. Cohen, "An FMRI Investigation of Emotional Engagement in Moral Judgment," *Science*, September 14, 2001, 2105–08; L. Neergaard, "Brain Scans Show Emotions Key to Resolving Ethical Dilemmas," *Houston Chronicle*, September 14, 2001, 13A.
39. George and Zhou, "Dual Tuning in a Supportive Context."
40. George and Zhou, "Dual Tuning in a Supportive Context."
41. R. C. Sinclair, "Mood, Categorization Breadth, and Performance Appraisal: The Effects of Order of Information Acquisition and Affective State on Halo, Accuracy, Informational Retrieval, and Evaluations," *Organizational Behavior and Human Decision Processes* 42 (1988), 22–46.
42. D. Goleman, *Emotional Intelligence* (New York: Bantam Books, 1994); J. D. Mayer and P. Salovey, "The Intelligence of Emotional Intelligence," *Intelligence* 17 (1993), 433–42; J. D. Mayer and P. Salovey, "What Is Emotional Intelligence?" in P. Salovey and D. Sluyter, eds., *Emotional Development and Emotional Intelligence: Implications for Education* (New York: Basic Books, 1997); P. Salovey and J. D. Mayer, "Emotional Intelligence," *Imagination, Cognition, and Personality* 9 (1989–1990), 185–211.
43. S. Epstein, *Constructive Thinking* (Westport, CT: Praeger, 1998).
44. "Leading by Feel," *Inside the Mind of the Leader*, January 2004, 27–37.
45. P. C. Early and R. S. Peterson, "The Elusive Cultural Chameleon: Cultural Intelligence as a New Approach to Intercultural Training for the Global Manger," *Academy of Management Learning and Education* 3, no. 1 (2004), 100–15.
46. George, "Emotions and Leadership"; S. Begley, "The Boss Feels Your Pain," *Newsweek*, October 12, 1998, 74; D. Goleman, *Working with Emotional Intelligence* (New York: Bantam Books, 1998).
47. J. Bercovici, "Remembering Bernie Goldhirsh," www.medialifemagazine.com/news2003/jun03/jun30/4_thurs/news1thursday.html, April 15, 2004.
48. B. Burlingham, "Legacy: The Creative Spirit," *INC.*, September 2003, 11–12.
49. Burlingham, "Legacy: The Creative Spirit"; "Inc. magazine," www.inc.com/magazine, May 28, 2006.
50. Burlingham, "Legacy: The Creative Spirit"; "Inc. magazine," www.inc.com/magazine, May 28, 2006; www.inc.com, February 5, 2008.
51. "Leading by Feel," *Inside the Mind of the Leader*, January 2004, 27–37.
52. George, "Emotions and Leadership."
53. J. Zhou and J. M. George, "Awakening Employee Creativity: The Role of Leader Emotional Intelligence," *Leadership Quarterly* 14 (2003), 545–68.

54. A. Jung, "Leading by Feel: Seek Frank Feedback," *Inside the Mind of the Leader,* January 2004, 31.
55. J. B. Sørensen, "The Strength of Corporate Culture and the Reliability of Firm Performance," *Administrative Science Quarterly* 47 (2002), 70–91.
56. "Personality and Organizational Culture," in B. Schneider and D. B. Smith, eds., *Personality and Organizations* (Mahway, NJ: Lawrence Erlbaum, 2004), 347–69; J. E. Slaughter, M. J. Zickar, S. Highhouse, and D. C. Mohr, "Personality Trait Inferences about Organizations: Development of a Measure and Assessment of Construct Validity," *Journal of Applied Psychology* 89, no. 1 (2004), 85–103.
57. T. Kelley, *The Art of Innovation: Lessons in Creativity from IDEO, America's Leading Design Firm* (New York: Random House, 2001).
58. "Personality and Organizational Culture."
59. B. Schneider, "The People Make the Place," *Personnel Psychology* 40 (1987), 437–53.
60. "Personality and Organizational Culture."
61. "Personality and Organizational Culture."
62. B. Schneider, H. B. Goldstein, and D. B. Smith, "The ASA Framework: An Update," *Personnel Psychology* 48 (1995), 747–73; J. Schaubroeck, D. C. Ganster, and J. R. Jones, "Organizational and Occupational Influences in the Attraction–Selection–Attrition Process," *Journal of Applied Psychology* 83 (1998), 869–91.
63. Kelley, *The Art of Innovation.*
64. www.ideo.com, February 5, 2008.
65. Kelley, *The Art of Innovation.*
66. "Personality and Organizational Culture."
67. Kelley, *The Art of Innovation.*
68. George, "Emotions and Leadership."
69. Kelley, *The Art of Innovation.*
70. Kelley, *The Art of Innovation.*
71. D. C. Feldman, "The Development and Enforcement of Group Norms," *Academy of Management Review* 9 (1984), 47–53.
72. G. R. Jones, *Organizational Theory, Design, and Change* (Upper Saddle River, NJ: Prentice-Hall, 2003).
73. H. Schein, "The Role of the Founder in Creating Organizational Culture," *Organizational Dynamics* 12 (1983), 13–28.
74. S. Covel, "Telemarketer Bucks High Turnover Trend," *The Wall Street Journal,* November 19, 2007, B4; "Ryla History & Culture!" www.rylateleservices.com/print.asp?level=2&id=166, January 24, 2008.
75. Covel, "Telemarketer Bucks High Turnover Trend."
76. Covel, "Telemarketer Bucks High Turnover Trend"; "Ryla History & Culture!"; Ryla, Inc., "Outsourced Customer Contact Center Solutions, about us," "The RYLA Difference," http://ryla.com/difference.html, February 5, 2010.
77. Covel, "Telemarketer Bucks High Turnover Trend"; Ryla, Inc., "Outsourced Customer Contact Center Solutions, about us," "The RYLA Difference," http://ryla.com/difference.html, February 5, 2010.
78. "Company Culture," www.rylateleservices.com/print.asp?level=2&id=98, January 24, 2008.
79. Covel, "Telemarketer Bucks High Turnover Trend."
80. Covel, "Telemarketer Bucks High Turnover Trend."
81. "A Great Career Is Waiting for You at Ryla," www.rylateleservices.com/print.asp?level=1&id=13, January 25, 2008.
82. Covel, "Telemarketer Bucks High Turnover Trend."
83. Covel, "Telemarketer Bucks High Turnover Trend."
84. "Ryla Named by The Wall Street Journal and Winning Workplaces as a Top Small Workplace in US," October 1, 2007, www.rylateleservices.com/print.asp?level=2&id=168, January 24, 2008.
85. "Ryla Named by The Wall Street Journal and Winning Workplaces as a Top Small Workplace in US."
86. Covel, "Telemarketer Bucks High Turnover Trend."
87. J. M. George, "Personality, Affect, and Behavior in Groups," *Journal of Applied Psychology* 75 (1990), 107–16.
88. J. Van Maanen, "Police Socialization: A Longitudinal Examination of Job Attitudes in an Urban Police Department," *Administrative Science Quarterly* 20 (1975), 207–28.
89. www.intercotwest.com/Disney; M. N. Martinez, "Disney Training Works Magic," *HRMagazine,* May 1992, 53–57.
90. P. L. Berger and T. Luckman, *The Social Construction of Reality* (Garden City, NY: Anchor Books, 1967).
91. H. M. Trice and J. M. Beyer, "Studying Organizational Culture through Rites and Ceremonials," *Academy of Management Review* 9 (1984), 653–69.
92. Kelley, *The Art of Innovation.*
93. H. M. Trice and J. M. Beyer, *The Cultures of Work Organizations* (Englewood Cliffs, NJ: Prentice-Hall, 1993).
94. Kelley, *The Art of Innovation.*
95. www.ibm.com; IBM Investor Relations–Corporate Governance, Executive Officers, "Executive Officers," http://www.ibm.com/investor/governance/executive-officers.wss, February 5, 2010.
96. K. E. Weick, *The Social Psychology of Organization* (Reading, MA: Addison Wesley, 1979).
97. B. McLean and P. Elkind, *The Smartest Guys in the Room: The Amazing Rise and Scandalous Fall of Enron* (New York: Penguin Books, 2003); R. Smith and J. R. Emshwiller, *24 Days: How Two Wall Street Journal Reporters Uncovered the Lies That Destroyed Faith in Corporate America* (New York: HarperCollins, 2003); M. Swartz and S. Watkins, *Power Failure: The Inside Story of the Collapse of ENRON* (New York: Doubleday, 2003).

Chapter 4

1. www.fda.org, press release, 2009.
2. Ibid.
3. B. J. Blackledge and S. Lindsey, "Peanut Plant Owner Becomes Recluse after Outbreak," ap.com, February 19, 2009.
4. A. E. Tenbrunsel, "Misrepresentation and Expectations of Misrepresentation in an Ethical Dilemma: The Role of Incentives and Temptation," *Academy of Management Journal* 41 (June 1998), 330–40.
5. www.yahoo.com, 2003; www.mci.com, 2004.
6. J. Child, "The International Crisis of Confidence in Corporations," *Academy of Management Executive* 16 (August 2002), 145–48.
7. T. Donaldson, "Editor's Comments: Taking Ethics Seriously–A Mission Now More Possible," *Academy of Management Review* 28 (July 2003), 463–67.
8. R. E. Freeman, *Strategic Management: A Stakeholder Approach* (Marshfield, MA: Pitman, 1984).
9. J. A. Pearce, "The Company Mission as a Strategic Tool," *Sloan Management Review,* Spring 1982, 15–24.
10. C. I. Barnard, *The Functions of the Executive* (Cambridge, MA: Harvard University Press, 1948).
11. Freeman, *Strategic Management.*
12. J. Perry, L. Di Leo, and S. Meichtry, "Mass Cuts of Temp Workers Pose a Tough Test for Europe," *The Wall Street Journal,* March 12, 2009, accessed at http://online.wsj.com/article/SB123680920862100627.html.
13. P. S. Adler, "Corporate Scandals: It's Time for Reflection in Business Schools," *Academy of Management Executive* 16 (August 2002), 148–50.

14. W. G. Sanders and D. C. Hambrick, "Swinging for the Fences: The Effects of CEO Stock Options on Company Risk Taking and Performance," *Academy of Management Journal* 53, no. 5 (2007), 1055–78.
15. "The Green Machine," *Newsweek,* March 21, 2005, E8–E10.
16. www.wholefoodsmarket.com, 2010.
17. "John Mackey's Blog: 20 Questions with Sunni's Salon," www.wholefoodsmarket.com, 2006.
18. Ibid.
19. T. L. Beauchamp and N. E. Bowie, eds., *Ethical Theory and Business* (Englewood Cliffs, NJ: Prentice-Hall, 1979); A. MacIntyre, *After Virtue* (South Bend, IN: University of Notre Dame Press, 1981).
20. R. E. Goodin, "How to Determine Who Should Get What," *Ethics,* July 1975, 310–21.
21. E. P. Kelly, "A Better Way to Think about Business" (book review), *Academy of Management Executive* 14 (May 2000), 127–29.
22. T. M. Jones, "Ethical Decision Making by Individuals in Organizations: An Issue Contingent Model," *Academy of Management Journal* 16 (1991), 366–95; G. F. Cavanaugh, D. J. Moberg, and M. Velasquez, "The Ethics of Organizational Politics," *Academy of Management Review* 6 (1981), 363–74.
23. L. K. Trevino, "Ethical Decision Making in Organizations: A Person–Situation Interactionist Model," *Academy of Management Review* 11 (1986), 601–17; W. H. Shaw and V. Barry, *Moral Issues in Business,* 6th ed. (Belmont, CA: Wadsworth, 1995).
24. T. M. Jones, "Instrumental Stakeholder Theory: A Synthesis of Ethics and Economics," *Academy of Management Review* 20 (1995), 404–37.
25. B. Victor and J. B. Cullen, "The Organizational Bases of Ethical Work Climates," *Administrative Science Quarterly* 33 (1988), 101–25.
26. D. Collins, "Organizational Harm, Legal Consequences and Stakeholder Retaliation," *Journal of Business Ethics* 8 (1988), 1–13.
27. R. C. Soloman, *Ethics and Excellence* (New York: Oxford University Press, 1992).
28. T. E. Becker, "Integrity in Organizations: Beyond Honesty and Conscientiousness," *Academy of Management Review* 23 (January 1998), 154–62.
29. S. W. Gellerman, "Why Good Managers Make Bad Decisions," in K. R. Andrews, ed., *Ethics in Practice: Managing the Moral Corporation* (Boston: Harvard Business School Press, 1989).
30. J. Dobson, "Corporate Reputation: A Free Market Solution to Unethical Behavior," *Business and Society* 28 (1989), 1–5.
31. M. S. Baucus and J. P. Near, "Can Illegal Corporate Behavior Be Predicted? An Event History Analysis," *Academy of Management Journal* 34 (1991), 9–36.
32. Trevino, "Ethical Decision Making in Organizations."
33. A. S. Waterman, "On the Uses of Psychological Theory and Research in the Process of Ethical Inquiry," *Psychological Bulletin* 103, no. 3 (1988), 283–98.
34. M. S. Frankel, "Professional Codes: Why, How, and with What Impact?" *Ethics* 8 (1989), 109–15.
35. J. Van Maanen and S. R. Barley, "Occupational Communities: Culture and Control in Organizations," in B. Staw and L. Cummings, eds., *Research in Organizational Behavior,* vol. 6 (Greenwich, CT: JAI Press, 1984), 287–365.
36. Jones, "Ethical Decision Making by Individuals in Organizations."
37. www.bbc.co.uk, press release, January 10, 2010.
38. A. Soke, "Jimmy Carter Helps Build 1000th and 1001st Home," www.typepad.com, May 22, 2007.
39. www.habitat.org, press release, March 2010.
40. E. Gatewood and A. B. Carroll, "The Anatomy of Corporate Social Response," *Business Horizons,* September–October 1981, 9–16.
41. M. Friedman, "A Friedman Doctrine: The Social Responsibility of Business Is to Increase Its Profits," *New York Times Magazine,* September 13, 1970, 33.
42. P. Engardio and M. Arndt, "What Price Reputation?" www.businessweek.com, July 9, 2007.
43. P. E. Murphy, "Creating Ethical Corporate Structure," *Sloan Management Review,* Winter 1989, 81–87.

Chapter 5

1. Shell International Limited, *Diversity and Inclusiveness at Shell,* Group Diversity and Inclusiveness, 2004, accessed at http://www.shell.com/static/enviro-soc-en/downloads/making_it_happen/our_commitments_and_standards/commitments/shell_diversity.pdf.
2. "Diversity and Inclusion–Environment & Society," Shell *Global home page,* accessed at http://www.shell.com/home/content/environment_society/performance/social/diversity_inclusion/.
3. W. B. Swann, Jr., J. T. Polzer, D. C. Seyle, and S. J. Ko, "Finding Value in Diversity: Verification of Personal and Social Self-Views in Diverse Groups," *Academy of Management Review* 29, no. 1 (2004), 9–27.
4. "Usual Weekly Earnings Summary," *News: Bureau of Labor Statistics,* April 16, 2004 (www.bls.gov/news.release/whyeng.nr0.htm); "Facts on Affirmative Action in Employment and Contracting," *Americans for a Fair Chance,s* January, 28, 2004 (fairchance.civilrights.org/research_center/details.cfm?id=18076); "Household Data Annual Averages," www.bls.gov, April 28, 2004.
5. J. Hempel, "Coming Out in Corporate America," *BusinessWeek,* December 15, 2003, 64, 72.
6. J. Files, "Study Says Discharges Continue under 'Don't Ask, Don't Tell,' " *The New York Times,* March 24, 2004, A14; J. Files, "Gay Ex-Officers Say 'Don't Ask' Doesn't Work," *The New York Times,* December 10, 2003, A14.
7. J. Gutierrez, "John deCourcey Evans, OPUS Hotels Founder, CEO and President," *Passport Magazine, The Insider's Guide to Gay Travel,* Q Communications Inc., accessed at http://www.passportmagazine.com/businessclass/JohnDecourceyEvans875.php.
8. Hempel, "Coming Out in Corporate America"; "DreamWorks Animation SKG Company History," www.dreamworksanimation.com/dwa/opencms/company/history/index.html, May 29, 2006; J. Chng, "Allan Gilmour: Former Vice-Chairman of Ford Speaks on Diversity," www.harbus.org/media/storage/paper343/news/2006/04/18/News/Allan.Gilmour.Former.ViceChairman.Of.Ford.Speaks.On.Diversity-1859600.shtml?nore write200606021800&sourcedomain=www.harbus.org, April 18, 2006.
9. S. E. Needleman, "More Programs Move to Halt Bias against Gays," *The Wall Street Journal,* November 26, 2007, B3.
10. Hempel, "Coming Out in Corporate America."
11. Needleman, "More Programs Move to Halt Bias against Gays."
12. Ibid.
13. "For Women, Weight May Affect Pay," *Houston Chronicle,* March 4, 2004, 12A.
14. V. Valian, *Why So Slow? The Advancement of Women* (Cambridge, MA: MIT Press, 2000).
15. S. T. Fiske and S. E. Taylor, *Social Cognition,* 2d ed. (New York: McGraw-Hill, 1991); Valian, *Why So Slow?*
16. Valian, *Why So Slow?*
17. S. Rynes and B. Rosen, "A Field Survey of Factors Affecting the Adoption and Perceived Success of Diversity

Training," *Personnel Psychology* 48 (1995), 247–70; Valian, *Why So Slow?*

18. V. Brown and F. L. Geis, "Turning Lead into Gold: Leadership by Men and Women and the Alchemy of Social Consensus," *Journal of Personality and Social Psychology* 46 (1984), 811–24; Valian, *Why So Slow?*
19. Valian, *Why So Slow?*
20. J. Cole and B. Singer, "A Theory of Limited Differences: Explaining the Productivity Puzzle in Science," in H. Zuckerman, J. R. Cole, and J. T. Bruer, eds., *The Outer Circle: Women in the Scientific Community* (New York: Norton, 1991), 277–310; M. F. Fox, "Sex, Salary, and Achievement: Reward Dualism in Academia," *Sociology of Education* 54 (1981), 71–84; J. S. Long, "The Origins of Sex Differences in Science," *Social Forces* 68 (1990), 1297–1315; R. F. Martell, D. M. Lane, and C. Emrich, "Male–Female Differences: A Computer Simulation," *American Psychologist* 51 (1996), 157–58; Valian, *Why So Slow?*
21. Cole and Singer, "A Theory of Limited Differences"; Fox, "Sex, Salary, and Achievement: Reward Dualism in Academia"; Long, "The Origins of Sex Differences in Science"; Martell, Lane, and Emrich, "Male–Female Differences: A Computer Simulation"; Valian, *Why So Slow?*
22. R. Folger and M. A. Konovsky, "Effects of Procedural and Distributive Justice on Reactions to Pay Raise Decisions," *Academy of Management Journal* 32 (1989), 115–30; J. Greenberg, "Organizational Justice: Yesterday, Today, and Tomorrow," *Journal of Management* 16 (1990), 399–402; "O. Janssen, "How Fairness Perceptions Make Innovative Behavior More or Less Stressful," *Journal of Organizational Behavior* 25 (2004), 201–15.
23. Catalyst, "The Glass Ceiling in 2000: Where Are Women Now?" www.catalystwomen.org, October 21, 2001; Bureau of Labor Statistics, 1999, www.bls.gov; Catalyst, "1999 Census of Women Corporate Officers and Top Earners," www.catalystwomen.org; "1999 Census of Women Board Directors of the *Fortune* 1000," www.catalystwomen.org; Catalyst, "Women of Color in Corporate Management: Opportunities and Barriers, 1999," www.catalystwomen.org, October 21, 2001.
24. "Household Data Annual Averages," www.bls.gov, April 28, 2004; U.S. Bureau of Labor Statistics, Economic News Release, Table 7. *Median Usual Weekly Earnings of Full-Time Wage and Salary Workers by Occupation and Sex, Annual Averages,* http://data.bls.gov/cgi-bin/print.pl/news.release/wkyeng.t07.htm, February 9, 2010.
25. "Household Data Annual Averages," www.bls.gov, April 28, 2004.
26. Greenberg, "Organizational Justice"; M. G. Ehrhart, "Leadership and Procedural Justice Climate as Antecedents of Unit-Level Organizational Citizenship Behavior," *Personnel Psychology* 57 (2004), 61–94; A. Colella, R. L. Paetzold, and M. A. Belliveau, "Factors Affecting Coworkers' Procedural Justice Inferences of the Workplace Accommodations of Employees with Disabilities," *Personnel Psychology* 57 (2004), 1–23.
27. G. Robinson and K. Dechant, "Building a Case for Business Diversity," *Academy of Management Executive* 3 (1997), 32–47.
28. A. Patterson, "Target 'Micromarkets' Its Way to Success; No 2 Stores Are Alike," *The Wall Street Journal,* May 31, 1995, A1, A9.
29. B. Frankel, "Measuring Diversity Is One Sure Way of Convincing CEOs of Its Value," *DiversityInc.com,* October 5, 2001.
30. A. Stevens, "Lawyers and Clients," *The Wall Street Journal,* June 19, 1995, B7.
31. H. R. Schiffmann, *Sensation and Perception: An Integrated Approach* (New York: Wiley, 1990).
32. McDonald's Corporation, 2008 Annual Report.
33. A. E. Serwer, "McDonald's Conquers the World," *Fortune,* October 17, 1994, 103–16.
34. S. T. Fiske and S. E. Taylor, *Social Cognition* (Reading, MA: Addison-Wesley, 1984).
35. J. S. Bruner, "Going beyond the Information Given," in H. Gruber, G. Terrell, and M. Wertheimer, eds., *Contemporary Approaches to Cognition* (Cambridge, MA: Harvard University Press, 1957); Fiske and Taylor, *Social Cognition.*
36. Fiske and Taylor, *Social Cognition.*
37. Valian, *Why So Slow?*
38. D. Bakan, *The Duality of Human Existence* (Chicago: Rand McNally, 1966); J. T. Spence and R. L. Helmreich, *Masculinity and Femininity: Their Psychological Dimensions, Correlates, and Antecedents* (Austin: University of Texas Press, 1978); J. T. Spence and L. L. Sawin, "Images of Masculinity and Femininity: A Reconceptualization," in V. E. O'Leary, R. K. Unger, and B. B. Wallston, eds., *Women, Gender, and Social Psychology* (Hillsdale, NJ: Erlbaum, 1985), 35–66; Valian, *Why So Slow?*
39. Valian, *Why So Slow?*
40. Serwer, "McDonald's Conquers the World"; P. R. Sackett, C. M. Hardison, and M. J. Cullen, "On Interpreting Stereotype Threat as Accounting for African American–White Differences on Cognitive Tests," *American Psychologist* 59, no. 1 (January 2004), 7–13; C. M. Steele and J. A. Aronson, "Stereotype Threat Does Not Live by Steele and Aronson," *American Psychologist* 59, no. 1 (January 2004), 47–55; P. R. Sackett, C. M. Hardison, and M. J. Cullen, "On the Value of Correcting Mischaracterizations of Stereotype Threat Research," *American Psychologist* 59, no. 1 (January 2004), 47–49; D. M. Amodio, E. Harmon-Jones, P. G. Devine, J. J. Curtin, S. L. Hartley, and A. E. Covert, "Neural Signals for the Detection of Unintentional Race Bias," *Psychological Science* 15, no. 2 (2004), 88–93.
41. M. Loden and J. B. Rosener, *Workforce America! Managing Employee Diversity as a Vital Resource* (Burr Ridge, IL: Irwin, 1991).
42. M. E. Heilman and T. G. Okimoto, "Motherhood: A Potential Source of Bias in Employment Decisions," *Journal of Applied Psychology* 93, no. 1 (2008), 189–98.
43. L. Roberson, B. M. Galvin, and A. C. Charles, "Chapter 13, When Group Identities Matter: Bias in Performance Appraisal," in J. P. Walsh and A. P. Brief, eds., *The Academy of Management Annals* 1 (New York: Erlbaum, 2008, 617–50).
44. A. Stein Wellner, "The Disability Advantage," *Inc. Magazine,* October 2005, 29–31.
45. A. Merrick, "Erasing 'Un' From 'Unemployable,'" *The Wall Street Journal,* August 2, 2007, B6.
46. Ibid.
47. Ibid.
48. "Habitat International: Our Products," www.habitatint.com/products.htm, April 6, 2006; "Habitat International Home Page," www.habitatint.com, April 6, 2006.
49. Wellner, "The Disability Advantage."
50. "Habitat International: Our People," Habitat International–Our People, http://www.habitatint.com/people.htm, February 10, 2010.
51. Wellner, "The Disability Advantage."
52. "Habitat International: Our People"; Wellner, "The Disability Advantage."
53. Ibid.
54. Ibid.
55. Ibid.
56. E. D. Pulakos and K. N. Wexley, "The Relationship among Perceptual

Similarity, Sex, and Performance Ratings in Manager Subordinate Dyads," *Academy of Management Journal* 26 (1983), 129–39.

57. Fiske and Taylor, *Social Cognition.*
58. "Nike Settles Discrimination Suit for $7.6 Million," *The Wall Street Journal,* July 31, 2007, B9.
59. Ibid.
60. Ibid.
61. M. Fackler, "Career Women in Japan Find a Blocked Path," *The New York Times,* August 6, 2007, A6.
62. Ibid.; www.un.org, February 11, 2008.
63. Fackler, "Career Women in Japan Find a Blocked Path."
64. www.nissanusa.com.
65. Fackler, "Career Women in Japan Find a Blocked Path."
66. A. G. Greenwald and M. Banaji, "Implicit Social Cognition: Attitudes, Self-Esteem, and Stereotypes," *Psychological Review* 102 (1995), 4–27.
67. A. Fisher, "Ask Annie: Five Ways to Promote Diversity in the Workplace," *Fortune,* April 23, 2004 (www.fortune.com/fortune/subs/print/0,15935,455997,00.html); E. Bonabeau, "Don't Trust Your Gut," *Harvard Business Review,* May 2003, 116–23.
68. A. P. Carnevale and S. C. Stone, "Diversity: Beyond the Golden Rule," *Training & Development,* October 1994, 22–39.
69. Fisher, "Ask Annie."
70. B. A. Battaglia, "Skills for Managing Multicultural Teams," *Cultural Diversity at Work* 4 (1992); Carnevale and Stone, "Diversity: Beyond the Golden Rule."
71. Swann et al., "Finding Value in Diversity."
72. Valian, *Why So Slow?*
73. A. P. Brief, R. T. Buttram, R. M. Reizenstein, S. D. Pugh, J. D. Callahan, R. L. McCline, and J. B. Vaslow, "Beyond Good Intentions: The Next Steps toward Racial Equality in the American Workplace," *Academy of Management Executive,* November 1997, 59–72.
74. Ibid.
75. Ibid.
76. Ibid.
77. B. Mandell and S. Kohler-Gray, "Management Development That Values Diversity," *Personnel,* March 1990, 41–47.
78. D. A. Thomas, "Race Matters: The Truth about Mentoring Minorities," *Harvard Business Review,* April 2001, 99–107.
79. Ibid.
80. S. N. Mehta, "Why Mentoring Works," *Fortune,* July 9, 2000.
81. Ibid.; Thomas, "Race Matters."
82. U.S. Equal Employment Opportunity Commission, "Facts about Sexual Harassment," www.eeoc.gov/facts/fs-sex.html, May 1, 2004.
83. R. L. Paetzold and A. M. O'Leary-Kelly, "Organizational Communication and the Legal Dimensions of Hostile Work Environment Sexual Harassment," in G. L. Kreps, ed., *Sexual Harassment: Communication Implications* (Cresskill, NJ: Hampton Press, 1993).
84. M. Galen, J. Weber, and A. Z. Cuneo, "Sexual Harassment: Out of the Shadows," *Fortune,* October 28, 1991, 30–31.
85. A. M. O'Leary-Kelly, R. L. Paetzold, and R. W. Griffin, "Sexual Harassment as Aggressive Action: A Framework for Understanding Sexual Harassment," paper presented at the annual meeting of the Academy of Management, Vancouver, August 1995.
86. B. S. Roberts and R. A. Mann, "Sexual Harassment in the Workplace: A Primer," www3.uakron.edu/lawrev/robert1.html, May 1, 2004.
87. S. J. Bresler and R. Thacker, "Four-Point Plan Helps Solve Harassment Problems," *HR Magazine,* May 1993, 117–24.
88. "Du Pont's Solution," *Training,* March 1992, 29.
89. Ibid.
90. Ibid.

Chapter 6

1. www.sony.com, press release, 2010.
2. L. J. Bourgeois, "Strategy and Environment: A Conceptual Integration," *Academy of Management Review* 5 (1985), 25–39.
3. M. E. Porter, *Competitive Strategy* (New York: Free Press, 1980).
4. "Coca-Cola versus Pepsi-Cola and the Soft Drink Industry," Harvard Business School Case 9-391-179.
5. www.splenda.com, 2010.
6. A. K. Gupta and V. Govindarajan, "Cultivating a Global Mind-Set," *Academy of Management Executive* 16 (February 2002), 116–27.
7. "Boeing's Worldwide Supplier Network," *Seattle Post-Intelligencer,* April 9, 1994, 13.
8. I. Metthee, "Playing a Large Part," *Seattle Post-Intelligencer,* April 9, 1994, 13.
9. "Business: Link in the Global Chain," *The Economist,* June 2, 2001, 62–63.
10. www.boeing.com, 2010.
11. www.hbi.com, 2010.
12. www.nokia.com, 2010.
13. M. E. Porter, *Competitive Advantage* (New York: Free Press, 1985).
14. T. Levitt, "The Globalization of Markets," *Harvard Business Review,* May–June 1983, 92–102.
15. "Dell CEO Would Like 40 Percent PC Market Share," www.dailynews.yahoo.com, June 20, 2001.
16. For views on barriers to entry from an economics perspective, see Porter, *Competitive Strategy.* For the sociological perspective, see J. Pfeffer and G. R. Salancik, *The External Control of Organization: A Resource Dependence Perspective* (New York: Harper & Row, 1978).
17. Porter, *Competitive Strategy;* J. E. Bain, *Barriers to New Competition* (Cambridge, MA: Harvard University Press, 1956); R. J. Gilbert, "Mobility Barriers and the Value of Incumbency," in R. Schmalensee and R. D. Willig, eds., *Handbook of Industrial Organization,* vol. 1 (Amsterdam: North Holland, 1989).
18. Press release, www.amazon.com, May 2001.
19. C. W. L. Hill, "The Computer Industry: The New Industry of Industries," in Hill and Jones, *Strategic Management: An Integrated Approach* (Boston: Houghton Mifflin, 2003).
20. J. Schumpeter, *Capitalism, Socialism and Democracy* (London: Macmillan, 1950), 68. Also see R. R. Winter and S. G. Winter, *An Evolutionary Theory of Economic Change* (Cambridge, MA: Harvard University Press, 1982).
21. N. Goodman, *An Introduction to Sociology* (New York: HarperCollins, 1991); C. Nakane, *Japanese Society* (Berkeley: University of California Press, 1970).
22. For a detailed discussion of the importance of the structure of law as a factor explaining economic change and growth, see D. C. North, *Institutions, Institutional Change, and Economic Performance* (Cambridge: Cambridge University Press, 1990).
23. R. B. Reich, *The Work of Nations* (New York: Knopf, 1991).
24. M. A. Carpenter and J. W. Fredrickson, "Top Management Teams, Global Strategic Posture, and the Moderating Role of Uncertainty," *Academy of Management Journal* 44 (June 2001), 533–46.
25. www.nestle.com, 2010.
26. 2009 Annual Report, www.nestle.com, 2010.
27. www.ikea.com, 2010.
28. J. Bhagwati, *Protectionism* (Cambridge, MA: MIT Press, 1988).

29. For a summary of these theories, see P. Krugman and M. Obstfeld, *International Economics: Theory and Policy* (New York: HarperCollins, 1991). Also see C. W. L. Hill, *International Business* (New York: McGraw-Hill, 1997), chap. 4.
30. A. M. Rugman, "The Quest for Global Dominance," *Academy of Management Executive* 16 (August 2002), 157–60.
31. www.wto.org.com, 2004.
32. www.wto.org.com, 2010.
33. C. A. Bartlett and S. Ghoshal, *Managing across Borders* (Boston: Harvard Business School Press, 1989).
34. C. Arnst and G. Edmondson, "The Global Free-for-All," *BusinessWeek,* September 26, 1994, 118–26.
35. W. Konrads, "Why Leslie Wexner Shops Overseas," *BusinessWeek,* February 3, 1992, 30.
36. E. B. Tylor, *Primitive Culture* (London: Murray, 1971).
37. For details on the forces that shape culture, see Hill, *International Business,* chap. 2.
38. G. Hofstede, B. Neuijen, D. D. Ohayv, and G. Sanders, "Measuring Organizational Cultures: A Qualitative and Quantitative Study across Twenty Cases," *Administrative Science Quarterly* 35 (1990), 286–316.
39. M. H. Hoppe, "Introduction: Geert Hofstede's Culture's Consequences: International Differences in Work-Related Values," *Academy of Management Executive* 18 (February 2004), 73–75.
40. R. Bellah, *Habits of the Heart: Individualism and Commitment in American Life* (Berkeley: University of California Press, 1985).
41. R. Bellah, *The Tokugawa Religion* (New York: Free Press, 1957).
42. C. Nakane, *Japanese Society* (Berkeley: University of California Press, 1970).
43. Ibid.
44. G. Hofstede, "The Cultural Relativity of Organizational Practices and Theories," *Journal of International Business Studies,* Fall 1983, 75–89.
45. Hofstede et al., "Measuring Organizational Cultures."
46. J. Perlez, "GE Finds Tough Going in Hungary," *The New York Times,* July 25, 1994, C1, C3.
47. www.ge.com, 2004, 2010.
48. J. P. Fernandez and M. Barr, *The Diversity Advantage* (New York: Lexington Books, 1994).

Chapter 7

1. D. Sacks, "The Catalyst," *Fast Company,* October 2006, 59–61.
2. About PUMA, http://about.puma.com/EN/1/, February 13, 2008.
3. Sacks, "The Catalyst."
4. About PUMA, "PUMA at a Glance," http://about.puma.com/?cat=4, February 16, 2010.
5. Sacks, "The Catalyst."
6. Ibid.
7. Ibid.
8. Ibid.; Fashion in Motion Africa 2005, Xuly Bet, www.vam.ac.uk/collections/fashion/fashion_motion/africa_05/index.html, February 14, 2008.
9. Sacks, "The Catalyst;" PUMA Online Shop, http://www.shop.puma.com/on/demandware.store/Sites-Puma-US-Site/en/Search-Show?q . . . , February 16, 2010.
10. G. P. Huber, *Managerial Decision Making* (Glenview, IL: Scott, Foresman, 1993).
11. Sacks, "The Catalyst."
12. H. A. Simon, *The New Science of Management* (Englewood Cliffs, NJ: Prentice-Hall, 1977).
13. D. Kahneman, "Maps of Bounded Rationality: A Perspective on Intuitive Judgment and Choice," Prize Lecture, December 8, 2002; E. Jaffe, "What Was I Thinking? Kahneman Explains How Intuition Leads Us Astray," *American Psychological Society* 17, no. 5 (May 2004), 23–26; E. Dane and M. Pratt, "Exploring Intuition and Its Role in Managerial Decision Making," *Academy of Management Review* 32 (2007), 33–54.
14. One should be careful not to generalize too much here, however; for as Peter Senge has shown, programmed decisions rely on the implicit assumption that the environment is in a steady state. If environmental conditions change, sticking to a routine decision rule can produce disastrous results. See P. Senge, *The Fifth Discipline: The Art and Practice of the Learning Organization* (New York: Doubleday, 1990).
15. Kahneman, "Maps of Bounded Rationality"; Jaffe, "What Was I Thinking?"
16. Ibid.
17. J. Smutniak, "Freud, Finance and Folly: Human Intuition Is a Bad Guide to Handling Risk," *The Economist* 24 (January 2004), 5–6.
18. Kahneman, "Maps of Bounded Rationality"; Jaffe, "What Was I Thinking?"
19. Ibid.
20. J. Pfeffer, "Curbing the Urge to Merge," *Business 2.0,* July 2003, 58; Smutniak, "Freud, Finance and Folly."
21. Kahneman, "Maps of Bounded Rationality"; Jaffe, "What Was I Thinking?"
22. Pfeffer, "Curbing the Urge to Merge"; Smutniak, "Freud, Finance and Folly."
23. M. Landler, "New Austerity for German Car Industry," *The New York Times,* September 29, 2005, C3; E. Taylor and C. Rauwald, "DaimlerChrysler to Cut 8,500 Jobs at Mercedes," *The Wall Street Journal,* September 29, 2005, A6; G. Edmondson, "On the Hot Seat at Daimler," *BusinessWeek Online,* February 17, 2006 (www.businessweek.com/autos/content/feb2006/bw20060217_187348.htm?campaign_id=search); Daimler AG News–*The New York Times,* http://topics.nytimes.com/topics/news/business/companies/daimler_ag/index.html., February 19, 2010.
24. "Hiring Freeze and Cost Cuts at Time Inc.," *The New York Times,* August 2005, B13.
25. Pfeffer, "Curbing the Urge to Merge."
26. Ibid.
27. H. A. Simon, *Administrative Behavior* (New York: Macmillan, 1947), 79.
28. H. A. Simon, *Models of Man* (New York: Wiley, 1957).
29. K. J. Arrow, *Aspects of the Theory of Risk Bearing* (Helsinki: Yrjo Johnssonis Saatio, 1965).
30. Ibid.
31. R. L. Daft and R. H. Lengel, "Organizational Information Requirements, Media Richness and Structural Design," *Management Science* 32 (1986), 554–71.
32. R. Cyert and J. March, *Behavioral Theory of the Firm* (Englewood Cliffs, NJ: Prentice-Hall, 1963).
33. J. G. March and H. A. Simon, *Organizations* (New York: Wiley, 1958).
34. H. A. Simon, "Making Management Decisions: The Role of Intuition and Emotion," *Academy of Management Executive* 1 (1987), 57–64.
35. M. H. Bazerman, *Judgment in Managerial Decision Making* (New York: Wiley, 1986). Also see Simon, *Administrative Behavior.*
36. Scott G. McNealy Profile–Forbes.com, http://people.forbes.com/profile/scott-g-mcnealy/75347, February 16, 2010; Sun Oracle, "Overview and Frequently Asked Questions," www.oracle.com, February 16, 2010.
37. "Sun Microsystems–Investor Relations: Officers and Directors," www.sun.com/aboutsun/investor/sun_facts/officers_directors.html, June 1, 2004; "How Sun Delivers Value to Customers," *Sun Microsystems–Investor Relations: Support & Training,* June 1, 2004 (www.sun.com/aboutsun/investor/sun_facts/core_strategies.html); "Sun at a Glance," *Sun Microsystems–Investor Relations: Sun Facts,* June 1, 2004 (www.sun.com/aboutsun/investor/sun_facts/index.html); "Plug in the System, and Everything Just Works," *Sun Microsystems–Investor Relations: Product Portfolio,* June 1, 2004 (www.sun.com/aboutsun/investor/sun_facts/portfolio/html).
38. N. J. Langowitz and S. C. Wheelright, "Sun Microsystems, Inc. (A)," Harvard Business School Case 686–133.

39. R. D. Hof, "How to Kick the Mainframe Habit," *BusinessWeek*, June 26, 1995, 102–104.
40. Bazerman, *Judgment in Managerial Decision Making;* Huber, *Managerial Decision Making;* J. E. Russo and P. J. Schoemaker, *Decision Traps* (New York: Simon & Schuster, 1989).
41. M. D. Cohen, J. G. March, and J. P. Olsen, "A Garbage Can Model of Organizational Choice," *Administrative Science Quarterly* 17 (1972), 1–25.
42. Ibid.
43. Bazerman, *Judgment in Managerial Decision Making.*
44. Senge, *The Fifth Discipline.*
45. E. de Bono, *Lateral Thinking* (London: Penguin, 1968); Senge, *The Fifth Discipline.*
46. Russo and Schoemaker, *Decision Traps.*
47. Bazerman, *Judgment in Managerial Decision Making.*
48. Russo and Schoemaker, *Decision Traps.*
49. J. Kingston, "A Crisis Made in Japan," *The Wall Street Journal*, February 5, 2010, http://online.wsj.com/article/SB10001424052748704533204575047370633234414.html.
50. D. Kahneman and A. Tversky, "Judgment under Uncertainty: Heuristics and Biases," *Science* 185 (1974), 1124–31.
51. C. R. Schwenk, "Cognitive Simplification Processes in Strategic Decision Making," *Strategic Management Journal* 5 (1984), 111–28.
52. An interesting example of the illusion of control is Richard Roll's hubris hypothesis of takeovers. See R. Roll, "The Hubris Hypothesis of Corporate Takeovers," *Journal of Business* 59 (1986), 197–216.
53. J. Pfeffer and R. I. Sutton, *Hard Facts, Dangerous Half-Truths, and Total Nonsense: Profiting from Evidence-Based Management* (Boston: Harvard Business School Press, 2006).
54. B. M. Staw, "The Escalation of Commitment to a Course of Action," *Academy of Management Review* 6 (1981), 577–87.
55. Russo and Schoemaker, *Decision Traps.*
56. Ibid.
57. I. L. Janis, *Groupthink: Psychological Studies of Policy Decisions and Disasters,* 2nd ed. (Boston: Houghton Mifflin, 1982).
58. C. R. Schwenk, *The Essence of Strategic Decision Making* (Lexington, MA: Lexington Books, 1988).
59. See R. O. Mason, "A Dialectic Approach to Strategic Planning," *Management Science* 13 (1969) 403–14; R. A. Cosier and J. C. Aplin, "A Critical View of Dialectic Inquiry in Strategic Planning," *Strategic Management Journal* 1 (1980), 343–56; I. I. Mitroff and R. O. Mason, "Structuring III–Structured Policy Issues: Further Explorations in a Methodology for Messy Problems," *Strategic Management Journal* 1 (1980), 331–42.
60. Mason, "A Dialectic Approach to Strategic Planning."
61. D. M. Schweiger and P. A. Finger, "The Comparative Effectiveness of Dialectic Inquiry and Devil's Advocacy," *Strategic Management Journal* 5 (1984), 335–50.
62. Mary C. Gentile, *Differences That Work: Organizational Excellence through Diversity* (Boston: Harvard Business School Press, 1994); F. Rice, "How to Make Diversity Pay," *Fortune,* August 8, 1994, 78–86.
63. B. Hedberg, "How Organizations Learn and Unlearn," in W. H. Starbuck and P. C. Nystrom, eds., *Handbook of Organizational Design,* vol. 1 (New York: Oxford University Press, 1981), 1–27.
64. Senge, *The Fifth Discipline.*
65. Ibid.
66. P. M. Senge, "The Leader's New Work: Building Learning Organizations," *Sloan Management Review,* Fall 1990, 7–23.
67. W. Zellner, K. A. Schmidt, M. Ihlwan, and H. Dawley, "How Well Does Wal-Mart Travel?" *BusinessWeek,* September 3, 2001, 82–84.
68. J. P. Walsh and A. P. Brief (eds.), "Creativity in Organizations," *The Academy of Management Annals,* Volume 1, New York: Erlbaum, 439–77.
69. Ibid.
70. C. Saltr, "FAST 50: The World's Most Innovative Companies," *Fast Company,* March 2008, 73–117.
71. R. W. Woodman, J. E. Sawyer, and R. W. Griffin, "Towards a Theory of Organizational Creativity," *Academy of Management Review* 18 (1993), 293–321.
72. T. J. Bouchard Jr., J. Barsaloux, and G. Drauden, "Brainstorming Procedure, Group Size, and Sex as Determinants of Problem Solving Effectiveness of Individuals and Groups," *Journal of Applied Psychology* 59 (1974), 135–38.
73. M. Diehl and W. Stroebe, "Productivity Loss in Brainstorming Groups: Towards the Solution of a Riddle," *Journal of Personality and Social Psychology* 53 (1987), 497–509.
74. D. H. Gustafson, R. K. Shulka, A. Delbecq, and W. G. Walster, "A Comparative Study of Differences in Subjective Likelihood Estimates Made by Individuals, Interacting Groups, Delphi Groups, and Nominal Groups," *Organizational Behavior and Human Performance* 9 (1973), 280–91.
75. N. Dalkey, *The Delphi Method: An Experimental Study of Group Decision Making* (Santa Monica, CA: Rand Corp., 1989).
76. T. Lonier, "Some Insights and Statistics on Working Solo," www.workingsolo.com.
77. I. N. Katsikis and L. P. Kyrgidou, "The Concept of Sustainable Entrepreneurship: A Conceptual Framework and Empirical Analysis," *Academy of Management Proceedings,* 2007, 1–6, web.ebscohost.com/ehost/delivery?vid=7&hid=102&sid=434afdf5-5ed9-45d4-993b-, January 24, 2008; "What Is a Social Entrepreneur?" http://ashoka.org/social_entrepreneur, February 20, 2008; C. Hsu, "Entrepreneur for Social Change," *U.S.News.com,* October 31, 2005, www.usnews.com/usnews/news/articles/051031/31drayton.htm; D. M. Sullivan, "Stimulating Social Entrepreneurship: Can Support from Cities Make a Difference?" *Academy of Management Perspectives,* February 2007, 78.
78. Katsikis and Kyrgidou, "The Concept of Sustainable Entrepreneurship"; "What Is a Social Entrepreneur?"; Hsu, "Entrepreneur for Social Change"; Sullivan, "Stimulating Social Entrepreneurship."
79. G. D. Bruton, S. Khavul, and H. Chavez, "Microfinance in Emerging Markets: Building a New Line of Inquiry from the Ground Up," *Journal of International Business Studies* (forthcoming).

Chapter 8

1. A. Chandler, *Strategy and Structure: Chapters in the History of the American Enterprise* (Cambridge, MA: MIT Press, 1962).
2. Ibid.
3. H. Fayol, *General and Industrial Management* (1884; New York: IEEE Press, 1984).
4. Ibid., 18.
5. F. J. Aguilar, "General Electric: Reg Jones and Jack Welch," in *General Managers in Action* (Oxford: Oxford University Press, 1992).
6. Ibid.
7. www.ge.com, 2010.
8. C. W. Hofer and D. Schendel, *Strategy Formulation: Analytical Concepts* (St. Paul, MN: West, 1978).
9. A. P. De Geus, "Planning as Learning," *Harvard Business Review,* March–April 1988, 70–74.
10. P. Wack, "Scenarios: Shooting the Rapids," *Harvard Business Review,* November–December 1985, 139–50.

11. R. Phelps, C. Chan, and S. C. Kapsalis, "Does Scenario Planning Affect Firm Performance?" *Journal of Business Research,* March 2001, 223–32.
12. J. A. Pearce, "The Company Mission as a Strategic Tool," *Sloan Management Review,* Spring 1992, 15–24.
13. D. F. Abell, *Defining the Business: The Starting Point of Strategic Planning* (Englewood Cliffs, NJ: Prentice-Hall, 1980).
14. C. Passariello, "Carrefour's Makeover Plan: Become IKEA of Groceries," *The Wall Street Journal,* September 15, 2010, http://online.wsj.com/article/SB100014240527487046521045754937721785448 84.html.
15. G. Hamel and C. K. Prahalad, "Strategic Intent," *Harvard Business Review,* May–June 1989, 63–73.
16. D. I. Jung and B. J. Avolio, "Opening the Black Box: An Experimental Investigation of the Mediating Effects of Trust and Value Congruence on Transformational and Transactional Leadership," *Journal of Organizational Behavior,* December 2000, 949–64; B. M. Bass and B. J. Avolio, "Transformational and Transactional Leadership: 1992 and Beyond," *Journal of European Industrial Training,* January 1990, 20–35.
17. J. Porras and J. Collins, *Built to Last: Successful Habits of Visionary Companies* (New York: HarperCollins, 1994).
18. E. A. Locke, G. P. Latham, and M. Erez, "The Determinants of Goal Commitment," *Academy of Management Review* 13 (1988), 23–39.
19. K. R. Andrews, *The Concept of Corporate Strategy* (Homewood, IL: Irwin, 1971).
20. www.campbellsoup.com, 2001.
21. "Campbell Completes $850M Godiva Sale," www.yahoo.com, March 18, 2008.
22. R. D. Aveni, *Hypercompetition* (New York: Free Press, 1994).
23. M. E. Porter, *Competitive Strategy* (New York: Free Press, 1980).
24. C. W. L. Hill, "Differentiation versus Low Cost or Differentiation and Low Cost: A Contingency Framework," *Academy of Management Review* 13 (1988), 401–12.
25. For details, see J. P. Womack, D. T. Jones, and D. Roos, *The Machine That Changed the World* (New York: Rawson Associates, 1990).
26. Porter, *Competitive Strategy.*
27. www.cott.com, 2010.
28. www.cocacola.com, 2010; www.pepsico.com, 2010.
29. M. K. Perry, "Vertical Integration: Determinants and Effects," in R. Schmalensee and R. D. Willig, *Handbook of Industrial Organization,* vol. 1 (New York: Elsevier Science, 1989).
30. "Matsushita Electric Industrial (MEI) in 1987," Harvard Business School Case 388-144.
31. P. Ghemawat, *Commitment: The Dynamic of Strategy* (New York: Free Press, 1991).
32. www.ibm.com, 2010.
33. E. Penrose, *The Theory of the Growth of the Firm* (Oxford: Oxford University Press, 1959).
34. M. E. Porter, "From Competitive Advantage to Corporate Strategy," *Harvard Business Review* 65 (1987), 43–59.
35. D. J. Teece, "Economies of Scope and the Scope of the Enterprise," *Journal of Economic Behavior and Organization* 3 (1980), 223–47.
36. www.3M.com, 2005, 2010.
37. www.3M.com, 2010.
38. C. Wyant, "Minnesota Companies Make *BusinessWeek*'s 'Most Innovative' List," *Minneapolis/St. Paul Business Journal,* April 18, 2008.
39. For a review of the evidence, see C. W. L. Hill and G. R. Jones, *Strategic Management: An Integrated Approach,* 5th ed. (Boston: Houghton Mifflin, 2003), chap. 10.
40. C. A. Bartlett and S. Ghoshal, *Managing across Borders* (Boston: Harvard Business School Press, 1989).
41. C. K. Prahalad and Y. L. Doz, *The Multinational Mission* (New York: Free Press, 1987).
42. "Gillette Co.'s New $40 Million Razor Blade Factory in St. Petersburg, Russia," *Boston Globe,* June 7, 2000, C6.
43. D. Sewell, "P&G Replaces Ex-Gillette CEO at Operations," www.yahoo.com, May 24, 2006.
44. R. E. Caves, *Multinational Enterprise and Economic Analysis* (Cambridge: Cambridge University Press, 1982).
45. B. Kogut, "Joint Ventures: Theoretical and Empirical Perspectives," *Strategic Management Journal* 9 (1988), 319–33.
46. "Venture with Nestlé SA Is Slated for Expansion," *The Wall Street Journal,* April 15, 2001, B2.
47. B. Bahree, "BP Amoco, Italy's ENI Plan $2.5 Billion Gas Plant," *The Wall Street Journal,* March 6, 2001, A16.
48. N. Hood and S. Young, *The Economics of the Multinational Enterprise* (London: Longman, 1979).
49. www.samsung.com, 2010.
50. Ibid.

Chapter 9

1. Suzanne Kapner, "The Unstoppable Fung Brothers," *CNNMoney.com,* December 9, 2009, http//:money.cnn.com/2009/12/07/news international/li_fung.fortune/index.htm.
2. See D. Garvin, "What Does Product Quality Really Mean?" *Sloan Management Review* 26 (Fall 1984), 25–44; P. B. Crosby, *Quality Is Free* (New York: Mentor Books, 1980); A. Gabor, *The Man Who Discovered Quality* (New York: Times Books, 1990).
3. D. F. Abell, *Defining the Business: The Starting Point of Strategic Planning* (Englewood Cliffs, NJ: Prentice-Hall, 1980).
4. According to Richard D'Aveni, the process of pushing price–attribute curves to the right is a characteristic of the competitive process. See R. D'Aveni, *Hypercompetition* (New York: Free Press, 1994).
5. www.ryanair.com/en, 2010.
6. S. Patel, "Tesco to Less CO: Can Tesco Save the World?" *Infosysblogs,* Supply Chain Management, December 31, 2009, http://www.infosysblogs.com/supply-chain/2009/12/tesco_to_less_co_can_tesco_sav.html.
7. Graham Technology, "Award-Winning CRM from Standard Bank," Interactive Technology–FST Europe/GDS Publishing, *European Financial Service Technology News,* October 5, 2010, http://www.fsteurope.com/article/Award-winning-CRM-from-Standard-Bank/.
8. The view of quality as reliability goes back to the work of Deming and Juran; see Gabor, *The Man Who Discovered Quality.*
9. See Garvin, "What Does Product Quality Really Mean?"; Crosby, *Quality Is Free;* Gabor, *The Man Who Discovered Quality.*
10. www.jdpa.com, 2009.
11. See J. W. Dean and D. E. Bowen, "Management Theory and Total Quality: Improving Research and Practice through Theory Development," *Academy of Management Review* 19 (1994), 392–418.
12. For general background information, see J. C. Anderson, M. Rungtusanatham, and R. G. Schroeder, "A Theory of Quality Management Underlying the Deming Management Method," *Academy of Management Review* 19 (1994), 472–509; "How to Build Quality," *The Economist,* September 23, 1989, 91–92; Gabor, *The Man Who Discovered Quality;* Crosby, *Quality Is Free.*
13. J. Bowles, "Is American Management Really Committed to Quality?" *Management Review,* April 1992, 42–46.
14. Gabor, *The Man Who Discovered Quality.*
15. "The Application of Kaizen to Facilities Layout," *Financial Times,* January 4, 1994, 12. Reprinted by permission of Financial Times Syndication, London.

16. R. Gourlay, "Back to Basics on the Factory Floor," *Financial Times,* January 4, 1994, 12.
17. P. Nemetz and L. Fry, "Flexible Manufacturing Organizations: Implications for Strategy Formulation," *Academy of Management Review* 13 (1988), 627–38; N. Greenwood, *Implementing Flexible Manufacturing Systems* (New York: Halstead Press, 1986).
18. M. Williams, "Back to the Past," *The Wall Street Journal,* October 24, 1994, A1.
19. For an interesting discussion of some other drawbacks of JIT and other "Japanese" manufacturing techniques, see S. M. Young, "A Framework for Successful Adoption and Performance of Japanese Manufacturing Practices in the United States," *Academy of Management Review* 17 (1992), 677–701.
20. G. Stalk and T. M. Hout, *Competing against Time* (New York: Free Press, 1990).
21. B. Dumaine, "The Trouble with Teams," *Fortune,* September 5, 1994, 86–92.
22. See C. W. L. Hill, "Transaction Cost Economizing as a Source of National Competitive Advantage: The Case of Japan," *Organization Science* 2 (1994); M. Aoki, *Information, Incentives, and Bargaining in the Japanese Economy* (Cambridge: Cambridge University Press, 1989).
23. J. Hoerr, "The Payoff from Teamwork," *BusinessWeek,* July 10, 1989, 56–62.
24. Vimolwan Yukongdi, "Teams and TQM: A Comparison between Australia and Thailand," *International Journal of Quality and Reliability Management* 18 (2001), 387–403.
25. M. Hammer and J. Champy, *Reengineering the Corporation* (New York: HarperBusiness, 1993), 35.
26. Ibid., 46.
27. Ibid.
28. K. Capell, "Zara Thrives by Breaking All the Rules," *BusinessWeek,* October 20, 2008.
29. www.google.com, 2010.
30. Ibid.

Chapter 10

1. N. Byrnes, "Avon: More Than Just Cosmetic Changes," www.businessweek.com, March 12, 2007.
2. www.avon.com, 2010.
3. G. R. Jones, *Organizational Theory, Design, and Change: Text and Cases* (Upper Saddle River: Prentice-Hall, 2003).
4. J. Child, *Organization: A Guide for Managers and Administrators* (New York: Harper & Row, 1977).
5. P. R. Lawrence and J. W. Lorsch, *Organization and Environment* (Boston: Graduate School of Business Administration, Harvard University, 1967).
6. R. Duncan, "What Is the Right Organizational Design?" *Organizational Dynamics,* Winter 1979, 59–80.
7. T. Burns and G. R. Stalker, *The Management of Innovation* (London: Tavistock, 1966).
8. D. Miller, "Strategy Making and Structure: Analysis and Implications for Performance," *Academy of Management Journal* 30 (1987), 7–32.
9. A. D. Chandler, *Strategy and Structure* (Cambridge, MA: MIT Press, 1962).
10. J. Stopford and L. Wells, *Managing the Multinational Enterprise* (London: Longman, 1972).
11. C. Perrow, *Organizational Analysis: A Sociological View* (Belmont, CA: Wadsworth, 1970).
12. F. W. Taylor, *The Principles of Scientific Management* (New York: Harper, 1911).
13. R. W. Griffin, *Task Design: An Integrative Approach* (Glenview, IL: Scott, Foresman, 1982).
14. Ibid.
15. J. R. Hackman and G. R. Oldham, *Work Redesign* (Reading, MA: Addison-Wesley, 1980).
16. J. R. Galbraith and R. K. Kazanjian, *Strategy Implementation: Structure, System, and Process,* 2nd ed. (St. Paul, MN: West, 1986).
17. Lawrence and Lorsch, *Organization and Environment.*
18. Jones, *Organizational Theory.*
19. Lawrence and Lorsch, *Organization and Environment.*
20. R. H. Hall, *Organizations: Structure and Process* (Englewood Cliffs, NJ: Prentice-Hall, 1972); R. Miles, *Macro Organizational Behavior* (Santa Monica, CA: Goodyear, 1980).
21. Chandler, *Strategy and Structure.*
22. G. R. Jones and C. W. L. Hill, "Transaction Cost Analysis of Strategy–Structure Choice," *Strategic Management Journal* 9 (1988), 159–72.
23. www.gsk.com, 2006.
24. www.gsk.com, 2010.
25. www.nokia.com, 2010.
26. S. M. Davis and P. R. Lawrence, *Matrix* (Reading, MA: Addison-Wesley, 1977); J. R. Galbraith, "Matrix Organization Designs: How to Combine Functional and Project Forms," *Business Horizons* 14 (1971), 29–40.
27. L. R. Burns, "Matrix Management in Hospitals: Testing Theories of Matrix Structure and Development," *Administrative Science Quarterly* 34 (1989), 349–68.
28. C. W. L. Hill, *International Business* (Homewood, IL: Irwin, 2003).
29. Jones, *Organizational Theory.*
30. P. Blau, "A Formal Theory of Differentiation in Organizations," *American Sociological Review* 35 (1970), 684–95.
31. S. Grey, "McDonald's CEO Announces Shifts of Top Executives," *The Wall Street Journal,* July 16, 2004, A11.
32. www.mcdonalds.com, 2010.
33. Child, *Organization.*
34. Evan Ramstad, "Pulling Rank Gets Harder at One Korean Company," *The Wall Street Journal,* August 20, 2007.
35. P. M. Blau and R. A. Schoenherr, *The Structure of Organizations* (New York: Basic Books, 1971).
36. Jones, *Organizational Theory.*
37. T. V. Mahalingam, "The Elephant Learns to Dance," *Business Today,* September 5, 2010, http://businesstoday.intoday.in/index.php?option=com_content&tltemid=1&task=view&id=15967§ionid=25&issueid=90&page=archieve.
38. Lawrence and Lorsch, *Organization and Environment,* 50–55.
39. J. R. Galbraith, *Designing Complex Organizations* (Reading, MA: Addison-Wesley, 1977), chap. 1; Galbraith and Kazanjian, *Strategy Implementation,* chap. 7.
40. Lawrence and Lorsch, *Organization and Environment,* 55.
41. S. D. N. Cook and D. Yanow, "Culture and Organizational Learning," *Journal of Management Inquiry* 2 (1993), 373–90.
42. Guy Chazan, "*The Wall Street Journal:* CEO Hayward to Streamline," *Royal Dutch Shell Plc.com,* October 11, 2007, http://royaldutchshellplc.com/2007/10/11/the-wall-street-journal-ceo-hayward-to-streamline/.
43. Economy & Business News, "BP Shares Up on Restructuring Plan," *Trend–News from the Caspian, South Caucasus and Central Asia–Politics, Economics, Society,* October 13, 2007, http://en.trend.az/capital/empty/1043953.html.
44. Richard Blackden, "BP's Tony Hayward: The Right Man in the Right Place at the Wrong Time?" *Telegraph.co.uk,* September 30, 2010, http://www.telegraph.co.uk/finance/newsbysector/energy/oilandgas/8033366/BPs-Tony-Hayward-the-right-man-in-the-right-place-at-the-wrong-time.html.
45. B. Schneider, "The People Make the Place," *Personnel Psychology* 40 (1987), 437–53.
46. J. E. Sheriden, "Organizational Culture and Employee Retention," *Academy of Management Journal* 35 (1992), 657–92.

47. M. Hannan and J. Freeman, "Structural Inertia and Organizational Change," *American Sociological Review* 49 (1984), 149–64.
48. C. A. O'Reilly, J. Chatman, and D. F. Caldwell, "People and Organizational Culture: Assessing Person–Organizational Fit," *Academy of Management Journal* 34 (1991), 487–517.
49. T. L. Beauchamp and N. E. Bowie, eds., *Ethical Theory and Business* (Englewood Cliffs, NJ: Prentice-Hall, 1979); A. MacIntyre, *After Virtue* (Notre Dame, IN: University of Notre Dame Press, 1981).
50. A. Sagie and D. Elizur, "Work Values: A Theoretical Overview and a Model of Their Effects," *Journal of Organizational Behavior* 17 (1996), 503–14.
51. G. R. Jones, "Transaction Costs, Property Rights, and Organizational Culture: An Exchange Perspective," *Administrative Science Quarterly* 28 (1983), 454–67.
52. C. Perrow, *Normal Accidents* (New York: Basic Books, 1984).
53. H. Mintzberg, *The Structuring of Organizational Structures* (Englewood Cliffs, NJ: Prentice-Hall, 1979).
54. G. Kunda, *Engineering Culture* (Philadelphia: Temple University Press, 1992).
55. www.nokia.com, 2010.
56. K. E. Weick, *The Social Psychology of Organization* (Reading, MA: Addison-Wesley, 1979).
57. Copyright © 2006, Gareth R. Jones.

Chapter 11

1. Philip D. Broughton, "Jérôme Kerviel: Tricks of the Trader," *The Sunday Times* (London), Business.timesonline.co.uk, February 15, 2009, http://business.timesonline.co.uk/tol/business/industry_sectors/banking_and_finance/article5716179.ece.
2. W. G. Ouchi, "Markets, Bureaucracies, and Clans," *Administrative Science Quarterly* 25 (1980), 129–41.
3. P. Lorange, M. Morton, and S. Ghoshal, *Strategic Control* (St. Paul, MN: West, 1986).
4. H. Koontz and R. W. Bradspies, "Managing through Feedforward Control," *Business Horizons,* June 1972, 25–36.
5. E. E. Lawler III and J. G. Rhode, *Information and Control in Organizations* (Pacific Palisades, CA: Goodyear, 1976).
6. C. W. L. Hill and G. R. Jones, *Strategic Management: An Integrated Approach,* 6th ed. (Boston: Houghton Mifflin, 2003).
7. E. Flamholtz, "Organizational Control Systems as a Management Tool," *California Management Review,* Winter 1979, 50–58.
8. W. G. Ouchi, "The Transmission of Control through Organizational Hierarchy," *Academy of Management Journal* 21 (1978), 173–92.
9. W. G. Ouchi, "The Relationship between Organizational Structure and Organizational Control," *Administrative Science Quarterly* 22 (1977), 95–113.
10. Ouchi, "Markets, Bureaucracies, and Clans."
11. W. H. Newman, *Constructive Control* (Englewood Cliffs, NJ: Prentice-Hall, 1975).
12. J. D. Thompson, *Organizations in Action* (New York: McGraw-Hill, 1967).
13. R. N. Anthony, *The Management Control Function* (Boston: Harvard Business School Press, 1988).
14. Ouchi, "Markets, Bureaucracies, and Clans."
15. Hill and Jones, *Strategic Management.*
16. R. Simons, "Strategic Orientation and Top Management Attention to Control Systems," *Strategic Management Journal* 12 (1991), 49–62.
17. G. Schreyogg and H. Steinmann, "Strategic Control: A New Perspective," *Academy of Management Review* 12 (1987), 91–103.
18. B. Woolridge and S. W. Floyd, "The Strategy Process, Middle Management Involvement, and Organizational Performance," *Strategic Management Journal* 11 (1990), 231–41.
19. J. A. Alexander, "Adaptive Changes in Corporate Control Practices," *Academy of Management Journal* 34 (1991), 162–93.
20. Hill and Jones, *Strategic Management.*
21. G. H. B. Ross, "Revolution in Management Control," *Management Accounting* 72 (1992), 23–27.
22. P. F. Drucker, *The Practice of Management* (New York: Harper & Row, 1954).
23. S. J. Carroll and H. L. Tosi, *Management by Objectives: Applications and Research* (New York: Macmillan, 1973).
24. R. Rodgers and J. E. Hunter, "Impact of Management by Objectives on Organizational Productivity," *Journal of Applied Psychology* 76 (1991), 322–26.
25. M. B. Gavin, S. G. Green, and G. T. Fairhurst, "Managerial Control–Strategies for Poor Performance over Time and the Impact on Subordinate Reactions," *Organizational Behavior and Human Decision Processes* 63 (1995), 207–21.
26. www.cypress.com, 2001, 2005, 2010.
27. B. Dumaine, "The Bureaucracy Busters," *Fortune,* June 17, 1991, 46.
28. www.microsoft.com, 2006, 2010.
29. O. Thomas, "Microsoft Employees Feel Maligned," www.money.cnn.com, March 10, 2006.
30. J. Nightingale, "Rising Frustration with Microsoft's Compensation and Review System," www.washtech.org, March 10, 2006.
31. "Microsoft's Departing Employees," www.yahoo.news.com, May 6, 2006.
32. D. S. Pugh, D. J. Hickson, C. R. Hinings, and C. Turner, "Dimensions of Organizational Structure," *Administrative Science Quarterly* 13 (1968), 65–91.
33. B. Elgin, "Running the Tightest Ships on the Net," *BusinessWeek,* January 29, 2001, 125–26.
34. P. M. Blau, *The Dynamics of Bureaucracy* (Chicago: University of Chicago Press, 1955).
35. J. McGregor, "The World's Most Innovative Companies," www.businessweek.com, May 4, 2007.
36. http://corporate.disney.go.com, 2010.
37. Ouchi, "Markets, Bureaucracies, and Clans."
38. Ibid.
39. This section draws heavily on K. Lewin, *Field Theory in Social Science* (New York: Harper & Row, 1951).
40. L. Chung-Ming and R. W. Woodman, "Understanding Organizational Change: A Schematic Perspective," *Academy of Management Journal* 38, no. 2 (1995), 537–55.
41. D. Miller, "Evolution and Revolution: A Quantum View of Structural Change in Organizations," *Journal of Management Studies* 19 (1982), 11–151; D. Miller, "Momentum and Revolution in Organizational Adaptation," *Academy of Management Journal* 2 (1980), 591–614.
42. C. E. Lindblom, "The Science of Muddling Through," *Public Administration Review* 19 (1959), 79–88; P. C. Nystrom and W. H. Starbuck, "To Avoid Organizational Crises, Unlearn," *Organizational Dynamics* 12 (1984), 53–65.
43. L. Brown, "Research Action: Organizational Feedback, Understanding, and Change," *Journal of Applied Behavioral Research* 8 (1972), 697–711; P. A. Clark, *Action Research and Organizational Change* (New York: Harper & Row, 1972); N. Margulies and A. P. Raia, eds., *Conceptual Foundations of Organizational Development* (New York: McGraw-Hill, 1978).
44. W. L. French and C. H. Bell, *Organizational Development* (Englewood Cliffs, NJ: Prentice-Hall, 1990).
45. "Concepts for Tomorrow's World," *Research,* 2007, 72–73; *Bayer Science for a Better Life,* October 23, 2007, http://www.bayer.com/.
46. W. L. French, "A Checklist for Organizing and Implementing an OD Effort," in W. L. French, C. H. Bell,

and R. A. Zawacki, eds., *Organizational Development and Transformation* (Homewood, IL: Irwin, 1994), 484–95.

Chapter 12

1. 100 Best Companies to Work For 2010: Zappos.com–AMZN–from FORTUNE, "15. Zappos.com," http://money.cnn.com/magazines/fortune/bestcompanies/2010/snapshots/15.html, February 22, 2010.
2. R. Wauters, "Amazon Closes Zappos Deal, Ends Up Paying $1.2 Billion," TechCrunch, November 2, 2009, http://techcrunch.com/2009/11/02/amazon-closes-zappos-deal-ends-up-paying-1-2-billion/, February 22, 2010.
3. J. McGregor, "Zappo's Secret: It's an Open Book," *BusinessWeek*, March 23 & 30, 2009, 62; "About.zappos.com," Tony Hsieh–CEO, http://about.zappos.com/meet-our-monkeys/tony-hsieh-ceo, February 22, 2010; M. Chafkin, "Get Happy," *Inc.*, May 2009, 66–73.
4. Chafkin, "Get Happy"; "Keeper of the Flame," *The Economist*, April 18, 2009, 75.
5. "Happy Feet–Inside the Online Shoe Utopia," *The New Yorker*, September 14, 2009, http://about.zappos.com/press-center/media-coverage/happy-feet-inside-online-shoe-utopia, February 22, 2010.
6. Ibid.
7. Chafkin, "Get Happy"; "Keeper of the Flame."
8. Ibid.
9. Zappos Core Values/about.zappos.com, http://about.zappos.com/our-unique-culture/zappos-core-values, February 22, 2010.
10. "From Upstart to $1 Billion Behemoth, Zappos Marks 10 Years," *Las Vegas Sun*, Tuesday, June 16, 2009, http://about.zappos.com/press-center/media-coverage/upstart-1-billion-behemoth-zappos- . . . , February 22, 2010; Chafkin, "Get Happy"; "Keeper of the Flame."
11. "Keeper of the Flame"; Chafkin, "Get Happy."
12. Chafkin, "Get Happy."
13. J. E. Butler, G. R. Ferris, and N. K. Napier, *Strategy and Human Resource Management* (Cincinnati: Southwestern Publishing, 1991); P. M. Wright and G. C. McMahan, "Theoretical Perspectives for Strategic Human Resource Management," *Journal of Management* 18 (1992), 295–320.
14. J. B. Quinn, P. Anderson, and S. Finkelstein, "Managing Professional Intellect: Making the Most of the Best," *Harvard Business Review*, March–April 1996, 71–80.
15. Ibid.
16. C. D. Fisher, L. F. Schoenfeldt, and J. B. Shaw, *Human Resource Management* (Boston: Houghton Mifflin, 1990).
17. J. McGregor and E. Gibson, "The World's Most Influential Companies," *Bloomberg Businessweek*, December 11, 2008, http://images.businessweek.com/ss/08/12/1211_most_influential/1.htm.
18. Wright and McMahan, "Theoretical Perspectives."
19. L. Baird and I. Meshoulam, "Managing Two Fits for Strategic Human Resource Management," *Academy of Management Review* 14, 116–28; J. Milliman, M. Von Glinow, and M. Nathan, "Organizational Life Cycles and Strategic International Human Resource Management in Multinational Companies: Implications for Congruence Theory," *Academy of Management Review* 16 (1991), 318–39; R. S. Schuler and S. E. Jackson, "Linking Competitive Strategies with Human Resource Management Practices," *Academy of Management Executive* 1 (1987), 207–19; P. M. Wright and S. A. Snell, "Toward an Integrative View of Strategic Human Resource Management," *Human Resource Management Review* 1 (1991), 203–225.
20. "Who's in Charge Here? No One," *The Observer*, April 27, 2003 (http://observer.guardian.co.uk/business/story/0,6903,944138,00.html); "Ricardo Semler, CEO, Semco SA," cnn.com, June 29, 2004 (http://cnn.worldnews.printthis.clickability.com/pt/cpt&title=cnn.com); D. Kirkpatrick, "The Future of Work: An 'Apprentice' Style Office?" *Fortune*, April 14, 2004 (www.fortune.com/fortune/subs/print/0,15935,611068,00.html); A. Strutt and R. Van Der Beek, "Report from HR2004," www.mce.be/hr2004/reportd2.htm, July 2, 2004; R. Semler, "Seven-Day Weekend Returns Power to Employees," workopolis.com, May 26, 2004 (http://globeandmail.workopolis.com/servlet/content/qprinter/20040526/cabooks26); "SEMCO," http://semco.locaweb.com.br/ingles, May 31, 2006; "Ricardo Semler, Semco SA: What Are You Reading?" cnn.com, May 31, 2006. (www.cnn.com/2004/BUSINESS/06/29/semler.profile/index.html).
21. R. Semler, *The Seven-Day Weekend: Changing the Way Work Works* (New York: Penguin, 2003); "SEMCO."
22. Semler, *The Seven-Day Weekend;* "SEMCO"; G. Hamel, *The Future of Management* (Cambridge, MA: Harvard Business Press, 2007).
23. A. Strutt, "Interview with Ricardo Semler," *Management Centre Europe*, April 2004 (www.mce.be/knowledge/392/35).
24. Semler, *The Seven-Day Weekend.*
25. Ibid.
26. R. Semler, "How We Went *Digital* without a *Strategy*," *Harvard Business Review* 78, no. 5 (September–October 2000), 51–56.
27. Semler, *The Seven-Day Weekend.*
28. S. L. Rynes, "Recruitment, Job Choice, and Post-Hire Consequences: A Call for New Research Directions," in M. D. Dunnette and L. M. Hough, eds., *Handbook of Industrial and Organizational Psychology*, vol. 2 (Palo Alto, CA: Consulting Psychologists Press, 1991), 399–444.
29. J. Perry, L. DiLeo, and S. Meichtry, "Mass Cuts of Temp Workers Pose a Tough Test for Europe," *The Wall Street Journal*, March 12, 2009, http://online.wsj.com/article/SB123680920862100627.html.
30. R. L. Sullivan, "Lawyers a la Carte," *Forbes*, September 11, 1995, 44.
31. E. Porter, "Send Jobs to India? U.S. Companies Say It's Not Always Best," *The New York Times*, April 28, 2004, A1, A7.
32. D. Wessel, "The Future of Jobs: New Ones Arise; Wage Gap Widens," *The Wall Street Journal*, April 2, 2004, A1, A5; "Relocating the Back Office," *The Economist*, December 13, 2003, 67–69.
33. The Conference Board, "Offshoring Evolving at a Rapid Pace, Report Duke University and The Conference Board," August 3, 2009, http://www.conference-board.org/utilities/pressPrinterFriendly.cfm?press_ID=3709, February 24, 2010; S. Minter, "Offshoring by U.S. Companies Doubles," *Industry Week*, August 19, 2009, http://www.industryweek.com/PrintArticle.aspx?ArticleID=19772&SectionID=3, February 24, 2010; AFP, "Offshoring by U.S. Companies Surges: Survey," August 3, 2009, http://www.google.com/hostednews/afp/article/ALeqM5iDaq1D2KZU16YfbKrMPdborD7 . . . , February 24, 2010; V. Wadhwa, "The Global Innovation Migration," *BusinessWeek*, November 9, 2009, http://www.businessweek.com/print/technology/content/nov2009/tc2009119_331698.htm, February 24, 2010; T. Heijmen, A. Y. Lewin, S. Manning, N. Perm-Ajchariyawong, and J. W. Russell, "Offshoring Research the C-Suite," 2007–2008 ORN Survey Report, *The Conference Board*, in collaboration with Duke University Offshoring Research Network.
34. The Conference Board, "Offshoring Evolving at a Rapid Pace"; Minter, "Offshoring by U.S. Companies Doubles"; AFP, "Offshoring by U.S. Companies Surges"; V. Wadhwa, "The Global

Innovation Migration"; Heijmen et al., "Offshoring Research the C-Suite."

35. R. J. Harvey, "Job Analysis," in Dunnette and Hough, *Handbook of Industrial and Organizational Psychology,* 71–163.
36. E. L. Levine, *Everything You Always Wanted to Know about Job Analysis: A Job Analysis Primer* (Tampa, FL: Mariner Publishing, 1983).
37. R. L. Mathis and J. H. Jackson, *Human Resource Management,* 7th ed. (Minneapolis: West, 1994).
38. E. J. McCormick, P. R. Jeannerette, and R. C. Mecham, *Position Analysis Questionnaire* (West Lafayette, IN: Occupational Research Center, Department of Psychological Sciences, Purdue University, 1969).
39. Fisher et al., *Human Resource Management;* Mathis and Jackson, *Human Resource Management;* R. A. Noe, J. R. Hollenbeck, B. Gerhart, and P. M. Wright, *Human Resource Management: Gaining a Competitive Advantage* (Burr Ridge, IL: Irwin, 1994).
40. Fisher et al., *Human Resource Management;* E. J. McCormick, *Job Analysis: Methods and Applications* (New York: American Management Association, 1979); E. J. McCormick and P. R. Jeannerette, "The Position Analysis Questionnaire," in S. Gael, ed., *The Job Analysis Handbook for Business, Industry, and Government* (New York: Wiley, 1988); Noe et al., *Human Resource Management.*
41. Rynes, "Recruitment, Job Choice, and Post-Hire Consequences."
42. R. Sharpe, "The Life of the Party? Can Jeff Taylor Keep the Good Times Rolling at Monster.com?" *BusinessWeek,* June 4, 2001 (*BusinessWeek* Archives); D. H. Freedman, "The Monster Dilemma," *Inc.,* May 2007, 77–78; P. Korkki, "So Easy to Apply, So Hard to Be Noticed," *The New York Times,* July 1, 2007, BU16.
43. Jobline International–Resume Vacancy Posting, Employment Resources, Job Searches, http://www.jobline.net, February 25, 2010.
44. S. L. Premack and J. P. Wanous, "A Meta-Analysis of Realistic Job Preview Experiments," *Journal of Applied Psychology* 70 (1985), 706–19; J. P. Wanous, "Realistic Job Previews: Can a Procedure to Reduce Turnover also Influence the Relationship between Abilities and Performance?" *Personnel Psychology* 31 (1978), 249–58; J. P. Wanous, *Organizational Entry: Recruitment, Selection, and Socialization of Newcomers* (Reading, MA: Addison-Wesley, 1980).
45. R. M. Guion, "Personnel Assessment, Selection, and Placement," in Dunnette and Hough, *Handbook of Industrial and Organizational Psychology,* 327–97.
46. J. Wirtz, L. Heracleous, and N. Pangarkar, "Managing Human Resources for Service Excellence and Cost Effectiveness at Singapore Airlines," *Managing Service Quality* 18 (2008), 4–19.
47. T. Joyner, "Job Background Checks Surge," *Houston Chronicle,* May 2, 2005, D6.
48. Joyner, "Job Background Checks Surge"; "ADP News Releases: Employer Services: ADP Hiring Index Reveals Background Checks Performed More Than Tripled since 1997," *Automatic Data Processing, Inc.,* June 3, 2006 (www.investquest.com/iq/a/aud/ne/news/adp042505background.htm).
49. "ADP News Releases."
50. Noe et al., *Human Resource Management;* J. A. Wheeler and J. A. Gier, "Reliability and Validity of the Situational Interview for a Sales Position," *Journal of Applied Psychology* 2 (1987), 484–87.
51. Noe et al., *Human Resource Management.*
52. J. Flint, "Can You Tell Applesauce from Pickles?" *Forbes,* October 9, 1995, 106–8.
53. Ibid.
54. "Wanted: Middle Managers, Audition Required," *The Wall Street Journal,* December 28, 1995, A1.
55. Wirtz et al., "Managing Human Resources for Service Excellence and Cost Effectiveness at Singapore Airlines."
56. I. L. Goldstein, "Training in Work Organizations," in Dunnette and Hough, *Handbook of Industrial and Organizational Psychology,* 507–619.
57. Metalúrgica Gerdau S.A., *Management Report, Doc. 1, Report 1* (Porto Alegre, Brazil: Metalúrgica Gerdau, 2004).
58. T. D. Allen, L. T. Eby, M. L. Poteet, E. Lentz, and L. Lima, "Career Benefits Associated with Mentoring for Protégés: A Meta-Analysis," *Journal of Applied Psychology* 89, no. 1 (2004), 127–36.
59. J. A. Byrne, "Virtual B-Schools," *BusinessWeek,* October 23, 1995, 64–68; Michigan Executive Education Locations around the Globe, http://exceed.bus.umich.edu/InternationalFacilities/default.aspx, February 25, 2010.
60. Fisher et al., *Human Resource Management.*
61. Fisher et al., *Human Resource Management;* G. P. Latham and K. N. Wexley, *Increasing Productivity through Performance Appraisal* (Reading, MA: Addison-Wesley, 1982).
62. T. A. DeCotiis, "An Analysis of the External Validity and Applied Relevance of Three Rating Formats," *Organizational Behavior and Human Performance* 19 (1977), 247–66; Fisher et al., *Human Resource Management.*
63. J. Muller, K. Kerwin, D. Welch, P. L. Moore, D. Brady, "Ford: It's Worse Than You Think," *BusinessWeek,* June 25, 2001 (*BusinessWeek* Archives).
64. J. S. Lublin, "It's Shape-Up Time for Performance Reviews," *The Wall Street Journal,* October 3, 1994, B1, B2.
65. C. Borman and D. W. Bracken, "360 Degree Appraisals," in C. L. Cooper and C. Argyris, eds., *The Concise Blackwell Encyclopedia of Management* (Oxford, England: Blackwell Publishers, 1998), 17; D. W. Bracken, "Straight Talk about Multi-Rater Feedback," *Training and Development* 48 (1994), 44–51; M. R. Edwards, W. C. Borman, and J. R. Sproul, "Solving the Double Bind in Performance Appraisal: A Saga of Solves, Sloths, and Eagles," *Business Horizons* 85 (1985), 59–68.
66. M. A. Peiperl, "Getting 360 Degree Feedback Right," *Harvard Business Review,* January 2001, 142–47.
67. A. Harrington, "Workers of the World, Rate Your Boss!" *Fortune,* September 18, 2000, 340, 342; www.ImproveNow.com, June 2001.
68. Lublin, "It's Shape-Up Time for Performance Reviews."
69. S. E. Moss and J. I. Sanchez, "Are Your Employees Avoiding You? Managerial Strategies for Closing the Feedback Gap," *Academy of Management Executive* 18, no. 1 (2004), 32–46.
70. J. Flynn and F. Nayeri, "Continental Divide over Executive Pay," *BusinessWeek,* July 3, 1995, 40–41.
71. A. Borrus, "A Battle Royal against Regal Paychecks," *BusinessWeek,* February 24, 2003, 127; "Too Many Turkeys," *The Economist,* November 26, 2005, 75–76; G. Morgenson, "How to Slow Runaway Executive Pay," *The New York Times,* October 23, 2005, 1, 4; S. Greenhouse, *The Big Squeeze: Tough Times for the American Worker* (New York: Alfred A. Knopf, 2008).
72. "Executive Pay," *BusinessWeek,* April 19, 2004, 106–110.
73. "Home Depot Chief's Pay in 2007 Could Reach $8.9m," *The New York Times,* Bloomberg News, January 25, 2007, C7; E. Carr, "The Stockpot," *The Economist, A Special Report on Executive Pay,* January 20, 2007, 6–10; E. Porter, "More Than Ever, It Pays to Be the Top Executive," *The New York Times,* May 25, 2007, A1, C7.
74. K. K. Spors, "Top Small Workplaces 2007," *The Wall Street Journal,* October 1, 2007, R1–R6; K. K. Spors, "Guerra DeBerry Coody," *The Wall Street Journal,* October 1, 2007, R5; "Guerra

DeBerry Coody Named One of the Nation's 15 Top Small Workplaces of 2007," *Business Wire,* http://findarticles.com/p/articles/mi_m0EIN/is_2007_Oct_1/ai_n20527510/print, March 6, 2008; "Guerra DeBerry Coody," www.gdc-co.com/, March 6, 2008; "Frank Guerra '83, Trish DeBerry-Mejia '87, and Tess Coody '93," *Trinity University, Alumni–Profiles,* www.trinity.edu/alumni/profiles/0503_guerra_deberry_coody.htm, March 6, 2008.

75. Spors, "Top Small Workplaces 2007"; Spors, "Guerra DeBerry Coody"; "Guerra DeBerry Coody Named One of the Nation's 15 Top Small Workplaces of 2007."
76. Spors, "Top Small Workplaces 2007"; Spors, "Guerra DeBerry Coody"; Guerra DeBerry Coody: Day Care, http://www.gdc-co.com/, February 25, 2010.
77. Spors, "Top Small Workplaces 2007"; Spors, "Guerra DeBerry Coody."
78. Ibid.
79. "Guerra DeBerry Coody Named One of the Nation's 15 Top Small Workplaces of 2007."
80. S. Shellenbarger, "Amid Gay Marriage Debate, Companies Offer More Benefits to Same-Sex Couples," *The Wall Street Journal,* March 18, 2004, D1.

Chapter 13

1. D. A. Pitta, "Creating a Culture of Innovation at Portugal Telecom," *Journal of Product & Brand Management* 18, no. 6 (2009), 448–451, http://www.emeraldinsight.com, Emerald Group Publishing Limited.
2. R. Kanfer, "Motivation Theory and Industrial and Organizational Psychology," in M. D. Dunnette and L. M. Hough, eds., *Handbook of Industrial and Organizational Psychology,* 2nd ed., vol. 1 (Palo Alto, CA: Consulting Psychologists Press, 1990), 75–170.
3. G. P. Latham and M. H. Budworth, "The Study of Work Motivation in the 20th Century," in L. L. Koppes, ed., *Historical Perspectives in Industrial and Organizational Psychology* (Hillsdale, NJ: Laurence Erlbaum, 2006).
4. N. Nicholson, "How to Motivate Your Problem People," *Harvard Business Review,* January 2003, 57–65.
5. A. M. Grant, "Does Intrinsic Motivation Fuel the Prosocial Fire? Motivational Synergy in Predicting Persistence, Performance, and Productivity," *Journal of Applied Psychology* 93, no. 1 (2008), 48–58.
6. Grant, "Does Intrinsic Motivation Fuel the Prosocial Fire?"; C. D. Batson, "Prosocial Motiviation: Is It Ever Truly Altruistic?" in L. Berkowitz, ed., *Advances in Experimental Social Psychology,* vol. 20 (New York: Academic Press, 1987), 65–122.
7. Grant, "Does Intrinsic Motivation Fuel the Prosocial Fire?"
8. J. P. Campbell and R. D. Pritchard, "Motivation Theory in Industrial and Organizational Psychology," in M. D. Dunnette, ed., *Handbook of Industrial and Organizational Psychology* (Chicago: Rand McNally, 1976), 63–130; T. R. Mitchell, "Expectancy Value Models in Organizational Psychology," in N. T. Feather, ed., *Expectations and Actions: Expectancy Value Models in Psychology* (Hillsdale, NJ: Erlbaum, 1982), 293–312; V. H. Vroom, *Work and Motivation* (New York: Wiley, 1964).
9. N. Shope Griffin, "Personalize Your Management Development," *Harvard Business Review* 8, no. 10 (2003), 113–119.
10. T. J. Maurer, E. M. Weiss, and F. G. Barbeite, "A Model of Involvement in Work-Related Learning and Development Activity: The Effects of Individual, Situational, Motivational, and Age Variables," *Journal of Applied Psychology* 88, no. 4 (2003), 707–24.
11. "Nokia Connects HR Policy with Company Success: Firm Seeks to Defend Its No. 1 Slot in Market Share and Profit Margins," *Human Resource Management International Digest* 12, no. 6 (2004), 30–32, http://www.emeraldinsight.com, Emerald Group Publishing Limited.
12. A. H. Maslow, *Motivation and Personality* (New York: Harper & Row, 1954); Campbell and Pritchard, "Motivation Theory in Industrial and Organizational Psychology."
13. Kanfer, "Motivation Theory and Industrial and Organizational Psychology."
14. S. Ronen, "An Underlying Structure of Motivational Need Taxonomies: A Cross-Cultural Confirmation," in H. C. Triandis, M. D. Dunnette, and L. M. Hough, eds., *Handbook of Industrial and Organizational Psychology,* vol. 4 (Palo Alto, CA: Consulting Psychologists Press, 1994), 241–69.
15. N. J. Adler, *International Dimensions of Organizational Behavior,* 2nd ed. (Boston: P.W.S. Kent, 1991); G. Hofstede, "Motivation, Leadership, and Organization: Do American Theories Apply Abroad?" *Organizational Dynamics,* Summer 1980, 42–63.
16. C. P. Alderfer, "An Empirical Test of a New Theory of Human Needs," *Organizational Behavior and Human Performance* 4 (1969), 142–75; C. P. Alderfer, *Existence, Relatedness, and Growth: Human Needs in Organizational Settings* (New York: Free Press, 1972); Campbell and Pritchard, "Motivation Theory in Industrial and Organizational Psychology."
17. Kanfer, "Motivation Theory and Industrial and Organizational Psychology."
18. F. Herzberg, *Work and the Nature of Man* (Cleveland: World, 1966).
19. N. King, "Clarification and Evaluation of the Two-Factor Theory of Job Satisfaction," *Psychological Bulletin* 74 (1970), 18–31; E. A. Locke, "The Nature and Causes of Job Satisfaction," in Dunnette, *Handbook of Industrial and Organizational Psychology,* 1297–1349.
20. D. C. McClelland, *Human Motivation* (Glenview, IL: Scott, Foresman, 1985); D. C. McClelland, "How Motives, Skills, and Values Determine What People Do," *American Psychologist* 40 (1985), 812–25; D. C. McClelland, "Managing Motivation to Expand Human Freedom," *American Psychologist* 33 (1978), 201–10.
21. D. G. Winter, *The Power Motive* (New York: Free Press, 1973).
22. M. J. Stahl, "Achievement, Power, and Managerial Motivation: Selecting Managerial Talent with the Job Choice Exercise," *Personnel Psychology* 36 (1983), 775–89; D. C. McClelland and D. H. Burnham, "Power Is the Great Motivator," *Harvard Business Review* 54 (1976), 100–10.
23. R. J. House, W. D. Spangler, and J. Woycke, "Personality and Charisma in the U.S. Presidency: A Psychological Theory of Leader Effectiveness," *Administrative Science Quarterly* 36 (1991), 364–96.
24. G. H. Hines, "Achievement, Motivation, Occupations, and Labor Turnover in New Zealand," *Journal of Applied Psychology* 58 (1973), 313–17; P. S. Hundal, "A Study of Entrepreneurial Motivation: Comparison of Fast- and Slow-Progressing Small Scale Industrial Entrepreneurs in Punjab, India," *Journal of Applied Psychology* 55 (1971), 317–23.
25. R. A. Clay, "Green Is Good for You," *Monitor on Psychology,* April 2001, 40–42.
26. J. S. Adams, "Toward an Understanding of Inequity," *Journal of Abnormal and Social Psychology* 67 (1963), 422–36.
27. Adams, "Toward an Understanding of Inequity"; J. Greenberg, "Approaching Equity and Avoiding Inequity in Groups and Organizations," in J. Greenberg and R. L. Cohen, eds., *Equity and Justice in Social Behavior* (New York: Academic Press, 1982), 389–435; J. Greenberg, "Equity and Workplace Status: A Field Experiment," *Journal of Applied Psychology* 73 (1988), 606–13;

R. T. Mowday, "Equity Theory Predictions of Behavior in Organizations," in R. M. Steers and L. W. Porter, eds., *Motivation and Work Behavior* (New York: McGraw-Hill, 1987), 89–110.

28. E. A. Locke and G. P. Latham, *A Theory of Goal Setting and Task Performance* (Englewood Cliffs, NJ: Prentice-Hall, 1990).
29. Locke and Latham, *A Theory of Goal Setting and Task Performance;* J. J. Donovan and D. J. Radosevich, "The Moderating Role of Goal Commitment on the Goal Difficulty–Performance Relationship: A Meta-Analytic Review and Critical Analysis," *Journal of Applied Psychology* 83 (1998), 308–15; M. E. Tubbs, "Goal Setting: A Meta Analytic Examination of the Empirical Evidence," *Journal of Applied Psychology* 71 (1986), 474–83.
30. E. A. Locke, K. N. Shaw, L. M. Saari, and G. P. Latham, "Goal Setting and Task Performance: 1969–1980," *Psychological Bulletin* 90 (1981), 125–52.
31. P. C. Earley, T. Connolly, and G. Ekegren, "Goals, Strategy Development, and Task Performance: Some Limits on the Efficacy of Goal Setting," *Journal of Applied Psychology* 74 (1989), 24–33; R. Kanfer and P. L. Ackerman, "Motivation and Cognitive Abilities: An Integrative/Aptitude–Treatment Interaction Approach to Skill Acquisition," *Journal of Applied Psychology* 74 (1989), 657–90.
32. W. C. Hamner, "Reinforcement Theory and Contingency Management in Organizational Settings," in H. Tosi and W. C. Hamner, eds., *Organizational Behavior and Management: A Contingency Approach* (Chicago: St. Clair Press, 1974).
33. B. F. Skinner, *Contingencies of Reinforcement* (New York: Appleton-Century-Crofts, 1969).
34. H. W. Weiss, "Learning Theory and Industrial and Organizational Psychology," in Dunnette and Hough, *Handbook of Industrial and Organizational Psychology,* 171–221.
35. Hamner, "Reinforcement Theory and Contingency Management."
36. F. Luthans and R. Kreitner, *Organizational Behavior Modification and Beyond* (Glenview, IL: Scott, Foresman, 1985); A. D. Stajkovic and F. Luthans, "A Meta-Analysis of the Effects of Organizational Behavior Modification on Task Performance, 1975–95," *Academy of Management Journal* 40 (1997), 1122–49.
37. A. D. Stajkovic and F. Luthans, "Behavioral Management and Task Performance in Organizations: Conceptual Background, Meta Analysis, and Test of Alternative Models," *Personnel Psychology* 56 (2003), 155–94.
38. Stajkovic and Luthans, "Behavioral Management and Task Performance in Organizations"; Luthans and A. D. Stajkovic, "Reinforce for Performance: The Need to Go beyond Pay and Even Rewards," *Academy of Management Executive* 13, no. 2 (1999), 49–56; G. Billikopf Enciina and M. V. Norton, "Pay Method Affects Vineyard Pruner Performance," www.cnr.berkeley.edu/ucce50/ag-labor/7research/7calag05.htm.
39. A. Bandura, *Principles of Behavior Modification* (New York: Holt, Rinehart and Winston, 1969); A. Bandura, *Social Learning Theory* (Englewood Cliffs, NJ: Prentice-Hall, 1977); T. R. V. Davis and F. Luthans, "A Social Learning Approach to Organizational Behavior," *Academy of Management Review* 5 (1980), 281–90.
40. A. P. Goldstein and M. Sorcher, *Changing Supervisor Behaviors* (New York: Pergamon Press, 1974); Luthans and Kreitner, *Organizational Behavior Modification and Beyond.*
41. Bandura, *Social Learning Theory;* Davis and Luthans, "A Social Learning Approach to Organizational Behavior"; Luthans and Kreitner, *Organizational Behavior Modification and Beyond.*
42. A. Bandura, "Self-Reinforcement: Theoretical and Methodological Considerations," *Behaviorism* 4 (1976), 135–55.
43. K. H. Hammonds, "Growth Search," *Fast Company,* April, 2003, 74-81.
44. B. Elgin, "Managing Google's Idea Factory," *BusinessWeek,* October 3, 2005, 88–90.
45. A. Bandura, *Self-Efficacy: The Exercise of Control* (New York: W.H. Freeman, 1997); J. B. Vancouver, K. M. More, and R. J. Yoder, "Self-Efficacy and Resource Allocation: Support for a Nonmonotonic, Discontinuous Model," *Journal of Applied Psychology* 93, no. 1 (2008), 35–47.
46. A. Bandura, "Self-Efficacy Mechanism in Human Agency," *American Psychologist* 37 (1982), 122–27; M. E. Gist and T. R. Mitchell, "Self-Efficacy: A Theoretical Analysis of Its Determinants and Malleability," *Academy of Management Review* 17 (1992), 183–211.
47. E. E. Lawler III, *Pay and Organization Development* (Reading, MA: Addison-Wesley, 1981).
48. "The Risky New Bonuses," *Newsweek,* January 16, 1995, 42.
49. P. Dvorak and S. Thurm, "Slump Prods Firms to Seek New Compact with Workers," *The Wall Street Journal,* October 19, 2009, A1, A18.
50. D. Mattioli, "Rewards for Extra Work Come Cheap in Lean Times," *The Wall Street Journal,* January 4, 2010, B7.
51. Motivation: Case Study–EasyJet, Employee Benefits, September 3, 2008, Centaur Communications Limited, http://www.accessmylibrary.com.
52. Lawler, *Pay and Organization Development.*
53. Ibid.
54. Ibid.
55. "Stock Option," *Encarta World English Dictionary,* June 28, 2001 (www.dictionary.msn.com); personal interview with Professor Bala Dharan, Jones Graduate School of Business, Rice University, June 28, 2001.
56. Personal interview with Professor Bala Dharan.
57. Ibid.
58. C. D. Fisher, L. F. Schoenfeldt, and J. B. Shaw, *Human Resource Management* (Boston: Houghton Mifflin, 1990); B. E. Graham-Moore and T. L. Ross, *Productivity Gainsharing* (Englewood Cliffs, NJ: Prentice-Hall, 1983); A. J. Geare, "Productivity from Scanlon Type Plans," *Academy of Management Review* 1 (1976), 99–108.
59. K. Belson, "Japan's Net Generation," *BusinessWeek,* March 19, 2001 (*BusinessWeek* Archives, June 27, 2001).
60. K. Belson, "Taking a Hint from the Upstarts," *BusinessWeek,* March 19, 2001 (*BusinessWeek* Archives, June 27, 2001); "Going for the Gold," *BusinessWeek,* March 19, 2001 (*BusinessWeek* Archives, June 27, 2001); "What the Government Can Do to Promote a Flexible Workforce," *BusinessWeek,* March 19, 2001 (*BusinessWeek* Archives, June 27, 2001).

Chapter 14

1. www.viacom.com/2006/pdf/Viacom_Fact_Sheet_4_5_06.pdf, June 9, 2006; M. Gunther, "Mr. MTV Grows Up," CNNMoney.com, April 13, 2006, http://money.cnn.com/magazines/fortune/fortune_archive/2006/04/17/8374305/index.htm; "Viacom Completes Separation into CBS Corporation and 'New' Viacom," Viacom.com, January 1, 2006, www.viacom.com/view_release.jhtml?inID=10000040&inReleaseID=126683; "MTV Networks," http://www.viacom.com/ourbrands/medianetworks/mtvnetworks/Pages/default.aspx, March 3, 2010.
2. J. H. Higgins, "A Rockin' Role: McGrath Keeps MTV Networks Plugged In and Focused," www.broadcastingcable.com, April 10, 2006, www.broadcastingcable.com/article/CA6323342.html?display=Search+

Results&text=judy+mcgrath; "*Fortune* 50 Most Powerful Women in Business 2005," CNNMoney.com, November 14, 2005, http://money.cnn.com/magazines/fortune/mostpowerfulwomen/snapshots/10.html; E. Levenson, "Hall of Fame: Digging a Little Deeper into the List, We Salute the Highfliers and Share Some Facts to Inspire and Amuse," CNNMoney.com, November 14, 2005, http://money.cnn.com/magazines/fortune/fortune_archive/2005/11/14/8360698/index.html; "50 Most Powerful Women 2007: The Power 50," CNNMoney.com, *Fortune,* The Power 50–Judy McGrath (18)–FORTUNE, http://money.cnn.com/galleries/2007/fortune/0709/gallery.women_mostpowerful.fortune/18 . . . , April 2, 2008; "50 Most Powerful Women in Business," "All-Stars," http://money.cnn.com/magazines/fortune/mostpowerfulwomen/2009/allstars/index.html, March 3, 2010; "50 Most Powerful Women in Business 2009" Full List–*FORTUNE on CNNMoney.com,* http://money.cnn.com/magazines/fortune/mostpowerfulwomen/2009/full_list/, March 3, 2010.

3. "The 100 Most Powerful Women," *Forbes,* http://www.forbes.com/lists/2009/11/power-woman-09_Judy-McGrath_6J9A.html, March 3, 2010; "MTV Networks Chairman and CEO Judy McGrath Tops the 2009 Billboard Women in Music Power Players List," *Hip Hop Press,* October 2, 2009, http://www.hiphoppress.com/2009/10/mtv-networks-chairman-and-ceo-judy-mcgrath-tops-t . . . , March 3, 2010; "MTV Network's Chairman and CEO Judy McGrath to Receive Foundation of AWRT Achievement Award at 34th Annual Gracies Gala," May 21, 2009, *Gracies,* http://www.awrt.org/Gracies/pdfs/Press_Release_McGrath_2009.pdf, March 3, 2010.
4. T. Lowry, "Can MTV Stay Cool?" *BusinessWeek,* February 20, 2006, 51–60.
5. "The 2006 National Show Mobile Edition–Judy McGrath," www.thenationalshoe.com/Mobile/SpeakerDetail.aspx?ID=199, June 9, 2006.
6. Lowry, "Can MTV Stay Cool?"
7. "Real World XX: Hollywood/Main," Real World XX: Hollywood/Show Cast, Episode Guides, Trailers, Aftershow & Preview . . . , www.mtv.com/ontv/dyn/realworld-season20/series.jhtml, April 2, 2008; New Music Videos, Reality TV Shows, Celebrity News, Top Stories / MTV, http://www.mtv.com, March 3, 2010.
8. Lowry, "Can MTV Stay Cool?"; "Viacom's MTV Networks Completes Acquisition of Xfire, Inc.," www.viacom.com/view_release.jhtml?inID=10000040&inReleaseID=227008, June 9, 2006; Nick.com/Kids Games, Kids Celebrity Video, Kids Shows/Nickelodeon, http://www.nick.com, March 3, 2010.
9. "MTV Networks Unveils URGE Digital Music Service on Microsoft's New Windows Media Player 11 Platform," *Microsoft,* May 17, 2006, www.microsoft.com/presspass/press/2006/may06/05-17URGEPR.mspx.
10. Lowry, "Can MTV Stay Cool?"
11. G. Yukl, *Leadership in Organizations,* 2nd ed. (New York: Academic Press, 1989); R. M. Stogdill, *Handbook of Leadership: A Survey of the Literature* (New York: Free Press, 1974).
12. Lowry, "Can MTV Stay Cool?"
13. W. D. Spangler, R. J. House, and R. Palrecha, "Personality and Leadership," in B. Schneider and D. B. Smith, eds., *Personality and Organizations* (Mahwah, NJ: Lawrence Erlbaum, 2004), 251–90.
14. W. D. Spangler, R. J. House, and R. Palrecha, "Personality and Leadership," in B. Schneider and D. B. Smith, eds., *Personality and Organizations* (Mahwah, NJ: Lawrence Erlbaum, 2004), 251–90; "Leaders vs. Managers: Leaders Master the Context of Their Mission, Managers Surrender to It," www.msue.msu.edu/msue/imp/modtd/visuals/tsld029.htm, July 28, 2004; "Leadership," Leadership Center at Washington State University; M. Maccoby, "Understanding the Difference between Management and Leadership," *Research Technology Management* 43, no. 1 (January–February 2000), 57–59, www.maccoby.com/articles/UtDBMaL.html; P. Coutts, "Leadership vs. Management," www.telusplanet.net/public/pdcoutts/leadership/LdrVsMgnt.htm, October 1, 2000; S. Robbins, "The Difference between Managing and Leading," www.Entrepreneur.com/article/0,4621,304743,00.html, November 18, 2002; W. Bennis, "The Leadership Advantage," *Leader to Leader* 12 (Spring 1999), www.pfdf.org/leaderbooks/121/spring99/bennis/html.
15. Spangler et al., "Personality and Leadership"; "Leaders vs. Managers"; "Leadership"; Maccoby, "Understanding the Difference between Management and Leadership"; Coutts, "Leadership vs. Management"; Robbins, "The Difference between Managing and Leading"; Bennis, "The Leadership Advantage."
16. "Greenleaf: Center for Servant Leadership: History," *Greenleaf Center for Servant Leadership,* www.greenleaf.org/aboutus/history.html, April 7, 2008.
17. "What Is Servant Leadership?" *Greenleaf: Center for Servant Leadership,* http://www.greenleaf.org/whatissl/index.html, April 2, 2008.
18. "What Is Servant Leadership?"; Review by F. Hamilton of L. Spears and M. Lawrence, *Practicing Servant Leadership: Succeeding through Trust, Bravery, and Forgiveness* (San Francisco: Jossey-Bass, 2004), in *Academy of Management Review* 30 (October 2005), 875–87; R. R. Washington, "Empirical Relationships between Theories of Servant, Transformational, and Transactional Leadership," *Academy of Management,* Best Paper Proceedings, 2007, 1–6.
19. "Greenleaf: Center for Servant Leadership: History"; "What Is Servant Leadership?"; "Greenleaf: Center for Servant Leadership: Our Mission," *Greenleaf Center for Servant Leadership,* www.greenleaf.org/aboutus/mission.html, April 7, 2008.
20. B. Burlingham, "The Coolest Small Company in America," *Inc.,* January 2003, www.inc.com/magazine/20030101/25036_Printer_Friendly.html, April 7, 2008.
21. Burlingham, "The Coolest Small Company in America"; "Zingerman's Community of Businesses," *About Us,* www.zingermans.com/AboutUs.aspx, April 7, 2008; L. Buchanan, "In Praise of Selflessness," *Inc.,* May 2007, 33–35; Zingerman's Community of Businesses, http://www.zingermanscommunity.com, March 3, 2010.
22. Burlingham, "The Coolest Small Company in America"; "Zingerman's Community of Businesses"; Buchanan, "In Praise of Selflessness."
23. Buchanan, "In Praise of Selflessness."
24. Ibid.
25. Burlingham, "The Coolest Small Company in America"; "In a Nutshell," *food gatherers,* www.foodgatherers.org/about.htm, April 7, 2008; Food Gatherers, "In a Nutshell," http://www.foodgatherers.org/about.htm, March 3, 2010.
26. "In a Nutshell."
27. Buchanan, "In Praise of Selflessness."
28. R. Calori and B. Dufour, "Management European Style," *Academy of Management Executive* 9, no. 3 (1995), 61–70.
29. Ibid.
30. H. Mintzberg, *Power in and around Organizations* (Englewood Cliffs, NJ: Prentice-Hall, 1983); J. Pfeffer, *Power in Organizations* (Marshfield, MA: Pitman, 1981).
31. R. P. French, Jr., and B. Raven, "The Bases of Social Power," in D. Cartwright and A. F. Zander, eds., *Group Dynamics* (Evanston, IL: Row, Peterson, 1960), 607–23.

32. R. L. Rose, "After Turning Around Giddings and Lewis, Fife Is Turned Out Himself," *The Wall Street Journal,* June 22, 1993, A1.
33. A. Grove, "How Intel Makes Spending Pay Off," *Fortune,* February 22, 1993, 56–61; "Craig R. Barrett, Chief Executive Officer: Intel Corporation," *Intel,* July 28, 2004, www.intel.com/pressroom/kits/bios/barrett/bio.htm; Craig R. Barrett Bio, http://www.intel.com/pressroom/kits/bios/barrett.htm, March 3, 2010.
34. Craig R. Barrett Bio, www.intel.com/pressroom/kits/bios/barrett.htm, April 8, 2008; Microsoft Press Pass–Microsoft Board of Directors, www.microsoft.com/presspass/bod/default.mspx, April 8, 2008; "Tachi Yamada Selected to Lead Gates Foundation's Global Health Program," Announcements–Bill & Melinda Gates Foundation, February 6, 2006, www.gatesfoundation.org/GlobalHealth/Announcements/Announce-060106.htm, April 8, 2008; Microsoft PressPass–Microsoft Executives and Images, "Microsoft Board of Directors," http://www.microsoft.com/presspass/bod/bod.aspx, March 3, 2010; Tachi Yamada–Bill & Melinda Gates Foundation, http://www.gatesfoundation.org/leadership/Pages/tachi-yamada.aspx, March 3, 2010.
35. M. Loeb, "Jack Welch Lets Fly on Budgets, Bonuses, and Buddy Boards," *Fortune,* May 29, 1995, 146.
36. T. M. Burton, "Visionary's Reward: Combine 'Simple Ideas' and Some Failures; Result: Sweet Revenge," *The Wall Street Journal,* February 3, 1995, A1, A5.
37. L. Nakarmi, "A Flying Leap toward the 21st Century? Pressure from Competitors and Seoul May Transform the Chaebol," *BusinessWeek,* March 20, 1995, 78–80.
38. B. M. Bass, *Bass and Stogdill's Handbook of Leadership: Theory, Research, and Managerial Applications,* 3rd ed. (New York: Free Press, 1990); R. J. House and M. L. Baetz, "Leadership: Some Empirical Generalizations and New Research Directions," in B. M. Staw and L. L. Cummings, eds., *Research in Organizational Behavior,* vol. 1 (Greenwich, CT: JAI Press, 1979), 341–423; S. A. Kirpatrick and E. A. Locke, "Leadership: Do Traits Matter?" *Academy of Management Executive* 5, no. 2 (1991), 48–60; Yukl, *Leadership in Organizations;* G. Yukl and D. D. Van Fleet, "Theory and Research on Leadership in Organizations," in M. D. Dunnette and L. M. Hough, eds., *Handbook of Industrial and Organizational Psychology,* 2nd ed., vol. 3 (Palo Alto, CA: Consulting Psychologists Press, 1992), 147–97.
39. E. A. Fleishman, "Performance Assessment Based on an Empirically Derived Task Taxonomy," *Human Factors* 9 (1967), 349–66; E. A. Fleishman, "The Description of Supervisory Behavior," *Personnel Psychology* 37 (1953), 1–6; A. W. Halpin and B. J. Winer, "A Factorial Study of the Leader Behavior Descriptions," in R. M. Stogdill and A. I. Coons, eds., *Leader Behavior: Its Description and Measurement* (Columbus Bureau of Business Research, Ohio State University, 1957); D. Tscheulin, "Leader Behavior Measurement in German Industry," *Journal of Applied Psychology* 56 (1971), 28–31.
40. E. A. Fleishman and E. F. Harris, "Patterns of Leadership Behavior Related to Employee Grievances and Turnover," *Personnel Psychology* 15 (1962), 43–56.
41. P. Crush, "Interview with Stephen Battalia HR Director at Nestlé Human Resources," *HR Magazine,* December 1, 2009, http://www.hrmagazine.co.uk/news/968663/Interview-Stephen-Battalia-HR-director-Nestle/.
42. R. Likert, *New Patterns of Management* (New York: McGraw-Hill, 1961); N. C. Morse and E. Reimer, "The Experimental Change of a Major Organizational Variable," *Journal of Abnormal and Social Psychology* 52 (1956), 120–29.
43. R. R. Blake and J. S. Mouton, *The New Managerial Grid* (Houston: Gulf, 1978).
44. P. Hersey and K. Blanchard, *Management of Organizational Behavior: Utilizing Human Resources* (Englewood Cliffs, NJ: Prentice-Hall, 1982).
45. F. E. Fiedler, *A Theory of Leadership Effectiveness* (New York: McGraw-Hill, 1967); F. E. Fiedler, "The Contingency Model and the Dynamics of the Leadership Process," in L. Berkowitz, ed., *Advances in Experimental Social Psychology* (New York: Academic Press, 1978).
46. J. Fierman, "Winning Ideas from Maverick Managers," *Fortune,* February 6, 1995, 66–80; "Laybourne, Geraldine, U.S. Media Executive," *Laybourne, Geraldine,* http://museum.tv/archives/etv/L/htmlL/laybournege/laybournege.htm, April 8, 2008.
47. M. Schuman, "Free to Be," *Forbes,* May 8, 1995, 78–80; "Profile–Herman Mashaba," *SAIE–Herman Mashaba,* www.entrepreneurship.co.za/page/herman_mashaba, April 8, 2008.
48. House and Baetz, "Leadership"; L. H. Peters, D. D. Hartke, and J. T. Pohlmann, "Fiedler's Contingency Theory of Leadership: An Application of the Meta-Analysis Procedures of Schmidt and Hunter," *Psychological Bulletin* 97 (1985), 274–85; C. A. Schriesheim, B. J. Tepper, and L. A. Tetrault, "Least Preferred Co-Worker Score, Situational Control, and Leadership Effectiveness: A Meta-Analysis of Contingency Model Performance Predictions," *Journal of Applied Psychology* 79 (1994), 561–73.
49. M. G. Evans, "The Effects of Supervisory Behavior on the Path–Goal Relationship," *Organizational Behavior and Human Performance* 5 (1970), 277–98; R. J. House, "A Path–Goal Theory of Leader Effectiveness," *Administrative Science Quarterly* 16 (1971), 321–38; J. C. Wofford and L. Z. Liska, "Path–Goal Theories of Leadership: A Meta-Analysis," *Journal of Management* 19 (1993), 857–76.
50. S. Kerr and J. M. Jermier, "Substitutes for Leadership: Their Meaning and Measurement," *Organizational Behavior and Human Performance* 22 (1978), 375–403; P. M. Podsakoff, B. P. Niehoff, S. B. MacKenzie, and M. L. Williams, "Do Substitutes for Leadership Really Substitute for Leadership? An Empirical Examination of Kerr and Jermier's Situational Leadership Model," *Organizational Behavior and Human Decision Processes* 54 (1993), 1–44.
51. Kerr and Jermier, "Substitutes for Leadership"; Podsakoff et al., "Do Substitutes for Leadership Really Substitute for Leadership?"
52. G. Spreitzer, K. H. Perttula, and K. Xin, "Traditionality Matters: An Examination of the Effectiveness of Transformational Leadership in the U.S. and Taiwan," University of Michigan, http://webuser.bus.umich.edu/spreitze/traditionalitymatters.pdf.
53. B. M. Bass, *Leadership and Performance beyond Expectations* (New York: Free Press, 1985); Bass, *Bass and Stogdill's Handbook of Leadership;* Yukl and Van Fleet, "Theory and Research on Leadership."
54. N. D. Schwartz, "Europeans Revitalize Plants to Save Jobs," *The New York Times,* February 3, 2010, http://www.nytimes.com/2010/02/04/business/global/04iht-euecon.html.
55. J. A. Conger and R. N. Kanungo, "Behavioral Dimensions of Charismatic Leadership," in J. A. Conger, R. N. Kanungo, and Associates, *Charismatic Leadership* (San Francisco: Jossey-Bass, 1988).
56. Bass, *Leadership and Performance beyond Expectations;* Bass, *Bass and Stogdill's Handbook of Leadership;* Yukl and Van Fleet, "Theory and Research on Leadership"; J. Reingold, "You Got Served," *Fortune,* October 1, 2007, 55–58.
57. Bass, *Leadership and Performance beyond Expectations;* Bass, *Bass and Stogdill's Handbook of Leadership;* Yukl and Van Fleet, "Theory and Research on Leadership."

58. Bass, *Leadership and Performance beyond Expectations.*
59. Bass, *Bass and Stogdill's Handbook of Leadership;* B. M. Bass and B. J. Avolio, "Transformational Leadership: A Response to Critiques," in M. M. Chemers and R. Ayman, eds., *Leadership Theory and Research: Perspectives and Directions* (San Diego: Academic Press, 1993), 49–80; B. M. Bass, B. J. Avolio, and L. Goodheim, "Biography and the Assessment of Transformational Leadership at the World Class Level," *Journal of Management* 13 (1987), 7–20; J. J. Hater and B. M. Bass, "Supervisors' Evaluations and Subordinates' Perceptions of Transformational and Transactional Leadership," *Journal of Applied Psychology* 73 (1988), 695–702; R. Pillai, "Crisis and Emergence of Charismatic Leadership in Groups: An Experimental Investigation," *Journal of Applied Psychology* 26 (1996), 543–62; J. Seltzer and B. M. Bass, "Transformational Leadership: Beyond Initiation and Consideration," *Journal of Management* 16 (1990), 693–703; D. A. Waldman, B. M. Bass, and W. O. Einstein, "Effort, Performance, Transformational Leadership in Industrial and Military Service," *Journal of Occupation Psychology* 60 (1987), 1–10.
60. R. Pillai, C. A. Schriesheim, and E. S. Williams, "Fairness Perceptions and Trust as Mediators of Transformational and Transactional Leadership: A Two-Sample Study," *Journal of Management* 25 (1999), 897–933.
61. "50 Most Powerful Women–1. Indra Nooyi (1)–*Fortune,*" http://money.cnn.com/galleries/2009/fortune/0909/gallery.most_powerful_women.fortune/i . . . , March 5, 2010.
62. "50 Most Powerful Women–5. Andrea Jung (5)–*Fortune,*" http://money.cnn.com/galleries/2009/fortune/0909/gallery.most_powerful_women.fortune/5 . . . , March 5, 2010.
63. L. Tischler, "Where Are the Women?" *Fast Company,* February 2004, 52–60.
64. I. P. Johnson, "EU Threat to Impose Female Quotas Gets Mixed Response in Germany," *Deutsche Welle,* September 17, 2010, http://www.dw-world.de/dw/article/0,,6015660,00.html.
65. A. H. Eagly and B. T. Johnson, "Gender and Leadership Style: A Meta-Analysis," *Psychological Bulletin* 108 (1990), 233–56.
66. Ibid.
67. The Economist, "Workers Resent Scoldings from Female Bosses," *Houston Chronicle,* August 19, 2000, 1C.
68. Ibid.
69. Ibid.
70. Ibid.
71. A. H. Eagly, S. J. Karau, and M. G. Makhijani, "Gender and the Effectiveness of Leaders: A Meta-Analysis," *Psychological Bulletin* 117 (1995), 125–45.
72. Ibid.
73. J. M. George and K. Bettenhausen, "Understanding Prosocial Behavior, Sales Performance, and Turnover: A Group-Level Analysis in a Service Context," *Journal of Applied Psychology* 75 (1990), 698–709.
74. T. Sy, S. Cote, and R. Saavedra, "The Contagious Leader: Impact of the Leader's Mood on the Mood of Group Members, Group Affective Tone, and Group Processes," *Journal of Applied Psychology* 90(2), (2005), 295–305.
75. J. M. George, "Emotions and Leadership: The Role of Emotional Intelligence," *Human Relations* 53 (2000), 1027–55.
76. Ibid.
77. J. Zhou and J. M. George, "Awakening Employee Creativity: The Role of Leader Emotional Intelligence," *The Leadership Quarterly* 14, no. 45 (August–October 2003), 545–68.
78. Ibid.
79. Ibid.
80. D. Fenn, "My Bad," *Inc.,* October 2007, 37–38; *Creative Display Solutions: About Us,* www.creativedisplaysolutions.com/pages/about/about.html, April 4, 2008; *Creative Display Solutions: About Us,* http://www.creativedisplaysolutions.com/pages/about/about.html, March 5, 2010.
81. Fenn, "My Bad"; *Creative Display Solutions: About Us,* www.creativedisplaysolutions.com/pages/about/about.html, April 4, 2008.
82. Fenn, "My Bad."
83. Ibid.
84. Ibid.
85. Ibid.
86. Ibid.
87. Ibid.; C. Mason-Draffen, "Inside Stories," "Feeling Like a Million," *Creative Display Solutions: CDS News,* www.creativedisplaysolutions.com/pages/about/news6.html, April 4, 2008.
88. D. Sonnenberg, "Mother Load: How to Balance Career and Family," July 30, 2007, *Creative Display Solutions: CDS News,* www.creativedisplaysolutions.com/pages/about/news8.html, April 4, 2008; C. Mason-Draffen, "Partnership at Work: Couples in Business Together Have Their Share of Sweet Rewards and Unique Challenges," February 13, 2007, *Creative Display Solutions, CDS News,* www.creativedisplaysolutions.com/pages/about/news7.html, April 4, 2008; "Client List," *Creative Display Solutions: About Us,* www.creativedisplaysolutions.com/pages/about/clients.html, April 8, 2008; Fenn, "My Bad;" "Client List," *Creative,* http://www.creativedisplaysolutions.com/pages/about/clients.html, March 5, 2010.
89. Fenn, "My Bad."

Chapter 15

1. G. Edmonson, "The Secret of BMW's Success," *BusinessWeek,* October 16, 2006, http://www.businessweek.com/magazine/content/06_42/b4005078.htm.
2. T. M. Mills, *The Sociology of Small Groups* (Englewood Cliffs, NJ: Prentice-Hall, 1967); M. E. Shaw, *Group Dynamics* (New York: McGraw-Hill, 1981).
3. E. Greb, "Is JIT Manufacturing the Right Prescription?" *Pharmaceutical Technology* 33, no. 3 (March 2009), 72–78.
4. J. A. Pearce II and E. C. Ravlin, "The Design and Activation of Self-Regulating Work Groups," *Human Relations* 11 (1987), 751–82.
5. B. Dumaine, "Who Needs a Boss?" *Fortune,* May 7, 1990, 52–60; Pearce and Ravlin, "The Design and Activation of Self-Regulating Work Groups."
6. Dumaine, "Who Needs a Boss?"; A. R. Montebello and V. R. Buzzotta, "Work Teams That Work," *Training and Development,* March 1993, 59–64.
7. C. Matlack, R. Tiplady, D. Brady, R. Berner, and H. Tashiro, "The Vuitton Machine," *BusinessWeek,* March 22, 2004, 98–102; "America's Most Admired Companies," *Fortune.com,* August 18, 2004, www.fortune.com/fortune/mostadmired/snapshot/0,15020,383,00.html; "Art Samberg's Ode to Steel," *Big Money Weekly,* June 29, 2004, http://trading.sina/com/trading/rightside/bigmoney_weekly_040629.b5.shtml; "Nucor Reports Record Results for First Quarter of 2004," www.nucor.com/financials.asp?finpage=news releases, August 18, 2004; "Nucor Reports Results for First Half and Second Quarter of 2004," www.nucor.com/financials.asp?finpage=newsreleases; J. C. Cooper, "The Price of Efficiency," *BusinessWeek Online,* March 22, 2004, www.businessweek.com/magazine/content/04_12/b3875603.htm; "LVHM–Fashion & Leather Goods," www.lvmh.com, June 18, 2006; C. Matlack, "Rich Times for the Luxury Sector," *BusinessWeek Online,* March 6, 2006, www.businessweek.com/globalbiz/content/mar2006/gb20060306_296309.htm? campaign_id=search; N. Byrnes, "The Art of Motivation," *BusinessWeek,* May 1, 2006, 56–62; "Nucor Steel," http://www.nucor.com/indexinner.aspx?finpage=aboutus,

April 16, 2008; "Annual General Meetings–Group Investor Relations–Corporate Governance," http://www.lvmh.com/comfi/pg_home.asp?rub=6&srub=0, March 16, 2008.

8. Matlack et al., "The Vuitton Machine."
9. M. Arndt, "Out of the Forge and into the Fire," *BusinessWeek*, June 18, 2001, *BusinessWeek* Archives; Byrnes, "The Art of Motivation."
10. S. Baker, "The Minimill That Acts Like a Biggie," *BusinessWeek*, September 30, 1996, 101–104; S. Baker, "Nucor," *BusinessWeek*, February 13, 1995, 70; S. Overman, "No-Frills at Nucor," *HRMagazine*, July 1994, 56–60.
11. www.nucor.com, November 21, 2001; "Nucor: About Us."
12. Baker, "The Minimill That Acts Like a Biggie"; Baker, "Nucor"; Overman, "No-Frills at Nucor"; www.nucor.com; Byrnes, "The Art of Motivation"; "Nucor: About Us."
13. N. Byrnes, "A Steely Resolve," *BusinessWeek*, April 6, 2009, 54.
14. Matlack et al., "The Vuitton Machine"; "About Nucor"; "America's Most Admired Companies"; "Art Samberg's Ode to Steel"; "Nucor Reports Record Results for First Quarter of 2004"; "Nucor Reports Results for First Half and Second Quarter of 2004"; Byrnes, "The Art of Motivation."
15. T. D. Wall, N. J. Kemp, P. R. Jackson, and C. W. Clegg, "Outcomes of Autonomous Work Groups: A Long-Term Field Experiment," *Academy of Management Journal* 29 (1986), 280–304.
16. J. S. Lublin, "My Colleague, My Boss," *The Wall Street Journal*, April 12, 1995, R4, R12.
17. W. R. Pape, "Group Insurance," *Inc.* (Technology Supplement), June 17, 1997, 29–31; A. M. Townsend, S. M. DeMarie, and A. R. Hendrickson, "Are You Ready for Virtual Teams?" *HR Magazine*, September 1996, 122–126; A. M. Townsend, S. M. DeMarie, and A. M. Hendrickson, "Virtual Teams: Technology and the Workplace of the Future," *Academy of Management Executive* 12, no. 3 (1998), 17–29.
18. Townsend et al., "Virtual Teams."
19. Pape, "Group Insurance"; Townsend et al., "Are You Ready for Virtual Teams?"; L. Gratton, "Working Together . . . When Apart," *The Wall Street Journal*, June 16–17, 2007, R4.
20. D. L. Duarte and N. T. Snyder, *Mastering Virtual Teams* (San Francisco: Jossey-Bass, 1999); K. A. Karl, "Book Reviews: *Mastering Virtual Teams*," *Academy of Management Executive*, August 1999, 118–19.
21. B. Geber, "Virtual Teams," *Training* 32, no. 4 (August 1995), 36–40; T. Finholt and L. S. Sproull, "Electronic Groups at Work," *Organization Science* 1 (1990), 41–64.
22. Geber, "Virtual Teams."
23. E. J. Hill, B. C. Miller, S. P. Weiner, and J. Colihan, "Influences of the Virtual Office on Aspects of Work and Work/Life Balance," *Personnel Psychology* 31 (1998), 667–83; S. G. Strauss, "Technology, Group Process, and Group Outcomes: Testing the Connections in Computer-Mediated and Face-to-Face Groups," *Human Computer Interaction*, 12 (1997), 227–66; M. E. Warkentin, L. Sayeed, and R. Hightower, "Virtual Teams versus Face-to-Face Teams: An Exploratory Study of a Web-Based Conference System," *Decision Sciences* 28, no. 4 (Fall 1997), 975–96.
24. S. A. Furst, M. Reeves, B. Rosen, and R. S. Blackburn, "Managing the Life Cycle of Virtual Teams," *Academy of Management Executive* 18, no. 2 (May 2004), 6–20.
25. Ibid.
26. Gratton, "Working Together . . . When Apart."
27. Ibid.
28. Ibid.
29. Ibid.
30. A. Deutschman, "The Managing Wisdom of High-Tech Superstars," *Fortune*, October 17, 1994, 197–206.
31. J. D. Thompson, *Organizations in Action* (New York: McGraw-Hill, 1967).
32. Ibid.
33. Lublin, "My Colleague, My Boss."
34. R. G. LeFauve and A. C. Hax, "Managerial and Technological Innovations at Saturn Corporation," *MIT Management*, Spring 1992, 8–19.
35. B. W. Tuckman, "Developmental Sequences in Small Groups," *Psychological Bulletin* 63 (1965), 384–99; B. W. Tuckman and M. C. Jensen, "Stages of Small Group Development," *Group and Organizational Studies* 2 (1977), 419–27.
36. C. J. G. Gersick, "Time and Transition in Work Teams: Toward a New Model of Group Development," *Academy of Management Journal* 31 (1988), 9–41; C. J. G. Gersick, "Marking Time: Predictable Transitions in Task Groups," *Academy of Management Journal* 32 (1989), 274–309.
37. J. R. Hackman, "Group Influences on Individuals in Organizations," in M. D. Dunnette and L. M. Hough, eds., *Handbook of Industrial and Organizational Psychology*, 2nd ed., vol. 3 (Palo Alto, CA: Consulting Psychologists Press, 1992), 199–267.
38. Ibid.
39. Ibid.
40. Lublin, "My Colleague, My Boss."
41. L. Festinger, "Informal Social Communication," *Psychological Review* 57 (1950), 271–82; Shaw, *Group Dynamics*.
42. J. Wirtz, L. Heracleous, and N. Pangarkar, "Managing Human Resources for Service Excellence and Cost Effectiveness at Singapore Airlines," *Managing Service Quality* 18, no. 1 (2008), 4–19.
43. Hackman, "Group Influences on Individuals in Organizations"; Shaw, *Group Dynamics*.
44. D. Cartwright, "The Nature of Group Cohesiveness," in D. Cartwright and A. Zander, eds., *Group Dynamics*, 3rd ed. (New York: Harper & Row, 1968); L. Festinger, S. Schacter, and K. Black, *Social Pressures in Informal Groups* (New York: Harper & Row, 1950); Shaw, *Group Dynamics*.
45. T. F. O'Boyle, "A Manufacturer Grows Efficient by Soliciting Ideas from Employees," *The Wall Street Journal*, June 5, 1992, A1, A5.
46. Lublin, "My Colleague, My Boss."
47. P. C. Earley, "Social Loafing and Collectivism: A Comparison of the United States and the People's Republic of China," *Administrative Science Quarterly* 34 (1989), 565–81; J. M. George, "Extrinsic and Intrinsic Origins of Perceived Social Loafing in Organizations," *Academy of Management Journal* 35 (1992), 191–202; S. G. Harkins, B. Latane, and K. Williams, "Social Loafing: Allocating Effort or Taking It Easy," *Journal of Experimental Social Psychology* 16 (1980), 457–65; B. Latane, K. D. Williams, and S. Harkins, "Many Hands Make Light the Work: The Causes and Consequences of Social Loafing," *Journal of Personality and Social Psychology* 37 (1979), 822–32; J. A. Shepperd, "Productivity Loss in Performance Groups: A Motivation Analysis," *Psychological Bulletin* 113 (1993), 67–81.
48. George, "Extrinsic and Intrinsic Origins"; G. R. Jones, "Task Visibility, Free Riding, and Shirking: Explaining the Effect of Structure and Technology on Employee Behavior," *Academy of Management Review* 9 (1984), 684–95; K. Williams, S. Harkins, and B. Latane, "Identifiability as a Deterrent to Social Loafing: Two Cheering Experiments," *Journal of Personality and Social Psychology* 40 (1981), 303–11.
49. S. Harkins and J. Jackson, "The Role of Evaluation in Eliminating Social Loafing," *Personality and Social Psychology Bulletin* 11 (1985), 457–65; N. L. Kerr and S. E. Bruun, "Ringelman

Revisited: Alternative Explanations for the Social Loafing Effect," *Personality and Social Psychology Bulletin* 7 (1981), 224–31; Williams et al., "Identifiability as a Deterrent to Social Loafing."

50. M. A. Brickner, S. G. Harkins, and T. M. Ostrom, "Effects of Personal Involvement: Thought-Provoking Implications for Social Loafing," *Journal of Personality and Social Psychology* 51 (1986), 763–69; S. G. Harkins and R. E. Petty, "The Effects of Task Difficulty and Task Uniqueness on Social Loafing," *Journal of Personality and Social Psychology* 43 (1982), 1214–29.
51. B. Latane, "Responsibility and Effort in Organizations," in P. S. Goodman, ed., *Designing Effective Work Groups* (San Francisco: Jossey-Bass, 1986); Latane et al., "Many Hands Make Light the Work"; I. D. Steiner, *Group Process and Productivity* (New York: Academic Press, 1972).

Chapter 16

1. M. Chong, "The Role of Internal Communication and Training in Infusing Corporate Values and Delivering Brand Promise: Singapore Airlines' Experience," *Corporate Reputation Review* 10, no. 3 (2007), 201–12.
2. C. A. O'Reilly and L. R. Pondy, "Organizational Communication," in S. Kerr, ed., *Organizational Behavior* (Columbus, OH: Grid, 1979).
3. "World's First Volume Computed Tomography (VCT) System, Developed by GE Healthcare, Scanning Patients at Froedtert," www.gehealthcare.com/company/pressroom/releases/pr_release_9722.html, June 18, 2004; "GE Healthcare Fact Sheet," *GE Healthcare Worldwide*, June 20, 2006, www.gehealthcare.com/usen/about/ge_factsheet.html; WTN News, "GE Healthcare Names New CEO," *Wisconsin Technology Network*, January 25, 2006, http://wistechnology.com/printarticle.php?id=2639, June 20, 2006; "About GE Healthcare," *GE Healthcare-Brochure–About GE Healthcare*, www.gehealthcare.com/usen/about/about.html, April 25, 2008; "About GE Healthcare," *GE Healthcare-Brochure–About GE Healthcare*, http://www.gehealthcare.com/usen/about/about.html, March 15, 2010.
4. S. Kirsner, "Time [Zone] Travelers," *Fast Company*, August 2004, 60–66; "LightSpeed VCT Series," *GE Healthcare Worldwide*, June 20, 2006, www.gehealthcare.com/usen/ct/products/vct.html.
5. "New CT Scanner by GE Healthcare Advances Imaging Technology," *Wisconsin Technology Network*, June 21, 2004, www.wistechnology.com.
6. Kirsner, "Time [Zone] Travelers."
7. Ibid.
8. Ibid.
9. E. M. Rogers and R. Agarwala-Rogers, *Communication in Organizations* (New York: Free Press, 1976).
10. D. A. Adams, P. A. Todd, and R. R. Nelson, "A Comparative Evaluation of the Impact of Electronic and Voice Mail on Organizational Communication," *Information & Management* 24 (1993), 9–21.
11. R. Winslow, "Hospitals' Weak Systems Hurt Patients, Study Says," *The Wall Street Journal*, July 5, 1995, B1, B6.
12. B. Newman, "Global Chatter," *The Wall Street Journal*, March 22, 1995, A1, A15.
13. R. L. Daft, R. H. Lengel, and L. K. Trevino, "Message Equivocality, Media Selection, and Manager Performance: Implications for Information Systems," *MIS Quarterly* 11 (1987), 355–66; R. L. Daft and R. H. Lengel, "Information Richness: A New Approach to Managerial Behavior and Organization Design," in B. M. Staw and L. L. Cummings, eds., *Research in Organizational Behavior* (Greenwich, CT: JAI Press, 1984).
14. R. L. Daft, *Organization Theory and Design* (St. Paul, MN: West, 1992).
15. "Lights, Camera, Meeting: Teleconferencing Becomes a Time-Saving Tool," *The Wall Street Journal*, February 21, 1995, A1.
16. Daft, *Organization Theory and Design.*
17. A. S. Wellner, "Lost in Translation," *Inc.*, September 2005, 37–38.
18. Ibid.
19. P. Dvorak, "Frequent Contact Helps Bridge International Divide," *The Wall Street Journal*, June 1, 2009, B4.
20. T. J. Peters and R. H. Waterman, Jr., *In Search of Excellence* (New York: Harper & Row, 1982); T. Peters and N. Austin, *A Passion for Excellence: The Leadership Difference* (New York: Random House, 1985).
21. "Lights, Camera, Meeting."
22. R. Kirkland, "Cisco's Display of Strength," *Fortune*, November 12, 2007, 90–100; "Cisco TelePresence Overview," Overview *(TelePresence)–Cisco Systems*, www.cisco.com/en/US/solutions/ns669/networking_solutions_products_genericcont . . . , April 25, 2008.
23. R. Kirkland, "Cisco's Display of Strength."
24. Kirkland, "Cisco's Display of Strength"; "Cisco TelePresence Overview."
25. Dvorak, "Frequent Contact Helps Bridge International Divide."
26. C. Hymowitz, "Missing from Work: The Chance to Think, Even to Dream a Little," *The Wall Street Journal*, March 23, 2004, B1.
27. D. Beizer, "Email Is Dead . . . ," *Fast Company*, July–August 2007, 46; "The Radicati Group, Inc.," www.radicati.com, April 28, 2008.
28. J. Sandberg, "Employees Forsake Dreaded E-mail for the Beloved Phone," *The Wall Street Journal*, September 26, 2006, B1.
29. Beizer, "Email Is Dead . . ."
30. Sandberg, "Employees Forsake Dreaded E-mail for the Beloved Phone."
31. Ibid.
32. K. Byron, "Carrying Too Heavy a Load? The Communication and Miscommunication of Emotion by E-mail," *Academy of Management Review* 33, no. 2 (2008), 309–27.
33. "There's a Message in Every E-mail," *Fast Company*, September 2007, 43; Byron, "Carrying Too Heavy a Load?"
34. Byron, "Carrying Too Heavy a Load?"
35. "Telecommuters Bring Home Work and Broadband," www.emarketer.com/Article.aspx?1002943, July 20, 2004; "Annual Survey Shows Americans Are Working from Many Different Locations outside Their Employer's Office," *International Telework Association & Council*, May 10, 2006, www.workingfromanywhere.org/news; "Itac, the Telework Advisory Group for Worldat Work," www.workingfromanywhere.org, May 10, 2006; "Virtual Business Owners Community–FAQ Center: Telecommuting/Telework," www.vsscyberoffice.com/vfaq/25.html, May 10, 2006; T. Schadler, "US Telecommuting Forecast, 2009 to 2016: Telecommuting Will Rise to Include 43% of US Workers by 2016," March 11, 2009, http://www.forrester.com/rb/Research/us_telecommuting_forecast%2C_2009_to_2016/q/i . . . , March 15, 2010.
36. E. Baig, "Taking Care of Business–Without Leaving the House," *BusinessWeek*, April 17, 1995, 106–7.
37. "Life Is Good for Telecommuters, but Some Problems Persist," *The Wall Street Journal*, August 3, 1995, A1.
38. "The Most Important Part of an E-mail System Isn't the Software. It's the Rules You Make About Using It," *Inc. Magazine*, October 2005, 119–22.
39. Ibid.
40. Ibid.
41. "Study: Workers Are Surfing on Company Time," www.medialifemagazine.com/news2004/may04/may03/3_wed/

news8wednesday.html, May 5, 2004; "Company Profile," *Websense,* www.websense.com/global/en/About Websense/, April 25, 2008.

42. "Study: Workers Are Surfing on Company Time."
43. Ibid.
44. ClikZ Stats staff, "U.S. Web Usage and Traffic, July 2004," www.clickz.com/stats/big_picture/traffic_patterns/article.php/3395351, August 23, 2004.
45. L. Conley, "The Privacy Arms Race," *Fast Company,* July 2004, 27–28; "Migrating to Microsoft Exchange . . . or Another Mail System?" www.stellarim.com, June 20, 2006; "About Stellar Technologies, Inc.," www.stellartechnologies.com/about_us.cfm, June 20, 2006.
46. Conley, "The Privacy Arms Race"; "2007 Electronic Monitoring & Surveillance Survey"; M. Villano, "The Risk Is All Yours in Office E-Mail," *The New York Times,* March 4, 2007, BU17.
47. "2007 Electronic Monitoring & Surveillance Survey."
48. J. Pfeffer, "It's Time to Start Trusting the Workforce," *Business 2.0,* December 2006, 68.
49. Conley, "The Privacy Arms Race."
50. "P & G Who We Are: Purpose, Values, and Principles," www.pg.com/company/who_we_are/ppv.jhtml, August 25, 2004; L. Conley, "Refusing to Gamble on Privacy," *Fast Company,* July 2004, http://pf.fastcompany.com/magazine/84.essay_hughes.html; "Who We Are," *P&G Global Operations,* June 20, 2006, www.pg.com/company/who_we_are/index.jhtml; "Company Who We Are," P&G, *PG .com–Who We Are,* www.pg.com/company/who_we_are/index.jhtml, April 28, 2008.
51. Conley, "The Privacy Arms Race;" "Privacy: Our Global Privacy Policy," *P&G,* http://www.pg.com/en_US/sustainability/point_of_view/privacy.shtml, March 15, 2010.
52. J. O'Neil, "E-Mail Doesn't Lie (That Much)," *The New York Times,* March 2, 2004, D6.
53. "Employee-Newsletter Names Include the Good, the Bad, and the Boring," *The Wall Street Journal,* July 18, 1995, A1.
54. W. M. Bulkeley, "Playing Well with Others," *The Wall Street Journal,* June 18, 2007, R10.
55. E. White, J. S. Lublin, and D. Kesmodel, "Executives Get the Blogging Bug," *The Wall Street Journal,* July 13, 2007, B1, B2.
56. *Blog–Wikipedia, the free encyclopedia,* http://en.wikipedia.org/wiki/Blog, April 28, 2008; White et al., "Executives Get the Blogging Bug."
57. *Blog–Wikipedia, the free encyclopedia;* White et al., "Executives Get the Blogging Bug"; "GM FastLane Blog: Lutz Biography," http://fastlane.gmblogs.com/archives/2005/01/lutz_biography_1.html, April 28, 2008.
58. "2006 Workplace E-Mail, Instant Messaging & Blog Survey: Bosses Battle Risk by Firing E-Mail, IM & Blog Violators," New York, July 11, 2006, *AMA Press Room,* http://press.amanet.org/press-releases/28/2006-workplace-e-mail-instant-messaging-blog-s . . . April 28, 2008.
59. Bulkeley, "Playing Well with Others."
60. Ibid.
61. D.M. Boyd and N.B. Ellison, "Social Network Sites: Definition, History, and Scholarship," *Journal of Computer-Mediated Communication* 13, no. 1 (2007), article 11, http://jcmc.indiana.edu/vol13/issue1/boyd.ellison.html, March 15, 2010; "Social Networking Site Definition from PC Magazine Encyclopedia," http://www.pcmag.com/encyclopedia_term/0,2542,t=social+networking&i=55316,00.asp, March 15, 2010; "Factsheet/Facebook," http://www.facebook.com/press/info.php?factsheet, March 15, 2010; "Statistics / Facebook," http://www.facebook.com/press/info.php?statistics, March 15, 2010; "Twitter News–*The New York Times,*" http://topics.nytimes.com/top/news/business/companies/twitter/index.html, March 15, 2010; "Twitter," http://twitter.com/about, March 15, 2010; "Facebook, Inc.: Private Company Information–*Business Week,*" http://investing.businessweek.com/research/stocks/private/snapshot.asp?privcapId=207654 . . . , March 15, 2010.
62. J. E. Vascellaro, "Why E-mail No Longer Rules," *The Wall Street Journal,* October 12, 2009, R1–3.
63. "Study: 54 Percent of Companies Ban Facebook, Twitter at Work/Epicenter/Wired.com," October 9, 2009, http://www.wired.com/epicenter/2009/10/study-54-of-companies-ban-facebook-twitter-at-. . . March 16, 2010.
64. Ibid.
65. B. Bates, "Changing of the Guard," *Smart Business Orange County* 5, no. 6 (2010), 10–15.
66. O. W. Baskin and C. E. Aronoff, *Interpersonal Communication in Organizations* (Santa Monica, CA: Goodyear, 1989).
67. T. Gutner, "Move Over, Bohemian Grove," *BusinessWeek,* February 19, 2001, 102.
68. "Top 15 Countries in Internet Usage, 2002," www.infoplease.com/ipa/A0908185.html, August 25, 2004; "Top 20 Countries with the Highest Number of Internet Users," http://www.internetworldstats.com/top20.htm, April 29, 2008; "Top 20 Countries with the Highest Number of Internet Users," http://www.internetworldstats.com/top20.htm, March 15, 2010.
69. J. Sandberg, "Internet's Popularity in North America Appears to Be Soaring," *The Wall Street Journal,* October 30, 1995, B2.
70. "How to Research Companies," *Oxford Knowledge Company,* www.oxford-knowledge.co.uk, September 16, 2004.
71. "Survey: Denmark Is Web-Savviest Nation," MSNBC.com, April 19, 2004, www.msnbc.msn.com/id/4779944/1/displaymode/1098; L. Grinsven, "U.S. Drops on Lists of Internet Savvy," *Houston Chronicle,* April 20, 2004, 6B.
72. M. J. Cronin, "Ford's Intranet Success," *Fortune,* March 30, 1998, 158; M. J. Cronin, "Intranets Reach the Factory Floor," *Fortune,* June 10, 1997; A. L. Sprout, "The Internet inside Your Company," *Fortune,* November 27, 1995, 161–68; J. B. White, "Chrysler's Intranet: Promise vs. Reality," *The Wall Street Journal,* May 13, 1997, B1, B6.
73. White, "Chrysler's Intranet: Promise vs. Reality."
74. G. Rifkin, "A Skeptic's Guide to Groupware," *Forbes ASAP,* 1995, 76–91.
75. Ibid.
76. Ibid.
77. "Groupware Requires a Group Effort," *BusinessWeek,* June 26, 1995, 154.
78. M. Totty, "The Path to Better Teamwork," *The Wall Street Journal,* May 20, 2004, R4; "Collaborative Software," *Wikipedia,* August 25, 2004, en.wikipedia.org/wiki/Collaborative_software; "Collaborative Groupware Software," www.svpal.org/~grantbow/groupware.html, August 25, 2004.
79. Totty, "The Path to Better Teamwork"; "Collaborative Software."
80. Totty, "The Path to Better Teamwork"; "Collaborative Software"; "Collaborative Groupware Software."
81. Totty, "The Path to Better Teamwork"; "Collaborative Software."
82. Ibid.
83. Microsoft Windows SharePont Services Developer Center, "Windows SharePoint Service," http://msdn.microsoft.com/sharepoint, June 21, 2006.
84. Totty, "The Path to Better Teamwork"; "Collaborative Software."
85. M. Conlin, "E-mail Is So Five Minutes Ago," *BusinessWeek,* November 28, 2005, 111–12; D. Dahl, "The End of E-mail," *Inc.,* February 2006, 41–42;

"Weaving a Secure Web around Education: A Guide to Technology Standards and Security," http://nces.ed.gov/pubs2003/secureweb/glossary.asp, June 21, 2006; "Wikis Make Collaboration Easier," *InformationWeek*, June 20, 2006, www.informationweek.com/shared/printableArticleSrc.jhtml?articleID=170100392.

86. "Postini," www.postini.com, April 28, 2008.
87. Conlin, "E-mail Is So Five Minutes Ago."
88. Ibid.
89. Ibid.
90. Ibid.
91. Dahl, "The End of E-mail"; "Wikis Make Collaboration Easier;" V. Vara, "Wikis at Work," *The Wall Street Journal*, June 18, 2007, R11.
92. Dahl, "The End of E-mail."
93. D. Dahl, "Connecting the Dots," *Inc.*, June 2009, 103–4; "Project Management, Collaboration, and Task Software: Basecamp," http://basecamphq.com/, March 15, 2010.
94. Conlin, "E-mail Is So Five Minutes Ago."
95. Ibid.
96. Bulkeley, "Playing Well with Others."
97. Ibid.
98. Conlin, "E-mail Is So Five Minutes Ago"; Dahl, "The End of E-mail"; "Weaving a Secure Web around Education."
99. Wakizaka, "Faxes, E-Mail, Help the Deaf Get Office Jobs," *The Wall Street Journal*, October 3, 1995, B1, B5.
100. S. E. Needleman, "Business Owners Try to Motivate Employees," *The Wall Street Journal*, January 14, 2010, B5.
101. Ibid.
102. D. Tannen, "The Power of Talk," *Harvard Business Review*, September–October 1995, 138–148.
103. Ibid.
104. Ibid.
105. D. Tannen, *Talking from 9 to 5*. (New York: Avon Books, 1995).
106. J. Cohen, "He Writes, She Writes," *Houston Chronicle*, July 7, 2001, C1–C2.
107. Ibid.
108. Ibid.
109. Tannen, "The Power of Talk," 148.

Chapter 17

1. B. Becht, "Building a Company without Borders," *Harvard Business Review*, April 2010, 103–6; "Board of Directors," http://www.rb.com/RB-worldwide/The-Board, March 17, 2010.
2. "The Power behind the Powerbrands: A Quick Guide to Reckitt Benckiser," *Reckitt Benckiser*, http://www.rb.com, March 17, 2010.
3. Becht, "Building a Company without Borders"; "The Power behind the Powerbrands"; "Corporate Factsheet: ($ information)," *Reckitt Benckiser*, http://www.rb.com, March 17, 2010.
4. J. Pfeffer and R. I. Sutton, *Hard Facts, Dangerous Half-Truths, and Total Nonsense: Profiting from Evidence-Based Management*, (Boston: Harvard Business School Press, 2006).
5. Becht, "Building a Company without Borders."
6. Ibid.
7. Ibid.
8. Ibid.
9. Ibid.
10. Ibid.
11. J. A. Litterer, "Conflict in Organizations: A Reexamination," *Academy of Management Journal* 9 (1966), 178–86; S. M. Schmidt and T. A. Kochan, "Conflict: Towards Conceptual Clarity," *Administrative Science Quarterly* 13 (1972), 359–70; R. H. Miles, *Macro Organizational Behavior* (Santa Monica, CA: Goodyear, 1980).
12. S. P. Robbins, *Managing Organizational Conflict: A Nontraditional Approach* (Englewood Cliffs, NJ: Prentice-Hall, 1974); L. Coser, *The Functions of Social Conflict* (New York: Free Press, 1956).
13. K. A. Jehn, "A Qualitative Analysis of Conflict Types and Dimensions in Organizational Groups," Cornell University, 1997; K. A. Jehn, "A Multimethod Examination of the Benefits and Detriments of Intragroup Conflict," Cornell University, 1995.
14. L. L. Putnam and M. S. Poole, "Conflict and Negotiation," in F. M. Jablin, L. L. Putnam, K. H. Roberts, and L. W. Porter, eds., *Handbook of Organizational Communication: An Interdisciplinary Perspective* (Newbury Park, CA: Sage, 1987), 549–99.
15. L. R. Pondy, "Organizational Conflict: Concepts and Models," *Administrative Science Quarterly* 2 (1967), 296–320; R. E. Walton and J. M. Dutton, "The Management of Interdepartmental Conflict: A Model and Review," *Administrative Science Quarterly* 14 (1969), 62–73.
16. G. R. Jones and J. E. Butler, "Managing Internal Corporate Entrepreneurship: An Agency Theory Perspective," *Journal of Management* 18 (1992), 733–49.
17. J. A. Wall, Jr., "Conflict and Its Management," *Journal of Management* 21 (1995), 515–58.
18. Walton and Dutton, "The Management of Interdepartmental Conflict."
19. Pondy, "Organizational Conflict."
20. W. F. White, *Human Relations in the Restaurant Industry* (New York: McGraw-Hill, 1948).
21. R. L. Pinkley and G. B. Northcraft, "Conflict Frames of Reference: Implications for Dispute Processes and Outcomes," *Academy of Management Journal* 37 (February 1994), 193–206.
22. K. W. Thomas, "Conflict and Negotiation Processes in Organizations," in M. D. Dunnette and L. M. Hough, eds., *Handbook of Industrial and Organizational Psychology*, 2nd ed., vol. 3 (Palo Alto, CA: Consulting Psychologists Press, 1992), 651–717.
23. "Ravi Kant: Executive Profile & Biography," *BusinessWeek*, http://investing.businessweek.com/businessweek/research/stocks/people/person.asp?person. . ., March 18, 2010; "Ravi Kant Profile," Forbes.com, http://people.forbes.com/profile/print/ravi-kant/76754, March 18, 2010.
24. M. Kripalana, "Tata: Master of the Gentle Approach," *BusinessWeek*, February 25, 2008; "Ravi Kant," *Tata Group*, www.tata.com/scripts/print.asp, May 2, 2008; "Ravi Kant: Executive Profile & Biography," *Business Week*, http://investing.businessweek.com/businessweek/research/stocks/people/person.asp?person . . . , March 18, 2010; "Ravi Kant Profile," Forbes.com, http://people.forbes.com/profile/print/ravi-kant/76754, March 18, 2010.
25. Kripalana, "Tata: Master of the Gentle Approach"; "Profile," Tata Motors, www.tatamotors.com/our_world/profile.php, May 2, 2008; "Our Companies: Tata Motors," www.tata.com/tata_motors/index.htm, May 2, 2008.
26. Kripalana, "Tata: Master of the Gentle Approach."
27. Ibid.
28. Ibid.
29. K. Chae, "CEO Message," *Tata Daewoo*, www.tata-daewoo.com/ver3/eng/03_company/01_ceo.html, May 7, 2008; "Events and Happenings," *Tata*, www.tata.com/scripts/print.asp, May 7, 2008.
30. Kripalana, "Tata: Master of the Gentle Approach."
31. Ibid.
32. Ibid.
33. Kripalana, "Tata: Master of the Gentle Approach;" Tata Group/Our Businesses/Tata Companies/The Tata Daewoo Commercial Vehicle Co . . . , "Tata Daewoo Commercial Vehicle Company," http://www.tata.com/company/profile.aspx?sectid=HckEHljxqtM=, March 18, 2010.
34. "Sales Activities," *Tata Daewoo*, www.tata-daewoo.com/ver3/eng/08_center/

01_faq.html, May 7, 2008; "Company," *Tata Daewoo,* www.tata-daewoo.com/ver3/eng/03_company/02_tata.html, May 7, 2008.

35. Kripalana, "Tata: Master of The Gentle Approach."
36. Thomas, "Conflict and Negotiation Processes in Organizations."
37. Pinkley and Northcraft, "Conflict Frames of Reference."
38. N. Heintz, "In Spanish, It's *Un Equipo,*" *Inc.,* April 2008; S. McAdams, "Putting Culture on the Map," *Ragan Report,* June 11, 2007, www.xplane.com/#/news/; S. Powers, "12 Revolutionary Companies Transforming the City That Works (and Yes, They're Hiring), *Portland Monthly,* October 2007, www.xplane.com/#/news/; About XPLANE/The visual thinking company, http://www.xplane.com/company/about/, March 18, 2010.
39. Heintz, "In Spanish, It's *Un Equipo.*"
40. Ibid.
41. Ibid.
42. Ibid.
43. Ibid.
44. Ibid.
45. Ibid.
46. XPLANE Expands, Opens Amsterdam Office/XPLANE/The Visual Thinking Company, March 17, 2010, http://www.xplane.com/company/news/2010/03/17/xplane-expands-opens-amsterdam-offi . . . , March 18, 2010.
47. P. R. Lawrence, L. B. Barnes, and J. W. Lorsch, *Organizational Behavior and Administration* (Homewood, IL: Irwin, 1976).
48. R. J. Lewicki and J. R. Litterer, *Negotiation* (Homewood, IL: Irwin, 1985); G. B. Northcraft and M. A. Neale, *Organizational Behavior* (Fort Worth, TX: Dryden, 1994); J. Z. Rubin and B. R. Brown, *The Social Psychology of Bargaining and Negotiation* (New York: Academic Press, 1975).
49. C. Bendersky, "Organizational Dispute Resolution Systems: A Complementarities Model," *Academy of Management Review* 28 (October 2003), 643–57.
50. R. E. Walton, "Third Party Roles in Interdepartmental Conflicts," *Industrial Relations* 7 (1967), 29–43.
51. "Meaning of Arbitrator," www.hyperdictionary.com, September 4, 2004; "Definitions of Arbitrator on the Web," www.google.com, September 4, 2004.
52. Nestlé UK, "Nestlé Partners with TFT (The Forest Trust) to Combat Deforestation," Nestlé UK home page, May 17, 2010, http://www.nestle.co.uk/PressOffice/PressReleases/May/NestlePartnerswithTFT; M. Hickman, "Online Protest Drives Nestlé to Environmentally Friendly Palm Oil," *The Independent,* May 19, 2010, http://www.independent.co.uk/environment/green-living/online-protest-drives-nestl-to-environmentally-friendly-palm-oil-1976443.html; K. Tabacek, "Nestle Uses NGO to Clean Up Palm Oil Supply Chain," *The Guardian,* May 17, 2010, http://www.guardian.co.uk/sustainable-business/nestl-ngo-clean-up-palm-oil-supply-chain.
53. L. Thompson and R. Hastie, "Social Perception in Negotiation," *Organizational Behavior and Human Decision Processes* 47 (1990), 98–123.
54. Thomas, "Conflict and Negotiation Processes in Organizations."
55. R. J. Lewicki, S. E. Weiss, and D. Lewin, "Models of Conflict, Negotiation, and Third Party Intervention: A Review and Synthesis," *Journal of Organizational Behavior* 13 (1992), 209–52.
56. Northcraft and Neale, *Organizational Behavior.*
57. Lewicki et al., "Models of Conflict, Negotiation, and Third Party Intervention"; Northcraft and Neale, *Organizational Behavior;* D. G. Pruitt, "Integrative Agreements: Nature and Consequences," in M. H. Bazerman and R. J. Lewicki, eds., *Negotiating in Organizations* (Beverly Hills, CA: Sage, 1983).
58. R. Fischer and W. Ury, *Getting to Yes* (Boston: Houghton Mifflin, 1981); Northcraft and Neale, *Organizational Behavior.*
59. P. J. Carnevale and D. G. Pruitt, "Negotiation and Mediation," *Annual Review of Psychology* 43 (1992), 531–82.
60. A. M. Pettigrew, *The Politics of Organizational Decision Making* (London: Tavistock, 1973); Miles, *Macro Organizational Behavior.*
61. D. J. Hickson, C. R. Hinings, C. A. Lee, R. E. Schneck, and D. J. Pennings, "A Strategic Contingencies Theory of Intraorganizational Power," *Administrative Science Quarterly* 16 (1971), 216–27; C. R. Hinings, D. J. Hickson, J. M. Pennings, and R. E. Schneck, "Structural Conditions of Interorganizational Power," *Administrative Science Quarterly* 19 (1974), 22–44; J. Pfeffer, *Power in Organizations* (Boston: Pitman, 1981).
62. Pfeffer, *Power in Organizations.*
63. Ibid.
64. M. Crozier, "Sources of Power of Lower Level Participants in Complex Organizations," *Administrative Science Quarterly* 7 (1962), 349–64; A. M. Pettigrew, "Information Control as a Power Resource," *Sociology* 6 (1972), 187–204.
65. Pfeffer, *Power in Organizations;* G. R. Salancik and J. Pfeffer, "The Bases and Uses of Power in Organizational Decision Making," *Administrative Science Quarterly* 19 (1974), 453–73; J. Pfeffer and G. R. Salancik, *The External Control of Organizations: A Resource Dependence View* (New York: Harper & Row, 1978).
66. B. Morris, Senior Editor, "The Pepsi Challenge," *Fortune,* "What Makes Pepsi Great?" February 19, 2008, http://cnnmoney.printthis.clickability.com/pt/cpt?action=cpt&title=What+makes+Pepsi+gre . . . , April 8, 2008.
67. "The 100 Most Powerful Women #5 Indra K. Nooyi," Forbes.com, August 30, 2007, www.forbes.com/lists/2007/11/biz-07women_Indra-K-Nooyi_1S5D_print.html, April 23, 2008; "Indra K. Nooyi Profile," Forbes.com, http://people.forbes.com/profile/indra-k-nooyi/62917, March 17, 2010.
68. "PepsiCo–Investor Overview," http://phx.corporate-ir.net/phoenix.zhtml?c=78265&p=irol-irhome, May 2, 2008; "Indra Nooyi–News, Articles, Biography, Photos," WSJ.com, http://topics.wsj.com/person/n/indra-k-nooyi/247, March 17, 2010.
69. Morris, "The Pepsi Challenge"; D. Brady, "Indra Nooyi: Keeping Cool in Hot Water," *BusinessWeek,* June 11, 2007, www.businessweek.com/print/magazine/content/07_24/b4038067.htm?chan=gl, April 30, 2008; P. Maidment, "Re-Thinking Social Responsibility," Forbes.com, January 25, 2008, www.forbes.com/2008/01/25/davos-corporate-responsibility-lead-cx_pm_0125notes . . . , April 23, 2008; B. Saporito, "Indra Nooyi," *TIME in Partnership with CNN,* Monday, April 30, 2007, www.time.com/time/specials/2007/printout/0,29239,1595326_1615737_1615996,00 . . . , April 23, 2008.
70. "The World's Most Influential People," *The 2008 TIME 100,* www.time.com/time/specials/2007/0,28757,1733748,00.html, May 2, 2008.
71. "25 Most Powerful People in Business," *Fortune,* http://money.cnn.com/galleries/2007/fortune/0711/gallery.power_25.fortune/22.html, April 30, 2008; "50 Most Powerful Women 2007, The Power 50," CNNMoney.com, *Fortune,* http://money.cnn.com/galleries/2007/fortune/0709/gallery.women_mostpowerful.fortune/i . . . , April 23, 2008; "PepsiCo CEO Indra Nooyi Is the Queen of Pop," September, 10, 2009, http://cnnmoney.printthis.clickability.com/pt/cpt?action=cpt&title=PepsiCo+CEO+Indra+ . . . , March 17, 2010; "50 "Most Powerful Women–1. Indra Nooyi (1)," *Fortune,* http://money.cnn.com/galleries/2009/fortune/0909/gallery.most_powerful_women.fortune/ . . . , March 17, 2010.

72. Morris, "The Pepsi Challenge"; "PepsiCo's Board of Directors Appoints Indra K. Nooyi as Chief Executive Officer Effective October 1, 2006, Steve Reinemund to Retire as Chairman in May 2007," *PEPSICO,* News Release, http://phx.corporate-ir.net/phoenix.zhtml?c=78265&p=irol-newsArticle_print&ID=895346 . . . , May 8, 2008.
73. Morris, "The Pepsi Challenge."
74. Ibid.
75. Ibid.
76. "PEPSICO Officers and Directors," *PepsiCo,* http://www.pepsico.com/PEP_Company/OfficersDirectors/index.cfm, May 2, 2008.
77. Morris, "The Pepsi Challenge."
78. "PepsiCo Announces Upcoming Retirement of Michael White Chairman and PepsiCo International CEO," http://www.pepsico.com/PressRelease/PepsiCo-Announces-Upcoming-Retirement-of-Mic . . . , March 17, 2010.
79. A. Moore, MarketWatch, "Indra Nooyi's Pepsi challenge, CEO puts her own brand on new products and global goals," December 6, 2007, www.marketwatch.com/news/story/indra-nooyi-puts-her-brand/story.aspx?guid=%7 . . . , April 23, 2008.
80. Morris, "The Pepsi Challenge."
81. Ibid.
82. Ibid.
83. Pfeffer, *Power in Organizations.*
84. Ibid.
85. Ibid.
86. L. Kramer, "Doing Well and Good: How Social Responsibility Helped One Coffee Grower Land a Deal with Starbucks," *Inc.,* June 2006, 55–56.
87. Kramer, "Doing Well and Good"; "Corporate Social Responsibility," www.starbucks.com/aboutus/csr.asp, June 25, 2006.
88. "The Exceptional Cup Participating Farms Finca El Faro," www.guatemalancoffees.com/GCContent/GCeng/auction_tec_fincas/FincaElFaro.asp, June 25, 2006.
89. Kramer, "Doing Well and Good."
90. Ibid.
91. Ibid.
92. Ibid.

Chapter 18

1. A. S. Jum'ah, "Session Four: The Impact of Upstream Technological Advances on Future Oil Supply," Third OPEC International Seminar, September 12–13, 2006, Vienna, Austria, http://www.opec.org/opec_web/en/press_room/256.htm; "Saudi Aramco: Technology and Innovation," *Aramco ExPats Online Community for Saudi Aramco Expatriates,* July 7, 2008, http://www.aramcoexpats.com.
2. N. B. Macintosh, *The Social Software of Accounting Information Systems* (New York: Wiley, 1995).
3. C. A. O'Reilly, "Variations in Decision Makers' Use of Information: The Impact of Quality and Accessibility," *Academy of Management Journal* 25 (1982), 756–71.
4. G. Stalk and T. H. Hout, *Competing against Time* (New York: Free Press, 1990).
5. www.iata.com, 2010.
6. R. Cyert and J. March, *Behavioral Theory of the Firm* (Englewood Cliffs, NJ: Prentice-Hall, 1963).
7. E. Turban, *Decision Support and Expert Systems* (New York: Macmillan, 1988).
8. W. H. Davidow and M. S. Malone, *The Virtual Corporation* (New York: Harper Business, 1992); M. E. Porter, *Competitive Advantage* (New York: Free Press, 1984).
9. S. M. Dornbusch and W. R. Scott, *Evaluation and the Exercise of Authority* (San Francisco: Jossey-Bass, 1975).
10. J. Child, *Organization: A Guide to Problems and Practice* (London: Harper & Row, 1984).
11. www.dhl.com, 2010.
12. Macintosh, *The Social Software of Accounting Information Systems.*
13. www.cypress.com, 2010.
14. Miya Knights, "Fit-for-Purpose IT Breeds Profit for Clothing Retailer," *Computerweekly.com,* January 8, 2007, http://www.computerweekly.com/Articles/2007/01/08/221018/Fit-for-purpose-IT-breeds-profits-for-clothing-retailer.htm.
15. www.boeing.com, 2010.
16. P. Bradley, "Global Sourcing Takes Split-Second Timing," *Purchasing,* July 20, 1989, 52–58.
17. J. A. Schumpeter, *Capitalism, Socialism, and Democracy* (New York: Harper, 1942).
18. V. P. Buell, *Marketing Management* (New York: McGraw-Hill, 1985).
19. See M. M. J. Berry and J. H. Taggart, "Managing Technology and Innovation: A Review," *R & D Management* 24 (1994), 341–53; K. B. Clark and S. C. Wheelwright, *Managing New Product and Process Development* (New York: Free Press, 1993).
20. www.ebay.com, March 2010.
21. See Berry and Taggart, "Managing Technology and Innovation"; M. Gort and J. Klepper, "Time Paths in the Diffusion of Product Innovations," *Economic Journal,* September 1982, 630–53. Looking at the history of 46 products, Gort and Klepper found that the length of time before other companies entered the markets created by a few inventive companies declined from an average of 14.4 years for products introduced before 1930 to 4.9 years for those introduced after 1949–implying that product life cycles were being compressed. Also see A. Griffin, "Metrics for Measuring Product Development Cycle Time," *Journal of Production and Innovation Management* 10 (1993), 112–25.
22. C. W. L. Hill and J. F. Pickering, "Divisionalization, Decentralization, and Performance of Large United Kingdom Companies," *Journal of Management Studies* 23 (1986), 26–50.
23. O. E. Williamson, *Markets and Hierarchies: Analysis and Antitrust Implications* (New York: Free Press, 1975).
24. Turban, *Decision Support and Expert Systems.*
25. www.merck.com, 2008.
26. N. A. Nichols, "Scientific Management at Merck: An Interview with CFO Judy Lewent," *Harvard Business Review,* January–February 1994, 88–91.
27. Turban, *Decision Support and Expert Systems.*
28. E. Rich, *Artificial Intelligence* (New York: McGraw-Hill, 1983).
29. F. Brandt, "Agents and Artificial Life." *BusinessWeek,* June 13, 1994, 55–56.
30. Rich, *Artificial Intelligence.*
31. Ibid., 346.
32. G. R. Jones, "SAP and the Enterprise Resource Planning Industry," in C. W. L. Hill and G. R. Jones, *Strategic Management: An Integrated Approach,* 6th ed. (Boston: Houghton Mifflin, 2003).
33. B. Kogut, "Joint Ventures: Theoretical and Empirical Perspectives," *Strategic Management Journal* 9 (1988), 319–32.
34. G. S. Capowski, "Designing a Corporate Identity," *Management Review,* June 1993, 37–38.
35. J. Marcia, "Just Doing It," *Distribution,* January 1995, 36–40.
36. Davidow and Malone, *The Virtual Corporation.*
37. T. A. Stewart, "Managing in a Wired Company," *Fortune,* July 11, 1994, 44–56.
38. www.lucasarts.com, 2010.
39. B. Hindo, "The Empire Strikes at Silos," www.businessweek.com, August 20, 2007.

Photo Credits

Chapter 1

43 Bloomberg via Getty Images; **48** AP Photo/Harry Cabluck; **50** Courtesy of Xerox Corporation; **51** AP Photo/Junji Kurokawa; **65** (t)AP Photo/Marco Vasini, (b)Photo by James Berglie/ZUMA Press. © 2006 by James Berglie

Chapter 2

73 (t)Austrian Archives/Corbis, (b)Chad Ehlers/International Stock; **77-78** Bettmann/Corbis; **79** charistoone-images/Alamy; **80** 20th Century Fox/Courtesy The Kobal Collection/Picture Desk; **81** Hulton Archive/Getty Images; **83** The Granger Collection, New York; **85** Jacques Boyer/Roger Viollet/The Image Works; **89** (t)Courtesy Regina A. Greenwood & Henley Management College, (b)Fox Photos/Getty Images; **92** AP Photo/HO/Hewlett Packard; **93** JEAN-CHRISTOPHE VERHAEGEN/AFP/Getty Images

Chapter 3

103 AP Photo/Jennifer Graylock; **109** AP Photo/Gillian Allen; **111** Digital Vision; **113** Courtesy of Gentle Giant Moving Company; **115** Flying Colours Ltd./Getty Images; **118** BananaStock/age footstock; **121** Courtesy of IDEO; **124** Ken Hawkins Photography; **125** PHILIPPE LOPEZ/AFP/Getty Images

Chapter 4

133 Mark Wilson/Getty Images; **136** The Granger Collection, New York; **141** AP Photo/Damian Dovarganes, file; **146** Jon Hicks/Corbis; **150** Darren McCollester/Getty Images; **151** Jin Lee/Bloomberg via Getty Images; **154** AP Images/John Todd; **157** Courtesy of Google

Chapter 5

163 Courtesy of Shell Oil Company; **168** Courtesy of Chubb Group of Insurance Companies; **176** (t)Habitat International, Inc./Photo by Jim Madden, (b)Zia Soleil/Iconica/Getty Images; **181** Somos/Veer/Getty Images

Chapter 6

187 AP Photo/Shizuo Kambayashi; **191** AP Photo/The News Tribune, Lui Kit Wong; **193** © Nokia 2010; **196** AP Photo/Itsuo Inouye; **198** Getty Images; **201** imagebroker/Alamy; **203** AP Photo/Matt Houston

Chapter 7

215 AP Photo/Christof Stache; **218** Andersen Ross/Blend Images/Getty Images; **230** Digital Vision/Punchstock; **234** Marc Romanelli/Workbook Stock/Getty Images; **236** AP Photo/Pavel Rahman; **237** Radius Images/Getty Images

Chapter 8

243 AP Photo/Itsuo Inouye; **246** Ryan McVay/Getty Images; **250** AP Images/Tom Mihalek; **255** AP Photo/Mel Evans; **259** Courtesy of Cott Corporation; **260** The McGraw-Hill Companies, Inc./Jill Braaten, photographer; **264** Bill Varie/Corbis; **266** (t)AP Images/Kasumi Kasahara, (b)Pablo Bartholomew/Getty News/Liaison; **269** Gene Blevins/LA Daily News/Corbis

Chapter 9

275 Daniel J. Groshong/Bloomberg via Getty Images; **280** Jeff Greenberg/PhotoEdit, **281** Denis Doyle/Getty Images; **282** Nelson Ching/Bloomberg via Getty Images; **290** Junko Kimura/Getty Images; **294** OJO Images Ltd/Alamy; **297** Erin Siegal/Redux Pictures

Chapter 10

303 Photo by Kevin Mazur/WireImage for Avon/Getty Images; **309** Jeffrey Allan Salter/Corbis; **313** © Z5327/_Sören Stache/dpa/Corbis; **315** Kim Steele/Photodisc Green/Getty Images; **316** Gene Blevins/LA Daily News/Corbis; **329** Fabrizio Costantini/The New York Times/Redux Pictures

Chapter 11

339 Jean-Claude Coutausse/Bloomberg via Getty Images; **343** vario images GmbH & Co.KG/Alamy; **349** AP Images/Harry Cabluck; **355** AP Images/Alyssa Hurst; **357** AP Photo/Disney, Gene Duncan; **358** STAFF/Reuters/Corbis

Chapter 12

369 Ronda Churchill/Bloomberg via Getty Images; **373** James Leynse/Corbis; **376** Amy Etra/PhotoEdit; **379** Cabruken/Taxi/Getty Images; **382** Reza Estakhrian/Photographer's Choice/Getty Images; **384** Helen Ashford/Workbook Stock/Getty Images; **390** AP Images/Ann Heisenfelt; **391** Photo by Jess Haessler/Courtesy Guerra DeBerry Coody; **392** Malte Christians/dpa/Corbis

Chapter 13

399 Mario Proenca/Bloomberg via Getty Images; **401** Jupiterimages/Comstock Images/Getty Images; **405** Shaul Schwarz/Getty Images; **412** Stockbyte/Punchstock Images; **416** vario images GmbH & Co. KG/Alamy; **418** Simon Dawson/Bloomberg via Getty Images

Chapter 14

425 Neilson Barnard/Getty Images; **428** Courtesy of Zingerman's; **433** Yun Suk Bong/Reuters/Corbis; **435** Christophe Bosset/Bloomberg via Getty Images; **438** Tim Pannell/Corbis; **446** Courtesy of Creative Display Solutions, Inc.

Chapter 15

453 © BMW AG; **455** image100/Alamy; **459** Comstock Images/PictureQuest; **460** AP Images/Alexandra Boulat/VII; **463** David P. Hall/Corbis; **466** Getty Images/Digital Vision

Chapter 16

481 AP Photo/Wong Maye-e; **484** Doug Menuez/Getty Images; **486** Allan Danahar/Getty Images; **490** Blend Images/Getty Images; **492** David Lee/Alamy; **495** Royalty-Free/Corbis; **501** NetPhotos/Alamy; **504** Duncan Smith/Getty Images; **505** Photodisc/Alamy

Chapter 17

511 Jiri Rezac 2008/All rights reserved; **513** avatra images/Alamy; **516** BananaStock/Jupiterimages; **517** KIM JAE-HWAN/AFP/Getty Images; **520** Doug Menuez/Getty Images; **523** Compassionate Eye Foundation/Robert Kent/Getty Images; **527** Andrew Harrer/Bloomberg via Getty Images; **530** Courtesy of El Faro Estate Coffee

Chapter 18

535 Reza/Getty Images; **539** Bill Freeman/PhotoEdit; **543** Lourens Smak/Alamy; **544** Website screenshot courtesy of Ebay; **549** REUTERS/China Newsphoto/Landov; **550** Louie Psihoyos/Corbis; **557** AP Images/Matt Sayles

INDEX

Names

A

Abell, D. F., 571
Ackerman, P. L., 577
Adams, D. A., 582
Adams, J. S., 576
Adler, N. J., 576
Adler, P. S., 565
Agarwal, R. S., 325
Agarwala-Rogers, R., 582
Aguilar, F. J., 570
al Falih, Khalid, 535
Alderfer, Clayton, 407, 576
Alexander, J. A., 573
Allen, T. D., 575
Amodio, D. M., 567
Ancona, D. G., 562
Anderson, C., 562
Anderson, J. C., 571
Anderson, P., 574
Andrews, K. R., 566, 571
Anthony, R. N., 573
Aoki, M., 572
Aplin, J. C., 570
Argyris, C., 575
Ariishi, Takako, 177–178
Armstrong, Bob, 484
Arndt, M., 566, 581
Arnst, C., 569
Aronoff, C. E., 583
Aronson, J. A., 567
Arrow, K. J., 569
Aveni, R. D., 571
Avolio, B. J., 571, 580
Ayman, R., 580

B

Baetz, M. L., 579
Bahree, B., 571
Baig, E., 582
Bailey, J. R., 563
Bain, J. E., 568
Baird, L., 574
Bakan, D., 567
Baker, S., 581
Ballmer, Steve, 431
Banaji, M., 568
Bandura, A., 577
Barbeite, F. G., 576
Barley, S. R., 566
Barnard, C. I., 565
Barnes, L. B., 585
Baron, R. A., 564
Barr, M., 569
Barrett, Craig, 431
Barrick, M. R., 563
Barry, V., 562, 566
Barsaloux, J., 570
Bartlett, C. A., 569, 571
Baskin, O. W., 583
Bass, B. M., 571, 579, 580
Bates, B., 583
Battaglia, B. A., 568
Baucus, M. S., 566
Bava, Zeinal, 399, 400, 402
Bazerman, M. H., 569, 570
Beauchamp, T. L., 566, 573
Becht, Bart, 511, 512, 584
Becker, T. E., 566
Begley, S., 564
Beizer, D., 582
Bell, C. H., 573
Bellah, R., 569
Belliveau, M. A., 567
Belson, K., 577
Bendersky, C., 585
Bennis, W., 578
Bensen, Peter, 320
Benz, Karl, 81
Bercovici, J., 564
Berger, P. L., 565
Berkowitz, L., 579
Berner, R., 580
Berry, L. L., 562
Berry, M. M. J., 586
Bertone, Antonio, 216
Bettenhausen, K., 564, 580
Beyer, J. M., 565
Bhagwati, J., 568
Bish, Reynolds, 496
Black, K., 581
Blackburn, R. S., 581
Blackden, Richard, 572
Blackledge, B. J., 565
Blake, Robert, 436, 579
Blanchard, Kenneth, 436, 579
Blau, P., 572, 573
Bohr, J., 563
Bonabeau, E., 568
Borman, C., 575
Borman, W. C., 575
Borrus, A., 575
Borzacchiello, Maureen, 445–446

Bouchard, T. J., Jr., 570
Bourgeois, L. J., 568
Bowen, D. E., 571
Bowie, N. E., 566, 573
Bowles, J., 571
Boyd, D. M., 583
Boyle, Dennis, 126
Brabeck-Latmathe, Peter, 201–202
Bracken, D. W., 575
Bradley, P., 586
Brady, D., 575, 580, 585
Brandt, F., 586
Branson, Richard, 103–104
Bresler, S. J., 568
Brett, J. B., 115
Brickner, M. A., 582
Brief, A. P., 118, 564, 567, 568, 570
Brin, Sergey, 297, 298
Brockner, J., 563, 564
Broughton, Philip D., 573
Brown, B. R., 585
Brown, D. J., 563
Brown, L., 573
Brown, V., 567
Bruer, J. T., 567
Bruner, J. S., 567
Bruton, G. D., 570
Buchanan, L., 578
Buckley, George, 264
Budworth, M. H., 576
Buell, V. P., 586
Buffett, Warren, 137
Bulkeley, W. M., 583, 584
Burdick, Denise, 125
Burke, M. J., 118
Burlingham, B., 564, 578
Burnett, D. D., 563
Burnham, D. H., 563, 576
Burns, L. R., 572
Burns, Tom, 96, 97, 563, 572
Burns, Ursula, 49, 50
Burton, T. M., 579
Butler, J. E., 574, 584
Buttram, R. T., 568
Buzzotta, V. R., 580
Byrne, J. A., 575
Byrnes, N., 572, 580, 581
Byron, Kristin, 491, 582

C

Caldwell, D. F., 573
Callahan, J. D., 568
Calori, R., 578
Caltabiano, Greg, 489, 490
Campbell, J. P., 562, 576
Capell, K., 572
Capowski, G. S., 586
Carey, A., 563
Carnevale, A. P., 568
Carnevale, P. J., 585
Carpenter, M. A., 568
Carr, E., 575
Carroll, A. B., 566
Carroll, J. S., 562
Carroll, S. J., 562, 573
Carter, Jimmy, 154
Cartwright, D., 578, 581
Cavanaugh, G. F., 566
Caves, R. E., 571
Chae, Kwang-Ok, 518, 584
Chafkin, M., 574
Chambers, John, 489
Champy, J., 572
Chan, C., 571
Chandler, A., 570, 572
Chaplin, Charlie, 78
Charles, A. C., 567
Chatman, J., 573
Chavez, H., 570
Chazan, Guy, 572
Chemers, M. M., 580
Child, J., 565, 572, 586
Chng, J., 566
Chong, M., 582
Choon, Choi, Jai, 518
Chua, Micheline, 557
Chung-Ming, L., 573
Clark, K. B., 586
Clark, K. D., 562
Clark, P. A., 573
Clay, R. A., 576
Clegg, C. W., 581
Clegg, S., 563
Cohen, J., 584
Cohen, J. D., 564
Cohen, M. D., 570
Cohen, R. L., 576
Cole, J., 567
Colella, A., 567
Colihan, J., 581
Collins, C. J., 562
Collins, D., 566
Collins, J., 571
Colquitte, J. A., 563
Conant, Douglas, 254–256
Conger, J. A., 579
Conley, L., 583
Conlin, M., 583, 584
Connolly, T., 577
Cook, J. D., 117
Cook, S. D. N., 572
Coons, A. I., 579
Cosier, R. A., 570
Costa, P. T., 563
Cote, S., 580
Coutts, P., 578
Covel, S., 565
Covert, A. E., 567
Cronin, M. J., 583
Crosby, P. B., 571
Crozier, M., 585

Crush, P., 579
Cullen, J. B., 566
Cullen, M. J., 567
Cummings, L. L., 564, 579, 582
Cuneo, A. Z., 568
Curtin, J. J., 567
Cyert, R., 569, 586

D

Daft, R. L., 569, 582
Dahl, D., 584
Daimler, Gottlieb, 80
Daimler, Paul, 80
Dalkey, N., 570
Dane, E., 569
Darley, J. M., 564
D'Aveni, Richard, 571
Davidow, W. H., 586
Davis, S. M., 572
Davis, T. R. V., 577
Dawley, H., 570
de Bono, Edward, 225, 570
De Geus, A. P., 570
de Janasz, S. C., 562
Dean, J. W., 571
Dechant, K., 567
DeCotiis, T. A., 575
Dekkers, Marijn E., 365
Delbecq, A., 570
Dell, Michael, 48, 49, 51, 52, 53, 56, 57, 58, 237, 349
DeMarie, S. M., 581
Deming, W. E., 563
Deutschman, A., 581
Devine, P. G., 567
Dewett, T., 563
Dharan, Bala, 577
Di Leo, L., 565, 574
Dickson, W. J., 563
Diehl, M., 570
Digman, J. M., 563
Dobson, J., 566
Donaldson, T., 562, 565
Donovan, J. J., 577
Dornbusch, S. M., 586
Doz, Y. L., 571
Drauden, G., 570
Drucker, P. F., 562, 573
Duarte, D. L., 581
Duchinsky, Brian, 484
Dufour, B., 578
Dumaine, B., 572, 573, 580
Duncan, R., 572
Dunham, Randall B., 115
Dunnette, M. D., 562, 574, 576, 577, 579, 581, 584
Dutton, J. M., 584
Dvorak, P., 577, 582

E

Eagly, A. H., 580
Earley, P. C., 577, 581
Early, P. C., 564
Ebbers, Bernie, 136
Eby, L. T., 575
Eccles, R. E., 563
Edmondson, G., 569
Edmonson, G., 580
Edwards, M. R., 575
Ehrhart, M. G., 567
Einstein, W. O., 580
Ekegren, G., 577
Elfenbein, H. A., 564
Elgin, B., 573, 577
Elizur, D., 573
Elkind, P., 565
Ellison, N. B., 583
Emrich, C., 567
Emshwiller, J. R., 565
Enciina, G. Billikopf, 577
Engardio, P., 566
Epstein, S., 564
Erez, M., 571
Evan, John deCourcey, 168
Evans, M. G., 579

F

Fackler, M., 568
Fairhurst, G. T., 573
Falkvinge, Rickard, 145
Fayol, Henri, 47, 84–87, 246–247, 562, 563, 570
Feather, N. T., 576
Feldman, D. C., 565
Fenn, D., 580
Fernandez J. P., 569
Ferris, G. R., 563, 574
Festinger, L., 581
Fiedler, Fred E., 437, 579
Fields, Jan, 321
Fierman, J., 579
Fife, William J., 431
Files, J., 566
Filo, David, 235
Finger, P. A., 570
Finholt, T., 581
Finkelstein, S., 574
Fiorina, Carly, 92
Fischer, R., 585
Fisher, A., 568
Fisher, C. D., 574, 575, 577
Fiske, S. T., 566, 567, 568
Flamholtz, E., 573
Fleishman, E. A., 579
Flint, J., 575
Floyd, S. W., 573
Flynn, J., 575
Folger, R., 567
Follett, Mary Parker, 88–89, 563
Ford, Henry, 73, 78
Forgas, J. P., 564
Fox, M. F., 567
Frankel, B., 567
Frankel, M. S., 566
Fredrickson, J. W., 568

Freedman, D. H., 575
Freeman, R. E., 565
French, R. P., Jr., 578
French, W. L., 573
Friedman, M., 566
Fry, L., 562, 572
Fuller, Millard and Linda, 154
Fung, Victor, 275
Fung, William, 275, 276
Furst, S. A., 581

G

Gabor, A., 571
Gael, S., 575
Galbraith, J. R., 572
Galen, M., 568
Galvin, B. M., 567
Ganster, D. C., 565
Gant, A. M., 576
Garvin, D., 571
Gates, Bill, 125, 137, 431
Gatewood, E., 566
Gavin, M. B., 573
Geare, A. J., 577
Geber, B., 581
Geffen David, 168
Geis, F. L., 567
Gellerman, S. W., 566
Gentile, Mary C., 570
George, J. M., 118, 563, 564, 565, 580, 581
Gerhart, B., 575
Gersick, C. J. G., 581
Gerstner, Lou, 127
Gerth, H. H., 562
Ghemawat, P., 571
Ghoshal, S., 569, 571, 573
Gibson, E., 574
Gier, J. A., 575
Gilbert, R. J., 568
Gilbreth, Frank, 80, 562
Gilbreth, Lillian, 80, 562
Gist, M. E., 577
Goenka, R. S., 325
Goldberg, Lewis R., 107
Goldhirsh, Bernard (Bernie), 119
Goldstein, A. P., 577
Goldstein, H. B., 565
Goldstein, I. L., 575
Goleman, D., 564
Gomez-Mejia, L., 562
Goodheim, L., 580
Goodin, R. E., 566
Goodman, N., 568
Goodman, P. S., 564, 582
Gort, M., 586
Gourlay, R., 572
Govindarajan, V., 568
Graham, P., 563
Gratton, Lynda, 462, 581
Gray, Dave, 519, 520
Greb, E., 580
Green, S. G., 573
Greenberg, J., 567, 576
Greene, J. D., 564
Greenleaf, Robert, 427–428
Greenwald, A. G., 568
Grey, S., 572
Griffin, A., 586
Griffin, N. Shope, 576
Griffin, R. W., 568, 570, 572
Grove, A., 579
Gruber, H., 567
Guerra, Frank, 392
Guest, R. H., 562
Guion, R. M., 575
Gupta, A. K., 562, 568
Gustafson, D. H., 570
Gutierrez, J., 566
Gutner, T., 583

H

Hackman, J. Richard, 310–311, 572, 581
Hales, C. P., 562
Hall, R. H., 572
Halpin, A. W., 579
Hambrick, D. C., 562, 566
Hamel, G., 571
Hamilton, F., 578
Hammer, M., 572
Hammonds, K. H., 577
Hamner, W. C., 577
Hannan, M., 573
Hardison, C. M., 567
Harkins, S. G., 581, 582
Harmon-Jones, E., 567
Harrington, A., 575
Harris, E. F., 579
Hartke, D. D., 579
Hartley, S. L., 567
Harvey, R. J., 575
Hastie, R., 585
Hater, J. J., 580
Hax, A. C., 581
Hayward, Tony, 328
Hedberg, B., 570
Hee, Lee Kun, 269
Heijmen, T., 574
Heilman, M. E., 567
Heintz, N., 585
Helmreich, R. L., 567
Hempel, J., 566
Hendrickson, A., 581
Hepworth, S. J., 117
Heracleous, L., 575, 581
Herring, Susan, 506
Hersey, Paul, 436, 579
Herzberg, F., 576
Hewlett, William, 92, 128, 489
Hickman, M., 585
Hickson, D. J., 573, 585
Higgins, J. H., 577
Highhouse, S., 565

Hightower, R., 581
Hill, C. W. L., 563, 568, 569, 571, 572, 573, 586
Hill, E. J., 581
Hill, L., 562
Hindo, B., 586
Hines, G. H., 563, 576
Hinings, C. R., 573, 585
Hoerr, J., 572
Hof, R. D., 570
Hofer, C. W., 570
Hofstede, Geert, 208, 569, 576
Hollenbeck, J. R., 575
Hood, N., 571
Hopkirk, Paddy, 288–289
Hoppe, M. H., 569
Hough, L. M., 574, 576, 577, 579, 581, 584
House, Robert, 439, 563, 576, 578, 579
Hout, T., 572, 586
Hsieh, Tony, 369
Hsu, C., 570
Huber, G. P., 569
Hughes, Sandy, 492
Hundal, P. S., 563, 576
Hunter, J. E., 573
Hurd, Mark, 92
Hymowitz, C., 564, 582

I

Iger, Bob, 357
Ihlwan, M., 570
Immelt, Jeffrey, 246–247
Isen, A. M., 564
Ito, Takanobu, 51

J

Jackson, J., 581
Jackson, J. H., 575
Jackson, P. R., 581
Jackson, S. E., 574
Jaffe, E., 569
Janis, I. L., 570
Janssen, O., 567
Jeannerette, P. R., 575
Jehn, K. A., 584
Jellinek, 80
Jensen, M. C., 581
Jerdee, T. H., 562
Jermier, J. M., 579
Jimenez, Joe, 432
Jobs, Steve, 43–44, 46, 52, 56, 63
Johnson, B. T., 580
Johnson, I. P., 580
Jones, D. T., 571
Jones, G. R., 562, 563, 565, 571, 572, 573, 581, 584, 586
Jones, J. R., 565
Jones, T. M., 566
Joyner, T., 575
Jum'ah, A. S., 586
Jung, Andrea, 303–304, 444, 565
Jung, D. I., 571

K

Kahn, Robert, 95, 563
Kahneman, Daniel, 219, 228, 569, 570
Kamprad, Ingvar, 203
Kanfer, R., 576, 577
Kant, Ravi, 517, 518
Kanungo, R. N., 579
Kapner, Suzanne, 571
Kapsalis, S. C., 571
Karau, S. J., 580
Karl, K. A., 581
Kasparov, Garry, 550
Katsikis, I. N., 570
Katz, Daniel, 95, 563
Katz, R. L., 562
Kazanjian, R. K., 572
Kelley, David, 121, 122
Kelley, T., 565
Kelly, E. P., 566
Kemp, N. J., 581
Kerr, S., 579, 582
Kerviel, Jerome, 339–340
Kerwin, K., 575
Kesmodel, D., 583
Khavul, S., 570
King, N., 576
Kingston, J., 570
Kirkland, R., 582
Kirkpatrick, D., 574
Kirkpatrick, S. A., 579
Kirsner, S., 582
Kleisterlee, Gerard, 158
Klepper, J., 586
Knight, Philip, 555
Knights, Miya, 586
Ko, S. J., 566
Kochan, T. A., 584
Kogut, B., 571, 586
Kohler-Gray, S., 568
Komar, J. A., 563
Komar, S., 563
Konovsky, M. A., 567
Konrads, W., 569
Koppes, L. L., 576
Korkki, P., 575
Kotter, J., 562
Kramer, L., 586
Kraul, A. I., 562
Kreitner, R., 415, 577
Kripalana, M., 584, 585
Kroc, Ray, 125, 126, 127
Krugman, P., 569
Kunda, G., 573
Kuznetsov, Ivan, 137
Kyrgidou, L. P., 570

L

Labich, K., 562
Landler, M., 569
Lane, D. M., 567

Langowitz, N. J., 569
Latane, B., 581, 582
Latham, Gary, 411, 571, 575, 576, 577
Law, K., 120
Lawler, E. E., III, 573, 577
Lawrence, M., 578
Lawrence, P. R., 572, 585
Lawrence, Paul, 96, 572
Laybourne, Geraldine, 437
Lee, C. A., 585
LeFauve, R. G., 581
Lengel, R. H., 569, 582
Lennard, Darren, 500
Lentz, E., 575
Levenson, E., 578
Lever, William, 205, 206
Levine, E. L., 575
Levitt, T., 568
Lewent, Judy, 549
Lewicki, R. J., 585
Lewin, A. Y., 574
Lewin, D., 585
Lewin, K., 573
Lewis, Randy, 175
Libby, Ryan, 113
Likert, R., 579
Lilly, Dave, 356
Lima, L., 575
Lindblom, C. E., 573
Lindsey, S., 565
Liska, L. Z., 579
Litterer, J. A., 562, 584, 585
Locke, Ed, 411, 571, 577, 579
Loden, M., 567
Loeb, M., 579
Long, J. S., 567
Lonier, T., 570
Lorange, P., 573
Lorsch, Jay, 96, 562, 572, 585
Lowry, T., 578
Lublin, J. S., 575, 581, 583
Lucas, George, 557
Luckman, T., 565
Luthans, F., 415, 577

M

Maccoby, M., 578
Macintosh, N. B., 586
MacIntyre, A., 566, 573
MacKenzie, P. M., 579
Mackey, John, 141
Madoff, Bernard, 151
Mahalingam, T. V., 572
Mahony, T. A., 562
Makhijani, M. G., 580
Malone, M. S., 586
Mandell, B., 568
Mann, Richard A., 182, 568
Manning, S., 574
Mao Zedong, 78
March, James, 220, 223, 562, 569, 570, 586
Marcia, J., 586
Margulies, N., 573
Martell, R. F., 567
Martin, Ricky, 154
Martinez, M. N., 565
Mashaba, Herman, 438
Maslow, Abraham, 406, 576
Mason, P. A., 562
Mason, R. O., 570
Mason-Draffen, C., 580
Mathieu, J. E., 564
Mathis, R. L., 575
Matlack, C., 580, 581
Mattioli, D., 577
Maurer, T. J., 576
Maybach, Wilhelm, 80
Mayer, J. D., 564
Mayo, Elton, 90, 563
McCann, J., 562
McCauley, Jim, 65
McClelland, David, 110, 408, 563, 576
McCline, R. L., 568
McCormick, E. J., 575
McCormick, Jim, 151–152
McCrae, R. R., 563
McGirt, E., 563
McGrath, Judy, 425–426, 444
McGregor, Douglas, 90, 91, 563
McGregor, J., 573, 574
McInnes, Mark, 181
McKenna, D. D., 562
McLean, B., 565
McMahan, G. C., 574
McNealy, Scott, 223
McWilliams, G., 562
Mecham, R. C., 575
Mehta, S. N., 568
Meichtry, S., 565, 574
Merrick, A., 567
Meshoulam, I., 574
Metthee, I., 568
Miles, R., 572
Miller, B. C., 581
Miller, D., 572, 573
Milliman, J., 574
Mills, C. W., 562
Mills, T. M., 580
Minter, S., 574
Mintzberg, Henry, 53, 562, 573, 578
Mische, Justus, 429
Mitchell, T. R., 576, 577
Mitroff, I. I., 570
Mittal, Lakshmi Niwas, 93
Moberg, D. J., 566
Mobley, W. H., 564
Mohr, D. C., 565
Montebello, A. R., 580
Moore, A., 586
Moore, P. L., 575
More, K. M., 577
Morgenson, G., 575
Morris, B., 585, 586

Morris, David, 175, 176
Morse, N. C., 579
Morton, M., 573
Moss, S. E., 575
Mount, M. K., 563
Mouton, Jane, 436, 579
Mowday, R. T., 577
Mulcahy, Anne, 49–51, 56, 58
Muller, J., 575
Mullinax, Harrison, 175
Murname, Mike, 506
Murphy, P. E., 566

N

Nakane, C., 569
Nakarmi, L., 579
Napier, N. K., 574
Nathan, M., 574
Nayeri, F., 575
Neale, M. A., 585
Near, J. P., 566
Needleman, S. E., 566, 584
Neergaard, L., 564
Nelson, R. R., 582
Nemetz, P., 572
Neuijen, B., 569
Nevijen, B., 208
Newman, B., 582
Newman, W. H., 573
Nichols, N. A., 586
Nicholson, N., 576
Niehoff, B. P., 579
Nightengale, J., 573
Noe, R. A., 563, 575
Nogues, Thierry, 460
Nohira, N., 563
Nooyi, Indra, 444, 526–527
Nord, W. R., 562
North, D. C., 568
Northcraft, G. B., 584, 585
Norton, M. V., 577
Nystrom, L. E., 564
Nystrom, P. C., 570, 573

O

O'Boyle, T. F., 581
Obstfeld, M., 569
O'Flynn, Stephen, 520
Ohayv, D. D., 208, 569
Okimoto, T. G., 567
Oldham, Greg R., 310–311, 572
O'Leary, V. E., 567
O'Leary-Kelly, A. M., 568
Olsen, J. P., 570
O'Neil, J., 583
O'Reilly, C. A., 573, 582, 586
Organ, D. W., 563
Ostrom, T. M., 582
O'Toole, Larry, 113, 114
Ouchi, William, 86, 573
Overman, S., 581

P

Packard, David, 92, 128, 489
Paetzold, R. L., 567, 568
Page, Larry, 297, 298
Page, R. C., 562
Palmisano, Samuel, 127
Palrecha, R., 578
Pangarkar, N., 575, 581
Pape, W. R., 581
Parker, L. D., 563
Parnell, Stewart, 133, 134
Passariello, C., 571
Patel, S., 571
Patterson, A., 567
Pearce, J. A., 565, 571, 580
Pedigo, P. R., 562
Peiperl, M. A., 575
Pencer, Gerald, 259–260
Pennings, D. J., 585
Pennings, J. M., 585
Penrose, E., 571
Perlez, J., 569
Perm-Ajchariyawong, N., 574
Perrow, Charles, 307, 562, 572, 573
Perry, J., 565, 574
Perry, M. K., 571
Perttula, K. H., 579
Peters, L. H., 579
Peters, Tom, 86, 87, 563, 582
Peterson, R. S., 564
Pettigrew, A. M., 585
Petty, R. E., 582
Pfeffer, Jeffrey, 86, 219, 568, 569, 570, 578, 583, 584, 585, 586
Phelps, R., 571
Pickering, J. F., 586
Pillai, R., 580
Pinkley, R. L., 584, 585
Pitta, D. A., 576
Pitta, J., 563
Podsakoff, P. M., 579
Pohlmann, J. T., 579
Pollard, H. R., 562
Polzer, J. T., 566
Pondy, L. R., 582, 584
Poole, M. S., 584
Porras, Estuardo, 529
Porras, J., 571
Porter, C. O. L. H., 563
Porter, E., 574, 575
Porter, L. W., 117, 577, 584
Porter, Michael, 254, 256–258, 568, 571
Poteet, M. L., 575
Powers, S., 585
Prahalad, C. K., 571
Pratt, M., 569
Premack, S. L., 575
Presnell, Connie, 176
Pritchard, R. D., 576
Provitera, M. J., 562
Pruitt, D. G., 585

Pugh, D.S., 573
Pugh, S. D., 568
Pulakos, E. D., 567
Putnam, L. L., 584

Q

Quinn, J. B., 574

R

Radosevich, D. J., 577
Raia, A. P., 573
Ramstad, Evan, 572
Rangaswani, J. P., 500
Rapp, Karl Friedrich, 453
Rauwald, C., 569
Raven, B., 578
Ravlin, E. C., 580
Reckford, Jonathan, 154
Reeves, M., 581
Reich, Robert, 150, 568
Reimer, E., 579
Reinhardt, Joerg, 432
Reizenstein, R. M., 568
Rhode, J. G., 573
Rice, F., 570
Rich, E., 586
Rifkin, G., 583
Roach, Andy, 500
Robbins, S., 578, 584
Roberson, L., 567
Roberts, Barry S., 182, 568
Roberts, K. H., 584
Robie, C., 563
Robinson, B., 118
Robinson, G., 567
Robinson, L., 118
Rockowitz, Bruce, 275
Roddick, Anita, 109
Rodgers, R., 573
Rodgers, T. J., 353, 540
Roethlisberger, F. J., 90, 563
Rogers, E. M., 582
Rogers, Simon, 167
Rokeach, Milton, 111, 112, 563
Roll, Richard, 570
Ronen, S., 576
Roos, D., 571
Rose, R. L., 579
Rosen, B., 566, 581
Rosener, J. B., 567
Ross, G. H. B., 573
Roth, G., 562
Roy, D., 562, 563
Rubin, J. Z., 585
Rubino, Alan, 388
Rugman, A. M., 569
Rungtusanatham, M., 571
Russell, J. W., 574
Russo, J. E., 570
Rynes, S., 566, 575
Rynes, S. L., 574

S

Saari, L. M., 577
Saavedra, R., 580
Sackett, P. R., 567
Sacks, D., 569
Sagie, A., 573
Saginaw, Paul, 428–429
Salancik, G. R., 568
Salovey, P., 564
Saltr, C., 570
Sanchez, J. I., 575
Sandberg, J., 582, 583
Sander, Jil, 216
Sanders, G., 208, 569
Sanders, W. G., 566
Sawin, L. L., 567
Sawyer, J. E., 570
Sayeed, L., 581
Schacter, S., 581
Schadler, T., 582
Schaubroeck, J., 565
Schein, H., 565
Schendel, D., 570
Schiffmann, H. R., 567
Schmalensee, R., 568, 571
Schmidt, Eric, 298
Schmidt, K. A., 570
Schmidt, S. M., 584
Schneck, R. E., 585
Schneider, Benjamin, 121, 565, 572, 578
Schoemaker, P. J., 570
Schoenfeldt, L. F., 574, 577
Schoenherr, R. A., 572
Schreyogg, G., 573
Schriesheim, C. A., 579, 580
Schroeder, R. G., 571
Schuler, R. S., 574
Schuman, M., 579
Schumpeter, J., 568, 586
Schwartz, N. D., 579
Schweiger, D. M., 570
Schwenk, C. R., 570
Scott, W. R., 586
Seiders, K., 562
Seltzer, J., 580
Semler, Ricardo, 373, 374, 574
Senge, Peter, 225, 232, 569, 570
Senkbiel, Liz, 468
Serwer, A. E., 567
Sewell, D., 571
Seyle, D. C., 566
Shama, A., 562
Sharpe, R., 575
Shaw, J. B., 574, 577
Shaw, K. N., 577
Shaw, W. H., 562, 566
Shellenbarger, S., 576
Shepperd, J. A., 581
Sheriden, J. E., 572
Shulka, R. K., 570
Silver, David, 506

Simmering, M. J., 563
Simon, Herbert, 220, 223, 562, 569
Simons, R., 573
Sinclair, R. C., 564
Singer, B., 567
Skinner, B. F., 413, 577
Skinner, Jim, 320
Slaughter, J. E., 565
Smith, Adam, 76, 562
Smith, D. B., 565, 578
Smith, F. J., 117
Smith, R., 565
Smutniak, J., 569
Snell, S. A., 574
Snyder, N. T., 581
Soke, A., 566
Soloman, R. C., 566
Sommerville, R. B., 564
Song, L., 120
Sonnenberg, D., 580
Sorcher, M., 577
Sorensen, J. B., 565
Spangler, W. D., 563, 576, 578
Spears, L., 578
Spence, J. T., 567
Spors, K. K., 563, 564, 575, 576
Spreitzer, G., 579
Sproul, J. R., 575
Sproull, L. S., 581
Sprout, A. L., 583
Stahl, M. J., 563, 576
Stajkovic, A. D., 577
Stalk, G., 572, 586
Stalker, G., 96, 97, 563, 572
Starbuck, W. H., 570, 573
Staw, B. M., 564, 570, 579, 582
Steele, C. M., 567
Steers, R. M., 577
Steiner, I. D., 582
Steinmann, H., 573
Stevens, A., 567
Stewart, R., 562
Stewart, T. A., 586
Stogdill, R. M., 578, 579
Stone, S. C., 568
Stopford, J., 572
Stratton, Jeff, 321
Strauss, S. G., 581
Stringer, Howard, 187–188
Stroebe, W., 570
Strutt, A., 574
Sullivan, D. M., 570
Sullivan, R. L., 574
Sullivan, S. E., 562
Sun Tzu, 79
Sutton, R. I., 570, 584
Swann, W. B., Jr., 566
Swartz, M., 565
Sy, T., 580

T

Tabacek, K., 585
Taggart, J. H., 586
Taiichi, Ohno, 73
Tannen, Deborah, 506, 584
Tanzi, Calisto, 65
Tashiro, H., 580
Taylor, E., 569
Taylor, Frederick W., 77–78, 562, 572
Taylor, S. E., 566, 567, 568
Teece, D. J., 571
Tellegen, Auke, 108, 564
Tenbrunsel, A. E., 565
Tepper, B. J., 579
Terrell, G., 567
Tetrault, L. A., 579
Tett, R. P., 563
Thacker, R., 568
Tharenou, P., 562
Thomas, D. A., 568
Thomas, K. W., 584
Thomas, O., 573
Thompson, Don, 320
Thompson, J. D., 563, 573, 581
Thompson, James, 95
Thompson, L., 585
Thurm, S., 577
Tiplady, R., 580
Tischler, Linda, 444, 580
Todd, P. A., 582
Tosi, H. L., 573, 577
Totty, M., 583
Townsend, A. M., 581
Trevino, L. K., 566, 582
Triandis, H. C., 576
Trice, H. M., 565
Tscheulin, D., 579
Tsuda, Miiko, 178
Tubbs, M. E., 577
Tuckman, B. W., 581
Turban, E., 586
Turner, C., 573
Tversy, Amos, 219, 228, 570
Tzu, Sun, 79

U

Unger, R. K., 567
Ury, W., 585

V

Valian, Virginia, 170, 174, 566, 567, 568
Van Der Beek, R., 574
van der Veer, Jeroen, 163
Van Fleet, D. D., 579
Van Maanen, J., 565, 566
Vancouver, J. B., 577
Vascellaro, J. E., 583
Vaslow, J. B., 568
Velasquez, M., 566
Victor, B., 566

Von Glinow, M., 574
von Pierer, Heinrich, 441
Vroom, Victor H., 402

W

Wack, P., 570
Wadhwa, V., 574
Wakizaka, Y., 584
Waldman, D. A., 580
Wall, J. A., Jr., 584
Wall, T. D., 117, 581
Waller, M. J., 562
Wallston, B. B., 567
Walsh, J. P., 564, 567, 570
Walster, W. G., 570
Walton, R. E., 584, 585
Wanous, J. P., 575
Warkentin, M. E., 581
Warr, P. B., 117
Washington, R. R., 578
Waterman, A. S., 566
Waterman, Robert, 87, 563, 582
Watkins, S., 565
Watson, D., 564
Wauters, R., 574
Weber, J., 568
Weber, Max, 82, 83, 562
Webster, J., 118
Weick, K. E., 565, 573
Weiner, S. P., 581
Weinzweig, Ari, 428–429
Weiss, D. J., 115
Weiss, E. M., 576
Weiss, H. W., 577
Weiss, S. E., 585
Welch, D., 575
Welch, Jack, 372, 432
Wellner, A. Stein, 567, 582
Wells, L., 572
Wertheimer, M., 567
Wessel, D., 574
Wexley, K. N., 567, 575
Wheeler, J. A., 575
Wheelright, S. C., 569
Wheelwright, S. C., 586
White, E., 583
White, Michael, 526, 527
White, W. F., 584
Whiting, V., 562
Williams, E. S., 580
Williams, K., 581
Williams, M., 572, 579
Williamson, O. E., 586
Willig, R. D., 568, 571
Wilson, Mark, 124
Winer, B. J., 579
Winslow, R., 582
Winter, D. G., 563, 576
Winter, R. R., 568
Wirtz, J., 575, 581
Witt, L. A., 563
Wittich, C., 562
Wofford, J. C., 579
Womack, J. P., 571
Wood, Aric, 520
Woodman, R. W., 570, 573
Woolridge, B., 573
Woycke, J., 563, 576
Wozniak, Steven, 43
Wren, D., 562
Wright, P. M., 574, 575
Wyant, C., 571
Wysocki, B., 562

X

Xin, K., 579

Y

Yamada, Tachi, 431
Yang, Jerry, 235
Yanow, D., 572
Yoder, R. J., 577
Young, S., 571, 572
Yukl, G., 578, 579
Yukongdi, Vimolwan, 572
Yunus, Mohammed, 236

Z

Zajac, D. M., 564
Zander, A. F., 578, 581
Zanna, M., 564
Zawacki, R. A., 574
Zedong, Mao, 78
Zeitz, Jochen, 215, 216
Zellner, W., 570
Zhou, J., 564, 580
Zickar, M. J., 565
Zuckerman, H., 567

Organizations

A

Accenture, 46, 556
Acer, 49, 52, 190, 194
ADP Employer Services, 379
Affilips N. V., 311-313
All Nippon Airways (ANA), 243
Alliance Unichem, 388
Amazon.com, 195, 369, 543, 544
AMD, 157, 197
AOL, 219
Apple, 43–44, 46, 49, 62, 63, 97, 146, 188, 191–192, 194, 221, 233, 261, 358–359, 536, 542–543
ArcelorMittal, 93
A.S. Watson & Company, 431
AT&T, 380, 542
Avon, 303–304

B

Bank of Montreal, 498
Bayer, 330, 364–365
Benz & Cie, 81
Black Like Me, 438
Blackberry, 192
BMW, 138, 157, 259, 453–454, 459
Body Shop, 108, 109
Boeing, 191, 192, 294, 541
Bonlat, 65
Boots Group, 433
Bose, 541
BP Amoco, 268
British Petroleum (BP), 328–329, 462
Burger King, 173

C

Campbell Soup, 255–256, 261
Carrefour, 46, 60–61, 194, 252, 258, 345, 431
Chevron, 497
Chrysler, 73, 219, 380
Chubb Corporation, 168
Cisco Systems, 246, 251, 292, 489, 493
Citibank, 120, 285
Coca-Cola, 180, 191, 198, 200, 259, 262, 263, 268, 279
Cott Corporation, 259–260
Creative Display Solutions, 445–446
Cypress Semiconductor, 353, 540, 548

D

Daewoo, 433
Daimler AG, 80–81, 219
Daimler Financial Services, 80
Dell Computer, 49, 52, 53, 57–58, 60, 194, 317, 349
Deutsche Bank, 236
DHL, 192, 193, 539–540, 548
Donna Karan, 544
Dresdner Kleinwort Wasserstein, 500, 501
DuPont, 182, 267, 268, 327

E

Eastman Kodak, 168, 279, 500
EasyJet, 418
eBay, 544–545
El Faro, 529–530
Emami Group, 325
EMI, 104
ENI, 268
Enron, 128–129, 136
Ernst & Young, 168
ExxonMobil, 120

F

Facebook, 233, 493
FedEx, 192, 279
Fiat, 74, 96
Fireman's Fund Insurance, 499-500
Ford Motor Company, 73, 74, 223, 281, 291–292, 380, 386, 459
Foxconn, 192, 358
Franklin Motor Company, 79

G

Gap Inc., 139, 140
Gateway, 356
G.D. Searle, 190–191
GE Healthcare, 484
General Electric (GE), 96, 210, 247–249, 291
General Mills, 256, 417
General Motors (GM), 73, 268, 281, 380
Gentle Giant Moving Company, 113–114
Gerdau S. A., 383
Gillette, 266
GlaxoSmithKline, 314–315, 332–333
Global Reporting Initiative (GRI), 222
Goodyear, 497
Google, 93, 97, 157, 192, 195, 233, 238, 296, 417, 536
Grameen Bank, 236
Greenleaf Center for Servant Leadership, 428
Greenpeace, 522
Guerra DeBerry Coody, 391–392

H

Habitat for Humanity, 46, 154–155
Habitat International, 175–176
Hallmark Cards, 472
Hanes Brands (HBI), 192
Hanjin, 46
HCL Technologies, 372
Hewlett-Packard (HP), 49, 52, 56, 92–93, 128, 194, 489, 490
Hilton Hotels, 267
Hissho Iwai, 420
Hitachi, 65
Hoffmann-La Roche, 388, 389
Home Depot, 175
Hon Hai, 358, 359

Honda, 51, 201, 279, 555
Honeywell, 500
HSBC, 236
Hugo Boss, 544
Hyundai, 74, 251, 433

I

IBM, 56, 65, 127, 149, 168, 194, 197, 208, 262–263, 493, 501, 553, 554
IDEO, 120–122, 126, 127
IG Metall, 392
Igus, 290
IKEA, 202–203, 252
ImproveNow.com, 388
INC., 119
Inditex, 294, 540, 541
Innocent Drinks, 263
Intel, 46, 157, 197

J

Japan Air System (JAS), 243, 244
Japan Airlines (JAL), 243–244
JobLine International, 376
Johnsonville Foods, 466

K

Kao Corporation, 153
Kellogg's, 139, 265
Kelon, 60
Ken's Kids, 175
Kentucky Fried Chicken, 173
Ketchum, 499–500
Kodak, 168, 279, 500
Kofax, 496

L

Lands' End, 206
Lehman Brothers, 156
Lehman Brothers Holdings Inc., 168
Leninets Concern, 266
Lenovo, 194
Levi Strauss, 191, 497
Li & Fung, 192, 275–276, 541
LinkedIn, 493
L.L.Bean, 285
Lockheed Corporation, 238
L'Oréal, 109
Louis Vuitton, 460
Lucas Arts, 557–558
Lucent Technologies, 168
Lundberg Family Farms, 196

M

Magellan, 298
Marks & Spencer, 258
Matsushita, 262, 265, 266
Mazda, 291, 431
McDonald's, 45, 46, 83, 126–127, 142, 173, 261, 262, 293, 308, 320–322
McKinsey & Co., 556
McNeil Nutritionals, 191
Medtronic, 112
Mercedes-Benz, 80, 81
Merck, 151, 168, 548–549
Metalurgica, 382
Metro, 431
Microsoft, 57, 63, 65, 168, 197, 199, 238, 331, 354–355, 372, 465, 474, 553
Mitsubishi, 317–318
Monster.com, 376
Motorola, 63, 223, 497
MTV Networks, 425–426
MySpace, 493

N

Napster, 146
Nestlé, 139, 201–202, 265, 268, 435, 522
NEXT, 43, 44
Nike, 62, 177, 555–556
Nippon Restaurant Enterprise Co., 196
Nokia, 63, 192–193, 268, 315–317, 332, 405, 462
Novartis, 432, 457
Nucor, 460–461

O

Ogilvy & Mather, 462
Openfind, 298
Oracle, 493, 553, 554

P

Palm, 63
Parkdale, 192
Parmalat Lehman Brothers, 136
Parmalat SpA, 64–65
Peanut Corporation of America (PCA), 133–134
PepsiCo, 198, 200, 259, 262, 279, 526–527
Perrier, 279
Pfizer, 497
Philips NV, 249
Pirate Party *(Piratpartiet),* 146
Pixar, 43
Pizza Hut, 173
Portugal Telecom, 399–400
Primark, 493
Procter & Gamble (P&G), 268, 492
PUMA, 215–216

Q

Quaker Oats, 198

R

Radacati Group, 491
Raytheon, 168
Reckitt Benckiser, 511–512
Rosas del Ecuador, 100
Royal Dutch Shell, 163–164, 250–251
Royal Philips, 158
Ryannair, 281
Ryla, 124–125

S

Samsung, 194, 269–270, 433
SAP, 57, 330, 331, 551–552, 553, 554
SAS, 411
Saudi Aramco, 535–536
S.C. Johnston & Sons, 168
Semco, 373–374
Siemens, 64, 96, 442
Singapore Airlines, 378, 470, 481–482
SiteDesign, 420
siteROCK, 356
SK Telecom, 323–324
Société Générale, 339–340
Sony, 187–188, 229, 260, 290, 542, 543
Sprint, 542
Standard Bank, 283
Standard Charter, 236
Stellar Technologies, 492
Subway, 309
Sun Microsystems, 223–224, 226
Sunflower Electric Power, 332

T

Tata Chemical, 483
Tata Daewoo, 518
Tata Motors, 517–518
Tate & Lyle, 191
Teknovus, 489, 490
Telefonica, 315, 316
Tesco, 282
The Body Shop, 108, 109
The Forest Trust (TFT), 522
The Gap, 139, 140
3M, 58, 238, 263–264, 294, 331
Time Warner, 219
Tokio Marine and Fire Insurance, 420
Toronto-Dominion Bank, 168
Toshiba, 194, 330
Toyota, 73, 74, 155–156, 201, 228, 258, 259, 279, 290, 342, 344, 357
Transstroi, 137
Tungsram, 210
Twitter, 493
Tyco, 128

U

Unilever, 205–206, 265, 266
United Parcel Service (UPS), 65, 433

V

Virgin Group, 103–104
Volvo, 431

W

W. N. Procter, 541
Walgreens, 175
Walmart, 44, 45, 60, 83, 158–159, 207, 233, 291, 542
Walt Disney Company, 43, 125, 154, 357, 500
Waterford Technologies, 491
Western Electric Company, 89
Whole Foods, 140–141, 142
WorldCom, 128, 136

X

Xerox, 49–51, 58, 62, 97
Xplane, 519–520

Y

Yahoo!, 500
Young & Rubicam, 498

Z

Zappos, 369–370
Zara, 294, 544
Zingerman's Delicatessen, 428–429

Glossary/Subjects

A

Ability tests, 380

Accommodation *An ineffective conflict-handling approach in which one party, typically with weaker power, gives in to the demands of the other, typically more powerful, party,* 518

Accommodative approach *Companies and their managers behave legally and ethically and try to balance the interests of different stakeholders as the need arises,* 157

Achievement orientation *A worldview that values assertiveness, performance, success, and competition,* 209

Achievement-oriented behaviors, 439, 440
Action plan, 412
Activity ratios, 348
Ad hoc committee, 327, 459
Adaptive cultures, 331–333
Adjourning, 467
Administrative barriers, 196

Administrative management *The study of how to create an organizational structure and control system that lead to high efficiency and effectiveness,* 81

Administrative management theory, 81–88

Administrative model *An approach to decision making that explains why decision making is inherently uncertain and risky and why managers usually make satisfactory rather than optimum decisions,* 220–223

Agreeableness *An approach to decision making that explains why decision making is inherently uncertain and risky and why managers usually make satisfactory rather than optimum decisions,* 106, 107

Alderfer's ERG theory *The theory that three universal needs–for existence, relatedness, and growth–constitute a hierarchy of needs and motivate behavior. Alderfer proposed that needs at more than one level can be motivational at the same time,* 407–408

All-channel network, 494, 495
Allocating authority, 320–324

Ambiguous information *Information that can be interpreted in multiple and often conflicting ways,* 222–223

Answering machine, 490
AOL-Time Warner merger, 219
Applications software, 545

Arbitrator *A third-party negotiator who can impose what he or she thinks is a fair solution to a conflict that both parties are obligated to abide by,* 393, 521

Art of War, The, 79

Artificial intelligence *Behavior performed by a machine that, if performed by a human being, would be called "intelligent,"* 550

ASA framework, 121, 122
Assessment centers, 380
Asynchronous technologies, 462

Attitude *A collection of feelings and beliefs,* 114

Attraction-selection-attrition (ASA) framework *A model that explains how personality may influence organizational culture,* 121, 122

Authority *The power to hold people accountable for their actions and to make decisions concerning the use of organizational resources,* 82, 320

Autonomy, 310

Avoidance *An ineffective conflict-handling approach in which the parties try to ignore the problem and do nothing to resolve their differences,* 518

B

B2B commerce, 553

B2B marketplace *An Internet-based trading platform set up to connect buyers and sellers in an industry,* 553

B2B network structure *A series of global strategic alliances that an organization creates with suppliers, manufacturers, and distributors to produce and market a product,* 555

B2C commerce, 553
Background check, 379
Background information, 378
Backward vertical integration, 261
Bank wiring room experiments, 90

Barriers to entry *Factors that make it difficult and costly for an organization to enter a particular task environment or industry,* 195–196

BARS, 385, 386
Behavior appraisals, 384–385
Behavior management theory, 88–93
Behavior model of leadership, 434–436

Behavioral management *The study of how managers should behave to motivate employees and encourage them to perform at high levels and be committed to the achievement of organizational goals,* 88

Behavioral observation scale (BOS), 385, 386
Behaviorally anchored rating scale (BARS), 385, 386
Belongingness needs, 406

Benchmarking *The process of comparing one company's performance on specific dimensions with the performance of other, high-performing organizations,* 365

Benefits, 390–391
Best sales practices, 283
Betamax, 229
BHAGs, 253

Bias *The systematic tendency to use information about others in ways that result in inaccurate perceptions,* 176–177, 228–230, 486

Big, hairy, audacious goals (BHAGs), 253
Big five personality traits, 105–110

Blog *A Web site on which an individual, group, or organization posts information, commentary, and opinions and to which readers can often respond with their own commentary and opinions,* 493

Bonus, 419
BOS, 385, 386

Bottom-up change *A gradual or evolutionary approach to change in which managers at all levels work together to develop a detailed plan for change,* 364

Boundaryless organization *An organization whose members are linked by computers, faxes, computer-aided design systems, and video teleconferencing and who rarely, if ever, see one another face-to-face,* 556

Bounded rationality *Cognitive limitations that constrain one's ability to interpret, process, and act on information,* 220–221

Brainstorming, 234

Brand loyalty *Customers' preference for the products of organizations currently existing in the task environment,* 195

Built to Last, 253

Bureaucracy *A formal system of organization and administration designed to ensure efficiency and effectiveness,* 82–83

Bureaucratic control *Control of behavior by means of a comprehensive system of rules and standard operating procedures,* 355

Bureaucratic red tape, 83
Business ethics. *See* Ethics and social responsibility
Business groups, 317

Business-level plan *Divisional managers' decisions pertaining to divisions' long-term goals, overall strategy, and structure,* 247

Business-level strategy *A plan that indicates how a division intends to compete against its rivals in an industry,* 247, 257–260

Business-to-business (B2B) commerce *Trade that takes place between companies using IT and the Internet to link and coordinate the value chains of different companies,* 553

Business-to-customer (B2C) commerce *Trade that takes place between a company and individual customers using IT and the Internet,* 553

Buyer beware, 139

C

Cafeteria-style benefit plan *A plan from which employees can choose the benefits they want,* 390

Capital, 204
Car-making history, 73–75
Carbon footprint, 222
Casual dress, 127
CEI, 483

Centralization *The concentration of authority at the top of the managerial hierarchy,* 85, 324

CEO, 55
CEO compensation, 138
Ceremonies and rites, 125–126
Chaebol, 317
Chain network, 494, 495
Chain of command, 320

Charismatic leader *An enthusiastic, self-confident leader who can clearly communicate his or her vision of how good things could be,* 442

Cheaper by the Dozen, 80
Chernobyl nuclear power plan meltdown, 66
Chief executive officer (CEO), 55
Chief operating officer (COO), 55
Child care, 401
Child labor, 150
Chiselers, 90
Chrysler-Daimler merger, 219
Circle network, 494, 495

Clan control *The control exerted on individuals and groups in an organization by shared values, norms, standards of behavior, and expectations,* 359–360

Classical decision-making model *A prescriptive approach to decision making based on the assumption that the decision maker can identify and evaluate all possible alternatives and their consequences and rationally choose the most appropriate course of action,* 220

Classroom instruction, 381–382

Closed system *A system that is self-contained and thus not affected by changes occurring in its external environment,* 95

Coercive power *The ability of a manager to punish others,* 431

Coldbath Fields Prison, 136

Collaboration *A way of managing conflict in which both parties try to satisfy their goals by coming up with an approach that* *leaves them both better off and does not require concessions on issues that are important to either party,* 517

Collaboration software *Groupware that promotes and facilitates collaborative, highly interdependent interactions and provides an electronic meeting site for communication among team members,* 499–500

Collective bargaining *Negotiations between labor unions and managers to resolve conflicts and disputes about issues such as working hours, wages, benefits, working conditions, and job security,* 393

Collectivism *A worldview that values subordination of the individual to the goals of the group and adherence to the principle that people should be judged by their contribution to the group,* 208

Command group *A group composed of subordinates who report to the same supervisor; also called* department *or* unit, 459

Commission pay, 420

Communication *The sharing of information between two or more individuals or groups to reach a common understanding,* 483. *See also* Promoting effective communication

Communication networks *The pathways along which information flows in groups and teams and throughout the organization,* 494–497

Communication process, 484–485
Communications effectiveness index (CEI), 483

Competition *An ineffective conflict-handling approach in which each party tries to maximize its own gain and has little interest in understanding the other party's position and arriving at a solution that will allow both parties to achieve their goals,* 518

Competitive advantage *The ability of one organization to outperform other organizations because it produces desired goods or services more efficiently and effectively than they do,* 58, 61, 277–278

Competitors *Organizations that produce goods and services that are similar to a particular organization's goods and services,* 194–195

Complex mental models, 232

Compromise *A way of managing conflict in which each party is concerned about not only its own goal accomplishment but also the goal accomplishment of the other party and is willing to engage in a give-and-take exchange and make concessions,* 517

Concentration on a single industry *Reinvesting a company's profits to strengthen its competitive position in its current industry,* 261

Conceptual skills *The ability to analyze and diagnose a situation and to distinguish between cause and effect,* 56

Concurrent control *Control that gives managers immediate feedback on how efficiently inputs are being transformed into outputs so managers can correct problems as they arise,* 344

Confidence, 111
Conflict. *See* Organizational conflict

Conscientiousness *The tendency to be careful, scrupulous, and persevering,* 106–107

Consideration *Behavior indicating that a manager trusts, respects, and cares about subordinates,* 434

Contingency models of leadership, 436
Contingency planning, 250

Contingency theory *The idea that the organizational structures and control systems managers choose depend on (are contingent on) characteristics of the external environment in which the organization operates,* 96–97

Contract book *A written agreement that details product development factors such as responsibilities, resource commitments, budgets, time lines, and development milestones,* 295

Control systems *Formal target-setting, monitoring, evaluation, and feedback systems that provide managers with information about how well the organization's strategy and structure are working,* 342–343

Controlling *Evaluating how well an organization is achieving its goals and taking action to maintain or improve performance; one of the four principal tasks of management,* 52, 128, 341. *See also* Organizational control

COO, 55
Coordinating mechanisms, 326–327

Core competency *The specific set of departmental skills, knowledge, and experience that allows one organization to outperform another,* 58

Core members *The members of a team who bear primary responsibility for the success of a project and who stay with a project from inception to completion,* 296

Corporate blog, 493

Corporate-level plan *Top management's decisions pertaining to the organization's mission, overall strategy, and structure,* 247

Corporate-level strategy *A plan that indicates in which industries and national markets an organization intends to compete,* 247, 257–268

Corporate scandals, 128
Crafts production, 76

Creativity *A decision maker's ability to discover original and novel ideas that lead to feasible alternative courses of action,* 232

- entrepreneurship, 235–238
- group, 234–235
- individual, 233–234

CRM, 281–284
Cross-cultural team, 458
Cross-departmental responsibility, 55

Cross-functional team *A group of managers brought together from different departments to perform organizational tasks,* 296, 319–320, 326, 327, 458

Cultural values and norms, 207–208
Current ratio, 348

Customer relationship management (CRM) *A technique that uses IT to develop an ongoing relationship with customers to maximize the value an organization can deliver to them over time,* 281–284

Customer service function, 279
Customer structure, 317
Customer wants, 280

Customers *Individuals and groups that buy the goods and services an organization produces,* 194

D

Data *Raw, unsummarized, and unanalyzed facts,* 537

Days sales outstanding, 348
Debt-to-assets ratio, 348

Decentralizing authority *Giving lower-level managers and nonmanagerial employees the right to make important decisions about how to use organizational resources,* 324

Decision making *The process by which managers respond to opportunities and threats by analyzing options and making determinations about specific organizational goals and courses of action,* 220–231

- administrative model, 220–223
- bias, 228–230
- classical model, 230
- group, 230–231
- Japan, 227–228
- opportunities, 217
- programmed/nonprogrammed, 217–218
- steps in process, 223–227
- threats, 217

Decision-making process, 223–227

Decision support system *An interactive computer-based management information system that managers can use to make nonroutine decisions,* 548–550

Decisional roles, 54, 170

Decoding *Interpreting and trying to make sense of a message,* 485

Defensive approach *Companies and their managers behave ethically to the degree that they stay within the law and strictly abide by legal requirements,* 156

Defining the business, 251–252

Delphi technique *A decision-making technique in which group members do not meet face-to-face but respond in writing to questions posed by the group leader,* 235

Demand forecasts, 375

Demographic forces *Outcomes of changes in, or changing attitudes toward, the characteristics of a population, such as age, gender, ethnic origin, race, sexual orientation, and social class,* 199

Department *A group of people who work together and possess similar skills or use the same knowledge, tools, or techniques to perform their jobs,* 53, 459

Derivatives, 64

Development *Building the knowledge and skills of organizational members so they are prepared to take on new responsibilities and challenges,* 381

Developmental consideration *Behavior a leader engages in to support and encourage followers and help them develop and grow on the job,* 443

Devil's advocacy *Critical analysis of a preferred alternative, made in response to challenges raised by a group member who, playing the role of devil's advocate, defends unpopular or opposing alternatives for the sake of argument,* 231

Dialectical inquiry *Critical analysis of two preferred alternatives in order to find an even better alternative for the organization to adopt,* 231

Differentiation strategy *Distinguishing an organization's products from the products of competitors on dimensions such as product design, quality, or after-sales service,* 258

Difficult goals, 412
Digital piracy, 145–146
Directive behaviors, 439, 440
Disabled employees, 175

Discipline *Obedience, energy, application, and other outward marks of respect for a superior's authority,* 86

Disney University, 125
Disseminator, 54, 170
Distortion, 323

Distributive justice *A moral principle calling for the distribution of pay raises, promotions, and other organizational resources to be based on meaningful contributions that individuals have made and not on personal characteristics over which they have no control,* 171

Distributive negotiation *Adversarial negotiation in which the parties in conflict compete to win the most resources while conceding as little as possible,* 522

Distributors *Organizations that help other organizations sell their goods or services to customers,* 193–194

Disturbance handler, 54, 170
Diverse workforce, 162–183
  bias, 176–177
  disabled employees, 175
  economic imperative, 172
  ethical imperative, 170–172
  EU, 166
  gender. *See* Gender
  managerial roles, 169–170
  managing diversity effectively, 178–181
  other kinds of diversity, 168–169
  overt discrimination, 177–178
  perception, 172–177
  sexual harassment, 181–183
  sexual orientation, 168
  sources of diversity, 165
  why important, 165
  women, 163–164, 170, 171

Diversification *Expanding a company's business operations into a new industry in order to produce new kinds of valuable goods or services,* 263–265

Diversity *Differences among people in age, gender, race, ethnicity, religion, sexual orientation, socioeconomic background, and capabilities/disabilities,* 165

Diversity awareness, 179
Diversity skills, 179
Diversity training, 180
Division, 313

Division of labor *Splitting the work to be performed into particular tasks and assigning tasks to individual workers,* 84, 308, 463

Divisional manager, 247

Divisional structure *An organizational structure composed of separate business units within which are the functions that work together to produce a specific product for a specific customer,* 312–317

Dress, 127

E

E-commerce *Trade that takes place between companies, and between companies and individual customers, using IT and the Internet,* 553

E-commerce system, 553–554
E-mail, 490–492, 500, 506
Economic feasibility, 225

Economic forces *Interest rates, inflation, unemployment, economic growth, and other factors that affect the general health and well-being of a nation or the regional economy of an organization,* 197

Economies of scale *Cost advantages associated with large operations,* 195

Effectiveness *A measure of the appropriateness of the goals an organization is pursuing and of the degree to which the organization achieves those goals,* 46

Efficiency *A measure of how well or how productively resources are used to achieve a goal,* 45

  communication, 483
  competitive advantage, 277
  facilities layout, 287–288
  flexible manufacturing, 289–290
  information systems, 292
  Internet, 292–293
  JIT inventory system, 290–291
  process engineering, 291–292
  self-managed work teams, 291

Emotional intelligence *The ability to understand and manage one's own moods and emotions and the moods and emotions of other people,* 118–119, 120, 445

Emotions *Intense, relatively short-lived feelings,* 116–118

Empathy, 504
Employee-centered behaviors, 436

Employee stock option *A financial instrument that entitles the bearer to buy shares of an organization's stock at a certain price during a certain period or under certain conditions,* 419

Employee stock ownership plans (ESOPs), 331
Employment interview, 379–380

Empowerment *The expansion of employees' knowledge, tasks, and decision-making responsibilities,* 433

Encoding *Translating a message into understandable symbols or language,* 485

Energy drinks, 198

Enterprise resource planning (ERP) systems *Multimodule application software packages that coordinate the functional activities necessary to move products from the design stage to the final customer stage,* 550–553

Entrepreneur *An individual who notices opportunities and decides how to mobilize the resources necessary to produce new and improved goods and services,* 54, 170, 235

Entrepreneurship *The mobilization of resources to take advantage of an opportunity to provide customers with new or improved goods and services,* 235–237

Entropy *The tendency of a closed system to lose its ability to control itself and thus to dissolve and disintegrate,* 95

Equity *The justice, impartiality, and fairness to which all organizational members are entitled,* 86, 409–410

Equity theory *A theory of motivation that focuses on people's perceptions of the fairness of their work outcomes relative to their work inputs,* 409–411

ERG theory, 407–408
ERP systems, 550–553

Escalating commitment *A source of cognitive bias resulting from the tendency to commit additional resources to a project even if evidence shows that the project is failing,* 229

Esprit de corps *Shared feelings of comradeship, enthusiasm, or devotion to a common cause among members of a group,* 87

Esteem needs, 406

Ethical dilemma *The quandary people find themselves in when they have to decide if they should act in a way that might help another person or group even though doing so might go against their own self-interest,* 135

Ethics *The inner guiding moral principles, values, and beliefs that people use to analyze or interpret a situation and then decide what is the right or appropriate way to behave,* 135

Ethics and social responsibility, 63–64, 132–161
  approaches to social responsibility, 156–157
  changes in ethics over time, 136
  community, society, and nation, 141–142
  customers, 139
  effects of ethical/unethical behavior, 147
  employees, 139
  ethical dilemmas, 135
  ethics and the law, 135–136
  failures in professional ethics, 152
  forms of socially responsible behavior, 155
  Gap Inc.'s code of vendor conduct, 140
  individual ethics, 151–152
  managers, 137–138
  nonprofit organizations, 138
  occupational ethics, 151
  organizational culture, 158
  organizational ethics, 152–153
  rules for ethical decision making, 143–145
  societal ethics, 148–150
  stockholders, 137
  suppliers and distributors, 139
  why be socially responsible?, 157
  why behave ethically?, 146–148

Ethics ombudsperson *A manager responsible for communicating and teaching ethical standards to all employees and monitoring their conformity to those standards,* 158

European Union (EU)
  diversity, 166
  foreign citizens, 167
  law, 149
  Microsoft, and, 199
  reporting requirements, 221–222
Evolution of management thought, 72–100
  administrative management theory, 81–88
  behavior management theory, 88–93
  bureaucracy, 82–83
  contingency theory, 96–97
  Fayol's principles of management, 84–87
  Follett, 88–89
  Gilbreths, 80
  Hawthorne studies, 89–90
  human relations movement, 90
  job specialization/division of labor, 77–78
  management science theory, 94
  open-systems view, 95–96
  organizational environment theory, 94–97
  scientific management theory, 75–78
  Taylor's principles, 77–78
  Theory X/Theory Y, 90–93

Evolutionary change *Change that is gradual, incremental, and narrowly focused,* 361

Excellent companies, 87–88
Executive compensation, 138

Executive support system *A sophisticated version of a decision support system that is designed to meet the needs of top managers,* 549

Existence needs, 407

Expectancy *In expectancy theory, a perception about the extent to which effort results in a certain level of performance,* 403

Expectancy theory *The theory that motivation will be high when workers believe that high levels of effort lead to high performance and high performance leads to the attainment of desired outcomes,* 402–405

Expert power *Power that is based on the special knowledge, skills, and expertise that a leader possesses,* 431–432

Expert system *A management information system that employs human knowledge, embedded in a computer, to solve problems that ordinarily require human expertise,* 550

Exporting *Making products at home and selling them abroad,* 267

External locus of control *The tendency to locate responsibility for one's fate in outside forces and to believe that one's own behavior has little impact on outcomes,* 110

External networks, 496–497
External recruitment, 376–377

Extinction *Curtailing the performance of dysfunctional behaviors by eliminating whatever is reinforcing them,* 414

Extraversion *The tendency to experience positive emotions and moods and to feel good about oneself and the rest of the world,* 105–106, 107

Extravert, 105

Extrinsically motivated behavior *Behavior that is performed to acquire material or social rewards or to avoid punishment,* 401

F

Face-to-face communication, 487–490
Facebook, 233, 493
Faces scale, 115

Facilities layout *The strategy of designing the machine–worker interface to increase operating system efficiency,* 287–288

Fayol's principles of management, 84–87
Feedback, 227, 310, 412

Feedback control *Control that gives managers information about customers' reactions to goods and services so corrective action can be taken if necessary,* 344

Feedforward control *Control that allows managers to anticipate problems before they arise,* 343

Feelings, 116–118
Fiedler's contingency theory of leadership, 437–439, 441
Figurehead, 54, 170

Filtering *Withholding part of a message because of the mistaken belief that the receiver does not need or will not want the information,* 503

Financial capital, 204

First-line manager *A manager who is responsible for the daily supervision of nonmanagerial employees,* 53, 56

Five forces model, 254–257
Fixed-position layout, 288
Flat organization, 322

Flexible manufacturing *The set of techniques that attempt to reduce the costs associated with the product assembly process or the way services are delivered to customers,* 287, 289–290

Focused differentiation strategy *Serving only one segment of the overall market and trying to be the most differentiated organization serving that segment,* 259

Focused low-cost strategy *Serving only one segment of the overall market and trying to be the lowest-cost organization serving that segment,* 258

Folkways *The routine social conventions of everyday life,* 208

Force-field theory of change, 361
Forced ranking, 386
Foreign citizens, 167
Foreign Corrupt Practices Act, 149

Formal appraisal *An appraisal conducted at a set time during the year and based on performance dimensions and measures that were specified in advance,* 388

Formal business attire, 127

Formal group *A group that managers establish to achieve organizational goals,* 458

Formal leader, 466
Forming, 466
Formulating strategy. *See* Strategy formulation
Forward vertical integration, 261, 262
Founders' values, 123–125

Franchising *Selling to a foreign organization the rights to use a brand name and operating know-how in return for a lump-sum payment and a share of the profits,* 267

Free trade, 205, 206–207

Free-trade doctrine *The idea that if each country specializes in the production of the goods and services that it can produce most efficiently, this will make the best use of global resources,* 205

Friendship group *An informal group composed of employees who enjoy one another's company and socialize with one another,* 462–463

Function, 311
Functional conflict resolution, 517

Functional-level plan *Functional managers' decisions pertaining to the goals that they propose to pursue to help the division attain its business-level goals,* 249

Functional-level strategy *A plan of action to improve the ability of each of an organization's functions to perform its task-specific activities in ways that add value to an organization's goods and services,* 249, 278

Functional manager, 247

Functional structure *An organizational structure composed of all the departments that an organization requires to produce its goods or services,* 311–312

G

GATT, 205
Gays and lesbians, 168, 392
Gender
  leadership, 443–445
  linguistic styles, 506
  old boys' network, 497
  Royal Dutch Shell, 163–164
  weekly earnings, 171
  women at disadvantage, 170

Gender schemas *Preconceived beliefs or ideas about the nature of men and women, their traits, attitudes, behaviors, and preferences,* 174

General Agreement on Tariffs and Trade (GATT), 205
General and Industrial Management (Fayol), 47

General environment *The wide-ranging global, economic, technological, sociocultural, demographic, political, and legal forces that affect an organization and its task environment,* 190, 196–200

Geographic structure *An organizational structure in which each region of a country or area of the world is served by a self-contained division,* 314, 315–317

Global crisis management, 65–66

Global environment *The set of global forces and conditions that operate beyond an organization's boundaries but affect a manager's ability to acquire and utilize resources,* 186–213

barriers to entry, 195–196
competitors, 194–195
customers, 194
declining barriers, 204–206
demographic forces, 199
distributors, 193–194
economic forces, 197
free trade, 205, 206–207
national culture, 207–210
political and legal forces, 199–200
process of globalization, 202–204
regional trade agreements, 206–207
sociocultural forces, 198
suppliers, 190–192
technological forces, 197

Global geographic structure, 315, 316

Global organization *An organization that operates and competes in more than one country,* 60, 188

Global outsourcing *The purchase or production of inputs from overseas suppliers to lower costs and improve product quality or design,* 191–192

Global product structure, 315, 316

Global strategy *Selling the same standardized product and using the same basic marketing approach in each national market,* 265

Globalization *The set of specific and general forces that work together to integrate and connect economic, political, and social systems across countries, cultures, or geographical regions so that nations become increasingly interdependent and similar,* 202

Goal, 252–253, 350

Goal-setting theory *A theory that focuses on identifying the types of goals that are most effective in producing high levels of motivation and performance and explaining why goals have these effects,* 411–412

Government regulation, 195

Grapevine *An informal communication network along which unofficial information flows,* 496

Graphic rating scale, 386
Grievance procedure, 393

Group *Two or more people who interact with each other to accomplish certain goals or meet certain needs,* 454. *See also* Groups and teams

Group cohesiveness *The degree to which members are attracted to or loyal to their group,* 469–473

Group creativity, 234–235
Group decision making, 230–231

Group decision support system *An executive support system that links top managers so they can function as a team,* 550

Group development, 466–467
Group leadership, 466

Group norms *Shared guidelines or rules for behavior that most group members follow,* 467

Group role *A set of behaviors and tasks that a member of a group is expected to perform because of his or her position in the group,* 465–466

Group size, 463–464, 472, 475
Group tasks, 464–465
Grouping jobs into functions/divisions, 311–320
Grouping tasks into jobs, 308–311
Groups and teams, 452–478

communication networks, 494–495
conflict, 476
conformity and deviance, 468–469
diversity, 472
group cohesiveness, 469–473
group goal accomplishment, 471
group identity, 472–473
group leadership, 466
group norms, 467
group roles, 465–466
group size, 463–464, 472, 475
group tasks, 464–465
innovation, 456
level of participation within group, 470–471
motivation, 457, 473–474
performance enhancers, as, 455–456
responsiveness to customers, 456
social loafing, 474–475
stages of group development, 466–467
types, 458–463

Groupthink *A pattern of faulty and biased decision making that occurs in groups whose members strive for agreement among themselves at the expense of accurately assessing information relevant to a decision,* 230

Groupware *Computer software that enables members of groups and teams to share information with one another,* 498–499

Growth needs, 407

H

Hawthorne effect *The finding that a manager's behavior or leadership approach can affect workers' level of performance,* 90

Hawthorne studies, 89–90

Herzberg's motivator-hygiene theory *A need theory that distinguishes between motivator needs (related to the nature of the work itself) and hygiene needs (related to the physical and psychological context in which the work is performed) and proposes that motivator needs must be met for motivation and job satisfaction to be high,* 408

Heuristics *Rules of thumb that simplify decision making,* 228

Hierarchy of authority *An organization's chain of command, specifying the relative authority of each manager,* 320

Hierarchy of needs, 406–407
High-performing organizations, 46
High-power-distance societies, 209
Historical overview. *See* Evolution of management thought
Hofstede's model of national culture, 208–209
Horizontal communication, 495

Hostile work environment sexual harassment *Telling lewd jokes, displaying pornography, making sexually oriented remarks about someone's personal appearance, and other sex-related actions that make the work environment unpleasant,* 181–182

House's path–goal theory, 439–440, 441
HP Way, 92, 128
Human capital, 204

Human relations movement *A management approach that advocates the idea that supervisors should receive behavioral training to manage subordinates in ways that elicit their cooperation and increase their productivity,* 90

Human resource management (HRM) *Activities that managers engage in to attract and retain employees and to ensure that they perform at a high level and contribute to the accomplishment of organizational goals,* 368–395

background information, 378–379
classroom instruction, 381–382
collective bargaining, 393
components, 371, 372–373
culture, and, 330–331
external recruiting, 376–377
formal education, 383
honesty in recruiting, 371
internal recruiting, 377
interview, 379–380
job analysis, 375–376
labor relations, 392–393
on-the-job training, 382–383
organizational structure, and, 307–308
paper-and-pencil tests, 380
pay and benefits, 389–392
performance appraisal and feedback, 384–389
performance tests, 380
physical ability tests, 380
planning, 374–375
recruitment and selection, 374–381
references, 380
selection process, 378–381
strategic HRM, 371–372
training and development, 381–383
unions, 392–393
varied work experiences, 383

Human resource planning *Activities that managers engage in to forecast their current and future needs for human resources,* 374–375

Human skills *The ability to understand, alter, lead, and control the behavior of other individuals and groups,* 57

Hygiene needs, 408

Hypercompetition *Permanent, ongoing, intense competition brought about in an industry by advancing technology or changing customer tastes,* 257

I

Illusion of control *A source of cognitive bias resulting from the tendency to overestimate one's own ability to control activities and events,* 229

Impersonal written communication, 493
Implementing strategy, 270

Importing *Selling products at home that are made abroad,* 267

Incomplete information, 221

Incremental product innovation *The gradual improvement and refinement of existing products that occur over time as existing technologies are perfected,* 293

Individual ethics *Personal standards and values that determine how people view their responsibilities to others and how they should act in situations when their own self-interests are at stake,* 151–152

Individualism *A worldview that values individual freedom and self-expression and adherence to the principle that people should be judged by their individual achievements rather than by their social background,* 208

Inequity *Lack of fairness,* 410

Inert cultures, 331

Informal appraisal *An unscheduled appraisal of ongoing progress and areas for improvement,* 389

Informal group *A group that managers or nonmanagerial employees form to help achieve their own goals or meet their own needs,* 458

Informal leader, 466

Informal organization *The system of behavioral rules and norms that emerge in a group,* 90

Information *Data that are organized in a meaningful fashion,* 537

ambiguous, 222–223
attributes, 537–538
complete/incomplete, 221, 538
control, and, 539–540
coordination, and, 540–541
decisions, and, 539

Information costs, 223

Information distortion *Changes in the meaning of a message as the message passes through a series of senders and receivers,* 503

Information overload *The potential for important information to be ignored or overlooked while tangential information receives attention,* 493

Information richness *The amount of information that a communication medium can carry and the extent to which the medium enables the sender and receiver to reach a common understanding,* 487

Information technology (IT) *The set of methods or techniques for acquiring, organizing, storing, manipulating, and transmitting information,* 65, 534–560

artificial intelligence, 550
B2B network structures, 555–556
communication, 498–500
communication media, 489–490
control systems, 343–344
delayering of the organizational hierarchy, 556
effects of advancing IT, 541–542
IT revolution, 541–546
limitations, 556–557
MIS. *See* Management information system (MIS)
network of computer power, 545–546
organizational structure, 307
product life cycle, 542–544
strategic alliance, 555

Informational roles, 54, 170

Initiating structure *Behavior that managers engage in to ensure that work gets done, subordinates perform their jobs acceptably, and the organization is efficient and effective,* 435

Initiative *The ability to act on one's own without direction from a superior,* 86

Innovation *The process of creating new or improved goods and services or developing better ways to produce or provide them,* 62

communication, 483
competitive advantage, 277
improving, 293–298
incremental product, 293
quantum product, 293
teams and groups, 456

Input *Anything a person contributes to his or her job or organization,* 402

Instrumental value *A mode of conduct that an individual seeks to follow,* 111

Instrumentality *In expectancy theory, a perception about the extent to which performance results in the attainment of outcomes,* 403–404

Integrating mechanisms *Organizing tools that managers can use to increase communication and coordination among functions and divisions,* 326–327

Integrating role, 326, 327

Integrative bargaining *Cooperative negotiation in which the parties in conflict work together to achieve a resolution that is good for them both,* 522–523

Intellectual stimulation *Behavior a leader engages in to make followers be aware of problems and view these problems in new ways, consistent with the leader's vision,* 443

Interest group *An informal group composed of employees seeking to achieve a common goal related to their membership in an organization,* 463

Intergroup conflict, 515
Intermediate-term plan, 249

Internal locus of control *The tendency to locate responsibility for one's fate within oneself,* 110

Internal recruiting, 377
International expansion, 265–268

Internet *A global system of computer networks,* 497

Interorganizational conflict, 515
Interpersonal conflict, 513–514
Interpersonal roles, 54, 170
Intragroup conflict, 514

Intranet *A companywide system of computer networks,* 497–498

Intrapreneur *A manager, scientist, or researcher who works inside an organization and notices opportunities to develop new or improved products and better ways to make them,* 235

Intrapreneurship and organizational learning, 237–238

Intrinsically motivated behavior *Behavior that is performed for its own sake,* 400

Introvert, 105

Intuition *Feelings, beliefs, and hunches that come readily to mind, require little effort and information gathering, and result in on-the-spot decisions,* 218

Inventory *The stock of raw materials, inputs, and component parts that an organization has on hand at a particular time,* 286

Inventory turnover, 348
iPhone, 543

Islamic Sabbath, 210
IT. *See* Information technology (IT)
iTunes, 146

J

Japanese rice market, 196

Jargon *Specialized language that members of an occupation, group, or organization develop to facilitate communication among themselves,* 502

JIT inventory system, 74, 286, 290–291

Job analysis *Identifying the tasks, duties, and responsibilities that make up a job and the knowledge, skills, and abilities needed to perform the job,* 375–376

Job description, 375

Job design *The process by which managers decide how to divide tasks into specific jobs,* 308

Job enlargement *Increasing the number of different tasks in a given job by changing the division of labor,* 309

Job enrichment *Increasing the degree of responsibility a worker has over his or her job,* 309

Job interview, 379–380
Job-oriented behaviors, 436

Job satisfaction *The collection of feelings and beliefs that managers have about their current jobs,* 114–115

Job simplification *The process of reducing the number of tasks that each worker performs,* 309

Job specialization *The process by which a division of labor occurs as different workers specialize in different tasks over time,* 76

Job specifications, 375

Joint venture *A strategic alliance among two or more companies that agree to jointly establish and share the ownership of a new business,* 268

Just-in-time (JIT) inventory system *A system in which parts or supplies arrive at an organization when they are needed, not before,* 74, 286, 290–291

Justice rule *An ethical decision distributes benefits and harms among people and groups in a fair, equitable, or impartial way,* 144

K

Kanban, 290
Keiretsu, 317
Knowbot, 550

Knowledge management system *A company-specific virtual information system that systematizes the knowledge of its employees and facilitates the sharing and integrating of their expertise,* 556

L

Labor relations *The activities managers engage in to ensure that they have effective working relationships with the labor unions that represent their employees' interests,* 392–393

LAN, 545

Lateral move *A job change that entails no major changes in responsibility or authority levels,* 377

Layoffs, 138

Leader *An individual who is able to exert influence over other people to help achieve group or organizational goals,* 54, 170, 427

Leader-member relations *The extent to which followers like, trust, and are loyal to their leader; a determinant of how favorable a situation is for leading,* 437

Leader substitutes model, 440, 441

Leadership *The process by which an individual exerts influence over other people and inspires, motivates, and directs their activities to help achieve group or organizational goals,* 424–448

- behavior model, 434–436
- characteristics of effective leaders, 434
- charismatic, 442
- contingency models, 436–441
- cross-cultural differences, 429–430
- emotional intelligence, 445
- empowerment, 433
- Fiedler's contingency model, 437–439
- gender, 443–445
- groups and teams, 466
- House's path–goal theory, 439–440
- leader substitutes model, 440
- personal leadership style, 427–428
- power, 430–432
- trait model, 433–434
- transactional, 443
- transformational, 441–443

Leadership substitute *A characteristic of a subordinate or of a situation or context that acts in place of the influence of a leader and makes leadership unnecessary,* 440

Leading *Articulating a clear vision and energizing and enabling organizational members so that they understand the part they play in achieving organizational goals; one of the four principal tasks of management,* 51, 128

Lean manufacturing, 73, 74

Learning *A relatively permanent change in knowledge or behavior that results from practice or experience,* 413

Learning organization *An organization in which managers try to maximize the ability of individuals and groups to think and behave creatively and thus maximize the potential for organizational learning to take place,* 232–233

Learning theories *Theories that focus on increasing employee motivation and performance by linking the outcomes that employees receive to the performance of desired behaviors and the attainment of goals,* 413–417

Least preferred coworker (LPC), 437

Legitimate power *The authority that a manager has by virtue of his or her position in an organization's hierarchy,* 430

Lesbian, gay, bisexual, and transgender (LGBT) people, 168, 392
Level of rivalry, 256
Levels of management, 53–56
Leverage ratios, 348
Lewin's force-field theory of change, 361
Lexus, 284
LGBT people, 168, 392
Liaison, 54, 170
Liaison roles, 326

Licensing *Allowing a foreign organization to take charge of manufacturing and distributing a product in its country or world region in return for a negotiated fee,* 267

Line manager *Someone in the direct line or chain of command who has formal authority over people and resources at lower levels,* 320

Line of authority *The chain of command extending from the top to the bottom of an organization,* 85

Linguistic style *A person's characteristic way of speaking,* 506–507

LinkedIn, 493
Linux, 146
Liquidity ratios, 348
Listening, 504
Local area network (LAN), 545
Locus of control, 110
Long-distance learning, 383

Long-term orientation *A worldview that values thrift and persistence in achieving goals,* 209

Long-term plan, 249

Low-cost strategy *Driving the organization's costs down below the costs of its rivals,* 257

Low-power-distance countries, 209
LPC, 437

M

Manage by exception, 324

Management *The planning, organizing, leading, and controlling of human and other resources to achieve organizational goals efficiently and effectively,* 45

- challenges, 60–66
- entrepreneurship, 237
- historical overview. *See* Evolution of management thought
- levels, 53–56
- required skills, 56–57
- tasks, 47–56
- turnaround, 63
- why studied, 46–47

Management by objectives (MBO) *A goal-setting process in which a manager and each of his or her subordinates negotiate specific goals and objectives for the subordinate to achieve and then periodically evaluate the extent to which the subordinate is achieving those goals,* 352–354

Management by wandering around *A face-to-face communication technique in which a manager walks around a work area and talks informally with employees about issues and concerns,* 489

Management information system (MIS) *A specific form of IT that managers utilize to generate the specific, detailed information they need to perform their roles effectively,* 94, 538, 546–554

- decision support system, 548–550
- e-commerce system, 553–554
- ERP system, 550–553
- executive support system, 549
- expert system, 550
- operations information system, 547–548
- transaction-processing system, 547

Management science, 94

Management science theory *An approach to management that uses rigorous quantitative techniques to help managers make maximum use of organizational resources,* 94

Manager
- communication skills, 501–507
- diversity, 169–170
- divisional, 247
- ethics, 137–138
- free trade, 205–206
- functional, 247
- line/staff, 320–321
- organizational culture, 121–122
- overconfidence, 219
- self-managed work teams, 459–460
- types, 53–56

Managerial Grid, 436
Managerial overconfidence, 219
Managerial perception, 173–174
Managerial power, 430–432
Managerial roles, 54, 169–170
Managerial skills, 56–57
Managerial tasks
- controlling, 52
- leading, 51–52
- organizing, 51
- planning, 47–49

Market structure *An organizational structure in which each kind of customer is served by a self-contained division; also called* customer structure, 314, 317

Marketing function, 278–279

Maslow's hierarchy of needs *An arrangement of five basic needs that, according to Maslow, motivate behavior. Maslow proposed that the lowest level of unmet needs is the prime motivator and that only one level of needs is motivational at a time,* 406–407

Mass-production manufacturing, 73
Materials management function, 279

Matrix structure *An organizational structure that simultaneously groups people and resources by function and by product,* 318, 319

MBO, 352–354
McLanguage, 127

Mechanistic structure *An organizational structure in which authority is centralized, tasks and rules are clearly specified, and employees are closely supervised,* 97

Mediator *A third-party negotiator who facilitates negotiations but has no authority to impose a solution,* 393, 521

Medium *The pathway through which an encoded message is transmitted to a receiver,* 485

Mentoring *A process by which an experienced member of an organization (the mentor) provides advice and guidance to a less experienced member (the protégé) and helps the less experienced member learn how to advance in the organization and in his or her career,* 181, 383

Mergers, 219

Merit pay plan *A compensation plan that bases pay on performance,* 417–420

Message *The information that a sender wants to share,* 485

Microlending, 236

Middle manager *A manager who supervises first-line managers and is responsible for finding the best way to use resources to achieve organizational goals,* 53, 55, 56

Military theory, 79
Minimum chain of command, 323
Mintzberg's typology, 53, 54
MIS, 94
Mission, 251

Mission statement *A broad declaration of an organization's purpose that identifies the organization's products and customers and distinguishes the organization from its competitors,* 245, 251

Modern Times, 78
Monitor, 54, 170
Monitoring e-mail and Internet use, 492

Mood *A feeling or state of mind,* 116–118

Moral rights rule *An ethical decision is one that best maintains and protects the fundamental or inalienable rights and privileges of the people affected by it,* 144

Mores *Norms that are considered to be central to the functioning of society and to social life,* 207

Motivation *Psychological forces that determine the direction of a person's behavior in an organization, a person's level of effort, and a person's level of persistence,* 400

Motivation and performance, 400–420
  Alderfer's ERG theory, 407–408
  equity theory, 409–411
  expectancy theory, 402–405
  goal-setting theory, 411–412
  groups and teams, 457, 473–474
  Herzberg's motivation-hygiene theory, 408
  learning theories, 413–417
  Maslow's hierarchy of needs, 406–407
  McClelland's needs for achievement, affiliation, and power, 408–409
  motivation equation, 402
  nature of motivation, 400–402
  need theories, 406–409
  OB MOD, 415–416
  operant conditioning theory, 413–416
  pay and motivation, 417–420
  social learning theory, 416–417
Motivation equation, 402
Motivator needs, 408

Multidomestic strategy *Customizing products and marketing strategies to specific national conditions,* 265, 266

MySpace, 493

N

NAFTA, 206–207

National culture *The set of values that a society considers important and the norms of behavior that are approved or sanctioned in that society,* 198, 207–210

Need *A requirement or necessity for survival and well-being,* 406

Need for achievement *The extent to which an individual has a strong desire to perform challenging tasks well and to meet personal standards for excellence,* 110, 408

Need for affiliation *The extent to which an individual is concerned about establishing and maintaining good interpersonal relations, being liked, and having other people get along,* 110, 408

Need for power *The extent to which an individual desires to control or influence others,* 111, 408

Need theories *Theories of motivation that focus on what needs people are trying to satisfy at work and what outcomes will satisfy those needs,* 406–409

Needs assessment *An assessment of which employees need training or development and what type of skills or knowledge they need to acquire,* 381

Negative affectivity *The tendency to experience negative emotions and moods, to feel distressed, and to be critical of oneself and others,* 106, 108

Negative emotions and moods, 117–118

Negative reinforcement *Eliminating or removing undesired outcomes when people perform organizationally functional behaviors,* 413

Negotiation *A method of conflict resolution in which the parties consider various alternative ways to allocate resources to come up with a solution acceptable to all of them,* 521–523

Negotiator, 54, 170
Nemawashi, 227

Network *Interlinked computers that exchange information,* 545

New ventures, 237

Noise *Anything that hampers any stage of the communication process,* 485

Nominal group technique *A decision-making technique in which group members write down ideas and solutions, read their suggestions to the whole group, and discuss and then rank the alternatives,* 234–235

Nonprogrammed decision making *Nonroutine decision making that occurs in response to unusual, unpredictable opportunities and threats,* 218

Nonroutine technology, 307

Nonverbal communication *The encoding of messages by means of facial expressions, body language, and styles of dress,* 485–486

Norming, 467

Norms *Unwritten, informal codes of conduct that prescribe how people should act in particular situations and are considered important by most members of a group or organization,* 83, 111, 207, 327–328, 467

North American Free Trade Agreement (NAFTA), 206–207

Nurturing orientation *A worldview that values the quality of life, warm personal friendships, and services and care for the weak,* 209

NutraSweet, 190–191

O

OB MOD, 415–416

Objective appraisal *An appraisal that is based on facts and is likely to be numerical,* 385

Observational learning, 416

Obstructionist approach *Companies and their managers choose not to behave in a socially responsible way and instead behave unethically and illegally,* 156

OCBs, 114

Occupational ethics *Standards that govern how members of a profession, trade, or craft should conduct themselves when performing work-related activities,* 151

Offshoring, 375
Old boys' network, 497

On-the-job training *Training that takes place in the work setting as employees perform their job tasks,* 382–383

Open system *A system that takes in resources from its external environment and converts them into goods and services that are then sent back to that environment for purchase by customers,* 95

Open-systems view, 95–96

Openness to experience *The tendency to be original, have broad interests, be open to a wide range of stimuli, be daring, and take risks,* 107, 108

Operant conditioning theory *The theory that people learn to perform behaviors that lead to desired consequences and learn not to perform behaviors that lead to undesired consequences,* 413–416

Operating budget *A budget that states how managers intend to use organizational resources to achieve organizational goals,* 350–351

Operating margin, 347–348
Operating system software, 545

Operations information system *A management information system that gathers, organizes, and summarizes comprehensive data in a form that managers can use in their nonroutine coordinating, controlling, and decision-making tasks,* 547–548

Operations management, 94

Optimum decision *The most appropriate decision in light of what managers believe to be the most desirable consequences for the organization,* 220

Order *The methodical arrangement of positions to provide the organization with the greatest benefit and to provide employees with career opportunities,* 86

Organic structure *An organizational structure in which authority is decentralized to middle and first-line managers and tasks and roles are left ambiguous to encourage employees to cooperate and respond quickly to the unexpected,* 97

Organization chart, 495
Organization structure, 81

Organizational architecture *The organizational structure, control systems, culture, and human resource management systems that together determine how efficiently and effectively organizational resources are used,* 305

Organizational behavior *The study of the factors that have an impact on how individuals and groups respond to and act in organizations,* 90

Organizational behavior modification (OB MOD) *The systematic application of operant conditioning techniques to promote the performance of organizationally functional behaviors and discourage the performance of dysfunctional behaviors,* 415–416

Organizational change *The movement of an organization away from its present state and toward some desired future state to increase its efficiency and effectiveness,* 360–365

- assessing need for change, 362–363
- deciding on change to make, 363
- evaluating the change, 364–365
- evolutionary change, 361
- implementing the change, 363–364
- Lewin's force-field theory of change, 361
- managing change, 362–365
- revolutionary change, 362
- steps in process, 362
- top-down/bottom-up change, 363–364

Organizational change process, 362–365

Organizational citizenship behaviors (OCBs) *Behaviors that are not required of organizational members but that contribute to and are necessary for organizational efficiency, effectiveness, and competitive advantage,* 114

Organizational commitment *The collection of feelings and beliefs that managers have about their organization as a whole,* 116

Organizational communication networks, 495–496

Organizational conflict *The discord that arises when the goals, interests, or values of different individuals or groups are incompatible and those individuals or groups block or thwart one another's attempts to achieve their objectives,* 513

- conflict management strategies, 517–521
- integrative bargaining, 522–523
- negotiation, 521–523
- organizational performance, and, 514
- sources of conflict, 515–517
- strategies focused on individuals, 519–521
- strategies focused on organization, 521
- types of conflict, 513–515

Organizational control, 341–360
- behavior control, 352–359
- bureaucratic control, 355–358
- clan control, 359–360
- control process, 344–347
- control system, 342–343
- direct supervision, 352
- financial measures of performance, 347–349
- importance, 341–342
- IT, 343–344
- MBO, 352–354
- operating budget, 350–351
- organizational goals, 350
- output control, 347–351, 359

Organizational culture *The shared set of beliefs, expectations, values, norms, and work routines that influence the ways in which individuals, groups, and teams interact with one another and cooperate to achieve organizational goals,* 119–129, 327–333

- adaptive vs. inert cultures, 331–333
- ceremonies and rites, 125–126
- controlling, 128
- ethics and social responsibility, 158
- founders' values, 123–125
- leading, 128
- managers, 121–122
- organizing, 128
- planning, 127
- socialization, 125
- sources of, 328–331
- stories and language, 126–127
- values/norms, 122–127

Organizational design *The process by which managers make specific organizing choices that result in a particular kind of organizational structure,* 305

Organizational environment *The set of forces and conditions that operate beyond an organization's boundaries but affect a manager's ability to acquire and utilize resources,* 94, 305–306

Organizational environment theory, 94–97

Organizational ethics *The guiding practices and beliefs through which a particular company and its managers view their responsibility toward their stakeholders; the moral values, beliefs, and rules that establish the appropriate way for an organization and its members to deal with each other and with people outside the organization,* 152–153, 330. *See also* Ethics and social responsibility

Organizational identity, 473
Organizational language, 126–127

Organizational learning *The process through which managers seek to improve employees' desire and ability to understand and manage the organization and its task environment,* 232–238

Organizational performance *A measure of how efficiently and effectively a manager uses resources to satisfy customers and achieve organizational goals,* 45

Organizational politics *Activities that managers engage in to increase their power and to use power effectively to achieve their goals and overcome resistance or opposition,* 523–529

- exercising power, 527–529
- gaining/maintaining power, 524–527
- importance, 524

Organizational rites, 126

Organizational socialization *The process by which newcomers learn an organization's values and norms and acquire the work behaviors necessary to perform jobs effectively,* 125

Organizational structure *A formal system of task and reporting relationships that coordinates and motivates organizational members so they work together to achieve organizational goals,* 51, 305–327

culture, and, 331
coordinating functions and divisions, 320–327
factors to consider, 306
grouping jobs into functions/divisions, 311–320
grouping tasks into jobs, 308–311
human resources, 307–308
job characteristics model, 310–311
job enlargement/job enrichment, 309
organizational environment, 305–306
strategy, 306–307
technology, 307

Organizations *Collections of people who work together and coordinate their actions to achieve a wide variety of goals or desired future outcomes,* 45

Organizationwide goal setting, 350

Organizing *Structuring working relationships in a way that allows organizational members to work together to achieve organizational goals; one of the four principal tasks of management,* 51, 128

Outcome *Anything a person gets from a job or organization,* 401

Outsource *To use outside suppliers and manufacturers to produce goods and services,* 375

Outsourcing *Contracting with another company, usually abroad, to have it perform an activity the organization previously performed itself,* 60

Overconfidence, 219
Overlapping authority, 516

Overpayment inequity *The inequity that exists when a person perceives that his or her own outcome–input ratio is greater than the ratio of a referent,* 410

Overt discrimination *Knowingly and willingly denying diverse individuals access to opportunities and outcomes in an organization,* 177

P

Paper-and-pencil tests, 380
PAQ, 376
Participative behaviors, 439, 440

Path–goal theory *A contingency model of leadership proposing that leaders can motivate subordinates by identifying their desired outcomes, rewarding them for high performance and the attainment of work goals with these desired outcomes, and clarifying for them the paths leading to the attainment of work goals,* 439–440, 441

Pay and benefits, 389–392
Pay and motivation, 417–420

Pay level *The relative position of an organization's pay incentives in comparison with those of other organizations in the same industry employing similar kinds of workers,* 390

Pay structures *The arrangement of jobs into categories reflecting their relative importance to the organization and its goals, levels of skill required, and other characteristics,* 390

PC industry, 194
Peer appraisal, 387
People with disabilities, 175

Perception *The process through which people select, organize, and interpret what they see, hear, touch, smell, and taste to give meaning and order to the world around them,* 172–177, 486

Performance appraisal *The evaluation of employees' job performance and contributions to their organization,* 384

Performance appraisal and feedback, 384–389

Performance feedback *The process through which managers share performance appraisal information with subordinates, give subordinates an opportunity to reflect on their own performance, and develop, with subordinates, plans for the future,* 384

Performing, 467
Personal mastery, 232
Personal selling, 279
Personality tests, 380

Personality traits *Enduring tendencies to feel, think, and act in certain ways,* 105–111

Personally addressed written communication, 490–492
Physical ability tests, 380
Physiological needs, 406
Piece-rate pay, 420

Planning *Identifying and selecting appropriate goals and courses of action; one of the four principal tasks of management,* 47–49, 245–253

culture, 128
effective plans, 245–247
formulating strategy. *See* Strategy formulation
implementing strategy, 270
importance, 246–247
levels/types, 247–249
missions/goals, 251–252
scenario planning, 250–251
single-use plans, 250
standing plans, 250
three-step process, as, 245, 270
time horizon, 249

Policy, 250

Political and legal forces *Outcomes of changes in laws and regulations, such as deregulation of industries, privatization of organizations, and increased emphasis on environmental protection,* 199–200

Political capital, 204

Political strategies *Tactics that managers use to increase their power and to use power effectively to influence and gain the support of other people while overcoming resistance or opposition,* 524

Pooled task interdependence *The task interdependence that exists when group members make separate and independent contributions to group performance,* 464–465

Porter's business-level strategies, 257
Porter's five forces model, 256
Portfolio strategy, 264
Position analysis questionnaire (PAQ), 376

Position power *The amount of legitimate, reward, and coercive power that a leader has by virtue of his or her position in an organization; a determinant of how favorable a situation is for leading,* 438

Positive emotions and moods, 117

Positive reinforcement *Giving people outcomes they desire when they perform organizationally functional behaviors,* 413

Potential competitors *Organizations that presently are not in a task environment but could enter if they so choose,* 195

Potential for entry, 256
Power, 430–432

Power distance *The degree to which societies accept the idea that inequalities in the power and well-being of their citizens are due to differences in individuals' physical and intellectual capabilities and heritage,* 209

Power of large suppliers, 256

Practical rule *An ethical decision is one that a manager has no reluctance about communicating to people outside the company because the typical person in a society would think it is acceptable,* 145

Practicality, 225
Premium price, 257
Price fixing, 194
Principle of the minimum chain of command, 323

Prior-hypothesis bias *A cognitive bias resulting from the tendency to base decisions on strong prior beliefs even if evidence shows that those beliefs are wrong,* 228

Proactive approach *Companies and their managers actively embrace socially responsible behavior, going out of their way to learn about the needs of different stakeholder groups and using organizational resources to promote the interests of all stakeholders,* 157

Procedural justice *A moral principle calling for the use of fair procedures to determine how to distribute outcomes to organizational members,* 171–172

Process layout, 287–288

Process reengineering *The fundamental rethinking and radical redesign of business processes to achieve dramatic improvement in critical measures of performance such as cost, quality, service, and speed,* 291

Product champion *A manager who takes "ownership" of a project and provides the leadership and vision that take a product from the idea stage to the final customer,* 238

Product development *The management of the value chain activities involved in bringing new or improved goods and services to the market,* 278, 294

Product development plan *A plan that specifies all of the relevant information that managers need to decide whether to proceed with a full-blown product development effort,* 295

Product layout, 287, 288

Product life cycle *The way demand for a product changes in a predictable pattern over time,* 542–544

Product structure *An organizational structure in which each product line or business is handled by a self-contained division,* 313–315

Product team structure *An organizational structure in which employees are permanently assigned to a cross-functional team and report only to the product team manager or to one of his or her direct subordinates,* 318, 319

Production blocking *A loss of productivity in brainstorming sessions due to the unstructured nature of brainstorming,* 234

Production function, 279
Profit ratios, 347–348
Profit sharing, 420

Programmed decision making *Routine, virtually automatic decision making that follows established rules or guidelines,* 217–218

Programs, 250
Projects, 250
Promoting effective communication, 480–509
  collaboration software, 499–500
  communication networks, 494–497
  communication process, 484–485
  cross-cultural differences, 505–506
  dangers of ineffective communication, 486–487
  e-mail, 490-492, 500, 506
  face-to-face communication, 487–490
  gender differences, 506
  groupware, 498–499
  impersonal written communication, 493
  importance of good communication, 483
  Internet, 497
  intranet, 497–498
  linguistic style, 506–507
  managers, communication skills, 501–507
  perception, 486
  personally addressed written communication, 490–492
  spoken communication electronically transmitted, 490
  vertical/horizontal communication, 495
Promoting from within, 331

Prosocially motivated behavior *Behavior that is performed to benefit or help others,* 401

Punishment *Administering an undesired or negative consequence when dysfunctional behavior occurs,* 414

Q

Quality
  communication, 483
  competitive advantage, 277
  information, 538
  organizational performance, 284
  Six Sigma, 286–287
  TQM, 284–287
Quantitative management, 94

Quantum product innovation *The development of new, often radically different, kinds of goods and services because of fundamental shifts in technology brought about by pioneering discoveries,* 293

Quick ratio, 348

Quid pro quo sexual harassment *Asking for or forcing an employee to perform sexual favors in exchange for receiving some reward or avoiding negative consequences,* 181

R

Ratebusters, 90

Real-time information *Frequently updated information that reflects current conditions,* 538

Realistic job preview (RJP) *An honest assessment of the advantages and disadvantages of a job and organization,* 377

Reasoned judgment *A decision that requires time and effort and results from careful information gathering, generation of alternatives, and evaluation of alternatives,* 218

Receiver *The person or group for which a message is intended,* 485

Reciprocal task interdependence *The task interdependence that exists when the work performed by each group member is fully dependent on the work performed by other group members,* 464, 465

Recruitment *Activities that managers engage in to develop a pool of qualified candidates for open positions,* 374

Recruitment and selection, 374–381
References, 380

Referent power *Power that comes from subordinates' and coworkers' respect, admiration, and loyalty,* 432

Regional trade agreements, 206–207

Related diversification *Entering a new business or industry to create a competitive advantage in one or more of an organization's existing divisions or businesses,* 263

Relatedness needs, 407

Relationship-oriented leaders *Leaders whose primary concern is to develop good relationships with their subordinates and to be liked by them,* 437

Relay assembly test experiments, 89

Reliability *The degree to which a tool or test measures the same thing each time it is used,* 380–381

Representativeness bias *A cognitive bias resulting from the tendency to generalize inappropriately from a small sample or from a single vivid event or episode,* 229

Reputation *The esteem or high repute that individuals or organizations gain when they behave ethically,* 148, 157

Research and development *A team whose members have the expertise and experience needed to develop new products,* 458

Resource allocator, 54, 170
Resource capital, 204
Responsiveness to customers, 456, 483

Restructuring *Downsizing an organization by eliminating the jobs of large numbers of top, middle, and first-line managers and nonmanagerial employees,* 59

Results appraisals, 385
Return on investment (ROI), 347

Revolutionary change *Change that is rapid, dramatic, and broadly focused,* 362

Reward power *The ability of a manager to give or withhold tangible and intangible rewards,* 430

Rewards for innovation, 238

Risk *The degree of probability that the possible outcomes of a particular course of action will occur,* 221

Rite of enhancement, 126
Rite of integration, 126
Rite of passage, 126
RJP, 377
Roboticized car plant, 74

Role making *Taking the initiative to modify an assigned role by assuming additional responsibilities,* 466

Role playing, 382
Rolling plan, 249
Routine technology, 307

Rules *Formal written instructions that specify actions to be taken under different circumstances to achieve specific goals,* 83, 250

Rumors *Unofficial pieces of information of interest to organizational members but with no identifiable source,* 503

S

Safety needs, 406
Salary increase, 419
Sales function, 279
Salience effect, 177
Same-sex partner benefits, 392

Satisficing *Searching for and choosing an acceptable, or satisfactory, response to problems and opportunities, rather than trying to make the best decision,* 223

Scanlon plan, 420
Scarce resources, 516

Scenario planning *The generation of multiple forecasts of future conditions followed by an analysis of how to respond effectively to each of those conditions,* 250

Schema *An abstract knowledge structure that is stored in memory and makes possible the interpretation and organization of information about a person, event, or situation,* 173

Scientific management *The systematic study of relationships between people and tasks for the purpose of redesigning the work process to increase efficiency,* 77–79

Scientific management theory, 75–78

Selection *The process that managers use to determine the relative qualifications of job applicants and their potential for performing well in a particular job,* 374

Selection process, 378–381
Selection tools, 378
Self-actualization needs, 406

Self-efficacy *A person's belief about his or her ability to perform a behavior successfully,* 417

Self-esteem *The degree to which individuals feel good about themselves and their capabilities,* 110

Self-managed work team *A group of employees who supervise their own activities and monitor the quality of the goods and services they provide,* 291, 459–460

Self-management of behavior, 417
Self-reinforcement, 416–417

Self-reinforcer *Any desired or attractive outcome or reward that a person gives to himself or herself for good performance,* 416

Sender *The person or group wishing to share information,* 485

Senge's principles for creating a learning organization, 232–233

Sequential task interdependence *The task interdependence that exists when group members must perform specific tasks in a predetermined order,* 464, 465

Servant leader *A leader who has a strong desire to serve and work for the benefit of others,* 428

Sexual harassment, 181–183
Sexual orientation, 168
Shared vision, 233

Short-term orientation *A worldview that values personal stability or happiness and living for the present,* 209

Short-term plan, 249
Similar-to-me effect, 176
Simulations, 382
Single-use plan, 250
Situational interview questions, 379

Six Sigma *A technique used to improve quality by systematically improving how value chain activities are performed and then using statistical methods to measure them,* 286–287, 371–372

Skill variety, 310

Skunkworks *A group of intrapreneurs who are deliberately separated from the normal operation of an organization to encourage them to devote all their attention to developing new products,* 238

Slavery, 135
Small-batch production, 73

Social entrepreneur *An individual who pursues initiatives and opportunities and mobilizes resources to address social problems and needs in order to improve society and well-being through creative solutions,* 235

Social learning theory *A theory that takes into account how learning and motivation are influenced by people's thoughts and beliefs and their observations of other people's behavior,* 416–417

Social loafing *The tendency of individuals to put forth less effort when they work in groups than when they work alone,* 474–475

Social networking site *A Web site that enables people to communicate with others with whom they have some common interest or connection,* 493

Social responsibility *The way a company's managers and employees view their duty or obligation to make decisions that protect, enhance, and promote the welfare and well-being of stakeholders and society as a whole,* 153. *See also* Ethics and social responsibility

Social status effect, 176

Social structure *The arrangement of relationships between individuals and groups in a society,* 198

Socialization, 125

Societal ethics *Standards that govern how members of a society should deal with one another in matters involving issues such as fairness, justice, poverty, and the rights of the individual,* 148–150

Sociocultural forces *Pressures emanating from the social structure of a country or society or from the national culture,* 198

Soft drink business, 259–260
Softbot, 550
Software agent, 550
SOPs, 83, 250
Spam, 500

Span of control *The number of subordinates who report directly to a manager,* 320

Specific goals, 412
Splenda, 191
Spoken communication electronically transmitted, 490
Spokesperson, 54, 170

Staff manager *Someone responsible for managing a specialist function, such as finance or marketing,* 320

Stage-gate development funnel *A planning model that forces managers to choose among competing projects so organizational resources are not spread thinly over too many projects,* 294, 295

Stakeholders *The people and groups that supply a company with its productive resources and so have a claim on and stake in the company,* 136

Standard operating procedures (SOPs) *Specific sets of written instructions about how to perform a certain aspect of a task,* 83, 250

Standing committee, 459
Standing plan, 250
Status inconsistencies, 516–517

Stereotype *Simplistic and often inaccurate beliefs about the typical characteristics of particular groups of people,* 174–175, 486

Stock options, 419
Stories and language, 126–127
Storming, 466

Strategic alliance *An agreement in which managers pool or share their organization's resources and know-how with a foreign company, and the two organizations share the rewards and risks of starting a new venture,* 268, 555

Strategic human resource management *The process by which managers design the components of an HRM system to be consistent with each other, with other elements of organizational architecture, and with the organization's strategy and goals,* 371–372

Strategic leadership *The ability of the CEO and top managers to convey to their subordinates a compelling vision of what they want the organization to achieve,* 252

Strategy *A cluster of decisions about what goals to pursue, what actions to take, and how to use resources to achieve goals,* 49, 245, 306–307

Strategy formulation *The development of a set of corporate-, business-, and functional-level strategies that allow an organization to accomplish its mission and achieve its goals,* 253–268

- business-level strategy, 257–260
- corporate-level strategy, 257–268
- five forces model, 254–257
- SWOT analysis, 253–254

Strategy implementation, 270
Strong adaptive cultures, 331–332
Stuck in the middle, 257

Subjective appraisal *An appraisal that is based on perceptions of traits, behaviors, or results,* 385

Superordinate goals, 522
Supervisor, 53

Suppliers *Individuals and organizations that provide an organization with the input resources it needs to produce goods and services,* 190–192

Supply forecasts, 375
Supportive behaviors, 436, 439, 440

SWOT analysis *A planning exercise in which managers identify organizational strengths (S) and weaknesses (W) and environmental opportunities (O) and threats (T),* 253–254

Synchronous technologies, 462

Synergy *Performance gains that result when individuals and departments coordinate their actions,* 96, 263, 455

Systematic errors *Errors that people make over and over and that result in poor decision making,* 228

Systems thinking, 233

T

Tall organization, 322

Tariff *A tax that a government imposes on imported or, occasionally, exported goods,* 204

Task analyzability, 307

Task environment *The set of forces and conditions that originate with suppliers, distributors, customers, and competitors and affect an organization's ability to obtain inputs and dispose of its outputs because they influence managers daily,* 190–196

Task force *A committee of managers or nonmanagerial employees from various departments or divisions who meet to solve a specific, mutual problem; also called ad hoc committee,* 326, 327, 459

Task identity, 310

Task interdependence *The degree to which the work performed by one member of a group influences the work performed by other members,* 464, 516

Task-oriented behaviors, 436

Task-oriented leaders *Leaders whose primary concern is to ensure that subordinates perform at a high level,* 437

Task significance, 310

Task structure *The extent to which the work to be performed is clear-cut so that a leader's subordinates know what needs to be accomplished and how to go about doing it; a determinant of how favorable a situation is for leading,* 437–438

Task variety, 307
Taylor's principles, 77–78

Team *A group whose members work intensely with one another to achieve a specific common goal or objective,* 454. *See also* Groups and teams

Team learning, 232

Technical skills *The job-specific knowledge and techniques required to perform an organizational role,* 57

Technological forces *Outcomes of changes in the technology that managers use to design, produce, or distribute goods and services,* 197

Technology *The combination of skills and equipment that managers use in designing, producing, and distributing goods and services,* 197. *See also* Information technology (IT)

Telecommuter, 491

Terminal value *A lifelong goal or objective that an individual seeks to achieve,* 111

Theory X *A set of negative assumptions about workers that leads to the conclusion that a manager's task is to supervise workers closely and control their behavior,* 91

Theory Y *A set of positive assumptions about workers that leads to the conclusion that a manager's task is to create a work setting that encourages commitment to organizational goals and provides opportunities for workers to be imaginative and to exercise initiative and self-direction,* 91

Thermostat, 346

Third-party negotiator *An impartial individual with expertise in handling conflicts and negotiations who helps parties in conflict reach an acceptable solution,* 521

Threat of substitute products, 256

360-degree appraisal *A performance appraisal by peers, subordinates, superiors, and sometimes clients who are in a position to evaluate a manager's performance,* 387–388

Time constraints, 223

Time horizon *The intended duration of a plan,* 249

Times-covered ratio, 348

Top-down change *A fast, revolutionary approach to change in which top managers identify what needs to be changed and then move quickly to implement the changes throughout the organization,* 363

Top management team *A group composed of the CEO, the COO, the president, and the heads of the most important departments,* 55, 458

Top manager *A manager who establishes organizational goals, decides how departments should interact, and monitors the performance of middle managers,* 55, 56

Total quality management (TQM) *A management technique that focuses on improving the quality of an organization's products and services,* 62, 94, 284–287

Tragedy of the commons, 146

Training *Teaching organizational members how to perform their current jobs and helping them acquire the knowledge and skills they need to be effective performers,* 381

Training and development, 381–383
Trait appraisals, 384
Trait model of leadership, 433–434

Transaction-processing system *A management information system designed to handle large volumes of routine, recurring transactions,* 547

Transactional leadership *Leadership that motivates subordinates by rewarding them for high performance and reprimanding them for low performance,* 443

Transformational leadership *Leadership that makes subordinates aware of the importance of their jobs and performance to the organization and aware of their own needs for personal growth and that motivates subordinates to work for the good of the organization,* 441–443

Trust *The willingness of one person or group to have faith or confidence in the goodwill of another person, even though this puts them at risk,* 147

Turnaround management *The creation of a new vision for a struggling company based on a new approach to planning and organizing to make better use of a company's resources to allow it to survive and prosper,* 63

Twitter, 493
Two-boss employee, 319
Two-person rule, 356

U

Uncertainty *Unpredictability,* 221, 524–525

Uncertainty avoidance *The degree to which societies are willing to tolerate uncertainty and risk,* 209

Underpayment inequity *The inequity that exists when a person perceives that his or her own outcome-input ratio is less than the ratio of a referent,* 410

Unions, 392–393
Unit, 459

Unity of command *A reporting relationship in which an employee receives orders from, and reports to, only one superior,* 85

Unity of direction *The singleness of purpose that makes possible the creation of one plan of action to guide managers and workers as they use organizational resources,* 86

Unrelated diversification *Entering a new industry or buying a company in a new industry that is not related in any way to an organization's current businesses or industries,* 264–265

Unstructured interview, 379
Uruguay Round, 205

Utilitarian rule *An ethical decision produces the greatest good for the greatest number of people,* 144

V

Valence *In expectancy theory, how desirable each of the outcomes available from a job or organization is to a person,* 404

Validity *The degree to which a tool or test measures what it purports to measure,* 381

Value chain *The coordinated series or sequence of functional activities necessary to transform inputs such as new product concepts, raw materials, component parts, or professional skills into the finished goods or services customers value and want to buy,* 278

Value chain management *The development of a set of functional-level strategies that support a company's business-level strategy and strengthen its competitive advantage,* 278–280

Value system *The terminal and instrumental values that are guiding principles in an individual's life,* 112

Values *Ideas about what a society believes to be good, right, desirable, or beautiful,* 111–113, 207, 327

Verbal communication *The encoding of messages into words, either written or spoken,* 485

Vertical communication, 495

Vertical integration *Expanding a company's operations either backward into an industry that produces inputs for its products or forward into an industry that uses, distributes, or sells its products,* 261

Vicarious learning *Learning that occurs when the learner becomes motivated to perform a behavior by watching another person performing it and being reinforced for doing so; also called* observational learning, 416

Videoconference, 489
Vioxx, 151

Virtual team *A team whose members rarely or never meet face-to-face but, rather, interact by using various forms of information technology such as e-mail, computer networks, telephone, fax, and videoconferences,* 461–462

Voice mail system, 490

W

Weber's principles of bureaucracy, 82–83
Wheel network, 494–495

Wholly owned foreign subsidiary *Production operations established in a foreign country independent of any local direct involvement,* 268

Wiki, 500–501
Women. *See* Gender
World Trade Organization (WTO), 205